BIRDS OF THE
WORLD

A PHOTOGRAPHIC GUIDE

ANDREW GOSLER General Editor

FIREFLY BOOKS

A Firefly Book

Published by Firefly Books Ltd. 2007

First printing

Publisher Cataloging-in-Publication Data (U.S.)

Gosler, Andrew.
    Birds of the world : a photographic guide /
Andrew Gosler, general editor.
[384] p. : col. photos., maps ; cm.
Includes index.
Summary: General information covering bird
evolution, classification, anatomy and conservation,
and species articles covering description, behavior,
habitat and distribution.
ISBN-13: 978-1-55407-241-5
ISBN-10: 1-55407-241-7
1. Birds — Pictorial works. 2. Birds — Identification. I.
Title.
598 dc22   QL674.G67 2007

Library and Archives Canada Cataloguing in
Publication data is available on request

Published in the United States by
Firefly Books (U.S.) Inc.
P.O. Box 1338, Ellicott Station
Buffalo, New York 14205

Published in Canada by
Firefly Books Ltd.
66 Leek Crescent
Richmond Hill, Ontario L4B 1H1

Printed in Hong Kong

*This page: Left to right, Greater Prairie Chicken,
Great Philippine Eagle, Fischer's Lovebird, African Penguin,
Australian Pelican, Anna's Hummingbird, King Vulture,
Eurasian Tree Sparrow*

*The list of birds is taken from the 6th edition of Clements
Checklist of the Birds of the World (by permission from
Cornell University Press).*

BIRDS OF THE WORLD

CONTENTS

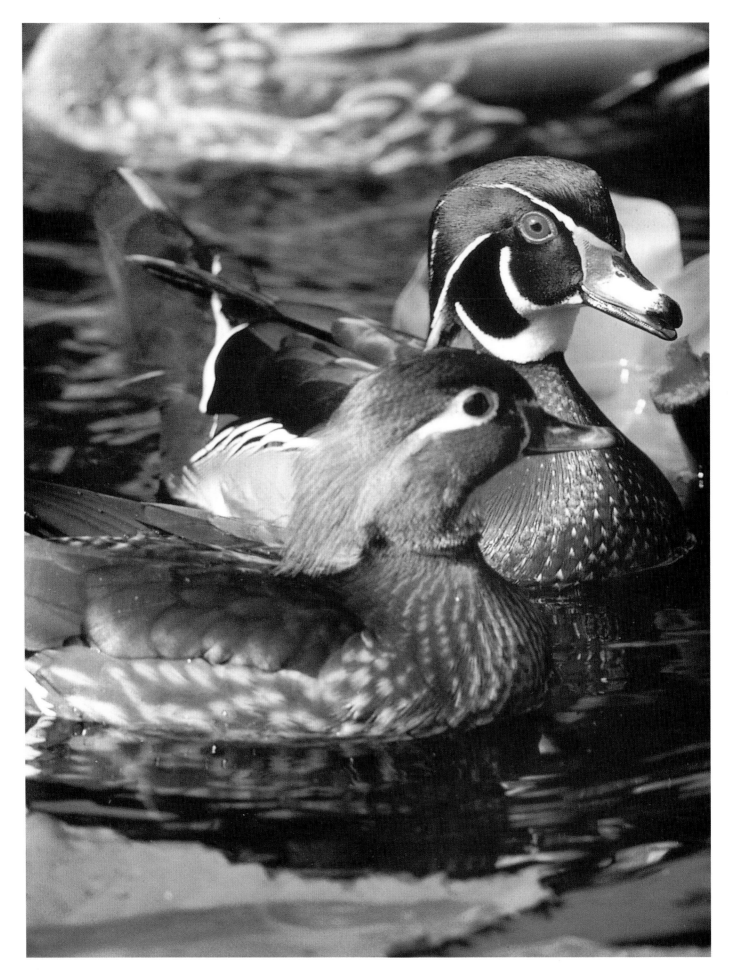

FOREWORD

Birds are the most popular group of animals; many more people go bird-watching than mammal-watching. This is perhaps surprising when one considers that we are mammals! Yet we are rather unusual mammals, not least because we rely, for our perception of the world, mainly on sight and sound; many mammals rely much less on sight and much more on their sense of smell, a sense in which we perform poorly in comparison with most other mammals. Further, the majority of mammals seem to be largely color-blind while we have very good color vision. Such senses, of course, match the "needs" of the organism concerned, having been developed by natural selection. Many mammals live underground or are mainly active after dark, when vision, especially color vision, is of little use, but the sense of smell is extremely important.

In contrast to most mammals, but not humans, birds are largely diurnal. Since they fly, they need good early warning of approaching objects. Hence they see well; good color vision heightens this perception and aids them in their search for food. Hearing is a very useful sense for communication since, especially in thick woodland, it is not always easy to keep in visual contact with other birds. Birds have developed the sense of hearing, together with the matching transmitter, voice, to a high degree. Many species communicate with each other largely by voice and their songs can be very intricate. To our ears, some of these songs are very beautiful. Poets such as Shelley and Wordsworth have immortalized the songs of the Skylark and the Nightingale.

Most birds have less need for a well-developed sense of smell since this is less useful to a creature moving rapidly through the air. So, like us, most birds rely mainly on sight, with sound as their second sense and smell a poor third. It is not surprising therefore that, because we can perceive more of their world than we can of our fellow mammals, we find birds more enjoyable to watch than mammals.

Birds are not merely enjoyable to watch; because we can perceive more of their world, they are in this sense easier to study than mammals. Much scientific knowledge, especially in the fields of behavior and ecology, has come from observations of birds. We must, however, be careful not to fall into a trap. We must not assume that, because we can perceive some aspects of the birds' world, it follows that we necessarily "see" such things in the same way that birds do. For example, the bird songs that we regard as beautiful are not necessarily beautiful to birds; to them, they function to identify others of their species and the song of one male may be perceived not as beautiful but as threatening by other males.

Nevertheless, we do find many birds and their songs to be beautiful, and so this book is first and foremost a celebration of birds. Although this is its main purpose, the editors intend that it will also enable us to get a much better idea of the birds of the world, and so enable us to better enjoy and understand the birds we see. It describes a wide range of species from all over the world, emphasizing, in the main, those species that we are most likely to encounter. The text is written by experienced ornithologists and gives an authoritative account of the birds and the ways in which they live. Most accounts are illustrated by color photographs which show the birds in their natural habitats. Modern bird photographers have attained such a high standard that most of us might as well just throw our cameras away! The exception to this lies in the many tropical regions where the threatened flora and fauna is still poorly known.

Whether we make intensely detailed studies of their lives or merely enjoy their antics at the bird table, birds are an important part of the make-up of our planet and one that we can ill-afford to lose. Yet that is just what we are in danger of doing. We are not in imminent danger of losing all our birds, of course, but we are in danger of losing a very high proportion of them. BirdLife International list 1,204 species as threatened with extinction, roughly one in eight of all the 9,704 or so bird species in the world! Many of these are birds that live in the great tropical rainforests, which are, together with all their other fauna and flora, being destroyed at such a great rate at the present time. Indeed, even this 1,204 is not a complete list of those birds that we could lose; many others, although not in immediate danger, could become so if most of these forests are removed. Human greed and over-population, leading to such extensive over-exploitation of our planet, is a threat, not only to the birds, but eventually to us also. So there are compelling reasons for trying to bring this plundering to a halt.

More subtle effects of humans on birds have proved useful to us. It was the crash of Peregrine Falcon populations and those of other birds of prey which prompted the studies that showed the hazards of the widespread use of pesticides and how they built up in animals until they reached dangerous levels; we are not immune from accumulating high levels of these dangerous compounds in ourselves. These studies on birds led to restrictions on the use of certain chemicals and greater monitoring of the introduction of new ones. This lesson, important as it was, has not yet been fully heeded. Many developing countries have not yet listened to these warnings and many so-called developed ones still do not have the controls necessary to avoid all major pollution problems. Somehow many people still tend to think of pesticides as killing organisms that we do not want, but having no effect on those we do, or on ourselves. Would that life was as simple as that! Often, as with the Peregrines, the outcome is unintentional, but serious for all that. In India in just over a decade three species of vultures have shown at least a 98% decline, due it turns out, to the use of a veterinary drug Diclofenac used to treat cattle. While vultures may not top everybody's list of favorite birds, they probably should top the list of ecologically important ones, especially in India where, depending on one's religion, they can be the human undertaker or the consumer of dead cows; their absence has caused a serious social problem in the first and has lead to an upsurge in dangerous packs of feral dogs in the second.

This book enables us to better understand the problems facing birds today, to recognize the species and it encourages us to learn more about what they are doing. Hopefully also it will lead to yet greater understanding and appreciation of our world and greater support for saving the environment. Birds and the planet need our concern.

Prof. Christopher Perrins
Edward Grey Institute of Field Ornithology

INTRODUCTION

This book has three main aims. The first is, overwhelmingly, to be a celebration of birds. As such, we hope to present the reader with an overview of the world of birds—a world of diverse sights and sounds, which is often colorful and exciting, but which is always intriguing. The second is to provide, in one volume, a guide that will give a feeling for the diversity of birds worldwide. The birds are presented by regions so that the relationships and similarities between the species of any region and those of any other might be recognized; in short, to place each species in a global context. Details are also provided on how to identify, at least, many of the commoner species in each region, but while we hope that the book will have some value for this, it is not our main purpose. No single volume can cover all of the world's birds adequately for identification purposes, and this is not a fieldguide. Furthermore, the biology of some species (in terms of diet, nest, or even plumages), particularly in the tropics, is very poorly known, and in many cases the geographical distribution has been described only vaguely, but we hope that emphasizing such issues will contribute to our third aim, which is to highlight the threat of extinction faced by so many species today, and to stimulate both a greater interest in, and concern for, birds and their environment. In so doing, we hope to contribute to their conservation.

We live on a shrinking planet. The ease with which birdwatchers can travel in search of birds increases almost annually as more of our world becomes accessible to tourism. The irony is, however, that often the opening up of areas that previously could be reached only after a long journey on foot or by boat has been possible because of development, such as timber extraction, carried out at the expense of the very habitat needed by the birds. While the majority of birdwatchers live in the developed world, the majority of bird species don't. They live in the primary habitats of the subtropics. Of 9,704 species recognized in this book, some 70% occur wholly or partly in tropical regions and many others that breed at temperate northern latitudes migrate to the tropics to winter. Many of the resident tropical species are highly specialized ecologically with particular requirements for feeding and breeding. Indeed in some respects it is this which allows such great species diversity in these areas, and particularly in the rainforests where 300 species may occur together in 1 sq km (0.3 sq mile). But this also makes them vulnerable, since they are unable to survive when these complex and diverse ecosystems are changed or lost. Habitat loss is the major threat to birds worldwide and because of the former inaccessibility of such areas, it is often the most endangered species that we know least about. Many species have become extinct in recent times—birds about whose ecology and behavior we can only guess. The very richness of life, *biodiversity*, is threatened as never before.

The evolution of birds

The introductory pages briefly describe the *evolution* of birds from their reptilian ancestors, and discuss how the great diversity of birds which we see today has developed over time through natural selection and *adaptation*. We shall also see how this process has resulted in patterns which we can use to unravel the evolutionary

The six zoogeographical regions used in this book. The Palaearctic is subdivided into Western and Eastern.

WP Western Palaearctic including N Africa & Middle East
EP Eastern Palaearctic including Japan & N China
AF Afrotropical region including Red Sea
OR Oriental region including Himalayas, Philippines, to Wallace's Line
AU East of Wallace's Line to E New Guinea, Australia, New Zealand
NA Nearctic, south to Rio Grande
NT Neotropical, Latin and S America, West Indies

history of birds. These may be patterns of similarities between related species which indicate a common ancestry, or patterns in space in the form of a particular geographical distribution shown by a species or group of species. We shall then see how these patterns can be used to produce a *classification* of birds that reflects that evolutionary history. The next section introduces the 173 families of birds into which the species are grouped, and gives an overview of characteristics shared by the various members of each family, and states how many species. Throughout the book the families are

generally arranged in the order introduced in this section. The remainder, and bulk of the book, presents a representative selection of species by regions, followed by a complete checklist of the world's birds indicating each species that is currently considered by *Birdlife International* (the conservation association that monitors the status of birds worldwide) to be globally threatened.

Ornithologists recognize six major zoogeographical regions of the world. Each is defined by the kinds of birds that are found there so that, although there is naturally some overlap in species between these areas, many will be distinct or *endemic* to that region. The regions are the Nearctic (North America), the Palaearctic (Eurasia), the Neotropical (South America), the Afrotropical (Africa south of the Atlas mountains), the Oriental (India and Southeast Asia), and the Australasian (Australia, New Guinea, the Pacific Islands, and New Zealand and here also including Antarctica). In addition, the Caribbean is sometimes recognized as distinct from the Neotropical Region, and the Madagascan from the Afrotropical Region, because the bird communities or *avifaunas* of these areas contain many endemic species and indeed some endemic families. The Palaearctic shares about 12.5% of its breeding species (particularly those with circumpolar distributions) and about 35% of its genera with the Nearctic, so that they are sometimes referred to together as the Holarctic.

Birds by region

The birds of the six major regions are described by recognized authorities on the birds of each area. Each region is introduced by a short essay that describes the avifauna, its origins, and relationships to the other regions; the principal habitats and threats to them; and organizations involved in the study and conservation of birds in the region. Each bird is identified by both its scientific name and an English or vernacular name. A short description then appears facing its photograph, together with details of its distribution and status worldwide. Where a species occurs in more than one region, this is mentioned in the text although it occurs only once in the book. Similar species, either in the same or a different region, whether they are illustrated in the book or not, are also listed, and where appropriate, a page reference is given. Wherever possible, the photographs have been selected to show not just the plumage of the bird, but also some aspect of its biology. Photographs show adult males unless otherwise stated.

King Penguin (Aptenodytes patagonicus) breeding colony. The diversity of birds reflects variation on a theme. In penguins this variation is pushed to the limit.

BIRD EVOLUTION

In a steamy world of cycads, tree ferns, giant dinosaurs, and flying reptiles, and which will later become Bavaria, a bird about the size of a small crow dies and drops from its perch into the warm waters of a tropical lagoon. It is rapidly covered by fine, calcareous silt, so reducing the rate of decay, and it is fossilized. Here it lies for the next 150 million years. The sediments of the lagoon are moved hundreds of miles north by continental drift and raised hundreds of feet above sea level by mountain-building forces which divide continents as if they were paper. Then, in 1861, the limestone matrix in which the bird rested for so many years is split by workmen quarrying stone for the lithographic printing industry.

Birds and dinosaurs

The fossil, which is named *Archeopteryx lithographica*, is quickly recognized as one of the most significant in the history of paleontology, for it is no bird with which we in modern times are familiar and it shows numerous characteristics which link birds with their reptilian ancestors. The whole skeleton is essentially like that of a small dinosaur. The jaws are not modified into a beak as in modern birds, but are bony and carry numerous undifferentiated teeth. There is no fusion of vertebrae or reduction of the tail, which consists of a series of vertebral elements tapering to a point. The breast bone (sternum) carries no keel for the attachment of the huge breast muscles necessary for powered flight. So why is it so obviously a bird? Because around the bones of the forelimbs and tail are the unmistakable impressions of feathers which are structurally identical to those of modern birds, and feathers are unique to birds. Indeed it is the possession of feathers which defines birds as a class, so that any organism bearing feathers is by definition a bird.

From the fossil record, which is generally poor for small, terrestrial vertebrates, we know that birds evolved rapidly from those early beginnings. The Cretaceous period (130-65 million years ago), which saw the peak of development and extinction of the dinosaurs, and the rise of flowering plants, also saw the rise and extinction of many toothed birds. Because of the conditions needed for fossilization we know only of aquatic species such as the flightless, diverlike *Hesperornis* or the ternlike *Ichthyornis* (which might not have been toothed), but there must have been many terrestrial forms also. Both of these birds show much reduction of the tail, and *Ichthyornis* also shows a well-developed sternal keel indicative of strong flight. However, the evolution of toothless, beaked birds must also have occurred rapidly during the Cretaceous as by the start of the Eocene Period, 65 million years ago, many modern groups such as divers, grebes, cormorants, pelicans, flamingos, ibises, rails, and sandpipers had already appeared. Again there is the bias in the fossil record toward aquatic forms. By the end of the Eocene, 36 million years ago, at least 20 modern orders (see p 14) had appeared. Fossils show that modern flightless birds, the ratites (Ostriches and so on), first appeared during the Eocene. However, they must in fact have arisen before the break-up of the southern supercontinent of Gondwanaland about 100 million years ago, since the closely related Emu (p 282), Ostrich (p 186), and the rheas (p 96) must have evolved in isolation in Australia, Africa, and South America respectively. This discrepancy between the fossil record and theory is almost certainly due to the fact that these are birds of arid habitats in which conditions are rarely suitable for fossilization.

Fossils also show that before the Jurassic there were no birds. Many species appeared and went extinct over the next 100 million years. There can be no doubt that evolution occurred. For example, the Cretaceous fossils show that conditions were suitable for the preservation of marine species at that time and yet important marine families such as penguins (Spheniscidae), gannets (Sulidae), shearwaters (Procellariidae) and petrels (Hydrobatidae) do not appear in the record until the Eocene or even later. But how does evolution occur?

To understand this we need to recognize that each species shows characteristics that fit it for a particular lifestyle. These are called *adaptations*. So, for example, all modern birds show numerous adaptations for flight, swimming birds have webbed feet and marine species have special salt-secreting glands. In the next section we shall look in more detail at the adaptations of birds, but for now it is sufficient to realize that the need to adapt in a changing world is the key to evolution. Observation shows that in the wild many individuals of any species produce more offspring than can ultimately survive to breed, and given that there is variation among individuals which reflects variation in the genetic blueprint (the DNA that is inherited from their parents), we should expect that some individuals will be more likely to survive by virtue of their inherited characteristics than will others. This differential survival, which can be observed in real, wild, evolving populations, is called *natural selection* (the survivors being "selected" by their environment) to differentiate it from the related *artificial selection* carried out for centuries by human breeders of plants and animals.

Natural selection

If environmental conditions change, or if there is little competition from other species, for example during a period of colonization, then different individuals in a population may survive better in slightly different habitats. Natural selection will then emphasize the differences between these subpopulations, resulting in new adaptations. Hybrids which are intermediate in form may be at a disadvantage because they are less well adapted to discretely differing habitats, so that there will be selection for distinct breeding groups. From this point they are genetically isolated and are effectively new species. This process of *speciation* can occur whenever populations are isolated genetically (that is, they are prevented from interbreeding). Another important form of selection in bird evolution, is sexual selection, in which certain characteristics of a potential mate, for example indicating his "fitness," are favored over other characteristics by the selecting sex (usually females in birds). Sexual selection is largely responsible for the exquisite or ornamental (noncryptic) plumages of male birds, especially where this contrast with that of the female. Selection, be it natural or sexual, can only act on

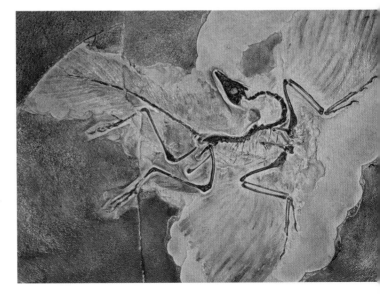

The fossil of **Archaeopteryx lithographica** *reveals evidence of early feathers.*

existing variation, it cannot create it. The origin of the variation through which selection can cause evolution is genetic mutation which occurs randomly in time and space through the population. Although the origin of variation is random, the selection of traits, either by the environment or a mate, is not random. If it were, evolution would not occur. Nor is it goal directed. There is no "purpose" to evolution, it is simply the inevitable outcome of genetic variation and nonrandom mortality.

Genetic isolation is considered the major cause of speciation in birds, and is called *allopatric* speciation. If speciation occurs from within a population it is said to be *sympatric* but there is little evidence for this in birds. Examples of the great *adaptive radiation* which can occur when species are free to adapt to unfilled ecological niches can be seen today in the finches of the Galapagos and the Hawaiian honeycreepers. We shall consider adaptive radiation in more depth in the next section.

ADAPTATIONS OF BIRDS

In the last section we saw how natural selection has adapted birds to their environment. Some adaptations, such as the webbed feet of aquatic species, are so obvious as to be hardly worthy of mention, but birds show a great diversity of adaptations, many of which are superbly subtle and should leave the greatest human designers dumbstruck with awe.

It is easy for the ornithologist to be overwhelmed by the apparent diversity of birds and yet, despite the diversity of color and other features, the class shows remarkable consistency of structure. It is useful, for example, to compare birds with mammals, which range in size from the Pygmy Shrew, weighing 2.3 g (0.08 oz) to the Blue Whale at 136,200 kg (134 tons), some 59 million times heavier. In contrast, birds range in size from the Scintillant Hummingbird (p 118) weighing 2.25 g (0.08oz) to the Ostrich (p 186) at about 150 kg (330 lb), only about 66,000 times heavier. Even the largest extinct bird does not bring the upper limit for the class to anywhere near that of mammals. Nor is there more variation in form than in mammals which, apart from those already mentioned, include the bats that can be every bit as agile on the wing as most birds. But birds, more than any other vertebrate group, are supremely adapted for flight and it is the need to reduce weight, without a loss of structural strength, which has been the overriding constraint in the evolution of birds.

Honeycomb bones

The principle in bird structure of high strength to low weight is seen at its best in the skeleton itself. The bones are generally hollow and extremely light but strengthened internally by cross-bracing or by a honeycomb structure of bone. There has been considerable fusing of bones to reduce flexibility and increase strength. This has been most apparent in the spinal column, but the bones of the hand also are greatly fused and there are only three digits. Further cross-bracing occurs across the ribs, each of which shows a backward-pointing projection—the uncinate process, which overlies the next rib. In some diving birds such as auks (Alcidae), which endure great external pressures at depths of more than 150 m (490 ft), these processes are very long to prevent the rib-cage from collapsing. Movement of the wing is reduced at the shoulder to just that necessary for flight and this has allowed a reduction in the mass of some muscles on the back.

The skull has been greatly modified. The bony, toothed jaws of *Archeopteryx* have been replaced by a slender beak of bone over which sits a horny covering which in most birds is continuously growing and wearing away. The beak or bill can be enormously strong for its light weight. For example, in the Hawfinch (p 180), a small bird that cracks olive and cherry stones in its bill, point pressures of more than 50 kg (110 lb) must be generated. The muscle mass of the jaws is also reduced and concentrated near to the center of gravity of the head. Much of the space in the head is taken up by the huge eyes, which are separated only by a thin sheet or *septum* of bone. The position of the eyes in the head varies between species depending on the relative importance of binocular vision for accurate distance judgement and

Great Spotted Woodpecker (Dendropcopos major). *All birds show adaptations to their specific ecology. In woodpeckers the bill, skull, tongue, feet, and tail all show adaptation for wood-boring.*

monocular vision allowing a wide field of view. Hence, in predators, the eyes typically face forward, giving a rather human appearance in owls (Strigidae) or downward under the bill in herons (Ardeidae), while they point to the sides in more vulnerable species. The ultimate such development is probably seen in the Eurasian Woodcock (p 160) which has a 360° field of view. Despite this, accurate distance judgement is essential for any fast-flying animal, especially one that inhabits dense cover, and in fact all birds have some binocular vision since in most species the eyes can move in their orbits. All diurnal species see the world in color, and in all birds the optical resolution is at least as good as ours, and in many cases better, for example including perception of UV coloration that occurs in the plumage of some species.

A fuller appreciation of the quality of eyesight in birds is gained by considering, for example, what a fishing Northern Gannet (p 142) actually has to do to survive. From a height of up to 40 m (130 ft), traveling at 30 km/h (20 mph) above a strong sea with a heavy swell and with a near gale-force wind blowing, it must spot fish less than 30 cm (12 in) in length, allow for refraction and dive headlong like a missile into the water among its prey. Even allowing for the fact that fish are probably caught on the bird's way back to the surface, there is little room for error. Faced with this prospect, it is probably not surprising that they prefer to fish shoals within 25 m (80 ft) of the surface.

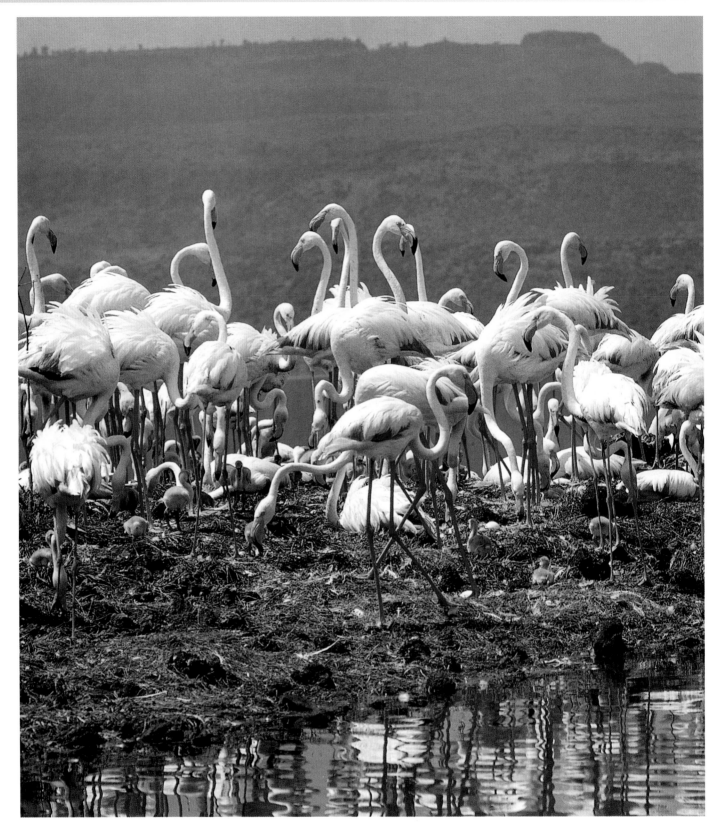

Birds' sense of hearing is also acute, for while the total frequency range of sensitivity is often similar to our own, the resolution (the ability to differentiate sounds in time) can be ten times better than ours. This means in practice that some species can distinguish two sounds which are only a ten-thousandth of a second apart. In addition, many can distinguish between two sounds that differ in frequency by less than 1%. Generally, songbirds (families 116–173, pp 37–47) have a higher upper limit to their frequency range than do other birds.

Although none is sensitive to ultrasonic vibration, some can hear extremely low-frequency sounds, well below human receptive ability. The auditory ability of birds, especially songbirds, means that they can receive a great deal of information from complex songs. We still can only guess at the full information content of songs such as that produced by the Reed Warbler (Sylviidae, p 172). The eyesight and hearing of birds compensate them for their senses of taste and smell which in general are rather poor.

Greater Flamingo (Phoenicopterus roseus). *The breeding biology of flamingos shows many adaptations, such as the production of a milk to feed the young until the highly modified bill has developed fully.*

The musculature and internal organs also show numerous adaptations both to save weight and to concentrate the mass close to an optimum center of gravity that lies beneath the wings when in flight. Hence, food is ground not by teeth, which would require a heavy jaw for support, but in the gizzard, a modification of the anterior part of the stomach containing grit, which the bird ingests for the purpose. This lies very close to the center of gravity. The major parts of the wing and leg muscles lie close to the body, and rely on long tendons to transmit their power to the extremities of the limbs. The reproductive system can be regarded in terms of weight saving since not only does the female shed the weight of each egg shortly after its development, but the gonads shrink outside the breeding season to a fraction of their weight when breeding. In some species, even the gut can be shrunk during migration when not required, so as to reduce weight further. There have also been extreme modifications of the respiratory and vascular systems to such a peak of efficiency that active flight is possible at altitudes where any mammal would quickly suffocate if it had not already died of the extreme cold. For example, geese (Anatidae) and waders (Scolopacidae) have been recorded migrating at altitudes of 7,500–9,000 m (25,000–30,000 ft).

The role of feathers

Despite all these modifications, perhaps the most striking is still that uniquely avian invention—the feather. There has been much speculation as to the origins of this remarkable structure. This is mainly because it didn't seem obvious what purpose it might have served in an animal lacking the power of flight. Remember that the lack of a sternal keel in *Archeopteryx* suggested that it was not capable of prolonged powered flight, and yet it had a wing essentially the same as a modern bird. Indeed the asymmetry of the primary flight quills (see p 16) is only satisfactorily explained if the bird was capable of flapping flight. Of course, feathers serve the four roles of providing an airfoil for flight, contouring the body into a streamlined shape, providing a surface for the colors of birds and insulating the body against the cold by trapping a layer of air between them and the skin. As anyone who has ever slept beneath a down-filled cover will know, feathers are extremely efficient in this last role. The feather consists of a central shaft or *rachis* off which run numerous parallel barbs. Each barb carries numerous tiny hooks or *barbules* which latch the barb securely to those alongside it. The feather is a triumph of design. It is light, strong and flexible so that it tends to bend rather than break, and when damaged the barbs are simply zipped together by stroking it quickly through the bill.

So far only adaptations that are general to all birds have been considered, but there are many striking adaptations related to particular ways of life. Indeed, birds provide biologists with so many fine examples of adaptation that we risk expecting to find adaptive explanations for avian features, even where none might exist. However, the rest of this section describes a few specific examples of adaptation whose validity is not questioned.

Evolutionary radiation

When a population evolves to exploit a new kind of food, or a new area such as an island, there is often rapid evolutionary radiation into a series of distinct adaptive forms to fill the many newly available niches. When this happens in birds, the features most closely related to feeding, and particularly the bill and legs, are those which evolve most rapidly. Some examples of this were briefly mentioned in the last section, but one of the best examples is that of the hummingbirds (Trochilidae, pp 74, 118) of the Neotropics and Nearctic. Here, a novel form of locomotion has given access to a vast array of new and unexploited feeding opportunities in the form of nectar from flowers inaccessible to other birds. In fact this "high octane" fuel is necessary to meet the considerable energy demands of hummingbird flight! This adaptation has resulted in a great array of bill lengths and shapes and a radiation into 335 species in 105 genera (see p 14 for an explanation of these terms). A parallel development has occurred in the passerine family of sunbirds (Nectariniidae, p 230) of the Old World where adaptation to the same resource has produced similar or *convergent* characteristics from very different origins and a radiation into 130 species.

Milk production

Variation in adaptation of the bill and feet tends, of course, to be greater between the orders of birds, which differ much more in ecology, than between closely related species. Examples of this are the strong, hooked bills and powerful talon-bearing feet of raptors (p 22), the spoonlike sifting bill and long wading legs of the Spoonbill (p 144) and the diversity of shape of bill and length of leg and bill in the waders or shorebirds (Scolopacidae and others). A remarkable suite of adaptations is seen in the flamingos (p 21). Here, the bill and tongue are greatly modified for filter-feeding and the birds specialize on microscopic plants and animals suspended in the water. In addition, the legs are extremely long, enabling them to feed in deeper water. However, adaptation to this specialized niche has required the development of a further adaptation, namely, the production of a "milk" from the parents' crop. This is because the chicks do not develop their unique bills until they are close to fledging and are therefore unable to feed for themselves. The Greater and Lesser Flamingo chicks may be fed for up to 75 days. Milk production is very rare in birds. Only one other group of birds—the pigeons (Columbidae, p 28)—has evolved the production of milk (though undoubtedly for different reasons than the flamingos) and this has allowed some members of that group to breed almost throughout the year even at temperate latitudes.

Adapted for drilling

Another group with extensive modification for a specialized niche is the woodpeckers (Picidae, p 35), which feed on wood-boring invertebrates in timber. Here, radiation into some 200 species has occurred because the resource (dead wood) is found worldwide, rather than because it offers diverse opportunities for the evolution of different species. Hence the major structural variation is in size— small species feed on smaller branches than large species. However, the adaptations for exploiting this niche, which are general to the family, are noteworthy. The bill is straight, is sharpened to a fine, chisellike point and is reinforced along its length. The bone of the skull is reinforced at the base of the bill to withstand the immense forces incurred by the cranium while drilling into the timber of live hardwood trees. The tongue is extremely long, sticky and often barbed for extracting insect larvae from their chambers. The bony base of the tongue, called the *hyoid apparatus*, which is used to project the rest of the tongue, is so long that it curves back over the top of the cranium. The legs are short and strong and the *zygodactyl* feet (two toes facing forward, two back) are armed with strong, sharp, curved claws which allow the bird to grip the vertical surface of the tree. The tail feathers are pointed and stiffened so that, together with the feet, they act as a tripod which supports the bird when feeding. Woodpeckers are typical of the kind of ecological adaptation seen in birds, where modification occurs not to a single characteristic, but to a whole array or suite of characteristics.

This account has generally been restricted to adaptations of morphology, that is, form. In fact one sees adaptation in every area of bird biology—in breeding, migration, feeding, and in behavior, and the reader will find many more examples throughout this book.

BIRD CLASSIFICATION

Wanting to name the birds we see is our common experience. It is also essential before we can say anything more interesting about them, but to do so we need to recognize the limits of each species. How else, for example, would we know that the small, long-tailed, yellow, blue-headed bird in the field is a race of the Yellow Wagtail (p 170) rather than a separate species?

Living organisms do not come in *all possible* shapes and sizes. For example, consider the variation between hummingbirds and Ostriches. There are not, and never have been, all possible intermediate forms, but discrete groups which we know, for example, as ducks, owls, thrushes and warblers. There are many reasons for this, including adaptive and genetic constraints. So we attempt to identify these different, discrete entities and to group them according to similarities, and separate them according to dissimilarities—in short, to classify them. This natural process is sometimes called "box-in-box" classification because we arrange species together in groups or boxes which are similarly arranged into larger more inclusive groups to form a hierarchy. The science of classification is called taxonomy or systematics, and the different boxes in the hierarchy are called *taxa* (singular, *taxon*). The "latinized" scientific names of organisms identify two levels of boxes (species and genera).

However, the tidy world of the human taxonomist's box-in-box system is disrupted the moment we try to fit the diversity of nature, which was caused by the complex and varied evolutionary histories of each lineage, into it. Thus any classification has an element of artificiality about it, which causes disagreement between practitioners, and so discrepancies between one system of classification and another. But before we consider that, we should review the essential issues. The *species* is the basic unit of taxonomy. It is significant because it is the only grouping that has any biological reality (i.e. the birds themselves distinguish between members of their own species and those of any other). All taxonomic groupings above that of the species are artificial constructions that may be more or less "natural" (defined below) groupings. However, despite this biological reality, it is difficult to define the term in such a way that it covers all known situations. Hence we have a series of species "concepts," such as the Biological Species Concept (BSC), the Phylogenetic Species Concept (PSC), and Ecological Species Concept (ESC). For birds, the BSC has proved to be most reliable generally; it defines species as groups of similar organisms that are, under natural circumstances, capable of interbreeding, and which would not normally interbreed with members of other species similarly defined. Hence BSC species are ultimately defined by genetic similarity, a fact shared with the PSC ("PSC" species share a common evolutionary history) but not necessarily the ESC ("ESC" species share a common ecology). In some cases, "BSC" species might be interfertile, but because of behavior or geography are effectively isolated genetically and would not normally form hybrids. Sometimes humans have broken down these isolating mechanisms, allowing hybridization, which has obscured the species' limits, and even sometimes created problems surrounding conservation. Within the species we might recognize geographical races or subspecies. Subspecies are completely interfertile and produce fertile offspring but are usually geographically isolated when breeding. These may partially overlap geographically to form a hybrid zone such as that of the Hooded and Carrion Crows, though these are now regarded as full species.

Species are grouped into *genera* (singular, *genus*). Each species is recognized by a unique name within its genus and the two together form the scientific name of the species. The genus is always given first with the first letter a capital, the species second in lower-case letters. Scientific names are latinized constructions and are given in a distinct typeface, usually in italics. Because it is unique to the species, it is unambiguous. The scientific name is called a *binomial*. A third name is added to identify each subspecies. For example, the Yellow Wagtail is *Motacilla flava*, but there are several races; the blue-headed race flava may be recognized by the trinomial *Motacilla flava flava* to distinguish it from, say, the black-headed race *Motacilla flava feldegg* of the Balkans and Middle East. Genera are grouped into families, which are recognized by the ending "-idae." Wagtails are members of the family *Motacillidae* (Wagtails and Pipits). Families are grouped into orders (28 are recognized in this book), distinguished by the ending "-iformes," in the wagtail case the *Passeriformes* (perching birds). Orders are grouped into classes. Birds form the class *Aves*. A taxon may be defined which contains only one species, in which case it is said to be *monotypic*.

This sounds straightforward, but how do we go about grouping species? Fortunately, there is a "correct" answer to this. Similarities between species exist either because they reflect a common ancestry, or because they are adapted to a similar lifestyle (ecology). In the latter case such characteristics are said to be *convergent* and are of no use in classification, but if we classify so as to reflect evolutionary history (a *phylogenetic* classification) there can be only one correct answer, and the groups so produced are said to be "natural" groups. So modern taxonomy aims to reflect the evolutionary relationships between taxa. However, although a "correct" answer, indicating the evolutionary history, must exist, there is still much scope for uncertainty. Hence classifications differ. For example, modern classifications (i.e. those including DNA evidence) have recognized as few as 142 families or as many as 204 (as presented in the *Birds of the World Checklist* (see pp 324–371). The 173 families listed in our *Bird Families of the World* (see pp 18–47) represents a deliberate compromise between these.

DNA and classification

Where does uncertainty arise in classification? To produce a natural classification, we should look for characteristics that are not likely to change with time through adaptation to slight differences in environment (which might result in convergence). Hence while bill size and shape and leg length are poor characteristics on which to form groups (see, for example, Scolopacidae, p 26), subtle differences in the arrangement of bones in the palate or the type of syrinx (voice-box) should be of greater use. But the best evidence should come from direct comparisons of the DNA for genes that also are not likely to be under selection, because variation here should reflect the random, undirected process of mutation, the rate of which should be more or less constant over time. Differences in appropriate DNA between taxa therefore indicate the length of time since they shared a common ancestor, and the more similar is the DNA of two taxa, the more closely related they should be.

From the principle that classification reflects evolutionary history, a successful classification is one that groups together all descendants of a common ancestor, and it has predictive power. That is, if new characteristics (say feather chemistry) are studied, perhaps because new techniques are available, a natural classification should give similar groupings based on the new characteristics while an unnatural classification would show poorer correspondence between groups derived according to different character sets. For this reason, as new information is obtained, classifications may change, and new groups, possibly requiring name changes, may be formed. Hence while scientific names may be more standard than the vernacular, they are still liable to change. This should not be resented as "change for change's sake," but accepted as essential to the dynamic science of taxonomy. Some issues in current bird taxonomy, reflecting new information, are highlighted in the section *Bird Families of the World*.

This diagram explains the classification of birds by tracing one species, the Yellow Wagtail, through the classification system.

ORDERS The class *Aves* is here divided into 28 orders. Some examples are given below

Ostriches	Penguins	Full-webbed Swimmers	Diurnal Birds of Prey	Kingfishers and allies	Perching Birds
Struthioniformes	*Sphenisciformes*	*Pelecaniformes*	*Falconiformes*	*Coraciiformes*	*Passeriformes*

FAMILIES The *Passeriformes* are the largest order with 74 families. Some examples are given below.

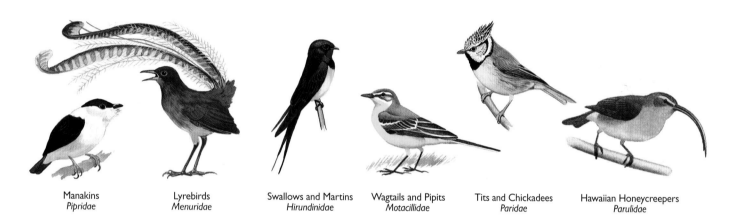

Manakins	Lyrebirds	Swallows and Martins	Wagtails and Pipits	Tits and Chickadees	Hawaiian Honeycreepers
Pipridae	*Menuridae*	*Hirundinidae*	*Motacillidae*	*Paridae*	*Parulidae*

GENERA The *Motacillidae* family contains 5 genera. Some examples are given below.

Tree Pipit
Anthus trivialis

Yellow Wagtail
Motacilla flava

SPECIES The genus *Motacilla* contains 11 species. An example is given below.

Yellow Wagtail
Motacilla flava

The diagrams below show body parts that may be referred to within the individual species descriptions.

CHART OF UNDERWING

CHART OF UPPERWING

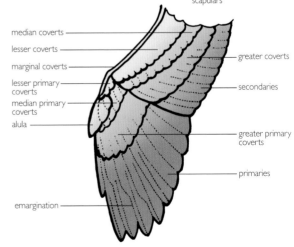

Illustration by permission of *British Birds*

BIRD CONSERVATION

Life has a massive effect on our planet. But no other species has had so negative an impact on biodiversity than has our own. For example, we humans now use nearly half of all the energy captured globally by green plants for our own use as food or fuel. The tropical forests, in which more than half of all known species are found, are being degraded by timber extraction or clear-felled for ranching. Such is the rate of habitat loss, that our best estimates suggest that the rate of extinction today is more than a thousand times greater than the "background" rate of extinction (i.e. the rate in the absence of humans). Furthermore, global oceanic and atmospheric circulations mean that no ecosystem remains unaffected by the human enterprise; even in the Arctic, animals have been reported carrying substantial quantities of agricultural pesticides, thousands of miles from any possible source. So, if biodiversity is to continue to thrive in the presence of humans, the need to conserve has never been greater.

The significance of birds

Faced with such a crisis, it might seem arbitrary to single out birds as particularly significant for conservation. Noting, for example, that *most* animals are *invertebrates* (there are millions of species of insect in the world, many of which have not yet been described) one might ask what importance should be placed on one class of *vertebrates* containing fewer than 10,000 species. And yet, birds play an immensely important role in the global human strategy to conserve biodiversity. The reasons for this are important. They have to do with the very features of birds, mentioned earlier, that give us cause to celebrate them in this book. They are diurnal, colorful, noisy, in short: conspicuous; and people not only *can* observe, and count, them, but they enjoy doing so. Is it any wonder that it was the decline in farmland bird species in Europe over the last 30 years, rather than dwindling aphid or earthworm populations, that drew to the attention of governments the fact that something was going seriously wrong in our countryside? And so, we might celebrate birds for the litmus test that they provide of the state of our environment. The issue is not that other species are not also affected (they might be affected even more than birds are); it is that birds are uniquely amenable to accurate study at a geographic scale appropriate for national or international monitoring.

So in Europe and North America, species population monitoring, conservation and protection are now at an advanced stage. We have a good idea of what is happening to the numbers and distributions of each species, and because the biology of these birds is so well known, in many cases we also know the causes of decline, and can take remedial action. But the temperate northern latitudes are not where birds are under the most intense threat; few of the species found there are actually threatened globally. As with other, non-avian, taxa, it is in the tropics, often in the poorest countries on Earth, and on oceanic islands, that the pressures are most acute. Some 1,204 species out of the 9,704 recognized in this book are considered by *Birdlife International* to be globally threatened, and a swift perusal of the *Bird Families of the World* section (pp 18–47), shows that these are not evenly distributed across taxa. There are particularly high numbers of threatened species in certain groups, and most of them are tropical, or chiefly so. Examples of especially threatened families include: kiwis (3/3 or 100%), albatrosses (36/72 or 50%), wildfowl (27/157 or 17%), parrots (75/279 or 26.8%), pheasants and partridges (52/211 or 24.6%), rails (32/134 or 23.8%), bustards (5/25 or 20%), pigeons (59/308 or 19%), and white-eyes (23/94 or 24.5%). Many high-risk families, of which this is not an exhaustive list, face particular kinds of threat, and in some cases these are quite specific to those groups, and arise from the particular ecology of the birds concerned.

The high-risk families offer a useful overview of the threats faced by birds globally. For kiwis and rails the issue, as it has been for many flightless island endemics, is predation by introduced "commensal" animals such as rats, stoats, and cats. This is because such birds evolved without exposure to predators, and have no appropriate defense behavior. For wildfowl, pheasants, and partridges, bustards and pigeons, direct persecution through overhunting is the key issue. Some wildfowl species are also threatened by hybridization with closely related species introduced, usually unwittingly, into their area by humans. For parrots, excessive exploitation for the pet trade, which also involves the destruction of the birds' nest-trees (an increasingly scarce resource), is the threat. The numbers of albatrosses of many species have declined by more than 20% since 1950 because of increased mortality caused by the birds being caught and killed on long-lines set to catch fish in the southern oceans. The impact of this fishery has been so severe because of the low reproductive rates of these, normally long-lived, birds such that they cannot replace their losses quickly enough through breeding. The white-eyes highlight a specific issue shared with many tropical species that makes them vulnerable to human activities such as deforestation. This is that many of these species have tiny geographic ranges, in some cases being endemic to just a single valley or forest. Hence human development that might be tolerated by the species, if it were more widely distributed, can be catastrophic if it affects their small part of the globe. However, despite the threats faced by these specific taxa, it is notable that there are a few families of birds that do not have a single threatened species, and for the rest, the overwhelming threat comes from habitat degradation (e.g. through overgrazing or pollution) or loss (e.g. through deforestation).

Endemic Bird Areas (EBAs)

From all this it should be clear that conservation priorities arise through a combination of potentially damaging human activities, and the ecology and evolutionary histories of the birds. Unique species (e.g. monotypic families) such as the Kagu, or species with small isolated populations, have high priority. They are likely to be found in areas where prolonged isolation has promoted speciation. The relatively large numbers of unique species found in such *Endemic Bird Areas* (EBAs), of which 218 have been identified globally, mean that they should have high priority for conservation, and the fact that EBAs tend also to hold endemics of other taxa (78% of EBAs overlap with general *Biodiversity Hotspots*), means that conserving EBAs also benefits the conservation of biodiversity more generally. But it would be simplistic to think that our problems would be solved if we simply focused on such areas.

The road to recovery starts with human concern. Human concern is fired by our sense of awe at the world. Uniquely, birds have inspired that sense of awe for many thousands of people worldwide. We hope that this book helps you also to be awe-inspired by birds.

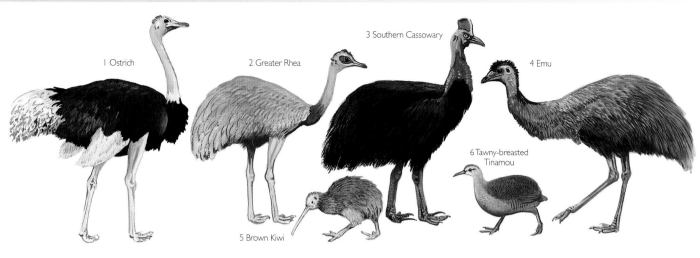

1 Ostrich
2 Greater Rhea
3 Southern Cassowary
4 Emu
6 Tawny-breasted Tinamou
5 Brown Kiwi

BIRD FAMILIES OF THE WORLD

In the following descriptions of bird families, information under certain headings is omitted where no information is available. Information on recent taxonomic changes can be found under the heading "Systematics."
• indicates globally threatened species (**IUCN** classes: *critically endangered, endangered, vulnerable*).
For an explanation of terms used in this section see Glossary on p 372

OSTRICHES Struthioniformes

Massive, flightless, unkeeled sternum, 2 (ostriches) or 3 (others) toes, 5 families.

1 Ostriches Struthionidae *Struthio camelus* (monotypic). See p 186.

2 Rheas Rheidae 2 species, 1 genus, e.g. Greater Rhea *Rhea Americana*
Description: largest birds of New World, standing 90 cm (35 in) high, Wt: c.l0 kg (22 lb). Massive, flightless, powerful running birds (up to 50 km/h, 30 mph), long neck and legs, 3 toes, thighs feathered, very short wings, tail absent. Plumage soft and filmy, gray or gray-brown. Monomorphic, females smaller. **Systematics:** Formerly classified in their own order before DNA analysis placed them firmly with other ratites. **Range and habitat:** NT. Dry plains and scrubland. **Migration:** nonmigratory. **Breeding:** polygamous. Nest is a scrape surrounded by twigs. Eggs: 20–50 laid by 2–12 females. Incubation by male for 35–40 days. Broods: 1. Young are precocial, defended by male. **Food:** mostly vegetable, also some small animals.

3 Cassowaries Casuariidae 3 species (2•), 1 genus, e.g. Southern Cassowary *Casuarius casuarius*
Description: massive flightless birds standing 110–80 cm (43–71 in), Wt: up to 54 kg (120 lb). Head carries bony casque arising from skull. Head and neck bare, brightly colored and often wattled. Plumage largely black, coarse, heavy, and drooping, wing feathers reduced to bare quills, tail more or less absent. Legs powerful, 3 toes—innermost armed with long sharp nail. Monomorphic, females larger. **Systematics:** Formerly classified in their own order with the emus before DNA analysis placed them with other ratites. **Range and habitat:** AU. Dense tropical forest. **Migration:** nonmigratory. **Breeding:** nest is a clearing on forest floor. Eggs: 3–6 pale to dark green, smooth or rough. Incubation by male, 30–50 days. Broods: 1. Young are precocial, attended by male or both, for c.4 months. **Food:** uses casque as a shovel to find plant shoots and fruit, insects and small vertebrates on forest floor.

4 Emus Dromaiidae *Dromaius novaehollandiae* (monotypic). See p 282.
Description: massive, flightless birds (2nd largest ratites). Long neck and legs, 3 toes, neck partly bare, colored, closely related to cassowaries.

5 Kiwis Apterygidae 3 species (3•), 1 genus, e.g. Brown Kiwi *Apteryx australis*
Description: medium-sized, flightless strangely mammal-like birds. L: 45–84 cm (18–33 in), 30 cm (12 in) high, Wt: 1.3–4 kg (2 lb 14 oz–8 lb 13 oz). Plumage coarse, hairlike. Wings rudimentary, 4–5 cm (1½–2 in), tailless, legs short and stout, 3 toes. Bill long, slightly decurved and flexible with open nostrils at tip. Brown or grayish, monomorphic but female larger than male. **Systematics:** Formerly classified in their own order before DNA analysis placed them with other ratites. **Range and habitat:** AU. Forest and scrub. **Migration:** nonmigratory. **Breeding:** nest is a burrow dug largely by male. Eggs: 1–2 huge and yolky, 0.5 kg (1 lb 2 oz) (18–25% female wt). Incubation by male, 74–84 days. Broods: 1. Young are precocial. **Food:** uses well-developed sense of smell to find plant seeds, fruit and a wide range of soil invertebrates.

TINAMOUS Tinamiformes

Primitive ground birds, keeled sternum, 3 or 4 toes, 1 family. Superficially like gamebirds (Galliformes).

6 Tinamous Tinamidae 47 species (7•), 9 genera, e.g. Tawny-breasted Tinamou *Nothocercus julius*
Description: small to medium, ground-dwelling, primitive palate. L: 15–49 cm (6–19 in), Wt: 450 g–2.3 kg (1–5 lb). Legs short, poor and reluctant fliers, neck curved in flight. Bill thin, slightly curved. Tail short and soft, often covered by rump feathers. Plumage barred brownish, mottled. Monomorphic, females larger. **Range and habitat:** NT. Dense forest, scrub and grasslands below 4,000 m (13,000 ft). **Migration:** nonmigratory. **Breeding:** nest is a scrape. Eggs: 1–12, large—21–68 g (¾–2½ oz)—glossy, unicolored but variable in color. Incubation by male for 19–20 days. Broods: 1. Young are precocial, protected by male. **Food:** fruit, seeds, insects and small vertebrates.

PENGUINS Sphenisciformes

Highly modified flightless swimming seabirds, 1 family.

7 Penguins Spheniscidae 17 species (10•), 6 genera, e.g. Rockhopper Penguin *Eudyptes chrysocome*
Description: medium to large flightless seabirds with paddlelike wings, used for propulsion under water, and heavy webbed feet set far back on body. L: 40–115 cm (16–45 in), Wt: 1–30 kg (2 lb 3 oz–66 lb). Strong swimmers (up to 20 knots). Bill medium-sized, stout. Plumage very uniform, generally blue-gray or blue-black above and white below, short, dense, lacking defined tracts. Most species more or less monomorphic. Some species suffer dramatic weight

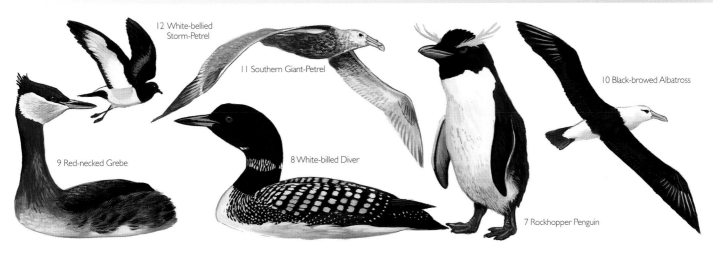

12 White-bellied Storm-Petrel

11 Southern Giant-Petrel

10 Black-browed Albatross

9 Red-necked Grebe

8 White-billed Diver

7 Rockhopper Penguin

loss during incubation. **Range and habitat:** AF, AN, AU, NT. Marine, breeding on ice, rock and sandy shorelines. **Migration:** some migratory species, those of warmer waters are nonmigratory. **Breeding:** varies greatly between species. Nest is on ground, in burrow or none. Eggs: 1–2, whitish. Incubation by male or both for 33–62 days. Broods: 1. Young are semi-altricial, creched. **Food:** fish, squid and crustacea.

DIVERS Gaviiformes

Swimming and diving birds, well-developed tail, neck stripes, 1 family.

8 Divers Gaviidae 5 species, 1 genus, e.g. White-billed Diver *Gavia adamsii*
Description: large swimming and diving birds, 3 front toes fully webbed, legs set far back, walk clumsily. L: 53–69 cm (21–7 in), Wt: 1–2.4 kg (2 lb 3 oz–5 lb 5 oz). Good, strong swimmers. Tarsi laterally compressed. Bill medium-sized, sharply pointed. Body long, neck long and thin. Wings relatively short, pointed. Tail short but well developed. Plumage dense, soft and velvety on head and neck, hard and compact on body, black, white, grays above, white below. Breeding and winter plumages differ. Monomorphic, males larger. Young have 2 coats of nestling down. **Range and habitat:** Holarctic: WP, EP, NA. Breeds on inland freshwater habitats, winters on the sea. **Migration:** strongly migratory. **Breeding:** little courtship. Nest is of little or no material, by water, site chosen by male. Eggs: 2 (rarely 3), olive-green/brown. Incubation by both male and female, 27–9 days. Broods: 1. Young are precocial, fledge at 50–65 days. **Food:** mainly fish, also frogs and aquatic invertebrates.

GREBES Podicipediformes

Swimming and diving birds, tail reduced to a tuft, 1 family.

9 Grebes Podicipedidae 19 species (5 ●), 5 genera, e.g. Red-necked Grebe *Podiceps grisegena*
Description: small-medium to medium-large swimming and diving birds, 4 toes lobed, legs set far back. L: 23–76 cm (9–30 in), Wt: 150 g–1.5 kg (5¼ oz–3 lb 5 oz). Tarsi laterally compressed. Bill short-medium to long, sharply pointed, nostril: a narrow slit. Body short to medium, neck long and thin. Wings short, pointed, flight often poor; some flightless. Tail vestigial. Plumage dense. Breeding and winter plumages usually differ. Breeding: grays, browns, reds, black and white above, tufts and crests on head used in courtship. Winter: usually gray and white. Monomorphic, males slightly larger. **Range and habitat:** worldwide except PA and AN. Open freshwater habitats, some winter on the sea. **Migration:** some strong migrants. **Breeding:** courtship highly ritualized. Nest is colonial or territorial, floating platform of weed. Eggs: 2–6, whitish but stain rapidly. Incubation by both, 21–8 days. Broods: 1–2 (rarely 3). Young are precocial, fledge at 44–80 days. **Food:** fish and aquatic invertebrates.

TUBE-NOSED SWIMMERS Procellariiformes

Marine, tubelike nostril (tubinares), good sense of smell. Come to land only to breed, care of young shared. 4 families.

10 Albatrosses Diomedeidae 14 species (13 ●), 4 genera, e.g. Black-browed Albatross *Thalassarche melanophrys*
Description: very large gliding seabirds. L: 68–135 cm (27–53 in), Wt: 3–12 kg (6 lb 10 oz–26 lb 7 oz). Bill medium-long, strong, plated and hook-tipped. Nostril tubes open laterally. Wings very long, slender, and pointed. Wingspan: 178–350 cm (70–138 in). Many secondary flight feathers. Legs short-medium, 3 forward toes fully webbed. Tail short and round to long and pointed. Monomorphic, some brown or gray, others white with dark upperparts. **Range and habitat:** EP, AF, AU, NT, PA, AN. Oceanic, breeding on oceanic islands. **Migration:** strongly migratory. **Breeding:** courtship ritualized. Nest is colonial, mound of soil or vegetation, or none. Eggs: 1 white. Incubation by both for 65–79 days. Broods: 1. Young are semi-altricial, fledge at 120–278 days. **Food:** fish and crustacea.

11 Petrels and Shearwaters Procellariidae 72 species (36 ●), 14 genera, e.g. Southern Giant-Petrel *Macronectes giganteus*
Description: small to large gliding seabirds with long, slender wings—up to 2 m (79 in) wingspan. L: 28–90 cm (11–35 in), Wt: 130 g–4 kg (4Ωoz–8 lb 13 oz). Tail short. Bill short to medium-long, stout or slender, hook-tipped, nostril tubes dorsal. Legs short, 3 toes fully webbed. Plumage black, white, brown, gray or a combination with dark upperparts, light underparts. Monomorphic but males generally larger than females. **Range and habitat:** oceanic worldwide, breeding on oceanic islands. **Migration:** migratory, some strongly so. **Breeding:** more or less colonial. Nest on cliff ledges or in underground burrows. Eggs: 1, 25–237 g (1–8 oz). Incubation by both for 43–60 days. Broods: 1. Young are semi-altricial, fledge at 70–105 days. **Food:** fish, squid, and crustacea.

12 Storm-Petrels Hydrobatidae 20 species (4 ●), 8 genera, e.g. White-bellied Storm-Petrel *Fregetta grallaria*
Description: the smallest seabirds, with relatively long, pointed wings. L: 14–26 cm (5½–10 in), Wt: 25–68 g (1–2 oz). Wingspan: 32–56 cm (13–22 in). Fluttering or batlike flight especially when feeding. Legs medium-sized, slender. 3 toes fully webbed. Bill short to medium, slender, plated, nostril tubes mounted on top of bill. Tail short to medium, rounded, square or forked. Plumage dense, dark browns, grays, and white. Monomorphic apart from size which varies with species. **Range and habitat:** oceans worldwide except Arctic seas, breeding on oceanic islands. **Migration:** most are migratory. **Breeding:** nest is more or less colonial, in burrows and rock crevices. Eggs: 1, white/whitish. Incubation by both for 40–50 days. Broods: 1. Young are semi-altricial, fledge at 56–73 days. **Food:** fish, squid, and plankton taken from surface of water.

14 White-tailed Tropicbird

17 Galapagos Cormorant

18 Anhinga

15 Great White Pelican

13 Common Diving-Petrel

16 Cape Gannet

13 Diving-Petrels Pelecanoididae 4 species (1 ●), 1 genus, e.g. Common Diving-Petrel *Pelecanoides urinatrix*

Description: in southern oceans ecologically analogous to northern Auks (Alcidae). Medium-sized diving seabirds with chunky bodies, short wings, tail and legs. L: 18–25 cm (7–10 in), Wt: 105–46 g (3¾–5 oz). Wingspan: 30–8 cm (12–15 in). 3 toes fully webbed. Bill short, stout, hooked. Nostril tubes open upward. Plumage black or gray above, white below. Monomorphic. **Range and habitat:** AU, NT, AN. Marine, breeding on coasts and islands. **Migration:** nonmigratory. **Breeding:** nest is colonial in burrows. Eggs: 1, whitish. Incubation by both parents for 45–53 days. Broods: 1. Young are semi-altricial. **Food:** small marine animals which they chase under water.

FULL-WEBBED SWIMMERS Pelecaniformes

Seabirds with 4 toes webbed (totipalmate), more or less expandable throat (gular) pouch. Care of young shared. 6 families.

14 Tropicbirds Phaethontidae 3 species, 1 genus, e.g. White-tailed Tropicbird *Phaethon lepturus*

Description: large white seabirds with black on head and wings. L: 80–110 cm (31–43 in) including tail streamers of 40–55 cm (16–22 in), Wt: 430–730 g (15 oz–1 lb 10 oz). Legs short. Bill red or yellow, long, pointed, strong and slightly decurved. Strong fliers with long, slender wings. Wingspan: 90–110 cm (35–43 in). Swim and walk poorly. Monomorphic, males larger. **Range and habitat:** tropical oceans and oceanic islands worldwide. **Migration:** partly migratory. **Breeding:** elaborate courtship display including undulation of tail streamers. Nest is colonial, on bare ground or in cliff or tree-holes. Eggs: 1, red-brown, blotched. Incubation by both for 40–6 days. Broods: 1. Young are altricial, fledge at 77–100 days. **Food:** fish (flying fish) and squid caught by plunge-diving.

15 Pelicans Pelecanidae 8 species (2 ●), 1 genus, e.g. Great White Pelican *Pelecanus onocrotalus*

Description: large waterbirds with long necks and flattened, hooked bills with huge, extensible gular pouch. L: 127–70 cm (50–67 in), Wt: 2.5–15 kg (5 lb 8 oz–33 lb). Legs short but feet large and strong. Tail short. Plumage of most species white with black wing tips, often with a wash of pink or orange on body, 1 species brown. Strong fliers, soarers, wings long and broad. Wingspan: 2–2.8 m (79–110 in). Monomorphic but males larger than females. **Range and habitat:** WP, EP, AF, OR, AU, NA, NT. Coasts and inland lakes. **Migration:** some migratory. **Breeding:** nest is colonial, of sticks in tree or on ground. Male collects material, female builds nest. Eggs: 1–4, white. Incubation by both for 30–7 days. Broods: 1. Young are altricial, cared for by both for 50–70 days. **Food:** fish caught by plunge-diving or surface fishing, scooping prey into pouch. Sometimes birds fish cooperatively.

16 Gannets and Boobies Sulidae 9 species (2 ●), 3 genera, e.g. Cape Gannet *Morus capensis*

Description: large powerful seabirds, with long, strong bill. L: 66–100 cm (26–39 in), Wt: 900 g–3.5 kg (2–7 lb 15 oz). Long, pointed wings. Wingspan: 1.4–1.7 m (55–67 in); short legs, large feet. Generally adapted for plunge-diving. Small gular pouch. Bare skin on face and throat often highly colored, as are feet. Plumage white and black or brown, juveniles brown and adult plumage acquired after several molts. Monomorphic, females usually larger. **Range and habitat:** WP, AF, OR, AU, NA, NT, PA. Oceanic and oceanic islands. **Migration:** migratory in temperate latitudes, in tropics more sedentary. **Breeding:** much ritual display at colonies. Most nests are in dense colonies, of weed on ground or sticks in trees depending on species. Eggs: 1–4 depending on species, whitish. Incubation by both for 42–55 days. Broods: 1. Young are altricial, fledge at c.90 days. **Food:** fish and squid, often caught by plunge-diving from great height.

17 Cormorants Phalacrocoracidae 39 species (10 ●), 2 genera, e.g. Galapagos Cormorant *Phalacrocorax harrisi*

Description: large, often powerful, waterbirds with long tubular hooked bill, and long necks and tails. L: 50–100 cm (20–39 in), Wt: 900 g–4.9 kg (2–11 lb). Legs short, set far back, feet large. Strong swimmers, swimming low in water. Often crested. Strong fliers, wings medium-sized, broad. Wingspan: 80–160 cm (31–63 in). 1 flightless. Plumage black, white, grays and browns. Northern species tend to be darker. Wings held out to dry. Monomorphic. **Range and habitat:** WP, EP, AF, OR, AU, NA, NT, few at high latitudes. A wide variety of coastal and inland wetland habitats. **Migration:** northern species migratory. **Breeding:** nest is colonial, large mound of twigs or weed collected by male, built by female on cliff or in tree. Eggs: 1–6, chalky blue. Incubation on feet by both for 22–6 days. Broods: 1. Young are altricial: 50–70 days. **Food:** chases fish, amphibia, and aquatic invertebrates under water.

18 Anhingas Anhingidae 2 species, 1 genus, e.g. Anhinga *Anhinga anhinga*

Description: also known as snakebirds or darters, these large birds strongly resemble cormorants (Phalacrocoracidae) but neck very long and sinuous, body longer and bill long, straight and sharply pointed. L: 85–90 cm (33–5 in), Wt: 900 g–2.6 kg (2–5 lb 12 oz). Legs short and set far back, with large feet. Strong swimmers, often swimming with only head and neck showing. Strong fliers and soarers. Wings long and broad. Wingspan: 120–7 cm (47–50 in) Tail very long. As in cormorants the wings are held out to dry after swimming as the bird lacks a preen gland. Dimorphic, males with black and white on neck and wings, females with light brown. **Range and habitat:** AF, OR, AU, southern NA, NT. A variety of freshwater habitats. **Migration:** migratory in Nearctic. **Breeding:** nest is colonial, bulky nest of sticks in tree near water. Eggs: 4 (rarely 2–6), elliptical, pale green, chalky and streaked red. Incubation by both for 26–30 days. Broods: 1. Young are altricial, fledge at 35–49 days. **Food:** chases fish which it spears with bill under water, amphibia, and aquatic invertebrates.

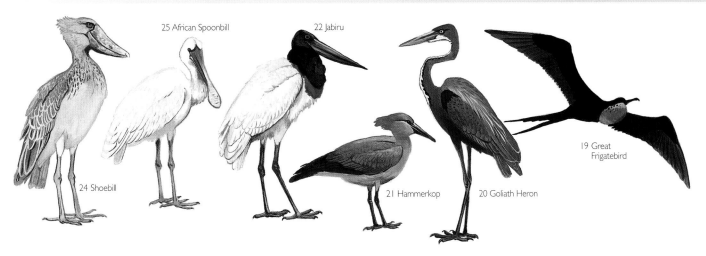

25 African Spoonbill

22 Jabiru

19 Great Frigatebird

24 Shoebill

21 Hammerkop

20 Goliath Heron

19 Frigatebirds Fregatidae 5 species (2 ●), 1 genus, e.g. Great Frigatebird *Fregata minor*
Description: large, extremely light, maneuverable seabirds with extremely long, slender wings. L: 79–104 cm (31–41 in), Wt: 750 g–1.63 kg (1 lb 10 oz– 3 lb 9 oz). Wingspan: 176–230 cm (69–90 in). Legs very short. Feet small, webs reduced, especially to hind toe. Plumage has poor waterproofing and birds cannot swim. Bill long, hooked. Tail long, forked. Despite their expertise in the air they are relatively helpless on land. Dimorphic, males 25–30% lighter than females, generally brownish black with distensible, red throat (gular sac) inflated and vibrated in impressive courtship display. Female generally brown with variable white underparts and without gular sac. Gregarious. **Range and habitat:** tropical oceans and oceanic islands worldwide. **Migration:** local wandering but nonmigratory. **Breeding:** nest is colonial, mostly of sticks accumulated by both during courtship, built in tree or sometimes on ground. Eggs: 1, large, white. Incubation by both for 55 days. Broods: 1. Young are altricial, dependent for 6–11 months. **Food:** fish and squid, also frequently kleptoparasites of pelicans and boobies.

HERONS AND ALLIES Ciconiiformes

Long bill, neck, legs, feet unwebbed or front toes partially so. 7 families in 6 suborders.

20 Herons and Bitterns Ardeidae 63 species (8 ●), 18 genera, e.g. Goliath Heron *Ardea goliath*
Description: small-medium to very large waterbirds with long, spear-shaped bill, long neck and legs. L: 30–140 cm (12–55 in), Wt: 100 g–c.3 kg (3 oz–6 lb 10 oz). Narrow-bodied. Some nocturnal. 4 long toes, unwebbed, middle claw has comb. Strong, maneuverable fliers, large, broad, rounded wings. Flies with neck bent in "S" shape. Tail short. Plumage loose, soft, powder down. Head may carry long plumes. Breeding plumage may include long display plumes. Patterned simply in browns (some highly cryptic), black, white (some entirely white) and grays. Monomorphic but males larger. **Range and habitat:** worldwide except AN. Fresh and salt wetland habitats. **Migration:** migratory in temperate latitudes. **Breeding:** nest is solitary or colonial, pile of sticks in tree or on ground, built by female. Eggs, depending on species: 2–7, whitish to blue, sometimes streaked. Incubation by both for 18–30 days. Broods: 1. Young are semi-altricial, fledge at 35–56 days. **Food:** fish, also small vertebrates and insects. Hunts by stalking, usually in water.

21 Hammerkop Scopidae
Scopus umbretta (monotypic). See p 186.
Description: medium-sized, heronlike bird with anvil-shaped head.

22 Storks Ciconiidae
19 species (5 ●), 5 genera, e.g. Jabiru *Jabiru mycteria*
Description: large to very large birds with long, pointed heavy bills varying in shape, color and patterning. L: 70–150 cm (28–59 in), Wt: 2–9 kg (4 lb 7 oz– 19 lb 13 oz). Long necks and legs. Front toes partly webbed. Tail short, rounded. Body heavy. Plumage variously black, white and grays, boldly patterned, face and neck bare in some. Strong fliers, wings large, and broad. Wingspan: 145–320 cm (57–126 cm). Neck level in flight. Monomorphic. **Range and habitat:** WP, EP, AF, OR, AU, NA, NT. A wide variety of habitats, usually open and often near water. **Migration:** northern species are strongly migratory. **Breeding:** nest is colonial or solitary, of sticks in tree or on cliff. Eggs: 3–5 (rarely 1), white becoming stained. Incubation by both for 30–50 days. Broods: 1. Young are altricial, fledge at 50–126 days. **Food:** fish, small vertebrates, insects, and carrion depending on species.

23 New World Vultures Cathartidae 7 species (1 ●), 5 genera, e.g. Californian Condor *Gymnogyps californianus* (see illustration p 22)
Description: large to very large scavengers. L: 60–130 cm (24–51 in), Wt: 900 g–14 kg (2–30 lb 13 oz). The bill is heavy, rounded and hooked, forest species have good sense of smell to find food. Others follow these to carcass. Head bare, often colored, sometimes wattled. Condors have a ruff. Wings long and broad for soaring. Wingspan: 1.5–3.2 m (59–126 in). Legs and toes moderately strong, claws weak. Plumage usually black or brown, 1 species also white. Monomorphic except in condors in which the male is larger, also male Andean Condor has a caruncle on its head, lacking in female. Gregarious at roost and at food, but nests solitarily **Systematics:** Formerly classified with Falconiformes, but DNA analysis shows them to be highly modified storks, the similarity with Old World vultures is a dramatic evolutionary convergence in form under selection for the same ecological niche. **Range and habitat:** NA, NT. A variety of open and in tropics also forest habitats. **Migration:** migratory in high latitudes. **Breeding:** nest is not built, but located in variety of sites such as rocky ledge, in caves or on bare ground. Eggs: 1–3. Incubation by both for 32–58 days. Broods: 1. Young are semi-altricial, fledge at 70–175 days. **Food:** carrion and animal waste.

24 Shoebill Balaenicipitidae *Balaeniceps rex (monotypic ●). See p 188.
Description: large, storklike bird with massive bill. Neck carried in heronlike "S" shape in flight.

25 Ibises and Spoonbills Threskiornithidae 33 species (8 ●), 18 genera, e.g. African Spoonbill *Platalea alba*
Description: medium to large long-legged birds with highly modified long bills spoon-shaped (spoonbills), or slender and decurved (ibises). L: 48–110 cm (19–43 in) Wt: 1.4–c.3 kg (3 lb 1 oz–6 lb 10 oz). Neck moderately long, level in flight. Flight strong and direct, wings broad and rounded. Tail short. Front toes webbed at base. May show bare skin on face or head, some crested. Plumage generally white, black, browns or reds. Monomorphic, males often larger. **Range and habitat:** WP, EP, AF, OR, AU, southern NA, NT. Plains, savannah grasslands, swamps and lakeside habitats. **Migration:** some species are strongly nomadic, others migratory. **Breeding:** most nests are colonial. Eggs: 2–5, white

26 Greater Flamingo 28 Hawaiian Goose 23 Californian Condor 30 Bonelli's Eagle 29 Osprey 27 Northern Screamer

or blue, sometimes spotted. Incubation by both or mostly female for 21 days. Broods: 1. Young are altricial, fledge at 20–30 days. **Food:** aquatic animals, some seeds depending on species.

26 Flamingos Phoenicopteridae 5 species (1 ●), 1 genus, e.g. Greater Flamingo *Phoenicopterus ruber*
Description: large, long-lived wading birds with very long legs and necks and highly modified bills adapted for filter feeding. L: 80–145 cm (31–57 in), Wt: 2–3 kg (4 lb 7 oz–6 lb 10 oz). The feet are small, hind toe reduced, front toes fully webbed. Slender, graceful birds, fly rapidly with long neck outstretched, legs trailing behind. The wings are relatively short and pointed. Swim well when necessary. Plumage white to red depending on species and diet. Monomorphic. **Systematics:** Formerly classified in three genera before DNA analysis. **Range and habitat:** WP, EP, AF, OR, NT. Fresh and salt water, shallow lagoons, lakes and estuaries. **Migration:** some migratory. **Breeding:** monogamous. Nest is colonial, of mud. Eggs: 1–2, white. Incubation by both for 28 days. Broods: 1. Young are precocial, cared for by both parents for 75 days and raised on "milk" from parent's crop. **Food:** minute suspended aquatic plants and animals sieved by drawing water through filtering lamellae inside bill using muscular tongue.

WATERFOWL Anseriformes

A well-defined order of semi-aquatic birds in 2 markedly different families. All share round, open nostrils, a feathered preen gland, well-developed down, 11 primaries and no incubation patch.

27 Screamers Anhimidae 3 species, 2 genera, e.g. Northern Screamer *Chauna chavaria*
Description: large, heavy-bodied birds with medium-length neck, crested or spiked head and small fowl-like bill. Medium-heavy legs with large, partially webbed feet to walk on floating vegetation. L:70–90 cm (28–35 in), Wt: 2–5 kg (4 lb 7 oz–11 lb). Bones are highly pneumatized and they have many subcutaneous air sacs. Strong but slow fliers and soarers, the broad, rounded wings carry 2 large spurs at the bend of the wing. Plumage ranges from black to gray, brown. Monomorphic. Rather gregarious. **Range and habitat:** NT. Shallow ponds, marshes, wet grasslands. **Migration:** nonmigratory. **Breeding:** nest is large platform on ground near water built by both parents. Eggs: 4–7, whitish with buff or green tinge. Incubation probably shared, takes 40–5 days. Young are precocial, fledge at 60–70 days. **Food:** largely aquatic plants.

28 Ducks, Geese, and Swans Anatidae 157 species (27 ●), 46 genera, e.g. Hawaiian Goose *Branta sandvicensis*
Description: a large and rather diverse family with at least five sub-families. Small-medium to very large aquatic or semi-aquatic birds. L: 30–150 cm

(12–59 in), Wt: 250 g–15 kg (9 oz–33 lb). Bill usually short, flat, broad, blunt with rounded serrations along edges. Neck medium to very long. Legs short, strong, 4 toes, front toes fully webbed, hind toe reduced, sometimes webbed. Good swimmers and fliers. Wings narrow and pointed. Tail short. Plumage either dimorphic: when female cryptic, male conspicuous; or monomorphic. Plumage highly variable. Most flightless during wing molt. Male may molt into cryptic temporary or "eclipse" plumage at this time. **Range and habitat:** worldwide except AN. Wide variety of habitats, usually near water. **Migration:** many strongly migratory species, especially northern Holarctic breeders. Some have special molt migration. **Breeding:** ritualized display in many species, territorial. Nest is variable, platform of vegetation near water, rocky ledge, tree-holes or crown, often lined with down from female. Eggs: 4–14, white or pale. Incubation by female for 18–39 days. Broods: 1. Young are precocial, fledge at 21–110 days. **Food:** wide range of aquatic plants and animals (mostly invertebrate).

DIURNAL BIRDS OF PREY Falconiformes

A large order of diurnal raptorial birds. 4 families.

29 Osprey Pandionidae *Pandion haliaetus* (monotypic). See p 150.
Description: a large fish-eating hawk which catches fish in its talons. Underside of foot especially rough to aid grip.

30 Hawks and Eagles Accipitridae 236 species (38 ●), 56 genera, e.g. Bonelli's Eagle *Hieraaetus fasciatus*
Description: medium to large diurnal raptors and scavengers. L: 25–115 cm (10–45 in), Wt: 100 g–12.5 kg (3 oz–27 lb 9 oz). Nostrils in bare fleshy cere. Head and neck may be bare in scavengers allowing them to reach into carcass without soiling plumage. Eyesight often exceptional with good binocular vision. Neck usually short. Bill hooked and strong, claws hooked as talons and strong in most, comparatively weak in vultures. Legs medium-sized, tarsus bare. Powerful fliers, especially soaring, wings broad and rounded, often long. Tail medium to long. Mostly monomorphic but females generally larger. Color varied, most browns, black, white and grays. **Range and habitat:** worldwide except AN. A wide variety of habitats. **Migration:** many strongly migratory species, especially Holarctic breeders. **Breeding:** solitary. Nest is a large mass of sticks in a tree or on a cliff ledge. Eggs: 1–7, white or marked with brown. Incubation depending on species: by both male and female (usually female does most of incubating) or female for 32–50 days. Broods: 1. Young are semi-altricial, fledge at 26–120 days. Allocation of parental duties between sexes differs among species. **Food:** a wide range of live animal prey killed with talons, or carrion depending on species.

31 Secretary Bird Sagittariidae *Sagittarius serpentarius* (monotypic). See p 192.
Description: large, long-legged raptors, hunting on foot, weak toes and claws.

31 Secretary Bird   32 Laggar Falcon   36 Hoatzin   34 Great Curassow   33 Malleefowl   35 Common Pheasant

32 Falcons and Caracaras Falconidae 62 species (5 ●), 10 genera, e.g. Laggar Falcon *Falco jugger*
Description: small to large diurnal raptors. L: 15–63 cm (6–25 in), Wt: 110–2 kg (3 oz–4 lb 7 oz). Bill hooked, strong and usually notched. Nostrils in bare fleshy cere. Eye-ring bare. Eyesight often exceptional with good binocular vision. Neck short. Legs medium to long, tarsus bare. Feet strong with sharp talons. Flight often very rapid and expert, wings medium-sized and pointed. Tail medium to long. Plumage varies but usually dull upperparts, paler barred underparts. Males usually brighter and smaller than females. **Range and habitat:** worldwide except AN. A wide variety of habitats. **Migration:** many strongly migratory species, especially Holarctic breeders. **Breeding:** solitary or colonial. Nest is of sticks in tree or on cliff, sometimes old crows' nest. Eggs: 2–6. Incubation by both but mostly by female for 25–49 days. Broods: 1. Young are semi-altricial. Male parent brings most food, female tends young for 25–49 days in nest, 14–60 days after fledging. **Food:** a wide range of live animal prey caught with talons (falcons) or carrion (caracaras).

FOWL-LIKE BIRDS Galliformes

Chickenlike birds. 7 families.

33 Megapodes Megapodiidae 21 species (9 ●), 6 genera, e.g. Malleefowl *Leipoa ocellata*
Description: medium to large ground-dwelling birds with large body, medium to long tail, sometimes vaulted, legs and feet large and strong, 4 toes with strong nails. L: 25–75 cm (10–29 in), Wt: 900 g–8 kg (2 lb–17 lb 10 oz). Head small, bill short, strong and overlapping at tip. 1 crested species, others bare-headed, colored skin, with wattles or casques. Wings short, rounded, rarely fly. Plumage somber, brownish or black. 1 species has pink underparts. **Range and habitat:** OR, AU. Forests and dry scrublands. **Migration:** nonmigratory. **Breeding:** 6–24 eggs are buried in sand, in volcanic ash or in great mound of rotting vegetation. Incubation is achieved by heat from sun or bacterial action. In some species the temperature in the mound is regulated by the male. Young are precocial, receiving no care after hatching. **Food:** wide variety of invertebrates, seeds, fruit and roots.

34 Curassows and Guans Cracidae 50 species (15 ●), 8 genera, e.g. Great Curassow *Crax rubra*
Description: medium to large, the most arboreal Galliformes, feed on ground until disturbed. L: 50–100 cm (20–39 in), Wt: 470 g–4.8 kg (1 lb 1 oz–10 lb 9 oz). Most crested with curved feathers. Some with other head ornaments. Lores bare, throat bare and wattled in some. Bill heavy and bent, sometimes with shiny cere, often with enlarged base to bill. The wings are short, rounded, flight fast but labored. Legs long and strong and the toes heavy, long and with bent claws. Strong runners. Tail long. Most monomorphic, some differ in iris color. Plumage somber browns, black, white. **Range and**

habitat: NT and southern NA. Mostly lowland forest. **Migration:** nonmigratory. **Breeding:** varies between species but mostly nest is simple pile of sticks on tree branch or rarely on the ground. Eggs: 2–3 (rarely 4), large, white, rough or smooth-shelled. Incubation by female for 22–34 days. Young are precocial, flying after 3 or 4 days, fed mostly animal matter. **Food:** largely seeds and fruit, some insects.

35 Pheasants and Partridges Phasianidae (see Systematics below) 211 species (52 ●), 61 genera, e.g. Common Pheasant *Phasianus colchicus*
Description: a large family containing many gamebird and domesticated species and some breathtakingly beautiful forms. Small (quail) to large (turkeys) birds. L: 12–110 cm (4–43 in), Wt: 43 g–18 kg (1 oz–39 lb 11 oz). Feed and nest on ground, most roost in trees. Body bulky, head small with short neck. Bill short, strong, decurved. Head often wattled, sometimes bare. Wings short, round, broad. Strong maneuverable fliers. Tail short, rounded or square to very long, graduated. Some with exaggerated tail or uppertail-coverts (peacock). Legs medium-sized, strong, tarsus sometimes carries 1 or more spurs. 4 toes, strong, hind toe reduced and elevated, adapted for scratching soil and litter. Legs and feet bare or feathered (grouse). Plumage and size monomorphic or strikingly dimorphic with male larger than female. **Systematics:** Formerly classified together as a single family, the Phasianidae, this group has now been split on the basis of DNA evidence as follows: turkeys (Meleagridae 2 spp.), grouse (Tetraonidae 17 spp. 3 ●), new-world quail (Odontophoridae 31 spp. 4 ●), pheasants and partridges (Phasianidae 155 spp. 44 ●) and guineafowl (Numididae 6 spp. 1 ●). These families were formerly recognized as subfamilies of the Phasianidae, and for simplicity, and because of their many morphological similarities, we have continued to group them together here. **Range and habitat:** WP, EP, AF, OR, AU, NA, NT. A wide variety of both open and forest habitats. **Migration:** some migratory species. **Breeding:** there is a great diversity of breeding systems including leks, polygyny and solitary nesting, and ritualized display. Nest is generally a scrape, and is rarely in trees. Eggs: 2–22, whitish, light brown or olive. Incubation by female (rarely both) for 16–28 days. Broods: 1. Young are precocial, tended generally by female (rarely both) for 30–100 days. **Food:** a variety of invertebrates, seeds, fruit and roots.

HOATZIN Opisthocomiformes

36 Hoatzin Opisthocomidae *Opisthocomus hoazin* (monotypic). See p 114.
Description: strangely reminiscent of *Archeopteryx*, the Hoatzin is an extraordinary, large inhabitant of riverine forests of NT. Combination of apparently primitive features such as claws on carpal of young birds, and specialized (derived) features adapted to feeding on tough leaves and fruits of a limited range of plants has led to great debate as to its true evolutionary and systematic relationships. It is certainly advanced rather than primitive. Wt: 700–900 g (1 lb 9 oz–2 lb) **Systematics:** In the past it has variously been included within 8 different orders, including the Gruiformes, Galliformes,

37 Brown Mesite

41 Pale-winged Trumpeter

40 Limpkin

39 Red-crowned Crane

38 Little Buttonquail

42 Common Moorhen

Columbiformes and Cuculiformes, the last of which may be supported by DNA evidence, however we have chosen to recognize its anatomical uniqueness here by treating it as a monotypic order.

CRANES, RAILS, AND ALLIES Gruiformes

A diverse order traditionally (i.e. classified together because they share a number of anatomical characteristics) containing 11 families, ranging from forms similar to Ciconiiformes and Galliformes to others similar to Charadriiformes. Although previously thought probably to be polyphyletic, DNA evidence now largely supports this arrangement (but see buttonquails below).

37 Mesites Mesitornithidae 3 species (3 ●), 2 genera, e.g. Brown Mesite *Mesitornis unicolor*
Description: medium-sized, mostly terrestrial, gregarious birds which run well and take flight only when disturbed. L: 25–8 cm (10–11 in), Wt: c.103–111 g (3–4 oz). Reduced collar bones, fly poorly. Bill slender, straight or decurved. Medium-sized, strong legs and feet, 4 level toes, wings short and rounded, tail rounded, long and broad. Plumage mostly browns and grays with 5 pairs of powder down patches. Monomorphic, or dimorphic with female brighter. Complex social organization and breeding systems but little known. **Range and habitat:** Madagascar (AF). Forests and scrublands. **Migration:** nonmigratory. **Breeding:** rarely observed. Nest is of sticks low in a bush. Eggs: 1–3. Incubation by female, male or both. Young are precocial. **Food:** seeds, insects and some fruit.

38 Buttonquails Turnicidae 16 species (3 ●), 2 genera, e.g. Little Buttonquail *Turnix sylvaticus*
Description: small ground-dwellers characterized by absence of hind toe. L: 11–18 cm (4–7 in), Wt: c.50–80 g (1–2 oz). Superficially like quails (Galliformes). Like true quails, the bill is short and slender, the wings short and rounded, tail very short. No crop, preen gland is feathered, feathers have aftershaft. Plumage brown, gray and black. Monomorphic but females larger, brighter and more aggressive. **Systematics:** DNA evidence has suggested a much earlier origin of the buttonquails, so that they might occupy their own order, the Turniciformes, within a major new group (Parvclass: Turnicae). However, as this is disputed we have not recognized it here. **Range and habitat:** AF, OR, AU, southern WP and EP. Open forest and grasslands. **Migration:** mostly nonmigratory. **Breeding:** reversed, courtship by female. Nest is usually a lined scrape, some more elaborate. Eggs: 4 (rarely 2). Incubation by male for 12–13 days. Young are precocial, tended by male, fledge at c.14 days. **Food:** seeds and insects.

39 Cranes Gruidae 15 species (9 ●), 4 genera, e.g. Red-crowned Crane *Grus japonensis*
Description: large, superficially like Ciconiiformes. L: 76–152 cm (30–60 in), Ht: 90–180 cm (35–71 in), Wt: 2.7–10.5 kg (5 lb 15 oz–23 lb 2 oz). Neck carried level in flight, feet trailing behind. Long neck and legs, terrestrial (never perch in trees). Bill straight, medium to long. Some with bare colored patches on head and neck. Flight powerful and easy. Wings long and broad. Wingspan: 1.5–2.7 m (59–106 in) with elaborate secondaries overhanging tail (which is short) used in display. Feet moderate with 4 toes, hind toe raised. Monomorphic, males larger. Plumage largely white, black, gray and browns. **Range and habitat:** WP, EP, AF, OR, AU, NA. Mostly shallow wetlands (breeding), short grasslands (winter). **Migration:** northern species migratory. **Breeding:** elaborate courtship displays. Nest is usually bulky of aquatic vegetation on marshy ground, rarely placed low in tree. Eggs: 2 (rarely 3–4), oval. Incubation by both for 30–40 days. Broods: 1. Young are precocial, usually only 1 fledged, cared for by both for 55–105 days. **Food:** a wide range of small animals, seeds, fruits, roots.

40 Limpkin Aramidae *Aramus guarauna* (monotypic). See p 60.
Description: medium-sized wading bird with long bill and legs from marshlands of NT and southern NA.

41 Trumpeters Psophiidae 3 species, 1 genus, e.g. Pale-winged Trumpeter *Psophia leucoptera*
Description: medium to large gregarious and noisy birds with small heads, short, stout, curved bills, medium-sized necks and long legs. L: 43–53 cm (17–21 in), Wt: 1–1.5 kg (2 lb 3 oz–3 lb 5 oz). Hind toe reduced and elevated. Fast runners. Tail stumpy. Feed on ground but nest and roost in trees. Wings broad. Laborious flight. Monomorphic. Plumage: chiefly black and velvety, especially on head and neck which have glossy purplish, green or bronze sheen. Outer webs of secondaries and tertials form hairlike filaments over back. **Range and habitat:** NT. Lowland rainforest. **Migration:** nonmigratory. **Breeding:** little information available. Nest is in tree-hole or palm crown. Eggs: 6–10, whitish. Incubation by female. Young are precocial. **Food:** fallen fruit and insects on ground.

42 Rails and Coots Rallidae 134 species (32 ●), 34 genera, e.g. Common Moorhen *Gallinula chloropus*
Description: small to large, mostly secretive (many nocturnal), aquatic or semi-aquatic. L: 10–60 cm (4–24 in), Wt: 30 g–3.3 kg (1 oz–7 lb 4 oz). Most strong fliers, some flightless island endemics (many such flightless species extinct since human arrival). Typically narrow-bodied, legs long and strong, 4 toes, sometimes lobe-webbed. Head may carry a frontal shield, usually colored. Bill short to long, generally strong. Wings rounded, tail short and soft, sometimes almost absent. Flightless during wing molt. Plumage loose in texture. Monomorphic, males sometimes much larger. Colors vary from black and dark blue or purple to browns, reds and grays. Some cryptic spotted patterning. **Range and habitat:** worldwide except AN. A wide variety of wetland habitats, also damp forest and meadows. **Migration:** some strongly migratory species. **Breeding:** often strongly territorial, sometimes with nest-helpers. Nest is a pile of sticks or aquatic vegetation on ground or floating, usually hidden. Eggs: 1–14, variable in color and pattern. Incubation by female or female and male, 20–30 days. Broods: 1–3. Young are precocial, raised by both (rarely female alone), c.60 days. **Food:** small animals, seeds, fruit, and aquatic vegetation depending on species.

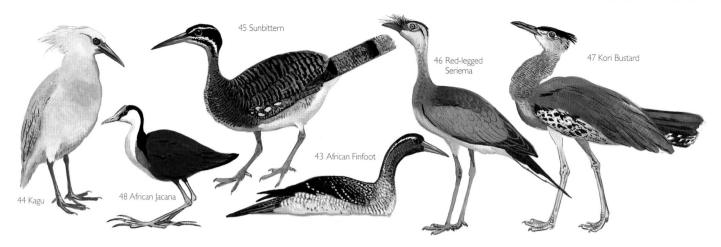

45 Sunbittern

46 Red-legged Seriema

47 Kori Bustard

43 African Finfoot

44 Kagu

48 African Jacana

43 Sungrebes or Finfoots Heliornithidae 3 species (1 ●), 3 genera, e.g. African Finfoot *Podica senegalensis*

Description: distribution indicates antiquity. Medium-large aquatic, elongated body, long neck and pointed bill; short, strong legs. L: 30–60 cm (12–24 in) Wt: 120–880 g (4 oz–2 lb). Toes broadly lobed and brightly colored. Tail long, graduated and stiff. The wings bear a thornlike claw on the first digit of the hand. Plumage rail-like, brownish above, lighter below. Male usually larger and brighter. Solitary, shy, secretive, reminiscent of Anhingidae. Well adapted for diving though usually seen swimming or walking, or perched on branch over water. Flight is labored and close to water. **Range and habitat:** 1 species in each of AF, OR, NT. Tropical forest lakes and rivers. **Migration:** nonmigratory or partially migratory (OR). **Breeding:** nest is shallow twiggy platform lined with leaves on branch just above water. Eggs: 2–4 (rarely 5–6), cream or reddish brown. Incubated by both for 11 days (short for size of bird). Broods: 1. Young are altricial, cared for by both or male who carries them in skin pouches between flank feathers and underwing, even in flight. **Food:** fish, amphibia, aquatic invertebrates, leaves, and seeds.

44 Kagu Rhynochetidae *Rhynochetos jubatus* (monotypic)
● Threatened (only a few hundred remain).
Description: superficially resembles herons (Ardeidae) but recent DNA evidence places it closest to the Sun-bittern (Eurypigidae). L:55 cm (22 in), Wt: 700–1100 g (1 lb 9 oz–2 lb 7 oz). Bill: L: 6.3 cm (2½ in). Bill and legs long, red. The head is loosely and copiously crested and the ash-gray plumage is also generally loose and barred with darker gray and browns. Powerful and beautiful predawn song. Monomorphic, males slightly larger. Wings broad, rounded but short, more or less flightless. Feet strong, hind toe reduced, fast runner. Move in loose flocks. **Range and habitat:** New Caledonia (PA). Dense montane forests, near still water and in rocky ravines. **Migration:** nonmigratory. **Breeding:** nest is thin layer of dead leaves on ground. Eggs: 1, blotched. Probably incubated by both, for 35–40 days. Young are precocial but semi-dependent for nearly 100 days. **Food:** taps ground to find invertebrates, especially earthworms, which it digs up with its strong bill.

45 Sunbittern Eurypygidae *Eurypyga helias* (monotypic). see p 108.
Description: a large, semi-arboreal wading bird from wet forests of Central and South America Wt: 200 g (7 oz). Long legs, bill and neck. Remarkable dance and display.

46 Seriemas Cariamidae 2 species, 2 genera, e.g. Red-legged Seriema *Cariama cristata*
Description: large, ground-dwelling, long legs, small semi-palmate feet (reduced and elevated hind toe). L: 80–90 cm (31–5 in), Wt: 1.2–1.5 kg (2 lb 4 oz–3 lb). Run fast with head down when disturbed, otherwise stalk prey slowly in small flocks. Bill: short, strong, decurved and broad. Bill and legs red or black. Head carries erectile crest (negligible in 1 species). Wings short, rounded, tail long. Flies reluctantly. Plumage is soft and hairy on neck, brownish gray and barred. Underparts paler. More or less monomorphic. **Range and habitat:** NT.

Grasslands and brush forest. **Migration:** nonmigratory. **Breeding:** nest is platform of sticks up to 3 m (10 ft) above ground. Eggs: 2, whitish and blotched. Incubation by both for 25–6 days. Broods: 1. Young are semi-altricial, tended by both in the nest till well grown. **Food:** diverse, but largely fruits and small animals.

47 Bustards Otididae 25 species (5 ●), 9 genera, e.g. Kori Bustard *Ardeotis kori*
Description: large, bulky, ground-dwelling, family includes the heaviest flying bird (Kori Bustard). L: 40–120 cm (16–47 in), Wt: 500 g–18 kg (1 lb 2 oz–39 lb 11oz). Legs stout, hind toe absent. 3 toes broad, nails flattened. Bill usually short, blunt and flattened. Neck long, tail short and wings broad. Wingspan: 1–2.5 m (39–98in). No preen gland, but produce dense powder down. Upperparts generally cryptic, browns, grays, buff, black, white, underparts generally white. Males generally larger, sometimes strikingly so. Males also often brighter. Often gregarious, shy in areas where persecuted for game, otherwise approachable. May take several years to reach maturity. **Range and habitat:** WP, EP, AF, OR, AU. Open plains, grasslands, scrublands. **Migration:** some migratory. **Breeding:** diverse mating systems. Nest is a scrape made by female. Eggs: 1–2 or 2–6 depending on species, olive to reddish. Wt: 41–146 g (1 oz–5 oz). Incubated by female for 20–5 days. Broods: 1. Young are cared for by female for 35–55 days. **Food:** omnivorous.

SHOREBIRDS, GULLS, AUKS Charadriiformes

A diverse group of aquatic/semi-aquatic, often marine birds, often web-footed with reduced and elevated or absent hind toe. The order shows great adaptive diversity of bill form. 19 families.

48 Jacanas Jacanidae 8 species, 6 genera, e.g. African Jacana *Actophilornis africanus*
Description: small to medium-large rail-like (Rallidae) birds with long legs and 4 very long toes. L: 15–30 cm (6–12 in), 1 is 50 cm (20 in), Wt: 40–230 g (1–8 oz). Walks on floating vegetation such as lily pads. Runs, swims and dives well. Wings short, rounded, and carrying a carpal spur, flight labored. Bill short, head sometimes has frontal shield or wattles. Plumage very varied, browns, black, white, greens, yellow, often darker below. Monomorphic but females larger. **Range and habitat:** AF, OR, AU, NT. Lake and riverside marshes. **Migration:** largely nonmigratory, 1 strong migrant. **Breeding:** roles reversed, some polyandrous. Nest is simple platform built by male on floating vegetation. Eggs: 3–4, polished, streaked and lined. Incubated by male for 21–6 days. Broods: 1. Young are precocial, tended by male (carried under wings) for 85–110 days. **Food:** small animals and seeds of aquatic plants.

49 Painted-Snipe Rostratulidae 2 species, 2 genera, e.g. Greater Painted-Snipe *Rostratula benghalensis*
Description: small-medium, long-legged, secretive waders. L: 20–5 cm (8–10 in), Wt: 76–165 g (2–5 oz). Bill medium-sized, L: 36–54 mm (1–2 in) slightly decurved, swollen tip. Wings short, rounded, flight weak. Plumage greens,

50 Crab Plover
54 Eurasian Thick-knee
52 Ibisbill
53 Pied Avocet
51 Eurasian Oystercatcher
49 Painted-Snipe

browns, reds and white in exquisite pattern, round yellow spots on wing feathers shown in display. Females brighter and larger, otherwise similar. **Range and habitat:** EP, AF, OR, AU, NT. Reedy swamps and paddy-fields. **Migration:** locally or partially migratory. **Breeding:** depending on species, females may be polyandrous. Nest is pad of woven plant material built by male in dense cover. Eggs: 1–2 or 4 (rarely 5–6) depending on species, cream to buff, spotted black and brown. Incubation by male, possibly also female, for 19 days. Young are precocial, tended by male. **Food:** small swamp invertebrates and seeds.

50 Crab Plover Dromadidae *Dromus ardeola* (monotypic). See p 202.
Description: unusual, medium-large, long-legged, black and white wader with massive, compressed, heronlike bill. Wt: 230–325 g (8–11 oz). Coasts of Indian Ocean.

51 Oystercatchers Haematopodidae 11 species (1 ●), 1 genus, e.g. Eurasian Oystercatcher *Haematopus ostralegus*
Description: large black or pied waders with long, straight, powerful red bill which varies with diet. L: 40–5 cm (16–18 in), Wt: 400–700 g (14 oz–1 lb 8 oz). Monomorphic but female usually larger with longer bill than male. **Range and habitat:** WP, EP, AF, OR, AU, NA, NT. Variety of coastal habitats, sometimes inland. **Migration:** some strongly migratory, most movements local or sedentary. **Breeding:** nest is a scrape. Eggs: 2–4, cryptic. Incubation shared for 24–7 days. Broods: 1. Young are precocial, fledge at 35–42 days. **Food:** invertebrates, chiefly bivalves.

52 Ibisbill Ibidorhynchidae *Ibidorhyncha struthersii* (monotypic). See p 248.
Description: unusual medium-large wader with long, decurved red bill. Found in mountain riverbeds above 1,700 m (5,500 ft) in central southern Asia. Wt: 270–320 g (9 oz–11 oz) **Systematics:** DNA evidence suggests that this species might be a highly modified form of stilt, and therefore can be placed in the Recurvirostridae.

53 Avocets and Stilts Recurvirostridae 10 species (1 ●), 3 genera, e.g. Pied Avocet *Recurvirostra avosetta*
Description: medium-sized waders with long, slender legs and bills, straight (stilts) or upcurved (avocets). L: 30–50 cm (12–20 in), Wt: 140–435 g (5–15 oz). Wings long and pointed, tail short, 3 toes partly webbed, hind toe vestigial. Plumage chiefly white, black, gray, brown. Monomorphic. **Range and habitat:** WP, EP, AF, OR, AU, NA, NT. Open marshes near fresh and brackish water. **Migration:** northern populations migratory. **Breeding:** colonial. Nest is a scrape. Eggs: 4 (rarely 2–5), cryptic. Incubation by both for 22–8 days. Broods: 1. Young are precocial, fledge at 28–42 days. **Food:** aquatic invertebrates and small vertebrates. Feeds by sweeping water with bill (avocets) or probing (stilts).

54 Thick-knees Burhinidae 9 species, 1 genus, e.g. Eurasian Thick-knee *Burhinus oedicnemus*
Description: medium to large semi-aquatic waders with large head and very

large yellow or orange eyes (partially nocturnal). L: 32–55 cm (13–22 in), Wt: c.1 kg (2lb 3oz). Bill medium to large, L: 33–79 cm (13–31 in), straight or upcurved, stout to massive, according to ecology. Wings long, broad, rounded and boldly patterned, strong flight. Legs long and thick. 3 partially webbed toes. Ecologically similar to bustards (Otidae). Plumage generally brown, streaked and cryptic. Monomorphic. **Range and habitat:** WP, AF, OR, AU, NT. Open, sparsely vegetated sites both near water and in arid or semiarid areas. **Migration:** northern populations migratory, nomadic in tropics. **Breeding:** nest is a shallow scrape. Eggs: 2, whitish to brown. Incubation shared, 25–7 days. Broods: 1, rarely 2. Young are precocial with large legs, attended by both parents for c.40 days. **Food:** small vertebrates, terrestrial and coastal invertebrates, partly depending on species.

55 Coursers and Pratincoles Glareolidae 17 species (2 ●), 5 genera, e.g. Black-winged Pratincole *Glareola nordmanni*
Description: extraordinary medium-sized waders in 2 distinct groups: coursers—long-legged, ground-dwellers, 3 toes, run fast, rarely fly, bill medium-sized, thin, decurved, tail short, square; pratincoles—short-legged, strong fliers, long, pointed wings, forked tail, swallowlike, bill short, stout, wide gape. L: 15–30 cm (6–12 in), Wt: 70–100 g (2½–3½ oz). Plumage browns, white, black and grays. Monomorphic. **Range and habitat:** WP, EP, AF, OR, AU. Arid or semiarid open or sparsely scrubby areas, usually near water. **Migration:** generally nomadic outside breeding season. **Breeding:** nest is a scrape. Eggs: 2–3, cryptic. Incubation by female or shared, 17–31 days. Broods: 1. Young are precocial, fledge at 25–35 days. **Food:** insects and some other invertebrates, aerial insects in pratincoles.

56 Plovers Charadriidae 67 species (8 ●), 11 genera, e.g. Ringed Plover *Charadrius hiaticula*
Description: small to medium, semi-aquatic, compact, thick neck, large eyes. L: 14–41 cm (5–16 in), Wt: 34–296 g (1¼–10½ oz). Bill short to medium, stout, straight. Wings long, pointed, sometimes spurred at carpal, flight strong and fast. Tail short, legs medium to long. Hind toe vestigial or absent. Fast runners. Plumage variable, contrasting, black, white, grays, browns, yellows, greens. Monomorphic, males often brighter (sometimes female). **Systematics:** Note that on DNA evidence, the Magellanic Plover *Pluvianellus socialis* may be elevated to its own, montypic, family: Pluvianellidae, but this is disputed. **Range and habitat:** worldwide except AN. Wide variety of coastal and inland open habitats. **Migration:** most species are strongly migratory. **Breeding:** varied mating systems: monogamy, polyandry, sex reversal, polygyny. Nest is a scrape. Eggs: 4 (rarely 2–5), cryptic. Incubation shared (or male or female) for 18–38 days. Broods: 1–3. Young are precocial, fledge at 21–42 days. **Food:** wide range of invertebrates, some plant matter.

57 Sandpipers and Snipe Scolopacidae 87 species (10 ●), 22 genera, e.g. Dunlin *Calidris alpina*
Description: small to large waders. L: 13–66 cm (5–26 in), Wt: 18–1,040 g

58 Plains Wanderer
57 Dunlin
56 Ringed Plover
60 Snowy Sheathbill
59 Rufous-bellied Seedsnipe
55 Black-winged Pratincole

(¾ oz–2 lb 5 oz). Short-medium to very long, straight or curved bill and medium to very long legs. Bill and leg length related to ecology. Generally monomorphic but females usually larger with longer bill than male. Plumage browns, grays and reds and often with distinct breeding plumage. **Range and habitat:** worldwide except AN. Wide variety of coastal and inland open habitats, usually near water. **Migration:** many Arctic breeders and most species strongly migratory. **Breeding:** mostly monogamous, also leks and polygamy. Nest is a scrape, in grass tussock or rarely in tree-hole. Eggs: 4 (rarely 2–3), cryptic. Incubation by female or shared by male and female for 18–30 days. Broods: 1, rarely 2. Young are precocial, fledge at 16–50 days. **Food:** wide range of invertebrates, rarely some plant matter.

58 Plains Wanderer Pedionomidae *Pedionomus torquatus* (monotypic ●)
Description: like buttonquails but foot with 4 toes though hind toe reduced and raised slightly. Also differences in internal anatomy which cause doubt of its correct taxonomic position—some grouping it with buttonquails, others taking it out from the Gruiformes altogether. Female much larger and brighter. L: male: 150 cm (59 in), female: 170 cm (67 in), Wt: 40–95 g (1–3 oz). Plumage reds and browns, cryptic. Legs longer than buttonquails, bill weaker and moderate length. Wings short and round, tail very short. Flies reluctantly with whirring flight. Often stands elevated on toes. **Range and habitat:** AU. Short grasslands. **Migration:** probably nomadic. **Breeding:** nest is scantily lined depression on ground. Eggs: 3–4, white and blotched. Incubated by male for 23 days. Young are precocial, raised by male. **Food:** invertebrates, seeds, and other vegetable matter.

59 Seedsnipe Thinocoridae 4 species, 2 genera, e.g. Rufous-bellied Seedsnipe *Attagis gayi*
Description: small to medium-sized, ground-dwelling, gregarious. L: 15–27 cm (6–10 in), Wt: 60–400 g (2–14 oz). Plump, short legs. Bill short, stout, conical, nostril protected by shieldlike covers. Wings long, pointed. Flight strong, agile, fast. Tail medium-sized. Hind toe short, front toes long. Plumage generally browns, grays, cryptic. Monomorphic, males brighter. **Range and habitat:** NT. Sparsely vegetated highlands and fields. **Migration:** some species migratory. **Breeding:** nest is a lined scrape. Eggs: 4, cryptic. Incubation by female, c.26 days. Eggs covered by female on departure. Young are precocial, fly at 49 days. **Food:** seeds, succulent vegetation, and some insects.

60 Sheathbills Chionididae 2 species, 1 genus, e.g. Snowy Sheathbill *Chionis alba*
Description: medium-sized, pigeonlike shorebirds most closely related to Lari. L: 38–41 cm (15–16 in), Wt: 290–550 g (10 oz–1 lb 3 oz). Named after saddle-shaped, horny, yellowish sheath covering the base of the short, stout bill. Generally found in association with penguin colonies. Generally walk on ground. Fly and swim strongly. Legs short, strong. Front toes slightly webbed, hind toe reduced, elevated. Plumage pure white, monomorphic. Gregarious, very social and tame. **Range and habitat:** AN. Rocky coasts. **Migration:** locally nomadic. **Breeding:** solitary, though still feeding socially.

Nest is well hidden in rock crevices. Eggs: 2–4, brown, flecked. Incubation shared by male and female for 28–32 days. Broods: 1. Young are precocial, fledge at 50–60 days. Most pairs raise only 1 or 2 chicks. **Food:** omnivorous, especially scavenging.

61 Jaegers Stercorariidae 7 species, 2 genera, e.g. Parasitic Jaeger *Stercorarius parasiticus* (see illustration p 28.)
Description: medium to large, slender to bulky. L: 40–60 cm (16–24 in), Wt: 250 g–1.9 kg (9 oz–4 lb 3 oz). Bill strong, hooked, nostrils in cere. Wings long, pointed. Flight strong, fast, stiffer-winged than gulls, light and agile to heavy. Tail medium to long with elongated central tail feathers—generally longer in the lighter species. Legs medium-sized. 4 toes, 3 webbed, hind toe reduced and elevated. Lighter species white with dark upperparts (light and dark phases), heavy species uniform brown. White primary bases show in flight. Monomorphic. **Range and habitat:** oceans worldwide. Marine, breeds on tundra and barren coasts. **Migration:** strongly migratory or nomadic. **Breeding:** monogamous, pairing for life, or rarely polygamous, rarely colonial. Nest is a scrape. Eggs: 2 (rarely 1, 3. Clutches of 3 rarely hatch as skuas have 2 brood patches). Cryptic. Incubation shared for 30 days. Broods: 1. Young are semi-precocial, fledge at 45–55 days. **Food:** wide range offish, Crustacea, small mammals, eggs and young of other birds, also kleptoparasites of terns and other seabirds.

62 Gulls and Terns Laridae 95 species (9 ●), 13 genera, e.g. Black-legged Kittiwake *Rissa tridactyla* (see illustration p 28.)
Description: generally white to gray, often with darker head and black wing tips. 3 webbed toes, hind toe reduced. Monomorphic, males larger. Wings long, pointed, flight strong. Distinct immature and subadult plumages. **Systematics:** Although DNA evidence for this is equivocal, some recent classifications recognise two families: the Gulls (Laridae 51 spp. 6 ●): medium to large, more bulky, good swimmers, tail generally medium-sized, squarish. L: 25–78 cm (10–31 in), Wt: 90 g–2 kg (3¼ oz–4 lb 7 oz). Bill heavy, hooked, medium-sized; and the Terns (Sternidae 44 spp. 3 ●): small to large-sized, more slender, swim rarely. L: 20–56 cm (8–22 in), Wt: 50–700 g (1¾–1 lb 8½ oz). Tail generally forked, medium to long, flight more buoyant, bill long, more slender, pointed. **Range and habitat:** coasts worldwide (fewer in tropics). **Migration:** many strongly migratory species (especially terns), the Arctic Tern, p 162, migrating further than any other species. **Breeding:** colonial. Nest is a lined scrape or grassy platform on cliff ledge. Eggs: 1–4, cryptic. Incubation shared for 18–35 days. Broods: 1, Young are precocial, fledge at 21–56 days. **Food:** omnivorous, including scavenging and kleptoparasitism, (gulls) or fish (terns—caught by plunge-diving).

63 Skimmers Rhynchopidae 3 species (1 ●), 1 genus, e.g. Black Skimmer *Rhynchops niger*
Description: large, ternlike birds with specialized bill. L: 40–50 cm (16–20 in), Wt: 300–400 g (10½–14 oz). Bill straight, deep, blunt and laterally compressed,

63 Black Skimmer

61 Parasitic Jaeger

65 Black-bellied Sandgrouse

64 Brunnich's Guillemot

62 Black-legged Kittiwake

lower mandible up to 25% longer than upper (see Food). Unique among birds in that in bright light the pupil of the eye closes to a vertical slit. Wings long, pointed, broad-based. Flight powerful. Tail short to medium, forked. 3 toes webbed, small. Plumage dark gray to brown upperparts, white underparts. Monomorphic, males 25% larger: **Systematics:** DNA evidence suggests a very close affinity with the Laridae, in which they might be included. **Range and habitat:** AF, OR, NT. Sheltered sandy coasts, estuaries and large rivers. **Migration:** partly migratory. **Breeding:** colonial. Nest is a scrape on ground. Eggs: 3 or 4, cryptic. Incubation shared for 21 days. Young are precocial, 25–30 days. Young fly at about 35 days by which time the difference between mandibles is sufficient for them to feed. **Food:** chiefly small fish, also aquatic invertebrates. Fish caught by flying low over water with lower mandible cutting surface. This is snapped shut and up on contact with prey.

64 Auks Alcidae 23 species (5 ●), 10 genera, e.g. Brunnich's Guillemot *Uria lomvia*
Description: small to medium-large seabirds with bulky, compact bodies, short necks, small, pointed wings. L: 16–45 cm (6½–18 in), Wt: 90 g–l kg (3¼ oz–2 lb 3 oz). Powerful flight with rapid wingbeat due to heavy wing loading. Legs short, strong, set far back—especially in cliff-ledge nesters which shuffle on tarsi rather than walking. 3 webbed toes often with sharp claws, no hind toe. Strong swimmers and divers (using wings under water), some diving to great depths to fish. Bills diverse, always strong, pointed and shallow (e.g. guillemot) to blunt and very deep (e.g. puffins). Bill may vary seasonally with bright or contrasting bill sheath developed in breeding season, lost after breeding. Plumage generally dark gray or black upperparts, white underparts. Head sometimes crested. Monomorphic. **Range and habitat:** northern oceans and coasts outside tropics worldwide. Mostly off rocky coasts. **Migration:** partly migratory or nomadic. **Breeding:** most are colonial. Nest on cliff ledges, in rock crevices or burrows. Eggs: 1–2, white, ovoid (burrows) or cryptic, pear-shaped (ledge nesters), Wt:16–110 g (½–3¾ oz), incubated by female or shared for 29–42 days. Broods: 1. Young are precocial or semi-precocial, nestling period very variable depending on species' ecology: 2–50 days. **Food:** fish and crustacea.

SANDGROUSE Pterocliformes

Chunky land birds with long, pointed wings, short legs, small feet, small heads and bills. Limited distribution of down. Young fed by regurgitation. 1 family formerly included within the Columbiformes.

65 Sandgrouse Pteroclididae 16 species, 2 genera, e.g. Black-bellied Sandgrouse *Pterocles orientalis*
Description: medium-sized, ground-dwelling, long, plump-bodied birds with powerful, straight flight. L: 27–48 cm (10½–19 in), Wt: 150–400 g (5¼–14 oz). Short, feathered legs. Toes short, sometimes partially webbed. Fast runners. Hind toe reduced or absent. Body and bill base insulated by dense

down undercoat. Tail pointed, often with very long center tail feathers. Plumage: dimorphic, males cryptic upperparts of barred browns, grays, orange; underparts banded black, chestnut or white. Females smaller and barred, more cryptic. Highly gregarious. **Range and habitat:** southern WP and EP, AF, OR. Sandy or rocky deserts and sparsely vegetated plains. **Migration:** some migrate irruptively. **Breeding:** nest is a scrape. Eggs: 3, cryptic. Incubation shared (male at night): 21–31 days. Broods: 1–3. Young are precocial, fly at 28–35 days. Males provide water to chicks by soaking modified belly feathers in water and carrying it to chicks which drink directly from these. **Food:** chiefly small seeds, also some other plant matter and small invertebrates. Drinks by sucking water into bill.

PIGEONS Columbiformes

Chunky land birds with long, pointed wings, short legs, small feet, small heads and bills. Limited distribution of down. Young fed by regurgitation. 1 large family.

66 Doves and Pigeons Columbidae 308 species (59 ●), 40 genera, e.g. Rock Dove *Columba livia*
Description: small to large, arboreal and/or ground-dwelling, generally plump-bodied with powerful, straight flight. L: 15–82 cm (6–32 in), Wt: 30 g–2.4 kg (1–5 lb 5 oz). Nostrils in fleshy cere. Legs and feet short. 4 level, bare and unwebbed toes. Tail short, square to long, pointed. Plumage highly varied in color and pattern, some crested. Most monomorphic. **Range and habitat:** worldwide except far northern latitudes and AN; many island endemic species have gone extinct since arrival of humans. Mostly forest and scrublands, some in more open habitats and cliffs. **Migration:** some (especially northern) species strongly migratory. **Breeding:** nest is twig platform, sometimes in tree-hole. Eggs: 2 (rarely 1), white. Incubation shared for 14–28 days. Broods: 2–3. Young are altricial or semi-altricial, in nest up to 35 days fed on pigeon "milk," formed from sloughed cells of the crop lining. This allows many species to have protracted breeding seasons. **Food:** vegetable matter: fruit, leaves, and seeds.

PARROTS AND ALLIES Psittaciformes

Tropical land birds defined by: powerful hooked bill with cere, upper mandible articulates with skull, short tarsus covered in granular scales, 4 toes—2 front, 2 hind (zygodactyl), distinctive distribution of feathers and molt. Often long-lived and some good mimics. Eggs: white, incubated for 16–32 days. Young altricial in nest: 21–90 days. In some classifications, based on DNA evidence, the family Psittacidae is enlarged by inclusion of the lories or of all three of the families recognized here. We have chosen to split them to emphasize their distinct morphological differences.

67 Cockatoos Cacatuidae 21 species (6 ●), 6 genera, e.g. Sulfur-crested Cockatoo *Cacatua galerita*
Description: medium to large parrots, simply colored, white to blackish, pinks

70 Green Turaco

69 Rose-ringed Parakeet

68 Black-capped Lory

66 Rock Dove

67 Sulfur-crested Cockatoo

and yellow with an erectile crest, sometimes very large. L: 33–69 cm (13–27 in), Wt: 280 g–1 kg (10 oz–2 lb 3 oz). Bill medium to massive with thick, fleshy tongue. Some with a brightly colored bare facial patch. Wings long, pointed. Tail medium-sized, square or rounded. Monomorphic or dimorphic, male larger. Some highly gregarious, noisy. **Range and habitat:** OR, AU, PA. A wide variety of forest, scrub and grassland habitats. **Migration:** generally nonmigratory or nomadic, some partly migratory. **Breeding:** nest is a tree-hollow. Eggs: 1–3. Incubation shared for c.30 days. Young in nest for up to 90 days. **Food:** a wide range of plant matter, fruits, buds, shoots, seeds, corms, and some invertebrates.

68 Lories Loridae 52 species (12 ●), 12 genera, e.g. Black-capped Lory *Lorius lory*
Description: small to medium parrots much modified for feeding on nectar and pollen on which they specialize. L:15–32 cm (6–13 in), Wt: 45–260 g (1 oz–9 oz). The tongue is modified and brush-tipped allowing them to reach into flowers. In so doing, they are important pollinators for some plant species. The gut is also modified. Wings medium-sized, pointed, flight fast, direct. Tail short, square to long, pointed. Plumage bright greens, reds, blues in bold patches. Monomorphic. Noisy and social. **Systematics:** This family is sometimes included within the Psittacidae, but we feel that the distinct anatomy, associated with their distinct diet, justifies the treatment given here. **Range and habitat:** OR, AU, PA. A wide variety of forest and scrubland habitats including gardens. **Migration:** many species migratory or nomadic. **Breeding:** little known, solitary or colonial. Nest is generally a tree-hole. Eggs: 2–4. Incubation by female. **Food:** nectar, pollen, plant shoots, and fruits.

69 Parrots Psittacidae 279 species (75 ●), 65 genera, e.g. Rose-ringed Parakeet *Psittacula krameri*
Description: a diverse family of small to large parrots including 1 flightless form (Kakapo). L: 9–100 cm (3½–39 in), Wt: 11 g–1.7 kg (½ oz–3 lb 13 oz). Wings medium-sized, rounded to long, pointed. Tail short, square to very long, pointed. Bill small to massive, with thick fleshy tongue. Lores often bare. Plumage varied and gaudy greens, reds, blues, yellows in bold patches. Generally monomorphic or male larger. Solitary to highly social, noisy. **Range and habitat:** AF, OR, AU, NT. A wide variety of forest, scrub and grassland habitats. **Migration:** most nonmigratory. **Breeding:** nest is generally a tree-hollow. Eggs: 1–12. Incubation by female, 17–35 days. Young in nest for 21–70 days. **Food:** a wide range of plant matter, fruits, buds, shoots, seeds, corms, and some invertebrates.

CUCKOOS AND ALLIES Cuculiformes

Land birds defined by: 4 toes—2 front, 2 hind (zygodactyl), 8–10 tail feathers, upper mandible unmovable, not hooked, no cere.

70 Turacos Musophagidae 23 species (2 ●), 6 genera, e.g. Green Turaco *Tauraco persa*
Description: medium to large, elongated arboreal birds. L: 35–75 cm (14–29 in),

Wt: 230–950 g (8 oz–2 lb 1 oz). Bill short, stout, pointed with diverse location and shape of nostril. Head small, often crested, neck medium-sized. Wings short and rounded, flight weak, tail long and broad. Legs medium-sized, walks with great agility through tree canopy. Plumage soft, variously: greens, blues, reds, white, brown and gray. Monomorphic. **Range and habitat:** AF. Dense forests and forest edge. **Migration:** nonmigratory. **Breeding:** nest is a flat platform of twigs at 5–20 m (16–66 ft) height. Eggs: 2–3, glossy white or pale green/blue. Incubation shared for 21–4 days. Young are semi-altricial with well-developed carpal claw, leave nest after 10–12 days, fly after about 30 days. **Food:** chiefly fruit, also seeds, buds, and invertebrates.

71 Cuckoos Cuculidae 138 species (9 ●), 28 genera, e.g. Great Spotted Cuckoo *Clamator glandarius* (see illustration p 30.)
Description: a diverse family of medium to large arboreal or rarely ground-dwelling (roadrunner) birds, including many nest parasites, especially in Old World (1 in New World). L: 17–65 cm (6–26 in), Wt: 30–700 g (1 lb–1 lb 8 oz). Slender birds with long tail. Legs short to medium. Bill stout, medium-sized, decurved, pointed, sometimes deep. Plumage generally streaked grays, browns, sometimes black, green or yellow. Most monomorphic. **Systematics:** DNA evidence suggests a deeper split than recognized here, placing the New World cuckoos and anis, and Old World coucals in their own families: Coccizidae, Croptophagidae and Centropodidae respectively. On the basis of DNA evidence, the Hoatzin, here recognized as a distinct order, is probably a highly modified cuculiform. **Range and habitat:** a variety of woodland, scrub and marsh habitats. **Migration:** northern species strongly migratory. **Breeding:** nest is a simple platform of sticks in tree or on ground, or that of host. Eggs: 10–15, possibly more, in parasitic species, color often mimics that of host eggs, very small relative to body-size in parasites. In nonparasites, 2–5, bluish or whitish. Incubation shared or by host for 11–16 days. Young are altricial, fledge at 16–24 days, may kill or evict host young or unhatched eggs in nest. **Food:** chiefly insects, especially prey considered toxic by other birds (e.g. hairy caterpillars). In some species also small vertebrates and plant matter.

OWLS Strigiformes

Raptorial species, often nocturnal with many adaptations for silent hunting, e.g. exceptional hearing, soft plumage allowing silent flight. Large eyes, face forward, set in facial disc, cannot move within socket. Feet strong with sharp claws. 4 toes, the last reversible. Bill short, strongly hooked. Resemblance to raptors (Falconiformes) is superficial. 2 families.

72 Barn Owls Tytonidae 16 species (5 ●), 2 genera, e.g. Barn Owl *Tyto alba*
Description: medium-sized owls with characteristic heart-shaped facial disc and relatively small eyes but mainly nocturnal. L: 23–53 cm (9–21 in), Wt:180–1,280 g (6½ oz–2 lb 13 oz). Head large, body slender but loose plumage gives deceptive impression of size. Legs long, tarsus feathered but feet bare, middle toe has comb claw. Wings very broad, rounded, hence light,

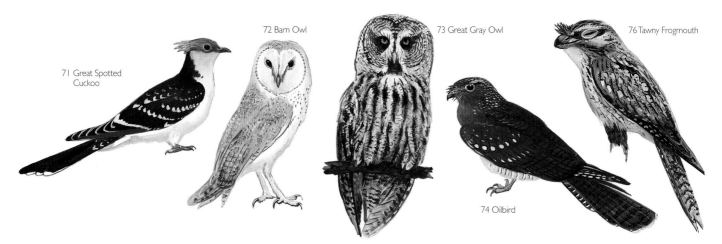

71 Great Spotted Cuckoo

72 Barn Owl

73 Great Gray Owl

76 Tawny Frogmouth

74 Oilbird

buoyant flight. Tail medium-sized, shorter than legs, feathers emarginated, primary flight feathers not emarginated. Plumage brown to golden brown, gray above, whitish underparts. Monomorphic but females often larger. **Range and habitat:** WP, AF, OR, AU, NA, NT. A variety of forest and open (including cultivated) habitats. **Migration:** largely nonmigratory. **Breeding:** nest is in tree-hole, building or ground, will use nestboxes. Eggs: 4–7, white. Incubation by female for 27–34 days. Broods: 1–2. Young are semi-altricial in nest, fledge at 49–56 days. **Food:** a wide range of small vertebrates caught with talons and generally swallowed whole, also large insects.

73 Owls Strigidae 188 species (23 ●), 25 genera, e.g. Great Gray Owl *Strix nebulosa*
Description: small to large owls with both nocturnal and diurnal forms. L:12–71 cm (4½–28 in), Wt: 40 g–4 kg (1½ oz–8 lb 13 oz). Eyes very large. Facial disk(s) rounded. Head large, sometimes carries ear-tufts. Legs medium to long but shorter than tail, tarsus and often feet feathered, except in fishing species which have roughened feet. Claws often very long. Arboreal and ground-dwelling species. Flight strong and silent on large, broad wings. Flight feathers fringed to reduce sound, especially in nocturnal species. Plumage soft, dense, gives false impression of size, generally cryptic mottled and barred browns, grays. Monomorphic, female often larger. **Range and habitat:** worldwide except AN. A wide range of forest, grassland, desert and tundra habitats. **Migration:** most species sedentary. **Breeding:** nest is in tree-hollows or old nests of other birds, e.g. crows (Corvidae). Eggs: 1–7, white. Incubation by female or shared for 15–35 days. Broods: 1. Young are semi-altricial, in nest for 24–52 days but may leave nest before they can fly. **Food:** a wide range of small vertebrates including fish, also earthworms and large insects. Prey caught with talons, generally swallowed whole.

NIGHTJARS AND ALLIES Caprimulgiformes

A well-defined (natural) order of nocturnal or crepuscular, mostly insectivorous, cryptic birds with very wide gape. Flight light and batlike. Feet small and weak. Intermediate in form (and systematic order) between owls and swifts. 5 families. DNA evidence indicates a common ancestor with the owls, with which they may be classified.

74 Oilbird Steatornithidae *Steatornis caripensis* (monotypic). See p 116.
Description: a largely frugivorous species, with a longer and more decurved bill than others of the order, but still retaining the rictal bristles indicative of its insectivorous ancestry. Wt: 350–485 g (12½ oz–1 lb 1 oz). The Oilbird is the only nocturnal frugivorous bird. It breeds in large, noisy colonies in caves on Trinidad and NT.

75 Owlet-nightjars Aegothelidae 9 species (1 ●), 1 genus, e.g. Mountain Owlet-nightjar *Aegotheles albertisi*
Description: small to medium, solitary, nocturnal birds closely related to

frogmouths (Podargidae). L: 20–30 cm (8–12 in), Wt: 45–115 g (1½–4 oz). The bill is similar to frogmouths but smaller and weaker and is largely hidden by forehead feathering. Includes rictal bristles. Plumage cryptic, generally like frogmouths but includes many stiff, partly erectile filoplumes on forehead and lores, and some on chin. Wings long, rounded. Flight strong and direct. Tail long and pointed. Feet small and weak, toes and claws long, slender, lacking comb-claw. Foraging seems intermediate between frogmouths and nightjars, and includes both hawking and (probably a majority) ground feeding. Monomorphic. **Range and habitat:** AU. Tropical forest, also scrublands in Australia. **Migration:** nonmigratory. **Breeding:** little known. Nest is in tree-hollow. Eggs: 3–4, white. Young are semi-altricial. **Food:** aerial insects and ground invertebrates.

76 Frogmouths Podargidae 12 species, 2 genera, e.g. Tawny Frogmouth *Podargus strigoides*
Description: medium to large with broad, rounded wings and tail, the latter longish. L: 23–54 cm (9–21 in), Wt: 130–600 g (4 oz–1 lb 5 oz). Owl-like patterning, superb cryptic coloration of browns and grays. Eyes very large and colored in some. Flight strong for short periods. The bill is boat-shaped with a huge gape and rictal bristles which led to the earlier belief that they hunted aerial insects on the wing. However, this is not the case: most prey are caught on the ground or from branches. Despite apparent evidence of their ancestry from nightjars, there are numerous internal anatomical differences such as the number of cervical vertebrae, toe bones, type of syrinx and palate. Feet small with long middle toe (3 forward, 1 hind). Monomorphic. At roost during the day some adopt a posture making best use of their crypsis and mimicking a broken branch. **Range and habitat:** OR, AU. Mostly tropical forest. **Migration:** partly migratory. **Breeding:** nest is a platform of sticks and feathers on a horizontal bough of a tree. Eggs: 1–3, white. Incubation by female or shared for 30 days. Young are semi-altricial, in nest for 30 days. **Food:** chiefly insects but according to species; also small vertebrates.

77 Potoos Nyctibiidae 7 species, 1 genus, e.g. Common Potoo *Nyctibius griseus*
Description: medium to large, long, slender birds. L: 23–50 cm (9–20 in), Wt: 45–620 g (1 oz–1 lb 6 oz). Solitary, nocturnal. Small bill is terminally decurved. Has a tooth on the edge of the upper mandible. Lacks rictal bristles. The mouth is very large. Eyes very large, iris sometimes yellow or dark brown but reflecting orange at night. Wings long and rounded, tail long and pointed. Legs very short. Feet small and weak, toes long and slender, lacking comb-claw. Highly cryptic plumage of browns and grays. Monomorphic. Flight strong and direct. **Range and habitat:** NT and southern NA. Forest. **Migration:** nonmigratory. **Breeding:** little known. Nest is a small depression in tree-hollow. Eggs: 1 (rarely 2), white. Incubated in rather upright posture for at least 33 days. Young are semi-altricial, leave nest at c.25 days but fly at 47–51 days. **Food:** aerial insects.

77 Common Potoo

75 Mountain Owlet-nightjar

79 Alpine Swift

81 Sword-billed Hummingbird

80 Crested Tree Swift

78 African Dusky Nightjar

78 Nightjars Caprimulgidae 89 species (7 ●), 15 genera, e.g. African Dusky Nightjar *Caprimulgus pectoralis*
Description: medium-sized, mostly solitary, nocturnal or crepuscular. L: 19–29cm (7–11in), Wt: 40–120g (1–4oz). Head flattened. Bill short, weak with very wide gape and usually also rictal bristles. Eyes large. Legs short, sometimes feathered. Wings long, pointed. Flight light, agile, batlike. Tail medium to long, square or forked. 2 species with long pennant feathers on wing or tail. Feet small, weak with comb-claw on middle toe. Plumage cryptic, barred browns and grays. Often dimorphic, males having white patches shown in display flight. 1 species hibernates. **Range and habitat:** worldwide except far northern Holarctic and AN. A wide variety of forest, scrub, and semiarid habitats. **Migration:** some species strongly migratory, migrating in loose flocks. **Breeding:** nest is on ground, no material. Eggs: 1–2, cryptic, white to pinkish, marbled or blotched black, brown or violet. Incubation shared for 16–19 days. Broods: 1–2. Young are semi-altricial, in nest for 16–20 days. **Food:** aerial insects.

SWIFTS AND HUMMINGBIRDS Apodiformes

An uneasy grouping of species in 2 natural groups or suborders (Apodi and Trochili) i.e. sharing many well-defined or unique characteristics. All are highly agile fliers with small feet but there are many internal differences between the suborders, and DNA evidence suggests two order: Apodiformes and Trochiliformes. 3 families in 2 suborders or orders.

79 Swifts Apodidae 98 species (6 ●), 18 genera, e.g. Alpine Swift *Tachymarptis melba*
Description: small to medium, fast-flying aerial birds with long, scythe-shaped wings, and short to medium-sized forked tails, sometimes spiny. L: 10–30 cm (4–12 in), Wt: 9–150g (¼–5¼ oz). Feet tiny with very sharp, curved claws. Many have reversible hind toe and perch with difficulty. Bill very small but gape wide. Body slender and short-necked. Plumage dense, dark browns, black and sometimes white throat, flanks or rump. Monomorphic. Often gregarious and noisy with screaming display flights. Probably the most aerial of birds, even copulation taking place on the wing. **Range and habitat:** worldwide except high latitudes, PA and AN. Aerial feeders coming to rest only to nest. **Migration:** many long-distance migrants. **Breeding:** solitary or colonial, some with nest-helpers. Nest is aerial flotsam cemented together with saliva. The nest of 1 species considered edible. Eggs: 1–6, white. Incubation shared for 17–28 days. Broods: 1–2. Young are altricial, in nest for 34–72 days, becoming torpid when conditions are unfavorable for the parents to hunt. **Food:** aerial insects.

80 Tree Swifts Hemiprocnidae 4 species, 1 genus, e.g. Crested Tree Swift *Hemiprocne longipennis*
Description: small to medium swifts, less highly adapted to an aerial lifestyle than the Apodidae, and superficially resembling swallows (Hirundinidae) because of their outer tail streamers, more maneuverable flight and their

perching abilities. L:17–33 cm (6–13 in), Wt: 70–120 g (2–4 oz). General body form is like true swifts but the head carries a long erectile crest, the eyes are large and the hind toe of the tiny foot is not reversible. Perches and roosts high in trees. Plumage dense, soft, glossy blue-grays to browns. Dimorphic. **Range and habitat:** OR, AU. Open woodland and forest edges. **Migration:** nonmigratory. **Breeding:** habits poorly known. Eggs: 1, white, cemented into a tiny cup-shaped nest, itself cemented to the side of a lateral tree branch. Incubation shared. **Food:** aerial insects.

81 Hummingbirds Trochilidae 335 species (28 ●), 105 genera, e.g. Sword-billed Hummingbird *Ensifera ensifera*
Description: a huge but natural group showing diverse adaptive radiation into an otherwise unexploited ecological niche. Tiny to small, the family includes the smallest birds known. L: 5.5–21.5 cm (2–8 in), Wt: 2–20 g (2¼–8½ oz). Hummingbirds show a number of adaptations giving them access to flowers from which they suck nectar (in so doing they are important pollinators for some plant species). In particular, a modified arrangement of the wing bones means birds make more than 70 wing-beats/sec allowing precision hovering in any direction including backward. They are also capable of very fast flight. In addition, a long, thin bill and protrusible tongue allows access to the nectaries at the base of the flower's corolla tube. The family shows great diversity of bill size and shape, which are adapted to feeding from different flower types. Plumage dimorphic, often brilliantly colored in metallic greens and reds, sometimes crested in males, females more drab. Tail short, square to long, forked. Feet tiny, weak, allow perching but not walking. **Range and habitat:** NA, NT. Forest, savannah scrublands and desert. **Migration:** some strongly migratory species. **Breeding:** polygynous, highly territorial, or lek. Nest is either a deep cup of plant fibers and spiders' webs astride a stem or twig, or a pendant nest attached by a cobweb to the underside of a leaf and counter-weighted by debris at the base. Eggs: 2, white. Incubation and care by female (except 1 recorded case) for 14–23 days. Young are altricial, in nest for 18–38 days. **Food:** nectar and small insects.

COLIES OR MOUSEBIRDS Coliiformes

A monotypic order showing no close affinity to any other.

82 Mousebirds Coliidae 6 species, 2 genera, e.g. Speckled Mousebird *Colius striatus*
Description: small birds with long, pointed, graduated tails. L: 30–5 cm (12–14 in) including tail which constitutes 66% of length, Wt: 45–55 g (1½–2 oz). Wings short, rounded, flight fast and level for short distances. Legs short with stout feet. 4 toes usually directed forward but outer toe is reversible. Bill short, stout, decurved and hooked. Usually perch hanging vertically but can also perch normally. Hop and run fast on ground also. Plumage soft, crested, variously marked grays and browns. Diverse molt patterns. Monomorphic. Highly gregarious. **Range and habitat:** AF. Scrublands and forest edges, also

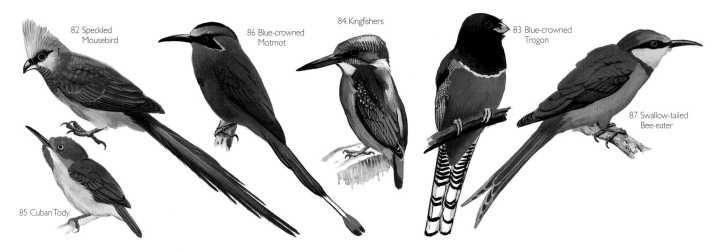

82 Speckled Mousebird

86 Blue-crowned Motmot

84 Kingfishers

83 Blue-crowned Trogon

87 Swallow-tailed Bee-eater

85 Cuban Tody

gardens and cultivation. **Migration:** nonmigratory. **Breeding:** solitary or loosely colonial. Nest is open cup, usually in thorn bush, sometimes bulky and untidy. Eggs: 3 (rarely 1–8), whitish streaked blackish or brownish. Incubation shared, sitting tightly for 11–14 days. Young are altricial, in nest for 15–20 days, fed by regurgitation. Care by female or shared. **Food:** a variety of plant matter including seeds, fruit, shoots, and leaves.

TROGONS Trogoniformes

Among the most beautiful of birds, no clear relationships with other orders.

83 Trogons Trogonidae
39 species (1 ●), 6 genera, e.g. Blue-crowned Trogon *Trogon curucui*
Description: medium-sized solitary, arboreal birds showing remarkably little variation considering their widespread distribution and movements. L: 23–38 cm (9–15 in), Wt: 38–210 g (1⅓–7½ oz). The legs and feet are small and weak, the latter unique in that, although zygodactyl, it is the 1st and 2nd toes which point backward rather than the 1st and 4th. Bill short, stout, decurved (serrated in NT species) and very broad-based with rictal bristles. Wings short, roundish. Tail long, truncated. Plumage bright and soft, metallic except in OR, greens, blues, reds, yellows, black and white. Dimorphic, females duller. **Range and habitat:** pantropical: AF, OR, NT. Tropical forest up to 3,000 m (10,000 ft). **Migration:** nonmigratory. **Breeding:** nest is a hole in tree, stump or termite mound. Eggs: 2–3 (rarely 4), unmarked glossy white, cream, buff, brown, pale blue or green. Incubation shared for 17–19 days. Young are altricial in nest for 17–18 days. **Food:** chiefly insects, in NT also fruit.

KINGFISHERS AND ALLIES Coraciiformes

A large diverse order of carnivorous land birds, usually brightly colored with large bills and usually with 2 front toes (of 4) joined for all or part of their length (syndactyl). 7 families. Little or no nest sanitation is practised.

84 Kingfishers Alcedinidae
93 species (12 ●), 18 genera, e.g. (Eurasian) Kingfisher *Alcedo atthis*
Description: small to large, compact birds with large head, long, stout and pointed bill. L: 10–45 cm (4–18 in), Wt: 8–500 g (¼ oz–1 lb 2 oz). Neck short. Wings short, rounded. Flight fast, direct. Tail short to medium, square to rounded. Legs and feet short and weak. The 3rd and 4th toes are joined for most of length, the 2nd and 3rd partially joined. The 2nd toe is vestigial or absent in some species. Plumage generally bright and conspicuous, sometimes metallic, blues, greens, reds, orange, sometimes cryptic. Most more or less monomorphic. Generally solitary. Piscivores, hunt by diving into water to take prey. **Systematics:** DNA evidence suggests that the kingfishers might be split into three families: Alcedinidae, Dacelonidae, and Cerylidae. We have followed the traditional grouping in line with *Birdlife International*. **Range and habitat:**

worldwide except high latitudes and AN. A wide variety of forest, scrub and savannah habitats, often near water. **Migration:** mostly nonmigratory. **Breeding:** some with nest-helpers. Nest is a chamber at end of long tunnel excavated in river-bank, or tree-hole. Eggs: 2–4 in tropics, 6–10 in temperate latitudes, white. Incubation shared for 18–22 days. Broods: 1–2. Young are altricial, in nest for 20–30 days. **Food:** fish, small vertebrates, or insects depending on species.

85 Todies Todidae
5 species, 1 genus, e.g. Cuban Tody *Todus multicolor*
Description: exquisite tiny, compact, short-necked birds with long, flattened, broad, red bill. L: 9–12 cm (3½–4½ in), Wt: 5.4g (⅕oz). Wings short, rounded. Tail short, square. Plumage varies little, green upper-parts, white underparts with yellow and pink patches, and red throat patch. Some with small blue patch below ear. Fossil evidence indicates that present distribution is a remnant of a formerly widespread range. Monomorphic. Tame, arboreal, usually paired. **Range and habitat:** endemic to Caribbean (NT). Forests, often near water. **Migration:** nonmigratory. **Breeding:** highly territorial, may have nest-helpers. Nest is a chamber in bank at end of 30 cm (12 in) tunnel. Eggs: 2–5, white, 25% of female weight. Incubation shared for rather long period: 21–2 days. Young are altricial in nest for 19–20 days, emerge sooner if helpers present. Fed extremely frequently. **Food:** insects, very high feeding rate.

86 Motmots Momotidae
10 species (1 ●), 6 genera, e.g. Blue-crowned Motmot *Momotus momota*
Description: small to medium birds most closely related to Todidae. L: 17–45 cm (6½–18 in), Wt: 27–150 g (1–5⅓oz). Unlike todies, the bill is strong, decurved, long and pointed. Wings short, rounded. Tail long, stiff, sometimes with bare shaft for part of its length, giving a racket-tip. Legs and feet short, toes as kingfishers (Alcedinidae). Plumage loose textured, bright greens, blues, browns, often with a black breast-spot and black eye stripe. More or less monomorphic. Solitary or paired, perch motionless for long periods. **Range and habitat:** NT. Tropical forest, often near streams. **Migration:** nonmigratory. **Breeding:** nest is a chamber at end of a very long tunnel. Eggs: 3–4, white. Incubation shared for 15–22 days. Young are altricial, in nest for 24–38 days. **Food:** insects caught by flying out from a perch (sallying), also some reptiles and fruit.

87 Bee-eaters Meropidae
26 species, 3 genera, e.g. Swallow-tailed Bee-eater *Merops hirundineus*
Description: small to medium but long, slender, gregarious birds with long, pointed, decurved bills. L: 17–35 cm (6½–14 in), Wt: 15–85 g (½–3 oz). Wings large, pointed, flight strong and agile. Tail long, usually with elongated center tail feathers. Legs short, feet small and weak. Feet syndactyl. Perch on branches and telegraph wires from which to hunt. Plumage brilliant greens, blues, yellows and reds, in bold patches with a black mask and often a contrasting throat patch. Monomorphic, males brighter. **Range and habitat:** southern WP and EP, AF,

90 Cuckoo Roller
89 Long-tailed Ground-Roller
93 Abyssinian Ground-Hornbill
91 Hoopoe
88 Indian Roller
92 Green Woodhoopoe

OR, AU. Open country including open forest and scrub, 6 species in rainforest. **Migration:** temperate breeders are migratory. **Breeding:** colonial or solitary (forest species), some with nest-helpers. Nest is a chamber at end of tunnel up to 3 m (10ft) long in sandbank. Eggs: 2–7 (2–4 in tropics), white. Incubation shared for 18–23 days. Broods: 1. Young are altricial, in nest for 27–32 days. **Food:** aerial insects, especially venomous worker bees which are rubbed on a branch to remove the sting.

88 Rollers Coraciidae
12 species (1 ●), 2 genera, e.g. Indian Roller *Coracias benghalensis*
Description: probably most closely related to Bee-eaters. Medium to large, thickset birds with powerful, medium to long or short, broad, hooked bills. L: 25–45 cm (10–18 in), Wt: c.100–200 g (c.3½–7 oz). Head large. Wings long, pointed. Flight strong, agile. Tail usually short to medium, square, sometimes with long outer feathers. Legs short with small, weak feet. Inner toes syndactyl but outer toe free. Plumage gaudy blues, greens and grays. More or less monomorphic. Generally solitary, arboreal. Noisy. **Range and habitat:** WP, EP, AF, OR, AU. Forests, scrublands and grasslands, including cultivation. **Migration:** some migratory species. **Breeding:** rolling courtship display flight. Nest is in tree-hollows, burrows, old walls. Eggs: 4, glossy white, Wt: 10–17g (¼–½ oz). Incubation shared for 17–19 days. Young are altricial, in nest for 25–30 days. **Food:** insects by sallying, also small vertebrates.

89 Ground-Rollers Brachypteraciidae
5 species (3 ●), 3 genera, e.g. Long-tailed Ground-Roller *Uratelornis chimaera*
Description: medium-sized. L: 24–45 cm (9½–18 in), 4 species less than 30 cm (12 in), Wt: 77–217 g (2¾–7¾ oz), solitary or in small groups, crepuscular ground-dwelling birds closely related to (and often treated with) rollers (Coraciidae). However, the legs are much longer and the wings shorter and rounder than in that family. Tail very long and truncated. Bill long, decurved, stout and hooked as rollers. Flight is strong and rolling in display, but birds tend to run rather than fly when disturbed. Plumage more cryptic than rollers with streaked browns, yellow, greens, but also patches of blue. **Range and habitat:** Madagascar (AF). Dense forest and scrub. **Migration:** nonmigratory. **Breeding:** little known. Nest is a chamber at end of sloping tunnel in bank. Eggs: 3–4, white. Incubation probably shared. **Food:** insects and small vertebrates on ground.

90 Cuckoo Roller Leptosomatidae
Leptosomus discolor (monotypic).
Description: large, noisy, rather gregarious, arboreal rollerlike bird. L: 42cm (17 in), Wt: 192–270 g (7–9½ oz). It is unusual in the presence of powder down patches on either side of the rump, and the 4th toe which is rotated to the side. Feathers of the lores face forward and upward, so concealing the base of the bill. Dimorphic: male iridescent green, head gray, underparts white. Female greenish with brown head and underparts spotted. **Range and habitat:** Madagascar and the Comoro Islands (AF). Evergreen forests. **Migration:**

nonmigratory. **Breeding:** poorly known. Nest is in tree-cavity. Eggs: 2 cream-buff. **Food:** insects and small vertebrates.

HOOPOES AND WOODHOOPOES Upupiformes

An order of medium-sized to large birds with long, decurved bills, and sharing some characteristics (e.g. syndactyly) with the Coraciiformes, in which they have traditionally been classified, but DNA evidence indicates a distinct evolutionary history.

91 Hoopoe Upupidae
Upupa epops (monotypic or 2 species). See p 166.
Description: common bird of open habitats in central and southern WP, and AF except Sahara. Wt: 50–90 g (2–3 oz) Feeds on ground on invertebrates and small vertebrates. Long, decurved bill used to probe ground. Feet syndactyl. Its systematic relationships are unclear as it shares some characteristics with Passeriformes rather than Coraciiformes, and hence its separate classification with the woodhoopes in a new grouping supported by DNA evidence.

92 Woodhoopoes Phoeniculidae
8 species, 2 genera, e.g. Green Woodhoopoe *Phoeniculus purpureus*
Description: medium to large, arboreal, solitary or in small groups. L: 23–46 cm (9–18 in), Wt: 20–100 g (¾–3½ oz). Bill long, thin, slightly to strongly decurved. Legs short, thick, sometimes feathered. Toes with long, curved claws, toes 3 and 4 fused at base. Bill and legs vary: red, orange, yellow or black depending on species, population and age. Tail very long and graduated. Wings rounded. Hops on ground unlike Hoopoe (Upupidae) which walks but generally flies strongly from tree to tree. Plumage generally black or dark green/purple with metallic sheen. **Range and habitat:** AF. Forest, wooded savannah. **Migration:** nonmigratory. **Breeding:** solitary to cooperative with nest-helpers. Nest is in tree-hollows. Eggs: 2–4 (rarely 5), blue, spotted. Incubation by female for 17–18 days. Young are altricial, in nest for 28–30 days. **Food:** insects and small fruits.

HORNBILLS AND GROUND-HORNBILLS Bucerotiformes

An order of medium-sized to very large birds sharing some characteristics with the Coraciiformes, in which they have traditionally been classified.

93 Hornbills Bucerotidae
57 species (9 ●), 9 genera, e.g. Abyssinian Ground-Hornbill *Bucorvus abyssinicus*
Description: a distinct group with many unique features. Medium to very large, arboreal or ground-dwelling birds with massive bills, often carrying a horny casque which may be as large as the bill itself. L: 38–160 cm (15–63 in), Wt: 85 g–4k g (3 oz–8 lb 13 oz). The casque is light and hollow but supported internally by bone. Bill generally long, pointed, powerful and gently decurved. Bill and casque usually colored red or yellow. Colors vary with age.

33

95 Spotted Puffbird

97 Red-billed Toucan

98 Black-throated Honeyguide

99 Gray-faced Woodpecker

96 Crimson-breasted Barbet

94 Rufous-tailed Jacamar

Fused axis and atlas vertebrae help to support the weight of the bill. Hornbills have eyelashes and sometimes colored (according to sex) bare facial skin and wattles. Neck medium to long. Wings long, broad. Flight strong but labored, especially in larger species. Tail long, broad, rounded. Legs short to medium (shorter in arboreal species). Plumage coarse, loose-webbed, generally browns, grays, black, boldly marked. Monomorphic or female duller; males up to 10% larger with 15–20% larger bill. Females generally molt during incubation. **Range and habitat:** AF, OR, New Guinea (AU). Forests and wooded savannah. **Migration:** nonmigratory. **Breeding:** may have nest-helpers. Nest is usually a hollow tree (except ground hornbills) into which the female is sealed so that only a vertical slit remains. She is fed through this by the male during incubation and until the young are half-grown. Eggs: 1–7 (fewer in larger species), white. Incubation is for 25–40 days. Young are altricial, in nest for 45–86 days. **Food:** chiefly insects, fruit, and small vertebrates.

WOODPECKERS AND ALLIES Piciformes

An order generally defined by zygodactyl foot and internal anatomy. 6 families in 2 suborders.

94 Jacamars Galbulidae 18 species (2 ●), 5 genera, e.g. Rufous-tailed Jacamar *Galbula ruficauda*
Description: small to medium, slender, graceful, highly active exciting birds with long, thin, swordlike bills. L: 15–31 cm (6–12 in) but largest has long tail, Wt: 20–70 g (¾–2½ oz). Legs short. Feet small, 1 species has 3 toes only (having lost the inner hind toe). Tail long, truncated or pointed. Wings short, rounded. Plumage loose-webbed, usually metallic green, bronze or purple above, rufous orange (most) or black below, often with white throat. Slight dimorphism, males brighter. **Range and habitat:** NT. Forest and wooded savannah. **Migration:** nonmigratory. **Breeding:** known for few species. Solitary. Nest is a nest-burrow in bank or rootplate of fallen tree. Eggs: 3–4, glossy white. Incubation shared during day, female at night for 20–30 days. Young are semi-altricial (unlike others of the order), in nest for 19–26 days. **Food:** insects caught by sallying.

95 Puffbirds Bucconidae 33 species, 10 genera, e.g. Spotted Puffbird *Bucco tamatia*
Description: small to medium, stolid, rather inactive, generally arboreal birds with large head and short neck. L: 14–29 cm (5½–11½ in), Wt: 30–90 g (1–3¾ oz). Bill medium-sized, strong, decurved or hooked, flat, with prominent rictal bristles. Legs short, feet zygodactyl. Wings short, rounded. Tail medium to long, square. Plumage soft and often puffed out when perched, dull browns, grays and white, sometimes streaked or spotted and often with a breast band. More or less monomorphic. **Range and habitat:** NT. Forest and wooded savannah. **Migration:** nonmigratory. **Breeding:** poorly known. No nest sanitation practised. Nest is a tunnel dug by both parents in a bank, termite mound or ground, or, more rarely, a tree-hole. Eggs: 2–3 (rarely 4), white.

Incubation shared for unknown period. Young are altricial, in nest for 20–1 days. **Food:** chiefly insects caught on the wing by sallying, or on ground.

96 Barbets Capitonidae 83 species (2 ●), 13 genera, e.g. Crimson-breasted Barbet *Megalaima haemacephala*
Description: small to medium, generally solitary or paired, arboreal and sometimes rather inactive birds with large heads, short necks. L: 9–33 cm (3½–13 in), Wt: 24–295 g (1–10 oz). Bill large, stout, decurved, pointed and often sharply toothed along the edge. Rictal bristles prominent, forming "beard" in some. Legs generally short. Feet strong and zygodactyl. Hops clumsily on ground. Wings short and rounded, flight rather weak and for short distances. Tail short and square. Plumage brightly colored in contrasting patches of greens, reds, blues and yellows. More or less monomorphic. **Range and habitat:** AF, OR, NT. A variety of forest, savannah and semiarid habitats. **Migration:** nonmigratory. **Breeding:** sometimes with helpers at the nest. Nest is a hole in a bank, termite mound or rotten tree-stump dug by both parents, or old woodpecker hole. Eggs: 2–5, white. Incubation shared for 12–19 days. Young are altricial, in nest for 20–35 days. In smaller species, young fed by regurgitation. **Food:** fruit, flowers, buds, insects. Larger species also take small vertebrates.

97 Toucans Rhamphastidae 41 species (1 ●), 6 genera, e.g. Red-billed Toucan *Rhamphastos tucanus*
Description: medium to large, generally solitary, arboreal birds with massive, brightly colored bill, superficially resembling hornbills of the Old World but these are quite unrelated. L: 33–66 cm (13–26 in), Wt: 100–750 g (3 oz–1 lb 11 oz). Bill generally long, deep and with a markedly decurved culmen (ridge of upper mandible) with nostrils at base. The cutting edges of the bill (tomia) are sometimes saw-toothed. Although sometimes as long as the bird's body, the bill is extremely light and strengthened internally by numerous bony filaments. The tongue is also much modified. Bare skin round eye is brightly colored. Legs medium to long, strong with stout zygodactyl feet. Wings short, rounded. Flight rather ungraceful. Tail long, graduated or rounded. Plumage coarse, gaudily patterned in contrasting patches of black, yellow, greens, blues and red. Most are monomorphic but male bill larger. **Range and habitat:** NT. Rainforest and more open wooded foothills. **Migration:** some altitudinal migrants. **Breeding:** nest is in tree-hollow. Eggs: 2–4, white. Incubation shared for 15–16 days. Young are altricial with thick heel pads to protect feet (which bear chicks' weight) against rough nest interior. In nest for 43–51 days, develop very slowly, e.g. eyes do not open until day 14. **Food:** chiefly fruit and insects, also other small animals.

98 Honeyguides Indicatoridae 17 species, 4 genera, e.g. Black-throated Honeyguide *Indicator indicator*
Description: small to medium, solitary arboreal birds, some showing a unique relationship with man (see Food). L: 10–20 cm (4–8 in), Wt: 10–55 g (¼–2 oz). Bill short, stout or thin, pointed. Legs short with strong, zygodactyl feet. Wings long,

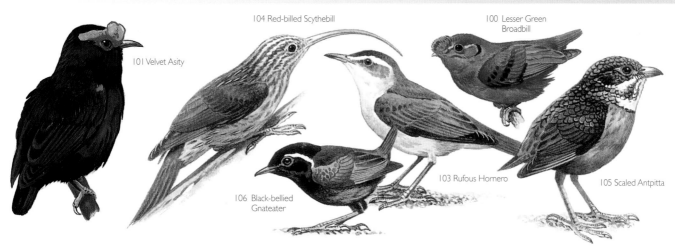

101 Velvet Asity

104 Red-billed Scythebill

100 Lesser Green Broadbill

106 Black-bellied Gnateater

103 Rufous Hornero

105 Scaled Antpitta

pointed. Flight strong, undulating. Tail graduated, rather long. Plumage generally drab grays and browns, paler underparts, some with yellow or orange patches or white outer tail feathers. Most more or less monomorphic. **Range and habitat:** AF, OR. Forest and wooded savannahs. **Migration:** seasonal short-distance movements. **Breeding:** nest parasites of hole-nesters such as barbets and woodpeckers, and of some flycatchers. Eggs: 1 per nest, white or blue (in 1 species to mimic host). Incubation 12–13 days. Young are altricial, in nest for 38–40 days, some have tooth on bill to kill host chicks if present. **Food:** insects and wax, especially beeswax. The Black-, or Greater, and the Scaly-throated Honeyguides instinctively lead man and other large mammals to the nests of honey-bees. The "helper" then opens the nest to obtain honey. Some human tribes leave beeswax for the bird. It is not clear to what extent the birds depend on wax obtained in this way since attempts to study them are bedevilled by the fact that the birds switch to "guiding" behavior on the approach of any human observer.

99 Woodpeckers Picidae 217 species (10 ●), 28 genera, e.g. Gray-faced Woodpecker *Picus canus*
Description: a well-defined group with many shared characteristics which adapt them to wood-boring. Small to medium-large, generally solitary, mostly arboreal birds. L: 8–55 cm (3–22 in), Wt: 8–563 g (4¼ oz–1 lb 4 oz). Bill chisel-like, straight, pointed, and strong. Skull strengthened. Tongue very long, protrusible and often brush-tipped. Tail stiffened as a support while hopping up tree-trunk except in piculets. Wings rather long, broad, pointed. Flight undulating. Head sometimes crested. Plumage generally rather coarse, boldly marked black, white, greens, browns, grays, yellow, and red. Often barred. Generally dimorphic in size and with small color differences between sexes. Wrynecks (Jynx species) superbly cryptic with fine barring. **Range and habitat:** WP, EP, AF, OR, AU, NA, NT. Wide range of forest, scrub and grasslands including cultivation. **Migration:** most nonmigratory. **Breeding:** usually solitary, sometimes with nest-helpers. Nest is in excavated tree-hole. Eggs: 3–11 (rarely 2–14), glossy white. Incubation shared for 9–20 days. Broods: 1, rarely 2. Young are altricial, in nest for 18–25 days. **Food:** chiefly insects extracted from beneath tree bark or ground. Also fruit, seeds, sap and honey depending on species.

PERCHING BIRDS Passeriformes

Perching land birds with 4 unwebbed, level toes—3 forward, 1 hind. Toes generally separate. Most fly strongly. Characteristic internal anatomy and spermatozoa. Eggs usually incubated by female but young usually fed by both. Young altricial. Often dimorphic, with males larger and brighter. The largest order, with 74 families in the present arrangement, but as few as 46, or as many as 100, may be recognized in other recent DNA-based classifications.

100 Broadbills Eurylaimidae 15 species (3 ●), 8 genera, e.g. Lesser Green Broadbill *Calyptomena viridis*
Description: small to medium, chunky, rounded wings, wide, colored

bill, wide head, large eyes, strong feet, short or graduated tail. L: 13–28 cm (5–11 in), Wt: 20.5–160 g (¾–5½ oz). Strikingly colored—reds, pinks, greens, blues, 1 wattled. Most dimorphic. **Range and habitat:** AF, OR. Tropical forests. **Migration:** nonmigratory. **Breeding:** nest is pear-shaped, hanging bag with porched entrance. Eggs: 2–8, color varied. Little known. **Food:** fruit, insects, and small vertebrates.

101 Asities Philepittidae 4 species (1 ●), 2 genera, e.g. Velvet Asity *Philepitta castanea*
Description: small, compact, arboreal. L: 9–16.5 cm (3½–6½ in). Wings and tail short, rounded. Strong flight. Legs and feet short and weak or long and strong. Bill various, generally pointed, stout, broad-based, medium-sized and slightly decurved. Plumage soft. Dimorphic: males blue and yellow or black with yellow on wing. Orbital ring area bare or with extraordinary wattle in breeding season. Females greenish. **Range and habitat:** Madagascar (AF). Forests. **Migration:** nonmigratory. **Breeding:** largely unknown. The nest of the Velvet Asity is pear-shaped, suspended. Eggs: 3, white. **Food:** (all species) fruit and some insects.

102 Pittas Pittidae 32 species (9 ●), 1 genus, e.g. Hooded Pitta *Pitta sordida* (see illustration on p 36.)
Description: small, compact, short necked, ground-dwelling but roost in trees. L: 15–28 cm (6–11 in), Wt: 42–218 g (1½–7½ oz). Fly strongly. Wings short, rounded. Tail very short. Long legs, large feet. Stout, slightly decurved, hook-tipped bill. Plumage loose, soft and brightly colored. Colors vary but are often contrasting in bold patches and brighter on underparts. Dimorphic. **Range and habitat:** AF, OR, AU. Chiefly tropical forest and scrublands. **Migration:** some migratory species. **Breeding:** nest is a huge, untidy, domed cup of twigs, lined. Eggs: 3–5 (rarely 2–7), whitish, spotted. Incubation shared for 15–17 days. Young in nest for 14–21 days. **Food:** small animals on ground.

103 Ovenbirds Furnariidae 240 species (26 ●), 56 genera, e.g. Rufous Hornero *Furnarius rufus*
Description: a diverse family. Front toes joined at base. Small to medium, wings short to long, round to pointed. L: 10–26 cm (4–10 in), Wt: 9–46 g (¼–1½ oz). Bill short to long, slender, pointed. Browns, grays, white, very varied pattern. Monomorphic. **Range and habitat:** NT. A wide variety of forest, scrub and grassland habitats. **Migration:** most species nonmigratory. **Breeding:** nest is diverse including domed mud "ovens," burrows and large twiggy nests. Eggs: 2–3, whitish. Incubation shared for 15–20 days. Young are in nest for 13–18 days. **Food:** invertebrates on ground or in trees.

104 Woodcreepers Dendrocolaptidae 51 species (1 ●), 12 genera, e.g. Red-billed Scythebill *Campylorhamphus trochilirostris*
Description: small to medium, arboreal. L: 13.5–35 cm (5½–14 in), Wt: 12–120 g (½–4 oz). Stiff tail, strong claws, short legs, round wings. Bill short, straight to long, decurved. Plumage dull browns, cryptic, monomorphic. **Range and**

112 Eastern Kingbird

110 Andean Cock of the Rock

109 Chilean Plantcutter

102 Hooded Pitta

111 White-bearded Manakin

107 Black-throated Huet-huet

habitat: NT. In forest and forest edge. **Migration:** nonmigratory. **Breeding:** nest is in tree-holes. Eggs: 2–3, white. Incubation shared for 15–20 days. Young are in nest for c.20 days. **Food:** invertebrates and small vertebrates taken largely from bark.

105 Antbirds, Antthrushes, and Antpittas Formicariidae 269 species (38 ●), 52 genera, e.g. Scaled Antpitta *Grallaria guatimalensis* (see illustration on p 35.) **Description:** a diverse family, (see Systematics). Front toes joined at base. Small to medium, arboreal or ground foragers. L: 8–35 cm (3–14 in), Wt: 9–75 g (¼–2¾ oz). Wings short, round. Tail short to long. Legs short to long. Bill medium-sized, stout, hook-tipped. Eyes red to yellow. Soft plumage generally drab but diverse patterns, many have white patches exposed in disputes. Dimorphic. **Systematics:** Modern DNA evidence suggests a split into two closely related families: Thamnophilidae (typical antbirds) and Formicariidae (antthrushes and antpittas). We have retained the traditional grouping in line with *Birdlife International*. **Range and habitat:** NT. A wide variety of forest and scrubland habitats. **Migration:** nonmigratory. **Breeding:** nest is an open cup in bush. Eggs: 2 (rarely 3), white, spotted. Incubation shared for 14–20 days. Young are in nest for 9–18 days. **Food:** fruit and small animals, especially ants.

106 Gnateaters (or antpipits) Conopophagidae 8 species, 1 genus, e.g. Black-bellied Gnateater *Conopophaga melanogaster*
Description: small, compact; short, round wings. L: 11–14 cm (4½–5½ in), Wt: 20–3 g (¾–1 oz). Long toes, front 3 joined at base, legs long. Tail very short. Bill short. Plumage generally browns, drab, soft. Dimorphic. **Range and habitat:** NT. Forest undergrowth. **Migration:** nonmigratory. **Breeding:** little known. Nest is a cup. Eggs: 2 (rarely 3), yellowish, spotted. Incubation shared. **Food:** insects.

107 Tapaculos Rhinocryptida 56 species (4 ●), 12 genera, e.g. Black-throated Huet-huet *Pteroptochos tarnii*
Description: family defined by nostril covered by movable flap. Small to medium, ground-dwelling, walk fast, legs and feet long, strong. L: 11–25 cm (4½–10 in), Wt: c.20 g (c¾ oz). Fly rarely. Wings short, rounded; tail short to long, often held erect. Bill short, stout. Plumage soft, loose, drab red-browns. Monomorphic. **Range and habitat:** NT. Dense forest and scrubland undergrowth. **Migration:** nonmigratory. **Breeding:** little known. Nest is on ground, domed cup or in tree-hole. Eggs: 2–4, white. Incubation shared. **Food:** chiefly invertebrates, some plant matter.

108 Sharpbill Oxyruncidae *Oxyruncus cristatus* (monotypic). See p 132.
Description: small, close to Tyrannidae but bill conical, sharp. L: 16.5–18 cm (6½–7 in), Wt: 42 g (1 oz). Front toes joined at base. Nostrils elongated, covered by flap. Rictal bristles replaced by fine bristly feathers. Monomorphic. Ecologically rather like tits. **Range and habitat:** NT. Rainforest. **Migration:** probably nonmigratory. **Breeding:** little known. Nest first described in 1980: cup on branch. Eggs: Probably 2. Incubation probably by female for 14–24 days. Young are in nest for 25–30 days. **Food:** small fruits and invertebrates.

109 Plantcutters Phytotomidae 3 species (1 ●), 1 genus, e.g. Chilean Plantcutter *Phytotoma rara*
Description: small, bill short, strong, conical, serrated. L: 17–20 cm (6½–8 in). Legs short, large feet, front toes partly joined. Wings short, pointed, tail longish. Plumage gray or brown, reddish below. Eyes bright yellow or amber. Dimorphic. **Range and habitat:** western and southern NT. Scrub, low woodland and cultivation. **Migration:** partly migratory. **Breeding:** nest is a flat, untidy platform of root fibers. Eggs: 2–4, blue-green, spotted brown. Incubation by female. **Food:** a range of plant matter including young leaves, buds, seeds and fruit.

110 Cotingas Cotingidae 68 species (17 ●), 27 genera, e.g. Andean Cock of the Rock *Rupicola peruviana*
Description: small to medium, most arboreal. L: 9–46 cm (3½–18 in), Wt: 6–400 g (¼–14 oz). Bill often flattened, short to long. Legs short, feet large, 2 front toes joined at base, wings and tail short to long. Some crested, wattled, very diverse patterns and colors, monomorphic or dimorphic, females duller. Some with powder downs. In the Passeriformes only these and the Artamidae have such feathers. **Range and habitat:** NT. Forest at all levels. **Migration:** nonmigratory. **Breeding:** little known, many polygynous, ritualized courtship. Nest is varied, usually cupped. Eggs: 1–3, buff or olive, spotted. Incubation by female for 19–28 days. Young in nest for 21–44 days. **Food:** insects and fruit.

111 Manakins Pipridae 52 species (4 ●), 15 genera, e.g. White-bearded Manakin *Manacus manacus*
Description: small, L: 9–19 cm (3½–7½ in), Wt: 10–25 g (¼–1 oz). Front toes partly joined at base. Wings short, tail short to long, bill short, broad, hook-tipped. Males bright black, white, reds, blues and yellows; females greenish. **Range and habitat:** NT. Tropical forest. **Migration:** nonmigratory. **Breeding:** polygynous, sometimes leks. Nest is a frail cup. Eggs: 2. All care by female for 17–21 days. Young are in nest 13–15 days. **Food:** insects and fruit.

112 Tyrant Flycatchers Tyrannidae 425 species (27 ●), 106 genera, e.g. Eastern Kingbird *Tyrannus tyrannus*
Description: ecologically diverse. Small to medium-sized, L: 6–50 cm (2¼–20 in), Wt: 4.5–80 g (¼–2¾ oz). Bill broad, flat, hook-tipped, rictal bristles. Large head, sometimes crested. Wings short to long, pointed. Tail medium-sized, sometimes forked. Legs and feet generally short, weak. Usually greens, browns and grays. Most monomorphic. **Range and habitat:** NA, NT. A wide range of terrestrial habitats. **Migration:** temperate species are migratory. **Breeding:** nest is diverse, includes cups (sometimes domed), purses in diverse sites. Eggs: 3–4 (rarely 2–8), whitish. All care by female for 14–20 days. Young are in nest 14–23 days. **Food:** aerial insects by sallying, tropical fruits, and small vertebrates.

113 Scrubbirds Atrichornithidae 2 species (1 ●), 1 genus, e.g. Rufous Scrubbird *Atrichornis rufescens*
Description: small to medium, ground-dwelling, fast runners with tail

114 Superb Lyrebird

117 Swallow

115 Rifleman

108 Sharpbill

116 Shore Lark

113 Rufous Scrubbird

erect, but flight very poor and rarely seen. L: 16–21 cm (6–8 in), Wt: 30–50 g (1–1¾ oz). None-the-less it roosts in trees. Bill medium-sized, strong, pointed, curved culmen. Wings very short, rounded. Tail long, graduated. Legs and feet large and strong. Plumage rufous above, paler below, finely barred. Monomorphic, male larger. Good mimics. **Range and habitat:** AU. Forest edge and scrubland. **Migration:** nonmigratory. **Breeding:** monogamous (may be polygamous in captivity). Nest is a loosely woven domed cup on or near ground. Eggs: 1, pinkish. All care by female. Incubation for 36–8 days. Young are in nest for 25 days. Stay with female till following year. **Food:** chiefly invertebrates, some small vertebrates, and seeds.

114 Lyrebirds Menurida 2 species (1 ●), 1 genus, e.g. Superb Lyrebird *Menura novaehollandiae*
Description: large, ground-dwelling, fast runners, poor flight but roost in trees. L: male: 89–100 cm (35–9 in), Wt: 1.15 kg (2 lb 9 oz); female: 76–86 cm (30–4 in), 950 g (2 lb 1oz). Solitary. Tail long and trainlike, of 3 types of highly modified feathers in male; simpler in female. Legs long, feet large with long claws. Bill pointed, sharp and conical. Plumage dark brown above with bluish orbital ring, underparts paler. Highly dimorphic. Good mimics. **Range and habitat:** AU. Montane forest. **Migration:** nonmigratory. **Breeding:** males polygynous, complex courtship and mating system. Nest is massive lined chamber of twigs up to 22 m (72 ft), Wt: c.14 kg (30 lb 13 oz). Eggs: 1, gray, mottled, Wt: 49–72 g (1¾–2½ oz). Incubated by female for 50 days. Young are in nest for 47 days, all care by female but independent after 8 months. **Food:** a wide range of invertebrates from soil and rotting wood.

115 New Zealand Wrens Xenicidae 2 species (1 ●), 2 genera, e.g. Rifleman *Acanthisitta chloris*
Description: very small, compact. L: 8–10 cm (3–4 in), Wt: 6.3–9 g (c.¼ oz). Fly weakly but run around logs, tree roots, rocks. Wings short, rounded. Tail very short. Long legs with large feet. Bill medium-sized, very thin, pointed. Plumage soft, brownish or green, yellow, white. Monomorphic, males brighter; or dimorphic when male smaller (unusual in Passeriformes). **Range and habitat:** New Zealand (AU). Forest. **Migration:** nonmigratory. **Breeding:** nest is a dome of loosely woven, abundant material, side entrance. Eggs: 2–5 (20% female wt), white, laid at 2–day intervals. Incubation shared for 19–21 days. Young are in nest for 24 days, slow growth rate. **Food:** invertebrates and some fruit.

116 Larks Alaudidae 91 species (8 ●), 19 genera, e.g. Shore Lark *Eremophila alpestris*
Description: small, ground-dwelling. Legs and toes longish, claws long and straight. Back of tarsus rounded and with scales. L: 12–24 cm (4½–9½ in), Wt: 15–75 g (½–2¾ oz). Wings pointed, innermost secondaries very long (sometimes as long as primaries). Tail medium-sized. Bill medium-sized, stout, pointed. Plumage generally variously streaked browns and grays, cryptic, white outer tail feathers. Underparts generally paler. Head often with small crest.

Monomorphic, males larger. Excellent songsters, many singing on the wing in towering song-flights. **Range and habitat:** WP, EP, AF, OR, AU, NA and NT (1 species). A variety of open habitats including shorelines. **Migration:** many strong migrants. **Breeding:** nest is a cup on ground, some domed. Eggs: 2–6, speckled. Incubation by female for 11–16 days. Broods: 1–3. Young leave nest before they can fly at about 10 days. **Food:** seeds and invertebrates.

117 Swallows and Martins Hirundinidae 90 species (7 ●), 15 genera, e.g. Swallow *Hirundo rustica*
Description: small, slender birds superbly adapted to an aerial lifestyle, hence superficially resemble swifts (Apodidae). L: 11.5–21.5 cm (4½–8 in), Wt: 10–55 g (¼–2 oz). Wings long, pointed. Tail short to long, forked, often with outer tail streamers. Legs and feet very small, reduced, but still used for perching. Bill short, flattened, pointed, broad-based with rictal bristles. Plumage usually darker above. Most more or less monomorphic, males larger with longer tail streamers when present. Flight rapid and agile, much time spent on the wing. Gregarious with twittering or buzzing songs and contact calls. **Range and habitat:** worldwide except high latitudes. Diverse. A wide range of open habitats and over forests and streams. **Migration:** many strong migrants, particularly in temperate latitudes. Traditional herald of spring in northern temperate regions. Diurnal migrants. **Breeding:** often colonial. Nest is a variety of mud hivelike structures cemented to a rock overhang, with or without entrance passage, or mud and straw cup. Several species nest on buildings or in tree-holes or burrows in sand cliff. Eggs: 3–8 (rarely 1–2), white or white with red spots. Incubation by female or shared for 13–16 days. Broods: 1–3. Young are in nest for 16–24 (rarely 28) days. **Food:** aerial insects caught on the wing.

118 Wagtails and Pipits Motacillidae 62 species (5 ●), 5 genera, e.g. Yellow Wagtail *Motacilla flava* (see illustration p 38.)
Description: small, slender-bodied, mostly ground-dwelling birds with long tails and longish legs. L: 12.5–22 cm (5–8½ in), Wt: 12–50 g (½–1¾ oz). Toes medium-sized, hind toe often long, nails short to long. Walk, never hop. Bill medium-sized, thin, pointed. Tail usually with paler outer feathers. Wings medium-sized, pointed. Flight strong and undulating. Plumage contrasting, boldly marked: black, white, yellow, blue, grays in wagtails, dimorphic; in pipits monomorphic, variously streaked browns. Many are gregarious and some form large communal roosts. **Range and habitat:** worldwide except PA and AN. A variety of open habitats including shorelines. **Migration:** many strong or partial migrants. **Breeding:** nest is an open cup on ground, in tree or rock cavity. Eggs: 2–7, white, gray or brown, speckled. Incubation by female (pipits) or shared (wagtails) for 12–20 days. Broods: 1–2. Young are in nest for 12–20 days. **Food:** chiefly insects, some small snails, seeds.

119 Cuckooshrikes Campephagidae 82 species (5 ●), 5 genera, e.g. Ground Cuckooshrike *Coracina maxima*
Description: small to medium, solitary or gregarious, chiefly arboreal birds.

118 Yellow Wagtail

121 Asian Fairy-Bluebird

123 Palm Chat

120 Yellow-vented Bulbul

125 Wren

119 Ground Cuckoo Shrike

L: 14–36 cm (5½–14 in), Wt where known: 20–111 g (¾–4 oz). Bill medium-sized, stout, slightly decurved, notched, and hook-tipped, nostrils partly hidden by bristles. Legs short with weak feet. Wings medium-sized, pointed. Flight strong but unsustained. Tail long, graduated or rounded. Plumage soft. In males chiefly light and dark gray, black, white or black and red. Females paler or browner. Feathers of back and rump thickly matted, spiny and readily lost, possibly in defence. 1 species has seasonally varying plumages achieved by 2 molts each year. **Range and habitat:** EP, AF, OR, AU. Dense forest and some forest edge habitats. **Migration:** most nonmigratory. **Breeding:** known for few species. Nest is a shallow cup of fine plant fibers, high in a fork or on a branch of a tree. Eggs: 2–5, pale green, marked with brown, gray or purple. Incubation by female or shared for 14–23 days. Young are in nest for 12–25 days depending on species. **Food:** insects, fruit, and small vertebrates depending on species.

120 Bulbuls Pycnonotidae 130 species (13 ●), 20 genera, e.g. Yellow-vented Bulbul *Pycnonotus barbatus*
Description: small to medium, generally gregarious, arboreal birds, either secretive and skulking (forests) or noisy and conspicuous (gardens). L: 15–28 cm (6–11 in), Wt: 20–65 g (¾–2¼ oz). Bill medium-sized, slender, pointed and slightly decurved with well-developed rictal bristles. Legs medium-sized. Head sometimes crested and with brightly colored eyes. Wings short, concave. Tail medium to long. Plumage soft, long and fluffy especially on lower back. Nape feathers hairlike. Usually browns, grays, yellow or greens, sometimes with white, yellow or red patches on head and undertail-coverts. Most monomorphic, males sometimes brighter. **Range and habitat:** AF, OR. Forest and scrub, also some species have occupied cultivated and suburban habitats. **Migration:** northern species are migratory. **Breeding:** males may lek, may have helpers at the nest. Nest is shallow cup in tree fork, often lined. Eggs: 2–5 (rarely 1), pink or white, marked purple, brown or red. Incubation usually shared for 11–14 days. Young are in nest for 14–18 days. **Food:** fruit and buds, some insects.

121 Fairy-bluebirds, leafbirds, and ioras Irenidae 14 species (1 ●), 3 genera, e.g. Asian Fairy-Bluebird *Irena puella*
Description: small to medium, arboreal, gregarious birds resembling bulbuls (Pycnonotidae) in fluffy texture of plumage, tendency to shed feathers on handling and presence of hairlike nape feathers. L: 14–27 cm (5½–10½ in), Wt: 10–90 g (¼–3¼ oz). Bill medium to long, pointed, decurved. Legs short, strong or slender. Wings short, rounded, but flight fast. Tail medium-sized, square or rounded, sometimes with long uppertail-coverts. Plumage generally brighter than bulbuls, blues, greens, yellows with contrasting black patches on throat or wings. Dimorphic, males brighter. **Systematics:** The 8 species of leafbird and 4 species of iora, are sometimes considered to be separate families: Chloropseidae and Aegithinidae respectively, although DNA evidence indicates close relationship between fairy-bluebirds and leafbirds, with ioras being most distantly related. We have retained the traditional grouping in line with *Birdlife International*. **Range and habitat:** OR. A range of forest and scrubland habitats.

Migration: nonmigratory. **Breeding:** little known, some with elaborate courtship. Nest is an open cup of plant fibers or rough platform of sticks in tree. Eggs: 2–3, pinkish or pale green marked with red and purple. Incubation by female or shared. **Food:** fruit, buds, seeds, nectar, and some insects.

122 Waxwings and allies Bombycillidae 8 species, 5 genera, e.g. Waxwing *Bombycilla garrulus*
Description: small to medium, highly gregarious, arboreal birds, most showing adaptations for fruit-eating. L: 8–24 cm (3–9½ in), Wt: 40–70 g (1½–2½ oz). Bill short, stout, slightly hooked with very wide gape. Legs and feet short, stout. Head often crested. Wings short to long, rounded to pointed. Tail short, square to long. Plumage soft, silky, vinaceous to grayish browns, yellow, black, red or grays. More or less monomorphic or highly dimorphic (Silky-Flycatcher). **Systematics:** Silky-Flycatchers and Hypocolius are sometimes placed in separate families: Ptilognatidae and Hypocoliidae respectively, however, DNA evidence indicates very close relationships between these three families, and with the Palm Chat (Dulidae). We have retained the traditional grouping in line with *Birdlife International*. **Range and habitat:** largely temperate WP, EP, NA, OR. Forest and scrubland habitats. **Migration:** some species irruptive. **Breeding:** solitary or loosely colonial. Nest is a cup of twigs and moss, finely lined, usually in conifer or thorn bush. Male may help in construction. Eggs: 5 (rarely 3–7), gray-blue finely spotted with black. Incubation shared for 12–18 days. Broods: 1. Young are in nest for 19–25 days, fed by regurgitation. **Food:** (waxwings) the most frugivorous northern temperate birds. Fruit, buds and some insects or (silky-flycatchers) insects caught by spectacular sallying flights.

123 Palm Chat Dulidae *Dulus dominicus* (monotypic).
Description: medium-sized, noisy, gregarious, arboreal species closely related to waxwings (Bombycillidae). L: 20 cm (8 in) Wt: 41–52 g (1½–2 oz). Upperparts olive, underparts buff, heavily spotted. **Range and habitat:** Hispaniola and Gonave Islands in West Indies (NT). Open woodlands and cultivation. **Migration:** nonmigratory. **Breeding:** the nest is a large, communal, compartmented structure of twigs, lined with grass, in palm or pine trees. Eggs: 2–4, white, spotted gray. **Food:** fruits and flowers.

124 Dippers Cinclidae 5 species (1 ●), 1 genus, e.g. Dipper *Cinclus cinclus*
Description: the only fully aquatic Passerine family, showing remarkably few obvious adaptations to this lifestyle. Small, solitary (but may roost communally), compact, short-necked birds. L: 15–17.5 cm (6–7 in), Wt: 60–80 g (2–2¾ oz). Bill slender, straight, compressed with slitlike nostrils. Legs medium length, with strong feet and claws. Often bobs while perched on rocks by water. Wings short, pointed, used in swimming underwater. Flight strong, direct. Tail short, square. Plumage soft and dense with thick layer of down. Uniform brown, gray or black, often with large white patch on throat, breast, head or back. Monomorphic. **Range and habitat:** WP, EP, OR, western NA and NT. Fast-flowing streams, usually in mountains. **Migration:** nonmigratory.

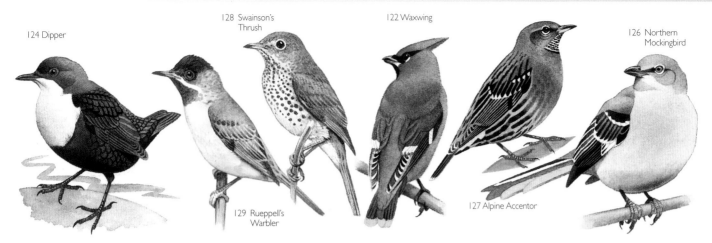

124 Dipper

128 Swainson's Thrush

122 Waxwing

126 Northern Mockingbird

129 Rueppell's Warbler

127 Alpine Accentor

Breeding: nest is a large domed structure with side entrance of moss generally under ledge over running water. Eggs: 5 (rarely 4–6), white. Incubation by female for 16–17 days. Broods: 2. Young are in nest for 19–25 days. **Food:** chiefly aquatic insects for which it dives. Also other invertebrates, some small fish and tadpoles.

125 Wrens Troglodytidae 79 species (7 ●), 17 genera, e.g. Wren *Troglodytes troglodytes*
Description: small, highly territorial, aggressive, compact birds. Most L: 7.5–12.5 cm (3–5 in), Wt: 8–15 g (¼–½ oz); 1 larger L:16–22 cm (6½–8½ in). Bill long, thin, pointed. Legs rather long, feet strong. Wings and tail short, rounded. Tail often cocked. Flight strong, direct. Plumage soft, generally browns and grays, barred and spotted. Monomorphic, males larger. Polygynous species with very loud, complex songs. Monogamous species with simple buzzing songs. **Systematics:** DNA evidence shows very close affinities of the wrens with the creepers, which may even place them in the family Certhidae. **Range and habitat:** WP, EP, NA, NT. Generally dense, low vegetation in a wide variety of habitats. **Migration:** some northern species migratory. **Breeding:** monogamy and polygyny. Nest is a domed structure with side entrance of twigs and grass suspended in vegetation, or in a cavity, may be bulky, usually constructed by male who may make several nests from which the female chooses. Eggs: 2–11 (fewer in tropics). Incubation by female for 12–20 days. Broods: 1–4 (in polygynous species, male may raise more broods than females). Young are in nest for 12–18 days. **Food:** small invertebrates.

126 Mockingbirds and Thrashers Mimidae 35 species (6 ●), 11 genera, e.g. Northern Mockingbird *Mimus polyglottos*
Description: medium-sized, slender, arboreal and ground-dwelling, solitary. L: 20–30 cm (8–12 in) Wt: 20–142 g (1–5 oz). Bill medium to long, slender, pointed, straight to decurved. Legs long. Wings short to medium, rounded. Flight mostly rather weak. Tail long, often graduated. Plumage browns, grays, black and white. Paler underparts, often streaked, or uniform, some with black and white wings and tail. Good songsters, many mimic. **Range and habitat:** NA, NT. Scrublands and forest edge. **Migration:** northern species migratory. **Breeding:** monogamous and aggressively territorial, helpers may be present at the nest. Nest is a lined cup of twigs in dense bush or tree. Eggs: 2–5, varied pale and spotted or streaked. Incubation by female (rarely shared) for 12–13 days. Young are in nest for 12–13 (rarely longer) days. **Food:** insects, fruit, and seeds on or near ground.

127 Accentors Prunellidae 13 species, 1 genus, e.g. Alpine Accentor *Prunella collaris*
Description: small, solitary to gregarious, inconspicuous, drably colored, ground-dwelling birds. L: 13–18 cm (5–7 in), Wt: 18–26 g (¾–1 oz). Mostly known from Palaearctic species. Biochemical evidence suggests that they may be closest to the weavers (Ploceidae). In general appearance they are rather like sparrows in that family though the bill is longer and more slender. Legs medium-sized, feet weak. Wings medium-sized, rounded to pointed, flight generally rapid. Tail medium-sized, square. Plumage grays, browns, streaked. Monomorphic, males larger. **Range and habitat:** WP, EP, northern AF, OR. Scrub, forest edges, cultivation. Most species at high altitudes. **Migration:** many altitudinal migrants. **Breeding:** diverse and flexible mating systems. Nest is an open cup of fine plant material low in vegetation or rock crevice. Eggs: 3–6, bluish. Incubation by female or shared for 11–15 days. Broods: 2–3. Young are in nest for 12–14 days. Some species parasitized by cuckoos (Cuculidae). **Food:** chiefly insects, also seeds and fruit in winter.

Note: families 128–35 are often treated as subfamilies (Turdinae to Pachycephalinae) of an enlarged family Muscicapidae. Such grouping is not well supported by DNA evidence.

128 Thrushes and Chats Turdidae 328 species (37 ●), 52 genera, e.g. Swainson's Thrush *Catharus ustulatus*
Description: small to medium, arboreal or ground-feeding. L:11–33 cm (4½–13 in), Wt: 8–220 g (¼–8 oz). Solitary when breeding, often gregarious in winter or on migration. Structurally similar. Bill medium to slender, pointed, straight, usually with well-developed rictal bristles. Legs medium to long. Feet strong to weak. Wings rounded to pointed. Flight strong, direct. Tail medium to long, square. Plumage very varied, browns, grays, black, white, reds and yellows. Males larger. Monomorphic or dimorphic in which females generally plain. Many good songsters. **Systematics:** The old world chats may be more closely related to old world flycatchers than to thrushes, but we have followed a traditional practice of grouping them with thrushes here in line with *Birdlife International*. **Range and habitat:** worldwide except AN. A wide range of terrestrial habitats from tropical forest to desert. **Migration:** many migratory species, especially in northern latitudes, many nocturnal migrants. **Breeding:** monogamous. Nest is an open cup of grasses and twigs in vegetation, sometimes with mud lining, sometimes a tree-hole or rock cavity, built by female. Eggs: 2–6 (rarely 7), whitish, blue to green or buff, often spotted or streaked. Incubation by female for 12–15 days. Broods: 1–3. Young are in nest for 11–18 days, usually fledge with spotted first plumage. **Food:** invertebrates and fruit, especially in winter.

129 Old World Warblers Sylviidae 362 species (40 ●), 60 genera, e.g. Rueppell's Warbler *Sylvia rueppelli*
Description: very small to medium. L: 9–16 cm (3½–6½ in), Wt: 5–20 g (¼– ¾ oz) mostly. Bill medium-sized, pointed. Legs medium-sized, with strong or weak feet. Wings short, rounded to long, pointed. Tail medium to long, square to rounded. Plumage browns, grays, green or yellow, often streaked darker, some with black on head. Males usually larger. Generally monomorphic, some dimorphic. Many good songsters. **Systematics:** DNA evidence suggests that the 6 species of kinglet and 111 species of cisticola, and their allies, might occupy their own families: Regulidae and Cisticolidae respectively. We have retained the traditional grouping in line with *Birdlife International*. **Range and**

135 Golden Whistler

130 Blue-gray Gnatcatcher

136 White-necked Bald Crow

137 Chestnut-backed Scimitar Babbler

138 Bearded Reedling

139 Spotted Quail Thrush

habitat: WP, EP, AF, OR, AU. A variety of forest, scrub and marshland habitats depending on species. **Migration:** many strongly migratory species, especially WP to AF and EP to OR. Nocturnal migrants. Some nonmigratory. **Breeding:** monogamous or more rarely polygynous. Nest is elaborate, cupped or domed, usually placed low in dense vegetation. Eggs: 2–7, semi-cryptic. Incubation by female or shared for 12–14 days. Broods: 1–2. Young are in nest for 11–15 days. Some species heavily parasitized by cuckoos (Cuculidae). **Food:** chiefly insects, some fruit in autumn/winter.

130 Gnatcatchers Polioptilidae 15 species, 3 genera, sometimes treated within the Sylviidae, e.g. Blue-gray Gnatcatcher *Polioptila caerulea*
Description: tiny, restless, arboreal and solitary birds. L: 10–12 cm (4–4½ in), Wt: less than 7g (¼ oz). Long tails and slender, pointed bills. Legs long, thin. Wings pointed. Plumage mostly blue-gray or brown upperparts, white underparts. Some with black on head, many with white outer tail feathers. More or less monomorphic. **Range and habitat:** NA, NT. Forest understorey, open forest and semiarid habitats. **Migration:** 1 migratory species, most nonmigratory. **Breeding:** nest is an open cup of plant fibers bound with spiders' web, attached at base and side. Eggs: 3–5. Incubation shared for 13–15 days. Broods: 2 (may overlap in time). Young are in nest for 11–14 days. **Food:** chiefly insects gleaned from leaves.

131 Old World Flycatchers Muscicapidae 108 species (17 ●), 9 genera, e.g. Spotted Flycatcher *Muscicapa striata*
Description: small, solitary, arboreal birds analogous to the tyrant flycatchers (Tyrannidae) of the New World. L: 10–21 cm (4–8 in), Wt: 6–20 g (¼–¾ oz). Head and eyes rather large. Bill flattened, slightly hook-tipped, broad-based with well-developed rictal bristles. Legs short. Feet small and weak. Wings short to long and pointed. Flight strong, agile. Tail short to medium, square. Plumage varied, uniform browns to pied, bright blue, yellow or red. Males often larger. Monomorphic to strongly dimorphic. **Systematics:** DNA evidence suggests that the Old World flycatchers should be a sub-family and sister-group (i.e. similar age) of the Old World chats. However, we have retained the traditional groupings here in line with *Birdlife International*. **Range and habitat:** WP, EP, AF, OR, AU, PA. Forest and scrublands. **Migration:** many strong migrants, nocturnal migrants. **Breeding:** monogamy and polygyny. Nest is an open cup on branch or in tree-hole or crevice. Eggs: 2–6 (fewer in tropics), whitish, greenish or buff, spotted. Incubation by female or shared for 10–15 days. Broods: 1–2. Young are in nest for 10–15 days. **Food:** insects taken by sallying (especially larger species) and gleaning.

132 Wattle-eyes and Puff-back Flycatchers Platysteirida 31 species (1 ●), 6 genera, often treated within the Muscicapinae, e.g. Brown-throated Wattle-eye *Platysteira cyanea*
Description: tiny to small, arboreal, solitary birds. L: 8–16 cm (3–6½ in), Wt: c.5–20 g (¼–¾ oz). They differ in several respects from the Muscicapidae. The bill is similar but sometimes stouter. Bill slightly hook-tipped, and with prominent rictal bristles. The back feathers are often long and fluffy and raised in alarm. Several species show blue or red wattles around the eyes. Females tend to differ more between species than males and are believed in some species to take a more dominant role in courtship. Legs, feet and wings as Muscicapidae, tail very short to medium, square. Plumage generally contrasting blues, black or violet upperparts, white underparts, often with red or orange breast band. Some with white wing patches. Generally dimorphic, immature plumage sometimes distinct. **Range and habitat:** AF. A wide variety of forest, forest edge and savannah habitats. **Migration:** nonmigratory. **Breeding:** little known. Nest is a small cup of plant fibers and cobwebs on a branch. Eggs: 2–3, pale green to blue, spotted or blotched gray, brown, violet or red. Incubation shared for 12–14 days. Young are in nest for 12–14 days. Some species are heavily parasitized by honeyguides (Indicatoridae) and cuckoos (Cuculidae). **Food:** chiefly insects.

133 Monarchs and Fantails Monarchidae 141 species (21 ●), 18 genera, e.g. Pied Monarch *Arses kaupi*
Description: small, striking birds. L: 12–30 cm (4½–12 in), Wt: 15–40 g (½–1½ oz). Solitary or paired, arboreal. Bill medium-sized, often flattened, notched and with a wide gape and small hook at tip. Rictal bristles prominent. Legs and feet small, weak. Wings medium to long, pointed. Tail square or graduated, medium to very long. Plumage often metallic black or gray, or chestnut with white underparts. Sometimes crested, frilled or wattled. Most are strongly dimorphic. **Systematics:** Recent classifications have split the 43 fantail species into their own family: Rhipiduridae. Although DNA evidence supports a split, it is at a much lower taxonomic level than the family, and so we have retained the traditional grouping. **Range and habitat:** AF, OR, AU. A variety of forest habitats. **Migration:** nonmigratory. **Breeding:** little known. Some with elaborate courtship displays. Nest is a small cup of plant fibers bound by cobwebs on branch or in fork, built by female or both. Eggs: 2–4, white, spotted brown. Incubation by female or shared for 14–17 days. Young are in nest for 12–18 days. **Food:** insects flushed from vegetation or by sallying, also some fruit.

134 Australasian Robins Petroicidae 44 species (1 ●), 13 genera, often treated as Muscicapinae, e.g. Lemon-breasted Flycatcher *Microeca flavigaster*
Description: small, usually solitary, arboreal birds, probably so named as they reminded early settlers of the European robin: they are plump little birds often with red underparts and take their food from the ground. L: 10–16.5 cm (4–6½ in). Characteristic upright posture with occasional flicks of drooping tail. Bill medium-sized, broad-based, flattened, slightly hook-tipped and with rictal bristles. Legs medium-sized, weak. Wings medium to long, pointed. Flight agile. Tail medium to long, square. Plumage black, brown or greenish upperparts, red, pink, white, yellow or gray underparts. Varying amounts of white on wings and tail. More or less monomorphic, females more drab and less variable. **Systematics:** Members of this family have traditionally been placed, variously, within the Muscicapinae and Turdinae, but DNA evidence clearly identifies them as a distinct lineage. **Range and habitat:** AU, PA. A variety of scrubland and forest

133 Pied Monarch

134 Lemon-breasted Flycatcher

131 Spotted Flycatcher

140 Long-tailed Tit

132 Brown-throated Wattle-eye

habitats. **Migration:** many partial migrants. **Breeding:** nest is a tiny shallow, lined cup of moss bound with cobwebs on a branch up to 20 m (65 ft) and sometimes decorated. Eggs: 2–4, pale blue or green, spotted with red-brown to violet. Incubation by female for 12–14 days. **Food:** chiefly insects and their larvae caught on ground by dropping from a perch (robins) or by sallying (flycatchers).

135 Whistlers and allies Pachycephalidae 57 species (1 ●), 12 genera, e.g. Golden Whistler *Pachycephala pectoralis*
Description: small to medium, solitary or gregarious, arboreal, often conspicuous. L: 12–25 cm (4½–10 in), Wt: 15–100 g (½–3 oz). Head rounded, heavy with chunky body. A few are wattled. Bill medium-sized, stout, straight to decurved, softie hook-tipped and with or without rictal bristles. Legs medium-sized, strong. Wings medium to long, pointed. Flight strong, undulating. Tail medium-sized, square. Plumage generally dull rufous browns and grays, with some green, white and black. Some with bright yellow underparts. Monomorphic or dimorphic, in most the male is brighter. Juvenile plumage sometimes distinct. Many with explosive songs. **Range and habitat:** AU, PA. Forest, scrublands, savannah and mangroves. **Migration:** some migratory species. **Breeding:** little known. Nest is a cup of sticks, plant fibers and cobwebs, in a tree-fork or cavity. Eggs: 2–4, glossy white to pinkish, spotted brown and gray. Incubation shared fore. 17 days. Broods: 1–3. Young are in nest for 13–16 days. **Food:** insects and fruit.

136 Rockfowl Picathartidae 2 species (2 ●), 1 genus, e.g. White-necked Bald Crow *Picathartes gymnocephalus*
Description: little is known about these extraordinary birds. Our understanding of their natural history owes much to the descriptions of native Africans as few ornithologists have witnessed them at first hand. Medium-sized, L: 39–50 cm (15–20 in). Bill is long, strong, and crowlike. Legs long. Head bare and colored red, black and blue or black and yellow. Upperparts black or gray with black wings. Underparts white or gray and white. Wings rounded, tail long, graduated. Monomorphic. Chiefly ground-dwelling, weak flight, rather quiet though gregarious. **Range and habitat:** western AF. Rainforests up to 2,100m (6,900ft), especially in caves. **Migration:** nonmigratory. **Breeding:** little information available, colonial, possibly with nest-helpers. Nest is a massive lined cup of mud cemented to rock faces 2–4 m (6½–13 ft) high in caves, or in rock crevice. Eggs: 2, profusely spotted and blotched in brown and gray. Incubation shared by male and female. **Food:** chiefly invertebrates, also frogs near streams.

137 Babblers Timaliidae 270 species (24 ●), 51 genera, e.g. Chestnut-backed Scimitar Babbler *Pomatorhinus montanus*
Description: a large and diverse assemblage with uncertain relationships. Small to medium, arboreal or ground-dwelling, solitary or highly gregarious. The latter with complex social organization. L: 10–35 cm (4–14 in), Wt: 5–150 g (¼–5¼ oz). Bill slender but strong, often decurved and with rictal bristles sometimes prominent. Legs medium to long, strong. Feet stout. Wings short, rounded. Flight rather weak. Tail medium-sized, square to long, graduated.

Plumage soft, usually drab browns, also white, and a few boldly patterned. Most monomorphic. **Systematics:** The Australo-Papuan *Pomastomus* babblers may constitute a distict family: Pomatostomidae, which is supported by DNA evidence, but we have retained the traditional grouping in line with *Birdlife International.* **Range and habitat:** AF, OR, AU, western NA (1 species). A very wide range of terrestrial habitats. **Migration:** most species nonmigratory. **Breeding:** solitary or in groups. In the latter, helpers often present at the nest. Nest is an open cup or domed with side entrance in diverse sites. Eggs: 2–6, usually white or blue. Incubation by female or shared for 14–15 days. Young are in nest for 13–16 days. **Food:** invertebrates.

138 Parrotbills Paradoxornithidae 20 species (3 ●), 3 genera, e.g. Bearded Reedling *Panurus biarmicus*
Description: small to medium, lively, gregarious birds especially outside breeding season. L: 9–29 cm (3½–11½ in), Wt: 5–36 g (¼–1¼ oz). Bill short, stout, decurved and laterally compressed, nostrils covered by bristles. Legs short, feet strong, 1 species unique among Passerines in having 3 toes only (outer toe is a stump syndactyl with the middle toe). Wings short, rounded. Flight strong, direct but some species fly reluctantly. Tail long, graduated. Plumage varied, usually shades of gray-brown with paler or white underparts, some with black on head, patterns sometimes complex. Dimorphic or monomorphic. **Range and habitat:** WP, EP, OR. Swamps, grass and bamboo thickets. **Migration:** nonmigratory or only local movements. **Breeding:** little information. Nest is a deep cup of grass and hair bound with cobwebs, placed low in vegetation or reeds. Eggs: 2 –7, pale, spotted red-brown. Incubation shared for 12–13 days. Broods: 2. Young in nest for 9–12 days. **Food:** insects, small seeds and fruits.

139 Logrunners, whipbirds, and quail-thrushes Orthonychidae 17 species, 7 genera, e.g. Spotted Quail Thrush *Cinclosoma punctatum*
Description: small to medium, dumpy birds. L: 10–30 cm (4–12 in), Wt: 20–80 g (¾–2¾ oz). Poorly known because of their secretive ground-dwelling behavior. Bill medium to stout, straight, pointed. Legs and feet robust. Wings short and rounded, tail medium-sized, some with spiny bare quill at feather tips. Plumage mostly brown, black or white or blue and white. Monomorphic or dimorphic. Noisy in breeding season. **Systematics:** DNA evidence suggests that the whipbirds and quail-thrushes may constitute a distinct family, Eupetidae; but we have retained the traditional grouping in line with *Birdlife International.* **Range and habitat:** OR, AU. Dense forest and scrubland. **Migration:** nonmigratory or locally nomadic. **Breeding:** incompletely known. Nest is usually a cup or dome of plant fibers, placed low in vegetation, or a lined scrape. Eggs: 1–3, white or pale blue. Incubation: 17–21 days. Young in nest for 12–14 days. **Food:** invertebrates and seeds.

140 Long-tailed Tits Aegithalidae 8 species, 3 genera, e.g. Long-tailed Tit *Aegithalos caudatus*
Description: tiny birds, 66% of whose length is tail. L: 9–14 cm (3½–5½ in), Wt: 5–7 g (¼ oz). Recent evidence suggests that they are most closely related

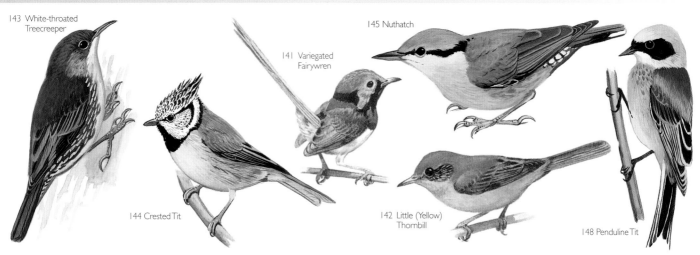

143 White-throated Treecreeper

141 Variegated Fairywren

145 Nuthatch

144 Crested Tit

142 Little (Yellow) Thornbill

148 Penduline Tit

to babblers (Timalidae). Gregarious with complex social organization, often in large flocks. Arboreal, moving with agility through vegetation. Bill short, stout, conical and laterally compressed. Legs and feet small. Wings medium-sized. Flight undulating, light. Tail long, graduated, especially in juveniles. Plumage soft, black, greys, pinks, white and browns. Upperparts darker than underparts. Monomorphic, males slightly larger. **Range and habitat:** WP, EP, OR, NA. Forest, forest edge and scrub habitats. **Migration:** non-migratory. **Breeding:** defend clan territories, and have helpers at the nest. Nest is a purse-shaped globe of moss, lichens and cobwebs, feather-lined with side entrance in vegetation. Eggs: 6–10, white, spotted red. Incubation by female for 13–14 days. Broods: 1. Young in nest for 16–17 days. **Food:** chiefly insects.

141 Fairywrens Maluridae 25 species (2 ●), 5 genera, e.g. Variegated Fairywren *Malurus lamberti*
Description: small, active, gregarious birds with long tails carried cocked over back. L: 14–22 cm (5½–8½ in), Wt: 7–37 g (¼–1¼ oz). Bill generally thin, pointed, slightly decurved, weak. Legs medium-sized, thin. Wings short, rounded. Tail feathers may be sparsely barbed or 'decomposed'. Highly dimorphic in breeding season. Male plumage duller outside this time. Plumage basically browns, rufous and white. Breeding males often bright metallic blues, purples, red, chestnut and white. Females may also show blue. **Range and habitat:** AU. Forest and scrublands. **Migration:** non-migratory. **Breeding:** may be helped by young from earlier broods, and by unpaired males. Nest is usually domed with porched side entrance, of plant fibres, sometimes bulky; or a cup. Eggs: 2–5, white speckled red-brown. Incubation by female for 12–15 days. Broods: 2, may overlap. Young are in nest for 10–12 days. Some species are heavily parasitized by cuckoos (Cuculidae). **Food:** small insects taken by gleaning.

142 Thornbills and Flyeaters Acanthizida 70 species (6 ●), 17 genera, e.g. Little (Yellow) Thornbill *Acanthiza nana*
Description: tiny to small, restless, arboreal to semi-terrestrial, solitary or gregarious birds often living in extended family groups or clans. L: 8–20 cm (3–8 in), Wt: 7–40 g (¼–1½ oz). Bill short to medium, stout to thin. Legs medium-sized, thin. Wings short, round to pointed. Tail medium-sized, broad and rounded. Plumage variously patterned, mostly browns, greys, greens, yellows, often with white in the tail. Monomorphic. **Systematics:** The 5 Australian chat species have variously been placed in the Acanthizidae, as here, the Maluridae, and in their own family: Epthianuridae. DNA comparison actually suggests close affinity with the Meliphagidae. **Range and habitat:** AU, PA. Wide variety of forest and arid scrubland habitats. **Migration:** most non-migratory, a few nomadic. **Breeding:** little known. Monogamous, some helped at the nest by failed breeders. Nest is a neat dome with side entrance, often porched, of plant fibres. Eggs: 2–3 (rarely 4), white, sometimes spotted. Incubation is for 15–20 days. Young are in nest for 15–20 days. **Food:** insects and seeds.

143 Australian Creepers Climacteridae 7 species, 2 genera, e.g. White-throated Treecreeper *Climacteris leucophaea*

Description: small, solitary or in small groups, arboreal and ground-foraging birds. L: 12–19 cm (4½–7½ in). Wt: 20–40 g (¾–1½ oz). Bill long, decurved, pointed. Legs and feet strong, with long, curved claws. Wings pointed. Tail short, square, soft and not used in support. Plumage: brown to black upperparts with broad, pale wing-bar, underparts rufous or streaked. Most monomorphic. **Range and habitat:** Au. Forests. **Migration:** non-migratory. **Breeding:** solitary or communal with helpers at the nest. Nest is a cup of plant fibres and hair in tree-hole. Eggs: 2–3, white or pinkish with reddish spots. Incubation by female for 16–23 days. Broods: 1–2. Young are in nest for 25–6 days. **Food:** insects (especially ants), flowers, pollen and nectar.

144 Tits and Chickadees Paridae 55 species (1 ●), 12 genera, e.g. Crested Tit *Parus cristatus*
Description: among the best studied of birds. Small, compact, acrobatic and arboreal, inquisitive and gregarious birds forming mixed-species flocks. L: 11.5–14 cm (4½–5½ in), Wt: 6–20 g (¼–¾ oz). Bill short to medium, thin to stout, generally strong. Nostrils covered by bristles. Legs medium-sized. Feet strong. Wings medium-rounded to pointed. Flight strong. Tail medium-sized. Plumage varied. Generally, brown, white, grey, black and white, some with yellow, green and blue. Underparts generally paler. Most monomorphic, males larger and brighter. **Range and habitat:** WP, EP, AF, OR, NA. A variety of forest, forest edge and scrub habitats including cultivation and suburbia. **Migration:** some partial migrants. **Breeding:** monogamous, territorial. Nest is a cup of moss and hair in tree-hole, excavated by some species. Some readily accept nestboxes. Eggs: 4–12 (rarely 18), white, spotted red-brown. Incubation by female: 13–14 days. Broods: 1, rarely 2. Young are in nest for 17–20 days. **Food:** a wide variety of invertebrates, also buds and seeds, especially of trees, feeding from ground to canopy.

145 Nuthatches Sittidae 27 species (4 ●), 3 genera, e.g. Nuthatch *Sitta europaea*
Description: small, compact, arboreal, agile and acrobatic, though less so than tits (Paridae), they can run swiftly up and down tree-trunks. L: 9.5–20 cm (3¾–8 in), Wt: 10–60 g (¼–2 oz). Many are highly territorial – some establishing territories within a few weeks of fledging. Bill long, straight or decurved and pointed. Legs short, stout. Feet strong with long, curved, strong nails. Wings longish, pointed. Flight strong. Tail short, square, not used in support. Plumage chiefly grey to blue above, white, brownish below. Some also with red. Head often striped. More or less monomorphic, males slightly larger. **Systematics:** The Wallcreeper is sometimes classified in the monotypic family: Tichodromidae, but this is probably not supported by DNA evidence. We have included the 2 sitellas following Birdlife International, although they should constitute a family: Neosittidae **Range and habitat:** WP, EP, OR, AU, NA. Natural and semi-natural forest habitats, also rocky habitats. **Migration:** most species non-migratory, some partial migrants. **Breeding:** monogamous, highly territorial. Nest is usually of dry leaves in a tree-hole or rock crevice. Several species reduce

146 Common Treecreeper
151 Oriental White-eye
149 Southern White-bellied Sunbird
147 Stripe-headed creeper
150 Thick-billed Flowerpecker
152 Fuscus Honeyeater

the entrance size by plastering it with mud. Eggs: 4–10, white with reddish spots. Incubation by female for 15–18 days. Broods: 1. Young are in nest for 23–5 days. **Food:** chiefly invertebrates gleaned from bark and leaves, also seeds.

146 Creepers Certhiidae 7 species (1 ●), 2 genera, e.g. Common Treecreeper *Certhia familiaris*

Description: small, slender, arboreal and solitary (though sometimes roost communally and often join mixed-species flocks). L: 12–15 cm (4½–6 in), Wt: 7–16 g (¼–½ oz). Bill long, thin, pointed and decurved. Legs short. Toes with long, decurved claws. Wings short. Flight fast. Tail long, of stiff, pointed feathers used in support when foraging on bark. Plumage: upperparts brown, streaked with buff; underparts white. Monomorphic, males slightly larger. **Range and habitat:** WP, EP, AF, OR, NA. Forests. **Migration:** generally short-distance partial migrants. **Breeding:** nest is a lined cup of twigs and plant fibers in a crevice, e.g. behind tree bark, or on branch. Eggs: 5–6 (rarely 2–9), white, reddish spots. Incubation chiefly by female; 14–15 days. Broods: 1–2. Young in nest for 15–16 days. **Food:** small invertebrates gleaned from bark.

147 Philippine Creepers Rhabdornithida 3 species, 1 genus, e.g. Stripe-headed Creeper *Rhabdornis mystacalis*

Description: among the least known of birds. Many geographical races are recognized. Usually in small flocks, sometimes with other species. Small birds with brown, streaked upperparts, underparts white with dark streaking on flanks. L: 13–15 cm (5–6 in). Males grayer. 1 species with a black mask and white streaking on the head. Bill straight and slightly hook-tipped or decurved, stouter than in Certhiidae. Tongue brush-tipped. Legs rather long, elongated hind toe. Wings medium or long, pointed. Tail medium-sized, square with broad feathers. **Range and habitat:** OR. A variety of forest habitats. **Migration:** nonmigratory. **Breeding:** unknown. Nest is a tree-hole. **Food:** insects from ground or gleaned from bark; birds also feed from flowers in the open.

148 Penduline Tits Remizidae 13 species, 5 genera, e.g. Penduline Tit *Remiz pendulinus*

Description: small, compact, arboreal birds behaviorally similar to the true tits (Paridae), moving acrobatically with great agility through vegetation. L: 10–11 cm (4–4½ in), Wt: 8–11 g (¼–½ oz). Solitary or gregarious. Bill small, conical with straight culmen, pointed. Legs medium-sized, feet strong. Wings medium-sized. Flight strong. Tail medium-sized, square. Plumage pale buff, chestnut, black, brown, gray and yellow depending on species. More or less monomorphic. **Range and habitat:** WP, EP, AF, NA. Sparsely wooded habitats, from semiarid to marshland depending on species. **Migration:** nonmigratory. **Breeding:** breeding groups, may have helpers at the nest. Nest is a pendulous purse of flower pappus, some with a false entrance. Built by male and female. Family named after their nests. Eggs: 5–10, white. Incubated by female for 12–14 days. Broods: 1. Young in nest for 16–18 days. **Food:** insects and small seeds.

149 Sunbirds and spiderhunters Nectariniidae 130 species (6 ●), 15 genera, e.g. Southern White-bellied Sunbird *Nectarinia talatala*

Description: small birds analogous to the hummingbirds (Trochilidae) of the New World. L: 9–30 cm (3½–12 in) including long tail, Wt: 5–20 g (¼–¾ oz). Solitary or paired, arboreal. Bill long, slender, decurved and pointed, serrated near tip. Nostrils covered by operculum, rictal bristles absent. Bills vary greatly between species which may specialize on different flowers. Tongue protrusible, tubular and divided at tip (not brush-tipped) for sucking nectar. Legs short to medium, strong. Wings short, rounded to pointed. Flight fast, dashing, sometimes hovering. Tail often sexually dimorphic: short, square (females) to very long, pointed or graduated (males). Plumage generally dimorphic. Males dark metallic purples, greens with red, yellow or orange underparts. Females duller olive, gray-green. **Range and habitat:** WP (1 species), AF, OR, AU. Forest, scrubland, cultivation and gardens. **Migration:** most nonmigratory. **Breeding:** strictly monogamous unlike hummingbirds, highly territorial. Nest is an elaborate hanging purse with porched side entrance of plant materials and cobwebs (cup-shaped in spiderhunters). Eggs: 2 (rarely 3), white or bluish, heavily spotted. Incubation chiefly by female (shared in spiderhunters) for 13–15 days. Broods: 1–5. Young are in nest for 14–19 days. Some species are parasitized by cuckoos (Cuculidae). **Food:** nectar and small invertebrates, sometimes fruit. Perch while feeding.

150 Flowerpeckers Dicaeidae 60 species (3 ●), 7 genera, e.g. Thick-billed Flowerpecker *Dicaeum agile*

Description: small, compact, with short neck, active and arboreal. L: 8–15 cm (3–6 in), Wt: 5–20 g (¼–¾ oz); 1 species 21 cm (8 in), 42 g (1½ oz). Bill short, stout and straight or long, thin and decurved. Distal 3rd of bill notched. Tongue tip tubular for nectar-feeding. Legs short. Wings medium-sized, pointed. Outermost primary sometimes vestigial. Flight fast, darting. Tail short, square. Plumage monomorphic, dull gray-green; or dimorphic with males glossy bright blues above yellows below, with patches of red and yellow, females duller. **Systematics:** Following *Birdlife International*, we include the pardalotes and berrypeckers and tit berrypeckers, which may be distinguished in families: Pardalotidae, Melanocharitidae and Parymythiidae respectively **Range and habitat:** OR, AU. Treetops in forest and scrubland habitats. **Migration:** nonmigratory. **Breeding:** nest is a lined cup in a tree-hole or dense vegetation, or pendant with a side entrance, all of plant fibers and cobwebs built by female; or a tunnel in a bank dug by both. Eggs: 1–3 (rarely 1–5), white, sometimes blotched. Incubation by female for c.12 days. Young are in nest for c.15 days. **Food:** small fruits (especially mistletoe berries, whose seeds the birds disperse), nectar, and invertebrates.

151 White-eyes Zosteropidae 94 species (23 ●), 12 genera, e.g. Oriental White-eye *Zosterops palpebrosa*

Description: small, arboreal, restless and gregarious in flocks. L: 10–14 cm (4–5½ in), Wt: 8–31 g (¼–1 oz). Little variation across whole family. Bill slender, decurved and pointed. Tongue brush-tipped. Legs medium-sized, strong. Wings

155 Blue Vanga

158 Magpie Lark

153 African Golden Oriole

157 Saddleback

154 Great Gray Shrike

short, rounded, with outermost primary absent. Flight dashing. Tail moderate. Plumage green above, white/ yellow below. Most with white eye-ring of tiny feathers, varying in size between species. Always monomorphic, but males often larger. **Range and habitat:** AF, OR, AU, PA. Forest, scrublands and gardens. **Migration:** mostly nonmigratory. **Breeding:** monogamous, paired for life, communal species may have nest-helpers. Can have very rapid breeding cycle—3 weeks from nest construction to fledging. Nest is a deep cup of plant material, suspended in a fork near the canopy. Eggs: 2–4, whitish. Incubation shared for 10–12 days. Broods: 2–4. Young are in nest for 10–12 days. **Food:** insects, fruit, and nectar.

152 Honeyeaters Meliphagidae 172 species (1 ●), 39 genera, e.g. Fuscus Honeyeater *Meliphaga fusca* (see illustration on p 43.)
Description: a diverse group showing evolution parallel to many other groups. Small to medium-large, arboreal, often gregarious and pugnacious birds. L: 8–45 cm (3–18 in), Wt: 6.5–150 g (¼–5¼ oz) Bill slender, pointed, medium to long and decurved. Tongue elaborate, protrusible and brush-tipped. Head sometimes with areas of bare skin and wattles. Legs short to medium. Wings long, pointed. Flight direct and dashing in small species to slow and rather clumsy in larger species. Tail medium to long. Plumage varied, of drab greens, browns, grays, yellows (monomorphic) or bold reds, black and white (dimorphic). Many have a conspicuous colored patch behind the ears. **Systematics:** The sugarbirds (2 spp.) may form a distinct family: Promeropidae **Range and habitat:** southern AF, AU. Forest and scrublands. **Migration:** some migratory species. **Breeding:** many colonial breeders with nest-helpers. Nest is cup-shaped or pendulous with a side entrance, of plant materials and cobwebs, often high in tree. Eggs: 2 (rarely 1–4), white to pale buff, spotted reddish. Incubation by female or shared for 13–17 days. Broods: rarely more than 2. Young in nest for 10–16 days. **Food:** nectar, insects and some fruit, both generalist and specialist species.

153 Orioles Oriolidae 29 species (3 ●), 2 genera, e.g. African Golden Oriole *Oriolus auratus*
Description: medium-sized, arboreal, with strong, pointed bill, legs and feet, bright plumage—yellows, greens and black. L: 20–30 cm (8–12 in), Wt: c.70 g (2½ oz). Wings pointed, tail medium to long. Solitary. Dimorphic, males larger. **Range and habitat:** WP (1 species), EP, AF, OR, AU. Forests and dense scrublands. **Migration:** some migratory species. **Breeding:** nest is a deep, grassy cup high in tree. Eggs: 2–5, green with reddish markings. Incubation sometimes shared for 14–15 days. Broods: 1. Young are in nest for 14–15 days. **Food:** insects and fruit.

154 Shrikes Laniidae 84 species (9 ●), 13 genera, e.g. Great Gray Shrike *Lanius excubitor*
Description: a large family containing a number of distinct groups. Small to medium, solitary (gregarious in helmet shrikes), arboreal birds with large heads. L: 15–38 cm (6–15 in), Wt: 10–87 g (¼–3 oz). Sharp, stout, notched and

hooked bills with partly covered nostrils and well-developed rictal bristles; some have weaker bills. Aggressive predators analogous to raptors. Legs medium-sized, strong claws sharp. Wings rather rounded, tail medium to long. Flight strong. Plumage varied, often soft, grays and browns with black and white markings on wings and head, or bright reds, greens and yellows. Pronounced dimorphism to monomorphic. **Systematics:** Following *Birdlife International*, we here include the bushshrikes (Malaconotidae) and Helmetshrikes (Prionopidae) and their allies, and the monotypic Pityriaseidae. **Range and habitat:** WP, EP, AF, OR, NA. A wide range of forest, savannah and savannah woodland, grassland and cultivated habitats. **Migration:** some strongly migratory species, especially in northern latitudes. **Breeding:** nest is a varied, open cup of twigs and finer material, often lined. Eggs: 2–7, white, spotted. Incubation by female (sometimes shared) for 12–18 days. Broods: 1–2. Young are in nest for 16–20 days. **Food:** insects and other invertebrates, also small vertebrates depending on species.

155 Vanga Shrikes Vangidae 14 species (4 ●), 12 genera, e.g. Blue Vanga *Leptopterus madagascarinus*
Description: a poorly known group of small to medium, rather gregarious, arboreal shrikelike birds. L: 13–32 cm (5–13 in). Varied bill-shapes, bill of most is relatively massive, notched and hooked. In 1 it is thin and curved for probing, in several it is high, laterally compressed or inflated. In bill form they are a good example of adaptive radiation in isolation. Otherwise like shrikes but wings and tail rather long. Monomorphic or dimorphic. **Range and habitat:** Madagascar (AF). Forest, scrublands and mangrove swamps. **Migration:** nonmigratory. **Breeding:** little known, nest-helpers may be present. Nest is a cup of twigs in a tree. Eggs: 2–3 (rarely 4), white or pale green, heavily spotted. Incubation probably shared. **Food:** chiefly insects.

156 Drongos Dicruridae 23 species (2 ●), 2 genera, e.g. Lesser Racquet-tailed Drongo *Dicrurus remifer* (see illustration on p 46.)
Description: medium-sized, solitary, active and arboreal birds with elaborate tails. L: 18–64 cm (7–25 in) including up to 30 cm (12 in) tail, Wt: c.40–50 g (1½–1¾ oz). Often crested. Bill stout, arched and slightly hooked with prominent rictal bristles. Nostrils sometimes concealed by dense feathering. Legs and feet strong. Wings long, pointed. Flight strong but unsustained. Tail medium to very long, outer feathers splayed outward or developed into racquet shape. Plumage generally black with green to purple iridescence. **Range and habitat:** AF, OR, AU. Open wooded habitats, savannah, forest edges and cultivation. **Migration:** some migratory species. **Breeding:** little known for many. Nest is a shallow cup in fork of a branch. Eggs: 2–4, often white speckled brown. Incubation by female or shared for 16 days. Broods: 2–3. **Food:** follow large mammals for disturbed insects. Also nectar.

157 Wattlebirds Callaeidae 2 species (1 ●), 2 genera, e.g. Saddleback *Creadion carunculatus*
Description: medium-sized, largely ground-dwelling birds. L: 22–50 cm

159 Dusky Woodswallow

163 Common Raven

162 Satin Bowerbird   161 Superb Bird of Paradise

160 Gray Butcherbird

(8½–20 in), Wt: 77–240 g (2¾–8½ oz). Exceptional for the sexual dimorphism of their bills. The extinct Huia of this family was the most extreme in this regard, the female's long, decurved bill being twice the length of the male's stout, conical bill. The gape carries orange or blue wattles of varying size. In the extant species: bill short, stout and hooked to long and decurved. Legs long, strong. Feet strong. Hops on ground. Wings short. Flight weak. Tail long, slightly vaulted. Plumage black, blue-gray or brown. **Range and habitat:** New Zealand (AU). Dense native forest. **Migration:** nonmigratory. **Breeding:** elaborate courtship. Nest is a shallow, lined cup of sticks, on or near ground. Eggs: 2–3, gray, spotted and blotched purple and brown. Incubation by female for 18–25 days. Broods: 1. Young in nest for 27–8 days. **Food:** fruit, nectar, and insects.

158 Magpie Larks Grallinidae 4 species, 3 genera, e.g. Magpie Lark *Grallina cyanoleuca*
Description: medium-sized, highly gregarious, rather graceful birds. L: 20–50 cm (8–20 in), Wt: 40–350 g (1½–12½ oz). Bill medium-sized, pointed, straight with uncovered nostrils. Legs long. Wings pointed. Flight poor. Tail long, square. Plumage gray or pied. Dimorphic in head patterns. Juvenile plumage distinct. **Systematics:** Following *Birdife International*, we include the Corcoracidae (2 spp.) here. ion, often near water. **Migration:** nonmigratory or nomadic migrants. **Breeding:** strongly territorial. Nests are deep bowls of mud strengthened with hair and plant fibers on a high tree branch, Wt: up to 1 kg (2 lb 3 oz). Eggs: 3–5 (rarely 8), white to pink, blotched red, brown or gray. Incubation shared for 17–18 days. Broods: 1–3. Young are semi-altricial, in nest for 19–23 days. **Food:** invertebrates, some seeds.

159 Woodswallows Artamidae 11 species, 1 genus, e.g. Dusky Woodswallow *Artamus cyanopterus*
Description: medium-sized, chunky, and highly gregarious birds. L: 12–23 cm (4½–9 in), Wt: 14–73 g (½–2½ oz). Bill stout, slightly decurved with a wide gape and without rictal bristles. Legs and feet short and strong. Wings very long and pointed. Flight agile and graceful. Sometimes soars. Tail short and square. Plumage solid colors of browns, grays, and black. Paler below. Monomorphic. Has powder down plumes which break up to dress feathers. In the Passeriformes, only these and Cotingidae have such feathers. **Range and habitat:** OR, AU. Wooded open country, often near water. **Migration:** some species migratory. **Breeding:** colonial. May have nest-helpers. Nest is a fragile cup high in a bush or cavity in tree or rock. Eggs: 2–4, white, spotted red-brown. Incubation shared for 12–16 days. Young are semi-altricial, in nest for 16–20 days. **Food:** aerial insects.

160 Butcherbirds Cracticidae 12 species, 4 genera, e.g. Gray Butcherbird *Cracticus torquatus*
Description: medium to large, solitary or gregarious and arboreal but often feed on ground. L: 25–50 cm (10–20 in), Wt: 80–140 g (2¾–5 oz). Bill large, straight, more or less hooked, with bare nostrils and prominent rictal bristles. Legs medium to long, strong. Wings long, pointed. Flight strong. Tail long, square.

Plumage gray or pied. Monomorphic or dimorphic. **Range and habitat:** AU. Open forests, scrublands and grasslands. **Migration:** nonmigratory or partial altitudinal migration. **Breeding:** rather poorly known. Strongly territorial. Nest is a large, lined, open cup of sticks high in a tree. Eggs: 3–5, green or blue, blotched and streaked brown. Incubated chiefly by female for 20 days. Broods: 1. Young are in nest for 28 days. **Food:** omnivorous but chiefly insects.

161 Birds-of-Paradise Paradisaeidae 44 species (4 ●), 17 genera, e.g. Superb Bird-of-Paradise *Lophorina superba*
Description: medium to large, stunningly beautiful, solitary, arboreal birds with diverse and spectacular plumage. L: 15–110 cm (6–43 in). Bill medium to long, straight to decurved, stout. Legs medium-sized, stout. Wings medium-sized, rounded. Flight weak. Tail short, square to very long, highly modified. Plumage highly dimorphic. Females generally dull browns and grays. Males enormously varied, often metallic with elaborated flank, back, tail or tail-covert feathers depending on species. Colors from red, yellow, orange to blues and greens. Some with colored wattles or bare skin on head. **Range and habitat:** AU. Tropical forests, wooded savannahs. **Migration:** nonmigratory. **Breeding:** little known for several species. Most polygynous, a few monogamous. Fantastic species-specific courtship displays, especially in polygynous species. Wild hybrids occur indicating genetic similarity. Nest is a bulky, shallow cup of plant material on a foundation of twigs, in a tree. Eggs: 1–2 (rarely 3), pale and streaked. Incubation by female for 17–21 days. Young in nest for 17–30 days. All care by female in polygynous species. **Food:** fruit, insects depending on species, also leaves, buds, and small vertebrates.

162 Bowerbirds Ptilonorhynchidae 20 species (1 ●), 7 genera, e.g. Satin Bowerbird *Ptilonorhynchus violaceus*
Description: medium-sized; solitary, ground-dwelling birds. L: 21–38 cm (8–15 in), Wt: 70–230 g (2½–8 oz). Bill stout, strong, sometimes slightly decurved and hooked. Nostrils covered. Wings, tail and legs tend to be short. Legs strong, hind toe short. Plumage usually dramatically dimorphic. Females drab, cryptic, greens and browns. Males metallic, beautiful blues, yellow, orange or red. Some with crest on the nape. **Range and habitat:** AU. Forest and semi-forest. **Migration:** nonmigratory. **Breeding:** highly polygynous, a few monogamous. In polygynous species, the male builds an elaborate stage or "bower" in which he displays to the female. This is often decorated with colored artifacts. The bower is totally independent of the nest in which the male takes no interest. Nest is a bulky cup of twigs and plant fibers in fork or crevice. Eggs: 1–2 (rarely 3), whitish to buff, plain, or blotched at end. Incubation by female: 19–24 days. Broods: females, 1; males, several. Young are in nest for 18–21 days. Care by female alone in all polygynous species. **Food:** fruit, invertebrates (especially insects), small vertebrates.

163 Crows and Jays Corvidae 117 species (14 ●), 26 genera, e.g. Common Raven *Corvus corax*
Description: medium to large, family includes the largest Passeriformes.

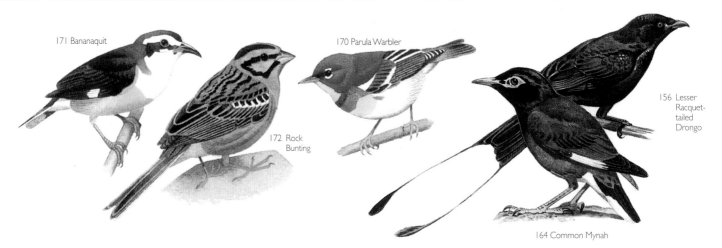

171 Bananaquit

170 Parula Warbler

172 Rock Bunting

156 Lesser Racquet-tailed Drongo

164 Common Mynah

L: 15–71 cm (6–28 in), Wt: 80 g–1.5 kg (2¾ oz–3 lb 5 oz). Strong black bill. Legs and feet medium-sized, strong. Crows: black/gray and white. Tail short to medium, long, broad wings. Jays: smaller, tail medium to long, graduated, brightly colored black and white, grays, browns, blues. Nostrils covered by bristles. Monomorphic, males larger. **Range and habitat:** worldwide except high Arctic and AN. Very diverse. **Migration:** most nonmigratory. **Breeding:** some colonial, some with nest-helpers. Nest is a platform of sticks in tree, sometimes domed, sometimes a tree-hole. Eggs: 3–10, pale. Incubation by female or shared for 16–22 days. Broods: 1. Young in nest for 20–45 days. **Food:** most omnivorous.

164 Starlings Sturnidae 114 species (8●), 28 genera, e.g. Common Mynah *Acridotheres tristis*

Description: small to medium, arboreal or ground-feeding, highly gregarious birds with complex social behavior. L: 16–45 cm (6½–18 in), Wt: 45–170 g (1½–6 oz). Bill long, strong and pointed, slightly arched. Stout and strong legs and feet. Walk on ground. Wings pointed. Flight strong and direct. Tail short to medium, square. Plumage diverse from gray and pied to purples, greens, yellows, often with glossy, metallic sheen. Juvenile plumages sometimes distinct. Eyes sometimes bright yellow. Some fine mimics. **Range and habitat:** WP, EP, AF, OR, PA, introduced into NA and AU. Forest, scrublands, grasslands, cultivation and suburbia. **Migration:** many migrants or partial migrants. **Breeding:** many colonial or loosely so. Nest is chiefly a cup of plant material in tree-hole, some species make domed, open cup, or pendulous nests. Eggs: 3–7, blue to white, sometimes spotted. Incubation by female or shared for 11–18 days. Broods: 1–2. Young are in nest for 18–30 days. **Food:** a wide range of plant and animal foods.

165 Weavers and Sparrows Ploceidae 168 species (14●), 21 genera, e.g. Paradise Whydah *Vidua paradisaea*

Description: small to medium birds, the largest having long tails. L: 10–65 cm (4–26 in), Wt: c.11–64 g (½–2¼ oz). Largely ground feeding, generally highly gregarious with complex social behavior. Bill stout, conical, slightly decurved and without rictal bristles. Legs medium-sized, feet weak. Wings medium-rounded to pointed. Flight strong, rapid. Tail medium-square to very long and elaborate, used in display (whydahs). Plumage varied, streaked browns, grays to bold black, white, yellow, orange and red. Monomorphic to highly dimorphic. Males larger. **Systematics:** We follow *Birdlife International* in including the Old World sparrows (Passeridae) and indigobirds (Viduidae) here. **Range and habitat:** WP, EP, AF, OR, introduced to NA and AU. Wide range of habitats from desert to forest. Several species associate with man. **Migration:** nonmigratory. **Breeding:** many colonial, polygamous, some parasitic and with elaborate courtship. Nest varies, generally a large, untidy structure (though sometimes intricately woven) of plant stems in hole or tree. Sometimes complex colonial nests. Eggs: 2–8, white to heavily spotted and varying greatly in color. Incubation by female or shared for 10–17 days. Broods: 1–3. Young are in nest for 15–24 days. **Food:** chiefly seeds, also fruit, buds and insects.

166 Waxbills Estrildidae 140 species (9●), 28 genera, e.g. Zebra Finch *Poephila guttata*

Description: tiny to small, highly gregarious, active, largely ground-feeding birds with complex social behavior. L: 9–14 cm (3½–5½ in) Wt: 6–13 g (¼–½ oz). Bill short, stout, pointed. Legs short to medium. Wings short, rounded to medium, pointed with reduced outermost primary. Flight fast, direct. Tail short to medium, square to rounded, some with extended, pointed central tail feathers. Plumage very varied in bright colors, usually dimorphic. **Range and habitat:** AF, OR, AU, introduced to Caribbean (NT). Chiefly grasslands, reedy marshes, tropical forests and forest edges. **Migration:** nonmigratory. **Breeding:** many are colonial, have complex courtship and pair for life. Nest is a large, untidy, dome of plant material with a side entrance, built by both. Rarely, a tree-hole. Eggs: 4–8, white. Incubation usually shared for 10–14 days. Broods: opportunistic. Young are in nest for 14–21 days. Several species parasitized by whydahs (Ploceidae). **Food:** chiefly small seeds taken on ground, some fruit and insects (especially young).

167 Vireos Vireonidae 52 species (3●), 4 genera, e.g. Red-eyed Vireo *Vireo olivaceus*

Description: small, arboreal and largely solitary birds, sometimes with mixed-species flocks with warblers (Parulidae) from which they are distinguished by chunkier appearance, less active behavior and the bill form. L: 10–16.5 cm (4–6½ in), Wt: 9–39 g (¼–1¼ oz). Tropical species flock throughout the year. Bill adapted to insect-eating but rather heavy, notched and hook-tipped, unlike warblers. Rictal bristles present. Species vary in bill size and shape. Legs short and strong. Wings rounded to pointed, outermost primary vestigial. Flight strong. Tail medium-sized, squarish. Plumage essentially greens, yellows, grays and white, often with wing-bars, eye-rings and eye stripes. Monomorphic. **Range and habitat:** NA, NT. Forests and scrublands. **Migration:** temperate species are migratory. Nocturnal migrants. **Breeding:** nest is an open cup suspended from fork in a branch, often low down. Eggs: 4–5 (2 in tropics), whitish, spotted brownish. Incubation shared (or, less usually, by female) for 11–13 days. Young are in nest for 11–13 days. Some species heavily parasitized by cowbirds (Icteridae). **Food:** insects and fruit.

168 Finches Fringillidae 134 species (11●), 19 genera, e.g. American Goldfinch *Carduelis tristis*

Description: small, arboreal and ground-feeding, solitary or gregarious birds adapted to seed-eating. L:11–19 cm (4½–7½ in), Wt: 9–100 g (¼–3½ oz). There are 2 well-defined subfamilies: Fringillinae (3 species) and Carduelinae (121 species) Bill always strong, short to medium, conical, often pointed, sometimes crossed depending on diet. Rictal bristles may be reduced. Legs and feet short to medium, often slender, generally weak. Wings medium to long, rounded to pointed. Flight strong, undulating. Tail medium-sized, often notched. Plumage varies from cryptic streaked browns and greens to bright yellows, pink, reds. Monomorphic or dimorphic, males usually larger and brighter. **Range and habitat:** WP, EP, AF, OR, NA, NT, introduced to New Zealand (AU). Wide

167 Red-eyed Vireo

166 Zebra Finch

165 Paradise Whydah

173 Common Grackle

169 Akiapolaau

168 American Goldfinch

variety of terrestrial habitats, especially open forest, scrub and cultivation. **Migration:** many migratory species. **Breeding:** courtship and territoriality differ between subfamilies, some loosely colonial. Nest is an open cup of plant fibers in tree or shrub built by female. Eggs: 3–5, whitish to dark green, spotted. Incubation by female for 12–14 days. Broods: 1–2, rarely 3. Young are in nest for 11–17 days. **Food:** chiefly seeds, nestlings may be fed on insects from parents' bill (Fringillinae) or seeds by regurgitation with or without insects (Carduelinae).

169 Hawaiian Honeycreepers Drepanididae 23 species (another 16 recently extinct, 18 ●), 12 genera, e.g. Akiapolaau *Hemignathus munroi*
Description: small, mostly arboreal birds, solitary or in loose flocks. L: 10–20 cm (4–8 in), Wt: 10–45 g (¼–1½ oz). The family gives one of the best examples of adaptive radiation (comparable with Darwin's finches, Emberizidae, of Galapagos Islands) since their bills and ecology vary from heavy, hooked, seed-cracking bills to long, thin, decurved and pointed nectar-feeding bills (these also with tubular tongues). Bill never notched or serrated. Believed to have evolved from cardueline finches (Fringillidae). The family is threatened by human habitat destruction. Legs medium-sized. Wings pointed, outermost primary vestigial. Flight strong. Tail medium-sized. Plumage usually dimorphic, males brighter but nonmetallic. Colors include black, white, red, green, brown, yellow and dazzling orange. **Range and habitat:** Hawaiian Islands (PA). Native forest and scrublands. **Migration:** nonmigratory. **Breeding:** little known for many. Nest is an open cup of twigs lined with plant fibers in a tree, shrub or grass clump, rarely in cavities. Eggs: 2–4, whitish, streaked red-brown. Incubation by female for 13–14 days. Young are in nest for 15–22 days. **Food:** chiefly insects and nectar, also fruit and seeds depending on species. Young fed seeds or seeds and insects.

170 New World Warblers Parulidae 117 species (16 ●), 26 genera, e.g. Parula Warbler *Parula americana*
Description: an important family of active, small, arboreal insectivores, analogous to the Sylviid warblers of the Old World but more closely related to the Emberizidae. L:10–18 cm (4–7 in), Wt: 7–25 g (¼–1 oz). Generally solitary, flocking at certain times of the year. Bill thin, pointed, usually with rictal bristles. Legs medium-sized. Wings medium-sized, pointed, outermost primary absent. Tail medium-sized, rounded or square. Plumage varied, often bright blues, greens, yellows, orange, black and white. Temperate species most dimorphic and with seasonal variation. Some monomorphic. **Systematics:** We include the Olive Warbler (Peucedramidae). **Range and habitat:** NA, NT. Forests and scrublands. **Migration:** northern species are strong, nocturnal migrants. **Breeding:** nest is a cup in tree or bush (most); domed with side entrance and on ground or in tree-hole. Eggs: 4–5 (rarely 2–8), white to green, spotted brown. Incubation by female for 10–14 days. Broods: 1. Young are in nest for 8–12 days. **Food:** chiefly insects and other invertebrates, also some fruit and seeds.

171 Bananaquit Coerebidae *Coereba flaveola* (monotypic). See p 138.
Description: abundant arboreal nectar and insect feeder of Caribbean and NT, found in a wide variety of wooded and garden habitats. Solitary, highly active,

small birds. **Systematics:**. DNA evidence places it close to the tanagers; despite its range, with 41 subspecies, it is one of the most varied species in the world.

172 Buntings, Cardinals, and Tanagers Emberizidae 622 species (56 ●), 150 genera, e.g. Rock Bunting *Emberiza cia*
Description: a large family with 5 well-defined subfamilies:
a. Buntings Emberizinae 321 species (35 ●), 72 genera
b. Plush-capped Finch Catamblyrhynchinae monotypic
c. Cardinals and Grosbeaks Cardinalinae 43 species, 13 genera
d. Tanagers Thraupinae 256 species (21 ●), 63 genera
e. Swallow Tanager Tersininae monotypic
Generally small, arboreal to terrestrial, solitary to gregarious. L: 9–28 cm (3–11 in), Wt: 8.5–40 g (¼–1½ oz). Bills heavy with or without rictal bristles, short to medium, conical, pointed or hook-tipped (tanagers). Legs short to medium, feet often weak. Wings long, pointed, outer primary absent. Flight strong, direct, but not dashing. Tail medium to longish. Plumage varies from cryptic streaked browns (buntings) to stunning bright reds, blues, yellows and black (cardinals and tanagers). Monomorphic or dimorphic, males often larger. **Systematics:** Following *Birdlife International*, and supported by DNA evidence, we include Cardinals (Cardinalidae) and Tanagers (Thraupidae) here. **Range and habitat:** worldwide except AU, PA, AN. Chiefly open habitats, desert, grassland, tundra, alpine meadows and cultivation, also open forest and forest edge. **Migration:** many strong migrants, especially northern species. **Breeding:** monogamous and polygamous. Nest is usually a woven cup of plant material in vegetation, often low down. Rarely a domed structure with a side entrance or in tunnel. Eggs: 4–5 (rarely 2–6), pure white to colored and spotted. Incubation by female (or, less usually, shared) for 10–18 days. Broods: 1–3. Young are in nest for 9–24 days. **Food:** chiefly seeds and some fruits, nestlings fed largely on arthropods (especially insects).

173 New World Blackbirds Icteridae
97 species (11 ●), 25 genera, e.g. Common Grackle *Quiscalus quiscula*
Description: small to large, arboreal or ground-dwelling, usually gregarious and noisy birds with complex social organization. L: 15–53 cm (6–21 in), Wt: 20–454 g (¾ oz–1 lb). Bill unnotched, conical, long and pointed or short and stout. Legs medium to long, strong. Wings long, pointed, outermost primary absent. Flight strong. Tail medium to long, square or graduated and vaulted. Plumage generally dark glossy purples, black or browns; or boldly colored in black, yellow, orange, red. Usually dimorphic, males larger. May have distinct immature plumage. **Range and habitat:** NA, NT. Forests, scrublands, grasslands and marshes. **Migration:** temperate species mostly nocturnal migrants. **Breeding:** varied mating systems: monogamous, polygynous, some species colonial, some with nest-helpers, some parasitic, e.g. on vireos (Vireonidae). Nests are extremely varied, from an open cup to long pendant purses, in reeds, shrubs, trees or on the ground. Eggs: 2–6, variable in colors and spotting. Incubation by female (rarely shared) or by host for 12–15. days. Broods: 1, rarely 2. Young are in nest for 9–35 days. **Food:** wide range of fruit and small animals.

THE NEARCTIC REGION

The Nearctic Region extends from Alaska and the Aleutian Islands in the west to Greenland in the east, and from Ellesmere Island in the high Arctic to the northern edge of the tropical rainforest in central Mexico. It is bordered by the Arctic Ocean to the north, the Bering Sea and Pacific Ocean to the west and south-west, the Atlantic to the east, and the Caribbean Sea and Mexican rainforest to the south. The biological similarities of the Nearctic and Palaearctic are often emphasized by referring to them as the Holarctic. Similarities to the Neotropics are occasionally stressed by referring to the "New World Region." The zoogeography of the Nearctic is best understood in terms of a Nearctic avifauna interacting with a Palaearctic avifauna to the northeast and northwest and a Neotropical avifauna to the south.

Prior to the Mesozoic era North America was located at the equator of Pangaea, a single landmass containing all the modern continents. About 200 million years ago Pangaea broke apart, with North America and Eurasia forming the continent of Laurasia. North America and Eurasia separated early in the Tertiary Period of the Cenozoic Era (about 50 million years ago), but a European connection through Greenland persisted during the early Tertiary and an Asian connection has been renewed repeatedly across the Bering Strait until as recently as the last ice age. To the south three large islands with four substantial water gaps separated North America from South America throughout most of the Tertiary period, until about three million years ago. During this separation the southern half of North America was subtropical or tropical; even late in the Tertiary, as the climate cooled, southernmost North America remained tropical. Thus throughout most of the Tertiary two tropical avifaunas evolved in parallel, one in the Nearctic Region and one in the Neotropical. Elimination of the water gaps between the Nearctic and Neotropics coincided with climatic cooling, which eliminated all tropical habitat from the Nearctic. The change in habitat and formation of a land bridge led to an extensive interchange of tropical species between the Nearctic and Neotropics and explosive radiation of several families and subfamilies, such as wrens, wood warblers, mimic thrushes and vireos from the tropical Nearctic, and tyrant flycatchers, blackbirds, tanagers and hummingbirds from the Neotropics.

Geographic features

The major geographic features of the Nearctic are oriented longitudinally. The western mountains extend from Alaska to central Mexico and include the Rockies and lesser ranges. The central plains extend from Canada to the Gulf of Mexico. Several remote, minor mountain ranges in the north-east coalesce into the Appalachians, which extend south from Pennsylvania to Georgia and Alabama. Florida and Mexico project south toward the Neotropics and the Mississippi River flows south from Minnesota to the Gulf of Mexico.

The Nearctic is home to about 750 bird species in 62 families, three of which are introduced and none of which is endemic. These families can be divided into six groups: *1* waterbirds, which include the oceanic skuas, partially oceanic pelicans and cormorants, and the freshwater grebes; herons and bitterns; storks; ibises; flamingos; ducks, geese and swans; and rails, coots and gallinules; *2* cosmopolitan families, such as the albatrosses, shearwaters, fulmars and petrels; gulls and terns; hawks, eagles and falcons; swifts; and swallows; *3* an indigenous element that evolved during the Tertiary isolation:

Wood Stork colony. Their massive nests are placed at various heights above water from a few feet to the tree tops.

wrens, mimic thrushes, vireos, wood warblers and American sparrows, also several small families and subfamilies: the New World vultures, quails and turkeys, dippers, gnatcatchers, waxwings, silky flycatchers, motmots, todies and the palmchat; *4* an old Holarctic element that evolved and dispersed during the Eocene when North America and Europe were connected through Greenland: cranes, pigeons, cuckoos, certain owls and caprimulgids, kingfishers, the blue jay group, cardueline finches and certain thrushes belong to this group; *5* a recent Holarctic element that has crossed the Bering

Strait land bridge from Asia and includes the Barn Owl, larks, tits, nuthatches, creepers, kinglets, the Wrentit, pipits, some swallows and some corvids; 6 immigrants from the Neotropics such as the hummingbirds, tyrant flycatchers, tanagers and blackbirds.

Biotic Communities

Within the Nearctic are nine major biotic communities characterized by their dominant vegetation.

Tundra is the northernmost community, also found above 3,000 m (10,000 ft) in the western mountains. It is characterized by lichens, mosses, grasses and dwarf willow. Winters are very cold and precipitation is moderate to heavy. Birds include ptarmigans, Snowy Owl, Horned Lark, Water Pipit and Lapland and Smith's Longspurs and Snow Bunting.

Northern coniferous (boreal) forest is dominated by pines, spruces, hemlocks, firs and cedars. The forest may be dense with little or no understory, or more open with an understory of shrubs and herbaceous plants. Winters are cold, summers cool, and rainfall moderate to heavy. Characteristic birds include Northern Goshawk, Olive-sided Flycatcher, Red-breasted Nuthatch, Winter Wren, Golden-crowned Kinglet, Hermit Thrush, Yellow-rumped Warbler, Dark-eyed Junco, White-winged Crossbill and Pine Siskin.

The eastern deciduous forest extends from the southern edge of the coniferous forest, with which it mixes, south into the south-eastern Nearctic. It is dominated by beech, maple, basswood, oak, hickory and walnut. The understory includes small shrubs and herbaceous plants. Winters are cool, summers warm, and rainfall moderate to heavy. Birds of the eastern deciduous forest include Red-shouldered and Broad-winged Hawks, Barred Owl, Downy Woodpecker, Eastern Wood-Pewee, Carolina Chickadee, White-breasted Nuthatch, Wood Thrush, Yellow-throated Vireo and Cerulean Warbler.

Grasslands occur in the interior and are characterized by abrupt seasonal changes with cold to very cold winters, warm to hot summers, and moderate to low rainfall. Swainson's and Ferruginous hawks, Greater Prairie Chicken, Sharp-tailed Grouse, Long-billed Curlew, Burrowing Owl, Lark Bunting, Grasshopper Sparrow and Western Meadowlark are found throughout the grasslands; Sprague's Pipit, Baird's Sparrow, McCown's Longspur and Chestnut-collared Longspur are found only on the northern prairies.

In the western mountains above the grasslands and below the coniferous forest is the pinyon-juniper woodland, a parklike woodland of small trees, pinyon pines, several species of juniper and yuccas. The woodland has warm summers, cool winters and little rainfall. Its birds include the Gray Flycatcher, Pinyon Jay, Juniper Titmouse, Plain Bushtit and Bewick's Wren.

Oaks (Quercus) characterize the south-western oak woodland. Trees are widely spaced, with grass and shrubs covering the ground. Summers are warm, winters cool, with moderate to low rainfall. Characteristic birds include Nuttall's Woodpecker, Bridled and Oak Titmice, Hutton's Vireo and Virginia's and Black-throated Gray Warblers.

South-western California with its mild climate, dry summers and wet winters is characterized by large areas of dense brush and stunted trees. This is the chaparral. Occasional rock outcroppings and grassy areas provide relief from the brush, which is inhabited by the Wrentit, California Thrasher, Gray Vireo, Orange-crowned Warbler and Black-chinned, Sage and White-crowned Sparrows.

Further north in the Great Basin Plateau between the Rocky mountains and the Sierra Nevada-Cascade mountains is another brushy habitat dominated by sagebrush. Summers are very hot and dry. Winters are cool and dry. Sage Grouse, Sage Thrasher and Brewer's and Sage sparrows are characteristic of the Great Basin Plateau.

Lowlands throughout the south-western Nearctic are very dry and hot with widely spaced plants, 1–2 m (3–6 ft) high. Creosote bush is the dominant plant, but mesquite, paloverde, catclaw, ironwood, ocotillo, agaves, cacti, yuccas and grasses are also present. A surprising variety of birds including Gambel's Quail, Greater Roadrunner, Elf Owl, Lesser Nighthawk, Costa's Hummingbird, Gila Woodpecker, Vermilion Flycatcher, Verdin, Cactus Wren, Black-tailed Gnatcatcher, Bendire's, Crissal and LeConte's Thrashers and Phainopepla occur here.

Parts of these areas have not reached the characteristic community structure. Because of poor soil and frequent fires the south-eastern Nearctic remains coniferous rather than deciduous. Characteristic of the south-eastern pines are the Red-cockaded Woodpecker, Brown-headed Nuthatch and Bachman's Sparrow. Large areas of south-western Texas and nearby New Mexico are dominated by mesquite rather than creosote bush; Golden-fronted Woodpecker and Black-crested Tufted Titmouse are characteristic species. The coniferous forest of the northwest coast is unusually wet and Chestnut-backed Chickadee and Varied Thrush are confined to this temperate rainforest.

Throughout these relatively stable communities are ephemeral communities that will develop toward the characteristic vegetation of the region. Such communities are frequent enough to have names and characteristic species. Beaches are inhabited by plovers, gulls and terns. Lakes are used by loons, swans, ducks and geese. Pied-billed Grebes and Black Terns feed on the open water of ponds, whereas bitterns, moorhens, rails, Sedge and Marsh Wrens and Red-winged Blackbirds nest in the cattails and sedges bordering the water. Shrublands are inhabited by Common Yellowthroats and Field Sparrows. Riparian woodlands, characteristic of streams and bottomlands in the western plains and desert southwest, are often inhabited by species characteristic of deciduous forest.

Throughout the Nearctic many natural biotic communities have been and continue to be disrupted by human activities, such as agriculture, forestry, flooding caused by dams, and deserts caused by overgrazing. However, these habitats may contain a rich variety of species that includes American Kestrel, Mourning Dove, kingbirds, American Crow, American Robin, bluebirds, Song Sparrow and blackbirds.

Nearctic ornithological societies

Several societies focus on Nearctic birds. The National Audubon Society (700 Broadway, New York, NY 10003, USA [www.audubon.org, join@audubon.org]) emphasizes birds but addresses broad conservation issues. The American Birding Association (4945 N. 30th St., Suite 200, Colorado Springs, CO 80919, USA [www.americanbirding.org, member@aba.org]) is devoted to birds and bird-watching. Enquiries about other societies should be directed to the Ornithological Societies of North America, (OSNA Business Office, 5400 Bosque Blvd Ste 680, Waco, TX 76710, USA [www.osnabirds.org, business@osnabirds.org]).

DIVERS Gaviiformes

Common Loon

Gavia immer (Gaviidae) 71–89 cm/28–35 in.
Black head, white necklace barred with black; black above with white checks on back and white spots on the sides, white below; long, black, daggerlike bill. Sexes alike, female smaller. Winter and immature plumages gray above, shading to white below; bill light, bluish cast. Sits low in water. Feet far back on body; walking posture upright, shuffling, awkward. Flight rapid with head and feet outstretched, body slightly hunched. Voice: loud yodeling; echoing quality. **Range and habitat:** Holarctic. Breeds on freshwater lakes, winters in coastal bays, estuaries, open lakes. **Similar species:** other divers, especially White-billed Diver (see p 142).

GREBES Podicipediformes

Western Grebe

Aechmophorus occidentalis (Podicipedidae) 51–61 cm/20–24 in.
Largest of Nearctic grebes. Distinctive long thin neck, long straight, slender bill and red eyes. Black crown, back of neck, and back; chin, throat, foreneck and breast white. Similar Clark's Grebe has a yellow-orange bill; white face surrounding the eye and speckled white flanks, whereas the Western Grebe has dark greenish yellow bill, dark face and flanks. Courtship behavior includes spectacular aquatic displays. Voice: a shrill "creet-creet" in the Western Grebe, a single "creet" in Clark's Grebe. **Range and habitat:** reeds and rushes along edges of freshwater lakes, west-central NA and PA coast. **Similar species:** Clark's Grebe, winter plumage Horned and Red-necked Grebes.

Horned Grebe

Podiceps auritus (Podicipedidae) 30–38 cm/12–15 in.
In breeding plumage both sexes have chrome-yellow "horns" that extend from behind the eye to beyond the crown; head and back dark green; neck, breast and flanks rich chestnut; belly white. In winter "horns" absent, dark above with white cheek, chin, throat, breast and belly. Slender, straight bill, dark in summer, paler in winter. Red eye. Sexes alike. Voice: series of loud, weird croaks and chattering, followed by several prolonged shrieks. In flight shows white speculum. **Range and habitat:** Holarctic. Breeds on northern marshes, ponds, quiet rivers. Winters along coasts and open lakes. **Similar species:** Black-necked Grebe; in winter plumage, Red-necked and Western Grebes.

Pied-billed Grebe

Podilymbus podiceps (Podicipedidae) 30–38 cm/12–15 in.
Most widespread NA grebe. Small, stocky, short-necked brown grebe with a fluffy white rear; named for its cream-colored, chickenlike bill encircled with a black band; narrow white eye-ring, black throat. In winter bill unmarked and throat brown. Sexes alike. Juvenile is conspicuously striped on head, less so on body. Often swims with only head above water. Voice: frequent, lengthy series of whinnying sounds, slowing to a mellow "cow-cow-cow-cowp-cowp." **Range and habitat:** freshwater with emergent vegetation, north, central and southern NA, winters on saltwater bays, southern NA into NT. **Similar species:** all other grebes have slender bills (see pp 96, 142, 282).

TUBE-NOSED SWIMMERS Procellariiformes

Black-footed Albatross

Phoebastria nigripes (Diomedeidae) 68–78 cm/27–31 in, wingspan 193–213 cm/76–84 in.
White around base of bill, under and behind eye, and white-shafted primary feathers, otherwise sooty brown; bill greenish brown, feet black. Individuals whiten with age, white spreads to forehead and over crown, belly becomes pale, rump may become white; bill fades to yellowish or pinkish and feet become dusky yellow. Sexes alike. Voice: groans, squeals and shrieks. **Range and habitat:** PA, pelagic except when breeding on Hawaiian islands and Torishima off Japan. Seen along western NA coast all year, most common in summer, autumn. **Similar species:** Short-tailed Albatross.

Great Shearwater

Puffinus gravis (Procellariidae) 48 cm/19 in.
Dark, gray-brown cap and back, pale feather-edgings give scaly appearance; flight feathers black; white throat, collar and underparts, diagnostic dark smudge on belly; underwings white with dark outline; narrow white rump patch; tail short, rounded with dark undertail-coverts; bill dark, long, slender and hooked. In flight, wings held straight and stiff, long glides punctuated by bouts of slow flapping. Sexes alike. Generally silent, occasional groans and squeals. **Range and habitat:** pelagic, except when nesting in burrows on Tristan da Cunha, migrates north along Atlantic coast. **Similar species:** Cory's Shearwater; Black-capped Petrel.

Sooty Shearwater

Puffinus griseus (Procellariidae) 40–45 cm/16–18 in.
Uniformly sooty brown with white wing-linings; slender, black bill; black feet. More widespread than Great Shearwater, less apt to occur in flocks. In flight wings appear crescent-shaped, several quick flaps followed by curving glide. Dives more frequently than other shearwaters, swims under water with feet and folded wings. Sexes alike. Voice: nasal, bleating call when competing for fish at sea. **Range and habitat:** nests in burrows on islands in southern Southern Hemisphere, migrates north along Atlantic and PA coasts. Pelagic on continental shelf. **Similar species:** Northern Fulmar, Pale-footed and Short-tailed Shearwaters, dark jaegers (see pp 68, 142, 284).

Wilson's Storm-Petrel

Oceanites oceanicus (Hydrobatidae) 18 cm/7 in.
Head and body black with square white rump patch that extends to the undertail-coverts; long legs with yellow webbing between toes. In flight feet extend beyond tail, which is square or slightly rounded. Sexes alike. Glides only occasionally. Wings rounded and wing-beat swallowlike. Feeds with wings raised in a V and feet paddling on the ocean surface. **Range and habitat:** nests in burrows or rock crevices on AN and nearby islands. Migrates north into Atlantic, Indian and PA oceans. Pelagic. **Similar species:** other all dark or white-rumped storm petrels (see p 142).

FULL-WEBBED SWIMMERS Pelecaniformes

Brown Pelican

Pelecanus occidentalis (Pelecanidae) 106–137 cm/42–54 in.
Long gray bill with large black pouch suspended from bill and throat. Bare skin around eyes, base of bill gray to black. Adults: white head, yellowish forehead, chestnut neck, gray-brown body. Nonbreeding birds: less yellow, no chestnut. Sexes alike, male slightly larger. Catches fish by plunging head-first from the air or scooping with the bill while on the surface. Immatures: gray-brown, white underparts. Usually silent, occasional croaks. Nestlings squeal. **Range and habitat:** coastal, south-eastern and western NA, western NT. **Similar species:** white pelicans (see pp 142, 186, 238, 286). Although the population as a whole is increasing, the Brown Pelican is endangered on Pacific coast.

American White Pelican

Pelecanus erythrorhynchos (Pelecanidae) 137–178 cm/54–70 in.
Long, salmon-colored bill with pouch suspended below mark this as a pelican. Plumage entirely white, except for black primaries, coverts, and outer secondaries; bill brighter during breeding season; legs and feet orange-red. Develops vertical horny plate projecting from midway along upper mandible during breeding season, also pale yellow patch on chest and pale yellow crest on nape that turns to gray by the end of the season. On water folded wings often elevated. In flight head rests on chest. Sexes alike. Immatures dusky with dark, streaked crown. Voice: in colony low groan, nestlings whining grunts. **Range and habitat:** nests in widely scattered colonies on isolated lakes in central NA. Winters along coast of south-eastern and south-western NA. **Similar species:** Brown Pelican, other white pelicans (see pp 142, 186, 238, 286).

Common Loon

Western Grebe (in courtship display)

Horned Grebe

Pied-billed Grebe

Great Shearwater

Black-footed Albatross

Wilson's Storm-Petrel

Sooty Shearwater

Brown Pelican

American White Pelican

Anhinga

Anhinga anhinga (Anhingidae) 81–91 cm/32–36 in.
Small head, long neck and tail; long, stiletto bill used to spear fish; unique curve in neck resulting from hinge mechanism of vertebrae; black plumage. Male: uniformly black, white plumes on back and wings, yellow bill. Female: buff-colored head, neck and breast, black body, white plumes. Immature browner than female. In flight neck outstretched, alternately flaps and glides, may soar to great height. Often swims with only head and neck above water. **Range and habitat:** cypress swamps, wooded ponds, rivers of south-eastern NA, eastern NT. **Similar species:** cormorants, darters (see pp 186, 238, 286).

Double-crested Cormorant

Phalacrocorax auritus (Phalacrocoracidae) 66–81 cm/26–32 in.
Small head; long, slender, often crooked neck; long tail; dark plumage, iridescent green and purple on back; yellow-orange throat pouch; bill long, narrow, black. During spring feather tufts project from crown. When perched, often spreads wings. Sexes alike. Immatures: brown above, pale below. In flight neck outstretched, body horizontal. Often swims with bill and head tilted up. Voice: grunts at nest, otherwise silent. **Range and habitat:** coasts, freshwater lakes, rivers of northern and central NA. Winters along central and southern NA rivers and coasts. **Similar species:** other cormorants, darters (see pp 186, 238).

Magnificent Frigatebird

Fregata magnificens (Fregatidae) 94–114 cm/37–45 in.
Long pointed wings, angled at wrist; tail scissorlike, often folded in a point. Glides effortlessly. Wingbeats infrequent, deep, deliberate, may soar to great heights, dives at high speed. Male black with red, inflatable throat pouch during breeding season, dorsal feathers long, purple. Female: black, white breast. Immature: black, white head and breast. Bill long, slender, hooked. Hoarse cackles; with pouch inflated, whistling whinny. **Range and habitat:** oceanic coasts and islands of south-eastern NA, tropical Atlantic, eastern PA. **Similar species:** other frigatebirds (see pp 238, 286).

HERONS AND ALLIES Ciconiiformes

American Bittern

Botaurus lentiginosus (Ardeidae) 58–68 cm/23–27 in.
Medium-sized secretive, heron most often seen flying low over marsh, uniformly brown back and dark brown wing tips are diagnostic. Occasionally seen standing at water's edge with bill pointing straight up, light brown underparts streaked with dark brown blending with cattail background. Sexes alike. Immatures lighter brown. Usually silent, but during spring a resonant "pump-per-lunk" repeated from 3 to 5 times. When flushed "kok-kok-kok." **Range and habitat:** fresh-water or brackish marshes of northern and central NA. Winters central and southern NA into Central America. **Similar species:** immature night-herons, Eurasian Bittern (see p 144).

Green Heron

Butorides virescens (Ardeidae) 38–56 cm/15–22 in.
Adults: rich chestnut head and sides, white streaks down throat, white underparts; black crown, dark bill, white eye-line and moustache; green-black wings and back; conspicuous orange-yellow legs. Sexes alike. Immature: browner, heavily streaked below wing-coverts buff edged. Voice: loud "skeeowp." **Range and habitat:** wet woodlands, streams, lakeshores, marshes and swamps from east-central to south-central NA, also west-central NA south along Pacific coast. In winter southern NA to northern NT, AF, OR. **Similar species:** American Bittern, Least Bittern, Little Blue Heron.

Great Egret

Ardea alba (Ardeidae) 94–104 cm/37–41 in.
Large; entirely white plumage, yellow bill, black legs and feet. In breeding plumage up to 54 long lacy plumes extend down back and beyond tail. Nonbreeding lacks plumes, bill less yellow. Sexes similar. Hoarse croak, also "cuk-cuk-cuk." **Range and habitat:** fresh and saltwater marshes, east-central, west-central, south-eastern NA.

Winters southern NA south into NT. Also occurs in AF, EP, OR, AU. **Similar species:** other white egrets, white morph of Great Blue Heron, immature Little Blue Heron.

Snowy Egret

Egretta thula (Ardeidae) 56–66 cm/22–26 in.
Small white egret; bill black, facial skin yellow; legs black with brilliant yellow toes. When breeding has lacy, recurved plumes on head, back, breast. Feet and toes contrast less in immature, may have yellow stripe up rear of legs. Forages by rushing about, stabbing into water or stirring water with 1 foot then stabbing into the turbulence. **Range and habitat:** wetlands, east-central NA south to southern NT, local in south-central and south-western NA. Winters in southern part of range. **Similar species:** other white egrets especially Little Egret, immature Little Blue Heron (see p 144).

Black-crowned Night-Heron

Nycticorax nycticorax (Ardeidae) 58–66 cm/23–26 in.
Short-billed, short-necked, short-legged nocturnal heron; black crown and back; narrow white plumes extend backward from crown; striking red eye; face, underparts white, wings gray. Sexes similar. Immature gray-brown with light spots above, light streaks below. Hunched profile when perched. Deep wingbeats, head retracted forming straight line with back, toes extend beyond tail. Voice: flat "kwawk." **Range and habitat:** wetlands, central, east- and west-central NA to southern NT, southern WP, EP into AF, OR. **Similar species:** American Bittern, immature Yellow-crowned Night-Heron.

Yellow-crowned Night-Heron

Nyctanassa violacea (Ardeidae) 56–71 cm/22–28 in.
Less common than Black-crowned Night-Heron, more diurnal. Adult pale gray with black head, white patch behind eye; yellowish forehead fades to white on crown. Stout, thick, pinkish bill. Sexes similar. Immature: slate-brown, scattered small, light spots dorsally, fine light streaks ventrally; yellowish legs. Loud high-pitched "quak." **Range and habitat:** cypress and mangrove swamps, lush marshes, east- and south-central NA to northern NT. Winters in southern part of range. **Similar species:** American Bittern, immature Black-crowned Night-Heron.

Great Blue Heron

Ardea herodias (Ardeidae) 127–137 cm/50–54 in.
Yellow bill, white forehead and crown, bordered with black; short dark plumes project backward from black nape; white face, neck cinnamon-gray with white ventral stripe spotted with dark; body and wings blue-gray; legs long, dark. Sexes similar; male larger. Immature pale; black crown lacks plumes. Wingbeat deep, slow. All-white morph with yellow bill and legs in Florida. Harsh, guttural croaks. **Range and habitat:** wetlands of central and southern NA. Winters southern NA to north-western NT. **Similar species:** other dark herons, Great Egret, Sandhill Crane (see p 60).

Little Blue Heron

Egretta caerulea (Ardeidae) 63–73 cm/25–29 in.
Slate-blue, with maroon head and neck; bluish bill has dark tip; blue-gray, unfeathered lores; legs bluish green. Slow, deliberate foraging behavior. Sexes similar. Immature: dark-tipped, bluish bill, blue-gray lores, plumage entirely white; legs pale. Molting immatures pied blue and white. Voice: low clucks, screams when fighting. **Range and habitat:** coastal and freshwater marshes, swamps; south-eastern NA to southern NT. **Similar species:** immature resembles white egrets. Adult resembles Reddish Egret, Tricolored Heron.

Tricolored Heron

Egretta tricolor (Ardeidae) 61–71 cm/24–28 in.
Long bill and neck, slim profile. Slate-blue body, white belly, flanks, underwings, rump; head and neck dark, red-brown stripe mottled white, from chin to breast, short white plumes project from nape. In breeding plumage cinnamon to buff plumes extend over rump. Sexes similar. Immature lacks plumes. In shallow water runs after small fish, in deep water stalks prey slowly. Noisy, harsh croaks, groans. **Range and habitat:** coastal, south-eastern NA to northern NT. **Similar species:** Little Blue Heron, Reddish Egret.

Anhinga (drying wings)

Double-crested Cormorant (juvenile)

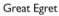

Magnificent Frigatebird (male, left and female)

American Bittern

Green Heron

Great Egret

Snowy Egret

Black-crowned Night-Heron

Yellow-crowned Night-Heron

Great Blue Heron

Little Blue Heron

Tricolored Heron

Wood Stork

Mycteria americana (Ciconiidae) 89–114 cm/35–45 in.
Large, long-legged wading bird, white plumage, black primaries, secondaries and tail; naked skin of head and neck black, scaly; bill black and decurved toward tip; legs black, feet pink. Sexes similar. Flies with neck extended, legs trailing, often soaring in large flocks. Immature: yellow bill, grayish brown, feathered head, neck. Nesting adults hiss, young noisy. Threatened by habitat destruction. **Range and habitat:** fresh and saltwater coastal marshes from south-eastern NA to southern NT. Nests in cypress. **Similar species:** White Ibis, white pelicans, Whooping Crane (see pp 50, 60).

White Ibis

Eudocimus albus (Threskiornithidae) 56–71 cm/22–28 in.
Adult white, primaries tipped black; facial skin, decurved bill red; legs red during breeding season, gray otherwise. Sexes similar. Immature: brown above, finely white marks on head, neck; white belly and rump; bill brown to red. Flies with head and neck extended, feet trailing, rapid wingbeats alternate with gliding, often in large flocks that assume a V or linear formation. **Range and habitat:** coastal wetlands, also grassy and ploughed fields from south-eastern NA to northern NT. **Similar species:** Wood Stork, immature resembles Tricolored Heron, immature Glossy Ibis.

Turkey Vulture

Cathartes aura (Cathartidae) 66–81 cm/26–32 in.
Large, soars with wings in shallow V, outer primaries separated, often wobbles in turbulent air, rarely flaps; silvery gray flight feathers, but blackish brown plumage on wings and body; long tail. Small, naked head, red in adults, gray in immatures. Lighter wing loading than Black Vulture so can live in cooler areas where thermals less strong. Grunts and hisses when disturbed. **Range and habitat:** central NA to southern NT. Winter in subtropical parts of range. **Similar species:** Black Vulture, eagles.

American Black Vulture

Coragyps atratus (Cathartidae) 58–68 cm/23–27 in.
Large, all-black with short, broad wings and a short broad tail. Hold wings horizontal, soars in tight circles quite often, makes 4 or 5 labored wingbeats between glides. White patches at base of primaries are conspicuous in flight. Head gray, feet pale. Sexes alike. Occasional grunts, hisses. **Range and habitat:** south-eastern NA to southern NT. Less common than Turkey Vulture where both present. **Similar species:** Turkey Vulture. **Not illustrated.**

WATERFOWL Anseriformes

Black-bellied Whistling-Duck

Dendrocygna autumnalis (Anatidae) 47–51 cm/18–20 in.
Tall duck, identified by distinctive red bill, pink feet and white wing patches; edges of mandibles salmon-colored. Most arboreal of whistling-ducks. Immature gray bill, adult pattern in subdued grays, browns. Mate for life. Often lays eggs in nests of conspecific Flight call, a repeated whistle "pe-che-che-ne." **Range and habitat:** nests locally along western Gulf coast, south-eastern Arizona, and coastal Central America. Nests in natural cavities. **Similar species:** Fulvous Whistling-Duck.

Trumpeter Swan

Cygnus buccinator (Anatidae) 150–183 cm/59–72 in.
Largest NA swan. Primarily white except long, flat, black bill and forehead profile (Tundra Swan has rounded profile); edges of mandibles salmon-colored. When alert neck held erect, otherwise slightly curved and drooped with kink at base. Autumn immature: dusky with black bill that is salmon on mid-dorsal surface. Deep, sonorous, rasping "ko-ko," trumpetlike. **Range and habitat:** nests locally in north-western and north-central NA. Winters in southern part of range. The species was almost extinct, but is now recovering. **Similar species:** other swans (see p 144).

Canada Goose

Branta canadensis (Anatidae). Eleven subspecies range from small "Cackling" Canada Goose, 56–68 cm/22–7 in, to "Giant" Canada Goose, 81–122 cm/32–48 in.
All have black head and neck with white chin-strap. Gray-brown body, darker on wings and back; belly, flanks, tail-coverts white; rump, tail black. Sexes similar, males larger. Fly in V formation. Deep musical honking in larger subspecies, high-pitched yelping in smaller subspecies. **Range and habitat:** breeds throughout northern and central NA, locally to the south. Winters as far north as open water persists. **Similar species:** Brent Goose, Barnacle Goose (see p 146).

Snow Goose

Chen caerulescens (Anatidae) 71–84 cm/28–33 in.
Two color morphs: all white and gray-bodied with white head and upper neck. Immature white morphs sooty above, white below. Immature dark morphs brownish gray, lighter below, with white chin spot. All have black primaries, red legs, feet and bills. Sexes similar, males larger. Noisy, shrill notes, also a soft honk. **Range and habitat:** Breeds from EP to northern NA. Winters from west-central NA to eastern coastal NA. **Similar species:** Ross's Goose, immature White-fronted Goose (see p 146).

Brent Goose

Branta bernicla (Anatidae) 56–66 cm/22–26 in.
Head, neck, breast, back black with whitish patch on both sides of neck below throat. In "Black" subspecies on Pacific coast, white patch may encircle neck: sides, underparts much darker than in Atlantic subspecies. Extreme lower belly, flanks, undertail-coverts white in both subspecies; legs and short bill black. Sexes similar, males larger. Drawn-out, rolling, throaty "r-r-ronk, rr-ronk." **Range and habitat:** breeds along Holarctic coasts, winters on coasts further south. Abundant in bays in winter. **Similar species:** Canada Goose, Barnacle Goose (see p 146).

American Black Duck

Anas rubripes (Anatidae) 51–63 cm/20–25 in.
Similar size and shape to Mallard, with which it may hybridize. Body dark sooty brown, lighter brown neck, head; in flight, white wing-linings contrast with dark body. Purplish blue speculum bordered with black. Feet and legs orange, brighter in male than female. His bill yellowish, hers mottled with black, immature's olive-green. Quacks. **Range and habitat:** favors brackish marshes and estuaries of north-eastern and north-central NA. Winters in south-central and south-eastern NA. **Similar species:** female Mallard (see p 146).

Gadwall

Anas strepera (Anatidae) 45–57 cm/18–22 in.
Nondescript gray-bodied duck with rusty scapulars, black tail-coverts, light brown head, neck. Female mottled brown. In flight both sexes show white belly, wing-linings outlined in dark feathers, and distinctive white speculum. Usually in small flocks, dives more than other dabbling ducks. In WP often with coots. Male gives low "bek-bek," also whistles. Female quacks. **Range and habitat:** freshwater wetlands of north-western, central and west-central NA, eastern and northern WP. Winters in central and southern NA, AF, southern EP. **Similar species:** male and female resemble many other female ducks (see pp 146, 240, 288).

American Wigeon

Anas americana (Anatidae) 45–58 cm/18–23 in.
Prominent white forehead, crown, green patch from eye around nape; lower face, neck brown; pinkish buff breast and flanks contrast with white rear flank feathers and black tail-coverts. Male in eclipse and female brownish gray. Blue bill tipped black. Rapid, erratic flight shows elliptical white belly, white wing-linings, large white wing patches. Voice: male, 3 whistles, higher middle note; female, low quack. **Range and habitat:** ponds and marshes of northern and central NA. In winter coastal and southern NA and Central America. **Similar species:** Green-winged Teal, Eurasian Wigeon, Gadwall.

Wood Stork

White Ibis

Turkey Vulture

Black-bellied Whistling-Duck

Trumpeter Swan

Canada Goose

Snow Goose

Brent Goose

American Black Duck

Gadwall

American Wigeon

Ruddy Duck

Oxyura jamaicensis (**Anatidae**) 38–40 cm/15–16 in.
Short body and neck; large head; long, stiff tail are distinctive. Male chestnut with black neck and head; white cheek patch; bright, pale blue bill; gray in autumn and winter, but the light cheek patch contrasts with the gray head. Female gray, less strongly contrasting cheek crossed by dark line. More apt to dive than fly. Voice: nasal sounds during breeding. **Range and habitat:** breeds on marshy lakes and ponds throughout plains, also west-central NA. Winters coast to coast from central NA to northern NT. Resident populations in West Indies and northern NT. **Similar species:** Masked Duck (see p 102).

Wood Duck

Aix sponsa (**Anatidae**) 38–53 cm/15–21 in.
Head green, iridescent green crest edged in white; bill and eye red-orange; white from chin and throat extends on to cheek and around neck; breast maroon, flecked with white; belly white, flanks golden; back and wings dark, secondaries with white trailing edge. Female brownish green with light spots, unmarked gray crest, white around eye and on belly. Both sexes have long tails. Male gives high-pitched, rising "jeeeee;" female a squealing "ww-e-e-ek." **Range and habitat:** wooded swamps, rivers, ponds from east-central NA south, also west-central NA south along Pacific coast.

Blue-winged Teal

Anas discors (**Anatidae**) 35–42 cm/14–17 in.
Small size; fast, erratic flight; china-blue wing patches are distinctive in both sexes. Male's white crescent-shaped face patch contrasts with blue-gray head. Body tan with brown spots. White flank patch contrasts with black undertail-coverts. Female small, mottled brown. Male in eclipse resembles female, but regains breeding plumage in mid-November. Male has peeping whistle, female faint quack. **Range and habitat:** nests in grass near prairie potholes and shallow marshes; northern and central NA. Winters from southern NA to central NT. **Similar species:** other teal (see pp 146, 240).

Cinnamon Teal

Anas cyanoptera (**Anatidae**) 37–43 cm/15–17 in.
Head and body of male are cinnamon-red. Feathers of back brown, buff highlights; red eyes. Females mottled brown. Both sexes have large chalky blue patches on upper surface of wings, paler than in Blue-winged Teal. Eclipse male resembles female. Flies in smaller flocks than other teal. Male gives low "chuk-chuk-chuk," female weak quack. **Range and habitat:** marshes from west-central and central NA south, also central and southern NT. Winters southwestern NA to northern NT. **Similar species:** other teal, Ruddy Duck (see pp 146, 190, 240).

Canvasback

Aythya valisineria (**Anatidae**) 48–56 cm/19–22 in.
Male's white body framed by black tail, tail-coverts and breast; head and neck copper-red. Bill black; sloping profile diagnostic. Female and juvenile have brown heads and necks, but the light body and sloping profile are distinctive. Canvasbacks fly faster than most ducks; the flicker created by the rapidly beating wings crossing the white body is distinctive. Male coos, growls; female quacks, purrs. **Range and habitat:** large inland lakes, coastal freshwater bays, north-western to central NA. Winters on coastal and southern NA. **Similar species:** Redhead, male Greater and Lesser Scaups (see p 148).

Redhead

Aythya americana (**Anatidae**) 45–56 cm/18–22 in.
Male's copper-red head has a rounded profile; bill blue, black tip; gray body; black breast, tail and tail-coverts. Female uniformly brown, lighter than female scaup and Ring-necked Duck; white belly and gray bill tipped in black. Often occur singly, in pairs or in small flocks on migration. Flight rapid, low, straight. Lays eggs in nests of other ducks. Male, catlike "whee-oogh," purr; female, harsh "squak." **Range and habitat:** freshwater marshes of central and west-central NA. Winters from east-central and south-western NA south. **Similar species:** Canvasback, female scaup and Ring-necked Duck. **Not illustrated.**

Lesser Scaup

Aythya affinis (**Anatidae**) 38–45 cm/15–18 in.
Endemic to western hemisphere. Dark head, neck, breast; gray back; white flanks, dark tail and tail coverts; purple gloss on head; pale blue bill. Back darker with darker vermiculations on flanks than in Greater Scaup; white stripe extends only across secondaries. Female dark brown with white belly. Gray bill with white around base. Soft "whee-ooo" by courting male, otherwise loud whistles, scolding. **Range and habitat:** northwest to central NA. Winters along coasts and rivers, central NA to northern NT. More frequent in central NA and protected coastal areas than Greater Scaup. **Similar species:** Greater Scaup, Ring-necked Duck, Tufted Duck.

Ring-necked Duck

Aythya collaris (**Anatidae**) 35–45 cm/14–18 in.
Male's head, neck, back and tail black; bill gray, tipped black, encircled with white ring; flanks gray; white wedge separates chest from flank. Female's bill less marked; head and body brown, darker on crown and back. Head of both peaks toward back of crown. Forms large flocks on migration. Dabbles and dives. Male whistles; female growls. **Range and habitat:** small freshwater ponds, marshes, bogs northern and central NA. Winters from central NA south on both coasts into Central America, also interior southeast. **Similar species:** scaup, Tufted Duck.

King Eider

Somateria spectabilis (**Anatidae**) 53–61 cm/21–24 in Stocky.
White foreparts, black rear parts, white patches in wings. Modified scapulars project like sails. Pearl-gray crown, green cheeks, red bill, orange bill shield unmistakable. Convex bill shield and rounded crown offer distinctive profile. Female warm brown, heavily barred. Immature male dusky with white foreparts. Gregarious, but smaller flocks than other eiders. Dives up to 60 m (180 ft), only Long-tailed Duck dives more deeply. Courting male coos, female a low "kuck." **Range and habitat:** Coasts of north-western and north-central NA. Winters on the ocean and along north-western and north-eastern coasts. **Similar species:** Common Eider (p 148).

Barrow's Goldeneye

Bucephala islandica (**Anatidae**) 40–51 cm/16–20 in.
Black head with purple sheen; white crescent between black bill and golden eye; long nape feathers form partial crest; neck, breast, forward flanks white; back, tail, rear flanks black with white markings. Female, juvenile: brown heads with pale gray to white neck, breast, belly; darker back, flanks, tail; bill yellow to pinkish orange. White on wings, which whistle in flight. Mews, grunts during courtship. **Range and habitat:** breeds in western mountains and north-eastern NA, western Iceland. Winters western, north-eastern and east-central coasts. **Similar species:** Common Goldeneye.

Harlequin Duck

Histrionicus histrionicus (**Anatidae**) 35–48 cm/14–19 in.
Short-billed duck. Male blue-gray, bold white and chestnut pattern; in eclipse gray with white crescent at base of bill, traces of white breast band and white in wings. Female, autumn immatures: gray-brown, white cheek and ear patches. Flight fast, erratic, low. Appear small, long-tailed, lack obvious white on wing. Squeaks and whistles. **Range and habitat:** north-eastern, north-western and west-central NA in turbulent streams. Winters along rocky coasts. **Similar species:** female Bufflehead, female scaup, female Surf Scoter.

Bufflehead

Bucephala albeola (**Anatidae**) 33–39 cm/13–15 in.
Smallest diving duck, large iridescent black head; large white semicircle wrapping over the nape from eye to eye; back and rump black; breast, flanks, belly white. Large white wing patches in flight. Female has dark head with long white patch below eye, dark back, gray flanks, white chest and belly. White wing patches small. Male whistles; female croaks. **Range and habitat:** nests in old woodpecker holes from north-western to west-central and central NA. Winters in small flocks in protected coastal areas and ice-free lakes. **Similar species:** Hooded Merganser, Ruddy Duck, female Harlequin Duck.

Ruddy Duck

Wood Duck (drake behind)

Blue-winged Teal

Cinnamon Teal

Canvasback

Lesser Scaup

Ring-necked Duck

King Eider

Barrow's Goldeneye

Harlequin Duck (drake, left, and duck)

Bufflehead

Hooded Merganser

Lophodytes cucullatus (Anatidae) 40–48 cm/16–19 in.
Thin bill, crest give distinctive profile. Male has black head, white patch from behind eye to black-bordered crest; white breast separated from rusty flanks by 2 vertical black bars. In flight, male shows large white wing patches, female smaller patches, both appear long-tailed. Brownish gray female has rust-orange crest. Eclipse male like female, juveniles with small crest. Froglike croak when courting. **Range and habitat:** nests in tree-cavities near fresh water in west-central NA, also north-eastern, east-central NA. Winters on coasts, ice-free lakes. **Similar species:** Bufflehead.

Surf Scoter

Melanitta perspicillata (Anatidae) 43–53 cm/17–21 in.
Male has large black head, white patches on forehead and nape; deep orange, red, white and black bill; body and wings black. Female brown with large bill and 2 light patches below eye. Juveniles 2 light facial patches, pale breast. First-winter males blacker than females, some bill color, white nape. When diving uses partially folded wings in underwater "flight." Low whistles and grunts during courtship. **Range and habitat:** nests on ground near freshwater marsh or pond in north-western, also north-eastern NA. Winters on coasts. **Similar species:** other scoters, female Harlequin Duck (see p 148).

DIURNAL BIRDS OF PREY Falconiformes

Bald Eagle

Haliaeetus leucocephalus (Accipitridae) 76–109 cm/30–43 in.
Large, fish-eating, scavenging eagle; long, broad wings; stout, hooked, yellow bill, eyes and feet also yellow; white head and tail; blackish brown body. Immature brown mottled with white, bill brownish, eyes pale yellow, feet yellow. Head and tail turn white in 4th or 5th year. Sexes alike. Hunts from perches overlooking water, occasionally on wing. Harsh, high cackle. **Range and habitat:** breeds and winters on large bodies of water from north-eastern EP throughout NA. **Similar species:** African Fish Eagle (see p 150). Severely reduced by pesticides, the species is now recovering.

Sharp-shinned Hawk

Accipiter striatus (Accipitridae) Male 25–29 cm/10–11½ in; female: 30–34 cm/12–13 in.
Preys on small to medium-sized birds. Long legs, short rounded wings, long notched or squared tail. Adults blue-gray above, white below barred with rufous. Eyes yellow-orange, redder with age. Immatures brown above, white spots on mantle, cream below, brown streaks on breast, barring on flanks. Eyes pale yellow. Voice: shrill "kik-kik-kik." **Range and habitat:** nests throughout NA, winters central and southern NA, Central America. Western subspecies smaller. **Similar species:** Cooper's Hawk.

Cooper's Hawk

Accipiter cooperii (Accipitridae) Male 38–44 cm/15–17 in; female 43–49 cm/17–19 in.
Ambushes medium-sized birds and mammals. Short rounded wings; long rounded tail; blue-gray above, white barred with rufous below; yellow-orange eyes, redder with age. Immature brown, white spots on mantle, white underparts, streaked with brown; eyes pale yellow. Proportionately shorter wings, larger head than Sharp-shinned Hawk. Immature less heavily streaked than Sharp-shinned Hawk. Voice: flickerlike "kek-kek-kek." **Range and habitat:** breeds in central and southern NA. Winters in southern part of range to Central America. Western subspecies smaller. **Similar species:** Sharp-shinned Hawk.

Red-tailed Hawk

Buteo jamaicensis (Accipitridae) 48–63 cm/19–25 in.
Large, stocky, broad-winged, broad-tailed hawk with several subspecies. Light-phase adults dark head, throat and dorsum; brick-red tail; white breast, heavily barred belly. White wing-linings with dark wrists and patagial stripes. Dark phase: dark above and below with reddish tail and breast. Immature darker than adult with longer wings and tail. Voice: asthmatic, descending "keeerrrrrr." **Range and habitat:** NA and West Indies. Winter from central NA south. **Similar species:** Red-shouldered Hawk, Swainson's Hawk, dark-phase Ferruginous and Rough-legged Hawks.

Red-shouldered Hawk

Buteo lineatus (Accipitridae) 43–61 cm/17–24 in.
Slim with narrow wings, long tail. Dark above, head tinged rufous; back with white chequering; breast and shoulder rufous, belly and flanks barred rufous; tail with wide dark bands, narrow white bands. Sexes similar. Immature brown above mottled with white, light below streaked with brown. White patch at base of outer primaries. Voice: loud "kee-yar," pitch drops. **Range and habitat:** moist woodlands of east-central and south-central NA. Winters southern NA. **Similar species:** Broad-winged, Red-tailed, Cooper's Hawks.

Broad-winged Hawk

Buteo platypterus (Accipitridae) 35–48 cm/14–19 in.
Both sexes stocky, dark brown above, whitish below with rufous barring. Tail has black and white stripes of equal width, narrow white terminal band. Wing-lining white with dark border. Immatures: dark above, often spotted white, light below with brown streaks, tail crossed by 5 or 6 narrow dark bands. Often hunt from perch at edge of clearing. Voice: high, whistled "pweeeee," constant pitch, diminuendo. **Range and habitat:** deciduous forests of central and eastern NA. Winters Central America south to Brazil. **Similar species:** Red-shouldered Hawk.

Swainson's Hawk

Buteo swainsoni (Accipitridae) 48–56 cm/19–22 in.
When perched, folded wings extend beyond long tail. Light phase: brown above; tail gray-brown with from 5 to 7 narrow dark bands; throat white, breast brown; flanks, belly and legs cream; white wing-linings, dark flight feathers. Dark phase: dark with buff undertail-coverts. Immature dark brown above, white to buff below streaked and spotted with brown. Soars with wings in shallow V. Voice: shrill, plaintive "kreeeeer." **Range and habitat:** plains and sparse forest, central and west-central NA south. Winters in NT. Numbers declining. **Similar species:** Red-tailed Hawk, dark-phase Rough-legged and Ferruginous Hawks.

Ferruginous Hawk

Buteo regalis (Accipitridae) 55–68 cm/22–27 in.
Light phase; reddish brown above, pale head, white below, rufous barring on flanks; wing-linings white with dark crescent and narrow chestnut patagial stripe; legs feathered to toes with heavily barred chestnut feathers; tail white, reddish near tip. Melanistic phase (2–5%): clove-brown body, light tail. Immature dark above, mottled white with cinnamon on breast, white belly and tarsi. Tail white proximally, brownish distally. Voice: "kree-a-ah." **Range and habitat:** arid, open prairies central, west-central NA south. Winters in south-western NA. **Similar species:** Red-tailed, Swainson's and Rough-legged Hawks.

American Kestrel

Falco sparverius (Falconidae) 19–20 cm/7½–8 in.
Male rufous above, black barred back, blue-gray wings, black primaries spotted with white; tail tipped with black band; forehead, eyebrows blue-gray, throat and face white crossed by 2 vertical black bands; 2 black spots on nape; cinnamon below with black spotting, heavier on flanks and mid-section. Female: rufous wings, black barring on back, wings, tail. Voice: high-pitched "klee-klee-klee." **Range and habitat:** common throughout NA along roadsides. Winters in southern NA **Similar species:** Sharp-shinned Hawk, Merlin (see p 152).

Prairie Falcon

Falco mexicanus (Falconidae) 35–45 cm/14–18 in.
Dark wing-linings distinctive. Adults sandy brown above with buff feather-edgings. Underparts buff to cream with brown spotting on breast and belly, barring on thighs. Sexes similar. Juveniles darker above and below with heavier streaking. Nests on cliff ledges. Hunts from perch or low rapid flight. Captures prey on or near ground. Call a sharp "kik, kik, kik," wails and whines during spectacular aerial courtship. **Range and habitat:** arid interior, west-central and central NA south. **Similar species:** Peregrine Falcon (see p 152).

Hooded Merganser

Surf Scoter

Bald Eagle

Sharp-shinned Hawk

Cooper's Hawk

Red-tailed Hawk
(eating rattlesnake)

Red-shouldered Hawk

Broad-winged Hawk

Swainson's Hawk
(pale phase)

Ferruginous Hawk

American Kestrel
(female)

Prairie Falcon (with ground squirrel as pr

FOWL-LIKE BIRDS Galliformes

Northern Bobwhite

Colinus virginianus (Phasianidae) 25 cm/10 in.
Brown above, chestnut streaks; under-parts white mottled with black. Male: black crown bordered by white stripe from bill over the eye to side of black neck; a contrasting black stripe extends from bill under the eye; throat white. Female's head pattern similar, but brown replaces black and buff replaces white. When frightened usually runs to heavy cover, freezes in group; if threat persists, flushes with whirr of short rounded wings. In cool weather aggregate in coveys of 8–25 birds. Voice: clear, whistled "bob-white," rising at end. **Range and habitat:** open woodlands and brushy fields, east-central and south-central NA. **Similar species:** Gray Partridge (see p 154). The population is declining at 3% per year.

Wild Turkey

Meleagris gallopavo (Phasianidae) 122–127 cm/48–50 in.
Large, shy, ground-dwelling bird. Flies weakly. Body plumage iridescent bronze; primaries, secondaries dark brown and white barred; tail rust-colored, finely barred, black subterminal band and pale rust tip. Head unfeathered; in male, bluish with red wattles on throat and foreneck. Male also has "beard" of feathers projecting from the breast. Female smaller, slimmer, less iridescent, smaller head, no "beard." Male gobbles and struts with wings drooped, tail fanned. Female clucks. **Range and habitat:** open woods and clearings, east-central and southern NA.

Sage Grouse

Centrocercus urophasianus (Phasianidae) 68–86 cm/27–34 in.
For most of year larger male and smaller female brown with pointed tails, black bellies and partially white undertail-coverts. Breeding male has large buff air sacs on upper breast, a black bib lies above and white collar surrounds the air sacs. Males display on communal leks, strutting with air sacs inflated and white collars expanded to contrast with drooping brown wings and black head. The tail forms a spiked backdrop. Male during courtship gives a "plop-plop," female "quak, quak." **Range and habitat:** wherever big sagebrush occurs in western NA. **Similar species:** other grouse, all of which are smaller (see p 152).

Greater Prairie Chicken

Tympanuchus cupido (Phasianidae) 43–45 cm/17–18 in.
Both sexes brown and white barred, short brown tail. In spring male has elongated feathers that it erects to form earlike structures above bright orange-red air sacs, which can be inflated. Orange combs above eyes are erected and male leans forward, stamps his feet, bobs and utters a booming, cooing sound, similar to blowing across the top of an empty bottle. Displays occur on traditional lek usually in early spring, from shortly before dawn to mid-morning. **Range and habitat:** prairies of central and south-central NA. **Similar species:** Lesser Prairie Chicken, Sharp-tailed Grouse. Some populations endangered.

Spruce Grouse

Falcipennis canadensis (Phasianidae) 33–40 cm/13–16 in.
Unusually tame. Male: black breast, throat; black tail tipped with rust, white-tipped undertail-coverts, finely barred gray and black on back and rump; scarlet comb over each eye; sides, lower chest and belly finely barred dark brown and buff with white mottling. Male Franklin's, a Rocky mountain subspecies, lacks rust tail tips, but has white-tipped uppertail-coverts. Female is brown with black barring, short fan-shaped tail with terminal buff band. Courtship includes strutting with spread tail oscillating side to side, short flights on whirring wings. **Range and habitat:** boreal forest of NA. **Similar species:** Ruffed Grouse, female Blue Grouse.

CRANES, RAILS AND ALLIES Gruiformes

Sandhill Crane

Grus canadensis (Gruidae) Greater: 102–127 cm/40–50 in; Lesser and Cuban: 51–76 cm/20–30 in.
Long neck, legs. Both sexes pale gray; smaller southern subspecies darker than migratory larger northern subspecies. Dark green bill, yellow eye, unfeathered red crown; black legs. In spring adults smear iron-containing mud on feathers, giving plumage rusty cast. Juveniles reddish brown. Flies with neck and feet outstretched. Voice: loud, rolling, bell-like rattle that carries well. **Range and habitat:** shallow open wetlands and grassy uplands from eastern EP to north-central NA. South in scattered populations through central and western NA. Winters in south-western NA. Resident subspecies in south-eastern NA. Mississippi population endangered. **Similar species:** Whooping Crane.

Whooping Crane

Grus americana (Gruidae) 127–152 cm/50–60 in.
The tallest North American flying bird has white plumage except for black primaries; naked crown and cheeks are red; eyes yellow, bill greenish, legs black. Juveniles: cinnamon-brown, white belly and secondaries, black primaries and legs, pale bill, feathered crown. Voice: exceptionally loud, higher-pitched and more continuous than that of Sandhill Crane. **Range and habitat:** breeds in Wood Buffalo National Park near Arctic circle in Northwest Territories, Canada and winters in Aransas National Wildlife Refuge in Texas. Introduced population in Florida. **Similar species:** Sandhill Crane. Endangered, but increasing from a low of 15 in 1937.

Limpkin

Aramus guarauna (Aramidae) 63–68 cm/25–27 in.
Dull brown, heavily streaked and spotted with white; bill pale at base, dark at tip, long, slender, slightly decurved; neck long, legs long and dark. Flies with neck and feet extended. Wingbeat slow, with cranelike upward flick. Slinks quietly through marsh, often pumps tail when walking. Voice: loud, wailing scream, like cries of lost child, usually at twilight, at night and on cloudy days. **Range and habitat:** locally common in freshwater marshes with open water channels, along marshy river-banks from south-eastern NA, West Indies, to southern NT. **Similar species:** immature night-herons and ibises (see p 52).

American Coot

Fulica americana (Rallidae) 33–40 cm/13–16 in.
Distinctive white bill and frontal shield against the black head and slate-gray body. Sides of undertail-coverts white, forming distinctive pattern from the rear. Legs greenish lobes around each toe-bone. Head oscillates when swimming. Feeds on vegetation by dipping or diving. Runs across water when taking off. Chick has orange head and breast. Immature like adult, but paler with dusky bill. Voice: loud cackles, whistles, croaks, grunts, also loud "kuk-kuk-kuk." **Range and habitat:** freshwater marshes, north-western and central NA in mountains to north-western NT. Winters, often in flocks, on ice-free fresh and salt water. **Similar species:** other coots, Moorhen, Purple Gallinule (see pp 154, 196).

American Purple Gallinule

Porphyrula martinica (Rallidae) 30–35 cm/12–14 in.
Both sexes have deep purple head, neck and underparts blending through blue to bronze-green on back and wings; undertail-coverts white; bill red with yellow tip and pale blue frontal shield; legs yellow, long toes spread weight as it walks across floating vegetation. Immature: buff head, dark brown back and wings, copper-colored underparts, white undertail-coverts; legs yellow, bill dark. In flight legs and feet dangle. Associates with coots, moorhens, but more apt to stay in cover. **Range and habitat:** uncommon resident of freshwater marshes from south-eastern NA, West Indies, to central NT. Winters in tropical and subtropical parts of range. **Similar species:** Moorhen, immature American Coot (see p 154).

Northern Bobwhite

Wild Turkey

Sage Grouse (male in courtship display)

Greater Prairie Chicken (male in courtship display)

Spruce Grouse (female)

Sandhill Crane

Whooping Crane

Limpkin

American Coot

American Purple Gallinule

Virginia Rail

Rallus limicola (**Rallidae**) 23 cm/9 in.
Only small North American rail with long bill. Crown, back olive, feathers of back edged in buff, gray face, rust-colored throat, breast; flanks strongly barred black and white; undertail-coverts white; long orange and black bill; legs brown with long toes. Immature: olive crown and back, blackish below, bill and legs dark. Distinctive "kidick-kidick," also descending laugh, grunts. **Range and habitat:** local breeder in freshwater marshes from central NA to south-eastern NT. Winters in coastal saltmarshes. **Similar species:** Clapper Rail.

Clapper Rail

Rallus longirostris (**Rallidae**) 35–40 cm/14–16 in.
Gray-brown with dark streaks above, gray cheeks, flanks with vertical gray and white bars, white undertail-coverts. Bird of Atlantic coast gray-brown throat and breast. Gulf and Pacific coast birds have rusty throat and breast, generally richer color. Bill orange and dark, long, slightly drooped. Voice: distinctive "kek kek kek" repeated 20–25 times. Noisiest at dusk when emerges to feed on mudflats. **Range and habitat:** Atlantic and Pacific saltmarshes, central NA to northern NT, West Indies. **Similar species:** Virginia Rail. Stable, but California populations endangered

King Rail

Rallus elegans (**Rallidae**) 38–48 cm/15–19 in.
Cinnamon replaces gray-brown of Clapper Rail. Rust-colored cheeks; shoulders, breast bright rust, flanks barred black and white; dark streaks on back and tail more contrasting than in Clapper Rail; white undertail-coverts. Like Clapper Rail often cocks tail. Toes not webbed, but swims well. Flies rarely and with legs dangling. Low, grunting "bup-bup." **Range and habitat:** freshwater marshes throughout east-central and south-eastern NA. Winters along coast in saltmarshes south to Cuba. **Similar species:** Clapper and Virginia Rails.

Sora (Sora Crake)

Porzana carolina (**Rallidae**) 20–25 cm/8–10 in.
Often feeds at edge of marsh openings. Olive-brown crown, back and wings with black spots; face black; cheeks, foreneck, upper breast gray, belly white, flanks barred white and brown; undertail-coverts white; bill short and yellow. When walking, flicks short tail up. Immature brown above, buff below, barred flanks. Voice rising "ker-wee," sharp "keek," descending whinny. Usually noisiest at twilight. **Range and habitat:** marshes and wet meadows, north-central, central and south-western NA. Winters from southern NA to northern NT, also West Indies. **Similar species:** Virginia and Yellow Rails.

SHOREBIRDS, GULLS, AUKS Charadriiformes

Killdeer

Charadrius vociferus (**Charadriidae**) 23–28 cm/9–11 in.
Only North American plover with 2 black breast bands. White forehead bordered by black; crown, back, wings brown; white eyebrow; black moustache; white collar and underparts; uppertail-coverts rufous, tail rufous edged in black and white. Sexes alike. Young and immatures have single black breast band. Ringing, repeated "kill-dee" or cries of "deer-deer-deer." **Range and habitat:** meadows, pastures and dry uplands of NA; also west-central NT. Winters from central NA into north-western NT. **Similar species:** other belted plovers (see pp 110, 156, 200, 294).

Semipalmated Plover

Charadrius semipalmatus (**Charadriidae**) 16–19 cm/6½–7½ in.
Single black breast band, stubby orange and black bill. Forehead white surrounded with black; nape, back, wings color of wet sand; white collar encircles neck, underparts white; legs orange. In flight white stripe along wings. Winter birds have brown breast bands, dark bills, dull legs. Sexes similar. Immature: black bill, brown breast band. Voice: plaintive, rising "too-li;" on breeding grounds a liquid rattle. **Range and habitat:** tundra of NA. Winters on coasts from southern NA to southern NT. **Similar species:** all belted plovers (see pp 110, 156, 200, 294).

American Golden-Plover

Pluvialis dominica (**Charadriidae**) 24–28 cm/9½–11 in.
Upperparts spotted black, yellow and gold; face, foreneck, underparts black; forehead, eyebrow, sides of neck, breast white. In winter speckled brown above, pale below. Juveniles heavily spotted with golden brown dorsally, underparts streaked and barred, eyebrow white, rump and tail dark. No wing-bar. Voice: plaintive "queedle," dropping at end. **Range and habitat:** smaller, more brightly colored western subspecies breeds from eastern EP to western Alaska, migrates to Hawaii, South Pacific islands; larger subspecies breeds across northern NA, winters in southern NT. **Similar species:** European Golden Plover (see p 156).

Upland Sandpiper

Bartramia longicauda (**Scolopacidae**) 28–32 cm/11–13 in.
Small head with large eyes on long, thin neck; large body, long tail projecting well beyond folded wings; long yellow legs; straight yellow bill. Brown above, feathers edged with buff; light below. In flight wings long, pointed, dark. Flaps below horizontal. After landing often extends wings vertically. Runs in spurts, often perches on rocks or hillocks. Voice: mellow, whistled "kip-ip-ip," song collection of reedy whistles and trills. **Range and habitat:** grassy prairies, open meadows north-western to central and east-central NA. Winters in Patagonia. **Similar species:** yellowlegs, Solitary Sandpiper.

Greater Yellowlegs

Tringa melanoleuca (**Scolopacidae**) 32–38 cm/13–15 in.
Long, chrome-yellow legs. Both sexes mottled black, gray, white above; white below, heavily to lightly barred; bill slightly upturned; wings dark; rump white. In winter brownish gray above, throat and breast finely streaked with gray; white below. Juvenile: dark brown above, dense white spotting; white below with dark bars. Voice: 3 whistled syllables, in spring a yodeling "whee-oodle." **Range and habitat:** muskeg of northern NA. Winters along coasts central NA to southern NT. **Similar species:** Lesser Yellowlegs, Solitary Sandpiper, Common Greenshank, Common Redshank (see p 158).

Lesser Yellowlegs

Tringa flavipes (**Scolopacidae**) 24–28 cm/9½–11 in.
Often feeds in large loose flocks, unlike Greater Yellowlegs. Most distinctive feature is thin, straight black bill, about same length as head or slightly longer. Legs proportionately longer, giving distinctly long-legged appearance. Belly white. Juveniles: fine gray streaks on breast, browner above than adults. Voice: high, flat soft "tew" or "tew tew." **Range and habitat:** marshes, bogs of northwest and north-central NA. Winters on coast from southern NA to southern NT. **Similar species:** Greater Yellowlegs, Solitary Sandpiper, Common Redshank, Common Greenshank (see p 158). The population is decreasing by around 9% per year.

Solitary Sandpiper

Tringa solitaria (**Scolopacidae**) 19–23 cm/7½–9 in.
Conspicuous white eye-ring; dark olive above flecked with white; dark tail, outer feathers barred with white; neck, breast heavily streaked with black; throat and belly white; short, straight, olive bill. Juveniles, winter adults: washed with brown, faintly streaked below, grayer above. Dark rump distinguishes it from yellowlegs. Swallowlike flight. Voice: whistled "peet!" or "peet-weet-weet!," higher than Spotted Sandpiper. **Range and habitat:** streamsides, wooded swamps, ponds, marshes throughout boreal NA. Winters from southern NA to south-eastern NT. **Similar species:** Lesser Yellowlegs.

Spotted Sandpiper

Actitis macularia (**Scolopacidae**) 18–20 cm/7–8 in.
Breeding adults gray-brown above, flecked with dark; whitish eyebrow, dark eye stripe; white below with conspicuous dark spots; bill stout, pale orange, dark tip, droops slightly. Teeters. Stiff-winged flight, shows white wing stripe, rounded tail with outer feathers barred white and black. Winter plumage, juvenile: white below without spots, gray-brown above. Voice: whistled "peet weet," 2nd note often repeated. **Range and habitat:** pebbly freshwater shores throughout NA, except southern extreme. Winters from southernmost NA to southern NT, has bred in WP. **Similar species:** Common Sandpiper, Solitary Sandpiper (see p 158).

Virginia Rail

Clapper Rail

King Rail

Sora

Killdeer

Semipalmated Plover

American Golden-Plover

Upland Sandpiper

Greater Yellowlegs

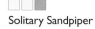

Lesser Yellowlegs

Spotted Sandpiper

Solitary Sandpiper

Semipalmated Sandpiper

Calidris pusilla (Scolopacidae) 14–18 cm/5½–7 in.
Most common of "peeps"—small sandpipers. Above grayish brown and black feathers rufous-edged; white below, dark brown streaks across upper breast, along flanks. In winter gray-brown above, whitish eyebrow, dusky face and sides of breast, white below. Sexes similar. Juveniles scaly buff, black above, scapulars rufous-edged, wing-coverts light-edged. Upper-parts white, buff band across upper breast. Legs, feet and bill black. Voice: harsh "chit." **Range and habitat:** arctic tundra of NA. Winters along southern coasts of NT. **Similar species:** other "peeps" (see pp 158, 250).

Western Sandpiper

Calidris mauri (Scolopacidae) 15–18 cm/6–7 in.
In breeding plumage, separated from Semipalmated Sandpiper by rusty-margined scapulars; slightly longer bill, drooped at tip; rusty tinge to crown, ear-coverts and back; V-shaped spots across breast, along flanks. Feeds in deeper water than Semipalmated. After late September distinguished from Semipalmated only by call, a high-pitched "cheep." Juvenile has bright rusty-edged scapulars, but molts rapidly. **Range and habitat:** arctic tundra of north-western NA. Winters along both coasts from central NA to NT. **Similar species:** other "peeps" (see pp 158, 250).

Least Sandpiper

Calidris minutilla (Scolopacidae) 13–15 cm/5–6 in.
Dull yellow or greenish legs and feet separate it from other "peeps." Sooty brown above, narrow chestnut and buff feather-edges wear away leaving sooty brown appearance. In flight, wing-bar faint. Foreneck and upper breast pale buff with coarse brown streaking. Winter plumage dusky gray. Sexes similar. Juveniles: rufous edges to feathers of crown, back incomplete white V on back. Voice: thin, drawn-out "kreeeet." **Range and habitat:** wet muddy or grassy areas in northern NA. Winters from southern and coastal NA to northern NT. **Similar species:** other "peeps" (see pp 158, 250).

White-rumped Sandpiper

Calidris fuscicollis (Scolopacidae) 18–20 cm/7–8 in.
Folded wings extend beyond tail. In flight shows white wing-bar, white rump. Crown, ear-coverts edged chestnut; dorsal feathers edged buff and chestnut; white below; dark brown streaks on breast and flanks. Winter birds gray-brown; white eyebrow, rump and underparts. Sexes similar. Juveniles like breeding birds but with incomplete white V on the sides of the back. Feet black. Voice: high-pitched, mouselike "jeet." **Range and habitat:** tundra of north-western and north-central NA. Winters in southern NT. **Similar species:** other "peeps" (see pp 158, 250).

Baird's Sandpiper

Calidris bairdii (Scolopacidae) 18–19 cm/7–7½ in.
Folded wings extend beyond tail. Face, foreneck, upper breast buff, thinly streaked with brown; back blotchy gray-brown; underparts white; legs black; bill black, straight, slightly tapered. Winter plumage like White-rumped Sandpiper, but dark rump. Juvenile: more scaly than blotchy. Voice: low, soft "krrrit," also a rolling trill. **Range and habitat:** tundra from north-central EP to north-western NA. Small flocks of migrants frequent muddy, sandy or grassy areas. Winters in southern NT. **Similar species:** other "peeps," Buff-breasted and Pectoral Sandpipers, Sanderling (see p 158).

Stilt Sandpiper

Calidris himantopus (Scolopacidae) 19–23 cm/7½–9 in.
In flight white rump and tail and no wing-bar distinctive. Black mottled with white above; ear-coverts, nape tinged chestnut, underparts white, heavily barred with black; legs grayish green to yellow; bill black, long, outer 3 rd drooped. Winter plumage brownish gray above, whitish eyebrow and underparts. Sexes alike. Juvenile blackish brown above, buff feather-edges, foreneck, breast cream, faintly streaked with brown. Voice: monosyllabic "querp." **Range and habitat:** tundra of northern NA. Winters from extreme southern NA to southern NT. **Similar species:** Lesser Yellowlegs (see p 62).

Pectoral Sandpiper

Calidris melanotos (Scolopacidae) 23–24 cm/9–9½ in.
Dorsal feathers sooty brown, buff edges; dark brown streaking on foreneck and breast ends abruptly at lower breast, contrasts with white belly, flanks, undertail-coverts. Winter plumage grayer. Legs, feet yellow, occasionally green or brown; bill black. Sexes similar. Juveniles brighter than adults, incomplete buff V on sides of back, pectoral streaking suffused with buff. Voice: reedy "trrrip trrrip." **Range and habitat:** tundra from EP to north-central NA. Migrants favor grassy wetlands. Winters in southern NT. **Similar species:** Least and Sharp-tailed Sandpipers.

Buff-breasted Sandpiper

Tryngites subruficollis (Scolopacidae) 19–21 cm/7½–8½ in.
Large eye set off by white eye-ring in buffy face; dorsal feathers dark brown, buff edges give scaly appearance; underparts buff; crown speckled; short, tapered bill, pale base; feathering extends onto bill; legs yellow. In flight buff body contrasts with white wing-linings, no wing-bar. Juveniles, dorsal scaly appearance enhanced by white edges to feathers. Voice: low trill "prr-r-r-rret," sharp "tik." **Range and habitat:** tundra of northernmost NA. Favors grassy areas on migration. Winters in southern NT. **Similar species:** Upland Sandpiper, juvenile Baird's Sandpiper.

Short-billed Dowitcher

Limnodromus griseus (Scolopacidae) 27–30 cm/10½–12 in.
Characteristic chunky body, long straight bill, white triangle on back. Subspecies: *hendersoni* (reddish brown below, some white on belly, lightly spotted with black from throat to undertail-coverts), *griseus* and *caurinus* (reddish below with dense spotting on breast, often including scalloped bars, white belly). All forms have barred flanks and tail feathers. Long-billed Dowitchers differ by salmon-red bellies, black tail feathers. Voice of Short-billed staccato "tu-tu-tu." Range and habitat: north-western (*caurinus*), north-central (*hendersoni*) and north-eastern (*griseus*) na. Winter along southern coasts to central NT. Similar species: Long-billed Dowitcher, Common Snipe (see p 160). The population is decreasing by around 5% per year.

Willet

Catoptrophorus semipalmatus (Scolopacidae) 36–41 cm/14–16 in.
Black and white wings, white rump. Breeding plumage: eastern subspecies gray-brown finely barred with black; western, larger, paler, grayer, often pinkish on breast. Bill long, straight, heavy, pale pink or blue-gray with black tip. Sexes similar. Voice: musical "pill-will-willet," loud "kay-ee," repeated "kip-kip-kip." **Range and habitat:** western subspecies breeds in central NA, eastern along east-central and south-eastern coasts. Winters from central coasts south. **Similar species:** Greater Yellowlegs, winter plumage Hudsonian Godwit (see p 66).

Long-billed Curlew

Numenius americanus (Scolopacidae) 51–66 cm/20–26 in.
Exceptionally long, sickle-shaped bill. Warm brown mottled with black above; crown, head unstriped; underparts buff. Cinnamon wing-linings conspicuous in flight. Female much larger. Juvenile: shorter bill. Call a loud, clear, rising "cur-lee," repeated. **Range and habitat:** breeds in grasslands of central and west-central NA, migrants frequent marshes, mudflats, shorelines. Winters southern NA to north-western NT. **Similar species:** Marbled Godwit, Whimbrel (has crown stripes), Western Curlew (see p 160).

Marbled Godwit

Limosa fedoa (Scolopacidae) 40–51 cm/16–20 in.
Smaller than Long-billed Curlew; bill upturned, long, salmon-colored with dark tip; dark back, heavily mottled with buff; wing-linings, secondaries and inner primaries cinnamon. Outer primaries, primary coverts blackish; underparts cinnamon-buff and barred; tail finely barred black and cinnamon to buff. Juveniles, winter adults: underparts unmarked, may look paler or grayer. Voice: accented "godwit," also "raddica, raddica." **Range and habitat:** breeds in wet meadows of central NA. Winters on southern coasts to west-central NT. **Similar species:** other godwits, Western Curlew (see p 160).

Semipalmated
Sandpiper

Western Sandpiper

Least Sandpiper

White-rumped
Sandpiper

Baird's Sandpiper

Stilt Sandpiper

Pectoral Sandpiper

Buff-breasted
Sandpiper

Short-billed
Dowitcher

Willet
(eastern subspecies)

Long-billed Curlew

Marbled Godwit

Hudsonian Godwit

Limosa haemastica (**Scolopacidae**) 35–40 cm/14–16 in.
Long, slightly upturned bill. In flight shows black axillaries and wing-linings, narrow white stripe along wing, white tail, terminal black band. Mottled brownish black above, chestnut below barred with black and white. In winter brownish gray; white lower breast, belly. Juvenile brownish black feathers edged with cinnamon, buff below. Bill salmon, tipped with black; paler in juveniles. Voice: loud high-pitched "godwit!." **Range and habitat:** breeds in north-western and north-central NA. Winters in southern NT. **Similar species:** other godwits, Willet (see pp 64, 160).

American Woodcock

Scolopax minor (**Scolopacidae**) 25–30 cm/10–12 in.
Plump shorebird of wet thickets, alder swales. Rusty gray forehead, face; black crown crossed by 4 rusty bars; back mottled rust, black, brown and gray; underparts rusty buff; legs short, pale; bill long, pale. Eyes high on head, providing binocular vision forward and backward. Performs courtship dance and flight in meadows during spring. Narrowed outer primaries produce twittering sound in flight. Voice: nasal "peent," liquid song during courtship flight. **Range and habitat:** east-central and south-eastern NA. Winters in south-eastern NA. **Similar species:** Snipe, other woodcocks (see p 160).

Surfbird

Aphriza virgata (**Scolopacidae**) 25 cm/10 in.
Breeding plumage: black and white streaked, spotted above with chestnut, black scapular feathers; blackish spots and bars on white underparts, belly white; short, dark ploverlike bill, yellow base on lower mandible. Winter adults, juveniles: brownish gray head, back, breast; dark spotting along flanks, white belly. All plumages show prominent white wing stripe and white tail in flight. Voice: "kee-wee" or "ke-wee-ek." **Range and habitat:** breeds in north-western NA. Winters on Pacific coast from north-western NA to southern NT. **Similar species:** Black Turnstone, Rock Sandpiper.

Black Turnstone

Arenaria melanocephala (**Scolopacidae**) 23 cm/9 in.
Black head, breast, back; white spot between eye and bill; white flecks across forehead, crown, sides of head, neck, breast; belly white. Winter adults and juveniles lack white flecks; head, breast, flanks somewhat brownish. In flight shows white shoulders, white stripe across secondaries and inner primaries, white lower back and base of tail. Short dark bill, slightly upturned. Legs short, dark. Voice: grating rattle. **Range and habitat:** frequents rocky shores, also rotting kelp, north-western NA. Winters along western coasts of NA. **Similar species:** Ruddy Turnstone, Surfbird (see p 156).

Wilson's Phalarope

Phalaropus tricolor (**Scolopacidae**) 21–24 cm/8½–9½ in.
Slim phalarope with white rump, tail, no wing stripe. Breeding female, gray crown, nape; dark stripe through eye, down neck, white below; chestnut wash across foreneck, breast; back lead gray with chestnut stripes. Bill black, needlelike, longer than head. Male paler. Juveniles brown mottled with buff above, buff wash on sides of breast. In winter, white forehead, dark eye-line, pale gray above, white below with yellow legs. Pronounced sex-role reversal. **Range and habitat:** shallow lakes and marshes in central and west-central NA. Winters in southern NT. **Similar species:** other phalaropes.

Black-necked Stilt

Himantopus mexicanus (**Recurvirostridae**) 34–39 cm/13–15 in.
Black above; white forehead, patch behind eye, lower face, foreneck, underparts; needlelike black bill, long pinkish red legs. In flight wings black above and below, axillaries and tail white, neck and legs extended. Female, juvenile: brownish black where male is black. Strides along shores or wades up to its belly picking insects off surface of water. Sharp yipping call. **Range and habitat:** freshwater and brackish ponds, open marshes, wet meadows along coasts from central NA to southern NT; local in central, south-western NA. Winters along southern coasts of NA, south. **Similar species:** Black-winged Stilt, Australian Stilt (see pp 156, 294).

American Avocet

Recurvirostra americana (**Recurvirostridae**) 43–47 cm/17–18 in.
White; large black patches on wings and back; head and neck cinnamon; black bill tapers to fine point and turns up, more so in females; legs long, gray-blue. In flight wing-linings white, outer half of wing, greater and median coverts black, secondaries white. Juvenile, winter plumages: head, neck grayish white. When feeding, sweeps bill back and forth over muddy water. **Range and habitat:** freshwater marshes, saline lakes and marshes, west-central and central NA, south. Winters along southern coasts, south **Similar species:** Avocet (see p 156).

Laughing Gull

Larus atricilla (**Laridae**) 40–43 cm/16–17 in.
Slim, long-winged gull with lead-gray mantle, black wing tips, white body, black head, white crescents above and below eye; bill red, legs dark. In winter head white, mottled with gray, bill black. Subadult gray, darker above, brown in mantle. Juvenile brown, back scaly. Both have white tail with black band. Voice: "hah-ha-ha-ha-hah-haah-haaaaa," ends in wail. **Range and habitat:** saltmarshes, coastal bays, beaches, east-central and southern NA, visits south-western NA. Winters southern NA to central NT. **Similar species:** other black-headed gulls (see pp 162, 250).

Franklin's Gull

Larus pipixcan (**Laridae**) 33–38 cm/13–15 in.
Small, compact. White stripe separates gray mantle from black outer primaries, which have white tips. White body, black head, white crescents above and below eye; bill scarlet. In winter half-hood covers head, eye crescents visible. Subadults have half-hood, eye crescents, gray mantle mottled with brown, grayish tail with black band, incomplete in 1st-year birds. Voice: shrill "kuk-kuk-kuk," mewing, laughing cry. **Range and habitat:** prairie marshes of central NA. Winters along coasts of extreme southern NA to central NT. **Similar species:** other black-headed gulls (see pp 162, 250).

Ring-billed Gull

Larus delawarensis (**Laridae**) 45–51 cm/18–20 in.
Black band encircles yellow bill. Yellow-green legs; head, body, tail white; mantle pale gray; wing tips black with white spots; eyes yellow. In winter neck streaked. Immature white with dusky spots, gray mantle mottled brown, incomplete tail band. Juvenile lighter than Herring Gull, mantle gray with brown carpal bar, dark secondary bar. Tail white with mottled base and incomplete band. Voice: "kree-kree-kree" when squabbling. **Range and habitat:** central NA. Winters on Great Lakes, along Mississippi, both coasts and southern NA. **Similar species:** other gulls.

Bonaparte's Gull

Larus philadelphia (**Laridae**) 30–35 cm/12–14 in.
Pointed wings; square tail; black head; narrow white eye crescents; white body; gray mantle with black tips to primaries; bill dark, legs red. White wedge in outer primaries in all plumages. Winter: head white, black ear patch, legs pink. First winter: blackish red bill; wing, black trailing edge, narrow white border, dark secondary bar, narrow black tail band. Voice: nasal "cheer," conversational notes. **Range and habitat:** nests in conifer trees, north-western and north-central NA. Winters along central, southern coasts and rivers. **Similar species:** other black-headed gulls (see pp 162, 250).

Glaucous Gull

Larus hyperboreus (**Laridae**) 53–66 cm/21–26 in.
Large, heavy-bodied gull with heavy yellow bill, yellow eye and legs. Head, body, tail white; mantle pale gray; primaries white, 1st-winter birds white mottled with pale gray-buff; bill pink, dark tip; legs pink. 2nd-year birds some gray in mantle, by 3rd year mantle gray, some buff mottling in body plumage, bill dark-tipped. Voice: hollow "cowp," deep "err-ul." **Range and habitat:** nests colonially around sea cliffs along Holarctic coasts. Winters from arctic south along coasts to mid-latitudes, also Great Lakes. **Similar species:** other white-winged gulls (see p 162).

Hudsonian Godwit

American Woodcock

Black-necked Stilt

American Avocet

Surfbird

Black Turnstone

Wilson's Phalarope

Laughing Gull

Franklin's Gull

Ring-billed Gull

Bonaparte's Gull

Glaucous Gull

Western Gull

Larus occidentalis (**Laridae**) 51–58 cm/20–23 in.

White-bodied gull with yellow bill, dark eye, pink legs, slate-gray (southern California) to medium gray (central and northern California) mantle with white trailing edge, and black wing tips with white spots. Underside of wing shows pronounced dark shadow. In winter dusky on head. First-winter birds mottled gray-brown. Second winter, mottled brown, whiter below, some gray in mantle. Third winter, white with dusky smudges, mantle gray-brown. Voice: gutteral "kuk-kuk-kuk," also "whee whee whee" and "ki-aa." **Range and habitat:** west-central and south-western Pacific coast. Winters in southern part of range. **Similar species:** Slatey-backed and Lesser Black-backed Gulls (see p 162).

California Gull

Larus californicus (**Laridae**) 45–51 cm/18–20 in.

Gray mantle, darker than that of Herring Gull. Black wing tips with white spots; head and body white; yellow bill has black and red spots; legs yellow-green; eyes dark. Sexes similar. First winter: mottled gray-brown above, lighter below; dark primaries; pink legs; pink bill, dark-tipped. Second winter: white mottled with gray-brown, gray mantle mottled brown, primaries dark, legs gray-green, bill gray-pink. Third winter: more gray in mantle, less gray-brown mottling in white. Voice: squealing "kiarr." **Range and habitat:** lakes, rivers, farmland, central to south-western NA. Winters on Pacific coast from west-central south NA. **Similar species:** other gray-backed gulls (see p 162).

Pomarine Jaeger

Stercorarius pomarinus (**Laridae**) 51 cm/20 in.

Flight slow, even, direct; wingbeats shallow. Large head and bill, broad wings give bulky appearance. Light phase: pale bill, dark cap, yellow wash to nape and cheeks, white below, mottled brown breast band and flanks, dark back and wings; blunt-tipped, twisted central tail feathers project beyond rest of tail; in flight base of primaries shows white. Dark phase recognized by tail feathers, flight pattern, bulky appearance. Sexes similar. Juveniles brown, heavily barred below, lack distinctive rectrices; subadults similar to adults, but straight rectrices. **Range and habitat:** Holarctic tundra. Winters at sea. **Similar species:** other jaegers, skuas (see pp 160, 296).

Forster's Tern

Sterna forsteri (**Laridae**) 35–42 cm/14–17 in.

Silvery white upper surface of primaries, paler than light gray mantle; tail gray, darkest on inner edge of fork, outer web of outermost tail feathers white; black cap, white body, orange bill with black tip, orange legs. Sexes similar. In winter crown white, black covers eye and ear, nape varies from pale gray to blackish. Juvenile has same mask with brownish upperparts. Bill brownish black, legs yellow. Voice: "zreep," raspy buzz like that of a nighthawk, shrill "pip-pip, pip, pip." **Range and habitat:** breeds on interior marshes of across central NA, also south-eastern coast. Winters along southern coasts. **Similar species:** Common Tern (see p 162).

Royal Tern

Sterna maximus (**Laridae**) 45–53 cm/18–21 in.

Large white-bodied tern with gray mantle and black cap, spotted with white on forehead, black crest projecting from nape. In nonbreeding and immature plumage forehead is white. Western subspecies: white of forehead extends behind eye. Bill large, orange to yellow-orange. In flight underside of primaries light. Plunge-dives for fish. Voice: "dhirrup," "keer" and "kaak." **Range and habitat:** saltwater habitats of east-central, south-eastern, south-western NA, west AF. Nests on sandy beaches with other colonial water birds. Parents recognize their own eggs. Winters along southern NA coasts, coastal NT, also west AF. **Similar species:** Caspian and Elegant Terns.

Black Skimmer

Rynchops niger (**Laridae**) 40–51 cm/16–20 in.

Lower mandible longer than upper, laterally flattened to form blade; upper mandible shorter, wider; both are red at base, black toward tip. Feeds by flying swiftly and evenly just above surface, with lower mandible slicing through water, flipping small fish and crustaceans into mouth. Black above with white forehead, foreneck, wing-lining and underparts; tail short, slightly notched.

Sexes similar. Juvenile similar to adult, but with mottled brown upperparts. Voice: nasal barking notes, soft "keow, keow." **Range and habitat:** nests with other seabirds on sand spits, barrier beaches and dredge-spoil islands from east-central and south-western NA south. Winters from southern NA to central NT. **Similar species:** African Skimmer (see p 202).

Pigeon Guillemot

Cepphus columba (**Alcidae**) 30–35 cm/12–14 in.

Thin neck, rounded head, long pointed bill contribute to distinctive profile. In all plumages, large white wing patches with 1, sometimes 2, black wedges; bill dark red to black, mouth and feet brilliant orange-red. Breeding birds black. In winter, mottled gray and white with dark wing-linings. Sexes similar. Immatures dusky gray above, wing patches small, crossed by indistinct dark bar. Voice: whistled "peeee." **Range and habitat:** nests in natural cavities above intertidal zone from north-eastern EP and north-western NA to east-central EP and west-central NA. Winters at sea south of arctic. **Similar species:** Black Guillemot, winter murrelets (see p 164).

Tufted Puffin

Fratercula cirrhata (**Alcidae**) 38–40 cm/15–16 in.

Large, laterally compressed, orange and green bill; white face, red eye-ring; long yellow tufts behind eyes; black crown and body; orange legs. Sexes similar. Winter: tufts reduced to short gray feathers, face dark, bill narrowed at base, orange only at tip. Subadults: mottled face, yellowish bill. Juveniles have dark bill, underparts dark gray to white. Voice: growling "errrr." **Range and habitat:** nests on islands in burrows atop cliffs or steep sea-facing slopes, north-eastern and east-central EP, north-western and west-central NA. Winters at sea. **Similar species:** Rhinoceros Auklet.

Rhinoceros Auklet

Cerorhinca monocerata (**Alcidae**) 38 cm/15 in.

Large alcid, sooty brown above, grayish brown throat, foreneck, breast and flanks, belly white. White plumes run from above eye past ear, 2nd line of white plumes form moustache. Reddish orange bill longer, narrower, shallower than other puffins. Pale knob projecting from base of bill absent in winter, as are facial plumes. Sexes similar. Immature like winter-plumage adult but darker, bill smaller and darker. Voice: low growl. **Range and habitat:** nests on sea-facing slopes in burrows, coming out only at night, north-eastern and east-central EP, north-western and west-central NA. Winters on inshore and offshore waters in breeding range south to south-western NA. **Similar species:** immature Tufted Puffin.

Thick-billed Murre

Uria lomvia (**Alcidae**) 43–48 cm/17–19 in.

Possibly the most abundant bird of the Northern Hemisphere. Slightly larger than the Common Murre, bill shorter, thicker with white line along base of upper mandible. Dark above, white underparts rise to acute angle on foreneck. In winter lower cheek and foreneck white, white line at base of upper mandible faint or lacking. Sexes similar. Uses wings under water in pursuit of fish prey. Voice: low, purring. **Range and habitat:** nests on sea cliffs, north-eastern EP to east-central EP, northern NA. Winters on open water near breeding range and somewhat further south. **Similar species:** Common Murre, Razorbill (see p 164).

Western Gull

California Gull

Pomarine Jaeger
(pale phase)

Forster's Tern
(first winter plumage)

Royal Tern
(with Sandwich Terns in background)

Black Skimmer

Pigeon Guillemot

Tufted Puffin

Rhinoceros Auklet

Thick-billed Murre

PIGEONS Columbiformes

Common Ground Dove
Columbina passerina (Columbidae) 16–18 cm/6½–7 in.
Size of sparrow. Male light gray-brown with black spots on upperwing-coverts. Primaries flash rufous in flight. Short rounded tail black and brown with narrow white corners; legs, bill pinkish orange. Female and young paler, grayer, less strongly spotted. When flushed, flies erratic course with rapid wing-beat, drops to ground or alights suddenly after short distance. Voice: soft, repeated "woo-oo." **Range and habitat:** frequents open dry areas, but occurs in broad range of habitat from forest edges to gardens, extreme southern NA and Bermuda south through Lesser Antilles to central NT. **Similar species:** Inca Dove (see p 112).

Band-tailed Pigeon
Columba fasciata (Columbidae) 35–38 cm/14–15 in.
Similar to Rock Dove but tail longer, black at base with broad pale terminal band; body gray to bluish-gray, iridescent nape and white crescent on back of neck; head, upper breast gray-brown in females, pink or purple in males; yellow bill, black tip; yellow feet, black nails. Immature: gray to yellow bill and feet; plumage gray; buff to brown edging on wing-coverts, primaries; lacks iridescence. Voice: deep, owl-like "whoo-whooooo." **Range and habitat:** north-western to south-western and south-central NA into north-western NT. **Similar species:** Red-billed Pigeon, also Mourning, Rock and White-winged Doves (see p 164).

Mourning Dove
Zenaida macroura (Columbidae) 28–33 cm/11–13 in.
Very common bird in North America. Gray-brown above with some dark spots, pinkish buff on head, foreneck and underparts; long diamond-shaped tail with white feather tips; slim neck, small head with blue eye-ring, dark spot below ear, purplish iridescence on sides of neck (barely noticeable in female); legs red. Wings whistle on take-off. Immature browner than adults, scaly upperparts. Mournful cooing, often begins before dawn. **Range and habitat:** towns, roadsides, farms, open woods, scrub from west-central, NA central and east-central NA south to north-western NT. **Similar species:** other doves.

CUCKOOS AND ALLIES Cuculiformes

Yellow-billed Cuckoo
Coccyzus americanus (Cuculidae) 28–33 cm/11–13 in.
Long tail, slender profile. Brown above with rufous primaries visible along edge of folded wing and outer half of wing in flight; cheek, throat, underparts white; upper mandible dark, lower mandible yellow; inconspicuous yellow eye-ring; tail feathers graduated, round, white terminal spots visible along underside of folded tail. Voice: rapid, guttural "ka-ka-ka-ka-ka-ka-ka-kow-kow-kowlp-kowlp-kowlp-kowlp," slowing at end. **Range and habitat:** woodlands, forest edges, thickets, orchards and farmlands central and southern NA, more common east of Rockies. Winters in north-eastern NT. **Similar species:** Black-billed and Mangrove Cuckoos.

Black-billed Cuckoo
Coccyzus erythropthalmus (Cuculidae) 30 cm/12 in.
Slender, with long tail. Gray-brown above, no rufous in wings; white cheeks, throat and underparts, black bill slightly decurved; red eye-ring surrounds dark eye; tail feathers graduated, narrow white tips visible along underside of folded tail. Feet gray; 2 toes forward, 2 backward. Eye-ring of immature yellowish. Raises own young. Voice: fast rhythmic "cucucu, cucucu, cucucu." **Range and habitat:** deciduous woodlands, forest edges, orchards and thickets central and east-central NA. Winters in north-western NT. **Similar species:** Mangrove and Yellow-billed Cuckoos.

Greater Roadrunner
Geococcyx californianus (Cuculidae) 51–61 cm/20–24 in.
Large ground-dwelling cuckoo; can run 24–32 kph (15–20 mph) to escape predation or pursue lizards, snakes, birds, invertebrates. Dark brown with narrow white streaks; belly, undertail-coverts cream; bushy crest; very long tail; bright blue and red patches behind eyes; large, long pointed bill; legs long, sturdy, blue-gray.

Sexes similar. Immature has lighter, wider streaks, lighter underparts. Voice: hoarse, throaty "coo, coo, coo, ooh, ooh, ooh." **Range and habitat:** deserts, chaparral, grasslands, open woodlands and agricultural areas of south-central and south-western NA. **Similar species:** Lesser Roadrunner.

Smooth-billed Ani
Crotophaga ani (Cuculidae) 35 cm/14 in.
Large black bill with raised curved culmen, long tail, distinctive. Black with bronze-brown edges to feathers of head, neck; iridescent green crescents in scapulars, lesser wing-coverts, feathers of upper back; purple gloss on flight feathers of wings, tail. Immature browner, especially on wings and tail. From 1 to 3 pairs build communal nest; females share incubation. Young fed by all parents. Whining whistle "quee-ick, quee-ick," also chuckling notes. **Range and habitat:** dense brush near fields or marshes from south-eastern NA to east-central NT. Resident. **Similar species:** Groove-billed Ani (see p 114).

OWLS Strigiformes

Short-eared Owl
Asio flammeus (Strigidae) 33–43 cm/13–17 in.
Active at twilight. Flies low, coursing back and forth on long wings with buoyant, mothlike flaps. Round head; small facial discs; neck, upper breast heavily streaked with brown; buff belly with narrow, vertical brown streaks. Brown above, mottled with buff. In flight shows buff patch on upper wing-surface, black wrist mark on wing-lining. Feeds on small mammals. Voice: rasping "wak, wak, wak," also "toot-toot-" repeated 15–20 times. **Range and habitat:** grasslands, marshes, dunes, moors, tundra of northern and central NA, WP and EP. Winters in central, southern NA, southern part of Eurasian range. **Similar species:** Barn Owl, Long-eared Owl (see p 166). The population is decreasing by around 5% per year.

Snowy Owl
Nyctea scandiaca (Strigidae) 51–68 cm/20–27 in.
Arctic predator. Adults white with yellow eyes, no ear-tufts; feet feathered to talons; feathers project onto bill. Most show dusky bars on white plumage, females more than males. Vagrants to south tend to be lightly to heavily barred. Feeds on mammals and birds up to size of Arctic Hare and Common Eider. Croaks, growls, whistles and hoots. **Range and habitat:** circumpolar Holarctic, throughout Arctic. Southward movement in winter erratic, depending on food supply. **Similar species:** white phase of Gyrfalcon, Arctic subspecies of Great Horned Owl. Cycles with lemmings.

Great Horned Owl
Bubo virginianus (Strigidae) 45–63 cm/18–25 in.
Very large, widely spaced prominent ear-tufts, large yellow eyes, white throat contrasts with dark brown mottled upperparts. White to buff underparts crossed by narrow dark brown bars; long, broad wings dark above, lined with buff. Color varies from nearly white in Arctic to very dark forms of Pacific northwest. Diet of skunks, opossums, ducks, hawks and Great Blue Herons. Nests early, often in old hawk nests. Voice: deep, low hoots "hoo-hoo-hoooo hoo-hoo." **Range and habitat:** resident in forests, open country and city parks throughout NA and NT. **Similar species:** Barred, Great Gray, Long-eared, Spotted and Snowy Owls (see p 166).

Great Gray Owl
Strix nebulosa (Strigidae) 60–84 cm/24–33 in.
Brownish gray, "earless," small yellow eyes set in prominent gray facial discs marked with concentric dark brown rings; body gray with heavy dark gray-brown streaks. White "bow-tie" on the upper breast readily visible. Long tail distinctive. Sexes similar. Low-pitched hoots, slowing toward end of series, infrequent, audible only at close range. **Range and habitat:** resident in northern coniferous forests of western and northern NA. Occasionally invades eastern Canada and northern United States in large numbers. **Similar species:** Barred, Great Horned and Spotted Owls (see p 72).

Common Ground Dove

Band-tailed Pigeon

Mourning Dove

Yellow-billed Cuckoo

Black-billed Cuckoo

Greater Roadrunner

Smooth-billed Ani

Short-eared Owl

Snowy Owl (female on nest)

Great Horned Owl

Great Gray Owl

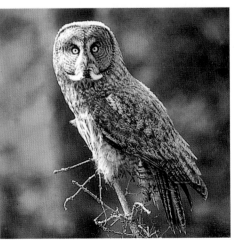

Barred Owl

Strix varia (Strigidae) 43–60 cm/17–24 in.
A large owl distinguished by its large round head, lack of ear-tufts and 9-note hoot "Who cooks for you, who cooks for you-all," pitch dropping on "all." Gray-brown plumage crossed by transverse bars on neck, upper breast; by vertical streaks on lower breast, belly. Brown eyes distinctive. Wings broad and short. Sexes similar. **Range and habitat:** wooded swamps and deep forest, where nests in tree-cavities and old hawk nests, in west-central, central, east-central and south-eastern NA, recently south into south-western mountains. **Similar species:** Great Gray and Spotted Owls (see p 70).

Northern Saw-whet Owl

Aegolius acadicus (Strigidae) 18–21 cm/7–8½ in.
Large round head. Large yellow eyes in facial discs that lack the black edge of most owls. Dark above flecked with white, buff below streaked with brown; short tail. Sexes similar. Juveniles chocolate brown above, cinnamon-buff belly, white triangle on forehead. Hard to find, but uses same roost for days. Voice: "too-too-too-too-too." Can be whistled into view by imitation of its song. **Range and habitat:** common resident of boreal forests of central NA and montane forests of mountains in central and south-western NA. Winters in and just south of breeding range. **Similar species:** Tengmalm's, Elf and Flammulated Owls, Ferruginous and Northern Pygmy-owls.

Burrowing Owl

Athene cunicularia (Strigidae) 20.5–3 cm/8–9 in.
Sandy-colored head, back, wings. White throat, upper breast, latter crossed by single dark line; barred lower breast, belly; no ear-tufts on broad head; long legs, unfeathered lower portion, short tail. Sexes similar. Occupies abandoned rodent burrows, which it modifies by digging with wings, beak, feet. When disturbed, bobs, bows, chatters. Active during day. Voice: high, mournful "coo-coo-coo," or "co-hoo." **Range and habitat:** deserts, open grasslands of west-central, central and south-western NA south into NT, resident in Florida. Winters from south-western NA south.

Eastern Screech-Owl

Otus asio (Strigidae) 18–25 cm/7–10 in.
Only small owl of eastern North America with ear-tufts. Red morph: cinnamon rufous above; rufous facial discs; white below streaked, barred with rufous. Gray morph: gray-brown above streaked with brown, white eyebrows, lores, underparts, heavily streaked with dark brown. Both morphs have yellow eyes surrounded by facial discs bordered by a broad black stripe that continues across throat. Sexes similar. Juveniles barred brown and white, red morph having rufous edges to bars. Voice: tremulous whinny on same pitch or descending. **Range and habitat:** woodlands and groves from central and south-eastern NA south. Nests in cavities. **Similar species:** Western Screech Owl.

NIGHTJARS AND ALLIES Caprimulgiformes

Common Nighthawk

Chordeiles minor (Caprimulgidae) 21–25 cm/8½–10 in.
Long pointed wings with conspicuous white patches just beyond bend of wing, identify this widespread species. Mottled upperparts, barred underparts; white throat patch; contrasting white subterminal tail band. Males gray and black, females brownish, with throat and wing patches buff-white and no white in tail. Juveniles may lack throat patch. Feed in evening and at night when nasal "peent" only evidence of their presence. During day perch lengthwise on tree limbs, fence-posts, roofs. **Range and habitat:** open country, open woods throughout NA, except northernmost areas. Winters in northern and central NT. **Similar species:** Antillean Nighthawk, Lesser Nighthawk and other nightjars (see pp 116, 166, 212, 254, 304).

Whip-poor-will

Caprimulgus vociferus (Caprimulgidae) 23–25 cm/9–10 in.
Known for its ringing "whip-poor-will," accented on the first and last syllables, repeated over and over. Widespread species of deciduous woodlands, feeds on flying insects, caught on wing at night, roosts on ground or lengthwise on limb by day. Mottled gray-brown plumage; black chin; narrow white throat patch; rounded wings; large white patches on corners of tail. **Range and habitat:** central and east-central NA, also south-western NA south. Winters in south-central NA into north-western NT. **Similar species:** Chuck-will's-widow, Buff-collared Nightjar, other nightjars (see pp 116, 166, 212, 254, 304).

Common Poorwill

Phalaenoptilus nuttallii (Caprimulgidae) 18–21 cm/7–8½ in.
Smallest North American nightjar. Brown upperparts mottled with silver-gray and black; underparts black and gray with faint bars; throat white, contrasting with black face, upper breast; wings rounded; short tail has white corners. Sexes similar. Juveniles: less distinct throat, tail patches and buff wash. Migratory status unknown, but can enter torpor to survive adverse weather. Voice: "pooooor-will," accent on 2 nd syllable. **Range and habitat:** upland arid areas of west-central and south-western NA south. Winters from south-western NA south, but wintering range poorly known. **Similar species:** Lesser Nighthawk, Whip-poor-will, other nightjars (see pp 116, 166, 212, 254, 304).

SWIFTS AND HUMMINGBIRDS Apodiformes

Chimney Swift

Chaetura pelagica (Apodidae) 14 cm/5½ in.
Small, brown, darkest above and on wings, lighter below, lightest on throat, upper breast. Wings long, narrow, mostly hand and primaries; tail short, stiff, slightly rounded when fanned, central shaft of each rectrix projects beyond webbing as a spine; small dark bill, but large mouth. Nest small, of sticks glued together with saliva, inside chimney or hollow tree. Rapid flight, bouts of shallow wingbeats interspersed with gliding, appears to beat wings alternately. Often flies in small, vociferous groups. Voice: rapid series of staccato chips. **Range and habitat:** open sky from central and south-central NA east. Winters in upper Amazon basin. **Similar species:** other swifts (see pp 116, 166, 216, 254, 304).

Vaux's Swift

Chaetura vauxi (Apodidae) 11 cm/4½ in.
Small, brown, dark above and on wings, lighter below, lightest on throat and upper breast, tail with spines. Sexes similar. Western equivalent of Chimney Swift, but smaller, much lighter below. Common over woods where it nests in hollow redwood stumps. Gradually adopting chimneys as forests are destroyed. Voice: similar to Chimney Swift, but somewhat higher-pitched, less vocal. **Range and habitat:** north-central NA. Winters from south-central NA to north-central NT. **Similar species:** other swifts (see pp 116, 166, 216, 254, 304).

White-throated Swift

Aeronautes saxatalis (Apodidae) 15–18 cm/6–7 in.
Large swift with bold black and white pattern. Throat, upper breast white, extending down midline to lower belly; white patches on flanks just behind wings; prominent broad white band across trailing edge of secondaries; rest of bird black; tail slightly forked and without projecting spines. Voice: drawn out, descending "skeeeeee." **Range and habitat:** rocky cliffs of western mountains and desert canyons from north-central to south-central NA and Central America. Winters from south-western into south-central NA. **Similar species:** other swifts, Violet-green Swallow (see pp 116, 166, 216, 254, 304).

Barred Owl

Northern Saw-whet Owl

Burrowing Owl

Eastern Screech Owl (red phase)

Common Nighthawk

Whip-poor-will

Common Poorwill

Chimney Swift

Vaux's Swift

White-throated Swift

Ruby-throated Hummingbird

Archilochus colubris (Trochilidae) 8–9 cm/3–3½ in.
Only hummingbird in eastern North America. Iridescent green above, white below. Male has ruby-red gorget, can appear black; olive-buff flanks; forked tail. Female white throat, sides, flanks; tail rounded with white feather tips. Bill long, dark. Male: looping, pendular courtship flight. Voice: high squeaks. **Range and habitat:** woodlands, parks, gardens from central and east-central NA south. Winters from southernmost NA to north-central NT. Similar species: Rufous Hummingbird.

Calliope Hummingbird

Stellula calliope (Trochilidae) 7 cm/2¾–3 in.
Short bill; short, broad, unforked tail. Male: gorget of elongated rose-purple rays on white background; olive-buff flanks. Female lacks gorget, throat covered with dusky spots. Buff wash on sides, breast; white corners on tail. Display flight, shallow U-shaped arc. Voice: brief "pfft" at bottom of display, high "tsip" when foraging. **Range and habitat:** meadows, thickets, brush in coniferous forests of west-central and south-western mountains of NA. Winters in Mexico. **Similar species:** female and juvenile Rufous and Allen's Hummingbirds.

Black-chinned Hummingbird

Archilochus alexandri (Trochilidae) 7–9 cm/3–3½ in.
In western NAreplaces Ruby-throated Hummingbird, which male resembles, but gorget black bordered below by iridescent purple-violet. Both sexes have white spot behind eye. Display flight: broad U-shaped arc. High-pitched warble; high, buzzy notes; wings make distinctive dry buzz. **Range and habitat:** semiarid country near water; west-central through south-western to south-central NA. Winters in south-western NA. **Similar species:** females like female Costa's or Ruby-throated Hummingbirds.

Broad-tailed Hummingbird

Selasphorus platycercus (Trochilidae) 9–10 cm/3½–4 in.
Male: only western hummingbird with green crown, rose gorget. Female: white throat spotted with brown, bright buff sides, outer rectrices rufous near base. Tail broad in both sexes. Deep U-shaped display flight. Voice: sharp "tew;" wings of male produce distinctive loud, rattling trill, except during molt. **Range and habitat:** meadows, patches of flowers within conifer and aspen forests of south-western and south-central NA. Winters from south-central NA into Central America. **Similar species;** female Calliope, Rufous and Allen's Hummingbirds, also Ruby-throated Hummingbird.

Anna's Hummingbird

Calypte anna (Trochilidae) 9–10 cm/3½–4 in.
Unique, rose red gorget elongated at sides, rose red crown. Females have red spots on throat, are green above and gray below; tail white at corners. Juveniles show white, unspotted throat. Long steep display dive ends with loud explosive popping in front of female. Voice: squeaky phrases; soft "chick" when foraging, rapid "chee-chee-chee." **Range and habitat:** gardens, canyons, foothills and riparian woodlands, west-central and south-western NA. **Similar species:** female resembles female Black-chinned and Costa's Hummingbirds.

Rufous Hummingbird

Selasphorus rufus (Trochilidae) 8–9 cm/3–3½ in.
Adult males orange-rufous above, iridescent orange-red gorget, white upper breast, orange-rufous wash on sides. Female green above, rufous sides, tail; white below, small red to golden green spots on throat. White tips on outer tail feathers. Young male some red on throat, green back. Vertical circular display with trilling buzz from male's wings. Soft "tchup;" excited, buzzy squeal "zeeee-chuppity-chup." **Range and habitat:** north-western and north-central NA. Winters in south-central NA. **Similar species:** Allen's Hummingbird, female Calliope and Broad-tailed Hummingbirds.

KINGFISHERS AND ALLIES Coraciiformes

Belted Kingfisher

Ceryle alcyon (Alcedinidae) 30–35 cm/12–14 in.
Long, stout bill; large head; bushy crest. Male blue-gray above; white

---

throat, collar; underparts with blue-gray breast band. Female similar, with rufous on flanks and chest below blue-gray band. In flight white patch visible on upper surface of dark primaries. Fishes by diving from a branch or from hovering flight. Distinctive rattle, often given in flight. **Range and habitat:** deep, irregular streams, lakes, sea coasts of NA. Nests in burrow. Winters along coasts, Mississippi valley, southern NA, West Indies and Bermuda. **Similar species:** other kingfishers (see pp 120, 208, 256, 304).

WOODPECKERS AND ALLIES Piciformes

Northern Flicker

Colaptes auratus (Picidae) 28–35 cm/11–14 in.
Barred black and brown above, white rump, buff-white below with black spots and black pectoral band. Eastern subspecies: crown gray, red nape; face, foreneck buff, black moustaches (male); wings and tail yellow below. Western: crown and nape brown, face gray, red moustaches (male); wings and tail salmon below. Forages on ground, especially for ants. Voice: loud "wicka, wicka, wicka, wicka," also sharp "klee-yer." **Range and habitat:** throughout NA south of arctic, also Cuba. Winters throughout central and southern NA. **Similar species:** Gila Woodpecker, Gilded Flicker

Downy Woodpecker

Picoides pubescens (Picidae) 15–16 cm/6–6½ in.
Black and white barred wings; white back; black crown, eye stripe and moustache; white eyebrow and lower face to nape; white below; black tail, white outer tail feathers with 2 or more black bars. Male has red nape. Short bill. Forages on branches and smaller trees. Voice: weak "pik;" rapid rattle. **Range and habitat:** forests, woodlots, shade trees throughout NA, except extreme south-western and south-central NA. Leaves northernmost parts of range in winter. **Similar species:** other spotted woodpeckers (see pp 74, 168, 258).

Yellow-bellied Sapsucker

Sphyrapicus varius (Picidae) 18–20 cm/7–8 in.
Black and white barred above with white rump and distinctive white patches in wings; upper breast and belly yellowish; red crown; throat red in males, white in females. Immature, distinctive white rump and wing patches. Drills pits in trees, returns to collect sap and insects. Voice: nasal mewing note, downward "cherrrr." Drumming syncopated. **Range and habitat:** aspen woodlands, western, central and east-central NA. Winters in south-eastern, south-central NA south in eastern Central America. **Similar species:** immature Red-breasted and Williamson's Sapsuckers, other black and white woodpeckers (see pp 74, 168, 258).

Pileated Woodpecker

Dryocopus pileatus (Picidae) 42–48 cm/17–19 in.
Large, black, with scarlet crest, white face. Black eye stripe extends to nape; black moustache turns down and connects to breast. Male has red on forehead and at base of moustache. Female: dark forehead. White wing-linings conspicuous in undulating flight. Immature grayish, streaked throat, orange crest, sexual distinctions as in adults. Voice: hollow, slow "wuk, wuk, wuk." **Range and habitat:** resident in mixed conifer-hardwood forests from north-western to west-central, central and eastern NA. **Similar species:** Ivory-billed Woodpecker.

Ivory-billed Woodpecker

Campephilus principalis (Picidae) 48–53 cm/19–21 in.
Very large, glossy almost blue-black plumage, broad, chisel-shaped ivory-white bill. White stripe extends from below eye down neck onto back; white inner flight feathers create white shield on back . Male has sides and back of crest scarlet. Female has dark crest, often upturned. Voice: single or double "toot", loud, deliberate double knock on tree with bill. **Range and habitat:** bottomland swamp forests of south-eastern United States and upland pine forests of Cuba.NA. **Similar species:** Pileated Woodpecker. Thought extinct, but recently sighted in south-eastern Missouri.

Ruby-throated Hummingbird

Calliope Hummingbird

Black-chinned Hummingbird

Broad-tailed Hummingbird

Anna's Hummingbird

Rufous Hummingbir

Belted Kingfisher (female)

Nortern Flicker

Downy Woodpeck

Yellow-bellied Sapsucker

Pileated Woodpeck (female)

Ivory-billed Woodpecker (model)

PERCHING BIRDS Passeriformes

Horned Lark
Eremophila alpestris (Alaudidae) 16–17 cm/6–6½ in.
Rather uniformly colored lark. In breeding plumage, face pale yellow with black forehead and two upswept "horns," black moustache and breast band. Rest of head and back rusty-brown, lightly streaked black. Underparts whitish, tinged rusty-brown on sides of breast. Tail brown in center, black sides, white edges. Head pattern mostly lost in winter. Gregarious in winter, running and walking on ground. Short warbling song mainly from ground, also "tseep" call. **Range and habitat:** breeds circumpolar Holarctic tundra, open habitats in NA, WP and EP. Northern populations migrate to central, southern NA for the winter. **Similar species:** other larks (see p 168).

Eastern Kingbird
Tyrannus tyrannus (Tyrannidae) 21–23 cm/8½–9 in.
Head black, dorsum dark bluish-black; 2 indistinct whitish wing-bars; white below, gray wash on flanks and upper breast; tail dark, terminal white band; narrow red crown patch (seldom visible); bill broad, black. Sexes similar. Lives in open habitats with emergent perches from which it sallies after insects. Flies with shallow wingbeats. Nest in top of tree. Parents very aggressive. Voice: "dzee-dzee-dzee" and "dzeet," given frequently. **Range and habitat:** wood edges, fencerows, roadsides throughout most of NA except far north and desert south-west. Winters in NT. **Similar species:** Gray Kingbird.

Western Kingbird
Tyrannus verticalis (Tyrannidae) 20–24 cm/8–9½ in.
Elongate profile, heavy black bill. Head, nape ash-gray; throat, breast pale gray; lores, ear-coverts darker creating narrow mask; back and wings gray-green, yellow below, tail black with white outer webs in outermost feathers; orange-red crown patch, usually concealed. Sexes similar. Voice: sharp "whit" or "whit-ker-whit." Flight song "pkit-pkit-deedle-ot," with emphasis on high "deedle." **Range and habitat:** open country with scattered trees, often on wire fences or telephone lines from central and west-central NA southward. Winters extreme south-central NA into Central America. **Similar species:** Cassin's, Couch's and Tropical Kingbirds (see p 130).

Great Crested Flycatcher
Myiarchus crinitus (Tyrannidae) 18–20 cm/7–8 in.
Common in eastern deciduous forests, more often heard than seen. Olive-brown above; gray throat and breast, bright yellow belly; wings dark brown; 2 white wing-bars, cinnamon rufous in primaries; tail brown, cinnamon rufous on inner web of tail feathers, visible when spread in flight. Sexes similar. When searching for insect prey or encountering other birds erects head feathers, leans forward with outstretched neck and bobs head slowly. Voice: loud, harsh, ascending "wheeep." **Range and habitat:** eastern and south-eastern NA west to prairies. Winters from extreme south-eastern NA to north-western NT. **Similar species:** Ash-throated, Brown-crested and Olivaceous Flycatchers.

Eastern Phoebe
Sayornis phoebe (Tyrannidae) 16–18 cm/6½–7 in.
1st flycatcher to return to streams, bridges and farms that are its summer home. Upright posture. Wags tail. Grayish black above; head, wings and tail slightly darker than back; whitish below, washed in pale yellow; bill black; no eye-ring, no wing-bars. Sexes similar. Immature: rufous wing-bars, yellow wash below. Voice: hoarse, clear "fee-bee, fee-bee" with 2nd syllable alternately rising and falling, also soft chip" note. **Range and habitat:** eastern, central and north-western NA. Winters in south-eastern and south-central NA. **Similar species:** *Empidonax* flycatchers, wood-pewees.

Willow Flycatcher
Empidonax traillii (Tyrannidae) 13–16 cm/5–6½ in.
Olive-brown above with brown wings and 2 prominent wing-bars; white below with olive wash on flanks; tail dark. Eye-ring narrow in eastern birds, usually lacking in western birds. Voice: an explosive "fitz-bew" or "fritz-be-yew," vaguely 3-syllabled, but emphasis always on 1st syllable, 2nd syllable lower. May be shortened to dry, burry "rrrrrip." also a thick "whit." **Range and habitat:** brushy fields, willow thickets, prairie woodlots, woodland edges across central, and into south-western NA. Uses drier, smaller, more open areas than Alder Flycatcher. Winters south to central NT. **Similar species:** other *Empidonax* flycatchers, wood-pewees. South-western subspecies endangered.

Alder Flycatcher
Empidonax alnorum (Tyrannidae) 16 cm/6½ in.
Olive-green above, greener than Willow Flycatcher, 2 wing-bars on brown wing; olive wash on flanks, white throat and underparts, brown tail; eye-ring indistinct; bill long, broad, dark above, orange-yellow below. Sexes similar. Voice: burry, 2-syllable "rrree-beea," 2nd syllable higher, stressed; ending faint, often inaudible. Occasionally shortened to ascending "rrrreeee," also flat "peep." **Range and habitat:** alder swamps, aspen thickets from northern and east-central NA. Wetter habitat than Willow Flycatcher. Winters in NT. **Similar species:** other *Empidonax* flycatchers, wood-pewees. **Not illustrated**.

Least Flycatcher
Empidonax minimus (Tyrannidae) 12–14 cm/5–6 in.
Grayest of the eastern *Empidonax*: Whitish underparts, occasionally a yellow wash on flanks, lower belly; 2 light wing-bars, prominent eye-ring. Sexes similar. 1st Empidonax to come north in spring and last to migrate south. Voice: sharp, often repeated "ch-bek," 2nd syllable stressed. Call a flat "wit." Sings during spring migration. **Range and habitat:** open woods, aspen groves, orchards, shade trees across northern and central NA, in mountains to south-eastern NA. Winters from south-central NA to north-central NT. **Similar species:** other *Empidonax* flycatchers, wood-pewees.

Scissor-tailed Flycatcher
Tyrannus forficatus (Tyrannidae) 30–38 cm/12–15 in.
Pearl-gray flycatcher; very long pairs of outer tail feathers, strikingly patterned in white and black; central tail feathers shorter and black; wings and uppertail-coverts black; flanks, belly, under-tail-coverts washed in salmon pink, wing-linings bright salmon pink. Female has shorter tail, is less colorful. Immature: short tail, brownish back. Voice: "keck," also "ka-leep," harsh kingbirdlike sounds. **Range and habitat:** semiopen country of south-central NA. Often perched on wire fences or dead exposed branches. Winters from south-central, south-eastern NA to north-central NT. **Similar species:** Fork-tailed Flycatcher, immature similar to Western Kingbird (see p 130).

Olive-sided Flycatcher
Contopus cooperi (Tyrannidae) 18–20 cm/7–8 in.
Perches on high, conspicuous dead branches where its olive flanks with white ventral stripe give it a distinctive vested appearance. White, cottony tufts behind wing diagnostic. General color is dark grayish-olive with no eye-ring, no wing-bars. Larger, stouter than pewee, larger head. Voice: vigorous, whistled "quick three beers," 1st note abrupt, inaudible at a distance. Call, low "pip, pip, pip." **Range and habitat:** conifers of northern and western NA. Winters in NT. **Similar species:** Smoke-colored Pewee, wood-pewees. The population is decreasing by around 4% per year, and the species is considered near threatened.

Western Wood-Pewee
Contopus sordidulus (Tyrannidae) 12–15 cm/5–6 in.
Replaces Eastern Wood-Pewee in west. Grayish olive above and on flanks, 2 prominent white wing-bars (buff in 1st-winter birds); lacks eye-ring; underparts whitish, tail dark; upper mandible dark, lower paler. Sexes similar. Voice: emphatic "pheer-reet" alternating with less harsh, somewhat rolling "phee-rr-reet." Call burry, slightly descending "pheeer" or more emphatic "pheer-reet," repeated every 5–10 sec. **Range and habitat:** open deciduous or mixed forest from north-western into south-central NA. Winters in northern and central NT. **Similar species:** Eastern Wood-Pewee (distinguishable only by voice), Smoke-colored Pewee, Olive-sided Flycatcher.

Horned Lark

Eastern Kingbird

Western Kingbird

Great Crested Flycatcher

Eastern Phoebe

Willow Flycatcher

Least Flycatcher

Scissor-tailed Flycatcher

Olive-sided Flycatcher

Western Wood-Pewee

Purple Martin

Progne subis (Hirundinidae) 18–22 cm/7–8½ in.
Largest North American swallow. Proportionately shorter, broader wings than other swallows. Male uniformly blue-black. Female and immatures gray below, lighter belly. Female with grayish forehead and collar, blue-black crown and back, black wings and tail. Tail in both sexes long, broad, forked. Glides in circles, alternating quick flaps and glides. Voice: complex, low gurgling. Call "swee-swuh," 2nd note lower, in flight a rich, descending "tyu." **Range and habitat:** open or semiopen country, often near water, central and southern NA except in western mountains. Winters in NT. **Similar species:** flight resembles European Starling (see p 182).

Northern Rough-winged Swallow

Stelgidopteryx serripennis (Hirundinidae) 12–14 cm/5–6 in.
Widespread, common, but small, solitary and inconspicuous. Brown above with dusky throat, white breast and belly; medium tail, slightly notched. Deep wingbeats with wing tips pulled back at end of each stroke, little gliding. Sexes similar. Voice: rough, rasping "brrrt." **Range and habitat:** near running water where it nests in drainpipes, cracks in bridges, old burrows, central and southern NA. Winters from south-central NA to northern NT. **Similar species:** immature Tree Swallow, Southern Rough-winged Swallow.

American Cliff Swallow

Hirundo pyrrhonota (Hirundinidae) 12–15 cm/5–6 in.
Chunky swallow, square tail. Cream forehead, blue-black crown and back, narrow white stripes on back, rust-colored rump; throat chestnut shading to black at breast, below dull white to grayish along sides and at collar. Sexes similar. Juvenile: darker forehead, white feathers mixed into throat. May soar on flattened wings. Voice: low "chur," harsh "keer," and series of grating, squeaking notes in flight. **Range and habitat:** NA except southeast and extreme north. Winters in NT. Nest juglike, on wall or cliff under overhang. **Similar species:** Cave Swallow.

Tree Swallow

Tachycineta bicolor (Hirundinidae) 12–15 cm/5–6 in.
Male metallic blue-green above, white below. First-year female brown, some metallic green above, white below. Second-year female metallic green above, some brown. Juvenile gray-brown above, white below. Only NA songbird with delayed plumage maturity in female. Females breed in 1st year. First swallow to return in spring, last to leave in autumn. **Range and habitat:** forage and nest near water from treeline to central NA. Winters in southern NA. **Similar species:** Violet-green Swallow; Northern Rough-winged Swallow resembles immature Tree Swallow (see p 168).

Loggerhead Shrike

Lanius ludovicianus (Laniidae) 20–25 cm/8–10 in.
Predatory songbird. Large head; black, almost conical, hooked beak; gray above; wings, tail black; white at wrists, corners of tail; grayish white below; black mask extends over bill. Sexes similar. Juvenile grayish, finely barred below. Often drops low after take-off, flies low to ground, swoops up to next perch. Caches prey, often by impaling it. Voice: harsh, deliberate, repetitive notes, also single "shack." **Range and habitat:** semiopen country, central and southern NA. Winters in southern NA. **Similar species:** Northern Mockingbird, Northern Shrike (see p 170). The population is decreasing by around 4% per year.

Cedar Waxwing

Bombycilla cedrorum (Bombycillidae) 16–20 cm/6½–8 in.
Appears sculpted. Crested, cinnamon to gray-brown, black face edged in white; chin glossy black (male), dull black (female); conical black bill. Yellowish flanks and belly; undertail-coverts white; tail gray, yellow terminal band; secondaries tipped with scarlet. Juvenile grayer than adult, diffusely streaked, especially below; black mask and throat incomplete or lacking. Feeds on berries, but will flycatch. Gregarious. Voice: lisping "hiss, sse, ssee." **Range and habitat:** open woodlands, orchards across central NA. Winters in central and southern NA to NT and West Indies. **Similar species:** (Bohemian) Waxwing (see p 170).

North American Dipper

Cinclus mexicanus (Cinclidae) 18–21 cm/7–8½ in.
Stout, wrenlike bird, thrush-size, short tail. Slate-gray with brownish wash on head; thin white crescents above and below eye; black bill. Sexes similar. Winter adults, juveniles have pale-tipped feathers on wings, underparts. Juvenile tinged rust, pale grayish throat, mottled below, bill yellow. Voice: rich, musical runs and trills, much repetition of phrases, also loud "bzeet." **Range and habitat:** resident western NA to north-western NT. Inhabits cold, rushing streams. Forages along edges and under water on bottom of stream for insect larvae, small fish. When flushed flies low along stream.

Sedge Wren

Cistothorus platensis (Troglodytidae) 10–11 cm/4–4½ in.
Dark brown crown faintly streaked with tan. Lacks white eye stripe of Marsh Wren and white dorsal stripes less prominent. Flanks orange-buff fading to buff on undertail-coverts, white below. Sexes similar. Voice: 2–3 deliberate notes followed by staccato chatter that descends at the end. Call, sharp "slap." **Range and habitat:** low shrubs of wet meadows, marsh edges; central NA. Winters in south-eastern, south-central NA. **Similar species:** Marsh Wren.

House Wren

Troglodytes aedon (Troglodytidae) 11–14 cm/4½–5½ in.
Small, aggressive, energetic wren, gray-brown above with dusky bars on wings and tail; underparts grayish white, lightest on throat, faint bars on flanks; tail cocked over back. Sexes similar. Male usually builds several nests from which female chooses one, lines it and lays eggs. Voice: musical gurgling; pitch rises, then falls in bubbling glis-sando. Scolding note a rapid grating sound. When singing, male perches with tail straight down. **Range and habitat:** common in bird houses, thickets, woodland openings and gardens throughout central NA. Winters in southern NA, throughout NT. **Similar species:** Winter Wren (see p 178).

Carolina Wren

Thryothorus ludovicianus (Troglodytidae) 14–15 cm/5½–6 in.
Large wren with rufous crown and back, dark barring in wings, tail. White throat, buff-rust underparts; prominent white eyebrow; tail long, often cocked or switched back and forth; bill dark, long, slightly decurved. Sexes similar. Seldom still. Voice: loud, clear, "tea-kettle, tea-kettle, tea-kettle, tea;" also loud descending trill, "tiirrrr;" scolding and twitters. Vocal in all kinds of weather throughout the year. **Range and habitat:** resident in yards and undergrowth near water of east-central and south-eastern NA. **Similar species:** Bewick's and Marsh Wrens.

Cactus Wren

Campylorhynchus brunneicapillus (Troglodytidae) 18–22 cm/7–8½ in.
Largest North American wren, similar to small thrasher in size, shape. Rust-brown crown, broad white stripe over each eye; body brown, darker above, barred and spotted with black and white. Sexes similar. Feeds on ground, flies slowly with rapid wing-beats. Sings from top of cactus. Tail rarely cocked. Voice: throaty "choo-choo-choo-choo" or "chug-chug-chug-chug," much like a stalled car. **Range and habitat:** resident in south-western deserts, especially those with large cholla cactus, mesquite, palo verde, also desert residential areas. **Similar species:** desert thrashers (see p 80).

Purple Martin

Northern Rough-winged Swallow

American Cliff Swallow

Tree Swallow
(at nest hole)

Loggerhead Shrike

Cedar Waxwing

North American Dipper

Sedge Wren

House Wren

Carolina Wren

Cactus Wren

Gray Catbird

Dumetella carolinensis (**Mimidae**) 23 cm/9 in.
Slim, long-tailed profile characteristic of mimic thrushes; slate-gray above and below, black crown, chestnut undertail-coverts. Tends to hold tail above horizontal. Sexes similar. Juvenile brownish gray, rufous undertail-coverts pale. Voice: disjointed phrases, without repetitions characteristic of thrashers and Northern Mockingbird. Catlike mew, may flick tail and lean forward when calling, also grating "tchek-tchek." **Range and habitat:** undergrowth, brush, gardens; always near dense cover, central into south-eastern NA. Winters in south-eastern and south-central NA into Central America. **Similar species:** female Brewer's and Rusty Blackbirds (see p 91).

Northern Mockingbird

Mimus polyglottos (**Mimidae**) 28 cm/11 in.
Gray above, paler below; 2 white wing-bars contrast with black flight feathers, also large white patch across base of primaries visible in flight. Wingbeats slow, buoyant. Tail long, black, white outer feathers. Sexes similar. Juvenile: faint spotting on breast. Voice: varied medley of notes and phrases, many of imitations of birds and local noises, each repeated 3 or more times. Sings from exposed perch, often at night. Call a loud "tchak." **Range and habitat:** thickets, woodland edges, towns, roadsides, gardens of central and southern NA. Northernmost birds may withdraw south in winter. **Similar species:** Townsend's Solitaire, shrikes (see p 170).

Sage Thrasher

Oreoscoptes montanus (**Mimidae**) 20–23 cm/8–9 in.
Smallest thrasher. Short, straight, slender bill. Gray-brown above, darker on wings and tail; 2 white wing-bars; white corners in tail. Eye yellow, pale eyebrow above, moustache below; cream below blends to buff on lower belly, undertail-coverts; small wedges of brown on throat and breast grow to streaks on flanks. Sexes similar. Immatures browner, with more diffuse streaking and dark eye. Voice: medley of sweet, warbling notes, also a throaty "chuck." Sings from top of sagebrush and in flight. **Range and habitat:** open sage and scrub country of western NA. Winters in deserts of south-western NA. **Similar species:** Bendire's and Curve-billed Thrashers.

Curve-billed Thrasher

Toxostoma curvirostre (**Mimidae**) 24–29 cm/9½–11½ in.
Pale gray-brown above, gray-buff below with dark gray spots arranged in longitudinal streaks. White corners on long tail. White wing-bars may be lacking in some individuals, particularly those of southern and western Arizona. Long, decurved bill. Bright orange-red eye. Runs, hops on ground; digs with bill; low, swift flight between bushes. Voice: loud, caroling from top of cholla cactus; low trills; wrenlike chattering; call loud, liquid "whit-wheet." **Range and habitat:** common resident in sparse brush, cacti of arid south-western and south-central NA. **Similar species:** Bendire's and Crissal thrashers.

Brown Thrasher

Toxostoma rufum (**Mimidae**) 29 cm/11.5 in.
Rufous above, 2 cream wing-bars. Face gray-brown; underparts white, washed with buff, heavily streaked with dark brown; eye yellow to orange; bill dark, with pale base on lower mandible and slightly decurved. Forages for insects in leaf litter by tossing leaves over its back with bill. Voice: musical couplets, rich and melodious. Usually sings from prominent, exposed perch. Call a harsh "chack," also a 3-note whistle. **Range and habitat:** dry thickets, brushy pastures, second-growth woods, sometimes garden shrubbery; central and east-central NA south. Winters in south-eastern NA. **Similar species:** brown-backed thrushes, Long-billed Thrasher.

Hermit Thrush

Catharus guttatus (**Turdidae**) 19 cm/7½ in.
Olive-brown above with rufous tail; face gray-brown, thin whitish eye-ring; whitish buff below, large dark brown spots on breast form narrow streaks on sides of throat and flanks; belly white. Sexes similar. Juveniles buff below. When perched often jerks tail up, slowly drops it. Often flicks wings. Voice: clear, flutelike, echoing; 3 or 4 phrases at different pitches, separated by pauses. Calls "tuk, tuk, tuk," soft "chuck," harsh "pay." **Range and habitat:** coniferous and mixed forests of northern NA south in western and eastern mountains. Winters in west-central and southern NA. **Similar species:** Fox Sparrow, other thrushes, Veery (see pp 88, 134, 176).

Eastern Bluebird

Sialia sialis (**Turdidae**) 15–16 cm/6–6½ in.
Bright blue crown, face, back, wings and tail; white chin; chestnut throat, breast, flanks; white belly and undertail-coverts. Female has brownish back, blue wings and tail; indistinct buff eye-ring; pale rust throat, breast, flanks; white belly and undertail-coverts. Juveniles heavily speckled gray, blue in wings and tail. Perches in hunched, vertical posture on exposed posts, branches. Makes short foraging flights to ground and back to perch. Voice: rich 3-or 4-note warble. Call a musical "tru-ly." **Range and habitat:** open woodlands from central and east-central NA south, also south-eastern Arizona. Winters in southern part of breeding range into Central America. **Similar species:** Mountain and Western Bluebirds.

Wood Thrush

Hylocichla mustelina (**Turdidae**) 19–21 cm/7½–8½ in.
Cinnamon rufous crown, fading to olive-brown on uppertail-coverts, tail; narrow white eye-ring; ear-coverts finely-streaked with white and brown; white underparts with extensive dark brown round spots on throat, breast, flanks, belly. Sexes similar. Juveniles similar, but tawny olive or buff spots on head and upperparts; on wing-coverts may form indistinct wing-bars. Voice: rising, flutelike "eee-lee-o-lay." Calls, occasional guttural notes, liquid "pip, pip, pip, pip," low "quirt." **Range and habitat:** deciduous woods, central and east-central NA south. Winters from south-central NA to northwest NT. **Similar species:** other thrushes, Veery (see p 134).

Swainson's Thrush

Catharus ustulatus (**Turdidae**) 16–19 cm/6½–7½ in.
Olive-brown (east) to russet (west) above; face, throat and breast buff, appears spectacled; breast densely patterned with black round spots, becoming wedge-shaped on sides of throat; belly white, flanks washed olive-gray. Sexes similar. Juveniles darker above, buff spots on back. Voice: rising, breezy series of flutelike phrases. Call a liquid "whoit." Night migrants give sharp "queep." **Range and habitat:** spruce forests of northern NA, south in western and eastern mountains. Winters from south-central NA to southern NT. **Similar species:** other thrushes, Veery (see pp 134, 176).

Varied Thrush

Ixoreus naevius (**Turdidae**) 25 cm/10 in.
Black crown, orange eyebrow above a black mask; dorsum black with 2 conspicuous orange wing-bars and orange and black flight feathers; brick-red below; black breast band. Female duller, gray breast band incomplete or lacking. Immature: indistinct breast band mottled with orange, eyebrow and wing-bars rusty, underparts have dusky spots. Voice: prolonged, melancholy, quavering whistle, a pause, and another note on a lower or higher pitch fading away at the end. Call, "chuk." **Range and habitat:** thick, wet coniferous forest of north-western and west-central NA. Winters from west-central to south-western NA. **Similar species:** American Robin.

American Robin

Turdus migratorius (**Turdidae**) 23–28 cm/9–11 in.
Gray back, rusty red breast, white chin streaked with black, white lower belly and undertail-coverts. Male, black head, white crescents above and below dark eye, black tail with white corners in eastern subspecies. Female paler. Juvenile, pale rust breast with large black spots, white throat, gray back with faint white stripes, pale wing-bars. Voice: loud, short, caroling phrases alternately rising and falling. More than 10 distinctly different calls, "tut, tut, tut" most common. **Range and habitat:** woodland openings, has adapted well to suburban lawns throughout NA, local in south. Winters in central and southern NA. **Similar species:** Eyebrowed, Rufous-backed and Varied Thrushes.

Gray Catbird

Northern Mockingbird

Sage Thrasher

Curve-billed Thrash

Brown Thrasher

Hermit Thrush

Eastern Bluebird

Wood Thrush

Swainson's Thrush

Varied Thrush

American Robin

Blue-gray Gnatcatcher

Polioptila caerulea (Polioptilidae) 11–12 cm/4½–5 in.
Tiny, slender bird; thin black bill; bluish gray above, dark wings edged in white; paler below; long black tail, underside and outermost feathers white, often cocked and flicked. Narrow white eye-ring in both sexes. Male, black forehead and eyebrow. Voice: thin, banjolike twang "zpee;" song insectlike notes followed by warbled ditty. **Range and habitat:** treetops of moist forests, oak woods, chaparral, open pinyon and juniper woods of central and southern NA. Winters from southern NA south. **Similar species:** Black-tailed and Black-capped Gnatcatchers.

Golden-crowned Kinglet

Regulus satrapa (Sylviidae) 9–10 cm/3½–4 in.
Tiny. Crown orange (males), yellow (females); in both sexes bordered with black, white eyebrow. Body olive-gray, lighter below, brown wings, 2 white wing-bars; short tail. Forages quickly, may hover briefly. Nervous wing-flicking characteristic. Juveniles: dark crown. Voice: high-pitched "tsee-tsee-tsee." Song, series of high notes rising in pitch then descending into chatter. **Range and habitat:** breeds in cool coniferous forests of eastern, central and western NA. Winters in forests of central and southern NA. **Similar species:** Ruby-crowned Kinglet, Firecrest.

Ruby-crowned Kinglet

Regulus calendula (Sylviidae) 11 cm/4½ in.
Olive-green, darker above, prominent white eye-ring, 2 white wing-bars (buffy in juvenile), lower wing-bar bordered with black. Short tail. Scarlet crown patch (male), usually hidden. Forages rapidly, often hovers. Frequently flicks wings. Voice: musical; 3 or 4 high notes, several low notes, then a rollicking chant, "tee, tee, tee, tew, tew, tew, tew, ti-dadee, ti-dadee, ti-dadee;" wrenlike "cack," husky "zhi-dit." **Range and habitat:** coniferous forests of western and northern NA. Winters along east- and west-central coasts and throughout southern NA to Central America. **Similar species:** Golden-crowned Kinglet, Goldcrest.

Tufted Titmouse

Baeolophus bicolor (Paridae) 11–14 cm/4 i–5½ in.
Small; gray crest, black forehead; mouse-gray above, pale gray to white below; peach-colored sides; large dark eye, conical black bill. Sexes similar. Juveniles lack peach color. Forages actively and acrobatically, often in mixed flocks. Visits feeders. Voice: clear, whistled "peter, peter, peter. . .," repeated 6–10 times. Calls nasal, wheezy, complaining. **Range and habitat:** resident in coniferous and deciduous forests of east-central, south-central and south-eastern NA. Nests in cavities, including bird houses. **Similar species:** Juniper, Oak and Black-crested Titmice.

Black-capped Chickadee

Poecile atricapillus (Paridae) 14 cm/6 in.
Black cap, black bib with ragged lower edge, white cheeks. Gray above, white below, buff flanks; wing-coverts edged white. Often forages in mixed flocks. Visits feeders. Voice: pure, whistled "fe-bee," 2nd note lower. Call "chick-adee-dee-dee," other gargles and hisses. **Range and habitat:** mixed and deciduous woods, willow thickets, shade trees. Nests in cavities including bird houses. Resident of northern and central NA. **Similar species:** Boreal, Carolina and Mountain Chickadees, Marsh and Willow tits (see p 178).

Mountain Chickadee

Poecile gambeli (Paridae) 15 cm/6 in.
Black cap, throat. White forehead, eyebrow, cheeks. Gray above, white below. Birds of Rockies browner back, cinnamon sides; those of Great Basin more buff, further west grayer. Cavity nester, will use nestbox. Visits feeders. Voice: sweet, whistled song "fee-bee-bay" like "Three blind mice." Call "chick-a-dee-a-dee-a-dee." **Range and habitat:** open coniferous forests of west-central and south-western mountains. Winters in oaks, cottonwoods, willows where it forages with migrating wood-warblers and vireos. **Similar species:** Black-capped and Carolina Chickadees.

Verdin

Auriparus flaviceps (Remizidae) 10–11 cm/4–4½ in.
Very small; gray, paler below; bright yellow head in male, dull yellow in female, rufous at bend of wing (brighter in male than female); sharply pointed black bill. Immature brownish gray, paler below, lacks

yellow head, rufous wing patch. Forages among terminal twigs, underside of leaves, flits about. Voice: loud "tsee, seesee," call emphatic "see-lip." **Range and habitat:** resident in south-western deserts with mesquite, palo verde and thorny scrub, also riparian woodlands. **Similar species:** Common Bushtit, penduline tits (see pp 176, 272). The population is decreasing by around 5% per year. **Not illustrated.**

White-breasted Nuthatch

Sitta carolinensis (Sittidae) 15 cm/6 in.
Crown and nape glossy black (male) contrasting with bluish gray back; female dull black with dull gray back. Tail stubby with white corners visible in flight and display. Face and underparts white. Undertail-coverts rusty. Forages on tree-trunks, often creeping head downward. Visits feeders. Voice: series, nasal notes "to-what, what, what,.. .;" also "yank, yank," soft "kit, kit" while foraging. **Range and habitat:** resident in forests, woodlots, shade trees in central and southern NA. **Similar species:** other nuthatches, Black-capped, Carolina and Mountain Chickadees (see pp 176, 272).

Red-breasted Nuthatch

Sitta canadensis (Sittidae) 11–12 cm/4½–5 in.
Small. Crown, nape glossy black (male), lead-colored or dull black (female). Prominent white eyebrow, black eye stripe; upperparts blue-gray; throat, lower face white, underparts rusty (paler in females), white on undertail-coverts. Stubby tail, large head, jerky flight between trees; may visit feeders. Voice: slow, nasal "enk, enk, enk." **Range and habitat:** resident in coniferous forests of central, south-western, north-eastern NA. Irregular irruptions south of breeding range. Nests in cavities of dead conifers, smears hole with pitch. **Similar species:** other nuthatches (see pp 176, 272).

Blue-headed Vireo

Vireo solitarius (Vireonidae) 12–15 cm/5–6 in.
Gray head, olive-green back. White eye stripe and eye-ring; 2 white wing-bars. White below, yellow and olive-gray wash on flanks. Sexes similar. Voice: like Red-eyed Vireo, but more deliberate; 2- to 6-note phrases higher, sweeter; may burst into warble of 15–20 notes; also nasal "see-a" or "see-weep." **Range and habitat:** mixed northern hardwoods of central NA, south in eastern mountains. Winters in south-eastern and south-central NA and Central America. **Similar species:** Black-capped, Gray, Plumbeous, Cassin's and White-eyed Vireos.

Red-eyed Vireo

Vireo olivaceus (Vireonidae) 14–16 cm/5½–6½ in.
Gray crown bordered with black, olive above; red eye, white eyebrow, black eye stripe; white below with yellowish olive wash on flanks. Sexes similar. Immatures have brown eyes. Central American subspecies yellower. Voice: short, robinlike phrases separated by deliberate pauses: "cherries? (pause) Have some, (pause) Take a few." Up to 40 phrases per minute. Call harsh "chway." Sings through heat of day well into mid-summer. **Range and habitat:** mixed and deciduous woods of north-western, central, south-central and south-eastern NA, Central America. Winters in Amazon basin. **Similar species:** Black-whiskered, Philadelphia and Warbling Vireos.

Warbling Vireo

Vireo gilvus (Vireonidae) 12–15 cm/5–6 in.
Light gray tinged olive-green above, crown and nape paler; white below, usually with greenish yellow wash on flanks, particularly in immatures. Sexes similar. Juveniles often buffy with faint buff wing-bar. Voice: husky, languid warble, pitch rises, tempo increases: "one, two, three, four, fivesixseveneight," also wheezy, catlike "twee." **Range and habitat:** deciduous woods, roadsides, aspen groves, riparian and alder thickets of north-western, central, eastern NA. Winters from south-central NA to north-western NT. **Similar species:** Philadelphia and Red-eyed Vireos, Tennessee Warbler.

Blue-gray Gnatcatcher

Golden-crowned Kinglet (female)

Ruby-crowned Kinglet

Tufted Titmouse

Black-capped Chickadee

Mountain Chickadee

White-Breasted Nuthatch

Red-Breasted Nuthatch

Blue-headed Vireo

Red-eyed Vireo

Warbling Vireo

Black-and-white Warbler

Mniotilta varia (Parulidae) 11–14 cm/4½–5½ in.
Boldly striped black and white above and below. Male has black facial striping, black throat, black streaks on sides, black spots on undertail-coverts. Female dull black, with brownish wash; face, throat, underparts white; flanks thinly streaked with black. Immature like female. Creeps over branches probing cracks. Voice: high, lisping "wee-wee," repeated 6 to 8 times, sharp "pit" and thin "seet." **Range and habitat:** deciduous and mixed forests from north-central and north-eastern NA south almost to Gulf coast. Winters south-eastern NA to northern NT. **Similar species:** Blackpoll and Black-throated Gray Warblers (see p 86).

Yellow-rumped Warbler

Dendroica coronata (Parulidae) 12–15 cm/5–6 in.
"Myrtle" subspecies blue-gray above streaked with black; yellow on crown, rump, shoulders; white tail spots; white eyebrow and eye-ring in black face; throat white; black upper breast, black streaked flanks. Female, winter male similar, but grayish brown. Winter female, immature browner, may lack yellow. "Audubon" subspecies similar, but slate-gray, yellow throat, black breast, upper flanks, white wing patch; female, winter male, immature browner. Loose musical trill, loud "check." **Range and habitat:** conifer and mixed forests of northern and north-central NA, south in western mountains to south-central NA. Winters from east- and west-central NA through southern NA into Central America. **Similar species:** Cape May, Magnolia and Palm Warblers.

Magnolia Warbler

Dendroica magnolia (Parulidae) 11–13 cm/4½–5½ in.
Gray crown, black back, yellow rump, black tail with rectangular white patches; white eyebrow, black face, white crescent below eye; 2 wide white wing-bars. Throat and underparts yellow streaked black, undertail-coverts white. Female similar, duller. Immature, autumn adult as female, head grayish with narrow white eye-ring, back olive-green, streaking faint on underparts, grayish breast band. Voice: short, rising "weeta, weeta, weetsee," also "tlep." **Range and habitat:** small conifers of northern and east-central NA. Winters south-central NA to north-western NT, also West Indies. **Similar species:** Yellow-rumped Warbler, immature Prairie Warbler.

Northern Parula

Parula americana (Parulidae) 11 cm/4½ in.
Blue-gray above with greenish yellow patch on back, white wing-bars and white patches on outer tail feathers; broken white eye-ring, yellow throat and breast; black and orange band across upper breast; belly and undertail-coverts white. Female duller, lacks breast band. Immature dull. Voice: buzzy trill that climbs, falls "zzzzzzzzurp." **Range and habitat:** humid woods with hanging mosses for nest, east-central and south-eastern NA. Winters south-central and south-eastern NA, Central America, West Indies. **Similar species:** Yellow-throated Warbler, immature Nashville Warbler, Tropical Parula.

Chestnut-sided Warbler

Dendroica pensylvanica (Parulidae) 11–13 cm/4½–5 in.
Lemon-yellow crown, yellow-green back streaked with black, white in outer tail feathers; dark wings, yellow wing-bars; face black and white, underparts white with narrow chestnut stripes along flanks. Female paler. Immature yellow-green above, grayish white below, yellow wing-bars, gray face, prominent white eye-ring. Autumn adult yellow-green above without black face, chestnut flanks. Voice: loud, "pleased, pleased, pleased to meet cha," accent on "meet;" also "chip." **Range and habitat:** brushy pastures, slashings central and east-central NA, south in mountains. Winters in Central America. **Similar species:** immature Bay-breasted Warbler; immature resembles Ruby-crowned Kinglet (see p 82).

Palm Warbler

Dendroica palmarum (Parulidae) 11–14 cm/4½–5½ in.
Often wags tail. Chestnut crown; olive-brown face and back with dusky streaks; greenish yellow rump. Faint wing-bars. Dark tail has white corners. Eyebrow, throat, upper breast, undertail-coverts yellow. Subspecies *palmarum*: lower breast, belly grayish white; *hypochrysea*: bright yellow below. Both streaked with chestnut below. Sexes similar. Immature brown above, yellow undertail-

coverts. Voice: weak, buzzy trill, also "check." **Range and habitat:** wooded borders of muskeg, north-central and north-eastern NA. Winters in south-eastern, south-central NA, Central America. Forages in low bushes, weedy fields on migration. **Similar species:** Prairie and Yellow-rumped Warblers.

Black-throated Green Warbler

Dendroica virens (Parulidae) 11–14 cm/4½–5½ in.
Yellow face contrasts with yellow-green crown and back, black throat, breast and flanks. Greenish eye stripe and ear-coverts. White wing-bars, white in outer tail feathers. White below. Female similar, less black; chin and throat mostly yellow. Autumn: all have yellow face, dusky throat, breast, flanks. Voice: lazy "zee, zee, zee, zoo, zee;" also high "tsip." **Range and habitat:** mixed and coniferous forest (birch and aspen in north, cypress in south), north-central and eastern NA. Winters in south-central and extreme south-eastern NA into Central America, Greater Antilles. **Similar species:** Golden-cheeked and Townsend's Warblers.

Yellow Warbler

Dendroica petechia (Parulidae) 11–13 cm/4½–5 in.
Yellow below, greenish-yellow above; yellow wing-bars; yellow patches in outermost tail feathers; breast and flanks with narrow chestnut streaks; dark eye in yellow face. Female, immature male yellow below, yellowish green above; immature females drab olive-green. Subspecies: density of chestnut streaks, amount of chestnut on crown varies. Voice: lively "sweet, sweet, oh so sweet;" also soft "chip." **Range and habitat:** willow and alder thickets bordering wetlands, cleared woodland, brushy fields, suburban gardens, northern NA to northern NT. Winters from south-central NA to central NT. **Similar species:** Wilson's and Prothonotary Warblers (see p 86).

Orange-crowned Warbler

Vermivora celata (Parulidae) 11–14 cm/4½–5½ in.
Olive-green above, olive washed in yellow below; yellow undertail-coverts; greenish yellow eyebrow, thin broken yellow eye-ring; dusky olive streaking on breast; orange crown patch, rarely visible. Western subspecies more yellow than eastern. Staccato trill. **Range and habitat:** brushy clearings, northern and west-central NA, south in western mountains, more common in west. Winters along both coasts from central to south-central NA and Central America. **Similar species:** Tennessee and Arctic warblers, female Yellow and Wilson's Warblers (see p 86).

Nashville Warbler

Vermivora ruficapilla (Parulidae) 11–13 cm/4½–5 in.
Crown, nape, face gray, concealed chestnut crown patch, conspicuous white eye-ring; olive-green back, wings and tail; yellow throat and underparts, belly whitish. Female, autumn male, immature pale gray or brownish gray head, pale yellow underparts, buff eye-ring. Voice: 2-parted, 1st part higher, slower, "sebit, seebit, seebit, seebit, tititititititi;" also sharp, metallic "clink." **Range and habitat:** cool, open, mixed woods, forest edges, bogs central NA south in western mountains. Winters in extreme south-central and south-eastern NA. **Similar species:** Connecticut, MacGillivray's, Mourning, Virginia's and Wilson's Warblers (see p 86).

Black-throated Blue Warbler

Dendroica caerulescens (Parulidae) 12–14 cm/4½–5½ in.
Male gray-blue above; black face, throat, upper breast, flanks; lower breast, belly white; wing, tail feathers dark; white patch in wing, white in outer tail feathers. Female olive-gray above, traces of blue on crown, uppertail-coverts; olive-yellow below; white eyebrow and wing patch. Immatures resemble adults. Voice: slow, buzzy "I am so lazeeee," last note rising, juncolike "smack." **Range and habitat:** undergrowth of deciduous and mixed woodlands of east-central NA, south in mountains. Winters in West Indies. **Similar species:** female Cerulean and Tennessee Warblers, Philadelphia Vireo.

Black-and-white Warbler

Yellow-rumped Warbler

Magnolia Warbler

Northern Parula

Chestnut-sided Warbler

Palm Warbler

Black-throated Green Warbler (autumn plummage)

Yellow Warbler

Orange-crowned Warbler

Nashville Warbler

Black-throated Blue Warbler

Blackpoll Warbler

Dendroica striata (**Parulidae**) 12–15 cm/5–6 in.
Black cap contrasts with white cheek. Back olive-gray streaked with black; 2 white wing-bars; white tail spots; white below, streaked with black on sides of neck and flank. Female greenish cap, pale eyebrow, olive-gray above with dusky streaks, white below, washed in yellow. Autumn adults and immatures resemble female, but greener above, greenish yellow below with faint streaks. Legs pinkish or straw-colored. Voice: extremely high, deliberate "zi-zi-zi-zi-zi-zi-zi-zi," crescendo followed by decrescendo, also loud "smack." **Range and habitat:** northern spruce-fir forest. Winters in central NT. **Similar species:** Black-and-White and Black-throated Gray warblers, in fall immature Pine and Bay-breasted Warblers.

Bay-breasted Warbler

Dendroica castanea (**Parulidae**) 12–15 cm/5–6 in.
Chestnut crown, black face bordered on neck with buff patches, chestnut throat, upper breast, flanks; greenish gray above, streaked with black, 2 white wing-bars, white tail spots; lower breast, belly, undertail-coverts buff. Female similar, chestnut reduced to wash, buff neck patch inconspicuous. Immature and autumn adult gray above with dusky streaks, buff below without streaks, trace of chestnut on flanks, dark legs (unlike pinkish legs of similar species Blackpoll Warbler). Voice: similar to Black-and-white Warbler but shorter, thinner, single pitch; also mellow "chip." **Range and habitat:** follows outbreaks of spruce budworm across northern coniferous forests. Winters in northern NT. **Similar species:** Chestnut-sided Warbler, immature Blackpoll Warbler (see p 84).

Wilson's Warbler

Wilsonia pusilla (**Parulidae**) 11–12 cm/4–5 in.
Black cap bordered by yellow forehead and eyebrow; olive-green above, yellow below; dark eye. Female, immature: olive-green above, yellow forehead and eyebrow, but black cap absent or obscured by green feather-edging, yellow below. Rarely forages above 3 m (10 ft). May twitch tail in circular motion, flicks wings like kinglet. Voice: thin, rapid chatter "chi, chi, chi, chi, chet, chet," pitch dropping at end, also flat "chuck." **Range and habitat:** moist tangles, thickets along wooded streams from treeline across northern NA, south in western mountains. Winters south-central and extreme south-western NA to north-western NT. **Similar species:** Yellow Warbler, female Hooded Warbler (see p 84).

Canada Warbler

Wilsonia canadensisb (**Parulidae**) 12–15 cm/5–6 in.
Bluish gray above, yellow below. Face, sides of neck black, yellow "spectacles" around eyes; necklace of black spots across breast; white undertail-coverts. Female similar, face gray, necklace faint. Immature like female, necklace further reduced, back often washed with olive-brown. Darts after insects, rarely higher than 3 m (10 ft). Voice: explosive burst of staccato notes, irregularly arranged, but with "ditchety" phrase and ending with single "chip," also a loud "chick." **Range and habitat:** moist undergrowth of mature northern and eastern woodlands, central, north-eastern and east-central NA, south in eastern mountains. Winters in NT. **Similar species:** Kentucky Warbler.

Common Yellowthroat

Geothlypis trichas (**Parulidae**) 11–14 cm/4½–5½ in.
Broad black mask across forehead, face, on to sides of neck, bordered above by pale gray; brownish olive above; bright yellow chin, throat, upper breast; flanks buff-brown, belly off-white; undertail-coverts yellow. Female similar, lacks mask, has faint eye-ring, ill-defined eye stripe, grayer above. Immature male browner than adult male, mask incomplete. Immature female browner than adult female, only hint of yellow throat. Voice: rollicking "witchity-witchity-whitch," noticeable geographic variation. Flight song a jumble of notes ending with "witchity-whitch." Husky "tchek." **Range and habitat:** marshes, wet thickets, brushy fields throughout NA, except extreme north. Winters east-central, southern coasts to northern NT, West Indies. **Similar species:** Kentucky Warbler, female Nashville Warbler, other species of yellowthroat found throughout Caribbean region (see p 84).

Northern Waterthrush

Seiurus noveboracensis (**Parulidae**) 12–15 cm/5–6 in.
Yellowish buff eyebrow diagnostic. Olive-brown above, yellowish buff below, small dark brown spots on throat, larger dark brown spots and streaks on breast, flanks, belly. Forages on ground, walks with teetering gait. Voice: vigorous, clear "sweet, sweet, sweet, swee-wee-wee, chew, chew, chew," accelerating staccato ending. Call a sharp "chip." **Range and habitat:** cool, dark wooded swamps, brush bogs, wooded lakes and streamsides from treeline across NA, south in eastern mountains. Winters from south-central NA to northern NT, also West Indies. **Similar species:** Louisiana Waterthrush, Ovenbird, Spotted Sandpiper, thrushes (see pp 62, 80).

Ovenbird

Seiurus aurocapillus (**Parulidae**) 14–16 cm/5½–6½ in.
Orange crown bordered with dark brown, olive-brown above, white below, densely marked with elongate brown spots on breast and flanks. Prominent white eye-ring. Legs pink. Female similar, paler. Juveniles: 2 buff wing-bars. Walks. Voice: emphatic crescendo of "teacher, teacher, teacher, teacher" always emphasizes the 1st syllable. Evening flight song a rapid jumble of bubbling, warbling notes ending in "teacher, teacher." Note, sharp "chock." **Range and habitat:** forages on ground in deciduous forest of central, north-eastern, east-central NA. In winter, south-eastern and south-central NA to northern NT. **Similar species:** thrushes, water thrushes (see p 80).

Mourning Warbler

Oporornis philadelphia (**Parulidae**) 12–14 cm/5½–6½ in.
Gray hood covers head, nape, throat, becoming black on upper breast; some black by the eyes; olive above, yellow below. In fall, black veiled in gray. Female: dull gray-brown hood with broken eye-ring, olive above, yellow below. Immature: hood brownish olive, yellow tinge on throat, broken eye-ring, olive above, pale yellow below. Voice: loud, liquid chant "chirry, chirry, chirry, chorry, chorry," loud, low-pitched "tcheck." **Range and habitat:** shrubby undergrowth in woods, old fields from west-central to north-eastern NA south in the eastern mountains. Winters from extreme south-central NA to northern NT, also West Indies. **Similar species:** Connecticut, MacGillivray's and Orange-crowned Warblers, female Common Yellowthroat.

Yellow-breasted Chat

Icteria virens (**Parulidae**) 19 cm/7½ in.
Black lores contrast with white "spectacles" and white whisker; bill large, heavy, black; olive-green above; long tail; bright yellow chin, throat, breast; white belly and undertail-coverts. Sexes similar. Juvenile brownish or grayish olive above, no yellow below; throat, breast spotted. Elusive, foraging and singing from within brush. Voice: clear whistles, alternating with mews, grunts, rattles, cackles, squeaks, suggests mimic thrush but longer pauses between phrases. Often sings at night. Call "whoit" or "kook." **Range and habitat:** brushy tangles, thickets and briars in wet areas across central and southern NA. Winters south-central NA to north-western NT.

American Redstart

Setophaga ruticilla (**Parulidae**) 11–13 cm/4½–5½ in.
Black above, also on throat, breast, lower belly white. Broad orange patch in wings and across all but central tail feathers; orange flanks. Female gray-brown head, olive-gray, dingy white below with yellow flanks; wing, tail patterns like male, but yellow. Male in 1st spring like female, but black patches and orange tinge in yellow markings. Voice: strident, sibilant "zee, zee, zee, zee, zwee" (last note rising), alternating with "zee, zee, zee, zee, zawaah" (last note slurring downward), sharp "chick." **Range and habitat:** 2nd-growth deciduous woodlands across northern, west-central, most of eastern NA. Winters from southern NA to central NT.

Blackpoll Warbler

Bay-breasted Warbler

Wilson's Warbler

Canada Warbler

Ovenbird

Common Yellowthroat

Northern Waterthrush

Mourning Warbler

Yellow-breasted Chat

American Redstart
(immature male)

Rose-breasted Grosbeak

Pheucticus ludovicianus (Emberizidae) 18–21 cm/7–8½ in.
Black above; rose red triangle on breast, enlarges with age; wings, tail black with white patches; white rump, flanks, belly, undertail-coverts; wing-linings rose. Female brown above, prominent light crown and eyebrow stripes; white wing patches, saffron wing-linings; gray-white below, streaked with brown. Winter male like female, but pink chest, black and white wings, rose wing-linings. Immature male paler than winter male. Voice: like American Robin, more mellow, more rapid; squeaky "ink." **Range and habitat:** deciduous woods, thickets, north-central, central, and east-central NA. Winters south-central to northern NT. **Similar species:** female Black-headed Grosbeak, female Purple Finch (see p 90).

Northern Cardinal

Cardinalis cardinalis (Emberizidae) 19–23 cm/7½–9 in.
Brilliant red, crested; red bill, surrounded by black face, throat. Female warm brown, shading to red on wings and tail; red bill, less black on face, throat. Immature: gray-brown, dark bill, little or no red in wings, tail. Voice: loud, throaty variable whistle. Female sings softer, less often than male. Call, metallic "tsink." **Range and habitat:** brushy undergrowth, resident east-central and southern NA. Expanding range north. Visits feeders. **Similar species:** Pyrrhuloxia, Summer and Scarlet Tanagers (see p 90).

Indigo Bunting

Passerina cyanea (Emberizidae) 14 cm/5½ in.
Brilliant blue, almost violet on head. Female brown, lighter below with faint streaking on breast. 1st-year male often mottled blue and olive-brown; Immature like female; but streaked on breast. Voice: high, strident, with phrases sung in couplets, each on different pitch; also sharp, thin "spit." **Range and habitat:** brushy pastures, woodland edges east-central, south-western, and southern NA. Winters south-central NA to northern NT. **Similar species:** Blue Grosbeak, females of other buntings (see pp 178, 274).

Spotted Towhee

Pipilo maculatus (Emberizidae) 18–22 cm/7–8½ in.
Black back, throat, breast; rufous flanks, white belly; white spots on back and wings. Red eyes. Female similar, but brown where male black. Males, females darkest in Pacific northwest, palest on Great Plains. Juvenile brown above, light below, heavily streaked. Voice: musical "chup, chup, zeeee." Call "chweee" in west. **Range and habitat:** undergrowth of west-central and south-western NA, except short grass prairies. In winter withdraws from northern rocky mountains, appears in south-central NA. **Similar species:** Eastern Towhee, extensive variation among towhees poorly understood.

Savannah Sparrow

Passerculus sandwichensis (Emberizidae) 12–16 cm/5–6½ in.
Gray-brown above, cream below; dark brown streaks over all, usually form central spot on breast; white stripe across mid-crown, yellowish eyebrow diagnostic; tail short, notched; legs pink. Western subspecies darker than eastern. Voice: lisping, rising notes then descending trill, also high "tsip." **Range and habitat:** meadows, prairies, dunes, wet grasslands; northern and central NA. Winters along east-and west-central coasts and across southern NA into Central America. **Similar species:** Lincoln's, Song and Vesper Sparrows.

Song Sparrow

Melospiza melodia (Emberizidae) 14–18 cm/5½ 7 in.
Brown above, streaked black and gray; white below, dark brown streaks on breast, flanks, forming spot on breast; crown brown with central gray stripe, broad grayish eyebrow, gray–brown ear coverts. Tail long, rounded; pumped in flight. Immatures may lack breast spot. Voice: variable, musical or buzzy, usually starts with 3 or 4 clear notes. Call, nasal "tchep." **Range and habitat:** widespread in brush, wooded edges north-western, central, south-western and south-eastern NA. Winters Alaskan coast, central and southern NA. **Similar species:** Lincoln's, Savannah and Swamp Sparrows.

Chipping Sparrow

Spizella passerina (Emberizidae) 12–14 cm/5–5½ in.
Rufous cap, white eyebrow, black eye stripe, brown back streaked with black; gray cheeks, underparts, rump. Winter adult has black streaks in cap, often with light median stripe; eyebrow, eye stripe less contrasting; brown grayer. Juvenile browner, finely streaked on breast and flanks; retains this plumage well into autumn. Voice: mechanical trill on 1 pitch, also high, sweet "tsip." **Range and habitat:** open woods; conifers, farms; towns throughout NA, except Alaska and extreme southern United States. Winters in south-central NA and Central America. **Similar species:** other rufous-capped sparrows.

Vesper Sparrow

Pooecetes gramineus (Emberizidae) 14–16 cm/5½–6½ in.
White outer tail feathers in dark tail are diagnostic. Pale gray-brown above, with dark brown streaks; gray-white below, with buff wash on breast, flanks; fine dark streaks on throat, breast, flanks; whitish eye-ring; chestnut at bend of wing. Immature finely streaked. Voice: sweet, throaty, usually opens with 2 minor notes, then 2 higher-pitched notes followed by descending series of trills. Call, sharp "chirp." **Range and habitat:** prairies, meadows, roadsides; central, south-western NA. Winters in east-central, southern NA. **Similar species:** pipits, Savannah and Song Sparrows.

Fox Sparrow

Passerella iliaca (Emberizidae) 16–19 cm/6½–7½ in.
Eastern subspecies: rufous tail, rust on gray head, back, and wings. Intermountain subspecies: gray head and back, rufous tinged with gray; west coast subspecies: dusky brown. All subspecies: breast heavily streaked, often with central spot. Voice: melodious, usually introductory whistle, then series of sliding whistles and clear notes. Call, "click" or "chip." **Range and habitat:** undergrowth across northern NA, south in western mountains. Winters along west-central and south-western coast, east-central and south-eastern NA. **Similar species:** thrushes, especially Hermit Thrush (see p 80).

Dark-eyed Junco

Junco hyemalis (Emberizidae) 12–16 cm/5–6½ in.
All subspecies have pink bill, white outer tail feathers, white belly, dark eyes. "Slate-colored" (3 subspecies): slate-gray head, breast, flanks, back, wings, tail. "White-winged" (1) similar, but 2 white wing-bars, more white in tail. "Oregon" (2): black hood, brown back, pink sides. "Pink-sided" (1): pale gray head, breast; dark lores; brownish back; pink flanks. "Gray-headed" (2): light gray head, breast, flanks, dark lores; rusty back. Female: paler or browner. Juvenile: breast streaked. Voice: loose, musical trill, and "smack." **Range and habitat:** conifer and mixed woods; northern, western, east-central NA, south-eastern mountains. Winters central and southern NA. **Similar species:** Mexican Junco, Vesper Sparrow.

White-throated Sparrow

Zonotrichia albicollis (Emberizidae) 16–19 cm/6½–7½ in.
Polymorphic. 1 morph: black and white head stripes, gray face, white throat; other: tan and dark brown head stripes, gray-brown face, white throat. Both chestnut-brown above, wings streaked with black, yellow lores, gray breast, faintly streaked olive-brown flanks, white belly and wing-bars. Pure whistled notes: "Old Sam Peabody, Peabody, Peabody;" loud "chink." **Range and habitat:** coniferous forests, north-central, north-eastern and east-central NA. Winters in east-central and southern NA, along west coast. **Similar species:** White-crowned Sparrow, immature Swamp Sparrow.

White-crowned Sparrow

Zonotrichia leucophrys (Emberizidae) 14–18 cm/5½–7 in.
Large; black and white striped crown; pearl-gray cheeks, neck, breast; back and wings brown with white and black streaks; long tail. Juveniles similar, but with cinnamon-brown and buff head striping. Voice: clear whistles in minor key, followed by husky, trilled whistles; many dialects; call, high "seeet." **Range and habitat:** shrubby areas, northern, west-central and south-western NA. Winters along Pacific coast, central, southern NA. **Similar species:** Golden-crowned Sparrow.

Rose-breasted Grosbeak

Northern Cardinal

Indigo Bunting (male singing)

Spotted Towhee

Savannah Sparrow

Song Sparrow

Chipping Sparrow

Vesper Sparrow

Fox Sparrow

Dark-eyed Junco

White-throated Sparrow

White-crowned Sparrow

Summer Tanager

Piranga rubra (Emberizidae) 18–19 cm/7–8 in.
Male orange-red. Female and immature pale yellow below, yellowish olive above, more olive on wings, tail and back. Bill large, pale in both sexes, darker during nonbreeding season. First-spring males similar to females, washed or blotched with red. Second-spring males similar to adult males, but paler, more yellowish. Forages high in foliage; particularly fond of bees. Voice: series of sweet, clear phrases similar to American Robin, but deliberate, also staccato "pi-tuk." **Range and habitat:** deciduous forest, especially oak groves of southern and east-central NA. Winters from south-central NA to central NT. **Similar species:** Northern Cardinal, Scarlet Tanager; female resembles female Northern Oriole.

Scarlet Tanager

Piranga olivacea (Emberizidae) 16–19 cm/6½–7½ in.
Male glowing scarlet with black wings and tail. First-spring males duller orange-red; wings, tail brownish black. Female, immature: green above, yellow below, gray-brown to blackish brown wings, tail. Autumn males resemble females, but green brighter, some yellow on crown, yellow underparts have faint orange wash. Juveniles resemble female, but with yellow wing-bars. Forages high in foliage. Courting males display from low perches. Voice: hoarse caroling of 4 or 5 phrases, like an American Robin with a sore throat, also hoarse "chip-burr." **Range and habitat:** deciduous forests, especially oak groves of east-central and south-eastern NA. Winters from northern to central NT. **Similar species:** Northern Cardinal, other tanagers (see p 136).

Bobolink

Dolichonyx oryzivorus (Icteridae) 15–20 cm/6–8 in.
Black head and body; golden nape; white scapulars, lower back and rump. Female buff-olive above with dark brown streaks, dark brown wings and tail with buff edges on wing-coverts. Buff-white below, finely streaked with dark brown on flanks and undertail-coverts; head grayish white with brown crown stripes and brown stripe behind dark eye; breast warm buff. Immatures similar, but yellowish below. Winter male like female, but darker above with yellow face. Voice: reedy introduction followed by bubbly, twanging jumble of notes, often given in flight. Call, sharp "pink." **Range and habitat:** open grassy areas of central NA. Winters in central NT. **Similar species:** female Red-winged Blackbird, Savannah Sparrow (see p 88).

Western Meadowlark

Sturnella neglecta (Icteridae) 20–25 cm/8–10 in.
Buff; streaked and mottled brownish black above, on flanks; head with prominent stripes; throat, breast and belly yellow; black V across breast; yellow in eyebrow; long conical bill. In flight several rapid wingbeats alternate with short glides, white outer tail feathers prominent. Voice: flutelike, double-noted, gurgling, unlike slurred whistles of Eastern Meadowlark. Sings from atop tall weeds, fence-posts, tree or in flight. Call, "chupp." **Range and habitat:** prairies, meadows, drier habitat than Eastern Meadowlark, central and south-central NA west. Withdraws southward in winter. **Similar species:** Eastern Meadowlark.

Red-winged Blackbird

Agelaius phoeniceus (Icteridae) 19–24 cm/7½–9½ in.
Male black, scarlet epaulettes bordered with buff. Female smaller, dark brown above streaked with buff, light below heavily streaked with dark brown. Buff eyebrow and throat. First-spring male darker than female, epaulette orange flecked with black, buff eyebrow, light cheek and throat. Immature similar to female, more buff. Voice: liquid "konk-a-ree." Call, low "chuck." Males establish territories in marshes, wet meadows, thickets. Females choose territories; many males polygamous. **Range and habitat:** marshes, wet meadows, NA except northernmost areas. Winters in central and southern NA. **Similar species:** Tricolored Blackbird.

Brown-headed Cowbird

Molothrus ater (Icteridae) 15–20 cm/6–8 in.
Male: coffee-brown head, glossy black body. Female: uniform gray-brown. Juvenile: brown, lighter below, often streaked dark brown. Bill short, conical. Known to parasitize 100+ North American species; has reduced populations of vireos, wood-warblers, tanagers, orioles.

Eggs not mimetic. Chicks hatch earlier than host, grow faster and larger, crowd out host chicks. Courtship includes a sleeked posture with bill pointed up and a bowing posture with wings spread, plumage fluffed. Voice: high-pitched, bubbly, with glissando in middle. Female: a loud harsh chatter. **Range and habitat:** north-central, central and southern NA. Winters in southern NA. **Similar species:** Bronzed Cowbird, other blackbirds (see p 136).

Brewer's Blackbird

Euphagus cyanocephalus (Icteridae) 20–25 cm/8–10 in.
Black with purple iridescence on head, green iridescence on body; bill conical, sharply pointed; eyes creamy white to pale yellow. Female gray-brown, lighter on head and neck; eyes dark. Juveniles like females. First-winter males: blackish with gray eyebrows, gray barring on back and chest. Often in large monospecific flocks, or with Red-winged Blackbirds. Voice: a creaking "ksheeik," also metallic "cheek." **Range and habitat:** wherever trees and open space available together; northwest and central, south-central NA west. Winters in west-central and south-central NA. **Similar species:** other blackbirds, Common Grackle, European Starling (see pp 136, 182).

Common Grackle

Quiscalus quiscula (Icteridae) 28–34 cm/11–13 in.
Large, with long profile; long, conical, slightly decurved bill; long, wedge-shaped, keeled tail, larger in male than female. Adults black; variable iridescence, blue sheen on head contrasting with a bronze sheen on back in the other. Eyes of both subspecies, both sexes, yellow. Juvenile sooty; dark eyes. Gregarious. Male lowers wings, puffs plumage, bows before female. Voice: scraping, ascending "kogubaleek." Call, loud "tchack." **Range and habitat:** common in towns, croplands, groves, streamsides; central and eastern NA. Winters entirely in eastern NA. **Similar species:** blackbirds, cowbirds, other grackles, European Starling (see pp 136, 182).

Boat-tailed Grackle

Quiscalus major (Icteridae) 33–42 cm/13–16 in.
Very large; long, wedge-shaped, keeled tail; all-black with iridescent blue, blue-green on back and breast. Eye color: yellow on Atlantic coast, dark brown in peninsular Florida and north-western Gulf coast; medium brown outlined with yellow along central Gulf coast. Female much smaller than male, dark brown, buff throat and breast, dark eye. Polygynous. Courting male spreads wings and tail; bobs, bows in front of female. Voice: harsh whistles and clucks. **Range and habitat:** resident in coastal areas near salt water, saltmarshes east-central and south-eastern NA. **Similar species:** Common and Great-tailed Grackles, Fish Crow.

Bullock's Oriole

Icterus bullockii (Icteridae) 18–20 cm/7–8 in.
Flame-orange and black with large white wing patches; pale lower mandible; black crown, nape, eye-stripe and bib with orange eyebrow, cheeks and sides of neck. Female and young gray above with 2 white wing-bars; yellow-orange face, throat, upper breast; gray-white belly. First-year male: black eye-stripe and bib; crown, nape, back olive-gray, dark steaks on back, 2 white wing-bars; gray to white flanks and belly. Voice: rich, piping whistles, somewhat disjointed. Call, low, whistled "hew-li" ("Baltimore"); clear sweet "kleek" ("Bullock's"). **Range and habitat:** open deciduous woodland of west-central and south-western NA. Winters from south-central NA to northern NT. **Similar species:** other orioles (see p 136).

Bobolink

Western Meadowlark

Red-winged Blackbird

Brown-headed Cowbird

Brewer's Blackbird

Common Grackle

Bullock's Oriole

Scarlet Tanager

Boat-tailed Grackle

Summer Tanager

Pine Siskin

Carduelis pinus (Fringillidae) 11–13 cm/4½–5½ in.
Brown above, white below, finely streaked with dark brown; wings and tail dark brown, yellow at base of flight feathers and sides and base of tail feathers; tail deeply notched; bill thin, sharply pointed cone. Voice: long, rapid jumble of notes including a rising, buzzy, diagnostic "zzzhrrreee." Call "sweeeet." **Range and habitat:** coniferous forest. north-western and central NA, in western mountains to south-western NA. Winters in central, southern NA. Visits feeders. **Similar species:** female House Finch and Goldfinch, Spruce Siskin (see p 180).

American Goldfinch

Carduelis tristis (Fringillidae) 11–14 cm/4½–5½ in.
Breeding male brilliant yellow with black cap, wings and tail; white in wings and tail, white tail-coverts; bill, legs pink. Female, similar pattern in yellow-olive, black and white. Autumn and winter male resembles female, but whiter below; male has more yellow about head, female less. Juvenile like female, cinnamon-buff above and on wing-bars; wings and tail brownish black. Voice: sweet jumbled twittering. Flight call "potato chip, potato chip" given between wingbeats. **Range and habitat:** weedy fields, streamsides, willow thickets across central NA, along Pacific coast. Winters along Pacific coast, across southern and central NA, many leave interior. **Similar species:** immature Indigo Bunting, Lawrence's and Lesser Goldfinches, Pine Siskin (see p 188).

House Finch

Carpodacus mexicanus (Fringillidae) 12–14 cm/4½–5½ in.
Male: red to orange forehead, crown, eyebrow, throat and rump; face and upper body gray-brown streaked with brown; off-white below with brown streaks. Female lacks reddish color, head unpatterned brown. Tail brown, square in both sexes. Voice: melodious, jumble of notes lasting more than 3 sec, ending with ascending note. Call, sweet "cheet." **Range and habitat:** abundant resident throughout central and southern NA; native to west-central, south-western and south-central NA. Introduced into New York City in 1940. Spread north, south and west to join native population. **Similar species:** Cassin's and Purple Finches.

Purple Finch

Carpodacus purpureus (Fringillidae) 14–15 cm/5½–6 in.
Male raspberry red head, throat, breast, back with underlying dark cheek, whisker and dorsal streaks; belly white, dark streaks, highlighted with red. Female streaked gray-brown above, prominent white eyebrow and cheek patch, white below with brown streaks. Both sexes: notched tail. Immature like buff female. Voice: rich, bubbling outburst of melodious notes; usually in couplets or triplets. Call, soft "pick." **Range and habitat:** north-western, central and north-eastern coniferous forests, south in far west coastal forests. Winters from central and east-central NA south, far west-central south along coast. **Similar species:** Cassin's and House Finches.

White-winged Crossbill

Loxia leucoptera (Fringillidae) 15–17 cm/6–7 in.
Male bright pink, lightest on belly; wings, tail black; white wing-bars. Female and juvenile gray with olive streaks, more heavily streaked above, white wing-bars; yellowish wash on breast, rump. Mandibles cross in both sexes, upper mandible to left. Voice: succession of long, loud trills at different pitches, often given in flight. Call, "wink-wink-wink" with upward, inflection. **Range and habitat:** northern coniferous forests of Holarctic. Wanders south in winter to central NA, where it may visit feeders. **Similar species:** Pine Grosbeak, other crossbills.

Pine Grosbeak

Pinicola enucleator (Fringillidae) 20–25 cm/8–10 in.
Male pink with black wings, tail; white wing-bars; gray flanks, belly. Female gray; dull yellow-orange head and rump; black wings, tail; white wing-bars. Immature male similar to female, but head and rump reddish. All have stubby bill. Flight undulating. Voice: varied warble similar to Purple Finch's song. Call, whistled "tee-tew-tew." **Range and habitat:** coniferous forests of Northern Hemisphere; south in North America in western mountains. May wander south in winter. Visits feeders. **Similar species:** White-winged Crossbill.

Evening Grosbeak

Coccothraustes vespertinus (Fringillidae) 18–21 cm/7–8½ in.
Yellow forehead and eyebrow, black crown; throat, face, neck and nape rich yellow-brown, becoming yellow on breast, flanks, belly, back and rump; wings and tail black, large white wing patches. Large bill apple-green (spring), chalky white (winter). Female gray, darker above, yellow wash on flanks; white in wings, tail. Voice: wandering warble. Call, ringing "cleer" or "clee-ip." **Range and habitat:** coniferous forests, central and western NA. Winters in deciduous and fruiting trees, central and southern NA. **Similar species:** American Goldfinch, Hawfinch.

Steller's Jay

Cyanocitta stelleri (Corvidae) 33 cm/13 in.
Crested jay, black on head, back, throat, breast; deep blue wings, rump, tail, belly. Inland form has conspicuous white eyebrow, absent in those along Pacific coast. Bill, legs black. Voice: loud "waah, waah, shack, shack, shack;" variety of calls and notes; soft, sweet song similar to "whisper song" of American Robin; imitates Red-shouldered Hawk and Golden Eagle. **Range and habitat:** resident in conifer and pine-oak forests of western NA. **Similar species:** Blue, Gray and Pinyon Jays.

Western Scrub Jay

Aphelocoma californica (Corvidae) 28–33 cm/11–13 in.
Crestless, long, slim jay, rich blue above with gray-brown on back; gray ear-coverts and underparts; white throat and upper breast with fine blue streaks and blue-gray necklace extending onto breast; undertail-coverts whitish to bluish. Voice: harsh, repeated "ike, ike, ike," slight upward inflection; longer, rough, slightly metallic, sharply rising "iennk;" rough, rapidly repeated "quick-quick-quick." **Range and habitat:** dry, open oak-juniper woods, south-western and south-central NA. **Similar species:** Island and Florida Scrub Jays, Gray-breasted and Pinyon Jays.

Blue Jay

Cyanocitta cristata (Corvidae) 28–32 cm/11–13 in.
Blue crest, back, wings, tail; black bars across wings, tail, white wing-bars, white edging on tail feathers; black band across breast around neck and nape; face, throat, underparts white, washed gray; black eye and eye stripe. Voice: harsh, slurring "jaaay;" musical, belllike "queedle, queedle;" guttural rattling "trrrr;" mimics Red-shouldered and Red-tailed Hawks. **Range and habitat:** common in oak-pine forests, suburbs, city parks and bird feeders from plains to east coast. Withdraws from northern areas in winter. **Similar species:** Steller's Jay.

Clark's Nutcracker

Nucifraga columbiana (Corvidae) 30–33 cm/12–13 in.
Profile resembles Northern Flicker. Ash-gray body; black wings, white in secondaries, tail white with black central feathers; forehead, throat, undertail-coverts white, bill black, long, heavy, pointed. Young birds browner, especially wing-coverts. Noisy, bold, often in small groups, walking and feeding on human scraps. Voice: harsh, grating "khaaa." **Range and habitat:** resident coniferous forests near treeline in west-central and south-western NA; occasional invasions of lower elevations. **Similar species:** Gray Jay, Northern Mockingbird, shrikes (see pp 78, 80, 170).

American Crow

Corvus brachyrhynchos (Corvidae) 43–53 cm/17–21 in.
Black, slight purplish gloss; square tail; bill large, stout, black; legs black. Juvenile brownish. Often in small groups, typically with a sentinel; wary of humans. Voice: distinctive "caw" or "cah," singly or in series; young birds more nasal than adults; mimics other birds, mammals and noises. **Range and habitat:** woodland, agricultural fields, river groves, recently suburbs and towns throughout NA except extreme north and extreme south-central. Winters in central and southern NA. **Similar species:** Chihuahuan and Common Ravens, other crows (see pp 182, 228, 278, 322).

Pine Siskin

American Goldfinch

House Finch

Purple Finch

White-winged Crossbill

Pine Grosbeak

Evening Grosbeak

Stellar's Jay

Western Scrub Jay

Blue Jay

Clark's Nutcracker

American Crow

THE NEOTROPICAL REGION

South of the cool Mexican plateau lies tropical rainforest, marking the northern boundary of the zoogeographical zone known as the Neotropical Region, which extends from 20° N to Cape Horn at 57° S. There are three main faunistic subdivisions: South America, Central America (Mexico to Panam,a) and the West Indies. The latter two are much influenced by recent geological and biogeographical events. South America holds the key to the unequaled species richness of the region.

South America

The South American continent lies mainly within the tropics and subtropics. However, the Andes, the world's longest mountain chain, spanning 10,000 km (6,200 miles) from the Sierra Nevada of Santa Marta in the north to the continent's southernmost tip, introduces climatic diversity at all latitudes. Thus a chain of vegetation zones runs the length of the continent, providing a pathway for temperate species into equatorial latitudes. The Andes are geologically part of the mountain chain running through western North America and Central America, resulting from uplift as an oceanic plate pushes below a continental plate. This activity is still taking place: the Santa Marta massif is only a million years old and the Andes hosts much volcanic and earthquake activity. The Andean chain is complex with several *cordilleras* with inter-Andine valleys which isolate highland areas. Thus habitat types such as Alpine *paramo* are discontinuous and this has provided scope for speciation. Some bird species are only found on certain "highland islands" surrounded by valleys with tropical vegetation which presumably they cannot cross. Rivers drain the Andes eastward and westward, but there is also a huge area of inner drainage, once a vast lake, now the *altiplano* or *puna* in Peru and Bolivia with large lakes such as Titicaca—8,300 sq km (3,200 sq miles)—and salt-plains which host endemic grebes, coots, and flamingos.

As well as providing a north-south pathway, the Andes act as an east-west barrier for many tropical and subtropical species, resulting in significant differences between the avifaunas in the foothills and lowlands to either side.

The narrow Pacific slope and lowlands boast great extremes of rainfall. In western Colombia and northern Ecuador, the annual rainfall can exceed 10 m (33 ft). This region of wet forest, extending from the tropical lowlands into montane cloud forest, has very high biodiversity and is notable for the large number of tanager species, forming colorful mixed-species flocks: one of the most spectacular of bird-watching experiences. Farther south, the cold Humboldt Current causes the precipitation to fall offshore and seasonal sea mists provide the only moisture to the deserts which run southward to northern Chile. This arid zone extends inland, crossing the Andes into central Argentina. The Humboldt Current causes upwellings of nutrient-rich water, making the inshore waters highly productive and able to support huge numbers of seabirds.

Farther south still are the southern beech forests of Chile which have a very distinctive but depauperate avifauna. The birds are, however, of Neotropical provenance, such as tapaculos and furnariids; unlike the plants and insects, which show Australasian affinities.

East of the Andes are two mountain blocks: the Tepui or Guianan-Venezuelan highlands and the Serra do Mar with the Atlantic forests of eastern Brazil. Both support distinctive endemic avifaunas. Vegetation types in the eastern lowlands are also determined by rainfall. High annual rainfall with no long dry season gives rise to humid forest. The greatest of all of these is the vast Amazon rainforest which originally covered about 6 million sq km (nearly 2½ million sq miles), approximately the land area of the United States. Far from being one vast uniform forest, rainfall variation (wetter in the west), soils and relief produce very different vegetation types, each with a distinctive bird community. This patchwork of different habitats is one reason why Amazonia supports the world's richest avifauna. Other factors are natural changes which enhance this mosaic, from small-scale tree falls opening up niches to specialists such as jacamars, to changes in the courses of rivers which leave "shadows" of their former routes in the form of a continuum of successional stages in the forest. In the longer term, climatic changes affect forest cover and cause fragmentation and conglomeration of habitat, increasing opportunities for speciation.

Western Amazonia

The richest area of all is western Amazonia, where over 500 species of birds can be found in a single locality, including over 20 species of parrot, 14 woodpeckers, over 45 antbirds, and 15 cotingas. Despite this wealth, finding these birds can be a frustrating task. In the semidarkness of the great forest, periods of stillness alternate with encounters with mixed-species flocks when a bewildering variety of birds may present themselves for an all-too-short moment.

More seasonal areas may have open grassland, flooded for parts of the year. Both the *llanos* of Venezuela and Colombia and the *pantanal* in south-west Brazil and northern Argentina are examples of these wet-dry tropics. Large concentrations of waterbirds, such as storks and ibises, may be found there. Strips of gallery forest and stands of *Mauritia* palm provide important refuges for parrots. Where rainfall is less, deciduous woodland, scrub, or open grassland predominates. These habitats are particularly important in the south. The natural vegetation of much of central Brazil is savannah (including *campos* and *cerrado*), home of the Greater Rhea and Red-legged Seriema. Pampas takes over in eastern Argentina, while to the south lies the bleak steppe of Patagonia.

More than 3,100 species of birds (including migrants from the Nearctic) occur in South America and there are new species described each year. In all, 88 families of birds breed in the Neotropics, of which 25 are endemic to the region. This high endemicity is partly because South America remained isolated from North America until just three million years ago, when the land bridge between Panama and Colombia formed, and many Neotropical families have not spread beyond the region. A major feature of the Neotropical avifauna is the predominance of the Deutero-oscines. Fewer than 50 species in this group occur in the Old World tropics, whereas over 500 are found in South America, including furnariids, woodcreepers, antbirds, cotingas, and tyrant flycatchers.

Central America has a mixed avifauna. The northern half had, until recent geological time, been a tropical peninsula of North America with an island arc extending southward. These islands were colonized by North American families (such as thrushes) moving south and hummingbirds and tyrant flycatchers moving north. Once established, the isthmus

Montezuma Oropendola. Related to the New World blackbirds and orioles, breeding colonies of oropendolas are a spectacular sight in the Neotropics.

provided a route for the movement of other forest species northward and the radiation of northern families such as wrens and wood warblers southward, facilitating the spread of such families into South America. The eastern and western coastal lowlands of Central America are isolated from each other by mountains. This barrier has led to the development of distinctive Pacific slope and Caribbean slope avifaunas. Central America also attracts many Nearctic migrants.

The West Indies

The West Indies are oceanic islands, never connected to continental landmasses, and have an avifauna based on mobile families derived from the Nearctic, Central American, and South American elements. These are typified by thrushes, vireos, wood warblers, tanagers, finches, icterids, tyrant flycatchers, hummingbirds, parrots, and pigeons. It is noteworthy that not one species of antbird or furnariid is represented. Successful colonists island-hopped and distinctive island forms evolved. There is a very high level of endemicity, including one endemic family, the Todidae. Many of the endemic species are rare and extinctions have occurred, such as the Cuban Macaw. A turnover of species is an ecological phenomenon on small islands, but by far and away the most important threat now comes from the action of man, directly through hunting or trapping, or indirectly through habitat

change. Although some island species are adaptable, their small population sizes increase their vulnerability greatly.

Elsewhere in the Neotropics, there are awesome threats to many species. In Brazil alone, *BirdLife International* have identified 114 species at threat, about two-thirds of which only occur in Brazil. The highest densities of threatened species occur in the Atlantic Forests of eastern Brazil, as well as the northern Andes of Colombia and Ecuador. Demand for land in these highly populated areas is making the future of these forests extremely precarious. Discontinuities in forest cover in these areas can fragment bird populations already restricted ecologically into narrow altitudinal belts and disrupt vertical migration, which may be important to the annual cycles of more Andean birds than we at present imagine. In the lowlands, the rate of forest clearance for logging and ranching is causing great alarm. The formerly large tracts of grasslands in southern South America, home of species such as the Black-and-white Monjita, have been degraded by heavy grazing and agricultural conversion.

The Neotropics remain the poorest known of all the avifaunal regions. The arrival in recent years of several excellent national and regional bird books will do much to facilitate study. These texts also point out the enormous gaps in our knowledge and will certainly stimulate the next generation of field ornithologists.

RHEAS Rheiformes

Greater Rhea

Rhea americana **(Rheidae)** 125 cm/49 in.
Very large, flightless bird. Blackish crown, nape and upper back. Upperparts otherwise gray, whitish below. Neck sometimes has white patches. Females are smaller and darker. Normally in small groups, readily run off when alarmed. Several females usually lay eggs in same scrape on ground. **Range and habitat:** NT, eastern Brazil south to central Argentina. Lowland to mid-elevation grassy plains. Near-threatened from hunting and most recently habitat loss. **Similar species:** Lesser Rhea.

TINAMOUS Tinamiformes

Solitary Tinamou

Tinamus solitarius **(Tinamidae)** 46 cm/18 in.
Large tinamou. Brownish above, darker on crown, with wings, back and rump heavily barred black. Ochrous head and neck, speckled on side of head, whiter on throat and buff line on side of neck. Foreneck and breast gray, whiter on belly with vermiculated flanks. Usually solitary, very wary. **Range and habitat:** NT, eastern Brazil to north-east Argentina. Lowland humid forest. Near-threatened from habitat loss. **Similar species:** White-throated Tinamou.

Undulated Tinamou

Crypturellus undulatus **(Tinamidae)** 28 cm/11 in.
Medium-sized tinamou with grayish bill and legs. Rather uniform grayish brown plumage with whitish throat and dark barring on flanks. At close quarters, fine black vermiculations on upperparts visible. Although wary, this ground-dwelling bird can be quite easy to see because it often "freezes" when alarmed. Calls frequently, particularly at dawn and dusk, a melancholic 3–4-note whistle. **Range and habitat:** NT, Guiana to western Argentina. Common in seasonally flooded forest. **Similar species:** Little Tinamou.

Brown Tinamou

Crypturellus obsoletus **(Tinamidae)** 28 cm/11 in.
Small. Unmarked dark chestnut-brown above, crown blackish, sides of head brownish gray with grayer throat. Underparts rufous brown barred black on flanks. Legs yellowish gray. Shy, ground-dwelling bird which flies reluctantly, usually seen running away. Call, usually heard at dawn and dusk, a crescendo of tremulous whistles. **Range and habitat:** NT, Andean chain from Venezuela to Argentina, and Brazil. Occurs over a large range from tropical lowlands to edge of temperate zone in forest edge and secondary vegetation. **Similar species:** Little and Highland Tinamous.

PENGUINS Sphenisciformes

Humboldt Penguin

Spheniscus humboldti **(Spheniscidae)** 68 cm/27 in.
Medium-sized with stout blackish bill, fleshy at base. Head mainly black with narrow white line forming loop from base of bill, around sides of crown to throat. Single black horseshoe across top of breast and extending down flanks to thighs, otherwise underparts mainly white. Upperparts blackish gray. Juvenile has brownish head, gray cheeks, lacks white head stripe and underparts entirely whitish. **Range and habitat:** NT, Pacific coast of Peru and Chile to 33° S. Vulnerable, mainly from over-fishing and some loss of nesting habitat from guano over exploitation. **Similar species:** Magellanic Penguin.

Magellanic Penguin

Spheniscus magellanicus **(Spheniscidae)** 71 cm/28 in.
Medium-sized with blackish bill. Head mainly black with white line forming loop from base of bill, around sides of crown to throat. Upperparts blackish gray, broad black band across upper breast, with narrower black horseshoe below, with sides extending down flanks to thighs; rest of underparts mainly white. Juvenile has pale gray cheeks and a single broad, but diffuse, breast band. **Range and habitat:** NT, on Pacific and Atlantic coasts. Mainly to south of Humboldt Penguin, but overlaps in winter when range extends northward. Near-threatened, mainly from oil pollution. **Similar species:** Humboldt Penguin.

Galapagos Penguin

Spheniscus mendiculus **(Spheniscidae)** 50 cm/20 in.
Small. Bill blackish upper mandible, yellow lower. Head blackish with narrow white line extending from eye around side of cheeks to throat. Upperparts blackish gray. Underparts mainly white with broad blackish breast band and narrower lower band forming horseshoe which extends down sides of flanks to thighs. Juvenile duller, with grayish cheeks, lacks striped pattern. Call is donkey-like. **Range and habitat:** NT, restricted to Galapagos. Endangered small population fluctuates from El Niño effects, also impact of introduced predators and over-fishing..

GREBES Podicipediformes

Short-winged Grebe

Rollandia microptera **(Podicipedidae)** 40 cm/16 in.
Flightless. Adult in breeding plumage has blackish forehead and crown, giving crested appearance. Bill yellow with reddish tip. Ear-coverts tufted black. Hindneck chestnut. Rest of upperparts dark brown with blackish streaks. Rump rather chestnut. Underparts white with brownish flecks on flanks. Nonbreeding birds paler. Often in family groups. Runs across water if alarmed, sometimes exposing wing. Calls include squeals and whines, also a repeated "gaeck." **Range and habitat:** NT, series of lakes on border of Peru and Bolivia, including Titicaca. High Andean lakes with access to reed-beds or floating vegetation. Endangered from habitat degradation and drowning in gill nets. **Not illustrated.**

Great Grebe

Podiceps major **(Podicipedidae)** 61 cm/24 in.
Large with very long blackish bill. In breeding plumage, head blackish, grayer on ear-coverts, lores and throat. Hindneck blackish, rest of neck chestnut. Upperparts dark brown, glossed blackish green. Underparts white, tinged chestnut-brown on both flanks and breast. Upperwings as upperparts, with whitish secondaries and bases of inner primaries. Underwing whitish. Nonbreeding birds rather paler, with whitish cheeks. **Range and habitat:** NT, Peruvian coast and southern Chile, southern Brazil southward to Tierra del Fuego. Breeds on lowland lakes, moves to coastal areas outside breeding season.

Least Grebe

Tachybaptus dominicus **(Podicipedidae)** 23 cm/9 in.
Very small, dumpy grebe with black bill and yellow eye. Breeding plumage shows black crown and throat. Rest of head and neck dark gray. Upperparts gray-brown, paler below. Speculum white. Nonbreeders have entire head dark gray. Normally solitary or in pairs. Usually silent. Calls include short, nasal hoot and high-pitched chattering. **Range and habitat:** NA and NT, southern USA to Argentina. Freshwater habitats with aquatic vegetation. **Similar species:** Pied-billed Grebe (see p 50).

Junin Grebe

Podiceps taczanowksi **(Podicipedidae)** 35 cm/14 in.
Flightless. Medium-sized, long-necked grebe with slender gray bill, slightly uptilted. Breeding birds show crest. Crown gray-brown. Nape blackish. Rest of upperparts brownish gray, paler on rump. Underparts whitish, particularly on flanks. Nonbreeders lack crest and black on nape. Usually in small groups. Call a whistling note. **Range and habitat:** NT, restricted to Lake Junin in Peru .Remains in open water, entering edges of reed marsh to breed. Critically Endangered with severe population declines caused by mining activities and climatic fluctuations. **Similar species:** Silvery Grebe.

Greater Rhea

Solitary Tinamou

Undulated Tinamou

Brown Tinamou

Humboldt Penguin

Magellanic Penguin
(with juvenile)

Galapagos Penguin

Great Grebe

Least Grebe

Junin Grebe

NEOTROPICAL

TUBE-NOSED SWIMMERS Procellariiformes

Waved Albatross
Phoebastria irrorata (Diomedeidae) 89 cm/35 in.
Large. Uniform yellow bill and bluish legs. Head and neck white, with buffish tinged crown and hindneck. Upperparts chestnut-brown with fine paler bars, most prominent on rump and uppertail coverts. Uppersurface of wings and tail brown. Underparts as upperparts, with white of neck extending down to upper breast. Underwings pale, bordered by brown. Flaps more and soars less than other albatrosses. **Range and habitat:** NT, PA. Breeding restricted to Galapagos and Las Platas, Ecuador. Outside breeding season off Peruvian and Ecuador coasts, with nonbreeders present all year. Only truly tropical albatross. Vulnerable from longline fishing and nest predation. **Similar species:** Wandering Albatross, Giant Petrel (see p 284).

Southern Fulmar
Fulmarus glacialoides (Procellariidae) 46–50 cm/18–20 in.
Rather long-winged, stocky-bodied seabird. Tube-nose bill is stout, mainly pink with dark tip. Body plumage white, with grayer tone on nape, breast and flanks. Lores darker. Mantle, rump and tail bluish gray as are upperwings. Black trailing edge to inner wing. Outer wing shows variable amounts of black. Underwing mainly white. Flies in characteristic stiff-winged gliding manner. Often in groups. **Range and habitat:** southern oceans. Regularly occurs during austral winter off western coast of South America to 10° S. **Similar species:** Fulmar (see p 142).

Galapagos Petrel
Pterodroma phaeopygia (Procellariidae) 43 cm/17 in.
Large, long-winged petrel. Upperparts entirely dark brown apart from white forehead and (sometimes) white sides of rump. Dark cap extends downward behind eye. Underside white apart from dark patch on axillaries and dark margin to wing, with diagonal bar crossing from carpel joint toward axillaries. Bill dark, legs pink. Has distinctive bounding flight of downward glide followed by short series of wing-flaps. **Range and habitat:** Pacific and NT. Breeds on Galapagos. Outside breeding season, dispersal to offshore regions between Mexico and northern Peru. Critically Endangered from nest predation and nest-site destruction by introduced animals. **Similar species:** Hawaiian Petrel.

Audubon's Shearwater
Puffinus lherminieri (Procellariidae) 30 cm/12 in.
Small, stocky shearwater with broad wings. Bill dark, legs pink. Upperparts, tail and vent brown. Rest of underparts white with brown on nape extending downward on to sides of breast. Underwing broadly margined brown with white center, sometimes with very little white. Can occur in large flocks. Flight rapid followed by short glides. **Range and habitat:** tropical oceans. Breeds on Pacific islands including Galapagos, West Indies, Indian ocean islands including Seychelles and Maldives. Movements off eastern seaboard of USA to 40° S, Gulf of Mexico and off coast of Ecuador. **Similar species:** Little and Manx Shearwaters (see p 142).

South Georgia Diving-Petrel
Pelecanoides georgicus (Peleca-noididae) 18–21 cm/7–8 in.
Very small, dumpy bird with short wings. Bill black, legs blue with black webs. Dark head with whitish throat. Upperparts black with distinctive grayish white scapulars. Black upperwings, browner tone on primaries. Trailing edge of secondaries white. Underparts whitish, some gray on sides of breast and flanks. Underwing linings whitish, axillaries and flight feathers darker. Fly low over waves, wings whirring. Visit breeding sites at night. **Range and habitat:** subantarctic. Breeds on South Georgia and other subantarctic islands. Probably sedentary. **Similar species:** other diving-petrels.

FULL-WEBBED SWIMMERS Pelecaniformes

Blue-footed Booby
Sula nebouxii (Sulidae) 76–84 cm/30–3 in.
Medium-sized with bright blue feet. Pale brown head, white patch on top of back, scaly brown and white back, pale band across rump and brown lower rump and tail. Upperwings uniform dark brown.

Underparts whitish with brown tail and extensive white patch at base of underwing, extending as 2 white bars toward carpel joint. Rest of underwing brown. Immature has dull gray feet, darker head and breast but shows characteristic underwing pattern. Flight direct and powerful. Feeds in small groups close to shore by plunge-diving typical of gannets and boobies. Males give whistling call, female has hoarser call. **Range and habitat:** NT, Pacific coast from Mexico to Peru. Breeds on offshore islands. Normally stays close to land. Wanders beyond normal range when food supplies short. **Similar species:** Brown, Blue-faced and Peruvian Boobies.

Peruvian Booby
Sula variegata (Sulidae) 74 cm/29 in.
Small booby with white head and underparts. Black bare skin at base of bill. Upperparts brown with pale feather edgings and whitish uppertail-coverts and center tail feathers. Underwing dark with white bar extending across wing from axillaries. Immature has pale brown body plumage. Sometimes in very large flocks with other seabirds. **Range and habitat:** NT, in Humboldt current region off Peruvian and Chilean coast, breeding on islands. Remains close to shore throughout year; periodic changes in sea currents change food supplies and cause dispersal beyond normal range. **Similar species:** Blue-footed Booby.

Red-footed Booby
Sula sula (Sulidae) 66–77 cm/26–30 in.
Variable species with several plumage forms. All have red legs and grayish bills with pink bases. White form is entirely white apart from black flight feathers and black patch on undersurface of wing at carpel joint. On the Galapagos, this form also has dark tail. Brown form is completely grayish brown. Also forms with white heads and/or white tails. Almost always in groups, frequently follows ships. **Range and habitat:** NT, PA, OR, AF and AU. Breeds on islands, but wanders far on feeding trips. **Similar species:** Blue-faced Booby.

Neotropic Cormorant
Phalacrocorax brasilianus (Phalacrocoracidae) 64–73 cm/25–9 in.
Large cormorant appearing all-black at distance. Long hooked bill is dark brown. Dull yellow naked skin on face bordered behind by narrow white margin. Breeding plumage shows white tufts on side of head. Immature grayish brown, paler on underparts, with breast whitish on younger birds. Rather long-tailed. Often in small flocks. **Range and habitat:** NT and southern NA. Marine and freshwater habitats, estuaries, lakes and rivers. Mainly lowland. May show some seasonal movements. Immatures wander. **Similar species:** Double-crested Cormorant (see p 52), Magellan Cormorant.

Guanay Cormorant
Phalacrocorax bougainvillii (Phalacrocoracidae) 76 cm/30 in.
Large cormorant with blue-black upperparts and neck, white chin and underparts. Nonbreeding birds are browner. Immatures are less pure white below. Breeds in huge colonies, sometimes of millions of birds. Large feeding flocks assemble, with other species such as boobies, at great height to search for shoals of fish. **Range and habitat:** NT. Occurs along the cold, food-rich Humboldt current off the Peruvian and Chilean coasts. Breeds on islands and some mainland sites. As with other seabirds endemic to this region, will disperse if food supplies fail. Near-threatened from over-fishing and over-exploitation of guano. **Similar species:** Magellan Cormorant.

Imperial Shag
Phalacrocorax atriceps (Phalacrocoracidae) 72 cm/28 in.
Striking-looking cormorant with crest and dark blue-black upperparts contrasting with underparts entirely white from chin to undertail-coverts apart from dark thighs. Amount of white on face variable. White tips of scapulars in breeding plumage and white patch on center of back, which the Falklands form lacks. Breeds in colonies and often forms large flocks outside breeding season. **Range and habitat:** NT and southern oceans. Northernmost populations breed southern tip of South America. Breeding sites may be used as roost sites during austral winter, although some dispersal to sea takes place. **Similar species:** Magellan Cormorant.

Waved Albatross

Southern Fulmar

Galapagos Petrel

Audubon's Shearwater

Blue-footed Booby

Peruvian Booby

South Georgia Diving-Petrel

Neotropic Cormorant

Red-footed Booby (white phase adult and immature)

Guanay Cormorant (juveniles at colony)

Imperial Shag

HERONS AND ALLIES Ciconiiformes

Stripe-backed Bittern
Ixobrychus involucris (**Ardeidae**) 30–3 cm/12–13 in.
Very small heron. Yellowish green bill and legs. Plumage generally straw-colored with back boldly streaked with black. Crown black. White throat with some white streaking on underparts. In flight, primaries show rufous with dark patch at base. Shy bird which clambers through marsh vegetation and tends to "freeze" to spot to avoid detection. Flies at low height with rather slow wingbeats. **Range and habitat:** NT, Venezuela to southern Brazil. Lowland bird of both freshwater and brackish marshes. **Similar species:** Least Bittern, Zigzag Heron.

Rufescent Tiger-Heron
Tigrisoma lineatum (**Ardeidae**) 66–76 cm/26–30 in.
Stocky heron with long, thickset neck. Yellowish powerful bill, rather short greenish legs. Adult plumage, attained after about 5 years, with rich chestnut head, neck and chest. Rest of upperparts finely barred black and buff. White and buff stripes extending from throat to belly, which is dull buff. Immature plumage strikingly different, boldly barred dark brown and golden buff above with underparts paler and less strongly marked. Calls include a series of hoots. Hunts alone. When flushed usually flies upward to a tree perch. **Range and habitat:** NT, in lowland forests, freshwater lakes and open country in proximity of tree cover. **Similar species:** Fasciated Tiger and Bare-throated Tiger-Herons.

Capped Heron
Pilherodius pileatus (**Ardeidae**) 58 cm/23 in.
Small stocky heron. Bluish bill and bright blue bare facial skin on lores and around eye contrast with white plumage, apart from black crown. Breeding birds show creamy tone on neck and breast. Immature plumage very similar, with crown streaked black and white. Mainly silent. Shy and usually solitary, often perches in trees. **Range and habitat:** NT, from Panama to southern Brazil and Paraguay. Occurs along river-banks and edges of small lakes. **Similar species:** Black-crowned Night-Heron (see p 52), Cattle Egret (see p 186).

Cocoi Heron
Ardea cocoi (**Ardeidae**) 102–30 cm/40–51 in.
Large, slender, long-necked heron. Crown black, rest of head, neck and upper breast white with some fine black streaking on front of neck. Upperparts whitish with blackish flight feathers. Belly black with white thighs. Immature browner above with underparts largely white. Usually solitary. Stands motionless beside shallow water, but wary. Often seen perched in trees. Flight slow and heavy. Call a croak. **Range and habitat:** NT, from Panama southward, mainly in lowlands in marshes, lakes and rivers, also coastal sites. **Similar species:** Great Blue Heron (see p 52).

Boat-billed Heron
Cochlearius cochlearius (**Ardeidae**) 46–51 cm/18–20 in.
Small but thickset heron with enormously broad, shovel-like bill. Black on crown and crest, extending to upper back, but forehead and cheeks white. Rest of upperparts pale gray (Central American form is darker gray). Breast whitish (buffish in Central America) and belly rufous with blackish flanks. Immature has no crest and is rufous brown above and buffish white below. Deep croaking call. Feeds at night, leaving tree cover at dusk. Roosts in groups but probably feeds mainly alone. **Range and habitat:** NT, locally from Mexico to northern Argentina. In lowland freshwater marshes, lagoons and mangrove swamps. **Similar species:** Black-crowned Night-Heron (see p 52).

Maguari Stork
Ciconia maguari (**Ciconiidae**) 97–102 cm/38–40 in.
Large stork with straight gray bill tipped dark red. Long orange legs. Unfeathered loral region orange-red. Rest of plumage white apart from black lower back, tail, greater coverts and flight feathers. Pale iris. Juveniles black. Usually solitary or in small parties, sometimes with other species. Soaring flight. Largely silent apart from a double light whistle. **Range and habitat:** NT, mainly east of the Andes from Guianas to southern Argentina and Chile. Lowlands in open country. **Similar species:** Wood Stork (see p 54), King Vulture (see p 102).

Jabiru
Jabiru mycteria (**Ciconiidae**) 122–40 cm/48–55 in.
Very large stork with heavy, slightly upturned black bill and long black legs. Head and neck bare black skin apart from tuft of white feathers on crown and reddish region of skin on lower neck. Rest of plumage white. Immature mainly grayish. Individuals wander widely, but large congregations also occur. Prey is captured by stalking. Silent apart from bill-clappering at nest. **Range and habitat:** NT, southern Mexico to northern Argentina. Local. Mainly occurs in open lowland wetlands. Individuals wander to coastal estuaries and large rivers.

Sharp-tailed Ibis
Cercibis oxycerca (**Threskiornithidae**) 71–81 cm/28–32 in.
Large stocky ibis with long, decurved dusky bill. Bare skin of lores and around eye is red. Orange bare skin on throat. Forehead and malar region pale gray. Rest of plumage blackish, glossy green. Thick-necked appearance from tuft of feathers running down hindneck. Proportionately long tail. Short reddish legs. Usually solitary or in small groups. Tends to fly just short distances. Call a loud double-noted nasal "tur-dee." **Range and habitat:** NT, lowland areas east of Andes from Guyana south to south-west Brazil. Open wet areas, including ricefields. **Similar species:** Green Ibis. **Not illustrated.**

Green Ibis
Mesembrinibis cayennensis (**Threskiornithidae**) 56 cm/22 in.
All-dark glossy green ibis, with greenish bill and short legs. Dark gray bare facial skin. Rather thick-necked appearance from feather tufts on hindneck. Immature is much duller. Usually solitary or in pairs. Wary, feeds on muddy patches on forest floor or edge of open water. Frequently perches in trees. Flight is stiff and jerky. Calls mainly at dusk and before dawn, often in flight, with loud, rolling, fluty "clu-clu-clu" repeated several times. **Range and habitat:** NT, Honduras to northern Argentina. Occurs in forested areas close to rivers, gallery forest and swamps. Infrequent in open marshes. **Similar species:** Whispering and Glossy Ibises.

Scarlet Ibis
Eudocimus ruber (**Threskiornithidae**) 56–61 cm/22–4 in.
Adult has bare parts reddish (or bill black when breeding) and plumage entirely scarlet apart from black wing tips. Immature grayish brown upperparts with white rump and underparts, tinged pink with age, and whitish brown head and neck. Often in large, spectacular flocks, sometimes mixed with other species. Call a high-pitched, plaintive "tior-tior," given mainly at nest or roost sites. **Range and habitat:** NT, lowlands of Colombia east to Guianas, including Trinidad, south to eastern Brazil. Wanders into Central America and West Indies. Marshes, ricefields, and mangroves. **Similar species:** immature very similar to White Ibis.

White-faced Ibis
Plegadis chihi (**Threskiornithidae**) 56 cm/22 in.
Adult has reddish bill and brownish legs. Bare facial skin usually reddish, bordered by white feathers during breeding season. Rest of plumage chestnut with glossy greenish tone on upperparts when breeding. Outside breeding season, much duller with fine whitish streaking on head and neck. Red iris of adult is diagnostic. Immature has brownish eye, grayish brown bill and legs, and dull dark gray-brown plumage with greenish tone on wing. Usually solitary or in small groups. Flight is strong with periods of gliding between flaps. Normally silent. **Range and habitat:** NA and NT, USA to central Mexico, wintering southward to El Salvador. Locally in South America south to central Argentina. Mainly freshwater marshes and flooded areas. **Similar species:** Glossy Ibis.

Stripe-backed Bittern

Rufescent Tiger-Heron

Capped Heron

Cocoi Heron

Boat-billed Heron

Maguari Stork

Jabiru

Scarlet Ibis

Green Ibis

White-faced Ibis

WATERFOWL Anseriformes

Horned Screamer

Anhima cornuta (**Anhimidae**) 86–94 cm/34–7 in.
Huge, turkeylike bird. When perched, appears largely glossy black with white belly and white scaling on head and neck. At close quarters, horny quill visible on forehead. In flight, note large white patch on upperwing-coverts. Feeds on marsh vegetation, but spends a lot of time perched on top of bushes or even tall trees. Flies powerfully and adeptly, sometimes gliding at great height. Call an extraordinary loud deep braying sound. **Range and habitat:** NT, Venezuela south to central Brazil. Typical bird of swampy and lakeside vegetation of Amazon basin, locally elsewhere. **Similar species:** 2 other screamers.

Flying Steamerduck

Tachyeres patachonicus (**Anatidae**) 66–71 cm/26–8 in.
Large stocky duck. Plumage variable but generally mottled black and gray body with white belly and vent. Head of male is usually whitish in breeding season, variable but often mainly brownish afterward and grayish brown with narrow white "spectacle" during rest of year. Bill is orange during breeding season, but otherwise grayish. Female also shows great variation, but head generally shows some rufous on cheeks and white "spectacle." Broad white speculum on wing. Unlike other steamer ducks, can fly although some individuals and populations may do so only rarely, if at all. **Range and habitat:** NT, southern tip of South America and Falklands. Occurs both along coast and on lakes and rivers. Tends to leave inland sites during winter. **Similar species:** 3 other steamer ducks.

Muscovy Duck

Cairina moschata (**Anatidae**) 66–84 cm/26–33 in.
Large stocky duck, ancestor to familiar domestic bird. All-black plumage, rather glossy on upperparts, apart from white upper and lower wing-coverts which are striking in flight views. Female is smaller version of male. Immature is duller and lacks white wing markings. Shy bird, normally solitary or in small groups, which feeds in shallow water or at water's edge. Frequently perches on trees and usually nests in tree-holes. Generally silent, apart from quiet hisses or quacks. **Range and habitat:** NT, Mexico to northern Argentina. Lowland freshwater marshes, rivers, and lakes, in forested areas.

Torrent Duck

Merganetta armata (**Anatidae**) 46 cm/18 in.
Small, stream-lined duck with long tail. Male has striking black and white striped head pattern. Upperparts dark, finely barred. Elongate black-centerd feathers on scapular and mantle. Speculum green with narrow white leading and trailing edge. Underparts variable according to geographical race. Female bluish gray above, cinnamon below. Juveniles grayish, paler below with barring on flanks. Usually in pairs or family groups. Agile swimmer and diver in fast-flowing water. Call a loud, shrill "wheet." **Range and habitat:** NT, fast-flowing rivers along entire Andean chain. Some altitudinal migration, although generally resident.

Chiloe Wigeon

Anas sibilatrix (**Anatidae**) 43–54 cm/17–21 in.
Medium-sized grazing and dabbling duck. Plumage of both sexes very similar. Dark, glossy greenish black head with extensive white area on face and smaller spot behind and below eye. Scaly breast, rufous flanks, and pale fringed dark scapulars. In flight, note white greater coverts and glossy greenish black speculum. Rump white and tail black. Pale underwing and white belly. Immature is much duller. Usually in small flocks and very vocal, producing whistling notes. **Range and habitat:** NT, Argentina, southern Chile and Falklands. Common in freshwater lakes and marshes. Molt migration may occur and populations migrate northward in austral winter.

Silver Teal

Anas versicolor (**Anatidae**) 38–43 cm/15–17 in.
Small dabbling duck. Both sexes have similar plumage. Bill rather large and bluish with yellow at base, crown dark and creamy sides of head. Rest of body feathers dark with pale fringes, giving spotted effect on breast and barring on flanks. Vermiculated rump. Greenish speculum bordered by white. Andean race is larger and paler. Usually in small groups. Generally quiet, calls include whistles and quacks. **Range and habitat:** NT; breeds in southern South America, moving northward into Brazil in winter. Fairly common in freshwater marshes and lakes with fringing vegetation. Andean race occurs in high altitude lakes in southern Bolivia southward.

Masked Duck

Nomonyx dominica (**Anatidae**) 30–35 cm/12–14 in.
Small, stiff-tailed duck with bluish bill, dark at tip. Male has black face and crown which contrasts with rufous chestnut nape and breast. Rest of body mottled black and chestnut. Female has distinctive head pattern with dark crown and whitish cheeks crossed by 2 dark lines. Male eclipse plumage similar to female. In flight, white panel on wing of both sexes is diagnostic. Usually in pairs or small groups. **Range and habitat:** NT, thinly distributed from southern Texas to central Argentina. Mainly east of Andes. Occurs in marshes and small pools with floating vegetation. **Similar species:** Ruddy Duck (see p 56).

DIURNAL BIRDS OF PREY Falconiformes

Lesser Yellow-headed Vulture

Cathartes burrovianus (**Cathartidae**) 58–66 cm/23–6 in.
Medium-sized vulture with bare yellow head and blackish plumage. Flight feathers are slightly paler than rest of wing, giving 2-toned appearance. Quills of outer primaries are whitish, producing pale panel on upperwing surface. Flies in buoyant manner, normally at low height over open country, rarely in groups. **Range and habitat:** NT, Mexico to northern Argentina. Common in lowland savannah and other open terrain. May show seasonal movements. **Similar species:** Greater Yellow-headed and Turkey Vultures (see p 58).

King Vulture

Sarcoramphus papa (**Cathartidae**) 71–81 cm/28–32 in.
Large with 2 m (6½ ft) wingspan. Adult is white with black flight feathers, tail and rump. Unfeathered head and neck brightly colored. Ruff grayish. Immatures dark brown, increasingly white with age on wing-linings and body. Broad wings and very short, square-ended tail. Soars steadily, often at great height and rarely with other species. **Range and habitat:** NT, southern Mexico to northern Argentina. Widely distributed in tropical forest zones. **Similar species:** Wood and Maguari Storks (see pp 54, 100).

Andean Condor

Vultur gryphus (**Cathartidae**) 102–30 cm/40–51 in.
Very large with 3 m (10 ft) wingspan. Black plumage with most of upperwing surface bright white. White ruff and reddish unfeathered head. Immature dark dull brown. Soaring flight with wings flattened, tips of primaries spread and upward-pointing, from cliff sides to great heights. Normally silent. Groups may congregate at carcasses. **Range and habitat:** NT, from Venezuela to Tierra del Fuego along Andes. In north of range, very localized and mainly above 3,000 m (9,850 ft), occurs at lower elevations in south. Near-threatened from human persecution..

Horned Screamer

Flying Steamerduck

Muscovy Duck
(domestic bird with
white breast)

Chiloe Wigeon

Silver Teal

Torrent Duck

Masked Duck

King Vulture

Lesser Yellow-headed
Vulture

Andean Condor

Hook-billed Kite

Chondrohierax uncinatus (Accipitridae) 41–6 cm/16–18 in.
Confiding raptor usually seen perched. Hooked bill, greenish cere, bare skin in front of whitish eye. Males usually gray above, barred below, 2 broad pale bands on tail. Female usually brown above with rufous collar and barred rufous below. There is a melanistic form. Rather long-winged and long-tailed in flight, barred flight feathers visible from below. Generally perches below canopy. Call a musical whistle. Diet mainly snails. **Range and habitat:** NT, Mexico to northern Argentina. Lowland humid forest and wooded marshy areas. **Similar species:** several, including Gray Hawk.

Swallow-tailed Kite

Elanoides forficatus (Accipitridae) 56–66 cm/22–6 in.
Graceful, elegant raptor with deeply forked tail and pointed wings. White apart from black flight feathers, tail, uppersurface of wings and back. Usually in small groups, feeding on flying insects or small animals from canopy. Call a high-pitched "klee-klee-klee," but normally silent. **Range and habitat:** NT and NA, from southern USA to northern Argentina. Northern populations migratory. Mainly lowlands and foothills, usually over forest.

Plumbeous Kite

Ictinia plumbea (Accipitridae) 36 cm/14 in.
Small long-winged raptor. Almost wholly dark gray with rufous patch on base of primaries and 2 or 3 narrow white bands at base of tail, which are difficult to see. Immature paler, with streaks below. Perches on bare branches at treetops, wings extending beyond tip of tail. Often in groups, sometimes in large flocks during migration. Catches insects and other small animals in air or from canopy. **Range and habitat:** NT, Mexico to northern Argentina. Central American populations mainly migratory. Common in tropical and subtropical zones in wide range of habitats from forest to open, wooded areas. **Similar species:** Mississippi Kite.

White Hawk

Leucopternis albicollis (Accipitridae) 46–56 cm/18–22 in.
Distinctive raptor with underparts entirely white, black wing tips and band across tail. Amount of black on upperwing and back variable according to race. Wings and tail rather broad. Usually solitary, soars low over canopy but most frequently encountered perched below canopy. Diet consists of snakes and other reptiles. Call a hoarse "ker-wee." **Range and habitat:** NT, southern Mexico to central Brazil. Widespread but generally uncommon in lowland forest. **Similar species:** Black-faced Hawk.

Savanna Hawk

Buteogallus meridionalis (Accipitridae) 46–61 cm/18–24 in.
Medium-sized raptor with very long wings and short tail. At rest appears almost uniformly rufous with rather faint dusky bars. In flight, grayish toned back contrasts with rich brown head and wings, latter with a bold black trailing edge. Black tail has white tip and median band. Immature is browner with buff mottling. Conspicuous bird which hunts from a perch or whilst soaring. Groups gather at grass fires or follow agricultural activities. **Range and habitat:** NT, Panama to northern Argentina. Common in open country, ranchland, sometimes along seashore. **Similar species:** Black-collared Hawk.

Roadside Hawk

Buteo magnirostris (Accipitridae) 33–8 cm/13–15 in.
Common raptor. Prominent yellow cere and eyes. Gray head, upperparts and chest. Rest of underparts barred brown and white. In flight, rufous base to primaries contrasts with rest of gray upperwing. Immatures brown above, buffy below with some streaking on breast. Rather short-winged, most often seen perched on exposed branches or posts. Flies sluggishly, with glides interspersed with flaps. Call a loud, drawn-out mew. **Range and habitat:** NT, Mexico to central Argentina. Widespread in forest edge and open habitats in lowlands and mid-elevations. **Similar species:** Broad-winged Hawk (see p 58), Gray Hawk.

Crested Eagle

Morphnus guianensis (Accipitridae) 79–89 cm/31–5 in.
Large, slim eagle with small crest. 2 plumage phases. Pale phase has pale gray head, neck and breast, dark lores, white belly, dark brown above and long tail with 3 pale bands. Underwing whitish with flight feathers barred. Dark phase has head, neck and breast dark gray, rest of underparts and wing-linings barred black and white. Like most large raptors, spends most of day perched. Call a high-pitched whistle, sometimes disyllabic. **Range and habitat:** NT, central America to northern Argentina. Rare and poorly known lowland forest species. Near-threatened from deforestation and hunting. **Similar species:** Harpy Eagle.

Harpy Eagle

Harpia harpyja (Accipitridae) 89–102 cm/35–40 in.
Huge with black, forked crest, gray head and powerful bill. Black chest band and white underparts with barred thighs. Upperparts blackish, slightly scaled with gray. 3 gray bands on black tail. Underwing barred. Immatures lack dark chest band. Rarely soars above canopy, normally hunts within cover, twisting and turning between trees to take monkeys and other large prey by surprise. Call a drawn-out wail. **Range and habitat:** NT, southern Mexico to northern Argentina. Rare forest species, mainly restricted to lowland area, requiring large tracts of suitable habitat. Near-threatened from deforestation and hunting. **Similar species:** Guiana Crested Eagle.

Ornate Hawk-Eagle

Spizaetus ornatus (Accipitridae) 58–64 cm/23–5 in.
Hawk eagles have rather oval-shaped wings and longish tails. Adult Ornate has black crown and crest, chestnut sides of head and breast, bordered anteriorly by narrow black margin to white throat. Upperparts blackish, underparts barred. Tail has 3 gray bands. Underwings show barred flight feathers and spotted wing-linings. Immature is white on head and underparts. Does not usually soar at great height, tending to capture prey on short flights from subcanopy perch. Call a loud series of whistles. **Range and habitat:** NT, Mexico to northern Argentina. Uncommon in humid forest, mainly in lowlands. **Similar species:** Gray-bellied Goshawk.

Black Caracara

Daptrius ater (Falconidae) 43–8 cm/17–19 in.
Slim, long-winged all-black raptor with white base of tail and conspicuous extensive bare orange skin on face. Yellow legs. Immature is duller with barred underparts and tail. Often in small groups, perched on exposed branches or on ground beside rivers in forested areas. Flies rapidly and directly. Call an eerie, rather hoarse, scream. **Range and habitat:** NT, Venezuela to central Brazil. Lowland forest, particularly along watercourses. **Similar species:** Red-throated Caracara.

Southern Caracara

Caracara plancus (Falconidae) 51–61 cm/20–4 in.
Large caracara with powerful bill. Red cere and bare facial skin. Black crown and bushy crest. Rest of head and neck white. Breast barred with rest of underparts black. Upperparts dark with barring on back and pale patches on outer primaries. Pale rump and lightly barred tail with subterminal band. Often in pairs or family groups walking on ground, hunting for carrion or small prey. Flight is direct, rarely soars. Call a harsh cackle. **Range and habitat:** NT and NA, Brazil and Chile southward. Open country in lowlands and mid-elevations. **Similar species:** Crested Caracara.

Yellow-headed Caracara

Milvago chimachima (Falconidae) 41–6 cm/16–18 in.
Slender-looking caracara with small pale bill. Creamy body plumage apart from brownish back and narrow line behind eye. Wings brown with pale patch on outer primaries. Pale rump and lightly barred tail with subterminal band. Immature shows some streaking on head and underparts. Usually solitary or in pairs, walking on ground or perched on exposed situations. Quarters ground with slow, deliberate flight and short glides. Call a long, harsh hiss. **Range and habitat:** NT, Central America to northern Argentina. Common in lowland and mid-elevation open country and beside large rivers.

Hook-billed Kite

Swallow-tailed Kite

Plumbeous Kite (immature)

White Hawk

Savanna Hawk

Roadside Hawk

Black Caracara

Harpy Eagle

Ornate Hawk-Eagle

Crested Eagle

Southern Caracara

Yellow-headed Caracara

Laughing Falcon

Herpetotheres cachinnans (Falconidae) 46–56 cm/18–22 in.
Medium-sized raptor with large head and long tail. Very distinctive appearance with creamy head and underparts contrasting with bold dark "bandit" mask and upperparts. Tail banded. Usually seen perched in exposed branches, often at top of isolated tree. Flies with series of wingbeats and glides, directly but slowly. Typical call a loud "gua-co" repeated endlessly, often in duet, and especially after sunset. **Range and habitat:** NT, Mexico to northern Argentina. Mainly a lowland species in wooded areas and forest edges.

Lined Forest-Falcon

Micrastur gilvicollis (Falconidae) 30–6 cm/12–14 in.
Forest falcons are typically short-winged, long-legged raptors which are agile hunters of small birds within forests. Lined Forest Falcon has orange cere, bare facial skin, yellow legs and whitish eyes. Upperparts are dark gray, underparts white with fine black barring. Black tail has 2 narrow white bands and white tip. Immatures are brown above. Call is loud 2-note bark. **Range and habitat:** NT, Amazonia. Uncommon in lowland tropical forest. **Similar species:** Barred and Slaty-backed Forest-Falcons.

Bat Falcon

Falco rufigularis (Falconidae) 23–30 cm/9–12 in.
Small falcon. Appearing very dark with blackish hood and upperparts. Creamy throat extends along base of cheeks. Underparts black with fine white bars, rusty thighs, and vent. Often in pairs, seen perched on exposed branches on tops of trees. Dashing flight with rapid wingbeats, dives, and occasional soars, catching insects, small birds, and bats on wing. Somewhat crepuscular. Call a high-pitched "ki-ki-ki-ki-ki." **Range and habitat:** NT, Mexico to northern Argentina. Mainly a lowland species in forest borders and wooded areas. **Similar species:** Orange-breasted and Aplomado Falcons.

Aplomado Falcon

Falco femoralis (Falconidae) 36–43 cm/14–17 in.
Rather slim-built, long-tailed falcon. General plumage tone pale, with gray upperparts, creamy ring around head, dark moustachial stripe. Creamy cheeks and breast, finely barred blackish underparts and pale rusty thighs. Tail is barred. Immature is browner and streaked below. Usually solitary. Tends to use low perches, sometimes hovers but normally catches prey in fast sallies, often attracted to bush fires. **Range and habitat:** NT and NA, southern USA to Tierra del Fuego. Mainly in dry open country at low elevations. **Similar species:** Bat and Orange-breasted Falcons.

FOWL-LIKE BIRDS Galliformes

Speckled Chachalaca

Ortalis guttata (Cracidae) 53 cm/21 in.
Rather small, slim and long-tailed cracid. A variable species, generally brownish above, paler below with a speckled breast. Tail dark brown with chestnut outer tail feathers. Head and neck brown or grayish depending on race. Reddish bare malar region and gray bare skin around eye. Noisy bird, usually encountered in small groups in canopy beside small clearings and in secondary vegetation. **Range and habitat:** NT, Western Amazonia. Mainly a lowland species of forest edges and woodland. **Similar species:** Andean Guan.

Andean Guan

Penelope montagnii (Cracidae) 61 cm/24 in.
Rather short-tailed guan with bare red skin on chin inconspicuous. Plumage generally warm brown, although head and breast grayer with fine whitish markings. Usually in small groups. Timid bird normally keeping to tops of trees but may move into more open situations to find fruit. Produces a honking call and a mechanical rattle with its wings during display flights. **Range and habitat:** NT, along Andean chain from Venezuela to Argentina, in highland forest. **Similar species:** Band-tailed Guan, Speckled (Variable) Chachalaca.

Spix's Guan

Penelope jacquacu (Cracidae) 89 cm/35 in.
Large guan with ample flap of red bare skin on chin. Overall has dark plumage tone, glossed green on wings and tail, brown edged with white on head and breast, warmer brown on belly. Usually in pairs. Shy bird which normally stays close to canopy, occasionally coming to lower levels, and making a loud deep trumpeting when disturbed. Like other guans, produces mechanical wing rattle during displays. **Range and habitat:** NT, basins of Amazon and Orinoco rivers. Lowland forest, gallery forest and wooded areas. **Similar species:** Crested Guan.

Blue-throated Piping Guan

Pipile cumanensis (Cracidae) 69 cm/27 in.
Very distinctive cracid with bluish bare skin on chin and normally paler skin around face, bushy white crest and bold white patches on wing. Otherwise plumage wholly blackish. Usually in small groups, moving through treetops, often perched in open. Produces series of whistling notes and wing rattles during displays. **Range and habitat:** NT, Venezuela to Peru. Lowland humid forest.

Black Guan

Chamaepetes unicolor (Cracidae) 64 cm/25 in.
All-glossy black guan, duller below, with red legs and blue bare facial skin. Usually in pairs or family groups, normally in trees but sometimes coming to ground to feed on fallen fruit. Has harsh alarm call and also produces whistling notes and wing rattles during display. Like other guans, flies with series of flaps followed by glide. **Range and habitat:** NT, Central America. Occurs in high-elevation cloud forest and in patchy forest where not hunted. Near-threatened from deforestation and hunting..

Razor-billed Curassow

Crax tuberosa (Cracidae) 89 cm/35 in.
Large, stocky bird with long tail. Plumage mainly glossy black with belly and vent chestnut and tail broadly tipped white. Black crest and heavy red bill with greatly enlarged upper mandible, forming upward keel. Sexes alike. Normally recorded in small groups, on ground, but flying to trees if disturbed. Produces a humming song from a perch. **Range and habitat:** NT, Amazon basin in lowland forest. **Similar species:** Wattled, Salvin's and Lesser Razor-billed Curassows.

Great Curassow

Crax rubra (Cracidae) 91 cm/36 in.
Both sexes have curly crest, but male is black apart from yellow swollen base to bill and white belly and vent, whereas female is generally chestnut-brown with barred wings and tail and closely barred black and white head. However, female plumage is variable and can be much darker. Both sexes have grayish legs. Usually alone or in pairs and seen on ground. Normally runs off rather than flies if disturbed. Alarm calls include a high-pitched whistle. Males produce a deep humming song. **Range and habitat:** NT, Mexico to Ecuador. Humid lowland forest. Near-threatened by habitat loss and hunting. **Similar species:** Blue-billed Curassow.

Red-billed Curassow

Crax blumenbachii (Cracidae) 89 cm/35 in.
Another crested curassow. Males have red base to bill, swollen to produce small knob and 2 wattles. Plumage glossy black, white belly and vent in males, chestnut in females. Females have white barring on crest and rufous mottling on wings. Usually in pairs, feeding in fruiting trees or shrubs or on fallen fruit on ground, fly to mid-level branches if disturbed. Male produces deep, far-carrying booming call. **Range and habitat:** NT, southeastern Brazil. Extremely rare in lowland primary forest. Endangered due to hunting and forest destruction.. **Similar species:** Wattled Curassow.

Laughing Falcon

Lined Forest Falcon

Bat Falcon

Aplomado Falcon
(male and female)

Speckled Chachalaca

Andean Guan

Spix's Guan

Blue-throated Piping Guan

Black Guan

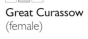

Razor-billed Curassow

Great Curassow
(female)

Red-billed Curassow

Crested Bobwhite

Colinus cristatus (Odontophoridae) 20–3 cm/8–9 in.
Common small terrestrial bird, both sexes with crest. Male has pale buff crest and head with darker crown and line behind eye. Upperparts vermiculated dark brown and black. Underparts heavily spotted white. Female duller. Usually in pairs or small groups, tending to run if alarmed or fly a short distance into cover. Often seen on roadsides. Call a rapid "bob-bob-wheet," frequently heard. **Range and habitat:** NT, Central America to northern Brazil. Quite common, except at high elevations, in dry open country. **Similar species:** Northern Bobwhite (see p 60).

Starred Wood-Quail

Odontophorus stellatus (Odontophoridae) 24 cm/9½ in.
Dumpy, terrestrial bird with conspicuous crest. Crown and crest bright chestnut. Upperparts grayish with lower back more olive-brown. Dark brown wings, spotted buff on wing-coverts. Throat gray, rest of underparts rufous with black barring on vent. Bare red skin around eye. Female has blackish brown crest. Groups walk in single file, scattering or "freezing" if alarmed, only reluctantly flying. Call a far-carrying, rhythmic, rollicking chorus. **Range and habitat:** NT, western Amazonia. Lowland humid forest. **Similar species:** Marbled Wood-Quail. **Not illustrated.**

CRANES. RAILS AND ALLIES Gruiformes

Gray-winged Trumpeter

Psophia crepitans (Psophiidae) 48–56 cm/19–22 in.
Shy, ground-dwelling bird with hunched appearance. Plumage blackish with long pale gray feathers covering back. Normally in groups, extremely wary, giving soft humming notes or harsh calls in alarm. Kept by forest Indians as "guard dogs." **Range and habitat:** NT, lowland Amazonian forest. **Similar species:** Pale-winged Trumpeter.

Gray-necked Wood-Rail

Aramides cajanea (Rallidae) 36–8 cm/14–15 in.
Large rail, frequently heard. Rather powerful yellow bill, red eye and long red legs. Head and neck gray. Upperparts olive-brown, rump, tail and vent black. Breast and flanks rufous. Rufous primaries visible in flight. Generally solitary but forms noisy duets at dusk with loud cackling calls. Usually on ground but sometimes climbs into shrubs. **Range and habitat:** NT, Mexico to northern Argentina. Low to mid-elevations in forest and woodland close to water, including mangroves. **Similar species:** Rufous-necked and Brown Wood Rails.

Blackish Rail

Pardirallus nigricans (Rallidae) 28 cm/11 in.
Medium-sized rail with long yellowish bill and red legs. Rather plain plumage, dark gray below and brown-toned above. Whitish chin and black undertail-coverts and tail. Immature is browner. Shows typical rallid behavior, generally keeping under cover in dense vegetation, rarely venturing out to edge of patches of open ground and flying just short distances. Gives short metallic call and mew. **Range and habitat:** NT, patchy distribution from Venezuela to northern Argentina in tropical and subtropical zones. Uncommon in freshwater marshes and in damp vegetation. **Similar species:** Plumbeous Rail.

Gray-breasted Crake

Laterallus exilis (Rallidae) 15 cm/6 in.
Tiny crake with gray bill, bright greenish at base. Head and foreparts grayish, darker on crown, with conspicuous rufous nape. Belly whitish with bold blackish bars on flanks. Upperparts dark brown with pale barring on wing-coverts and rump. Immatures lack rufous on nape. Denizen of dense, wet grassy vegetation. Very difficult to flush, keeping to tunnel-like runs on ground. Has trilling call and series of repeated "keek" notes. **Range and habitat:** NT, Central America to Paraguay. Uncommon in wet grassland. **Similar species:** Paint-billed Crake.

Red-gartered Coot

Fulica armillata (Rallidae) 44 cm/17 in.
Medium-sized coot with angled profile of head from bill-tip to top of shield. Shield and bill yellowish with red on base of culmen. Legs orange with red "garter." Plumage dark gray with 2 white patches on undertail. Usually in groups, but territorial when breeding.

Feeds by up-ending or diving. Several call-notes including short whistles and clicks. **Range and habitat:** NT, southern Argentina and Chile, migrating to southern Brazil. Common in lowlands and mid-elevations in marshland and shallow lakes. **Similar species:** several coots.

Giant Coot

Fulica gigantea (Rallidae) 55 cm/22 in.
Huge, stocky coot with black knobs on forehead protruding either side of yellow shield. Bill mainly red with yellow sides and white culmen. Legs red. Plumage blackish gray with very indistinct white streaks on undertail. Immature is grayer below with duller bare parts. Usually in family groups; territorial disputes can be seen frequently. Adults practically flightless because of huge bulk. Calls a range of loud growls and gobbling sounds. **Range and habitat:** NT, Peru, Bolivia and Chile. High altitude lakes with extensive areas of waterplants.

Sungrebe

Heliornis fulica (Heliornithidae) 30 cm/12 in.
Small, shy bird with black and white striped head and neck and reddish bill. Male has white cheek, female buff. Rest of upperparts olive-brown. Tail tipped white, underparts whitish. Swims low in water, close to well-vegetated banks and in inundated forest. Flies short distances, low over water, when disturbed. Call a series of loud, barking honks. **Range and habitat:** NT, from southern Mexico to northern Argentina in tropical lowlands on slow-flowing rivers, flooded forest and small areas of freshwater. **Similar species:** ducks, grebes, Peter's Finfoot (see p 198).

Sunbittern

Eurypyga helias (Eurypgidae) 48 cm/19 in.
Slender, long-bodied bird with disproportionately small black and white striped head. Upperparts closely barred black, brown and gray. Vermiculated breast, rest of underparts pale buff, becoming whiter on belly. Vermiculated tail also boldly barred brown. Flight reveals bright orange patches on wings, also shown during elaborate dancing display. Moves slowly and elegantly on ground. Flies to nearby branch if disturbed. Call a high whistle which rises and falls slightly in pitch. **Range and habitat:** NT, from southern Mexico to northern Argentina in tropical lowlands, in forests close to water.

Red-legged Seriema

Cariama cristata (Cariamidae) 69 cm/27 in.
Large terrestrial bird with long red legs and raptorlike head and frontal crest. Finely vermiculated plumage is grayish-brown, with black and white barring on primaries and tail. Paler underparts are lightly streaked. Hunts various prey, including snakes, on ground and tends to run rather than fly if alarmed. Nest is placed on top of small bushes. Often give away presence by their loud call. **Range and habitat:** NT, central Brazil to northern Argentina. Lowland grassy plains with scattered bushes. **Similar species:** Black-legged Seriema.

Crested Bobwhite

Gray-winged Trumpeter

Gray-necked Wood-Rail

Blackish Rail

Gray-breasted Crake

Red-gartered Coot

Giant Coot (on nest)

Sungrebe

Sunbittern

Red-legged Seriema

SHOREBIRDS, GULLS, AUKS Charadriiformes

Wattled Jacana
Jacana jacana (Jacanidae) 25 cm/10 in.
Long-legged with very long toes. Bill yellow with red basal lobes. Adult black with dark brown back and wings with yellow flight feathers. Immature white below, brown above with blackish crown, eye stripe and long white supercilium. Wades in damp vegetation or walks on floating waterplants. Noisy with loud "kee-kick" call. **Range and habitat:** NT, common in lowlands from Panama to northern Argentina, mainly east of Andes in southern part of range. Freshwater marshes, lakes, and slow-flowing rivers. **Similar species:** other jacanas (see pp 198, 248, 294).

Double-striped Thick-Knee
Burhinus bistriatus (Burhinidae) 46 cm/18 in.
Large thick-knee with white supercilium bordered black above. Large yellow eye and long yellow legs. Plumage generally brownish with paler feather edgings, giving streaked effect, and white belly. Flight feathers dark with broken white wing-bar. Spends most of day resting, active at dusk and at night. Usually solitary or in small groups. Call a rapid chattering. **Range and habitat:** NT, Central America and northern South America. Fairly common in dry open country. **Similar species:** other thick-knees (see pp 160, 198, 294).

Southern Lapwing
Vanellus chilensis (Charadriidae) 36 cm/14 in.
Large wader with black-tipped red bill and red legs. Gray head with black on face, bordered behind and above by white, extending to throat and breast. Rest of underparts white. Back brownish with bronzy shoulders. White rump and black subterminal tail band. Flight feathers black and long white wing patch. Rather slow flight. Usually in singles or small groups. Very vocal, usual call is loud "keek-keek-keek." **Range and habitat:** NT, common throughout South America, although largely absent from Amazonia, western Colombia, Ecuador and Peru. Open short grassland. **Similar species:** Andean Lapwing.

Collared Plover
Charadrius collaris (Charadriidae) 15 cm/6 in.
Small dainty wader with dark bill and pale yellowish legs. Black lores and bar across crown. White forehead, patch behind eye and underparts, apart from black breast band. Chestnut hindcrown and nape. Upperparts gray-brown. In flight shows narrow white wing-bar and white tail edges. Usually single or in pairs. Gives short "cheet" call but generally silent. **Range and habitat:** NT, Mexico southward to northern Argentina. Beside large rivers, beaches, and fields. **Similar species:** Semipalmated and Snowy Plovers (see p 62).

Tawny-throated Dotterel
Oreopholus ruficollis (Charadriidae) 27 cm/10½ in.
Large plover with long, thin bill. Sides of face pale buff with narrow black line through eye. Dark crown. Neck and breast brownish gray. Throat orange-buff. Upper belly and flanks buff, black belly patch and rest of underparts white. Upperparts streaked brown and rufous. Narrow white bar on primaries. Forms flocks outside breeding season. Flight call a descending, tremulous note. **Range and habitat:** NT, Andes from Peru southward and southern Argentina. High grasslands, arid zones, coastal areas in Peru. Some altitudinal migration and movement of southern birds northward during austral winter. **Similar species:** American Golden Plover (see p 62), Dotterel (see p 156).

Giant Snipe
Gallinago undulata (Scolopacidae) 40 cm/16 in.
Very large snipe with rounded wings. Plumage similar to other snipes but markings more blackish than brown. Rich brown edgings on scapular and mantle feathers. Rump and uppertail cinnamon with fine dark bars. Unique among snipes in having barred flight feathers, but this is barely visible in field. Gives harsh "kek-kek" when flushed. Display calls, probably only given at night, include a buzzing call and guttural "HO-go go." Very poorly known species. **Range and habitat:** NT, 2 distinct populations: Colombia and northern Brazil, and southern Brazil and Paraguay. Lowland grassland. **Similar species:** several snipes (see pp 110, 160, 202, 250). Not illustrated.

Least Seedsnipe
Thinocorus rumicivorus (Thinocoridae) 17 cm/6½ in.
Small, dumpy bird. Males have gray faces, necks, and breasts. White chin bordered by black, and black line runs down center of breast to black border between breast and white underparts. Upperparts cryptically patterned buff and dark brown. Narrow white wing-bar and trailing edge. Females streaked brownish on head and breast. Ground-dwelling bird, often in large flocks. Gives a short harsh note when flushed. Song an endlessly repeated but variable series of notes, given either in flight or from perch. **Range and habitat:** NT, southern South America and coastal southern Ecuador to northern Chile. Southernmost populations migrate north in austral winter. Sandy areas with scattered vegetation at low elevations. **Similar species:** Gray-breasted Seedsnipe.

Brown-hooded Gull
Larus maculipennis (Laridae) 36–8 cm/14–15 in.
Small gull with chocolate-brown hood, replaced by dusky patches behind eye and on crown in winter. Bill and legs red. Upperwing pale gray, outer primaries white, with some black on outer web. Immatures have complex upperwing pattern and dark subterminal tail band. Rather long, narrow wings; flies with rapid wingbeat. Gregarious, noisy bird with harsh high-pitched calls. **Range and habitat:** NT, southern South America, dispersal to coasts of Brazil and northern Chile in austral winter. Breeding colonies on coast and inland lakes and marshes. **Similar species:** Andean and Gray-headed Gulls (see p 202).

Swallow-tailed Gull
Creagrus furcatus (Laridae) 53–8 cm/21–3 in.
Distinctive gull with long wings and forked tail. Black bill, tipped yellow, and pink legs. Breeding adult has dark gray hood and white underparts. Striking upperwing pattern with black outer primaries contrasting with white triangle on hindwing and gray forewing and mantle. Nonbreeders have white heads with dark eye patch. Mainly nocturnal feeder on squid and fish, often in large groups. Calls include a harsh scream and a rattle. **Range and habitat:** NT, breeds on the Galapagos and Malpelo Island. Pelagic wanderer throughout Humboldt current region, sometimes north to Panama. **Similar species:** Sabine's Gull.

Large-billed Tern
Phaetusa simplex (Sternidae) 38 cm/15 in.
Large tern with heavy yellow bill. Black crown and white underparts. Striking wing pattern with black primaries, white triangle formed across secondaries and gray tertials and forewing. Upperparts and shallowly forked tail gray. Outside breeding season, forehead is mottled white. Immatures brownish above. Seen singly or in small, dispersed groups. Breeds on sandbanks on large rivers. Noisy birds, giving a harsh "skee-er." **Range and habitat:** NT, rivers and lakes east of Andes.

South American Tern
Sterna hirundinacea (Sternidae) 40–4 cm/16–17 in.
Medium-sized tern with red bill and legs. Breeding adults have black crowns bordered by white, pale gray underparts, whiter on belly, gray upperparts and wing with outer web of outer primary black. Rump and forked tail white. Nonbreeders have whitish foreheads. Immatures have brownish tips to back and forewing with dusky wing tips. Usually in groups. Calls include high-pitched screech and metallic note. **Range and habitat:** NT, breeding colonies on coasts south from Peru and southern Brazil. Dispersal northward during austral winter. **Similar species:** Antarctic, Common and Arctic Terns (see pp 162, 296).

Inca Tern
Larosterna inca (Sternidae) 40–2 cm/16–17 in.
Striking graceful tern with blue-gray plumage, blacker on crown, with long white "moustache" and white trailing edge to wing, shallowly forked tail black. Large red bill with yellow base. Browner immature has shorter moustache. Like many Humboldt Current seabirds, huge flocks gather to feed, often in association with marine mammals. **Range and habitat:** NT, from Ecuador to Chile along Humboldt current. Rocky coastlines, beaches and harbours. Near-threatened by El Niño effects leading to food shortages.

Wattled Jacana

Southern Lapwing

Collared Plover

Double-striped Thick Knee

Brown-hooded Gull

Least Seedsnipe

Swallow-tailed Gull

Tawny-throated Dotterel

Large-billed Tern

South American Tern

Inca Tern

NEOTROPICAL

PIGEONS AND SANDGROUSE Columbiformes

Scaled Pigeon

Patagioenas speciosa (Columbidae) 30 cm/12 in.
Medium-sized pigeon with distinctive scaled pattern on neck, upper back and breast. Bill red, tipped white. Upperparts purplish chestnut, underparts buffy, becoming paler on lower belly and vent. Tail and wings blackish brown. A fruit-eater, normally seen singly or in pairs, frequently perches on high, exposed branches. Flight fast and direct. Call a short series of deep "whoo" calls. **Range and habitat:** NT, southern Mexico to northern Argentina. Fairly common in lowland forest and woodland. **Not illustrated.**

Ruddy Pigeon

Patagioenas subvinacea (Columbidae) 28 cm/11 in.
Small dark pigeon with black bill and reddish legs. Plumage generally dark reddish brown, slightly paler on head, neck and underparts. Wing-linings tinged cinnamon. Fruit-eater, normally seen alone or in pairs, perched close to canopy. Calls a far-carrying, 4-syllabled coo and a harsh growl. **Range and habitat:** NT, Costa Rica to central Brazil. Generally common in lowland forest. **Similar species:** Plumbeous and Short-billed Pigeons.

Ruddy Ground-Dove

Columbina talpacoti (Columbidae) 16.5 cm/6½ in.
Small, distinctive-looking dove. Male has gray cap, rufous upperparts, slightly paler below with whitish throat. Bold black spots on wing-coverts. Female quite different, with grayish brown upperparts, paler below, and rufous wings. Usually in pairs but groups aggregate on ground at rich sources of food. Call a soft double-noted hoot, repeated several times. **Range and habitat:** NT, southern Mexico to northern Argentina. Found mainly at low elevations, where common in secondary vegetation, cultivations, towns, and gardens. **Similar species:** Plain-breasted Ground-Dove.

Inca Dove

Columbina inca (Columbidae) 20 cm/8 in.
Small, mainly ground-dwelling dove with long tail. Sexes similar. Plumage generally pale gray with scaly pattern. Primaries rufous with dark tips, underwing mainly rufous. Outer tail feathers edged white. Immatures are browner. Rather tame, usually in pairs or small groups, feeding on seeds and spilt grain. Males give a double-noted coo, often rendered as "no-hope!," from exposed perches. **Range and habitat:** NT and NA, southern USA to Costa Rica. Common in open country, cultivated areas, farmyards, and gardens in lowland areas. **Similar species:** Scaly Dove.

Ruddy Quail-Dove

Geotrygon montana (Columbidae) 23 cm/9 in.
Small, plump, skulking dove. Bill, bare skin on lores and eye-ring red. Rufous brown above, with purplish gloss to hindneck and upper back. Cheeks and underparts pale cinnamon with rufous brown stripe across side of face. Female is darker with less pronounced facial pattern. Shy ground-dwelling bird, feeding on fallen fruit, but sometimes uses high perches. Call is soft coo, repeated after short pauses. **Range and habitat:** NT, Mexico to northern Argentina. Common in humid forest, secondary vegetation and plantations, mainly in lowlands. **Similar species:** Violaceous Quail Dove.

PARROTS AND RELATIVES Psittaciformes

Hyacinth Macaw

Anodorhynchus hyacinthinus (Psittacidae) 100 cm/39 in.
World's largest parrot. Rich cobalt-blue plumage, darker on flight feathers and underside of tail. Yellow bare skin on base of lower mandible and eye-ring. Bill grayish black. Perches on treetops, also descends to ground to collect fallen fruit. Usually in pairs or small groups. Impressive on the wing, flying high with long, streamerlike tail, constantly giving guttural contact calls. **Range and habitat:** NT, central Brazil and eastern Bolivia. Rare in lowland gallery forest, woodland, forest edge and palms. Endangered from illegal trade, hunting and habitat loss.. **Similar species:** Indigo and Glaucous Macaws.

Spix's Macaw

Cyanopsitta spixii (Psittacidae) 54 cm/21 in.
Small, beautiful macaw. Dark blue plumage with paler, grayer head

and neck, underparts tinged green. Blackish bare skin on lores and around yellow eye. Seen in pairs, formerly in small groups. Very timid, readily flies off in alarm, giving a sharp "kraa-ark" call. **Range and habitat:** NT, endemic to north-east Brazil in gallery woodland. Critically Endangered, possibly extinct in the wild.. Population probably declined with habitat loss, then exterminated by trapping.

Blue-and-yellow Macaw

Ara ararauna (Psittacidae) 84 cm/33 in.
Large, spectacular-looking macaw, bright blue above and yellow below. Bare white skin on face, lined with black and bordered below by black bar across chin. Usually in pairs, but sometimes in broken groups of 25 or more, flying strongly with slow wingbeats. Flight call a rather nasal "aaak." Flights generally made early morning and late afternoon, with birds spending most of day feeding quietly in canopy, when they can be remarkably inconspicuous. **Range and habitat:** NT, Panama to southern Brazil. Lowland forest and gallery woodland.

Scarlet Macaw

Ara macao (Psittacidae) 89 cm/35 in.
Large, gaudy macaw with bicolored bill and white bare facial skin. Scarlet body plumage, yellow greater coverts and deep blue flight feathers, rump, tail-coverts and outer tail feathers. Red inner tail. Usually in pairs or small groups, but may form larger flocks, sometimes with other species. Roosts communally. Flight call a loud, very harsh "raaaaaak." **Range and habitat:** NT, southern Mexico to eastern Brazil. Lowland forest and woodland. **Similar species:** Green-winged Macaw.

Dusky-headed Parakeet

Aratinga weddellii (Psittacidae) 28 cm/11 in.
Medium-sized parakeet with long tail. Plumage generally green with dull grayish head with conspicuous whitish bare skin around eye. Underparts have yellowish tone. Bluish flight feathers and tail tip. Usually in small noisy groups, often congregating to take nectar at flowering trees. Calls are loud harsh squawks. **Range and habitat:** NT, Amazonia. Common in riverside vegetation, forest edge and beside swamps. **Similar species:** White-eyed Parakeet.

Brown-throated Parakeet

Aratinga pertinax (Psittacidae) 25 cm/10 in.
Small parakeet with generally green plumage apart from pale brown face and breast. Toned yellowish on underparts and undertail. Eastern race has yellow eye-ring. Occurs in noisy flocks which fly rapidly, twisting and turning. Flight call a high-pitched screech. **Range and habitat:** NT, from southern Panama to northern Brazil. Common in lowland open country, woodland, dry scrub and mangroves. Populations may show movements, following passage of rains. **Similar species:** Blue-crowned Parakeet.

Ruddy Pigeon

Ruddy Ground-Dove

Inca Dove

Ruddy Quail-Dove

Hyacinth Macaw

Blue-and-yellow Macaw

Scarlet Macaw

Brown-throated Parakeet

Spix's Macaw

Dusky-headed Parakeet

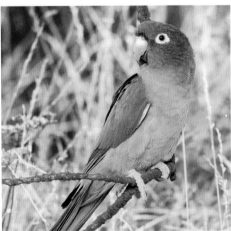

Monk Parakeet

Myiopsitta monachus (Psittacidae) 29 cm/11½ in.
Medium-sized parakeet with gray forehead, face and breast. Bright green nape, duller green upperparts, blackish blue flight feathers, lower breast tinged yellowish, becoming greener on belly. Forms large noisy flocks and can be agricultural pest. Flight low and direct. **Range and habitat:** NT, mainly in lowland areas of southern Brazil, Bolivia to central Argentina. Dry open country.

White-winged Parakeet

Brotogeris versicolurus (Psittacidae) 23 cm/9 in.
Small parakeet with pointed tail. Plumage mainly green apart from conspicuous whitish flight feathers, with yellow on inner wing and blue outer primaries. Usually in noisy, chattering groups, often in large flocks before sunset, which fly fast above canopy, sometimes at great height. **Range and habitat:** NT, Amazon basin, south to northern Argentina. Forest edge and secondary growth beside rivers, sometimes common close to human settlements.

Cobalt-winged Parakeet

Brotogeris cyanoptera (Psittacidae) 16.5 cm/6½ in.
Small parakeet with short, pointed tail. Plumage generally green apart from yellow forehead, orange spot on chin and blue primaries. Occurs in small, noisy flocks, sometimes visiting flowering trees to feed on nectar. **Range and habitat:** NT, Amazonia. Common bird of river-banks, secondary growth, forest edge and woodland. **Similar species:** Tui Parakeet.

Black-headed Parrot

Pionites melanocephala (Psittacidae) 23 cm/9 in.
Small stocky parrot with bull-necked appearance. Dark crown, yellow-orange nape and face. Underparts whitish with yellow-orange thighs and vent. Upperparts bright green. Usually in small groups, feeding on fruit from mid-level to canopy. Gives a high-pitched call in flight and often noisy when perched. **Range and habitat:** NT, Venezuela to northern Brazil. Lowland forest. **Similar species:** White-bellied Parrot.

Scaly-headed Parrot

Pionus maximiliani (Psittacidae) 29 cm/11½ in.
Medium-sized parrot with black and yellow bill. Dull green plumage, with bronzy tone below. Head rather dark with dusky-edged feathers, giving scaly effect, and white-edged feathers on cheeks. Undertail-coverts and base of tail red. Bare whitish eye-ring. Usually in groups, seen flying from 1 forest patch to another. Feed in treetops, when very inconspicuous. Noisy flight call a resonant "choik-choik." **Range and habitat:** NT, north-east Brazil to northern Argentina. Common in low and mid-elevation humid forest and woodland. **Similar species:** several in genus.

Festive Parrot

Amazona festiva (Psittacidae) 36 cm/14 in.
Large parrot with mainly green plumage apart from narrow red line on forehead and lores and red patch on lower back which can be surprisingly difficult to see. Primaries dark blue and bluish tinge behind eye. Often forms large flocks, particularly at roosting sites when very noisy. Flight call a nasal "wah-wah." Feeds in canopy, often at forest edge. **Range and habitat:** NT, Venezuela to central Brazil. Lowland swampy or seasonally flooded forest, river-banks, and islands. **Similar species:** Short-tailed Parrot.

Red-fan Parrot

Deroptyus accipitrinus (Psittacidae) 36 cm/14 in.
Large, aberrant parrot with long-tailed and heavy-headed appearance. Whitish forehead, brownish streaked head, dark reddish scaly nape and underparts. Nape feathers sometimes raised to form ruff. Upperparts bright green with blackish primaries. Curious undulating gliding flight for a parrot. Normally in small groups, perched on open branches. Flight call consists of quiet "chacks," followed by short series of loud, high-pitched calls. **Range and habitat:** NT, Venezuela to central Brazil. Lowland forest on sandy soils. **Not illustrated.**

CUCKOOS AND ALLIES Cuculiformes

Squirrel Cuckoo

Piaya cayana (Cuculidae) 43 cm/17 in.
Large, long-tailed cuckoo with yellowish green bill. Rufous brown head, breast and upperparts. Pale grayish belly, becoming darker toward vent. Underside of tail dark rufous with bold white tips. Seen singly or in pairs from mid-level to canopy, clambering through vegetation and along branches in squirrel-like manner, making short gliding flights between trees. Calls include loud nasal "chi-kara." **Range and habitat:** NT, Mexico to northern Argentina. Tropical to temperate areas in forest, secondary vegetation and woodland. **Similar species:** Black-bellied Cuckoo.

Groove-billed Ani

Crotophaga sulcirostris (Cuculidae) 28–30 cm/11–12 in.
Medium-sized cuckoo with rather shaggy black plumage. Upper mandible has raised compressed ridge arching from base to tip of bill and grooves on sides. Gregarious species found in small dispersed groups, moving from bush to bush with uneasy gliding flight. Calls include a dry "hwilk" and a liquid, slurred series of "tee-ho" notes. Communal breeder with several females sometimes laying in same bulky nest. **Range and habitat:** NT and NA, southern USA to northern Argentina. Common in lowland dry country and scrub. **Similar species:** Smooth-billed Ani (see p 70).

Pheasant Cuckoo

Dromococcyx phasianellus (Cuculidae) 38 cm/15 in.
Large parasitic cuckoo with small head and long tail. Rufous crown which is slightly crested. Narrow white line behind eye. Rest of head and breast buffy with black spots, underparts white. Dark brown above with wing-coverts appearing spotted. Dark grayish brown tail feathers narrowly tipped white. Stays low down but very skulking. Call a thin 3-note whistle, 3rd drawn out and tremulous, heard mainly at night. **Range and habitat:** NT, southern Mexico to northern Argentina. Uncommon in lowland riverside vegetation, secondary growth and forest edge. **Similar species:** Pavonine Cuckoo.

Rufous-vented Ground-Cuckoo

Neomorphus geoffroyi (Cuculidae) 46 cm/18 in.
Large, terrestrial cuckoo. Bill greenish yellow. Flattened crest blackish, bluish bare skin around eye. Upperparts generally bronzy rufous, with long tail bronzy or greenish depending on race. Underparts buffish with black band across breast and rufous flanks. Very wary, but runs off rather noisily with bounding paces. Can be approachable when attracted to swarm of army ants. Has subdued, drawn-out hoot and frequently bill-snaps. **Range and habitat:** NT, Central America to Bolivia. Rare, probably overlooked, in lowland and foothill humid forest. **Similar species:** Scaled Ground Cuckoo. **Not illustrated.**

HOATZIN Opisthocomiformes

Hoatzin

Opisthocomus hoazin (Opisthocomidae) 61–6 cm/24–6 in.
Extraordinary bird with long wispy crest and hunchbacked appearance. Red eyes, bluish bare facial skin and brownish upperparts, streaked buff on nape and back. Breast buffy, rest of underparts chestnut. Wing-coverts and tail tipped pale buff, rufous primaries. Rather clumsy bird which flies weakly and tends to clamber through branches. Quite noisy, producing loud hissing sounds. Foliage-eater and only known bird to have ruminantlike system of digestion. Juvenile has clawed wing, used to clamber through trees. **Range and habitat:** NT, Guianas to Brazil. Lowland swamps, gallery forest and oxbow lakes in forested areas.

Monk Parakeet

White-winged Parakeet

Cobalt-winged Parakeet

Black-headed Parrot

Squirrel Cuckoo

Scaly-headed Parrot

Festive Parrot

Groove-billed Ani

Pheasant Cuckoo

Hoatzin

OWLS Strigiformes

Spectacled Owl

Pulsatrix perspicillata (**Strigidae**) 46 cm/18 in.
Large, striking owl. Dark brown upperparts, head and chest with broad whitish face markings and yellow eyes. Underparts pale buff. Immature is creamy white with black, heart-shaped mask and brown wings. Largely nocturnal, but sometimes hunts in daylight. Catches prey by swooping down from a perch, normally roosts in thick cover. Call a series of deep, accelerating hoots. **Range and habitat:** NT, southern Mexico to northern Argentina. Mainly in lowlands in forest, secondary vegetation and gallery woodland. **Similar species:** Band-tailed Owl.

Tropical Screech-Owl

Megascops choliba (**Strigidae**) 23 cm/9 in.
Small owl with ear-tufts and yellow eyes. Plumage is toned brownish gray with well-spaced black streaks on underparts, finely streaked and vermiculated above. Facial disc is boldly outlined black. Scapulars and wing-coverts tipped white. Wholly nocturnal, spending day roosting in thick vegetation, often close to tree-trunk. Call is hesitant, tremulous trill, mainly at dusk and before dawn. **Range and habitat:** NT, Costa Rica to northern Argentina. Common in low to mid-elevations in forest edge, secondary vegetation, woodland and gardens. **Similar species:** Pacific Screech Owl.

Striped Owl

Pseudoscopus clamator (**Strigidae**) 36 cm/14 in.
Medium-sized owl with brownish eyes and ear-tufts. Whitish facial disc rimmed by black, underparts pale buff boldly patterned with dark streaks. Upperparts and wings tawny brown, with dark markings. Underwing shows blackish carpel patches. Immature has darker, buffy face. Often active at dusk, hunting over open ground. Searches for prey from wing or from a low perch. Has a variety of hooting and barking calls. **Range and habitat:** NT, southern Mexico to northern Argentina. Lowland open country, fields, and marshes, particularly with scattered thickets or trees. **Similar species:** Short-eared Owl (see p 78).

NIGHTJARS AND ALLIES Caprimulgiformes

Oilbird

Steatornis caripensis (**Steatornithidae**) 48 cm/19 in.
Curious nocturnal fruit-eating bird. Hooked bill, long wings and tail. Plumage reddish brown above, boldly spotted with black-rimmed white spots on wing feathers. Underparts buff with small white spots. Breeds in caves, only emerging at night to fly, sometimes long distances, to fruiting trees. Fruit are taken on the wing. Nests consist of mound of regurgitated seeds. Extremely noisy in cave with a range of screams and snarls. Clicking calls used for echo-location. Flight call outside is a "kuk-kuk." **Range and habitat:** NT, Panama south to Bolivia and east to Trinidad. Colonies are situated in caves in mountains or on coast. Undertakes seasonal movements in search of food.

Great Potoo

Nyctibius grandis (**Nyctibiidae**) 51 cm/20 in.
Large, pale nocturnal bird. Some variation in plumage but generally pale grayish buff above, vermiculated with black. Whiter below with fine dark vermiculations. Bolder spotting on scapulars, broken markings on breast. Wings and tail barred. Perches on high bare branches, flying out over canopy to catch flying insects and even bats, on aerial sallies. Call a drawn-out growl. **Range and habitat:** NT, southern Mexico to southern Brazil. Lowland forest and gallery woodland. **Similar species:** Common and Long-tailed Potoos.

Gray Potoo

Nyctibius griseus (**Nyctibiidae**) 36–41 cm/14–16 in.
Large nocturnal bird with eyes which reflect orange in torchlight. Grayish brown above heavily streaked and vermiculated black and buff. Paler and grayer below with fine streaking and blotchy "necklace" of darker markings across breast. Tail barred. Makes sallies from a perch such as an exposed branch, telegraph pole or fence-post. Spends day motionless. Call an evocative series of mournful whistles. Northern populations produce a more guttural call. **Range and habitat:** NT, Mexico to northern Argentina. Lowland and mid-elevation in forest edge and scattered woodland. **Similar species:** Great and Long-tailed Potoos.

Short-tailed Nighthawk

Lurocalis semitorquatus (**Caprimulgidae**) 20 cm/8 in.
Long-winged, short-tailed nighthawk. Very dark brown with white chevron on throat. Racial variation with some birds showing slightly paler, unbarred bellies. Some birds show pale band across base of upperwing. Active at dusk, flying batlike at treetop height in pursuit of flying insects. Calls vary according to race but include an inflected "whick," a mellow hoot and a "tot-ta-quirrt." **Range and habitat:** NT, Central America to northern Argentina. Widespread from lowland forest and forest edge to temperate woodland. **Similar species:** Band-tailed Nighthawk. **Not illustrated.**

Pauraque

Nyctidromus albicollis (**Caprimulgidae**) 28 cm/11 in.
Medium-sized, long-winged nightjar. Typically cryptically marked with vermiculations of brown, buff and black. White chevron on throat. Male has white band on primaries; outer 2 tail feathers black and next 2 mainly white. Female has buff wing marking and pale tips to outer 3 tail feathers. Scapulars boldly marked with black and buff. Rests on ground during day. Active at night catching insects on aerial sallies. Calls include a hollow, whistling "ker-whee-oo" and a nasal "waa-oo." **Range and habitat:** NT and NA, southern USA to northern Argentina. Widespread from lowlands to subtropical zone in forest edge, secondary vegetation, and scattered woodland. **Similar species:** White-tailed and Band-winged Nightjars.

Scissor-tailed Nightjar

Hydropsalis torquata (**Caprimulgidae**) 48 cm/19 in.
Large nightjar with very long outer tail feathers, tipped white. Rest of tail feathers have white notches and edging, with central tail feathers also elongate. Otherwise plumage typically cryptic with distinctive rufous collar. **Range and habitat:** NT, Brazil to central Argentina. Low and mid-elevation woodland and savannah. **Similar species:** Swallow-tailed Nightjar.

SWIFTS AND HUMMINGBIRDS Apodiformes

White-collared Swift

Streptoprocne zonaris (**Apodidae**) 20 cm/8 in.
Large swift with powerful flight. Black with white collar, widest on chest, and notched tail. Immatures have broken collar. Usually in flocks, sometimes of hundreds of birds, flying at considerable height but also coming down low and sweeping down canyons at great speed. Breed on damp cliffs, sometimes behind waterfalls; forage over great distances. Call a nasal chattering. **Range and habitat:** NT, Mexico to northern Argentina. Over mountains and foothills. **Similar species:** Biscutate Swift.

Chapman's Swift

Chaetura chapmani (**Apodidae**) 13 cm/5 in.
Medium-sized swift with short square-ended tail and rather uniform appearance. Blackish plumage, rather glossy above, with dark brownish rump and dark gray underparts. Usually in small groups and almost always with other species of swifts. Rather poorly known. **Range and habitat:** NT, Central America to central Brazil, east to Guianas and Trinidad. Low to mid-elevation, over forest and open areas with scattered woodland. **Similar species:** Chimney Swift (see p 72). **Not illustrated.**

Lesser Swallow-tailed Swift

Panyptila cayennensis (**Apodidae**) 13 cm/5 in.
Slender with long forked tail, normally appearing pointed. Black with white throat, collar and patch on side of rump, visible from below. Usually seen singly or in pairs, sometimes in mixed species groups of swifts, but generally flying somewhat higher. Nest a long downward-pointing tube of plant down, fixed by saliva to tree-trunks, below branches, rock faces or even buildings. **Range and habitat:** NT, Mexico to Brazil. Widespread at low and mid-elevations over forest and wooded areas. **Similar species:** White-tipped and Fork-tailed Palm-swifts. **Not illustrated.**

Spectacled Owl
(juvenile and adult)

Tropical Screech-Owl

Striped Owl

Oilbird

Great Potoo

Gray Potoo

White-collared Swift

Pauraque

Scissor-tailed Nightja

Eastern Long-tailed Hermit
Phaethornis superciliosus (Trochilidae) 13 cm/5 in.
Hummingbird of understorey with long, decurved bill and elongated white-tipped central tail feathers. Plumage generally brownish with bronzy green tinge to upperparts and buffy rump. Buff stripes on face. Paler below. Visits isolated flowers, traveling considerable distance, sometimes more than I km (over ½ mile), between feeds. Also collects small invertebrates from foliage. Nest hangs on underside of a broad leaf. Males assemble to sing in courtship leks. **Range and habitat:** NT, northern South America to central Brazil. Lowland forest understorey and nearby secondary growth, often close to streams. **Similar species:** several other hermits.

Swallow-tailed Hummingbird
Eupetomena macrourus (Trochilidae) 19 cm/7½ in.
Large hummingbird with long, deeply forked dark blue tail. Bill black and slightly decurved. Head, throat and breast deep purplish blue, rest of body shining green. Agile flier which frequently glides. Call a repeated "shep-shep-shep-shep." **Range and habitat:** NT, Guianas and central Brazil to Bolivia. Mainly mid-elevation scrub and savannah.

White-necked Jacobin
Florisuga mellivora (Trochilidae) 12 cm/4½ in.
Medium-sized hummingbird with rather short bill. Male boldly patterned with dark blue head and throat, upperparts, breast and central tail bright green; rest of underparts, outer tail and nape white. Tail feathers narrowly edged black. Female green above, scaled bluish on throat, white belly and greenish blue tail, tipped white on sides. Mainly a canopy or forest edge species, visiting flowering trees. **Range and habitat:** NT, Mexico to central Brazil. Lowland species of forest borders and clearings.

Black-throated Mango
Anthrocothorax nigricollis (Trochilidae) 10 cm/4 in.
Medium-sized hummingbird with slightly decurved bill. Male blackish below, dark greenish above with dark maroon tail. Female quite different, having white underparts with bold black stripe passing from center of chin to belly. Encountered at flowering trees. **Range and habitat:** NT, Central America to northern Argentina. Mainly in lowlands at forest edge, secondary vegetation, cleared areas, and gardens. **Similar species:** Green-breasted Mango.

Festive Coquette
Lophornis chalybeus (Trochilidae) 7.5 cm/3 in.
Tiny hummingbird with short, straight bill. Dark greenish plumage with brilliant green on side of head, extending behind as tuft with white spots. White bar across rump. Female lacks tufted appearance and whitish plumage on chin, which extends back to side of face. Feeds mainly at flowering trees, flight is beelike. **Range and habitat:** NT, Venezuela to Brazil. Lowland species of forest edge and open areas with shrubs or trees. **Similar species:** several other coquettes.

Violet-capped Woodnymph
Thalurania glaucopis (Trochilidae) 12 cm/4½ in.
Medium-sized hummingbird with slightly decurved black bill. Male has violet crown and bronzy green back. Underparts golden green. Forked tail steel blue. Female grayish white below with green discs on sides, forked dark blue tail with white tips. Usually solitary at lower levels in forest. **Range and habitat:** NT, south-east Brazil. Very common in lowland forest and scrub. **Similar species:** Fork-tailed Woodnymph.

Green-throated Carib
Eulampis holosericeus (Trochilidae) 12 cm/4½ in.
Medium-sized hummingbird with long, black, slightly decurved bill. Mainly green with bright green throat, violet-blue breast patch and blackish belly. Tail is bluish black. Sexes alike. A pugnacious bird which defends flowering trees and shrubs from other nectar feeders. **Range and habitat:** NT, Caribbean islands. Common at low elevations, mainly in cultivated areas and secondary growth, sometimes forest. **Similar species:** Purple-throated Carib.

Green-crowned Brilliant
Heliodoxa jacula (Trochilidae) 13 cm/5 in.
Large hummingbird with straight black bill. Green with inconspicuous, violet spot on throat. Long bluish black tail is forked. Female white below, heavily spotted green. Upperparts green with white spot behind eye and white malar stripe. Tail tipped white.

Usually perches on inflorescence to feed. Visits flowers from mid-level to canopy, sometimes defending nectar sources. **Range and habitat:** NT, Costa Rica to Ecuador. Mainly in highland forest, although may descend to lower altitude outside breeding season. **Similar species:** Violet-fronted Brilliant.

Giant Hummingbird
Patagona gigas (Trochilidae) 23 cm/9 in.
Huge hummingbird with long wings and characteristic flight. Dull bronze-green above and buffy below, whitish rump and undertail-coverts. Female has spotted underparts. Flies like a swallow with frequent glides. Hovers slowly but often perches to feed. Aggressive, frequently seen chasing other species away from flowers. **Range and habitat:** NT, along Andean chain from Ecuador to central Chile. Mainly in dry shrubby highland areas. Some populations show altitudinal migration. **Similar species:** Great Sapphirewing.

Sword-billed Hummingbird
Ensifera ensifera (Trochilidae) 14 cm/5½ in.
Hummingbird with extraordinary long bill, about 11 cm/4½ in. Rather dark bronzy green plumage and forked tail. Female has heavily spotted and streaked underparts. Singles visit fuchsias and other tubular flowers, approaching from below. Usually perch with bill pointing upward. **Range and habitat:** NT, along Andean chain from Venezuela to Bolivia. Widespread in humid montane forest up to treeline.

Scintillant Hummingbird
Selasphorus scintilla (Trochilidae) 6.5 cm/2½ in.
Smallest bird in the world. Tiny hummingbird with straight black bill. Male has orange-red gorget with incomplete white collar. Mainly buffish below with green spots. Upperparts bronzed green with rufous and black striped tail. Female is buffy on throat and has dark subterminal tail band. Territorial in breeding season. Usually visits small flowers on shrubs. **Range and habitat:** NT, Costa Rica and Panama. Widespread at mid-elevations in plantations, secondary vegetation and gardens. **Similar species:** Volcano Hummingbird.

Black-eared Fairy
Heliothryx aurita (Trochilidae) 10 cm/4 in.
Elegant hummingbird with short black bill. Male brilliant green above, blackish ear-coverts and spotless white below. Female has some grayish markings on throat. Very active feeder with rapid, darting flight, visiting flowers at mid-level to canopy. Also hawks insects. Sometimes apparently associated with mixed species flocks. **Range and habitat:** NT, east of Andes from Guianas to southern Brazil. Lowland humid forest. **Similar species:** Purple-crowned Fairy.

Eastern Long-tailed Hermit (at Passion Flower)

Swallow-tailed Hummingbird

White-necked Jacobin

Black-throated Mango

Festive Coquette

Violet-capped Woodnymph

Green-throated Carib

Green-crowned Brilliant (female)

Giant Hummingbird

Sword-billed Hummingbird

Scintillant Hummingbird

Black-eared Fairy

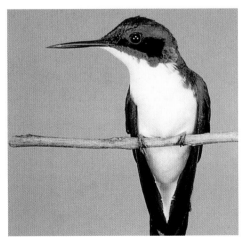

TROGONS Trogoniformes

Resplendent Quetzal

Pharomachrus mocinno (**Trogonidae**) 36 cm/14 in.
Spectacular-looking male has 60 cm/24 in) long streamers formed from uppertail-coverts. Male has flattened bushy green crest, extended forward over yellow bill. Bright green above and on breast. Rest of underparts red with white undertail. Female lacks crest and such extravagant streamers, has gray belly, red undertail coverts and black and white barred tail. Usually solitary or in pairs, although a group may assemble at a fruiting tree. Also feed on large insects plucked from leaves in swooping sallies. Song a series of mellow, deep notes. **Range and habitat:** NT, Central America. Humid montane forest. Near-threatened by deforestation.

Collared Trogon

Trogon collaris (**Trogonidae**) 25 cm/10 in.
Smallish trogon. Male has yellow bill, is green above and on chest with white chest band and red underparts. Tail narrowly barred white and black. Brown replaces green on female, which has a broken white eye-ring and bicolored bill, she is rather pinker below with a finely vermiculated tail which appears grayish. Solitary or in pairs at low to mid-height, feeding in typical trogon fashion of peering from a perch and flying out to snatch small animals such as insects or fruit from nearby trees. Song a slow, rather sad series of notes, "cow cu-cu cu-cu....." **Range and habitat:** NT, Mexico to Brazil. Low to mid-elevation in humid forest and secondary vegetation. **Similar species:** several other trogons.

Violaceous Trogon

Trogon violaceus (**Trogonidae**) 24 cm/9½ in.
Small trogon. Male has yellow eye-ring and pale grayish bill. Upperparts glossy green, becoming bluish on head and chest. Narrow white chest band and deep yellow underparts. Tail barred black and white. Female gray above with smudged boundary between chest and belly, broken eye-ring is white. Generally perches at mid-level. Song a series of even-pitched, rather fast "kew-kew-kew" notes. **Range and habitat:** NT, Mexico to Brazil. Mainly in lowlands in forest edges, clearings, and woodland. **Similar species:** Black-throated and White-tailed Trogons.

KINGFISHERS AND ALLIES Coraciiformes

Ringed Kingfisher

Ceryle torquata (**Alcedinidae**) 38 cm/15 in.
Large, rather noisy kingfisher with untidy crest. Male bluish above, white on sides of neck and throat and rufous below. Female has bluish and white chest band. Usually seen alone or in pairs, on high perches. Flies high, giving a loud "klek" call. Calls also include a hard rattle. Nests in banks, often in colonies. **Range and habitat:** NT, NA, southern USA to Tierra del Fuego. Common, mainly in lowlands, beside rivers and lakes, also in coastal areas. **Similar species:** Belted Kingfisher (see p 74).

Green Kingfisher

Chloroceryle americana (**Alcedinidae**) 19 cm/7½ in.
Small kingfisher with dark green upperparts, white spots on wing and white collar. Male has rufous chest band, female 2 green bands, rest of underparts white. Usually solitary, flying low or perched close to water. Flight call a low "choot," often repeated as a chatter. **Range and habitat:** NT and NA, southern USA to Argentina. Fairly common beside rivers and lakes, marshes and woodland streams, from low to mid-elevations. **Similar species:** Amazon Kingfisher.

Puerto Rican Tody

Todus mexicanus (**Todidae**) 10 cm/4 in.
Small attractive bird with long, wide-based bill with red lower mandible. Emerald green above, grayish below with red throat patch and yellow flanks. Watch from exposed perches for insects which are captured, in flight, from substrates such as undersides of leaves. Whilst perched constantly move heads in jerky fashion. Rattling sound produced in flight. **Range and habitat:** NT, endemic to Puerto Rico. Rather widespread from drier coastal areas to more humid mountain slopes. **Similar species:** 4 other todies, none of which also occurs on Puerto Rico.

Rufous Motmot

Baryphthengus martii (**Momotidae**) 46 cm/18 in.
Large motmot with long tail, sometimes with racket-tips, which is swayed from side to side when bird is alarmed. Blackish face-mask with rest of head and underparts to lower belly rufous. Rest of underparts and upperparts greenish. Small black spot on chest. Usually solitary, perched at mid-level to subcanopy. Makes sudden flights to new perches and large insect prey are plucked off vegetation in flight. Call is series of owl-like hoots, often given before dawn. **Range and habitat:** NT, Central America to northern Argentina. Lowland and foothill species of humid forest. **Similar species:** Broad-billed Motmot.

Blue-crowned Motmot

Momotus momota (**Momotidae**) 41 cm/16 in.
Medium-sized with long tail, usually with rackets. Black face-mask and red eyes, with center of crown black, broadly bordered by brilliant turquoise-blue. Greenish above and dull buff below with small black chest spots usually visible. Sits still singly or in pairs on mid-level perches and easily overlooked unless seen in flight. Call a low, double-noted hoot. **Range and habitat:** NT, Mexico to northern Argentina. Common from lowlands to mid-elevations in secondary vegetation, cacao plantations, forest edge and woodland. **Similar species:** Turquoise-browed Motmot.

WOODPECKERS AND ALLIES Piciformes

Rufous-tailed Jacamar

Galbula ruficauda (**Galbulidae**) 23 cm/9 in.
Medium-sized jacamar with long bill and tail. Metallic green above and on breast. White throat and rest of underparts, including tail, rufous. Female has buffy throat. Perch, usually in pairs, on exposed branch which they leave to hawk large flying insects such as butterflies. Usually return to same or nearby perch. Call a high-pitched "peee," normally given in accelerating series. **Range and habitat:** NT, Mexico to southern Brazil. Common, mainly at low elevations, in forest edge habitats, secondary growth and shrubby vegetation. **Similar species:** White-chinned and Great Jacamars.

Great Jacamar

Jacamerops aureus (**Galbulidae**) 30 cm/12 in.
Stout-billed, heavily built jacamar with metallic green upperparts and chin. White throat band (buffy in female) and rufous underparts. Underside of tail blackish. Bill appears slightly decurved. Usually solitary and easily overlooked, perches for long periods at mid-levels within forest. Call a hawklike whistle. **Range and habitat:** NT, Costa Rica to central Brazil. Uncommon in lowland and humid forest of foothills. **Similar species:** Rufous-tailed Jacamar.

White-necked Puffbird

Notharchus macrorhynchus (**Bucconidae**) 25 cm/10 in.
Large puffbird with heavy black bill. White forehead, throat, sides of face and collar. Underparts white apart from black breast band and some barring on flanks. Black on hindcrown, eye-stripe and upperparts. Sits on high exposed perches and, like other puffbirds, appears very lethargic. Makes short flights to collect insect prey from nearby vegetation, usually returning to original perch. Generally silent. In breeding season gives bubbling trill. **Range and habitat:** NT, southern Mexico to northern Argentina. Widespread in lowland forest edge, secondary vegetation and woodland. **Similar species:** Brown-banded Puffbird.

Spotted Puffbird

Bucco tamatia (**Bucconidae**) 18 cm/7 in.
Medium-sized puffbird with stout black bill and red eyes. Dull brown above, grayish on face with white malar bordered below by broad black patch and warm buff throat. Underparts whitish, heavily scalloped with black. Seen singly or in pairs, on a low perch and usually remarkably confiding. Call an accelerating series of whistles. **Range and habitat:** NT, Orinoco and Amazon basins. Fairly common in seasonally inundated forest and riverside woodland. **Similar species:** Chestnut-capped Puffbird.

Resplendent Quetzal

Collared Trogon

Violaceous Trogon

Ringed Kingfisher

Green Kingfisher

Puerto Rican Tody

Rufous Motmot

Blue-crowned Motmot

Rufous-tailed Jacamar

Great Jacamar

White-necked Puffbird

Spotted Puffbird

Black Nunbird

Monasa atra (**Bucconidae**) 27 cm/10½ in.
Large puffbird with long, slender, red bill, slightly decurved. Generally grayish black, paler on rump and underparts, apart from blackish throat. Wing-coverts on inner wing white. Usually in pairs or small groups, perched confidingly at low to mid-level. Plucks insects and small reptiles from vegetation on short sallies or from ground in swooping flight. Nests in burrows. Loud call, often given in choruses. **Range and habitat:** NT, north-eastern South America. Lowland humid forest, gallery forest and clearings. **Similar species:** Black-fronted Nunbird.

Swallow-wing

Chelidoptera tenebrosa (**Bucconidae**) 15 cm/6 in.
Small aberrant puffbird with rather short bill and broad wings. Plumage mainly black with white rump and undertail-coverts and rufous belly. Usually in pairs or small groups perched on exposed treetop branches, making aerial sallies for flying insects. Generally silent. **Range and habitat:** NT, Venezuela to Brazil. Lowland species common along sandy river-banks, forest borders, and gallery woodland.

Black-spotted Barbet

Capito niger (**Capitonidae**) 19 cm/7½ in.
Large barbet with stout black bill. Upperparts black with dull yellow crown and brighter yellow supercilium from behind eye extending down back to form V. Yellow wing-bar and spotting on tertials. Underparts yellow with red or orange throat (depending on race) and black spots on flanks. Female much more heavily marked black below. Usually in pairs and often in mixed species flocks from mid-level to canopy. Feeds on fruit and also searches foliage for large insects. Call a deep double hoot. **Range and habitat:** NT, Guianas to central Brazil. Common in lowland humid forest. **Similar species:** Lemon-throated Barbet.

Emerald Toucanet

Aulacorhynchus prasinus (**Ramphastidae**) 33 cm/13 in.
Small toucan with black bill with yellow ridge on upper mandible and white base. Plumage mainly green with chestnut vent and undertail. Throat color variable according to race. Usually in small groups, constantly on move. Normally adopts horizontal stance, when alarmed nods head and cocks tail. Call a series of "churt" notes. **Range and habitat:** NT, Central America and along Andean chain from Venezuela to Bolivia. Common at mid to high elevations in humid, montane forest and secondary vegetation. **Similar species:** several toucanets.

Curl-crested Araçari

Pteroglossus beauharnaesii (**Ramphastidae**) 36 cm/14 in.
Small slender toucan with long graduated tail. Upper mandible black with orange-brown culmen, lower mandible white. Upperparts black apart from red back and rump. Underparts yellow with red band across upper breast. Crest of curly feathers. Usually in small groups in canopy. Has rather harsh call-note. **Range and habitat:** NT, south of Amazon in Peru and Brazil. Lowland Amazon forest. **Similar species:** several araçaris.

Gray-breasted Mountain-Toucan

Andigena hypoglauca (**Ramphastidae**) 46 cm/18 in.
Medium-sized toucan with strikingly patterned bill. Upper mandible mainly orange-red, lower mandible black. Large yellow region with black vertical bar in basal half of bill. Bluish bare skin around eye, black hood, blue-gray collar and underparts apart from red vent. Olive-green upperparts with conspicuous yellow rump and blackish tail tipped chestnut. Often in pairs or small parties, generally in canopy but visits shrubs in fruit. Mainly silent but gives loud nasal call at dawn. **Range and habitat:** NT, Andean chain from Colombia to Peru. Montane forest to treeline. Near-threatened by deforestation. **Similar species:** Plate-billed Mountain-Toucan.

Channel-billed Toucan

Ramphastos vitellinus (**Ramphastidae**) 53 cm/21 in.
Large toucan with bill mainly black with light blue base. Bare facial skin around eye bluish. Black upperparts apart from red uppertail-coverts. Throat white, becoming yellowish on breast. Red border between breast and black belly. Undertail-coverts red. Seen singly, in pairs or small groups, mainly in canopy but sometimes at lower levels. Hops energetically along branches. Flight is heavy and undulating. Very vocal with far-carrying yelping call. **Range and habitat:** NT, northern South America. Low to mid-elevations in humid forest and forest edge. **Similar species:** several other large toucans.

Toco Toucan

Ramphastos toco (**Ramphastidae**) 62 cm/24 in.
Large toucan with enormous orange bill, with black oval patch at tip of upper mandible. Black line at base of bill. Plumage black apart from white throat and rump, and red undertail-coverts. Seen singly or in small groups, usually in treetops. **Range and habitat:** NT, Guianas to northern Argentina. Mainly in lowland woodland, stands of palms and secondary vegetation.

Plain-breasted Piculet

Picumnus castelnau (**Picidae**) 9 cm/3½ in.
Tiny, dumpy bird with very short tail. Male has black crown with red spots, replaced by white spots on hind-crown. Female has all-black crown. Nape is scaled gray, rest of upperparts brownish olive, lightly barred yellowish with yellow edgings to primaries. Unmarked underparts have a yellowish olive wash. Black tail with sides and inner web of central feathers white. Usually solitary and unobtrusive at low to subcanopy level. Call a high-pitched trill. **Range and habitat:** NT, western Amazonia. Uncommon in lowland swamp forest, secondary vegetation close to rivers and river islands. **Similar species:** White-bellied Piculet.

Campo Flicker

Colaptes campestris (**Picidae**) 29 cm/11½ in.
Large woodpecker. Crown and nape black. Brown and buff barred upperparts with whitish rump. White around eye, otherwise ear-coverts golden yellow, extending on to chest. Reddish malar, throat white or black according to race. Underparts buffy white with well-spaced dark bars. Feeds, often in groups, on ants collected from ground. Nests in dead trees or in burrows in ground or termite nests. Repertoire of several calls including series of "keep" notes. **Range and habitat:** NT, eastern South America. Lowland fields, grasslands, and clearings. **Similar species:** Andean Flicker (no altitudinal overlap).

Blond-crested Woodpecker

Celeus flavescens (**Picidae**) 22 cm/8½ in.
Medium-sized woodpecker. Head and long crest creamy white or buff. Male has red malar, female blackish or white. Very variable species with upperparts varying from blackish barred with pale gold to creamy buff with bold black spots (depending on race). Underparts either black or brownish with buff scaling. Diet probably mainly consists of ants, collected from twigs and branches. **Range and habitat:** NT, central Brazil to northern Argentina. Lowland and foothill forest, woodland and scrub. **Similar species:** Pale-crested Woodpecker.

Helmeted Woodpecker

Dryocopus galeatus (**Picidae**) 29 cm/11½ in.
Large black and white woodpecker with large red crest and ivory-colored bill. Ear-coverts finely barred black and buff, red malar (in male) and buffy throat. Upperparts and neck black with white stripe on side of neck and white rump and uppertail-coverts. Underparts barred black and white. Extremely poorly known species. **Range and habitat:** NT, southern Brazil, Paraguay and northern Argentina. Very rare species of lowland primary forest. Vulnerable from habitat loss. **Similar species:** several in genus. **Not illustrated.**

Black Nunbird

Swallow-wing

Black-spotted Barbe

Emerald Toucanet

Curl-crested Araçar

Gray-breasted
Mountain-Toucan

Channel-billed Touca

Toco Toucan

Plain-breasted Picule

Campo Flicker

Blond-crested
Woodpecker

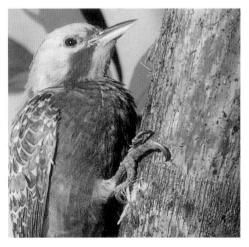

PERCHING BIRDS Passeriformes

Wedge-billed Woodcreeper

Glyphorynchus spirurus (Dendrocolaptidae) 14 cm/5½ in.
Tiny woodcreeper with short bill. Brown plumage with warmer-toned rump and tail. Buff bases to flight feathers visible in flight. Buff supercilium and spotting on head and breast. Orange-buff chin. Usually solitary or in pairs, often in mixed species parties. Creeps up tree-trunk to about mid-level, thence flying to base of nearby tree. Call is short "cheef." **Range and habitat:** NT, Mexico to Brazil. Lowland and mid-elevation humid forest. **Similar species:** Fulvous-dotted Treerunner.

Striped Woodcreeper

Xiphorhynchus obsoletus (Dendrocolaptidae) 20 cm/8 in.
Medium-sized woodcreeper with pale buff stripes on dull brown underparts and mantle. More solidly pale buff throat. Warm brown wings, rump and tail. Bill slightly decurved. Usually solitary or in pairs, frequently in mixed species parties at low to mid-levels. Call an excited trill. **Range and habitat:** NT, lowland Amazon forest in seasonally inundated forest and swampy woodland. **Similar species:** several other woodcreepers.

Red-billed Scythebill

Campylorhamphus trochilirostris (Dendrocolaptidae) 23 cm/9 in.
Medium-sized woodcreeper with remarkable long, deeply decurved reddish bill. Plumage generally brown, warmer on wings and tail with buff streaks on head, breast and mantle. Found singly or in pairs, usually in mixed species flocks. Uses long bill to probe in bases of epiphytes and crevices in bark. Normally at low to mid-levels. Calls include a high-pitched trill. **Range and habitat:** NT, Panama to northern Argentina. Uncommon in lowland forest edge and woodland. **Similar species:** Curve-billed Scythebill.

Rufous Hornero

Furnarius rufus (Furnariidae) 19 cm/7½ in.
Large terrestrial furnariid. Slightly decurved bill and rather long dark legs. Plumage uniformly dull brown, more rufous on tail and paler on throat. Walks confidently in open areas, collecting insects and seeds from ground. Call a high-pitched chattering. Horneros build domed nests of mud on posts or on horizontal branches. **Range and habitat:** NT, southern Brazil to northern Argentina. Mainly lowlands, but range extends into highlands of Bolivia. Common in drier woodland, open country and gardens. **Similar species:** Pale-legged Hornero.

Plain-mantled Tit-Spinetail

Leptasthenura aegithaloides (Furnariidae) 15 cm/6 in.
Small furnariid with very long, pointed tail and small, stubby bill. Dark crown, finely streaked brown. Unstreaked back grayish brown and rufous patch on wing. Throat whitish, rest of underparts buff or pale gray. Usually in pairs or small groups searching, in an engaging acrobatic manner, clusters of leaves and flower heads for insects and seeds. **Range and habitat:** NT, fairly common in arid zone of southern South America. **Similar species:** Brown-capped Tit-spinetail.

Dark-breasted Spinetail

Synallaxis albigularis (Furnariidae) 15.5 cm/6 in.
Small furnariid with rather short, ragged-looking tail. Olive brown above with rufous hind-crown and shoulders. Underparts dark gray with whitish belly. Throat white with bases of feathers black so that when feathers are raised throat appears blackish. Skulking, usually in pairs, in tangled vegetation and grass close to ground. Large stick nest placed low in bushes. Call a conversational "di-dududu." **Range and habitat:** NT, western Amazonia. Common in secondary vegetation and shrubby growth. **Similar species:** Dusky and Pale-breasted Spinetails.

Rusty-backed Spinetail

Cranioleuca vulpina (Furnariidae) 14.5 cm/5½ in.
Small spinetail with rather dingy gray underparts, slightly paler on throat. Upperparts rusty brown. Pale supercilium and narrow dark eye stripe, with fine dark streaking on sides of head. Usually in pairs, seen clambering up vine tangles and thick-stemmed tall grasses, searching for insect prey. Calls include a high-pitched whinny and a hard rattle. **Range and habitat:** NT, Amazonia. Fairly common in lowland secondary vegetation with tall grass and bushes, particularly on river islands. **Similar species:** Crested Spinetail.

Striped Woodhaunter

Hyloctistes subulatus (Furnariidae) 16.5 cm/6½ in.
Small foliage-gleaner with quite slender, slightly decurved bill. Plumage generally dull brown, slightly more olive below, with buff throat and streaks on head, underparts and mantle. Extent of streaking depends on subspecies. Usually in mixed species flocks, keeping fairly low down and searching for insect prey in vine tangles and clusters of dead leaves. Song a series of whistles followed by trill; usual call a loud, nasal "chook." **Range and habitat:** NT, Central America to central Brazil. Lowland and foothill species of humid forest. **Similar species:** several foliage-gleaners.

White-browed Foliage-Gleaner

Anabacerthia amaurotis (Furnariidae) 16 cm/6½ in.
Small foliage-gleaner with bold white supercilium behind eye. Upperparts dark brown, tail rufous. Crown finely spotted white. White throat, buffy below with bold white breast markings. Usually in mixed species flocks at mid-level to subcanopy. Active forager, hopping along branches, peering and poking acrobatically into clusters of dead leaves. **Range and habitat:** NT, southeast Brazil and northern Argentina. Lowland forest. Near-threatened by deforestation. **Similar species:** several similar foliage-gleaners.

Streaked Xenops

Xenops rutilans (Furnariidae) 11.5 cm/4½ in.
Small busy bird with lower mandible upturned. Conspicuous white crescent on cheek and pale supercilium. Plumage generally brown, paler below, with narrow buff streaks on head, back and below. Bold cinnamon wing-bar. Usually in pairs, frequently in mixed species flocks. Climbs along branches, poking into rotten stumps, balancing on tiny twigs. Call a high-pitched series of shrill notes. **Range and habitat:** NT, Central America to Argentina. Widespread at mid-elevations in humid forest. **Similar species:** Slender-billed Xenops.

Plain Xenops

Xenops minutus (Furnariidae) 12 cm/4½ in.
Small with short bill with upturned appearance. Plumage dull olive-brown with buff supercilium and white crescent on side of face, sometimes slightly streaked on breast. Bold cinnamon wing-bar and black streak on side of rufous tail. Forages actively at low to mid-levels, usually in mixed species flocks. Call a high-pitched "cheet," song a chattering trill. **Range and habitat:** NT, southern Mexico to northern Argentina. Species of lowland and mid-elevations in humid forest and secondary growth. **Similar species:** Spectacled Spinetail.

Tawny-throated Leaftosser

Sclerurus mexicanus (Furnariidae) 15 cm/6 in.
Rather plump terrestrial bird with long bill which distinctly droops at tip. Dark brown plumage with bright rufous throat and rump. Tail blackish. Usually solitary, hopping on ground and tossing over leaf litter, hence its alternative name, "leaftosser." Difficult to see, normally flies off if disturbed, giving a sharp "chick" call. **Range and habitat:** NT, southern Mexico to southern Brazil. Lowland and mid-elevation humid forest. **Similar species:** several other leafscrapers.

Wedge-billed Woodcreeper

Striped Woodcreeper

Red-billed Scythebill

Rufous Hornero

Plain-mantled Tit-Spinetail

Dark-breasted Spinetail

Rusty-backed Spinetail (adult and juvenile)

Striped Woodhaunter

White-browed Foliage-Gleaner

Streaked Xenops

Plain Xenops

Tawny-throated Leaftosser

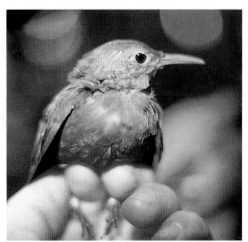

Giant Antshrike

Batara cinerea (Thamnophilidae) 32 cm/13 in.
Huge antshrike with very heavy, hooked bill. Male has black crest and crown with upperparts black with fine white barring. Underparts grayish. Female has chestnut crown, black upperparts with buff barring and dull pale brown underparts. Usually in pairs in dense forest undergrowth, foraging on large arthropods and small vertebrates. **Range and habitat:** NT, eastern Brazil, Paraguay, southern Bolivia and northern Argentina. Low and mid-elevation forest. **Similar species:** Undulated Antshrike.

Black-hooded Antshrike

Thamnophilus bridgesi (Thamnophilidae) 16.5 cm/6½ in.
Medium-sized dark plumaged antshrike. Male black, slightly grayer on belly, with small white spots on wing-coverts, white tips to outer 3 tail feathers and white wing-linings. Female has black head with fine white streaks, blackish brown above with white tips to wing-coverts and on tail. Underparts dirty olive with white streaks. Usually in pairs, actively gleaning insects from vegetation. Call a series of nasal notes. **Range and habitat:** NT, Costa Rica and Panama. Lowlands and foothills in secondary vegetation and forest borders. **Similar species:** male similar to several antshrikes elsewhere.

Amazonian Antshrike

Thamnophilus amazonicus (Thamnophilidae) 15 cm/6 in.
Medium-sized antshrike with rather stout bill. Male gray with black wings boldly tipped white to coverts and white edgings to scapulars and tertials. Black tail tipped white. Crown gray or black according to race. Female has rufous buff head and breast, paler below, with dark wings and tail similarly well marked with white. Usually in pairs, foraging actively at low levels, sometimes in mixed species flocks. **Range and habitat:** NT, Guianas to central Brazil. Fairly common at edge of swampy forest and open woodland in Amazonia. **Similar species:** Slaty Antshrike.

Plain Antvireo

Dysithamnus mentalis (Thamnophilidae) 11.5 cm/4½ in.
Small, rather plump bird with stout bill and short tail. Male gray above, darker on crown and ear-coverts, paler below. Wing-coverts narrowly tipped white. Female has chestnut crown, olive-brown above with indistinct buff tips to wing coverts. Paler below with grayish tinge on ear-coverts and narrow white eye-ring. In pairs or family groups and sometimes in mixed species flocks. Hop along branches at low levels, gleaning prey of adjacent foliage. Song a series of rising and falling whistles. **Range and habitat:** NT, Mexico to northern Argentina. Common at mid-elevations in humid forest. **Similar species:** Spot-crowned Antvireo, some antshrikes.

Amazonian Antwren

Myrmotherula multostriata (Thamnophilidae) 9.5 cm/4 in.
Very small, active antbird with very short, stubby tail. Male heavily streaked black and white with 2 bold white wing-bars. Female has rufous crown with black streaks. Underparts warm buff and virtually unstreaked. Wings dark with 2 white wing-bars and white edgings to scapulars. Usually in pairs, constantly moving, often hovering, as they glean foliage for small insects. Song a ringing trill. **Range and habitat:** NT, Amazonian basin. Common in lowlands and foothills in forest edges and secondary vegetation, often close to water. **Similar species:** Pacific and Guianan Antwrens.

Pygmy Antwren

Myrmotherula brachyura (Thamnophilidae) 8 cm/3 in.
Tiny antbird with very short stubby tail. Black and white streaked above, apart from grayish rump and darker tail. Pale cheeks, black malar stripe and white throat. Rest of underparts lemon-yellow. Female is buffy on head. Family parties actively search for insect prey from canopy to mid-level, incessantly giving their accelerating short trilling call. Sometimes join mixed species flocks. **Range and habitat:** NT, Panama to Brazil. Common in lowland humid forest and on forest edge. **Similar species:** Short-billed Antwren.

Banded Antwren

Dichrozona cincta (Thamnophilidae) 10.5 cm/4 in.
Small, terrestrial antbird. Long bill and short tail. Brown above with white bar across lower back and pale grayish rump. Wing-coverts tipped white, with greater coverts tipped golden, forming bold wing-bars. Underparts whitish with necklace of bold black spots.

Female has buffer barring. Walks on forest floor in crakelike fashion. Usually solitary, giving high-pitched series of rising drawn-out whistles. **Range and habitat:** NT, Amazonia. Uncommon, but probably overlooked in lowland humid forest. **Similar species:** Spot-backed Antbird.

Dot-winged Antwren

Microrhopias quixensis (Thamnophilidae) 13 cm/5 in.
Large antwren with long, graduated tail. Male black with white dots on wing-coverts, bold wing-bar, and white tips to tail. Female similar to male above but underparts entirely rufous, or with black throat (depending on race). Usually in pairs and in mixed species flocks. Actively search for insect prey in clusters of dense foliage. Song a rapid series of whistles. **Range and habitat:** NT, Mexico to Brazil. Mainly in lowland humid forest and secondary vegetation.

Scaled Antbird

Drymophila squamata (Thamnophilidae) 11 cm/4½ in.
Small antbird with longish tail. Upperparts black with white supercilium and bold white spots on back, wing-coverts and white bars on tail. Underparts white with black spots. Female brown above with buffy spots on back, tail black with buff bars and underparts white with fine black streaking. Rather wrenlike in behavior, hopping through dense tangles of vegetation. **Range and habitat:** NT, eastern coastal Brazil. Lowland humid forest. **Similar species:** several in same genus.

Blackish Antbird

Cercomacra nigrescens (Thamnophilidae) 15 cm/6 in.
A slim, long-tailed medium-sized antbird. Male is uniform blackish gray with wing-coverts tipped white and white edging to bend of wing. Female is brown above with warm rufous forehead, cheeks, and underparts. Pairs reside in thick tangled vegetation. Calls include a rising series of nasal notes and a trill. **Range and habitat:** NT, Guianas to Brazil. Lowland forest edge and secondary vegetation, particularly in seasonally flooded areas. **Similar species:** Dusky Antbird.

White-shouldered Antbird

Myrmeciza melanoceps (Thamnophilidae) 18 cm/7 in.
Large antbird with stout black bill. Male all-black apart from bluish bare skin around eye and white flash on shoulder (visible in flight). Female has black head and chest, rest of plumage rufous chestnut. Usually solitary or in pairs, sometimes attending swarms of army ants with other species. Keeps close to ground, often in thick undergrowth, "pumping" tail when perched. Loud song a series of double notes repeated. **Range and habitat:** NT, Amazonia. Common mainly in seasonally inundated forest. **Similar species:** Sooty Antbird.

Black-spotted Bare-Eye

Phlegopsis nigromaculata (Thamnophilidae) 18 cm/7 in.
Large, distinctive antbird with red bare facial skin. Head and underparts blackish, upperparts olive-brown heavily spotted black. Wings and tail rufous-toned. Sexes similar. Perch close to ground in typical hunchbacked fashion. Usually in family groups and associates with other species at swarms of army ants. Drop from low perches to ground to collect large arthropods flushed by ants. Call a drawn-out, nasal squeal. **Range and habitat:** NT, Amazonia. Common mainly in seasonally inundated forest. **Similar species:** Reddish-winged Bare-eye.

Giant Antshrike (female)

Black-hooded Antshrike (immature male)

Amazonian Antshrike

Plain Antvireo

Amazonian Antwren

Pygmy Antwren

Banded Antwren

Dot-winged Antwren

Scaled Antbird

Blackish Antbird

White-shouldered Antbird

Black-spotted Bare-Eye

Brazilian Antthrush

Chamaeza ruficauda (**Formicariidae**) 19 cm/7½ in.
Large, plump terrestrial antbird. Dark rufescent brown above with bold white stripe behind eye. Whitish buff below with feathers edged black, giving strongly streaked effect. Sexes similar. Usually solitary, walks with tail cocked across forest floor and fallen branches. Song a single "cu" repeated as a trill for almost a minute. **Range and habitat:** NT, southeast Brazil. Humid montane forest. **Similar species:** Short-tailed Antthrush.

Wing-banded Antbird

Myrmornis torquata (**Thamnophilidae**) 16.5 cm/6½ in.
Large, plump terrestrial antbird with very short tail and long bill. Male warm brown above with blackish scaling. Wings dark brown with several bold bright buff bars, more extensive panel on flight feathers. Throat and chest black, bordered by fine barring of black and white. Rest of underparts dull gray with buff vent. Female has rufous throat patch. Usually in pairs, hopping on ground, tossing over leaf litter in search of prey. Song a series of loud whistles. **Range and habitat:** NT, Central America to central Brazil. Lowland humid forest. **Not illustrated.**

Chestnut-belted Gnateater

Conopophaga aurita (**Conopophagidae**) 13 cm/5 in.
Small plump bird with short tail and long legs. Attractive male is dark brown above with blackish scaling, has a white tuft of feathers behind eye which can sometimes be obscured. Black face and chin, rufous chestnut breast and whitish belly. Female has rufous on face. Usually in pairs perched close to ground, dropping down to collect insect prey or toss over leaves. Quiet and unobtrusive. **Range and habitat:** NT, Amazonia. Uncommon in lowland humid forest.

Rufous-vented Tapaculo

Scytalopus femoralis (**Rhinocryptidae**) 14 cm/5½ in.
Small mainly terrestrial bird with fairly long cocked tail. Dark gray plumage with browner tone on wings and back. Some pale scaling on belly and flanks, vent chestnut with black bars. Some individuals show diagnostic white spot on crown. Very difficult to see as it hops through tangles of vegetation close to ground. Song a long series of rapidly repeated "chuock" or "chu-ock" notes. **Range and habitat:** NT, Andes from Colombia to Peru. Fairly common, mainly at mid-level, in undergrowth of humid forest. **Similar species:** several very similar in genus.

Purple-breasted Cotinga

Cotinga cotinga (**Cotingidae**) 19 cm/7½ in.
Medium-sized, plump cotinga with short black bill. Male dark blue with black wings and tail and dark purple throat and breast. Female brown with feathers edged pale buff, giving wholly scaled appearance. Usually solitary, although small groups may gather at a fruiting tree. Remain perched for long periods, making short sallies to pluck fruit. Often perch in exposed treetop branches. Silent though mechanical whirring sound produced in flight. **Range and habitat:** NT, southern Venezuela to northern Brazil. Uncommon in lowland forest on sandy soils. **Similar species:** Banded Cotinga. **Not illustrated.**

Plum-throated Cotinga

Cotinga maynana (**Cotingidae**) 19 cm/7½ in.
Medium-sized, stocky cotinga with yellow eyes. Male is turquoise-blue with black on primaries and underside of tail. Neat dark purple throat patch appears almost black at a distance. Female is grayish brown, wholly scaled with pale buff. Vent and underwing-coverts are cinnamon. Perches high on exposed branches. Usually solitary but several may gather at fruiting tree. Fruit are plucked on a sally, the bird normally sitting quietly in tree after each feed. In direct flight a whirring whistle is produced by wings, otherwise silent. **Range and habitat:** NT, western Amazonia. Uncommon in lowland forest and woodland. **Similar species:** Spangled Cotinga.

Black-necked Red Cotinga

Phoenicircus nigricollis (**Cotingidae**) 24 cm/9½ in.
Large, brilliantly colored cotinga. Striking male is black with a scarlet crown, breast and belly, rump and tail (tipped black). Female has duller brown and reddish plumage. Usually seen alone in subcanopy and visits fruiting canopy trees. Males are smaller than females and congregate in courtship leks, about which very little is known. More often heard than seen, far-carrying call is rather crowlike. **Range and habitat:** NT, western Amazonia. Fairly common in lowland humid forest. **Similar species:** Guianan Red Cotinga.

Bare-necked Fruitcrow

Gymnoderus foetidus (**Cotingidae**) 30–4 cm/12–13 in.
Rather large, long-tailed, small-headed cotinga. Male black with silvery gray uppersurface to wings and bluish bare skin on neck. Female dark gray with smaller area of bare skin on neck. Usually in dispersed groups often seen flying high. Mainly silent. **Range and habitat:** NT, Amazonia. Common in lowlands, mainly at forest edge and usually close to water. **Not illustrated.**

Red-ruffed Fruitcrow

Pyroderus scutatus (**Cotingidae**) 38–43 cm/15–17 in.
Very large cotinga. Plumage black with extensive area of "crinkled" red feathers on throat. Underparts show variable amount of chestnut, depending on race. Usually solitary visitors to fruiting trees. Males gather in small communal leks, producing a deep booming call. **Range and habitat:** NT; different races in northern Andes, Guianas and south-east Brazil to northern Argentina. Uncommon in low to mid-elevation cloud forest, woodland and forest edge.

Amazonian Umbrellabird

Cephalopterus ornatus (**Cotingidae**) 46–51 cm/18–20 in.
Large, peculiar cotinga with long feathered wattle hanging from throat and thick tuft of feathers on crown. Plumage glossy bluish black. Eyes are white. Sexes similar, although female has smaller adornments. Usually solitary or in small groups, often seen flying with deep undulating flight across rivers and swamps. Perches high in trees, hopping heavily through branches. Males give deep booming sound. **Range and habitat:** NT, Amazonia. Fairly common in lowlands and foothills, mainly at forest edge and close to water. **Similar species:** Long-wattled Umbrellabird.

Three-wattled Bellbird

Procnias tricarunculata (**Cotingidae**) 25–30 cm/10–12 in.
Large, stout cotinga. Male has white head, neck and chest, rest of plumage chestnut. 3 long wormlike wattles hang from base of very broad bill. Female olive-green above, yellow below with olive streaks. Usually solitary, feeding at mid-level upward. Snatches fruit in flight or plucked from a perch. Male calls from a canopy perch, producing very loud, explosive "BOK." **Range and habitat:** NT, Central America. During breeding season in montane forest, then migrates to lower elevation woodland and secondary vegetation. Vulnerable from deforestation..

Bearded Bellbird

Procnias averano (**Cotingidae**) 28 cm/11 in.
Large cotinga with very wide-based bill. Male has brown head, black wings; otherwise whitish gray. Cluster of black wattles hangs from throat. Female olive-green above, yellowish below heavily streaked green. Males spend most of day on canopy perches giving very loud, far-carrying "BOK" call, or occupy mid-level perches carrying out stereotyped displays to conspecifics. Fruit mainly taken in flight. **Range and habitat:** NT, northern South America. Quite common in low to mid-elevation humid forest, shows vertical migration.

Brazilian Antthrush

Plum-throated Cotinga

Chestnut-belted Gnateater (female)

Rufous-vented Tapaculo

Black-necked Red Cotinga

Red-ruffed Fruitcrow

Amazonian Umbrellabird

Bearded Bellbird

Three-wattled Bellbird

Guianan Cock-of-the-Rock

Rupicola rupicola (Cotingidae) 32 cm/13 in.

Large, stocky bird. Male bright orange with brownish black wings with white speculum and short dark tail. Compressed crest arches above crown and almost covers short orange bill. Female dark brown with smaller crest and grayish orange eye. Males spend most of day gathered at communal lek, displaying within individual "courts" on or close to ground. Call a buglelike "kawaooh." **Range and habitat:** NT, southern Venezuela and Guianas. Widespread in rocky forest on Guianan shield. **Similar species:** Andean Cock-of-the-Rock.

Andean Cock-of-the-Rock

Rupicola peruviana (Cotingidae) 32 cm/13 in.

Very similar in appearance to Guianan species. Body plumage of male may be scarlet or orange-red (depending on race). Wings and tail black with white tertials enlarged and flattened. Female is dark reddish brown with white eyes and small crest. Male courtship leks differ from former species, being at mid-level to subcanopy. Away from leks, usually solitary, visiting fruiting trees. **Range and habitat:** NT, fairly common at low to mid-altitudes on slopes of Andes from Venezuela to Bolivia. Occurs in wooded ravines, often close to rivers. **Similar species:** Guianan Cock-of-the-rock.

Sulfur-bellied Tyrant Manakin

Neopelma sulphureiventer (Pipridae) 12 cm/4½ in.

Rather large-billed, long-tailed flycatcherlike manakin with semiconcealed yellow crown patch. Olive-green above, dirty white throat with sides of underparts grayish olive and a clean yellow belly. Usually solitary, perched at low levels and partially insectivorous, flying out on short sallies to collect airborne prey or insects from foliage. **Range and habitat:** NT, eastern Peru to northern Bolivia. Lowland forest and woodland. **Similar species:** Pale-bellied and Saffron-crested Tyrant Manakins. **Not illustrated.**

Orange-collared Manakin

Manacus aurantiacus (Pipridae) 10 cm/4 in.

Medium-sized manakin with orange legs and black bill. Dumpy, bull-necked appearance. Male has black crown, nape and upper back and wings, olive-green rump and tail. Rest of head and breast bright orange, forming a collar. Rest of underparts bright yellow. Female is dull olive above, yellower below. Usually solitary but groups of males gather in undergrowth in courtship leks. Calls include loud "chee-pooh" and various mechanical whirring and clicking sounds. **Range and habitat:** NT, Costa Rica and Panama. Common in lowlands and foothills in humid secondary forest and forest edge. **Similar species:** White-bearded Manakin.

White-bearded Manakin

Manacus manacus (Pipridae) 10 cm/4 in.

Medium-sized manakin with orange legs and black bill. Male has black crown, nape, wings, back and tail. Otherwise white with gray rump. Female dull olive-green, paler below. Males form large lekking groups, active throughout year, with each male occupying individual court. 6 types of stereotyped display, generally involving jumps and slides along perches. Noisy, producing several calls including soft trill and mechanical sounds. **Range and habitat:** NT, Venezuela to Argentina. Common in lowland and foothill secondary vegetation and forest edge. **Similar species:** Golden-collared Manakin.

Wire-tailed Manakin

Pipra filicauda (Pipridae) 10.5 cm/4 in.

Large manakin with white eyes. Male has spectacular plumage with red crown and nape, yellow face, rump and underparts, black back, wings, and tail. Wing has white flash on flight feathers. Long filaments extend from tail. Female olive-green, yellower on belly with shorter tail filaments. Perches at low levels, usually solitary although several may gather at fruiting shrub. Males form dispersed leks. Complicated display involves jumps and short flights and culminates with male brushing female's face with tail filaments. **Range and habitat:** NT, Venezuela to Brazil. Lowlands in seasonally inundated forest, woodland and secondary growth.

Black-and-white Monjita

Xolmis dominicanus (Tyrannidae) 19 cm/7½ in.

Large, long-tailed flycatcher. White body with black wings and tail. Primaries tipped white. Females brownish tinged on crown, nape

and back. Uses exposed perches as vantage posts to search for invertebrate prey, dropping from perch to collect prey from ground. **Range and habitat:** NT, south-east Brazil to north-east Argentina. Uncommon species of lowland open scrub, usually near water or swamps. Vulnerable to habitat modification. **Similar species:** several in same genus.

Fork-tailed Flycatcher

Tyrannus savana (Tyrannidae) 28–38 cm/11–15 in.

Medium-sized flycatcher with enormously long forked tail. Black hood and tail, rest of upperparts gray, wings dark gray, white underparts. Makes aerial sallies from exposed perches such as fence-posts to catch insects, also visits fruiting trees. Migrants form large communal roosts, sometimes thousands strong: a spectacular sight as flock gathers in air. Call a short "tik." **Range and habitat:** NT, Mexico to central Argentina. Widespread at low and mid-elevations in open country or beside large rivers in forested regions. Has several migratory populations. **Similar species:** Scissor-tailed Flycatcher (see p 76).

Tropical Kingbird

Tyrannus melancholicus (Tyrannidae) 22 cm/8½ in)

Large flycatcher with slightly forked tail. Rather heavy black bill. Gray head with concealed reddish crown stripe, dusky on ear-coverts. Olive-green back and dull brown wings and tail. Whitish throat, olive smudge on chest, rest of underparts yellowish. Perches out in open on treetops, wires, and posts. Makes aerial sallies for flying insects. Has high-pitched trilling call. **Range and habitat:** NT, Mexico to Argentina. Common widespread species from lowlands to temperate zones in open terrain, woodland and forest edge. Some populations migratory. **Similar species:** several kingbirds (see p 76).

Social Flycatcher

Myiozetetes similis (Tyrannidae) 16.5 cm/6½ in.

Medium-sized flycatcher with rather stubby black bill. Head dark olive-brown apart from white throat, broad white supercilium which does not quite encircle head and concealed crimson crown patch. Upperparts olive-brown, underparts yellow. Immature has rufous edgings to wing and tail. Usually in noisy family groups, giving nasal "teeer." Feeds on small insects and fruit, the latter usually collected in a brief hovering flight. **Range and habitat:** NT, Mexico to Argentina. Common bird of lowland forest borders, secondary vegetation and gardens. **Similar species:** Rusty-margined Flycatcher.

Great Kiskadee

Pitangus sulphuratus (Tyrannidae) 22 cm/8½ in.

Large, noisy, rather stocky flycatcher. Quite a heavy black bill. Crown black with concealed yellow center. Broad white supercilium completely encircling head and blackish ear-coverts. White throat, rest of underparts yellow. Brown upperparts with rufous edgings to wing and tail feathers. Perches in open, making aerial sallies or swoops to ground to collect food. Boisterous manner, calling its name triumphantly "Kiska-dee." **Range and habitat:** NT and NA, southern USA to Argentina. Common in tropical and subtropical zones in forest borders, secondary vegetation and gardens. **Similar species:** Lesser Kiskadee, Boat-billed Flycatcher.

Grayish Mourner

Rhytipterna simplex (Tyrannidae) 20 cm/8 in.

Large flycatcher. Plumage generally gray with slight brown tone to wings and tail. Usually solitary, but sometimes joins mixed species flocks, perched inconspicuously on branch at mid-level or Subcanopy. Makes short flights to snatch insects from nearby foliage. Has loud song consisting of rising series of notes which terminate abruptly. **Range and habitat:** NT, Venezuela to southern Brazil. Uncommon in lowland humid forest. **Similar species:** Screaming Piha.

Guianan Cock-of-the Rock

Andean Cock-of-the Rock

Orange-collared Manakin

White-bearded Manakin

Fork-tailed Flycatcher

Wire-tailed Manakin (on display perch)

Black-and-white Monjita

Tropical Kingbird

Social Flycatcher

Great Kiskadee

Grayish Mourner

Northern Royal Flycatcher

Onychorhynchus mexicanus (Tyrannidae) 16.5 cm/6½ in.

Medium-sized, slender flycatcher with hammer-headed appearance at rest. Long black bill, plumage generally dull brown, more rufous on tail and pale tips to wing-coverts. Paler below with whitish chin and dark mottling on breast. Spectacular crest forms brilliant fan of red feathers (more orange in females) tipped inky blue; it is rarely seen fully expanded in field and its function is not fully understood. Usually solitary and inconspicuous at low levels. Call a low squeaky disyllabic whistle. **Range and habitat:** NT, southern Mexico to northern South America. Uncommon in lowland humid forest. **Similar species:** Northern Royal Flycatcher sometimes treated as separate species.

Gray-crowned Flycatcher

Tolymomyias poliocephalus (Tyrannidae) 11.5 cm/4½ in.

Small flycatcher with pale eyes and blackish bill. Crown grayish, rest of upperparts bright olive-green with yellow edgings to wing feathers. Under-parts yellowish green, slightly smudged olive on breast. Active at mid-level and subcanopy, sometimes in mixed species flocks, searching for small insects in foliage. Call a wheezy whistle. **Range and habitat:** NT, Venezuela to south-east Brazil. Uncommon in lowland humid forest and forest edge. **Similar species:** other members of same genus.

Rufous-tailed Flatbill

Ramphotrigon ruficauda (Tyrannidae) 16 cm/6½ in.

Medium-sized, large-headed flycatcher with wide-based bill. Dark olive-green above with rufous wing edgings and tail. Yellowish underparts with heavy olive diffuse streaking, buff vent. Usually solitary or in pairs, sometimes in mixed species flocks, perched at low levels. Remains motionless on perch before making short flight to new branch. Call consists of 2 or 3 drawn-out whistles. **Range and habitat:** NT, Amazonia. Uncommon in humid forest. **Not illustrated.**

Spotted Tody Flycatcher

Todirostrum maculatum (Tyrannidae) 9.5 cm/4 in.

Very small flycatcher with long tail and long flattened bill. Gray head with prominent yellow eye and whitish lores. Olive-green above with yellow wing edgings. Throat whitish with fine black spotlike streaks, rest of underparts yellowish. Solitary or in pairs, keeping low down in foliage, usually detected by loud "peep" call. **Range and habitat:** NT, Venezuela to northern Bolivia. Common in lowland secondary vegetation and river-banks. **Similar species:** Johannes' Tody Tyrant.

Large Elaenia

Elaenia spectabilis (Tyrannidae) 18 cm/7 in.

Medium-sized flycatcher. Crown, sides of head and upper-parts gray-olive. Throat and upper breast medium gray, contrasting with yellowish gray underparts. 3 whitish wing-bars. Usually solitary, perched in open situations at low to mid-levels. Call is soft "wheeoo." **Range and habitat:** NT, breeds in Brazil and northern Argentina, migrating to Amazonia during austral winter. Occurs in secondary vegetation, gardens, and clearings, often close to rivers on wintering quarters. **Similar species:** Small-billed Elaenia.

Sooty-headed Tyrannulet

Phyllomyias griseiceps (Tyrannidae) 10 cm/4 in.

Small flycatcher with stubby black bill. Rather bushy cap is dusky, obviously darker than olive upperparts. Darker wings, flight feathers with pale edgings but no wing-bars. Narrow whitish supercilium. Underparts tinged pale olive on breast, cleaner yellow below. Usually solitary at mid-level to canopy, actively searching foliage for small insects. Call a short trill. **Range and habitat:** NT, Panama to central Peru. Fairly common at low and mid-elevations in woodland, shrubby areas, and forest borders. **Similar species:** several similar tyrannulets.

White-winged Becard

Pachyramphus polychopterus (Tyrannidae) 14 cm/5½ in.

Medium-sized flycatcher, showing close affinities to cotingas. Male gray with black crown, mantle, tail and wings or all-black according to race. Wing-coverts, secondaries, scapulars, and tail broadly edged white. Female quite different with olive-brown upperparts, pale below with whitish spectacles and buff wing and tail markings.

Usually in pairs and often in mixed species flocks at mid-level or subcanopy. Song a series of descending soft whistles. **Range and habitat:** NT, Central America to northern Argentina. Common in lowland and mid-elevation secondary vegetation and woodland. **Similar species:** several becards.

Masked Tityra

Tityra semifasciata (Tyrannidae) 20 cm/8 in.

Rather stout, heavy-billed flycatcher, showing close affinities to cotingas. Red bare facial skin and bill with dusky tip. Male mainly white with front of head black, black wings and tail (tipped white) and with grayish tone to back. Female has brown crown and mantle. Usually in pairs, hopping heavily in canopy and reaching out to collect fruit. Also makes short flights to seize fruit or insect prey from vegetation. Call a dry croak. **Range and habitat:** NT, Mexico to Argentina. Common at low and mid-elevations in forest edge and woodland. **Similar species:** Black-tailed Tityra.

Sharpbill

Oxyruncus cristatus (Cotingidae) 16.5 cm/6½ in)

Rather curious bird with sharp pointed bill and reddish eye. Black crown with concealed red crest. Olive-green above, pale yellowish below. Black scaling on face and throat, rest of underparts heavily spotted black. Generally solitary in canopy and subcanopy, searching in acrobatic fashion for insects, using sharp bill to poke into leaf clusters and buds. Also takes fruit. Males gather in small leks to produce trilling song. **Range and habitat:** NT, patchily distributed from Central America to Paraguay in foothill montane forest.

Rufous-tailed Plantcutter

Phytotoma rara (Cotingidae) 18 cm/7 in.

Finchlike with stout bill. Male has rufous crown and streaked brown underparts. Blackish wings have white bar across median coverts and buff edgings to inner wing. Tail has black subterminal band and central feathers, with rufous on inner webs and rest of feathers, conspicuous in flight. Underparts pale rufous. Female is streaked brownish with buffy wing-bars. Usually in pairs or small groups, perching in exposed places such as telegraph wires and tops of bushes. Feed on fruit, buds, and leaves and can cause damage in orchards. Has a croaking call. **Range and habitat:** NT, southern Chile and Argentina. Low to mid-elevation in scrub, orchards, and gardens. **Similar species:** other plantcutters.

White-winged Swallow

Tachycineta albiventer (Hirundinidae) 14 cm/5½ in.

Medium-sized swallow. Bluish green above with white rump and patch on inner wing. Underparts white. Immatures are grayer. Usually seen in pairs flying low over water or perched on emergent bare branches. Nests in cavities close to water. Call a short trill. **Range and habitat:** NT, Venezuela to Argentina. Common in lowland lakes and large rivers. **Similar species:** Mangrove, White-rumped and Chilean Swallows.

Blue-and-white Swallow

Notiochelidon cyanoleuca (Hirundinidae) 13 cm/5 in.

Small slender swallow. Dark blue above, white below with black undertail-coverts. Immature browner above with buffish underparts. Often in small groups, with darting, flittering flight. Often seen perched on telegraph wires. Nests in crevices under roofs, in trees or cliffs or excavates hole in bank. Song a thin twittering trill. **Range and habitat:** NT, Central America to Tierra del Fuego. Common at mid-elevations to treeline in open areas and villages. Southern populations are migratory. **Similar species:** Tree Swallow (see p 78), Pale-footed Swallow.

Northern Royal Flycatcher

Gray-crowned Flycatcher

Large Elaenia

Spotted Tody Flycatcher

Sooty-headed Tyrannulet

White-winged Becard

Masked Tityra

Sharpbill

Rufous-tailed Plantcutter

White-winged Swallow

Blue-and-white Swallow

Azure-hooded Jay

Cyanolyca cucullata (Corvidae) 29 cm/11½ in.
Small jay with stiffened feathers on forehead. Head, upper back and breast black apart from light blue crown and nape. Rest of plumage dark blue. Usually in small, noisy groups moving through trees, searching in epiphytes and crevices for large invertebrate prey. Call a loud "jeet-jeet." **Range and habitat:** NT, Central America. Uncommon in mid-elevation mountain forest and forest edge. **Similar species:** White-collared Jay.

Plush-crested Jay

Cyanocorax chrysops (Corvidae) 35 cm/14 in.
Large jay with rather stiff bushy crest. Head and breast black with yellow eye and bright blue patches around eye. Nape whitish blue, rest of upperparts violet-blue with white tip to tail. Underparts creamy white. Usually in small noisy groups, sometimes with other species of jay, rather inquisitive. Calls include loud "cho-cho-cho." **Range and habitat:** NT, Brazil to northern Argentina. Common at low and mid-elevations in forest and woodland. **Similar species:** White-naped and Black-chested Jays.

Thrushlike Wren

Campylorhynchus turdinus (Troglodytidae) 20 cm/8 in.
Large long-tailed wren. Dull brown above with narrow whitish supercilium. Underparts white, heavily spotted dark brown. Southern race unmarked below and grayer above. Family parties clamber about in epiphyte clumps and vine tangles in subcanopy, peering downward and probing into detritus. Song, often given in duet, a loud repeated "chooka-cookcook." **Range and habitat:** NT, western and southern Amazonia, south-west and eastern Brazil. Lowland humid forest and forest border.

Moustached Wren

Thryothorus genibarbis (Troglodytidae) 15 cm/6 in.
Medium-sized wren. Grayish brown crown and nape. Rest of upperparts warmer brown, unmarked wings, tail brown with bold dark bars. White supercilium, ear-coverts streaked black and white, white malar, black submalar and white throat. Rest of underparts dull buff. Usually in pairs in undergrowth. Song, often delivered as duet, a series of rapid phrases. Andean populations have more liquid song and may be separate species. **Range and habitat:** NT, southern Amazonia to eastern Brazil, lowlands, and foothills in bamboo thickets and forest undergrowth. Andean population south to Ecuador occurs at mid-elevations in forest borders and old clearings. **Similar species:** Coraya Wren.

Scaly-breasted Wren

Microcerculus marginatus (Troglodytidae) 11.5 cm/4½ in.
Small, terrestrial wren. Long bill and short, cocked tail. Upperparts dark, grayish brown, white underparts with flanks and vent brownish, faintly or boldly scaled black. Walks furtively, crakelike, on forest floor and over fallen logs. Memorable song consists of opening flourish followed by tantalizing series of whistles, descending in pitch and with increasing intervals. **Range and habitat:** NT, Amazonia. Common at low and mid-elevations in humid forest. **Similar species:** several, sometimes all considered to be races of single species, the Nightingale Wren.

Black-capped Mockingthrush

Donacobius atricapilla (Troglodytidae) 22 cm/8½ in.
Striking slender bird with long mobile tail. Upperparts dark brown with yellow eye. White wing flash and tips to tail. Underparts creamy with dark scaling on flanks. Usually seen in pairs, perched on tops of waterside grassy vegetation or shrubs. Often set up antiphonal duets, with pair facing each other, tails wagging from side to side. Other calls include loud whoops. **Range and habitat:** NT, Panama to northern Argentina. Common in lowlands beside rivers and lakes. **Similar species:** Bicolored Wren.

Black-billed Thrush

Turdus ignobilis (Turdidae) 24 cm/9½ in.
Dark thrush with blackish bill. Dull brown plumage with whitish throat, streaked black. Some races have white crescent on lower throat. Underparts pale grayish brown becoming whiter on center of belly. Usually solitary, seen hopping on open ground or perched on telegraph wires or roofs. Song a subdued series of fluty notes. **Range and habitat:** NT, Colombia to Bolivia. Common in lowland and mid-elevations in forest borders, secondary vegetation, open areas, and gardens. **Similar species:** several similar thrushes.

Lawrence's Thrush

Turdus lawrencii (Turdidae) 23 cm/9 in.
Large thrush with bright orange-yellow bill and eye-ring. Dark brown above, paler below with pale throat streaked black and whitish belly and vent. Female has blackish bill and weaker eye-ring. Feeds on ground but also visits fruiting canopy trees. Song, delivered from canopy, shows remarkable mimicry of wide range of forest species. Will sing from 1 perch, then fly away to continue from another and can be very difficult to see. **Range and habitat:** NT, western Amazonia. Fairly common in lowland humid forest. **Similar species:** Pale-vented and Bare-eyed Thrushes.

Cocoa Thrush

Turdus fumigatus (Turdidae) 23 cm/9 in.
Large thrush with brown bill. Plumage generally uniform rufous brown. Underparts slightly paler with pale streaked throat and buffy center of belly and vent. Usually in pairs, usually on or close to ground, sometimes higher. Rather shy. Gives rich, musical song consisting of repeated phrases. **Range and habitat:** NT, Venezuela to central Brazil, southeast Brazil and Caribbean. Mainly in lowlands, in humid forest and wooded areas. **Similar species:** Pale-vented Thrush. Not illustrated.

Clay-colored Thrush

Turdus grayi (Turdidae) 23 cm/9 in.
Thrush with yellowish bill and reddish eye. Dull olive-brown above, buffier below with paler throat, lightly streaked. Immatures, as in most thrushes, retain some pale-tipped wing-coverts from juvenile plumage. Forages on ground, searching in leaf litter for earthworms and other small prey. Also visits fruiting trees. Pleasant musical song is rather varied with trills, whistles, and warbling notes. **Range and habitat:** NT, Mexico to Colombia. Fairly common in low to mid-elevations in gardens, secondary vegetation and, especially outside breeding season, in forest. **Similar species:** Pale-breasted Thrush.

Tropical Gnatcatcher

Polioptila plumbea (Polioptilidae) 11.5 cm/4½ in.
Small bird with long, slender tail and fine bill. Male has glossy black cap, gray above with blackish wings edged white and black tail with outer tail feathers white. Underparts whitish, smudged gray on breast. Female lacks black cap, apart from in Peruvian race when similar to male. Engagingly active bird, often in mixed species flocks, which constantly twitches its tail whilst searching for insects on tips of small twigs. Call a nasal mew, song a series of thin, high-pitched notes. **Range and habitat:** NT, Mexico to Peru and eastern Brazil. Common at low and mid-elevation forest edge, secondary growth and drier woodland. **Similar species:** Slate-throated, Guianan and Blue-gray Gnat-catchers (see p 82).

Yellowish Pipit

Anthus lutescens (Motacillidae) 13 cm/5 in.
Slender, small terrestrial bird with thin bill. Brown above with buff and dusky streaks. Tail blackish with white outer tail feathers. Narrow eye-ring. Underparts washed whitish yellow with brown streaks on breast. Walks on ground and difficult to see unless in flight. Usually occur in loose groups. Sings in flight, starting with series of "tsits," then glides back to ground with long "zeeeeeeeeeu." **Range and habitat:** NT, Panama, eastern South America and Pacific coast of Peru. Common in lowland grassland. **Similar species:** Chaco Pipit.

Azure-hooded Jay

Plush-crested Jay

Thrushlike Wren

Moustached Wren

Lawrence's Thrush
(immature)

Scaly-breasted Wren

Black-capped
Mockingthrush

Black-billed Thrush

Clay-colored Thrush

Tropical Gnatcatcher
(female)

Yellowish Pipit

Rufous-browed Peppershrike

Cyclarhis gujanensis (Vireonidae) 14–15 cm/5½–6 in.
Large, stocky vireo with heavy bill. Olive-green above, grayer on crown, with rufous supercilium and forehead, and gray cheeks with brownish eyes. Underparts yellow with white center to belly and vent. Plumage rather variable between races. In pairs, often in mixed species flocks, rather sluggish, keeping under cover of foliage from mid-level to canopy. Short, musical song frequently repeated. **Range and habitat:** NT, Mexico to Argentina. Fairly common at low and mid-elevations in forest borders and secondary vegetation, mainly in drier areas. **Similar species:** Black-billed Peppershrike.

Rufous-crowned Greenlet

Hylophilus poicilotis (Vireonidae) 12.5 cm/5 in.
Small, warblerlike vireo. Distinctive plumage with rufous crown, extending down to nape, olive-green upperparts, whitish face and throat with fine blackish streaking on ear-coverts (depending on race). Rest of underparts yellowish with buffy tinge on breast. Often in mixed species flocks, mainly foraging at mid-level. Has loud, ringing song: **Range and habitat:** NT, south-east Brazil, northern Argentina and Paraguay. Common in low and mid-elevation humid forest, secondary vegetation and scrub.

Crested Oropendola

Psarocolius decumanus (Icteridae) 33–43 cm/13–17 in.
Large oropendola with white bill. Plumage essentially black with chestnut on rump and vent and all but central tail feathers yellow. At close quarters, wirelike crest of male visible. Usually solitary, but sometimes in flocks with other oropendolas; breed in colonies. Spectacular display by male, seemingly about to topple from perch while producing extraordinary series of loud gurgling and tearing sounds. **Range and habitat:** NT, Panama to northern Argentina. Low to mid-elevation humid forest and partially cleared areas. **Similar species:** Chestnut-headed Oropendola.

Montezuma Oropendola

Gymnostinops montezuma (Icteridae) 38–50 cm/15–20 in.
Very large oropendola with black bill, tipped orange. Black head and chest, otherwise deep chestnut with black tips to flight feathers and yellow tail, apart from black central tail feathers. Bare facial skin blue, pinkish at base of bill. Usually in small groups in canopy, searching for invertebrates in crevices and also feeding on fruit. Nests in colonies in isolated trees. Male display involves deep bowing, producing loud liquid gurgling call with accompanied screeches. **Range and habitat:** NT, Central America. Common in lowlands and foothills in forest borders and cultivated areas. **Similar species:** Chestnut-mantled and Olive Oropendolas.

Yellow-rumped Cacique

Cacicus cela (Icteridae) 24–8 cm/9½–11 in)
Medium-sized icterid with whitish bill and eyes. Mainly black with yellow rump, base of tail, vent and flash on upper wing. Often in noisy groups, but sometimes solitary. Forages from canopy to low levels, searching for invertebrates and fruit. Nests colonially, invariably in an isolated tree close to human habitation or surrounded by water, often associated with wasp nests. Several loud barking calls. Song of nominate race is highly mimetic. **Range and habitat:** NT, Panama to central Brazil. Common in lowlands in forest edge and partially cleared areas. **Similar species:** Band-tailed Oropendola.

Venezuelan Troupial

Icterus icterus (Icteridae) 23 cm/9 in.
Small icterid with pale eye. Rather variable, some races may be separate species. Essentially orange and black. Black bib always appears to have ragged border with orange underparts. Head wholly black or with orange crown, back may be black or orange depending on race. Usually some white on wing. Normally in pairs, foraging mainly at low levels. Musical song consists of several long fluid whistles delivered from high perch, usually broken off by flight. Takes over nests of other species. **Range and habitat:** NT, Colombia to Paraguay. Common in lowland forest edge, woodland and scrub. **Similar species:** several orioles (see p 90).

Giant Cowbird

Molothrus oryzivous (Icteridae) 28–36 cm/11–14 in.
Medium-sized icterid with small-headed, bull-necked appearance.

Male wholly glossy black. Female slimmer, blackish brown with pale eye. Has undulating flight and long-tailed, heavy-bodied profile is characteristic. Usually alone or in small groups, walking on ground or in attendance at an oropendola or cacique colony, the nests of which are parasitized. Apart from some grating flight calls, mainly silent. **Range and habitat:** NT, southern Mexico to northern Argentina. Uncommon at low and mid-elevations in forest borders, cleared areas and river banks. **Similar species:** Great-tailed Grackle.

Red-crowned Ant-Tanager

Habia rubica (Thraupidae) 18 cm/7 in.
Medium-sized tanager with blackish bill. Male reddish brown with inconspicuous scarlet crown patch, bordered by black. Paler and rosier below, with brighter throat. Female olive-brown above with orange-yellow crown patch. Dull olivaceous buff below, cleaner on throat. Family parties are noisy, chattering components of low-level mixed species flocks. **Range and habitat:** NT, Mexico to northern Argentina. Fairly common in lowland humid forest. **Similar species:** Red-throated Ant-tanager.

Silver-beaked Tanager

Ramphocelus carbo (Thraupidae) 18 cm/7 in.
Medium-sized tanager with bold, swollen silvery white lower mandible. Male mainly black with velvety maroon tone to upperparts and tinged dark crimson on throat and chest. Female has duller bill, with reddish brown plumage and redder tone on rump. Immature similar to female. Noisy conspicuous groups move through bushes, feeding on fruit and insects. Call a loud, metallic "chink." **Range and habitat:** NT, common in lowlands east of Andes, south to southern Brazil. Forest borders and secondary vegetation. **Similar species:** female similar to Red-crowned Ant-tanager.

Blue-gray Tanager

Thraupis episcopus (Thraupidae) 16.5 cm/6½ in.
Medium-sized tanager. Pale bluish gray head and underparts which contrast with darker blue back, wings and tail. Lesser wing-coverts bright blue or white with white wing-bar (depending on race). Usually in small groups which forage actively in treetops and shrubs. Has rather squeaky call. **Range and habitat:** NT, Mexico to central South America. Very common at low and mid-elevation in wide range of habitats from humid forest borders and open woodland to gardens. **Similar species:** Sayaca Tanager.

Palm Tanager

Thraupis palmarum (Thraupidae) 16.5 cm/6½ in.
Rather dingy, grayish olive medium-sized tanager. Darker and glossier above, forehead tinged yellowish. Most obvious feature is 2-toned wing with paler wing-coverts contrasting with flight feathers which, apart from bases, are blackish. Pairs or small groups often seen in palms or tops of other trees, searching for insects in acrobatic fashion. Call rather squeaky. **Range and habitat:** NT, Central America to southern Brazil. Common in lowlands in forest borders, shrubby vegetation and settled areas. **Similar species:** Golden-chevroned Tanager.

Thick-billed Euphonia

Euphonia laniirostris (Thraupidae) 11 cm/4½ in.
Small tanager with stubby bill and short tail. Forecrown and underparts yellow, rest of upperparts blackish blue with white spots on outer 2 tail feathers. Female is olive-green with yellower tone below. Usually in pairs or family parties, sometimes in mixed species flocks of frugivores at mid-level to canopy. A remarkable mimic of other species' calls. **Range and habitat:** NT, Costa Rica to Brazil. Common in lowland woodland, secondary growth and forest edge. **Similar species:** several euphonias.

Rufous-browed Peppershrike

Rufous-crowned Greenlet

Crested Oropendola

Montezuma Oropendola

Yellow-rumped Cacique

Venezuelan Troupial

Giant Cowbird

Red-crowned Ant-Tanager

Silver-beaked Tanager (female)

Blue-gray Tanager

Palm Tanager

Thick-billed Euphonia

Paradise Tanager

Tangara chilensis (Thraupidae) 15 cm/6 in.
Multi-colored gem. Apple-green head with black on nape and around eye. Black upperparts with bright red or red and orange rump. Turquoise wing-coverts and underparts, more violet on throat and black center of belly and vent. Common in mixed species canopy flocks, visits fruiting trees and actively searches branches with epiphytes. Call a high-pitched twitter. **Range and habitat:** NT, Amazonia. Lowland humid forest and forest borders.

Opal-rumped Tanager

Tangara velia (Thraupidae) 14 cm/5½ in.
Small dark tanager. Black upper-parts with opal-colored lower back and rump and shining blue uppertail-coverts. Wings, head and underparts purplish blue with chestnut belly and vent. Some races have pale blue forehead and eastern Brazilian race has pale blue, not purple-blue, on underparts. Usually in mixed canopy flocks with other tanagers. **Range and habitat:** NT, Amazonia and eastern coast of Brazil. Fairly common in lowland humid forest and forest edge. **Similar species:** Opal-crowned Tanager.

Black-faced Dacnis

Dacnis lineata (Thraupidae) 11.5 cm/4½ in.
Small honey creeper with short, pointed bill. Black mask contrasting with yellow eye and blue crown. Rest of upperparts black with blue rump, scapulars and edges to tertials. Underparts turquoise-blue with white belly and vent. Western race has yellow replacing white, also evident as tuft in front of wing. Female drab olivaceous, paler below with yellow belly in western race. Usually in pairs and often in mixed species flocks with other tanagers. Searches foliage for small insects and visits fruiting trees. **Range and habitat:** NT, Amazonia and northern Andean valleys and foothills. Common in lowland humid forest and secondary growth. **Similar species:** Turquoise Dacnis.

Bananaquit

Coereba flaveola (Coerebidae) 10 cm/4 in.
Very small bird with fine, decurved bill. Blackish brown. above with bold white supercilium, white speculum and tips to outer tail. Yellow rump and underparts apart from gray throat and whitish vent. All-black forms occur on some Caribbean islands. Active, highly energetic bird usually alone or in pairs. Can be very tame. Visits flowers for nectar and takes fruit from low levels to canopy. Call a shrill twitter. **Range and habitat:** NT, Mexico to northern Argentina, throughout Caribbean. Low to mid-elevation, locally abundant in gardens, secondary vegetation and woodland.

Buff-throated Saltator

Saltator maximus (Cardinalidae) 20 cm/8 in.
Large finch with heavy bill. Bright olive-green above with grayer head and short white supercilium. Black malar and white chin, bordered buffy below. Underparts grayish olive with belly and vent buff. Usually solitary or in pairs and rather wary. Mainly keeps to low or mid-levels, visiting fruiting trees or shrubs. Pleasant, repetitive song is thrushlike. **Range and habitat:** NT, Mexico to southern Brazil. Common in low and mid-elevation secondary vegetation and wooded areas. **Similar species:** Grayish Saltator.

Yellow Cardinal

Gubernatrix cristata (Emberizidae) 20 cm/8 in.
Large, boldly marked, crested finch. Male has black-fronted crest and throat, yellow supercilium and malar. Otherwise olive-green above with blackish centers to back feathers, yellower below. Female grayer with white replacing yellow on face. In pairs and small groups, perched in open on shrubs. Feeds mainly on ground. Attractive musical song. **Range and habitat:** NT, southern Brazil, Uruguay and northern Argentina. Rare in lowland woodland and scrub. Endangered by trapping for pet trade.

Blue-black Grosbeak

Cyanocompsa cyanoides (Cardinalidae) 16 cm/6½ in.
Medium-sized, heavy-billed finch. Plumage of male wholly deep dark blue, rather brighter on forehead and around black bill. Female dark chocolate brown. Usually in pairs which remain furtively in undergrowth. Call a metallic "chink." Song a rich jumble of ascending and descending notes. **Range and habitat:** NT, Mexico to Bolivia. Fairly common, mainly in lowlands, in forest edge and secondary woodland. **Similar species:** Ultramarine Grosbeak.

Sooty Grassquit

Tiaris fuliginosa (Emberizidae) 11.5 cm/4½ in.
Small finch with conical dark bill, pinkish on gape. Male uniformly dull blackish. Female drab olive-brown above, paler below. Usually in pairs or small groups, not associated with other species, foraging in grass or low down in shrubs. Builds grass domed nest, close to ground. Song a thin, high-pitched short series of notes. **Range and habitat:** NT, locally from Venezuela and Trinidad to eastern Brazil. Uncommon in lowland forest borders, drier scrub and woodland. **Similar species:** female in particular may be confused with several small finches.

Yellow-bellied Seedeater

Sporophila nigricollis (Emberizidae) 11.5 cm/4½ in.
Small finch. Male has pale bill, black hood, dark olive-green above, sometimes with inconspicuous white speculum on wing, and whitish yellow below. Female has dark bill and is olive-brown, paler and warmer below. Often in small flocks mixed with other small finches. Usually on or close to ground, although male often perches high on telegraph wires. Gives short, musical song. **Range and habitat:** NT, Central America to southern Brazil. Common at low and mid-elevations in open grassy areas, woodland and forest edge. **Similar species:** Black-and-white and Dubois' Seedeaters.

Saffron Finch

Sicalis flaveola (Emberizidae) 14 cm/5½ in.
Small bright yellow finch. Male almost wholly yellow with orange crown. Upperparts slightly olive-tinged, with faint streaking. Female similar but somewhat duller. Immature pale grayish brown, streaked above, with yellow restricted to collar and vent. Usually in flocks, foraging on ground or perched in small trees or bushes. Has musical, repetitive song. **Range and habitat:** NT, patchily distributed throughout South America and introduced to Panama and Jamaica. Common in lowland savannah, parks and gardens. **Similar species:** Orange-fronted Yellow-Finch.

Cinereous Warbling-Finch

Poospiza cinerea (Emberizidae) 13 cm/5 in.
Small finch. Gray upperparts with dark gray cheeks. White underparts. Flight feathers edged gray and tail feathers tipped white. Poorly known . **Range and habitat:** NT, southern Brazil (*cinerea*). Scarce and local in open deciduous woodland and shrubby areas. Vulnerable owing to rapid habitat loss.

Great Pampa-Finch

Embernagra platensis (Emberizidae) 20.5-23 cm/8-9 in.
Large, stocky finch with orange bill with dark culmen. Dull olive-gray upperparts, slightly grayer on rump. Fine blackish streaking on crown and back (or unstreaked depending on race), yellowish wing edgings. Gray face, duskier around eye, and underparts with buffy flanks and whitish belly. Immature heavily streaked. Usually in pairs, sometimes in small groups, foraging on ground close to cover, or perched on fence-posts or bushes. Rather jerky flight with broad tail slightly cocked. Has short, spluttering song. **Range and habitat:** NT, southern Brazil to northern Argentina. Common from lowlands to mountains in cultivated areas, grasslands and marshes. **Similar species:** Buff-throated Pampa-Finch.

Paradise Tanager

Opal-rumped Tanager

Black-faced Dacnis

Bananaquit

Buff-throated Saltator

Yellow-bellied Seedeater

Sooty Grassquit

Blue-black Grosbeak

Yellow Cardinal

Saffron Finch

Cinereous Warbling-Finch

Great Pampa-Finch

THE PALAEARCTIC REGION

The Palaearctic Region comprises all of Europe, those parts of Africa north of the Sahara Desert and all of Asia north of the Himalayas. Among offshore islands and island groups included in the region are Iceland, the Faroes, the Azores, the Canaries, the Selvagens and the Cape Verde Islands. The northern boundary is formed by the Arctic Ocean, to the west lies the Atlantic, while the eastern boundary is the Pacific Ocean. To the south, the boundaries with the Afrotropical and Oriental Regions are less well defined, though there is a nearly continuous chain of mountainous regions from the Atlas in the west to the Himalayas in the east, to the north of which lies a more or less continuous line of deserts.

Within the vast extent of this region there is, naturally enough, great diversity of geography, topography, climate and vegetation. The last great influence on all of these was the sequence of at least four Pleistocene glaciations, the final one of which ended some 10,000 years ago. The climatic regime now affecting the Palaearctic is still postglacial, although it has been described as interglacial.

During the last glaciation, ice-sheets extended quite well south in the western half of the region, but hardly at all in the eastern. The effect of the glaciation was to push the major climatic zones some thousands of miles southward, thus completely altering the situation in the western Palaearctic, though much less so in the eastern. As the ice retreated there was a steady expansion northward and north-westward of the birds that had been forced south and south-east by the onset of the glaciation. This expansion is still going on with several examples of species extending their ranges during this century, the Eurasian Collared-Dove being the most spectacular.

As mentioned above, the boundaries between the Palaearctic and the Afrotropical and Oriental Regions are relatively poorly defined and consequently there are occurrences in the extreme south of the Palaearctic Region of what are really species of the latter more southerly regions, such as the sandgrouse. However, to the west the Atlantic Ocean has formed a very effective barrier to avian spread, with no known colonizations from the Nearctic, though the Spotted Sandpiper has bred just once, and this despite hundreds of vagrants crossing from west to east every year. The Pacific Ocean is also a complete barrier except in the far north, where the chain of islands stretching between Siberia and Alaska has allowed some species to colonize in either direction.

The faunal zones

The enormous size and diversity of the region demands some method of subdivision so that the main climatic and vegetational zones can be described. An accepted scheme is through the concept of faunal type, with from five to seven zones designated. Here five have been distinguished, running from north to south, namely Arctic, boreal, temperate, Mediterranean and desert.

The northern latitudes comprising the Arctic zone are characterized by a very short summer during which large numbers of comparatively few species of birds breed, and very long winters, often with extremely cold temperatures, making the area hardly suitable for any bird life. Thus, virtually all breeding birds of the region are migrants.

Much of the Arctic zone has comparatively low precipitation. Vegetation is classified as tundra, with few if any plants reaching 50 cm (20 in) in height. Trees and shrubs are restricted to creeping varieties. The underlying permafrost greatly impedes drainage, leading to the formation of extensive marshes, in part compensating for the low precipitation. Such marshes provide nesting and feeding areas for many birds. Among these are the Brent and Greater White-fronted Geese, King Eider, Sanderling, Red Knot, Gray Phalarope and Glaucous Gull. Land birds are scarce but include the Hoary Redpoll and Snowy Owl.

The more southerly part of the Arctic zone includes a region of greater precipitation and less cold temperatures. Here there are often patches or larger extents of scrub, growing fairly high and thus providing nest shelter and food for a greater variety of birds. Marshy areas also abound. Characteristic birds include the Willow Ptarmigan, Lapland Longspur and Spotted Redshank.

The seas in the Arctic zone are generally shallow and fertile and, in summer, support vast numbers of seabirds which nest on coastal cliffs, including auks, the Black-legged Kittiwake and the Northern Fulmar. The conditions of weather and vegetation found on the upper regions of the higher mountains in more southerly latitudes show distinct similarities to those in the Arctic, and for this reason are usually included in that zone. Some breeding birds undertake a purely vertical migration between summer and winter, breeding on the high tops and wintering lower down; examples are the Rock Ptarmigan and Snow Bunting.

To the south of the Arctic zone lies a broad continuous belt of coniferous forest comprising the boreal zone. The northern limit of trees merges with the low Arctic scrub, with maximum penetration of trees northward along more sheltered river valleys. Clearings and river valleys within the forest zone are frequently wet and boggy, or filled with lakes, providing a sheltered habitat for wetland birds in addition to the forest birds that occur. Birds of this zone can be residents or migrants. They include the Smew, Spotted Redshank and Wood Sandpiper around the marshy pools, and the Northern Goshawk, Redwing, Brambling and Eurasian Siskin in the forests.

Small areas similar to the boreal zone occur around the lower slopes of the larger mountain massifs further south. The Western Capercaillie is a typical species.

The temperate zone was formerly a zone of deciduous forests, once more or less continuous but now much reduced and fragmented by man, with the bulk of the cleared areas converted into agricultural land, though with considerable urbanization, too. This type of habitat is more or less confined to the Western Palaearctic, with isolated pockets further east and also further south on higher ground. It reappears in the Eastern Palaearctic in, for example, China. Species diversity is much greater than in the coniferous forests of the boreal zone. The Eurasian Green Woodpecker, various tits, European Robin, Eurasian Blackbird and several different finches are characteristic groups found in deciduous woodland, while ground-nesting birds such as the Northern Lapwing and the Eurasian Skylark breed in the cleared areas.

Wetlands in the temperate zone support a great number of different breeding species including many ducks—such as Mallard and Common Teal—as well as Common Coot, Common Moorhen, Spotted Redshank and various gulls.

Seabirds are numerous on coastal cliffs, especially the Northern Gannet, Atlantic Puffin and Common Murre. Also of vital importance to birds are the many estuaries providing feeding and wintering grounds for enormous numbers of mainly Arctic breeding waders such as the Red Knot, Dunlin and Common Ringed and Gray Plovers.

The more southerly latitudes of the Palaearctic Region are characterized by a much warmer, drier climate known as the Mediterranean zone. Here evergreen trees and shrubs flourish in some areas, while in others—for example, the Russian steppes—the natural vegetation is open grassland. Several species of warblers, such as the Subalpine and Dartford, are typical of this zone, as are larger woodland birds such as the African Golden Oriole and Eurasian Hoopoe. Wetlands hold the Purple Heron, Little Egret and Little Bittern and the drier areas attract bustards and larks.

The desert zone contains deserts that extend not quite continuously right across the southern part of the Palaearctic from the northern half of the Sahara, through those of northern Arabia and thence eastward into Mongolia and the Gobi.

The avifauna of the Palaearctic Region is estimated to contain just under 950 species of which about 450 are nonpasserines and 500 passerines. Because of the effect of the last glaciations, mentioned above, species diversity increases very markedly from west to east.

Palaearctic ornithological societies

Ornithologists in the Palaearctic Region are well served by societies. Most countries have one or more devoted to birds, some to conservation, others to research, while in western Europe the hobby of bird-watching, usually linked to conservation, has enabled some societies to attract very large memberships. Further information on birds in the UK can be obtained from the Royal Society for the Protection of Birds (RSPB), The Lodge, Sandy, Bedfordshire SG19 2 DL.

Seabird city, Norway. Here cliff ledges provide nest sites for many thousands of seabirds, notably Common Murres and Black-legged

Kittiwakes. Each species has slightly different nesting requirements so that almost the entire cliff face is occupied.

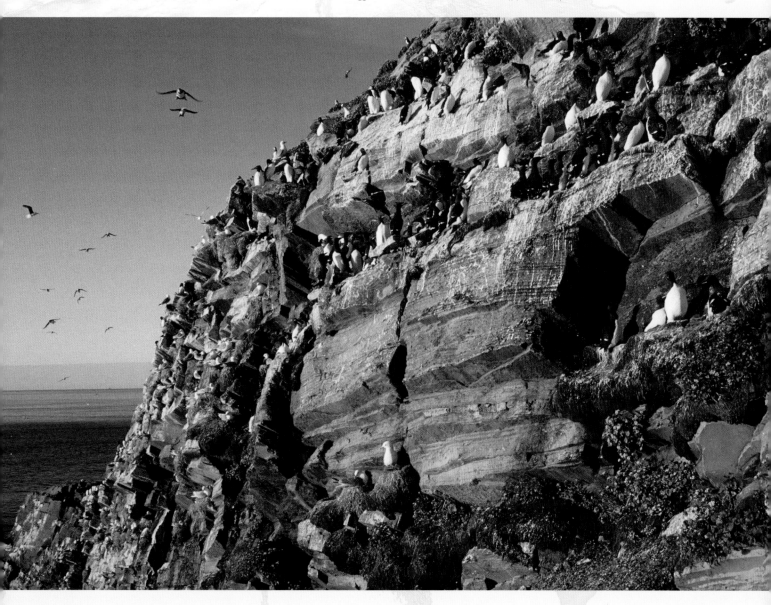

DIVERS Gaviformes

Arctic Loon
Gavia arctica (Gaviidae) 60–70 cm/24–8 in.
Large, stream-lined diving bird with slender, pointed bill. In breeding plumage, head and nape soft gray, with black throat patch. Back black, finely patterned with white. Sides of throat and chest white, streaked black. Underparts white. Winter plumage gray-black above, whitish below. Loud, wailing calls in breeding season; deep "kwuk-kwuk" in flight. **Range and habitat:** widespread circumpolar Holarctic. Breeds on freshwaters in arctic and northern temperate zones. Winters in coastal waters from breeding range south to temperate zone. Declining in a few areas through disturbance. **Similar species:** Red-throated Loon.

Red-throated Loon
Gavia stellata (Gaviidae) 50–60 cm/20–4 in.
Slender diving bird with thin upturned bill. Gray head and black and white streaked neck in breeding plumage, with patch of red on throat. Back dark gray, underparts whitish. In winter, overall pale gray above, whitish below. In flight, shows typical narrow wings of diver, head, neck and legs held below line of back. Wailing calls in breeding season; "kuk-kuk-kuk" in flight. **Range and habitat:** widespread circumpolar Holarctic. Breeds freshwaters in arctic and northern temperate zones. Winters in coastal waters from breeding range south to temperate zone. Vulnerable to oil spills at sea. **Similar species:** Arctic Loon.

GREBES Podicipediformes

Great Crested Grebe
Podiceps cristatus (Podicipedidae) 48 cm/19 in.
Largest grebe with long thin neck and fine, pointed bill. In summer plumage, highly distinctive black ear-tufts and chestnut and black plumes on side of head, raised in elaborate courtship display. In winter, white face and neck, cap remaining blackish, and gray-brown body. Far-carrying barking call, variety of crowing and moaning sounds making up song. **Range and habitat:** locally common breeder in fertile waters in temperate Holarctic, also AF (few areas) and AU, wintering within and to south of range on freshwaters, estuaries and sheltered coasts. **Similar species:** Red-necked Grebe.

Little Grebe
Tachybaptus ruficollis (Podicipedidae) 27 cm/10½ in.
Smallest grebe of WP, dumpy, very short-necked with short, stout bill. Pale patch at gape obvious from distance. In summer, chestnut throat and cheeks distinctive, rest of upperparts dark brown, paler below. Winter plumage lacks chestnut, paler all over with whitish throat and cheeks. Song a shrill trill. Calls include sharp "whit-whit."
Range and habitat: widespread breeder on ponds, lakes and slow-moving rivers of temperate Holarctic, also AF and OR, wintering mainly within breeding range on freshwaters and estuaries. Vulnerable to severe winters. **Similar species:** Black-necked Grebe, Pied-billed Grebe (see p 50).

TUBE-NOSED SWIMMERS Procellariiformes

Northern Fulmar
Fulmarus glacialis (Procellaridae) 47 cm/18 in.
White or gray-white gull-like shearwater, with gliding flight on stiff wings. Upperparts—back, wings and tail—gray (dark gray in "blue" northern color phase), underparts pure white (pale gray in "blue" phase). Distinctive yellow bill, short and thick with prominent tubed nostrils on upper mandible. Rarely lands except on nest-ledge. Mainly glides in flight, often soaring close to cliffs, rarely flapping. Call a hoarse, chuckling grunt. **Range and habitat:** extremely numerous. Breeds on cliff ledges in north temperate and arctic WP, eastern NA, Pacific coasts of NA and EP. Winters at sea.

Manx Shearwater
Puffinus puffinus (Procellaridae) 37 cm/15 in.
Medium-sized shearwater showing contrasting black upperparts and pure white underparts. Black cap extending to below eye. Black border to underside of wings. Glides on stiff wings low over waves, showing alternately black and white. Mediterranean races have dark brown upperparts and brown-washed underparts. Calls only at colony with wild caterwauling and crooning. **Range and habitat:** colonial nester in underground burrows on offshore islands in temperate and southern WP; other races in PA and AU. Winters at sea, WP birds reaching coasts of NT. Introduced rats a threat at some colonies. **Similar species:** Cory's Shearwater.

European Storm-Petrel
Hydrobates pelagicus (Hydrobatidae) 15 cm/6 in.
Tiny petrel, smallest seabird in WP. Blackish overall with conspicuous white rump. Square-ended tail. Faint whitish wing-bar. Small black bill and very short black legs. Latter dangle and feet patter on surface of sea during weak, fluttering flight. Only comes to land to breed. Silent at sea but loud churring call in nest-burrow, rising and falling and ending with characteristic "hiccup." **Range and habitat:** numerous colonial breeder in rock crevices on offshore islets of temperate and Mediterranean WP. Winters at sea south to southern AF. Disturbance and rats threaten some colonies. **Similar species:** Leach's Storm-petrel.

FULL-WEBBED SWIMMERS Pelecaniformes

Great White Pelican
Pelecanus onocrotalus (Pelecanidae) 140–80 cm/55–71 in.
Huge waterbird with long bill and extensible throat pouch. Body white with black tips to broad white wings and black trailing edges below. Bill" yellowish, legs and feet pink. In breeding plumage, slight crest to head and rosy tinge to plumage. Flies with alternate gliding and slow wingbeats, head held back into shoulders. Flies in lines or Vs. Growling and grunting calls at nest. **Range and habitat:** nests in colonies in shallow freshwaters and deltas of southern WP and AF. Some migrate south for winter. Vulnerable, as concentrated in very few colonies. **Similar species:** Dalmatian Pelican, Pink-backed Pelican (see p 186).

Northern Gannet
Morus bassanus (Sulidae) 90 cm/35 in.
Large, powerful seabird. Body and wings white, extensive black wing tips and yellow tinge to head of adult. Dark brown juveniles molt through stages of increasing whiteness. Large, bluish daggerlike bill, dark legs and feet. In flight, body cigar-shaped, wings narrow and pointed, flaps with short glides. Feeds by spectacular vertical dive with half-closed wings. Harsh barking calls at nest. **Range and habitat:** large colonies on cliffs and stacks, confined to northern Atlantic coasts of WP and NA. Winters at sea, including to south of breeding range. **Similar species:** Boobies (see pp 98, 286).

Great Cormorant
Phalacrocorax carbo (Phalacrocoracidae) 90 cm/35 in.
Large waterbird. Breeding adult black, glossed purple-blue, except for white cheeks, chin and thigh patch (last-named lost in winter). Other WP races have more white on throat and head. Long, hooked bill, gray above, yellowish below, with yellow skin at base. Juveniles brownish, paler beneath. Flies with outstretched long neck. Accomplished diver. Characteristic upright stance with wings half-extended. Gutteral calls at nest, otherwise silent. **Range and habitat:** Widespread breeder on coasts and large inland freshwaters in temperate Holarctic, eastern NA, OR, AF and AU. Some human persecution. **Similar species:** European Shag.

European Shag
Phalacrocorax aristotelis (Phalacrocoracidae) 76 cm/30 in.
Medium-sized waterbird. Breeding adult black, glossed bluish green, with short upright crest at front of head. Long, hooked beak dark, paler at base. Crest lost in winter, plumage browner and throat whitish brown. Juveniles brown, paler beneath. Flies with neck outstretched, dives easily. Stands upright on rocks, often with wings half-outstretched. Only vocal at nest, with croaks and grunts, hisses if approached. **Range and habitat:** colonial breeder on cliffs and among boulders of virtually all WP coasts. Winters in adjacent maritime waters. Sensitive to marine algal blooms. **Similar species:** Great Cormorant.

Arctic Loon

Red-throated Loon

Great Crested Grebe (pair)

Little Grebe (with young on nest)

Northern Fulmar

Manx Shearwater

European Storm-Petrel

Great White Pelican

Northern Gannet (nesting)

Great Cormorant (pair; calling at nest)

European Shag (courtship)

HERONS AND ALLIES Ciconiiformes

Gray Heron

Ardea cinerea (**Ardeidae**) 90 cm/35 in.

Very tall, long-legged, long-necked wading bird with heavy, daggerlike bill. Soft blue-gray upperparts, whitish head, neck and underparts. Black crest and streaks down neck. Bill yellow and legs brown, both turning orangey red in spring. Slow, flapping flight on very broad wings with black flight feathers. Voice a loud, harsh "fraank," only in flight. **Range and habitat:** widespread WP, EP, AF and OR, breeding in trees and reeds or on cliffs near marshes, lakes and estuaries. Some resident, others migrate and disperse, particularly to coasts. Sensitive to habitat destruction and severe weather. **Similar species:** Purple Heron.

Purple Heron

Ardea purpurea (**Ardeidae**) 80 cm/31 in.

Tall, long-legged and long-necked wading bird with gray upperparts, glossed purple, and rufous neck and chest. Slight black crest, dark streaking to head and neck. Some rufous tips to elongated wing plumes. Flies with slow, flapping flight of broad wings, showing very dark above, lacking contrast. Calls only in flight, a high-pitched "fraank." **Range and habitat:** southern temperate and subtropical WP, EP, AF and OR, in wetlands with dense vegetation. Winters mainly within breeding range, some dispersal. Drought in West Africa main threat through increased winter mortality. **Similar species:** Gray Heron.

Little Egret

Egretta garzetta (**Ardeidae**) 56 cm/22 in.

Slightly built, slim, long-legged heron. All-white in plumage, with long, thin black bill, long black legs and unexpected bright yellow feet. Very rarely black all over instead of white. In breeding season, adult develops 2 head plumes c. 16 cm/6½ in) long, also many elongated plumes on upper breast, mantle and wings (known as "aigrettes"). Silent away from nesting colony, where gives variety of harsh and bubbling calls. **Range and habitat:** southern temperate and subtropical WP, EP, AF, OR and AU, in marshes, lakes and estuaries, some winter dispersal. Susceptible to severe winters. **Similar species:** Snowy Egret (see p 52).

Little Bittern

Ixobrychus minutus (**Ardeidae**) 35 cm/14 in.

Diminutive, black and pinky buff or streaky brown heron. Male pinky buff neck and body, with black cap and back. Large pinky buff patch on black wings. Female duller and streaked brown. Very skulking, climbing among reeds. Rapid flight with shallow wingbeats, quickly drops into cover. Croaking call in flight; male gives regular barking croak in spring. **Range and habitat:** southern temperate WP and EP; subtropical AF, OR and AU, in densely vegetated freshwater marshes, WP and EP breeding birds migrate south for winter, remainder nonmigratory. Threatened by droughts in African wintering ground and by habitat loss in breeding range.

Great Bittern

Botaurus stellaris (**Ardeidae**) 76 cm/30 in.

Bulky, thick-necked heron with daggerlike bill. Overall golden brown in color, heavily marked with dark brown and black spots, streaks and mottles. Black cap. Flight rather owl-like, on broad, rounded wings. Principal call of adult male a far-carrying booming, preceded by a few short grunts, audible up to 3–5 km (2–3 miles). **Range and habitat:** temperate WP and EP, also AF. Mainly migratory to south for winter. Almost always in dense reed-beds, fresh and brackish. Severely threatened by habitat degradation, but habitat restoration can be successful. **Similar species:** American Bittern (see p 52).

Eurasian Spoonbill

Platalea leucorodia (**Threskiornithidae**) 86 cm/34 in.

Large, white, long-legged heron with elongated black bill ending in distinctive spatulate tip. Overall white plumage with bare yellowish skin round chin, throat and eyes. In breeding season, develops crest plumes and yellow gorget. Wing tips of immature blackish. In flight, neck sags below line of back, legs trail. Mostly silent, apart from low grunts at nesting colonies. **Range and habitat:** southern temperate and subtropical WP, EP, AF and OR. Some nonmigratory, others migrate south for winter. Inhabits marshes and estuaries, more

marine in winter. Habitat loss, pollution and disturbance are main threats. **Similar species:** African Spoonbill (see p 188).

White Stork

Ciconia ciconia (**Ciconiidae**) 102 cm/40 in.

Very large black and white, long-legged and long-necked bird with long, pointed red bill. Body and inner part of wings pure white; outer part of wings, including trailing edge, black. Long red bill and legs. Graceful flight on slow wingbeats with frequent and often prolonged soaring. Silent except for noisy bill-clappering between adults at nest. **Range and habitat:** widespread breeder in WP and EP, migrating south to AF and OR for winter. Inhabits open, shallow wetlands and farmland, frequently nesting on buildings. Modern agriculture leading to loss of habitat, plus droughts in Sahel wintering areas, have caused substantial declines. **Similar species:** Yellow-billed Stork (see p 188).

Black Stork

Ciconia nigra (**Ciconiidae**) 97 cm/38 in.

Very large, mainly black stork, long neck and legs. Overall black upperparts, also head, neck and chest. Belly pure white. Long, pointed bill, eyes and legs red. Flies well on broad wings, also soars frequently. Silent away from nest, but bill-clappering between pair at nest, also variety of whistling and hissing calls. **Range and habitat:** widespread temperate and southern WP and EP, also AF, in forests with streams and pools. Migratory from WP and BP south to AF and OR for winter, in well-vegetated wetlands. Current status favorable, but still reliant on enough good breeding habitat.

WATERFOWL Anseriformes

Mute Swan

Cygnus olor (**Anatidae**) 152 cm/60 in.

Huge, long-necked waterbird. Pure white plumage in adult, with enlarged black knob at base of orange-red bill, larger in male. Juvenile gray-brown with gray bill, lacking knob. Nesting pairs strongly territorial, also in flocks. Variety of grunting and hissing calls. Wings make musical throbbing in flight. **Range and habitat:** widespread in lowland WP and EP; introduced AF, AU and NA. Mainly fresh and brackish waters of all types. Partial migrant moving south for winter. Culled in some areas. Has recovered well in, e.g., Britain, following ban of poisonous lead fishing weights. **Similar species:** Trumpeter (see p 54) and Whooper Swans.

Whooper Swan

Cygnus cygnus (**Anatidae**) 152 cm/60 in.

Huge, long-necked waterbird. Adult plumage completely white, with extensive yellow on upper mandible of black bill. Juvenile gray, with pink and gray bill, becoming white after 1 year. Flight powerful and direct. Loud and far-carrying musical trumpeting calls, produced on ground and in flight. **Range and habitat:** breeds northern temperate and subarctic WP and EP, on shallow freshwater pools in tundra, taiga and steppe. Migrates south for winter to large freshwaters and sheltered coasts. Has benefitted from increased protection, including provision of reserves; few other threats. **Similar species:** Trumpeter (see p 54) and Tundra Swans.

Tundra Swan

Cygnus columbianus (**Anatidae**) 122 cm/48 in.

Smallest all-white swan, with yellow and black bill. Smaller and shorter-necked than Whooper Swan. Adult plumage pure white, with variable yellow on upper mandible of black bill. Legs and feet gray-black. Juvenile gray with pink and gray bill, becoming like adult at about 1 year. High-pitched musical honking and baying notes given in flight and on ground. **Range and habitat:** breeds arctic regions of WP and EP on marshy tundra pools and beside rivers. Migrates south to winter on temperate marshes and estuaries. Dependent on shallow freshwaters, always under threat of drainage. **Similar species:** Whooper Swan.

Gray Heron

Purple Heron

Little Egret (at nest)

Little Bittern

Great Bittern

Eurasian Spoonbill

White Stork (pair; at nest)

Black Stork (and young)

Mute Swan

Whooper Swan (pair)

Tundra Swan

Graylag Goose

Anser anser (**Anatidae**) 80 cm/31 in.

Large, heavy gray goose with big head, thick neck and triangular bill. Overall gray body, paler below, a few scattered black marks on belly, white undertail. Western race has orange bill, eastern has pink bill and is overall paler and larger. Legs pink. Very pale gray forewings conspicuous in powerful flight, often in large flocks. Loud cackling honks, particularly in flight. **Range and habitat:** breeds northern and temperate WP and EP marshes and open wetlands. Winters to south, reaching OR, often feeding on farmland. Heavily shot to prevent crop damage. **Similar species:** Pink-footed Goose.

Pink-footed Goose

Anser brachyrhynchus (**Anatidae**) 70 cm/28 in.

Medium-sized compact gray goose with round head and fairly short neck. Overall pinky brown, grayer on back, paler below; white undertail and dark brown head and neck. Bill dark brown and pink, legs pink. Usually in large flocks. Powerful flight, often in V skeins. Forewing paler gray than hindwing in flight. Call a musical "wink-wink." **Range and habitat:** breeds on tundra of Iceland, Greenland, Svalbard; winters Britain, Netherlands, Belgium, roosting on lakes and estuaries, feeding on farmland. Some Iceland breeding areas at risk from development. **Similar species:** Graylag Goose.

Greater White-fronted Goose

Anser albifrons (**Anatidae**) 70 cm/28 in.

Medium to large long-necked goose, darker gray-brown on back, paler below. Adult has conspicuous white forehead and variable black barring on breast and belly, absent in juvenile, white undertail; pink bill. All-dark upperwings lack contrast in flight. Greenland race has orange bill, is larger and darker. Legs orange. Musical, laughing "lyo-lyok" calls, especially in flight. In large and small flocks. **Range and habitat:** circumpolar Holarctic, breeding on tundra marshes, wintering lowland marshes and farmland of NA, WP and EP. Better protection needed in some countries. **Similar species:** other gray geese.

Barnacle Goose

Branta leucopsis (**Anatidae**) 63 cm/25 in.

Small goose with short neck and compact, round body. Gray above, narrowly barred black on upperparts, paler whitish gray belly and white undertail. Black breast, neck and head; creamy white cheeks, thin black line from bill through eye. Small black bill. Legs black. Occurs in large flocks, flying rapidly, when wings show overall gray above. Yapping call, not unlike small dog's. **Range and habitat:** breeds tundra of Greenland, Svalbard, north-west Siberia; winters farmland and coasts of Britain, Ireland, Netherlands. **Similar species:** Canada Goose (see p 54).

Red-breasted Goose

Branta ruficollis (**Anatidae**) 51–8 cm/20–3 in.

Tiny goose boldly patterned in black, white and russet red. Crown and back of neck black, large russet cheek patch, throat and chest, with narrow white borders. Belly and back black with broad white flank stripe and white undertail. 2 narrow white wing-bars. Walks fast, flight agile. High-pitched "kee-kwa" calls. Gregarious, often flocking in winter with White-fronted Geese. **Range and habitat:** breeds tundra of extreme north-western EP, wintering on open steppes and farmland of south-eastern WP. Vulnerable to land-use changes in wintering areas.

Common Shelduck

Tadorna tadorna (**Anatidae**) 61 cm/24 in.

Boldly marked gooselike duck. Body white, head and upper neck greenish black. Broad chestnut breast band, blackish stripe down center of belly. Blackish scapulars, forming black bar either side of white back when wings closed. Bill red, knob at base larger in male, absent in juvenile, which is overall duller. Legs pink. In flight, outer wings black, inner forewing white, trailing edge green and chestnut. Male whistles, female quacks. **Range and habitat:** temperate coasts and larger wetlands of WP and EP, some nonmigratory, others migrate to more southern coasts and wetlands. Risk of pollution of molting areas.

Mallard

Anas platyrhynchos (**Anatidae**) 58 cm/23 in.

Large dabbling duck, big head and bill. Male has green head, yellow bill, white neck-ring, red-brown chest, pale gray back and flanks, black and white tail with curled central feathers. Female overall pale brown, marked with black. Rapid flight, showing white-edged blue speculum. Male has nasal "raab," female loud quack. Commonest duck in WP, semidomesticated in urban areas. **Range and habitat:** breeds throughout Holarctic, except far north, on great variety of wetlands, winters within range and to south, including OR. Introduced to AU. **Similar species:** female, other female dabbling ducks.

Eurasian Wigeon

Anas penelope (**Anatidae**) 46 cm/18 in.

Medium-sized dabbling duck. Male has chestnut head with buff crown stripe, pinkish breast, gray body with white stripe above flanks, black and white tail, conspicuous white forewings in flight. Female overall rufous or gray-brown, forewing pale gray. Highly gregarious, feeding on land in dense flocks, flight rapid and twisting. Male has loud whistling "whee-oo" call. **Range and habitat:** breeds WP and EP in arctic and northern temperate marshes. Migrates to southern temperate coasts and marshes, including in AF and OR. **Similar species:** American and Chiloe Wigeons (see pp 54, 102).

Common Teal

Anas crecca (**Anatidae**) 35 cm/14 in.

Smallest dabbling duck, compact body and very short neck. Male has chestnut and green head, dark gray body, white flank line (absent in North American race, which has vertical white line either side of breast), creamy yellow undertail. Female brown, mottled and streaked darker. Gregarious, flight rapid, performing aerial maneuvers like waders. Male has high-pitched whistle, female quacks. **Range and habitat:** circumpolar Holarctic tundra and northern temperate marshes, migrating south for winter including to AF and OR. Drainage threatens some breeding areas. **Similar species:** female, other small female dabbling ducks.

Garganey

Anas querquedula (**Anatidae**) 38 cm/15 in.

Small dabbling duck; male has chestnut-brown head and neck, conspicuous white eye stripe curving down to nape. Upperparts dark with elongated white scapulars, flanks gray. Pale blue forewing prominent in flight. Female brown, whitish throat and pale spot at base of bill. Occurs in huge flocks in winter, more scattered in summer. Flight rapid and direct. Call of male harsh rattle, female quacks. **Range and habitat:** breeds temperate marshland of WP and EP. Migrates to open wetlands of AF and OR for winter. Declining from loss of summer and winter habitat. **Similar species:** female, other small female dabbling ducks.

Northern Pintail

Anas acuta (**Anatidae**) 56–66 cm/22–6 in.

Long-necked slender dabbling duck. Pointed tail, c. 10 cm/4 in) long in male, which has chocolate brown head and nape, clear white neck, gray body streaked black and white on back, yellow and black undertail. Female pale brown, slightly elongated tail. Flight fast, often in Vs. Not very vocal; male has soft whistle, female soft quack. **Range and habitat:** breeds circumpolar Holarctic tundra and northern temperate marshes. Migrates south to coasts and marshes within Holarctic and to AF and OR. **Similar species:** female, other medium-sized female dabbling ducks.

Northern Shoveler

Anas clypeata (**Anatidae**) 51 cm/20 in.

Very heavy-headed dabbling duck with broad, spatulate bill. Male has dark green head, conspicuous white breast, chestnut flanks with white line above, dark back, black and white undertail. In flight, shows blue forewing. Female pale brown, pale blue forewing. Very large bill immersed as bird feeds while swimming; gives top-heavy appearance in flight. Male has quiet "took-took" call, female soft quack. **Range and habitat:** circumpolar Holarctic tundra and northern temperate marshes, migrating south to marshes within Holarctic and also AF and OR. Some breeding areas threatened by drainage. **Similar species:** other shovelers.

Graylag Goose

Pink-footed Goose

Greater White-fronted Goose

Barnacle Goose

Red-breasted Goose

Common Shelduck

Mallard

Eurasian Wigeon

Common Teal

Garganey

Northern Pintail

N orthern Shoveler

Tufted Duck

Aythya fuligula (Anatidae) 43 cm/17 in.

Compact diving duck with round head and drooping crest. Male mainly black, glossed purple on head, white flanks and underparts. Female dark brown, paler mottled flanks and whitish underparts, occasionally some white round base of bill. Both have white wing-bar in flight. Swims buoyantly and dives with preliminary leap. Flight rapid, wings making whistling sound. Male has soft whistle, female low growl, but not very vocal. **Range and habitat:** northern temperate and arctic tundra and marshes of WP and EP; migrates to temperate and southern open freshwaters and coasts of WP and EP, also to AF and OR. Vulnerable to disturbance from water-borne leisure pursuits. **Similar species:** other black and white or brown diving ducks (see pp 56, 288).

Greater Scaup

Aythya marila (Anatidae) 48 cm/19 in.

Bulky diving duck with large bill. Male has black head, glossed green, black breast and tail, pale gray back and white flanks. Bill blue-gray with black tip. Female mainly dark brown, paler on flanks, variable white patch at base of bill. White wing-bar shows in flight, which is strong but heavy. Swims buoyantly and dives easily. Not very vocal; female has harsh growl. **Range and habitat:** breeds circumpolar Holarctic tundra and northern marshes. Migrates to temperate WP, EP and NA, where normally on sheltered coasts and some large inland brackish or freshwater wetlands. At risk from marine pollution of wintering areas. **Similar species:** other black and white or brown diving ducks (see pp 56, 288).

Common Pochard

Aythya ferina (Anatidae) 46 cm/18 in.

Large, long-billed diving duck with high-domed head. Male has chestnut head and black breast, pale gray upperparts and flanks, black tail. Female yellow-brown on head and breast, gray-brown on back and flanks. In strong, fast flight, pale wing stripe shows on hindwing. Round-backed shape on water, where dives freely. Generally silent, though wings whistle in flight and female has growling note. **Range and habitat:** breeds northern temperate WP and EP marshes and pools, migrating south to marshes, open wetlands and coasts, including AF and OR. Threatened by habitat loss in some breeding areas. **Similar species:** other redheaded and brown diving ducks (see pp 56, 288).

Common Eider

Somateria mollissima (Anatidae) 58 cm/23 in.

Heavily built, short-necked seaduck. Male has white face with pale green patches at rear, pinkish breast, white back with elongated scapulars trailing over black flanks and tail, round white patch at sides of rump. Long sloping forehead leading into long wedge-shaped greenish bill. Female cinnamon brown, paler on head, mottled darker on body. Heavy flight on broad wings, low over water, flocks usually flying in lines. During courtship display, male utters musical cooing, female has guttural "gok-gok." **Range and habitat:** circumpolar arctic and temperate coasts of Holarctic, wintering within range and coasts to south. Winter concentrations at risk from marine pollution. **Similar species:** other eiders.

Black Scoter

Melanitta nigra (Anatidae) 48 cm/19 in.

Stockily built seaduck. Male is only all-black duck, has large head with prominent black knob at base of yellow bill. Knob is also yellow in North American race. Female dark brown, slightly paler on flanks and breast, head capped dark brown, cheeks and throat buff-white. Bill green-black with small basal knob. No wing-bars in flight, which is fast and strong and low over water. Swims buoyantly with tail occasionally cocked, dives frequently. **Range and habitat:** breeds arctic tundra and northern temperate freshwater wetlands of WP and EP, locally also in NA. Winters predominantly coasts to south. Vulnerable to oil spills and through conflict with shellfish industry. **Similar species:** other scoters (see p 56).

Common Goldeneye

Bucephala clangula (Anatidae) 46 cm/18 in.

Dumpy, large-headed seaduck. Male has large, round black head, glossed green, round white patch in front of eye. Back black with extensive black-outlined white panels, breast and underparts white.

Female brown-headed with gray back and brown flanks, showing traces of white at top of flanks. Both sexes show double white wing-bar in flight, which is fast and direct. Swims buoyantly and dives readily and frequently. Mostly silent, with soft, nasal calls during display. **Range and habitat:** circumpolar arctic tundra and northern temperate Holarctic lakes and rivers, wintering on coasts and freshwater wetlands to south. Lack of trees with suitable nest holes limits numbers in some regions. **Similar species:** Barrow's Goldeneye (see p 56).

Long-tailed Duck

Clangula hyemalis (Anatidae) 41–53 cm/16–21 in.

Slim, elegant seaduck with greatly elongated tail in male. Plumage of both sexes undergoes complex changes during year. Breeding male has dark brown head, with white cheeks, brown chest and black and white flanks. Winter male white-headed and white on back. Central tail feathers project c. 13 cm/5 in. Breeding female has dark brown and white head, dark brown back, whitish underparts. Winter female browner and duller. Dark wings in rapid, swinging flight. Male has yodeling display call, female soft quack. **Range and habitat:** breeds circumpolar Holarctic tundra, winters coasts to south. Large wintering concentrations very vulnerable to oil pollution. **Similar species:** female, female or juvenile Harlequin Duck (see p 56).

Common Merganser

Mergus merganser (Anatidae) 62 cm/24 in.

Large, bulky sawbill. Male has green-glossed black head, shaggy at back, with long, narrow bright red bill ending in slightly hooked tip. Back black; neck, breast and flanks white, tinged with pink or cream in front. In flight, which is powerful and fast, whole forewing is white. Female has rufous head, shaggy at back, red bill, whitish throat and underparts; gray upperparts and flanks. In flight, rear of forewing is white. Silent except in courtship when variety of harsh notes. **Range and habitat:** breeds circumpolar Holarctic by rivers and freshwaters, mainly in forests. Winters mainly to south on fresh and brackish open waters. Culled in some areas because of perceived conflict with angling interests. **Similar species:** Red-breasted Merganser.

Red-breasted Merganser

Mergus serrator (Anatidae) 55 cm/22 in.

Medium-sized, slender sawbill. Male has green-black head with double crest and long, narrow red bill ending in a hook. White neck-ring above reddish breast spotted with black. Upperparts black with broad white flank stripe, underparts and flanks gray. Female has reddish head with double crest, gray-brown upperparts and gray underparts. Both sexes have white on inner wing in flight, which is fast and direct. Swims low in water and dives smoothly. Both sexes have low calls during courtship. **Range and habitat:** breeds circumpolar boreal and northern temperate Holarctic wooded lakes and rivers. Migrates south, mainly to coasts, for winter. Some culling in areas with strong angling interests. **Similar species:** Common Merganser.

Smew

Mergus albellus (Anatidae) 41 cm/16 in.

Small and compact sawbill. Male mainly white on head, breast and upperparts, with fine black markings around eye, and black lines along flanks and back. Flanks and tail gray. Female has chestnut cap to white face, blackish round eye, chestnut down back of neck. Body gray, darker above. Male appears black and white in flight with white markings on inner part of dark wings. Female has less white. Flies very fast, with great agility. Swims high on water, dives frequently. Rarely calls in winter, whistles in courtship. **Range and habitat:** northern forests of WP and EP nesting beside still or running water. Winters on large freshwaters and shallow, sheltered coasts to south.

Tufted Duck

Greater Scaup

Common Pochard

Common Eider

Black Scoter

Common Goldeneye

Long-tailed Duck

Common Merganser (pair)

Red-breasted Merganser

Smew

DIURNAL BIRDS OF PREY Falconiformes

Osprey

Pandion haliaetus (Pandionidae) 51–9 cm/20–3 in.
Medium-sized raptor, normally found close to water. Small white head with dark streak through the eye and down nape to dark brown back and wings. Underparts strikingly white including feathered upper legs. In flight, looks dark above, white beneath. Wings long and narrow, often angled at carpal joint. Head protrudes quite noticeably, tail comparatively short. Call a shrill whistle. **Range and habitat:** widespread northern Holarctic, also AF, OR and AU, breeding and wintering at wetlands of all types. Local persecution only threat. **Similar species:** pale morph of Booted Eagle.

Red Kite

Milvus milvus (Accipitridae) 58–64 cm/23–5 in.
Long, angular-winged medium-sized raptor with deeply forked tail. Rich chestnut overall, darker above, prominent nearly white head. Flight very free with wings and tail constantly flexed. Upperwings with blackish flight feathers, blackish and chestnut shoulders. Underwings show large white patch toward tip. Long tail chestnut with white band at tip, conspicuously notched. Call a shrill mew. **Range and habitat:** open woodland and farmland of central and southern WP. Northern populations mostly migrate to within breeding range of southern nonmigratory populations. Main threat loss of habitat. **Similar species:** Black Kite.

Black Kite

Milvus migrans (Accipitridae) 53–9 cm/21–3 in.
Medium-sized, bulky raptor. Upperparts dark brown, head paler and grayer. Underparts similar, toning to rufous on belly and undertail. In flight, long wings arched and held at angle. Upper- and underwings dark brown or blackish toward leading edge with a pale panel toward tip. Dark tail slightly forked. Very vocal with high-pitched trilling calls. **Range and habitat:** widespread, often near wetlands, in temperate and southern WP and EP, also almost throughout AF, OR and AU. At risk from habitat loss and persecution. **Similar species:** Red Kite, Western Marsh-harrier (see p 152).

Short-toed Snake-Eagle

Circaetus gallicus (Accipitridae) 63–9 cm/25–7 in.
Small eagle. Upperparts brown, tinged with pale buff. Underparts paler, usually with dark brown breast spots. Head rounded, like owl's, often with dark hood. Wings long and broad, light brown above, with whitish patch; underwings and underparts appear almost white, contrasting with black outer half of primaries. Buzzardlike mewing call. **Range and habitat:** open lowlands and forest edges of southern WP and western EP migrating to winter in equatorial AF. Resident in Indian subcontinent (OR). Suffers from habitat loss. **Similar species:** Osprey and buzzards.

Eurasian Sparrowhawk

Accipiter nisus (Accipitridae) 28–38 cm/11–15 in.
Small raptor. Male has slate-gray upperparts with rufous patches on cheeks, whitish below with narrow orange barring (also on underwings). Larger female has dark brown or gray-brown upperparts, barred brown on paler underparts and underwings. Tail with dark brown bands. Long tail and shortish rounded wings obvious in low, dashing flight. Chattering "kew-kew" call. **Range and habitat:** widespread in wooded areas of WP and EP, also northern OR. EP population migratory to OR. **Similar species:** Northern Goshawk.

Northern Goshawk

Accipiter gentilis (Accipitridae) 48–58 cm/19–23 in.
Medium-sized raptor. Upperparts of male gray-brown with darker crown and whitish stripe over eye. Underparts paler, heavily barred brown. Female larger, upperparts browner with more obvious white stripe over eye, underparts paler, barred brown. Both sexes have barred underwings and tails. Long tail and broad, rounded wings. Flight fast and dashing. Calls shrill and screaming. **Range and habitat:** widespread in wooded areas of northern and temperate Holarctic, mostly nonmigratory, but northern breeding birds move south for winter. Some persecution. **Similar species:** Eurasian Sparrowhawk.

Common Buzzard

Buteo buteo (Accipitridae) 50–6 cm/20–2 in.
Medium-sized raptor, not unlike small eagle with rounded wings ending in "fingers" when soaring. Very variable, typically dark brown upperparts, slightly paler below, but often paler or even whitish on head and body and sometimes wings. In flight, always darker above and paler below, with dark carpal patches on underwings and dark trailing edge. Call a high-pitched "mew." **Range and habitat:** open and wooded country in temperate WP and EP, partially migratory to AF and OR. **Similar species:** other buzzards (see pp 58, 194).

European Honey-Buzzard

Pernis apivorus (Accipitridae) 50–8 cm/20–3 in.
Medium-sized raptor with long, pointed wings and relatively small head. Upperparts gray-brown; male grayer, female browner. Underparts vary from dark brown to very pale, almost white, with variable darker barring. In flight, wings show 3 dark bars toward trailing edge and dark carpal patches below. Tail has 2 narrow dark bars at base, 1 broad bar close to tip. Shrill whistling calls. **Range and habitat:** mainly temperate woodland and semiopen areas of WP and western EP. Wholly migratory to southern AF. Severe persecution. **Similar species:** other buzzards (see pp 58, 194).

Booted Eagle

Hieraeetus pennatus (Accipitridae) 45–53 cm/18–21 in.
Small eagle with 2 very different color phases. Commoner pale phase rufous above and strikingly white below on body, wings and tail. White forewing contrasts with dark flight feathers and trailing edge. Dark phase is rich dark rufous brown above and below with paler rufous tail. In flight, slight pale patch toward wing tips. Flight buoyant. Shrill "kee-kee" call. **Range and habitat:** southern woodlands of WP and EP, migrating AF and OR. Also breeds extreme south AF. Habitat loss is main threat. **Similar species:** other small eagles (see p 242).

Golden Eagle

Aquila chrysaetos (Accipitridae) 76–90 cm/30–5 in.
Large eagle with prominently protruding head in flight and long tail. Body and wings dark red-brown to blackish above, dark brown below. Crown of head and nape golden brown. Immature shows variable white (for 1st 4–5 years) on rump and outer wings. Soars with wing feathers extended. Has mewing cry and barking call. **Range and habitat:** mountainous areas and woodland in WP, EP and NA; many resident, northerly birds moving south for winter. Persecution and habitat loss both serious. **Similar species:** other large eagles (see pp 58, 242).

Egyptian Vulture

Neophron percnopterus (Accipitridae) 58–66 cm/23–6 in.
Small vulture. Body white with yellow tinge to head and neck and bare yellow skin on head and throat. Shaggy ruff at back of head also tinged yellow. Bill small. Main wing feathers black, so black wing tips and trailing edge in flight, rest of wings white. Wings straight, tail longish and wedge-shaped. Normally silent. **Range and habitat:** open country from lowlands to mountains in southern WP and EP, also AF and OR. WP and EP populations migrate south in winter to AF and OR. Suffers serious persecution.

Eurasian Griffon

Gyps fulvus (Accipitridae) 97–104 cm/38–41 in.
Huge vulture. Body and wing-coverts uniform ginger-buff. Flight feathers and tail dark brown or blackish; contrast in flight between dark wing tips and trailing edge and pale forewings. Head and neck down-covered, whitish ruff at base of neck. Soaring flight on broad straight-edged wings with extended "fingers." Usually silent. **Range and habitat:** open, often mountainous, areas of southern WP and south-western EP, also AF and OR, some moving short distances south for winter. Threatened by persecution. **Similar species:** other large vultures (see p 192).

Osprey

Red Kite

Black Kite

Short-toed Snake Eagle

Eurasian Sparrowhawk (at nes'

Northern Goshawk (female)

Common Buzzard (a nest)

European Honey-Buzzard (in light colo phase)

Booted Eagle (feedin young)

Golden Eagle (at nes'

Egyptian Vulture

Eurasian Griffon

Western Marsh-Harrier

Circus aeruginosus (Accipitridae) 48–56 cm/19–22 in.
Large, broad-winged harrier. Male's upperparts brown, shoulders creamy. Paler head and rufous underparts streaked brown. Extensive gray on rear half of wing, contrasting with dark wing tip and creamy leading edge. Female all-dark brown except for creamy head, shoulders and breast. Broad dark stripe through eye. In flight, dark except for leading edge to wing and head. Heavy flapping flight; slow glides with wings in shallow V. Shrill calls during courtship. **Range and habitat:** shallow wetlands and lowlands of temperate WP and EP, migrating in winter to AF and OR. Also resident in AF and AU. Threatened by habitat destruction. **Similar species:** other harriers (see p 242).

Northern Harrier

Circus cyaneus (Accipitridae) 43–51 cm/17–20 in.
Medium-sized harrier. Male pale gray above, whitish below, with small white rump and black primaries contrasting sharply with all-gray upper and white underwings in flight. Much larger female dark brown above, pale streaky brown below. White rump and strongly barred tail. Flight buoyant with rapid beats interspersed with gliding, wings held in shallow V. Chattering and whistling calls in display. **Range and habitat:** breeds in wide variety of open habitats in circumpolar northern temperate Holarctic, mostly migrating south for winter reaching OR. Also widespread resident in NT. Main threats are habitat destruction and persecution. **Similar species:** other harriers (see p 242).

Peregrine Falcon

Falco peregrinus (Falconidae) 38–48 cm/15–19 in.
Medium to large falcon with prominent black crown and moustache. Male gray-backed with well-barred paler underparts and barred tail. Much larger female generally dark gray-brown above, paler brown below, more heavily barred than male with large drop-shaped spots on breast. Flight swift and powerful on pointed wings, stooping from considerable height. Also soars on stiff slightly swept-back wings. Harsh chattering and whining calls. **Range and habitat:** widespread in open habitats in northern and central Holarctic, also widespread in OR and AU, and parts of AF and NT. Some populations migratory. Some local persecution, also restricted by available nest-sites. **Similar species:** other large falcons (see pp 58, 242).

Eurasian Hobby

Falco subbuteo (Falconidae) 30–6 cm/12–14 in.
Small, slim falcon with long swept-back wings and shortish tail giving silhouette similar to Swift. Upperparts of adult very dark slate-gray, tail slightly paler, with broad buff-white collar, very dark cap and obvious blackish moustache. Underparts very pale whitish buff, heavily streaked and spotted black. Thighs and undertail rufous, conspicuous in flight. Aerially active, soaring on stiff wings, catching prey on wing by stooping and hawking. Shrill "kew-kew" note. **Range and habitat:** widespread in lowlands with scattered small woodlands throughout WP and EP, also parts of OR. Completely migratory, south to AF and OR. Some declines linked to prey numbers. **Similar species:** other small falcons, especially Red-footed.

Merlin

Falco columbarius (Falconidae) 27–33 cm/10½–13 in.
Small falcon with few obvious markings. Male has slatey blue upperparts, broad black tip to slightly paler tail. Head with dark crown and rufous nape, moustachial streak faint. Underparts rusty, heavily streaked black. Rusty underwings. Female dark brown above, with paler streaks and brown-streaked underparts, with brown tail barred with cream. Outer wing feathers of both sexes darker in flight. Shrill and chattering "kee-kee" call. Dashing flight. **Range and habitat:** widespread in open habitats throughout circumpolar Holarctic arctic and north temperate. Migrates south for winter, some reaching OR and NT. **Similar species:** other small falcons (see pp 58, 196).

Common Kestrel

Falco tinnunculus (Falconidae) 33–6 cm/13–14 in.
Long-winged, long-tailed falcon with characteristic prolonged hovering flight when hunting. Male has blue-gray head with narrow black moustache, chestnut upperwings and back spotted with black, blue-gray tail with black band at tip, and buff underparts, spotted and streaked with black. Female is rufous brown above, streaked and barred black, paler below, also streaked and spotted. Both sexes show dark wing tips in flight. Hovers head to wind with sloping body and fanned tail. Shrill "kee-kee" calls. **Range and habitat:** widespread in great variety of habitats throughout WP and EP, also widespread in AF and parts of OR. Partially migratory. Has declined in areas of intensive agriculture. **Similar species:** other falcons (see pp 58, 196).

FOWL-LIKE BIRDS Galliformes

Willow Ptarmigan

Lagopus lagopus (Phasianidae) 38–41 cm(15–16 in.
Smallish round-bodied gamebird with small head and very variably patterned plumage. Male has red wattle over eye. Summer male has dark rufous upperparts, barred with black. Both sexes underparts and most of wings white. Summer females paler rufous brown with more obvious black barring. Both sexes all-white in winter. Particolored birds occur in spring and autumn. British/Irish race (Willow Ptarmigan lagopus) has no white in summer or winter. Call a loud "kok-kok" and "goback-goback." **Range and habitat:** widespread in circumpolar Holarctic tundra, scrubby taiga, moorland and other open habitats. Short distance movements in winter to less exposed areas. Habitat quality crucial to maintenance of populations. **Similar species:** Rock Ptarmigan.

Rock Ptarmigan

Lagopus muta (Phasianidae) 33–6 cm/13–14 in.
Small mountain gamebird. Male has red wattle above eye. Upperparts of summer male darkish gray-brown, mottled blackish and buff. Underparts and wings white, as are feathered legs. Summer female browner than male with golden and blackish markings and less white below; wings white. Both sexes have distinct autumn plumage, darker than in summer, though retaining white underparts and wings, before changing to all-white in winter. Flight conspicuous because of white wings. Usually very tame. Makes hoarse cackles and croaks as well as crowing song during display. **Range and habitat:** circumpolar Holarctic tundra and mountains. Nonmigratory. **Similar species:** Willow Ptarmigan.

Black Grouse

Tetrao tetrix (Phasianidae) 41–56 cm/16–22 in.
Bulky gamebird. Much larger male has glossy black plumage with a white wing-bar and white undertail. Tail feathers extended into lyre-shaped curves. Female mostly rufous brown, barred black on upperparts and dark brown on underparts. Small white bars on wings. Male has red wattles above eyes, enlarged in spring. Flight on rapid wingbeats and then gliding. Male has sneezing call, female a harsh "kok-kok." Often perches on low trees or scrub. **Range and habitat:** widespread in northern wooded and scrub regions of WP and EP. Mainly nonmigratory. In decline over much of range, mainly linked to habitat degradation. **Similar species:** Western Capercaillie.

Western Capercaillie

Tetrao urogallus (Phasianidae) 58–90 cm/23–35 in.
Huge gamebird, much larger male reminiscent of turkey with shaggy head and broad tail. Upperparts of male blue-gray, with brown on back and wings. Darker head with throat feathers erected when calling, and red wattle over eye. Breast black with green gloss, gray underparts with pale barring. Tail dark-tipped, fanned in display. Female orange-buff to brown overall, heavily barred black above, with chestnut breast and buff-barred whitish underparts. Calls of both sexes raucous. Display song of male quickening rattle ending in pop and gurgle, like bottle being uncorked and poured. **Range and habitat:** northern forests of WP and EP where resident. Widespread declines as a result of modern forestry practices. **Similar species:** Black Grouse.

Western Marsh-Harrier

Northern Harrier (pair, at nest)

Peregrine Falcon (at nest)

Eurasian Hobby (at nest)

Merlin

Common Kestrel (pair, at nest)

Willow Ptarmigan

Rock Ptarmigan

Black Grouse (in male lek)

Western Capercaillie

Common Pheasant

Phasianus colchicus (**Phasianidae**) 52–90 cm/20–35 in.
Gamebird. Male purple-chestnut all over, marked with black, except for bottle green head, short brown wings and black belly. Bare skin round eye bright red. Tail up to half overall length. Much plumage variation, some dark all over, some with white neck-ring. Female pale buff-brown all over, chestnut on back and breast, elongated tail. Flies with explosive burst of flapping followed by glide. Voice a harsh "kok-kok" and cackles. **Range and habitat:** widespread in mixed wooded and open habitats of temperate WP, EP and OR, also introduced to NA and AU. Nonmigratory. Distribution largely dictated by man. **Similar species:** other pheasants (see pp 244, 246).

Red-legged Partridge

Alectoris rufa (**Phasianidae**) 30 cm/12 in.
Medium-sized, bulky gamebird with upright stance. Sexes similar with olive to chestnut upperparts, white stripe above eye, black through eye, bold white cheeks and chin. Blackish collar above gray breast, flanks barred chestnut, black, gray and white. Underparts buff-orange. Legs and bill red. Main call a loud "chuka-chuka," also wheezing notes. Usually in pairs or family groups (coveys). Runs freely, flies fast and low, gliding on down-bent wings. **Range and habitat:** confined to open habitats, including farmland, of warm temperate south-west WP where resident; introduced Britain. Habitat loss affecting some populations. **Similar species:** other partridges (see pp 196, 244).

Gray Partridge

Perdix perdix (**Phasianidae**) 30 cm/12 in.
Medium-small stocky gamebird with round head and short neck. Male has brown upperparts, streaked buff; gray mantle, neck and breast. Face orange. Flanks gray,-barred with chestnut. Prominent broad dark brown horseshoe mark on pale belly. Female duller, less well marked, paler face and indistinct horseshoe mark on belly. Lives in family groups (coveys) through autumn and winter. Flies fast and low, often gliding on wings held down-curved. Runs freely with neck outstretched. Voice a creaking "keev-it." **Range and habitat:** widespread in open, vegetated habitats, including farmland, of temperate WP and eastern EP, where resident. Introduced to NA. Some declines through habitat loss. **Similar species:** other partridges (see pp 196, 244).

Common Quail

Coturnix coturnix (**Phasianidae**) 18 cm/7 in.
Very small, dumpy gamebird with comparatively long, thin wings. Male has buff upperparts marked with both black and pale streaks, particularly along flanks. Breast rufous shading to pale buff belly. Head variably chestnut with bold black throat and neck stripes, sometimes indistinct; white stripe above eye. Female much duller, black bands on throat and neck broken into spots, blackish spots on side of chest. Main call a plaintive "wet-my-lips." Flies reluctantly. **Range and habitat:** open vegetated habitats of central and southern WP and EP, also parts of OR and AF. Migratory in Palaearctic. Main threat is intensive agriculture. **Similar species:** juvenile partridges and other quail (see pp 196, 244, 292).

CRANES, RAILS AND ALLIES Gruiformes

Common Crane

Grus grus (**Gruidae**) 106–14 cm/42–5 in.
Tall, elegant, long-legged and long-necked bird. Body gray all over, becoming gray-brown with wear, except black upper neck and head with broad white patch round eye, trailing down hindneck. Small red patch of bare skin on crown and lores. Long, red-brown bill. Long inner wing feathers form trailing cloak over tail. In flight, dark outer wing feathers contrast with paler inner areas. Strong flight, neck and legs outstretched. Voice a loud "kroo." **Range and habitat:** breeds in marshy clearings among forested taiga and steppe woodlands of WP and EP, migrating south to open marshlands of AF and OR. Dependent on continued protection. **Similar species:** other cranes (see pp 60, 198, 246).

Great Bustard

Otis tarda (**Otididae**) 75–105 cm/29–41 in.
Huge running bird, male up to 50% larger than female. Male has gray head and neck with, in breeding season, long white moustachial bristles. Upperparts cinnamon barred black, underparts white with rufous breast band. In flight and display, shows much white on black-tipped wings. Female duller, neck thinner, no breast band, less white on wings. Flight steady with slow regular wingbeats. Walks with stately gait. Mostly silent. **Range and habitat:** patchily distributed in open plains and plateaux of southern WP and EP, those in latter region migratory. At risk from agricultural change.

Water Rail

Rallus aquaticus (**Rallidae**) 27–9 cm/10½–11½ in.
Small gray and brown rail with long and slightly decurved, reddish bill. Crown and upperparts dark brown, streaked paler. Face, throat and breast blue-gray apart from tiny white chin spot and dark stripe through eye. Black flanks narrowly barred white. Whitish undertail, with buff markings. Long flesh-colored legs dangled in weak flight. Secretive but occasionally feeds in open. Loud squealing and grunting calls, and regular "kipp-kipp-kipp" song. **Range and habitat:** dense aquatic vegetation in fens and lakes of WP and EP. Resident in western WP, otherwise migratory to south for winter. Threatened by wetland drainage. **Similar species:** other rails (see pp 62, 108, 196, 248, 292).

Spotted Crake

Porzana porzana (**Rallidae**) 22–4 cm/8½–9½ in.
Medium-sized rail. Male has green-brown upperparts and olive-brown underparts strongly tinged with gray. Some black spotting above, with white spotting above and below. Flanks barred black and white. Buff undertail, longish green legs. Short bill yellow with red spot at base. Female more spotted, particularly on throat and underparts. Very secretive and skulking. Presence announced by far-carrying whiplash call "hwit-hwit-hwit." **Range and habitat:** marshes and bogs of central and southern WP and EP, migrating for winter to wetlands of AF and OR. Threatened by wetland drainage. **Similar species:** other rails (see pp 62, 108, 248).

Corncrake

Crex crex (**Rallidae**) 25–8 cm/10–11 in.
Dumpy land-based rail. Sexes similar with dull yellowy buff upperparts tinged with gray, especially on head, neck and breast, and streaked on back with black. Underparts pale red-brown, flanks barred with chestnut. Forewings chestnut, remainder red-brown. Weak, fluttering flight with dangling legs. Call a 2-note rasping "crex-crex," heard more at night. Secretive. **Range and habitat:** lowland well-vegetated areas including pastures and crops in temperate WP and EP, migrating to eastern AF for winter. Declining because of agricultural intensification. **Similar species:** other brown crakes or rails (see pp 62, 108, 248).

Common Moorhen

Gallinula chloropus (**Rallidae**) 31–5 cm/12–14 in.
Bulky waterbird with distinctive habit of flicking white undertail. Dark blackish brown upperparts, slate-gray below. White line along flanks and conspicuous white undertail. Bill red with yellow tip, extending into red frontal shield. Swims jerking head and tail, flies weakly with dangling legs. Walks readily and climbs reeds and bushes. Normally wary but tame in urban parks. Main call a croaking "cur-ruc." **Range and habitat:** widespread in varied freshwater habitats in temperate and southern WP and EP, in southern NA, most of OR, also parts of AF and NT. Some resident, others migratory. **Similar species:** other gallinules (see p 60).

Common Coot

Fulica atra (**Rallidae**) 36–40 cm/14–16 in.
Round-bodied waterbird. Body plumage very dark slaty black, varying from glossy black head and neck to more gray tone on flanks and underparts. Short, pointed bill and frontal shield white and very conspicuous. White-tipped inner flight feathers show as pale wing-bar in flight when gray-green legs trail behind. Gregarious, forming large winter flocks. Swims buoyantly, making frequent brief dives. Also feeds on land. **Range and habitat:** widespread on varied freshwaters with emergent or marginal vegetation in temperate and southern WP and EP, also widespread in OR and AU. Some populations migratory and found in winter on brackish and freshwater. **Similar species:** other coots (see pp 60, 108, 196).

Common Pheasant

Red-legged Partridge

Gray Partridge

Common Quail

Common Crane
(pair)

Great Bustard

Water Rail

Spotted Crake

Corncrake

Common Moorhen

Common Coot

SHOREBIRDS, GULLS, AUKS Charadriiformes

Eurasian Oystercatcher

Haematopus ostralegus (Haematopodidae) 41–5 cm/16–18 in.
Large, robust wading bird with conspicuous bill. Glossy black upperparts, head, neck and upper breast. Pure white lower breast and rest of underparts, also rump and band across trailing edge of wings. Variable white collar present in winter. Long, stout orange-red bill. Pink legs and feet. Highly gregarious outside breeding season. Shrill "kleep-kleep" call, loud piping display notes. **Range and habitat:** breeds northern and temperate WP and EP, particularly on coasts, also inland along river valleys and by larger freshwaters. Winters coasts of WP and EP, also AF and OR. **Similar species:** other oystercatchers (see pp 200, 294).

Pied Avocet

Recurvirostra avosetta (Recurvirostridae) 41–5 cm/16–18 in.
Long-legged wading bird with distinctive long, thin, upturned bill. Body plumage pure white, with black cap to head and black nape, black wing tips, black bar across center of wings and black bar at wing roots. Bill c. 8 cm/3 in) long, delicately upcurved and tapering to point. Used in highly distinctive side-to-side sweeping movement through shallow water. Flight graceful, with legs and feet trailing behind tail. Chief call "kloo-eet." **Range and habitat:** shallow brackish and saline wetlands of western and southern WP, central EP and scattered through AF, wintering similar habitats in WP, AF and OR. Colonies threatened by disturbance and predation. **Similar species:** other avocets (see pp 66, 296).

Black-winged Stilt

Himantopus himantopus (Recurvirostridae) 36–40 cm/14–16 in.
Slender wading bird on exceptionally long, thin legs. Cheeks, neck, underparts and tail pure white, crown blackish or white. Back black, also both wing surfaces. Needlelike black bill c. 6 cm/2¼ in) long. Bright pink legs 12.5–16.5 cm/5–6½ in) long. Rapid flight action on pointed wings, with legs trailing far beyond tail. "Kik-kik-kik" call used mainly in alarm or when mobbing predator. **Range and habitat:** discontinuous distribution in shallow fresh and brackish open wetlands of southern WP and EP, also widespread in southern AF, and almost throughout NT, AF, OR and AU. Palaearctic populations migratory, to AF. **Similar species:** other stilts (see pp 66, 294).

Common Ringed Plover

Charadrius hiaticula (Charadriidae) 18–20 cm/7–8 in.
Plump, pale sandy brown and white shorebird with head and neck banded black and white. Crown and upperparts sandy brown, rest of head and underparts white. Black bands through eyes and above bill and black collar. Prominent pale wing-bar. Short, stubby orange bill tipped black. Orange legs. Runs with very rapid steps, interspersed with pauses. Flies rapidly. Territorial when nesting, otherwise gregarious. Calls a liquid "too-ee" and sharper "queep." **Range and habitat:** arctic tundra and northern temperate shores of WP and EP, and also north-eastern arctic NA. Winters western coasts of WP, also widely in AF. Threatened by disturbance and predation when nesting. **Similar species:** other small plovers (see pp 62, 110, 200, 294).

Little Ringed Plover

Charadrius dubius (Charadriidae) 14–16 cm/5½–6½ in.
Small brown and white plover with black and white banding on head and chest. Upperparts and crown dull brown, remainder of head and underparts pure white. Black band through eyes, joining over white forehead. Very narrow black line from eyes to bill. Black collar below white throat. Thin dark bill, yellowish or pinkish legs. Runs freely, pausing at intervals. Flight fast, showing uniform brown upper surface of wings. High-pitched "pee-oo" call. Territorial breeder, not especially gregarious in winter. **Range and habitat:** widespread in lowland freshwaters of WP, EP and OR. Wintering in AF and OR. Few, if any, threats. **Similar species:** other small plovers (see pp 62, 110, 200, 294).

Eurasian Golden-Plover

Pluvialis apricaria (Charadriidae) 27–9 cm/10½–11½ in.
Medium to large short-billed wader with rounded head and bulky body. Crown, upperparts and upperwings blackish brown liberally speckled with gold, especially on nape. Face, chin, throat and center of underparts jet black, with white sides to neck, shoulders, flanks and undertail. Black less extensive in southerly breeding birds. Black lost in winter. Underwings whitish. Gregarious except when breeding. Liquid "tloo-ee" call. Rapid, agile flight; easy running gait. **Range and habitat:** arctic tundra and north temperate open mountain areas of WP and north-western EP, wintering in west and south WP on farmland and floodlands. **Similar species:** other golden plovers (see p 62).

Gray Plover

Pluvialis squatarola (Charadriidae) 28–31 cm/11–12 in.
Stoutly built medium to large short-billed wader. Upperparts finely barred and spotted black and white to give silvery appearance. Forehead, sides of nape and shoulders white; face, chin, throat and underparts black. Undertail white. In flight shows pale underwings with black at junction with body. Black lost in winter and upperparts paler. Call a plaintive "tlee-oo-ee." Gregarious. **Range and habitat:** breeds circumpolar Holarctic tundras, except Greenland. Winters on coasts of NA, NT, AF, OR and AU; a few remain on coasts of WP and EP. **Similar species:** golden plovers (see p 62).

Eurasian Dotterel

Eudromias morinellus (Charadriidae) 20–3 cm/8–9 in.
Plump, small-billed plover. In summer plumage upperparts are gray and brown with blackish crown and prominent white stripes above eyes forming V on nape. Gray breast separated from chestnut underparts by white line. Blackish belly and white undertail. Wings brown above, pale below. Female brighter. In winter, paler and browner, losing chestnut on underparts. Quiet "peep-peep" call. Wingbeats very rapid in fast and strong flight. **Range and habitat:** breeds arctic tundra and northern temperate mountain uplands, and rarely lowlands, of WP and EP, migrating to winter in dry open country in southern WP. **Similar species:** other larger plovers (see pp 110, 200, 250, 294).

Northern Lapwing

Vanellus vanellus (Charadriidae) 29–32 cm/11½–13 in.
Medium-large crested plover, black and white at distance. Upperparts dark glossy purple-green. Crown, crest and throat black, and black mark through eye. Lower face and nape whitish. Breast black, underparts white, undertail cinnamon, rump white. Rounded wings black above, black and white below. Distinctive slow erratic wing-beats and manoeuvrable tumbling flight in display making "lapping" sound. Call a loud "pee-wit." Very gregarious. Runs and pauses while feeding. **Range and habitat:** widespread in mainly temperate open habitats of WP and EP, including farmland and marshes. Partially migratory, reaching OR, and often on coasts in winter. Declines when farmland drained. **Similar species:** other lapwings (see pp 110, 200, 250, 294).

Ruddy Turnstone

Arenaria interpres (Scolopacidae) 22–4 cm/8½–9½ in.
Boldly marked small short-billed wader. Breeding plumage has white head and underparts, dark streaks on crown and black on face and breast. Upperparts chestnut with blackish stripes and mottlings. Underparts white. In winter, gray; blackish on back, head and breast. In flight, highly patterned with 2 bold white wing-bars, white rump and black band to tail. Gregarious outside breeding season. Call a rapid "kit-it-it." Flight fast. Walks among seaweed and stones flicking them over with bill. **Range and habitat:** breeds circumpolar Holarctic tundra, also northern temperate coasts of WP and NA. Winters coasts of WP, EP, NA, NT, AF, OR and AU. **Similar species:** Black Turnstone (see p 66).

Eurasian Oystercatcher

Pied Avocet

Black-winged Stilt (at nest)

Common Ringed Plover (brooding young)

Little Ringed Plover (shading eggs)

Eurasian Golden-Plover

Gray Plover (on tundra)

Eurasian Dotterel

Ruddy Turnstone (on nest)

Northern Lapwing

Curlew Sandpiper

Calidris ferruginea (Scolopacidae) 18–20 cm/7–8 in.
Slim, upright wader with prominent white rump. Breeding plumage dark chestnut-brown above, richer chestnut-red below, with black, brown and whitish markings. Whitish wing-bar, and rump and undertail conspicuously white in flight. In winter, brown-gray above and white below, upperparts with dark streaks and pale feather edgings. Thin decurved bill. Found singly or in small groups. Flight note a soft "chir-rup." **Range and habitat:** breeds arctic tundra of EP, migrating, some via WP, to coastal and inland wetlands of AF, and coasts of OR and AU. **Similar species:** Dunlin.

Dunlin

Calidris alpina (Scolopacidae) 16.5–19 cm/6½–7½ in.
Small and abundant shore wader with black legs and slightly decurved bill. Breeding plumage distinctive with reddish tinged dark upperparts and black belly patch on paler underparts. Winter plumage brown-gray above, paler below. White wing-bar, outer tail and outer rump show white in flight. Highly gregarious on passage and in winter. Call a grating "schreep." Trilling display song. **Range and habitat:** circumpolar Holarctic breeder on arctic tundra, and north temperate moorland and saltmarsh. Migrates in winter to NA, WP, AF and OR, on tidal mudflats and margins of open freshwaters. Some local declines of breeding pairs through agricultural change. **Similar species:** other small waders (see pp 64, 250).

Little Stint

Calidris minuta (Scolopacidae) 14–15.5 cm/5½–6 in.
Tiny, dumpy wader. Overall summer plumage dark above with rufous markings, speckled rufous chest and white belly. In winter, loses rufous tinge, becomes very pale gray-brown above, white below. Short black legs and short fine bill. Active, running and pecking, with fast flight when white wing-bar and white sides to rump show. Flight note a high "chik." **Range and habitat:** breeds arctic tundra of WP and EP, migrating to winter on coasts and inland freshwaters of south-east WP, and widely in AF and OR. **Similar species:** other small waders and stints (see pp 64, 250).

Red Knot

Calidris canutus (Scolopacidae) 24–7 cm/9½–10½ in.
Medium-small wader, uniform gray in winter. Breeding plumage chestnut above, marked with black, underparts rich cinnamon-pink. Flight feathers gray and black. Narrow white wing-bar also visible on winter plumage bird, which has all-gray body, whitish on lower belly and rump. Straight black bill, legs olive-green. Highly gregarious, often in very large flocks, wheeling and turning in unison. Call a low "knut." **Range and habitat:** widespread breeder on arctic tundra of NA and a few places in EP. Migrates to winter on coasts of NT, WP, AF, OR and AU. Vulnerable as high proportion of population dependent on very few migration stopovers. **Similar species:** Great Knot.

Sanderling

Calidris alba (Scolopacidae) 19–22 cm/7½–8½ in.
Small, very active wader of winter shorelines. Breeding plumage rufous buff on upperparts and breast, streaked and spotted white and black. White belly, short black bill and black legs. Winter plumage white over much of body, gray back and crown, black streaks on closed wings. Conspicuous white wing-bar in flight. Runs actively to and fro at tide edge. Gregarious. Calls "twick-twick" in flight. **Range and habitat:** breeds arctic tundras of EP and NA, migrating in winter to coasts of NA, NT, WP, AF, EP, OR and AU.

Purple Sandpiper

Calidris maritima (Scolopacidae) 20–2 cm/8–8½ in.
Small but stocky shorebird of rocky coasts. Dark uniform gray-brown above, paler beneath, with rufous spotting on upperparts in breeding plumage, more even gray in winter, mottled on breast and flanks. Belly white. Moderately long slightly decurved dark bill, yellow at base, and distinctive yellowish legs. Winters in small flocks. Tame at all seasons. Not very vocal, main call a low "weet-wit." **Range and habitat:** arctic tundras and upland plateaux of WP, EP and NA. Moves to coasts of WP and NA for winter.

Red-necked Phalarope

Phalaropus lobatus (Scolopacidae) 17–19 cm/6½–7½ in.
Slender, almost dainty swimming wader with needle-thin bill. Breeding female much brighter than male, slate-gray head, chest and back, last-named with buff lines. White chin, orange-red sides of neck and chest, white underparts. Winter plumage pale blue-gray above, white below, dark markings round eye and on wings. Prominent white wing-bar. Very tame. "Tirrick" call when alarmed. **Range and habitat:** breeds widely on circumpolar Holarctic tundra and north temperate freshwaters. Polyandrous. Winters at sea off coasts of west NT, OR and northern AD. Small colonies outside main range threatened by habitat loss. **Similar species:** Gray Phalarope.

Common Redshank

Tringa totanus (Scolopacidae)
6–30 cm/10–12 in.
Medium-sized shank with noticeable red legs and noisy calls. Gray-brown above, streaked breast and whitish underparts, lacking obvious markings. Longish bill red at base. In flight appears black and white, with dark wings and broad white trailing edge, white rump. Fast, active flight with jerky wingbeats. Alarm and flight calls, musical, ringing "tu-tu-tu" or "tewk." Gregarious outside breeding season. **Range and habitat:** widespread on coasts and wide variety of freshwater habitats of WP and EP, mostly migratory south to northern AF, OR and AU. Some local declines from agricultural changes and waterways management. **Similar species:** other shanks (see p 62).

Spotted Redshank

Tringa erythropus (Scolopacidae) 29–32 cm/11½–13 in.
Large shank, all-dark in summer. Breeding plumage black all over, relieved by white spotting on back and dusky tone to face, neck and chest. Base of bill and legs dull red. In winter, ash-gray above, paler below. In flight, wings dark, rump and lower back white. Gives diagnostic clear 2-note "chew-it" call on being flushed. **Range and habitat:** breeds by marshes and pools among scattered trees in northern WP and EP, migrating south reaching AF and OR. **Similar species:** none in summer, other large shanks in winter (see p 62).

Common Greenshank

Tringa nebularia (Scolopacidae) 29–32 cm/11½–13 in.
Large, long-legged shank. Dark gray above, spotted and streaked dark gray and black in summer. Paler gray on neck and breast, streaked darker in summer. Belly white. Long bill slightly upturned. Legs green. On taking flight, gives far-carrying "teu-teu-teu" call, and shows conspicuous white rump and white wedge up back. **Range and habitat:** breeds by marshes and pools often among trees in northern WP and EP, wintering south in WP and widely in AF, OR and AU. **Similar species:** other large shanks (see p 62).

Common Sandpiper

Actitis hypoleucos (Scolopacidae) 19–21 cm/7½–8 in.
Small, stocky wader. Upperparts olive-brown, underparts pure white with brown mark on either side of breast. White eye stripe, broad white wing-bar, barred white sides to tail. Call a shrill "twee-twee-twee," given in flight, when wings held down in short glides. Constantly wags rather long tail when walking or still. Usually solitary, or in pairs or small groups. **Range and habitat:** wide variety of freshwaters, often running water, almost throughout WP and EP, migrating to winter widely in AF, OR and AU. Some declines of breeding numbers through agricultural drainage. **Similar species:** Spotted Sandpiper (see p 62).

Green Sandpiper

Tringa ochropus (Scolopacidae) 22–4 cm/8½–9½ in.
Medium-small sandpiper, noticeably dark above. Upperparts dark olive-brown with small white spots present in summer, soon wearing away. Neck, breast and flanks spotted and streaked brown in summer, paler in winter, white on belly. Rises abruptly when flushed and towers, giving loud "weet-weet-weet" note before zig-zagging away. **Range and habitat:** breeds swamps and marshes often among trees in northern WP and EP, wintering south to southern WP, AF and OR. **Similar species:** other medium-small sandpipers (see pp 64, 250).

Curlew Sandpiper (coming into summer plumage)

Dunlin (in summer plumage)

Little Stint

Red Knot

Sanderling

Purple Sandpiper

Red-necked Phalarope

Common Redshank

Spotted Redshank (at nest)

Common Greenshank

Common Sandpiper

Green Sandpiper

Ruff

Philomachus pugnax (Scolopacidae) 22–31 cm/8½–12 in.
Wader with longish neck and small head, very variable in size. Larger male develops bizarre multi-colored ruff and ear-tufts, black, white, rufous or mixture, in spring. Female gray-brown marked with sepia. In winter both gray-brown, with scaly pattern on closed wing. In flight, narrow white wing-bar and conspicuous white oval either side of dark rump. Rarely calls. Elaborate displays by groups of courting males. Often singly, small flocks at other times. **Range and habitat:** breeds lowland marshes and wet scrubby areas of temperate and northern WP and BP. Migrates to fresh and brackish waters in southern WP, AF and OR. Declines with agricultural change. **Similar species:** Buff-breasted Sandpiper (see p 64).

Eurasian Curlew

Numenius arquata (Scolopacidae) 51–61 cm/20–4 in.
Very large, long-legged wader. Body overall pale gray-brown, variably streaked darker brown on head, neck and breast merging to produce ill-defined bib; paler on back and wings. Belly white, darker markings on flanks. Conspicuous white rump in flight. Bill 10–15 cm/4–6 in) evenly decurved; long, dark horn, very long legs blue-gray. Loud "cour-lee" call and bubbling musical song delivered in flight. Gregarious outside breeding season. **Range and habitat:** open habitats with some water, often upland, in temperate and northern WP and EP. Migrates to winter mainly on coasts of WP, EP, AF and OR. Sensitive to agricultural change. **Similar species:** Whimbrel.

Whimbrel

Numenius phaeopus (Scolopacidae) 39–43 cm/15–17 in.
Large, long-legged brown wader with decurved bill. Brown plumage, darker above, streaked and spotted buff. Dark crown split by broad buff stripe; buff stripes above eyes. Belly white, streaked brown on flanks. White rump shows in flight, absent in NA race. Long bill bent downward toward tip. Call a 7-note tittering trill "ti-ti-ti-ti-ti-ti-ti." Also bubbling song. Gregarious in small flocks. **Range and habitat:** discontinuous circumpolar breeding distribution through northern open forests, marshes and moorlands of WP, EP and NA. Winters south to coasts of NA, NT, AF, OR and AU. **Similar species:** other curlews (see p 64).

Bar-tailed Godwit

Limosa lapponica (Scolopacidae) 36–40 cm/14–16 in.
Medium to large slim wader. Summer adult has reddish chestnut underparts with fine black streaking on crown and nape and heavy black markings on rufous back. Wing-coverts gray-brown. In winter, pale gray-brown streaked above and toning to whitish below. Fine, tapering bill 8.5–10 cm/3¼–4 in) long, gently upcurved. In flight, whitish triangular rump above barred tail. Harsh "kirrik" flight call. Gregarious. **Range and habitat:** breeds subarctic tundra and marshes of WP and EP, and northwestern NA. Winters coasts of WP, AF, OR and AU. **Similar species:** other godwits (see p 64, 66).

Black-tailed Godwit

Limosa limosa (Scolopacidae) 38–43 cm/15–17 in.
Large, upright wader with fine straight bill, long legs trailing in flight. Breeding plumage pink-chestnut on head, breast and upper back; streaked and barred blackish on lower back and flanks. Belly whitish, wing-coverts gray-brown. In winter, uniform pale gray-brown above, white below, head and neck brownish. White rump and black-barred tail. Broad white wing-bar and blackish trailing edge in flight. Loud "wicka-wicka" flight call. Gregarious. **Range and habitat:** moist lowland areas of mainly temperate WP, also scattered in EP. Migrates to inland and coastal wetlands of WP, AF, OR and AU. Declines with agricultural drainage. **Similar species:** other godwits (see p 64, 66).

Eurasian Woodcock

Scolopax rusticola (Scolopacidae) 32–6 cm/13–14 in.
Large, heavily built wader with shortish legs and long, straight bill. Camouflaged plumage of reddish brown, darker above, mottled and marbled with black. Broad black bars on head and nape, face and throat buff. Rufous tail. Very broad, rounded wings, flies with bill angled downward. Solitary and wary, flying mainly at night or at dusk, weaving between trees. Silent except in "roding" display flight when gives grunting notes followed by "twisick." **Range and habitat:** widespread in moist woodlands with clearings throughout temperate and boreal WP and EP. Migrates to similar or scrub habitat in southern WP and EP, also OR. At risk from woodland clearance. **Similar species:** other woodcocks (see p 66).

Common Snipe

Gallinago gallinago (Scolopacidae) 25–8 cm/10–11 in.
Medium-sized wader, bill 6–7 cm/2¼–2¾ in) long. Upperparts dark brown mottled black; cream stripes on head and back. Pale buff cheeks and neck, streaked darker, belly white, boldly barred flanks. When flushed, gives "scaap" call and zig-zags, then towers. White trailing edge to wing. Display call a persistent "chip-er," also "drumming" with stiff outer tail feathers. Wary, sometimes in small groups. **Range and habitat:** very widespread in lowland wetlands and scrub of temperate and northern Holarctic, also NT and AF. Northern populations migratory to southern WP, EP, NA; also NT, AF and OR. At risk from loss of wetland breeding habitat. **Similar species:** other snipe (see pp 110, 202, 250).

Eurasian Thick-Knee

Burhinus oedicnemus (Burhinidae) 38–43 cm/15–17 in.
Robust, rather ungainly wader. Overall plumage sandy brown, streaked blackish on upperparts and breast, belly white. Large, staring yellow eyes, yellow and black bill, yellow legs. Slow and direct flight showing 2 white and 1 black wing-bars and white underwings. Walks or runs over ground, stopping at intervals. Has wild, wailing "coor-lee" call. Rather shy, most active at dusk and during night. **Range and habitat:** dry heathlands and steppes of southern WP and EP, also OR; wintering south into AF more often at or near wetlands. Threatened by loss of breeding habitat. **Similar species:** other thick-knees (see pp 110, 198, 294).

Collared Pratincole

Glareola pratincola (Glareolidae) 24–7 cm/9½–10½ in.
Slender ternlike wader with long wings and short legs, and short, stubby bill. Upperparts uniform darkish brown. Narrow black line outlines cream throat. Breast and flanks fawn, rest of underparts white. White rump conspicuous in flight, chestnut underwings not obvious alongside black wing feathers. Fast and erratic ternlike flight on long pointed wings; tail deeply forked. Ternlike call, "kir-rik." Gregarious and colonial breeder. **Range and habitat:** scattered breeder on steppes, dry floodplains and semideserts in southern WP and EP and throughout AF. Palaearctic populations winter AF. Maintenance of breeding habitat essential. **Similar species:** other pratincoles (see pp 202, 250).

Great Skua

Catharacta skua (Stercorariidae) 56–61 cm/22–4 in.
Very large and dark skua, more gull-like in shape than other skuas. Plumage dark brown on upperparts, gray-brown below, mottled with rufous. Yellowish streaks on head, lacking in winter. Stout, hooked bill. White patches toward tips of wings, both above and below, conspicuous in flight, which is fast and powerful when chasing other birds, slower and heavier at other times. Nests colonially, defending nest territory vigorously, striking intruders. Loud "kak-kak" and "ha-ha" calls. **Range and habitat:** breeds moorland and tundra in few localities northern WP, other races breeding NT and AN. Winters at sea. Some declines due to over-fishing. **Similar species:** South Polar Skua.

Parasitic Jaeger

Stercorarius parasiticus (Stercorariidae) 38–48 cm/15–19 in.
Medium-sized skua with narrow, pointed wings and projecting central tail feathers; 2 color phases plus intermediates. Dark phase dark brown all over, grayer below and with black cap. Pale phase underparts white, tinged yellow on cheeks and neck, gray-brown breast and flanks, sometimes breast band. Wings all-dark with pale patch toward tip. Graceful flight, fast and skilful when chasing other birds. Loud "kaa-aow" call when breeding. Colonial breeder. **Range and habitat:** circumpolar Holarctic tundra and moorland. Winters at sea and round coasts of WP, EP, AF, NA, NT, OR and AU. **Similar species:** Long-tailed and Pomarine Jaegers (see p 68).

Ruff

Eurasian Curlew (at nest)

Whimbrel (at nest)

Bar-tailed Godwit (tundra breeding grounds)

Black-tailed Godwit

Eurasian Woodcock (at nest)

Common Snipe

Eurasian Thick-Knee (pair with young)

Collared Pratincole (at nest)

Great Skua

Parasitic Jaeger

Common Black-headed Gull
Larus ridibundus (Laridae) 35–8 cm/14–15 in.
Small gull with chocolate brown head in summer. Nape and whole of underparts white. Back gray. Wings gray with prominent white leading edge and black tips. Winter adult white-headed with dusky black marks on head and behind eye. Thin bill and legs dark red. Flight buoyant. Gregarious, breeding colonially. Often tame. Harsh "kraah" call. **Range and habitat:** widespread on coasts, inland marshes and pools of temperate and northern WP and EP. Winters inland and coasts of WP, EP, also NA, AF and OR. **Similar species:** other small dark-headed gulls (see pp 62, 250).

Mediterranean Gull
Larus melanocephalus (Laridae) 37–40 cm/15–16 in.
Medium-sized gull with black head in summer. All-white neck and underparts, dove-gray wings and back. Stout reddish bill, with slightly drooping tip, and red legs. Black head, except in winter, when blackish mark behind eye and dusky areas over crown. In flight, white on outer half of upper wing and white underwing. Gregarious at all seasons; breeds colonially. Harsh "kee-ow kee-er" calls. **Range and habitat:** restricted as breeder to scattered lowland marshes of central and southern WP. Winters coasts, including to north. **Similar species:** other small dark-headed gulls (see pp 66, 250, 296).

Herring Gull
Larus argentatus (Laridae) 53–9 cm/21–3 in.
Abundant heavily built large gull. Head, neck, underparts and tail white. Back and upperwings variable slate-gray to silver-gray. Outer primaries black with white tips. White trailing edge to wings. Heavy yellow bill with red spot near tip of lower mandible. Legs pink or yellow. Gregarious, often tame. Many noisy calls, including "kee-yow" and "gah-gah-gah." **Range and habitat:** widespread in coastal WP and central and northern EP and NA. Winters coasts and some inland areas of WP, EP and NA. Human persecution. **Similar species:** other large gulls (see pp 66, 68, 296).

Lesser Black-backed Gull
Larus fuscus (Laridae) 51–6 cm/20–2 in.
Large gull with dark upperparts, varying from dark gray to black with race, also within races. Head, neck, underparts and tail white. Wings dark above, white below. White tips to primaries and white trailing edge. Stout yellow bill with red spot on lower mandible. Legs and feet yellow. Noisy calls, including "kyow-kyow" and "gar-gar-gar." Gregarious. **Range and habitat:** breeds coastal and some inland wetlands of western and northern WP and EP. Winters at sea and coasts of WP, NA and coasts and inland AF. Human persecution, also colony disturbance. **Similar species:** other large dark-backed gulls (see pp 68, 296).

Great Black-backed Gull
Larus marinus (Laridae) 64–79 cm/25–31 in.
Very large bulky gull. Back and upperwings slate-black. Head, neck, underparts and tail pure white. Trailing edge to wings and tips of outermost feathers white. Heavy, deep bill yellow with red spot on lower mandible. Legs flesh-colored. Black eye-mark gives scowling appearance. Harsh barking call, "yowk." **Range and habitat:** breeds temperate and northern coasts of WP and NA. Winters same coasts and to south, also at sea. Culled in some areas. **Similar species:** other large dark-backed gulls (see pp 68, 296).

Mew Gull
Larus canus (Laridae) 38–43 cm/15–17 in.
Medium-sized gray-backed gull. Head, neck, underparts and tail white, back and upperwings pale blue-gray. Outer half of primaries black, white spots at tips. Bill and legs yellow-green. Easy, graceful flight. High-pitched "kee-yaa" call. Very gregarious at all times, breeding in colonies. Often inland. **Range and habitat:** widespread breeder on coasts and inland temperate and northern WP and EP and western half of NA. Winters coasts and inland within southern part of breeding range and to south, reaching OR. Feral mink threaten some colonies. **Similar species:** other medium-sized gulls (see pp 66, 110).

Black-legged Kittiwake
Rissa tridactyla (Laridae) 38–43 cm/15–17 in.
Slim and dainty gull. Back and upperwings darkish gray, darker in NA race. Head, neck, underparts and tail pure white. Wings show black triangular tips and white trailing edge. Bill yellow-green, legs black. In winter, nape gray, blackish marks behind eye. Very buoyant, graceful flight. Gregarious at all times, breeding in dense, cliff-ledge colonies. Very noisy "kittee-wayke" call when nesting. **Range and habitat:** northern and arctic coasts, especially cliffs, of WP, EP and NA. Winters at sea in northern oceans. Sensitive to fish stocks being overfished. **Similar species:** small gulls (see pp 66, 110).

Sandwich Tern
Thalasseus sandvicensis (Laridae) 38–43 cm/15–17 in.
Medium-large tern with slim yellow-tipped black bill. Crown and shaggy crest black, pale ash-gray back and upperwings, latter fading to white at edges. Forehead and crown white in winter, white streaks in black crest. Black legs and feet, with yellow soles. Flight strong and buoyant on long pointed wings, forked tail. Harsh "kirrick" call. Gregarious, colonial breeder. **Range and habitat:** breeds on flat coasts of south and west WP, also scattered localities in NT. Winters coastal waters of WP, NA, AF and OR. Breeding colonies can be badly disturbed. **Similar species:** other medium to large terns (see pp 68, 110, 202, 250).

Common Tern
Sterna hirundo (Laridae) 30–6 cm/12–14 in.
Slender medium-small tern. Cap black, extending down nape. Upperparts and upperwings pale gray, sides of face and neck white, underparts and forked tail very pale gray-white. Underwings white. Longish bill deep red with black tip. Legs and feet red. In winter, forehead becomes white and bill black with reddish base. Harsh, grating "kee-yar" call. Colonial breeder. **Range and habitat:** widespread inland and coastal breeder in WP, EP and NA, also scattered in NT and AF. Winters at sea and coasts of WP, EP, NA, NT, AF, OR and AU. Nesting colonies subject to human disturbance. **Similar species:** other medium-small terns (see pp 68, 202, 250, 296).

Arctic Tern
Sterna paradisaea (Laridae) 30–9 cm/12–15 in.
Slender medium-small tern; tail deeply forked, 10–18 cm/4–7 in) long. Black cap and nape. Pale blue-gray upperparts, white cheeks and pale gray underparts. Longish, pointed bill blood-red. Short legs and feet red. Wings pale gray above, white below, appear translucent from beneath and edged blackish. Forehead whitish in winter. Graceful, buoyant flight, diving vertically. Colonial breeder. Harsh, grating "kee-errr" call. **Range and habitat:** circumpolar northern and arctic Holarctic coasts and tundra. Winters south polar seas. Some declines due to overfishing. **Similar species:** other medium-small terns (see pp 68, 250, 296).

Little Tern
Sterna albifrons (Laridae) 23–6 cm/9–10 in.
Tiny, short-legged tern. Black cap and nape, white forehead and streak over eye. Blue-gray upperparts shading to white rump and tail. Blue-gray and white upperwings. White face, underparts and underwings. Yellow bill with black tip, legs orangey. Black cap mostly lost in winter, grayer wings. Active, jerky flight, hovering before diving. Shrill "kik-kik" call. Colonial breeder. **Range and habitat:** widespread breeder on shingle coasts and inland in temperate and southern WP, EP and NA; also NT, AF, OR and AU. Winters coasts and shallow seas. Habitat loss and disturbance threaten many colonies. **Similar species:** other small terns (see pp 68, 250).

Black Tern
Chlidonias niger (Laridae) 23–6 cm/9–10 in.
Marsh tern with slightly forked tail. In summer, plumage very dark slate-gray, pale gray underwings and white at base of undertail. In winter, black-capped head, white underparts and much paler underwings. Restless flight on long wings, beating to and fro, dipping to surface. Thin squeaky calls. Gregarious, colonial breeder. **Range and habitat:** widespread breeder in south temperate freshwater wetlands in WP, EP and NA. Winters estuaries and coastal lagoons of AF and NT. At risk of agricultural drainage. **Similar species:** other marsh terns.

Common Black-headed Gull

Mediterranean Gull (coming into summer plumage)

Herring Gull

Lesser Black-backed Gull

Great Black-backed Gull

Mew Gull

Black-legged Kittiwake (pair, at nesting ledge)

Sandwich Tern

Common Tern

Arctic Tern

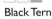

Little Tern (at nest)

Black Tern

Atlantic Puffin

Fratercula arctica (**Alcidae**) 29–31 cm/11½–12 in.
Stubby auk with round head and grotesque face and bill in summer. Upperparts black, underparts white. Face gray, red eye-ring and blue appendages above and below. Greatly enlarged triangular bill striped blue-gray, yellow and orange. Much reduced by molt and mostly yellow in winter and face much grayer. Legs and feet red-orange. Rapid whirring flight. Wings pure black above, white below. Colonial breeder. Deep growling "kaa-arr-arr" call at nest. **Range and habitat:** breeds coastal islands and stacks northwest WP and north-east NA, including arctic. Winters at sea. Numbers dependent on adequate fish stocks. **Similar species:** other auks (see p 68).

Razorbill

Alca torda (**Alcidae**) 39–43 cm/15–17 in.
Medium to large auk with deep, vertically flattened bill. Black head, neck and upperparts. Narrow white bar across folded wings, forming white trailing edge in flight. Underparts white, inner part of underwings white, outer gray. Vertical white line on black bill and white line from upper bill to eye. In winter, cheeks and throat whitish. Flight fast and whirring. Gregarious. Colonial breeder. Has variety of growling and snoring notes at colony. **Range and habitat:** northern and arctic cliff coasts of north-west WP and north-east NA. Winters at sea. Very vulnerable to oil spills. **Similar species:** other large auks (see p 68).

Common Murre

Uria aalge (**Alcidae**) 40–4 cm/16–17 in.
Large auk with longish, pointed black bill. Head, neck and upperparts blackish brown, more gray-brown in southern race. Thin white bar across folded wings shows as narrow white trailing edge in flight. Dark, indented furrow behind eye. White eye-ring and white line along furrow in proportion of birds ('bridled'). Dark marks on flanks, otherwise underparts white. Black of neck and cheeks becomes white in winter. Fast, whirring flight. Colonial breeder. Loud growling and trumpeting calls at colony. **Range and habitat:** northern and arctic cliff coasts of WP, EP and NA. Winters at sea. At risk from oil spills and fishing nets. **Similar species:** other large auks (see p 68).

Black Guillemot

Cepphus grylle (**Alcidae**) 33–5 cm/13–14 in.
Small, compact auk. Breeding plumage all-black except for large oval white patch on wings, highly visible at rest and in flight. Longish, pointed black bill and very obvious bright red legs and feet. In winter, becomes overall gray-white on head and body, retaining black tail and black and white wings. Rapid, whirring flight. Walks relatively easily. Solitary or in small groups. Call a shrill whistle. **Range and habitat:** northern and arctic coasts of WP, EP and NA, wintering at sea. Fishing nets a problem in some areas. **Similar species:** winter plumage confusable with male Smew (see p 148).

Dovekie

Alle alle (**Alcidae**) 20–2 cm/8–8½ in.
Tiny, stubby auk. Head, neck and breast chocolate brown, upperparts and tail glossy black. White streaks down back and across folded wings. Wings black above, with white trailing edge, underwing mainly dark. Tiny white mark above eye. Very short black bill. Highly gregarious, breeding in enormous colonies, though gale-blown vagrants often solitary. Very fast agile flight, flocks twisting and turning in unison. High-pitched laughing cries at breeding colony. **Range and habitat:** arctic coastal screes of north-west WP and extreme north-east NA. Winters at sea. **Similar species:** small auklets (see p 68).

SANDGROUSE Pterocliformes

Pin-tailed Sandgrouse

Pterocles alchata (**Pteroclididae**) 31–9 cm/12–15 in.
Short-legged and short-necked terrestrial birds with greatly elongated tail streamers. Male has greenish upperparts, spotted yellow in spring, yellow-chestnut face, black eye-line, chin and throat. Black-outlined broad chestnut-buff breast band, pure white belly and underwing. Female duller, more buff on upperparts, more yellow on face and chest. Highly gregarious. Groups undertake close aerial maneuvers and gather at drinking places. Ringing "cata-cata"

call in flight. **Range and habitat:** lowland plains of southern WP and south-west WP, most resident, some winter in south-west OR. Seriously threatened by agricultural change. **Similar species:** other sandgrouse (see p 204).

PIGEONS Columbiformes

Rock Pigeon

Columba livia (**Columbidae**) 31–5 cm/12–14 in.
Medium-sized plump dove with shortish tail, ancestor of highly variable domestic pigeons. Blue-gray head and body, with glossy purple breast and glossy green neck. Paler gray on back and closed wings, which have 2 black bars. Rump white, tail blue-gray with broad blackish band at tip. Bill dull gray with whitish cere. Dashing flight, often low with wheeling and gliding. "Coo-roo-coo" call in display. Gregarious. **Range and habitat:** widespread in cliff caves (domestics use buildings) throughout WP, EP, NA, OR and scattered in NT and AU. Nonmigratory. **Similar species:** other doves (see p 204).

Stock Pigeon

Columba oenas (**Columbidae**) 31–5 cm/12–14 in.
Medium-sized compact dove with shortish tail. Upperparts and underparts mostly gray, with blue tone on head and under body, slatey gray on back. Glossy green sides to neck, purplish tinge to breast. Forewing pale gray with 2 short black wing-bars. Outer wing dark gray. Tail with broad black band at tip. Bill yellowish, legs and feet pink. Active flier in small groups or pairs. Call a grunting repeated double "coo." **Range and habitat:** widespread in open woodland of temperate and southern WP and western EP. Some resident, others winter south, mainly within breeding range. At risk of habitat changes and hunting pressure. **Similar species:** other doves (see pp 204, 252).

Common Wood-Pigeon

Columba palumbus (**Columbidae**) 39–43 cm/15–17 in.
Large, bulky pigeon with rather small head and long tail. Head, back and upper tail blue-gray with lighter gray mantle and forewings. Glossy green sides and back of neck with bold white patch. Breast pinkish, belly blue-gray. White wing-bar shows on folded wing. Flight feathers and tail tip blackish. Fast, powerful flight, with clattering takeoff. Song a 5-note rhythmic cooing. Often in large flocks. **Range and habitat:** widespread in temperate and northern woodlands of WP and western part of EP. Nonmigratory or moves south within breeding range. Considerable pressure from hunting. **Similar species:** other large pigeons (see pp 204, 252).

Eurasian Collared-Dove

Streptopelia decaocto (**Columbidae**) 29–32 cm/11½–13 in.
Medium-sized long-tailed dove. Overall plumage dull gray-brown, pinkish on head and breast, becoming whitish buff on belly and undertail. Black collar round hindneck, edged white. Outer wings dark, inner wings paler underneath. Outer tail whitish above, clearer white below, contrasting with dark inner tail. Persistent 3-note cooing song. Rapid flight, often gliding or swooping. Gregarious, especially when feeding. **Range and habitat:** southern and temperate lowlands of WP, also OR and southern EP. Resident but much dispersal by juveniles, including colonization of WP this century. **Similar species:** other doves (see pp 204, 252).

European Turtle-Dove

Streptopelia turtur (**Columbidae**) 26–9 cm/10–11½ in.
Small, graceful dove. Gray-blue head and nape; pinky mauve neck and breast, former with black and white on sides, latter shading to whitish belly. Back rufous brown, mottled with black. Tail conspicuously black with white edgings above and white tip below. Wings chestnut and gray above, paler below. Some racial variation across range. Rapid and agile flight, particularly among trees. Long-drawn-out crooning "roorr" call. **Range and habitat:** breeds in open country with scattered trees in temperate and southern WP and EP, migrating south to central AF for winter. Threatened by hunting pressure in summer and drought in African wintering grounds. **Similar species:** other doves (see pp 204, 252).

Atlantic Puffin

Razorbill

Common Murre

Black Guillemot

Dovekie

Pin-tailed Sandgrou.

Rock Pigeon

Stock Pigeon

Common Wood-Pigeon

Eurasian Collared-Dove

European Turtle-Do

CUCKOOS AND ALLIES Cuculiformes

Common Cuckoo

Cuculus canorus (**Cuculidae**) 32–4 cm/12–13 in.
Long-tailed, hawklike bird. Male dull gray above, darker brown-gray on tail and flight feathers. Throat and breast gray, rest of underparts white narrowly barred brown-black except undertail. Some white spotting on tail. Adult female browner with less distinct barring beneath; rarely rufous above, pale below, barred with black. Direct flight on pointed wings. Familiar "cuck-oo" call from male; female has bubbling trill. **Range and habitat:** widespread throughout WP and BP, also southeast OR; migrates to southern AF and OR for winter. **Similar species:** other cuckoos (see pp 204, 252, 302).

OWLS Strigiformes

Barn Owl

Tyto alba (**Tytonidae**) 33–6 cm/13–14 in.
Medium-sized owl. Upperparts, including crown and hind-neck, orangey buff, finely mottled brown, gray and white. Pronounced facial disc white outlined with brown. Underparts pure white, with slight dark spotting and buff tone, more on female, or, in other races, grayer above and more buff below. Long, white feathered legs. Slow, wavering but buoyant flight. Mainly nocturnal and crepuscular. Shrieks in flight, snores at nest. **Range and habitat:** widespread in lowlands of temperate WP and NA, and almost throughout NT, AF, OR and AU. Habitat and nest site loss serious.

Little Owl

Athene noctua (**Strigidae**) 21–3 cm/8–9 in.
Small owl with broad head. Upperparts darkish brown (paler in some races), flecked and spotted white. Facial disc whitish with brown streaking round bright yellow eyes. Underparts white, heavily spotted brown forming band on breast, lighter on belly. Wings brown above, white below. Flight fast and bounding. Main call sharp "kee-oo." Solitary or in pairs. **Range and habitat:** widespread in lowland lightly wooded country, also dry uplands throughout temperate and southern WP and EP and parts of AF. Nonmigratory. Some habitat and nest site losses. **Similar species:** other small owls (see pp 72, 254).

Eurasian Tawny Owl

Strix aluco (**Strigidae**) 36–40 cm/14–16 in.
Medium-sized owl with rounded face. Facial disc pale gray-brown, paler between black eyes. Upperparts variable brown, red-brown or grayish, streaked and barred dark brown and white. Underparts paler brown to whitish, streaked darker brown. Broad rounded wings barred toward tips; wingbeats slow and deliberate. Nocturnal, roosts by day in hole or against trunk, calling sharp "kee-vick" as well as familiar hooting song. Solitary or in pairs. **Range and habitat:** in wooded areas, less often parks and towns, of much of WP and south and east EP. Nonmigratory. **Similar species:** other medium-sized owls.

Long-eared Owl

Asio otus (**Strigidae**) 34–7 cm/13–15 in.
Medium-sized owl with prominent ear-tufts. Overall plumage rufous brown slightly paler below, mottled and barred gray and buff above, streaked darker below. Elongated face buff, outlined in black, with dark brown patches around eyes. Nocturnal but may hunt by day, with few beats of broad rounded wings interspersed with long glides. Sharp barking and squealing calls, also double "oo-oo" song. **Range and habitat:** mainly wooded areas with clearings throughout temperate and northern WP, EP and NA, partially migratory to south, reaching OR. **Similar species:** other medium-sized owls.

NIGHTJARS AND ALLIES Caprimulgiformes

Eurasian Nightjar

Caprimulgus europaeus (**Caprimulgidae**) 26–8 cm/10–11 in.
Large-headed crepuscular and nocturnal bird with huge gape for catching aerial insects. Superbly camouflaged, brown streaked, spotted and barred with elaborate patterns of white, silver-gray, buff, rufous, dark brown and black. In buoyant flight, which includes swift turns and glides, prominent white spots visible near wing and tail tips (buff spots in female). Solitary or in pairs. "Koo-ick" flight call, song a prolonged churring trill. **Range and habitat:** lowland woods, plantations with open glades in temperate and southern WP and EP, migrating to AF for winter. Declining through habitat loss. **Similar species:** other nightjars and nighthawks (see pp 72, 116, 212, 254, 304).

SWIFTS AND HUMMINGBIRDS Apodiformes

Common Swift

Apus apus (**Apodidae**) 16–17 cm/6–6½ in.
Very long-winged, short-tailed all-dark swift. Overall plumage black-brown, some green gloss on back. Forehead gray, chin and throat white, sometimes brown tinged. Faint whitish markings on rump and underparts. Completely aerial, only landing at nest site. Scythe-shaped wings held stiffly and beaten rapidly between long glides. Screaming calls during group chases around buildings. **Range and habitat:** widespread round built-up areas, also mountain and cliff terrain throughout much of WP and EP, migrating south to southern AF for winter. **Similar species:** other swifts (see pp 72, 116, 216, 254, 304).

KINGFISHERS AND ALLIES Coraciiformes

European Bee-eater

Merops apiaster (**Meropidae**) 27–9 cm/10½–11½ in.
Brilliantly colored with long curved bill and extended inner tail feathers. Chestnut crown and nape, golden on back. White, blue, black and green stripes on head. Throat bright yellow, separated from green-blue underparts by narrow black line. Long tail green. Wings mainly green with chestnut inner areas. Flight a mixture of wheeling and gliding, interspersed with rapid wingbeats in pursuit of aerial prey. Distinctive liquid "quilp" call. Gregarious and colonial breeder. **Range and habitat:** varied open landscapes with soft-soiled nesting cliffs in southern WP and EP, also extreme southern AF. Migrates to AF for winter. Main threat from habitat loss. **Similar species:** other bee-eaters (see pp 210, 256, 304).

European Roller

Coracias garrulus (**Coraciidae**) 29–32 cm/11½–13 in.
Large, crowlike bird. Head, body and large panel on closed wing pale turquoise-blue, more purplish blue on lower back and rump. Whitish blue streaks on forehead, throat and breast. Upperwings and mantle chestnut-brown. Paler blue tail with dark central feathers and black tips. In powerful flight, upper wings show turquoise-blue and blackish blue. Harsh "rack-kack" calls. **Range and habitat:** breeds in open woodlands of temperate and southern WP and western EP, migrating to eastern AF for winter. Some habitat loss. **Similar species:** other rollers (see pp 208, 256).

Common Kingfisher

Alcedo atthis (**Alcedinidae**) 15–16 cm/6–6½ in.
Small and brilliantly colored. Crown, nape, moustache and upperparts bright blue, with paler sheen on back and darker tinge to wings and tip of short tail. Cheeks and underparts rich chestnut, whitish on throat and sides of neck. Long dagger-shaped bill black, with some orange at base (more in female). Fast, whirring flight, perches or hovers before plunging into water. Shrill "cheee" call. **Range and habitat:** freshwater wetlands in temperate and southern WP and EP, also OR and parts of AU, partially migratory to south. Main threats habitat loss and pollution. **Similar species:** other small kingfishers (see pp 120, 208).

Eurasian Hoopoe

Upupa epops (**Upupidae**) 27–9 cm/10½–11½ in.
Boldly patterned and crested with long, slightly decurved bill. Body pink-brown, brighter on head and upper back, paler below, with whitish belly. Long fan-shaped crest on head of pink-brown feathers tipped white and black. Wings and tail boldly barred black and white. Erratic jerking flight on broad rounded wings reminiscent of butterfly. Far-carrying song, "poo-poo-poo." **Range and habitat:** open country with scattered woods and trees in central and southern WP and EP, widespread throughout AF and OR, northern population migratory to south for winter. Declining through habitat loss.

Common Cuckoo

Barn Owl

Little Owl

Eurasian Tawny Owl

Long-eared Owl

Eurasian Nightjar

Common Swift

European Bee-eater

European Roller

Common Kingfisher

Eurasian Hoopoe

WOODPECKERS AND ALLIES Piciformes

Eurasian Green Woodpecker

Picus viridis (Picidae) 30–3 cm/12–13 in.
Large woodpecker often feeding on ground. Red crown extending down nape, mottled with gray. Upperparts dull greeny yellow, becoming bright yellow on rump, which is conspicuous in flight. Underparts pale gray-green, almost white on throat. Black patch round eye and black and red moustache. Powerful undulating flight on broad wings, outer part brownish faintly barred cream. Strong bill used for probing in ground as well as attacking trees. Hops in upright stance on ground. Loud, laughing "plue-plue-plue" call. Solitary. **Range and habitat:** woodland and open country with trees in temperate and southern WP. Resident. Very sensitive to cold winters. **Similar species:** other large woodpeckers (see pp 74, 122, 216, 258).

Great Spotted Woodpecker

Dendrocopos major (Picidae) 22–4 cm/8½–9½ in.
Medium-sized, boldly marked woodpecker. Glossy black cap with white forehead and cheeks, red on nape and black moustache. Black back, white shoulder patches, black tail. Underparts white or buff-white, except for red patch under tail. Some races have red and black breast band. Undulating flight with several wing-flaps alternating with complete closure of wings. White patch at base of wing. Climbs spirally round tree trunks. Drums loudly on dead wood, also abrupt, clear "tchick" call. **Range and habitat:** forests and open woodland of all but extreme southern WP and EP, also parts of OR. Nonmigratory. **Similar species:** other medium-sized woodpeckers (see pp 74, 122, 216, 258).

Lesser Spotted Woodpecker

Dendrocopos minor (Picidae) 14–15 cm/5½–6 in.
Very small boldly patterned woodpecker. Crown of male dull red, that of female browny white and black. Back and wings black boldly marked with white transverse bars. Forehead, face and underparts whitish tinged with buff, with black moustache, and sides of breast and flanks streaked black. Undulating flight. Climbs tree-trunks agilely, also feeds among outer twigs. Main call a slow, weak "pee-pee-pee," also quiet "chick." Drums with bill on dead wood. Shy and solitary. **Range and habitat:** widespread in forests and open woodlands of all but extreme southern WP and EP. Nonmigratory. Declines from habitat loss. **Similar species:** other small woodpeckers (see pp 74, 216).

Eurasian Wryneck

Jynx torquilla (Picidae) 15–16 cm/6–6½ in.
Small cryptically patterned woodland bird. Overall gray-brown plumage mottled and barred with dark brown and black, producing highly camouflaged effect. Darker above than below. Pale gray unmarked areas above eye and down back. Underparts pale yellowish buff, with light transverse barring. Longish tail with 3 dark bars. Hops on ground with tail raised, flies jerkily, sometimes climbs tree-trunks. At rest twists head and neck to and fro. Shrill "quee-quee" call. **Range and habitat:** breeds open woodlands, also parks and orchards, of central and southern WP and EP, extending into eastern OR. Migrates to winter in AF and OR. Declines from habitat loss and declining food.

PERCHING BIRDS Passeriformes

Crested Lark

Galerida cristata (Alaudidae) 16.5–17.5 cm/6½–7 in.
Plump, medium-sized lark with pointed crest. Overall buff-brown, well streaked above, much paler below, shading to whitish on belly and undertail. Diffuse streaks and elongated spots on upper breast. Darker crest and cheek patch, latter outlined with paler buff. Whitish chin. Relatively long bill and short tail, latter with buff outer feathers. In flight, wings broad with buff undersides. Conspicuous, often tame bird with plaintive song of short phrases delivered from ground or air. Clear "whee-whee-oo" call. **Range and habitat:** open ground, often arid, also around habitations of central and southern WP and EP, also northern AF and OR. Sedentary. **Similar species:** other larks (see pp 218, 260, 306).

Wood Lark

Lullula arborea (Alaudidae) 15–16 cm/6–6½ in.
Stocky medium-sized lark with slight crest. Overall buff plumage, shading to buffish white on belly. Streaked black on head with bold whitish shapes above eye which meet behind. Cheeks darker buff. Neck, throat and breast finely streaked black. Upperparts broadly streaked black. In flight, wings rounded and tail short. Black and white marks at bend in wing. Undulating hesitant flight. Song-flight spiral ascent then circling, song liquid and fluting. Flight call "tit-loo-eet." Solitary or in pairs. **Range and habitat:** breeds open habitats with scattered trees of temperate and southern WP. Northern populations winter within range of southern populations. **Similar species:** other larks (see pp 218, 260, 306).

Eurasian Skylark

Alauda arvensis (Alaudidae) 17–19 cm/6½–7½ in.
Medium-sized lark with prolonged aerial song. Buff-brown above, well streaked with dark brown or black. Crown streaked black with small erectile crest. Throat and breast warm buff, finely streaked black-brown. Rest of underparts whitish, streaked dark brown on flanks. Tail with white outer feathers. Rises vertically in song-flight, then hovers and sings for up to 5 minutes before dropping. Pointed wings and longish tail give cruciform shape when hovering. Liquid "chirrup" call. Gregarious outside breeding season. **Range and habitat:** open habitats throughout WP and EP. Northern populations winter south to AF and OR. Some declines through habitat loss. **Similar species:** other larks (see pp 218, 260, 360).

Barn Swallow

Hirundo rustica (Hirundinidae) 17–19 cm/6½–7½ in.
Medium-sized hirundine, with outer tail feathers elongated by 2–7 cm/¾–2¼ in. Shiny blue-black upperparts, also narrow breast band. Forehead and throat chestnut-red. Underparts creamy buff to red-brown, varying with race. Underside of forewings similar, rest of underwings dusky black. White spots at tips of tail feathers. Swooping flight in long curves, but jinking after insects. Song a mix of warbles and trills. Call a shrill "witt-witt-witt." Gregarious, especially on migration. Perches on wires, rarely on ground. **Range and habitat:** widespread breeder throughout all but southernmost WP, EP and NA, also OR. Winters AF, NT, OR and AU. Habitat and food reduction in some areas. **Similar species:** other hirundines (see pp 78, 132, 224, 260, 306).

Sand Martin

Riparia riparia (Hirundinidae) 12 cm/4½ in.
Small hirundine, nesting in holes. Dark sandy brown above, including head and cheeks, extending into broad breast band. Chin and throat white, rest of underparts white with smudgy brown marks on flanks. Underwings and undertail dusky brown with faint white spotting on some wing feathers. Fast and fluttering flight on narrow pointed wings. Tail only slightly forked. Weak twittering song of repeated harsh chirring notes. Gregarious and colonial breeder. **Range and habitat:** widespread breeder near freshwaters throughout all but southernmost WP, EP and NA and into OR. Migrates south to NT and AF for winter. Sensitive to drought in Sahel. **Similar species:** other hirundines (see pp 78, 132, 224, 260, 306).

Northern House-Martin

Delichon urbicum (Hirundinidae) 12–13 cm/4½–5 in.
Medium-sized round-headed hirundine with forked tail. Upperparts metallic blue-black with conspicuous white rump. Tail dull black. Underparts pure white. Undersides of wings gray near body, with dark gray flight feathers. Underside of tail dark gray. Rapid but fairly steady flight, not swooping. Often high-flying. Lands on ground to collect nest mud. Melodious chirruping song. Call a hard "chirrup." Gregarious, breeding colonially. Over much of range has deserted natural cliff sites for buildings. **Range and habitat:** widespread throughout WP and EP and parts of OR. Migrating to winter in AF and OR. **Similar species:** other hirundines (see pp 78, 132, 224, 260, 306).

Eurasian Green Woodpecker

Great Spotted Woodpecker

Eurasian Wryneck

Lesser Spotted Woodpecker

Crested Lark

Wood Lark

Eurasian Skylark

Barn Swallow

Sand Martin

Northern House-Martin

Tree Pipit

Anthus trivialis (Motacillidae) 15–16 cm/6–6½ in.
Medium-sized elegant pipit with quite large bill. Olive-brown upperparts streaked with black, finely on head, broader streaks on back. Rump and tail unstreaked. Underparts yellowish buff, becoming whitish on belly, with lines of bold spots on breast, fading on to flanks. Strong pinkish legs. Perches on trees. Runs and walks and wags tail on ground. Song-flight rising from tree and often dropping back in spirals. Song of several trilling phrases. High-pitched "tseep" call. Mostly solitary. **Range and habitat:** breeds in open habitats with trees of temperate and northern WP and EP, migrating south to AF and OR for the winter. **Similar species:** other medium-sized pipits (see pp 218, 260, 306).

Meadow Pipit

Anthus pratensis (Motacillidae) 14–15 cm/5½–6 in.
Medium-sized dumpy pipit. Generally dull olive-brown upperparts and paler underparts, shading to dull gray-white. Upperparts heavily streaked blackish. Breast has small, dense blackish streaks gradually reducing on flanks. Outer tail feathers white. Walks and runs on the ground. Brief song-flight has fluttering ascent and a parachuting descent, song a series of tinkling notes followed by a trill during descent. Gregarious outside breeding season. **Range and habitat:** open areas, including moorland and bogs among scrub, in temperate and north WP including low arctic. Partial migrant, moving to south of breeding range in WP and into south-west EP. **Similar species:** other medium-sized pipits (see pp 218, 260, 306).

Rock Pipit

Anthus petrosus (Motacillidae) 16–17 cm/6–6½ in.
Medium-large dark-legged pipit. Dark olive-gray upperparts with faint darker streaking on back. Underparts dirty buff, almost white on throat, usually with some darker streaking on pink-buff breast. Fairly obvious pale stripe above eye. Outer tail feathers pale gray, rest of tail dark brown. Flight buoyant and strong, ending in curving sweep on landing. Short upward song-flight accompanying musical and trilling song. Penetrating "feest" call. Mostly solitary or in small groups. **Range and habitat:** confined as breeder to rocky coasts of north-west WP, more northerly breeders migrating south-west for winter, mainly on coasts. Others nonmigratory. **Similar species:** other medium-sized pipits (see pp 218, 260, 306).

White Wagtail

Motacilla alba (Motacillidae)17–18 cm/6½–7 in.
Boldly marked wagtail. 2 races, 1 pale gray above, the other black (Pied Wagtail). Crown, chin and breast of both black, forehead and cheeks white. Wing feathers with prominent white edgings. Long tail black with white outer feathers. Flight bounding and easy; runs, walks and hops, head moving backward and forward, and tail wagging, especially after a run. Twittering song can be delivered from air. Call a shrill "tchizzick." Small flocks form on migration. **Range and habitat:** widespread in wide range of habitats, usually near water, in temperate and northern WP and EP and northern OR, northern populations migratory to south, reaching AF and OR. At risk from water pollution. **Similar species:** other wagtails (see pp 218, 260).

Yellow Wagtail

Motacilla flava (Motacillidae) 16–17 cm/6–6½ in.
Longish-tailed but small wagtail. Back and rump greeny yellow to olive-brown, underparts bright yellow in male, paler yellow in female. Very variable head color: heads of males of different races have crowns of black, gray, white or yellow, often with darker area round eye, and white or yellow chin. Females more similar and mostly gray or greeny brown. Long tail dark with white outer feathers, wagged constantly. Brief warbling song. Shrill, plaintive "schreep" call. Gregarious. **Range and habitat:** widespread in lowlands near wetlands throughout WP and EP, reaching extreme north-west NA. Migrates to AF, OR and AU for winter. Declines following agricultural improvement. **Similar species:** other wagtails (see pp 218, 260).

Gray Wagtail

Motacilla cinerea (Motacillidae) 18–19 cm/7–7½ in.
Very long-tailed and slender wagtail. Male gray above, including head, female duller gray. Whitish stripe through eye. Male has black bib outlined in white, female chin and throat whitish. Underparts lemon-yellow, duller in female, brightest on breast and undertail. White edgings to wing feathers. Very long tail black with white outer feathers. Very active, with darting and flitting movements. Tail wagged constantly. Trilling, warbling song. Call a staccato "tzitzi." Solitary or in small groups. **Range and habitat:** widespread breeder beside mainly running freshwater from lowland to altitude in temperate WP and EP. Mainly migratory south to AF, OR and AU. Suffers in severe winters. **Similar species:** other wagtails (see pp 218, 260).

Bohemian Waxwing

Bombycilla garrulus (Bombycillidae) 17–18 cm/6½–7 in.
Plump woodland bird with pronounced crest. Overall body color vinous brown to chestnut, pinker on crest, nape and breast, paler on belly, but darker under tail. Black bib outlined with white and black stripe through eye. Wings dark gray-black with white and yellow markings, plus bright red waxy tips to inner flight feathers. Rump and tail gray with yellow band at end of tail. Female generally duller than male with smaller waxy tips. Call a weak trill "sirrr." Gregarious. **Range and habitat:** northern forests of WP, EP and western NA. Migratory and eruptive south to open country with scattered trees and hedges. Modern forestry unsuitable for breeding. **Similar species:** Cedar Waxwing (see p 78).

Red-backed Shrike

Lanius collurio (Laniidae) 16–18 cm/6½–7 in.
Slimly built, boldly colored shrike. Male of western race has blue-gray head and nape contrasting with broad black mask running from base of bill through eye. Eastern race male has chestnut head. Cheeks and throat white. Back and upperwings chestnut. Underparts pale pinky white. Outer wings dark brown, tail black with white sides. Female rufous brown above, underparts paler with dark crescentic barring. Perches on bushes. Flight undulating, can hover. Warbling song with harsh "chack" calls. **Range and habitat:** wooded and open scrub areas in most of WP and EP except extreme north, also northern OR. Migrates south to AF and OR. Declined through loss of unimproved farmland habitat. **Similar species:** other shrikes (see pp 78, 226, 264).

Great Gray Shrike

Lanius excubitor (Laniidae) 23–5 cm/9–10 in.
Large shrike with long tail and longish bill. Head and mantle soft gray. Broad black mask extends back from base of stout, hooked bill through eye, narrowly bordered above with white. Underparts white. Wings and long, rounded tail black, with 1 or 2 small white wing-bars and white outer tail feathers. Solitary. Perches conspicuously on top of low trees and bushes, swooping down to catch prey. Harsh "chek-chek" call. **Range and habitat:** widespread in open areas with bushes of temperate, southern and desert regions of WP, EP, OR and northern AF, also NA. Mainly nonmigratory, with some dispersal southward of northerly breeding birds. Declines caused by habitat loss. **Similar species:** other shrikes (see pp 78, 226, 264).

Hedge Accentor

Prunella modularis (Prunellidae) 14–15 cm/5½–6 in.
Small, drably plumaged brown and gray ground-dwelling bird. Head and breast dark gray-brown, with brown streaking on crown and ear-coverts. Upperparts and wings rufous brown, inconspicuously streaked black; 2 faint white bars on closed wings. Belly whitish, flanks gray-brown streaked black. Thin, dark bill and quite noticeable red-brown eye. Main call a thin "tseep," song a nondescript squeaky warbling. Hops and walks on ground, creeps through bushes. Mainly solitary. **Range and habitat:** widespread in forested and open woodland, also parks and gardens, of boreal and temperate WP. Mainly nonmigratory, some southward migration within WP. **Similar species:** other accentors and sparrows (see pp 88, 182, 264).

Tree Pipit

Meadow Pipit

Rock Pipit

White Wagtail

Yellow Wagtail (at nest)

Gray Wagtail

Bohemain Waxwing

Red-backed Shrike

Hedge Accentor

Great Gray Shrike

Common Grasshopper-Warbler

Locustella naevia (Sylviidae) 12–13 cm/4½–5 in.
Medium-sized warbler. Olive-brown above, tinged yellowish and streaked darker brown, only slightly on rump. Underparts pale buff to white, sometimes yellowish, slightly streaked darker on chest sides. Longish tail broad and noticeably round-ended. Skulks and creeps among reeds and other undergrowth. More often heard than seen. Very high-pitched, far-carrying churring, long-sustained and ventriloquial song. Sharp "tchik" call. **Range and habitat:** temperate and southern wet or dry well-vegetated marshes, meadows and scrub of WP and western EP. Migrates to AF and OR. Habitat loss through agricultural improvements and Sahel droughts. **Similar species:** other *Locustella* warblers (see p 268).

Reed Warbler

Acrocephalus scirpaceus (Sylviidae) 12–13 cm/4½–5 in.
Medium-sized warbler. Upperparts warm brown tinged rufous, especially on rump. Underparts paler brown, deep buff on flanks. Faint pale stripe above eye. Tail rounded. Longish, thin bill and gray-brown legs. Skulks in reeds, sidling up stems. Flight jerky and low, with spread tail. Song a prolonged rhythmic series of repeated notes, "chur,r-churr-churr, chack-chack-chack." **Range and habitat:** reed-beds in wetlands of temperate and southern WP and south-western EP, wintering in tropical AF. Declined through habitat loss. **Similar species:** other *Acrocephalus* warblers (see pp 222, 310).

Sedge Warbler

Acrocephalus schoenobaenus (Sylviidae) 12–13 cm/4½–5 in.
Medium-sized streaky brown warbler. Overall brown upperparts, streaked with black, most densely on crown above conspicuous creamy stripe over eye. Rump rufous, unstreaked. Tail graduated. Skulks in thick vegetation, sidles up stems. Flight weak-looking with tail fanned. Prolonged song a mixture of harsh and musical notes, including mimicry. Also harsh churring note and anxious "tuc." **Range and habitat:** widespread in tall vegetation and thickets usually near water throughout WP, except south, and western EP. Migrates to subtropical and tropical AF. Habitat loss and droughts in Africa causing declines. **Similar species:** other *Acrocephalus* warblers (see pp 222, 310).

Common Whitethroat

Sylvia communis (Sylviidae) 13–15 cm/5–6 in.
Medium-sized gray-brown warbler. Head and cheeks of male gray, throat white. Upperparts gray-brown, streaked rufous on wings. Tail longish, with white sides. Breast pinkish buff. Head in some males and females browner, underparts less pink. Undulating flight between thick cover, but may perch conspicuously or flutter into air to deliver short, scratchy warbling song. Scolding "chack" and "wheet" calls. **Range and habitat:** widespread in scrub and hedgerows near cultivation throughout WP and western EP, migrating to tropical AF. Some habitat loss, but African droughts more important. **Similar species:** other *Sylvia* warblers.

Lesser Whitethroat

Sylvia curruca (Sylviidae) 13–14 cm/5–5½ in.
Small gray-brown warbler. Upperparts uniform gray-brown, grayer on head and rump, with noticeable dark mask extending below and behind eye. Throat white, breast and belly pinkish shading to buff on flanks and becoming whiter through summer. Outer tail feathers white. Legs dark gray. Solitary and skulking. Hard, rattling song preceded by soft warble. Harsh "chack" call-note. **Range and habitat:** widespread in scrub and open woodland of WP and central and western EP. Winters in subtropical AF and OR. **Similar species:** other *Sylvia* warblers.

Blackcap

Sylvia atricapilla (Sylviidae) c. 14 cm/5½ in.
Medium-sized gray-brown warbler with black or brown cap. Male upperparts gray-brown with glossy black cap and gray nape, cheeks and underparts, becoming paler on belly. Female olive-brown above, paler gray-brown below, with red-brown cap. Undulating flight and restless, skulking behavior. Pleasing warbling song, rich and varied, in short phrases, also a harsh "tak-tak" call. **Range and habitat:** widespread in broad-leaved and mixed woodlands, also parks and gardens, almost throughout WP and central EP. Winters from southern WP to subtropical AF. **Similar species:** other *Sylvia* warblers.

Garden Warbler

Sylvia borin (Sylviidae) c. 14 cm/5½ in.
Medium-sized warbler. Overall gray-brown to buff plumage, grayer on back, paler below especially whitish buff throat and lower belly. Trace of pale stripe over eye. Solitary and skulking, delivering musical and sustained warbling song (similar to Blackcap) from deep in bush. Also harsh "tak-tak" call. **Range and habitat:** widespread in mixed woodland with scrub layer in much of WP and western EP. Winters subtropical and tropical AF. **Similar species:** other *Sylvia* warblers.

Dartford Warbler

Sylvia undata (Sylviidae) 12–13 cm/4½–5 in.
Small, dark-headed warbler. Dark brown upperparts with slate-gray head, rufous underparts, small white spots on throat. Female browner above, paler pinky buff below. Eye prominently red. Short wings whirr in weak, low flight. Long tail, equals body length, often cocked. Mainly skulking but also perches on tops of bushes. Harsh, warbling song and scolding "chirr-ik." **Range and habitat:** confined to scrub and heath areas of south-west WP where resident. Populations affected by severe winters. **Similar species:** other small dark-headed warblers.

Willow Warbler

Phylloscopus trochilus (Sylviidae) c. 11 cm/4½ in.
Tiny greeny yellow or gray-brown leaf warbler. Upperparts of western race greeny brown, tinged olive, underparts tinged yellow, wearing whiter by late summer. Narrow, pale stripe above eye. Other races paler, less yellow, more brown above and white below. Legs mainly pale brown, sometimes darker. Restless, flitting among vegetation, flicking wings and tail. Song a gentle descending scale. Call a plaintive "hoo-eet." **Range and habitat:** widespread in temperate and northern woodlands and thickets of WP and EP. Winters widely in AF. **Similar species:** other leaf warblers (see p 268).

Common Chiffchaff

Phylloscopus collybita (Sylviidae) c. 11 cm/4½ in.
Tiny brown and buff or gray and buff leaf warbler. Western race upperparts olive-brown with pale yellowish stripe above eye. Underparts pale buff lightly tinged yellow, particularly on breast, belly whitish. Other races much browner or grayer, lacking much or all yellow. Legs normally dark brown. Wings rounded. Restless with much wing flicking. Song a monotonous "chiff-chaff, plus "hweet" call. **Range and habitat:** all types of forest and open woodland areas of much of WP and EP, wintering in south of range and in AF and OR. **Similar species:** other leaf warblers (see p 268).

Wood Warbler

Phylloscopus sibilatrix (Sylviidae) 12–13 cm/4½–5 in.
Small to medium-sized leaf warbler. Upper-parts greeny yellow with marked yellow stripe above eye. Throat and chest yellow, with contrasting white belly. During summer becomes duller and grayer with less yellow. Songs a repetition of call-note "pwee-ur," also a quick series of notes ending in a trill. Arboreal. **Range and habitat:** mainly beech or part beech woods of boreal and temperate WP. Migrates to subtropical and tropical AF. **Similar species:** other leaf warblers (see p 268).

Bonelli's Warbler

Phylloscopus bonelli (Sylviidae) 11–12 cm/4–4½ in.
Small gray and white leaf warbler with some yellow. Upperparts gray-brown, but grayer on head and mantle, with very faint pale stripe above eye. Rump and outer tail feathers yellowish, also edges of wing feathers. Underparts gray-white on breast tending to white on belly. Dark pink-brown legs. Short trilling song and "hoo-eet" call-note. **Range and habitat:** confined to broad-leaved and coniferous woodlands especially in hills of south-western WP. Migrates to winter in tropical AF. **Similar species:** other leaf warblers (see p 268).

Common Grasshopper-Warbler (at nest)

Reed Warbler (at nest)

Sedge Warbler (at nest)

Common Whitethroat

Lesser Whitethroat (at nest)

Blackcap

Garden Warbler at nest

Dartford Warbler (at nest)

Willow Warbler

Common Chiffchaff (at nest)

Wood Warbler

Bonelli's Warbler

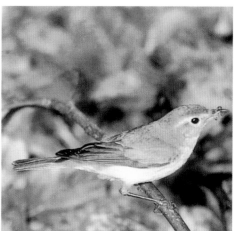

European Goldcrest

Regulus regulus (Reguliidae) 9 cm/3½ in.
Tiny arboreal bird. Overall plumage color dull green, paler shading to whitish below. Male has orange-yellow crown stripe, female's is yellow, both bordered with black. Pale area round eyes giving "surprised" expression; 2 white and 1 dark wing-bars. Restless, flitting, canopy feeder. Very high-pitched "zi-zi-zi" call and repeated "seeda-seeda-seeda" song. **Range and habitat:** widespread in coniferous and some broad-leaved forests and woodlands of WP, EP and northern OR, including montane. Northerly populations move south in winter. **Similar species:** Firecrest and kinglets (see p 82).

Firecrest

Regulus ignicapillus (Reguliidae) 9 cm/3½ in.
Tiny arboreal bird. Upperparts greenish, underparts whitish. Male crown orange and yellow, female yellow, bordered with black above prominent white stripe over eye, black stripe through eye. Bronze patch on shoulder; 2 white and 1 dark wing-bars. Restless, flitting, among scrub and trees. **Range and habitat:** coniferous and mixed forests and scrub of south-west WP and east and west NA, including montane. Mainly resident, some southerly movement of northern breeders. **Similar species:** Goldcrest and kinglets (see p 82).

Spotted Flycatcher

Muscicapa striata (Muscicapidae) 14 cm/5½ in.
Medium-sized flycatcher. Dull brown plumage, uniform darker above, paler to whitish below. Black streaks on crown, dark brown streaks on throat and breast. Broad bill, large dark eyes. Upright stance on twigs and wires, agile twisting flight to catch insects, returning to same perch. Thin squeaky song of 6 high notes, call a shrill "tzee." **Range and habitat:** widespread in open woodland and forest edges, also parks and gardens of WP and EP. Winters subtropical and tropical AF and northern OR. Habitat deterioration and reduced food supply a problem in some areas. **Similar species:** other flycatchers (see pp 220, 266).

European Pied Flycatcher

Ficedula hypoleuca (Muscicapidae) 12–13 cm/4½–5 in.
Small black and white or brown and white flycatcher. Male contrastingly colored black above with white forehead, chin and underparts, also white wing patches and outer tail feathers. Female olive-brown upper-parts, white to whitish buff below, smaller white wing patch, lacks white forehead. Upright stance on perch, restless flicking wings and tail, flying up to catch insects. "Whit" call and varied, jangling song. **Range and habitat:** deciduous and some mixed woodlands of WP and western EP, migrating to subtropical AF for winter. **Similar species:** other flycatchers (see pp 220, 266).

Common Stonechat

Saxicola torquatus (Muscicapidae) 12–13 cm/4½–5 in.
Dumpy, short-winged chat. Head and upperparts of western race summer male black with contrasting white neck patches, orange-red breast and white belly. White wing patch and rump. Eastern race brighter, larger orange or white rump. In winter, black mottled with rufous. Female dull brown streaked head and upperparts, pale rufous breast. Very upright stance, bobs constantly. Hard "tsak-tsak" call, squeaky warbling song, often in flight. **Range and habitat:** open moors, heaths and grasslands of WP, EP and AF, also northern OR. Suffers from habitat degradation and severe winters. **Similar species:** other chats (see pp 222, 268).

Whinchat

Saxicola rubetra (Muscicapidae) 12–13 cm/4½–5 in.
Upright, brown and white chat. Male dark brown, streaked black on upperparts, orangey buff below, becoming whitish on belly. Bold white eye stripe and black cheeks. White wing-bar and white sides to tail. Female dull brown, whitish below, less obvious eye stripe and wing-bar. Perches on bushes and wires, constantly bobbing and flicking wings. Scolding "tic-tic" call and short warbling song. **Range and habitat:** woodland clearings and open areas with bushes throughout most of WP and western EP, wintering in subtropical and tropical AF. Declines through agricultural intensification. **Similar species:** other chats (see pp 222, 268).

Northern Wheatear

Oenanthe oenanthe (Muscicapidae) c. 15 cm/6 in.
Medium-sized wheatear. Head and back of male soft gray with black mask through eye, bordered above by narrow white stripe. Underparts creamy buff, becoming white on belly. Blackish wings and tail tip, conspicuous white rump. Female duller, browner above, browner mask and wings. Very active, bobbing, wagging tail. Harsh "chack-chack" call and squeaky warbling song. **Range and habitat:** widespread in open habitats almost throughout WP and EP, including arctic, also northern NA. Winters in dry open areas of AF. Habitat loss a problem in a few areas. **Similar species:** other wheatears.

Black Redstart

Phoenicurus ochruros (Muscicapidae) 14–15 cm/5½–6 in.
Small, plump thrush. Summer male black all over except for white wing patches and orange-red rump and tail. Underparts of eastern races deep chestnut. Becomes gray-black in winter. Female gray-brown, paler below, with orange-red rump and tail. Active, shivers tail. Sharp calls "tsic," "tic" and "tucc-tucc," warbling song with rattling notes. **Range and habitat:** rocky and mountainous areas, also buildings, of central and southern WP and EP. Winters to south in WP, AF and OR. **Similar species:** other redstarts (see p 268).

Common Redstart

Phoenicurus phoenicurus (Muscicapidae) 14–15 cm/5½–6 in.
Slim thrush. Upperparts of summer male gray, with white forehead and black face and throat. Orange-red breast, flanks and tail, whitish on belly. White wing patch in eastern race. Winter male browner. Female gray-brown above, pale orange-buff below, orange-red tail. Restless, quivering tail. "Hoo-eet" and "hweet-tuc-tuc" calls, song a squeaky warble. **Range and habitat:** widespread in open broad-leaved and some conifer woodlands of most of WP and central western EP. Winters subtropical AF. Some loss of breeding habitat from modern forestry. **Similar species:** other redstarts (see p 268).

European Robin

Erithacus rubecula (Muscicapidae) c. 14 cm/5½ in.
Small, dumpy thrush. Upperparts and wings uniform olive-brown. Face, throat and breast orange-red edged with gray. Belly and undertail white. Races vary in plumage tone and breast color. Rounded appearance, lacking obvious neck. Alert, darting flight, often tame. Solitary. Repeated "tic-tic" alarm call. Pleasing but thin warbling song. **Range and habitat:** widespread in woodland and open areas with bushes or trees throughout WP except extreme south and in north-east EP. Northern populations migrate to south WP and EP in winter. **Similar species:** other small thrushes (see pp 222, 268).

Bluethroat

Erithacus svecica (Muscicapidae) c. 14 cm/5½ in.
Slim version of Robin with blue throat. Upperparts dark brown, underparts buff-white. White eye stripe. Metallic blue throat and breast of male contains white or red spot, according to race, and bordered in black, white and red. Female throat and breast whitish with slight blue and reddish markings. Chestnut patches at tail base. Skulking. Rich, varied warbling song and "hweet" and "tac" calls. **Range and habitat:** widespread in swampy woodland of temperate and northern WP and EP and extreme north-west NA, migrating south to subtropical AF and OR. Some local declines through habitat deterioration.

Common Nightingale

Erithacus megarhynchos (Muscicapidae) 16–17 cm/6–6½ in.
Medium-small brown thrush with chestnut tail. Overall body plumage russet-brown above, becoming brighter chestnut on rump and brightest on long, rounded tail. Paler gray-brown below, whitish on chin and vent. Skulking, rarely seen, singing from deep cover. Song rich, varied and loud, based on repeated clear notes, some guttural. Various harsh call-notes, "tak," "kerr," "charr." Solitary. **Range and habitat:** woodlands with thick undergrowth in central and southern WP and western EP, migrating to tropical AF for winter. Seriously at risk from habitat loss in some areas. **Similar species:** Thrush Nightingale.

European Goldcrest

Firecrest

Spotted Flycatcher

European Pied Flycatcher

Common Stonechat

Whinchat

Northern Wheatear

Black Redstart

Common Redstart

European Robin

Bluethroat

Common Nightingale

Eurasian Blackbird

Turdus merula (**Turdidae**) 24–6 cm/9½–10 in.
Medium-sized dark thrush. Male glossy black all over apart from very dark brown wings, some races duller black. Bill and eye-rings orangey yellow. Female dark brown above, slightly paler below, occasionally rufous tinged, and faintly streaked and mottled. Wings, rump and tail black-brown. Bill dark horn. Active on ground, hopping and running. Scolding "tchook-tchook" and "pink-pink;" rich, fluting song. **Range and habitat:** widespread in forests, open woodlands, parks and gardens of WP, parts of EP, OR and AU. Some movement south in winter by northerly breeding populations. **Similar species:** other dark thrushes (see pp 80, 134, 220, 266).

Ring Ouzel

Turdus torquatus (**Turdidae**) 23–5 cm/9–10 in.
Medium-sized dark thrush. Male dark sooty brown all over, except for broad white crescentic mark across breast and pale gray panel on wing, more conspicuously white in some races. Female dark brown, breast crescent narrower and less clear white. Underparts with pale feather edgings. Both sexes show more mottled or scaly plumage in winter due to paler feather edgings. Harsh scolding "tac-tac" and clear, shrill song of 3 to 4 notes. **Range and habitat:** upland woods, open moorland and heaths of northern and montane WP, migratory to southern WP for winter. **Similar species:** other dark thrushes (see pp 80, 134, 220, 266). Suffers from human disturbance in some breeding areas.

Fieldfare

Turdus pilaris (**Turdidae**) 25–7 cm/10–10½ in.
Large, gregarious thrush. Head and rump gray, back and upperwings chestnut-brown. Black marks on forehead and cheeks. Dirty yellow on breast heavily spotted with black, belly and black-spotted flanks white. Female less heavily spotted, duller on back. Wings dark brown, tail black. Hops and runs on ground, pausing upright. Gregarious in autumn and winter, in fields and on trees. Loud "chak-chak" call and squeaky, whistling song. **Range and habitat:** temperate and northern forests and scrub of WP and EP, migrating south within WP for winter. **Similar species:** other thrushes (see pp 80, 134, 220, 266).

Redwing

Turdus iliacus (**Turdidae**) 20–2 cm/8–8½ in.
Medium-small brown thrush. Upperparts uniform brown with bold white stripe above eye, brown cheeks bordered below with white, dark stripe running down from base of bill. Breast whitish, yellowish buff at sides, heavily spotted dark brown, belly whitish. Flanks and inner part of underwing chestnut-red. Highly gregarious in autumn and winter, in fields and berried trees and hedgerows. Thin "tseep" call in flight. Short repetitive warbling song. **Range and habitat:** northern woods and scrub of WP and EP, migrating south to temperate and southern WP for winter. **Similar species:** other medium-small thrushes (see pp 80, 134, 220, 266).

Song Thrush

Turdus philomelos (**Turdidae**) 22–4 cm/8½–9½ in.
Medium-sized brown thrush. Overall warm brown upperparts and upperwings, though variable from ochre-brown to gray-brown in different races. Faint eye stripe and patterning on cheeks. Throat, breast and flanks very pale buff or whitish liberally marked with black arrowhead spots. Belly white, unspotted. Yellowy buff underwings. Loud "chuk" alarm call, thin "tsip" in flight. Musical song of repeated 2- to 4-note phrases. **Range and habitat:** widespread in mixed forests, parks and gardens of temperate and boreal WP and western EP. Partially migratory to southern WP. Declines through habitat loss and hunting pressure. **Similar species:** other medium-sized thrushes (see pp 80, 134, 220, 266).

Mistle Thrush

Turdus viscivorus (**Turdidae**) 26–8 cm/10–11 in.
Large, pale thrush. Upperparts gray-brown, tinged olive, with pale edgings to back, rump and wing feathers. Underparts and underwings white with yellow-buff tinge to breast. Large, wedge-shaped black spots on throat and upper breast, rounder spots on lower breast and flanks. Upright stance on ground. In pairs or small groups. Defends fruit trees in winter. Grating chatter in flight. Loud, clear song comprises short ringing phrases. **Range and habitat:** woodlands, parks and gardens of much of WP and western EP, avoiding warmer south. More northerly and easterly populations move south in winter. At risk from loss of habitat and severe winters. **Similar species:** other large thrushes (see pp 80, 134, 220, 266).

Long-tailed Tit

Aegithalos caudatus (**Aegithalidae**) c. 14 cm/5½ in.
Tiny, black and white bird with extremely long tail. Head white with or without black or gray stripe above eye and down sides of nape, depending on race. Back, wings and tail black with variable white wing patch, depending on race, and white sides to tail. Underparts white, pinkish suffusion on inner wings, rump and belly. Tiny bill. Tail occupies more than half total length. Agile, restless, frequently in small flocks. Penetrating "zee-zee-zee" call, also "tsirrup." Rare song formed from call-notes. **Range and habitat:** widespread in woodland and scrub throughout temperate and southern WP and EP. Resident. Habitat loss and severe winters causes of declines.

Eurasian Penduline Tit

Remiz pendulinus (**Remizidae**) 10–11 cm/4–4½ in.
Tiny, long-tailed bird. Head and nape gray, with broad black mask across forehead and through eye. Eastern race has chestnut crown sometimes joining chestnut of back. Upperparts and inner wing chestnut, rest of wings and long tail black with white edgings. Throat pale gray, rest of underparts buff tinged pinkish on breast. Restless, agile bird, flicking tail and climbing among reed stems. Thin "tsee" and "tsi-tsi" calls. **Range and habitat:** reed marshes and thickets by water throughout central and southern WP and EP. Mainly resident but some dispersal southward after breeding.

Wood Nuthatch

Sitta europaea (**Sittidae**) c. 14 cm/5½ in.
Small, short-necked and short-tailed arboreal bird. Crown and upperparts blue-gray, fine black line through eye. Throat white, cheeks and rest of underparts vary: whitish all over in northern and western parts of range, deep orangey buff chest and flanks with white belly in southern and eastern races. Clambers up and down trees (head first), undulating flight. Ringing "chwit-chwit" call, loud "twee-twee-twee" and fast trill as song. **Range and habitat:** widespread in mainly coniferous forests and broad-leaved woods of boreal and temperate WP, EP and OR. Largely resident but some southward dispersal from northerly breeding areas. **Similar species:** other nuthatches (see pp 82, 272). Dependent on presence of mature trees so declines where these disappear.

Wallcreeper

Tichodroma muraria (**Sittidae**) 16–17 cm/6–6½ in.
Small bird of rocky places. Crown and upperparts charcoal gray, short tail black with gray tip. Throat and breast black, female and winter male with white throat, rest of underparts pale gray. Whole of forewings bright crimson, main wing feathers black with some white spotting near tips of outer flight feathers. Fine-pointed and decurved bill. Hops up rock faces, flicking wings. Butterflylike flight. High-pitched piping calls and song. **Range and habitat:** montane cliffs and gorges of southern WP and EP, resident but also descending to lower altitude in winter when may be found on buildings. Some threat from human disturbance.

Eurasian Treecreeper

Certhia familiaris (**Certhiidae**) 12–13 cm/4½–5 in.
Small brown and white arboreal bird with fine, decurved bill. Upperparts brown, heavily streaked with darker brown and buff, rump rufous. Whitish bar above eye, pale buff wing-bar and whitish underparts, buff on flanks. Northern races paler above, white on flanks. Climbs in spirals round trunks and along underside of branches, supported on tail, flitting down to base of next tree. High-pitched "tseee" call repeated to make song. **Range and habitat:** widespread in mainly coniferous forests of WP, EP, mainly resident with only local movements in some areas. **Similar species:** other treecreepers (see p 272).

Eurasian Blackbird

Ring Ouzel (at nest)

Fieldfare (at nest)

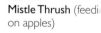

Redwing

Song Thrush

Mistle Thrush (feedi on apples)

Long-tailed Tit (feeding young)

Eurasian Penduline T (at nest)

Wood Nuthatch

Wallcreeper

Eurasian Treecreepe

Great Tit

Parus major **(Paridae)** c. 14 cm/5½ in.
Large tit. Head black with conspicuous white cheeks. Bib, and broad stripe down yellow breast and belly, black; wider in male than female. Yellowish nape, greeny back, blue-gray wings and tail, white wing-bar and white outer tail feathers. White undertail. Acrobatic, often in small flocks. Often tame. Many calls including hard "pink" and "teacher-teacher" song. **Range and habitat:** wooded and forested areas, also parks and gardens, throughout WP, EP and much of OR. Northern breeders move south for winter, others resident. **Similar species:** other large tits (see p 82).

Blue Tit

Cyanistes caeruleus **(Paridae)** 11–12 cm/4–4½ in.
Small tit. Crown blue, bordered with white. Black stripe through eye above white cheek. Small black bib. Nape and upper-wings blue, back green. Whole of underparts yellow except for narrow dark line down belly. Plumage brighter in summer than winter. Very agile and acrobatic, clinging upside-down to twigs. In parties in winter, often very tame. Main call and song based on "tsee-tsee-tsee" notes. No apparent threats apart from severe winters. **Range and habitat:** widespread in forests, scrub, parks and gardens throughout WP. Mainly resident. **Similar species:** other small tits and chickadees (see pp 82, 228, 272).

Coal Tit

Periparus ater **(Paridae)** c. 11 cm/4½ in.
Small tit with large head and thin bill. Crown and bib black, cheeks and center of nape white. Upperparts olive to slate-gray, depending on race, with 2 pale wing-bars. Underparts whitish to pale buff, darker on flanks, some races having white areas tinged yellow or even rufous. Agile and acrobatic, in small parties. High-pitched thin call, "tsee-tsee" and louder song, "weecha-weecha." **Range and habitat:** widespread chiefly in coniferous but also broad-leaved woodland of WP and EP, some altitudinal movement in winter. Some declines through woodland degradation. **Similar species:** other small tits and chickadees (see pp 82, 228, 272).

Marsh Tit

Poecile palustris **(Paridae)** 11–12 cm/4–4½ in.
Small tit. Crown, nape and bib glossy black, becoming browner during summer. Bib flecked with white, cheeks whitish. Upperparts uniform warm brown, underparts pale buff. Active and agile among trees, usually in pairs or families. Loud calls "pitchoo" and "tchay," with repeated "chip-chip-chip" song. **Range and habitat:** lowland broad-leaved, often damp, woodland of boreal and temperate WP and eastern EP. Resident, with some local dispersal. Declines follow loss of mature woodland. **Similar species:** other small tits and chickadees (see pp 82, 228, 272).

Crested Tit

Lophophanes cristatus **(Paridae)** 11–12 cm/4–4½ in.
Small tit with pronounced crest. Crown and stiff upswept pointed crest speckled black and white, becoming shorter and blacker during summer months through abrasion. Black bib. Dirty white cheeks outlined in black, with narrow black collar. Upperparts including nape dull brown, underparts buff to whitish. Agile and acrobatic among twigs, also creeps up trunks. Principal call thin 'tsee-tsee," also deep trill repeated to form song. **Range and habitat:** generally confined to tall coniferous forests, mainly upland, of WP. Resident. Loses habitat when mature pine plantations are felled. **Similar species:** other small tits and chickadees (see pp 82, 228, 272).

White-throated Dipper

Cinclus cinclus **(Cinclidae)** 17–18 cm/6½–7 in.
Plump, short-necked, short-tailed waterbird. Blackish brown above, chocolate on head. Clear white throat and breast with blackish belly. Chestnut band below white breast in 2 races. Constantly bobs, jerking tail, and flicking white inner eyelid across eye. Runs or plunges into water, including fast-flowing. Solitary. Metallic "clink-clink" call, also loud "zit-zit." Song of grating and warbling notes. **Range and habitat:** widespread but scattered through mainly montane WP and EP. Resident apart from some altitudinal movements. At risk from water pollution and acidification. **Similar species:** other dippers (see p 78).

Winter Wren

Troglodytes troglodytes **(Troglodytidae)** 9–10 cm/3½–4 in.
Tiny, short-tailed dumpy bird. Overall rufous brown above, paler below, barred darker brown especially on back, flanks and undertail. Pale stripe above eye. Tail usually cocked. Flight whirring, rarely far. Active and creeping among stones and vegetation. Scolding "tic-tic-tic" call and very loud (for size) warbling trilling song. **Range and habitat:** widespread in dense undergrowth of forests, parks and gardens throughout WP, eastern and southern EP and NA. Resident. Severe winters can cause major, if temporary, population reductions. **Similar species:** other wrens (see pp 78, 134).

Corn Bunting

Emberiza calandra **(Emberizidae)** 17–18 cm/6½–7 in.
Large, heavy-headed bunting. Overall gray-brown above, heavily streaked blackish. Streaked brown cheeks outlined in buff. Underparts whitish buff, more finely streaked on breast and flanks, belly whitish unstreaked. Bill deep and yellowish. Perches on bushes and wires, feeds on ground. Sometimes flies with legs dangling. Gregarious in winter. Harsh "chip" and "kwit" calls, and jangling trilling song. **Range and habitat:** open plains and agricultural land in southern WP and south-western EP, mainly resident. Large declines associated with agricultural intensification. **Similar species:** other buntings (see pp 88, 274).

Yellowhammer

Emberiza citrinella **(Emberizidae)** 16–17 cm/6–6½ in.
Slim bunting. Male has bright yellow head and underparts and chestnut upperparts streaked with black. Chestnut rump unstreaked, sides of tail white. In winter, head and throat streaked brownish, yellow underparts duller. Female much less yellow than male, duller chestnut on back and more streaked and patterned on head and underparts. Gregarious in winter, hopping on ground. Perches, flicking tail. Harsh "twit" call, high-pitched jangling song. **Range and habitat:** broad-leaved woodland edges and more open areas of temperate and northern WP. Mainly resident. Sensitive to agricultural change. **Similar species:** other buntings (see pp 88, 274).

Reed Bunting

Emberiza schoeniclus **(Emberizidae)** 14–16 cm/5½–6½ in.
Mainly brown bunting with conspicuous black head in male. Head, throat and bib of male black, with strongly contrasting broad white collar. Whitish moustache. Back and wings rufous brown streaked black. Underparts white, flanks slightly streaked brown. Head becomes brownish in winter. Female streaky brown, paler below, lacking marked head pattern. Perches on reeds and bushes, hops on ground. Gregarious. Varied calls including "tseep," and squeaky 2- to 5-note song. **Range and habitat:** widespread in marshy vegetation and scrub almost throughout WP and EP. Northerly breeders migrate reaching northern OR, remainder resident. Declines following wetland drainage and agricultural improvements. **Similar species:** other buntings (see pp 88, 274).

Lapland Longspur

Calcarius lapponicus **(Emberizidae)** 14–16 cm/5½–6½ in.
Boldly patterned northerly breeding bunting. Summer male has black head and bib, outlined in white and with chestnut nape. Upperparts brown, streaked black and chestnut, underparts white, flanks streaked chestnut. Becomes much paler and less colored in winter. Female like winter male, showing little black or chestnut. Gregarious, ground feeder. Distinctive "chew" call, also short trill and melodious warbling song. **Range and habitat:** circumpolar Holarctic breeder in tundra and scrub, winter ing on temperate coasts and open plains of WP, EP and NA. **Similar species:** other buntings (see pp 88, 274).

Snow Bunting

Plectrophenax nivalis **(Emberizidae)** 16–17 cm/6–6½ in.
Medium-large bunting. Summer male overall white, with black back, outer wings and center of tail. In winter, head and breast rufous buff, black areas mottled tawny and white. Summer female has gray and rufous head, brown streaks on black back, white body and large white wing patches. Becomes duller in winter. Gregarious in winter. Feeding on ground. Musical trilling song and rippling "tirrirripp" flight call. **Range and habitat:** circum polar Holarctic tundra and some montane areas, wintering on coasts and open plains to south.

Great Tit

Blue Tit

Coal Tit

Marsh Tit

Crested Tit

White-throated Dipper

Winter Wren

Corn Bunting

Yellowhammer (in winter)

Reed Bunting

Lapland Longspur (at nest)

Snow Bunting

Chaffinch

Fringilla coelebs (Fringillidae) 15–16 cm/6–6½ in.
Medium-sized finch with prominent white shoulder and wing-bars. Male has soft blue-gray head with small black forehead, chestnut back and yellow-green rump. Wings and tail brown. Cheeks, throat and breast pinkish, becoming paler on belly. White on shoulder, wing-bar and outer tail. Female gray-brown above, tinged yellow, paler below, white as in male. Undulating flight, hops and walks on ground. Highly gregarious in winter. Metallic "pink-pink" call, also "chip" in flight. Clear, rattling song. **Range and habitat:** widespread and common in forests, woods, parks and gardens of WP, northerly breeders migrating south within WP in winter. No apparent threats other than severe winters. **Similar species:** Brambling.

Brambling

Fringilla montifringilla (Fringillidae) 14–15 cm/5½–6 in.
Medium-sized finch. Summer male's head, upper cheeks and upper back black; throat, breast and shoulders orange. Wings and tail blackish with small white shoulder mark and narrow white wing-bar. Rump and underparts white. Black of head mottled buff in winter but breast and shoulders becoming richer orange. Female like winter male, grayer on head and paler on breast, with similar white markings on wings and white rump. Gregarious in winter. Call-notes "tsweek" and "chuc," song a drawn-out "dzweee." **Range and habitat:** northern scrub and birch woods of WP and BP, migrating to temperate areas for winter. **Similar species:** Chaffinch.

European Greenfinch

Carduelis chloris (Fringillidae) 14–15 cm/5½–6 in.
Large, thickset finch. Olive-green above, including crown, bright yellow-green underparts. Gray panel on closed wing, with bright yellow patch on outer wings and at sides of base of tail. In winter, tinged gray or gray-brown. Female gray-brown above, gray below, tinged yellow, becoming whitish on belly, overall green tone in summer. Stout and pale bill. Strong, undulating flight, gregarious in winter. Trilling flight call, nasal "dzwee" and twittering song. **Range and habitat:** widespread in woodlands and all open areas with trees in WP and extreme south-west EP, northerly breeders migrating south to winter within southern WP and EP. **Similar species:** other finches.

European Goldfinch

Carduelis carduelis (Fringillidae) c. 12 cm/4½ in.
Small, colorful finch. Red face extending back to behind eyes, less extensive in female. White cheeks extending up to black crown and nape, latter with whitish spot. Tawny brown back, whitish rump, dark forked tail with white tips. Wings blackish with broad bright yellow wing-bar and small white tips. Small, whitish bill. Active, with dancing flight. Gregarious, feeding agilely from thistle heads. Liquid "tswitt-twitt-twitt" flight note and trilling song. **Range and habitat:** widespread in open woodlands and open areas with trees throughout WP and western EP. Northerly breeders winter within southerly birds' breeding range. **Similar species:** other finches (see p 92).

Eurasian Bullfinch

Pyrrhula pyrrhula (Fringillidae) 14–15 cm/5½–6 in.
Stout, short-necked finch. Crown and small bib black, upperparts of male blue-gray, rump white. Cheeks and underparts deep pinky red, except for white lower belly. Wings and tail black, with broad white wing-bar. Female gray-buff above, pale pinky buff below, other markings as male. Very short, stout bill and large head, lacking discernible neck. Soft, low whistling "deu" call-note, used in short, creaky song. Secretive, in pairs or families. **Range and habitat:** widespread in coniferous forests, also some broad-leaved and more open treed areas of WP and EP. More northerly breeders move south for winter. **Similar species:** other finches (see p 92).

Hawfinch

Coccothraustes coccothraustes (Fringillidae) 16–17 cm/6–6½ in.
Stout, thick-necked finch with massive bill on large head. Head of male rufous, richer on nape, black round base of huge, stout bill. Gray collar, red-brown back, rufous rump, short rufous tail with white tip. Wings dark with broad white wing-bar. Underparts pale pinky brown. Female grayer brown on body and grayer wings. Rapid, undulating flight, perching in tree-tops. Solitary or in small parties, shy. Abrupt "tick" call, also high-pitched "tsip," rarely heard short scratchy

song. **Range and habitat:** scattered distribution in broad-leaved woodland in WP and parts of EP, northerly breeders moving south for winter. Some local declines following loss of mature woodland and old orchards. **Similar species:** other finches (see p 92).

Eurasian Siskin

Carduelis spinus (Fringillidae) c. 12 cm/4½ in.
Small, dumpy yellowish finch. Male has black crown and chin, otherwise bright yellow-green tinged gray above and bright yellow below, turning to white on belly. Dark streaking on flanks. Dark wings and short, forked tail with 2 yellow wing-bars and yellow at sides of base of tail. Female's upperparts grayer and underparts whiter, well streaked, tinged with yellow. Yellow wing-bars and tail base as male. Clear "tsuu" call-note and warbling, twittering song. Restless and acrobatic in trees. Gregarious. **Range and habitat:** mainly coniferous forests and woods of boreal and temperate WP and eastern EP, northerly breeders moving south in winter. **Similar species:** other finches (see p 92).

European Serin

Serinus serinus (Fringillidae) 11–12 cm/4–4½ in.
Tiny, yellowish finch with notched tail. Head, upperparts and breast of male yellow, streaked brownish on crown, cheeks, sides of breast and back. Rump pure yellow, unstreaked. Streaking heavier on head and back in winter, but less on flanks, overall less yellow. Belly whitish, flanks streaked brown. Wings and tail brown. Female paler brown, tinged yellow on upperparts and breast, green-yellow on head. Heavily streaked except for pale yellow rump. Trilling flight call and thin jangling song. Fast, undulating flight. Agile in trees. **Range and habitat:** forest edges, open habitats with trees throughout south-west WP. Northern breeders move south for winter. **Similar species:** other small finches (see p 92).

Common Redpoll

Carduelis flammea (Fringillidae) 12–13 cm/4½–5 in.
Small, dumpy finch with red forehead. Rest of head and upperparts tawny brown, heavily streaked dark brown; 2 pale wing-bars. Chin black. Rump, cheeks, throat, breast and flanks pink, brighter in summer. Some dark streaking on flanks. Forked tail. Female more streaked below, lacking much pink. Some races grayer above and with more white on wing and rump, which can be unstreaked, while flanks may be more heavily marked. Agile, acrobatic while feeding, gregarious. Hard "chuch-uch" and "err" flight notes, used in song. **Range and habitat:** circumpolar Holarctic tundra, open scrub and woods south to temperate zone, northern breeders winter further south. **Similar species:** other small finches (see p 92).

Red Crossbill

Loxia curvirostra (Fringillidae) 16–17 cm/6–6½ in.
Bulky, large-headed finch with long mandibles crossed at tip. Male crimson-orange, brighter on head, rump and breast, duller elsewhere, dark streaked on cheeks and mantle. Wings and notched tail dark brown. Female dull yellowy green tinged gray, sometimes a few golden or orange feathers. Dark streaking on head, upperparts and flanks. Crossed bill varies in size according to race. Fast, undulating flight. Agile, clambers about branches, clings to cones with 1 foot. Metallic "jip-jip" call in flight. Song of short, staccato trills. **Range and habitat:** in conifers in northern, temperate and montane WP, EP, NA and parts of OR. Resident or irruptive migrant southward. **Similar species:** other crossbills (see p 92).

Chaffinch

Brambling (at nest)

European Greenfinch

European Goldfinch

Eurasian Bullfinch
(male and female
feeding young)

Hawfinch

Eurasian Siskin

European Serin
(bathing)

Common Redpoll

Red Crossbill

House Sparrow

Passer domesticus (Passeridae) 14–15 cm/5½–6 in.
Small sparrow. Male has gray crown, white cheeks and large black bib. Dark stripe through eye. Mantle chestnut streaked black, rump gray. Wings and tail brown, former with short white wing-bar. Underparts dirty white. Duller in winter with white streaks in black bib. Female brown all over, paler beneath, buff stripe behind eye, 2 pale wing-bars. Very gregarious, lives in human settlements; rapid flight, hops and flicks tail. Many chirrups and cheeps, strung together into song. **Range and habitat:** widespread throughout WP, EP and OR, introduced to NA, NT, AF and AU. Mostly nonmigratory. Declined from loss of agricultural habitat and food. **Similar species:** other sparrows (see pp 88, 232, 234, 276).

House Sparrow

Eurasian Tree Sparrow

Eurasian Tree Sparrow

Passer montanus (Passeridae) c. 14 cm/5½ in.
Small sparrow. Crown and nape chestnut-brown. Black spot on white cheeks, small black bib. White collar round sides of neck. Back brown, streaked black, rump yellowish brown. Wings and tail brown, with 2 thin white wing-bars. Underparts whitish, buff under tail. Hard, high-pitched "chip-chip" call, "teck-teck" in flight. Song of rapid chirping. Gregarious with other sparrows and finches in winter, but shy. **Range and habitat:** widespread throughout lightly wooded and cultivated areas of WP, EP and OR. Mainly resident though some movement south by northerly breeders. Suffers from agricultural change. **Similar species:** other sparrows (see pp 88, 232, 234, 276).

Common Starling
(feeding on meat)

Common Starling

Sturnus vulgaris (Sturnidae) 21–2 cm/8–8½ in.
Male in summer black, glossed purple and green, brownish wings and tail with pale feather edgings. Female tends to have more pale spots on body, while both sexes in winter are well-spotted buff above, whitish below. Longish, pointed bill yellow in summer, brown in winter. Rapid direct flight, walks and runs on ground. Highly gregarious, often roosting in immense numbers. Song a mimetic combination of whistles, chatters, screams and clicks. **Range and habitat:** widespread in woodlands, cultivated land and urban areas of WP, south-western EP and parts of OR, introduced NA, AF and AU. Local declines from agricultural change. **Similar species:** other starlings (see pp 228, 276).

Eurasian Golden-Oriole

Oriolus oriolus (Oriolidae) 23–5 cm/9–10 in.
Large, brilliantly colored bird. Male bright yellow all over except for black wings and black base and center to tail and small black stripe from eye to base of reddish bill. Small yellow wing-bar. Female greenish yellow above, grayish below streaked with brown. Wings and most of tail dark brown. Shy, secretive birds, more often heard than seen. Squealing catlike call. Melodious and fluting song "weela-weelo." **Range and habitat:** widespread in broad-leaved woodlands and orchards of temperate and southern WP and EP, also OR. Nonmigratory in OR, remainder winter in tropical AF. Some habitat loss and persecution. **Similar species:** African Golden Oriole (see p 228).

Eurasian Golden-Oriole (at nest)

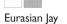

Eurasian Jay

Eurasian Jay

Garrulus glandarius (Corvidae) 33–6 cm/13–14 in.
Large, boldly colored bird. Pinky brown body, brighter on nape and back, paler below. Forehead and crown whitish, streaked black. Black moustache, white throat. Pure white rump and long black tail conspicuous in flight. Black wings, with pinky brown shoulders, white patch to rear and speckled blue and white forewing. Stout bill. Undulating flight, hops. Harsh scolding "skaak-skaak," also "kaa" and "keu." Soft, scratchy warbling song. Very wary. **Range and habitat:** in most types of woodland in temperate and southern WP and EP, also OR. Mainly nonmigratory, but irruptive movements southward by northern breeders. **Similar species:** other jays (see pp 92, 134).

Black-billed Magpie

Pica pica (Corvidae) 46–50 cm/18–20 in.
Large, very long-tailed black and white crow. Head, breast and back black, with purplish gloss. Wings black, glossed blue and green, with much white in black-tipped outer feathers. Large white patches at wing bases in flight. Very long, tapering tail (c. half overall length) black, glossed green to purple. Lower breast and belly pure white. Weak-looking flight, often gliding. Walks and hops. In pairs or small

flocks. Harsh chattering call and musical "chook-chook." No real song. **Range and habitat:** woodland and cultivated areas of WP, EP, OR and NA. Nonmigratory apart from some postbreeding dispersal. **Similar species:** Yellow-billed Magpie.

Carrion Crow

Corvus corone (Corvidae) 45–9 cm/18–19 in.
Large all-black or black and gray crow. Carrion Crow black all over, with green and purple gloss, former especially on head and neck. Hooded Crow has black head, throat, wings and tail, and gray body, very finely streaked black. Hybrids occur. Stout black bill with feathered base. Powerful, deliberate flight. Walks and hops. Solitary or in small flocks. Thrice-repeated calls of "kaaah" or "keerk." No song. **Range and habitat:** widespread wherever there are trees; Carrion Crow confined to south-west WP, Hooded Crow throughout WP and EP. Northern breeders winter to south. Some culling. **Similar species:** other crows (see pp 92, 228, 278, 322).

Rook

Corvus frugilegus (Corvidae) 44–7 cm/17–18 in.
Medium-sized crow. Black all over, glossed purple and green, mainly purple on head and neck. Adult has bare whitish skin round base of black bill including chin and below eyes. Shaggy feathers on upper leg. Highly gregarious, nesting in colonies. Flight rapid. Waddles on ground, also hops. No song, calls include "kaah," "kaa-aah" and higher-pitched "ki-ook." **Range and habitat:** widespread in broad-leaved and mixed woodlands and stands of trees in grassy and cultivated land in most of WP and EP. Some nonmigratory, but northern breeders move south for winter, reaching OR. **Similar species:** other crows (see pp 92, 228, 278, 322).

Eurasian Jackdaw

Corvus monedula (Corvidae) 32–4 cm/12–13 in.
Small and compact crow. Black all over except for ash-gray nape, which contrasts with glossy black of cap and throat. Northern race has paler silvery gray nape and some whitish feathers at base of neck. Short, stubby black bill. Gregarious, often mixing with Rooks. Nests in holes. Flight rapid on rather narrow, pointed wings, includes diving and tumbling. Brisk walk on ground. No song. High-pitched "chack" and shrill "kyow" calls. **Range and habitat:** open wooded areas almost throughout WP and western EP. Northern and eastern breeders move south and west for winter. **Similar species:** other small crows (see pp 92, 228, 278, 322).

Black-billed Magpie

Carrion Crow

Rook

Common Raven

Corvus corax (Corvidae) 60–7 cm/24–6 in.
Very large crow with very stout bill. Completely black all over, glossed green and purple. Large head emphasized by shaggy throat feathers and heavy, deep bill. Long tail wedge-shaped. Wings long and narrow, outer part slightly swept back in powerful flight. During display becomes aerobatic, tumbling, nose-diving, soaring, even flying upside-down. Walks on ground. Usually in pairs, but in small groups at roosts. Loud, deep croaking call "pruk-pruk." No song. **Range and habitat:** circumpolar Holarctic in wide variety of habitats almost throughout WP, EP and NA. Nonmigratory, but some wandering in winter by northern breeders. **Similar species:** other ravens (see pp 92, 228).

Red-billed Chough

Pyrrhocorax pyrrhocorax (Corvidae) 36–41 cm/14–16 in.
Medium-sized all-black crow with bright red bill and legs. Glossy blue-black all over, except for wings and tail which are glossed greenish. Long red bill pointed and decurved. Legs red. Very buoyant flight, often undulating, on broad wings with tips of flight feathers spread. Quite aerobatic, soaring and diving with closed wings. Agile on ground. Normally in pairs or small flocks. Main call a loud, far-carrying "chee-ow," also quieter "chuff and deeper "kaa." No song. **Range and habitat:** coasts and mountains of mainly south-western and southern WP and EP. Nonmigratory. Declines through agricultural change. **Similar species:** Alpine Chough.

Eurasian Jackdaw

Common Raven
(calling)

Red-billed Chough

THE AFROTROPICAL REGION

White-backed Vultures attend a wildebeest carcass in Kenya. Different vulture species feed on separate parts of the carcass so that it is swiftly consumed.

Africa was formed about 100 million years ago during the fragmentation of the southern supercontinent of Gondwana. It is the second largest of the world's landmasses after Eurasia, and unique in completely spanning the tropics, from the Mediterranean region far into the southern oceans.

Although a single landmass, Africa is not a single zoogeographical unit because its northern reaches are occupied by the Sahara, the greatest of the world's deserts. This immense sandy wilderness, over 1,500 km (930 miles) wide north-south, has long acted as a barrier to the movement of many lifeforms, and now forms the boundary between two of the Earth's major zoogeographical realms, the Palaearctic Region to the north, and the Afrotropical (formerly known as the Ethiopian) Region to the south. The Sahara is not a total barrier, however; for example, it is crossed or skirted twice a year by millions of migrant birds from the Palaearctic.

Although the bulk of the Afrotropics is within continental Africa, this region is often considered to include peninsular Arabia and the island of Madagascar.

Like sub-Saharan Africa, Arabia is divided from Eurasia by wide deserts, but its avifauna shows both Palaearctic and Afrotropical affinities. Madagascar separated from Africa's eastern coast over 30 million years ago and its fauna and flora possess numerous endemic elements, including many lower primates (dominated by the lemurs) and five families of birds, such that it is often considered a zoogeographical realm, the Malagasy Region, in its own right.

After extended periods as a stable landmass, Africa's surface has been eroded into vast peneplains. In the absence of mountains large enough to influence climate on a continental scale, the distribution of Africa's rainfall and vegetation is mainly decided by the annual movements of the Inter-Tropical Convergence Zone (ITCZ), a belt of low atmospheric pressure and resulting high rainfall that follows the sun on its annual progression north and south of the Equator.

Rainfall patterns

Areas within about 10° of the Equator receive the ITCZ (and thus wet seasons) at two well-separated times of the year. This produces high, evenly distributed rainfall, which results in the growth of forest; Africa's tropical rainforests are second in extent only to those of South America. They contain a wealth of birds, including the Congo Peafowl and many members of such families as hornbills, barbets and greenbuls.

Regions more than 10° from the Equator receive a single wet season each year, followed by a prolonged drought. Depending on the total amount of rainfall, which decreases away from the Equator into the tropics, this type of regime produces savannah woodland, semiarid bush or, at its driest, desert. For these reasons, Africa's basic types of vegetation are arranged in parallel east-west belts of decreasing luxuriance, on either side of the Equator.

The savannah woodlands consist of deciduous trees of moderate height, which provide numerous nest-holes for such groups as starlings, rollers and the smaller, open country hornbills. The arrival of the rainy season produces tall, lush growths of grass alive with displaying bishops and widowbirds. The semiarid bush is also largely deciduous, and is dominated by various acacias. This dry country supports a great variety of weavers, and the vegetation is often festooned with their hanging, grassy nests. Numerous ground-dwelling birds include the bustards, sandgrouse and pipits. Beyond these semiarid lands, the rainfall is insufficient to support much vegetation and the land is open desert, the

Sahara to the north and the Kalahari and Namib to the south. The diversity of birds in these two southern deserts is distinctly lower than that in the moister Afrotropical regions—hence the appearance of the phrase "apart from the far south-west" in many of the species' summaries given here.

Two other distinctive Afrotropical areas should be mentioned.

Africa's southernmost tip has a subtropical climate like that of the Mediterranean; this produces a low, mixed scrub known as *fynbos*, which is very similar to the maquis of the north. The many seabirds around these shores include the African Penguin.

Africa's Rift Valley is the surface expression of weaknesses in the African continent's crust. The soda-lakes found on the Rift's floor at such sites as Nakuru and Natron accommodate enormous concentrations of flamingos which are among the world's foremost wildlife spectacles. Dramatic uplifts that accompanied rifting produced the Ethiopian and East African highlands. The latter are of relatively restricted extent but they contain close conjunctions of diverse ecosystems that, in Kenya and Uganda, support the richest local avifaunas on the continent.

The Afrotropical avifauna consists of approximately 1,850 species in 95 families, and is exceeded in richness only by that of the Neotropics. One order (the mousebirds) and 12 families are endemic to the Afrotropical Region. Five of these families contain unique, single species: these are the Ostrich, the Shoebill, the Hammerkop, the Secretary Bird and, in the Malagasy area, the Cuckoo Roller. The Ostrich, a relic of Africa's Gondwanan days, has become confined to sub-Saharan Africa through human agencies, having been hunted to extinction in the Middle East, and virtually so in North Africa only recently.

The largest of the Afrotropical's unique families is the 20 turacos, an ancient group possibly related to owls and nightjars. The wood hoopoes and helmet shrikes are also endemic to the Afrotropical mainland, while the mesites, ground-rollers, asities and vangas are confined to the Malagasy area. The guineafowl are endemic to Africa as a whole, though fast declining north of the Sahara. Other uniquely Afrotropical groups, of but two species each, are the sugarbirds, the oxpeckers and the picathartes or rockfowl.

Families at their most diverse in the Afrotropics include the bustards, coursers, bee-eaters, rollers, barbets, honeyguides, larks, shrikes, sunbirds and weavers. The prolific speciation of the cisticola warblers (43 taxa), sunbirds (82) and weavers (81) is especially notable. The Afrotropical Region is also exceptionally rich in large diurnal raptors.

Families poorly represented in the Afrotropical Region relative to other tropical areas of the Old World include the parrots, trogons, (large) woodpeckers, broadbills, pittas, babblers, cuckooshrikes and white-eyes. Most of these attain their greatest diversity farther east, in the Oriental and Australasian Regions. The parrots are also diverse in South America and, like the Ostrich, probably represent Gondwanan stock.

Palaearctic migrants

Hundreds of millions of migrant birds of over 200 species breed in the Palaearctic and spend the northern winter in the Afrotropical Region. The aquatic species of migrants utilize all types of waters, but the land birds favor Africa's savannah woodlands and bush, and make very little use of the vast tropical rainforests.

Many of these birds, like the Common Pochard and Eurasian Turtle Dove, penetrate south only as far as Africa's northern tropics, but others like the Garganey and Barn Swallow reach the far south.

Much of the migration is on broad fronts but some takes place in bands as narrow as 30 km (20 miles) across, particularly where the birds' progress is channeled around highland regions. One such stream passes over Ngulia Lodge in Kenya, where spectacular "falls" of up to 100,000 birds have occurred.

Relatively small numbers of these Palaearctic migrants regularly remain in sub-Saharan Africa for the northern summer. The White Stork, Black Stork, Booted Eagle, Eurasian Bee-eater and House Martin have established resident breeding populations in the far south, where the annual variations in day-length and season most resemble those of the Palaearctic.

Intra-African migrants

Most Afrotropical birds were formerly considered nonmigratory, but in fact many frequently perform movements of some kind, ranging from local wandering to regular, trans-equatorial migration. Many dry country species are nomadic, moving erratically to avoid adverse climatic conditions and breeding opportunistically on entering areas that are green after recent rains. Intra-African migrants make regular movements between breeding and off-season ranges within Afrotropical Africa. This type of migration has been rather arbitrarily defined as involving journeys of more than 400 km (250 miles) in either direction, but species like Abdim's Stork cover many thousands of miles each year.

Almost 10% of Afrotropical bird species are threatened by such factors as desertification, deforestation and the destruction of wetlands, which are a consequence of the southward spread of the Sahara, and of the unsustainable exploitation of natural habitats by the large and rapidly increasing human populations. The vast international trade in captive birds, including bustards, is another serious problem.

Birds that benefit from the spread of man include those capable of utilizing dry, degraded environments (e.g. larks, sandgrouse), those that scavenge around habitation (e.g. crows, vultures) and those that have taken to nesting on buildings (e.g. swifts, swallows). Artificially introduced species like the Rock Pigeon, House Crow and House Sparrow have also spread widely.

Afrotropical ornithological societies

Various Afrotropical ornithological societies exist, and many produce good-quality publications. Further information can be obtained from: the Bird Committee of the East Africa Natural History Society, P.O. Box 44486, 00100 Nairobi, Kenya; the West African Ornithological Society, Zoological Gardens, Chester CH2 1LH, UK; and the Southern African Ornithological Society, PO Box 84394, Greenside, Johannesburg, South Africa. Currently, 145 site support groups have been established and actively involved in conserving over 50 Important Bird Areas (IBA's) across the continent.

OSTRICHES Struthioniformes

Ostrich
Struthio camelus (**Struthionidae**) 190–240 cm/75–94 in.
Flightless, unmistakably huge, the largest living bird. Adult male has mainly black plumage, skin of neck and legs pinkish in most races, bright blue-gray in Somali Ostrich of north-eastern AF. Female smaller, plumage mainly gray-brown, neck and legs grayer. Immature as female, plumage increasingly black in male. Usually silent; breeding male produces deep booming, like lion roaring. Found in pairs and small groups in open country; conspicuous, but resembling bushes at long range. **Range and habitat:** recently hunted to extinction in Arabia, almost so in North Africa; remains in 3 regions of AF: at 10–20° N; south from Sudan, Ethiopia to Tanzania; south of 15° S. Locally common. Resident; seasonal and nomadic movements known. **Similar species:** Greater Rhea (see p 96), Emu (see p 282).

PENGUINS Sphenisciformes

African Penguin
Spheniscus demersus (**Spheniscidae**) 63 cm/25 in.
Rather small penguin, black above and on face, with conspicuous broad white eyebrow extending back to broader white stripe down side of neck; pinkish skin above and around eye, bill black with subterminal pale band; underparts white, with black band across upper breast and down on to flanks. Immature has head and neck sooty, bare skin as adult. Call, frequently at night, is loud braying. Found singly or in flocks, foraging at sea. **Range and habitat:** only resident penguin in Africa, from Namibia to southern Mozambique. Locally common offshore, especially islands and on coasts. Resident, also wandering. Classified as vulnerable because of rapid population decline mainly resulting from egg-collection, habitat degradation, and oilspills. **Similar species:** Rockhopper and Macaroni Penguins.

FULL-WEBBED SWIMMERS Pelecaniformes

Long-tailed Cormorant
Phalacrocorax africanus (**Phalacrocoracidae**) 60 cm/24 in.
Rather small, long-tailed, blackish or dark brown cormorant with red eyes and yellow bill. Breeding adult has short crest on forehead and contrasting glossy feathers on upperwing; nonbreeding adult duller, lacking crest, rather blotchy below. Immature has ventral torso dusky whitish. Usually silent; occasionally croaking sounds; more vocal at nest. Found singly or in small parties, on open shores, perches or water; sometimes approachable. **Range and habitat:** widespread in AF south of 17° N. Locally common on all types of water except open sea, particularly near fringing vegetation. Resident, moving locally. **Similar species:** Great Cormorant, Darter.

Oriental Darter
Anhinga melanogaster (**Anhingidae**) 90 cm/35 in.
Medium-sized waterbird recalling slender cormorant, distinguished by long, thin, kinked neck, equally slim head and pointed (not hook-tipped) bill. Adult has black torso streaked white on wings, and bright chestnut-brown neck with white lateral stripe. Crown black in male, browner in female. Immature buff on neck and underparts. Usually silent; various grunts, croaks at nest. Found singly or in small groups, on water or nearby prominent perch, often swimming with only neck showing; often unobtrusive. **Range and habitat:** widespread in AF south of 15° N. Locally common on fresh, sluggish waters with fringing vegetation, also coastal inlets on occasion. Resident, moving locally. **Similar species:** other darters (see pp 52, 238, 286).

Pink-backed Pelican
Pelecanus rufescens (**Pelecanidae**) 140 cm/55 in.
Rather small, gray pelican, washed pinkish on torso when breeding; bill pouch pinkish or grayish, small spot of naked black skin in front of eye. In flight, slight contrast between underwing-coverts and browner flight feathers. Immature with head and wings brownish, otherwise whitish. Usually silent; harsh croaks at nest. Singly or in small groups, not fishing in coordinated parties; on water or open shores, often with Great White Pelican (*P. onocrotalus*); fairly approachable. **Range and habitat:** widespread in AF south of 15° N, apart from much of far south. Locally common on any freshwater with sufficient fish. Resident, but dispersing widely after breeding. **Similar species:** Great White Pelican (see p 142).

HERONS AND ALLIES Ciconiiformes

Black-headed Heron
Ardea melanocephala (**Ardeidae**) 95 cm/37 in.
Large gray heron with top of head, hindneck and legs black, and white throat. In flight, contrast between pale underwing-coverts and black flight feathers. Immature has hindneck and top of head grayish; foreneck white, tinged buff or rufous. Call is loud "oo-arrk;" also harsh sounds at nest. Found singly or in small groups, foraging on open ground or shores; moderately approachable. **Range and habitat:** widespread in AF south of 15° N. Common but seldom numerous, in variety of inland wetlands and also far from water in open country or cultivated land. Resident, with post-breeding dispersal; moves into arid country after rains. **Similar species:** Gray Heron (see p 144).

Goliath Heron
Ardea goliath (**Ardeidae**) 140 cm/55 in.
Very large, heavily built heron with massive bill, slate-gray wings and tail, and rich chestnut head, neck and underparts. Combination of great size and slow, deliberate wingbeats distinctive even at long range. Immature paler, gray-brown on back, underparts whitish with dark streaking. Call is loud "woork," often given when flushed. Found singly or in pairs, occasionally loose flocks, foraging in open; wary. **Range and habitat:** WP in Kuwait, Iraq, Red Sea; otherwise AF, where widespread south of 15° N, apart from far south-west. Rather uncommon around permanent waters, both fresh and saline, including running tide. Resident, dispersing after breeding. **Similar species:** Purple Heron (see p 144)

Black Heron
Egretta ardesiaca (**Ardeidae**) 66 cm/26 in.
Medium, slaty black heron with conspicuous yellow feet that turn reddish during breeding. Immature duller, browner. Usually silent; threat is raucous scream. Found singly or in small parties, seasonal flocks up to hundreds in some areas; fishes in open water, holding wings in canopy above head; bold. **Range and habitat:** widespread in AF south of 15° N, apart from far south-west and much of Congo basin. At best locally common, along open margins of lakes, marshes, coastal creeks, sometimes rivers. Some populations resident, dispersing after breeding; others possibly intra-African migrants. **Similar species:** Slaty Egret, dark phases of Little Egret and Western Reef-Egret (see p 144).

Cattle Egret
Bubulcus ibis (**Ardeidae**) 52 cm/20 in.
Rather small, short-necked egret, nonbreeding adult (most of year) white with yellowish bill and legs. Breeding adult has bill and legs more orange, with crown, breast and back buff-orange. Immature white, with bill, legs and feet black. Usually silent; occasional croaking calls. Found in small flocks, foraging on open ground; habitually takes insects flushed by large mammals, often approachable. **Range and habitat:** OR, southern WP, EP; widespread in AF south of 15° N, apart from far south-west; has recently spread to NA, NT, AU. Common, locally numerous, in open grassy country, often away from water. Some populations resident, others regular intra-African migrants. **Similar species:** other white egrets (see pp 52, 144, 286).

Hammerkop
Scopus umbretta **Scopidae**) 56 cm/22 in.
Unique brown waterbird, recalling short, squat stork, with black legs, stout, conical black bill and thick drooping crest on back of head. In buoyant flight, can be mistaken for ibis or raptor until longish neck and heavy bill are seen. Immature resembles adult. Call is series of loud, shrill whistles, again suggesting raptor, often rising to strained crescendo. Found singly or in pairs, sometimes small, loose flocks, foraging in shallow open water; massive nest on tree or rock face; bold, sometimes approachable. **Range and habitat:** widespread in AF south of 15° N, also south-west Arabia. Fairly common around slow inland waters, also estuaries. Basically resident, colonizing seasonal waters, nomadic in arid lands. **Similar species:** Hadada Ibis (see p 188).

Ostrich (in display)

African Penguin

Long-tailed Cormorant (drying wings)

Oriental Darter

Pink-backed Pelican

Black-headed Heron

Black Heron (fishing)

Goliath Heron

Cattle Egret (showing breeding plumes)

Hammerkop

Shoebill
Balaeniceps rex (Balaenicipitidae) 150 cm/59 in.
Very large, dark gray, storklike bird with unmistakable huge, pale, shoe-shaped bill and short tuftlike crest. Immature browner, with smaller bill. Mainly silent; occasional chuckling and shrill whistles; clatters bill. Found singly or paired, very rarely small, loose groups; shy, often in dense vegetation, can soar at great heights. **Range and habitat:** central AF, from south Sudan and Central African Republic south to Zambia, Botswana. Very local, often obscure, in *Miscanthidium* and papyrus swamps. Resident, possibly wandering very locally. Small and declining population owing to hunting, nesting disturbance and habitat degradation. **Similar species:** Marabou high overhead.

Woolly-necked Stork
Ciconia episcopus (Ciconiidae) 86 cm/34 in.
Rather small stork with glossy brownish black body and wings; contrasting white neck has peculiar, short "woolly" feathering, white patch at base of bill. In flight, shows conspicuous white abdomen. Immature browner, lacking patch at base of bill. Usually silent; makes harsh sounds and clatters bill at nest. Found singly, paired, or in small loose groups; not secretive. **Range and habitat:** east in OR from India to Philippines, Indonesia; widespread in AF south of 15° N, apart from far south-west. Local, often uncommon, in vicinity of water, usually in wooded country. Some populations resident, others intra-African migrants.

African Openbill
Anastomus lamelligerus (Ciconiidae) 92 cm/36 in.
Rather small, blackish brown stork; bill pale, with narrow gap between closed mandibles. Immature browner, gap reduced or absent. Usually silent; occasional honking or croaking sounds. Usually gregarious, foraging in open; bold, fairly approachable. **Range and habitat:** widespread in AF south of 15° N, apart from far south-west. Locally common, usually near wetland, where specialized bill extracts mollusks from shells. Some resident; most intra-African migrants, which can temporarily appear in any habitat. **Similar species:** Asian Openbill (see p 238).

Saddle-billed Stork
Ephippiorhynchus senegalensis (Ciconiidae) 145 cm/57 in.
Africa's largest stork, with black and white plumage and unmistakable huge, black and red bill with yellow "saddle" at base of upper mandible. Eye dark in male, yellow in female. In flight, white flight feathers conspicuous even at great range. Immature gray and mottled, bill black. Silent. Found singly or paired, foraging in open; shy. **Range and habitat:** widespread in AF between 15° N and 20° S. Local, thinly distributed, around inland wetlands. Resident.

Abdim's Stork
Ciconia abdimii (Ciconiidae) 76 cm/30 in.
Small stork with dark upperparts and white ventral torso; facial skin blue and red, bill tawny; legs pinkish gray with contrasting red tarsal joints and feet. In flight, large white patch on back and rump visible at great range. Immature browner, bill redder. Usually silent; occasional weak whistles; clatters bill. In flocks up to thousands, foraging in open; moderately approachable, nesting even in towns. **Range and habitat:** intra-African migrant that breeds during the rains in northern AF, from Senegal east to Ethiopia and extreme south-west Arabia, then migrates into southern AF for southern rainy season, south to South Africa. Seasonally common in open country, often far from water. **Similar species:** Black Stork (see p 144).

Marabou Stork
Leptoptilos crumeniferus (Ciconiidae) 152 cm/60 in.
Huge, unmistakable stork, dark above and white below, with bare pinkish head and neck, and similarly naked, pendulous air sac dangling over breast. In flight readily identified by massive bill and contrast between white belly and black wings and tail. Immature has whitish, "woolly" feathering on head. Usually silent, sometimes clattering bill; snores and grunts at nest. Single or in small parties, flocks at food or on migration; bold, moderately approachable. **Range and habitat:** widespread in AF between 15° N and 25° S. Common in small numbers in open, dry or wetland habitats, also scavenging at carrion and refuse. Resident or intra-African migrant.

Yellow-billed Stork
Mycteria ibis (Ciconiidae) 97 cm/38 in.
Medium-sized, mainly white stork with orange-yellow, slightly decurved bill, bare red facial skin and red legs; plumage tinged pinkish when breeding. In flight, white underwing-coverts contrast with black flight feathers. Immature gray-brown, bill and face duller, legs brown. Generally silent; clatters bill; various screams at nest. Single or in small groups, foraging in open; bold, moderately approachable. **Range and habitat:** widespread throughout AF between 15° N and 30° S. Fairly common at inland waters; local on coasts. Few entirely resident, substantial movements occur. **Similar species:** White Stork (see p 144).

Sacred Ibis
Threskiornis aethiopicus (Threskiornithidae) 89 cm/35 in.
Mainly white with elongate black plumes drooping over tail, decurved black bill and naked black head and neck; legs blackish. Immature lacks plumes; head and neck feathered. Usually silent; squeals and croaks at nest. Found singly or in flocks up to hundreds, foraging in open; not shy. **Range and habitat:** locally Middle East, in Iraq and Iran; widespread in AF south of 17° N, apart from far south-west. Common in wetlands, including sea coast; also on cultivated land, and scavenging at habitation. Some resident, others making regular movements.

Hadada Ibis
Bostrychia hagedash (Threskiornithidae) 76 cm/30 in.
Medium-sized gray-green ibis with metallic purplish green wash (often inconspicuous) on closed wing, and whitish stripe on cheek. In flight, wings distinctively broad and rounded, recalling Hammerkop. Immature duller, lacking metallic wash. Call (origin of name) is very loud, harsh "ark-ha, haaaaa," most frequent at twilight. Single, in pairs or small parties, larger flocks known, foraging in open; often approachable. **Range and habitat:** widespread in AF south of 15° N, apart from far south-west. Locally common on damp ground or near water, usually near woodland or forest. Basically nonmigratory. **Similar species:** Green and Glossy Ibises, Hammerkop (see pp 100, 186).

African Spoonbill
Platalea alba (Threskiornithidae) 91 cm/36 in.
White waterbird with long, gray and red spatulate bill, bare red facial skin and red legs. Immature with blackish wing tips, yellow bill and blackish legs. Usually silent; occasional grunts and croaks; clatters bill. Single or in small flocks, foraging in open, shallow water; rather retiring. **Range and habitat:** widespread in AF south of 17° N, apart from far south-west. Locally common at open waters. Few truly resident; regular intra-African movements. **Similar species:** other spoonbills (see pp 144, 288).

Greater Flamingo
Phoenicopterus roseus (Phoenicopteridae) 142 cm/56 in.
Tall, very pale flamingo with black-tipped pink bill and pink legs. In flight, scarlet wing-coverts contrast with black flight feathers. Call is loud, gooselike honk; flocks grunt and murmur. Very gregarious, often flocking in thousands, frequently alongside Lesser Flamingos. **Range and habitat:** NT, southern NA and Palaearctic; in AF, migrants from Palaearctic in north, AF-resident populations in east, and south of 15° S. Locally abundant on open, shallow waters, particularly if saline or brackish. Substantial dispersal from few major AF breeding sites; also erratic, nomadic. **Similar species:** Lesser Flamingo.

Lesser Flamingo
Phoenicopterus minor (Phoenicopteridae) 101 cm/40 in.
Medium-sized, distinctly pink flamingo with black-tipped, very dark maroon bill and red legs. In flight, pink and red wing-coverts contrast with black flight feathers. Immature distinct. Call is gooselike honk; flocks grunt and murmur. Extremely gregarious, in concentrations that can exceed a million, often alongside Greater Flamingos, wary, walking away into water. **Range and habitat:** Persian Gulf and north-west India, but mainly AF, especially on rift valley soda-lakes from Ethiopia to southern Tanzania; also west coast, and south of 15° S. Locally extremely abundant on saline and brackish waters; moribund wanderers elsewhere. Resident, dispersing after breeding, and erratic nomad. Its population decline is due to the restricted number of unprotected breeding sites. **Similar species:** Greater Flamingo.

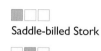

Shoebill

Woolly-necked Sto[rk]

African Openbill

Saddle-billed Stork

Abdim's Stork

Marabou Stork

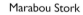

Yellow-billed Stork

Sacred Ibis

Hadada Ibis

African Spoonbill

Greater Flamingo

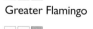

Lesser Flamingo
(in territorial displays[)]

WATERFOWL Anseriformes

Maccoa Duck

Oxyura maccoa (**Anatidae**) 45 cm/18 in.
Rather small diving duck, sole AF stifftail; breeding male with unmistakable combination of black head, vivid cobalt-blue bill and bright chestnut body. Nonbreeding male, female and immature brown, with conspicuous dark horizontal streak across white face. Usually silent; grunts in threat and courtship. In pairs, or small groups with fewer males than females; swims low in water, often with only head showing; rather retiring, dives if alarmed. **Range and habitat:** 2 areas of AF: north-east, in Tanzania, Kenya and Ethiopia, and south of 20° S. Rather local, on shallow inland waters with fringing vegetation. Resident. **Similar species:** Southern Pochard, other stifftails (see pp 56, 102).

White-backed Duck

Thalassornis leuconotus (**Anatidae**) 42 cm/17 in.
Rather small diving duck, mottled brown, fulvous and white, with conspicuous white spot on either side of face near base of bill. White back visible only in flight. Immature as adult. Usually silent; occasional soft whistles. In pairs or small parties, often swimming low in water, with tail submerged; unobtrusive, often close-sitting, inconspicuous when motionless among emergent vegetation. **Range and habitat:** widespread in southern AF, apart from far south-west, and north to Kenya, Ethiopia; also from Senegal to Chad in north. Local, on quiet fresh waters with fringing and floating vegetation. Nonmigratory, moves in response to changing water levels.

Southern Pochard

Netta erythrophthalma (**Anatidae**) 50 cm/20 in.
Medium-sized diving duck, distinctive male very dark brown, paler on flanks, with blue-gray legs and bill, and red eyes. Female paler brown, with curved white stripe on side of head. Immature as female, but paler. In flight, shows conspicuous white bar running length of dark upperwing. Usually silent; occasional purrs, quacks. Found paired, or in thousands; sometimes shy. **Range and habitat:** local tropical NT, declining significantly; widespread in AF south of 10° S, north to Uganda, Kenya, Ethiopia. Common on large, deep fresh waters. Resident or intra-African migrants, with annual nonbreeding influx September–October to northern AF, departs south in March. **Similar species:** female Maccoa Duck, African Black Duck.

Cape Teal

Anas capensis (**Anatidae**) 46 cm/18 in.
Rather small, pale, speckled brown and gray duck with pink bill, black at base. In flight, shows contrasting white and green speculum on dark brown wings. Immature as adult. Usually silent; occasional whistles. In pairs or small parties, flocks of hundreds known. Fairly approachable. **Range and habitat:** widespread in AF south of 15° S, and north through Bast Africa to Ethiopia; also scattered areas of north-west. Locally common, usually on shallow brackish or saline waters. Resident, but wandering and also making nomadic and possibly more regular movements. **Similar species:** Red-billed Duck.

Hottentot Teal

Anas hottentota (**Anatidae**) 35 cm/14 in.
Small, yellowish brown duck with dark speckling on breast and mantle, and distinctive dark cap above pale face; bill blue-gray. In flight, shows green speculum with white trailing edge, on dark brown wings. Immature browner, bill grayer. Usually silent; occasional low quacks, thin whistles. In pairs or small parties, often unobtrusive. **Range and habitat:** widespread in AF south of 15° S, apart from arid south-west, and north through East Africa to Ethiopia; also Chad. Locally common on sluggish, fresh or brackish waters, especially with surface vegetation. Resident or intra-African migrant. **Similar species:** Red-billed Duck

Red-billed Duck

Anas erythrorhyncha (**Anatidae**) 48 cm/19 in.
Medium-sized, speckled brown and white duck, readily identified by red bill and dark cap above white face. In flight, shows conspicuous creamy buff speculum on dark brown wings. Immature duller; bill pinkish brown. Usually silent; occasional barely audible whistles. In pairs, or flocks up to hundreds; not shy. **Range and habitat:** widespread in AF south of 10° S and north through East Africa to Ethiopia, Sudan. Common on fresh and alkaline waters, including temporary pools. Resident or intra-African migrant. **Similar species:** Hottentot Teal, Cape Wigeon.

White-faced Whistling-Duck

Dendrocygna viduata (**Anatidae**) 48 cm/19 in.
Medium-sized duck with white face (often stained by muddy water), bright chestnut lower neck, barred flanks and, when out of water, distinctly erect stance on rather long legs. Immature has face pale brown. Call is loud, shrill whistle "seeeee-oooooooo," uttered in flight. In pairs, or flocks up to hundreds; often noisy, not shy. **Range and habitat:** tropical NT, south to Uruguay, northern Argentina; widespread in AF south of 15° N, except far south-west and Congo basin. Common, locally numerous, on variety of quiet waters. Resident, flocking and moving in nonbreeding season; probably intra-African migrant. **Similar species:** female South African Shelduck.

Spur-winged Goose

Plectropterus gambensis (**Anatidae**) 80–101 cm/31–40 in.
Largest AF anatid, readily identified by reddish bill and facial skin, dark glossy upperparts and white belly. Mature male has fleshy knob on forehead, variably white face. Female smaller, browner, less facial white. In flight, white wing-coverts contrast with dark flight feathers. Immature as female but browner, face feathered. Usually silent; occasional soft whistles. Found in pairs, or in flocks of up to hundreds during off-season; rather shy and retiring. **Range and habitat:** widespread in AF south of 15° N, apart from Congo basin and far southwest. Locally common on fresh waters, particularly inundated areas around wetlands. Resident, or intra-African migrant. **Similar species:** Comb Duck.

Pygmy Goose

Nettapus auritus (**Anatidae**) 34 cm/13 in.
Small duck with dark green upperparts, white face and conspicuous bright rufous orange breast and flanks. Male has black-bordered green patch on side of head; female and immature have this area speckled grayish. In flight, short white speculum contrasts with dark upperwing. Male's call is soft whistle, female's is soft quack. Found in pairs or small parties, rarely in large flocks; not shy, but often still, unobtrusive,—easily overlooked among emergent vegetation. **Range and habitat:** widespread in AF between 15° N and 20° S. Local on quiet fresh waters, especially with much floating vegetation. Resident, probably also intra-African migrant. **Similar species:** other pygmy geese (see p 240).

Comb Duck

Sarkidiornis melanotos (**Anatidae**) 62–79 cm/24–31 in.
Large duck with speckled head and neck, and glossy blue-black upperparts contrasting with white underparts. Male has dark knob, enlarged when breeding, at base of upper mandible; female smaller, lacking knob. In flight, black underwings contrast with white body. Immature buffish below, more speckled above. Usually silent. Found in pairs or flocks of up to hundreds, perching on shores or trees; sometimes, shy. **Range and habitat:** tropical NT, from Venezuela south to Paraguay; OR, from India to China; widespread in AF south of 15° N, apart from far south-west. Locally or seasonally common on wide variety of fresh waters. Resident or intra-African migrant. **Similar species:** Spur-winged Goose.

Egyptian Goose

Alopochen aegyptiacus (**Anatidae**) 72 cm/28 in.
Large, gooselike duck, brown above, grayer below, with prominent patches of dark chestnut around eyes and in center of breast. In flight, shows conspicuous white wing-coverts. Immature duller, more uniform, chestnut patches reduced or absent. Frequent loud wheezing and honking calls. In pairs or family parties, molting flocks of hundreds, on open ground or water; noisy, bold. **Range and habitat:** in WP, resident Egypt, occasional Tunisia, Algeria, feral UK; in AF, 1 of commonest and most widespread of anatids south of 15° N, on all types of water except sea. Basically resident, with molt migrations and wandering. **Similar species:** Ruddy and South African Shelducks (see p 240).

Maccoa Duck

White-backed Duck

Southern Pochard

Cape Teal

Hottentot Teal

Red-billed Duck

White-faced Whistling-Duck

Spur-winged Goose

Pygmy Goose

Comb Duck

Egyptian Goose

DIURNAL BIRDS OF PREY Falconiformes

Secretary Bird

Sagittarius serpentarius (Sagittariidae) 120–50 cm/47–59 in.
Very large, black and pale gray raptor with bare red facial skin, lax crest of long black feathers on back of head, and long pinkish legs. In occasional soaring flights, recognized by contrast between pale wing-coverts and black flight feathers, long neck, and elongated central tail feathers. Immature has yellow facial skin. Generally silent; various coughs, croaks at nest. Singly or paired, or in rare small groups, walking purposefully; rather wary and shy. **Range and habitat:** widespread in AF south of 17° N. Common in open country. Resident, occasionally wandering.

Rueppell's Griffon

Gyps rueppellii (Accipitridae) 100 cm/39 in.
Large, speckled, brown plains vulture with yellow eyes and cream bill. In flight, shows slender pale bars on underwing-coverts; coarsely speckled ventral torso. Immature with underwing barring reduced. Harsh squeals and hisses when disputing carcasses. Highly gregarious; moderately approachable. **Range and habitat:** northern AF, from Senegal "east to Ethiopia, Kenya, northern Tanzania. Common over open dry country with good numbers of large mammals; roosts and nests on cliffs. Basically resident, making daily foraging flights of up to 150 km (95 miles). **Similar species:** African White-backed and Cape Vultures.

African White-backed Vulture

Gyps africanus (Accipitridae) 97 cm/38 in.
Large, rather plain, brown plains vulture with dark eyes and black bill. In flight, shows white back, and contrast between pale underwing-coverts and blackish flight feathers. Immature lacks white back, and has faintly streaked undertorso. Harsh squeals when disputing carcasses. Highly gregarious; quite approachable. **Range and habitat:** widespread in AF between 15° N and 30° S, apart from equatorial forest. Common over open country with good numbers of large mammals; roosts and nests on trees. Basically resident, but making long daily foraging flights and following migrations of wild ungulates, e.g. Wildebeest. **Similar species:** Rueppell's Griffon, Cape Vulture, Eurasian Griffon (see p 150).

Lappet-faced Vulture

Torgos tracheliotus (Accipitridae) 105 cm/41 in.
Largest and most powerful AF plains vulture, identified by naked crimson head with lateral skin folds and massive yellowish bill. In flight, white under-forewing-bar and thighs contrast with dark underparts. Immature has head duller, less white on thighs. Generally silent; harsh guttural sounds when disputing carcasses. Single or paired, sometimes 4 at carcass; moderately approachable. **Range and habitat:** widespread in AF at 15–30° S, and north through East Africa to areas of northern tropics and Arabia, reaching WP in Israel. Moderately common, never numerous, in open country with large numbers of big mammals. Resident, territorial, foraging locally. A small declining population remains in Africa, owing to poisoning and persecution. **Similar species:** White-headed Vulture.

Hooded Vulture

Necrosyrtes monachus (Accipitridae) 65–70 cm/26–8 in.
Small, dark brown vulture with bare pink facial skin, white downy feathering on hindneck and head, and white legs. In flight, overall brown coloration broken by pale feet and thighs, and pale area at base of flight feathers. Immature has brown down on head and neck, face as adult. Generally silent; squeals at carcasses and when nesting. Single or paired, occasionally small parties; sometimes approachable. **Range and habitat:** widespread in AF between 17° N and 22° S. Common in many habitats, from desert to forest edge; often around habitation in northern AF. Resident, making only local foraging flights. **Similar species:** immature Egyptian Vulture (see p 150).

Palm-nut Vulture

Gypohierax angolensis (Accipitridae) 60 cm/24 in.
Small, black and white vulture with yellowish bill and bare reddish facial skin; legs yellowish orange or pinkish. In flight, black secondaries, tail and primary tips contrast with white underparts. Immature brown, with yellowish facial skin and whitish legs. Generally silent;

occasional guttural and crowing calls. Found singly or in pairs; sometimes approachable. **Range and habitat:** widespread in AF south from Senegal, Sudan and Kenya to Botswana and Mozambique. Locally common in wooded areas, particularly near Raphia and Elaeis palms, whose fruit it eats. Nonmigratory, but wanderers known. **Similar species:** Egyptian Vulture (see p 150).

Black-shouldered Kite

Elanus caeruleus (Accipitridae) 32 cm/13 in.
Small, graceful raptor, pale gray above with red eyes, white tail and black carpal patches visible on closed wing; underparts white. One of very few AF raptors to hover frequently. Immature browner above, washed warm buff on breast, eyes yellowish. Usually silent; occasional weak whistles. Single or paired, perching prominently; moderately approachable. **Range and habitat:** OR and WP, including Spain, Portugal, North Africa; widespread in AF south of 16° N. Common, never numerous, in many open habitats. Nonmigratory or moving locally, e.g. to concentrations of rodent prey. **Similar species:** Scissor-tailed Kite, Australian Black-shouldered Kite (see p 290).

Scissor-tailed Kite

Chelictinia riocourii (Accipitridae) 37 cm/15 in.
Small, elegant, ternlike raptor with deeply forked tail; upperparts pale gray, underparts white with black carpal patch on underwing. Flight buoyant and graceful, hovering frequently. Immature browner above, streaked below, tail less deeply cleft. Usually silent; low mewing calls at nest. Single or in small flocks; rather shy. **Range and habitat:** mainly at 8–16° north in AF, east from west coast to Ethiopia, Somalia, Kenya. Locally common in dry, open country. Intra-African migrant, breeding March–June during northern tropics' rains and then moving south to avoid ensuing dry season. **Similar species:** black-shouldered kites (see p 290).

Bat Hawk

Macheiramphus alcinus (Accipitridae) 45 cm/18 in.
Medium-sized, very dark brown raptor with palish throat, large yellow eyes and whitish legs and feet. In flight, resembles thickset falcon *Falco* species, with narrow tail, tapered wings. Immature whitish on belly. Generally silent; occasional high whistles. Found singly; not especially shy, but spends day in dense Qanopies, emerging at dusk to hunt bats and small birds on wing. **Range and habitat:** OR east to New Guinea; widespread in AF south of Senegal and Somalia. Rather uncommon in densely wooded habitats and town centers, always near open areas to hunt. Basically nonmigratory, possibly dispersing after breeding.

Verreaux's Eagle

Aquila verreauxii (Accipitridae) 84 cm/33 in.
Very large, black eagle with boldly contrasting white V on back. In flight, shows distinctively narrow, "pinched" bases to wings, and white flash at base of underwing primaries. Immature rufous on mantle, nape and crown, otherwise heavily speckled and streaked buffish, blacker on breast and face. Generally silent; occasional yelping and mewing. In pairs, singly or with immature; often inconspicuous high on rock faces, not shy. **Range and habitat:** widespread in all but interior areas of AF south of 10° S, and north through East Africa to Ethiopia, southern Arabia; also Sudan, Chad. Reaches WP in southern Egypt, Sinai, Israel. Locally common around rocky hills, gorges, cliffs with hyrax, the main prey. Basically resident, immatures wander.

Tawny Eagle

Aquila rapax (Accipitridae) 65–75 cm/26–9 in.
Medium-sized eagle, varying from creamish to very dark brown, with blackish flight feathers and tail; long, yellow gape, extending back to level with center of eye. Immature has 2, diffuse, white wing-bars, and white crescent on rump. Usually silent, but various yelping and barking calls. Single, paired; sometimes in small parties; can be approachable. **Range and habitat:** widespread in AF south of 17° N, and north to south-western Arabia. Also Morocco and Algeria in WP, east to India, Burma. Locally common in scrub or woodland or scavenging at habitation. Some are resident, others local migrants. **Similar species:** Steppe Eagle, other brown eagles (see p 150).

Secretary Bird

Rueppell's Griffon

Lappet-faced Vulture

African White-backed Vulture

Verreaux's Eagle

Hooded Vulture

Palm-nut Vulture

Black-shouldered Kite

Bat Hawk

Scissor-tailed Kite

Tawny Eagle

Crowned Hawk-Eagle

Stephanoaetus coronatus (Accipitridae) 81–90 cm/32–5 in.
Very large, thickset eagle, dark above with crest on nape and barred tail; undertorso buffish or white, blotched and barred dark. In flight, shows underwings with rufous coverts, white flight feathers barred black, and broad black trailing edge. Immature gray above, white on head and ventral torso; underwing-coverts faintly rufous. Male loudly whistles "ki-wii ki-wii ki-wii..." during high undulating display flight; female a lower "kuu-kuu-kuu." Single or paired; shy. **Range and habitat:** AF from Senegal and Ethiopia south to South Africa. Sometimes common, often local, in forest and woodland. Nonmigratory. **Similar species:** immature Martial Eagle.

Martial Eagle

Polemaetus bellicosus (Accipitridae) 76–83 cm/30–3 in.
Large, powerful eagle with dark brown upperparts, head and breast; below white, rather inconspicuously spotted brown; short crest on nape. In flight shows contrast between white belly and dark head, tail and underwings. Immature gray above, white below; in flight, whitish underwing-coverts contrast with dark flight feathers. Generally silent; ringing "klow-eee," also barking. Single or paired; sometimes wary and shy. **Range and habitat:** widespread in AF south of 15° N, apart from forest regions and many areas of west. Moderately common in open habitats. Nonmigratory, making long daily foraging flights. **Similar species:** Short-toed Eagle (see p 150).

African Hawk-Eagle

Aquila spilogaster (Accipitridae) 60–70 cm/24–8 in.
Medium-sized eagle, blackish above, white below, with short dark streaks on breast. In flight, black underwing-coverts contrast with white flight feathers; black terminal band to tail. Immature browner above, with rufous head, undertorso and underwing-coverts. Usual call is "kloo-kloo-kloo," also various yelping and barking sounds. Found singly or in pairs; moderately approachable. **Range and habitat:** widespread in AF south of 15° N, apart from far south-west and equatorial forests. Locally common, never numerous, in scrub and woodland, often around rocky prominences. Mainly resident. **Similar species:** Ayres' Hawk Eagle, Booted Eagle (see p 150).

Long-crested Eagle

Lophaetus occipitalis (Accipitridae 52–8 cm/20–3 in.
Small, blackish eagle with long, loosely erect crest on rear of crown. In flight, shows black and white barred tail, white patch at base of upperwing primaries, and black underwing-coverts contrasting with white and gray flight feathers. Immature browner, crest shorter, some white speckling on neck and wings. Various high, sharp, repeated whistles, "ki-ki-ki-ki..." and drawn-out screams, "keeee-eeeer." Single or sometimes in pairs, perching conspicuously; often approachable. **Range and habitat:** widespread in AF south of 15° N, apart from far south-west. Locally common in wooded country, including forest edge and farmland. Basically resident, some wandering.

Lizard Buzzard

Kaupifalco monogrammicus (Accipitridae) 37 cm/15 in.
Small raptor with gray upperparts, head and breast, and white throat crossed by vertical black streak; belly finely barred gray on white; cere and legs red. In flight, shows 2 (sometimes 1) conspicuous white bars on dark tail. Immature buffer than adult, with less well-defined throat streak. Call is far-carrying, ringing whistle "keee-oo keee-oo," also "doo-doo-doo..." Single, sometimes paired, still-hunting from high perches; sometimes inconspicuous in dense canopies, sometimes shy. **Range and habitat:** AF within 15° of Equator, reaching 30° S in east. Quite common in well-wooded areas. Basically resident, moving locally or nomadically. **Similar species:** Gabar Goshawk.

Brown Snake-Eagle

Circaetus cinereus (Accipitridae) 71 cm/28 in.
Medium-sized eagle, darkish brown at rest, with large yellow eyes, large owl-like head and bare whitish legs. In flight, easily identified by heavily barred tail, and contrast between dark body plumage and silvery flight feathers. Immature paler, may have whitish mottling on undertorso, and streaking on crown. Call is drawn-out "zeee-oooo" whistle; also guttural "tok." Singly, usually perching conspicuously; sometimes retiring. **Range and habitat:** widespread in AF south of 15° N, except western equatorial forests and far south. Quite uncommon in dry, open scrub and woodland. Basically resident. **Similar species:** immature Bateleur, Short-toed Eagle.

Bateleur

Terathopius ecaudatus (Accipitridae) 60–70 cm/24–8 in.
Striking, medium-sized eagle, mainly black at rest, with large owl-like head, bright red legs and facial skin, and bright chestnut tail and mantle. In flight, readily identified by long pointed wings, virtual lack of tail and habitual sideways rocking action; underwings blazing white, with narrow black trailing edge in female and much broader edge in male. Immature brown, tail longer than adult's. Generally silent, sometimes barking. Single or paired, usually in conspicuous low gliding flight; not shy. **Range and habitat:** widespread in AF south of 15° N, except Congo forests and far south. Common in open habitats, including woodland. Basically resident. **Similar species:** Brown Snake-Eagle.

African Fish-Eagle

Haliaeetus vocifer (Accipitridae) 66–75 cm/26–9 in.
Large eagle with white head, mantle, breast and tail; shoulders and belly deep chestnut, flight feathers blackish. In flight, distinctive broad-winged, short-tailed silhouette. Immature initially brown, developing white areas of adult plumage with brown mottling and streaking. Call is loud, 3- or 4-part, ringing gull-like scream. Paired, sometimes Single, perching prominently, noisy, quite approachable. **Range and habitat:** widespread in AF south of 16° N. Locally common around fish-bearing waters. Some resident, most disperse after breeding to even small seasonal waters. **Similar species:** Palm-nut Vulture, Bald Eagle (see pp 58, 192).

Augur Buzzard

Buteo augur (Accipitridae) 45–53 cm/18–21 in.
Large buzzard with blackish upperparts, rather short reddish tail, and barred panel in upperwing secondaries; 2 distinct color phases occur; commoner pale morph mainly white below, rarer dark phase mainly black. Distinctive flight silhouette, with broad wings often held above body, and short, broad tail. Immature brown above and on tail, with dark markings below. Call is far-carrying high crowing. Single or paired; not shy. **Range and habitat:** eastern and southern AF, from Ethiopia to East Africa and scattered/areas at 10–25° S. Common in open habitats, usually near hills and rocky outcrops. Basically nonmigratory. **Similar species:** Red-backed Hawk and Jackal Buzzard.

Little Sparrowhawk

Accipiter minullus (Accipitridae) 23–5 cm/9–10 in.
Very small sparrowhawk, size only of oriole; gray above, with 2 conspicuous white spots on black tail; below white, finely barred rufous on breast and belly; eye, cere and legs yellow. White rump visible in flight. Immature brown above, with tail spots and narrow white rump; heavily spotted below. Often silent; call is repeated high "kee." Found singly, sometimes in pairs; small, unobtrusive, overlooked in dense canopies, often retiring. **Range and habitat:** AF, widespread in moist areas to south of Congo basin, and north to East Africa, Ethiopia. Usually uncommon, in dense woodlands. Basically nonmigratory. **Similar species:** Red-thighed Sparrowhawk.

Eastern-Chanting Goshawk

Melierax poliopterus (Accipitridae) 50–60 cm/20–4 in.
Large goshawk with upright stance and long orange or red legs; upperparts and breast pale gray, belly finely barred gray on white; cere yellow to orange-red. In flight, shows black wing tips and tail and white rump; shallow wing-beats. Immature browner, with streaked breast and more heavily barred belly. Chanting is loud, melodious piping, accelerating to crescendo then fading, given from perch or in flight in breeding season. Single or paired, perching prominently; not shy. **Range and habitat:** north-eastern AF, in East Africa, Ethiopia, Somalia. Common in open scrub and woodland. Basically nonmigratory. **Similar species:** Dark-Chanting Goshawk.

Crowned Hawk-Eagle

Martial Eagle

African Hawk-Eagle

Long-crested Eagle

Brown Snake-Eagle

Lizard Buzzard

Bateleur

African Fish-Eagle

Augur Buzzard

Eastern-Chanting Goshawk

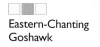

Little Sparrowhawk
female at nest

African Harrier-Hawk

Polyboroides typus (Accipitridae) 61–6 cm/24–6 in.
Quite large, blue-gray raptor with bare yellow facial skin, lax crest on rear of small head, and finely barred abdomen. In flight, shows black tips and trailing edges to broad wings, and white bar on black tail. Immature uniformly brown or mottled paler, sometimes warm buff below. Generally silent; long quavering whistle "keeeeeeeee" in flight. Single or sometimes paired, foraging on tree-trunks and cliff faces, thrusting long legs into holes and nests; quite retiring, unobtrusive. **Range and habitat:** widespread in AF south of 15° N, apart from dry south-west. At best locally common, in well-wooded areas. Basically nonmigratory. **Similar species:** Madagascar Harrier-Hawk.

Red-necked Falcon

Falco chicquera (Falconidae) 30–6 cm/12–14 in.
Small falcon with rufous crown and nape, and warm buff wash on cream breast; remainder of plumage blue-gray above and white below, with fine dark barring. In flight, shows dark subterminal bar to pale tail. Immature browner, some streaking below. Call is shrill "kee-kee-kee-kee. . .." Single, paired or in family parties; sometimes unobtrusive, shy. **Range and habitat:** widely distributed in India; widespread in AF south of 15° N, apart from Congo forests of west. Uncommon in low, open, mainly dry country, often near palm trees. Basically resident, and wandering. **Similar species:** Lanner Falcon.

Pygmy Falcon

Polihierax semitorquatus (Falconidae) 19 cm/7½ in.
Tiny falcon, only size of shrike, male gray above with white face and underparts, female with chestnut mantle. In flight, conspicuous white rump; tail and flight feathers black, spotted white. Immature as female, washed warm buff on breast. Call sharp and high-pitched "kee-kee-kee....," or "koo-koo-koo.. .." Single or paired, or in small, loose parties, perching conspicuously, mostly taking prey from ground; moderately approachable. **Range and habitat:** 2 regions of AF: in north-east, from Sudan, Ethiopia and Somalia south to Tanzania; in south, in Namibia, Botswana, South Africa. Fairly common in open, dry bushed and wooded country, breeding in old weaver nests. Basically resident. **Similar species:** White-rumped Falcon.

FOWL-LIKE BIRDS Galliformes

Stone Partridge

Ptilopachus petrosus (Phasianidae) 25 cm/10 in.
Unique medium-sized gamebird, resembling partridge; mainly dark brown inconspicuously speckled buff, with pale buff or cream lower breast and belly; legs red; walks and runs with tail cocked upward like bantam. Rarely flies. Immature as adult, barred above and below. Noisy; characteristic high, piping call "ooeeet-ooeeet-ooeeet." In small parties, running on rocks and cliffs; very shy, betrayed by calls. **Range and habitat:** northern AF, at 6–16° N, from Senegal east to Ethiopia, north-west Kenya. Locally common on rocky hills and cliffs in dry country. Very sedentary. **Similar species:** Crested Francolin.

Swainson's Francolin

Francolinus swainsonii (Phasianidae) 34–9 cm/13–15 in.
Rather large francolin, best identified by combination of streaked brown plumage, conspicuous red bare facial skin and neck, black legs and bill. Female smaller. Immature has face and neck feathered buffy white with white spotting elsewhere. A noisy bird, producing a loud crowing "krraa krraa" repeated several times and usually delivered at dusk from a branch or anthill. Otherwise shy, found on ground in pairs or small groups. **Range and habitat:** southern AF. Common on cultivated land, woodland edges and open secondary growth. Nonmigratory. **Similar species:** 34 other AF francolins.

Yellow-necked Francolin

Francolinus leucoscepus (Phasianidae) 33–6 cm/13–14 in.
Large francolin with upright stance, gray-brown above and buff below, finely streaked white; identified by bare yellow skin on throat, bare red skin around eye, and black legs. In flight, open wing shows large pale patch at base of primaries. Immature duller, bare skin paler, legs brown. Call is loud and frequently uttered, retching, grating "gruaaaark," often at twilight. Paired or small flocks, foraging openly

on ground; moderately approachable, bold. **Range and habitat:** north-eastern AF, in Ethiopia, Somalia, Kenya, Tanzania. Common in many less open habitats. Nonmigratory. **Similar species:** Gray-breasted and Red-necked Francolins.

Helmeted Guineafowl

Numida meleagris (Phasianidae) 52–7 cm/20–2 in.
Large, plump gamebird with fine white spotting on dark gray plumage, rendered unmistakable by combination of horny casque protruding from crown, and naked red and blue head and neck, with pendulous wattles near base of bill. Immature browner, casque reduced or absent, downy feathering on neck. Loud, frequent call is grating "keerrrrr." In flocks of up to hundreds, foraging on open ground; sometimes approachable, bold. **Range and habitat:** WP in Morocco, where fast declining; widespread in AF south of 15° N (including south-west Arabia), apart from Congo forests and extreme south-west. Common in many wooded habitats, usually near water. Resident. **Similar species:** other guineafowl in AF.

Vulturine Guineafowl

Acryllium vulturinum (Phasianidae) 58–61 cm/23–4 in.
Long-tailed guineafowl, with gray head and neck naked save for tuft of rich brown, downy feathering on nape; feathers of mantle and breast elongated and striped black, white and bright cobalt-blue; remainder of plumage "dark gray, finely spotted white. Immature browner, with more downy feathering on head. Often silent; loud, high-pitched alarm "chink chink…chickerr." Flocks on ground; not shy. **Range and habitat:** north-eastern AF, in Somalia, Ethiopia, Kenya, Tanzania. Common in open bushed and wooded areas, often far from water. Resident. **Similar species:** Helmeted Guineafowl.

CRANES, RAILS AND ALLIES Gruiformes

Small Buttonquail

Turnix sylvatica (Turnicidae) 14–15 cm/5½–6 in.
Small, quail-like bird with pale eyes, female brown above with rufous breast, white belly and heart-shaped spots on flanks. Male duller. In brief low flights, shows brown rump and pale upperwing-coverts. Immature duller; breast spotted. Call is ventrilo-quial hooting, "hoom." Single, paired or in small parties, foraging on ground; skulking and often overlooked. **Range and habitat:** WP in Portugal, Spain, North Africa, declining rapidly; also OR east to Philippines. Widespread in AF south of 15° N, apart from Congo forests and far south-west. Locally common in open grassy habitats. Resident or intra-African migrant. **Similar species:** Hottentot Buttonquail, true quails (see pp 154, 244, 246). **Not illustrated.**

Black Crake

Amaurornis flavirostris (Rallidae) 20–3 cm/8–9 in.
Medium-sized black crake with red eyes, legs and feet, and greenish yellow bill. Immature grayer with pale throat, duskier bill and legs. Call is deep, straining, growling grunt, repeated 2 or 3 times; also various clucking notes, and sharp "chik" alarm. Single, paired or in small, loose parties, foraging on ground; not secretive, sometimes approachable. **Range and habitat:** widespread in AF south of 15° N. Common, most easily seen crake, on swamp with open water and some vegetation. Basically nonmigratory. **Similar species:** Blackish Rail (see p 108).

Red-knobbed Coot

Fulica cristata (Rallidae) 42 cm/17 in.
Medium-sized, thickset black waterbird with conspicuous white bill and frontal shield, and 2 dark red knobs (often very inconspicuous) on forecrown; legs and lobed feet greenish to grayish. Immature gray-brown above, off-white below. Call is resonant, penetrating "kronnk." Single, paired or in flocks up to thousands, swimming, diving, seldom flying; not shy. **Range and habitat:** WP in Spain, Morocco, Algeria, Tunisia, but declining. Widespread in AF south of 10° S, and north through East Africa to Ethiopia. Common, seasonally abundant, on inland waters. Moves extensively when not breeding. **Similar species:** Moorhen, Red-fronted Coot (see p 154).

African Harrier-Hawk

Stone Partridge

Red-necked Falcon

Pygmy Falcon (female

Swainson's Francolir

Yellow-necked Francolin

Helmeted Guineafowl

Vulturine Guineafow

Black Crake

Red-knobbed Coot

Black Crowned-Crane

Balearica pavonina **(Gruidae)** 105 cm/41 in.

Medium-sized crane with golden crest on rear of crown, and bright red and white throat and face wattles; rest of plumage mainly gray, with large white patch in closed wing. In flight, distinctively drooping neck, and white wing-coverts. Immature smaller, browner, lacking wattles. Call is 2-note honk, "graa-oww." Paired when nesting, or flocks up to 200, foraging in open; moderately approachable. **Range and habitat:** widespread in AF south of 16° N, apart from Congo forests and far south-west. Locally common on marshes and other damp habitats. Resident, moving locally. Classified as near threatened because of population decline and dramatic range reduction in western subpopulation. Across range affected by habitat loss and degradation, pesticides and hunting. **Similar species:** South African Crowned-Crane.

Blue Crane

Grus paradisea **(Gruidae)** 105 cm/41 in.

Medium-sized, pale blue-gray crane with pinkish bill, white crown and elongated dark gray tertials curving down behind wings; legs black. In flight, dark flight feathers contrast with pale wing-coverts. Immature paler, lacking tertial elongation; crown warm brown. Call is loud, high-pitched "craaaaaarrk." Paired when breeding, or in flocks up to hundreds, foraging in open; not shy. **Range and habitat:** 2 areas of southern AF: Etosha, northern Namibia; South Africa, from Cape Province to Transvaal. Common in grasslands. Resident, moving outside breeding season. Classified as vulnerable because of rapid recent population decline due to poisoning and afforestation of its breeding habitat. **Similar species:** Demoiselle Crane.

Wattled Crane

Bugeranus carunculatus **(Gruidae)** 120 cm/47 in.

Large crane, gray above and black below, with white breast and neck, dark gray crown, and reddish and white wattle hanging from naked, dark reddish face; legs black. Flies reluctantly. Immature has wattles reduced or absent, crown white. Generally silent; occasional loud, ringing "horoonnk." Found in pairs, or in flocks up to hundreds, foraging in open; shy. **Range and habitat:** 3 areas of AF: Ethiopian highlands; central south, from Namibia to Zimbabwe; eastern South Africa. Uncommon around lakes and marshes, and on damp grasslands. Resident. Classified as vulnerable due to presumed population decline. Information on population trends, however, is conflicting.

African Finfoot

Podica senegalensis **(Heliornithidae)** 46–53 cm/18–21 in.

Cormorantlike waterbird with conspicuous red bill, legs and lobed feet, whitish stripe on side of neck and dark, white-spotted wings and back; underparts white. Male has head and neck dark blue-gray. Female smaller, chin and foreneck whitish. Immature as female but browner, less spotted. Generally silent; occasional hard "bak," weaker "kiiii." Single or paired, foraging beneath overhanging riverine vegetation; secretive, often overlooked. **Range and habitat:** widespread in AF south of 10° N. Uncommon on quiet inland waters with dense overhanging vegetation. Nonmigratory, moving locally. **Similar species:** other finfoots, Sungrebe (see p 108).

Kori Bustard

Ardeotis kori **(Otididae)** 120–50 cm/47–59 in.

Large, crested bustard, gray-brown above with black and white tips to wing-coverts; neck finely vermiculated gray-white, with peculiarly thick appearance due to loose feathering; underparts white. Female smaller. Flies reluctantly but strongly. Immature spotted above. Generally silent; displaying male produces deep grunting, "vum, vum, vum, vummmmmmm." Found singly, in pairs or small, loose parties, walking in open areas; quite retiring. **Range and habitat:** 2 regions of AF: widespread south of 15° S; also north-east, from Tanzania to Ethiopia. Locally common in open country. Mainly resident. **Similar species:** Arabian Bustard.

White-bellied Bustard

Eupodotis senegalensis **(Otididae)** 53 cm/21 in.

Small, handsome bustard, brown on back and wings, with white belly. Male has dark cap, white face, black throat and blue-gray foreneck; female has brown cap, with face, throat and foreneck white or pale brown. Immature resembles female. Call is far-carrying squawk, "aarwarka, aawarka." Paired or in family parties, walking; shy, betrayed by

call. **Range and habitat:** many areas of AF within 17° of Equator; also eastern South Africa. Rather local and uncommon in grassland and open bush. Resident. **Similar species:** 3 similar small bustards in AF.

Hartlaub's Bustard

Lissotis hartlaubii **(Otididae)** 53 cm/21 in. Small bustard.

Male has black underparts, foreneck, cheek patch and line behind eye; back and wings brown; in flight, wings white, rump and tail blackish. Female brown above, underparts and foreneck white, rump and tail grayish. Immature undescribed. Call is quiet "pop.. . hoooomm." Single, paired, occasionally loose groups; sometimes approachable. **Range and habitat:** north-eastern AF, from Tanzania to Sudan, Ethiopia. Local or uncommon in grassland and open bush, usually in dry areas. Resident. **Similar species:** 3 similar AF bustards.

Red-crested Bustard

Eupodotis ruficrista **(Otididae)** 53 cm/21 in. Small bustard.

Male brown above with whitish V markings; belly black; reddish pink crest on nape. Female similar, lower breast white; crest less developed. Immature not described. Male's call is series of piercing, mournful whistles; also croaking duet. Single or paired, on ground; secretive, retiring, betrayed by call. **Range and habitat:** 3 regions of AF: north-east, from Tanzania to Ethiopia; northern tropics, from Senegal to Sudan; at 15–30° S. Common in dry, densely bushed areas. Resident. **Similar species:** 3 similar AF bustards.

SHOREBIRDS, GULLS, AUKS Charadriiformes

Spotted Thick-knee

Burhinus capensis **(Burhinidae)** 43 cm/17 in.

Large stone-curlew, upperparts buff with profuse dark spotting; underparts white, washed buff on breast; legs, large eyes and base of blackish bill yellow. In flight, wings conspicuously black and white. Immature streaked dark above. Call, usually at night, is series of shrill whistles "chi-weee," increasingly loud then fading. Found paired on ground; mainly nocturnal, resting in shade by day; unobtrusive. **Range and habitat:** widespread in AF south of 16° N, apart from western forests. Sometimes common, never numerous, in open scrub and woodland. Resident, moving locally. **Similar species:** other thick-knees (see pp 110, 160, 294).

Senegal Thick-knee

Burhinus senegalensis **(Burhinidae)** 37 cm/15 in.

Medium-sized, upper-parts gray-brown, thinly streaked dark, with grayish panel in closed wing; underparts white, streaked on breast; legs, large eyes and base of bill yellow. In flight, black flight feathers contrast with pale wing-coverts. Immature more finely streaked. Call is series of high "pee" notes. Single, in pairs or small flocks, active by day and night; unobtrusive. **Range and habitat:** at 5–16° N in AF, reaching WP along Nile, in Egypt. Locally common near water in bushed or grassy habitats. Resident, and local migrant. **Similar species:** Other thick-knees (see p 110, 160, 294).

African Jacana

Actophilornis africanus **(Jacanidae)** 28 cm/11 in.

Striking gallinulelike bird, with chestnut-brown body, white foreneck and face; bill and frontal shield bright bluish white; long legs and elongated toes, grayish. Immature brown above, white below, tinged golden on breast; crown and hindneck blackish. Strident screeching, trilling and grating calls. Single, in pairs or flocks; noisy, somewhat retiring. **Range and habitat:** widespread in AF south of 16° N. Common on fresh waters with floating vegetation where they forage. Resident, or local migrant. **Similar species:** other jacanas (see pp 110, 248, 294).

Lesser Jacana

Microparra capensis **(Jacanidae)** 15 cm/6 in.

Sparrow-sized, brown above with black rear-neck, chestnut cap and white eyebrow; underparts white, long legs, toes greenish. In short flights, shows white trailing edge to blackish wings. Immature has crown dark, nape golden. Often silent; low grunt, "pruk." Found singly, in pairs or loose parties, foraging on floating vegetation or swampy shores; shy. **Range and habitat:** scattered areas of AF from Niger to Ethiopia, and through East Africa to Angola, South Africa. Local, usually uncommon, on fresh waters with floating vegetation. Resident or local migrant. **Similar species:** other jacanas (see pp 110, 248, 294).

Black Crowned-Crane

Blue Crane

Wattled Crane

African Finfoot

Kori Bustard

White-bellied Bustard

Hartlaub's Bustard (male displaying)

Red-crested Bustard

Spotted Thick-knee

Senegal Thick-knee

African Jacana

Lesser Jacana

Greater Painted-Snipe

Rostratula benghalensis (Rostratulidae) 24–8 cm/9½–11 in.
Medium-sized, snipelike wader; bill long, with slightly drooping tip. Female gray-green above with dark rufous head and neck, and conspicuous broad white stripes through eye and center-crown, and on mantle; underparts white with black breast band. Male smaller, grayer, lacking rufous coloration. Flight low, rail-like, with dangling legs and showing dark, rounded, buff-spotted wings. Immature as male, lacking breast band. Often silent; sharp "chek." Found singly or in pairs, unobtrusive in marshes; shy and often overlooked. **Range and habitat:** WP in Egypt; east through OR to Philippines, also AU. Widespread in AF south of 15° N, apart from Congo forests and far south-west. Local and uncommon along quiet swampy margins where vegetation provides refuge. Resident or migrant. **Similar species:** South American Painted-snipe.

African Oystercatcher

Haematopus moquini (Haematopodidae) 45 cm/18 in.
Large, thickset, glossy black wader with red eyes, long straight orange-red bill, and purplish red legs. Immature browner, legs grayish. Loud piping calls "tee-weeep, tee-weeep," with sharper "tik tik" alarm notes. Found singly or in small parties on open shores; somewhat shy. **Range and habitat:** far southern AF, on coasts of Namibia and South Africa. Locally common along coastline of mainland and offshore islands. Basically nonmigratory; breeds in more remote areas. **Similar species:** other black oystercatchers (see p 294).

White-fronted Plover

Charadrius marginatus (Charadriidae) 18 cm/7 in.
Small plover, sandy brown above with narrow white collar, white forehead and thin dark eye stripe; underparts white, sometimes washed buff on breast; bill and legs black. Male has darker crown than female. Immature paler on crown, all white below. Flight call is softly piped "twi-it," also sharp alarm. Found singly or in pairs, flocking in off-season, on open shores; sometimes approachable, can be unobtrusive. **Range and habitat:** widespread in AF south from Kenya, Zaire, Niger and Senegal. Common or locally so on open, sandy seashores, also around large inland waters. Basically resident. **Similar species:** other *Charadrius* plovers (see pp 62, 110, 156,294).

Kittlitz's Plover

Charadrius pecuarius (Charadriidae) 16 cm/6½ in.
Small plover, gray-brown above with conspicuous white stripe above eye extending back to form complete white collar around hindneck; bill, legs and eye stripe black; underparts white with buff or orangish breast. Immature has head brownish, underparts white. Flight call is plaintive piping, "chip-eeep." Single, paired or in loose flocks on open flats; can be approachable, sometimes overlooked. **Range and habitat:** WP in Egypt; widespread in AF south of 16° N, with exception of Congo forest regions. Locally common on bare or short grass flats adjacent to inland waters, sometimes marine coast. Resident or local migrant. **Similar species:** White-fronted Plover.

Three-banded Plover

Charadrius tricollaris (Charadriidae) 18 cm/7 in.
Small plover, brown above with white forehead, eyebrow and collar, red eye-ring, and black-tipped red bill; underparts white, with 2 black breast bands; legs pinkish. Immature speckled buff above, with brown head and incomplete breast bands. Flight call is plaintive piping. Single or paired, loosely flocking in some areas, on open shorelines; moderately approachable, can be unobtrusive. **Range and habitat:** widespread in southern AF, and north to East Africa, Sudan, Ethiopia; also Mali, Chad, Cameroon. Common but never numerous on shores of inland waters. Resident or local migrant. **Similar species:** other *Charadrius* plovers (see pp 62, 110, 156, 294).

Crowned Lapwing

Vanellus coronatus (Charadriidae) 30 cm/12 in.
Large plover, identified by conspicuous white ring encircling black crown; upperparts and breast grayish brown, latter with dark lower margin, below which belly is white; black-tipped red bill, conspicuous long red legs. Immature speckled buff above, lacking dark breast margin. Call is strident scream "streeep," rapidly repeated in flight. In pairs and small flocks on open ground; diurnal, but often active and calling at night; noisy, aggressive when nesting, otherwise somewhat retiring. **Range and habitat:** widespread in AF south of 10° S, and through East Africa to Ethiopia, Somalia. Common on open and bushed grasslands, mainly in drier country. Basically resident. **Similar species:** other *Vanellus* plovers (see pp 110, 156, 250, 294).

Spur-winged Plover

Vanellus spinosus (Charadriidae) 26 cm/10 in.
Medium-sized plover, gray-brown above with black cap, and conspicuous vertical black stripe from chin to center of white breast; upper belly black, abdomen white; bill and legs black; wing spur not fieldmark. In flight, prominent white rump and wing-bar. Immature speckled buff above. Call is loud screech, "dee-dee-durrr-it;" sharp "teck" alarm. Found in pairs or small, loose flocks on open ground; rather retiring. **Range and habitat:** WP in Egypt and Near East; widespread in AF at 5–16° N, from Senegal east to Somalia, Kenya. Common on open flats and short grassland near water; rare on exposed seashores. Resident or local migrant. **Similar species:** Long-toed Lapwing.

Blacksmith Plover

Vanellus armatus (Charadriidae) 29 cm/11½ in.
Large plover, black with contrasting white forehead, hindneck and belly, and pale gray mantle and wings; eye reddish brown, bill and legs black. Immature has conspicuous broad, vertical, dark brown stripe on side of white neck; head brown. Call is distinctive, hard, repeated "tink," often blending into scream. Found singly or in pairs, sometimes loose flocks, on open ground; noisy, rather retiring. **Range and habitat:** widespread in AF south of 10° S, and north through Tanzania to Kenya. Common on open flats and grassland near water, but rarely coastal. Resident, or wandering locally. **Similar species:** Long-toed Lapwing.

Wattled Lapwing

Vanellus senegallus (Charadriidae) 34 cm/13 in.
Large, gray-brown plover with conspicuous red and yellow wattles at base of black-tipped yellow bill, prominent white forehead and streaked neck; long yellow legs. In flight, shows prominent white patch on inner wing. Immature has wattles "and forehead white reduced. Call is sharp, shrill, repeated "kweep," often ascending and accelerating; frequently at night. Found singly or in pairs, flocking in off-season; somewhat retiring. **Range and habitat:** widespread in AF south of 15° N, apart from Congo forests, far south-west and much of far east. Locally common on bare ground or grassland, often near water. Resident or local migrant. **Similar species:** White-headed Lapwing.

Black-headed Lapwing

Vanellus tectus (Charadriidae) 25 cm/10 in.
Medium-sized plover, gray-brown above and white below, with upswept black crest on rear of black crown, red wattles at base of black-tipped red bill, vertical black median stripe on white breast, and long maroon legs. In flight, shows white wing-coverts, rump and black-tipped tail. Immature speckled buff and black above. Call is shrill, rasping "kerr, kerr, kerr," also "kerr-vick." Found in pairs or small flocks, on open ground; sometimes approachable. **Range and habitat:** widespread in AF at 10–17° N, from Senegal to Somalia, Kenya. Locally common in dry, open and bushed habitats. Nonmigratory, or moving locally. **Similar species:** Spur-winged Plover.

Long-toed Lapwing

Vanellus crassirostris (Charadriidae) 30 cm/12 in.
Large plover, brown above, with striking white face and throat contrasting with black hindneck and breast; eyes red, bill pinkish with dark tip; long, dull red legs with elongated toes. In flight, wings appear mostly white. Immature not described. Call is plaintive whistle, "wheeeet;" sharper "tickkk" alarm. Found in pairs or small groups, foraging on floating vegetation or open ground; wary, often retiring. **Range and habitat:** mainly eastern AF, from Mozambique and Zambia north to East Africa, south Sudan; also Angola, Chad. Uncommon to locally common around permanently swampy areas with floating vegetation. Nonmigratory or local migrant.

Greater Painted-Snipe

African Oystercatcher

White-fronted Plover

Kittlitz's Plover

Three-banded Plover

Crowned Lapwing

Long-toed Lapwing

Spur-winged Plover

Blacksmith Plover

Wattled Lapwing

Black-headed Lapwing

African Snipe

Gallinago nigripennis (Scolopacidae) 30 cm/12 in.
Medium-sized wader with long, straight bill; upper-parts blackish brown with buff streaking, underparts white. Flight fluttering. Immature less boldly marked. Generally silent; characteristic "ts-uck" when flushed; deep "drumming" produced by tail feathers during aerial display. Single, in pairs or loose parties, on mud in marshy vegetation; somewhat nocturnal; secretive and often overlooked. **Range and habitat:** widespread in AF south of 10° S, apart from dry south-west; also East Africa, Ethiopia. Locally common in marshes, inundated grassland. Resident **Similar species:** other snipe (see pp 110, 160, 250).

Crab Plover

Dromas ardeola (Dromadidae) 38 cm/15 in.
Large, thickset, white wader with black mantle, long grayish legs and heavy black bill. In flight, contrasting black flight feathers. Immature browner, with dark streaking on crown. Call is sharp "cheerook," also constant chatter and barking. In small parties, flocks reaching hundreds at times, on open shores; diurnal, active at night; retiring. **Range and habitat:** breeds in WP on shores of Arabia, then migrates August–April to western India, Indian ocean islands and east coast of AF south to Mozambique and (stragglers) South Africa. Locally common on sandy and muddy marine shores. **Similar species:** Pied Avocet (see p 156).

Temminck's Courser

Cursorius temminckii (Glareolidae) 20 cm/8 in.
Rather small, brown courser with bright chestnut cap, black and white eye stripes extending to nape, rufous upper belly, black central belly and white vent; legs long and gray-white. Immature streaked black on crown, speckled buff above, less black on belly. Generally silent; grating, metallic flight call "eerrrr-errr." In pairs or small flocks, on open ground; rather retiring. **Range and habitat:** widespread in AF south of 15° N, except equatorial forests and far south-west. Locally common on short grassland, including recently burnt ground. Mainly resident or nomadic. **Similar species:** other coursers (see p 248).

Double-banded Courser

Smutsornis africanus (Glareolidae) 21 cm/8 in.
Small, pale courser, mottled buff and black above, pale buff below with 2 black breast bands, long whitish legs. In flight, shows white rump and rufous patch in wing. Immature as adult, initially lacking breast bands. Generally silent; low piping "peee-peeee." Single, in pairs or scattered groups, on open ground; often active at night; unobtrusive. **Range and habitat:** 3 areas of AF: Ethiopia and Somalia; southern Kenya and Tanzania; far south-west. Locally common in dry, open or sparsely bushed plains. Resident. **Similar species:** Three-banded and Jerdon's Coursers.

Bronze-winged Courser

Rhinoptilus chalcopterus (Glareolidae) 27 cm/10½ in.
Large courser, brown above and white below, with broad dark streak across white face, brown breast band with blackish lower margin, and dull red legs. In flight, shows white rump, black flight feathers and violet primary tips. Immature speckled buff above, washed buff below. Call is piping "jee-koo-eet." Single, in pairs or small parties; nocturnal, spending day under bushes; retiring, often overlooked. **Range and habitat:** widespread in AF south of 15° N, except Horn, Congo forests and far south-west. Uncommon in bushed and wooded country. Resident and intra-African migrant. **Similar species:** Crowned Lapwing

Egyptian Plover

Pluvianus aegyptius (Glareolidae) 21 cm/8 in.
Squat, short-legged courser, gray above with black mantle and cap, and white eyebrows joining on nape; underparts buffish white with thin black breast band; legs grayish. In flight, black bar on pale wing. Immature as adult, speckled brown above, wing-coverts rusty. Call is loud, rapidly repeated "churrsk." Found in pairs or flocks on open ground; usually tame. **Range and habitat:** widespread in AF at 5–15° N from Senegal to Ethiopia, also south to Congo, Zaire. Locally common around those rivers and lakes with emergent bars and short vegetation. Resident and intra-African migrant.

Rock Pratincole

Glareola nuchalis (Glareolidae) 19 cm/7½ in.
Small pratincole, dark brown above, with conspicuous white collar (rufous some regions) from cheeks around hindneck; gray breast merges with white abdomen; legs red. In flight, shows stubby forked tail, white rump. Immature speckled, legs black, lacking collar. Call is shrill "pee-pee-pee-. . .;" alarm a faint "tip-tip-tip." In small flocks on open shores and rocks; approachable, can be unobtrusive. **Range and habitat:** widespread in AF from Sierra Leone and Angola east to Uganda, Zaire, Mozambique; also Niger, Chad, Ethiopia. Locally common on rivers and lakes with exposed rocks. Resident and intra-African migrant. **Similar species:** other pratincoles (see pp 160, 250).

Gray-headed Gull

Larus cirrocephalus (Laridae) 41 cm/16 in.
Medium-sized gull, breeding adult with pale gray hood and red bill and legs; upperwing gray with black tip and white flash toward base of primaries. Nonbreeding adult has hood indistinct. Immature has white head with dark spot on ear-coverts; dark tail band. Call is loud, raucous "kraaarr." In flocks up to thousands; not shy. **Range and habitat:** widely distributed NT; widespread in eastern AF from South Africa to Sudan, Ethiopia; also western coasts. Common on coasts and inland waters; scavenger at harbors, rubbish tips. Resident and intra-African migrant. **Similar species:** 3 similar red-billed gulls in AF.

Sooty Gull

Larus hemprichii (Laridae) 44 cm/17 in.
Medium-sized gull, breeding adult gray-brown above with blackish brown hood; collar, rump and tail white; bill yellow-green with black band and red tip; legs greenish yellow. Nonbreeding adult has paler hood, more diffuse collar. Immature has black tail, lacks collar. Call is loud scream, "kee-aawr." In flocks, up to hundreds, on open coasts; scavenges at harbors, not shy. **Range and habitat:** breeds coasts of Arabia and north-east AF south to Kenya, before moving down east AF coast to Tanzania October–May. Seasonally common. **Similar species:** White-eyed Gull.

White-cheeked Tern

Sterna repressa (Laridae) 32–7 cm/13–15 in.
Medium-sized tern, breeding adult dark gray, with black cap above conspicuous broad white streak extending from lores to nape; bill black with reddish base, legs red. Nonbreeding adult has whitish speckled forehead and whitish underparts. Immature as nonbreeding adult, dark leading edge to upperwing; underparts white. Call is harsh, loud "kee-errr" or "kee-leeek." In flocks on open coasts; retiring. **Range and habitat:** breeds coasts of western India, Arabia and north-east AF June–October then disperses, some south to Tanzania. Seasonally common. **Similar species:** Antarctic and Whiskered Terns (see p 296).

Greater-crested Tern

Sterna bergii (Laridae) 50 cm/20 in.
Breeding adult pale or dark gray above with white forehead, black cap and yellow bill; white below, legs black. Nonbreeding; cap flecked white, neck speckled grayish. In flight, shows gray rump and deeply forked tail uniform with wings. Immature heavily marked above, white below; bill yellowish. Often silent; hard "tik-tik," screamed "kreeee." Found in small parties, sometimes singly, on open coasts. **Range and habitat:** coasts of Arabia, east to OR, AU; eastern and far south-western AF coasts. Common. Resident or disperse after breeding. **Similar species:** Lesser Crested Tern, Sandwich Tern (see p 162).

African Skimmer

Rynchops flavirostris (Rynchopidae) 38 cm/15 in.
Medium-sized ternlike species, breeding adult blackish above, white below, long red bill with yellow tip and elongated lower mandible; legs red. Nonbreeding adult has pale hindneck collar. In flight, shows white rump and forked tail, dark wings. Immature speckled buff above, bill and legs yellow. Calls hard "tik," screaming "kreeep." Found in small parties, flocks of 1,000 known, on open shores; retiring. **Range and habitat:** widespread in AF from Senegal, Ethiopia south to Angola, Mozambique. Locally common on inland waters. Intra-African migrant, dispersing after breeding. Population decline resulting from loss of breeding habitat, pesticides, egg-collection, trapping, disturbance and reduced food supply. **Similar species:** other skimmers (see p 68).

African Snipe
(leaving nest)

Crab Plover

Temminck's Courser

Double-banded
Courser

Bronze-winged
Courser

Egyptian Plover

Rock Pratincole

Gray-headed Gull

Sooty Gull

White-cheeked Tern

Greater-crested
Tern (in courtship
display)

African Skimmer

SANDGROUSE Pterocliformes

Chestnut-bellied Sandgrouse

Pterocles exustus (Pteroclididae) 30 cm/12 in.
Medium-sized sandgrouse with long, central tail feathers. Male sandy, with black breast band and chestnut belly. Female vermiculated and streaked, with face and breast band plain buffish; belly dark. In flight, shows dark belly and underwings. Immature as female but grayer, no breast band. Call is musical "gutta gutta.. .." Found in small parties, larger drinking flocks, on open ground, but shy and often overlooked. **Range and habitat:** Egypt, east to Middle East, India; widespread in AF at 10–19° N, from Mauritania east to Somalia, southern Arabia. Locally common in dry, open country. Resident. **Similar species:** Spotted and Black-bellied Sandgrouse.

Yellow-throated Sandgrouse

Pterocles gutturalis (Pteroclididae) 33 cm/13 in.
Large sandgrouse, male gray-brown with custard yellow face and throat bordered by black gorget; belly chestnut-brown. Female with yellowish face, mottled buff and brown above and on breast, belly as male. In flight, shows dark underwing and wedge-shaped tail. Immature as female, more finely mottled above. Call is guttural "gutta;" also "weet-weet." In pairs or small parties, in hundreds when drinking or migrating, on open ground; shy. **Range and habitat:** 3 regions of AF: interior south of 14° S; from Zambia to Tanzania, southern Kenya; Ethiopia. Common or locally so on open grass plains. Resident; intra-African migrant in south.

PIGEONS Columbiformes

Red-eyed Dove

Streptopelia semitorquata (Columbidae) 30 cm/12 in.
Large, gray-brown dove with black collar on hindneck; forecrown pale gray; eye appears dark at any distance. In flight, tail shows terminal band grayish white above, white below. Immature speckled buff above, warm buff below, collar reduced or absent. Distinctive, far-carrying call "coo coo, coo-coo, coo-coo;" shrill "zeeee" when landing. Single or in pairs, small parties foraging on ground, perching in canopies; rather shy. **Range and habitat:** widespread in AF south of 12° N, except far south-west and Congo forests. Common in well-wooded country. Resident. **Similar species:** other *Streptopelia* doves (see pp 164, 252).

Laughing Dove

Streptopelia senegalensis (Columbidae) 24 cm/9½ in.
Small dove with pinkish head, rusty back and blue-gray closed wing; breast pinkish rufous, speckled black at base of neck; abdomen white. In flight, shows rump and wing-coverts blue-gray, flight feathers black; white sides and tip to tail. Immature browner above, grayer below. Call is soft chuckling, "ooooo coo-coo-oo." Single, in pairs or feeding flocks, foraging on ground; unobtrusive, often approachable. **Range and habitat:** widespread India, Middle East, North Africa; AF south of 20° N except Congo forests and arid south-west. Common in reasonably open habitats, including cities. Resident or intra-African migrant. **Similar species:** other *Streptopelia* doves (see pp 164, 252).

Madagascar Green-Pigeon

Treron australis (Columbidae) 30 cm/12 in.
Large, thickset, gray-green or yellow-green pigeon, with mauve carpal patch, red bill and red or yellow legs. Plump, bull-necked silhouette during fast, very direct flight. Immature duller, lacking carpal patch. Call is shrill whistling, "teea-weet teea-weet...," ending with quiet "tok" notes. Found in small parties, foraging parrotlike in dense canopies; camouflaged, often silent and unobtrusive, betrayed by call. **Range and habitat:** widespread in AF south from Senegal, northern Zaire, Ethiopia, Kenya, except far south-west. Common or locally so in wooded country. Resident, moving locally to fruiting trees. **Similar species:** 3 other green pigeons in AF.

Speckled Pigeon

Columba guinea (Columbidae) 33 cm/13 in.
Large gray pigeon with pale chestnut back and wings, latter spotted white; also bare red skin around eye. In flight, prominent pale gray rump. Immature brown, including facial skin. Call is rapid series of high notes, "coo-coo-coo. ..," becoming louder then fading. Found singly or in flocks, foraging on ground, often around habitation; can be approachable. **Range and habitat:** widespread in AF south of 16° N, apart from lowland forest and country between Congo basin and Botswana. Common or locally so near cliffs or buildings, including city centers; foraging in open country. Resident, making long foraging flights. **Similar species:** Rock Pigeon (see p 164).

Namaqua Dove

Oena capensis (Columbidae) 27 cm/10½ in.
Small size and long graduated tail unique among AF doves. Male gray above with black face, throat and breast, purple bill with yellow tip, and white underparts. Female with black bill, face to breast grayish. In rapid, direct flight, shows reddish flight feathers and black and white bars on lower back. Immature as female, heavily spotted above. Often silent; call is soft "cuh-hoooo." Single or in pairs, sometimes flocks, foraging on open ground; often approachable. **Range and habitat:** WP in Near East; widespread in AF (including Arabia) south of 20° N. Common in scrub or open woodland. Resident, local or intra-African migrant.

Emerald-spotted Wood-Dove

Turtur chalcospilos (Columbidae) 20 cm/8 in.
Small, short-tailed, gray-brown dove, paler below, with metallic green spots (often appearing black) visible in closed wing; bill blackish or reddish. In brief low flights, shows reddish flight feathers, black and white bands on back. Call is soft cooing, starting hesitantly, accelerating, dying: "coo-coo...coo...coo-coo...coo...coo . . . coocoocoocoocoocoocoocoocoocoo." Single or in pairs, foraging on ground, often in shade; shy, betrayed by call. **Range and habitat:** widespread in AF south of 15° S, apart from far south-west; and north to East Africa, Ethiopia, Somalia. Common in dry, bushed and wooded country. Resident. **Similar species:** 4 other AF wood doves.

Tambourine Dove

Turtur tympanistria (Columbidae) 23 cm/9 in.
Small dove, male dark brown above with white face, supercilium and underparts. Female grayer about face and breast. In low flight, shows reddish primaries. Immature barred above, gray-brown below with white belly. Call is prolonged, soft cooing, starting deliberately, accelerating, dying: "coo-coo. . .coo-coo. . .coo-coo. . xoocoocoocoocoo . . .." Single or in pairs, foraging on ground in shade, unobtrusive, shy. **Range and habitat:** widespread in AF between 9° N and 15° S, also south to eastern South Africa. Common in dense scrub or woodland. Nonmigratory.

CUCKOOS AND ALLIES Cuculiformes

Dideric Cuckoo

Chrysococcyx caprius (Cuculidae) 19 cm/7½ in.
Small cuckoo, male metallic green above with white eyebrow and red eye; underparts white, barred green on flanks. Female more coppery above, breast washed buff. Immature dull green or rusty above with coral bill; underparts white, streaked or spotted greenish. Call is shrill whistle, "dee-dee-dee deederick." Single, sometimes pairs, perching prominently; brood parasite of, e.g., various weavers; bold, moderately approachable, unobtrusive if not calling. **Range and habitat:** widespread in AF south of 16° N, apart from extreme south-west; summer visitor, southern Arabia. Common in open scrub and woodland. Resident equatorial areas or intra-African migrant. **Similar species:** African Emerald and Klaas' Cuckoos.

Pied Cuckoo

Clamator jacobinus (Cuculidae) 33 cm/13 in.
Large, long-tailed crested cuckoo, black above with white patch in closed wing; white or pale gray below; dark morph black apart from wing patch. Immature brownish above, buff below. Call is loud piping "tleeu" or "tleeu-ip." Single, in pairs or small groups; brood parasite of bulbuls; often noisy. **Range and habitat:** widespread in OR, from India to Burma; widespread in AF south of 16° N, except Congo forests and far south-west. Common in open scrub and woodland. Some resident; most migrant, either intra-African or from OR. **Similar species:** Levaillant's and Great Spotted Cuckoos.

Chestnut-bellied Sandgrouse

Yellow-throated Sandgrouse (two male in foreground)

Laughing Dove

Red-eyed Dove

Speckled Pigeon

Madagascar Green-Pigeon

Namaqua Dove

Emerald-spotted Wood-Dove

Tambourine Dove

Dideric Cuckoo (female)

Pied Cuckoo

Red-chested Cuckoo

Cuculus solitarius (**Cuculidae**) 29 cm/11½ in.
Medium-sized cuckoo, dark gray above with yellow eye-ring, rufous breast and whitish, thinly barred belly. Immature blackish above and about head, with white feather-edgings and nape patch; underparts whitish, thinly barred dark. Call, given day and night, is far-carrying whistle, "wheet wheet whou," rendered "it will rain." Single, sometimes several in same area, usually high in canopies; brood parasite of thrushes; inconspicuous, shy, sometimes approachable, betrayed by call. **Range and habitat:** widespread in AF south of 10° N, apart from Somali and far south-west arid areas. Common or seasonal in wooded country. Resident equatorial areas or intra-African migrant. **Similar species:** red-chested race of Black Cuckoo.

White-browed Coucal

Centropus superciliosus (**Cuculidae**) 44 cm/17 in.
Medium-sized coucal with red eye and long, broad, black tail; wings and back rufous red, underparts white. Some in southern AF have crown to upper mantle bluish black; rest have brownish crown and nape finely streaked white, and broad white eyebrow. Flight low, floundering. Immature has eyebrow and underparts buff. Call is distinctive melodic bubbling, falling in pitch then rising, like water poured from bottle. Single or paired, in dense herbage; skulking, sometimes approachable, betrayed by call. **Range and habitat:** widespread in AF south of 5° S except south-west; and through East Africa to Ethiopia, south-west Arabia. Common in dense grass and thickets, often near water. Mainly nonmigratory. **Similar species:** other coucals see pp 254, 302).

Senegal Coucal

Centropus senegalensis (**Cuculidae**) 40 cm/16 in.
Rather small coucal with red eye, black crown and nape, rufous back and wings, white underparts and long, broad, black tail; dark morph in west AF has brownish throat, rufous underparts. Immature brown and closely barred above with fine white streaking; buffish below. Call is melodic bubbling, descending in pitch then rising, like water poured from bottle. Single or in pairs, low in dense herbage; shy, betrayed by call. **Range and habitat:** southern AF from Botswana to Zambia, Malawi; also between 5° S and 15° N, east to Ethiopia, Kenya; also Nile delta in WP. Local, in dense grass, often away from water. Mainly nonmigratory. **Similar species:** other coucals (see pp 254, 302).

Hartlaub's Turaco

Tauraco hartlaubi (**Musophagidae**) 41 cm/16 in.
Medium-sized, green turaco with blue-black, subtly crested crown bordered below by thin white line extending from gape to ear-coverts; also prominent white spot in front of eye, and bare red circumorbital skin. Brilliant crimson flight feathers conspicuous during brief, flapping flights. Immature unknown. Call is loud, hoarse, high-pitched croaking, "caw-caw-caw-caw. ..," also sharp "chik," "chukkerrrr" and growling. Single or in pairs, small parties at fruiting trees, usually high in canopies, running silently along branches; cryptic, often unobtrusive, betrayed by call. **Range and habitat:** eastern AF, in Kenya, eastern Uganda, north-eastern Tanzania. Locally common in highland forest and adjacent well-timbered areas. Nonmigratory. **Similar species:** 10 similar green turacos in AF.

Ross' Turaco

Musophaga rossae (**Musophagidae**) 51 cm/20 in.
Large, deep violet-black turaco with short erect crimson crest and conspicuous yellow bill, frontal shield and circumorbital skin. Crimson flight feathers conspicuous during usually brief and clumsy flapping flights. Immature duller, crimson only in center of crown, forehead feathered, eye-ring black. Call, sometimes in chorus, is hoarse, quite high-pitched crowing, "caw caw caw. . .." In pairs or small parties, usually high in canopy, running silently along branches; dark, often unobtrusive, betrayed by call. **Range and habitat:** central AF around periphery of Congo basin forests from Angola to Zambia, Kenya, Central African Republic, Cameroon. Locally common in woodland. Nonmigratory. **Similar species:** Violet Turaco.

Great Blue Turaco

Corythaeola cristata (**Musophagidae**) 75 cm/29 in.
Largest and most spectacular turaco, bright gray-blue above with thick black crest, bright yellow bill with red tip, long broad tail with subterminal black band; breast blue merging to greenish yellow below, abdomen chestnut. Brief flapping, gliding flights, often losing height; no red in wings. Immature duller, crest reduced, breast grayish yellow. Loud, far-carrying call begins with deep bubbling trill, then rapid series of croaking "tok" notes. In small parties, high in canopy, climbing and running on branches; noisy or silent, unobtrusive. **Range and habitat:** west and central AF, east from Sierra Leone to the Congo basin and Uganda. Locally common in forest, sometimes near cleared areas. Nonmigratory.

White-bellied Go-away-bird

Corythaixoides leucogaster (**Musophagidae**) 51 cm/20 in.
Large, slim, gray turaco with long crest, white abdomen and long, broad tail. Brief flapping flight, shows conspicuous broad white bar on tail, also white wing-bar; can momentarily resemble raptor. Immature browner, with rather fluffy plumage on belly, head and neck. Call is loud, barking "back, back, go-back," also nasal "wayeerrr, go-wayeerrr. ..." Single, in pairs or small parties, often on elevated, prominent perches; noisy, not skulking but retiring. **Range and habitat:** northeastern AF, from Ethiopia and Somalia to Kenya, Tanzania. Common in dry, open scrub and woodland. Resident or wandering. **Similar species:** 4 other gray turacos.

PARROTS AND RELATIVES Psittaciformes

Gray Parrot

Psittacus erithacus (**Psittacidae**) 30 cm/12 in.
The largest African parrot, gray with boldly contrasting bright scarlet tail; bare whitish facial skin around yellow eyes; pale feather-edgings give overall scaly appearance to plumage. Flight fast, direct, often very high. Immature as adult but eyes gray, tail darker near tip. Calls are high clear whistles and screams, also raucous, screeching alarms. Found in flocks, foraging in canopies; shy. **Range and habitat:** central and western AF, from Kenya and Uganda, through Congo basin, to forests around Gulf of Guinea. Common, locally abundant, in well-wooded areas, including gardens. Nonmigratory, moving only to forage and roost.

Meyer's Parrot

Poicephalus meyeri (**Psittacidae**) 23 cm/9 in.
Medium-sized parrot, brown above with contrasting yellow shoulders and (sometimes) patch on crown; breast brown, abdomen bluish green. In low fast flight, shows conspicuous blue-green rump and yellow underwing-coverts. Immature as adult, but yellow absent on crown, reduced in wing. Calls are raucous screams and shrieks, including distinctive 2-note sound, apparently given in duet by pair. Found in pairs or small parties, foraging in dense canopies, sometimes perching conspicuously; wary, shy, often retiring, betrayed by calls. **Range and habitat:** interior AF, from Angola and Botswana north-east to south-eastern Zaire, East Africa and Ethiopia; also Sudan, Chad. Common or locally so in wooded areas and open country with scattered large trees. Resident. **Similar species:** 5 AF parrots.

Fischer's Lovebird

Agapornis fischeri (**Psittacidae**) 14 cm/½ in.
Sparrow-sized parrot, green above, paler below, with dull yellow collar, brown cap and conspicuous white eye-ring; bill, throat and forehead orange-red. Contrasting blue rump seldom seen in fast, direct, high flight. Immature as adult, duller. Calls are high shrill whistles and twittering. In small parties, occasionally larger numbers, foraging on ground and vegetation; rather wary and retiring, betrayed by calls. **Range and habitat:** eastern AF, in interior northern Tanzania, recently Rwanda, Burundi; also feral populations in Kenya and Tanzania, often hybridizing with Yellow-collared Lovebird A. personata. Common in open woodland and cultivation. Nonmigratory; apparently extending range in Rwanda, Burundi. Classified as near threatened because of major population decline caused by pet trade. **Similar species:** 7 other AF lovebirds and hybrids.

White-browed Coucal

Gray Parrot

Senegal Coucal

Red-chested Cuckoo

Hartlaub's Turaco

Ross' Turaco

White-bellied Go-away-bird

Great Blue Turaco

Meyer's Parrot

Fischer's Lovebird

KINGFISHERS AND ALLIES Coraciiformes

Lilac-breasted Roller
Coracias caudata (**Coraciidae**) 36 cm/14 in.
Medium-sized roller, readily identified by contrast between lilac throat and breast and azure blue abdomen (north-eastern race *lorti* has breast blue, lilac only on throat); forehead and eyebrow whitish, back brown; blue tail has outer 2 feathers elongated to form pointed streamers. In flight, bright blue coverts contrast with dark flight feathers. Immature duller, throat and breast buffish. Call is loud harsh squawk, "zaaak." Single or paired, perching prominently, takes prey from ground; aggressive, often noisy. **Range and habitat:** widespread in AF south of Congo basin, apart from extreme south; also north to East Africa, Ethiopia, Somalia. Common in open scrub and woodland. Resident or intra-African migrant. **Similar species:** 4 blue rollers in AF, European Roller (see p 166).

Rufous-crowned Roller
Coracias naevia (**Coraciidae**) 36 cm/14 in.
Rather large and thickset, square-tailed roller, with brown or greenish crown, white forehead and eyebrow, and maroon-brown underparts profusely streaked white; back and wings olive-gray or greenish, tail dark blue. In flight, shows glossy dark blue and purple wings. Immature browner, underparts more broadly streaked white. Call is loud but hardly strident "grerrr," also "ka-kaaaa." Single or paired, perching prominently, takes prey from ground. Still and quiet or noisy, active. **Range and habitat:** widespread in AF between 15° N and 30° S, apart from Congo forest areas. Rather uncommon or local in open, usually dry, scrub and woodland. Resident or intra-African migrant.

Broad-billed Roller
Eurystomus glaucurus (**Coraciidae**) 27 cm/10½ in.
Small, stocky roller, brown above, lilac below, with azure-blue tail and vent, and broad, bright yellow bill. In flight, brown wing-coverts contrast with dark blue flight feathers; overall appearance like falcon. Immature brownish above and on upper breast, belly and lower breast gray-blue, bill yellowish. Call is nasal "ke-aiow;" also chattering "tikk-k-k-k-r-r-r." Single or paired, sometimes flocks when foraging or migrating, hawking insects on wing, rather crepuscular; perching prominently, sometimes aggressive, noisy. **Range and habitat:** widespread in AF from 15° N south to Angola, eastern South Africa. Locally common in wooded areas. Resident or intra-African migrant. **Similar species:** Dollarbird (see p 256).

Giant Kingfisher
Megaceryle maxima (**Alcedinidae**) 46 cm/18 in.
Crow-sized, by far the largest African kingfisher, with massive black daggerlike bill, shaggy crest and black upperparts speckled white. Male has chestnut breast, white belly with black bars; female has heavily spotted breast, chestnut abdomen. Immature male as adult, speckled black on chestnut breast; immature female as adult, breast less heavily spotted. Call is loud, raucous, laughing or shrieking "tek-tek-tek. ..." Single or in pairs, often unobtrusive in leafy canopy, shy, betrayed by call. **Range and habitat:** widespread in AF south of 15° N, apart from far south-west and Somalia. At best locally common, along wooded edges of rivers and lakes, also coastal lagoons. Resident.

Pied Kingfisher
Ceryle rudis (**Alcedinidae**) 28 cm/11 in.
2 nd largest African kingfisher, strikingly black and white with substantial black bill and shaggy crest. Male has white underparts with thick black breast band above thinner; female similar, with single thick band, usually incomplete. Immature as female, throat and breast speckled dark brown. Call is high-pitched, squeaky chattering, "kweek-kweek-kweek. . .," often in chorus. In pairs or small, loose parties, perching prominently by water, hovering high and plunging for fish; noisy, often approachable. **Range and habitat:** from Near and Middle East to India, China; also Nile in North Africa; widespread in AF south of 15° N, apart from far south-west. Common, or locally numerous, around open fresh or sea water. Resident or intra-African migrant.

Malachite Kingfisher
Alcedo cristat (**Alcedinidae**) 14 cm/5½ in.
Small kingfisher, ultramarine above with often inconspicuous crest,

dark cap extending down to eyes, red bill and white patch on neck; underparts rufous orange with white throat. Immature darker above, browner below, speckled dark on breast, bill black. Flight call is sharp "teek;" chittering song, often in duet. Single or paired, perching openly at waterside, but often quiet, unobtrusive; moderately approachable. **Range and habitat:** widespread in AF south of 15° N, apart from far south-west and parts of Congo basin. Common in open fringing vegetation around water bodies. Resident or local migrant. **Similar species:** 5 similar kingfishers in AF, Kingfisher (see p 166).

African Pygmy-Kingfisher
Ispidina picta (**Alcedinidae**) 13 cm/5 in.
Small kingfisher, ultramarine above with rufous orange eyebrow and hindneck, diffuse mauve wash on ear-coverts, white spot on side of neck, and red bill; underparts rufous orange with white chin and throat. Immature as adult but speckled blackish above, paler below, bill blackish. Often silent; call, mainly in flight, is high squeak, "seep." Single or paired, often perched in low and inconspicuous situations; quiet, shy, overlooked. **Range and habitat:** widespread in AF between 15° N and 20° S, reaching 30° S along south-east coast. Locally common in variety of dense habitats, including forest far from water. Resident, or intra-African migrant. **Similar species:** 5 AF kingfishers.

Woodland Kingfisher
Halcyon senegalensis (**Alcedinidae**) 23 cm/9 in.
Medium-sized kingfisher, pale blue above with pale gray hood (latter can be washed pale blue or brown according to race) and extensive black "shoulder" in closed wing; large bill has upper mandible red, lower black; underparts whitish, legs black. In flight, striking black and brilliant azure contrast in open wings. Immature has breast and flanks washed buffish with dusky vermiculation, lower mandible sometimes patchily reddish. Loud distinctive call is high note followed by descending trill, "chi, chiiiiirrrr." Single or paired, often perching prominently, or unobtrusive. **Range and habitat:** widespread in AF between 15° N and 22° S, east to Ethiopia, Kenya and range of allopatric Mangrove Kingfisher *H. senegaloides*. Common in scrub and woodland, often near water. Mainly resident near Equator or intra-African migrant. **Similar species:** Mangrove, Blue-breasted and White-throated Kingfishers (see p 256).

Gray-headed Kingfisher
Halcyon leucocephala (**Alcedinidae**) 20 cm/8 in.
Medium-sized, red-billed kingfisher, with gray or light brown head and breast, black back and shoulders, brilliant cobalt-blue rump, tail and flight feathers; belly rich chestnut. Immature is rather duller, with buffy neck, face and breast mottled with dark gray, belly is buff and bill dusky red. Calls include a clear, repeated "piuu" and some chattering notes. Song is a rather weak trill. Single or paired, perches prominently, takes prey from the ground; sometimes quiet and unobtrusive. **Range and habitat:** AF, widespread but largely absent from Congo basin, South Africa and parts of East Africa. Common in woodland, riverine thickets, wooded grassland and forest edge. Resident and local migrant. **Similar species:** 6 AF kingfishers.

Striped Kingfisher
Halcyon chelicuti (**Alcedinidae**) 18 cm/7 in.
Rather dull smallish kingfisher, with streaked, gray-brown cap divided from brown back by whitish collar; bill black on upper mandible, dull reddish below; underparts white, finely streaked dark on breast and flanks. During wing-opening display, male shows black band on underwing. In flight, shows bright, pale blue rump. Immature buff below, speckled on breast. Call is ringing, far-carrying trill, "ki-kirrrir," often in series and duet, accompanied by wing-opening display. Single or paired, perches conspicuously, takes prey from ground; moderately approachable, located by call. **Range and habitat:** widespread in AF between 15° N and 22° S, except equatorial forest. Common in wooded areas, often far from water. Resident or migrant. **Similar species:** Brown-hooded Kingfisher.

Lilac-breasted Roller

Rufous-crowned Roller

Giant Kingfisher

Broad-billed Roller

Pied Kingfisher

Malachite Kingfisher

African Pygmy-Kingfisher

Woodland Kingfisher (prospecting for nest-hole)

Gray-headed Kingfisher

Striped Kingfisher

Northern Carmine Bee-eater

Merops nubicus (Meropidae) 36–8 cm/14–15 in.
Unmistakable, large, bright carmine-red bee-eater with elongated central tail feathers. North tropical race *nubicus* has vent and head dark greenish blue; southern tropics *nubicoides* (may be separate species) has chin and throat carmine. In flight, shows contrasting pale blue rump. Immature browner above, pinky brown below, lacking tail elongation. Call is deep, husky "turk." Found in flocks up to hundreds, perching prominently, hawking flying insects; conspicuous, moderately approachable. **Range and habitat:** widespread in AF from 15° N to Angola, Botswana, eastern South Africa, except equatorial forest. Seasonally common in open lowland scrub and woodland. Intra-African migrant; converges on Equator after breeding.

Little Bee-eater

Merops pusillus (Meropidae) 16 cm/6½ in.
Smallest AF bee-eater; green above with black mask, and yellow throat bordered below by black gorget; remainder of underparts buffish ochre. In low brief dashing flights, wings and tail appear mainly rufous orange. Immature washed greenish below, lacking gorget. Often silent; call is quiet "chip." In pairs or family parties, sometimes singly, perching low in open, hawking insects; sometimes unobtrusive, moderately approachable. **Range and habitat:** widespread in AF south of 15° N, apart from far south-west and Congo forest regions. Commonest AF bee-eater, in open scrub and woodland. Resident, moving locally. **Similar species:** 5 similar AF bee-eaters, Green Bee-eater.

White-fronted Bee-eater

Merops bullockoides (Meropidae) 23 cm/9 in.
Medium-sized, square-tailed bee-eater with black mask, white forehead, chin and cheeks, and bright red throat; upperparts green, with cinnamon nape; underparts cinnamon with dark blue vent. In flight, shows contrasting blue lower rump. Immature greenish below; paler red on crown and throat. Call is deep squeak, "qrrrrt." Single or in flocks, perches prominently, hawking insects from air or vegetation; conspicuous, sometimes approachable. **Range and habitat:** southern AF, east from Angola to Tanzania and north-east South Africa; also Kenya. Locally common in open country, often near gullies. Resident or wandering. **Similar species:** Red-throated Bee-eater.

Black Bee-eater

Merops gularis (Meropidae) 19 cm/7½ in.
Small, square-tailed, blackish bee-eater with scarlet throat and azure rump and belly. Immature lacks red throat and is generally duller. Normally silent, but gives a high-pitched "tssssp" and a liquid trill. Perches prominently in pairs or small parties but sometimes unobtrusive, not particularly tame. Forages at canopy height. **Range and habitat:** lowland forests of west and central AF, east from Guinea to Uganda, south to northern Angola. Uncommon or local in rainforest glades, streams and clearings. Probably mainly sedentary. **Similar species:** Blue-headed Bee-eater.

Trumpeter Hornbill

Ceratogymna bucinator (Bucerotidae) 59–66 cm/23–6 in.
Large, glossy black hornbill with white belly and bare purplish pink skin around eye. Male has casque running length of blackish bill; female smaller, casque reduced. In flight, shows white rump, white tips to secondaries and long, mainly black tail. Immature as female, brownish on face. Loud call is distinctive wailing, like crying of child, "waaaaaaaa, waaaaaaaa...." Usually in small flocks, foraging in canopy; bold, moderately approachable. **Range and habitat:** south-eastern AF, from Kenya and Tanzania to southern Zaire, Zambia, eastern South Africa. Locally common in wooded and forested areas. Basically resident. **Similar species:** 4 AF hornbills.

Silvery-cheeked Hornbill

Ceratogymna brevis (Bucerotidae) 75–80 cm/29–31 in.
Large, glossy black hornbill with white lower abdomen and bare blue skin around eye; silvery-tipped feathers on face. Male has brownish bill with pale basal band, surmounted by huge creamish casque; female smaller, casque reduced and darker. In flight, shows white rump; wings appear entirely dark. Immature has face brownish, casque reduced or absent. Call is loud, quacking or braying; also sharp barks, grunts. In pairs or flocks, foraging in canopies; often noisy, bold; quite approachable. **Range and habitat:** eastern AF, from north-east South Africa to Kenya, Ethiopia. Locally common in woodland. Apparently resident, but moving seasonally when foraging. **Similar species:** 4 AF hornbills.

African Gray Hornbill

Tockus nasutus (Bucerotidae) 44–9 cm/17–19 in.
Smallish hornbill, gray-brown above, white below, with white eyebrow and grayish upper breast. Male has black bill, cream at base of upper mandible; female smaller, bill creamy above, black below, with reddish tip. In flight, shows whitish streak on back, and white tip to tail. Immature as male, grayer; bill gray. Call is series of whistles, "peee peee peee peeeoow peeeoooow.. .." In pairs or flocks, bold, quite approachable. **Range and habitat:** at 7–17° N in AF, east to Ethiopia, south-west Arabia; also south through East Africa to Namibia, northern South Africa. Common, never numerous, in open wooded country. Resident, local migrant. **Similar species:** Pale-billed Hornbill.

Red-billed Hornbill

Tockus erythrorhynchus (Bucerotidae) 43–50 cm/17–20 in.
Smallish hornbill with slender red bill; crown and upperparts black, profusely spotted white on closed wing; face and underparts white. Immature has smaller, browner bill, wing-spots buffish. Call is loud high clucking, "tok-tok-tok...." In pairs or small to large flocks, foraging on open ground; conspicuous, often noisy, usually approachable. **Range and habitat:** at 9–17° N in AF east to Ethiopia, and thence south through East Africa to Namibia, Botswana, north-eastern South Africa. Common, sometimes local, in open scrub and woodland. Resident, moving locally. **Similar species:** 5 AF hornbills.

Eastern Yellow-billed Hornbill

Tockus flavirostris (Bucerotidae) 48–58 cm/19–23 in.
Medium-sized hornbill, black or dark brown above, boldly spotted white on closed wing, with unmistakable large yellow or orangish bill; underparts white. Male has massive bill, gular skin rosy; female smaller, bill reduced, gular skin black. Immature as female, bill mottled dusky; dark streaking on breast. Call is low staccato clucking, "tok-tok-tok.. .," often accelerating, then fading. Single, in pairs or small parties, foraging openly on ground or vegetation; moderately approachable. **Range and habitat:** 2 regions of AF: north-east from Tanzania to Ethiopia, Somalia; also widespread at 15–30° S (sometimes considered separate species). Common or local in open scrub and woodland. Resident. **Similar species:** Red-billed Hornbill.

Crowned Hornbill

Tockus alboterminatus (Bucerotidae) 50–4 cm/20–1 in.
Medium-sized, blackish brown hornbill with white belly, deep orange-red bill and white flecking on nape. Male has long casque-ridge, gular skin black; female smaller, casque reduced, gular skin greenish yellow. In flight, shows white-tipped outer tail feathers. Immature as adult, bill yellow, no casque. Call is loud piping, often rising and falling, "pee-pee-pee. ...." In pairs or small parties, foraging openly on vegetation; moderately approachable. **Range and habitat:** widespread in southern AF, from Angola to Tanzania and South Africa, avoiding south-west; also Kenya, Ethiopia. Common, local in wooded and forest edge habitats. Resident. **Similar species:** 4 AF hornbills.

Southern Ground-Hornbill

Bucorvus leadbeateri (Bucerotidae) 90–100 cm/35–9 in.
Huge, black, terrestrial hornbill with black bill surmounted by low basal casque-ridge. Male has bright red wattles on face and throat; female smaller, wattles bluish on throat. White primaries conspicuous during occasional low flights. Immature brownish, bill reduced and gray; wattles grayish or yellowish. Call is deep, rhythmic, lionlike grunting, "oo-oo-oo. ...," often in duet. In pairs or small parties, sedately walking; rather retiring. **Range and habitat:** widespread in AF south of Congo basin, apart from far south-west; also north to Uganda, Kenya. Locally common in open country. Resident, moving locally. **Similar species:** Abyssinian Ground-Hornbill.

Northern Carmine Bee-eater

Little Bee-eater

White-fronted Bee-eater

Black Bee-eater

Silvery-cheeked Hornbill

Trumpeter Hornbill

African Gray Hornbill

Red-billed Hornbill

Eastern Yellow-billed Hornbill

Crowned Hornbill

Southern Ground-Hornbill

Green Woodhoopoe

Phoeniculus purpureus (Phoeniculidae) 30–6 cm/12–14 in.
Large wood hoopoe with conspicuous long, decurved, red bill, red legs and long graduated tail; plumage generally blackish, glossed bright metallic green on head, mantle and underparts, deep violet on wings and tail. In flight, shows conspicuous white wing-bar and tail-spots. Immature duller, throat buffish; legs and short, straight bill black. Call is high hysterical cackling, accelerating to crescendo, usually in chorus. In small parties, foraging agilely on bark of tree-trunks and branches; active, often noisy, quite approachable. **Range and habitat:** widespread in AF south of 15° N, except equatorial forests, arid Horn and far south-west. Locally common in wooded country. Resident, wandering. **Similar species:** 6 other wood hoopoes in AF.

Common Scimitar-Bill

Rhinopomastus cyanomelas (Phoeniculidae) 25–8 cm/10–11 in.
Medium-sized wood hoopoe with thin, black, sharply decurved bill, black legs and long tail. Male generally black, glossed violet-blue; female with face and ventral torso dull dark brown. In flight, shows conspicuous white wing-bar and tips to outer 3 tail feathers. Immature as female, bill shorter, less curved. Call is low, mournful, repeated whistle, "phooee, phooee. . ." Single or paired, sometimes in small parties, foraging on bark of tree-trunks and branches; active but often quiet, quite approachable. **Range and habitat:** widespread in AF between 16° N and 30° S, apart from equatorial lowland forests. Moderately or locally common in open scrub and woodland. Resident. **Similar species:** 6 other wood hoopoes in AF.

Abyssinian Scimitar-Bill

Rhinopomastus minor (Phoeniculidae) 23 cm/9 in.
Small wood hoopoe with long, conspicuous, sharply decurved, bright orange-red bill, black legs and long graduated tail. Male generally black, glossed purple-blue and violet; female browner below. In flight, shows conspicuous white wing-bar (absent in southern race). Immature as female, browner below, bill brownish. Often silent; call is harsh chatter, "ki-ki-ki-ki.. .," rising and falling. Single or paired, occasionally in small groups, foraging agilely on tree-trunks, branches, flowers; active but sometimes unobtrusive, shy. **Range and habitat:** north-eastern AF, from Somalia, Ethiopia, southern Sudan to Tanzania. Sometimes common, never numerous, in mainly dry, open scrub and woodland. Nonmigratory. **Similar species:** 6 other AF wood hoopoes.

OWLS Strigiformes

Pearl-spotted Owlet

Glaucidium perlatum (Strigidae) 16–18 cm/6½–7 in.
Small owl with large yellow eyes, no "ear" tufts, and striking "false face" on nape; upperparts brown, profusely spotted white, especially boldly on relatively long tail; underparts white with coarse, irregular, dark brown streaking. Immature less spotted on crown and mantle. Call is loud distinctive series of whistles, very far-carrying and increasing in pitch and volume, culminating in several very extended descending notes: "keee, keee, keee.. .peeeooooo, peeeooooo. ..." Single or paired, often roosts unseen by day but frequently betrayed by combination of partly diurnal habits, mobbing by other birds and unique calls; often approachable. **Range and habitat:** widespread in AF south of 15° N, except Congo forests and far south-west. Common in open scrub and woodland. Nonmigratory. **Similar species:** 4 owls in AF, Spotted Owlet (see p 254).

Marsh Owl

Asio capensis (Strigidae) 36 cm/14 in.
Medium-sized owl, dark brown above, pale buff below, with conspicuous dark eyes set in pale facial disc; short "ear" tufts sometimes visible. In flight, appears long-winged, with prominent reddish buff primaries. Immature has facial disc darker, buff speckling on back. Call is loud tearing croak, "zirkk." Single, in pairs or flocks, nocturnal and crepuscular, often emerging on cloudy days to quarter open country like harrier; otherwise roosting unseen on ground; rather shy. **Range and habitat:** uncommon in Morocco; widespread in AF south of Congo basin, apart from south-west, also north to Ethiopia, Sudan, scattered parts of west. Locally common in open marshy and grassy areas. Resident, nomadic. **Similar species:** African Grass-Owls and Short-eared Owls (see p 70).

Verreaux's Eagle-Owl

Bubo lacteus (Strigidae) 61–5 cm/24–6 in.
Very large, finely vermiculated, milky gray owl with rather small (often inconspicuous) "ear" tufts and prominent black border to pale gray facial disc; large dark eyes with striking pink lids. Immature browner, more barred. Call is distinctively deep and gruff, often irregular, grunting, "hoo...hoo hoo...hoo. . .;" also extended, shrieking whistle, "seeeeeeeeeerr." Single or paired, sometimes with immature, nocturnal, roosting motionless in large shady tree by day; often unseen, sometimes approachable. **Range and habitat:** widespread in AF south of 14° N, apart from lowland equatorial forests and far south-west. Quite common in wooded habitats, particularly near water. Resident, immatures disperse locally. **Similar species:** 7 other large owls in AF, Great Horned Owl (see p 70).

Pel's Fishing-Owl

Scotopelia peli (Strigidae) 63–5 cm/25–6 in.
Very large owl, barred rufous brown above, paler buff with fine streaking below; large dark eyes in poorly defined facial disc; crown flattish, lacking "ear" tufts, feathering fluffed out when excited to give rounded head; legs bare, whitish, often concealed by body plumage. Immature whitish with rufous wash, becoming darker. Call is low booming grunt, "hoooommmmm-ut," far-carrying and often repeated for minutes at a time. Single or paired, sometimes with immature, taking surface fish at night, roosting unseen high in dense waterside canopy by day; moderately approachable. **Range and habitat:** widespread in AF from Senegal, Nigeria, Ethiopia south to Congo, Botswana, eastern South Africa. Local common to rare in riverine forest and swamps. Nonmigratory. **Similar species:** Rufous Fishing-Owl, 6 AF eagle owls, Buffy Fish-Owl (see p 254).

NIGHTJARS AND ALLIES Caprimulgiformes

Abyssinian Nightjar

Caprimulgus poliocephalus (Caprimulgidae) 24 cm/9½ in.
Medium-sized, square-tailed nightjar; streaked and mottled gray, brown and black above with diffuse rufous collar; underparts barred and vermiculated gray, brown and buff, with small white patch on side of throat. In flight, male shows white outer tail feathers and flash in primaries; female less white in tail, wing flash buff. Immature as female, more rufous brown. Call, at night, is loud whistle, "phee-oo-weet," followed by wavering, descending trill. Single or paired, nocturnal, roosting unseen on ground by day; betrayed by call. **Range and habitat:** mainly east AF, from Ethiopia to Malawi; also Angola. The only AF montane nightjar, locally common above 1,000 m (3,300 ft) in woods and forest edge. Resident. **Similar species:** 17 other square-tailed nightjars in AF, European Nightjar (see p 166).

Standard-winged Nightjar

Macrodipteryx longipennis (Caprimulgidae) 23 cm/9 in.
Medium-sized nightjar; breeding male with unmistakable elongated 2 nd primaries forming standards over twice body length, consisting of bare feather shaft with flaglike vane at tip, giving impression of 2 small birds following nightjar in flight; shed on reaching "wintering" range. Nonbreeding male brownish, throat pale buff, no standards. Female and immature as male, paler, no standards. Male's song is soft, high stridulation. In pairs or loose groups, active dusk and night, roosting unseen on ground by day; close-sitting. **Range and habitat:** widespread in AF at 5–15° N, from Senegal, Liberia to Ethiopia, Kenya. Seasonally common in bushed and open wooded country. Intra-African migrant, breeds December–June, then moves north. **Similar species:** when without standards, several nightjars (see pp 72, 116, 166, 254, 304).

Green Woodhoopoe

Common Scimitar-Bi

Abyssinian Scimitar-B

Pel's Fishing-Owl

Standard-winged Nightjar

Pearl-spotted Owlet

Marsh Owl

Abyssinian Nightjar

Verreaux's Eagle-Ow

COLIES OR MOUSEBIRDS Coliiformes

Speckled Mousebird

Colius striatus (Coliidae) 30–5 cm/12–14 in.
Medium-sized mousebird, brown above with grayish face, short crest and long, broad pointed tail; bare white skin behind eye in some races; underparts paler, barred on breast; legs red or purplish. In flight, short rounded wings, long tail and fast gliding like small pheasant. Immature duller, with slight crest, stubby tail. Call is soft "sioo" or "tooo;" sharper alarm "swik." In small parties, foraging openly and agilely on vegetation; usually conspicuous and approachable. **Range and habitat:** widespread in AF between 10° N and 10° S, apart from central Congo basin; also south in east to Cape. Common in fairly open scrub and woodland, gardens and forest edge. Nonmigratory. **Similar species:** 5 other mousebirds.

Blue-naped Mousebird

Urocolius macrourus (Coliidae) 30–5 cm/12–14 in.
Slender-tailed mousebird, gray-brown above with bare red skin around eye, red base to black bill and bright turquoise nape patch; underparts paler, legs pinkish. In flight, shows pale rump and long tail. Immature paler, lacking nape patch, facial skin pink. Call is thin but far-carrying whistle, "seeeee seeeeeeeeee;" also "treee-treee." In small parties, foraging openly on vegetation; rather shy. **Range and habitat:** widespread in AF at 10–20° N from Senegal to Ethiopia, Somalia, and south to East Africa. Common in dry, bushed and wooded country. Resident, wandering locally. **Similar species:** 5 other mousebirds.

TROGONS Trogoniformes

Narina Trogon

Apaloderma narina (Trogonidae) 30 cm/12 in.
Striking, long-tailed, pigeon-sized bird, male bright green with greenish yellow bill and scarlet abdomen; ventral tail white. Female pinkish brown on face and upper breast, grading to gray lower breast; abdomen pinker. Immature duller above with white-spotted wing-coverts; grayish below, lightly barred. Call is series of far-carrying ventrilo-quial hoots, "woo-hoo, woo-hoo.. .." Single or paired, occasionally in 3 s, motionless in canopy, unseen except during brief flights; moderately approachable, betrayed by call. **Range and habitat:** widespread in AF between 10° N and 20° S, also eastern South Africa. Moderately common, often local, in well-wooded areas. Resident, or local migrant. **Similar species:** 2 other AF trogons.

WOODPECKERS AND ALLIES Piciformes

White-headed Barbet

Lybius leucocephalus (Capitoni-dae) 16 cm/6½ in.
Medium-sized barbet, blackish brown above and white below, with white hood and heavy blackish bill. Of several distinctive races, 1 with white tail, another with blackish belly. In flight, white rump contrasts with dark back and wings. Immature has bill, and white of plumage, brownish. Call is loud, variable "chek-chek-shee-chip-chip...." Single, paired or in small parties, foraging on fruiting trees; sometimes unobtrusive, moderately approachable. **Range and habitat:** 3 areas of AF: from Nigeria to Chad, Central African Republic; from southern Sudan to Kenya, Tanzania; Angola. Quite common in open scrub and woodland. Resident, moving to fruiting trees.

Spot-flanked Barbet

Tricholaema lacrymosa (Capi-tonidae) 13 cm/5 in.
Smallish, black above with white eyebrow, yellow edging in wing, and black bill; underparts white, with dark spots on flanks and dark stripe from chin to breast. Male has eye pale yellowish, female dark brown. Immature duller, grayer above, eye dark. Call is loud hoot, "poop.. .poop;" also short croaks. Single or paired, foraging on bushes and trees; sometimes unobtrusive, not shy. **Range and habitat:** eastern AF, from southern Sudan and eastern Zaire to Uganda, Kenya, Tanzania, Zambia. Locally common, seldom numerous, in moist, bushed and wooded country. Resident, moving locally to fruiting trees. **Similar species:** Black-throated and Pied Barbets.

Red-and-yellow Barbet

Trachyphonus erythrocephalus (Capitonidae) 23 cm/9 in.
Large "ground barbet;" male has speckled black and yellow head with black crown and throat, and red, black and white flash on ear-coverts; rest of upperparts black, spotted white or yellowish; underparts yellow, with narrow black- and white-spotted breast band and red vent. Female has cap and ear-coverts orange-red, throat yellow. In brief low flights, shows red rump. Immature duller, browner above, male with crown darkening. Call is loud duet, "ka-shee-ka-chao, ka-shee-ka-chao." In pairs or small parties, foraging on low vegetation; noisy, active, approachable. **Range and habitat:** north-east AF, from Somalia, Ethiopia to Kenya, Tanzania. Locally common in dry scrublands, near termite hills. Nonmigratory. **Similar species:** 3 other "ground barbets."

D'Arnaud's Barbet

Trachyphonus darnaudii (Capitonidae) 16 cm/6½ in.
Medium-sized "ground barbet" with erectile crest on black or gray crown; rest of head yellow, finely speckled with black; remainder of upperparts dark brown, spotted white; underparts yellowish with variable black throat, merging to whitish belly and scarlet vent; bill pale, but blackish in west Kenya. Immature browner on crown and throat, grayer below. Call is prolonged loud "kerr-ta-te-doodle, kerr-ta-te-doodle.. .." In pairs, or 3 or 4 together, foraging on ground or low vegetation; noisy but sometimes shy, quite approachable. **Range and habitat:** north-eastern AF, from Somalia and Ethiopia to East Africa. Common in dry scrublands. Resident. **Similar species:** 3 other "ground barbets" in AF.

Red-fronted Tinkerbird

Pogoniulus pusillus (Capitonidae) 10 cm/4 in.
Small barbet, black upperparts streaked and speckled white and yellowish, with red forehead, black stripe through eye and thinner black malar stripe; underparts pale yellowish. In flight, shows yellowish rump. Immature has forehead black. Call is far-carrying hollow note, given for long periods, "tonk-tonk-tonk.. .;" also shrill trill. Single, or paired, foraging openly on bushes and trees; busy, active, sometimes retiring. **Range and habitat:** 2 areas of AF: eastern South Africa; north-east, from Tanzania and Kenya to Ethiopia, Somalia. Common in scrublands or forest edge. Resident. **Similar species:** Yellow-fronted Tinkerbird, Red-fronted Barbet.

Yellow-rumped Tinkerbird

Pogoniulus bilineatus (Capitonidae) 10 cm/4 in.
Small barbet, black above with yellow edge on wing, thin white eyebrow, white stripe from forehead to neck, and black malar stripe; bill black; underparts grayish, yellower on belly. In flight, shows yellow rump. Immature speckled yellow on mantle, bill paler. Call is far-carrying, hollow note, uttered for long periods in groups of 4 to 6 with brief pauses, "tonk-tonk-tonk-tonk ... tonk-tonk-tonk-tonk ...;" also short series of croaks. Single or paired, foraging openly on bushes and trees; busy, active, sometimes approachable. **Range and habitat:** widespread within 10° of equator, also south to Mozambique, eastern South Africa. Common in dense woodland, moist thicket. Nonmigratory. **Similar species:** 3 other "black" tinkerbirds in AF.

Greater Honeyguide

Indicator indicator (Indicatoridae) 20 cm/8 in.
Large honeyguide, male brown above, white below, with pink bill, black throat and whitish cheeks. Female with dark bill. In flight, shows white outer tail feathers and small yellow "shoulder" on wing. Immature brown above, bill black, with yellow throat and breast, belly white. Male's call is far-carrying "wheet-terrr.. .wheet-terrr...;" guides with chattering, "tik-tik-ik-ik-tik-ik.. .." Found singly on bushes and trees, often near bees" nests; brood parasite of e.g., bee-eaters, barbets; unobtrusive, can be shy. **Range and habitat:** in AF south of 15° N, except Congo forests, arid Horn, far south-west. Fairly common, often local, in scrublands. Resident. **Similar species:** 3 other large honey guides in AF, Yellow-rumped Honeyguide (see p 258).

Speckled Mousebird

Blue-naped Mousebird

Narina Trogon

White-headed Barbet

Spot-flanked Barbet

Red-and-yellow Barbet

D'Arnaud's Barbet

Red-fronted Tinkerbird

Yellow-rumped Tinkerbird

Greater Honeyguide (immature)

Ground Woodpecker

Geocolaptes olivaceus (Picidae) 26 cm/10 in.
Large, terrestrial woodpecker; male with gray hood, pinkish white eye, and dark, faintly reddish moustachial stripe; rest of upperparts dark greenish brown with fine pale spots and bars; pinkish red breast merging to crimson on abdomen, with barred flanks. Female lacks reddish tinge to moustache. In flight, shows prominent red rump. Immature paler, pinker below, eye white, often some red on nape. Call is harsh scream, "keeearrrgh;" also rhythmic 'tick-dee.' In pairs or small parties, foraging on ground; noisy, sometimes aggressive, can be inconspicuous. **Range and habitat:** far southern AF, in South Africa. Locally common on reasonably open, rocky or uneven ground, up to 2,100 m (6,900 ft). Resident, moving locally, seasonally.

Golden-tailed Woodpecker

Campethera abingoni (Picidae) 20–2 cm/8–9 in.
Medium-steed woodpecker; male with black and red speckled forecrown, red hindcrown and moustache; upperparts otherwise olive or gray-brown, barred and spotted white, and tail yellowish. Underparts whitish or buffy, streaked black (some populations spotted on breast, throat blackish). Female has black forecrown speckled white, lacks moustache. Immature as female, duller. Call is wailing "waaaa," occasional soft drumming. Found in pairs or singly, foraging on trunks and branches. Approachable, can be unobtrusive. **Range and habitat:** widespread in southern AF apart from far south-west, and north to East Africa, Sudan, Somalia. Locally common, never numerous, in bush, woods, forests. Resident. **Similar species:** 6 similar AF woodpeckers.

Gray Woodpecker

Dendropicos goertae (Picidae) 18 cm/7 in.
Medium-sized woodpecker; male with gray head and red hindcrown. Upperparts otherwise green, with red rump; underparts gray, usually with red patch on belly. Female has head entirely gray. Immature faintly barred below, rump paler, abdominal red reduced. Call is distinctive, high rattling "wikk-wikk-wikk. . .," rarely drums. Found in pairs or singly, foraging on trunks and branches. Moderately approachable, betrayed by call. **Range and habitat:** mainly at 5–17° N in AF east to Ethiopia, and south to East Africa. Also Congo, Zaire, Angola. Common or locally so in many wooded habitats. Resident. **Similar species:** Olive and Ground Woodpeckers.

Bearded Woodpecker

Dendropicos namaquus (Picidae) 24 cm/9½ in.
Large woodpecker; male with red hindcrown, and white face cut by broad dark stripe behind eye and similar black malar stripe; upperparts otherwise olive or gray-brown, barred and speckled white, tail yellowish; underparts yellowish olive, finely barred whitish. Female has hindcrown black. Immature as male, crown blackish red, speckled white. Call is loud, high chattering, "kik-kik-kik...;" also frequent loud, far-carrying, decelerating drumming, "trrrrrrrrr-tap-tap-tap." Single or paired, foraging on large tree-trunks and branches; noisy, often conspicuous, quite approachable. **Range and habitat:** widespread in AF south of 10° S, apart from far south-west, and north through East Africa to Ethiopia, Central African Republic. Somewhat local, never numerous, in open woodland. Nonmigratory. **Similar species:** 3 similar AF woodpeckers.

Rufous-necked Wryneck

Jynx ruficollis (Picidae) 18 cm/7 in.
Resembling smallish woodpecker, but gray-brown nightjarlike upperparts with fine mottling, speckling and vermiculation, and broken, black median stripe from crown to mantle; below, reddish rufous throat and breast, with whitish, finely streaked belly and rufous-washed vent (Ethiopian race *aequatorialis* has underparts mostly rufous). Immature darker above; less rufous, more barred, below. Call is loud series of high shrieks, "keek-keek-keek. . .." Single or paired, foraging on ground, tree-trunks and branches; unobtrusive, quite approachable. **Range and habitat:** fragmented distribution in AF, from Cameroon, southern Sudan, Ethiopia south to Angola, Zambia, eastern South Africa. Locally common in wooded areas. Resident, some dispersal; local migrant extreme south. **Similar species:** Eurasian Wryneck (see p 168).

SWIFTS AND HUMMINGBIRDS Apodiformes

Nyanza Swift

Apus niansae (Apodidae) 15 cm/6 in.
Medium-sized, dark brown swift with whitish throat, forked tail and in good light shows pale panel on upperwing secondaries. Flight fluttering, not powerful. Immature not described. Call is very thin, shrill screech. In flocks, foraging high, lower down around hills, cliffs, buildings, and after rain and storms; often with other swift species. **Range and habitat:** north-eastern AF, from Ethiopia and northern Somalia south to north-eastern Zaire, northern Tanzania. Locally common around cliffs, rocks and buildings in highland areas, also foraging over lowlands. Resident or intra-African migrant. **Similar species:** other dark swifts (see pp 72, 116, 166, 254, 304). Not illustrated.

Little Swift

Apus affinis (Apodidae) 13 cm/5 in.
Rather small, thickset, blackish swift with square tail, broad white rump extending down to flanks, and white throat. Flight fluttering, not strong and direct. Immature browner, washed olive. Call is frequent loud, twittering scream, "tri-i-i-i-i-i.. .." In flocks up to hundreds, foraging high, also low around cliffs, buildings and during storms; often with other swift species; noisy, often nesting on buildings, approachable. **Range and habitat:** WP in North Africa and Arabia, Near East, and east through OR to China, Borneo. Widespread in AF south of 16° N, except Horn and far south-west. Common away from arid country, particularly near buildings (in cities), rock faces. Resident in many areas, also local, partial and WP migrant. **Similar species:** other white-rumped swifts (see p 254).

Batlike Spinetail

Neafrapus boehmi (Apodidae) 9 cm/3½ in.
Very small, almost tail-less swift, black above with white rump; throat and breast pale brownish, merging in white abdomen. Like torso-less "flying wing" in erratic slow, batlike, often low flight; wings very broad-based, tapering sharply to tips. Immature duller. Often silent; call is shrill twittering, "tee-tee-tee-deep." Single, paired or in small parties, foraging low"", often with swallows. **Range and habitat:** mainly southern AF, in scattered areas from Angola, Zambia, Mozambique to Tanzania, Kenya. At best locally common, over woodland and forest edge. Resident or moving locally. **Similar species:** 3 other white-bellied spinetails in AF, White-throated Spinetail (see p 254). Not illustrated.

White-rumped Swift

Apus caffer (Apodidae) 15 cm/6 in.
Medium-sized, slim black swift with narrow white rump, deeply forked tail with slender outer, feathers and white throat. Immature speckled white on wings. Often silent. Call is low, twittering scream. Usually in pairs, sometimes loose groups, foraging low, often with other swift species; not shy. **Range and habitat:** WP in Morocco, southern Spain; widespread in AF south of Ethiopia, Chad, Senegal, apart from southern interior and equatorial forests. Locally common around buildings and cliffs or over open country, often near old nests of swallows, which it mainly uses. Resident and intra-African migrant. **Similar species:** Horus and Little Swifts.

African Palm-Swift

Cypsiurus parvus (Apodidae) 14–17 cm/5½–6½ in.
Small, slender, pale gray-brown swift with long, slender and tapering wings, and long, cleft tail with thin swallowlike streamers. Tail usually held closed during fast veering flight. Immature speckled warm buff, with shorter streamers. Call is muted, thin and high twitter; also quiet "si-ip." In pairs or loose flocks, foraging low; noisy, distinctive, often aggressive. **Range and habitat:** widespread in AF between 15° N and 20° S, apart from arid Horn; also south to eastern South Africa, north to south-west Arabia. Locally common over open, low-lying country with native or exotic palms, also nesting/roosting under bridges. Resident; wanders. **Similar species:** Asian Palm-Swift.

Ground Woodpeck (pair at nest-hole in b

Rufous-necked Wryneck

White-rumped Swif

Golden-tailed Woodpecker

Bearded Woodpecke

African Palm-Swift

Gray Woodpecker

Little Swift (at coloni nest site)

PERCHING BIRDS Passeriformes

Rufous-naped Lark

Mirafra africana (Alaudidae) 18 cm/7 in.

Medium-sized lark, brown streaked with black above, pale buff below, with fine black streaking on breast; some rufous in closed wing, but rufous nape not infallible fieldmark. In flight, shows short, rounded, conspicuously rufous wings, and short tail. Immature has breast streaking more diffuse, upperparts rather scaly. Call is mournful, clear whistle, "chi-wee," from perch. Single, sometimes paired, perching prominently on, e.g., bushes, termite hills; not shy. **Range and habitat:** widespread in AF south of 10° S, except far south-west, and north through east to Kenya; also west. Locally common on open and bushed grassland. Nonmigratory. **Similar species:** Red-winged Lark, Fawn-colored Bush Lark.

Fawn-colored Lark

Calendulauda africanoides (Alaudidae) 14 cm/5½ in.

Rather small lark, rufous brown streaked with black above, with conspicuous whitish eye stripe; underparts pale buff, streaked reddish to brown on breast. In flight, shows prominent white outer tail feathers. Immature spotted dark above, more extensively white in tail. Song is brief, staccato series of "chip" and "cheree" whistles, from perch or flight. Single or paired, perching prominently on trees and bushes; not shy. **Range and habitat:** widespread in AF south of 15° S; also north-east, from Tanzania to Ethiopia and Somalia. Locally common on open and bushed grasslands, mainly in areas with dry, sandy soils. Nonmigratory. **Similar species:** Rufous-naped Lark, Singing Bushlark (see p 306).

Red-capped Lark

Calandrella cinerea (Alaudidae) 15 cm/6 in.

Medium-sized lark, palish brown above with diffuse darker streaking and conspicuous bright orange rufous pectoral patches and crown; underparts unmarked white. Immature darker brown above with some white spotting; dark spotting on breast. Call is brief twittering; also trilling song, given in flight. In small flocks, or loose gatherings of hundreds when not breeding; perching and foraging on open ground; not shy. **Range and habitat:** widespread in AF south of 5° S, and north through East Africa to Ethiopia, Somalia. Locally common on open, short grassland and bare or burnt ground. Resident or nomadic. **Similar species:** Lesser Short-toed Lark.

Chestnut-backed Sparrow-Lark

Eremopterix leucotis (Alaudidae) 13 cm/5 in.

Small, thickset lark with heavy bill, male black with white ear coverts, hindneck collar and thighs, and chestnut back. Female mottled, with narrow white collar and blackish central belly. Immature as female, paler. Call is sharp "chirrup-chew," musical song. Found in flocks on open ground, often with Chestnut-headed Sparrow-Lark *E. signata* in north-eastern AF. Rather shy. **Range and habitat:** two regions of AF at 10–17° N and south of 15° S, apart from far south-west. Common to scarce on open plains with scattered bushes and trees. Resident, local migrant, nomad. **Similar species:** 4 other AF *Eremopterix*.

African Pied Wagtail

Motacilla aguimp (Motacillidae) 20 cm/8 in.

Conspicuously pied wagtail, mainly black above with prominent white eyebrow and much white in closed wing; underparts white, with prominent black breast band. Immature duller, browner and grayer. Call is frequent brisk "tissip;" also sustained jumbled song. Single or paired, sometimes small, loose parties, walking and running on open ground, habitually wagging tail; often tame. **Range and habitat:** widespread in AF south of 10° N, apart from far south-west. Commonest AF wagtail, found on flat, open ground, usually near water or habitation, including city centers. Resident; local migrant in subtropics. **Similar species:** 5 other wagtails in AF, White Wagtail (see p 170).

Cape Wagtail

Motacilla capensis (Motacillidae) 19 cm/7 in.

Shorter-tailed wagtail, grayish or olive-brown above with white eyebrow and outer tail. Underparts whitish with dark breastband (vestigial or absent in some). Immature browner, tail shorter. Call is loud "tseep" or "tsee-eep," also piping song. Found singly or in pairs, sometimes flocks, walking or running on open ground, often wagging tail. Can be tame. **Range and habitat:** south of 10° S in AF, and north to East Africa. Common to scarce in open, waterside habitats, forest clearings, also near habitation. Resident, moving locally, seasonally. **Similar species:** 5 other wagtails in AF.

Plain-backed Pipit

Anthus leucophrys (Motacillidae) 17 cm/7 in.

Medium-sized pipit, brown above with buffy eyebrow, virtually unmarked mantle and buffy outer tail, no moustachial stripe. Underparts cinnamon, extremely faintly streaked on breast. Bill dark with yellowish base, legs pinkish. Immature mottled above. Flight call is low "chiz-zick," sparrowlike, chirping song, from perch. Found singly, in pairs or flocks, foraging on open ground. Moderately approachable. **Range and habitat:** widespread south of 15° N in AF apart from much of Congo basin and south-west. Common to local in short grasslands, often near rocks, termite hills. Resident, nomad, migrant. **Similar species:** 5 similar AF pipits.

Yellow-throated Longclaw

Macronyx croceus (Motacillidae) 20 cm/8 in.

Large pipit, dark and mottled above, bright yellow below, with broad black breast band; hind claw elongate. White corners of tail conspicuous during low, jerky flight. Immature buffish below, breast band diffuse. Call is repeated loud, mewing whistle, "toooeeee," from perch; also vigorous whistled song. Usually in pairs, on ground or low perches; often approachable. **Range and habitat:** northern AF, from Gulf of Guinea east to Kenya, and thence south through eastern areas to eastern South Africa. Locally common in open, bushed and wooded grassland, also swampy areas. Resident with erratic local movements. **Similar species:** Golden Pipit, and 7 other longclaws.

Rosy-throated Longclaw

Macronyx ameliae (Motacillidae) 20 cm/8 in.

Large pipit, dark and mottled above, male deep salmon-red below with prominent black breast band. Female paler, more buffy, washed reddish below. Note white corners of tail in low flight. Immature as female but duller, scalloped buff above. Call is plaintive whistle, "chooitt," from perch; series of squeaking whistles during song-flight. Single or paired, on ground; shy, often unobtrusive. **Range and habitat:** mainly southern areas of AF, from eastern South Africa north to Angola, southern Zaire, Tanzania, Kenya. Local, never numerous, in open, often damp, grassland. Nonmigratory, but local movements frequent in some areas. **Similar species:** 7 other longclaws.

Arrow-marked Babbler

Turdoides jardineii (Timaliidae) 23 cm/9 in.

Medium-sized, rather dark gray-brown babbler with orange or yellow eyes and very small pale, arrow-shaped markings (produced by feather tips) on throat and breast. Immature lacks arrow-marks, has eyes dark. Call, often 1 st indication of presence, is loud 'churrr churrr churrr. . .," increasing to crescendo, usually in chorus. Almost invariably in small parties, flying low 1 after the other between bushes and trees; often noisy and extrovert, then quiet, shy. **Range and habitat:** widespread in AF south of 5° S, north to Uganda, Kenya. Locally common in bushed and wooded country. Resident. **Similar species:** Brown and Black-lored Babblers, other babblers (see p 270).

Rufous Chatterer

Turdoides rubiginosus (Timaliidae) 19 cm/7½ in.

Slender, rather long-tailed babbler, brown above, warm cinnamon below, with pale yellow eyes. Immature duller below, eyes dark. Loud churring and chattering calls, also whistles, usually in chorus, often 1 st indication of presence. Usually in small parties, flying low 1 after the other between patches of low cover; also hopping on ground with tail cocked; sometimes approachable, often rather shy. **Range and habitat:** north-eastern AF, from Tanzania to Sudan, Ethiopia, Somalia. At best locally common, in dense low cover, mainly in drier areas. Resident. **Similar species:** Fulvous and Scaly Chatterers.

Rufous-naped Lark

Fawn-colored Lark

Chestnut-backed Sparrow-Lark

Red-capped Lark

Cape Wagtail

African Pied Wagtail

Plain-backed Pipit

Yellow-throated Longclaw

Rosy-throated Longclaw

Arrow-marked Babbler

Rufous Chatterer

Common Bulbul

Pycnonotus barbatus (**Pycnonotidae**) 20 cm/8 in.
Jaunty, restless, thrushlike species, brown above, darker on head, with short erectile crest; below, paler brown breast grades to whitish abdomen, vent is bright yellow. Immature duller, paler, buffish above in some races. Call is frequent twittering "tchit...tchit..."; song is brief chattering "quick-doctor-quick." In pairs or loose parties foraging on ground or in vegetation; extrovert. **Range and habitat:** widespread North Africa and Middle East; outside forests, probably most ubiquitous bird in AF, in most areas south of 20° N except Cape and arid south-west. Common in scrub/wooded areas, even city centers. Resident. **Similar species:** other bulbuls (see p 262).

Yellow-whiskered Greenbul

Andropadus latirostris (**Pycnonotidae**) 18 cm/7 in.
Medium-sized greenbul, dark olive-green above, washed brownish on tail, and paler below, merging to yellowish on belly; easily identified by bright yellow moustaches on either side of throat. Immature lacks moustaches. Loud distinctive song, throughout day, from cover, is monotonous "chip chup chip chip chup," interspersed with high trill. Single or paired, in dense cover; shy. **Range and habitat:** mainly west and central AF, from Gulf of Guinea, east through Congo basin, to Sudan, Kenya, Tanzania. Common in forest, bamboo, even large urban gardens. Resident, moving to favored food sources. **Similar species:** 46 AF greenbuls, other bulbuls (see p 262).

Dusky Alseonax

Muscicapa adusta (**Muscicapidae**) 12 cm/4½ in.
Small, plump, short-tailed, gray-brown above, dusky brown below merging to whitish on throat and belly. Immature speckled and spotted buff above, brown spotting and streaking below. Generally silent; occasional long, sibilant, "tseeeet." Single or paired, hawking insects from low perches; often unobtrusive; usually approachable. **Range and habitat:** mainly eastern AF, from Ethiopia, south through East Africa to Cape; also Angola, Cameroon. Common in forest edge and moist well-wooded habitats, gardens. Nonmigratory; local migrant in southern subtro-pics. **Similar species:** other flycatchers (see pp 174, 266).

White-eyed Slaty-Flycatcher

Melaenornis fischeri (**Muscicapidae**) 15 cm/6½ in.
Plump, slate-gray above with white eye-ring; paler gray below merging to whitish on abdomen. Immature spotted white above, dark spotting below. Usually silent; call is sharp "tzit," also chattering, descending trill. Found singly or in pairs on low perches, taking insects from air and ground, most active at twilight; often approachable. **Range and habitat:** mainly highlands of eastern AF, from Malawi and Zambia north to East Africa and Ethiopia; also Angola. Common in forest edge and moist well-wooded sites, cultivation, gardens. Nonmigratory. **Similar species:** Abyssinian Slaty-Flycatcher.

Southern Black-Flycatcher

Melaenornis pammelaina (**Muscicapidae**) 20 cm/8 in.
Large, glossy bluish black flycatcher with dark brown eyes and slightly notched tail. Wings palish in flight. Immature blackish above with buff spots; profusely spotted and barred rusty below. Usually quiet; persistent "sweer" in twilight; also faint piping song. Single, paired or in small, loose parties, on exposed perches, taking insects from air or ground; frequently near very similar Drongo; often unobtrusive, rather shy. **Range and habitat:** widespread in AF south of 5° S, apart from dry south-west, north to Tanzania, Kenya. Common, often local, in bushed and wooded habitats. Resident. **Similar species:** Black-Flycatcher, 2 drongos, Black Cuckooshrike in AF (see p 224).

Silverbird

Empidornis semipartitus (**Muscicapidae**) 18 cm/7 in.
Slender, quite long-tailed flycatcher with silvery gray upperparts and bright rufous underparts. Immature spotted black and buff above, mottled black on buff below. Usually silent; soft thrushlike song. Found singly or in pairs, using perches and taking insects from air and ground; shy. **Range and habitat:** north-eastern AF, from interior northern Tanzania to Uganda, western Kenya, south Sudan and western Ethiopia. Locally common but never numerous in

many open, bushed and wooded habitats, in both dry and moist country, but absent from many apparently suitable areas. Nonmigratory; wandering.

Chinspot Batis

Batis molitor (**Platysteiridae**) 12 cm/4½ in.
Small, short-tailed flycatcher, male gray, white and black above with thick black eye stripe and contrasting pale yellow eye; underparts white, with conspicuous broad black breast band. Female similar, with chestnut breast band and chin-spot. Immature resembles female, washed buff or rufousish above. Song is soft but far-carrying, descending piping, "chin-spot" or "chin. . .spot.. . fly.. .cat-cher;" also harsh alarms. Single or paired, foraging in bushes and canopy; bold. **Range and habitat:** widespread in AF south of 5° S, apart from far south-west, and north through East Africa to south Sudan. Common but never numerous in wooded habitats. Generally nonmigratory. **Similar species:** other puff-back flycatchers.

African Blue-Flycatcher

Elminia longicauda (**Monarchidae**) 14 cm/5½ in.
Small, strikingly beautiful flycatcher with bright blue upperparts, paler breast and white abdomen; tail long, habitually fanned. Immature distinctly paler, with some buff spotting above. Call is loud chirp; also sunbirdlike twittering song. Single or paired, foraging from ground level to tree-tops, also pursuing insects in flight; conspicuous, not shy. **Range and habitat:** mainly west and central AF, from Senegal to Angola; also east to Sudan, Uganda, north-west Tanzania, western Kenya. Locally common, never numerous, in moist scrublands and forest edge. Resident. **Similar species:** White-tailed Blue-Flycatcher.

African Paradise-Flycatcher

Terpsiphone viridis (**Monarchidae**) 16–40 cm/6½–16 in.
Medium-sized, male unmistakable with rusty orange back, wings and long (over twice body length) tail, glossy blue-black head and breast, white abdomen; uncommon color phase, males only, has orange replaced by white. Female as male, tail shorter. Immature as female, less glossy on head. Call is sharp "schveit;" song a ringing whistle, "pee-pee, pee-pee-pee-pee, pee, pee, pee." Single or paired, hawking insects; not shy, sometimes unobtrusive. **Range and habitat:** widespread in AF south of 15° N (including southern Arabia), except far south-west. Locally common in scrub and woodland. Nonmigratory or intra-African migrant. **Similar species:** other paradise flycatchers (see pp 264, 308, 310).

Olive Thrush

Turdus olivaceus (**Turdidae**) 23 cm/9 in.
Large, dark olive-brown thrush with rufous orange belly and orange-yellow bill and legs. Immature spotted black on breast and flanks. Call is thin "weeeet," sharper alarm; loud melodious song, from perch. Single or paired, foraging on ground, perching in bushes, trees; generally shy. **Range and habitat:** eastern and southern AF, from Ethiopia and Kenya south to Mozambique and South Africa. Common in wide range of wood and forest habitats, including alpine heath, gardens and plantations. Basically resident, but moving locally, e.g. in postreproductive flocking or altitudinal migration. **Similar species:** 5 similar thrushes in AF; other *Turdus* thrushes (see pp 80, 134, 176, 266).

Groundscraper Thrush

Psophocichla litsitsirupa (**Turdidae**) 22 cm/8½ in.
Large thrush, gray-brown above, heavily spotted black on buff or white below, with curved black mark on ear-coverts. In flight, shows orange-buff patch in wing. Immature spotted whitish or buff above, finely spotted below. Alarm is chuckling "chee;" song a varied succession of shrill whistles, from perch. Single or paired, foraging on ground, perching in bushes, trees; usually approachable. **Range and habitat:** 2 populations in AF: Ethiopian highlands; from Angola and Tanzania south to northern South Africa. Generally common, sometimes local, in open scrublands, including near habitation. Basically resident. **Similar species:** Spotted Ground-Thrush.

Common Bulbul

Yellow-whiskered Greenbul

Dusky Alseonax

White-eyed Slaty-Flycatcher

Southern Black-Flycatcher

Silverbird

Chinspot Batis

African Blue-Flycatcher

African Paradise-Flycatcher
(male at nest)

Olive Thrush

Groundscraper Thrush

Northern Anteater-Chat

Myrmecocichla aethiops (Turdidae) 20 cm/8 in.

Medium-sized, rather thickset and erect thrush, entirely brownish black at rest, appearing black from any distance. In flight, open wings show conspicuous white patch on primaries. Immature brownish on wing-coverts. Call is piping whistle; song a strong and melodic whistling, from perch. In pairs or family parties, foraging on ground, sometimes perching prominently on low bushes, trees or termite hills; not skulking, approachable. **Range and habitat:** mainly at 10–15° N in AF, from Senegal east to southern Sudan; also Kenya, north-east Tanzania. Common in open grassy, bushed or wooded country, often near termite hills. Nonmigratory. **Similar species:** Southern Anteater-Chat, Sooty Chat, female White-winged Cliff-Chat.

White-browed Robin-Chat

Cossypha heuglini (Turdidae) 20 cm/8 in.

Medium-sized thrush with black cap cut by white eyebrow; underparts, rump and outer tail feathers bright rufous orange, back and wings grayish. Immature spotted buff above, mottled black and buff below, lacking eyebrow. Call is monotonously repeated whistle, "doo-doo, swee…doo-doo, swee…;" song, in duet from perch, most often at twilight, is loud and beautiful, often ventriloquial, whistled crescendo, usually incorporating much mimicry. Singly or paired, foraging on ground, perching in cover; shy, retiring. **Range and habitat:** widespread in AF at 10–25° S, north to East Africa, Chad, Somalia. Common in low cover of moist well-vegetated country. Resident. **Similar species:** 16 other robin chats in AF.

Red-backed Scrub-Robin

Cercotrichas leucophrys (Turdidae) 15 cm/6 in.

Small thrush, pale brown to rufous brown above, with bold white eyebrow and variable amount of white in wing; tail mainly rufous, white-tipped; underparts whitish, streaked dark on throat and breast. Immature mottled buff and dark brown. Harsh, chattering alarm calls; song is loud, penetrating, often ventriloquial series of whistles with much repetition, from perch; also mimicry. Single, sometimes paired, foraging on ground, perching in cover; shy, retiring. **Range and habitat:** widespread in AF south of 5° S, apart from far south-west; and north to East Africa, Sudan, Ethiopia, Somalia. Common in great variety of bushed and wooded habitats where some ground cover is present. Nonmigratory or moving locally. **Similar species:** other scrub-robins.

White-starred Robin

Pogonocichla stellata (Turdidae) 15–16 cm/6–6½ in.

Beautiful small thrush with slate-blue head, greenish back and wings, yellow-edged black tail and contrasting bright yellow underparts; the "stars" are small white spots in front of each eye and in the center of the breast. Immature initially dark, profusely spotted yellow; later unspotted, greenish above, lemon-yellow below. Harsh, grating alarm and 2-note piping call; song is soft fluting, 6-note whistle. Usually found singly, foraging on ground or vegetation; unobtrusive, retiring, in cover. **Range and habitat:** eastern AF, north from Cape to Malawi and East Africa. Locally common in low cover of forests (including bamboo) and dense woodland. Nonmigratory; regular altitudinal migration in far south. **Similar species:** Swynnerton's Robin.

Banded Warbler

Parisoma boehmi (Sylviidae) 11 cm/4½ in.

Medium-sized warbler, gray-brown" above with pale yellow eye, white feather-edging in wing and white sides to black tail; underparts white with fine black spotting on throat, conspicuous black breast band and rufous brown flanks and vent. Immature spotted with buff above, lacking breast band. Call is loud squeaking "tick-warra, tick-wurrr;" also brief repeated, trilling song. Single, sometimes paired, foraging openly on bushes and trees, especially acacia; not shy. **Range and habitat:** north-eastern AF, from eastern Tanzania to Kenya, Ethiopia, Somalia. Locally common, never numerous, in dry, bushed or wooded country. Basically resident, wandering to avoid drought. **Similar species:** Black-collared Apalis. **Not illustrated.**

African Reed-Warbler

Acrocephalus baeticatus (Sylviidae) 12 cm/4½ in.

Small warbler, unmarked brown above, darker on wings and tail, with faint pale stripe above pale brown eye; lower mandible yellowish; underparts white or buff-white, tinged warmer buff on breast and flanks; legs dark brown. Immature as adult, generally buffer. Call is sharp "tickk," also harsh "churrrrr" alarm; song is slow, scratchy, grating, with much repetition, resembling Eurasian Reed Warbler *A. scirpaceus*. Single or paired, foraging in dense vegetation; unobtrusive, shy, retiring. **Range and habitat:** widespread in AF south of 15° S, north to East Africa; also Senegal, Cameroon, Chad, Sudan, Somalia. Local, seldom common, in dense, moist, low vegetation. Resident or regular intra-African migrant. **Similar species:** other *Acrocephalus* warblers (see pp 172, 310).

African Yellow Warbler

Chloropeta natalensis (Sylviidae) 14 cm/6 in.

Medium-sized warbler, male greenish brown above with yellower rump, darker crown and dull yellow edging in wings and tail; underparts bright yellow. Female duller below. Immature as female, more buff below and in wings and tail. Hard "churr" alarm, shrill, hoarse song with brief, rapidly repeated phrases. Found singly or in pairs, foraging low in dense herbage but occasionally perching prominently. Generally unobtrusive, often retiring. **Range and habitat:** widespread in AF at 5° N–15° S; also Ethiopia, eastern South Africa. At best locally common, in moist, well vegetated hollows and forest edge, often near water. Resident. **Similar species:** Mountain Yellow Warbler and Papyrus Yellow Warbler.

Bar-throated Apalis

Apalis thoracica (Sylviidae) 12–13 cm/4½–5 in.

Small, long-tailed warbler, dark above with pale eye and white outer tail. Pale underparts cut by black breastband in male, band narrower or absent in female. Great racial variation, with upperparts grayish, greenish or brownish, belly white or yellow. Immature duller, breastband much reduced. Male's song is ringing clicking with galloping rhythm; female replies in duet, with high "cheek" calls. Found in pairs or singly, foraging in bushes and trees. Often tame. **Range and habitat:** eastern AF, from Kenya south to eastern South Africa. Common in bush, woodland and forests. Resident, some altitudinal migration. **Similar species:** 19 other *Apalis* in AF.

Red-faced Crombec

Sylvietta whytii (Sylviidae) 10 cm/4 in.

Tiny, plump, short-necked, short-tailed warbler, silvery-gray above, with face, ear coverts and underparts rufous. Immature browner above with some fawn speckling. Call is high, whistling "see-see-see-seeee," also sharp, far-carrying "chick" alarm, often rapidly repeated. Found in pairs or singly, foraging busily on bushes and trees, systematically searching bark and leaves for invertebrates. Bustling, not skulking or retiring. **Range and habitat:** eastern AF, from Sudan and Ethiopia south to East Africa, Zimbabwe, Mozambique. Locally common in diverse bushed and wooded habitats, including forest edge. Resident, moving locally. **Similar species:** 8 other crombecs in AF.

Green-backed Camaroptera

Camaroptera brachyura (Sylviidae) 11 cm/4½ in.

Plump, restless little warbler, gray above with dull green wings and moderately short tail, frequently cocked over rump; below, throat and breast gray merging to whitish belly, but underparts whitish to buffish in some races. In some areas, nonbreeding plumage is browner above, whiter below. Immature usually yellowish below, sometimes browner or greener above. Call is loud bleating "squeeeeeeeb;" song a loud deep clicking. Single or paired, foraging on shady ground or in dense vegetation; skulking, retiring. **Range and habitat:** widespread in AF south of 15° N, apart from far south-west. Common in dense, low vegetation. Resident, moving very locally.

White-browed Robin-Chat

Northern Anteater-Chat

African Reed Warbler

Red-backed Scrub-Robin

White-starred Robin

Red-faced Crombec

African Yellow Warbler

Bar-throated Apalis

Green-backed Camaroptera

Rattling Cisticola

Cisticola chiniana (Sylviidae) 12–13 cm/4½–5 in.
Large cisticola, streaked black or grayish on brown back and wings, with warmer brown cap (sometimes streaked black) and panel in closed wing; tail brown, tipped whitish, with subterminal black spots; underparts whitish. Male larger. Immature yellowish on breast; some races rustier above. Alarm is loud "swearing," "cheeeee-cheeee. . .;" song a similar "cheee-cheee-cheee-churrrrrr," often from prominent perch. In pairs or family parties, foraging in grass, bushes, trees, often in open; noisy. **Range and habitat:** widespread in AF south of 5° S, except far southwest, and north to Sudan, Ethiopia. Common in open bushed and wooded country. Nonmigratory. **Similar species:** other cisticolas, e.g. Fan-tailed Warbler (see p 310).

Singing Cisticola

Cisticola cantans (Sylviidae) 13 cm/5 in.
Large, unstreaked cisticola, brown to grayish above with contrasting warmer brown cap and panel in closed wing; dusky subterminal band and whitish tip to tail; underparts whitish, washed buff on breast. Some races have nonbreeding plumage, rustier or streaked darker above. Immature duller with faint streaking, or yellowish wash below. Alarm is extended "cheeeerr;" song a loud stuttering "pit-choo" or "pit-choo-chi." Single, in pairs or family parties, foraging in undergrowth; shy. **Range and habitat:** mainly eastern AF, north from Mozambique to East Africa and Ethiopia; also northern tropics, west to Senegal. Common in low, mainly moist, dense vegetation. Nonmigratory. **Similar species:** Fan-tailed Warbler (see p 310).

Tawny-flanked Prinia

Prinia subflava (Sylviidae) 12 cm/4½ in.
Small, slim, restless warbler, brown above with white eyebrow, and white below with warm buffish flanks; long tail frequently cocked vertically and wagged from side to side. Immature washed yellow below, bill yellowish. Call is sharp, far-carrying "sip, sip.. .," also harsh alarm "shzbeeeee;" piping song. In pairs and small parties, foraging low in vegetation but not skulking; often approachable. **Range and habitat:** east through OR to Java; widespread in AF south of 15° north, apart from far south-west. Locally common at low to medium levels in moist, dense scrubland. Nonmigratory. **Similar species:** other prinias (see p 268).

Mosque Swallow

Cecropis senegalensis (Hirundinidae) 24 cm/9 in.
Large, thickset swallow, glossy blue-black above with rufous rump and long tail streamers. Underparts rufous with white face and upper breast. Displays blazing white underwing coverts during falconlike flight. Immature duller; streamers shorter, brownish speckling on upperwing. Call is deep, nasal "harrrrp." Found singly or in pairs, occasionally small parties, hawking aerial insects. Not shy. **Range and habitat:** widespread at 15° N to 20° S in AF apart from equatorial forests. Locally common, never numerous, in open wooded areas. Resident, moving locally. **Similar species:** 14 similar swallows in AF.

Wire-tailed Swallow

Hirundo smithii (Hirundinidae) 13 cm/5 in.
Small swallow, glossy violet-blue above with rufous orange crown and long, thin tail streamers; underparts white. Immature gray-brown above, washed buff below, streamers very reduced. Usually silent; occasional low twitterings. Single or paired, sometimes loose parties while foraging, hawking aerial insects; often tame. **Range and habitat:** widespread in OR, east to Laos, Vietnam; widespread in AF south of 10° N, apart from far south-west and Congo basin forests. Locally common, never numerous, in open areas near water; often around habitation. Basically nonmigratory. **Similar species:** other swallows in AF.

Lesser Striped-Swallow

Cecropis abyssinica (Hirundinidae) 17 cm/6½ in.
Medium-sized swallow, blue-black above with rufous chestnut crown and rump, and long tail streamers; easily identified by coarse dark streaking on white ventral torso. Immature duller, washed buff below, tail streamers reduced. Call consists of loud, distinctive discordant squeaks; also discordant piping song. In pairs or small flocks, hawking aerial insects; often approachable, nesting on buildings. **Range and habitat:** widespread in AF south of 15° N,

apart from far south-west and Congo forest regions. Common in many open habitats, including forest edge; often around habitation. Nonmigratory, or local or intra-African migrant. **Similar species:** other AF swallows.

Plain Martin

Riparia paludicola (Hirundinidae) 13 cm/5 in.
Small martin with slightly forked tail; most brown with white abdomen, but a few entirely brown; north African race grayish white below with darker throat. Immature speckled dark buff above, washed buff on abdomen. Harsh alarm call, also weak twittering. In flocks up to thousands, hawking aerial insects; not shy, can be unobtrusive. **Range and habitat:** widespread resident in Morocco, and OR east to Philippines; widespread in AF south of 15° N, apart from Congo forests. Locally common, usually near inland wetlands. Resident; postbreeding dispersal and other movements. **Similar species:** 6 other brown martins in AF, Bank swallow, Dusky Crag-Martin (see pp 168, 260).

Banded Martin

Riparia cincta (Hirundinidae) 17 cm/6½ in.
Large, robust, sluggish martin, brown above with small white streak in front of eye, and square or slightly notched tail; ventral torso and underwing-coverts white, with brown breast band. Immature speckled buff above. Often silent; various twittering calls. In pairs or small parties, larger flocks after breeding season, hawking low-flying insects, perching on grass stems; not shy. **Range and habitat:** widespread in AF south of 10° N, except far southwest. Rather local, foraging low over open or lightly bushed grasslands. Sometimes resident, but mainly local or intra-African migrant. **Similar species:** 7 other brown martins in AF, Sand Martin, Dusky Crag Martin (see pp 168, 260).

Black Sawwing

Psalidoprocne holomelas (Hirundinidae) 17 cm/7 in.
Medium-sized, slightly glossy, black rough-wing swallow with long, deeply forked tail. In flight, white-winged birds show conspicuous white or pale underwing coverts. Immature as adult, duller. Weak twittering calls, but often silent. Found singly or in small flocks, sometimes with White-beaded Rough-wings, hawking aerial insects. Not shy. **Range and habitat:** widespread in AF south of Cameroon and Ethiopia, apart from arid Horn and far south-west. Locally common, sometimes numerous, in moist, open, bushed, wooded and forest edge habitats. Resident, intra-African migrant in south. **Similar species:** immature White-headed Sawwing.

Black Cuckooshrike

Campephaga flava (Campephagidae) 21 cm/8 in.
Male is medium-sized glossy, faintly bluish black, somewhat cuckoolike bird with rounded tail, orange-yellow gape wattles and, in some individuals, conspicuous yellow shoulders. Female brown with dark barring above, much bright yellow edging in wings and tail, and black, yellow and white barring below. Immature as female, more heavily barred. Generally silent; call is sharp "chup," also insectlike trill. Single or paired, foraging unobtrusively in mid-storey of vegetation; not shy. **Range and habitat:** widespread in AF south of 5° S, apart from far south-west; also north to Ethiopia. Seasonally common in bushed and wooded habitats. Some equatorial populations nonmigratory, others intra-African migrants. **Similar species:** 3 other cuckooshrikes (see p 262).

Fork-tailed Drongo

Dicrurus adsimilis (Dicruridae) 25 cm/10 in.
Medium-sized glossy black, rather shrikelike bird with reddish eye and deeply forked, diverging "fishtail." In flight, wings show pale grayish wash. Immature grayer above and below, tail less deeply cleft. Call is loud, strident "waank;" loud, strident song, also mimicry. Single or paired, on exposed perches, hawking insects, killing small birds; noisy, aggressive, extrovert; also unobtrusive forest race, the Velvet-mantled Drongo. **Range and habitat:** widespread in AF south of 15° N. Common in many nonforest habitats; Velvet-mantled is rarer, in interior of Congo forests. Basically nonmigratory. **Similar species:** other drongos (see pp 278, 322).

Rattling Cisticola

Singing Cisticola

Tawny-flanked Prinia

Mosque Swallow

Black Sawwing

Wire-tailed Swallow

Lesser Striped-Swallow

Plain Martin

Banded Martin

Black Cuckooshrike

Fork-tailed Drongo

White Helmetshrike

Prionops plumatus (Laniidae) 20 cm/8 in.

Medium-sized shrike, black and white above with yellow eyes and surrounding wattles, and bristly crest on forecrown; below white, with orange-yellow legs. Immature browner above, spotted on wing-coverts, lacking eye-wattles. Frequent loud, chattering calls and whistling, often in chorus; also bill-snapping. Habitually in small flocks, foraging through bushes and trees; often approachable. **Range and habitat:** widespread in AF south of 15° N, apart from far south-west and Congo forests. Locally common in generally dry scrublands. Resident, making extensive erratic, foraging movements; irrupts in south. **Similar species:** Gray-crested Helmetshrike.

White-rumped Shrike

Eurocephalus ruppelli (Laniidae) 24 cm/9½ in.

Distinctive, noisy, rather large shrike, brown above with white crown and nape; underparts white. White rump prominent during characteristically stiff-winged, gliding flight. Immature speckled buffish above, crown and nape grayish hrown. Calls are sharp, high-pitched, chattering squawks and whistles. Found in pairs or small parties, perching prominently, high on bushes and trees; often retiring. **Range and habitat:** north-eastern AF, from Tanzania to Kenya, Ethiopia, Somalia, southern Sudan. Common in generally dry scrublands. Basically nonmigratory. **Similar species:** White-rumped Shrike.

Brubru

Nilaus afer (Laniidae) 13 cm/5 in.

Small bush shrike, male boldly patterned black and white above with prominent white eyebrow; below white, with conspicuous rufous chestnut flanks. Female similar, black replaced by dark brown. Immature mottled dark above, with some irregular dark barring or streaking below. Male gives high, far-carrying trill, "trreeeeeeeee;" female often makes wheezing sounds in duet. Single or paired, restlessly foraging at mid-levels in vegetation; unobtrusive, not retiring. **Range and habitat:** widespread in AF south of 17° N, except Cape and Congo basin areas. Fairly common in scrublands, especially in acacia canopies. Nonmigratory. **Similar species:** *Batis* flycatchers (see p 220).

Gray-backed Fiscal

Lanius excubitoroides (Laniidae) 25 cm/10 in.

Medium-sized shrike with pale gray upper-parts and bold black streak across forehead and through eye, extending to side of neck. Wings black. Long tail is black with white basal region and tip. Underparts of male white, female has some chestnut on flanks. Immature is lightly barred dusky brown. Calls are varied, may be musical or harsh. Very gregarious, sometimes in large groups feeding on emerging flying ants; noisy, conspicuous, aggressive. **Range and habitat:** AF in southern Sudan, Ethiopia, Uganda, western Kenya and Tanzania. Fairly common in open bush country. Resident and local migrant. **Similar species:** in AF, other fiscals, puffback shrikes, also boubous.

Yellow-billed Shrike

Corvinella corvina (Laniidae) 30 cm/12 in.

Large, very long-tailed shrike, brown streaked with black above, with dark facial mask and conspicuous chrome-yellow bill; ventral torso buffish white, thinly streaked black. Male has pale chestnut flank patch. In flight, shows conspicuous rufous primaries. Immature mottled blackish above, barred blackish on breast. Typical call is monotonously repeated "scis-scis;" also shrill whistles, shrieks. In small parties, perching prominently, following each other like babblers; often approachable. **Range and habitat:** at 5–15° N in AF, east to southern Sudan and Kenya. Locally common in open scrublands, particularly near water and dense undergrowth. Resident.

Papyrus Gonolek

Laniarius mufumbiri (Laniidae) 20 cm/8 in.

Medium-sized, but robust bush shrike mainly black above with golden-yellow crown and nape with white tips to wing coverts. Underparts bright crimson with buff vent. Immature has a yellower crown. Call is a loud, mellow "yoyo." Single or paired; shy, retiring in dense cover, usually betrayed by calls. Often rather inquisitive to strange sounds. **Range and habitat:** AF in south and west Uganda, western Kenya and north-western Tanzania. Restricted to papyrus swamps, where locally common. Nonmigratory. Classified as near threatened because of high level of specialization to papyrus habitat which itself is under threat. **Similar species:** Black-headed, Common Gonolek.

Slate-colored Boubou

Laniarius funebris (Laniidae) 18 cm/7 in.

Medium-sized, rather rotund, dark slate to blackish bush shrike. Female slightly paler below. Immature indistinctly barred brown above; grayer below with fine blackish barring. Various whistles, harsh "churrs" and softer "plops;" but mainly loud, rapid, precisely synchronized duets between male and female, typically "hoo -hoo, hoooeeet," often repeated. Single or paired, skulking and retiring in or under low dense vegetation, betrayed by calls. **Range and habitat:** north-eastern AF, from Tanzania and Kenya to Sudan, Ethiopia, Somalia. Common in drier, dense scrublands. Nonmigratory. **Similar species:** other black boubous and black helmetshrikes.

Southern Boubou

Laniarius ferrugineus (Laniidae) 23 cm/9 in.

Large, rather robust bush shrike, glossy black above, sometimes with white wing-bar and/or whitish rump; below white, washed pink or peach, especially on vent. Immature spotted buffish above; washed buff below, sometimes with brown barring. Various whistling, snarling and churring calls, but characteristically an extensive vocabulary of loud, precisely synchronized duets, often incorporating pure, bell-like notes. Found in pairs, skulking in vegetation or in open, betrayed by calls; sometimes tame. **Range and habitat:** widespread in AF south of 10° N, apart from far south-west and Congo forests. Common in moist, dense cover. Nonmigratory, perhaps moving locally. **Similar species:** 2 similar boubous.

Black-backed Puffback

Dryoscopus cubla (Laniidae) 16 cm/6½ in.

Small, black and white bush shrike with crimson eyes; male glossy blue-black above, with downy white rump feathers puffed out during courtship. Female duller above, forehead and eyebrow white, rump gray. In flight, wings make buzzing "purrrrp." Immature as female, with pale plumage washed buff. Various clicks, whistles and bill-snapping; typical call is high shrill whistle, preceded by click. In pairs, foraging in canopies for insects; not retiring. **Range and habitat:** widespread in AF south from Angola, southern Zaire and Kenya, apart from far south-west. Common in moist woods and forest edges. Nonmigratory. **Similar species:** in AF 4 other puffbacks and black and white shrikes.

Black-crowned Tchagra

Tchagra senegala (Laniidae) 21 cm/8 in.

Medium-sized bush shrike with black cap cut by striking white eyebrow, rusty red wings, and longish black tail with white tip; underparts white, washed gray on breast. Immature has brownish crown. Usual call is far-carrying piping whistle, from flight or perch; also harsh alarm, "churr." Single or paired, foraging in or under low cover but also reaching higher, more exposed situations; shy. **Range and habitat:** WP in Morocco, Algeria, Tunisia; widespread in AF south of 15° N (including southern Arabia), apart from far south-west and Congo forests. Common in low cover and thickets, in scrublands. Nonmigratory. **Similar species:** other tchagras in AF.

Sulfur-breasted Bushshrike

Telophorus sulphureopectus (Laniidae) 18 cm/7 in.

Medium-sized, slim bushshrike, gray and yellow-green above with yellow forehead and eye stripe; underparts bright yellow, merging to bright orange on breast. Immature barred black, lacking orange breast and yellow forehead. Call is far-carrying ringing whistle, including characteristic "tee-tee too-toooo" and 'tee-tee-tee-teeeeee" phrases; also harsh alarms. Single or paired, foraging at medium to high levels in vegetation; sometimes skulking and retiring. **Range and habitat:** widespread in AF south of 10° N, apart from Congo basin and far southwest. Locally common in many scrub habitats. Apparently nonmigratory. **Similar species:** other bushshrikes.

White Helmetshrike

Black-crowned Tchagra

White-rumped Shrike

Brubru

Gray-backed Fiscal

Yellow-billed Shrike

Papyrus Gorolek

Slate-colored Boubou

Southern Boubou

Sulfur-breasted Bushshrike

Black-backed Puffback

White-bellied Tit
Melaniparus albiventris **(Paridae)** 14 cm/5½ in.
Noisy, active, mainly black tit, with much white edging in wing and conspicuous unmarked white belly. Male is glossy black; female duller, sooty black. Immature has some yellow in flight feathers. Characteristic call is loud, sharp "see see see;" song a repeated softer "dee dee dee durrr." In pairs, family groups or single, restlessly foraging at medium to high levels in bushes and trees; conspicuous, bold. **Range and habitat:** mainly eastern AF, in Tanzania, Kenya, Uganda, southern Sudan; also Cameroon in west. Fairly common but never numerous in generally moist bush and woodland. Nonmigratory. **Similar species:** other tits (see pp 82, 272).

African Golden Oriole
Oriolus auratus **(Oriolidae)** 24 cm/9½ in.
Medium-sized oriole, male golden yellow with dark pink bill and black eye stripe extending back to ear-coverts; much yellow edging in black wings. Female greener above, paler yellow with olive streaking below; eye stripe similar. Immature as female, greenish edging in wings. Characteristic call is liquid, melodious whistle, "weela-wooo;" also catlike mewing. Single, paired or in small parties, foraging high in dense canopy; shy, betrayed by calls. **Range and habitat:** widespread in AF between 15° N and 22° S, apart from Congo forests. Uncommon in woods. Intra-African migrant converging on Equator after breeding. **Similar species:** Eurasian Golden Oriole (see p 182). **Not illustrated.**

African Black-headed Oriole
Oriolus larvatus **(Oriolidae)** 24 cm/9½ in.
Medium-sized, bright golden yellow oriole, greenish on back and tail, with black hood; coral-pink bill, white and yellow edging in wing. Immature has blackish bill; streaked yellowish on head, black on breast and belly. Characteristic call is melodious, liquid whistle, "weeela-weeeoooo;" also harsh and mewing sounds. Single or paired, foraging high in dense canopy; shy, betrayed by calls. **Range and habitat:** widespread in AF south of 5° S, except far south-west; also north through East Africa to Sudan, Ethiopia. Common in well-wooded areas. Basically resident. **Similar species:** 6 similar orioles; various black-headed weavers (see pp 182, 232, 278).

White-necked Raven
Corvus albicollis **(Corvidae)** 54 cm/21 in.
Large, thickset, short-tailed, glossy black raven with massive black bill tipped with white, and white crescent on hindneck and upper mantle. Immature browner, white patch streaked dark; sometimes thin white breast band. Call is distinctively high croak, "kraaak." Single or paired, up to hundreds at good feeding sites; highly aerial, foraging on ground; approachable, extrovert. **Range and habitat:** highlands of eastern AF, from South Africa to eastern Zaire and East Africa. Locally common around cliffs and rocky hills, often scavenging boldly at carcasses and habitation. Nonmigratory, making long foraging flights, wandering. **Similar species:** other ravens.

Pied Crow
Corvus albus **(Corvidae)** 46 cm/18 in.
Large, glossy black crow with conspicuous white breast and collar. Immature duller, white feathering speckled dusky. Call is loud, raucous, frequently uttered "caww;" also subdued grunts, snoring. In pairs, also flocks up to hundreds, foraging boldly on ground; occasionally shy, usually approachable, opportunistic. **Range and habitat:** widespread in AF south of 20° N, apart from far southern interior; vagrants north to Algeria and Libya in WP. Common, omnivorous scavenger, mainly in and around settlements where sympatric with the Brown-necked Raven, more widespread south of latter's range. Basically resident.

Piapiac
Ptilostomus afer **(Corvidae)** 35 cm/14 in. Small, slender, noisy, glossy black crow, browner on wings and long graduated tail, with black bill and violet eye. Immature duller, with violet bill tipped with black. Shrill, frequently uttered, squeaking calls; also croaking alarms. In small parties, foraging on open ground; active, often shy. **Range and habitat:** northern AF, from Senegal and Guinea east to southern Sudan, Uganda, western Kenya. Common in open wooded grasslands, especially near *Borassus* palms; often seizing insects flushed by mammals; in towns in western AF. Resident or

moving extensively but erratically. **Similar species:** Rueppell's Glossy-Starling.

Cape Crow
Corvus capensis **(Corvidae)** 48 cm/19 in.
Large but not heavily built, glossy black crow with noticeably slender black bill. Immature duller, washed brownish. Call is frequently uttered, loud high-pitched "kraaah;" also lower liquid and growling sounds. Single or paired, more often small flocks, occasionally thousands, foraging on ground; not shy. **Range and habitat:** 2 separate areas of AF: widespread south of 10° S except the interior; and north-east, from East Africa to southern Sudan, Ethiopia, Somalia. Sometimes common or locally so in open country with scattered trees and cultivated land. Nonmigratory, moving locally to feeding sites, occasionally wandering. **Similar species:** Brown-necked Raven.

Wattled Starling
Creatophora cinerea **(Sturnidae)** 21 cm/8 in.
Medium-sized, drab gray-brown starling with black wings and tail, and pale or white rump. Breeding male unmistakable with bare yellow and black skin and long black wattles on head. Nonbreeding male has head feathered, without wattles; female similar, with black wing-coverts. Immature as female, browner. Often silent; alarm is nasal "raaah" also squeaky, high-pitched song. In flocks up to thousands, foraging on ground; not shy. **Range and habitat:** widespread in AF south of 5° S, and north to Ethiopia, Somalia and sometimes south Arabia. Locally common, irregularly abundant, in open scrublands, often foraging around large mammals. Resident, but frequently nomadic in search of food.

Greater Blue-eared Glossy-Starling
Lamprotornis chalybaeus **(Sturnidae)** 23 cm/9 in.
Medium-sized, thickset, metallic blue-green starling with bluish ear-coverts and conspicuous orange-yellow eyes; central tail feathers green, washed with blue. Immature sooty black, glossed green; eyes gray. Typical call is harsh "skeea-eeeear;" song a mixture of similar squawking and chattering notes. In pairs during breeding, then flocks up to hundreds, foraging on ground; often tame. **Range and habitat:** at 10–15° N in AF from Senegal to Ethiopia, and south through East Africa to Angola, eastern South Africa. Common in open scrublands, often around habitation. Resident or moving extensively when not breeding. **Similar species:** other glossy-starlings, New World grackles (see pp 90, 182, 276).

Violet-backed Starling
Cinnyricinclus leucogaster **(Sturnidae)** 18 cm/7 in.
Small starling, male unmistakable with brilliant, metallic crimson-violet head and upperparts, white under-parts. Female brown above; below white or buffish, with dusky spotting and streaking; eyes yellow. Immature as female, eyes brown. Often silent; twitters in flight, also twanging, whining song. In pairs when breeding; then mainly small flocks, often of 1 sex; foraging high in trees or on ground; often shy. **Range and habitat:** widespread in AF between 25° S and 15° N, apart from Congo forest areas; also north to south-west Arabia in northern summer. Seasonally common in wooded and forested country. Intra-African migrant converging on Equator after breeding. **Similar species:** female resembles spotted thrushes.

Rueppell's Long-tailed Glossy-Starling
Lamprotornis purpuropterus **(Sturnidae)** 35 cm/14 in.
Large, metallic blue and violet starling with long graduated tail and white eyes. Immature duller, blacker. Harsh alarm, "skaaaaa;" also squeaky chattering and whistling, and short, musical song. In pairs or small groups, foraging in trees or on ground; often tame. **Range and habitat:** north-eastern AF, from eastern Zaire and northern Tanzania to Somalia, Ethiopia, Sudan. Common in moist open bushed and wooded country; more local in arid areas, usually near water; often around habitation. Basically resident, wandering. **Similar species:** other glossy-starlings in AF. New World grackles (see p 90).

White-bellied Tit

African Black-headed Oriole

White-necked Raven

Pied Crow

Piapiac

Cape Crow

Greater Blue-eared Glossy-Starling

Wattled Starling
(display calling)

Violet-backed Starling

Rueppell's Long-tailed Glossy-Starling

Golden-breasted Starling

Lamprotornis regius (Sturnidae) 35 cm/14 in.
Slender starling with metallic turquoise-green head and neck, white eyes, blue-violet gloss on wings and long tail; underparts golden yellow. Immature duller, blackish above, brownish on face and breast. Call is loud chattering whistle. In pairs or small parties, foraging high in vegetation; shy. **Range and habitat:** north-eastern AF, from northern and eastern Tanzania to Kenya, Somalia, south-east Ethiopia. Locally common in open scrublands. Resident or moving locally, e.g. dispersing during rains. **Similar species:** structure as Ashy Starling.

Superb Starling

Lamprotornis superbus (Sturnidae) 18 cm/7 in.
Distinctive small starling, metallic blues and greens above, with blackish head and contrasting yellowish white eyes; below, conspicuous thin white band divides metallic blue breast from rufous chestnut abdomen; vent white. Immature duller, blacker; eyes dark; lacks breast band. Loud whining alarm, "weeeaaaaa;" also varied warbling song, with mimicry. In small parties, foraging on ground; tame. **Range and habitat:** north-eastern AF, from Tanzania to south Sudan, Ethiopia, Somalia. Common in many bush and woodland habitats and city centers. Basically resident. **Similar species:** 3 AF starlings (see p 228).

Red-winged Starling

Onychognathus morio (Sturnidae) 28 cm/11 in.
Slender, moderately long-tailed starling; male glossy blue-black; female gray on head and neck, streaked gray on breast. In flight, rufous primaries. Immature as male, lacking gloss. Call is loud, melodious, liquid whistle; harsher alarm. Nesting in pairs, otherwise flocks up to hundreds, foraging on trees or ground; often shy, but nests on buildings. **Range and habitat:** mainly eastern AF, from Cape to Ethiopia; also patchily in northern tropics. Locally common in wooded country, often around cliffs and buildings, including city streets. Resident. **Similar species:** other *Onychognathus* starlings.

Yellow-billed Oxpecker

Buphagus africanus (Sturnidae) 22 cm/9 in.
Slender, medium-sized starling, darkish brown on head and upperparts with red-tipped yellow bill and narrow yellow eye-ring. Underparts pale buff. In flight, prominent pale buff rump. Immature duller, bill dusky. Call is penetrating hiss "shssssss," also cackling, chattering. In small parties, gleaning parasites, flesh and blood from hides of large mammals, often with Red-billed Oxpecker. Shy. **Range and habitat:** widespread in AF between 15° N and 20° S apart from Congo forests. Common in open country. Resident. **Similar species:** Red-billed Oxpecker.

Cape Sugarbird

Promerops cafer (Meliphagidae) 24–44 cm/9½–17 in.
Distinctive, bulbul-sized species, like sunbird; male with long decurved bill, brown upperparts and long, graduated brown tail; underparts whitish, russet on breast, vent bright yellow. Female similar, tail shorter. Immature with tail shorter still, lacking yellow verit. Harsh alarm; song a sustained jumble of discordant twanging and grating notes, from perch. Single or paired, rarely in small parties, foraging at flowers; bold. **Range and habitat:** extreme southern AF, in south Cape Province, South Africa. Common in fynbos vegetation, often near proteas. Resident, moves seasonally to feed at protea flowers. **Similar species:** Gurney's Sugarbird, various sunbirds (see p 274).

African Yellow White-eye

Zosterops senegalensis (Zosteropidae) 10.5 cm/4 in.
Small white-eye, yellowish-green above with thin white eye-ring and bright yellow forehead. Underparts bright canary-yellow. Immature duller, initially lacking eye-ring. Usual call is frequent, high peeping whistle; also a soft, low warbling song. Nests in pairs, otherwise found in small parties, restlessly foraging through cover. Not shy, often tame. **Range and habitat:** widespread throughout most of AF, south to north-east South Africa. Common in scrubland, forest edge and gardens. **Similar species:** other white-eyes (see pp 272, 318).

Malachite Sunbird

Nectarinia famosa (Nectariniidae) 14–24 cm/5½–9½ in.
Large sunbird, breeding male unmistakable bright emerald green with inconspicuous yellow pectoral tufts, and blackish wings and tail, latter with greatly elongated central feathers. Nonbreeding male speckled green, yellow below, often lacking elongated tail. Female and immature grayish, with yellow malar stripe; white-edged tail. Shrill "tseee" and "siip" notes; also rapid twittering, jingling song, from perch. Single or paired, foraging at flowers; active, bold. **Range and habitat:** eastern AF, from South Africa to Ethiopia. Locally common, visiting flowers in many habitats. Resident or local migrant. **Similar species:** Red Malachite Sunbird.

Mariqua Flycatcher

Bradornis mariquensis (Nectariniidae) 13 cm/5 in.
Medium-sized, square-tailed sunbird, male with metallic green head and mantle, dark blue breastband shading downward to maroon, and black belly, wings, tail. No nonbreeding plumage. Female grayish above, yellowish below with dark streaking. Immature as female, male with throat blackish. Call is sharp "sip-sip;" high, rapid song. Found singly or in pairs, foraging at flowers. Not shy. **Range and habitat:** two regions of AF, north-east, in Ethiopia, East Africa, and at 15–25° S. Locally common in open, bushed and wooded habitats. Resident. **Similar species:** 14 AF sunbirds.

Variable Sunbird

Cinnyris venusta (Nectariniidae) 11 cm/4½ in.
Small sunbird, male metallic blue-green above with metallic purple breast and nonmetallic white, yellow or orange belly. Female gray-brown above, whitish to yellowish below. Immature as female, throat blackish in male. Harsh "cheer" alarm, softer "tsip" calls; short tuneful, twittering song, from perch. Usually found in pairs, small groups at favored feeding sites, foraging at flowers and leaves; often tame. **Range and habitat:** widespread in AF between 10° N and 17° S, apart from Congo basin. Common in bushed and wooded areas. Resident, some seasonal movement. **Similar species:** Collared and White-breasted Sunbirds.

Scarlet-chested Sunbird

Chalcomitra senegalensis (Nectariniidae) 15 cm/6 in.
Medium-sized sunbird, male always black with brilliant scarlet breast and metallic turquoise-green crown and throat. Female brown above, yellowish with dark mottling below. Immature as female, male developing scarlet breast. Harsh "chaak" alarm, squeaky song; characteristic call deliberate, monotonously repeated "sheep, ship, shop," from high perch. Single or paired, small groups at feeding sites, foraging at flowers; active, sometimes approachable. **Range and habitat:** widespread in AF between 15° N and 20° S, apart from Congo forests. Common in moist scrub and woodland. Resident, moving locally, seasonally. **Similar species:** Hunter's Sunbird.

Southern Double-collared Sunbird

Cinnyris chalybea (Nectariniidae) 12.5 cm/5 in.
Medium-sized, sunbird with long, decurved bill. Male has metallic green head, throat and mantle, narrow purple chest-band followed by broader red band. Rest of underparts dirty gray. Rump blue, wings and tail blackish. Female gray below with slight yellowish wash, dull brownish gray above. Calls include a harsh "zzik." Song a jumble of notes which rise and fall in pitch. Usually in pairs, sometimes in groups, foraging on nectar or insects. **Range and habitat:** southern AF, South Africa to southern Angola. Fairly common in forest and gardens. **Similar species:** several "double-collared" sunbirds.

Beautiful Sunbird

Cinnyris pulchella (Nectariniidae) 12–15 cm/4½–6 in.
Rather small sunbird, breeding male metallic green with elongated central tail feathers, and bright red breast bordered yellow on flanks; belly black in some races. Nonbreeding male metallic green on rump and tail, otherwise grayish above, whiter below. Female similar, yellowish below, with whitish eyebrow. Immature similar, throat black in male. Monotonous "sip" calls, soft song. Single, in pairs or small groups, feeds at flowers; not shy. **Range and habitat:** mainly at 8–17° N in AF, from Senegal to Ethiopia; also East Africa. Locally common in open bushed and wooded areas. Resident. **Similar species:** Olive-bellied and Black-bellied Sunbirds.

Golden-breasted Starling

Superb Starling

Red-winged Starling

Yellow-billed Oxpecker

Cape Sugarbird

African Yellow White-eye

Malachite Sunbird

Mariqua Flycatcher

Variable Sunbird

Scarlet-chested Sunbird

Southern Double-collared Sunbird

Beautiful Sunbird

Red-billed Buffalo-Weaver

Bubalornis niger (Ploceidae) 25 cm/10 in.
Large, stocky weaver, male black with white on flanks, and conspicuous large red bill. Female brown above, mottled and streaked dusky on white below, bill as male. White wing patch visible in flight. Immature as female, bill yellowish or brown. Loud, garrulous, falsetto chattering and croaking calls. In pairs or small parties, foraging on ground; not shy. **Range and habitat:** northeast AF, from Tanzania to Ethiopia, Somalia; south AF, from Angola, Zambia to South Africa. Common in dry, open scrublands. Nonmigratory, wandering; migrant far south. **Similar species:** White-billed Buffalo-Weaver.

White-browed Sparrow-Weaver

Plocepasser mahali (Ploceidae) 16 cm/6½ in.
Medium-sized, noisy weaver, brown above with broad white eyebrow, white edging in blackish wings; underparts white, sometimes spotted on breast. In flight, shows white rump. Immature with pinkish bill. Sharp "chuck" alarm; loud, chattering, liquid song with "chop" and "cheep" notes. In pairs or small parties, feeds on ground; not shy. **Range and habitat:** 2 regions of AF: northeast, in Kenya, Sudan, Ethiopia; south of 15° S, except far south-west. Locally common in dry, open, wooded country, near habitation. Resident. **Similar species:** Donaldson-Smith's Sparrow-Weaver.

Gray-headed Social-Weaver

Pseudonigrita arnaudi (Ploceidae) 13 cm/5 in.
Rather small and short-tailed grayish buff weaver, blacker on wings, with conspicuous gray or pale gray cap; tail black or dark, broadly tipped dirty gray. Immature buffer, including cap. Brief, piping flight call; also chattering and squeaking at nest. In small parties, feeds on ground; busy, often tame. **Range and habitat:** northeastern AF, from Tanzania north to Uganda, Sudan, Ethiopia. Locally common in mainly dry bushed and open wooded country, often on sandy soils; sometimes around habitation. Basically nonmigratory or wandering.

Chestnut Sparrow

Passer eminibey (Ploceidae) 11 cm/4½ in.
Small sparrow, breeding male warm chestnut-brown, wings and tail darker with some pale edging; bill black. Nonbreeding male, and female, grayer-brown above with pale brown eyebrow and some dark streaking; buffish or grayish below; bill horn. Immature similar, still grayer above. Low chirping calls. In small parties or larger flocks, feed on ground; sometimes shy. **Range and habitat:** northeastern AF, from Tanzania to Sudan, Ethiopia, southern Somalia. Locally common in open scrublands, often near habitation or water. Resident, wandering widely. **Similar species:** Chestnut Weaver.

White-headed Buffalo-Weaver

Dinemellia dinemelli (Ploceidae) 23 cm/9 in.
Large, stocky weaver with white head and underparts, striking reddish orange rump and vent, brown back, wings and tail. In flight, white patch at base of upperwing primaries. Immature has orange rump. Call is harsh squeal, also loud chattering. Found in pairs and small parties, foraging openly on ground; can be wary. **Range and habitat:** north-eastern AF, in Ethiopia, Somalia, East Africa. Common in dry, open bushed and wooded country. Resident. **Similar species:** White-rumped Shrike.

Golden Palm Weaver

Ploceus bojeri (Ploceidae) 15 cm/6 in.
Medium-sized weaver, male always bright yellow, greener above, with head and breast washed chestnut-orange; mantle unmarked; dark eye contrasts with pale face. Female yellow, dusky to greenish above, brighter below. Immature as female, paler below. High-pitched" chattering and sizzling calls, especially around nest. In small parties; feeds on ground; noisy, active, fairly tame. **Range and habitat:** north-east AF, in Tanzania, Kenya, southern Somalia. Common or locally so in open bushed and wooded areas, often around habitation or water. Nonmigratory, wandering. **Similar species:** 4 other golden weavers in AF.

Baglafecht Weaver

Ploceus baglafecht (Ploceidae) 15 cm/6 in.
Medium-sized weaver, male black above (some green) with pale eyes, yellow face cut by black mask (face black in some), and golden yellow edging in wing; underparts yellow (white in some). Female as male, face and crown all black. Immature as female, streaked dark on olive above. Call is sharp "chirp;" short chattering, sizzling song. In pairs or family parties; feeds on ground and vegetation; active, often tame. **Range and habitat:** mainly eastern AF, from Malawi to Ethiopia; also Cameroon. Common in moist woodland; often around habitation. Nonmigratory. **Similar species:** 5 similar AF weavers.

Black-headed Weaver

Ploceus melanocepalus (Ploceidae) 18 cm/7 in.
Large weaver with greatly varying races, breeding male yellow above with black hood or face, variably chestnut nape, and yellow edging in black wings and tail; underparts yellow, sometimes washed chestnut. Nonbreeding male gray-brown, with yellow breast, white belly. Female similar, greener and yellower when breeding. Immature as breeding female, browner above. Loud sizzling and chattering at nest. Found in flocks, foraging on ground and vegetation; noisy, approachable. **Range and habitat:** widespread in AF south of 15° N, apart from far south-west. Common in open bushed and wooded habitats, often around habitation or water. Resident and local migrant. **Similar species:** many similar yellow and black weavers (see p 276).

Red-headed Weaver

Anaplectes rubriceps (Ploceidae) 15 cm/6 in.
Medium-sized weaver, breeding male with bright red head and breast, white belly; some races red on mantle and wings. Nonbreeding male grayer above, some races dull orange on head, with yellow breast; female as latter races. Immature as female, buffish below. Often silent; calls "tink," also sizzling, squeaky song. Single or paired; feeds in trees; unobtrusive, not shy. **Range and habitat:** widespread in AF south of 13° N, apart from far south-west and much of west. Locally common, never numerous, in scrub and woodland. Mainly resident; local migrant in far south. **Similar species:** Cardinal and Red-headed Queleas.

Red Bishop

Euplectes orix (Ploceidae) 14 cm/5½ in.
Medium-sized bishop. Breeding male bright red above with pale brown wings and tail. Face (including forehead), lower breast and belly black. Nonbreeding male, female and immature are brown, sparrowlike, heavily streaked black, buff and brown above, buff below with fine streaking on breast and flanks. Sharp "chiz" flight call, rather wheezy twittering song. Found in flocks, foraging on the ground, busy and noisy. **Range and habitat:** widespread throughout AF. Common in bushed or open moist grassland, also cultivations and gardens. Basically resident, wandering. **Similar species:** 3 similar bishops in AF.

Yellow Bishop

Euplectes capensis (Ploceidae) 15 cm/6 in.
Large bishop, breeding male black with conspicuous, bright lemon-yellow shoulders and rump. Nonbreeding male retains yellow but otherwise sparrowlike, heavily streaked on upperparts and breast, belly white. Female and immature as nonbreeding male, rump and shoulders dull yellow-olive. Often quiet; sharp "tzeet" call; subdued twittering in courtship. Paired when breeding, flocks in off-season, foraging on, e.g., standing sedges; active, not shy. **Range and habitat:** local in AF, at 5–30° S north to Ethiopia; also Cameroon. Locally common in tall, bushed grassland and woodland edge. Basically resident. **Similar species:** Yellow-shouldered Widowbird, Yellow-crowned Bishop.

Jackson's Widowbird

Euplectes jacksoni (Ploceidae) 14–35 cm/9–14 in.
Medium-sized widowbird, breeding male black with brown shoulders; in flight, long tail is distinctively droop-tipped. Nonbreeding male sheds tail, and is brown, streaked, sparrowlike. Female and immature similar. Call is soft "cheeee," song "see-see-chip-chip-chip." In flocks, females outnumber males, foraging on ground. Unique courtship display; male performs jumping "dance" around grass tuft. Unobtrusive out of season. **Range and habitat:** eastern AF, in Kenya and Tanzania. Locally common in moist, open grassland. Resident, moving locally outside breeding season. Large-scale fragmentation and degradation of montane grassland habitat has reduced numbers. **Similar species:** 6 other AF widowbirds.

Red-billed
Buffalo-Weaver

White-browed
Sparrow-Weaver

Gray-headed
Social-Weaver

Chestnut Sparrow

White-headed
Buffalo-Weaver

Golden Palm Weaver
(male nest-weaving)

Baglafecht Weaver

Black-headed Weaver

Red-headed Weaver

Red Bishop

Jackson's Widowbird

Yellow Bishop
(in display)

Bronze Mannikin

Spermestes cucullatus (Estrildidae) 9 cm/3½ in.

Small mannikin, brown above with head, neck and breast blacker and inconspicuously glossed bottle-green; bill black above, blue-gray below; underparts white with fine dark barring along flanks. Immature brown, paler below, with blackish bill and black tail. Alarm call is hard "stik;" also low twittering song. Found in small parties, foraging on ground or standing grasses; busy, often tame. **Range and habitat:** widespread in AF south of 10° N, apart from far south-west. Common in open grassy scrub and woodland, often near habitation. Resident, wandering. **Similar species:** 5 other mannikins and silver-bills in AF.

Red-billed Firefinch

Lagonosticta senegala (Estrildidae) 10 cm/4 in.

Male is pinkish red, browner on back, wings and tail, with pinkish tinge to gray bill; small white spots on breast; pale vent. Female has pinkish red lores and rump, otherwise brown above, buffish below, bill as male. Immature as female, lores gray-brown, bill dark. Alarm is sharp "tzit;" also softer "hueet," and low fluting song. In pairs or small groups, foraging on ground; active, quite tame. **Range and habitat:** widespread in AF south of 20° N, except Congo forests and far south-west. Common in open scrublands, often around habitation. Basically resident, local migrant far south. **Similar species:** 7 other firefinches in AF.

Village Indigobird

Vidua chalybeata (Ploceidae) 11 cm/4½ in.

Breeding male glossy bluish, purplish or greenish black, with coral-pink legs and (depending on race) coral or white bill. Nonbreeding male, and female, sparrowlike, streaked above, paler below, with especially conspicuous buff streaks on crown. Immature as female, browner below, no crown streaks. Call is sharp "tikk;" mimics song of Red-billed Firefinch, of which it is brood parasite. Single in breeding season, otherwise in small flocks, foraging on ground; active, sometimes tame. **Range and habitat:** widespread in AF south of 20° N, apart from Congo forests and far south-west. Somewhat uncommon in open scrub or woodland. Resident, regular local movements. **Similar species:** 10 other AF indigobirds.

Purple Grenadier

Uraeginthus ianthinogaster (Estrildidae) 14 cm/5½ in.

Large, unmistakable waxbill, male with red bill, bright cinnamon head and neck, darker brown wings and tail, and conspicuous bright violet-blue rump, underparts and eye patch. Female with conspicuous white eye-ring and violet-blue rump, otherwise brown above, pale cinnamon below, merging to whitish on belly. Immature as female, lacking eye-ring. Usually quiet; low tinkling, chirping, trilling notes. In pairs or small parties, foraging on ground; sometimes unobtrusive, tame. **Range and habitat:** north-eastern AF, from Tanzania north to Ethiopia, southern Somalia. Locally common in open bush and wooded areas. Nonmigratory. **Similar species:** Common Grenadier.

Red-cheeked Cordonbleu

Uraeginthus bengalus (Estrildidae) 13 cm/5 in.

Male unmistakable bright sky blue, with red patch on ear-coverts; bill pinkish; crown, back and wings brown, belly buffish. Female as male but duller blue, lacking red ear-coverts. Immature as female, less extensively blue below. Usually quiet; low piping and squeaking; also subdued, monotonously repeated song, "tz, tz, seeee." In pairs or family groups, feeds on ground; busy, usually tame. **Range and habitat:** mainly at 10–15° N in AF, from Senegal east to Ethiopia; also south through East Africa to southern Zaire and Zambia. Common in scrub and woodland, often around habitation. Resident. **Similar species:** 2 other cordonbleus in AF.

Red-billed Quelea

Quelea quelea (Ploceidae) 13 cm/5 in.

Rather small weaver, breeding male with red bill, and black face surrounded by buff or rosy wash; upperparts heavily streaked buff and black; underparts whitish, lightly spotted on breast and flanks. Nonbreeding male, and female, lack black face and wash. Immature as female, bill pinkish gray. Often silent; sharp "chak" alarm, loud chattering at nest. In flocks up to millions, foraging on ground or on, e.g., cereal crops, hence Africa's main avian agricultural pest; bold.

Range and habitat: widespread in AF south of 17° N, apart from western forests and extreme south. Common, seasonally abundant, in dry, open, bushed grasslands. Few resident; most breed opportunistically, move in response to rain. **Similar species:** nonbreeding quelea resemble sparrows, weavers (see p 276).

Pin-tailed Whydah

Vidua macroura (Ploceidae) 12–34 cm/4½–13 in.

Breeding male has red bill, black cap and upperparts, white collar and underparts, and long, slender, black tail. Nonbreeding male short-tailed, sparrowlike, with red bill and especially broad black and buff streaks on crown. Female and immature similar, bill pinkish. Sharp "tseep" flight call; shrill, twittering song. In small parties with more females, foraging on ground; brood parasite of Common Waxbill; active, bold. **Range and habitat:** widespread in AF south of 15° N, except arid south-west. Common in open bushed and wooded habitats. Resident, moving locally. **Similar species:** Shaft-tailed Whydah.

Straw-tailed Whydah

Vidua fischeri (Ploceidae) 10–29 cm/4–11 in.

Breeding male has black head and upperparts, red bill, pale buff crown and underparts and straw-colored, slender, elongated, central tail feathers. Nonbreeding male, and female, brown, streaked above, sparrowlike, with red bill. Immature browner, less streaked, bill blackish. Call is sharp "sip;" short, much-repeated song. Found in small parties, females outnumbering males, foraging on ground. Brood parasite of Purple Grenadier. Active, sometimes shy. **Range and habitat:** north-eastern AF, from Tanzania to Ethiopia, Somalia. Locally common in dry bush. Resident, moving locally. **Similar species:** Shaft-tailed Whydah.

Brimstone Canary

Serinus sulphuratus (Fringillidae) 15 cm/6 in.

Large, thickset canary, greenish yellow streaked with black above, brighter yellow below, with diffuse, dusky moustachial stripe and, in some, dusky breast; heavy conical, grayish bill. Immature duller, some breast and flank streaking. Call is harsh "chirrup;" jumbled, deep, harsh, husky, rather tuneless song. Single or paired, sometimes small parties, foraging on ground and vegetation; unobtrusive, not shy. **Range and habitat:** widespread in AF south of 10° S, apart from arid south-west; also north through east to Kenya, Uganda. Sometimes common in open, moist bushed and wooded country. Resident or moving locally. **Similar species:** 14 similar canaries in AF, Serin (see p 180).

African Citril

Serinus citrinelloides (Fringillidae) 11 cm/4½ in.

Small, rather slender canary, yellowish green above with dark streaking on mantle and, sometimes, prominent yellow eyebrow; below yellow, sometimes lightly streaked. Male has black or grayish face; female lacks this coloration and is more distinctly streaked below. Immature as female but browner above, paler below. Low cheeping calls; song is sustained, far-carrying, shrill, tuneful whistle. In small parties, feeds on ground and vegetation; sometimes unobtrusive, but not shy. **Range and habitat:** eastern AF, from Malawi north to Ethiopia. Common in many moist, fairly open habitats, including gardens and forest edge. Basically resident, wandering. **Similar species:** 14 similar AF canaries, Serin (see p 180).

Cinnamon-breasted Bunting

Emberiza tahapisi (Fringillidae) 14 cm/6 in.

Medium-sized bunting, male streaked black on brown above, cinnamon below, with white-striped black hood. Female similar, hood browner, striped gray. Immature as female, duller. Call is 2-note "see-eeeeee;" song a high "chee-trrr, chee chee." Found singly or in pairs, sometimes small parties, foraging openly on ground. Often unobtrusive. **Range and habitat:** widespread south of 15° N in AF (including southern Arabia), apart from equatorial forests and far south-west. Locally common on open, rocky ground with some grass or bush. Resident and local migrant. **Similar species:** 8 *Emberiza* in AF.

Bronze Mannikin

Village Indigobird

Purple Grenadier

Red-cheeked Cordonbleu

Pin-tailed Whydah

Red-billed Quelea

Red-billed Firefinch

African Citril

Straw-tailed Whydah (nonbreeding male)

Brimstone Canary

Cinnamon-breasted Bunting

THE ORIENTAL REGION

The tropical mainland of Asia, together with the islands, or island groups, of Sri Lanka, Sumatra, Java, Borneo, Taiwan, Hainan and the Philippines, constitute the Oriental Region, though the boundaries are for the most part less distinct than those of some other zoogeographical regions. The most clearly defined one runs along the narrow arc of the Himalayan mountain chain, which forms both a physical and a climatic barrier between the subtropical forests on the south side and the cold, arid Tibetan Plateau to the north. The valley of the river Indus forms a convenient, if somewhat arbitrary, boundary on the western flank, in an area where the number of truly Oriental species diminishes, and Palaearctic forms become more noticeable. A much broader and more complex area of transition to a Palaearctic fauna skirts the edge of the Tibetan Plateau, and runs through the mountainous country of south-eastern Tibet and south-western China, north and east to include Szechuan, and then follows a latitude of about 30° N across China to the China Sea. South of this line, the Philippine Islands, with their somewhat specialized fauna, are included, though the whole archipelago of Wallacea, lying between Borneo and New Guinea, has a strong Australo-Papuan element, is highly transitional in nature, and is not incorporated in the Oriental Region in this analysis.

Regional variety

The total land area of some 9 million sq km (3.5 million sq miles) is only half that of South America, or about one-third of the African landmass, but is characterized by an astonishing variety of climate, vegetation and scenery. In the south-east of the region, the humid tropics, with their very uniform annual temperature, support one of the three largest areas of lowland rainforest in the world, with an immensely rich tree fauna, and an abundant though specialized avifauna, with many striking endemic species such as the Great Argus pheasant and the Rhinoceros Hornbill. There are two much smaller patches of rainforest, one in southwest India and the other in the slopes and foothills of the eastern Himalayas and Assam, which, despite the discontinuity, hold many bird species in common.

Tropical semievergreen forest covers a much larger total area in the region than the lowland evergreen forest, and especially in montane areas is equally rich in bird species, if not more so in some respects. Altitude and rainfall account for a great deal of variation, and some lowland forest is relatively dry, though much is moist, and hill forests often very wet. It is the home of many of the babblers and pheasants for which the region is notable. It is a biome in marked contrast with the vegetation in the west of the region, in north-west India and Pakistan, where semidesert conditions and dry thorn scrub support birds more characteristic of the arid lands which run from Morocco to the steppes of central Asia. However, it is worth noting that in quite recent times, even up to 200 years ago, this area was much wetter, with subtropical vegetation in Pakistan capable of supporting mammals such as rhinoceros. Human activity has been a major factor in modifying landscape and vegetation across the Oriental Region, and is now a more potent and threatening force than before, while the consequences of climate change might be even more dramatic.

Over most of the region outside the rainforest areas, the marked dry seasons constitute a monsoon regime, though

Painted Storks *feed against the backdrop of an Indian sunset.*

there are very marked variations locally in the pattern and extent of rainfall. Assam, in north-east India, has the highest annual rainfall in the world at over 9.5 m (400 in), while the hills of south-west India receive over 3 m (130 in) per annum. The monsoon is heavier and comes earlier in the year in the eastern half of the Himalayas, and decreasing rainfall westward is associated with a less rich flora and fauna, and a diminishing number of species typical of the eastern Himalayas and Southeast Asia. Many species whose ranges extend the length of the Himalayan chain have evolved darker forms in the eastern, wetter section, and paler forms in the west, and these are given subspecific status.

The total number of bird species in the region, at over 2,000, compares very favorably with any similar-sized tropical area in the world, although there are in fact only three endemic families, the Leafbirds, Ioras and Fairy-bluebirds totalling 14 species. Many bird families generally typical of the Old World tropics are well represented, such as trogons, hornbills, barbets, broadbills, pittas, bulbuls and sunbirds. Perhaps the outstanding features of Oriental bird life are the abundance of pheasants, and the great array of babblers, flycatchers, warblers and thrushes.

Avifauna

The distribution of birds in the region falls very clearly into three subregions, to such an extent that only 14% of the total number of species occur in all three of these. The richest in terms of species, which is probably best called Sino-Himalayan (the alternative name of Indo-Chinese sounds better but is less exact), comprises continental Southeast Asia, Taiwan, Hainan, southern and western China, and the southern faces and foothills of the Himalayas west to Kashmir. Around two-thirds of the total number of Oriental species, around 1300, are found in this area of nearly 4 million sq km (1.5 million sq miles), containing many of the highest mountains and the most spectacular scenery in the world. The spectacular pheasants and tragopans are the jewel of the avifauna, although many are gravely threatened by habitat destruction. Even more striking is the diversity of babblers, and this is true to a lesser extent in many other groups, for example, owls, bulbuls, warblers, thrushes, flycatchers and woodpeckers.

A feature that lends both interest and charm to birding in these hilly tracts is the perceptible vertical zonation of forest types and bird-life. A few hours' walk in Nepal can take one from dry evergreen on the valley floor, through wet hill evergreen, bamboo, broad-leaved deciduous woods with much oak and chestnut and finally pine forests, before the snowy peaks come clearly into view.

It was in this sub-region that a fascinating zoogeographical puzzle came to light in 1966 with the chance discovery of a species of swallow new to science. This was the White-eyed River-Martin, a very distinctive swallow, having only one close relative, and that a very similar-looking bird confined to the rivers of West Africa. Other previously unknown species recently discovered include the Mekong Wagtail and three babbler species.

Around 38% of the species found in the Sino-Himalayan subregion penetrate south through peninsular Thailand to another clearly defined faunal area, the Malaysian subregion. This comprises the southern tips of Myanmar and Thailand, Malaysia, and the great islands of Sumatra, Java and Borneo lying on the Sunda shelf, which are separated from the mainland by a uniformly shallow sea about 36 m (120 ft) deep, and which in recent geological time were part of continental Asia. Over 900 bird species occur in this mosaic of islands and rainforest, including some of the most typical Oriental birds. Of the 14 leafbirds and ioras, 13 are found here, and among the many species of pheasant are the quite spectacular Great Argus and a clutch of rare peacock-pheasants. All the Oriental broadbills occur here, and 24 of the 27 flowerpeckers, which, with eight of the region's 10 frogmouths, gives an Australo-Papuan flavor to the avifauna. Also well represented are pittas, cuckoos, bulbuls, babblers and flycatchers.

The great rainforests which are the glory of the subregion are fragile and highly threatened, and yet have huge potential for research. Bird life can seem almost absent at times in the forest, until one suddenly comes upon a "bird-band" or hunting party of many different species, which forage actively through the vegetation at all levels from the canopy to the forest floor. Often, before one can see and note down the birds present, they have moved on and all is quiet again.

The Philippines, though included in the sub-region in this analysis, have a specialized avifauna with some Bornean and also some Australo-Papuan elements. The endemic and rare Monkey-eating Eagle is arguably the most spectacular bird of prey in the world. Other endemic species in this group of over 7,000 large and small islands are a small parrot, the Guaiabero whose nearest relative is Malaysian, and the aberrant large tree-creepers of which there are two species remarkable for their brush-tipped tongues, plumage pattern and heavy, curved bills. Two species new to science—a rail and a woodcock—have recently been discovered in the Philippines, though among the 395 breeding species, little or nothing is known of the breeding habits of about 80 of the endemic species.

The third subregion, which within itself has several markedly differing faunal areas, comprises the Indian subcontinent south of the Himalayan foothills and west of the Brahmaputra River, Pakistan and Sri Lanka. In general, it is characterized by having many families of dry-country birds more typical of North Africa or Southwest Asia, such as bustards, coursers, larks, chats and sandgrouse. The total species list of the subregion at about 700 is markedly lower than that of the other two, and it is of interest to note that only 25% of the species in the Malaysian subregion also occur here. However, there are many interesting endemic species such as a flycatcher, a thrush, some bulbuls, barbets, a malcoha and a coucal, especially in the humid hills of south-west India and in Sri Lanka. Some recent fascinating additions to the avifauna have been a newly described Scops Owl from Sri Lanka, and the re-discovery of the Forest Owlet.

There are some striking similarities between birds which occur in the Sino-Himalayan subregion and again in the wet hill forests of south-west India, despite the gap of some 2,500 km (1,500 miles), indicating the loss of suitable habitat in the intervening area, probably with the recession of the last Ice Age. Notable species in this context include the Great Hornbill, Fairy-bluebird and Broad-billed Roller, and groups such as laughing thrushes, trogons and frogmouths have evolved distinct species. There are also interesting species in northern India, possibly relics of the ancient pre-Himalayan drainage systems, such as the recently extinct Pink-headed Duck, the Bristled Grass Warbler and the Sind Jungle Sparrow. Jerdon's Courser, thought to be extinct as it had not been sighted since 1900, was re-discovered in central India in 1986—a spectacular event in the history of Indian ornithology.

Oriental ornithological societies

Ornithology in the Oriental Region has had many illustrious students over the 170 years or so and a vast amount of information has been published in such journals as *Stray Feathers*, which appeared from 1873–99, and that of the Bombay Natural History Society, founded in 1886 and still in the forefront of research. A more recent development has been the establishment of the Oriental Bird Club (P. O. Box 324, Bedford, MK42 OWG, U.K.) which publishes news and research from the whole region in its highly respected journal *Forktail* and the bi-annual magazine *BirdingAsia*

FULL-WEBBED SWIMMERS Pelecaniformes

Spot-billed Pelican

Pelecanus philippensis (Pelecanidae) 150 cm/59 in.

Grayish upperparts and the pinkish tinge below give this species a dingier appearance than the White Pelican. Nonbreeding and young birds are markedly browner. Very buoyant in the air for such a heavy bird, whether in low flap-and-glide flight over the water or soaring in thermals. A colonial breeder, formerly in huge numbers in the region in swamps long since drained, though there are still large pelicanries in a few places. Voice a deep croak. **Range and habitat:** OR. Resident and locally migratory, in well-watered plains. Outside breeding season on large rivers and creeks. **Similar species:** White and Dalmatian Pelicans (see p 142).

Indian Cormorant

Phalacrocorax fuscicollis (Phalacrocoracidae) 62 cm/24 in.

A slim, medium-sized cormorant with a white tuft on the sides of the head in breeding plumage; yellow throat and slender bill distinguish it from Javanese Cormorant. Often occurs in large flocks and breeds colonially, often in company with other species, the timing of breeding dependent on the rains and water conditions. Mostly silent. **Range and habitat:** OR. Common resident, wandering locally, on lakes, rivers, reservoirs or on the coast. **Similar species:** Great and Little Cormorants.

Little Cormorant

Phalacrocorax niger (Phalacrocoracidae) 50 cm/20 in.

A small, stocky cormorant with a thickish bill, long tail and dark throat which becomes white outside the breeding season. The thicker neck and head help to distinguish it from similar species. Gregarious and often in huge numbers in suitable localities, though equally likely to be only 1 or 2 birds on a tiny patch of marsh or village pond. Shares tree nesting sites with other cormorant and heron species. Largely silent. **Range and habitat:** OR. Common resident in the plains in marshland, by lakes, ponds, rivers and reservoirs and at the coast. **Similar species:** Little Black and Indian Cormorants.

Oriental Darter

Anhinga melanogaster (Anhingidae) 90 cm/35 in.

The long, wedge-shaped tail is obvious when this cormorantlike species is seen soaring over marshes, though a more usual view just shows the thin, snaky head and neck as the bird swims semisubmerged. Fish are caught after an underwater chase with a spearlike thrust of the strong neck and sharp bill. The twig nest is in trees, often with other species nesting close by. **Range and habitat:** OR. Resident on lowland lakes, marshes and rivers, also on the coast in mangroves. **Similar species:** other darters and anhingas (see pp 52, 186, 286).

Christmas Island Frigatebird

Fregata andrewsi (Fregatidae) 100 cm/39 in.

Breeding only on Christmas Island in the southern Indian ocean, this species has one of the more restricted ranges of its family, and is certainly the smallest in terms of total population. Nests are placed in tall, isolated trees from which the bird has a clear, wind-assisted take-off; rising off a calm sea appears to be a major problem. In the air, though, frigatebirds are masters of the element, swooping to gather fish or offal from the surface. The voice is an occasional, harsh croak. **Range and habitat:** OR and PA, Christmas Island, dispersing presumably over adjacent seas: occurs off Javan and Bornean coasts. **Similar species:** Great, Lesser and Ascension Frigatebirds (see pp 52, 286).

HERONS AND ALLIES Ciconiiformes

Indian Pond-Heron

Ardeola grayii (Ardeidae) 52 cm/20 in.

A strikingly plumaged small heron in its breeding plumage of maroon and buff, though virtually indistinguishable from related species in the streaky brown winter dress. Common at the water's edge everywhere, whether a village pond or in mangrove swamps, the white wings suddenly become obvious as it flaps up. Nesting is in colonies in trees which are often, though not necessarily, near

water. The note is a heronlike croak, more varied and continuous during nesting activities. **Range and habitat:** OR, Indian subcontinent and Sri Lanka. Common resident, wandering locally, in open country by ponds, paddyfields or by the coast.

Asian Openbill

Anastomus oscitans (Ciconiidae) 80 cm/31 in.

One of the smaller storks, though common in its range, and sharing with a close relative in Africa the unique oval gap in the closed bill. The purpose of this is evidently to facilitate coping with the snails on which the birds feed. A strong flier and partial to soaring, but agile on the wing and capable of rushing, tumbling descents under complete control. Breeding colonies are sometimes very large, with thousands of birds standing on or by their tree nests, and a constant coming and going of birds feeding in nearby waterways. It makes a typical storklike clattering with the mandibles. **Range and habitat:** OR, except Indo-Malayan subregion, resident but also dispersing long distances, by lakes, rivers and marshes in the lowlands. **Similar species:** African Openbill (see p 188).

Black-necked Stork

Ephippiorhynchus asiaticus (Ciconiidae) 130 cm/51 in.

A majestic and striking species with its black daggerlike bill and scarlet legs—the female differs only in having a staring yellow eye as opposed to black in the male. Like many large, shy birds, it is not numerous, and is usually seen singly or in pairs. The large stick nest is placed high up in a tree, and the display is a ceremonial face-to-face affair, with wing-flapping and clattering of bills. **Range and habitat:** OR to north AU. Resident in lowland areas in marshes or by rivers.

Greater Adjutant

Leptoptilos dubius (Ciconiidae) 160 cm/63 in.

This huge, ugly scavenger is the Asian counterpart of the African Marabou, and is perhaps seen at its best when soaring majestically, often in company with vultures. Its powers of flight render it capable of wandering great distances, for although not known to breed now in India, it occurs regularly across northern India as far west as Sind. Burma and Indo-China are the main breeding areas. Nests are in tall trees, and breeding colonies were sometimes very large. Numbers are now thought to be dramatically reduced, though a colony has recently been located in Assam. **Range and habitat:** OR; except southern India, Sri Lanka and Indo-Malayan subregion. **Similar species:** Lesser Adjutant Stork.

Red-naped Ibis

Pseudibis papillosa (Threskiornithidae) 68 cm/27 in.

A somewhat solitary ibis which appears to be more tolerant of dry habitats such as stubble fields and cultivated areas than related species. The black plumage, bare scarlet skin on the head and red legs are distinctive, and unlike the Black-headed Ibis there are no plumes on neck or back in the breeding season. Often seen singly or in small parties at best, it shuns the noisy, crowded colonies of breeding waterbirds, and it is only rarely that more than 2 or 3 pairs nest in the same tree. It has a loud call when taking wing but is mostly a quiet species. **Range and habitat:** OR; northern India to Indo-China, in open country near rivers, lakes or marshes. **Similar species:** Glossy Ibis.

Spot-billed Pelican

Indian Cormorant with (left) Little Cormorant

Christmas Island Frigatebird

Little Cormorant

Oriental Darter

Indian Pond-Heron

Black-necked Stork

Asian Openbill

Greater Adjutant

Red-naped Ibis

WATERFOWL Anseriformes

Lesser Whistling-Duck

Dendrocygna javanica (Anatidae) 42 cm/17 in.
Deriving its whistling name from the constantly uttered flight call, it is one of the relatively few ducks which nest in cavities in trees, though occasionally nests are placed in waterside vegetation on the ground. A surface feeder in water with plenty of emergent vegetation, it has an unusually upright posture when standing, and walks well, though a poor flier on its rounded wings. In this connection, it is of note that Whistling Ducks have curious notches on the inner vane of the primary feathers. Usually found in flocks, sometimes large. The sexes are alike. **Range and habitat:** OR. Resident, wandering locally, on ponds, rivers or marshes on the plains.

Bar-headed Goose

Anser indicus (Anatidae) 75 cm/29 in.
A breeding bird in Central Asia, this goose migrates over the Himalayas, and the only wintering areas lie in the Indian subcontinent. Like all geese, it occurs in family parties which aggregate to form large flocks on stretches of water or rivers adjacent to cultivated areas where the birds can feed. Grazing the crops is a nocturnal activity, and by day the wary geese rest around river or lake shores. Said to be remarkably tame when on the remote and undisturbed breeding grounds, in contrast to alert behavior in winter. Call a musical honking. **Range and habitat:** EP, in winter to OR. Open country, lakes, rivers, crops.

Ruddy Shelduck

Tadorna ferruginea (Anatidae) 66 cm/26 in.
Orange plumage and pale head distinctive, the female lacking the black collar of breeding males; black flight feathers and a white wing patch are prominent when the birds are on the wing. More goose-than ducklike, it grazes on crops and grass as well as taking aquatic animal food. Not as gregarious as some relatives, it is usually seen in small parties which haunt rivers, sandbanks and lakes in the winter. It has a loud, gooselike honking call. **Range and habitat:** southern WP and EP, wintering to OR, occasional in AF. Open country, mountains, steppes, lakes and rivers. **Similar species:** Common Shelduck (see p 146).

Cotton Pygmy-Goose

Nettapus coromandelianus (Anatidae) 33 cm/13 in.
A diminutive duck, with a stubby bill and short legs, consequently a poor walker (and does not graze), though strong and agile in flight. It feeds on the surface on waterplants and small animal life, and is often to be seen in pairs or small groups. Prefers quite reedy ponds or even very small patches of water, and nests in tree-holes at heights from 2 m (6½ ft) to 30 m (98 ft). The female lacks the iridescence of the dark parts of the male's plumage, being browner, and the white underparts are dingier. **Range and habitat:** OR. Locally common and resident by ponds, marshes and wet paddyfields in the plains. **Similar species:** African Pygmy-Goose (see p 190).

Falcated Duck

Anas falcata (Anatidae) 50 cm/20 in.
The name is a reference to the sickle shape of the inner secondaries, which fall in a curve over the primaries on the folded wing. The drake is also adorned with a full, drooping crest behind the beautifully glossed head, and the duck has a vestigial crest, giving but a trace of the heavy-headed look. A wary bird, it mingles with the other wintering species in small numbers on lakes and rivers, occasionally on the sea. Females quack; males make a short, whistling note. **Range and habitat:** EP, in winter to OR, occasionally to WP. Rivers, lakes, flooded land. **Similar species:** Gadwall, Pintail, Wigeon (see p 146).

Spot-billed Duck

Anas poecilorhyncha (Anatidae) 60 cm/24 in.
The bright red spot at the base of the bill is nearly lacking in the female, and totally so in the Chinese subspecies, which also differs in being much browner, without such well-defined pale feather edges. Similar in lifestyle and voice to the Mallard, it is rather heavier and slower in flight. Frequenting shallow waters in which it can up-end for food, it is mostly resident, and both local movements and timing of breeding are governed by water conditions. **Range and habitat:** EP, OR in marshland, by ponds and reservoirs. **Similar species:** Pacific Black Duck (see p 288).

White-winged Duck

Cairina scutulata (Anatidae) 81 cm/32 in.
A rare, forest-haunting duck, and a close relative of the Muscovy Duck of South America. It has a bony knob on the wing similar to that of the Comb Duck, and the male has a swollen and reddish base to the bill when breeding, though not exaggerated as in the Muscovy. In flight, the large white wing patch is striking and prevents confusion with the Comb Duck. It is a little-known species as it is partly nocturnal and inhabits the sort of terrain which is very difficult to work. The call is a mournful honking, which is most often heard as the birds fly to and from their feeding grounds at dawn and dusk. **Range and habitat:** OR. Resident around boggy pools and streams in evergreen forest. **Similar species:** Comb Duck, Muscovy Duck (see p 102).

DIURNAL BIRDS OF PREY Falconiformes

Jerdon's Baza

Aviceda jerdoni (Accipitridae) 48 cm/19 in.
A sluggish, somewhat buzzardlike hawk with long wings and a crest which is raised vertically when the bird is sitting. Tending to be crepuscular, it is not one of the more obvious hawks in its habitat, and feeds on small prey such as insects and frogs, though quite a strong flier, especially in the soaring display above the tea-gardens or hill forest. There are several subspecies which vary in the saturation of color and the weight of the barring; there is a small variation in size in some races. Juveniles lack the broad barring on the underparts, which are much purer white. The call is a buzzardlike mewing. **Range and habitat:** OR to the Philippines and Celebes. Resident in forests up to 1,800 m (5,900 ft). **Similar species:** Crested Goshawk. **Not illustrated.**

Oriental Honey-Buzzard

Pernis ptilorhynchus (Accipitridae) 68 cm/27 in.
Closely related to the European Honey Buzzard and just as variable in plumage, though the populations of tropical forests are crested and sedentary. In flight, the long tail and slender head and neck are distinctive when the bird is seen soaring over a patch of forest, and the whistling call is frequently uttered. Although taking honeycombs and bee larvae, prey such as small mammals, reptiles and birds are also recorded. Quite a sociable hawk, gathering in numbers at roosts and, especially as regards the northern populations, when on migration. **Range and habitat:** EP and OR; in open country, deciduous woods and evergreen forests, to 1,700 m (5,500 ft) in the hills. **Similar species:** Eurasian Buzzard, Jerdon's Baza.

Brahminy Kite

Haliastur indus (Accipitridae) 48 cm/19 in.
The immature bird is quite unlike the handsome adult, being mainly brown with a pale patch under the wing at the base of the primaries, so somewhat buzzardlike. Always in the vicinity of water, whether rivers, reservoirs or coastal harbors, where it wheels about, flying with great ease and buoyancy, swooping to snatch food from the surface, or pick up a dead fish from the shore. When quartering flooded paddyfields, it behaves and flies much as a harrier. It is a gregarious bird, and large numbers congregate in good feeding areas and at roosts. As a species, it undoubtedly benefits from human activities such as rice-growing and fisheries, and is a common sight around towns and villages near water. **Range and habitat:** OR and AU. Resident in suitably watered areas and coasts, and up to 1,800 m (5,900 ft) in the hills. **Similar species:** Whistling Kite (see p 290).

Lesser Whistling-Duck

Bar-headed Goose

Ruddy Shelduck

Cotton Pygmy-Goose

Falcated Duck

Spot-billed Duck

White-winged Duck

Oriental Honey-Buzzard

Brahminy Kite

White-bellied Fish-Eagle

Haliaeetus leucogaster (Accipitridae) 70 cm/28 in.

A familiar sight around the coasts of tropical Asia, this is an impressive bird in flight on its broad white wings with black borders. The tail is short, and this with the heavy build gives it a somewhat vulturine aspect. The immature bird is dark brown, and becomes progressively lighter with age. Like many eagles, it spends much time perched, often in a prominent position commanding a wide view, which it will return to after a successful foray with a fish or snake. The prey is caught in a powerful dive to the surface either off the perch or more usually in flight, like an Osprey. In display, the pair soar high in the air, and call frequently with their loud, clanging, gooselike notes. **Range and habitat:** OR and AU, along sea coasts and inland, but not far, along major waterways. **Similar species:** Pallas' Fish Eagle, White-tailed Eagle.

White-rumped Vulture

Gyps bengalensis (Accipitridae) 90 cm/35 in.

The blackish plumage and white rump patch distinguish it from the Long-billed Vulture, the dark underside in flight contrasting with the white wing-lining. Usually seen perched hunched-up on treetops, or scrambling for food at carcasses or at slaughter houses. In the morning it remains perched on trees until about three hours after dawn and takes wing rather reluctantly. Once up however, it soars majestically on thermals as it searches for food. Vultures in India have undergone a dramatic decline in numbers as a result of poisoning from residues of the chemical diclofenac in carcasses. **Range and habitat:** OR. India to Indo-China; in cultivated and well-wooded country. **Similar species:** other vultures (see pp 150, 192).

Crested Serpent-Eagle

Spilornis cheela (Accipitridae) 75 cm/29 in.

The thick erectile crest, yellow eyes and bare yellow legs are constant features in all the races—over 20—of this variable species. Plumage differences concern size and clarity of the spots and barring, overall coloration and body size. The wings are noticeably rounded and heavily barred, making the bird easy to recognize in flight, when it is apt to be quite noisy, with a variety of whistling calls. It is a woodland bird, and when sitting quietly in some large leafy tree is inconspicuous, though soaring and calling above the canopy draw attention to its presence. It drops on its prey, mainly reptiles, from a perch, rather than in flight like some close relatives of open country. **Range and habitat:** OR; resident in wooded areas in the plains and hills up to 3,000 m (9,850 ft). **Similar species:** Short-toed Eagle (see p 150).

Pied Harrier

Circus melanoleucos (Accipitridae) 49 cm/19 in.

The male is one of the most strikingly marked of the harriers, with the black head, breast and back contrasting with pure white underparts, and silvery gray wings and tail. The female is a typical brownish hawk with streaked underparts and a barred tail. In low, though buoyant and airy, flight, it quarters the paddyfields on the look-out for frogs, lizards or small rodents, but does not apparently pose much of a threat to birds, though taking munias regularly in Borneo. It is a quiet bird in its winter quarters in tropical Asia, though on its breeding grounds makes a repeated alarm call and a chattering note. **Range and habitat:** EP, wintering across OR, resident in northern Myanmar and Assam. Open country, marshes, paddyfields, hill grasslands. **Similar species:** Pallid Harrier, Western Marsh-Harrier (see p 152).

Chinese Goshawk

Accipiter soloensis (Accipitridae) 30 cm/12 in.

The plain breast of the male, washed with rufous, is unusual among the sparrowhawks, as is the habit of feeding largely on frogs, on which it often stoops from a perch. As a result of specializing on this prey, it is a bird of more open country than its relatives, both in breeding quarters and when wintering southward through Southeast Asia. The tail lacking barring above, and white underside of the flight feathers renders it easier to tell in the field than some small hawks. It migrates northward in parties, but is more solitary and so less conspicuous on the return journey in the autumn. **Range and habitat:** EP, in winter to Indo-China, Borneo and the Greater Sundas. **Similar species:** Shikra. **Not illustrated.**

White-eyed Buzzard

Butastur teesa (Accipitridae) 42 cm/17 in.

One of a small group of 4 closely related hawks, 1 in Africa and the other 3 Asian, with rather pointed wings and a long, square-cut tail. Like the others, this species is a somewhat unspectacular bird, often walking about to pick up small prey off the ground, though also fond of using low perches, such as fence-posts, as a look-out. The sexes are alike, and immature birds are paler and streakier below, with pale edges to wing feathers. Not a gregarious bird, it is usually seen singly or in pairs. The call is a buzzardlike double note. **Range and habitat:** OR; Indian subcontinent to Burma. Resident in open country or sparse woodland in the plains to 1,200 m (3,900 ft) in the hills. **Similar species:** Rufous-winged and Grasshopper Buzzards.

Great Philippine Eagle

Pithecophaga jefferyi (Accipitridae) 95 cm/37 in.

One of the most spectacular of the world's eagles, and unfortunately high on the list of the world's most threatened species. Like several other large, rare eagles, it is a forest bird, and takes mammal prey such as flying lemurs and monkeys. The feet and claws are very powerful, and the bill laterally compressed and deeply arched. This, together with the full crest and pale blue eyes, gives the bird an impressive appearance. It builds a huge nest high in a forest tree and lays a single egg, which takes about 2 months to hatch. **Range and habitat:** OR, Mindanao Island, Philippines. Resident in heavy forest up to 1,300 m (4,300 ft).

Black Eagle

Ictinaetus malayensis (Accipitridae) 75 cm/29 in.

A somewhat aberrant eagle, adapted to a diet which largely features nestlings and eggs. The claws are notably long but only shallowly curved, which may well facilitate the snatching of nests, and the bird is capable of flying extremely slowly and buoyantly on its broad wings. It is particularly adept at following the contors of foliage and small clearings while making a close inspection of the surroundings for prey—which also includes small rodents and mammals on occasion. The sexes are alike in their black plumage, and the bright yellow feet are easily seen when the bird is soaring overhead. **Range and habitat:** OR. Resident in hill forests up to 2,700 m (8,900 ft). **Similar species:** Changeable Hawk-Eagle.

Changeable Hawk-Eagle

Spizaetus cirrhatus (Accipitridae) 72 cm/28 in.

Variable in plumage, this eagle has a somewhat hawklike profile with its broad wings and long tail, which must aid manoeuvrability in its forest habitat. There is a dark plumage phase, but more commonly the bird is brown above and white, heavily streaked, below. The Indian race has a long, floppy crest. Like many related species, it can become a determined killer of poultry, but usual prey is small mammals and birds. It is not a conspicuous species, though calls noisily during the soaring display flight above the forest. The nest is placed high in a forest tree, and a single egg is laid. **Range and habitat:** OR. Resident in open woodland and forest in the plains and foothills. **Similar species:** Mountain Hawk-Eagle, Black Eagle.

Laggar Falcon

Falco jugger (Falconidae) 45 cm/18 in.

Somewhat smaller than either Lanner or Saker Falcons, the 2 common, large, resident falcons of India. Distinct from the local race of the Peregrine, the Shaheen Falcon, by having white rather than cinnamon underparts. Though an accomplished flier, it is not as dashing as the Peregrine, and on occasion picks up dead birds, though quite capable of catching small mammals and birds with ease. Often seen in pairs which stay together the year round, and not infrequently in towns, where it perches conspicuously on buildings. **Range and habitat:** OR; Indian subcontinent to Burma. Resident in open or rocky country. **Similar species:** Lanner and Saker Falcons, Peregrine (see p 152).

White-bellied
Fish-Eagle

White-rumped
Vulture

Crested
Serpent-Eagle

Pied Harrier

White-eyed Buzzard

Great Philippine Eagle

Black Eagle

Changeable
Hawk-Eagle

Laggar Falcon

FOWL-LIKE BIRDS Galliformes

Painted Francolin
Francolinus pictus (Phasianidae) 30 cm/12 in.
The yellowish legs and chestnut face (though the female has a whiter throat) are quick pointers to identity, but otherwise the black back and underparts with white spotting are very like that of the Black Francolin. More active at dawn and dusk than in the heat of the day, it is a difficult bird to watch, though a pair may sometimes be seen foraging in cultivated fields or in thin bush. It feeds on seeds, shoots and insects, and nests on the ground in a patch of concealing vegetation. It has a typical partridge-type call in the breeding season, when the male ascends some small mound or other vantage point to proclaim his whereabouts. **Range and habitat:** OR; peninsular India and Sri Lanka. Resident in the plains in thin scrub, grasslands and also cultivation. **Similar species:** Black Francolin, Gray Francolin. **Not illustrated.**

Chinese Francolin
Francolinus pintadeanus (Phasianidae) 33 cm/13 in.
The male is best identified by the face pattern, with a black stripe dividing the white cheeks and throat. The black and white spotting on back and underparts recalls several related species, and the female is duller and more buff. It is the only species of francolin in China. A shy and rarely seen bird in grassy or lightly bushed country, though, like its relatives, noisy in the breeding season. It is not gregarious, and does not form coveys, though quite numerous in some localities. It runs with head lowered and tail cocked up when alarmed. **Range and habitat:** OR and south EP. Resident in dry, rocky or grassy hills, scrub jungle and cultivation. **Similar species:** Black Francolin. **Not illustrated.**

Gray Francolin
Francolinus pondicerianus (Phasianidae) 31 cm/12 in.
More reminiscent of the European Gray Partridge, with its rufous tail feathers, than the other Asian francolins with black in the tail. However, like the francolins, it has a spur above the hind toe. The tail color is noticeable when the bird is put up, though often a covey will escape danger by splitting up and running in different directions. Tolerant of most types of habitat except forest, it is often in coveys which break up with the onset of the breeding season. Commonly roosts in trees, and will also take refuge in a tree or bush when disturbed. **Range and habitat:** OR; India and Sri Lanka. Resident in scrub jungle and cultivated plains. **Similar species:** Chinese Francolin.

Jungle Bush-Quail
Perdicula asiatica (Phasianidae) 17 cm/6½ in.
The bush quails are a group of 4 species confined to the Indian subcontinent, differing from the true quails in having a heavier and deeper bill, and a spurred tarsus. In this and 1 other species, the male is closely barred on the underparts whereas the female is plain rufous. Keeps in small coveys which, when put up, rise with a startling fluster and disperse at once in all directions. The species is noted for only making very short flights when disturbed, and is in general very sedentary. It has developed several well-marked subspecies. The call in the breeding season is a somewhat partridgelike repetitive grating note. **Range and habitat:** OR; peninsular India and Sri Lanka. Resident in grasslands, cultivation and thin forest. **Similar species:** Rock Bush-Quail.

Hill Partridge
Arborophila torqueola (Phasianidae) 28 cm/11 in.
Typical of this group of 18 species of the Himalayas and Southeast Asia, though this and 1 other are only 2 species whose ranges extend to the western Himalayas. As with many Himalayan species, the race of the western, drier region is paler in coloration than those occurring further east. Keeping in family parties, it forages in dense undergrowth in ravines and hill gullies, often in deciduous forest. Roosts in trees, into which it will often fly when disturbed, and has a long, low whistle repeated at intervals. **Range and habitat:** OR; western Himalayas to Vietnam. Resident in broad-leaf or evergreen hill forest. **Similar species:** Rufous-throated Partridge.

Crested Partridge
Rollulus rouloul (Phasianidae) 25 cm/10 in.
The remarkable fanlike crest and dark green plumage are unique among gamebirds. Both male and female have a hairy crest growing from the crown, though the female lacks the bushy fan, is much lighter green in color than her glossy mate, and has a gray head. Like many of its relatives, it is often to be seen in coveys or family parties, which scratch about on the ground, often in clearings, in lowland forest. It appears to prefer fairly dry forest with plenty of bamboo or palm. The diet includes fallen fruits, seeds and insects, and the note is a repeated, low whistle. **Range and habitat:** OR. Resident in heavy forest in Malaysia, Sumatra and Borneo.

Red Spurfowl
Galloperdix spadicea (Phasianidae) 37 cm/15 in.
The spurfowl are a group of 3 species confined to India and Sri Lanka, somewhat resembling a domestic fowl in shape, but with a rather long, rounded and not arched tail, and 2 or 3 spurs on the leg in the male. Not a gregarious bird, it is usually seen singly or in small family parties, though it is in any case difficult to see, and a swift runner when disturbed. The dense cover which the birds frequent does not permit long flights, and sometimes they will take to the trees for refuge and for roosting purposes. The note is a henlike cackling. **Range and habitat:** OR. Resident in peninsular India in thick scrub and near cultivation in the lowlands and lower hills. **Similar species:** Painted and Ceylon Spurfowl.

Blood Pheasant
Ithaginis cruentus (Phasianidae) 46 cm/18 in.
A short-tailed, bushy-crested pheasant of high altitudes in the Himalayas. The female, in her brown plumage, is much dowdier than the male with his scarlet throat and eye-ring, and scarlet-streaked, lime-green breast. There are no fewer than 14 subspecies of this sedentary bird, differing mainly in the extent of red on the face and breast and in overall size. Usually in parties except in the breeding season, this pheasant lives at or near the snow-line, and is a notoriously tame bird. Roosts and finds shelter in the fir woods or bamboo, but feeds in the open, digging into the snow for seeds and leaves. **Range and habitat:** EP and OR, in southern Tibet, the Himalayas and north-west China, Resident in alpine scrub or forest above 3,500 m (11,500 ft).

Satyr Tragopan
Tragopan satyra (Phasianidae) 68 cm/27 in.
The 5 species of tragopan are bulky pheasants with a rounded but not elongated tail, and the males are remarkably ornamented for display with erectile fleshy horns and brilliantly patterned and inflatable throat lappet. The Satyr Tragopan is typical, being a sedentary species, not gregarious, and very shy and elusive. Entirely at home in trees, though also ground feeding, it is a mountain bird of steep, forested slopes, and, unlike most pheasants, is a tree-nester. It is a popular and confiding bird in captivity. **Range and habitat:** OR, central Himalayas, in hill forests up to 4,250 m (13,900 ft).

Sclater's Monal
Lophophorus sclateri (Phasianidae) 72 cm/28 in.
The 3 species of monal are heavy, brilliantly metallic pheasants, with an unusual tail for a pheasant, being flat and square. The lengthened upper mandible is effective in digging up roots and bulbs. Living at up to the tree limit in fir or rhododendron scrub, it is often solitary or in very small groups. Being a very sedentary bird, it is unfortunately all too easily snared, though little is known about its biology in the wild. It has a loud, whistling call, often uttered by a sentinel bird from its viewpoint on a rocky hillside. **Range and habitat:** OR; northern Myanmar and adjacent parts of Tibet and China. Resident in forest up to 4,000 m (13,000 ft). **Not illustrated.**

Gray Francolin

Jungle Bush-Quail

Hill Partridge

Red Spurfowl

Satyr Tragopan

Crested Partridge

Blood Pheasant

Red Junglefowl

Gallus gallus (Phasianidae) 65 cm/26 in.

The unmistakable ancestor of domestic fowl, it has 2 close relatives in India and Sri Lanka and 1 in Java. Unlike the domestic variety, the wild Junglefowl is noteworthy for having an eclipse plumage into which it molts after breeding, losing the neck hackles and long tail feathers. Gregarious birds, they have a similar crow to that of the barnyard cockerel, though shorter, and are difficult to observe, being very alert and shy. The usual view is of the backs of 3 or 4 birds as they jump up at the side of a track. **Range and habitat:** OR; India throughout Southeast Asia to the Philippines. Resident in light forest and scrub. **Similar species:** Gray Junglefowl, Green Junglefowl.

Silver Pheasant

Lophura nycthemera (Phasianidae) 67 cm/26 in.

A sedentary species dwelling in thick evergreen forest, it has developed no fewer than 14 subspecies, which differ in the intensity and pattern of the markings and also in size. The "true" Silver Pheasant, the race originally described from China, is the largest and also the whitest above, with very long, almost unmarked central tail feathers. It lives in small family parties in hill forests, especially bamboo, and though not shy and quite a noisy bird, is not easy to see. The striking appearance of the male has for centuries made them desirable birds in captivity. **Range and habitat:** southern EP and OR in south and west China and continental Southeast Asia, in hill forests. **Similar species:** Kalij Pheasant.

Great Argus

Argusianus argus (Phasianidae) Male up to 190 cm/75 in), female 63 cm/25 in.

The striking feature of this species is the great development and beautiful patterning of the secondaries and the immensely long central tail feathers. These are shown to advantage in display in which the male faces the female with wings spread and arched, hiding the head, and the tail standing vertically behind. For this purpose the cock maintains a scrupulously cleared patch on the forest floor. He spends much time here, advertising his presence vocally, ready to display to any female ready to breed. The call is a commonly heard, far-carrying and repeated bark. **Range and habitat:** OR; in Malaysia, Borneo and Sumatra. Resident in lowland forest. **Similar species:** Crested Argus.

Indian Peafowl

Pavo cristatus (Phasianidae) Male is up to 200 cm/79 in), female 85 cm/33 in.

The decorative splendor of this bird has made it a favorite in captivity and a familiar sight for more than 30 centuries, though presumably for all that time people have winced at the harsh double call, especially irritating at night. Persecution and hunting renders it a shy bird in the wild, though it is tame around villages. It is surprising how easily a cock with full train can fly up out of tall grass to perch in an isolated tree at the approach of danger. Always extremely alert, peafowl are particularly wary of the large cats which share their jungle home. **Range and habitat:** OR; in India and Sri Lanka. Resident in forests in the plains and foothills. **Similar species:** Green Peafowl.

CRANES, RAILS AND ALLIES Gruiformes

Barred Buttonquail

Turnix suscitator (Turnicidae) 15 cm/6 in.

This species is representative of the family of 16 species, which differ from true quails by lacking the hind toe and the crop, and also in that females are larger and more brightly colored, and leave incubation and care of the young to the male. The hen makes a loud drumming or booming call to attract a mate. Usually seen singly, it is an unobtrusive bird of grassy undergrowth, difficult to watch or even put up, though when it flies it looks like a typical quail, small rounded wings beating rapidly until it abruptly lands in cover and vanishes. **Range and habitat:** OR; throughout India and Sri Lanka. Resident in grassy places, cultivation or thin forest. **Similar species:** Small Buttonquail.

White-naped Crane

Grus vipio (Gruidae) 127 cm/50 in.

Of the 8 species of crane recorded from the OR, all but 1 are winter visitors. The White-naped Crane migrates as far south as Taiwan, on the north-eastern limits of the region, though the main wintering areas are on the lower Yangtse in eastern China, in Korea and Japan. It is one of the most beautiful of the family with its red face and legs, and dark stripe down the neck. Within the winter flocks, family groups tend to preserve their identity, and males attack other males which come too close to their own group. By the time the birds are back on their breeding grounds in Manchuria they are already paired up. **Range and habitat:** EP; wintering OR south to Taiwan, on marshes, crops and by rivers. **Similar species:** Common and Sarus Cranes.

Sarus Crane

Grus antigone (Gruidae) 150 cm/59 in.

A huge, pale gray crane, almost always to be seen in pairs, and very familiar to, and protected by, the country people generally in India. It is unusual among the cranes in being sedentary, and in its tameness, presumably a result of not being molested. Like all its relatives, though, it has a dancing display with much wing-flapping, bowing and noisy trumpeting. The pair also call together, with necks stretched up, when greeting or as a warning. The nest is a big heap of reeds and rushes built on swampy ground in a marsh or paddyfield. **Range and habitat:** OR; India to Southeast Asia. Resident in well-watered plains country. **Similar species:** Common Crane (see p 154).

Indian Bustard

Choriotis nigriceps (Otididae) 125 cm/49 in.

One of the rarest of the world's large bustards, and gravely threatened by hunting and habitat destruction. Very shy and wary and unapproachable on foot, it can however be easily shot from a vehicle. The male is a massive bird weighing up to 18 kg (40 lbs), though able to run with facility, and a powerful flier. Moves about in small groups which wander in search of suitable grasslands according to weather conditions, rendering demarcated reserves a problematical solution to the hunting threat. The clutch is a single egg, and the breeding season extended. **Range and habitat:** OR; north, west and central India. Rare resident and nomad in sparse grasslands and light scrub. **Similar species:** Kori Bustard, Arabian Bustard (see p 198).

Bengal Florican

Houbaropsis bengalensis (Otididae) 66 cm/26 in.

This species and the Lesser Florican are very reminiscent in appearance of several African bustards, and are among the most threatened species in the family. Highly valued for its eating qualities and hence still a target for the pot, the male is a conspicuous object during display when he flutters high into the air above the tall grass, making a humming noise while beating the air. Unusually in the family, he is slightly smaller than his mate. Usually found solitarily, these bustards forage in open, grassy areas at dusk and in the early morning, and keep to thicker cover during the day. **Range and habitat:** OR; Himalayan foothills and north-east India, possibly still in Kampuchea. Resident in areas of tall grassland and scattered bushes. **Similar species:** Lesser Florican.

Lesser Florican

Sypheotides indica (Otididae) 46 cm/18 in.

Smaller and more slender than the Bengal Florican, it has particularly long legs, and the male is unusual in having a form of eclipse plumage following the breeding season. The white inner wing and shoulder contrast in flight with the black neck and underparts, particularly in the jumping display flight, which is repeated with extraordinary regularity and persistence. When disturbed, prefers running to flying, when its wingbeats are rapid for a bustard, but is generally less shy than its relatives. Successful breeding very dependent on the rains allowing good grass growth. **Range and habitat:** OR; Pakistan and India. Resident and nomadic in grassy areas. **Similar species:** Bengal Florican.

Silver Pheasant

Great Argus

Red Junglefowl

Indian Peafowl (pair)

Barred Buttonquail

Bengal Florican

Lesser Florican

White-naped Crane

Sarus Crane (pair)

Indian Bustard

Slaty-breasted Rail

Gallirallus striatus (Rallidae) 28 cm/11 in.

The chestnut crown and nape contrasting with the grayish breast, and especially the finely banded upperparts, distinguish this species from related rails in its range. Like many other sedentary birds, it has developed a number of subspecies which differ both in size and in intensity of coloration. It is a difficult subject to study in its wetland habitat, taking cover at a quick run at any sign of danger, and is rarely seen in the open. In the highlands of Borneo it has been caught in numbers in rodent snares. It is generally solitary, and makes a sharp double call-note. **Range and habitat:** OR. Resident in swamps, mangroves or flooded fields from India to the Philippines. **Similar species:** Water Rail, Slaty-legged Crake (see p 154). **Not illustrated.**

Ruddy-breasted Crake

Porzana fusca (Rallidae) 23 cm/9 in.

A small, rich brown crake with noticeably red legs. Like many crakes, it has been able, despite apparently weak flight, to colonize quite remote islands, in this case the Andamans and Christmas Island. In the Andamans it has been found nesting in dense, wet forest, though in other parts of its range, a more usual site would be in waterside vegetation. It is particularly secretive and also rather quiet, and so a very unobtrusive species. It is apparently more migratory than many of its relatives, being a summer visitor to much of eastern China, and a winter visitor (as well as being resident) in Sri Lanka. **Range and habitat:** EP, OR; resident and migratory to some extent. Inhabits marshes and swamps. **Similar species:** Red-legged Crake.

White-breasted Waterhen

Amaurornis phoenicurus (Rallidae) 30 cm/12 in.

Not only one of the commonest of waterside birds in the OR, it also happens to be, with the Moorhen, one of the species in the family most adapted to feeding in the open. Although not particularly shy, it is nevertheless very wary, and runs rapidly into cover if disturbed. It is a noisy bird with a sharp double note which is often repeated for minutes on end. Like many of the family, it is pugnacious and quarrelsome. Breeding is during the rains in the monsoon areas, the nest on or by water, sometimes 1 m (39 in) or more above the ground in a bush or tree. **Range and habitat:** OR; India and Sri Lanka to the Philippines. Resident and local migrant, by ponds, marshes or wet areas in the plains and hills up to 2,400 m (7,900 ft). **Similar species:** Common Moorhen (see p 154).

Watercock

Gallicrex cinerea (Rallidae) 42 cm/17 in.

Owes its name to the pugnacious nature of the males, who battle furiously in the breeding season, and develop at this period a fleshy red horn above the frontal shield. Resembles an outsize Moorhen with red legs, but lacks the white undertail-coverts. Actions similar too, as it prospects with jerking tail round the margin of a pond, running into cover when alarmed. It is more active at dawn and dusk, and does not feed in the open, preferring to keep among lush waterside vegetation. The call, uttered for long periods at a stretch, is a rhythmic series of booming notes. **Range and habitat:** OR, and in summer to EP. Resident and migrant in well-watered lowlands.

SHOREBIRDS, GULLS, AUKS Charadriiformes

Pheasant-tailed Jacana

Hydrophasianus chirurgus (Jacanidae) 30 cm/12 in.

A striking and elegant adornment to any lotus-covered pond, over which the enormously elongated toes enable it to walk with ease. In the breeding season the male grows the 15 cm/6 in) arching tail, to which the bird owes its name. Often surprisingly inconspicuous when feeding among the tangle of waterplants, it is easily seen in flight when the white wings are striking and the long toes dangle awkwardly. Often congregates in quite large flocks in winter. The female is larger than the male, who incubates the eggs and rears the chicks. **Range and habitat:** OR, in summer to EP. Largely resident on lakes, marshes and ponds. **Similar species:** Bronze-winged Jacana.

Bronze-winged Jacana

Metopidius indicus (Jacanidae) 28 cm/11 in.

Unlike the Pheasant-tailed Jacana, this bird has no special breeding plumage, and the tail is short and rounded. It is even more addicted

to ponds where the emergent vegetation is really luxurious and there are bordering reeds and sedges. It is a rather shy bird, and can often be difficult to see among the curling lily leaves, and is an unwilling flier; it seems to be more adept at swimming and diving than its longer tailed relative, sinking the body to avoid being seen. The male incubates the eggs and rears the chicks. **Range and habitat:** OR. Resident on lakes and ponds in the lowlands. **Similar species:** African Jacana (see p 198).

Ibisbill

Ibidorhyncha struthersii (Ibidorhynchidae) 40 cm/16 in.

A strange shorebird with no obviously close relations, notable for its red, down-curved bill, rounded wings, and red legs and feet which lack a hind toe. The shape of the bill is well adapted for probing between the rounded boulders along the Himalayan rivers it frequents, and the bird also has a habit of wading in the water and tilting the whole head and neck underneath in the manner of a dipper. It has rather slow, lapwinglike wingbeats, and utters a clear, double whistle in flight, when the white patch on the wing is noticeable. Nowhere particularly common, usually seen in pairs or small parties. Nests in early spring before the snow has melted. **Range and habitat:** EP and OR. Resident by rocky rivers in Tibet and the Himalayas.

Great Thick-knee

Esacus recurvirostris (Burhinidae) 50 cm/20 in.

The heavy bill of this outsize stone curlew enables the bird to cope with the crabs and shellfish on which it feeds, and this feature is even further developed in the closely related species in Australia. The staring yellow eyes are a clue to the bird's nocturnal habits; the daytime is spent roosting on a river sand-bar or saltpan. Despite being nocturnal, it is accustomed to brilliantly sunny, hot conditions in the day, and nests on the bare ground completely in the open. Not a gregarious bird, though often in pairs. It has a loud, mournful cry like others of its family. **Range and habitat:** OR. Resident by rivers, saltpans and on the coast. **Similar species:** Eurasian Thick-knee (see p 160).

Indian Courser

Cursorius coromandelicus (Glareolidae) 26 cm/10 in.

Until recently, thought to be the only breeding courser in India, the family being more typical of dry grasslands in Africa. Usually in pairs or small groups, it is a bird well adapted for life on sandy, barren areas, being very fast on its legs. The feet lack a hind toe, in common with many other ground-dwelling species. It is also, however, strong and quick on the wing when forced to fly. Takes food from the ground by tilting the body down in a mechanical way, then runs a metre or two before stopping stock still, when it is often difficult to see. It nests in the hot weather before the ground is saturated by the monsoon. **Range and habitat:** OR; India and Sri Lanka. Resident in open country in the plains. **Similar species:** Cream-colored Courser.

Ruddy-breasted Crake

White-breasted Waterhen

Watercock

Pheasant-tailed Jacana

Bronze-winged Jacana

Ibisbill

Great Thick-knee

Indian Courser

Small Pratincole

Glareola lactea (Glareolidae) 17 cm/6½ in.

This dainty little pratincole is a common sight as it wheels about over the big rivers of southern Asia, congregating to rest and roost on the sandbanks. It is constantly active in the air, flying perhaps more erratically than its larger relatives, perhaps because of taking smaller, more agile flying insects. The sexes are alike, the black underwing and shallowly forked tail giving a distinctive appearance. Nests colonially on bare ground or sand along river-banks, dispersing after the breeding season to suitable stretches of water or coastal areas. It has a low, harsh note. **Range and habitat:** OR; the Indus river and Sri Lanka to Southeast Asia. Resident and nomadic by marshes and rivers in the lowlands. **Similar species:** Oriental Pratincole.

Yellow-wattled Lapwing

Vanellus malabaricus (Char-adriidae) 25 cm/10 in.

The plumage and yellow facial wattle recall a very similar African species, though in this species the wattle lies along the throat as opposed to being pendant. It is quieter and less frantic than its larger red-wattled relative in the OR, and prefers a much drier type of habitat, especially ploughed fields and arid or stony ground. Often to be seen foraging in small groups, which rise with a double piping call, showing the prominent white wing-bar, though when standing motionless, often difficult to detect against a grayish brown dried-up field. **Range and habitat:** OR; India and Sri Lanka. Resident in open country in the lowlands. **Similar species:** Red-wattled Lapwing.

Red-wattled Lapwing

Vanellus indicus (Charadriidae) 33 cm/13 in.

A noisy, demonstrating and vigilant bird, particularly relentless when mobbing predators near a nest or chicks. The heavy, floppy flight is transformed when the bird corkscrews down with great agility to discomfort its target, swooping up immediately to a safe height. Usually in pairs or small groups, it feeds in typical plover fashion, tilting down to take an insect, then running on a little way. The sexes are alike, and there is no seasonal change in the plumage as with the Lapwing. There are several subspecies, differing in size, coloration and extent of white on the neck. **Range and habitat:** WP and OR; South-west Asia to Sri Lanka and Southeast Asia. Resident near water, marshes or cultivation in the plains and lower hills. **Similar species:** Yellow-wattled Lapwing.

Gray-headed Lapwing

Vanellus cinereus (Charadriidae) 35 cm/14 in.

Strikingly patterned in flight, with the rather pointed, black-tipped wings having a broad white band along the trailing edge. The long, yellow legs project well beyond the tail tip. The muted plumage coloring renders the bird often difficult to see when standing quietly in the grass or on a paddyfield. Very noisy and demonstrative on the breeding grounds, mobbing intruders with a sharp, short note. Sociable in winter, when small parties gather by rivers or in the fields. The food is largely aquatic insects. **Range and habitat:** EP, in winter across OR, on marshes, grasslands and cultivation, river margins. **Similar species:** Yellow-wattled Lapwing.

Swinhoe's Snipe

Gallinago megala (Scolopacidae) 27 cm/10½ in.

Identification of Asiatic snipes in the field has been hindered by lack of critical data until the last few years, and museum criteria such as this species having 20 tail feathers compared with 28 in the Pintail Snipe are of little use to the modern birder who rarely has a bird in the hand. Swinhoe's may be commoner in the region in winter than previously thought, though already known to be common in the Philippines. Larger and with a longer bill than Pintail Snipe, it is also a duller and paler bird, and not as heavily striped on the back as Common. **Range and habitat:** EP, in winter to OR in marshes or wet paddyfields. **Similar species:** Pintail Snipe, Common Snipe (see p 160). **Not illustrated.**

Long-toed Stint

Calidris subminuta (Scolopacidae) 15 cm/6 in.

A bird of wet paddyfields and swampy or marshy ground rather than the open shore, and rather prone to stretch up while standing, maybe to get a clearer view over surrounding vegetation. A dark, well-streaked stint, it does in fact have a middle toe about

15% longer than that of the Little Stint. In its winter quarters in Southeast Asia, the birds tend to feed in loose groups through the marsh vegetation, and it is often surprising how many can be flushed from a comparatively small wet area. It rises with a dry trilling call. **Range and habitat:** EP, in winter to OR; in swampy places and wet paddyfields. **Similar species:** Rednecked Stint, Little Stint (see p 158).

Spoonbill Sandpiper

Eurynorhynchus pygmeus (Scolopacidae) 17 cm/6½ in.

In winter, when this species consorts with other small sandpipers on the mudflats, it is by no means easy to pick it out by the curious bill shape, although this can be obvious enough if the bird is close and head-on to the observer. Very active and sprightly, it dabbles the bill from side to side as it moves through shallow water, changing direction without lifting the head up. It also takes insects off the ground, these forming the main diet in the breeding season. The grayish upperparts of winter become more rufous in summer, as do the face and breast, much as in the Red-necked Stint. **Range and habitat:** EP, in winter to OR, on shores and mudflats. **Similar species:** Little Stint, Red-necked Stint (see p 158).

Brown-headed Gull

Larus brunnicephalus (Laridae) 46 cm/18 in.

Somewhat larger than the similar Black-headed Gull, and with a white spot in the black wing tip, it is common in winter around the coasts of southern Asia. At this season, the brown hood shrinks to a dark patch on the side of the whitish head. Often in large flocks which scavenge around harbors, lakes or estuaries in typical gull fashion. Also takes insect food from the surface while swimming. It is not a particularly noisy bird, but has various strident notes, and is especially vocal at breeding sites. The brown hood of summer is showing on most birds in late spring before they migrate north. **Range and habitat:** central PA, in winter to OR; on rivers, lakes and sea-coasts. **Similar species:** Black-headed Gull (see p 162).

River Tern

Sterna aurantia (Sternidae) 40 cm/16 in.

It is interesting that 2 species of tern, 1 being this species, are almost exclusively inland birds of rivers in southern Asia, and 2, also with yellow bills, in South America, but that no counterpart exists in Africa. The River Tern is among the largest of the "black-capped" terns and has a heavy yellow bill which becomes duller, with a dark tip, in winter. At this time, the crown is heavily streaked with white. It nests fairly early in the year before the monsoon rains swell the river levels and cover the sandbanks which are a usual nest-site. **Range and habitat:** OR, but not in Sri Lanka or the Indo-Malayan subregion. Resident and locally migratory, on rivers, reservoirs and sometimes sea coasts. **Similar species:** Black-bellied Tern.

Black-bellied Tern

Sterna melanogaster (Sternidae) 33 cm/13 in.

A long-tailed, more slender tern with a lighter bill than the River Tern, and with a conspicuous blackish belly in the summer plumage. Traces of the black underparts are often retained in winter. It is even more restricted to fresh water, living by large rivers or open stretches of water in the lowlands. A sociable bird, it is usually in flocks which rest on the river-bank or on sandy islands when not beating the water in their search for fish. This tern also hawks for insects on occasion, taking them off the surface or in aerial chase. **Range and habitat:** OR, from Pakistan to Southeast Asia. Not in Sri Lanka or the Indo-Malayan subregion. Resident along rivers in the plains. **Similar species:** River Tern. **Not illustrated.**

Small Pratincole

Yellow-wattled Lapwing

Red-wattled Lapwing

Gray-headed Lapwing

Long-toed Stint

Spoonbill Sandpiper

Brown-headed Gull

River Tern

PIGEONS Columbiformes

Yellow-footed Pigeon

Treron phoenicoptera (Columbidae) 33 cm/13 in.
Often concealed among dense foliage, it is often surprising how many birds can be beaten out of a tree, all bursting out with loud wing-clapping. Forages quietly but voraciously on ripe fruit, especially figs. The feet of green pigeons have swollen, padded soles as an adaptation for grasping twigs, and the bird is very nimble and agile when feeding, despite being quite bulky. Does not feed on the ground. Several races are distinguished by size and amount of yellow in plumage. **Range and habitat:** OR; India and Sri Lanka to Indo-China. Resident in forest, groves and gardens. **Similar species:** 17 species of green pigeon are broadly similar.

Oriental Turtle-Dove

Streptopelia orientalis (Columbidae) 33 cm/13 in.
Very similar to Eurasian Turtle-Dove, and its eastern counterpart, but larger and heavier and without white tail tips. Rufous, well-patterned upperparts distinguish it from other Asian doves and pigeons. Breeding pairs gather together in parties to migrate, and in winter resident birds of Indian peninsula share habitat with more northern breeders. Often seen along paths or forest tracks where it picks up grain or seeds, flying up with expanded tail. Several races over total range differ largely in richness of rufous and color of tail tip. **Range and habitat:** BP, OR, in winter to south of range, in forest, light woodland or cultivation. **Similar species:** Eurasian Turtle-Dove (see p 164).

Little Cuckoo-Dove

Macropygia ruficeps (Columbidae) 28 cm/11 in.
The long, graduated tail gives this rufous little dove its name. The sexes are alike, but the female lacks the metallic reflections. Like other doves, it is a ground feeder, coming into clearings and small patches of cultivation in the forest to forage in parties, which coo as they move about. It also takes berries, searching forest slopes for ripe fruit. It is a rapid flier when alarmed, showing the chestnut underwing. **Range and habitat:** OR, in Indo-Malayan and Sino-Himalayan subregions. Resident in hill evergreen forest. **Similar species:** Barred Cuckoo-Dove.

Spotted Dove

Streptopelia chinensis (Columbidae) 28 cm/11 in.
Very familiar throughout its range, often around villages and towns, it walks about fearlessly on tracks and paths, constantly searching for grain and seeds. If sufficiently alarmed, it jumps into the air almost vertically, with the widely fanned tail showing the white tips. Often in pairs, though will congregate in large numbers at suitable sources of food, such as reaped paddyfields. The pleasant cooing and gentle disposition make it a favorite cagebird everywhere. Plumage variations are responsible for the separation into 8 subspecies across the wide range. **Range and habitat:** OR; resident and common around villages, gardens and cultivation in the plains. **Similar species:** Oriental Turtle-Dove.

Emerald Dove

Chalcophaps indica (Columbidae) 26 cm/10 in.
A fast, low-flying dove, often seen hurtling across forest paths or clearings, for although quite familiar, it is a shy bird. Looks rather dark in flight, and shows the 2 white rump bars and short tail. The female is duller and browner than the male. Very much a ground bird, it is rarely far from cover, and the deep cooing may often be heard from amongst dense foliage. It is not a sociable species, usually being seen singly or in pairs. **Range and habitat:** OR, AU. Resident in mixed or evergreen forest in the hills and plains. **Similar species:** Green Imperial-Pigeon.

PARROTS AND RELATIVES Psittaciformes

Vernal Hanging-Parrot

Loriculus vernalis (Psittacidae) 15 cm/6 in.
Tiny, and difficult to see in thick foliage when climbing about searching for fruit or nectar. Flies from 1 tree to another with an undulating flight on whirring wings which are rather short and triangular. Often in small parties which keep in touch with a continuous distinctive squeaking which often draws attention to their presence. Remarkable for sleeping while hanging upside-down from a twig. Typically adept at clinging and clambering at all angles while feeding. **Range and habitat:** OR. Resident in forested areas. **Similar species:** Ceylon and Blue-crowned Hanging-Parrots. **Not illustrated.**

Alexandrine Parakeet

Psittacula eupatria (Psittacidae) 52 cm/20 in.
A popular cagebird whose numbers may have been reduced in the wild by nestlings being taken for pets. A heavy-headed, stream-lined bird in flight, it is destructive to crops and fruit, and keeps in small parties which congregate at roosts. It makes a loud scream when on the wing, but is not much of a talker in captivity. The nest-hole, in a tree, is carved out with the powerful bill, or an old hole is suitably enlarged. The birds pair for life, and are very affectionate. **Range and habitat:** OR; India and Sri Lanka to Indo-China. Resident in wooded country in the plains. **Similar species:** Plum-headed Parakeet.

Plum-headed Parakeet

Psittacula cyanocephala (Psittacidae) 36 cm/14 in.
The female lacks the beautiful rosy color of the male's head, and the black collar. A small, slim species, though with a long, narrow tail. The rapid wingbeats enhance the speedy impression in flight, and the birds are very adept at swerving and dodging in thick woodland. Like other parakeets, it is noisy in flight, with a scream which is less harsh than that of some relatives. The nest is a hole, often high in a dead tree, several pairs often choosing adjacent trees and forming a small colony. **Range and habitat:** OR; India and Sri Lanka. Resident in forests and cultivation in the plains and lower hills. **Similar species:** Alexandrine Parakeet.

CUCKOOS AND ALLIES Cuculiformes

Common Hawk-Cuckoo

Cuculus varius (Cuculidae) 33 cm/13 in.
Like many cuckoos, almost totally unobtrusive and silent in the colder months. It makes up for this by the endless and irritating repetition of its call in the hot weather and the rains—a 3-syllabled, frenzied and accelerating shout. It is parasitic on various babbler species and lays an egg of a beautiful turquoise color. Resembles a sparrow-hawk, even to the immature being streaked rather than barred on the underparts. The food is largely caterpillars. **Range and habitat:** OR; India and Sri Lanka. Resident and nomadic in wooded areas and cultivation or gardens. **Similar species:** Large Hawk-Cuckoo.

Oriental Cuckoo

Cuculus saturatus (Cuculidae) 31 cm/12 in.
Tends to parasitize even smaller host species than does the European Cuckoo, though both are much the same size, commonly laying in the nests of tiny warblers. It is very similar in plumage, though the barring on the underparts is broader and more widely spaced. The 4 notes of the call, however, all at the same pitch, render it easily identifiable. Movements outside the breeding season are difficult to study owing to its unobtrusive habits at that time, though some populations are certainly migratory. **Range and habitat:** BP, OR in central Asia, the Himalayas to southern China and the Greater Sundas. Resident or migratory in wooded hill country. **Similar species:** Common Cuckoo (see p 166). **Not illustrated.**

Plaintive Cuckoo

Cacomantis merulinus (Cuculidae) 23 cm/9 in.
An attractively colored, small cuckoo with its tawny underparts, and as with many other cuckoos, a reddish brown, barred phase is common among females. The name refers to the quality of a commonly heard call, though the song is a multi-note whistle. It has a rapid and agile flight on pointed wings, and is often quite easy to see as it haunts open woodland and gardens, and tends to call from treetops rather than in deep foliage. It parasitizes small warblers. **Range and habitat:** OR; from south China to Myanmar, Java and the Philippines. Resident or local migrant, in open wooded country. **Similar species:** Banded Bay Cuckoo, Lesser Cuckoo.

Yellow-footed Pigeon

Oriental Turtle-Dove

Little Cuckoo-Dove

Spotted Dove

Emerald Dove

Alexandrine Parakeet

Plum-headed Parakeet

Common Hawk-Cuckoo

Plaintive Cuckoo

Blue-faced Malkoha

Phaenicophaeus viridirostris (**Cuculidae**) 40 cm/16 in.

The dark gray plumage and skulking habits render this an inconspicuous bird in the tangled, dense foliage it frequents. It clambers, climbs or hops about rather like a squirrel, the long, white-tipped tail sticking out behind. It is a poor flier, soon diving into cover. The bright green bill and blue eye patch soon identify it when the head is pushed briefly through the leaves. Unlike many cuckoos, it builds its own nest and rears the young. **Range and habitat:** OR; Peninsular India and Sri Lanka. Resident in woodland in the plains and foothills. **Similar species:** Black-bellied Malkoha.

Greater Coucal

Centropus sinensis (**Cuculidae**) 48 cm/19 in.

Coucals are unlike other cuckoos in having a long, straight claw on the inner hind toe, and are much less arboreal. Rather ungainly birds, they clamber through dense grass or brushwood, the big tail flopping about or flicked or expanded, and sometimes perch in the open on a small bush to call. They forage for lizards, nestlings or small mammals on the ground, pushing through thick cover or under bushes, and are reluctant fliers. The large nest is made of twigs, and the call is a resonant, repeated booming. **Range and habitat:** OR. Resident in grassy, bushed areas, gardens and scrub. **Similar species:** Lesser Coucal.

OWLS Strigiformes

Buffy Fish-Owl

Ketupa ketupu (**Strigidae**) 41 cm/16 in.

Roosting in the daytime on a branch of a tall tree, often by the junction with the main trunk, it emerges in the late afternoon to patrol the ricefields or forest streams. The food is largely amphibians, fish or small mammals, and grasping slippery prey is facilitated by the prickly scales on the soles of the feet. The fish-owls enjoy bathing, and splash about with their wings at the edge of a shallow pool or stream. The call is a soft whistle or trilling sound. **Range and habitat:** OR; in Indo-Malayan subregion. Resident in lowland forest near streams or ricefields or at the coast. **Similar species:** Brown Fish-Owl.

Spotted Owlet

Athene brama (**Strigidae**) 20 cm/8 in.

Much more likely to be seen in daylight than some other owls, when its presence is often indicated by the noisy mobbing of various small birds. One of the most familiar owls because of its preferred habitat of groves or gardens, often around houses, but avoiding thick forest. The yellow eyes and heavily white-spotted plumage render identification easy. Often lives in small groups, usually at least 2 birds roosting together. When disturbed, bobs up and down and stares at intruder before flying off with undulating flight. Call a series of screeches. **Range and habitat:** OR; except Sri Lanka and Indo-Malayan subregion. Resident in light woodland, cultivation, villages. **Similar species:** other owlets.

Jungle Owlet

Glaucidium radiatum (**Strigidae**) 20 cm/8 in.

A much less familiar bird than its spotted cousin, as it is both more strictly nocturnal, and also haunts much denser vegetation in woods and thick forest. The lack of ear-tufts distinguishes it from other small owls of the same habitat. Spends the daytime roosting in a tree-hole, but is sometimes discovered and mobbed by other birds, and then flies off to deeper cover. It preys mainly on large insects and small animals and birds. The call is a repeated, musical hoot. **Range and habitat:** OR; India and Sri Lanka. Resident in forests up to 2,000 m (6,500 ft). **Similar species:** other owlets.

NIGHTJARS AND ALLIES Caprimulgiformes

Hodgson's Frogmouth

Batrachostomus hodgsoni (**Podargidae**) 26 cm/10 in.

The family name refers to the enormously wide gape, such that, seen from above, the bill is a rounded triangular shape, though the base is mostly covered with bristles. The feet are extremely small and weak. The food, mostly moths and insects, is probably taken as much from branches as in the air. Difficult to see, frogmouths spend the day perched on a dead branch or stump in thick forest, and have mottled, highly protective plumage. The call is a soft, descending whistle. **Range and habitat:** OR; Himalayas to Indo-China. Resident in evergreen hill forest. **Similar species:** other frogmouths (see p 304). Not illustrated.

Indian Nightjar

Caprimulgus asiaticus (**Caprimulgidae**) 24 cm/9½ in.

Most usually seen at night, either hawking noiselessly for insects, or resting on a path or track, when the eyes shine red in a car's headlights. The nightjars, of which there are 11 species in the OR, are best identified by the call, which in this bird is a repetition of 3 notes running into a throaty trill. Spends the day squatting quietly on the ground, almost invisible owing to the protective plumage, but starts to feed and call at dusk. Seasonal movements are difficult to study, as calling ceases after the breeding season. **Range and habitat:** OR; India and Sri Lanka to Indo-China. Resident in dry scrub, gardens, wasteland. **Similar species:** other nightjars (see pp 72, 116, 166, 212, 304).

SWIFTS AND HUMMINGBIRDS Apodiformes

White-throated Needletail

Hirundapus caudacutus (**Apodidae**) 20 cm/8 in.

The name is a reference to the shafts of the tail feathers, which project beyond the vane as a short spike. A large swift and a very powerful flier, which makes a loud, whooshing noise as it sweeps by. Often flies very high in the air, but when hawking insects at low levels the great size, with a wing spread of up to 53 cm/21 in) is apparent, as is the bulky body with a white patch at the rear. Often in small groups, the birds scream as they chase each other. **Range and habitat:** EP, OR, in winter to AU. Resident and migratory, wandering great distances. **Similar species:** Common Swift (see p 166).

Fork-tailed Swift

Apus pacificus (**Apodidae**) 18 cm/7 in.

A widely distributed swift in eastern Asia, wandering widely southward in winter. The forked tail and gleaming white rump patch facilitate identification even when the bird is flying at a great height, as it often does in fine weather. In Tibet, nests under eaves and in stonework of buildings, but outside breeding season almost continuously on the wing. Has a screaming note much as in Swift. **Range and habitat:** EP, OR, in winter to AU. Largely migratory. **Similar species:** Common Swift (see p 166).

Edible-nest Swiftlet

Aerodramus fuciphagus (**Apodidae**) 12 cm/4½ in.

One of a group of about 20 species, some of which make the nests which are used for birds's-nest soup. The best nests for this purpose consist entirely of coagulated saliva, looking a clear white in color, and the present species builds one of the purest and therefore most favored. In appearance it is a tiny, slim swift with a well-forked tail and a fluttery, batlike flight, which hawks for minute insects over beaches and around coconut trees. The nests are built in cliff or cave crevices. **Range and habitat:** OR. Resident around beaches, plantations or forest. **Similar species:** Common Swift (see p 166).

Asian Palm-Swift

Cypsiurus balasiensis (**Apodidae**) 13 cm/5 in.

A slim, small swift with a long, deeply forked tail which distinguishes this species from swiftlets. The name is derived from its habit of nesting in palm trees. Unlike swiftlets, palm swifts construct their nests from feathery seeds, often those of the kapok tree. These are glued together with saliva and stuck onto the upper surface of older, hanging palm fronds. Colonial breeder. Hawk flying insects on the wing, and congregate around the palms in which they breed. **Range and habitat:** OR; resident in open country with palm trees. **Similar species:** swiftlets.

Blue-faced Malkoha (feeding young)

Greater Coucal (feeding young)

Buffy Fish-Owl

Spotted Owlet

Jungle Owlet

Indian Nightjar

White-throated Needletail

Fork-tailed Swift

Edible-nest Swiftlet

Asian Palm-Swift

KINGFISHERS AND ALLIES Coraciiformes

White-throated Kingfisher

Halcyon smyrnensis (Alcedinidae) 28 cm/11 in.
The heavy red bill, and white breast contrasting with chocolate head and under-parts, are diagnostic of this familiar bird—one of the most noticeable kingfishers throughout the whole OR. In flight, shows a large, white wing patch. Perches in a characteristically exposed position, often on telephone wires or roadside posts, and equally at home in wet paddyfields or forest clearings, for it eats more insects and small animals than fish. Bobs nervously on its perch, and has a loud, rippling whistle. The 6 subspecies vary in saturation of plumage colors and size of the white bib. **Range and habitat:** WP, EP, OR; Iran to the Philippines. Resident in open country, thin forest, sea coasts, at up to 2,500 m (8,200 ft) in the Himalayas. Similar species: Black-capped Kingfisher.

Black-capped Kingfisher

Halcyon pileata (Alcedinidae) 30 cm/12 in.
Much more restricted to the neighborhood of water than the similar white-breasted bird, and easily distinguished by the black head, pale buffy underparts and blackish violet back. Also shows a large white wing patch in flight. Often seen on a post sticking out of a swampy area or in mangroves, it is mainly a fish- and crab-eater, well equipped for dealing with such prey with its formidable bill. A solitary and rather shy bird, not allowing a close approach. It has a shrill, whistling call. **Range and habitat:** OR; India to eastern China and the Philippines. Resident, wandering locally, on rivers, lakes and sea coasts. **Similar species:** White-throated Kingfisher.

Chestnut-headed Bee-eater

Merops leschenaulti (Meropidae) 20 cm/8 in.
The green back, and lack of elongated central tail feathers, distinguish it from the European Bee-eater, and it is also a much smaller bird. Young birds have heads the same color as the back and are duller. Often seen in small groups, it perches on exposed branches in forest glades or by the side of a track, swooping out now and then to chase a passing insect. Several birds sit side by side and change positions as 1 after another circles out and then returns to the perch. It is very vocal when on the wing, making a musical, liquid, rippling note. **Range and habitat:** OR; India to Indo-China and Java. Resident and migratory in wooded areas. **Similar species:** European Bee-eater (see p 166).

Blue-tailed Bee-eater

Merops philippinus (Meropidae) 30 cm/12 in.
The bright blue tail and rump distinguish it from the otherwise similar Blue-cheeked Bee-eater, and it shows the same beautiful, coppery underwing in flight. It is a highly gregarious species, many birds nesting together and migrating in parties. It is addicted to the neighborhood of water, whether forest streams, paddyfields or coastal estuaries, and spends much time on the wing in such areas hawking for food. The prey features the larger flying insects such as dragonflies, wasps and bees. The call is a soft, rippling whistle, often uttered in flight. **Range and habitat:** OR; India to Borneo. Migratory in northern parts of range. Open country, light woodland, seashores. **Similar species:** Blue-cheeked Bee-eater.

Blue-bearded Bee-eater

Nyctyornis athertoni (Meropidae) 36 cm/14 in.
The largest of the bee-eaters, and, with its red-bearded relative, a somewhat unusual one in behavior. It is entirely a forest bird, and forages through the foliage and branches for insects as well as catching them in flight. It seems possible that beetles form a good part of its diet. It is a shy bird, and does not gather in the large, noisy groups characteristic of some of the others of the family, usually being seen singly. The call is a loud, harsh croak, uttered with the long throat feathers fluffed forward. **Range and habitat:** OR; Himalayas and India to Southeast Asia. Resident in evergreen forest. **Similar species:** Red-bearded Bee-eater.

Red-bearded Bee-eater

Nyctyornis amicta (Meropidae) 28 cm/11 in.
A sedentary species which takes the place of its blue-bearded relative in the Indo-Malayan subregion of the OR. The male has much more extensive lilac coloring on the crown, but otherwise the female is similar, as with most bee-eaters. An unobtrusive and solitary bird, which, however, draws attention to its presence by the throaty, descending chuckle, which is often answered by a 2nd bird. Insects are caught in flight from perches often concealed in foliage, though it is a sluggish bird and is inactive for long periods. **Range and habitat:** OR; southern Myanmar to Borneo. Resident in forest. **Similar species:** Blue-bearded Bee-eater.

Great Hornbill

Buceros bicornis (Bucerotidae) 130 cm/51 in.
Like all large birds, now much threatened by habitat destruction and disturbance. A splendid hornbill, very impressive in flight, when the wingbeats make a loud throbbing noise, easily heard even when the bird is invisible over the forest canopy. Very buoyant and agile on its feet, bouncing along large boughs and nimble when foraging for fruit. Also takes small animals and reptiles. Needs a large tree cavity in which to nest, so selects only the biggest trees, which unfortunately are most likely to be felled for their timber. Quite a noisy bird with a variety of loud barking and bellowing noises. **Range and habitat:** OR; western India and Himalayas to Malaya. Resident in tall evergreen forest. **Similar species:** other hornbills (see p 210).

Helmeted Hornbill

Buceros vigil (Bucerotidae) 125 cm/49 in.
Remarkable for its solid, rather than hollow, casque, and also for its call. This is a familiar sound of the forest, a series of loud barks which gradually accelerate until they culminate in a cackling laugh. The casque, which is hard like ivory, used to be in great demand for carving into ornaments, and the long central tail feathers are still valued as ornaments. Hornbills play a large part in the folklore of Bornean tribes. Usually seen singly, these large birds have a flap-and-glide flight over the forest canopy, though often difficult to see through the dense vegetation. **Range and habitat:** OR; Malaysia, Sumatra and Borneo. Resident in tall primary forest. **Similar species:** other hornbills (see p 210).

Indian Roller

Coracias benghalensis (Coraciidae) 30 cm/12 in.
The flash of brilliant blue on the wings as it drops down from a perch is always surprising, as, at rest, this roller often looks a rather drab bird. It is a very familiar sight in open country, both for choosing conspicuous look-outs from which to see grasshoppers or other prey, and also for its noisy and acrobatic display. This takes the form of excited flapping and throwing itself about in the air, diving and rolling and swooping up again, with constant loud, harsh calls. The sexes are alike, and the several subspecies vary somewhat in color. **Range and habitat:** OR; except Greater Sunda, Borneo and the Philippines. Resident and locally migratory in open country in the plains. **Similar species:** European Roller (see p 166).

Dollarbird

Eurystomus orientalis (Coraciidae) 30 cm/12 in.
Known as the Dollarbird in reference to the circular silvery blue patch visible below the expanded wing. Most often seen sitting motionless at the extremity of some bare twig, it watches for insects which it catches in flight, only occasionally dropping to the ground like the Indian Roller. The bill is particularly short and broad, though the feet are small and weak. It is more of a forest bird, preferring clearings among tall trees, often in heavy jungle in the Himalayan foothills. The many subspecies vary in both size and intensity of the plumage colors. **Range and habitat:** EP, OR and AU; northern birds wintering southward. **Similar species:** Broad-billed Roller (see p 208).

White-throated Kingfisher

Black-capped Kingfisher

Chestnut-headed Bee-eater

Blue-tailed Bee-eater

Blue-bearded Bee-eater

Red-bearded Bee-eater

Great Hornbill

Helmeted Hornbill

Indian Roller

Dollarbird

WOODPECKERS AND ALLIES Piciformes

Coppersmith Barbet

Megalaima haemacephala (Capitonidae) 17 cm/6½ in.
Known as the Coppersmith owing to the metallic note, which is repeated with great regularity and persistence. Although brightly colored, its small size and habit of sitting quietly amongst foliage render it unobtrusive, but for the note. It feeds voraciously on ripe fruit, gathering in some numbers in suitable trees, often in company with other species. Often, however, it is quite solitary. The young bird is much greener overall, lacking the bright patches of color. Several subspecies occur, 1 in the Philippines having the throat and facial patches yellow. **Range and habitat:** OR; except southern China. Resident in light woodland in the plains and up to 2,000 m (6,500 ft) in the hills. **Similar species:** Blue-throated Barbet.

White-cheeked Barbet

Megalaima viridis (Capitonidae) 23 cm/9 in.
Typical of the family in structure, though it lacks brightly colored facial or breast patches, and in this resembles several larger, mainly green, barbets. It also has a similar call to these closest of its relatives, a resonant double note preceded by a metallic trill, and is extremely noisy in the breeding season. However, although the call is familiar, the bird itself, being leaf-green and staying mainly in the foliage, is not much seen. It is a fruit- and insect-eater. **Range and habitat:** OR; south-west India, resident in evergreen forest in the plains and hills. Similar species: Brown-headed Barbet.

Great Barbet

Megalaima virens (Capitonidae) 32 cm/13 in.
In spite of its bright colors, it usually looks a drab bird in the field, though the large, pale bill is noticeable. The mournful, double whistle is a very familiar sound, echoing across all the valleys of the hill country across southern Asia, though sighting the bird is not easy. In winter, there is a general move to lower levels, and the birds gather in small flocks. Although mainly a fruit-eater, insects and even small birds are sometimes taken. The powerful bill is useful for excavating the nest-hole, while the bird supports itself on the tail like a woodpecker. **Range and habitat:** OR; Himalayas to Indo-China and eastern China. Resident in hill forests. **Similar species:** Brown-headed Barbet.

Blue-throated Barbet

Megalaima asiatica (Capitonidae) 22 cm/8½ in.
A widely distributed bird, with several subspecies differing in plumage details. Often common around villages, especially in the Himalayan foothills, though it keeps entirely in the trees, moving around in search of fruit and sometimes large insects. When calling from an exposed perch, often high up, the bright blue of the throat is easily seen. A sedentary species, it is most vocal, and so most noticed, in the spring, and the constantly and rapidly repeated call is a hard, triple, rolling note, which soon becomes very familiar. **Range and habitat:** OR; Himalayas to Indo-China and Borneo. Resident in the hills up to 2,000 m (6,500 ft) in open or secondary forest. **Similar species:** Brown-throated Barbet.

Yellow-rumped Honeyguide

Indicator xanthonotus (Indicatoridae) 15 cm/6 in.
A particularly unobtrusive bird, it sits quietly in the foliage by some shady path, perching upright, and often with the wings drooped so exposing the brilliant yellow rump. It is neither very lively nor noisy, the only note being a short, quiet call uttered on the wing, so it is often overlooked. It is the only representative in India of a family of 14 characteristic of Africa and unique in their diet of honeycomb and wax. Parasitic in breeding habits, though it is not yet known which species, possibly barbets, the Indian bird chooses as a foster parent. **Range and habitat:** OR; in the Himalayas up to 3,500 m (11,500 ft). Resident in forests. **Similar species:** other honeyguides (see p 214). **Not illustrated.**

Speckled Piculet

Picumnus innominatus (Picidae) 10 cm/4 in.
A tiny woodpecker in habits, though instead of having stiff tail feathers to use as a support while climbing, it has a soft, rounded tail, and often sits across a branch like a perching bird. Usually, though, it is seen climbing around small branches or twigs, or foraging up bamboo stems, tapping away in its search for insects. Often in company with other species in hunting parties. It makes a short, sharp call, and also drums like larger woodpeckers. Makes a tiny hole in a rotten branch to excavate the nest. **Range and habitat:** OR; wide ranging but not in Sri Lanka. Resident in hill forests. **Similar species:** other piculets.

Sunda Woodpecker

Dendrocopos moluccensis (Picidae) 14 cm/5½ in.
The red streak on either side of the crown is lacking in the female, but both birds are in general quite typical in plumage of the pied woodpeckers, with white barring on the back and streaking on the underparts. This species has a wide geographical range, and a number of subspecies have been described, varying in the tone of the plumage and extent of the white marks. It is a tiny but quite common woodpecker, not unduly shy, and often seen in company with other foraging species such as tits and nuthatches. It makes a muted drumming, and has a quiet call-note. **Range and habitat:** OR; Malaysia to Borneo. Resident in thin forest and bamboo. **Similar species:** other pied woodpeckers (see pp 74, 168).

Greater Yellownape

Picus flavinucha (Picidae) 33 cm/13 in.
A splendid, bright green woodpecker, especially when the golden crest is expanded as the bird clings to a branch when calling. At this moment, the head is thrown back so that the bill points up vertically, and the throat is expanded. The female differs in having the throat brown, instead of bright yellow. Many subspecies have been listed, varying in both size and plumage details. It ascends tree-trunks jerkily, and has a bounding flight, but often forages at low levels or on the ground. **Range and habitat:** OR. Wide ranging except Sri Lanka, Java, Borneo and the Philippines. Resident in evergreen or deciduous woodland. **Similar species:** Lesser Yellownape.

Black-rumped Flameback

Dinopium benghalense (Picidae) 30 cm/12 in.
A widely distributed and common woodpecker, which shows a good deal of variation in the color of the upperparts and also the streaking on the throat and breast, and has been split into several subspecies accordingly. The female has a black, rather than crimson, crown. Feeds as much on the ground as in trees, where it is often accompanied by other species in hunting parties, and is more familiar than some woodpeckers owing to its preference for gardens, avenues and scattered trees round cultivation and houses. It has a loud, harsh scream. **Range and habitat:** OR; India and Sri Lanka. Resident in lightly wooded areas in the plains and foothills. **Similar species:** Greater Flameback

Bay Woodpecker

Blythipicus pyrrhotis (Picidae) 28 cm/11 in.
A large woodpecker, the rufous plumage and yellow bill being distinctive in the field. It is a noisy bird, with a loud, descending series of raucous notes. Often in groups of 2 or 3 birds, which chatter away until aware of an intruder, when they disappear silently. Favorite foraging places are low down in bamboo or dense vegetation in evergreen forest, which makes observation difficult. It less often ascends large trees in the usual woodpecker fashion. Several subspecies have been described, but the sexes differ only in the female lacking the crimson on the neck. **Range and habitat:** OR; Himalayas to south China and Malaysia. Resident in evergreen hill forest. **Similar species:** Rufous Woodpecker.

Coppersmith Barbet

Great Barbet

White-cheeked Barbet

Blue-throated Barbet

Sunda Woodpecker

Speckled Piculet

Greater Yellownape

Bay Woodpecker

Black-rumped Flameback

PERCHING BIRDS Passeriformes

Long-tailed Broadbill
Psarisomus dalhousiae (Eurylaimidae) 27 cm/10½ in.
A somewhat unobtrusive bird, and often difficult to see in the heavy foliage it frequents, as the bright coloring of the plumage blends exactly with the light and shade on the leaves. Often sits quietly, perched upright, for long periods, but also flutters about catching insects, and is more easily seen then or when flying through a clearing. Solitary or in small groups which are usually quiet, though the bird has a loud whistle which draws attention to its presence. Sexes are alike in this broadbill. **Range and habitat:** OR; Himalayas to Indo-China and Borneo. Resident in evergreen forest in the plains and hills. **Similar species:** other broadbills.

Indian Pitta
Pitta brachyura (Pittidae) 20 cm/8 in.
Gaudy bird with long, strong legs and short tail. Lives on the ground in forest or thick scrub. Not easy to see or study, though it is not especially shy, and has a loud, musical whistle, often heard at dusk. When calling, the head is thrown back, and the tail is slowly wagged if the bird is nervous. In the deep woodland shade, when the colors cannot be seen, the dumpy shape and upright posture are diagnostic. The sexes are alike. **Range and habitat:** OR; India to eastern China and Borneo. In evergreen or deciduous forest, the southern populations resident, northern ones migrate southward in winter.

Hooded Pitta
Pitta sordida (Pittidae) 20 cm/8 in.
The large, white wing patch is noticeable in flight, which is rapid, on whirring wings. The sexes are alike, though the young bird is paler and duller than the adults. Often quite common in parts of its range, may haunt quite open habitat, such as the margins of mangrove swamps. The food consists mainly of worms, caterpillars and small insects. It has a double, whistled note which is frequently uttered. Sedentary bird with 13 subspecies which vary in size and intensity of coloration. **Range and habitat:** OR. Widespread resident, wandering locally, in forest, scrub and mangroves. **Similar species:** other pittas.

Gurney's Pitta
Pitta gurneyi (Pittidae) 20 cm/8 in.
A pitta of very restricted distribution, and hence very vulnerable to habitat destruction, especially as its preferred lowland jungle is being logged even more extensively than the hill forests. Hardly seen in the wild for 50 years, it was rediscovered in 1986 as a result of investigating birds illegally held for sale in Bangkok, and a tiny population found in southern Thailand. Determined efforts to conserve the birds and their habitat ensued. More recently, a larger population has been found in southern Myanmar. **Range and habitat:** OR, in southern Myanmar and southern Thailand. Resident in dense, semievergreen rain forest. **Similar species:** other pittas.

Ashy-crowned Sparrow-Lark
Eremopterix grisea (Alaudidae) 13 cm/5 in.
A small, nondescript little lark which gathers in large flocks outside the breeding season. Even when large numbers are feeding over a dry field, they are quite inconspicuous, holding themselves very low to the ground as they search for seeds. The female lacks the black eye-line and underparts. In the breeding season, which can extend over many months, the male has a conspicuous song-flight, notable for the regular earthward dives followed by swoops upward to gain altitude and resume the song once more. **Range and habitat:** OR; India, Pakistan and Sri Lanka. Resident in the plains in dry, open countryside. **Similar species:** other larks.

Oriental Skylark
Alauda gulgula (Alaudidae) 18 cm/7 in.
Very reminiscent of the Skylark, though not as sweet a singer. Character of the song and type of song-flight extremely similar, however. It is a slightly smaller bird, with a shorter tail and more rounded wings, and sandy rather than white outer tail feathers, and has a quite different call-note in flight. Often in small parties which may mingle with wintering skylarks. Many subspecies have been described of this widely distributed lark. **Range and habitat:** EP and OR; northern birds wintering southward. Resident and migratory in open country and grasslands. **Similar species:** Skylark (see p 168). **Not illustrated.**

Dusky Crag-Martin
Hirundo concolor (Hirundinidae) 13 cm/5 in.
A sooty little swallow, with white spots on the square tail which show up as the bird banks in the air. Slow and buoyant flight, sailing to and fro around old buildings or rocky crags. The birds call with a low, soft, chipping note. The sexes are alike. Usually found in pairs or small groups, it is not a colonial nester and does not occur in large parties like some of the migratory swallows or the Cliff Swallow. **Range and habitat:** OR; India to Indo-China. Resident around cliffs, buildings or towns in the plains or lower hills. **Similar species:** Eurasian Crag Martin.

Streak-throated Swallow
Hirundo fluvicola (Hirundinidae) 13 cm/5 in.
The shallowly forked tail and rather fluttery flight recall the Sand Martin, with which this species often occurs, for it often nests colonially in the vicinity of water, over which the 2 species hawk together. The dull chestnut cap, streaked underparts and pale rump are diagnostic of this species; the sexes are alike, the young bird duller. Nesting colonies are often large, many nests being clustered together, the site selected as likely to be on a building as a cliff-face. **Range and habitat:** OR; Himalayas and northern and peninsular India. Resident but migratory in some areas, in the plains and lower hills. **Similar species:** Barn Swallow (see p 168). **Not illustrated.**

Olive-backed Pipit
Anthus hodgsoni (Motacillidae) 18 cm/7 in.
The softly streaked, olive upperparts and white stripe over the eye, and the dark streaking on the very pale underparts, are good pointers to its identity. Commonly seen in small parties in shady places and clearings in woodland, the birds fly up into trees when disturbed, and sit there with tails wagging nervously. Like the Tree Pipit, has a song-flight which starts from, and returns to, a perch in a tree. The call-note resembles that of the Tree Pipit. **Range and habitat:** EP and OR; northern populations wintering southward. Inhabits open woodland, grassy places, cultivation. **Similar species:** Tree Pipit (see p 170).

Nilgiri Pipit
Anthus nilghiriensis (Motacillidae) 18 cm/7 in.
A pipit of very limited distribution, and like many birds of high rainfall areas, of rather dark appearance, with heavy streaking on the underparts. Usually seen singly or in pairs in the breeding season, it is typical of grassy areas and coffee plantations in the hills, and though familiar in its range, little has been published about its habits or song. **Range and habitat:** OR. Resident above 1,000 m (3,300 ft) in the hills of south-west India. **Not illustrated.**

White-browed Wagtail
Motacilla maderaspatensis (Motacillidae) 22 cm/8½ in.
One of the largest of the wagtails, and in effect an Indian version of the large Pied Wagtail of Africa. A common and conspicuous bird, with its pied plumage, wagging tail and constant presence in the open along streams or around ponds. Often perches on houses or boats, where it sometimes nests, being quite a confiding bird. Usually in pairs, though sometimes parties gather outside the breeding season. **Range and habitat:** OR; Pakistan and India. Resident in the plains and hills by water. **Similar species:** White Wagtail (see p 170).

Forest Wagtail
Dendronanthus indicus (Motacillidae) 17 cm/6½ in.
A somewhat aberrant wagtail in habits, living in often dense evergreen forest, though always by streams, waterfalls or very wet paths and tracks. Easily identified by the double breast band, and 2 prominent white wing-bars. The sexes are alike. Has a curious trick of swaying the body and tail, as well as normal tail-wagging. Partial to perching in trees, in which it takes refuge if disturbed. The note is unusual for a wagtail—a sharp, single call. **Range and habitat:** EP, in winter to OR, in dry or wet forest and bamboo. **Similar species:** White Wagtail (see p 170).

Hooded Pitta

Long-tailed Broadbill

Indian Pitta

Ashy-crowned Sparrow-Lark

Dusky Crag-Martin

Olive-backed Pipit

Gurney's Pitta

White-browed Wagtail

Forest Wagtail

Black-faced Cuckooshrike

Coracina novaehollandiae (Campephagidae) 28 cm/11 in.
The female lacks the black eye patch, and has closely barred underparts. There are nearly 20 subspecies of this very widely distributed bird, varying in details of plumage and in size. Often seen in pairs or small parties which keep to the treetops, though conspicuous on account of the loud, shrill whistle which is frequently uttered. It is an active bird, constantly on the move in the search for the insects, caterpillars and fruit on which it feeds. **Range and habitat:** OR and Au. Resident, wandering locally, in open forest in the plains and lower hills. **Similar species:** Black-headed Cuckooshrike.

Black-headed Cuckooshrike

Coracina melanoptera (Campephagidae) 20 cm/8 in.
Female and young birds lack the black head of the male, and are browner, with barred underparts. Actively searches through foliage singly or in little parties, and often in company with other species. Keeps mostly in the trees, where it feeds on insects and berries. It has a variety of whistling notes, often 1 note being repeated several times at the same pitch, and is especially noisy in the breeding season. **Range and habitat:** OR; in India and Sri Lanka. Resident in open woodland in the plains and lower hills. **Similar species:** Black-winged Cuckooshrike.

Common Woodshrike

Tephrodornis pondicerianus (Campephagidae) 16 cm/6½ in.
An unobtrusive and quietly colored bird, not perching conspicuously like the true shrikes to watch for prey, but moving rather slowly and methodically through the foliage as it searches for insects. The sexes are much alike, the eye stripe being less well marked in the female. Usually in pairs, and difficult to see as it is often in thick foliage, but betrays its presence with repeated, descending whistle. The male also has a warbling song. **Range and habitat:** OR; India to Indo-China. Resident in open deciduous forest in the plains. **Similar species:** Large Woodshrike. **Not illustrated.**

Rosy Minivet

Pericrocotus roseus (Campephagidae) 18 cm/7 in.
The more northern populations of this species, in China, lack the rosy underparts and rump which make the Himalayan race such an attractive bird. A forest bird which keeps to the treetops, often in flocks in winter, when it moves well to the south of its breeding range in China. Usually seen perching in tall trees, or moving through the forest, the birds following each other over the canopy or across the clearings. The whistling calls are less musical than those of some of its relatives. **Range and habitat:** BP and OR. Resident or migratory, in hill forests. **Similar species:** Scarlet Minivet. **Not illustrated.**

Small Minivet

Pericrocotus cinnamomeus (Campephagidae) 15 cm/6 in.
Differs somewhat from its relatives in being a plains bird of quite open scrub and sparsely wooded places. However, similar in habits in its lively manner of hunting through foliage in parties. The birds keep in touch with a constant, quiet whistling. It has a very long breeding season, and builds a particularly beautiful and tiny nest about 25 mm (1 in) deep. The female lacks the dark throat, is browner above, and has paler, duller underparts. More than 10 subspecies have been described. **Range and habitat:** OR; India and Sri Lanka to Borneo. Resident in open woodland in the plains. **Similar species:** Scarlet Minivet.

Scarlet Minivet

Pericrocotus flammeus (Campephagidae) 20 cm/8 in.
The largest, best known and one of the most brightly colored of the minivets. It is a common bird of hill forests in southern Asia, conspicuous when flying over the treetops, the birds flashing red, yellow and black against the green foliage. Flocks keep in touch with a constant, liquid whistling, and the birds are very active as they chase insects among the leaves or in short, aerial flutters. Many subspecies occur, with variations in plumage intensity and pattern, and in size. **Range and habitat:** OR. A very widely distributed resident in hill forests. **Similar species:** Small Minivet.

Red-vented Bulbul

Pycnonotus cafer (Pycnonotidae) 20 cm/8 in.
One of the most familiar garden birds in all India, it is a noisy, friendly and active favorite, though capable of doing much damage to flowers and fruit. The sexes are alike, and the white tail tip and rump are seen even more easily than the red patch below the tail. The chirpy call is constantly uttered, but the bird is not much of a songster. Generally keeps in the trees, and often sits conspicuously on the top of a bush but rarely descends to the ground. The food is mainly insects, fruit and berries. **Range and habitat:** OR; India and Sri Lanka to Myanmar. Resident in the plains and hills, not in desert or dense forest. **Similar species:** Red-whiskered Bulbul.

Red-whiskered Bulbul

Pycnonotus jocosus (Pycnonotidae) 20 cm/8 in.
The long, pointed crest and red patch behind the eye are common to both sexes. A very common and well-known bird, gregarious and obvious around villages, gardens and neighboring scrub. It is cheerfully noisy, the calls being louder and more musical than those of its red-vented relation. On the whole, more partial to areas of higher rainfall, with a more easterly general distribution. Several subspecies occur, and the bird has been introduced in Australia and Florida. Some subspecies lack the white tail tip, and there are differences in back color and crest length. **Range and habitat:** OR; India to Hong Kong. Resident in open woodland and forest edge. **Similar species:** Red-vented Bulbul.

Ashy Bulbul

Hemixos flavala (Pycnonotidae) 20 cm/8 in.
The short, rounded crest and light brown cheeks are distinctive; the subspecies occurring in Malaya lacks the conspicuous yellow wing patch of the Himalayan and Indo-Chinese birds. A sociable and noisy bird outside the breeding season, the flocks foraging actively through the treetops for berries and insects. Has a musical, fluty call-note and a short song. Birds breeding at higher altitudes move to lower levels in the winter and to less densely forested areas. **Range and habitat:** OR; Himalayas to Indo-China and Borneo. Resident in hill forests:- **Similar species:** Chestnut Bulbul.

White-browed Bulbul

Pycnonotus luteolus (Pycnonotidae) 17 cm/6½ in.
A dull-colored bird, though the white stripe over the eye and the red eye can be noticed if one can get a good look, for it is a very skulking species. It inhabits dense shrubbery and thickets in predominantly dry countryside. It is a noisy bird, so that it is much more often heard than seen, and the song is a sudden jumble of loud notes. It also has a churring alarm note. Not one of the more sociable bulbuls, usually found in pairs. **Range and habitat:** OR; peninsular India and Sri Lanka. Resident in dry scrub. **Similar species:** Yellow-browed Bulbul. **Not illustrated.**

Black Bulbul

Hypsipetes leucocephalus (Pycnonotidae) 25 cm/10 in.
A widely distributed bird with many subspecies, some of which have the head and breast white. The red bill and legs are unique among bulbuls. A restless bird of treetops, highly gregarious and lively and often in large parties. The birds do not stay long in 1 place, and follow each other from tree to tree making a variety of squeaky whistles. It is a strong flier. It is attracted to flowering and fruiting trees, and also makes short flights after insects. **Range and habitat:** OR, where widespread except Malaysian subregion. Also AF (Madagascar and the Comoros). Resident in hill forests. **Similar species:** Ashy Bulbul.

Black-faced
Cuckooshrike

Black-headed
Cuckooshrike

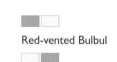

Small Minivet

Scarlet Minivet

Red-vented Bulbul

Red-whiskered Bulbul

Ashy Bulbul

Black Bulbul

Common Iora

Aegithina tiphia (Aegithinidae) 15 cm/6 in.
The most widely distributed member of its family, which is one of only three families peculiar to the OR. A small, active, tree-loving bird, with short wings and tail. The feathers on the rump are very thick and soft, and are fluffed out in display. A very variable species, especially in the amount of black on the upperparts. Females have greener wings and a green tail. Often in pairs, searching through the foliage for insects, sometimes in company with other species in a hunting party. The calls feature a variety of sweet whistles. **Range and habitat:** OR; from Pakistan to Borneo. Resident in the plains and lower hills in woodland, gardens and scrub. **Similar species:** White-tailed Iora.

Golden-fronted Leafbird

Chloropsis aurifrons (Chloropseidae) 19 cm/7½ in.
The shining orange forehead distinguishes this species from several similar-looking relatives. The sexes are much alike, the female just lacking the yellow border round the black chin patch. Always keeps in bushes and trees, where it searches for insects and probes flowers for nectar with the delicately curved and pointed bill. It is an active and agile bird, almost titlike when foraging, and fast and confident on the wing. It has a musical, whistling call-note and a pleasant song, but is also a versatile and inveterate mimic of other birds. **Range and habitat:** OR; Himalayas and India to Sumatra. Resident in woodland in the plains and hills up to 1,800 m (5,900 ft). **Similar species:** Orange-bellied Leafbird.

Orange-bellied Leafbird

Chloropsis hardwickii (Chloropseidae) 19 cm/7½ in.
The only leafbird with orange underparts. The female lacks the black and blue face-mask, and the young bird is entirely green. The commonest of its family in hill forests, ascending to 2,300 m (7,500 ft) in the Himalayas, though moving to lower levels with the onset of winter. Often to be seen at flowering trees with other nectar-seeking species, it is an important pollinator and also responsible for spreading parasitic plants of the mistletoe family, whose berries it eats. It has a fine song, and is also a great mimic. **Range and habitat:** OR; Himalayas to Hainan and Malaysia. Resident in hill evergreen forest. **Similar species:** Golden-fronted Leafbird.

Asian Fairy-bluebird

Irena puella (Irenidae) 27 cm/10½ in.
The brilliant metallic blue of the male's plumage is not always easy to see in the field while the bird is moving through dense evergreen forest in the shade, but becomes startlingly apparent once it shifts into the sunlight. The female is a duller, greener blue. The rich red eyes are obvious in a good view. Despite apparently liking the densest cover, it is quite a noisy and conspicuous bird, with a sharp, double whistle, constantly repeated and unmistakable. Numbers often gather in a fig tree to gorge on the fruit in company with such birds as barbets and green pigeons. **Range and habitat:** OR; south-west India, eastern Himalayas to Java. Resident in evergreen forest.

Black-throated Accentor

Prunella atrogularis (Prunellidae) 15 cm/6 in.
The black throat at once distinguishes it from the other members of the family, though the streaked plumage is otherwise similar. The sexes are alike. Usually in small groups, it is only a winter visitor to the Himalayas from its breeding grounds in central Asia. Keeps mostly to the ground, where it forages for insects, turning over the leaves and twiglets. Often perches in bushes and trees, where it usually flies on being disturbed. It is a quiet bird, but sometimes makes a short, soft, contact note. **Range and habitat:** BP, in winter to OR in the Himalayas. Frequents scrubby or grassy hillsides. **Similar species:** Rufous-breasted Accentor.

Ashy Woodswallow

Artamus fuscus (Artamidae) 19 cm/7½ in.
The most widespread of only 2 representatives in the OR of an Australo-Papuan family. A thickset bird with a strong bill, very long wings and a short tail. Most often seen above woodland glades where it wheels about, much like a bee-eater, on widely spread, triangular wings. Perches on bare or exposed twigs while on the look-out for the flying insects on which it feeds. It is a social bird, and frequently calls with a loud, harsh cry. **Range and habitat:** OR; India

and Sri Lanka to Indo-China. Resident in lowland wooded areas. **Similar species:** White-breasted Woodswallow (see p 320).

Long-tailed Shrike

Lanius schach (Laniidae) 25 cm/10 in.
A large and impressive shrike, it is somewhat variable in plumage. Some races have a gray, not rufous, back, and the head may be all-black, or gray with a black eye-stripe. The sexes are alike. Often conspicuous as it perches at the top of a bush, watching the surrounding grass for insects, small animals or fledgelings, which are killed by blows from the heavy bill. An aggressive and noisy bird, it makes a variety of harsh calls, but also mimics the calls of other birds. **Range and habitat:** OR; Himalayas to the Philippines. Resident and migratory, in open or bushy country in the plains and hills. **Similar species:** Bay-backed Shrike.

Bay-backed Shrike

Lanius vittatus (Laniidae) 18 cm/7 in.
A smart little shrike, the deep, rich color of the back at once distinguishing it. The sexes are alike. It does not have the plumage variation of the wider-ranging Rufous-backed Shrike. A common bird around field edges or cultivated patches, it watches from the edge of a bush or a fence for its prey, taking small items such as insects, sometimes mice or nestlings. Like many shrikes, it has a rather pretty warbling song, in contrast to the harsh call-note. **Range and habitat:** EP and OR; South-West Asia, Pakistan and India. Resident and locally migratory, in lightly wooded or open country. **Similar species:** Red-backed Shrike (see p 170).

Brown Shrike

Lanius cristatus (Laniidae) 19 cm/7½ in.
A rather dull-colored shrike which can be easily confused with some races of the Red-backed Shrike. As with other species, the young bird has wavy concentric barring on the underparts. A noisy bird with a harsh, chattering note, uttered as it sits on a bush or telephone wire, the tail switching about as it maintains its balance. It feeds voraciously on insects, especially large grasshoppers, and has been seen to catch frogs. **Range and habitat:** BP, wintering widely across OR. Frequents woodland glades, gardens, grassy scrub. **Similar species:** Red-backed Shrike (see p 170).

Asian Paradise-Flycatcher

Terpsiphone paradisi (Monarchidae) 20 cm/8 in.
Only males over the age of 4 years acquire the beautiful white plumage, and even then retain a glossy black head. Younger males resemble females, though these have shorter tails. A very familiar bird owing to its striking appearance and conspicuous habits. The long tail floats behind, fluttering and twisting, as the bird pursues its aerial prey; when on a perch, the stance is upright and the tail hangs down, curving gracefully. The call is a short, grating note. **Range and habitat:** EP and OR, Arabia and South-west Asia to Java. Resident and migratory in woodland, gardens and scrub. **Similar species:** Japanese Paradise-Flycatcher.

Black-naped Monarch

Hypothymis azurea (Monarchidae) 17 cm/6½ in.
The female is duller and lacks the black nape patch and breast band. Many subspecies are listed, showing small plumage differences. An active and sprightly bird, pirouetting on tree-trunks and fanning the tail, only to stop suddenly and flutter out after an insect, though food is taken as much off twigs and branches. Often seems to keep in quite shady places in trees, tall hedges or bamboo groves. Often joined in its foraging activities by other species in hunting parties. The food consists of small insects, and the call is a short, sharp little note. **Range and habitat:** OR; India and Sri Lanka to the Philippines. Resident in forests and groves. **Similar species:** other monarch flycatchers.

Common Iora

Golden-fronted Leafbird

Orange-bellied Leafbird

Asian Fairy-bluebird

Black-throated Accentor

Ashy Woodswallow

Long-tailed Shrike

Bay-backed Shrike

Brown Shrike

Asian Paradise-Flycatcher

Black-naped Monarch

Gray-headed Canary-Flycatcher

Culicicapa ceylonensis (Muscicapidae) 11 cm/4½ in.

A very common little flycatcher in woodland in southern Asia. Rarely high in the trees, it forages very like a warbler, flicking and fluttering among the leaves and darting out to take an insect, or hovering to take a morsel off a leaf. It is very vocal, with a characteristic double call-note and a trilling song. It is often a member of the hunting parties which move swiftly through the hillside trees in the Himalayas, where it breeds at up to 3,000 m (9,900 ft). **Range and habitat:** OR. Widely distributed in hill forests, wintering at lower altitudes. **Similar species:** Ashy-throated Warbler.

Tickell's Blue-Flycatcher

Cyornis tickelliae (Muscicapidae) 14 cm/5½ in.

A persistent songster as it moves about in the shady foliage above a stream gully, with a series of rather metallic notes. It also makes a ticking alarm note. Very similar in color and pattern to several other Asian flycatchers, though in this case the female is duller but similarly colored, while females of other species are brown. Often difficult to see in deep forest when it is perching, which it does very upright, the head turning as it scans the surroundings. **Range and habitat:** OR. Widespread resident in thick woodland. **Similar species:** Hill Blue-Flycatcher. **Not illustrated.**

Rufous-bellied Niltava

Niltava sundara (Muscicapidae) 17 cm/6½ in.

The shining blue patch on the sides of the neck is virtually the only distinguishing feature from a related, extremely similar species. The female also has this patch, but otherwise is brown with a white chest gorget. Despite the brilliance of the plumage when the bird is in a good light, it is by no means so obvious in the preferred habitat of a damp gully deep in evergreen forest. Keeps low down in the foliage, often taking food off the forest floor. One of those species with a discontinuous range in south-western India and again in the Himalayas. **Range and habitat:** OR; Himalayas to southern China. Resident in hill forests. **Similar species:** Vivid Niltava.

White-browed Fantail

Rhipidura aureola (Rhipiduridae) 17 cm/6½ in.

The very broad bill, surrounded by long bristles, and the long graduated tail are typical of this group of flycatchers. A very sprightly and restless bird, constantly twitching and pirouetting around tree-trunks, expanding and closing the tail all the time. It has a short, attractive little song, and with its posturing and indifference to man, is a very pleasing bird to watch. The food consists of small insects, which are snapped up continuously, caught in the air or picked off vegetation. The sexes are alike. **Range and habitat:** OR; India and Sri Lanka to Indo-China. Resident in bushy places, gardens and woodland. **Similar species:** other fantail flycatchers.

White-rumped Shama

Copsychus malabaricus (Muscicapidae) 27 cm/10½ in.

Probably more familiar as a cagebird than in the wild, it is highly prized for its beautiful, fluty song. Often quite difficult to see, as not only is it a shy bird, but it inhabits much denser cover than the garden-loving Magpie Robin. Its favorite habitat is among the undergrowth in fairly moist forest, often in ravines with small streams or in bamboo, and it feeds to a large extent on the ground. The female is like the male but duller, and in the race occurring in the Andamans, the male has a white, not chestnut, breast. **Range and habitat:** OR. Widespread resident in forests. **Similar species:** Oriental Magpie-Robin.

Oriental Magpie-Robin

Copsychus saularis (Muscicapidae) 22 cm/8½ in.

A very common and familiar bird almost throughout the whole region. It is a familiar sight in gardens where it hops tamely about, cocking the tail jauntily over the back. Although particularly favoring areas around human habitation, also occurs in open woodland or scrub almost anywhere. Feeds on the ground on insects, earthworms or vegetable matter. The song is an attractive whistling, very pleasing but not as rich as that of the Shama. The female is duller and grayer than the male. **Range and habitat:** OR. Widespread resident except in dense forest or semidesert. **Similar species:** White-rumped Shama.

Blue Whistling-Thrush

Myophonus caeruleus (Turdidae) 30 cm/12 in.

The deep blue-back of the plumage is suddenly seen to be brilliantly spangled with a shining, paler blue when the bird moves into a sunlit patch. Most of the time it is in dark shadow in the ravines and stream-sides it haunts. Hops surefootedly about on rocks in the tumbling water on its strong legs, or forages among the dead leaves on a nearby path, when it looks very like a Blackbird. Also has the habit of raising and flirting its tail. The call is a piercing, repeated whistle. **Range and habitat:** OR. Widespread resident by hill streams in forest. **Similar species:** Blue Rock-Thrush.

White-throated Rock-Thrush

Monticola gularis (Turdidae) 18 cm/7 in.

The female, though lacking the bright colors of the male, also has a conspicuous white throat patch. The white wing patch and rufous rump on the male distinguish it from similar related species. A beautiful little thrush, though somewhat inconspicuous in its usual haunts on the forest floor. Sometimes visits gardens and more open ground, especially on migration. Usually solitary and somewhat shy, it flies up into low branches if disturbed. **Range and habitat:** EP and OR, wintering widely in Southeast Asia, in woodland. **Similar species:** Blue Rock-Thrush.

Siberian Thrush

Zoothera sibirica (Turdidae) 23 cm/9 in.

A large white patch underneath the wing is noticeable in flight, and the male's slaty plumage with white eyebrow is diagnostic. The female is brown, barred darker below, with a buffy eyebrow. It is a shy bird, often in small groups in winter which quickly take alarm and fly up into trees. Much time is spent on the ground, turning over the leaf debris in the search for insects, worms and berries. It makes a quiet twittering. **Range and habitat:** EP, in winter to OR. Haunts shrubbery, thickets and woods, often near water.

Scaly Thrush

Zoothera dauma (Turdidae) 26 cm/10 in.

A beautiful and prominently marked thrush, showing a large pale patch under the wing in flight. A very widely distributed bird which has been divided into some 16 subspecies. Many of the races are sedentary birds in isolated areas of hill forest throughout the region, and even vary as to the number of tail feathers. Usually seen singly or in pairs, often in a clearing or by a small stream, it is a quiet bird and rather shy. Feeds on the ground, on insects, fallen berries or worms. **Range and habitat:** EP, OR and AU. Northern populations migratory. Haunts woodland and forested hillsides. **Similar species:** Long-tailed Thrush.

Dark-throated Thrush

Turdus ruficollis (Turdidae) 25 cm/10 in.

The black-throated race lacks chestnut in the tail, apart from the obvious difference in the throat. Both birds mix in winter flocks. Feeds on ground in usual manner of family, but also forages in bushes and trees for berries and also in flowering trees, possibly for insects. Has a loud, abrupt contact note and a chuckling alarm call. Early autumn migrants in the Himalayas move to lower levels with onset of winter. **Range and habitat:** EP, in winter to northern parts of OR, in woods, scrub and cultivation. **Similar species:** Siberian Thrush.

Gray-headed Canary-Flycatcher

Rufous-bellied Niltava

White-browed Fantail (at nest)

White-rumped Shama

Blue Whistling-Thrush

Oriental Magpie-Robin

White-throated Rock-Thrush

Siberian Thrush

Scaly Thrush (at nest)

Dark-throated Thrush

Gray Bushchat

Saxicola ferrea (Muscicapidae) 15 cm/6 in.

The female is browner than her mate, with a less marked eye patch and a brown tail. A common bird on grassy or scrubby hillsides where it perches conspicuously on a bush or bracken frond. It prefers rather taller and thicker scrub than do some of its relatives, even bamboo thickets, and quite often perches in trees. It has the usual hard alarm note of the stonechat family, but also has quite a pretty little song. It feeds on small insects which are caught after a short sally from the look-out perch, in the manner of a shrike. **Range and habitat:** OR; Himalayas east through southern China, wintering at lower altitudes. Scrub and cultivation in the hills. **Similar species:** Whinchat (see p 174).

Pied Bushchat

Saxicola caprata (Muscicapidae) 13 cm/5 in.

The female is brown and buff; the male, smart black and white. Sometimes when the male is sitting the white wing patches are concealed, but become obvious when he drops to the grass for an insect. A typical stonechat, liking cultivated terraces or hillsides dotted with bushes on which it perches, sometimes fluttering up to take an insect or in brief song-flight. Short, quiet song, and a hard alarm note. This species and the Gray Bushchat are often parasitized by cuckoos. **Range and habitat:** south EP, OR and AU, to New Guinea. Resident and migrant in open, bushy country. **Similar species:** Common Stonechat (see p 174).

Indian Blue Robin

Luscinia brunnea (Muscicapidae) 15 cm/6 in.

The female is a brown bird, paler on the underparts, quite unlike the colorful male. One of a group of 5 species of similar appearance, it is a skulking, unobtrusive bird of deep undergrowth. It keeps much to the ground or lowest levels of bushes, foliage and tangle of fallen branches and ferns in moist, shady forest. Hops about quietly, now and then flicking the wings or flirting its tail. Feeds on insects. Has a brief song, starting with 3 notes, which often draw attention to its presence. **Range and habitat:** OR. Breeds in southwest China and the Himalayas, wintering in south-west India and Sri Lanka. **Similar species:** Red-flanked Bluetail.

Indian Chat

Cercomela fusca (Muscicapidae) 17 cm/6½ in.

Modest appearance, but confiding behavior. Often in pairs, seen in old forts and temples, where it nests in crevices in the masonry, but also inhabits rocky hillsides away from habitation. Feeds on insects caught on the ground, often pouncing from a look-out on a wall or roof. Flies directly and strongly like a wheatear. Has a warbling song and a harsh alarm note. **Range and habitat:** OR, in Pakistan and northern India. Resident in dry countryside. **Similar species:** Northern Wheatear (see p 174).

Plumbeous Redstart

Rhyacornis fuliginosus (Muscicapidae) 14 cm/5½ in.

The female is much browner than the male, and instead of a chestnut tail, has this brown with a broad white base. Flits around boulders in rushing Himalayan rivers and streams, the tail constantly being wagged and fanned, as it searches for flies. Sometimes makes a little fluttering jump in the air or forages on the bank, soon returning to the center of the stream. Always on the move, it is a delightful bird to watch. It has a short song and a sharp little alarm note. **Range and habitat:** OR; Himalayas to western China. Resident by hill streams. **Similar species:** White-capped Redstart.

Daurian Redstart

Phoenicurus auroreus (Muscicapidae) 15 cm/6 in.

Both sexes share the white wing patch, by which the female can be told from the female Common Redstart—the males, apart from this feature, are very alike. Typical redstart behavior, with constant shivering of the tail, and active foraging in trees and bushes for insects. Sometimes flies down to the ground from a low perch, but is soon up in the foliage again. **Range and habitat:** EP and OR. Breeds in north and east China and the eastern Himalayas, wintering to Southeast Asia and the Himalayan foothills. Haunts groves, cultivation, open woodland. **Similar species:** Hodgson's Redstart.

Bar-winged Prinia

Prinia familiaris (Cisticolidae) 13 cm/5 in.

Small greenish-brown bird with 2 pronounced yellowish-white wing bars, a gray throat and lemon-yellow belly. Bill medium length and slightly decurved. Tail long and graduated with white tips to the feathers. Within its rather limited range it is a familiar bird with a remarkably loud and explosive song. **Range and habitat:** endemic to Java, Sumatra and Bali where it frequents a variety of open grassy habitats below 1,500 m (4,900 ft), including gardens around habitation. Especially common on Java. **Similar species:** other Prinias.

Gray-hooded Warbler

Seicercus xanthos-chistos (Sylviidae) 10 cm/4 in.

One of a group of warblers closely related to the willow-warblers, but with a broader bill surrounded with long bristles—hence the reference to flycatchers in the name. A tiny bird, constantly flitting about in foliage, flicking its wings, or hovering for a moment to pick an insect off a leaf. It is often in company with other warblers and babblers in the mixed hunting parties which forage through the woods. The call-note, which is frequently heard, is a thin, high note. **Range and habitat:** OR. Resident in hill forests in the Himalayas. **Similar species:** other flycatcher-warblers.

Tickell's Leaf-Warbler

Phylloscopus affinis (Sylviidae) 11 cm/4½ in.

The Himalayas and Southeast Asia are the headquarters of the leaf- or willow-warblers, with some 23 breeding species. This is easier than some to identify, with its bright yellow underparts, and dark, olive upperparts without a pale wing-bar. Typical of the group, it is an active little insectivorous bird, which searches the foliage in the constant quest for food. Often in the lower levels of trees or in low bushes and scrub near the ground. It is a particularly high altitude nester, at up to 4,500 m (14,800 ft). **Range and habitat:** OR; Himalayas and south-west China, wintering south in India, in woodland and scrub. **Similar species:** other willow-warblers (see p 173).

Blyth's Leaf-Warbler

Phylloscopus reguloides (Sylviidae) 11 cm/4½ in.

A distinct yellowish line along the crown and 2 white wing-bars, together with white borders to the tail, are the field-marks of this pretty little warbler. There are, however, several very similar species. A common and active small bird which hunts through the foliage, often with other species. It swings through the smallest twigs or makes brief flycatching sorties and never seems to be still, except perhaps when singing, though even this is often done on the move. The song is a short warble. **Range and habitat:** OR; Himalayas to Indo-China. Resident in evergreen forests. **Similar species:** other leaf-warblers (see p 173). **Not illustrated.**

Mountain Warbler

Phylloscopus trivirgatus (Sylviidae) 10 cm/4 in.

A sedentary species of montane forest, with a very wide distribution from Malaysia through all the islands south and eastward to New Guinea. The isolation of all the many populations has led to the evolution of 11 subspecies, which are differentiated by variations in the plumage color and markings. All races share the distinctly banded head pattern in black and yellow. A bird of the forest canopy, often feeding on the ferns and orchids which festoon the larger trees. It has a variety of call-notes, and a high-pitched song. **Range and habitat:** OR and AU. Resident in montane forest. **Similar species:** other leaf-warblers (see p 173).

Pallas' Warbler

Locustella certhiola (Sylviidae) 11 cm/4½ in.

An extremely skulking bird in thick waterside vegetation. Usually only seen briefly as it flies away, before dropping down, showing reddish brown rump and a very founded tail with whitish tips to the feathers. Runs along the ground like a rodent, and can slip with ease through the tangled stems and debris. Churring alarm note. **Range and habitat:** EP, in winter across OR, in wet paddyfields, marshes and wet thickets. **Similar species:** Grasshopper Warbler (see p 172).

Gray Bushchat

Indian Chat

Gray-hooded Warbler

Pied Bushchat

Indian Blue Robin

Tickell's Leaf-Warbler

Daurian Redstart

Pallas' Warbler

Mountain Warbler

Plumbeous Redstart

Bar-winged Prinia

Common Tailorbird

Orthotomus sutorius (Sylviidae) 13 cm/5 in.

A dull-looking little bird famed for its remarkable nest. Rufous on the crown. It has a rather long, sharp bill and a spiky tail, which is often carried cocked over the back. Some races develop longer tail feathers in the breeding season. Usually seen foraging for insects in shrubs in gardens or low scrub. Makes a loud, sharp, double call-note, which is more familiar to most people than its appearance. The nest is in a large leaf, or several smaller leaves, the edges of which are sewn together with fibers. **Range and habitat:** OR. Widespread in scrub or cultivation in the lowlands. **Similar species:** Rufous-fronted Prinia.

Rufous-fronted Prinia

Prinia buchanani (Cisticolidae) 13 cm/5 in.

The dark brown tail with conspicuous white tips, together with the rufous crown, distinguish it from several similar species. A slender little warbler with a conspicuously long tail, which shows the white tips when it is fanned. Often seen in small parties in low scrub, constantly active as they creep and flutter about through the stems, twitching or cocking the tail, or hop about on the ground below in their search for insects. Makes a double call-note, and has a twittering song. **Range and habitat:** OR; in Pakistan and India. Resident in dry scrub and semidesert. **Similar species:** other prinias.

Puff-throated Bulbul

Alophoixus pallidus (Pycnonotidae) 23 cm/9 in.

The puffed-out pure white beard, grayish breast and primrose yellow belly distinguish this species from similar bearded bulbuls. Live in pairs or small groups throughout the forests of Southeast Asia. Shyer than most bulbuls, they frequent the dark forest understorey, feeding on a variety of small fruits and insects. Often associate with other birds in mixed flocks, especially babblers and flycatchers. **Range and habitat:** OR. Hainan, Indo-China, northern Thailand and Myanmar; resident in undergrowth of evergreen forest. **Similar species:** White-throated Bulbul.

Streaked Laughingthrush

Garrulax lineatus (Sylviidae) 22 cm/8½ in.

A combination of the grayish body with rufous wings, tail and ear patch, and whitish shaft streaks on its back and breast distinguish this from other Laughing Thrushes. Small groups forage around scrub and rocks on open hillsides and around mountain villages. Rarely flying far, these noisy birds tend to glide downhill with bowed wings when disturbed, although around villages they are often tame and merely hop to cover. They are agile and strong on their feet as they hop around searching for berries and insects. **Range and habitat:** OR. Himalayas from Afghanistan to Bhutan, on sparsely vegetated hillsides and around villages to 3,050 m (10,000 ft). **Similar species:** Striped Laughingthrush.

White-crested Laughingthrush

Garrulax leucolophus (Sylviidae) 30 cm/12 in.

A typical species inhabiting dry deciduous woods and bamboo thickets in the lower foothills, it moves in parties through the undergrowth and lower branches, the bushy white crests held vertically. After a period of silence or quiet chattering, the flock may burst into wild, cackling laughter, repeating this at intervals until all the birds have left the vicinity. Forages vigorously among the fallen leaves like a thrush, bounding along on its strong legs, but keeps well under cover. **Range and habitat:** OR; Himalayas to Indo-China and Sumatra. Resident in forest in the lower hills. **Similar species:** White-throated Laughingthrush. **Not illustrated.**

Jungle Babbler

Turdoides striatus (Sylviidae) 25 cm/10 in.

A common and familiar bird, sociable and of undistinguished and untidy appearance. Brown, with a long, scrawny tail, and pale yellowish eyes and bill. The birds keep together in flocks of up to a dozen, hopping about below hedges or bushes, or flying jerkily after each other across a clearing, all the time maintaining a low conversation. When alarmed, the calls suddenly increase in volume to a noisy chatter. The flocks have a complex social structure, with nonbreeding birds assisting in the rearing of nestlings, and the same individuals staying together in the flock for long periods of time. **Range and habitat:** OR. Resident in India and Pakistan in light woodland and cultivation or gardens. **Similar species:** Common Babbler.

Common Babbler

Turdoides caudatus (Sylviidae) 23 cm/9 in.

Sociable like others of its family, and very much a ground-dwelling bird, the flocks foraging fussily about under bushes or scrub. The birds often cock up their straggly tails and bounce about after each other, now and then taking to wing with a low flap-and-glide flight to another patch of cover. The birds keep up a conversation of low whistles which become louder and shriller when they are alarmed. They feed on insects, berries and seeds, and also nectar. **Range and habitat:** OR. Resident in India in dry scrub or bushy country. **Similar species:** Jungle Babbler.

Yellow-eyed Babbler

Chrysomma sinense (Sylviidae) 18 cm/7 in.

A common babbler of grassy places and thickets in southern Asia, where it climbs about through the tangle of stems, now and then emerging into the open to utter a snatch of song, when the yellow eye and white eye stripe are noticeable. Flutters across open spaces with a weak, jerky flight and immediately vanishes into cover again. Often in small, loose groups in company with other small birds such as munias and warblers. It makes a loud, cheeping call-note which often advertises its presence when invisible in the vegetation. **Range and habitat:** OR. Widespread in the lowlands in grassy and bushy places. **Similar species:** Chestnut-capped Babbler.

Chestnut-backed Scimitar-Babbler

Pomatorhinus montanus (Sylviidae) 21 cm/8 in.

The name refers to the long, strongly curved bill which is characteristic of this little group of babblers. Very distinctive when once seen, its black crown and cheeks contrast with white supercilium and yellow bill. The mantle, rump and flanks are bright chestnut. However, it is a skulking bird of dense undergrowth which rarely allows itself to be watched in the open. Often, its presence in some jungly overgrown gully is given away by the beautiful mellow, fluty note often repeated several times. Also has a coarse, bubbling call. **Range and habitat:** OR, Greater Sundas, Malaysia. Resident in hill forest. **Similar species:** other scimitar-babblers.

Striped Tit-Babbler

Macronous gularis (Sylviidae) 14 cm/5½ in.

A very widely distributed babbler in southern Asia, with some 25 subspecies arising from the many isolated populations on islands. It is an easily distinguished species in the field with its rufous crown and dark streaking on the yellow underparts. A noisy little bird with a repeated mellow note, constantly uttered as it forages through the undergrowth. Often in small parties, which are often joined by various other kinds of small birds in hunting parties or "bird waves," which move rapidly onward in the forest at all levels in their quest for food. **Range and habitat:** OR. Resident in undergrowth and forest in the lowlands from south-west India to the Philippines. **Similar species:** Rufous-fronted Babbler.

Brown-cheeked Fulvetta

Alcippe poioicephala (Sylviiidae) 16 cm/6½ in.

This is a small, plain-colored babbler, with a gray head and brown wings. A common inhabitant of 2nd-growth and woods from western India to China in a number of subspecies, usually seen in small parties, foraging actively in the foliage of bushes and trees. The call-note is a repetition of double notes at alternately higher and lower pitches. Populations in some areas have a black band on the sides of the crown, and are confusingly like a related species. **Range and habitat:** OR; southern India to Indo-China. Resident in forest in the plains and foothills. **Similar species:** Gray-cheeked Fulvetta.

Common Tailorbird

Rufous-fronted Prinia

Puff-throated Bulbul

Jungle Babbler
(feeding young)

Yellow-eyed Babbler

Streaked Laughingthrush

Common Babbler

Chestnut-backed Scimitar-Babbler

Striped Tit-Babbler

Brown-cheeked Fulvetta

Whiskered Yuhina

Yuhina flavicollis (Sylviidae) 15 cm/6 in.

The short, black moustachial stripe is a more constant plumage feature in the various races of this bird than the collar, which may be yellow, rufous or almost absent. A characteristic of all yuhinas is the jaunty, pointed crest, and in its acrobatic foraging this bird resembles the familiar Crested Tit of Europe. It is always in the trees, swinging from a spray or fluttering out after an insect, moving through the foliage in company with other small insectivorous birds. **Range and habitat:** OR; Himalayas to Indo-China. Resident in hill forests, moving to lower altitudes in winter. **Similar species:** White-naped Yuhina.

Dusky Fulvetta

Alcippe brunnea (Sylviidae) 15 cm/6 in.

An active and sprightly babbler of tangled vegetation and dwarf bamboo in wet hill forests, often foraging among the leaf litter on the ground. Difficult to watch in these dense and dank surroundings" it does not make observation any easier by being quite shy. It makes a constant churring contact note and also has a short, jingling song in the breeding season. Often in small groups, and sometimes with other species hunting through the bushes in winter. **Range and habitat:** OR; in the Himalayas and southern China. Resident in forest and forest edge up to 2,400 m (7,900 ft). **Similar species:** Rufous-throated Fulvetta. **Not illustrated.**

Red-billed Leiothrix

Leiothrix lutea (Sylviidae) 14 cm/5½ in.

A loud burst of musical, rich song from the depths of a shady gully often betrays the presence of this beautifully colored but retiring babbler. It is, on account of the song, greatly valued as a cagebird, when the bright plumage is certainly easier to see than is often the case in the wild. The female bird lacks the crimson on the wing, this patch being all yellow. Outside the breeding season, behaves much as other babblers, hunting through foliage or rummaging about in the debris on the forest floor, usually in small parties. It makes a variety of harsh or piping call-notes. **Range and habitat:** OR; Himalayas to China. Resident in hill forest, moving to lower altitudes in winter. **Similar species:** Silver-eared Mesia.

Hoary-throated Barwing

Actinodura nipalensis (Sylviidae) 20 cm/8 in.

The barwings are a small group of 6 species, intermediate in size between the small babblers and the laughing thrushes, characterized by moplike crests and barred tails and wings. In winter, they forage in the higher levels of the hillside trees, hopping actively along the branches and searching the epiphytic ferns and mossy stems for insects. Their size, crests and long tails make them easy to identify among the mixed-species hunting parties so evident in the woods at this time of year. **Range and habitat:** OR, confined to the Himalayas. Resident in higher-level forests. **Similar species:** other barwings. **Not illustrated.**

Chestnut-tailed Minla

Minla strigula (Sylviidae) 15 cm/6 in.

One of the more colorful of the smaller babblers, with orange-yellow patches on the crown, wings and tail. It is a particularly noticeable species in the mixed hunting parties which roam through the woods in winter, in company with tits, nuthatches, creepers and other small babblers. It keeps in the trees all the time, hunting actively through the foliage for insects, berries and seeds. It has a short, 3- or 4-note song, and a simple, piping call-note. **Range and habitat:** OR; Himalayas to Southeast Asia and Malaya. Resident in hill forest. **Similar species:** Red-tailed Minla.

Black-backed Sibia

Heterophasia melanoleuca (Sylviidae) 23 cm/9 in.

Common in the hills in Southeast Asia, in loose bands which roam through the forest, exploring the branches and clumps of ferns, mosses and orchids which festoon the trees at higher altitudes. Active and restless, the birds flirt their tails and constantly call to each other with a variety of notes. A very characteristic song, evocative of these misty evergreen forests, is a sad, descending cadence of 6 notes. There are several subspecies in which the back color varies from black to brown and gray. **Range and habitat:** OR. Resident in hill evergreen forest. **Similar species:** Long-tailed Sibia.

Yellow-cheeked Tit

Parus spilonotus (Paridae) 14 cm/5½ in.

A noisy and sociable tit, easily recognized by the pointed yellow-tipped black crest, yellow cheeks, eyebrow and lores and streaked green back. Often in parties with other species, in particular babblers, when foraging through the trees. Typical in their actions, swinging upside-down at the tip of a twig, or searching around the bole of a tree near the ground. Like other tits, they nest in holes, and constantly repeat their short, cheery songs whilst searching for food. Food consists of insects, grubs and berries. **Range and habitat:** OR. Resident in pine and mixed woodlands from the eastern Himalayas to Indo-China, usually above 1520 m (5000 ft). **Similar species:** Black-lored Tit.

Black-throated Tit

Aegithalos concinnus (Aegithalidae) 10 cm/4 in.

A tiny, long-tailed tit, delightful to watch as it is often quite oblivious of the human observer. Always on the move, swinging and flitting through the bushes, clinging upside-down as it examines a leaf or fluttering to the next bush as the flock moves along the hillside. Often forages near the ground amongst the low vegetation in forest clearings, but sometimes high in the trees. Usually in company with a variety of other species of small insectivorous birds which keep a loose association as they hunt for food. The sexes are alike. **Range and habitat:** OR; Himalayas to Indo-China. Resident in hill scrub and forest edge. **Similar species:** Long-tailed Tit (see p 176).

Bar-tailed Treecreeper

Certhia himalayana (Certhiidae) 12 cm/4½ in.

Distinguished from the familiar creeper of Europe, which also occurs in the Himalayas, by the barring on the tail. Habits typical of those of the family. Usually seen ascending the trunk of a tree in jerky, hesitant fashion, probing into the cracks and crevices, or slipping round to the other side, only to reappear higher up, moving outward underneath a large branch. The food consists of tiny insects, grubs and spiders. The call is" a low, thin note, and it has a short, twittering song. **Range and habitat:** OR. Resident in woods in the Himalayas. **Similar species:** Eurasian Treecreeper (see p 176). Not illustrated.

Velvet-fronted Nuthatch

Sitta frontalis (Sittidae) 11 cm/4½ in.

A very widely distributed bird, in a number of races. The red bill and violet upperparts are diagnostic. A small nuthatch, and quite sociable, often being seen in 2 s and 3 s, and very often participating in the mixed-species hunting flocks. Usual nuthatch actions, hitching jerkily around branches and stems, stopping to tap here and there, or exploring a clump of fern. It is highly adaptable as regards habitat, and occurs in all kinds of woodland from dense evergreen to tea plantations or mangroves. It has a repeated, whistling call-note. **Range and habitat:** OR. Widespread resident in woodland in the hills and plains. **Similar species:** Eurasian Nuthatch (see p 176).

Oriental White-eye

Zosterops palpebrosa (Zosteropidae) 10 cm/4 in.

A tiny, green, warblerlike bird, with sharply pointed bill and a ring of white feathers around the eye. A sedentary species which has developed many subspecies across its wide range, especially in the numerous islands south and east of Malaya. Common in most types of woodland, where it forages, often high in the canopy, in company with other small birds. It feeds on small insects and nectar, so is often seen probing into the blossoms in flowering trees. It has a quiet, chirping call-note and a jingling song. **Range and habitat:** OR. Widespread resident in woodland in the hills and plains. **Similar species:** other white-eyes (see pp 230, 318).

Whiskered Yuhina

Chestnut-tailed Minla

Red-billed Leiothrix

Yellow-cheeked Tit

Black-backed Sibia

Oriental White-eye

Black-throated Tit

Velvet-fronted Nuthatch

Purple Sunbird

Cinnyris asiaticus (Nectariniidae) 10 cm/4 in.

An all-dark sunbird, often looking quite black until it is seen in a good light, with a short, square tail. Constantly active around flowering shrubs and trees, where it probes into the blossoms with its strongly curved bill. Although nectar is an important food item, many small flies and insects are taken as well. It has a loud, shrill call-note, and is usually seen singly, although sometimes consorting with other nectar-seeking species. Following the breeding season, the males molt into a duller plumage similar to that of the female, except for some blue patches. **Range and habitat:** EP and OR, from Arabia to Indo-China. Resident in light woodland and gardens. **Similar species:** Purple-rumped Sunbird.

Fork-tailed Sunbird

Aethopyga christinae (Nectariniidae) 10 cm/4 in.

The finely pointed central tail feathers on the male extend to 13 mm (½ in) beyond the rest, so the total tail length is markedly less than on some of its close relatives. The female has a rounded tail, and is a dull olive bird, yellower on the underparts. A beautiful little sunbird, which haunts the topmost boughs of tall trees. It has the active foraging habits of the family, seeking nectar or insects among blossom, and has a loud, metallic note and a quieter chirp. **Range and habitat:** OR; south China, Indo-China and Hainan. Resident in woodland in hill country. **Similar species:** Crimson Sunbird.

Crimson Sunbird

Aethopyga siparaja (Nectariniidae) 10 cm/4 in.

The scarlet back and breast and green tail readily separate the male bird from other sunbirds, though the female is similar to those of other species, being olive above and yellower below. Constantly fluttering around blossoms in the forest or in gardens, hovering to take nectar or insects for a moment, then darting off to explore an adjacent flower. It is often seen singly, and has a typical sunbird sharp call-note. There are several races of this bird, with minor plumage variations. **Range and habitat:** OR; India to the Philippines. Resident in moist evergreen forest. **Similar species:** Mrs Gould's Sunbird.

Plain Flowerpecker

Dicaeum concolor (Dicaeidae) 9 cm/3½ in.

A dully plumaged, tiny little bird, often seen in pairs which hunt through foliage and flowering trees in their search for nectar and insects. Flowerpeckers are important in assisting the spread of parasitic plants such as mistletoe, as the fruits are swallowed, and the undigested, sticky seeds deposited on branches wherever the birds happen to leave them. The birds make a loud, chipping note as they fly, often at considerable heights, from 1 treetop to another. **Range and habitat:** OR. Widespread resident in hill forests. **Similar species:** Pale-billed Flowerpecker.

Orange-bellied Flowerpecker

Dicaeum trigonostigma (Dicaeidae) 9 cm/3½ in.

The male is a tiny gem of a bird, bright blue head and wings contrasting with an orange rump and belly, but the female has only a vestige of these colors, being mostly a dull green-gray. It is an active bird, often frequenting the extreme tops of trees and turning with an almost mechanical flicking movement from side to side. Like other flowerpeckers, it feeds on the berries of parasitic plants, the seeds subsequently adhering to branches within the bird's droppings, and thereby colonizing fresh sites. Many subspecies have been described from the bird's wide range. **Range and habitat:** OR; from eastern India through southeast Asia to the Philippines. Resident in forests in the plains and lower hills. **Similar species:** Crimson-breasted Flowerpecker.

Thick-billed Flowerpecker

Dicaeum agile (Dicaeidae) 9 cm/3½ in.

A widely distributed bird in southern Asia, occurring in a number of subspecies which differ in plumage details. The swollen bill and red eyes are distinctive. A somewhat solitary species, sometimes in pairs, which hunts actively through foliage and flowers for nectar and insects. As with other flowerpeckers, also takes berries of tree parasites. However, instead of swallowing them whole, it strips the flesh off the berry, and discards the sticky seeds by wiping them off on the branch. It thus helps to concentrate the parasite on its

existing host-tree. **Range and habitat:** OR. Widespread resident in hill forests. **Similar species:** Pale-billed Flowerpecker. **Not illustrated.**

Crested Bunting

Melophus lathami (Emberizidae) 15 cm/6 in.

A soberly plumaged bunting with chestnut wings and tail and black head and body, but distinguished by the pointed crest. The female is a brown, sparrowlike bird with a vestigial crest. In the winter, often seen in small flocks which scratch about in the dust on jungle tracks or bare ground on hillsides, flying into nearby bushes when disturbed. It has a brief call-note and a typically dry and short song phrase. It is a resident species, and is not seen in large numbers like the migratory buntings in their winter quarters. **Range and habitat:** OR; Himalayas and north India to eastern China, on hillside clearings and open ground.

Black-headed Bunting

Emberiza melanocephala (Emberizidae) 18 cm/7 in.

The large flocks of this handsome bunting which visit the Indian plains in winter do a good deal of damage to the crops, particularly when the numbers are concentrated in the spring, before the return passage to their breeding areas. As with most buntings, the female is quite unlike the male, having a streaky brown, sparrowlike plumage. The call is a sweet, rather husky note, and the song a short jingle, sometimes heard just as the birds are about to depart. **Range and habitat:** EP, in winter to OR in Pakistan and western India. Open country and cultivation in the plains. **Similar species:** Red-headed Bunting.

Yellow-breasted Bunting

Emberiza aureola (Emberizidae) 15 cm/6 in.

One of the better songsters among the buntings. This fact, together with the beautiful plumage of the male, makes it a favorite cagebird in China. The song can be heard from males in the spring, when they are gathering for their northward migration. Often in very large numbers in the winter quarters in Southeast Asia, where they congregate in the ricefields and around villages, taking a great quantity of rice and grass seed. The bright, clean colors of the summer plumage appear as the buff feather tips of the winter dress wear off. **Range and habitat:** EP, in winter to OR, occasionally to WP, in open country and cultivation. **Similar species:** Black-headed Bunting.

Black-faced Bunting

Emberiza spodocephala (Emberizidae) 15 cm/6 in.

The female lacks the gray head and black mask, and has a pale yellow eyebrow, but is otherwise much like the male. It is scarcer than other buntings in winter, appearing in small groups, which frequent hedgerows, scrub and damp, grassy places. The birds feed on the ground, flying up into nearby bushes if disturbed, calling with a ticking note. Being rather shy, and not as conspicuous as those of its relatives which congregate in large numbers, it is probably often overlooked. There are several races of this bunting in China, varying somewhat in plumage coloring. **Range and habitat:** EP, wintering to northern parts of Southeast Asia and southern China. Frequents open country, wet scrub and crops. **Similar species:** Yellow-breasted Bunting.

Red-headed Bunting

Emberiza bruniceps (Emberizidae) 17 cm/6½ in.

A popular cagebird on account of the striking plumage and pleasant little song. Closely related to the Black-headed Bunting, with which it occurs in very large numbers in winter, feeding in crops. When scared off or otherwise disturbed, flies up in dense flocks which color the trees yellow. It is a variable species, the males sometimes having yellow crowns or heads, and hybridizes with the Black-headed Bunting where the breeding ranges overlap. **Range and habitat:** EP, in South-West Asia, wandering to western Europe, and in winter to OR.

Red-headed Bullfinch

Pyrrhula erythrocephala (**Fringillidae**) 17 cm/6½ in.

A quiet and unobtrusive species, often announcing its presence with a soft, low whistle. In small parties in winter, feeding slowly and methodically in bushes and trees, nipping off buds, or sometimes picking up seeds from the ground, where they favor patches of tall herbs under the trees. When disturbed, they flit off instantly into cover, showing the white rump patch. Female's head is yellowish green instead of red. **Range and habitat:** OR. Resident in the Himalayas at up to 4,000 m (13,100 ft). **Similar species:** Eurasian Bullfinch (see p 180). **Not illustrated.**

Red Avadavat

Amandava amandava (**Estrildidae**) 10 cm/4 in.

A favorite cagebird, being easy to keep and active and cheerful in captivity. In the wild, a sociable little bird, gathering in large numbers in grassy places, twittering as they cling to the seeding heads and stems. The tall grasses of moist ground and swamp margins are particularly favored. The birds roost communally in such places, and also in reed-beds. The female lacks the red underparts with white spotting, and the male has a similar plumage outside the breeding season. **Range and habitat:** OR; India to China and Java, in open country in the plains and lower hills. **Similar species:** Green Avadavat.

Nutmeg Mannikin

Lonchura punctulata (**Estrildidae**) 10 cm/4 in.

Like the avadavats, all the mannikins are familiar as cagebirds. This species has a very wide distribution in southern Asia, with many subspecies, although, very curiously, it is absent from Borneo. Always in flocks which feed in crops and grass, flying about in groups from place to place, or perching in nearby bushes or trees. The sexes are alike in this munia, though outside the breeding season the plumage is duller, lacking the speckled underparts. **Range and habitat:** OR; India to the Philippines. Resident in open country in the lowlands and foothills. **Similar species:** White-rumped Munia.

Pin-tailed Parrotfinch

Erythrura prasina (**Estrildidae**) 15 cm/6 in.

A colorful, small, finchlike bird, typical of this small group of mainly green and red members of the family. This is the only species with, in the male, an elongated and pointed tail. The sexes are similar apart from the tail shape, the female being duller. Sometimes feeds on bamboo seed-heads, but chiefly a rice-eater, and a serious pest in the paddyfields in the uplands of Borneo. Either migratory, or else wanders widely, though little is yet known about its movements. It has a short, high-pitched call-note. **Range and habitat:** OR; Southeast Asia to Malaya and Borneo. Resident or nomadic in cultivation, thickets and on the forest edge. **Similar species:** other parrotfinches.

Baya Weaver

Ploceus philippinus (**Ploceidae**) 15 cm/6 in.

A common bird of grassy places in the plains. The nesting colonies, with their woven grass nests hanging from the branches of bushes, are a familiar sight. When in breeding plumage, the male is easily told from other Asian weavers by its black mask and yellow breast. However, outside the breeding season, both sexes resemble sparrows. Timing of breeding is related to the onset of the monsoon, and males initiate the colony by building the nests. The females only appear later to approve a nest and mate with its builder. The nest has a long, downward-pointing entrance tunnel, up which the birds fly without a pause. **Range and habitat:** OR; Pakistan to Sumatra. Resident in cultivation and scrub in the plains. **Similar species:** Streaked Weaver.

Streaked Weaver

Ploceus manyar (**Ploceidae**) 15 cm/6 in.

The male in breeding plumage is easily distinguished by the heavy streaking on the breast and the yellow crown contrasting with the black head. The female is difficult to tell from other species, and both sexes look alike outside the breeding season. The construction of the nest differs from that of the Baya, in that it is supported from a bunch of stems, rather than tapering at the top to a single support point. Also, the entrance tube is much shorter. The nesting colonies often consist of only a few pairs, and are always located in tall reeds over water. **Range and habitat:** OR; Pakistan to Java. Resident in open, well-watered country in the plains. **Similar species:** Baya Weaver.

Sind Sparrow

Passer pyrrhonotu (**Passeridae**) 13 cm/5 in.

For many years after its initial discovery, this species was not recorded again, probably owing to confusion with the common House Sparrow. It is, however, a smaller and slimmer bird, and the male's black bib is much narrower and does not extend beyond the throat. Females are extremely similar. Its identity as a good species was not confirmed until it was found nesting close to House Sparrows. A bird of tall vegetation along watercourses in the region of the Indus river, it occurs in small groups, and is not as obviously gregarious as its larger relative. It nests in loose colonies in trees standing in or by water. **Range and habitat:** OR. Resident in waterside scrub in semidesert in Pakistan. **Similar species:** House Sparrow (see p 182). **Not illustrated.**

Brahminy Starling

Sturnus pagodarum (**Sturnidae**) 22 cm/8½ in.

A strikingly plumaged starling, with its long black crest, pink underparts and white-bordered tail. Sexes alike, but the female has a shorter crest. Often in parties which frequent flowering and fruiting trees, it is a common and familiar bird in India. It feeds on berries, nectar or insects, which it searches for in typical starling fashion on the ground, walking or running about in the grass or amongst grazing animals. It has a musical song and various other notes, and also mimics other bird calls. **Range and habitat:** OR; Pakistan, India and Sri Lanka. Resident in light woodland and cultivation in the plains and foothills. **Similar species:** Rosy Starling.

Asian Pied Starling

Gracupica contra (**Sturnidae**) 23 cm/9 in.

A smart black and white starling, the plumage set off by an orange bill and bare skin around the eye. The sexes are alike. A gregarious, noisy bird, often around gardens, fields and villages. It feeds on the ground in loose flocks, taking both insects and grubs as well as vegetable food, especially grain. It associates with other species such as the Common Myna, and shares the same noisy, packed roosts. Like other starlings, it is very vocal, with a variety of whistling notes, and is also a good mimic. **Range and habitat:** OR; India to Southeast Asia and Java. Resident in open, cultivated country. **Similar species:** Black-collared Starling. **Not illustrated.**

Common Myna

Acridotheres tristis (**Sturnidae**) 22 cm/8½ in.

Perhaps the most familiar bird in southern Asia, certainly in towns and around all human habitation. A bold, perky and yet wary bird, highly successful at taking advantage of the feeding and nesting opportunities which man's activities afford. It is as happy walking around small patches of grass in busy cities as foraging amongst cattle by a remote forest settlement. Often in noisy, active flocks, and roosts in huge numbers in groves of trees, reed-beds or on buildings. It takes a wide variety of food, both animal and vegetable, and is highly vocal, with a mixture of harsh and liquid notes. **Range and habitat:** OR, introduced into AF and Arabia. Resident except at the highest altitudes or in thick forest. **Similar species:** Bank Myna.

Common Hill Myna

Gracula religios (**Sturnidae**) 30 cm/12 in.

A striking species, the glossy black plumage set off by large white wing patches, and the bright yellow wattles and bare skin on the head and nape. The sexes are alike. A most familiar cagebird, owing to its wide vocal repertoire, which is as noticeable in the wild. Characteristic penetrating, short, descending whistle from which it derives its Bornean name of "Tiong." Often singly or in small groups in forest treetops, or gathering in fruiting trees with such birds as barbets and green pigeons. Insects and small animals are taken as well as berries and fruit. The nest is placed in a hole in a forest tree. **Range and habitat:** OR. Widespread resident in hill forests. **Similar species:** Ceylon Myna.

Red Avadavat

Pin-tailed Parrotfinch

Baya Weaver

Brahminy Starling

Streaked Weaver (building nest)

Nutmeg Mannikin

Common Myna

Common Hill Myna

Blue Magpie

Urocissa erythrorhyncha (**Corvidae**) 70 cm/28 in.
The long, gracefully curving tail is seen to advantage when several birds fly, after each other, across a Himalayan hillside. The flight is rather jerky, several flaps followed by a glide. The birds live in small groups in the hill woods, feeding around cultivated terraces or glades. Though feeding mainly in the trees, they do forage on the ground, and as they hop about, the tail is elevated, though drooping at the tip. They are noisy birds, with a variety of harsh and chattering calls, and are also good mimics. The attractive appearance makes them popular birds in aviaries. **Range and habitat:** OR; Himalayas to southern China. Resident in hill forests. **Similar species:** Gold-billed Magpie.

Green Magpie

Cissa chinensis (**Corvidae**) 39 cm/15 in.
A beautiful crow, the white tips to the tail and bright rufous wings noticeable in flight. The vivid green of the plumage, often highly cryptic in its forest environment, fades to a dull turquoise in museum specimens. Like many other crows, it is a noisy bird as well as being shy, so is often heard more than it is seen. It has a variety of loud whistles and raucous, chattering notes. Rarely more than 2 or 3 birds together, it stays well concealed in dense vegetation, where it forages for insects or small animals, sometimes in company with other species such as laughing thrushes. **Range and habitat:** OR; Himalayas to Borneo. Resident in hill forest. **Similar species:** Short-tailed Magpie.

Racket-tailed Treepie

Crypsirina temia (**Corvidae**) 34 cm/13 in.
One of 2 similar species, both having a curiously spatulate tail measuring up to 20 cm/8 in. Hunts through the forests singly or in small groups, almost always in company with other species such as laughing thrushes and other babblers or drongos. It has a variety of harsh notes, including a characteristic swearing note of 3 syllables. It is shy and unobtrusive but for the note, and always stays in the bushes or trees, appearing not to take food on the ground. **Range and habitat:** OR; southern Burma to Java. Resident in woodland. **Similar species:** Hooded Treepie.

Rufous Treepie

Dendrocitta vagabunda (**Corvidae**) 50 cm/20 in.
A typical magpie in habits, wary and inquisitive, adaptable, noisy and omnivorous. It is, as its name indicates, a woodland bird, moving about in small parties which attract attention with their distinctive, fluty, 3-note call. They climb about actively among the branches, or hop lightly up big boughs with the tail cocked, searching for insects or fruit. The range of food taken is very wide, as with most crows. A somewhat reluctant flier, it has a jerky flap-and-glide progress, 1 bird following another when the group is on the move, showing the bold white wing patch. It can be extremely shy and inconspicuous around human habitations, though daring in snatching food when opportunity offers. **Range and habitat:** OR; India to Indo-China. Resident in lightly wooded country. **Similar species:** Gray Treepie.

Black-hooded Oriole

Oriolus xanthornus (**Oriolidae**) 25 cm/10 in.
A common and beautiful bird, which keeps to leafy trees in gardens or light woodland, attracting attention with its melodious, fluty whistles. The sexes are alike. Largely a fruit-eater, though insects form a substantial part of the diet. Usually seen singly, sometimes in pairs, and not easily noticed in thick foliage despite the brilliant yellow plumage. However, it is not especially shy, and is conspicuous when flying from 1 tree to another. Often consorts with other species such as drongos, barbets, treepies and babblers at fruiting or flowering trees. **Range and habitat:** OR. Widespread resident in wooded areas in the plains and foothills. **Similar species:** Eurasian Golden Oriole (see p 182). **Not illustrated.**

Large-billed Crow

Corvus macrorhynchos (**Corvidae**) 48 cm/19 in.
Replaces the Raven in much of tropical Asia, being more of a forest species where the 2 birds overlap. However, also occurs in eastern Asia as far north as Manchuria. There are several subspecies, which vary in size, bill shape and details of gloss on the plumage. Often solitary or in small parties, only gathering in larger numbers at a suitably abundant food supply. It takes a wide variety of animal food and carrion, and scavenges habitually around villages and towns, though always very wary and quick to flap away if alarmed. It has the typical harsh cawing of the larger crows. **Range and habitat:** BP and OR. Widespread resident in wooded areas, cultivation or around towns and villages. **Similar species:** Carrion Crow (see p 182).

House Crow

Corvus splendens (**Corvidae**) 43 cm/17 in.
An abundant and successful species, with a distinctly urban lifestyle. It is, perhaps, the most specialized of all its family in profiting from man's activities, and is to be found around every village, city or settlement in large numbers. A highly gregarious bird, roosting in huge numbers, the locality being marked by the conspicuous morning and evening flight paths to and from feeding and foraging areas. Despite its boldness and confidence, it remains quick to take alarm, but as soon as any perceived danger is past, is back immediately to snatch a morsel of food. It is frequently parasitized by a large black cuckoo, the Koel. **Range and habitat:** OR, introduced into Arabia and AF. Widespread resident in the lowlands. **Similar species:** Eurasian Jackdaw (see p 182).

White-bellied Drongo

Dicrurus caerulescens (**Dicruridae**) 23 cm/9 in.
The combination of the black plumage, long forked tail and white belly (the white restricted to the vent in some races) is diagnostic. The shrikelike habit of perching on a conspicuous look-out, from which it can launch a chase after insect prey, makes it an easily noticed bird. It is particularly attracted to a food source such as a swarm of termites. It is a pugnacious bird, freely attacking much larger species which trespass on its nesting area, and can harass very effectively, being a superbly agile flier. It has a large variety of attractive, whistled calls, and is also a good mimic of other birds' calls. **Range and habitat:** OR. Resident in forests and forest edge in India and Sri Lanka. **Similar species:** Black Drongo.

Greater Racket-tailed Drongo

Dicrurus paradiseus (**Dicruridae**) 35 cm/14 in.
With a tail measuring up to another 30 cm/12 in), this is a conspicuous species in flight. The 2 spatulate barbs at the ends of the extended outer tail feather shafts look like 2 small birds fluttering along just behind, and make a distinct thrumming noise. Often seen in flight in open parts of forest, but easily located when perched in dense evergreen foliage by the constant babble of metallic and whistling calls. It is constantly calling, and when not practising its own repertoire, is mimicking other birds with great fidelity. Though not especially gregarious, a few birds at most being seen together, it is often in company with other species at flowering trees, where it takes nectar. Flying insects form the main part of the diet. **Range and habitat:** OR. Widespread resident in forest in the plains and foothills. **Similar species:** Lesser Racket-tailed Drongo.

Black Drongo

Dicrurus macrocercus (**Dicruridae**) 30 cm/12 in.
A very familiar bird around compounds or clearings, which swoops with great agility on flying insects or, like a shrike, pounces on a grasshopper or beetle on the ground. It chooses conspicuous perches, such as telephone wires, bare boughs or fences, and happily rides on the backs of cattle or buffaloes, which helpfully disturb insects from the grass. Usually in pairs, which are ferocious in defence of their nesting territory, unmercifully harrying any crow or cat which strays too close for comfort. Although it has several musical notes, and a good variety of harsh, chattering noises, it is not as accomplished vocally as some of its relatives. **Range and habitat:** OR, marginally EP in South-west Asia. Resident in wooded country in the plains from Iran to China. **Similar species:** Ashy Drongo.

Blue Magpie

House Crow

Green Magpie

Racket-tailed Treepie

Rufous Treepie

Large-billed Crow

White-bellied Drongo

Greater Racket-tailed Drongo

Black Drongo

THE AUSTRALASIAN REGION

The Australasian Region consists of the continental mass of Australia, the large islands of New Guinea and New Zealand and many smaller islands at the eastern end of Indonesia and throughout the western Pacific. It is separated from the Oriental Region by Wallace's Line, between Bali and Lombok, and Borneo and Sulawesi, with marsupials dominant on the Australian side and placental mammals in the Orient. Birds are more mobile than mammals and Malaysia and Indonesia are regions of gradual change-over. Antarctica is sometimes considered to be part of the Australasian Region.

Australia and Antarctica belonged to the massive southern continent of Gondwana. Africa and India separated from Gondwana about 100 million years ago, and South America somewhat later. Antarctica and Australia split some 45 million years ago, as Australia drifted northward. New Zealand and some of the larger Pacific islands were also separate by this time. The links between Australia and the other Gondwanan landmasses can be seen in the animals living in the southern continents today. For instance the ratites, large flightless birds, are found in South America (rheas), Africa (Ostrich), Australia (Emu and cassowaries) and New Zealand (kiwis). The extinct elephant-birds of Madagascar and the Moa of New Zealand also belonged to this group.

Australia

Australia is an ancient continent, characterized by poor soils and a mostly arid climate. Rainfall increases from the center to the coasts and the vegetation changes accordingly. Much of the interior is desert, or covered by grassland and scrub, whereas woodland and forest are found in the north, east and south-west.

Stony deserts or gibbers have a sparse cover of saltbush, while the sandy deserts are often well vegetated with shrubs and scattered small trees. Native chats (related to honeyeaters), grasswrens, parrots and pigeons are the most obvious birds in desert areas. Two widespread forms of semiarid woodland are the mulga and mallee. Mulga is acacia woodland and mallee consists of multi-stemmed eucalypts. Both have a rich bird fauna, including many kinds of parrots, and the Malleefowl.

Taller woodlands and forests are dominated to a remarkable degree by one genus of trees, Eucalyptus, and many types of birds have adapted to live in eucalypt woodlands and forests. Eucalypts come in many forms, differing most conspicuously in the type of bark they possess: smooth-barked gums; peppermints and boxes with flaky bark; and the aptly named stringybarks and ironbarks. Many insectivorous birds search for food on the leaves and bark of eucalypts, honeyeaters and lorikeets visit the flowers for nectar and pollen, parrots consume the seeds and a variety of species from tiny pardalotes to massive black-cockatoos nest in the holes that are frequent in old eucalypts. Eucalypt woodland also has a remarkably large number of cooperatively breeding species, in which nonbreeding birds help to rear the young of others.

Heathy vegetation predominates in parts of the south-west and east coast on rocky or sandy soils. There is a diverse flora with many of the species producing masses of nectar, which the honeyeaters harvest while pollinating the flowers. Perhaps surprisingly for such a dry continent, there are significant areas of rainforest, in north Queensland, the central east coast and Tasmania. The temperate rainforests in the south are remnants from the time when great moist forests of southern beeches clothed much of Gondwana. This kind of tree is now also found in New Zealand and South America, and used to occur in Antarctica. The tropical rainforests are very rich in tree species, and have an avifauna more akin to that of New Guinea, including bowerbirds and fruit-doves.

Australia is famed for its great sandy beaches, but these are mostly poor bird habitat. There are estuaries and mudflats, with good sites around the major cities, but the best wader sites are near Port Hedland and Broome in the north of Western Australia. These provide a home for migrant waders from the northern hemisphere. Extensive mangroves are found across the north, and these have their own group of bird species. The Great Barrier Reef, which extends along most of the coast of Queensland, is the breeding ground for boobies, frigate birds, tropicbirds and terns, whereas shearwaters (muttonbirds), albatrosses and gannets breed in the islands of the Bass Strait.

The Rainbow Lorikeet is a common occupant of various arboreal habitats in eastern Australia.

People arrived in Australia at least 40,000 years ago and had a major impact on the land. Their use of fire encouraged the spread of eucalypts at the expense of rainforest and fire-sensitive trees. They apparently exterminated many of the large mammal species: giant kangaroos, diprotodonts and the marsupial lion (Thylacoleo). It is probable that many large birds disappeared at this time. Others would of course have been favored by the environmental changes, especially those inhabiting grassland or profiting from eucalypts.

In the short time since Europeans settled Australia, a little over 200 years ago, they have cleared half of the remaining forests and woodlands and degraded much of the rest. The sheep, cattle and rabbits they introduced devastated the vegetation in semiarid regions, which had never before felt the impact of hard hooves, leading to the loss of many medium-sized marsupials. Foxes and cats now prey on ground-dwelling birds, which have become scarce in many areas. Australia has a small population (20 million) but people are concentrated near the coast, which is now feeling the effects of development and tourism.

Despite the damage caused by European settlement, probably only one species of bird, the Paradise Parrot has become extinct on the Australian mainland. Many more are Endangered or Vulnerable. The Noisy Scrub-birds, believed extinct until 50 years ago, has increased thanks to protection from fire and translocation. Regent Honeyeaters show complex movements depending on the flowering of eucalypts. Perhaps the most difficult to protect is the rarely sighted Night Parrot, from the extensive inland plains, hiding in dense spinifex and saltbush by day. Conservation now has a large popular following, and recent decades have seen a proliferation of national parks. Many of these are World Heritage listed, including the rainforests of eastern Australia, the wilderness of south-western Tasmania, the Kakadu wetlands in the north and the central desert. The large cities all have areas of bush near or within them, such as King's Park in Perth, Sherbrooke Forest near Melbourne and Royal National Park on the outskirts of Sydney.

Australia's birds fall into three main groups in terms of their origin. A few are ancient survivors from Gondwana days, including the ratites, and also the megapodes or mound-builders and probably the parrots. Most other groups evolved within Australia during the period of 30 million years or so when it was isolated from the other continents. The honeyeaters and Australian warblers, flycatchers, robins and wrens all have a long history in Australia. A few species are clearly recent arrivals, such as the Silvereye and a single bee-eater, pipit and lark, as their nearest relatives are found in Asia.

Altogether Australia has some 575 breeding species, somewhat over half being passerines. Only a handful of migrant land birds reach the country, such as the White-throated Needletail, which breeds in Japan. Numerous waders from the north and seabirds from the south also migrate to Australia.

New Guinea and New Zealand

New Guinea originated from the Australian plate colliding with the Asian plate. For much of its history it has been joined to northern Australia. It is a land of rainforest, with smaller areas of woodland and grassland. The richness of the forests, and perhaps lack of certain mammals, along with the great altitudinal range, has led to a highly diverse avifauna, with almost as many breeding birds as Australia. The parrots range from the pygmy parrots, scarcely larger than a wren, to the huge Palm Cockatoo. Fruit-doves abound and New Guinea has a greater variety of kingfishers than anywhere else. The two most remarkable groups of birds are the birds of paradise and the bowerbirds. These are not closely related to each other, but both feed on rich fruits, which has freed the males of many species from parental care. Sexual selection imposed by the females for males with the best genes has led to spectacular plumages and bizarre displays.

New Zealand has an even longer history of isolation than Australia. During this period it suffered volcanism, glaciation and the arrival of people, and thus has a depauperate avifauna, with only 42 breeding species of land bird. Some, like the kiwis and Rifleman are survivors from Gondwana; others, like the wattlebirds, are of uncertain origin. Many species are similar to Australian birds, suggesting a more recent origin. New Zealand was mostly forested, but burning by the Maoris and clearing by European settlers has replaced much forest by grassland. Sadly, many birds, like the Huia, have become extinct recently and many others teeter on the brink, like the Chatham Island Black Robin, which was once down to seven individuals. The Maoris exterminated the moas and a giant eagle that preyed on the moas, and decimated vast colonies of sea-birds. New Zealand has many national parks, encompassing volcanoes, snowy mountains, glaciers, fjords and forests, and has an excellent recent history of research on endangered bird species. However, native birds are hard to find and species from Europe, such as Chaffinches, dominate, even in native forests. Many endangered species clung to existence on off-shore islands free from the introduced mammals. An exciting development is predator-free reserves on the main islands, including Karori Wildlife Sanctuary in Wellington, which is surrounded by a mammalproof fence.

New Caledonia and Antarctica

New Caledonia has been a separate landmass for a long time, and although many of its birds are related to Australian species it has one oddity, the Endangered Kagu. The other islands of the Pacific show a decline in diversity of birds the further one travels from Australia and Southeast Asia. Fiji is quite rich, with a mixture of Australian and Asian birds, whereas Tahiti has few birds. Parrots and rails have been successful in reaching even the most distant islands, but many of these have become extinct following human settlement.

Antarctica is now almost covered in snow and ice and has no true land birds. The surrounding seas are rich in plankton and other sealife, so huge colonies of seabirds nest on the Antarctic mainland. Penguins are the best known of these, but there are skuas, terns and petrels as well. The subantarctic islands harbor vast seabird colonies, particularly of albatrosses, petrels and shearwaters. These are threatened by long-line fisheries in the Southern Ocean.

Australasian ornithological societies

Birds Australia (http://www.birdsaustralia.com.au) coordinates monitoring and conservation activities, has regional groups, and special groups for raptors, parrots, waders and seabirds. The Ornithological Society of New Zealand (www.osnz.org.nz) performs the same role in New Zealand.

OSTRICHES Struthioniformes

Emu
Dromaius novaehollandiae (Dromaiidae) 2 m/6½ ft.
Huge flightless bird with long neck, long powerful legs. Long, thick hairlike plumage appears soft and shaggy. Grizzled grayish brown, with short, black hairlike feathers on head and neck, bare blue skin on face and throat. Breeding birds have pale neck ruff. Downy chick striped brown and white, immature smaller and darker brown than adult. Runs with a bouncy, swaying motion. Call a deep, resonant booming or grunting. **Range and habitat:** AU. Common nomad in open habitats from woodland to desert in Australia, occasionally near coast. In southern inland, large groups make nomadic or migratory seasonal movements. Extinct populations on Kangaroo and King Island, may have been distinct species. Large scale decline in last 20 years. **Similar species:** immature Southern Cassowary, introduced Ostrich (see p 186).

Southern Cassowary
Casuarius casuarius (Casuariidae) 1.5–2 m/5–6½ ft.
Huge flightless bird with long neck, long legs, very long inner claw. Black plumage long and hairlike. Tall bony casque on head, bare blue skin on face and neck, red wattles on neck. Downy chick striped brown and yellow, immature brown with rusty head. Runs with head lowered, using bladelike casque to assist passage through vine tangles. Solitary. Call a loud, hollow booming or deep rumbling; also roaring, hissing and shrill whistle. **Range and habitat:** AU. Uncommon resident of tropical rainforest, often near streams and clearings, in New Guinea and northeast tip of Australia. Vulnerable overall, and Endangered in Australia, due to hunting, dogs, traffic accidents, and loss of habitat. **Similar species:** Emu.

Brown Kiwi
Apteryx australis (Apterygidae) 50 cm/20 in.
Fowl-sized, dumpy, flightless bird with hairy plumage, long decurved bill. Grizzled gray-brown with rusty tinge, grayer on head. Pale to dark brown feet. No tail, short legs. Nocturnal, powerful runner. Call a shrill double whistle, repeated sounds like "ki-wi," or a guttural hoarse cry. Snuffling noises when feeding, by probing into ground in search of earthworms. **Range and habitat:** AU. Uncommon resident of forest remnants and edge in New Zealand. Separate species on North and South Island. Vulnerable due to predation by introduced mammals, especially of young, but major recovery program underway. **Similar species:** Little Spotted Kiwi, Greater Spotted Kiwi, both of which are barred.

Little Spotted Kiwi
Apteryx oweni (Apterygidae) 40 cm/16 in.
Fowl-sized, dumpy, flightless bird with hairy plumage, moderately long, slightly decurved bill. Irregularly banded and mottled brownish black on pale buff-gray background. Head gray, feet pale brown to flesh-white. No tail, short legs. Nocturnal, powerful runner. Call a shrill, even trill or low rolling "churr." **Range and habitat:** AU. Rare resident of forest remnants on South Island of New Zealand. Main population on Kapiti Island where it was introduced. **Similar species:** Brown Kiwi, Greater Spotted Kiwi, which is more chestnut.

PENGUINS Sphenisciformes

Adelie Penguin
Pygoscelis adeliae (Spheniscidae) 70 cm/28 in.
Medium-sized black and white penguin with stubby bill, peaked crown, long stiff tail of pointed feathers. Head, chin and upperparts black, underparts and prominent eye-ring white. Short beak partly feathered. Call a trumpeting and braying, or guttural squawk. **Range and habitat:** AN. Oceanic and circumpolar; abundant breeder in coastal and peninsular Antarctica, South Shetland, Orkney and Sandwich Islands, Bouvet and Peter I Island. **Similar species:** other *Pygoscelis* penguins.

Chinstrap Penguin
Pygoscelis antarctica (Spheniscidae) 76 cm/30 in.
Medium-sized pied penguin with distinctive face pattern.

Upperparts black, face and underparts white with prominent black line encircling throat from ear to ear. Short unfeathered beak. Long tail. Call a loud braying, also low growling and hissing. **Range and habitat:** AN. Oceanic and circumpolar, common breeder in peninsular Antarctica, South Shetland, Orkney and Sandwich Islands, Bouvet and Peter I Islands, occasionally reaching more northerly landmasses. **Similar species:** other *Pygoscelis* penguins.

Emperor Penguin
Aptenodytes forsteri (Spheniscidae) 112 cm/44 in.
Large, fat gray and white penguin with brightly colored head pattern. Heaviest seabird at 25–45 kg (55–99 lb). Upperparts blue-gray, underparts white, slightly yellow on breast. Head black with orange-yellow throat and ear patch. Juvenile gray-brown. Rather small, slightly decurved bill with narrow pink gape and stripe on lower mandible. Grayish chicks with black and white head. Call is a resonant squawk, or shrill trumpeting or braying. **Range and habitat:** AN. Oceanic and circumpolar, breeds in winter on snow and sea-ice in Antarctica. **Similar species:** King Penguin.

King Penguin
Aptenodytes patagonicus (Spheniscidae) 95 cm/37 in.
Large gray and white penguin with brightly colored head pattern. Upperparts blue-gray, underparts white with yellow sides to breast. Head black with golden orange ear patches and throat. Long bill with prominent pink gape and broad stripe along lower mandible. Woolly brown juveniles. Call a squawk, or shrill trumpeting or braying. **Range and habitat:** AN. Oceanic and circumpolar, breeds on Macquarie, Marion, Prince Edward, Heard, Kerguelen and Crozet, South Sandwich Islands, South Georgia. **Similar species:** Emperor Penguin.

Fiordland Penguin
Eudyptes pachyrhynchus (Spheniscidae) 60 cm/24 in.
Medium-sized pied penguin with brightly colored bill and eye stripe. Head and upperparts glossy black with faint white streaks on cheeks, underparts white. Underflipper white with black border. Bill red, without bare pale skin at base. Black eye. Long, thin eyebrows of yellow filamentous feathers, ending in downward-drooping crest. Call a loud braying. **Range and habitat:** AU. Oceanic, breeds in south-western South Island, Stewart Island, New Zealand in coastal forest, small caves and overhangs; postbreeding movement to southern Australian seas. Vulnerable, due to predation by introduced mammals and wekas, breeding mostly on predator-free islands. **Similar species:** other *Eudyptes* penguins, which have bare skin at base of bill, different underflipper patterns, differently shaped crests.

Little Penguin
Eudyptula minor (Spheniscidae) 35 cm/14 in.
Small, plain penguin. Upperparts blue-gray to blue-black, face gray, underparts white. Flippers have white trailing edge. Small beak. Call is a yapping, braying and wailing. **Range and habitat:** AO. Common on the southern coasts of Australia, Tasmania, New Zealand. Some colonies are a major tourist attraction. Oceanic, coming ashore to molt and breed on rocks, dense shrubs or grass tussocks often on islands or base of cliff. **Similar species:** Yellow-eyed Penguin of New Zealand is larger, with pink bill, yellow eye and band across crown.

GREBES Podicipediformes

Hoary-headed Grebe
Podkeps poliocephalus (Podicipedidae) 27 cm/10½ in.
Small gray grebe. Upperparts dark gray, breast buff, underparts white. Broad white band through flight feathers. Breeding plumage distinctive, with thin, white hairlike plumes on black head and face. In nonbreeding plumage, dark cap extends below eye, hind-neck black. Nonbreeding birds form tight flocks, flee from danger with long, pattering take-off across water. Usually silent; call near nest is a soft churring. **Range and habitat:** AU. Common nomad on lakes, swamps and estuaries in Australia, New Zealand. **Similar species:** nonbreeding Australasian Grebe is darker with fleshy yellow or cream gape, usually dives to escape danger; New Zealand Dabchick is darker and glossier.

Emu

Southern Cassowary (with young)

Brown Kiwi

Little Spotted Kiwi

Adelie Penguin

Chinstrap Penguin

Fiordland Penguin

Little Penguin (on nest)

Emperor Penguin

King Penguin

Hoary-headed Grebe

TUBE-NOSED SWIMMERS Procellariiformes

Yellow-nosed Albatross

Diomedea chlororhynchos (Diomedeidae) 78 cm/31 in.
Small, slender albatross with black and yellow bill. White with black back, wings and tail. Underwing white with thin black border. Race in AU has gray cheeks, Atlantic race has gray head and neck, white cap. Bill black with yellow stripe from forehead to tip. Juvenile has white head, no yellow on bill. Most small albatrosses glide alternately showing pale underparts and dark wing and mantle. Call a croak at sea, braying at nest. **Range and habitat:** oceanic, breeding on subantarctic islands in Atlantic and Indian oceans. Common winter visitor off all southern continents. Vulnerable, due to long-line fisheries. **Similar species:** other small albatrosses (mollymawks), especially Gray-headed and Buller's, both of which have yellow stripe on bottom of bill as well as top.

Gray-headed Albatross

Diomedea chrysostoma (Diomedeidae) 88 cm/35 in.
Small albatross with gray head, black and yellow bill. White with black back, wings and tail. Underwing white with black border. Head gray, bill black with yellow stripe along top and bottom, pink tip. Juvenile has black bill, gray underwing. Call a croak at sea, braying whistle at nest. **Range and habitat:** oceanic and circum-polar, breeding on subantarctic islands in all southern oceans. Uncommon winter visitor off all southern continents. Vulnerable, due to long-line fisheries. **Similar species:** Sometimes split into several species. Atlantic Yellow-nosed Albatross, Black-browed Albatross, Buller's Albatross which has dark gray head, white cap.

Royal Albatross

Diomedea epomophora (Diomedeidae) 125 cm/49 in.
Large, mainly white albatross with black tips and hind border on underwings. Upperwings black in northern race, white with black tips and hind border in southern. Tail white. Juvenile has black upperwings, mottled back. Bill yellowish pink with black cutting edge. Call a guttural croaking, braying whistle and bill-clappering. **Range and habitat:** oceanic, breeding on islands off New Zealand, small colony on mainland near Dunedin can be visited. Uncommon winter-spring visitor to seas off AU, South America. Endangered, due to long-line fisheries. **Similar species:** Sometimes separated into two species, Northern and Southern Wandering Albatross.

Wandering Albatross

Diomedea exulans (Diomedeidae) 135 cm/53 in.
Large albatross, variable in color but mostly white with black tips and hind edges to wings, dark mottling on upperwings and fine vermiculations on underparts. Tail white with black edges. Juvenile dark brown with white face. Immatures paler and mottled with dark collar and breast band, becoming increasingly white. Bill pink, without black cutting edge. Soars gracefully with little flapping. Call a guttural croaking, hoarse braying whistle and bill-clappering. **Range and habitat:** oceanic and circumpolar, breeding on subantarctic islands in all southern oceans. Fairly common winter-spring visitor off all southern continents. Endangered, due to long-line fisheries. **Similar species:** Considered to consist of several distinct species. Royal Albatross, Southern Giant-Petrel.

Light-mantled Albatross

Phoebetria palpebrata (Diomedeidae) 70 cm/28 in.
Small, slender, all-dark albatross with long pointed tail. Brown with white eye-ring, gray nape and back. Bill black with light blue line near cutting edge. Soaring flight elegant and graceful, with little flapping. Ghostly trumpeting at sea; call at nest is a shrill "pee-ow," the second part deeper. **Range and habitat:** oceanic and circumpolar, breeding on antarctic and subantarctic islands in all southern oceans. Rare winter visitor to AU and South America. Vulnerable, due to long-line fisheries. **Similar species:** Sooty Albatross, which has dark upperparts, yellow line along bill; Southern Giant-Petrel.

Southern Giant-Petrel

Macronectes giganteus (Procellariidae) 90 cm/35 in.
Huge, dumpy petrel with bulbous horn-colored bill. Brown, mottled paler and grayer on head, face and underparts. Juvenile all-dark brown. White form is all-white with scattered brown spots. In flight shows short tail, ragged wing outline, more flapping and less graceful gliding than albatrosses. Call is a croaking at sea, hoarse whinnying and mewing at nest. Feeds on offal at sea and on land near breeding colonies. Occasionally kills petrels, penguins and albatrosses. **Range and habitat:** oceanic and circumpolar, breeding on Antarctica, antarctic and subantarctic islands. Common winter visitor off all southern continents. Vulnerable, due to long-line fisheries. **Similar species:** juvenile Wandering Albatross, sooty albatrosses. 2 species sometimes recognized—Northern and Southern, with pink and green bill tips respectively.

Short-tailed Shearwater

Puffinus tenuirostris (Procellariidae) 42 cm/17 in.
All-dark shearwater with dark feet, slender dark bill. Brown, with gray underwings, short rounded tail. Flies with a series of quick flaps then a long banking glide low over the water surface. Often in large flocks. Silent at sea; call at nest is a crooning, rising to crescendo, and harsher noises. Also called muttonbird, as young are still harvested for food. **Range and habitat:** oceanic. Abundant breeder on islands of southern Australia and Tasmania, migrates in winter to north Pacific ocean. **Similar species:** other dark *Puffinus* shearwaters (see p 50); Sooty has white underwing-coverts.

Flesh-footed Shearwater

Puffinus carneipes (Procellariidae) 45 cm/18 in.
Large all-dark shearwater with pink feet, large pale bill. Entirely brown, tail short and fan-shaped, feet do not project beyond tail in flight. Flies with a series of stiff, deep wingbeats and long banking glides on straight wings, low over the water surface. Silent at sea; call at nest is a mewing, crooning and cackling. **Range and habitat:** oceanic. Common breeder on islands off southern Australia, New Zealand, migrates north in winter to tropical and subtropical Indian and Pacific oceans. **Similar species:** other all-dark *Puffinus* shearwaters (see p 50).

Cape Petrel

Daption capense (Procellariidae) 40 cm/16 in.
Large, distinctively pied petrel. Head and upperparts black with white patches in upperwings, white chequering on back and rump, white base to tail. Underparts white, underwings white with black border. Flies with stiff-winged fluttering and gliding"follows ships. Call a raucous chattering, trilled "cooo." **Range and habitat:** oceanic and circumpolar, breeding in Antarctica, antarctic and subantarctic islands, islands off New Zealand. Common winter-spring visitor off all southern continents. **Similar species:** Antarctic Petrel is browner, more clear-cut dark and white without chequering.

Soft-plumaged Petrel

Pterodroma mollis (Procellariidae) 33 cm/13 in.
Medium-sized gray and white petrel with face pattern, breast band, dark upperwings. Head and upperparts gray with white face and throat, black eye patch. Upperwings with dark M pattern. Underparts white with gray breast band, underwings dark with pale leading edge near body. Feet pink. Occasional all-dark individuals occur. Flight rapid, with wheeling arcs on long, backswept swiftlike wings. Often in flocks. Call a shrill, trilling whistle or a moaning cry. **Range and habitat:** oceanic. Breeds on Atlantic islands off southern Africa and in Indian and south Pacific oceans, common winter visitor to seas off southern Australia, southern Africa. **Similar species:** other *Pterodroma* petrels (see p 98). **Not illustrated.**

Fairy Prion

Pachyptila turtur (Procellariidae) 25 cm/10 in.
Small blue-gray petrel. Upperparts with faint white eyebrow, dark M pattern across spread wings, broad dark tail tip. Underparts white. Bill narrow, with large nail at tip. Often in flocks. Flight swift and erratic, dips to "hydroplane" along water surface. Call a guttural cooing. **Range and habitat:** oceanic. Abundant breeder on islands off southern Australia and New Zealand, and some subantarctic islands in all southern oceans. Common winter visitor off southern Australia, southern Africa. **Similar species:** other prions; distinguished by bill shape and width, amount of black on tail.

Yellow-nosed Albatross

Gray-headed Albatross

Royal Albatross

Wandering Albatross

Cape Petrel

Light-mantled Albatross

Southern Giant-Petrel

Short-tailed Shearwater

Flesh-footed Shearwater

Fairy Prion

FULL-WEBBED SWIMMERS Pelecaniformes

Australian Pelican

Pelecanus conspicillatus (Pelecanidae) 150–180 cm/59–71 in.
Large, distinctively pied pelican. Head, neck and underparts white, with gray crested nape, yellow eye-ring. Wings black with white shoulders, tail black. Large pink bill and pouch. Feeds by plunging head below surface. Swimming flocks herd schools of fish. Call a deep grunt. **Range and habitat:** AU. Common resident or visitor on lakes, rivers and estuaries in Australia, New Guinea. Irruptive, breeding in large numbers when inland lakes fill, then disperses coastward when they dry out. Vagrants occasionally reach eastern Indonesia, New Zealand, islands in western PA. **Similar species:** none in AU.

Australian Gannet

Morus serrator (Sulidae) 90 cm/35 in.
Large, slender diving seabird with long bill, long pointed wings, long tail. White with golden-buff head, black tips and hind border to wings, black central tail feathers. Juvenile mottled dark brown, paler on underparts. Flies strongly and .heavily with series of quick beats and long glides, dives with closed wings into sea. Call a croak at sea, and a nasal chuckling and cackling at nest. **Range and habitat:** oceanic. Abundant breeder on islands of New Zealand, smaller colonies off southern Australia. Common in offshore waters, especially in winter. **Similar species:** other gannets and boobies; albatrosses (see pp 98, 142).

Australian Darter

Anhinga novaehollandiae (Anhingidae) 90 cm/35 in.
Large black or gray-brown fishing bird with long pointed bill, long snakelike neck. Male black with white neck stripe, rusty patch on foreneck, white patches and streaks on wings. Female paler, gray-brown; with white underparts. Bill yellow, slender. Flight labored, with series of quick beats and long glides, showing pale upperwing band and ample tail; soars well with distinctive "flying cross" shape. Swims with only head and neck above water, often submerges. Perches beside water with wings open, snakelike movements of head. Call a strident, descending and accelerating croaking. **Range and habitat:** common resident or visitor on mainly freshwater wetlands. **Similar species:** other *Anhingas* (see pp 52, 186, 238).

Pied Cormorant

Phalacrocorax varius (Phalacrocoracidae) 75 cm/29 in.
Large black and white cormorant with long, prominently hooked bill. Upperparts black, face and underparts white with black thighs. Yellow, blue and orange facial skin, bone-colored bill. Swims with bill slightly uptilted. Flies heavily with series of quick beats and glides, holding head slightly above plane of body, flocks often in V formation. Perches with wings open. Call a loud guttural cackling, croaking or screaming. **Range and habitat:** AU. Common resident of coastal waters and large lakes in Australia and New Zealand. **Similar species:** Black-faced Cormorant has black face and bill, Little Pied Cormorant has a short yellow bill.

Little Black Cormorant

Phalacrocorax sulcirostris (Phalacrocoracidae) 65 cm/26 in.
Small, entirely black cormorant with slender bill. Upperparts have bronze-green, scaled appearance. Flies with quick beats and glides, often in flocks in V formation. Often in large, tight fishing flocks which swim and submerge together. Perches in dead trees with wings open. Call a guttural croaking, ticking or whistling, mainly near nest. **Range and habitat:** OR, AU. Common resident or visitor to freshwater wetlands and estuaries in Indonesia, New Guinea, Australia and New Zealand. **Similar species:** Great Cormorant (see p 142).

Lesser Frigatebird

Fregata ariel (Fregatidae) 75 cm/29 in.
Large dark seabird with long pointed wings, forked tail. Male glossy black with inflatable red throat skin, small white patch at base of underwing. Female has white collar and breast, brown mottling on shoulders, no throat sac. Juvenile mottled brown with rusty head, white belly. Pale bill long and slender, with hook at tip. Soars effortlessly on large wings, harries other seabirds to give up food.

Call a grunting, cackling and bill rattling. **Range and habitat:** tropical coastal seas. Abundant breeder on tropical islands, islets and reefs in all oceans. **Similar species:** other frigatebirds (see pp 52, 238).

HERONS AND ALLIES Ciconiiformes

Pacific Heron

Ardea pacifica (Ardeidae) 90 cm/35 in.
Large pied heron. Upperparts sooty black glossed blue, with maroon lanceolate hackles on back in breeding plumage. Head, neck and breast white with line of dark spots down foreneck. White "headlights" on leading edge of wings in flight. Juvenile duller, with fawn-tinged, more heavily spotted neck and breast. Flies with slow, sweeping beats, neck retracted. Call a harsh croak. Sometimes soars. Uses stand-and-wait method to capture prey. **Range and habitat:** AU. Common resident or nomad on shallow freshwater wetlands in Australia; occasional vagrants reach New Guinea and New Zealand. **Similar species:** juvenile Pied Heron is much smaller, lacks wing "headlights."

White-faced Egret

Egretta novaehollandiae (Ardeidae) 65 cm/26 in.
Medium-sized, all-gray heron with white face and throat, gray hackles on back, rusty hackles on lower neck. Juvenile duller, lacking white face and hackles. Call a deep, hoarse cry, repeated. Commonest heron through most of range, in all kinds of habitats. **Range and habitat:** AU, PA. Abundant resident or nomad on shallow, fresh or saline wetlands and wet grasslands in eastern Indonesia, Australia, New Zealand, islands in western Pacific. **Similar species:** gray morph of Pacific Reef-Egret.

Intermediate Egret

Egretta intermedia (Ardeidae) 65 cm/26 in.
Medium-sized, all-white egret with stout bill, neck same length as body. In breeding plumage has long filamentous plumes on breast and back, green facial skin, red or orange bill, red upper legs. Nonbreeding birds lack plumes and have orange-yellow bill and face, black legs. Stalks prey slowly with neck straight, upright. Flies with slow beats, neck retracted; in flight looks broad-winged, with slight neck bulge. Call a, deep, rattling croak. **Range and habitat:** common resident, nomad or migrant on shallow, fresh and saline wetlands in AF, OR, AU. **Similar species:** other white egrets, spoonbills.

Rufous Night-Heron

Nycticorax caledonicus (Ardeidae) 59 cm/23 in.
Squat, dumpy heron with stout bill, short legs. Upperparts rufous with black cap, long white plumes on crown. Underparts pale rufous, shading to white on belly. Juvenile streaked and mottled brown, with white spots on back and wings. Nocturnal, roosting by day in hunched posture in leafy waterside trees. If disturbed, circles about before landing in another tree. Call a hollow, squeaky "kyok." **Range and habitat:** OR, AU, PA. Common resident, migrant or nomad of shallow, fresh and saline wetlands with nearby trees in Indonesia, New Guinea, Australia, islands in western Pacific. **Similar species:** rufous form of Striated Heron, lacks cap and plumes, more rufous and spotted ventrally; Australasian Bittern is yellowish brown with dark streaks and bars, lives in reeds.

Black Bittern

Ixobrychus flavicollis (Ardeidae) 60 cm/24 in.
Medium-sized, all-dark bittern. Dark brown to sooty black with yellow plumes down sides of neck, pale streaks from throat to breast. Juvenile paler, browner. Seldom seen unless flushed from trees. In flight looks compact, all-dark. Call a deep croak, cooing and booming. **Range and habitat:** OR, AU, PA. Uncommon resident or migrant of mangroves, trees fringing streams and wetlands in India, eastern Asia, New Guinea, coastal Australia, islands in western Pacific. **Similar species:** Striated Heron.

Australian Pelican

Australian Gannet
(colony)

Australian Darter
(male)

Pied Cormorant

White-faced Egret

Little Black Cormorant

Pacific Heron

Lesser Frigatebird
(female)

Black Bittern

Intermediate Egret

Rufous Night-Heron

Straw-necked Ibis

Threskiornis spinicollis (**Threskiornithidae**) 67 cm/26 in.
Pied ibis with strawlike plumes on neck. Upperparts black glossed blue-purple and green, with bald black head, white neck ruff, long yellow plumes on foreneck. Underparts and tail white. Juvenile duller with dusky feathered head, shorter bill, no plumes. Flies with quick, rhythmic beats and long glides, neck outstretched. Large flocks soar in circles or fly in V formation. Call a deep grunt. Often feeds well away from water, patrolling pasture in search of large insects. **Range and habitat:** AU. Abundant resident of grasslands and shallow freshwater wetlands in Australia. Partly nomadic or migratory, large flocks gathering at insect plagues and southern juveniles wintering in tropical northern Australia and occasionally New Guinea. **Similar species:** Pacific (White-necked) Heron, Pied Heron (see p 286).

Royal Spoonbill

Platalea regia (**Threskiornithidae**) 78 cm/31 in.
All-white spoonbill with black face, bill and legs. Long plumes on nape in breeding plumage. Flies with quick, rhythmic beats and long glides, neck outstretched. Call a deep grunt, bill-clappering. **Range and habitat:** OR, AU. Common resident of shallow, fresh and saline wetlands in Indonesia, New Guinea, Australia and New Zealand. **Similar species:** Yellow-billed Spoonbill has yellow bill and legs; white egrets (see pp 52, 144, 286).

WATERFOWL Anseriformes

Magpie Goose

Anseranas semipalmata (**Anseranatidae**) 70–90 cm/28–35 in.
Distinctively pied goose with knob on head, long unwebbed toes. Head, neck, wings and tail black. Back, shoulders and underparts white. Pink bill and face, long yellow or pink legs. Immature has white areas mottled brown. Large flocks gather on feeding grounds. Breeds colonially, occasionally as trios. Call a resonant honking. **Range and habitat:** AU. Abundant breeding resident or local nomad of swamps and flooded grasslands and crops in New Guinea and tropical Australia. Formerly abundant breeder in south-eastern Australia but now rare, though recovering slowly. **Similar species:** none in AU.

Black Swan

Cygnus atratus (**Anatidae**) 100–40 cm/39–55 in.
All-black swan with red bill, white wing tips revealed in flight. Immature gray-brown, white wing feathers mottled and tipped brown. Downy young gray. Call a plaintive bugling. Feeds from surface, by submerging bill and neck or upending. **Range and habitat:** AU. Abundant resident or nomad on both fresh and brackish wetlands in Australia, vagrant to New Guinea. Introduced to New Zealand, where now abundant.

Cape Barren Goose

Ceopsis novaehollandiae (**Anatidae**) 75–100cm/29-39in.
Large all-gray goose with bulbous yellow-green cere, white crown, black spots on wings, pink legs. In flight shows black wing-tips and tail. Call is a deep resonant grunting and honking, repeated. **Range and habitat:** AU. Uncommon breeder in heath and tusssock-grass on islands off southern Australia, dispersing to coast and pastures of southern Australian mainland and Tasmania. **Similar species:** none in AU.

Pacific Black Duck

Anas superciliosa (**Anatidae**) 55 cm/22 in.
Medium-sized, dark duck with striped face. Mottled dark brown with black crown, pale and dark horizontal lines through eye and face, buff throat, iridescent patch in wing which varies from green to purple depending on angle of light. In flight shows glossy green patch on rear of inner upperwing, large white patch on inner underwing. Call a deep, hoarse quack, sometimes repeated as a descending "laugh." **Range and habitat:** OR, AU, PA. Abundant resident or nomad of mainly freshwater wetlands in Indonesia, New Guinea, Australia, New Zealand and Pacific islands. Declining in New Zealand through genetic swamping by introduced Mallard, with which it hybridizes. **Similar species:** Gray Teal, female Mallard (see p 146).

Gray Teal

Anas gibberifrons (**Anatidae**) 42 cm/17 in.
Small duck, mottled gray-brown with pale face and white throat. In flight shows small green wing patch at rear of upperwing, white stripe along center of upperwing, small white patch on inner underwing. Call a descending "laugh" of soft cooing quacks, or whistled "peep." **Range and habitat:** OR, AU, PA. Abundant nomad of fresh and brackish wetlands from Andaman Islands and Indonesia to New Guinea, Australia, New Zealand and western Pacific islands. Irruptive in Australia, congregating on ephemeral inland wetlands after rain to breed and dispersing when they dry out. **Similar species:** Pacific Black Duck; female Chestnut-breasted Teal is darker without pale throat.

Pink-eared Duck

Malacorhynchus membranaceus (**Anatidae**) 40 cm/16 in.
Small, boldly barred duck with long bill. Upperparts brown, underparts white with broad dark bars, buff undertail. Distinctive head pattern of white face, black eye patch, small pink ear spot. Bill has flap of skin at each side of tip. Feeds on surface by filtering out small animals. Flight rapid and whirring, showing prominent bill, white crescent on rump. Often in flocks. Call is a liquid chirrup, often given in flight. **Range and habitat:** AU. Common nomad of freshwater wetlands in Australia. Breeds on ephemeral inland waters, disperses coastward during drought. **Similar species:** Gray Teal; female Australian Shoveller is plainer, has blue shoulders in flight.

Hardhead

Aythya australis (**Anatidae**) 55 cm/22 in.
Dark brown duck with white wing patch and undertail. Male with white iris, female dark iris. White underwing, stripe along upperwing, broader at tip. Smooth outline with no obvious tail in water. Has gray beak with blue tip. Dives. **Range and habitat:** Australia, deep lakes, flooded rivers, permanent swamps. **Similar species:** Blue-billed Duck has no white on wings.

Maned Duck

Chenonetta jubata (**Anatidae**) 47 cm/18 in.
Medium-sized, gray perching duck with small bill, brown head, white wing flashes in flight. Male gray with brown head, speckled neck and breast, dark plumes on back, black undertail. Female has white eyebrow and cheek stripe, underparts mottled brown and white. In flight shows black wing tips, broad white rear edge on inner upperwing, white underwing. Often perches on trees or stands on land. Nests in tree-holes. Call a nasal, querulous ascending mew. **Range and habitat:** AU. Abundant resident or local nomad of freshwater wetlands and pastures in Australia. **Similar species:** none in AU.

Musk Duck

Biziura lobata (**Anatidae**) 47–73 cm/18–29 in.
Dark, elongated diving duck that sits low in the water. Entirely dark brown with fine, pale vermiculations. Bill short and stout, head large, tail long and stiff. Male has large leathery flap below bill and throat. Female smaller, no leathery flap. Swims partly submerged, with only head and back above water, often dives. Rarely flies, walks with difficulty. Call by male in display is a shrill whistle and "plonk" made by feet in water, while head raised and tail cocked. **Range and habitat:** AU. Common resident of deep freshwater wetlands and coastal waters in southern Australia. **Similar species:** female/eclipse Blue-billed Duck is smaller with rounded head, flat bill.

Straw-necked Ibis

Royal Spoonbill

Magpie Goose

Black Swan

Cape Barren Goose

Pacific Black Duck

Gray Teal

Pink-eared Duck

Hardhead

Maned Duck

Musk Duck

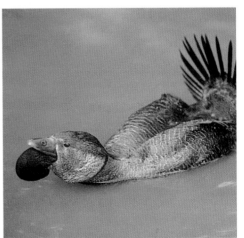

DIURNAL BIRDS OF PREY Falconiformes

Black-shouldered Kite

Elanus axillaris (Accipitridae) 35 cm/14 in.
Small, long-winged white hawk with pale gray back and wings, black shoulders, black spot near bend of underwing and dark wing tips. Juvenile washed rusty on head and breast, mottled on back and wings. Winnowing and hovering flight, glides on raised wings. Call a weak whistling note and harsh wheezing. **Range and habitat:** AU. Common in open woodland, grassland and farmland in Australia. Irruptive and nomadic, following mouse plagues. **Similar species:** Letter-winged Kite has black line along inner underwing, pale wing tips.

Black-breasted Buzzard

Hamirostra melanosternon (Accipitridae) 51–61 cm/20–4 in.
Robust, soaring hawk with white panels in wings, short pale tail. Adult black, with rufous nape, shoulder mottling, thighs and undertail. Juvenile/immature rufous to sandy brown with black streaks. Flight eaglelike gliding and soaring on raised wings, with sideways rocking motion. Call a repeated short, hoarse yelp. **Range and habitat:** AU. Uncommon resident of woodland in arid inland and tropical northern Australia. **Similar species:** Wedge-tailed Eagle; Square-tailed Kite is slender with long tail, barred flight feathers. **Not illustrated.**

Whistling Kite

Haliastur sphenurus (Accipitridae) 51–9 cm/20–3 in.
Medium-sized, untidy, soaring hawk. Mottled or streaked sandy brown with dark flight feathers, underwing pattern of pale leading edge and inner primaries, dark secondaries and outer primaries. Slow circling flight on bowed wings with splayed primaries, showing large pale area on upperwing and long rounded tail. Often gregarious. Call a loud whistle sliding down scale, accompanied by rapid up-scale chatter. **Range and habitat:** AU, PA. Common resident, migrant or nomad of open and lightly wooded country, often near water, in New Guinea, Australia and New Caledonia. **Similar species:** juvenile Brahminy Kite (see p 240); Little Eagle is chunkier with narrow pale upper-wing band, short tail, flat wings in flight, feathered legs.

Brown Goshawk

Accipiter fasciatus (Accipitridae) 37–55 cm/15–22 in.
Fierce, active, powerful hawk with rounded wings, long rounded tail, long yellow legs. Upperparts slate-gray washed brown, with rufous half-collar. Underparts finely barred dull rufous and white. Juvenile brown, with white underparts coarsely streaked and barred brown. Flight heavy, beats wings in rapid bursts, glides on flat wings. Call a rapid, shrill chatter or slower mewing notes. **Range and habitat:** AU, PA. Common but secretive resident and partial migrant of woodlands and open forests in eastern Indonesia, New Guinea, Australia and New Caledonia. Some southern birds winter in tropical AU. **Similar species:** Collared Sparrowhawk, Brown Falcon (see p 292).

Collared Sparrowhawk

Accipiter cirrhocephalus (Accipitridae) 29–38 cm/11½–15 in.
Small, fierce hawk with rounded wings, long square-tipped tail, long spindly legs, long middle toe. Upperparts slate-gray washed brown, with rufous half-collar. Underparts finely barred rufous and white. Juvenile brown, with white underparts coarsely streaked and barred brown. Flight agile and winnowing or flickering, beats wings in rapid bursts, glides on flat wings. Call a very rapid chittering or slower mewing. **Range and habitat:** AU. Uncommon, secretive resident of forests and woodlands in Australia and New Guinea. **Similar species:** Brown Goshawk.

Gray Goshawk

Accipiter novaehollandiae (Accipitridae) 33–55 cm/13–22 in.
Striking hawk with short rounded wings, long tail, long orange-yellow legs. Upper-parts gray, underparts either white (Australia) or rufous (New Guinea and islands). Also an all-white color form in both regions, and a dark gray form/sometimes with chestnut underparts) in New Guinea. Juveniles in New Guinea and islands are brown, with buff underparts streaked and barred brown. Flight powerful and agile, beats wings in rapid bursts, glides on bowed wings. Call a series of upslurred, ringing whistles. **Range and habitat:** AU, PA. Common but secretive resident of wet forests in Australia, New Guinea and islands from eastern Indonesia to Solomon Islands. **Similar species:** Brown Goshawk in New Guinea, Black-shouldered Kite, Gray Falcon in Australia.

Wedge-tailed Eagle

Aquila audax (Accipitridae) 85–104 cm/33–41 in.
Large dark eagle with lanky build, long wedge-shaped tail, baggy feathered legs. Sooty black with tawny nape, mottled gray-brown upperwing-bar, brown undertail, pale bases to flight feathers. Juvenile/immature dark brown with golden to reddish brown nape, back and upperwing-bar, pale undertail. Stable and controled soaring flight on long, upswept wings. Often gregarious at carrion. Call a weak yelp or squeal. **Range and habitat:** AU. Common resident or visitor, most habitats except intensively cultivated or settled areas, in Australia and New Guinea. **Similar species:** Black-breasted Buzzard Kite, juvenile White-bellied Sea Eagle; in New Guinea Gurney's Eagle has rounded tail, flat wings in flight.

Pacific Baza

Aviceda subcristata (Accipitridae) 35–46 cm/14–18 in.
Medium-sized crested hawk with long wings and tail, short legs. Upperparts slate-gray, underparts and flight feathers boldly barred. Underwing-coverts, thighs and undertail-coverts pale rufous. Juvenile much browner. Flight buoyant and agile, with slow beats, glides on flat wings. Active and acrobatic in tree canopy, sometimes gregarious. Call a reedy 2-note whistle, rising and falling. **Range and habitat:** AU, PA. Common resident or altitudinal migrant of forests and woodlands in Australia, New Guinea and islands from eastern Indonesia to Solomon Islands. **Similar species:** Brown Goshawk, Collared Sparrowhawk.

Black Falcon

Falco subniger (Falconidae) 45–56 cm/18–22 in.
Large, sleek, fierce falcon with small head, powerful shoulders, pointed wings, short legs. Dark brown to sooty gray or sooty black with inconspicuous black cheek stripe, white chin, and dark underwings. Flight is a kestrel-like winnowing or slower, crowlike flapping, glides on bowed wings. Often soars, showing long, square-tipped, usually furled tail. Fast and agile in stoop or pursuit. Usually silent; call a deep harsh chatter, slow whining or soft whistle. **Range and habitat:** AU. Uncommon resident or nomad of plains in inland Australia. Irruptive, into southern coastal areas. **Similar species:** Black Kite, Brown Falcon (see p 292).

Australian Hobby

Falco longipennis (Falconidae) 30–6 cm/12–14 in.
Small, slender, dusky falcon with small bill and feet, long scythe-shaped wings. Upperparts slate-gray with black mask, pale forehead and half-collar. Underparts rufous with fine dark streaks. Juvenile browner. Flight often low, fast and flickering, glides on flat wings with tips swept back. Aerobatic in pursuit of small aerial prey. Call a reedy chatter. **Range and habitat:** AU. Common resident or partial migrant of open woodland, towns and cities in Australia, winter migrant to eastern Indonesia and New Guinea. **Similar species:** Peregrine Falcon, Oriental Hobby (see p 152).

Gray Falcon

Falco hypoleucos (Falconidae) 33–43 cm/13–17 in.
Medium-sized, pale gray falcon with long pointed wings, short tail, short legs. Upperparts gray with faint cheek stripe, black wing tips. Underparts white with faint shaft streaks, wings and tail finely barred. Juvenile darker, and more boldly marked. Flight is a kestrel-like winnowing, glides on flat wings. In pursuit of birds, flies low and fast or stoops from a height. Call a hoarse chattering, clucking and whining. **Range and habitat:** AU. Rare in shrubland, grassland and woodland of arid inland Australia; some birds winter in northern Australia and rarely New Guinea. **Similar species:** Black-shouldered Kite, Gray Goshawk, Australian Hobby, Peregrine Falcon (see p 152). **Not illustrated.**

Black-shouldered K

Whistling Kite

Brown Goshawk

Collared Sparrowhawk

Gray Goshawk

Pacific Baza

Wedge-tailed Eagle

Black Falcon

Australian Hobby

Brown Falcon

Falco berigora (Falconidae) 41–51 cm/16–20 in.
Medium-sized, scruffy, loose-plumaged falcon with large head, round shoulders, long gray legs. Variable in plumage, from rufous brown on the upperparts and white on the underparts, with dark streaks and brown thighs, to uniformly dark brown. Double cheek stripe distinct on paler birds, barred underwings and tail visible on dark birds. Often perches sluggishly. Flight slow, heavy and erratic, glides on raised wings with rounded tail often fanned, sometimes hovers. Very vocal; call is a raucous cackling, chattering or screeching. **Range and habitat:** AU. Abundant resident and partial migrant in most open and lightly wooded habitats in Australia and New Guinea; some southern juveniles winter in northern Australia. **Similar species:** Brown Goshawk, Black Falcon (see p 290), Australian Kestrel.

New Zealand Falcon

Falco novaeseelandiae (Falconidae) 41–8 cm/16–19 in.
Medium-sized, dark, dashing and powerful falcon. Upperparts blue-black with pale bars, dark cheek stripe. Underparts cream to rufous with dark streaks, flanks barred. Juvenile duller and browner, without barring on flanks. Flight rapid and powerful, glides on flat wings. Soars, sometimes hovers or wind-hangs, makes fast, slanting dives at prey. Call a chattering, clucking or whining. **Range and habitat:** AU. Uncommon resident of wooded and open habitats in New Zealand. **Similar species:** none in New Zealand.

Australian Kestrel

Falco cenchroides (Falconidae) 30–5 cm/12–14 in.
Small, pale falcon with slender build, long tail. Upperparts pale rufous with indistinct cheek stripe, fine black markings, dark wing tips. Underparts buff with fine dark streaks. Flight winnowing, glides on flat wings. Often hovers, showing black band near tail tip. Call a shrill chatter. **Range and habitat:** AU. Abundant resident or partial migrant of most open and lightly wooded habitats in Australia and New Guinea. **Similar species:** pale-colored Brown Falcon.

FOWL-LIKE BIRDS Galliformes

Malleefowl

Leipoa ocellata (Megapodiidae) 60 cm/24 in.
Beautifully mottled fowl-like bird with large feet. Upper-parts gray-brown with chestnut, black and white mottling on back and wings. Underparts pale gray-brown with buff throat, black streak down breast. Walks or runs powerfully, flies heavily if pressed. Presence indicated by large nesting mounds of sand and leaf litter. Call a booming, grunting or soft cluck. Chicks are independent immediately after emerging from mound and can fly when very small. **Range and habitat:** AU. Vulnerable. Uncommon, localized and declining resident of remnant "mallee" in southern Australia—low, dense, multi-stemmed *Eucalyptus* scrub, acacia scrub. **Similar species:** none in AU.

Australian Brush-Turkey

Alectura lathami (Megapodiidae) 70 cm/28 in.
Turkeylike bird with vulturine head, large feet, tent-shaped or vaulted tail. Black, with bare red head, yellow neck wattles, gray scalloping on belly. Walks or runs powerfully, flies heavily if pressed. Call a deep grunt or loud booming. Male constructs huge mound by raking up leaf litter. Chicks independent on emerging. **Range and habitat:** AU. Common resident of wet forest, thick scrub and well-vegetated tropical gardens (even in suburbs), in coastal eastern Australia. **Similar species:** none in AU.

Stubble Quail

Coturnix pectoralis (Phasianidae) 18 cm/7 in.
Secretive, dumpy ground bird. Upperparts gray-brown with fine black and white vermiculations, prominent cream streaks. Underparts white with brown streaks. Male has rufous throat, dense black streaks on chest. Feet flesh-pink. Readily detected by call, seldom seen unless flushed. Flies suddenly with rapid whirring of pointed wings, in flight appears gray-brown with white streaks. Call a liquid 3-note whistle "pip-pee-whit" or a sharper 2-note "pip-pip" repeated. Range and habitat: AU. Common nomad of grassland and crops in Australia; extinct in Tasmania and New Zealand. Similar species: other quail and button-quail (see pp 154, 196, 244, 246).

Brown Quail

Coturnix ypsilophora (Phasia-nidae) 18 cm/7 in.
Secretive, dumpy ground bird. Upper-parts brown with fine chestnut, gray and black marbling, fine white streaks. Underparts light brown with fine, wavy black barring. Some birds with blue-gray suffusion. Female sandier brown and more coarsely marked than male. Feet orange-yellow. Readily detected by call, seldom seen unless flushed. Flies suddenly with rapid whirring of rounded wings, in flight appears rich brown. Call a mournful rising whistle of 2 notes "tu-whee" or shorter "whee-whit," not rising. **Range and habitat:** AU. Common resident or nomad of rank grass, swamps and heath in Indonesia, New Guinea, Australia; introduced to New Zealand and Fiji. **Similar species:** other quail and button-quail (see pp 154, 196, 244, 246). **Not illustrated.**

CRANES, RAILS AND ALLIES Gruiformes

Little Button-Quail

Turnix velox (Turnicidae) 13–15 cm/5–6 in.
Tiny quail-like bird with short, stout bill. Upperparts rufous, mottled gray-brown and black, streaked white on back and wings. Breast rufous, belly white. Male smaller, grayer and more mottled. Creeps hesitantly between clumps of grass, rocking backward and forward on toes, seldom seen unless flushed. Flies suddenly with rapid whirring of pointed wings, in flight appears rufous with white flanks and undertail. Call a low, disyllabic cooing. **Range and habitat:** AU. Common nomad of dry grassland and grassy woodland in Australia. **Similar species:** quail (see p 154); Red-chested Button-quail appears gray with rufous underparts.

Buff-banded Rail

Rallus philippensis (Rallidae) 31 cm/12 in.
Small, secretive waterbird of thick vegetation. Upperparts brown, mottled black and white. Head rufous, with white eyebrow. Flight feathers barred chestnut. Underparts barred black and white, with gray throat and buff patch on breast. Short, red-brown bill. Skulks through ground vegetation, runs into cover if startled. Calls varied—croaks, clicks, rattles and squeaky "swit-swit." **Range and habitat:** OR, AU, PA. Common but seldom-seen resident or partial migrant of swamps and rank grass in Indonesia, New Guinea, Australia and islands of Indian and western Pacific oceans. **Similar species:** Lewin's Rail has longer bill, no eyebrow or breast band, and is rarer.

Black-tailed Native-Hen

Gallinula ventralis (Rallidae) 35 cm/14 in.
Bantamlike waterbird with cocked, fan-shaped tail. Upperparts dark olive-brown, head and underparts dark blue-gray with white spots on flanks, black tail. Bill green with orange base, legs red. Runs rapidly with tail depressed. Often in large flocks. Call a sharp "kek" or low cackle. Range and habitat: au. Abundant breeding visitor to ephemeral wetlands of inland Australia; highly irruptive and nomadic, following rains and dispersing coastward when wetlands dry out. Similar species: Dusky Moorhen and Purple Swamphen have red bills and white undertails; Coot (see p 154).

Brolga

Grus rubicunda (Gruidae) 140 cm/55 in.
Large gray crane. Crown gray; face and band around nape scarlet, with gray ears; black dewlap under chin. Legs dark gray-brown to black. Performs bowing and leaping "dances." Flies slowly with neck extended, shallow flicking beats; soars well. Call a wild gurgling and trumpeting. **Range and habitat:** AU. Common breeding resident of shallow freshwater wetlands in northern Australia; uncommon and declining in the south. **Similar species:** Sarus Crane (see p 246) has more extensive red on head and upper neck, no dewlap, pink legs.

Brown Falcon

New Zealand Falcon

Australian Kestrel (female)

Malleefowl

Australian Brush-Turkey

Stubble Quail

Little Button-Quail

Black-tailed Native-Hen

Buff-banded Rail

Brolga (immature)

Australian Bustard

Choriotis australis (Otididae) 75–100 cm/29–39 in.
Large, heavily built ground bird with long neck and legs. Crown black, neck white finely vermiculated gray. Upperparts brown, with black and white chequering near bend of wing. Underparts white to pale gray with narrow black breast band. Stalks imperiously with bill uptilted, sometimes "freezes" in cryptic stance. Flight powerful and heavy with flicking beats, neck extended. Call a resonant grunting or croaking; in display male gives guttural roar with neck feathers fanned, tail raised. **Range and habitat:** AU. Uncommon nomad of plains and dry woodland in northern and inland Australia, now rare in south. **Similar species:** none in AU.

SHOREBIRDS, GULLS AND AUKS Charadriiformes

Comb-crested Jacana

Irediparra gallinacea (Jacanidae) 23 cm/9 in.
Small waterbird with very long, thin toes. Upperparts brown, underparts white with broad black breast band. Distinctive red chickenlike comb on head; face and throat buff. Immature duller, lacks comb and breast band. Walks on waterlilies and other floating vegetation without sinking. Flight low and fluttering, with long toes trailing. Call a weak piping whistle. **Range and habitat:** OR, AU. Common resident or nomad of freshwater wetlands with floating vegetation in Indonesia, New Guinea and Australia. **Similar species:** none in AU; other jacanas in OR (see p 248).

Bush Thick-Knee

Burhinus magnirostris (Burhinidae) 55 cm/22 in.
Large, long-legged ground bird with large yellow eyes. Upperparts mottled gray with pale shoulders. White eyebrow, forehead and throat. Underparts buff with dark streaks. Active at night; during day usually squats in cryptic posture, but if disturbed walks with stiff-legged gait or flies with stiff-winged, shallow beats, showing white patches in wings. Call a mournful wailing "wee-loo" repeated to crescendo, then wavering and dying away. **Range and habitat:** AU. Common resident or nomad of open forest to woodland (even in urban areas) with abundant ground litter in northern Australia and New Guinea; rare and declining in south, extinct in Tasmania.

Sooty Oystercatcher

Haematopus fuliginosus (Haematopodidae) 50 cm/20 in.
Robust, all-black shorebird with long red bill, red eye-ring, red legs. Clambers expertly over wave-washed rocks. Call a melodious piping "pip-peep" and longer series of notes. **Range and habitat:** AU. Uncommon resident of rocky shores, reefs and islands of Australian coastline. **Similar species:** Variable Oystercatcher of New Zealand almost identical in all dark plumage.

Wrybill

Anarhynchus frontalis (Charadriidae) 20 cm/8 in.
Small, squat gray and white plover with slender bill turned to the right at the tip. Head and upperparts gray, underparts white. In breeding plumage has white forehead and eyebrow, bordered by thin black line on forehead, and black breast band. Forms flocks and coordinated mass flights in autumn and winter. Call a short clear "weet," short harsh note or rhythmic churring. **Range and habitat:** AU. Uncommon breeder on shingle of large river-beds in South Island of New Zealand. Declining along many rivers due to predation by exotic mammals and disturbance by humans. Migrates in winter to open seashores of North Island. **Similar species:** migratory Charadrius plovers in nonbreeding plumage (see pp 62, 110, 156, 200).

Banded Lapwing

Vanellus tricolor (Charadriidae) 28 cm/11 in.
Large, boldly patterned plover of dry land. Upperparts soft brown with black cap, white stripe from eye to nape. Underparts white, with broad V-shaped black breast band extending up neck to face. Small red wattles on forehead. Flies with shallow, stiff-winged beats showing broad white band in wings. Call a strident but plaintive series of 3 or 4 high-pitched notes, slightly descending. **Range and habitat:** AU. Common resident or nomad of dry grassland and bare plains in Australia. **Similar species:** larger Masked Plover lacks breast band, has large

Red-kneed Dotterel

Erythrogonys cinctus (Charadriidae) 18 cm/7 in.
Small, boldly marked plover with dumpy, front-heavy appearance and long legs. Upperparts brown with black cap. Underparts white with broad black breast band, chestnut flanks. Bill red, knees red on otherwise dark legs. Juvenile duller and browner, without breast band or colored flanks. Sometimes wades. In flight shows white edges to tail, broad white trailing edge to wings. Call a liquid "wit-wit" or low trilling. **Range and habitat:** AU. Common resident or nomad on margins of shallow wetlands in Australia and New Guinea. **Similar species:** more slender Black-fronted Plover has brown cap, white eyebrow, narrower breast band, white flanks.

Red-capped Plover

Charadrius ruficapillus (Charadriidae) 15 cm/6 in.
Small, pale plover of sandy areas. Upperparts fawn, with rufous cap and half-collar, white forehead bordered black. Underparts white. Juvenile lacks rufous cap. Flight rapid and darting, showing narrow white wing-bar. Call a sharp "wit" or trill. **Range and habitat:** AU, OR. Common resident or nomad of margins of saline wetlands and beaches in Australia; breeds Timor, vagrant elsewhere in Indonesia, vagrant to New Zealand. **Similar species:** migratory Charadrius plovers in nonbreeding plumage, especially Kentish Plover (both species may co-occur in northern Australia and Lesser Sundas).

Inland Dotterel

Peltohyas australis (Charadriidae) 20 cm/8 in.
Small, sandy plover of dry country. Upperparts mottled brown, with black bar across crown to below eyes. Underparts fawn with chestnut belly, Y-shaped black breast band from nape to center of belly. Juvenile lacks black markings. Turns back to intruder, bobs head. Flight low and swift on long wings, showing buff upperwing patches. Call is a single metallic note or trill. **Range and habitat:** AU. Uncommon nomad of stony plains and bare ground in inland Australia. **Similar species:** Plains Wanderer is more quail-like, lacks black markings.

Banded Stilt

Cladorhynchus leucocephalus (Recurvirostridae) 41 cm/16 in.
Elegant brown and white wading bird with needlelike bill, long legs. White with blackish brown wings, chestnut breast band extending into black line along belly. Legs pink. Juvenile has no breast band. Broad white trailing edge to wings in flight. Swims; occurs in large flocks. Call is a puppylike yapping. **Range and habitat:** AU. Locally abundant nomad of saline wetlands, salt works and estuaries in inland and southern Australia. Highly irruptive, breeding in large colonies when inland salt lakes fill. **Similar species:** Black-winged Stilt, Red-necked Avocet (see p 156, 296).

Black Stilt

Himantopus novaezealandiae (Recurvirostridae) 38 cm/15 in.
Medium-sized, slender, all-black wader with needlelike bill, long pink legs. Upperparts glossed green. Juvenile white or mottled on head and underparts. In flight, long legs trail beyond tail. Call a puppylike yapping. **Range and habitat:** AU. Rare and highly endangered resident of dry shingle-beds and adjacent swamps in South Island, New Zealand. Under 100 birds remain. Hybridization with Black-winged Stilt could eliminate the species. Also suffers predation from exotic mammals. Some winter dispersal northward within New Zealand. **Similar species:** Black-winged Stilt; Sooty Oystercatcher is dumpier with stout red bill (see p 156).

Australian Bustard

Bush Thick-Knee

Inland Dotterel

Sooty Oystercatcher

Wrybill

Banded Lapwing

Red-kneed Dotterel

Red-capped Plover

Comb-crested Jacana

Banded Stilt

Black Stilt

Red-necked Avocet

Recurvirostra novaehollandiae (**Recurvirostridae**) 43 cm/17 in.
Elegant pied wading bird with long, slender upturned bill, long legs. White with dark chestnut head and neck, broad black bands in wings. White ring round eye. Legs blue-gray, partially webbed. Juvenile duller and paler. Legs extend beyond tail in floppy flight. Call a liquid "toot-toot," also yelps and wheezes. Gregarious. Swims or wades, sweeps beak from side to side, taking prey from surface of water or mud. **Range and habitat:** AU. Widespread and locally abundant nomad of shallow saline and freshwater wetlands in Australia. Breeds in Lake Eyre in vast numbers, when it fills. Vagrant to New Zealand. **Similar species:** Banded Stilt (see p 294).

Australian Pratincole

Stiltia Isabella (**Glareolidae**) 23 cm/9 in.
Elegant dry-country "wader" with very long wings, short unforked tail, long legs. Orange-buff head, breast and back, with black eye stripe and wing tips, dark chestnut belly patch, white undertail. Tail square, white with black tip, white rump. Bill red with black tip. Juvenile duller, more mottled, all-black beak. Stands erect, runs gracefully, bobs head, teeters rear end. Wings extend well beyond tail. Flight swift, erratic and graceful, swallowlike or ternlike. Call is a plaintive chirrup. **Range and habitat:** OR, AU. Common breeding migrant to lagoon edges and open plains near water in eastern, inland and northern Australia; occasionally near south coast in fields; winters in northern Australia, New Guinea and Indonesia. **Similar species:** Oriental Pratincole has a forked tail.

Snowy Sheathbill

Chionis alba (**Chionidae**) 41 cm/16 in.
Plump all-white gull-like bird with short, stout, pinkish yellow bill with dark tip, hard sheath over nostrils, flesh-pink warty skin on forehead and face. Feet black. Walks with a pigeonlike bobbing of head. Call a harsh, guttural caw or low muttering. Feeds on seashore or scavenges around seal and penguin colonies. **Range and habitat:** AN, oceanic and circumpolar. Common resident of seabird colonies on rocky coasts of peninsular Antarctica, South Georgia, South Orkney and Shetland Islands. Partial migrant, some birds wintering off South America. Generally not far from land. **Similar species:** Black-faced Sheathbill.

Silver Gull

Larus novaehollandiae (**Laridae**) 41 cm/16 in.
Small gray and white gull with red bill, eye-ring and legs. White with gray back and wings, black wing tips with white leading edge and white spots on trailing edge. Some African birds have faint lavender collar. Immature mottled brown on wings, with brown bill, eyes and legs. Call a variety of harsh, raucous notes, short and sharp or prolonged. Gregarious, colonial. **Range and habitat:** AF, AU, PA. Abundant and increasing resident or nomad of beaches, coastal and inland waters, parks, airfields, cricket pitches and rubbish dumps in southern Africa, Australia, islands in south-west Pacific. Breeding on islands, occasionally near freshwater, salt lakes. **Similar species:** Gray-headed Gull (see p 202); immature is like Black-billed Gull of New Zealand, which has more white in wing tips and thinner bills, and is more associated with freshwater.

Kelp Gull

Larus dominicanus (**Laridae**) 58 cm/23 in.
Large black and white gull with slender yellow bill. White with black back and wings, broad white hind border to wings and row of white spots along wing tips. No or slight black band on tail. Bill has red spot on lower mandible only. Juvenile mottled brown, with black bill. Call a prolonged yelping. **Range and habitat:** Circumpolar. Common resident of temperate, coastal and inland waters, rubbish dumps and farmland in AF, NT, AU, subantarctic islands; increasing in AU after colonising about 50 years ago. **Similar species:** Pacific Gull, other black-backed gulls elsewhere (see p 162).

Pacific Gull

Larus pacificus (**Laridae**) 63 cm/25 in.
Large black and white gull with massive bill. White with black back and wings, black band near tail tip, narrow white hind border to wings, no white spots on wing tips. Deep yellow bill with prominent red tips on both mandibles. Juvenile brown, mottled on back and wings, with pink-based bill. Call is a deep barking "owk-owk," or "kiaw." Strictly marine, may follow ships. **Range and habitat:** AU. Uncommon resident of coastal waters in southern Australia, perhaps declining. Breeds on offshore islands in small colonies. **Similar species:** Kelp Gull.

Antarctic Skua

Catharacta antarctica (**Stercorariidae**) 58 cm/23 in.
Large, heavily built, brown gull-like seabird with conspicuous white patches at primary bases, visible in flight. Central tail feathers project slightly. Upperparts uniform dark brown, with some light streaking. Underparts variable, dark to pale brown. Bill strongly hooked. Flight swift and powerful on broad, pointed wings. Predatory and piratical, chasing other seabirds. Scavenges, follows ships. Call a gull-like barking. Sometimes treated as a subspecies of the Great Skua (see p 160). **Range and habitat:** oceanic and circumpolar; breeds on southern oceanic islands and on the Antarctic peninsula. Winter visitor to all southern continents and into north Pacific ocean. **Similar species:** Great (see p 160) and South Polar Skuas, juvenile Pacific and Kelp (or Southern Black-backed) Gulls.

Antarctic Tern

Sterna vittata (**Laridae**) 38 cm/15 in.
Medium-sized marine tern with long tail streamers. Breeding plumage gray with black cap, white cheek stripe, rump and tail, red bill and feet. Nonbreeding birds have white forehead, mottled crown, paler underparts, dark bill and feet. Immature mottled, with white underparts. Flight graceful and undulating, often hovers. Call a shrill, high-pitched chatter or rattle. **Range and habitat:** oceanic and circumpolar. Common breeder on Antarctica, antarctic and subantarctic islands, also small islands near New Zealand, some winter movement northward to temperate waters. **Similar species:** many other terns, especially nonbreeding Arctic Tern (see p 162); Kerguelen Tern is darker gray, with gray tail.

Sooty Tern

Sterna fuscata (**Laridae**) 43 cm/17 in.
Medium-sized, pied marine tern. Upperparts blackish brown with white forehead and outer edges to forked tail, underparts white. Juvenile dark brown with pale spots on upperparts, pale underwings, white undertail. Flight graceful, buoyant and swooping; soars. Flocks skim and dip to water surface, often far from land. Occasionally feeds at night. Call a high-pitched, nasal "ker-wack-wack." Sometimes in huge colonies. **Range and habitat:** oceanic and pantropical. Breeds on islands in Atlantic, Indian and Pacific oceans off equatorial AF, OR, AU, eastern NT and NA. **Similar species:** Bridled Tern has more extensive white forehead, noddies; Gray-backed Tern has white eyebrows, grayer upperparts.

Black Noddy

Anous minutus (**Laridae**) 35 cm/14 in.
Small, dark brown seabird with white cap, black face, white crescent below eye, slender bill, short forked tail. Flight swift and erratic, low over water, dips to surface. May patter feet on surface. Generally close to shore. Often in large flocks. Call is a querulous, rattling "kirr," cackling "krik-krik-krik." Range and habitat: tropical coastal seas of au, pa and nt, breeding on islands in equatorial Pacific and western Atlantic oceans. Similar species: other noddies, juvenile Sooty Tern.

Red-necked Avocet

Australian Pratincole (juvenile)

Snowy Sheathbill

Silver Gull

Kelp Gull

Pacific Gull

Antarctic Skua

Black Noddy

Antarctic Tern

Sooty Tern

PIGEONS Columbiformes

New Zealand Pigeon

Hemiphaga novaeseelandiae (Columbidae) 51 cm/20 in.
Large, brightly colored fruit-pigeon, only native pigeon in New Zealand. Upperparts and breast iridescent green, bronze and purple, sometimes with blue-gray cast in certain lights. Underparts white. Eye, bill and feet red. Much swishing and clapping of wings as birds fly or move about tree-branches. Call a soft, penetrating coo. **Range and habitat:** AU. Common resident of forest and exotic fruiting trees and shrubs in New Zealand. **Similar species:** none in New Zealand.

Rose-crowned Fruit-Dove

Ptilinopus regina (Columbidae) 22 cm/8½ in.
Small, brightly colored pigeon of the forest canopy. Upperparts bright green, with rose-pink cap bordered yellow, gray nape, broad yellow tail tip. Throat and breast blue-gray, spotted white, with lilac patch on lower breast, belly and undertail orange. Female duller than male. Juvenile green with mottled yellow belly. Difficult to see; detection aided by falling fruits, rapid flight with whistling wings. Call is a double coo, and a long series of accelerating "hoo" notes. **Range and habitat:** AU. Common resident and partial migrant of tropical and subtropical rainforest in north-western and north-eastern Australia to mid-New South Wales, vagrant further south, eastern Indonesia and New Guinea. **Similar species:** other *Ptilinopus* fruit-doves.

Pink-spotted Fruit-Dove

Ptilinopus perlatus (Columbidae) 26 cm/10 in.
Medium-sized, brightly colored pigeon of the forest canopy. Upperparts bright green, with pink spots on shoulders, gray tail tip. Head all-gray or yellow-brown with gray collar, brown breast band. Underparts olive-green. Gregarious. Call is an accelerating, rising and falling series of "hoo" notes, or a series of coos alternating in pitch. **Range and habitat:** AO. Common nomad of rainforest and edge in New Guinea and satellite islands. **Similar species:** Ornate Fruit-Dove. **Not illustrated.**

White-bibbed Fruit-Dove

Ptilinopus rivoli (Columbidae) 25 cm/10 in.
Medium-sized, brightly colored pigeon of the forest canopy. Green with purple cap and belly, white breast band with yellow wash. Female green with yellow undertail. Island males have yellow belly and undertail. Solitary and inactive. Call is an accelerating and descending series of "hoo" notes, and single or repeated "hoo" notes. Range and habitat: au. Common nomad of hill and montane rainforest in New Guinea and satellite islands. Similar species: other *Ptilinopus* fruit-doves. **Not illustrated.**

Ornate Fruit-Dove

Ptilinops ornatus (Columbidae) 26 cm/10 in.
Medium-sized, brightly colored pigeon of the forest canopy. Upperparts bright green, with purple and gray shoulder patch, yellow tail tip. Head yellow-brown or purple with gray collar, brown breast band, olive-green underparts. Gregarious. Call is a series of ascending "hoo" notes, or a series of coos alternating in pitch. Range and habitat: au. Common nomad of rainforest and moss forest in New Guinea. Similar species: Pink-spotted Fruit-Dove. **Not illustrated.**

Wompoo Fruit-Dove

Ptilinopus magnificus (Columbidae) 30–40 cm/12–16 in.
Large, brightly colored, long-tailed pigeon of the forest canopy and subcanopy. Upperparts green with blue-gray head, yellow shoulder flash, orange-red bill. Throat and breast purple, belly and undertail yellow. Difficult to see; detection aided by falling fruits, calls. Flies swiftly, low to canopy, showing yellow in underwings. Call a deep, resonant far-carrying, "wom-poo" or "wollack-a-woo." Has declined in southern part of range due to loss of rainforest. **Range and habitat:** AU. Uncommon resident or partial migrant of tropical and subtropical rainforest in north-east Australia to central New South Wales, New Guinea and satellite islands. **Similar species:** none in AU.

Peaceful Dove

Geopelia placida (Columbidae) 22 cm/8½ in.
Tiny long-tailed dove. Upperparts gray-brown, barred darker. Head and breast finely barred gray and white, belly pale fawn. Pale blue-gray eye-ring. Feeds on ground. Flight rapid and undulating, with whistling wings; appears gray with white fringes to tail. Call is a melodious coo "doodle-doo" and low rattle. **Range and habitat:** OR, AU. Common resident of woodland in South-East Asia, New Guinea and satellite islands, north and east Australia. Has declined in some areas. Introduced Hawaii. **Similar species:** Diamond Dove.

Diamond Dove

Geopelia cuneata (Columbidae) 20 cm/8 in.
Tiny long-tailed dove. Upperparts gray-brown with white spots on wings, red eye-ring. Head and breast blue-gray, belly white. Juvenile browner, upperparts barred. Flight rapid and undulating, with whistling wings; shows rufous in spread flight feathers. Call is a soft, mournful cooing. Feeds on grass seeds on ground. Visits desert water holes. **Range and habitat:** AU. Common nomad of dry woodland in Australia. **Similar species:** Peaceful Dove.

Common Bronzewing

Phaps chalcoptera (Columbidae) 32 cm/13 in.
Medium-sized, plump, brown pigeon with pale forehead and chin, iridescent patch on wings. Upperparts brown with cream forehead, lilac neck, bronze-green bands on wings. Underparts pinkish fawn. Female, immature duller, browner. Feeds on ground, inconspicuously, then rockets up noisily. Often seen along roadsides in early morning. Flight swift and direct, showing buff in spread flight feathers. Call is a resonant "oom," repeated. **Range and habitat:** AU. Common resident of open forest and woodland with moderate understorey, occasionally farmland, crops, throughout Australia. **Similar species:** Brush Bronzewing is more blue-gray and chestnut with buff forehead, chestnut throat, rufous in spread flight feathers.

Crested Pigeon

Ocyphaps lophotes (Columbidae) 31–5 cm/12–14 in.
Medium-sized, pinkish gray pigeon with conspicuous vertical crest. Gray head, brownish gray back, light gray beneath, pink on sides of neck and breast. Wings barred with black, prominent green or purple patches. Eye-ring and legs red. Tall pointed crest is black. Longer tail than other crested pigeons in Australia. Raises tail on landing. Rapid flight makes loud whistling noise. Simple, low, soft cooing. In pairs or small flocks, often in farmland, along roads. Feeds on ground on seeds, green leaves and insects. **Range and habitat:** open habitats in most of Australia, except for forested coastal areas, has extended range with forest clearing.

Wonga Pigeon

Leucosarcia melanoleuca (Columbidae) 37 cm/15 in.
Large gray and white ground pigeon. Upper-parts blue-gray with white forehead. Breast blue-gray with V-shaped band of white, belly and undertail white spotted black. Bill and feet red. Feeds on seeds on ground in cover. Flies suddenly with very loud clatter of wings, lands on tree-branch with back to observer. Call a fast, penetrating, monotonous "wonk-wonk-wonk..." repeated for long periods. **Range and habitat:** AU. Common resident of dense, damp forest, or edge of rainforest in Australia from central Queensland to eastern Victoria.

New Zealand Pigeon

Rose-crowned Fruit-Dove

Wompoo Fruit-Dove

Peaceful Dove

Diamond Dove

Crested Pigeon

Common Bronzewing

Wonga Pigeon

PARROTS AND ALLIES Psittaciformes

Kea

Nestor notabilis (Psittacidae) 46 cm/18 in.
Large, short-tailed gray-green parrot with slender, elongated upper mandible. Scaly olive-green with red underwing patches, dull red rump. Inquisitive and approachable, attracted to humans and buildings. Call is a loud screech "keaa" given in flight. Normally feeds on plant material, but occasionally on carrion. May damage property, e.g. car windscreeen wipers. **Range and habitat:** AU. Common resident of mountain forests, scrub and alpine grassland on South Island, New Zealand. **Similar species:** Kaka.

Kaka

Nestor meridionalis (Psittacidae) 45 cm/18 in.
Large, short-tailed bronze-brown parrot with heavy bill. Scaly olive-brown to olive-green with red collar, rump, belly and underwings, pale crown, orange cheek patch. Flies low and fast through bush or high in the air, showing large head and bill. Call is a harsh "ka-aa" or ringing, musical whistle, given in flight. Tears up rotten wood in search of insects. **Range and habitat:** AU. Uncommon resident of native forest in New Zealand. Can be seen at Karori Sanctuary in Wellington. **Similar species:** Kea.

Red-tailed Black-Cockatoo

Calyptorhynchus banksii (Cacatuidae) 50–63 cm/20–5 in.
Large black cockatoo with red or orange in tail. Male black with large crest, broad scarlet band in tail. Female spotted yellow on head and barred yellow on breast, with fine black bars across orange tail band, white bill. Flight slow and labored, showing long wings and tail. Gregarious, wary. Call is a grating, discordant metallic screech. **Range and habitat:** AU. Common, but patchily distributed, resident of open forest, woodland, semiarid scrub in Australia. Subspecies in south-eastern Australia is endangered due to loss of buloke (Casuarina) woodlands. **Similar species:** smaller, tamer Glossy Cockatoo is duller with shorter crest, more bulbous bill; female has yellow blotches on head but little or no yellow spotting and barring, gray bill. It occurs in sheoak woodland near east coast.

Galah

Cacatua roseicapillus (Cacatuidae) 36 cm(14 in.
Small pink and gray cockatoo. Crest pale pink, head and underpays deep rose-pink. Upperparts gray, paler on rump. Byes brown in male, pink in female. Commonest cockatoo in southern Australia, gathers in large, noisy, wheeling flocks. Flies strongly with deep, rhythmic beats. Call is a shrill disyllabic screech, also harsh alarm squawks. **Range and habitat:** AU. Abundant resident or nomad of most open habitats, including parks and towns, in Australia; increasing and has spread with clearing of forests near coast. Sometimes a pest in crops. **Similar species:** Gang-gang Cockatoo is darker, all-gray with red head in males.

Little Corella

Cacatua sanguinea (Cacatuidae) 37 cm/15 in.
Small white cockatoo with short pale bill, short white crest, pink face. Bulbous blue-gray skin around and below eye, yellow wash on underwings and undertail. Gregarious, forms large, noisy wheeling flocks, often in crops. Flight strong and direct. Call is a wavering 2-note cry, harsh alarm shrieks. **Range and habitat:** AU. Abundant resident or nomad of woodland, open plains and farmland in Australia and New Guinea; increasing. **Similar species:** Long-billed Corella has pink forehead and throat, long upper mandible, Western (Muir's) Corella in south western Australia also has long mandible, larger Sulfur-crested Cockatoo has long yellow crest.

Major Mitchell's Cockatoo

Cacatua leadbeateri (Cacatuidae) 36 cm/14 in.
Pink and white cockatoo with multicolored crest. Upperparts white, head and underparts salmon pink. Long, filamentous crest shows bands of red and yellow when raised. Eyes brown in male, pink in female. Flight is a hesitant, shallow flapping and gliding, showing pink underwings. Call is a plaintive chuckling cry, harsh alarm screeches. Usually in smaller flocks than other cockatoos. **Range and habitat:** AU. Uncommon resident of woodland and plains in inland Australia.

Declining locally. **Similar species:** corellas; larger Sulfur-crested Cockatoo is all-white with yellow crest; Galah which has gray back, but is pale in Western Australia.

Rainbow Lorikeet

Trichoglossus haematodus (Loridae) 28 cm/11 in.
Medium-sized, spectacularly colored lory with long pointed tail. Upperparts bright green with blue head, yellow collar. Breast orange, belly blue, undertail yellow-green. Bill red. Gregarious, forming noisy flocks, among flowering eucalypts and other nectar-bearing trees and shrubs. Flight swift and whirring, showing yellow band across wing. Call a rolling or discordant screech, mellow whistle. **Range and habitat:** AU, PA. Abundant nomad or partial migrant of open forest, woodland, orchards and towns in eastern Indonesia, New Guinea, northern and eastern Australia and western Pacific islands. **Similar species:** Red-collared Lorikeet (probably a geographical race) has orange collar, blue nape, blue-black belly; Scaly-breasted Lorikeet is green with yellow scalloping on breast, red underwings.

Dusky Lory

Pseudeos fuscata (Loridae) 25 cm/10 in.
Medium-sized, short-tailed, dull lory sometimes appearing all-dark. Scaly brown with orange cap, bill, breast and belly patches, white rump. Yellow and orange in underwings and tail. Gregarious and vocal, forming huge communal roosts. Call a loud, harsh grating screech. **Range and habitat:** AU. Abundant nomad or migrant of forest, edge and plantations in New Guinea. **Similar species:** Rainbow Lorikeet; Duyvenbode's Lory is larger with black bill, longer tail.

Goldie's Lorikeet

Psitteuteles goldiei (Loridae) 19 cm/7½ in.
Small green lory with long tail. Upperparts green, underparts yellower with dark green streaks. Cap red, face purple with blue streaks. Yellow band through flight feathers. Flight rapid with backswept wings, pointed tail. Gregarious. Call a high-pitched shriek. **Range and habitat:** AU. Common nomad of montane forest in New Guinea. **Similar species:** Striated Lorikeet is darker, lacking red and purple on head.

Papuan King-Parrot

Alisterus chloropterus (Psittacidae) 38 cm/15 in.
Large, brightly colored, long-tailed parrot. Head and underparts red, upperparts green with blue nape and rump, yellow-green shoulder flash, black tail. Female and juvenile have green head, no shoulder flash. Flight agile and graceful with deep wing-beats. Call a sharp, metallic "keek" in flight or a high-pitched, longer whistling note "eeek" repeated when perched. **Range and habitat:** AU. Common resident of forest in New Guinea.

Red-winged Parrot

Aprosmictus erythropterus (Psittacidae) 32 cm/13 in.
Medium-sized green parrot with red wing flashes. Male bright green with black back, blue rump, red bill and shoulders. Female and juvenile duller, greener, with smaller red shoulder patches. Tail moderately long, square, with yellow tip. Strong, erratic flight on long wings, with deep, leisurely beats. Feeds on fruit and seeds of trees, sometimes on ground and in crops. Usually pairs or small flocks. Call a sharp, metallic "kik" in flight, or rolling "crillik." **Range and habitat:** AU. Common resident or nomad of woodland and mangroves in northern and eastern Australia to central New South Wales and southern New Guinea. **Similar species:** Superb Parrot is green with long pointed tail, yellow and red throat in males; Australian King Parrot is red below, has long dark tail.

Kea

Kaka

Red-tailed Black-Cockatoo

Galah

Little Corella

Major Mitchell's Cockatoo

Rainbow Lorikeet

Dusky Lory

Red-winged Parrot

Goldie's Lorikeet

Papuan King-Parrot

Cockatiel

Cockatiel

Nymphicus hollandicus (**Cacatuidae**) 32 cm/13 in.
Tiny, long-tailed cockatoo. Gray with yellow face and crest, orange ear patches, white shoulders. Female duller, tail finely barred, outer tail feathers yellow. Flight strong but erratic, with leisurely beats, showing pointed wings and long pointed tail. Call a rolling, upslurred "queel," softer plaintive wavering notes. **Range and habitat:** AU. Common migrant within Australia, moving north in autumn and south in spring, in woodland, farmland and plains.

Budgerigar

Melopsittacus undulatus (**Psittacidae**) 18 cm/7 in.
Tiny green and yellow parrot with long, pointed tail. Head yellow finely barred black, with black and blue spots on cheeks. Back and wings barred yellow, green and black. Rump and underparts green, tail blue. Cere blue in male, brown or pale blue in female. Flight rapid, whirring and undulating, showing yellow bands in wings and tail. Forms noisy, wheeling flocks. Call a warbling and chirruping, harsh scolding and alarm screeches. **Range and habitat:** AU. Abundant nomad or migrant of dry woodlands and grasslands in inland Australia, generally avoiding forested and coastal areas. Often in large flocks. Breeds prolifically after rain.

Crimson Rosella

Platycercus elegans (**Psittacidae**) 35 cm/14 in.
Medium-sized, long-tailed red and blue parrot. Rich red with blue cheeks, wings and tail, black scalloping on back. Juvenile green with red on forehead, breast and undertail. Geographical races vary in color: "Yellow Rosella" is yellow with tiny red patch on forehead, "Adelaide Rosella" is orange to brick red. Flight undulating. 3-note belllike whistle, middle note highest, and harsh alarm notes. **Range and habitat:** AU. Common resident of forest and woodland in eastern and southern Australia. Yellow Rosella is found along River Murray and Murrumbidgee. **Similar species:** Australian King Parrot is larger and greener, lacks blue cheeks.

Mulga Parrot

Psephotus varius (**Psittacidae**) 28 cm/11 in.
Small, brightly colored parrot with long tail. Male bright green with blue wings and tail, red nape, belly and rump patches, yellow forehead, shoulder and undertail. Female duller, with red shoulder. Flight low and undulating. Short, soft whistling notes. **Range and habitat:** AU. Uncommon resident of woodland in inland Australia. **Similar species:** Red-rumped Parrot is more simply colored, green and yellow with red rump; female is dull green without patches of color.

Bourke's Parrot

Neopsephotus bourkii (**Psittacidae**) 19 cm/7½ in.
Very small, softly colored parrot with long tail. Upperparts brown with blue forehead and wing edges, cream scalloping on wings. Underparts pink, undertail pale blue. Female and juvenile lack blue forehead. Flight low and fluttering, showing white edges to tail. Call is a chirrup, soft twitter or shrill alarm note. **Range and habitat:** AU. Uncommon resident or nomad of dry woodland and scrub in inland Australia. **Similar species:** Diamond Dove (see p 298).

CUCKOOS AND ALLIES Cuculiformes

Pallid Cuckoo

Cuculus pallidus (**Cuculidae**) 33 cm/13 in.
Medium-sized gray cuckoo with long, barred tail. Upper-parts gray with yellow eye-ring, pale eyebrow and nape, black eye stripe. Underparts pale gray. Juvenile mottled and barred black and white, immature mottled brown and buff. Perches in exposed positions with tail drooping. Flight undulating on pointed wings, flicks tail on alighting. Call a series of whistles ascending in semitones by male, harsh single whistle by female. **Range and habitat:** AU. Common resident and migrant of woodland and scattered trees in farmland in Australia; occasionally Timor, New Guinea. **Similar species:** Oriental Cuckoo, which has barred belly (see p 252).

Horsfield's Bronze Cuckoo

Chalcites basalts (**Cuculidae**) 17 cm/6½ in.
Tiny, glossy cuckoo with barred underparts. Upperparts dull bronze-green with white eyebrow, dark stripe through eye and ear;

rufous in spread tail. Underparts and undertail boldly barred brown and white, bars broken on belly. Juvenile duller, less barred. Flight rapid and undulating on pointed wings, showing white wing-bar. Call a high-pitched, descending whistle "see-oo," sparrowlike chirrup. **Range and habitat:** OR, AU, PA. Common resident or partial migrant of open forest and woodland in Australia; some birds winter in New Guinea, Indonesia and islands in eastern Indian ocean. **Similar species:** other bronze cuckoos. **Not illustrated.**

Koel

Eudynamys scolopacea (**Cuculidae**) 39–46 cm/15–18 in.
Large, long-tailed cuckoo. Male all-black with red eye, pale (AU) or green bill (OR). Female brown, barred and spotted buff and white; head rufous (New Guinea) or black (Australia) with white cheek stripe, finely barred underparts, heavily barred tail. Juvenile mottled rusty brown and buff, barred black. Flight shallow and fluttering. Far-carrying call a shrill "coo-ee" and rollicking notes by male, sometimes at night, series of piercing whistles by female. **Range and habitat:** OR, AU, PA. Common resident and migrant in India, east Asia, New Guinea, eastern and northern Australia, western Pacific islands. Southern birds winter in islands north of Australia. **Similar species:** Long-tailed Koel (AU, PA) is streaked on head and underparts.

Pheasant Coucal

Centropus phasianinus (**Cuculidae**) 60–80 cm/24–31 in.
Huge, ungainly ground cuckoo with barred plumage, long tail. In breeding plumage head and underparts black, upperparts rusty brown finely barred black and white, streaked cream, tail barred. In nonbreeding plumage head and underparts rusty with cream streaks. Byes red. Flight low and labored on short, rounded wings, tail fanning. Call a series of rapid, resonant hoots, falling then rising; also sharp, hissing alarm notes. **Range and habitat:** AU. Common resident of thick undergrowth in forest, woodland, farmland, swamps in Timor, New Guinea and eastern and northern Australia. **Similar species:** immature Greater and Lesser Coucals.

Brush Cuckoo

Cacomantis variolosus (**Cuculidae**) 23 cm/9 in.
Small, dull cuckoo. Head and eye-ring gray, upper-parts gray-brown. Breast buff, belly and undertail pale rufous. Juvenile richly mottled and barred brown and rufous, paler on underparts. Flight rapid and undulating on pointed wings, showing pale wing-bar and barred tail. Call a mournful series of downslurred whistles descending by semitones; urgent series of 3-note whistles, phrase repeated at increasing pitch; single loud, tremulous whistle. **Range and habitat:** OR, AU, PA. Common resident and migrant of forest and woodland in South-East Asia, New Guinea and Australia; southern birds winter in tropics. **Similar species:** Plaintive Cuckoo, Banded Bay Cuckoo in OR (see p 252); Fan-tailed Cuckoo has yellow eye-ring, more tapered tail and orange breast.

Greater Coucal

Centropus menbecki (**Cuculidae**) 64 cm/25 in.
Huge, pheasantlike ground cuckoo with stout, arched bill. All-black with short wings, long broad tail, pale bill, red eyes. Immature has barred tail. Secretive in dense vegetation, where it hops clumsily. Flies infrequently and heavily on rounded wings. Call a deep series of descending hooting notes, also croaks and rattles. **Range and habitat:** AU. Common resident of undergrowth in forest and edge in New Guinea and satellite islands. **Similar species:** smaller Lesser Coucal has dark eye and bill, immature barred brown. **Not illustrated.**

Cockatiel

Crimson Rosella

Budgerigar

Bourke's Parrot

Mulga Parrot

Pallid Cuckoo

Koel

Pheasant Coucal

Brush Cuckoo

OWLS Strigiformes

Boobook Owl

Ninox novaeseelandiae (**Strigidae**) 25–35 cm/10–14 in.
Small brown hawklike owl. Dark to light brown with white spots on wings, barred wings and tail. Under-parts streaked, marbled or spotted white on brown or rufous. "Mask" of dark eye patches on white face. Juvenile has downy white underparts, faintly streaked. Eyes gray-green or yellow. Falsetto double hoot "boo-book," 2nd note lower, and soft continuous hooting. **Range and habitat:** AU. Common resident of woodland in eastern Indonesia, New Guinea, Australia, New Zealand (sometimes considered a separate species). **Similar species:** Rufous Hawk Owl, Little Owl (see p 166); Sumba Boobook, Barking Owl.

Australian Masked-Owl

Tyto novaehollandiae (**Tytonidae**) 37–50 cm/15–20 in.
Large owl with prominent heart-shaped facial disc, feathered legs, large feet and claws. Upperparts mottled dark brown to gray-brown, speckled white, strongly barred on wings and tail. Facial disc has crisp black border, dark zone around black eyes. Considerable variation in plumage with dark, intermediate and pale morphs. Face chestnut, underparts rufous, coarsely spotted black in darkest birds; face and underparts white, breast sparsely spotted in palest birds. Very loud, deep rasping screech or shrill tremulous scream. **Range and habitat:** AU. Uncommon in forest, woodland, caves in New Guinea and Australia. Large Tasmanian race is Endangered, as is Melville Island race, other races are generally rare throughout range. **Similar species:** Barn Owl (see p 166); sooty owls.

NIGHTJARS AND ALLIES Caprimulgiformes

Tawny Frogmouth

Podargus strigoides (**Podargidae**) 34–46 cm/13–18 in.
Owl-like nocturnal bird with broad bill, large yellow eyes, weak feet, ragged tail. Large head, tuft of feathers above bill. Mottled gray, browner on shoulders; wings and tail barred. Less common rufous or brown forms. Perches by day on branches, cryptic. At night perches sluggishly, flies with quick shallow beats and long glides, appears pale. Monotonous, resonant "oom-oom-oom . . .." **Range and habitat:** AU. Common resident of forest and woodland in Australia, rare in New Guinea. **Similar species:** smaller Marbled Frogmouth has banded plumes, long tail; larger Papuan Frogmouth has red eyes, long tail, both are in rainforest.

Australian Owlet-Nightjar

Aegotheles cristatus (**Aegothelidae**) 23 cm/9 in.
Small nocturnal bird with fluttering, mothlike flight. Soft gray, finely barred, paler on belly; rufous color form occurs. Face mammal-like, with large dark eyes, black crown stripe, eye stripes and collar. Wings rounded, long tail and legs. Roosts in tree-hollows, often at entrance; if flushed, flies with undulating flight to another hole. At night active in trees, in air and on ground. Shrill, strident churring, often during the day. **Range and habitat:** AU. Common resident of forest and woodland in New Guinea and Australia. Tasmanian race is Vulnerable. **Similar species:** other owlet-nightjars.

Spotted Nightjar

Eurostopodus argus (**Caprimulgidae**) 30 cm/12 in.
Delicately mottled, well-camouflaged nocturnal bird with long wings, strong graceful flight. Mottled and spotted buff, gray and black with white throat, barred tail. Juvenile more rufous. Rounded wing tips, large white spot in wings. Roosts on ground, flies suddenly and silently. At night active in the air; red eye-shine. Call a hoarse 'haw-haw-haw, chokka-chokka-chokka" on same pitch. **Range and habitat:** AU. Open woodland in Australia; some north-south migration. Also in New Guinea, probably as a migrant from Australia. **Similar species:** White-tailed Nightjar; White-throated Nightjar has small white spot in wing, pointed wing tips.

SWIFTS AND HUMMINGBIRDS Apodiformes

Mountain Swiftlet

Aerodramus hirundinaceus (**Apodidae**) 13 cm/5 in.
Small uniform swift. Upperparts blackish brown, underparts silvery gray-brown, legs feathered. Flight rapid and fluttering, with long glides. Gregarious, flies high in the air over cave entrances. Call a rapid twittering. **Range and habitat:** AU. Montane New Guinea and satellite islands, aerial over hill and mountain forest to above treeline. **Similar species:** lowland Uniform Swiftlet has browner underparts, pale throat, unfeathered legs. **Not illustrated.**

KINGFISHERS AND ALLIES Coraciiformes

Laughing Kookaburra

Dacelo novaeguineae (**Alcedinidae**) 45 cm/18 in.
Giant brown and white kingfisher with loud "laughing" call. Head cream with brown streaks and ear patch. Upperparts brown with pale blue mottling on shoulders, rufous tail barred black. Rump pale blue in male, brown in female and juvenile. Underparts cream, faintly barred brown. Perched profile distinctive, with large head and bill, dropped tail. In flight shows white patches in wings, white tail tip; on alighting raises tail. Loud, rollicking and hooting "laughter," throaty chuckling. Lives in groups and breeds cooperatively. **Range and habitat:** AU. Common resident of forest and woodland in eastern Australia, introduced into south western Australia. **Similar species:** Blue-winged Kookaburra.

Red-backed Kingfisher

Halcyon pyrrhopygia (**Alcedinidae**) 20 cm/8 in.
Small, pale, dry-country kingfisher. Head streaked gray-green and white, with black eye stripe encircling nape, white collar. Upperparts gray-green, bluer on wings in male, with rufous rump. Underparts white. Call a single mournful whistle, or chattering and rattling. **Range and habitat:** AU. Common resident and also partial migrant of dry, open woodland in Australia; southern birds winter in northern and coastal areas. **Similar species:** Sacred Kingfisher.

Sacred Kingfisher

Halcyon sancta (**Alcedinidae**) 21 cm/8 in.
Small, bright woodland kingfisher. Upperparts glossy blue-green, bluer in male, with black eye stripe encircling nape, small buff "headlights" on forehead, buff to white collar. Underparts white to rich buff. Juvenile duller, faint buff scalloping on breast and wings. Call a strident 4-note squeak, slightly descending; also trilling, rattling and harsh scolding. **Range and habitat:** AU, PA. Common resident and migrant of open forest and woodland in eastern Indonesia, New Guinea, Australia, New Zealand, western Pacific islands. Southern birds winter in tropics. **Similar species:** Red-backed Kingfisher, White-collared Kingfisher; Forest Kingfisher has large white spot in wing.

Rainbow Bee-eater

Merops ornatus (**Meropidae**) 23–8 cm/9–11 in.
Brightly colored, with slender curved bill. Iridescent blue and green with orange nape and throat, black eye stripe and throat band, orange in wings revealed in flight. Tail black with thin, projecting central feathers. Juvenile duller, without throat band or tail wires. Flight erratic and undulating with extended wheeling glides; soars. Call a short trilling note repeated, also rippling and ticking notes. Nests in sand banks, sometimes behind beaches, and in holes in the ground. **Range and habitat:** AU. Common resident and migrant of woodland in Australia and New Guinea, southern birds winter in tropics, sometimes islands in western Pacific. **Similar species:** Blue-tailed Bee-eater (see p 256).

Boobook Owl

Australian Masked-Owl (dark phase)

Tawny Frogmouth

Australian Owlet-Nightjar

Spotted Nightjar

Sacred Kingfisher

Laughing Kookaburra

Rainbow Bee-eater

Red-backed Kingfisher

PERCHING BIRDS Passeriformes

Rifleman

Acanthisitta chloris (**Xenicidae**) 8 cm/3 in.
Tiny, with very short tail and long thin bill. Male bright yellowish green above, buff below, female browner and streaked above, pale eyebrow and wing-bars. Family parties, with immatures like female. Usually located by high-pitched call "zipt." Flicks wings while feeding by creeping along bark and moss on tree-trunks and branches. Monogamous, and cooperative, with adults and young of first broods may help to feed subsequent young. **Range and habitat:** all main islands of New Zealand, still fairly common in wide range of native forests occasionally in exotic vegetation. **Similar species:** Rock Wrens, which is above tree-line on South Island only.

Superb Lyrebird

Menura novaehollandiae (**Menuridae**) 74–98 cm/29–38 in.
Very large ground-dwelling passerine, with strong legs and feet. Usually glimpsed rushing off along the ground giving a loud "whisht" alarm call, though sometimes quite tame. Dark brown above, gray-brown below with rufous throat. Male has spectacular lyre-shaped tail, with large patterned outer feathers and fine filamentous central ones. The tail is spread and arched over the body during a courtship display on a cleared arena. Expert songster with powerful melodious phrases and complex and accurate mimicry of many other birds, and perhaps mechanical noises. Polygamous, with female caring for single young alone. **Range and habitat:** fairly common in damp forests of south-eastern Australia, even in outskirts of Sydney and Melbourne. **Similar species:** Albert's Lyrebird.

Singing Bushlark

Mirafra javanica (**Alaudidae**) 12–15 cm/4–6 in.
Rather undistinguished smallish brown bird, heavily streaked above and on breast. Rufous wing patch and deep finchlike bill help to separate it from similar species. Song is melodious, though less impressive than that of Skylark, may include mimicry, uttered in flight. Numerous subspecies, differing in color to match background, from gray to cinnamon and russet-brown. **Range and habitat:** AF, OR and AU, probably including several distinct species, fairly common in open grassland, but has also adapted well to farmland and crops. **Similar species:** other larks, and also pipits (see pp 168, 170, 218, 260).

White-backed Swallow

Cheramoeca leucosternum (**Hirundinidae**) 15 cm/6 in.
Striking black and white swallow, usually nesting colonially and roosting communally in holes in sandy banks or small cliffs. Black wings, tail and lower body, white back and breast, with grayish crown. Deeply forked tail and fluttering flight. **Range and habitat:** most of Australia, except for north and coastal areas. Typically found in open country, it originally nested in the burrows of small marsupials. These have since declined, but clearing of forests and activities related to roads and building have allowed the species to spread. Apparently not migratory but may enter torpid state in cold weather. **Not illustrated.**

Welcome Swallow

Hirundo neoxena (**Hirundinidae**) 15 cm/6 in.
A typical swallow, very like the Barn Swallow. Blue-black back, wings and tail, orange throat and forehead and white belly, but no dark breast band, very long tail streamers. A common and popular bird throughout its range, coping well with human activities. Twittering song. **Range and habitat:** eastern and southern Australia, Tasmania and New Zealand. Most habitats, except for deep in forest; nests commonly in human structures, but also in old Fairy Martin nests. **Similar species:** Barn Swallow (see p 168).

Tree Martin

Hirundo nigricans (**Hirundinidae**) 13 cm/5 in.
Glossy blue-black above and dirty white below and on rump, with tiny rufous patch on forehead. Tail barely forked. In loose groups, but gathers in larger flocks on telegraph wires and fences to migrate. Twittering call. **Range and habitat:** throughout Australia, mostly nesting south of the Tropic of Capricorn, migrating north in winter, also in New Caledonia, New Guinea and Indonesia. Common in open woodland, nesting and roosting in holes in large trees. **Similar species:** Fairy Martin.

Fairy Martin

Hirundo ariel (**Hirundinidae**) 12 cm/4½ in.
Small martin commonly seen feeding in groups along roadsides in open country. Black wings, tail and back, white underparts and rump, with rufous head. Square tail. Weak twittering call, and louder chirruping alarm call. **Range and habitat:** Australia, except Tasmania, in open habitats. Nests colonially, often with Welcome Swallow, placing its bottle-shaped mud nests under overhanging rocks and cliffs, but more typically now under bridges and road culverts. Some north-south migration. **Similar species:** Tree Martin.

Australasian Pipit

Anthus novaeseelandiae (**Motacillidae**) 17 cm/6½ in.
Large pipit, dark brown above, buff below, with heavy streaking on back and breast and pale eyebrow. Legs and beak are also pale. Some local variation in color of this widespread species. Wags tail up and down. Abrupt flight call "shreep," and monotonous song delivered from the ground or in flight. **Range and habitat:** EP, OR, AF and AU, uncommon visitor to WP. However, several distinct species may occupy this range. Common in short grassland, low heath, steppe, farmland, up to about 2,000 m (6,500 ft), also semiarid areas in Australia. **Similar species:** many larks and other pipits (see pp 168, 170, 260).

Black-faced Cuckooshrike

Coracina novaehollandiae (**Campephagidae**) 33 cm/13 in.
Smart-looking, large gray bird, with black face and upper breast and flight feathers. Juvenile has small black face patch, extending behind the eye. Small legs, rather heavy beak, dark eyes. Undulating flight, shuffles wings after landing. Call is a harsh "kaark," occasional sweeter notes. Also known as Gray Jay or Blue Jay. A sit-and-wait predator, snatching large larvae and beetles from the foliage. **Range and habitat:** AU and OR, widespread in all types of wooded country, even among scattered trees and in towns, some migration in Australia, with birds crossing Torres Strait. **Similar species:** White-bellied Cuckooshrike, Papuan Cicadabird.

Ground Cuckooshrike

Pteropodocys maxima (**Campephagidae**) 33–7 cm/13–15 in.
Largest cuckooshrike. Generally gray, with black tail and wings, lower breast, belly, rump and lower back barred dark gray. Tail slightly forked, bright yellow iris. Immature is barred all over body and has dark face and eye. Unlike other cuckooshrikes it feeds on the ground, walking like a pigeon. Flight direct. Metallic "ti-yew" call. Lives in family groups, with all birds helping to rear the young. **Range and habitat:** widespread, though rather uncommon, in dry woodland in inland Australia. Somewhat nomadic. **Similar species:** other cuckooshrikes (see p 262). **Not illustrated.**

White-winged Triller

Lalage sucrii (**Campephagidae**) 19 cm/7½ in.
The male is a striking pied bird, with black cap, back, tail and wings, clean white underparts and wing patches, and gray rump. Female gray-brown above and buff below. Male like female in nonbreeding season. Usually detected in late spring by loud trilling song, often given in an energetic song-flight. Loosely colonial, though males chase each other a lot early in breeding season. Also called Caterpillar-eater, as takes larvae snatched from foliage or pounced upon on the ground. **Range and habitat:** throughout Australia, except Tasmania, but avoids heavy forest, also New Guinea and Indonesia. Regular north-south migration, with late arrival and early departure in the south. **Similar species:** Varied Triller.

Rifleman

Superb Lyrebird

Singing Bushlark

Welcome Swallow

Fairy Martin (in nest)

Australasian Pipit

Tree Martin

White-winged Triller (female)

Black-faced Cuckooshrike (juvenile)

Red-capped Robin

Petroica goodenovii (Petroicidae) 11 cm/4½ in.
Male has black head, back, wings and tail, white belly and wing patch, and red breast and diagnostic red cap. Female very dull, gray-brown above and buff below, with hint of reddish on forehead. Young male is like female, and may breed in this plumage. Song a rattling trill. Perches on a low branch, flycatching and pouncing on insects on the ground. Flicks wings and tail. Australian robins are remarkably similar to Palaearctic flycatchers in appearance and behavior, but are not closely related. Red-capped Robin is the semiarid representative of its genus; 4 other red-breasted robins occupy progressively wetter and denser habitats. **Range and habitat:** inland Australia, in eucalypt, acacia and native pine woodland. Partly migratory, more common near coast during droughts. **Similar species:** other *Petroica* robins

Scarlet Robin

Petroica multicolor (Petroicidae) 13 cm/5 in.
Attractive red, black and white robin. Male has black head, throat, back, wings and tail, scarlet breast outlined in white, and white forehead, wing-bars and tail edges. Female is gray-brown with pale red breast. Rather weak twittering song. Perches on low branch, pouncing on ground prey, also hawks and snatches insects from tree-trunks in summer. **Range and habitat:** Southern Australia, Tasmania, and many Pacific islands, dry forest, with some understorey. Has declined in many parts of range. **Similar species:** Red-capped Robin, Flame Robin has more orange breast to throat.

White-winged Robin

Peneothello sigillatus (Petroicidae) 15 cm/6 in.
Black robin, with conspicuous white wing patch. Birds from the western part of distribution have another white patch on the shoulder. Juveniles are mottled brown and black. Perches on low mossy branches and pounces on ground prey. Calls a variety of piping trills. **Range and habitat:** forests of the central ranges of New Guinea, above 2,500 m (8,200 ft). **Similar species:** White-rumped Thicket Flycatcher has a white rump.

Jacky-Winter

Microeca fascinans (Petroicidae) 13 cm/5 in.
A dull brown flycatcher, with white outer tail feathers and eyebrow. Wags tail from side to side. Juvenile spotted with white above and brown below. Perches on trees and fence-posts, darting out after flying insects or pouncing on them on the ground. Loud song, described as "Jacky Winter," or more accurately as "Peter Peter." Tiny, inconspicuous nest. **Range and habitat:** woodland and scrub throughout Australia, but not Tasmania. Also southern New Guinea. Will occupy farmland, where few trees remain, and particularly on edge of woodland or forest. **Similar species:** female Hooded Robin.

Golden Whistler

Pachycephala pectoralis (Pachycephalidae) 17 cm/6½ in.
Usual male plumage is spectacular, with black head and gorget, white throat, bright yellow under-parts and collar, green back and black tail. Female is grayish brown above and buff below. Immature is like female but has rufous patch on wings. Numerous races of this widespread species, with great variety of plumage. Some females are brighter, some males duller. Males may take 2 or more years to attain bright plumage, but may breed in femalelike plumage. Powerful, melodious whistling song, sometimes ending in a whipcrack. Whistlers snatch and glean large insects from foliage. As sit-and-wait predators they can be unobtrusive in nonbreeding season. **Range and habitat:** in forests in southern and eastern Australia, moving into more open habitat in winter, and on numerous Pacific islands. **Similar species:** Black-tailed Whistler.

Rufous Whistler

Pachycephala rufiventris (Pachycephalidae) 17 cm/6½ in.
One of the most ubiquitous songsters in Australia. Male has gray back, wings, tail and head, white throat, outlined in black and pale rufous underparts. Female is gray above, with white throat and buff abdomen with vertical dark streaks. Immature and second year male resemble female. Loud whistling song, usually finishing with "ee-chong" or a series of "chews." Snatches and gleans large insects from foliage. **Range and habitat:** woodland and open forest, throughout Australia, except Tasmania and Kangaroo Island. **Similar species:** other whistlers.

Gray Shrike-Thrush

Colluricincla harmonica (Pachycephalidae) 24 cm/9½ in.
Well-named bird; gray, thrushlike with a slightly hooked beak, but really a large whistler. Eastern birds have a brownish back and western birds brownish underparts. Male has white lores with black eye-ring, female gray lores and white eye-ring. Immatures streaked on breast and some rufous on wings and face. Feeds by fossicking on ground, on horizontal branches and from foliage, for large insects. Occasionally takes small lizards, eggs and baby birds. Beautiful, melodious and whistling song, with neighboring birds frequently replying to each other with matched phrases. **Range and habitat:** New Guinea and Australia, wherever there are trees or shrubs. **Similar species:** other shrike-thrushes, which are more localized and generally browner.

Crested Bellbird

Oreoica gutturalis (Pachycephalidae) 22 cm/8½ in.
Striking bird with white face, black erectile crest and bib, gray-brown back and tail and white belly. Female is duller than male, has no crest and dark eyes, whereas male has orange eyes. Typically detected by haunting, ventriloquial bell-like call, and can usually be found hopping inoffensively along the ground, feeding amongst leaf litter. Attaches hairy caterpillars to nest, perhaps as a food supply or deterrent to predators. **Range and habitat:** throughout inland Australia, in dry woodland and scrub. Has declined markedly with clearing of native vegetation for growing crops. **Similar species:** none, though Bell Miner, a honeyeater, is usually called Bellbird.

Restless Flycatcher

Myiagra inquieta (Monarchidae) 18 cm/7 in.
Black above and white below, long tail and slight crest. Female has pinkish breast. Usually seen hovering above the ground before diving into long grass after insects. Also feeds by hawking, snatching insects from leaves and bark and gleaning on the ground. It utters a strange grinding, wheezing noise, whence its common name of Scissors-grinder, also grating sounds and loud whistling song. **Range and habitat:** open, grassy, eucalypt and paperbark woodland in northern, eastern and southwestern Australia. Birds in north are much smaller. And may be a separate species. **Similar species:** Willie Wagtail (see p 310), Satin and Leaden Flycatchers, which have dark or orange throats.

Black-faced Monarch

Monarcha melanopsis (Monarchidae) 17 cm/6½ in.
A gray flycatcher with bright rufous underparts. Adult has black forehead and throat, juvenile no black face. Calls range from loud whistles to harsh nasal rasps. Monarchs typically pursue active prey by hawking or snatching insects from foliage and branches. This species though spends much time searching leaves and twigs for insects. **Range and habitat:** Rainforest and eucalypt forest in eastern Australia. Some birds migrate over the Torres Strait in autumn. **Similar species:** Black-winged Monarch, Spectacled Monarch.

Mountain Peltops

Peltops montanus (Monarchidae) 20 cm/8 in.
A spectacular bird of the treetops. Black, with white patches on back and cheeks, and red rump and undertail-coverts. Typically sallies for insects from emergent trees, or at the edge of clearings, and roadsides. Call is a rapid, descending "tit tit tit...," reported to be like the sound of a finger being run over a comb, also "schweep." Although like a flycatcher, related to the Australian butcher birds. **Range and habitat:** rainforest in foothills and mountains of New Guinea. **Similar species:** Lowland Peltops Flycatcher, which replaces it below 550 m (1,800 ft). **Not illustrated.**

Red-capped Robin
(at nest)

Scarlet Robin
(at nest)

White-winged Robin

Jacky-Winter
(at nest)

Golden Whistler
(male) at nest

Gray Shrike-Thrush
(female)

Rufous Whistler
(at nest)

Crested Bellbird

Black-faced Monarch
(at nest)

Restless Flycatcher
(at nest)

Gray Fantail

Rhipidura fuliginosa (Monarchidae) 16 cm/6½ in.

A hyperactive gray flycatcher, with white throat, eyebrow and buff underparts. Long tail, frequently fanned while perching. Never still for long. Delicate legs and feet, short broad beak with obvious bristles around gape. Juvenile more buff on head and wings. Numerous races, vary in shade of gray and amount of white on tail probably separate species in Australia and New Zealand (where a black form occurs) and elsewhere in range. Pursues small flying insects aerobatically, occasionally feeds on ground. High-pitched twittering calls and song. **Range and habitat:** Australia, in woodland and forest, Pacific islands. Mangrove Fantail of northern Australia and New Guinea may be a distinct species. Partial migrant in southern parts of range, on migration in towns and open habitat. **Similar species:** other fantails (see p 266).

Friendly Fantail

Rhipidura albolimbata (Monarchidae) 15 cm/6 in.

Sooty gray fantail, with white chin, belly, eyebrow and spots on wings and tail. Repeated, staccato whistles. Like other fantails, it willingly approaches humans, perhaps attracted to insects associated with or flushed out by them. Hawks for flying insects in middle or lower levels of forest. **Range and habitat:** rainforest in New Guinea from 1,750 m (5,700 ft) to timberline. **Similar species:** other fantails (see p 266).

Willie Wagtail

Rhipidura leucophrys (Monarchidae) 20 cm/8 in.

Striking fantail. White eyebrow, can be raised when alarmed. Juvenile brownish on wings and eyebrow. One of Australia's best-known and popular birds. Bold and aggressive, even attacking much larger birds. Sweet, chattering song; harsh alarm notes; sometimes sings at night. Feeds on beetles, grasshoppers, on ground, cocking and wagging long tail from side to side, or by pursuing flying insects. Perches on sheep and takes ticks from cattle. **Range and habitat:** Australia, New Guinea, parts of Indonesia, in open woodland, grassland, farmland, gardens, city parks. **Similar species:** Restless Flycatcher (see p 308).

Chirruping Wedgebill

Psophodes cristatus (Eupetidae) 20 cm/8 in.

Light brown, medium-sized bird, with white outer tail feathers. Pointed crest, rather heavy black beak and long wedge-shaped tail. Feeds in bushes and on ground on seeds and insects. Wedgebills have been split into 2 distinct species by their distribution and calls. Chiming Wedgebill calls "why did you get drunk," and Chirruping Wedgebill "tootsie cheer." Otherwise appear identical. **Range and habitat:** Chiming Wedgebill in dense acacias and other shrubs in western central Australia, often along watercourses; Chirruping Wedgebill in eastern inland, in more open habitat. **Not illustrated.**

Clamorous Reed-Warbler

Acrocephalus stentoreus (Sylviidae) 17 cm/6½ in.

Clean-looking pale brown bird, warm brown above, buff below, white throat and eyebrow. Loud, continuous song with melodious quality, but some harsh notes. Usually heard from dense reed-beds, but will perch in view and sometimes pursues flying insects in the open. During droughts in bushes, gardens, away from water. **Range and habitat:** north-east Africa, southern Asia, New Guinea, eastern and south-west Australia, reed-beds. **Similar species:** other *Acrocephalus* warblers (see pp 172, 222).

Little Grassbird

Megalurus gramineus (Sylviidae) 14 cm/5½ in.

Inconspicuous small bird, dark brown above, gray-brown below, heavily streaked. Long graduated tail. Usually detected by high-pitched, 2- or 3-noted whistling call, then seen flitting from tussock to tussock at the edge of water. **Range and habitat:** eastern and south-western Australia, in grassy swamps, lake shores, saltmarshes, artesian bores and farm dams, vagrant to New Guinea. Migratory, or perhaps only silent and overlooked in winter. **Similar species:** Tawny Grassbird is larger, more rufous, in rank grassland or heath.

Golden-headed Cisticola

Cisticola exilis (Sylviidae) 10 cm/4 in.

Male has golden head and upperparts, with dark streaking on wings, white underparts and very short tail. Female and nonbreeding male less golden and streaked head, longer tail. Buzzing calls and songs. Can occur at high density and be conspicuous, at other times hard to see. **Range and habitat:** AU and OR, India, China, South-East Asia, New Guinea, north and east Australia. Swamps, wet grassland, crops, canefields, irrigated regions. May be migratory or irruptive. **Similar species:** other cisticolas (see p 224).

Rufous Songlark

Cinclorhamphus mathewsi (Sylviidae) 16–20 cm/6½–8 in.

Brown above, lightly streaked with obvious rufous rump, underparts pale with some darker smudging on breast, pale eyebrow. Male performs lively, melodious song-flight in breeding season, usually starting from and finishing on high branch. Female much smaller than male and less conspicuous. May be polygamous, but nests in dense grass are hard to observe. **Range and habitat:** Australia, except Tasmania. Open woodland and grassland with scattered trees, typically long grass, especially roadsides. Migratory. **Similar species:** female Brown Songlark, Australasian Pipit (see p 306).

Brown Songlark

Cinclorhamphus cruralis (Sylviidae) 18–25 cm/7–10 in.

Conspicuous dark brown bird of open country. Male is dark chocolate brown, streaked above, but uniform below, slight eyebrow. Female streaked above and pale, slightly marked below. Usually seen in creaky, clattering song-flight descending vertically with legs dangling, or perched on a fence-post, tail cocked. Male much bigger than female. Feeds on insects and seeds on ground. **Range and habitat:** Australia, generally not near coast, partly migratory, moves out of center during droughts. Grassland, crops. **Similar species:** female like Rufous Songlark. **Not illustrated.**

Splendid Fairywren

Malurus splendens (Maluridae) 14 cm/5½ in.

Fairywrens are small, lively ground feeding birds, with very long tails, often cocked. Male Splendid Fairywren is brilliant iridescent blue, paler in the face, with black eye stripe, nape and breast band, dark beak. Female gray-brown, rufous face patch and beak and blue tail. Male outside breeding season is brown with blue wings and tail, dark face and beak. Breeds in pairs or groups, with extra birds helping to rear nestlings and fledglings. Helpers are often young that have not dispersed, usually males. Voice high-pitched squeaks and trills. **Range and habitat:** 3 isolated populations in south-west, central and inland east Australia, perhaps separate species, eucalypt forest and woodland, arid scrub. **Similar species:** Superb Fairywren has white belly.

Variegated Fairywren

Malurus lamberti (Maluridae) 15 cm/6 in.

Male has light blue or purple crown, face, upper back and tail, black throat, breast and nape patch, chestnut saddle across back and white belly. Female is gray-brown above, pale below, with dark brown face and beak and bluish tail. Male also brown in nonbreeding season. Some races have much bluer female. Social, usually seen feeding among low shrubs. Metallic squeaks and trills. **Range and habitat:** distinct races occupy central, north-west, northeast and central east Australia. Heathlands, forests with dense understorey. **Similar species:** Blue-breasted and Red-winged Fairywrens.

White-winged Fairywren

Malurus leucopterus (Maluridae) 13 cm/5 in.

Male of race *leuconotus* is a brilliant deep blue with white wings. Female dull gray-brown above, white below with blue tail and no red eye-ring. Race *leucopterus* is velvety-black in male, with blue tail and white wings. Calls are high-pitched trills. Feeds on tiny insects taken from bushes and ground. Cooperative breeder, in groups of up to 10 birds. **Range and habitat:** inland Australia, reaching coast in west and south. Race *leucopterus* on Dirk Hartog and Barrow Islands off Western Australia. Shrub steppe with low, often scattered bushes. **Similar species:** other fairywrens.

Gray Fantail
(at nest)

Friendly Fantail

Willie Wagtail

Golden-headed
Cisticola

Clamorous Reed-
Warbler

Little Grassbird

Splendid
Fairywren

Brown Songlark

Variegated Fairywren
(at nest)

White-winged
Fairywren

Striated Grasswren

Amytornis striatus (Maluridae) 15–17 cm/6½–7 in.
Brown above, heavily streaked with white, black moustache, orange eyebrow and buff beneath. Female has chestnut patches on belly. Plumage varies between races, to match background. Long tail, frequently cocked. Thin squeaking call. Usually keeps close to the ground, often under grass thickets. Runs rather than flies. May shelter in burrows when hot. **Range and habitat:** patchy through inland Australia, in porcupine grass on sandy soil and scrub in more rocky areas. Range has contracted probably due to habitat loss, grazing by sheep and changes in fire frequency. **Similar species:** other grass wrens, which differ in shade of brown, facial markings, range and habitat.

Redthroat

Pyrrholaemus brunneus (Acanthizidae) 13 cm/5 in.
Only small brown bird in Australia with pale chestnut throat. Female has white throat, both sexes gray underparts, slightly scaly crown and white lores. Tip of tail white. Rich song, often with mimicry. Active birds, gleaning insects and seeds from ground and foliage of low shrubs. **Range and habitat:** inland Australia, in mallee, mulga, shrub-steppe and deserts. Has declined where habitat damaged by grazing. **Similar species:** female like thornbills. **Not illustrated.**

Striated Calamanthus

Calamanthus fuliginosus (Acanthizidae) 13 cm/5 in.
Varies from grayish brown, through olive-brown to reddish brown. Whitish belly. Heavily streaked black above and below. Usually glimpsed perched with tail cocked on top of a shrub, before darting under cover. Musical, twittering song. Sedentary, usually in pairs or small groups. **Range and habitat:** patchily distributed across southern Australia. Habitat varies from wet coastal and mountain heaths to saltbush and spinifex of arid plains, even edges of salt lakes. Perhaps 2 3 species, and many races. **Similar species:** heath wrens, Little Grassbird. **Not illustrated.**

Weebill

Smicrornis brevirostris (Acanthizidae) 8 cm/3 in.
Smallest Australian bird. Olive-brown above, buff below in south, paler in center, but northern race very yellow. Pale eyebrow and iris and very short, dumpy, pale beak. Clear high-pitched calls, loud for such a tiny bird, may resemble "I'm a Weebill." Social, often with other small birds, tame. Feeds on outer foliage, often hovering near or clinging to leaves to take scale insects. **Range and habitat:** most of Australia and Tasmania, in dry eucalypt forest and woodland and mallee. **Similar species:** thornbills, but identified by beak and call.

White-throated Gerygone

Gerygone olivacea (Acanthizidae) 10 cm/4 in.
Bright lemon-yellow underparts with white throat, gray above with white forehead and patches on tail. Eye bright red. Immatures are all-yellow below. Beautiful high-pitched wavering, descending song. Sometimes called Bush Canary, due to song and color. Australian warblers sometimes called Gerygones. Feeds by gleaning and dashing energetically amongst leaves for active insects. Nest constructed of shredded bark and spiders' webs, is pendant with long tail extending downward and small hood at side. **Range and habitat:** northern and eastern Australia, in open eucalypt forest and woodland, generally not far inland. Migratory, arriving in south in October, departing in April. **Similar species:** other *Gerygone* warblers, most of which are whiter below.

Inland Thornbill

Acanthiza apicalis (Acanthizidae) 10 cm/4 in.
Thornbills are tiny birds, filling the role of warblers in Australia. They have a reputation for being hard to identify, but calls and habits help. Gray-brown above, some populations with dark rufous rump, pale below with fine striations. Scalloped forehead, reddish brown eyes. Unlike very similar Brown Thornbill, often cocks tail. Rich warbling call, harsh churring. Feeds and nests in shrub layer. Usually in pairs or family groups. **Range and habitat:** inland Australia, typically replaces Brown Thornbill west and north of Great Dividing Range, dry woodland and scrub. Reaches coast in south-west, where also in eucalypt forest. **Similar species:** other thornbills. **Not illustrated.**

Brown Thornbill

Acanthiza pusilla (Acanthizidae) 10 cm/4 in.
Small, brown bird, identified by strong calls. Gray-brown above, with rich brown rump. Scalloped forehead and streaked throat, buff underparts. Usually solitary or in pairs, but will sometimes join other thornbills in mixed species feeding flocks. Warbling call, harsh chattering alarm call. Gleans small insects from shrubs. **Range and habitat:** south-eastern Australia and Tasmania, in rainforest and eucalypt forest with understorey. **Similar species:** other thornbills.

Southern Whiteface

Aphelocephala leucopsis (Acanthizidae) 10 cm/4 in.
Small, dull brown bird with white face. Gray-brown above, brown tail with white tip, whitish below, with buff flanks. White face bordered with black on crown and below eye. Pale iris. Tinkling, wistful calls and tuneful bell-like song. Sedentary, in small groups, often with thornbills. Feeds on insects and seeds on the ground, often turning over objects in its search. **Range and habitat:** inland Australia, near coast in south, in semiarid and arid scrub and grassland. Still found in farmland, though has declined in some regions. **Similar species:** other whitefaces.

Gray Gerygone

Gerygone igata (Acanthizidae) 11 cm/4½ in.
Small greenish gray bird of the outer foliage. Pale gray throat, white belly, yellowish flanks, pale eyebrow and patches on tail. Attractive trilling song. Searches for insects and spiders by gleaning and hovering among leaves. Pendant pear-shaped nest, frequently parasitized by Shining Bronze-cuckoo (*Chrysococcyx lucidus*). **Range and habitat:** throughout New Zealand, forests and woodland, one of the few native species to adapt well to exotic vegetation in farmland, parks and gardens.

Banded Whiteface

Aphelocephala nigricincta (Acanthizidae) 10 cm/4 in.
Chestnut-brown back and black breast band distinguish it from other whitefaces. White face bordered black, gray tail and wings, rufous flanks and pale iris. Musical, weak calls. Sometimes feeding on ground with other small birds. May be a cooperative breeder. **Range and habitat:** central Australia, in saltbush and spinifex in stony and sandy deserts with scattered trees. May be nomadic. **Similar species:** Southern Whiteface is more widespread, Chestnut-breasted Whiteface much rarer. **Not illustrated.**

Crimson Chat

Epthianura tricolor (Epthianuridae) 10–12 cm/4–4½ in.
Striking red, black and white bird of the Australian outback. Male has red cap, breast, belly and rump, black eye stripe, nape, back, wings and tail and white throat. Female is grayish brown above, buff below, with red smudges, also red rump. Slightly decurved beak. Bouncy flight, high-pitched calls. Short-tailed ground feeder taking mostly insects, but also visits flowers for nectar. Can be common, occurring in flocks with other chats. **Range and habitat:** inland and western Australia, nomadic and irruptive, sometimes well outside normal range, acacia scrub, shrub-steppe often near salt-lakes. Australian chats are closely related to honeyeaters.

White-fronted Chat

Epthianura albifrons (Epthianuridae) 11–12 cm/4–4½ in.
Male has white face, throat and upper breast, with thick black border. Gray back, white belly, black wings and tail. Female generally grayer, with narrow breast band, juvenile has faint breast band. Call "tang," rather like a Zebra Finch. Jerky flight. Wags short tail up and down. Strictly ground feeding, on insects. Loosely colonial in breeding season, flocks at other times. Commonest chat in southern Australia. **Range and habitat:** southern Australia and Tasmania, in damp grassland, edges of lagoons and salt-lakes, coastal saltmarshes, sometimes crops.

Striated Grasswren

Weebill

Southern Whiteface

White-throated Gerygone

Brown Thornbill

Gray Gerygone

Crimson Chat

White-fronted Chat (at nest)

White-browed Treecreeper

Climacteris affinis (Climacteridae) 14 cm/5½ in.
Grayish brown bird, heavily streaked below and in face. White throat and eyebrow, female with orange line over eyebrow. Flight somewhat undulating, but also glides showing conspicuous pale orange stripe across wing feathers. Longish decurved beak and long toes. Australian treecreepers are not closely related to treecreepers on other continents, but are an endemic group perhaps related to lyrebirds and bowerbirds. Typically work their way steadily up trunks and major branches in search of insects, especially ants. Also feed on ground. Hole-nesting and probably cooperative. Calls high pitched, somewhat shrill, less vocal than other treecreepers. **Range and habitat:** central Australia, uncommon in woodland dominated by sheoak (*Casuarind*) and trees other than eucalypts with declines in eastern and southern parts of range. **Similar species:** other treecreepers, which typically inhabit eucalypt woodland or forest. Not illustrated.

Red Wattlebird

Anthochaera carunculata (Meliphagidae) 31–9 cm/12–15 in.
Large, raucous, gray-brown honeyeater. White streaks over grayish brown body, darker head but whitish face. Yellow belly, wattle of red skin dangling from chin, which is small in juvenile and may be hard to see in adult. Longish beak and strong pink legs. Range of harsh rattling and clanking calls. Often in groups feeding in eucalypt flowers, with much noise and chasing. Highly aggressive to other honeyeaters and lorikeets. In territorial pairs in breeding season. **Range and habitat:** southern Australia, in woodland, open forest, heaths, common in town parks and gardens. Some local movements. **Similar species:** Little and Wetsern Wattlebirds have no wattle or yellow patch on belly.

Spiny-cheeked Honeyeater

Acanthagenys rufogularis (Meliphagidae) 22–7 cm/8½–10½ in.
Medium-sized grayish honeyeater. Scalloped or streaked above and below, with pale rufous throat and upper breast. Bare pink skin around eye, stretching to pink and black beak. Black through eye, with white spiny feathers below eye. Attractive warbling call, excellent songster at dawn. Feeds in flowers of trees and shrubs, on berries and hawks for insects. **Range and habitat:** inland Australia, occasionally up to coast, in dry woodland, mallee, scrub, stony shrub-steppe. **Similar species:** none, though can look like Yellow-throated Miner in flight.

Stitchbird

Notiomystis cincta (Meliphagidae) 15 cm/6 in.
Male a striking bird, female duller. Black head, upper back and breast bordered yellow, white tuft behind ears, grayish belly. Gray, yellow and white wings and tail in male. Female generally brown, more olive above, with white wing patch. Dark iris, prominent bristles, sometimes tilts tail. Calls "tzit," also "pek pek pek …." Is promiscuous with males pursuing females and forcing copulation in an exceptional face-to-face position, with female on her back on the ground. Feeds On nectar, fruit and insects from foliage, at all levels in the forest. Nests in tree-holes. **Range and habitat:** now restricted to forests of Little Barrier Island, where fairly common, but with introduced populations on some islands and also in Karori Wildlife Sanctuary in Wellington, from where it straggles into neighboring suburbs, formerly more widespread on North Island, New Zealand. Uncertain taxonomic status and probably not a honeyeater. **Similar species:** female like Bellbird.

Little Friarbird

Philemon citreogularis (Meliphagidae) 27 cm/10½ in.
Gray-brown above, silvery white below, with bald bluish facial skin. Longish tail and beak. Immature has yellow chin and throat. Raucous cackling calls. A noisy, active, aggressive bird, often feeding in groups in flowering trees. Also takes fruit and large insects. **Range and habitat:** in open, eucalypt forests and woodland, in northern and eastern Australia. **Similar species:** other friarbirds have knobs on top of their beaks.

Yellow-throated Miner

Manorina flavigula (Meliphagidae) 23–8 cm/9–11 in.
Medium-sized gray bird, with contrasting white or pale gray rump, conspicuous in flight. Black face, with yellow on forehead and side of throat and bare yellow patches on gape, chin streak and behind eye. White tips to tail. Beak and legs bright yellow. Social, living and breeding in groups. Loud ringing calls. **Range and habitat:** open woodland and scrub, inland Australia, reaching coast in south and west. Likes partly cleared country, where it may have replaced or hybridized with endangered Black-eared Miner. **Similar species:** other miners none of which has pale rump.

Noisy Miner

Manorina melanocephala (Meliphagidae) 24–8 cm/9½–11 in.
Bold, clamorous, gray bird with black on face and crown. No contrast between rump and back. Yellow beak, legs and bare patch behind eye. Slight yellow wash on wings and tail. Range of piping calls, with some harsh elements. Highly social, living in groups or colonies. Numerous individuals may help at one nest. Performs "corroboree" display where up to 20 individuals gather, call loudly and flutter wings. Vigorously drives away other birds, from tiny insectivores to large raptors. Loud alarm calls lead to common name of Soldier bird. Takes insects, lerps (scale insects), honeydew and some nectar. **Range and habitat:** eastern Australia, in open woodland, particularly where trees are scattered and unhealthy, also gardens. **Similar species:** other miners.

Tui

Prosthemadera novaeseelandiae (Meliphagidae) 28–30 cm/11–12 in.
Only large dark honeyeater in New Zealand. Iridescent green, with dark bronzy reflections on back and belly. Unusual white curls hanging from chin and filamentous feathers around neck, also white shoulder patch. Immature duller. Attractive bell-like calls, also strange harsher wheezes and chuckles. Mostly nectarivor-ous, but takes some insects and also fruit in autumn, usually in canopy. May feed lower on native flax and on garden flowers. **Range and habitat:** native forests in most of New Zealand, but will venture into settled districts. **Similar species:** Male Blackbird, Kokako, Saddleback (see p 320).

White-eared Honeyeater

Meliphaga leucotis (Meliphagidae) 20 cm/8 in.
Dark bottle-green honeyeater, with white facial patch surrounded by black. Gray crown, yellow belly and wash on wings and tail. Juvenile has yellowish face, less black. Birds in west and drier* country are small and pale. Loud "chok chok" call, also "pick-em-up." A rather solitary bird, typically probing amongst fibrous bark for insects and honeydew. Sometimes visiting flowers of eucalypts and shrubs. **Range and habitat:** central Queensland through south-east Australia, perhaps continuously to south-west Australia, in rather scrubby forest and mallee. **Similar species:** juvenile can be confused with other honeyeaters with yellow faces.

Smoky Honeyeater

Melipotes fumigatus (Meliphagidae) 22 cm/8½ in.
Nondescript gray bird, with large yellow patch of bare skin in face, which may flush bright red. Rather sluggish for a honeyeater, but sometimes aggressive. Short beak. Quiet "swit swit" call. Feeds mostly on fruit in taller shrubs and trees. **Range and habitat:** rainforests in mountain ranges of New Guinea. **Similar species:** subspecies Western Smoky Honeyeater has different range.

Helmeted Friarbird

Philemon buceroides (Meliphagidae) 30–7 cm/12–15 in.
Very large, gray, conspicuous honeyeater. Black bare face, silvery feathers on crown and chin, forming ruff on nape. Large, gently sloping knob where beak joins forehead. Brownish throat and breast. Harsh metallic cackling calls, e.g. "poor devil poor devil" "sergeant major." Noisy, aggressive flocks gather at flowering trees; also eats fruit, insects and spiders. **Range and habitat:** edge of monsoon forest, eucalypt woodland, mangroves, gardens in northern Australia, New Guinea and southern Indonesia. Probably several separate species. Somewhat nomadic. **Similar species:** other friarbirds, but note knob shape and pattern of silvery feathers.

Red Wattlebird

Spiny-cheeked Honeyeater

Stitchbird

Little Friarbird

Yellow-throated Miner

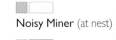

Noisy Miner (at nest)

Tui

White-eared Honeyeater

Smoky Honeyeater

Helmeted Friarbird

Brown Honeyeater

Lichmera indistincta (Meliphagidae) 12–16 cm/4½–6½ in.
Small, dull honeyeater, with yellow or black gape (breeding male only) and yellow patch of skin behind eye. Olive-brown above, buff grading to white below, yellow wash on wings. One of the best songsters among the honeyeaters, melodious and chattering notes resemble a reed-warbler. Active in treetops, sometimes lower, visiting nectar from flowers such as mistletoes, mangroves and paperbarks. Also captures small insects in flight. **Range and habitat:** most of Australia, but lacking from south and south-east. New Guinea, southern Indonesia. A wide range of habitat from mangroves, forest, heath to semiarid scrub. **Similar species:** like female Myzomela, but song is diagnostic.

Golden-backed Honeyeater

Melithreptus laetior (Meliphagidae) 15 cm/6 in.
Clean-looking gold and white bird, with distinctive head pattern. Head black, with white crescent extending across nape and broad white streak from beak on either side of small black chin. Bare greenish skin above eye. Juvenile has brown head, pale beak. Usually considered race of Black-chinned Honeyeater, which has olive back and blue eye patch. Feeds on insects and exudates in canopy of eucalyptus trees, often in small groups. Sometimes visits flowering trees and shrubs. Loud, churring and ringing call. **Range and habitat:** across northern Australia in eucalypt and paperbark woodland, Black-chinned in open woodland in south-east Australia, generally not near coast. **Similar species:** other *Melithreptus* honeyeaters, but note color of eye patch and calls. **Not illustrated.**

White-plumed Honeyeater

Lichenostomus penicillata (Meliphagidae) 15–19 cm/6–7½ in.
Lively, short-beaked, yellowish honeyeater. White line on side of neck, faintly bordered with black, is distinctive, but can be hard to see. Olive-gray with yellow in face and on wings and tail. Local races differ, very yellow in west, greener in south-east. Usual call "chick-a-wee," sometimes repeated and delivered in rising and descending song-flight. Takes insects and scales from leaves, and nectar from eucalypt flowers. Very common in suburbs, town parks in south-east Australia. **Range and habitat:** Australia, except south-west and north, and islands. Eucalypt woodland and especially red gums (*Eucalyptus camaldulensis*) along creeks in the outback. Occasionally in mallee or other scrub. **Similar species:** other *Meliphaga* honeyeaters, but yellow face, white plume and call diagnostic.

White-throated Honeyeater

Melithreptus albogularis (Meliphagidae) 13–15 cm/5–6 in.
Black head with white crescent across nape, olive-green back and very clean white underparts. White throat extending to chin and bluish white skin above eye. Very similar White-naped Honeyeater in eastern Australia has tiny black patch on chin and red above eye. A social bird that gleans among eucalypt foliage, and less often takes nectar. Call "tserp tserp." **Range and habitat:** northern Australia and southern New Guinea, in eucalypt and paperbark woodland. Overlaps with White-naped in south Queensland, north-east New South Wales, but usually nearer coast. **Similar species:** White-naped Honeyeater.

White-fronted Honeyeater

Phylidonyris albifrons (Meliphagidae) 16–18 cm/6½–7 in.
Fairly inconspicuous black and white honeyeater with yellow on wing. White forehead and chin stripe, black cheeks, throat and breast merging into blotches on white belly, gray back and yellow on primaries. Tiny red spot of skin behind eye. Juvenile washed-out, browner version of adult. Tuneful song. Visits flowers of eucalypts and desert shrubs like Eremophila. **Range and habitat:** inland southern Australia, in acacia and eucalypt scrub and woodland. Unpredictable and nomadic species. Sometimes very common in a locality, then not seen for years.

Black Honeyeater

Certhionyx niger (Meliphagidae) 10–12 cm/4–4½ in.
Very small black and white honeyeater. Male has black back, head and stripe down center of otherwise white breast. Female and nonbreeding male dull brown. Longish decurved beak. Thin "peee peee" call, often delivered in buoyant flitting flight. Feeds on flowers of desert shrubs and trees, especially Eremophila. **Range and** habitat: sparsely through inland Australia, with numbers fluctuating from year to year. Generally in south in spring and summer, a few records from north in autumn and winter. Arid woodland and scrub. **Similar species:** Pied Honeyeater, female like several other small honeyeaters. **Not illustrated.**

Pied Honeyeater

Certhionyx variegatus (Meliphagidae) 15–18 cm/6–7 in.
Black and white honeyeater. No black stripe down breast, but white on rump, side of tail and wings. Blue patch of skin below eye, bluish decurved beak. Female dull brown above, paler mottled below, conspicuous white scalloping on wings. Takes nectar of mistletoes and shrubs, also insects and saltbush fruit. Voice "tee titee tee tee," diving display flight. **Range and habitat:** sparse in central Australia, complex movements, in desert scrub and acacia and eucalypt woodland. **Similar species:** Black Honeyeater is much smaller, also plumage like Hooded Robin (see p 308), though behavior different.

Mistletoebird

Dicaeum hirundinaceum (Dicaeidae) 10–11 cm/4–4½ in.
Tiny brilliant bird, often located by high-pitched call. Male is glossy blue-black on top, red on throat, breast and undertail, white belly with black stripe along keel. Female is gray above, off-white below, with pink undertail. Very short tail, but long wings and strong flight. Short, broad beak, consumes mistletoe fruits leaving skin attached to plant. Seeds pass through in 20–30 minutes and are wiped onto a horizontal branch, on which they grow. As well as loud call-note, has a complex, varied song, with mimicry. Delicate hanging nest, with side entrance. **Range and habitat:** Australia, except Tasmania, Aru Island off New Guinea, associated with parasitic mistletoe in any habitat with trees or shrubs, migratory or nomadic.

Spotted Pardalote

Pardalotus punctatus (Pardalotidae) 9 cm/3½ in.
Tiny brightly colored bird with very short tail. Male has bright yellow throat and undertail coverts, red rump, black crown, wings and tail spotted white and white eyebrow. Female duller with cream throat and yellow spots on crown. Very short stumpy beak. Ringing two or three note call, quite loud for such a small bird. Feeds on small insects and scale in the treetops. Nests in holes in banks and slopes. **Range and habitat:** eastern Australia, Tasmania and extreme south-western Australia. Some movement north and inland in autumn. Eucalypt forest and woodland. **Similar species:** Yellow-rumped Pardalote (which may be conspecific).

Red-browed Pardalote

Pardalotus rubricatus (Dicaeidae) 10–12 cm/4–4½ in.
Rather dull pardalote of northern Australia. Fawn above and below, black crown with white spots, yellow eyebrow with small red spot near beak. Orangey wing patch and yellow on breast. Short beak and tail, but long wings; monotonous 5-note call. Mostly sedentary, in pairs or small groups. **Range and habitat:** inland and northern Australia, in eucalypt and paperbark woodland, scattered trees in deserts. **Similar species:** other pardalotes.

Brown Honeyeater

White-plumed Honeyeater

White-throated Honeyeater

White-fronted Honeyeater

Pied Honeyeater

Mistletoebird

Spotted Pardalote

Red-browed Pardalote

Silvereye

Zostereops lateralis (**Zosteropidae**) 12 cm/4½ in.

Small greenish bird, with conspicuous white eye-ring. Olive-green head, wings, rump and tail, ring of white feathers around eye, partly outlined in black. Generally gray to white below. Many races, which vary in details of plumage. Tasmanian race has very rufous flanks, western race green on back, some eastern races very yellow on throat and undertail. Sharp black beak, brown eyes. Call high-pitched weak "tsee-oow," lively warbling song. Flocks in winter. Very versatile in foraging behavior, taking insects, fruit and nectar. Tame, approachable. Successful in towns, suburbs, disturbed vegetation. **Range and habitat:** south-western, southern and eastern Australia, including Tasmania, southern islands, Barrier Reef islands (well-marked bright, large subspecies), New Zealand, islands through south-west Pacific. Southern races migrate, partial migrant elsewhere. Rainforest, eucalypt forest and woodland, scrub, heath, gardens, parks. **Similar species:** white-eyes (see pp 230, 272), but other species have different range or are much rarer.

Painted Firetail

Emblema pictum (**Estrildidae**) 10–12 cm/4–4½ in.

Small brown, red, black and white finch. Red face in male, red rump and mid-belly in both sexes. Brown back, and face in female, black underparts, boldly spotted white. Longish deep beak, tipped red. Call a loud "trut." Feeds on ground among rocks and tussocks, mostly in small groups. Visits water-holes, scooping up water. **Range and habitat:** patchily through central Australia, occasionally south or east of normal range. Arid, stony hills and gorges with acacia and spinifex arid plains. **Similar species:** other firetails in wetter habitats.

Zebra Finch

Taeniopygia guttata (**Estrildidae**) 10 cm/4 in.

Common, attractive, grayish brown finch. Male has gray head, orange cheek patch, bold black-white-black stripes between beak and cheeks, fine transverse black and gray stripes across breast. Chestnut sides with white spots, white belly, gray-brown back, black and white striped tail, white rump. Female more uniform grayish brown, with same facial stripes. Beak orange in both sexes, black in immature. Call a nasal "tang," twittering song. Feeds on seeds on ground in flocks, may pull down grass stems to reach seed-heads. Large flocks may visit water-holes, to suck up water. Popular cage bird and experimental subject. **Range and habitat:** most of Australia, though not generally near coast or islands (closely related species in Indonesia). Open habitats, breeds in introduced hawthorn scrub.

Double-barred Finch

Taeniopygia bichenovii (**Estrildidae**) 10–11 cm/4–4½ in.

Small brown and white finch. White face and underparts with 2 well-spaced black bands across throat and breast. Dark gray-brown back, black wings with fine white speckles, black undertail and tail. Rump white in south, black in north. Grayish beak and legs. Immature has faint breast bars. Call "tiaah," similar to Zebra Finch, but weaker, soft nasal song. **Range and habitat:** northern and eastern Australia, grassy woodland near water, disturbed areas, e.g. blackberry tangles. **Similar species:** Plum-headed Finch has many fine breast bands.

Streak-headed Munia

Lonchura tristissima (**Estrildidae**) 10 cm/4 in.

Dull blackish brown, with conspicuous yellow rump, black tail. Heavy gray beak. Call a buzzy "tseed." Occurs in flocks. Spherical nest of grass. **Range and habitat:** New Guinea lowlands to 1,400 m (4,600 ft), forest edge, secondary growth. **Similar species:** other munias differ in color of head, back and tail.

Olive-backed Oriole

Oriolus sagittatus (**Oriolidae**) 25 cm/10 in.

Medium-sized speckled greenish bird. Head and back olive-green, finely streaked, underparts white with bold spots. Tail and wings gray. Bill and eye red. Female somewhat duller than male. Immature more rufous with pale eyebrow. Strong, undulating flight. Call far-carrying "orry-orry-ole," complex song with mimicry, can only be fully appreciated at close quarters. Feeds in treetops on large insects and fruit. **Range and habitat:** northern and eastern Australia, New Guinea in open forest and woodland, rainforest,

occasionally in towns. Southern birds migrate north in autumn. **Similar species:** Australian Yellow and Brown Orioles, Figbird, can look like friarbirds in flight.

Brown Oriole

Oriolus szalayi (**Oriolidae**) 27 cm/10½ in.

Dull brown, streaky, medium-sized bird. Gray-brown, darker in face, heavily streaked on head and underparts. Red beak and eye. Immature has dark beak and eye and pale eyebrow. Loud musical warbling calls. Feeds in canopy on fruit, often with friarbirds. **Range and habitat:** New Guinea, up to 1,400 m (4,600 ft), in forest. **Similar species:** other orioles, also remarkably like friarbirds (see p 314), possibly as a result of convergence to avoid aggression. Not illustrated.

Great Bowerbird

Chlamydera nuchalis (**Ptilonorhynchidae**) 35 cm/14 in.

Large gray bowerbird. Pale gray below, gray with brownish scalloping above. Tail heavily spotted. Heavy, decurved, black beak. Harsh, grating, hissing calls, mimicry of predators' calls. Males build a large bower of sticks in a double avenue, decorated with various objects, such as snail-shells, pale stones, bleached bones and dung. Male displays at bower, revealing lilac crest on nape. Feeds on large insects and fruit, sometimes from the ground. Often in groups. **Range and habitat:** northern Australia, inhabits drier" habitat than most bowerbirds; riverine forest and thickets and open woodland. Occasionally in towns. **Similar species:** Spotted Bowerbird.

Fawn-breasted Bowerbird

Chlamydera cerviniventris (**Ptilonorhynchidae**) 25–30 cm/10–12 in.

Fawn and gray bowerbird. Gray-brown on back, head and throat, with feathers tipped white, buff-fawn below. Heavy black beak. Shortish tail, thick neck and heavy flight, typical of most bowerbirds. Harsh, rasping, churring calls, mechanical sounds, mimicry. Builds a large, 2-walled bower of sticks on a raised platform of sticks. Gregarious, can be noisy. **Range and habitat:** New Guinea, extreme north-east Australia, edge of rainforest, thickets in savannah. **Similar species:** Golden-fronted Bowerbird.

Satin Bowerbird

Ptilonorhynchus violaceus (**Ptilonorhynchidae**) 27–33 cm/10½–13 in.

Heavily built, greenish or glossy black bird. Males black with blue sheen, violet eyes, yellow beak and legs. Female and male up to age of 5–6 years dull green above, with rufous on wings and tail, pale underparts, heavily scalloped with olive-gray. Thick beak, short tail, rounded wings. Variety of whistling, wheezing, mechanical buzzing calls, with mimicry. Males, including some green birds, display at bowers consisting of a double avenue of sticks, typically decorated with blue objects (e.g. parrot feathers, drinking straws, bottle tops, clothes pegs) but also yellow and sometimes other colors. May paint bower with mixture of charcoal and saliva. **Range and habitat:** eastern Australia, in rainforest and wet eucalypt forest, quite tolerant of human activity occasionally in gardens.

Regent Bowerbird

Sericulus chrysocephalus (**Ptilonorhynchidae**) 24–8 cm/9½–11 in.

Spectacular male black, golden yellow on crown, nape, shoulders, most of wings; yellow beak and eyes. Female and young male dark grayish brown, scalloped white on back, pale on head and below, scalloped brown. More slightly built than most bowerbirds, with slender beak. Male displays at bower with double avenue of sticks, usually with few decorations. May paint bower yellow with saliva and juice from crushed leaves. Fairly quiet, scolding, chattering calls. **Range and habitat:** central eastern Australia, in rainforest and dense undergrowth.

Silvereye

Painted Firetail

Zebra Finch

Double-barred Finch

Streak-headed Munia

Olive-backed Oriole

Great Bowerbird

Fawn-breasted Bowerbird

Satin Bowerbird

Regent Bowerbird

White-breasted Woodswallow

Artamus leucorhynchus (**Artamidae**) 17 cm/6½ in.
Clean, gray and white, aerial bird. White rump and underparts, slaty-gray head, upper breast, back and tail. Juvenile mottled with buff. Call "pert pert." Woodswallows are smallish, dumpy birds, with short tails and long wings. They feed mostly by pursuing insects high in the air, in a manner similar to bee-eaters. **Range and habitat:** northern and eastern Australia, woodland, usually near water, swamps, mangroves. Some years move south of normal range. Also from Malaysia, through Indonesia, New Guinea to Fiji. **Similar species:** other woodswallows.

Masked Woodswallow

Artamus personatus (**Artamidae**) 19 cm/7½ in.
Black face and throat, edged with white, pale gray underparts and slate-gray crown, nape and back. White tips to tail. Female with less clear-cut division on throat. Blue beak with black tip. Immature mottled. Calls "chip chip." Occasionally feeds on ground or in trees. **Range and habitat:** throughout Australia, more common in west, generally not near coasts. Regular north-south migration, sometimes irrupts beyond normal range. Woodland, scrub and desert. **Similar species:** other woodswallows (see p 264). **Not illustrated.**

White-browed Woodswallow

Artamus superciliosus (**Artamidae**) 19 cm/7½ in.
Spectacular, gregarious bird, most distinct of woodswallows. Male is blue-gray on upper breast and upperparts, head black with a distinct white eyebrow and deep chestnut belly. Female similar, but head gray, less sharply marked. Beak blue with black tip and slightly decurved. Sparrowlike calls and chattering. Often heard passing over in flocks high in the air. Highly social, breeding in loose colonies. Numbers vary in a locality from year to year. Sometimes feeds on ground on locusts and snails, or in trees and shrubs on nectar. Often with Masked Woodswallow, with which it may hybridize. **Range and habitat:** common, inland Australia, especially in east, erupting toward coast in some years as well as regular migration. Woodland, scrub, desert.

Black-faced Woodswallow

Artamus cinereus (**Artamidae**) 18 cm/7 in.
Rather dull woodswallow. Smoky gray, paler below, with distinct black face. Undertail-coverts white in east, black elsewhere. White tip to tail. Different races vary in color around vent. Juvenile mottled. Similar Dusky Woodswallow is browner, with white leading edge to wing. Calls "chep chep" and chattering. Breeds opportunistically after rain, sometimes with helpers. **Range and habitat:** inland Australia, spreading to coast in west. Also vagrant to Timor and New Guinea. More sedentary than most woodswallows. Open habitat, often on telegraph wires in treeless farmland. **Similar species:** Dusky and Little Woodswallows.

Dusky Woodswallow

Artamus cyanopterus (**Artamidae**) 18 cm/7 in.
Grayish-brown woodswallow, rather darker in face, underparts fawnish. Wings and tail dark gray with white leading edge to wing and tip of tail. Slate-blue, rather deep, bill with black tip. Juvenile speckled brown. Breeding pairs may have helpers. In cold weather flocks may cluster on branches to roost. Feeds in flight, and sometimes on the ground. Call "sweep sweep," and harsh chattering when nest disturbed. **Range and habitat:** open woodland, throughout Australia, except for far north. Migratory in south. **Similar species:** Black-faced Woodswallow, Little Woodswallow has no white on wings. Many woodswallows appear to have declined in recent decades.

Kokako

Callaeas cinerea (**Callaeidae**) 37 cm/15 in.
Large dark, somewhat crowlike bird. Dark bluish gray, washed with olive-brown. Black lores and eye-ring. Circular wattle hanging down from gape, is bright blue on North Island and rich orange on South Island. Heavy, hooked beak. Wide variety of calls; song described as like 2 long rich organ notes, interspersed with whistles, can be heard far away. Hops up tree-branches, gliding flight is weak. **Range and habitat:** New Zealand, has declined since European settlement, quite widespread in small numbers on North Island (total population about 1,000), very rare or possibly extinct on South Island, in native forests. **Similar species:** Saddleback, Tui (see p 314).

Saddleback

Creadion carunculatus (**Callaeidae**) 25 cm/10 in.
Dark, somewhat starlinglike bird. Glossy black with iridescence on head and breast. Bright chestnut saddle across back, scapulars, wing-coverts and rump. Orange wattle hanging down from gape. Long slender beak. Calls "cheep te-te-te-te" and "che-che-u-che." Very vocal, also other musical and clicking calls. **Range and habitat:** New Zealand, used to be widespread on all islands, now restricted to forest on a small number of offshore islands that are free of cats and rats (Hen Island, islets off Stewart Island), where it is fairly common. Also in Karori Wildlife Sanctuary in Wellington. **Similar species:** Tui (Parson Bird) (see p 314) and Kokako are larger, different calls.

Magpie-Lark

Grallina cyanoleuca (**Grallinidae**) 27 cm/10½ in.
Boldly pied, ground-dwelling bird. Both sexes black back, wings and tail tip, with white underparts, rump, base of tail and shoulders. Male has black face, throat and breast, and white eyebrow and cheeks. Female has black line extending from eye downward to meet on chest, with white forehead, chin and throat and white from breast extending up to behind eye. Call a loud "pee-wee," giving common name of Peewee, often pairs call antiphonally. Builds large mud nest (another name is Mudlark). Walks strongly, bobbing head back and forth. Direct flapping flight. Often feeds along edge of water, taking snails. **Range and habitat:** throughout Australia, vagrant in Tasmania, also southern New Guinea. Open woodland, farmland with scattered trees, near water. **Similar species:** Black-backed Magpie, Black-throated Butcher Bird.

Apostlebird

Struthidea cinerea (**Grallinidae**) 29–32 cm/11½–13 in.
Medium-sized gray bird with long tail. Slate-gray with fine white striations, brown on wings. Heavy, finchlike black beak. Harsh chattering calls. Lives in tight groups of about 12 (hence name). All members contribute to building the mud nest and feeding the young. Feeds on ground on large insects, seeds and occasionally mice. Generally sedentary, but groups wander in nonbreeding season. **Range and habitat:** inland eastern Australia, open woodland near water.

Gray Butcherbird

Cracticus torquatus (**Cracticidae**) 24–30 cm/9½–12 in.
Medium-sized gray, black and white bird. Black cap, face, wings and tail, white lores, rump and underparts, gray back. Juvenile brownish. Heavy, hooked gray and black beak, strong claws. Fast, direct flight, often calling. Loud, musical call, with some harsh notes. Will vigorously attack intruders in breeding season, pecking humans on head. Young in 1st year occasionally help parents. Pounces on large insects, lizards and small mammals on ground, occasionally taking birds. Will wedge food in forks or impale prey on thorns. **Range and habitat:** most of Australia, scarce in northern inland, in woodland, scrub. **Similar species:** other butcherbirds.

Pied Butcherbird

Cracticus nigrogularis (**Cracticidae**) 32 cm/13 in.
Medium-sized black and white bird. Black head, throat and upper breast, back, wings, tail. White belly, collar across back, wing patches, rump and tail tips. Juvenile browner. Upright stance on wires, posts, branches. Beautiful flutelike song, resembling opening bars of Beethoven's 5th Symphony. Behavior similar to Gray Butcherbird, but more often in communal groups. **Range and habitat:** most of Australia, but absent from cooler parts of south-east, in woodland, mallee, scrub. **Similar species:** other butcherbirds, Magpie Lark.

White-breasted Woodswallow

White-browed Woodswallow

Kokako

White-browed Woodswallow (female)

Black-faced Woodswallow

Magpie-Lark

Saddleback

Dusky Woodswallow

Apostlebird

Gray Butcherbird

Pied Butcherbird

Pied Currawong

Strepera graculina (**Cracticidae**) 40–50 cm/16–20 in.
Large, dark, long-tailed bird. Black, with white patches on wings, base and tip of tail. Long heavy beak, with slight hook. Yellow eye. Loud, ringing call "curra-wong," musical whistles and fluting. Flocks in winter come into towns to feed on berries of exotic trees and shrubs. Major nest predator. **Range and habitat:** eastern Australia, in forest and woodland in breeding season, more open habitat in winter. **Similar species:** other currawongs, differ in amount of white and calls.

Hair-crested Drongo

Dicrurus hottentottus (**Dicruridae**) 30–2 cm/12–13 in.
Glossy black bird with long fish tail. Body black with iridescent spangles, white edging to undertail feathers. Bright red eye. Heavy black beak. Noisy, rasping, hissing calls. Agile flight rather like bee-eater in pursuit of insects. Also takes nectar and occasionally other birds. **Range and habitat:** southern Asia, New Guinea, northern and eastern Australia (probably representing several species). Forest, particularly edges, along streams or on emergent trees.

Magnificent Riflebird

Ptiloris magnificus (**Paradisaeidae**) 26–33 cm/10–13 in.
Male is black showing iridescent blue-green on crown, breast and tail. Filamentous plumes hanging from flanks. Female is gray-brown above, cinnamon on wings, pale below with fine dark bars. Long, curved beak. Male has spectacular display in which breast shield is spread. Growling call. Takes insects from bark, often chiseling into dead bark, also fruit. **Range and habitat:** rainforest in New Guinea and extreme north-east Australia. **Similar species:** other riflebirds, with different ranges.

Brown Sicklebill

Epimachus meyeri (**Paradisaeidae**) 100 cm/39 in.
Extremely long-tailed bird of paradise, with long slender, decurved beak. Male is gray-brown, with dark head and blue eyes. Also flank plumes of blue and brown. Female has chestnut crown, with finely barred underparts, light blue eyes. Male call is a loud, unmusical "tat at tat at tat at" or "tat at at at tat at at at at," described as having the quality of a pneumatic drill or machine gun. Also liquid gurgling notes. Display, in which breast feathers are spread, is from a traditional arboreal perch. Males occupy large, exclusive territories. Use long, curved beaks to extract insects from wood and occasionally fruits from capsules. **Range and habitat:** mid-mountain forest in Central Ranges of New Guinea, most common around 2,000 m (6,500 ft). **Similar species:** Black Sicklebill is darker, has red eyes.

Superb Bird-of-Paradise

Lophorina superba (**Paradisaeidae**) 25 cm/10 in.
Black or brown smallish bird of paradise. Male is black, with iridescent blue breast shield, which he spreads during display, also a velvety cape, which can be erected. Female brown above and barred below, like many other birds of paradise, but has rufous patch on wings, pale eye stripe and brown eyes. Males hold exclusive territories. Mostly insectivorous. **Range and habitat:** common, montane forests in New Guinea. **Similar species:** other birds-of-paradise, especially parotias.

King Bird-of-Paradise

Cicinnurus regius (**Paradisaeidae**) 16 cm/6½ in.
Male is a spectacular, small, red bird of paradise. White belly, dark wings, breast band and spot above eye, otherwise bright ruby-red. Very short tail with 2 long thin streamers ending in green discs. Female a more normal brown and barred plumage, with pale yellow beak. Male displays and calls "kraan kraan . . ." from vine tangles high in the canopy. Often display in pairs. May join mixed flocks. **Range and habitat:** New Guinea and neighboring islands up to 300 m (1,000 ft). **Similar species:** female like Magnificent Bird-of-Paradise.

Magnificent Bird-of-Paradise

Cicinnurus magnificus (**Paradisaeidae**) 18 cm/7 in.
Male is small and compact, generally dark, with golden back. Blue beak and streak behind eye, long, curved tail wires, from very short tail. Female brown above, barred below, with distinctive blue beak, legs and line of bare skin behind eye. Male sings from a cleared arena in a thicket to attract a female. Then he displays by raising feathers around his neck to form a shield and dancing mechanically, while clinging to a vertical stem, just above the ground. Calls range from trills to hisses. Feeds on complex fruits, like nutmeg. **Range and habitat:** forested foothills and lower mountain-sides in New Guinea and neighboring islands. **Similar species:** female like many other birds-of-paradise.

Raggiana Bird-of-Paradise

Paradisaea raggiana (**Paradisaeidae**) 33 cm/13 in.
One of the most familiar red and yellow birds of paradise. Male has yellow head and back, iridescent green throat and around ivory beak, chocolate brown underparts. Long red or orange flank plumes are spread in spectacular, inverted display by males at communal leks. Females are dark brown above and below, with yellow crown and nape. Promiscuous, females attracted to display grounds by loud "wau wau wau . . ." call of males. Mostly frugivorous, joins mixed-species flocks. **Range and habitat:** eastern New Guinea in rainforest. **Similar species:** other *Paradisaea* differ in color of plumes, breast in males and head and underparts in females.

Australian Magpie

Gymnorhina tibicen (**Cracticidae**) 36–44 cm/14–17 in.
Large, crowlike, pied bird. Black head, underparts, wings and tip of tail. Males in south-east (race *hypoleuca*) have white on shoulders and from nape to tail, females grayish on back. Western Magpie (race *dorsalis*) has male like *hypoleuca*, female heavily marked with black on back. Birds through rest of range (*tibicen*) have broad black band across back, females light gray on nape. Black-backed and white-backed birds hybridize to produce offspring with narrow or incomplete black bands. Lively caroling song and harsh squawking. Attack and sometimes terrify and injure humans during breeding season. Live in small breeding groups or larger nonbreeding flocks. **Range and habitat:** grassy forest, open woodland, farmland with scattered trees, towns, in most of Australia, southern New Guinea. **Similar species:** Magpie Lark, Pied Currawong.

Little Crow

Corvus bennetti (**Corvidae**) 48 cm/19 in.
Smallest Australian crow. Glossy black with white eyes. Bases of feathers white, short, hackle feathers pointed. Call fairly low, monotonous "ca ca ca . . . ." Social, rapid, agile flight, often soaring. Tame. **Range and habitat:** inland Australia, reaching coast in south and west. Woodland, arid and semiarid scrub, towns. **Similar species:** other crows and ravens, distinguished by call, size and throat feathers.

Torresian Crow

Corvus orru (**Corvidae**) 50 cm/20 in.
All-black, white eyes. Feather bases white, hackle feathers rounded. Slightly more heavily built than Little Crow, with shorter, broader tail. Shuffles wings on landing. Call is high-pitched, rapid cawing. Sometimes longer notes. Social, sometimes in flocks. **Range and habitat:** northern Australia, New Guinea, Moluccas, in most habitats. **Similar species:** other crows and ravens. **Not illustrated.**

Australian Raven

Corvus coronoides (**Corvidae**) 52 cm/20 in.
Large, black bird, with white eyes. Long, pointed throat hackles, gray bases to feathers. High-pitched, wailing calls, last note sounding as if strangled. Fans throat when calling. Usually solitary or in pairs or family groups. **Range and habitat:** southern and eastern Australia, most habitats, but not in dense forests. **Similar species:** other ravens and crows, distinguished by long call and throat hackles. **Not illustrated.**

Pied Currawong

Magnificent Riflebird

Hair-crested Drongo

Brown Sicklebill

Magnificent Bird-of-Paradise

King Bird-of-Paradise (female, left, and male)

Superb Bird-of-Paradise

Australian Magpie

Raggiana Bird-of-Paradise

Little Crow

WORLD CHECKLIST OF BIRDS

Ornithologists differ in their opinions of how many species exist and how to classify them. This is because, for example, some taxa recognized as sub-species (geographic races) by one ornithologist, are regarded as full species by another. Since these differences of opinion are often equally valid, it is impossible to adjudicate between them. The following list is the most extensive available, and recognizes 9,924 species in 204 families, rather than the 9,704 species in 173 families presented in the *Bird Families of the World* section of the book. Differences between these two classifications are specifically highlighted in the *Bird Families of the World* section where appropriate.

• denotes critical or endangered species

OSTRICHES Struthioniformes

Ostriches Struthionidae
Ostrich   *Struthio camelus*

Rheas Rheidae
Greater Rhea   *Rhea americana*
Lesser Rhea   *Rhea pennata*

Cassowaries Casuariidae
Southern Cassowary   *Casuarius casuarius*
Dwarf Cassowary   *Casuarius bennetti*
Northern Cassowary   *Casuarius unappendiculatus*

Emus Dromaiidae
Spotted Emu   *Dromaius novaehollandiae*

Kiwis Apterygidae
Tokoeka   *Apteryx australis*
Okarito Brown Kiwi   *Apteryx rowi*
Brown Kiwi   *Apteryx mantelli* •
Little Spotted Kiwi   *Apteryx owenii*
Great Spotted Kiwi   *Apteryx haastii*

TINAMOUS Tinamiformes

Tinamous Tinamidae
Gray Tinamou   *Tinamus tao*
Solitary Tinamou   *Tinamus solitarius*
Black Tinamou   *Tinamus osgoodi*
Great Tinamou   *Tinamus major*
White-throated Tinamou   *Tinamus guttatus*
Highland Tinamou   *Nothocercus bonapartei*
Tawny-breasted Tinamou   *Nothocercus julius*
Hooded Tinamou   *Nothocercus nigrocapillus*
Berlepsch's Tinamou   *Crypturellus berlepschi*
Cinereous Tinamou   *Crypturellus cinereus*
Red-footed Tinamou   *Crypturellus erythropus*
Little Tinamou   *Crypturellus soui*
Tepuí Tinamou   *Crypturellus ptaritepui*
Brown Tinamou   *Crypturellus obsoletus*
Undulated Tinamou   *Crypturellus undulatus*
Pale-browed Tinamou   *Crypturellus transfasciatus*
Brazilian Tinamou   *Crypturellus strigulosus*
Gray-legged Tinamou   *Crypturellus duidae*
Yellow-legged Tinamou   *Crypturellus noctivagus*
Black-capped Tinamou   *Crypturellus atrocapillus*
Slaty-breasted Tinamou   *Crypturellus boucardi*
Chocó Tinamou   *Crypturellus kerriae*
Variegated Tinamou   *Crypturellus variegatus*
Thicket Tinamou   *Crypturellus cinnamomeus*
Rusty Tinamou   *Crypturellus brevirostris*
Bartlett's Tinamou   *Crypturellus bartletti*
Small-billed Tinamou   *Crypturellus parvirostris*
Barred Tinamou   *Crypturellus casiquiare*
Tataupa Tinamou   *Crypturellus tataupa*
Red-winged Tinamou   *Rhynchotus rufescens*
Ornate Tinamou   *Nothoprocta ornata*
Chilian Tinamou   *Nothoprocta perdicaria*
Brushland Tinamou   *Nothoprocta cinerascens*
Andean Tinamou   *Nothoprocta pentlandii*
Curve-billed Tinamou   *Nothoprocta curvirostris*
Taczanowski's Tinamou   *Nothoprocta taczanowskii*
White-bellied Nothura   *Nothura boraquira*

Lesser Nothura   *Nothura minor*
Darwin's Nothura   *Nothura darwinii*
Spotted Nothura   *Nothura maculosa*
Chaco Nothura   *Nothura chacoensis*
Dwarf Tinamou   *Taoniscus nanus*
Elegant Crested Tinamou   *Eudromia elegans*
Quebracho Crested Tinamou   *Eudromia formosa*
Puna Tinamou   *Tinamotis pentlandii*
Patagonian Tinamou   *Tinamotis ingoufi*

PENGUINS Sphenisciformes

Penguins Spheniscidae
King Penguin   *Aptenodytes patagonicus*
Emperor Penguin   *Aptenodytes forsteri*
Gentoo Penguin   *Pygoscelis papua*
Adélie Penguin   *Pygoscelis adeliae*
Chinstrap Penguin   *Pygoscelis antarcticus*
Fiordland Crested Penguin   *Eudyptes pachyrhynchus*
Snares Crested Penguin   *Eudyptes robustus*
Erect-crested Penguin   *Eudyptes sclateri* •
Rockhopper Penguin   *Eudyptes chrysocome*
Royal Penguin   *Eudyptes schlegeli*
Macaroni Penguin   *Eudyptes chrysolophus*
Yellow-eyed Penguin   *Megadyptes antipodes* •
Little Penguin   *Eudyptula minor*
Jackass Penguin   *Spheniscus demersus*
Humboldt Penguin   *Spheniscus humboldti*
Magellanic Penguin   *Spheniscus magellanicus*
Galápagos Penguin   *Spheniscus mendiculus* •

DIVERS Gaviiformes

Divers Gaviidae
Red-throated Loon   *Gavia stellata*
Arctic Loon   *Gavia arctica*
Pacific Loon   *Gavia pacifica*
Common Loon   *Gavia immer*
Yellow-billed Loon   *Gavia adamsii*

GREBES Podicipediformes

Grebes Podicipedidae
Red-throated Little Grebe   *Tachybaptus ruficollis*
Australasian Little Grebe   *Tachybaptus novaehollandiae*
Madagascar Little Grebe   *Tachybaptus pelzelnii*
Least Grebe   *Tachybaptus dominicus*
Pied-billed Grebe   *Podilymbus podiceps*
White-tufted Grebe   *Rollandia rolland*
Short-winged Grebe   *Rollandia microptera* •
Hoary-headed Grebe   *Poliocephalus poliocephalus*
New Zealand Grebe   *Poliocephalus rufopectus*
Great Grebe   *Podiceps major*
Red-necked Grebe   *Podiceps grisegena*
Great Crested Grebe   *Podiceps cristatus*
Horned Grebe   *Podiceps auritus*
Black-necked Grebe   *Podiceps nigricollis*
Silvery Grebe   *Podiceps occipitalis*
Puna Grebe   *Podiceps taczanowskii* •
Hooded Grebe   *Podiceps gallardoi*
Western Grebe   *Aechmophorus occidentalis*
Clark's Grebe   *Aechmophorus clarkii*

TUBE-NOSED SWIMMERS Procellariiformes

Albatrosses Diomedeidae
Wandering Albatross   *Diomedea exulans*
Southern Royal Albatross   *Diomedea epomophora*
Short-tailed Albatross   *Phoebastria albatrus*
Waved Albatross   *Phoebastria irrorata*
Laysan Albatross   *Phoebastria immutabilis*
Black-footed Albatross   *Phoebastria nigripes* •
Gray-headed Mollymawk   *Thalassarche chrysostoma*
Black-browed Mollymawk   *Thalassarche melanophris* •
Buller's Mollymawk   *Thalassarche bulleri*
Shy Mollymawk   *Thalassarche cauta*
Yellow-nosed Mollymawk   *Thalassarche chlororhynchos* •
Sooty Mollymawk   *Phoebetria fusca* •
Light-mantled Mollymawk   *Phoebetria palpebrata*

Petrels and Shearwaters Procellariidae
Southern Giant Petrel   *Macronectes giganteus*
Northern Giant Petrel   *Macronectes halli*
Northern Fulmar   *Fulmarus glacialis*
Southern Fulmar   *Fulmarus glacialoides*
Antarctic Petrel   *Thalassoica antarctica*
Cape Petrel   *Daption capense*
Snow Petrel   *Pagodroma nivea*
Great-winged Petrel   *Pterodroma macroptera*
Mascarene Petrel   *Pterodroma aterrima*
Tahiti Petrel   *Pterodroma rostrata*
White-headed Petrel   *Pterodroma lessonii*
Black-capped Petrel   *Pterodroma hasitata* •
Bermuda Petrel   *Pterodroma cahow* •
Atlantic Petrel   *Pterodroma incerta*
Phoenix Petrel   *Pterodroma alba* •
Mottled Petrel   *Pterodroma inexpectata*
Providence Petrel   *Pterodroma solandri*
Murphy's Petrel   *Pterodroma ultima*
Kermadec Petrel   *Pterodroma neglecta*
Magenta Petrel   *Pterodroma magentae* •
Herald Petrel   *Pterodroma arminjoniana*
Henderson Petrel   *Pterodroma atrata* •
Soft-plumaged Petrel   *Pterodroma mollis*
Fea's Petrel   *Pterodroma feae*
Zino's Petrel   *Pterodroma madeira* •
Barau's Petrel   *Pterodroma baraui* •
Galápagos Petrel   *Pterodroma phaeopygia* •
Hawaiian Petrel   *Pterodroma sandwichensis*
Juan Fernández Petrel   *Pterodroma externa*
White-necked Petrel   *Pterodroma cervicalis*
Cook's Petrel   *Pterodroma cookii* •
De Filippi's Petrel   *Pterodroma defilippiana*
Gould's Petrel   *Pterodroma leucoptera*
Bonin Petrel   *Pterodroma hypoleuca*
Black-winged Petrel   *Pterodroma nigripennis*
Chatham Islands Petrel   *Pterodroma axillaris* •
Stejneger's Petrel   *Pterodroma longirostris*
Pycroft's Petrel   *Pterodroma pycrofti*
Fiji Petrel   *Pterodroma macgillivrayi* •
Vanuatu Petrel   *Pterodroma occulta*
Blue Petrel   *Halobaena caerulea*
Broad-billed Prion   *Pachyptila vittata*
Salvin's Prion   *Pachyptila salvini*
Antarctic Prion   *Pachyptila desolata*
Slender-billed Prion   *Pachyptila belcheri*

Fulmar Prion   *Pachyptila crassirostris*
Fairy Prion   *Pachyptila turtur*
Bulwer's Petrel   *Bulweria bulwerii*
Jouanin's Petrel   *Bulweria fallax*
Gray Petrel   *Procellaria cinerea*
White-chinned Petrel   *Procellaria aequinoctialis*
Parkinson's Petrel   *Procellaria parkinsoni*
Westland Petrel   *Procellaria westlandica*
Kerguelen Petrel   *Aphrodroma brevirostris*
Streaked Shearwater   *Calonectris leucomelas*
Cory's Shearwater   *Calonectris diomedea*
Cape Verde Islands Shearwater   *Calonectris edwardsii*
Pink-footed Shearwater   *Puffinus creatopus*
Flesh-footed Shearwater   *Puffinus carneipes*
Great Shearwater   *Puffinus gravis*
Wedge-tailed Shearwater   *Puffinus pacificus*
Buller's Shearwater   *Puffinus bulleri*
Sooty Shearwater   *Puffinus griseus*
Short-tailed Shearwater   *Puffinus tenuirostris*
Christmas Island Shearwater   *Puffinus nativitatis*
Manx Shearwater   *Puffinus puffinus*
Balearic Shearwater   *Puffinus mauretanicus* •
Yelkouan Shearwater   *Puffinus yelkouan*
Hutton's Shearwater   *Puffinus huttoni* •
Black-vented Shearwater   *Puffinus opisthomelas*
Townsend's Shearwater   *Puffinus auricularis* •
Fluttering Shearwater   *Puffinus gavia*
Little Shearwater   *Puffinus assimilis*
Audubon's Shearwater   *Puffinus lherminieri*
Persian Shearwater   *Puffinus persicus*
Heinroth's Shearwater   *Puffinus heinrothi*
Mascarene Shearwater   *Puffinus atrodorsalis*

Storm Petrels Hydrobatidae
Gray-backed Storm-Petrel   *Garrodia nereis*
Wilson's Storm-Petrel   *Oceanites oceanicus*
Elliot's Storm-Petrel   *Oceanites gracilis*
White-faced Storm-Petrel   *Pelagodroma marina*
Black-bellied Storm-Petrel   *Fregetta tropica*
White-bellied Storm-Petrel   *Fregetta grallaria*
White-throated Storm-Petrel   *Nesofregetta fuliginosa*
European Storm-Petrel   *Hydrobates pelagicus*
Least Storm-Petrel   *Oceanodroma microsoma*
Wedge-rumped Storm-Petrel   *Oceanodroma tethys*
Madeiran Storm-Petrel   *Oceanodroma castro*
Leach's Storm-Petrel   *Oceanodroma leucorhoa*
Swinhoe's Storm-Petrel   *Oceanodroma monorhis*
Tristram's Storm-Petrel   *Oceanodroma tristrami*
Markham's Storm-Petrel   *Oceanodroma markhami*
Matsudaira's Storm-Petrel   *Oceanodroma matsudairae*
Black Storm-Petrel   *Oceanodroma melania*
Ashy Storm-Petrel   *Oceanodroma homochroa* •
Hornby's Storm-Petrel   *Oceanodroma hornbyi*
Fork-tailed Storm-Petrel   *Oceanodroma furcata*

Diving Petrels Pelecanoididae
Peruvian Diving-Petrel   *Pelecanoides garnotii* •
Magellanic Diving-Petrel   *Pelecanoides magellani*
South Georgian Diving-Petrel   *Pelecanoides georgicus*
Common Diving-Petrel   *Pelecanoides urinatrix*

FULL-WEBBED SWIMMERS
Pelecaniformes

Tropicbirds Phaethontidae
Red-billed Tropicbird   *Phaethon aethereus*
Red-tailed Tropicbird   *Phaethon rubricauda*
White-tailed Tropicbird   *Phaethon lepturus*

Pelicans Pelecanidae
Great White Pelican   *Pelecanus onocrotalus*
Pink-backed Pelican   *Pelecanus rufescens*
Spot-billed Pelican   *Pelecanus philippensis*
Dalmatian Pelican   *Pelecanus crispus*

Australian Pelican   *Pelecanus conspicillatus*
American White Pelican   *Pelecanus erythrorhynchos*
Peruvian Pelican   *Pelecanus thagus*
Brown Pelican   *Pelecanus occidentalis*

Gannets and Boobies Sulidae
Northern Gannet   *Morus bassanus*
Cape Gannet   *Morus capensis*
Australasian Gannet   *Morus serrator*
Abbott's Booby   *Sula abbotti* •
Blue-footed Booby   *Sula nebouxii*
Peruvian Booby   *Sula variegata*
Masked Booby   *Sula dactylatra*
Nazca Booby   *Sula granti*
Red-footed Booby   *Sula sula*
Brown Booby   *Sula leucogaster*

Cormorants Phalacrocoracidae
Little Black Cormorant   *Phalacrocorax sulcirostris*
Double-crested Cormorant   *Phalacrocorax auritus*
Indian Cormorant   *Phalacrocorax fuscicollis*
Neotropical Cormorant   *Phalacrocorax brasilianus*
Great Cormorant   *Phalacrocorax carbo*
Cape Cormorant   *Phalacrocorax capensis*
Socotra Cormorant   *Phalacrocorax nigrogularis*
Bank Cormorant   *Phalacrocorax neglectus* •
Japanese Cormorant   *Phalacrocorax capillatus*
Brandt's Cormorant   *Phalacrocorax penicillatus*
European Shag   *Phalacrocorax aristotelis*
Pelagic Cormorant   *Phalacrocorax pelagicus*
Red-faced Cormorant   *Phalacrocorax urile*
Rock Shag   *Phalacrocorax magellanicus*
Guanay Shag   *Phalacrocorax bougainvillii*
Pied Cormorant   *Phalacrocorax varius*
Black-faced Cormorant   *Phalacrocorax fuscescens*
Rough-faced Cormorant   *Phalacrocorax carunculatus*
Bronze Shag   *Phalacrocorax chalconotus*
Chatham Islands Shag   *Phalacrocorax onslowi* •
Auckland Islands Shag   *Phalacrocorax colensoi*
Campbell Island Shag   *Phalacrocorax campbelli*
Bounty Islands Shag   *Phalacrocorax ranfurlyi*
Antarctic Shag   *Phalacrocorax bransfieldensis*
South Georgia Shag   *Phalacrocorax georgianus*
Imperial Shag   *Phalacrocorax atriceps*
Heard Shag   *Phalacrocorax nivalis*
Crozet Shag   *Phalacrocorax melanogenis*
Kerguelen Shag   *Phalacrocorax verrucosus*
Macquarie Shag   *Phalacrocorax purpurascens*
Red-legged Shag   *Phalacrocorax gaimardi*
Spotted Shag   *Phalacrocorax punctatus*
Pitt Island Shag   *Phalacrocorax featherstoni* •
Little Pied Cormorant   *Phalacrocorax melanoleucos*
Long-tailed Cormorant   *Phalacrocorax africanus*
Crowned Cormorant   *Phalacrocorax coronatus*
Little Cormorant   *Phalacrocorax niger*
Pygmy Cormorant   *Phalacrocorax pygmaeus*
Galápagos Cormorant   *Phalacrocorax harrisi* •

Anhingas Anhingidae
Anhinga/American Darter   *Anhinga anhinga*
Oriental Darter   *Anhinga melanogaster*

Frigatebirds Fregatidae
Ascension Island Frigatebird   *Fregata aquila*
Christmas Island Frigatebird   *Fregata andrewsi* •
Magnificent Frigatebird   *Fregata magnificens*
Greater Frigatebird   *Fregata minor*
Lesser Frigatebird   *Fregata ariel*

HERONS AND ALLIES Ciconiiformes

Herons and Bitterns Ardeidae
Whistling Heron   *Syrigma sibilatrix*
Capped Heron   *Pilherodius pileatus*

Gray Heron   *Ardea cinerea*
Great Blue Heron   *Ardea herodias*
Cocoi Heron   *Ardea cocoi*
Pacific Heron   *Ardea pacifica*
Black-headed Heron   *Ardea melanocephala*
Humblot's Heron   *Ardea humbloti* •
White-bellied Heron   *Ardea insignis* •
Great-billed Heron   *Ardea sumatrana*
Goliath Heron   *Ardea goliath*
Purple Heron   *Ardea purpurea*
Great Egret   *Ardea alba*
Reddish Egret   *Egretta rufescens*
Pied Heron   *Egretta picata*
Slaty Egret   *Egretta vinaceigula*
Black Heron   *Egretta ardesiaca*
Tricolored Heron   *Egretta tricolor*
Intermediate Egret   *Egretta intermedia*
White-faced Egret   *Egretta novaehollandiae*
Little Blue Heron   *Egretta caerulea*
Snowy Egret   *Egretta thula*
Little Egret   *Egretta garzetta*
Western Reef-Egret   *Egretta gularis*
Chinese Egret   *Egretta eulophotes*
Pacific Reef-Egret   *Egretta sacra*
Squacco Heron   *Ardeola ralloides*
Indian Pond-Heron   *Ardeola grayii*
Chinese Pond-Heron   *Ardeola bacchus*
Javan Pond-Heron   *Ardeola speciosa*
Madagascar Squacco Heron   *Ardeola idae* •
Rufous-bellied Heron   *Ardeola rufiventris*
Cattle Egret   *Bubulcus ibis*
Striated Heron   *Butorides striata*
Green Heron   *Butorides virescens*
Chestnut-bellied Heron   *Agamia agami*
Black-crowned Night-Heron   *Nycticorax nycticorax*
Rufous Night-Heron   *Nycticorax caledonicus*
Yellow-crowned Night-Heron   *Nyctanassa violacea*
White-backed Night-Heron   *Gorsachius leuconotus*
White-eared Night-Heron   *Gorsachius magnificus* •
Japanese Night-Heron   *Gorsachius goisagi* •
Malaysian Night-Heron   *Gorsachius melanolophus*
Boat-billed Heron   *Cochlearius cochlearius*
Bare-throated Tiger-Heron   *Tigrisoma mexicanum*
Fasciated Tiger-Heron   *Tigrisoma fasciatum*
Rufescent Tiger-Heron   *Tigrisoma lineatum*
Forest Bittern   *Zonerodius heliosylus*
White-crested Tiger-Heron   *Tigriornis leucolopha*
Zigzag Heron   *Zebrilus undulatus*
Stripe-backed Bittern   *Ixobrychus involucris*
Least Bittern   *Ixobrychus exilis*
Yellow Bittern   *Ixobrychus sinensis*
Black-backed Bittern   *Ixobrychus novaezelandiae*
Little Bittern   *Ixobrychus minutus*
Von Schrenck's Bittern   *Ixobrychus eurhythmus*
Cinnamon Bittern   *Ixobrychus cinnamomeus*
African Dwarf Bittern   *Ixobrychus sturmii*
Black Bittern   *Ixobrychus flavicollis*
Pinnated Bittern   *Botaurus pinnatus*
American Bittern   *Botaurus lentiginosus*
Great Bittern   *Botaurus stellaris*
Australasian Bittern   *Botaurus poiciloptilus* •

Hamerkop Scopidae
Hammerkop   *Scopus umbretta*

Storks Ciconiidae
Wood Stork   *Mycteria americana*
Milky Stork   *Mycteria cinerea*
Yellow-billed Stork   *Mycteria ibis*
Painted Stork   *Mycteria leucocephala*
Asian Openbill   *Anastomus oscitans*
African Openbill   *Anastomus lamelligerus*
Black Stork   *Ciconia nigra*
Abdim's Stork   *Ciconia abdimii*

Woolly-necked Stork *Ciconia episcopus*
Storm's Stork *Ciconia stormi* •
Maguari Stork *Ciconia maguari*
European White Stork *Ciconia ciconia*
Oriental White Stork *Ciconia boyciana* •
Black-necked Stork *Ephippiorhynchus asiaticus*
Saddle-billed Stork *Ephippiorhynchus senegalensis*
Jabiru *Jabiru mycteria*
Lesser Adjutant *Leptoptilos javanicus*
Marabou *Leptoptilos crumeniferus*
Greater Adjutant *Leptoptilos dubius* •

Shoebill Balaenicipitidae
Shoebill *Balaeniceps rex*

Ibises and Spoonbills Threskiornithidae
Sacred Ibis *Threskiornis aethiopicus*
Black-headed Ibis *Threskiornis melanocephalus*
Australian White Ibis *Threskiornis molucca*
Straw-necked Ibis *Threskiornis spinicollis*
Black Ibis *Pseudibis papillosa*
White-shouldered Ibis *Pseudibis davisoni* •
Giant Ibis *Pseudibis gigantea* •
Northern Bald Ibis *Geronticus eremita* •
Southern Bald Ibis *Geronticus calvus*
Crested Ibis *Nipponia nippon* •
Olive Ibis *Bostrychia olivacea* •
Spot-breasted Ibis *Bostrychia rara*
Hadada Ibis *Bostrychia hagedash*
Wattled Ibis *Bostrychia carunculata*
Plumbeous Ibis *Theristicus caerulescens*
Buff-necked Ibis *Theristicus caudatus*
Andean Ibis *Theristicus branickii*
Black-faced Ibis *Theristicus melanopis*
Sharp-tailed Ibis *Cercibis oxycerca*
Green Ibis *Mesembrinibis cayennensis*
Whispering Ibis *Phimosus infuscatus*
American White Ibis *Eudocimus albus*
Scarlet Ibis *Eudocimus ruber*
Glossy Ibis *Plegadis falcinellus*
White-faced Ibis *Plegadis chihi*
Puna Ibis *Plegadis ridgwayi*
Madagascar Crested Ibis *Lophotibis cristata*
Eurasian Spoonbill *Platalea leucorodia*
Royal Spoonbill *Platalea regia*
African Spoonbill *Platalea alba*
Black-faced Spoonbill *Platalea minor* •
Yellow-billed Spoonbill *Platalea flavipes*
Roseate Spoonbill *Platalea ajaja*

Flamingos Phoenicopteridae
Greater Flamingo *Phoenicopterus roseus*
Caribbean Flamingo *Phoenicopterus ruber*
Chilean Flamingo *Phoenicopterus chilensis*
Lesser Flamingo *Phoenicopterus minor*
Andean Flamingo *Phoenicopterus andinus*
Puna Flamingo *Phoenicopterus jamesi*

New World Vultures Cathartidae
American Black Vulture *Coragyps atratus*
Turkey Vulture *Cathartes aura*
Lesser Yellow-headed Vulture *Cathartes burrovianus*
Greater Yellow-headed Vulture *Cathartes melambrotus*
Californian Condor *Gymnogyps californianus* •
Andean Condor *Vultur gryphus*
American King Vulture *Sarcoramphus papa*

WATERFOWL Anseriformes

Screamers Anhimidae
Horned Screamer *Anhima cornuta*
Northern Screamer *Chauna chavaria*
Southern Screamer *Chauna torquata*

Ducks, Geese and Swans Anatidae
Magpie Goose *Anseranas semipalmata*
Spotted Whistling-Duck *Dendrocygna guttata*
Plumed Whistling-Duck *Dendrocygna eytoni*
Fulvous Whistling-Duck *Dendrocygna bicolor*
Wandering Whistling-Duck *Dendrocygna arcuata*
Lesser Whistling-Duck *Dendrocygna javanica*
White-faced Whistling-Duck *Dendrocygna viduata*
West Indian Whistling-Duck *Dendrocygna arborea*
Black-bellied Whistling-Duck *Dendrocygna autumnalis*
White-backed Duck *Thalassornis leuconotus*
Mute Swan *Cygnus olor*
Black Swan *Cygnus atratus*
Black-necked Swan *Cygnus melancoryphus*
Trumpeter Swan *Cygnus buccinator*
Whooper Swan *Cygnus cygnus*
Tundra Swan *Cygnus columbianus*
Coscoroba Swan *Coscoroba coscoroba*
Swan Goose *Anser cygnoides* •
Forest Bean Goose *Anser fabalis*
Pink-footed Goose *Anser brachyrhynchus*
Greater White-fronted Goose *Anser albifrons*
Lesser White-fronted Goose *Anser erythropus*
Graylag Goose *Anser anser*
Bar-headed Goose *Anser indicus*
Lesser Snow Goose *Chen caerulescens*
Ross's Goose *Chen rossii*
Emperor Goose *Chen canagica*
Brent Goose *Branta bernicla*
Barnacle Goose *Branta leucopsis*
Tundra Goose *Branta hutchinsii*
Canada Goose *Branta canadensis*
Hawaiian Goose *Branta sandvicensis*
Red-breasted Goose *Branta ruficollis*
Cape Barren Goose *Cereopsis novaehollandiae*
Freckled Duck *Stictonetta naevosa*
Blue-winged Goose *Cyanochen cyanoptera*
Andean Goose *Chloephaga melanoptera*
Upland Goose *Chloephaga picta*
Kelp Goose *Chloephaga hybrida*
Ashy-headed Goose *Chloephaga poliocephala*
Ruddy-headed Goose *Chloephaga rubidiceps*
Orinoco Goose *Neochen jubata*
Egyptian Goose *Alopochen aegyptiaca*
Ruddy Shelduck *Tadorna ferruginea*
South African Shelduck *Tadorna cana*
Australian Shelduck *Tadorna tadornoides*
Paradise Shelduck *Tadorna variegata*
Common Shelduck *Tadorna tadorna*
White-headed Shelduck *Tadorna radjah*
Magellanic Flightless Steamerduck *Tachyeres pteneres*
White-headed Steamerduck *Tachyeres leucocephalus*
Falkland Flightless Steamerduck *Tachyeres brachypterus*
Flying Steamerduck *Tachyeres patachonicus*
Spur-winged Goose *Plectropterus gambensis*
Muscovy Duck *Cairina moschata*
White-winged Duck *Cairina scutulata* •
Knob-billed Duck *Sarkidiornis melanotos*
Hartlaub's Duck *Pteronetta hartlaubii*
Green Pygmy-Goose *Nettapus pulchellus*
Cotton Pygmy-Goose *Nettapus coromandelianus*
African Pygmy-Goose *Nettapus auritus*
Ringed Teal *Callonetta leucophrys*
American Wood Duck *Aix sponsa*
Mandarin Duck *Aix galericulata*
Maned Duck *Chenonetta jubata*
Brazilian Teal *Amazonetta brasiliensis*
Blue Duck *Hymenolaimus malacorhynchos* •
Torrent Duck *Merganetta armata*
Salvadori's Teal *Salvadorina waigiuensis*
African Black Duck *Anas sparsa*
Eurasian Wigeon *Anas penelope*
American Wigeon *Anas americana*

Chiloe Wigeon *Anas sibilatrix*
Falcated Duck *Anas falcata*
Gadwall *Anas strepera*
Baikal Teal *Anas formosa*
Eurasian Teal *Anas crecca*
Green-winged Teal *Anas carolinensis*
Speckled Teal *Anas flavirostris*
Cape Teal *Anas capensis*
Madagascar Teal *Anas bernieri* •
Sunda Teal *Anas gibberifrons*
Andaman Teal *Anas albogularis*
Gray Teal *Anas gracilis*
Chestnut Teal *Anas castanea*
Auckland Island Teal *Anas aucklandica*
Campbell Island Teal *Anas nesiotis* •
Brown Teal *Anas chlorotis* •
Mallard *Anas platyrhynchos*
Laysan Duck *Anas laysanensis* •
Hawaiian Duck *Anas wyvilliana* •
Mottled Duck *Anas fulvigula*
American Black Duck *Anas rubripes*
Yellow-billed Duck *Anas undulata*
Meller's Duck *Anas melleri* •
Spot-billed Duck *Anas poecilorhyncha*
Pacific Black Duck *Anas superciliosa*
Philippine Duck *Anas luzonica*
Spectacled Duck *Anas specularis*
Crested Duck *Anas specularioides*
Northern Pintail *Anas acuta*
Eaton's Pintail *Anas eatoni*
South Georgian Teal *Anas georgica*
White-cheeked Pintail *Anas bahamensis*
Red-billed Duck *Anas erythrorhyncha*
Puna Teal *Anas puna*
Silver Teal *Anas versicolor*
Hottentot Teal *Anas hottentota*
Garganey *Anas querquedula*
Blue-winged Teal *Anas discors*
Cinnamon Teal *Anas cyanoptera*
Red Shoveler *Anas platalea*
Cape Shoveler *Anas smithii*
Australasian Shoveler *Anas rhynchotis*
Northern Shoveler *Anas clypeata*
Pink-eared Duck *Malacorhynchus membranaceus*
Marbled Duck *Marmaronetta angustirostris*
Red-crested Pochard *Netta rufina*
Rosy-billed Pochard *Netta peposaca*
Southern Pochard *Netta erythrophthalma*
Common Pochard *Aythya ferina*
Canvasback *Aythya valisineria*
Redhead *Aythya americana*
Ring-necked Duck *Aythya collaris*
Ferruginous Duck *Aythya nyroca*
Madagascar Pochard *Aythya innotata* •
Baer's Pochard *Aythya baeri*
Hardhead *Aythya australis*
Tufted Duck *Aythya fuligula*
New Zealand Scaup *Aythya novaeseelandiae*
Greater Scaup *Aythya marila*
Lesser Scaup *Aythya affinis*
Common Eider *Somateria mollissima*
King Eider *Somateria spectabilis*
Spectacled Eider *Somateria fischeri*
Steller's Eider *Polysticta stelleri*
Harlequin Duck *Histrionicus histrionicus*
Long-tailed Duck *Clangula hyemalis*
Common Scoter *Melanitta nigra*
Surf Scoter *Melanitta perspicillata*
Velvet Scoter *Melanitta fusca*
Common Goldeneye *Bucephala clangula*
Barrow's Goldeneye *Bucephala islandica*
Bufflehead *Bucephala albeola*
Smew *Mergellus albellus*
Hooded Merganser *Lophodytes cucullatus*

Brazilian Merganser   *Mergus octosetaceus* •
Red-breasted Merganser   *Mergus serrator*
Common Merganser   *Mergus merganser*
Scaly-sided Merganser   *Mergus squamatus* •
Black-headed Duck   *Heteronetta atricapilla*
Masked Duck   *Nomonyx dominica*
Ruddy Duck   *Oxyura jamaicensis*
Andean Ruddy Duck   *Oxyura ferruginea*
White-headed Duck   *Oxyura leucocephala* •
Maccoa Duck   *Oxyura maccoa*
Argentine Blue-billed Duck   *Oxyura vittata*
Australian Blue-billed Duck   *Oxyura australis*
Musk Duck   *Biziura lobata*

DIURNAL BIRDS OF PREY
Falconiformes

Osprey Pandionidae
Osprey   *Pandion haliaetus*

Hawks and Eagles Accipitridae
African Baza   *Aviceda cuculoides*
Madagascar Baza   *Aviceda madagascariensis*
Jerdon's Baza   *Aviceda jerdoni*
Pacific Baza   *Aviceda subcristata*
Black Baza   *Aviceda leuphotes*
Gray-headed Kite   *Leptodon cayanensis*
White-collared Kite   *Leptodon forbesi* •
Hook-billed Kite   *Chondrohierax uncinatus*
Long-tailed Honey-Buzzard   *Henicopernis longicauda*
Black Honey-Buzzard   *Henicopernis infuscatus*
European Honey-Buzzard   *Pernis apivorus*
Barred Honey-Buzzard   *Pernis celebensis*
Oriental Honey-Buzzard   *Pernis ptilorhynchus*
Square-tailed Kite   *Lophoictinia isura*
Black-breasted Kite   *Hamirostra melanosternon*
American Swallow-tailed Kite   *Elanoides forficatus*
Bat Hawk   *Macheiramphus alcinus*
Pearl Kite   *Gampsonyx swainsonii*
Black-shouldered Kite   *Elanus caeruleus*
Australian Black-shouldered Kite   *Elanus axillaris*
White-tailed Kite   *Elanus leucurus*
Letter-winged Kite   *Elanus scriptus*
African Swallow-tailed Kite   *Chelictinia riocourii*
Snail Kite   *Rostrhamus sociabilis*
Slender-billed Kite   *Rostrhamus hamatus*
Double-toothed Kite   *Harpagus bidentatus*
Rufous-thighed Kite   *Harpagus diodon*
Mississippi Kite   *Ictinia mississippiensis*
Plumbeous Kite   *Ictinia plumbea*
Red Kite   *Milvus milvus*
Black Kite   *Milvus migrans*
Whistling Kite   *Haliastur sphenurus*
Brahminy Kite   *Haliastur indus*
White-bellied Sea-Eagle   *Haliaeetus leucogaster*
Sanford's Sea-Eagle   *Haliaeetus sanfordi*
African Fish-Eagle   *Haliaeetus vocifer*
Madagascar Fish-Eagle   *Haliaeetus vociferoides* •
Pallas's Fish-Eagle   *Haliaeetus leucoryphus*
White-tailed Eagle   *Haliaeetus albicilla*
Bald Eagle   *Haliaeetus leucocephalus*
Steller's Sea-Eagle   *Haliaeetus pelagicus*
Lesser Fish-Eagle   *Ichthyophaga humilis*
Gray-headed Fish-Eagle   *Ichthyophaga ichthyaetus*
Palm-nut Vulture   *Gypohierax angolensis*
Hooded Vulture   *Necrosyrtes monachus*
Lammergeier   *Gypaetus barbatus*
Egyptian Vulture   *Neophron percnopterus*
African White-backed Vulture   *Gyps africanus*
Indian White-rumped Vulture   *Gyps bengalensis* •
Indian Long-billed Vulture   *Gyps tenuirostris* •
Long-billed Griffon   *Gyps indicus* •
Rueppell's Griffon   *Gyps rueppellii*
Himalayan Griffon   *Gyps himalayensis*

Eurasian Griffon   *Gyps fulvus*
Cape Griffon   *Gyps coprotheres*
Monk Vulture   *Aegypius monachus*
Lappet-faced Vulture   *Torgos tracheliotus*
White-headed Vulture   *Trigonoceps occipitalis*
Red-headed Vulture   *Sarcogyps calvus*
Short-toed Eagle   *Circaetus gallicus*
Beaudouin's Snake-Eagle   *Circaetus beaudouini*
Black-chested Snake-Eagle   *Circaetus pectoralis*
Brown Snake-Eagle   *Circaetus cinereus*
Southern Banded Snake-Eagle   *Circaetus fasciolatus*
Smaller Banded Snake-Eagle   *Circaetus cinerascens*
Bateleur   *Terathopius ecaudatus*
Great Nicobar Serpent-Eagle   *Spilornis klossi*
Sulawesi Serpent-Eagle   *Spilornis rufipectus*
Mountain Serpent-Eagle   *Spilornis kinabaluensis*
Crested Serpent-Eagle   *Spilornis cheela*
Philippine Serpent-Eagle   *Spilornis holospilus*
Andaman Serpent-Eagle   *Spilornis elgini*
Congo Serpent-Eagle   *Dryotriorchis spectabilis*
Madagascar Serpent-Eagle   *Eutriorchis astur* •
Eurasian Marsh Harrier   *Circus aeruginosus*
African Marsh Harrier   *Circus ranivorus*
Eastern Marsh Harrier   *Circus spilonotus*
Swamp Marsh Harrier   *Circus approximans*
Réunion Harrier   *Circus maillardi* •
Long-winged Harrier   *Circus buffoni*
Spotted Harrier   *Circus assimilis*
Black Harrier   *Circus maurus*
Cinereous Harrier   *Circus cinereus*
Hen Harrier   *Circus cyaneus*
Pallid Harrier   *Circus macrourus*
Pied Harrier   *Circus melanoleucos*
Montagu's Harrier   *Circus pygargus*
African Harrier-Hawk   *Polyboroides typus*
Madagascar Harrier-Hawk   *Polyboroides radiatus*
Lizard Buzzard   *Kaupifalco monogrammicus*
Dark Chanting-Goshawk   *Melierax metabates*
Eastern Chanting-Goshawk   *Melierax poliopterus*
Pale Chanting-Goshawk   *Melierax canorus*
Gabar Goshawk   *Micronisus gabar*
Gray-bellied Goshawk   *Accipiter poliogaster*
Crested Goshawk   *Accipiter trivirgatus*
Red-chested Goshawk   *Accipiter toussenelii*
Sulawesi Crested Goshawk   *Accipiter griseiceps*
African Goshawk   *Accipiter tachi ro*
Chestnut-flanked Sparrowhawk   *Accipiter castanilius*
Shikra   *Accipiter badius*
Nicobar Sparrowhawk   *Accipiter butleri*
Levant Sparrowhawk   *Accipiter brevipes*
Chinese Sparrowhawk   *Accipiter soloensis*
Frances' Sparrowhawk   *Accipiter francesii*
Spot-tailed Sparrowhawk   *Accipiter trinotatus*
Variable Goshawk   *Accipiter hiogaster*
Gray Goshawk   *Accipiter novaehollandiae*
Brown Goshawk   *Accipiter fasciatus*
Black-mantled Goshawk   *Accipiter melanochlamys*
Pied Goshawk   *Accipiter albogularis*
New Caledonia Sparrowhawk   *Accipiter haplochrous*
Fiji Goshawk   *Accipiter rufitorques*
Moluccan Goshawk   *Accipiter henicogrammus*
Blue-and-gray Sparrowhawk   *Accipiter luteoschistaceus*
Imitator Sparrowhawk   *Accipiter imitator*
Gray-headed Goshawk   *Accipiter poliocephalus*
New Britain Goshawk   *Accipiter princeps*
Tiny Hawk   *Accipiter superciliosus*
Semicollared Hawk   *Accipiter collaris*
Red-thighed Sparrowhawk   *Accipiter erythropus*
African Little Sparrowhawk   *Accipiter minullus*
Japanese Sparrowhawk   *Accipiter gularis*
Small Sparrowhawk   *Accipiter nanus*
Besra   *Accipiter virgatus*
Rufous-necked Sparrowhawk   *Accipiter erythrauchen*

Australian Collared Sparrowhawk   *Accipiter cirrocephalus*
New Britain Collared Sparrowhawk   *Accipiter brachyurus*
Vinous-breasted Sparrowhawk   *Accipiter rhodogaster*
Madagascar Sparrowhawk   *Accipiter madagascariensis*
Ovampo Sparrowhawk   *Accipiter ovampensis*
Eurasian Sparrowhawk   *Accipiter nisus*
Rufous-breasted Sparrowhawk   *Accipiter rufiventris*
Sharp-shinned Hawk   *Accipiter striatus*
Plain-breasted Hawk   *Accipiter ventralis*
Rufous-thighed Hawk   *Accipiter erythronemius*
Cooper's Hawk   *Accipiter cooperii*
Gundlach's Hawk   *Accipiter gundlachi* •
Bicolored Hawk   *Accipiter bicolor*
Chilean Hawk   *Accipiter chilensis*
Great Sparrowhawk   *Accipiter melanoleucus*
Henst's Goshawk   *Accipiter henstii*
Northern Goshawk   *Accipiter gentilis*
Meyer's Goshawk   *Accipiter meyerianus*
Chestnut-shouldered Goshawk   *Erythrotriorchis buergersi*
Red Goshawk   *Erythrotriorchis radiatus*
Doria's Hawk   *Megatriorchis doriae*
African Long-tailed Hawk   *Urotriorchis macrourus*
Grasshopper Buzzard   *Butastur rufipennis*
White-eyed Buzzard   *Butastur teesa*
Rufous-winged Buzzard   *Butastur liventer*
Gray-faced Buzzard   *Butastur indicus*
Crane Hawk   *Geranospiza caerulescens*
Plumbeous Hawk   *Leucopternis plumbeus*
Slate-colored Hawk   *Leucopternis schistaceus*
Barred Hawk   *Leucopternis princeps*
Black-faced Hawk   *Leucopternis melanops*
White-browed Hawk   *Leucopternis kuhli*
White-necked Hawk   *Leucopternis lacernulatus*
Semiplumbeous Hawk   *Leucopternis semiplumbeus*
White Hawk   *Leucopternis albicollis*
Gray-backed Hawk   *Leucopternis occidentalis* •
Mantled Hawk   *Leucopternis polionotus*
Rufous Crab Hawk   *Buteogallus aequinoctialis*
Common Black-Hawk   *Buteogallus anthracinus*
Mangrove Black-Hawk   *Buteogallus subtilis*
Great Black-Hawk   *Buteogallus urubitinga*
Savannah Hawk   *Buteogallus meridionalis*
Harris' Hawk   *Parabuteo unicinctus*
Black-collared Hawk   *Busarellus nigricollis*
Black-chested Buzzard-Eagle   *Geranoaetus melanoleucus*
Black Solitary Eagle   *Harpyhaliaetus solitarius*
Crowned Solitary Eagle   *Harpyhaliaetus coronatus* •
Gray Hawk   *Asturina nitida*
Roadside Hawk   *Buteo magnirostris*
Red-shouldered Hawk   *Buteo lineatus*
Ridgway's Hawk   *Buteo ridgwayi*
Broad-winged Hawk   *Buteo platypterus*
White-rumped Hawk   *Buteo leucorrhous*
Short-tailed Hawk   *Buteo brachyurus*
White-throated Hawk   *Buteo albigula*
Swainson's Hawk   *Buteo swainsoni*
White-tailed Hawk   *Buteo albicaudatus*
Galápagos Hawk   *Buteo galapagoensis*
Red-backed Hawk   *Buteo polyosoma*
Puna Hawk   *Buteo poecilochrous*
Zone-tailed Hawk   *Buteo albonotatus*
Hawaiian Hawk   *Buteo solitarius*
Red-tailed Hawk   *Buteo jamaicensis*
Rufous-tailed Hawk   *Buteo ventralis*
Common Buzzard   *Buteo buteo*
African Mountain Buzzard   *Buteo oreophilus*
Madagascar Buzzard   *Buteo brachypterus*
Long-legged Buzzard   *Buteo rufinus*
Upland Buzzard   *Buteo hemilasius*
Ferruginous Hawk   *Buteo regalis*

Rough-legged Buzzard *Buteo lagopus*
African Red-tailed Buzzard *Buteo auguralis*
Augur Buzzard *Buteo augur*
Archer's Buzzard *Buteo archeri*
Jackal Buzzard *Buteo rufofuscus*
Guiana Crested Eagle *Morphnus guianensis*
Harpy Eagle *Harpia harpyja*
New Guinea Eagle *Harpyopsis novaeguineae*
Great Philippine Eagle *Pithecophaga jefferyi* •
Asian Black Eagle *Ictinaetus malayensis*
Lesser Spotted Eagle *Aquila pomarina*
Indian Spotted Eagle *Aquila hastata*
Greater Spotted Eagle *Aquila clanga*
Tawny Eagle *Aquila rapax*
Steppe Eagle *Aquila nipalensis*
Spanish Imperial Eagle *Aquila adalberti*
Eastern Imperial Eagle *Aquila heliaca*
Wahlberg's Eagle *Aquila wahlbergi*
Gurney's Eagle *Aquila gurneyi*
Golden Eagle *Aquila chrysaetos*
Wedge-tailed Eagle *Aquila audax*
Verreaux's Eagle *Aquila verreauxii*
Bonelli's Eagle *Aquila fasciatus*
African Hawk-Eagle *Aquila spilogaster*
Booted Eagle *Aquila pennatus*
Little Eagle *Aquila morphnoides*
Ayres's Hawk-Eagle *Aquila ayresii*
Rufous-bellied Hawk-Eagle *Aquila kienerii*
Martial Eagle *Polemaetus bellicosus*
Black-and-white Hawk-Eagle *Spizastur melanoleucus*
Long-crested Eagle *Lophaetus occipitalis*
Cassin's Hawk-Eagle *Spizaetus africanus*
Changeable Hawk-Eagle *Spizaetus cirrhatus*
Flores Hawk-Eagle *Spizaetus floris* •
Mountain Hawk-Eagle *Spizaetus nipalensis*
Blyth's Hawk-Eagle *Spizaetus alboniger*
Javan Hawk-Eagle *Spizaetus bartelsi* •
Sulawesi Hawk-Eagle *Spizaetus lanceolatus*
Philippine Hawk-Eagle *Spizaetus philippensis*
Wallace's Hawk-Eagle *Spizaetus nanus*
Black Hawk-Eagle *Spizaetus tyrannus*
Ornate Hawk-Eagle *Spizaetus ornatus*
Crowned Hawk-Eagle *Stephanoaetus coronatus*
Black-and-chestnut Eagle *Oroaetus isidori*

Secretary Bird Sagittariidae
Secretary Bird *Sagittarius serpentarius*

Falcons and Caracaras Falconidae
Black Caracara *Daptrius ater*
Red-throated Caracara *Ibycter americanus*
Carunculated Caracara *Phalcoboenus carunculatus*
Mountain Caracara *Phalcoboenus megalopterus*
White-throated Caracara *Phalcoboenus albogularis*
Striated Caracara *Phalcoboenus australis*
Northern Crested Caracara *Caracara cheriway*
Southern Crested Caracara *Caracara plancus*
Yellow-headed Caracara *Milvago chimachima*
Chimango Caracara *Milvago chimango*
Laughing Falcon *Herpetotheres cachinnans*
Barred Forest-Falcon *Micrastur ruficollis*
Plumbeous Forest-Falcon *Micrastur plumbeus*
Lined Forest-Falcon *Micrastur gilvicollis*
Cryptic Forest-Falcon *Micrastur mintoni*
Slaty-backed Forest-Falcon *Micrastur mirandollei*
Collared Forest-Falcon *Micrastur semitorquatus*
Buckley's Forest-Falcon *Micrastur buckleyi*
Spot-winged Falconet *Spiziapteryx circumcincta*
African Pygmy Falcon *Polihierax semitorquatus*
White-rumped Falcon *Polihierax insignis*
Collared Falconet *Microhierax caerulescens*
Black-thighed Falconet *Microhierax fringillarius*
White-fronted Falconet *Microhierax latifrons*
Philippine Falconet *Microhierax erythrogenys*

Pied Falconet *Microhierax melanoleucos*
Lesser Kestrel *Falco naumanni*
Eurasian Kestrel *Falco tinnunculus*
Madagascar Kestrel *Falco newtoni*
Mauritius Kestrel *Falco punctatus*
Seychelles Kestrel *Falco araea*
Spotted Kestrel *Falco moluccensis*
Nankeen Kestrel *Falco cenchroides*
Greater Kestrel *Falco rupicoloides*
American Kestrel *Falco sparverius*
Fox Kestrel *Falco alopex*
Gray Kestrel *Falco ardosiaceus*
Dickinson's Kestrel *Falco dickinsoni*
Madagascar Banded Kestrel *Falco zoniventris*
Red-necked Falcon *Falco chicquera*
Red-footed Falcon *Falco vespertinus*
Amur Falcon *Falco amurensis*
Eleonora's Falcon *Falco eleonorae*
Sooty Falcon *Falco concolor*
Aplomado Falcon *Falco femoralis*
Merlin *Falco columbarius*
Bat Falcon *Falco rufigularis*
Orange-breasted Falcon *Falco deiroleucus*
Eurasian Hobby *Falco subbuteo*
African Hobby *Falco cuvierii*
Oriental Hobby *Falco severus*
Australian Hobby *Falco longipennis*
New Zealand Falcon *Falco novaeseelandiae*
Brown Falcon *Falco berigora*
Gray Falcon *Falco hypoleucos*
Black Falcon *Falco subniger*
Lanner Falcon *Falco biarmicus*
Laggar Falcon *Falco jugger*
Saker Falcon *Falco cherrug* •
Gyrfalcon *Falco rusticolus*
Prairie Falcon *Falco mexicanus*
Barbary Falcon *Falco pelegrinoides*
Taita Falcon *Falco fasciinucha*
Peregrine Falcon *Falco peregrinus*

FOWL-LIKE BIRDS Galliformes

Megapodes Megapodiidae
Australian Brush-Turkey *Alectura lathami*
Wattled Brush-Turkey *Aepypodius arfakianus*
Bruijn's Brush-Turkey *Aepypodius bruijnii*
Red-billed Brush-Turkey *Talegalla cuvieri*
Black-billed Brush-Turkey *Talegalla fuscirostris*
Brown Collared Brush-Turkey *Talegalla jobiensis*
Malleefowl *Leipoa ocellata*
Maleofowl *Macrocephalon maleo* •
Moluccan Scrubfowl *Megapodius wallacei*
Polynesian Scrubfowl *Megapodius pritchardii* •
Micronesian Scrubfowl *Megapodius laperouse* •
Nicobar Scrubfowl *Megapodius nicobariensis*
Philippine Scrubfowl *Megapodius cumingii*
Sula Scrubfowl *Megapodius bernsteinii*
Tanimbar Scrubfowl *Megapodius tenimberensis*
Dusky Scrubfowl *Megapodius freycinet*
Forsten's Scrubfowl *Megapodius forstenii*
Melanesian Scrubfowl *Megapodius eremita*
Vanuatu Scrubfowl *Megapodius layardi*
New Guinea Scrubfowl *Megapodius affinis*
Orange-footed Scrubfowl *Megapodius reinwardt*

Curassows and Guans Cracidae
Plain Chachalaca *Ortalis vetula*
Gray-headed Chachalaca *Ortalis cinereiceps*
Chestnut-winged Chachalaca *Ortalis garrula*
Rufous-vented Chachalaca *Ortalis ruficauda*
Rufous-headed Chachalaca *Ortalis erythroptera*
Rufous-bellied Chachalaca *Ortalis wagleri*
West Mexican Chachalaca *Ortalis poliocephala*
Chaco Chachalaca *Ortalis canicollis*

White-bellied Chachalaca *Ortalis leucogastra*
Little Chachalaca *Ortalis motmot*
Speckled Chachalaca *Ortalis guttata*
Buff-browed Chachalaca *Ortalis superciliaris*
Band-tailed Guan *Penelope argyrotis*
Bearded Guan *Penelope barbata*
Baudó Guan *Penelope ortoni*
Andean Guan *Penelope montagnii*
Marail Guan *Penelope marail*
Rusty-margined Guan *Penelope superciliaris*
Red-faced Guan *Penelope dabbenei*
Crested Guan *Penelope purpurascens*
Cauca Guan *Penelope perspicax* •
White-winged Guan *Penelope albipennis* •
Spix's Guan *Penelope jacquacu*
Dusky-legged Guan *Penelope obscura*
White-crested Guan *Penelope pileata*
Chestnut-bellied Guan *Penelope ochrogaster*
White-browed Guan *Penelope jacucaca*
Blue-throated Piping-Guan *Pipile cumanensis*
Trinidad Piping-Guan *Pipile pipile* •
Red-throated Piping-Guan *Pipile cujubi*
Black-fronted Piping-Guan *Pipile jacutinga* •
Wattled Piping-Guan *Aburria aburri*
Black Guan *Chamaepetes unicolor*
Sickle-winged Guan *Chamaepetes goudotii*
Highland Guan *Penelopina nigra*
Horned Guan *Oreophasis derbianus* •
Nocturnal Curassow *Nothocrax urumutum*
Crestless Curassow *Mitu tomentosum*
Salvin's Curassow *Mitu salvini*
Amazonian Razor-billed-Curassow *Mitu tuberosum*
Alagoas Curassow *Mitu mitu*
Helmeted Curassow *Pauxi pauxi*
Horned Curassow *Pauxi unicornis* •
Great Curassow *Crax rubra*
Blue-billed Curassow *Crax alberti* •
Yellow-knobbed Curassow *Crax daubentoni*
Black Curassow *Crax alector*
Bare-faced Curassow *Crax fasciolata*
Wattled Curassow *Crax globulosa*
Red-billed Curassow *Crax blumenbachii* •

Turkeys Meleagridae
Wild Turkey *Meleagris gallopavo*
Ocellated Turkey *Meleagris ocellata*

Grouse Tetraonidae
Spruce Grouse *Falcipennis canadensis*
Blue Grouse *Dendragapus obscurus*
Siberian Grouse *Dendragapus falcipennis*
White-tailed Ptarmigan *Lagopus leucura*
Willow Ptarmigan *Lagopus lagopus*
Rock Ptarmigan *Lagopus muta*
Black-billed Capercaillie *Tetrao parvirostris*
Western Capercaillie *Tetrao urogallus*
Eurasian Black Grouse *Tetrao tetrix*
Caucasian Black Grouse *Tetrao mlokosiewiczi*
Hazel Grouse *Bonasa bonasia*
Severtzov's Hazel Grouse *Bonasa sewerzowi*
Ruffed Grouse *Bonasa umbellus*
Greater Sage-Grouse *Centrocercus urophasianus*
Gunnison Sage-Grouse *Centrocercus minimus* •
Sharp-tailed Grouse *Tympanuchus phasianellus*
Greater Prairie Chicken *Tympanuchus cupido*
Lesser Prairie Chicken *Tympanuchus pallidicinctus*

New World Quail Odontophoridae
Bearded Tree-Quail *Dendrortyx barbatus*
Long-tailed Tree-Quail *Dendrortyx macroura*
Buffy-crowned Tree-Quail *Dendrortyx leucophrys*
Mountain Quail *Oreortyx pictus*
Scaled Quail *Callipepla squamata*
Elegant Quail *Callipepla douglasii*

California Quail   *Callipepla californica*
Gambel's Quail   *Callipepla gambelii*
Barred Quail   *Philortyx fasciatus*
Northern Bobwhite   *Colinus virginianus*
Black-throated Bobwhite   *Colinus nigrogularis*
Crested Bobwhite   *Colinus cristatus*
Marbled Woodquail   *Odontophorus gujanensis*
Spot-winged Woodquail   *Odontophorus capueira*
Black-eared Woodquail   *Odontophorus melanotis*
Rufous-fronted Woodquail   *Odontophorus erythrops*
Black-fronted Woodquail   *Odontophorus atrifrons*
Chestnut Woodquail   *Odontophorus hyperythrus*
Dark-backed Woodquail   *Odontophorus melanonotus*
Rufous-breasted Woodquail   *Odontophorus speciosus*
Tacarcuna Woodquail   *Odontophorus dialeucos*
Gorgeted Woodquail   *Odontophorus strophium* •
Venezuelan Woodquail   *Odontophorus columbianus*
Black-breasted Woodquail   *Odontophorus leucolaemus*
Stripe-faced Woodquail   *Odontophorus balliviani*
Starred Woodquail   *Odontophorus stellatus*
Spotted Woodquail   *Odontophorus guttatus*
Singing Quail   *Dactylortyx thoracicus*
Montezuma Quail   *Cyrtonyx montezumae*
Ocellated Quail   *Cyrtonyx ocellatus*
Tawny-faced Quail   *Rhynchortyx cinctus*

Pheasants and partridges Phasianidae
Snow Partridge   *Lerwa lerwa*
Verreaux's Monal-Partridge   *Tetraophasis obscurus*
Széchenyi's Monal-Partridge   *Tetraophasis szechenyii*
Caucasian Snowcock   *Tetraogallus caucasicus*
Caspian Snowcock   *Tetraogallus caspius*
Altai Snowcock   *Tetraogallus altaicus*
Tibetan Snowcock   *Tetraogallus tibetanus*
Himalayan Snowcock   *Tetraogallus himalayensis*
Rock Partridge   *Alectoris graeca*
Chukar   *Alectoris chukar*
Philby's Partridge   *Alectoris philbyi*
Rusty-necklaced Partridge   *Alectoris magna*
Barbary Partridge   *Alectoris barbara*
Red-legged Partridge   *Alectoris rufa*
Arabian Partridge   *Alectoris melanocephala*
See-see Partridge   *Ammoperdix griseogularis*
Sand Partridge   *Ammoperdix heyi*
Black Francolin   *Francolinus francolinus*
Painted Francolin   *Francolinus pictus*
Chinese Francolin   *Francolinus pintadeanus*
Indian Gray Francolin   *Francolinus pondicerianus*
Swamp Francolin   *Francolinus gularis*
Coqui Francolin   *Francolinus coqui*
White-throated Francolin   *Francolinus albogularis*
Schlegel's Francolin   *Francolinus schlegelii*
Latham's Francolin   *Francolinus lathami*
Crested Francolin   *Francolinus sephaena*
Ring-necked Francolin   *Francolinus streptophorus*
Finsch's Francolin   *Francolinus finschi*
Red-winged Francolin   *Francolinus levaillantii*
Gray-winged Francolin   *Francolinus africanus*
Moorland Francolin   *Francolinus psilolaemus*
Shelley's Francolin   *Francolinus shelleyi*
Orange River Francolin   *Francolinus levaillantoides*
Scaly Francolin   *Francolinus squamatus*
Ahanta Francolin   *Francolinus ahantensis*
Gray-striped Francolin   *Francolinus griseostriatus*
Nahan's Francolin   *Francolinus nahani* •
Hartlaub's Francolin   *Francolinus hartlaubi*
Double-spurred Francolin   *Francolinus bicalcaratus*
Heuglin's Francolin   *Francolinus icterorhynchus*
Clapperton's Francolin   *Francolinus clappertoni*
Harwood's Francolin   *Francolinus harwoodi*
Red-billed Francolin   *Francolinus adspersus*
Cape Francolin   *Francolinus capensis*
Natal Francolin   *Francolinus natalensis*
Hildebrandt's Francolin   *Francolinus hildebrandti*

Yellow-necked Francolin   *Francolinus leucoscepus*
Gray-breasted Francolin   *Francolinus rufopictus*
Red-necked Francolin   *Francolinus afer*
Swainson's Francolin   *Francolinus swainsonii*
Jackson's Francolin   *Francolinus jacksoni*
Handsome Francolin   *Francolinus nobilis*
Mount Cameroon Francolin   *Francolinus camerunensis* •
Swierstra's Francolin   *Francolinus swierstrai*
Chestnut-naped Francolin   *Francolinus castaneicollis*
Erckel's Francolin   *Francolinus erckelii*
Pale-bellied Francolin   *Francolinus ochropectus* •
Gray Partridge   *Perdix perdix*
Daurian Partridge   *Perdix dauurica*
Tibetan Partridge   *Perdix hodgsoniae*
Long-billed Partridge   *Rhizothera longirostris*
Madagascar Partridge   *Margaroperdix madagascarensis*
Black Wood-Partridge   *Melanoperdix niger*
Japanese Quail   *Coturnix japonica*
Common Quail   *Coturnix coturnix*
Harlequin Quail   *Coturnix delegorguei*
Rain Quail   *Coturnix coromandelica*
Stubble Quail   *Coturnix pectoralis*
Brown Quail   *Coturnix ypsilophora*
Blue-breasted Quail   *Coturnix chinensis*
African Blue Quail   *Coturnix adansonii*
Snow Mountain Quail   *Anurophasis monorthonyx*
Jungle Bush-Quail   *Perdicula asiatica*
Rock Bush-Quail   *Perdicula argoondah*
Painted Bush-Quail   *Perdicula erythrorhyncha*
Manipur Bush-Quail   *Perdicula manipurensis*
Udzungwa Forest-Partridge   *Xenoperdix udzungwensis* •
Common Hill-Partridge   *Arborophila torqueola*
Sichuan Hill-Partridge   *Arborophila rufipectus* •
Chestnut-breasted Hill-Partridge   *Arborophila mandellii*
White-necklaced Partridge   *Arborophila gingica*
Rufous-throated Hill-Partridge   *Arborophila rufogularis*
White-cheeked Hill-Partridge   *Arborophila atrogularis*
Taiwan Hill-Partridge   *Arborophila crudigularis*
Hainan Hill-Partridge   *Arborophila ardens*
Chestnut-bellied Tree-Partridge   *Arborophila javanica*
Gray-breasted Hill-Partridge   *Arborophila orientalis*
Barred Hill-Partridge   *Arborophila brunneopectus*
Orange-necked Hill-Partridge   *Arborophila davidi* •
Chestnut-headed Tree-Partridge   *Arborophila cambodiana*
Red-breasted Tree-Partridge   *Arborophila hyperythra*
Red-billed Hill-Partridge   *Arborophila rubrirostris*
Scaly-breasted Partridge   *Arborophila chloropus*
Annam Hill-Partridge   *Arborophila merlini*
Chestnut-necklaced Hill-Partridge   *Arborophila charltonii*
Ferruginous Partridge   *Caloperdix oculeus*
Crimson-headed Wood-Partridge   *Haematortyx sanguiniceps*
Crested Partridge   *Rollulus rouloul*
Stone Partridge   *Ptilopachus petrosus*
Mountain Bamboo-Partridge   *Bambusicola fytchii*
Chinese Bamboo-Partridge   *Bambusicola thoracicus*
Red Spurfowl   *Galloperdix spadicea*
Painted Spurfowl   *Galloperdix lunulata*
Sri Lanka Spurfowl   *Galloperdix bicalcarata*
Blood Pheasant   *Ithaginis cruentus*
Western Horned Tragopan   *Tragopan melanocephalus*
Satyr Tragopan   *Tragopan satyra*
Blyth's Tragopan   *Tragopan blythii*
Temminck's Tragopan   *Tragopan temminckii*
Cabot's Tragopan   *Tragopan caboti*
Koklass Pheasant   *Pucrasia macrolopha*
Himalayan Monal   *Lophophorus impejanus*
Sclater's Monal   *Lophophorus sclateri*
Chinese Monal   *Lophophorus lhuysii*
Red Junglefowl   *Gallus gallus*
Gray Junglefowl   *Gallus sonneratii*
Sri Lanka Junglefowl   *Gallus lafayetii*

Green Junglefowl   *Gallus varius*
Kalij Pheasant   *Lophura leucomelanos*
Imperial Pheasant   *Lophura imperialis*
Edwards's Pheasant   *Lophura edwardsi* •
Vietnamese Pheasant   *Lophura hatinhensis* •
Swinhoe's Pheasant   *Lophura swinhoii*
Salvadori's Pheasant   *Lophura inornata*
Silver Pheasant   *Lophura nycthemera*
Crestless Fireback   *Lophura erythrophthalma*
Crested Fireback   *Lophura ignita*
Siamese Fireback   *Lophura diardi*
Bulwer's Pheasant   *Lophura bulweri*
White Eared-Pheasant   *Crossoptilon crossoptilon*
Brown Eared-Pheasant   *Crossoptilon mantchuricum*
Blue Eared-Pheasant   *Crossoptilon auritum*
Cheer Pheasant   *Catreus wallichi*
Elliot's Pheasant   *Syrmaticus ellioti*
Mrs Hume's Pheasant   *Syrmaticus humiae*
Mikado Pheasant   *Syrmaticus mikado*
Copper Pheasant   *Syrmaticus soemmerringii*
Reeves' Pheasant   *Syrmaticus reevesii*
Common Pheasant   *Phasianus colchicus*
Green Pheasant   *Phasianus versicolor*
Golden Pheasant   *Chrysolophus pictus*
Lady Amhurst's Pheasant   *Chrysolophus amherstiae*
Bronze-tailed Peacock-Pheasant   *Polyplectron chalcurum*
Mountain Peacock-Pheasant   *Polyplectron inopinatum*
Germain's Peacock-Pheasant   *Polyplectron germaini*
Gray Peacock-Pheasant   *Polyplectron bicalcaratum*
Malaysian Peacock-Pheasant   *Polyplectron malacense*
Bornean Peacock-Pheasant   *Polyplectron schleiermacheri* •
Palawan Peacock-Pheasant   *Polyplectron napoleonis*
Crested Argus   *Rheinardia ocellata*
Great Argus   *Argusianus argus*
Indian Peafowl   *Pavo cristatus*
Green Peafowl   *Pavo muticus*
Congo Peafowl   *Afropavo congensis*

Guineafowl Numididae
White-breasted Guineafowl   *Agelastes meleagrides*
Black Guineafowl   *Agelastes niger*
Helmeted Guineafowl   *Numida meleagris*
Plumed Guineafowl   *Guttera plumifera*
Crested Guineafowl   *Guttera pucherani*
Vulturine Guineafowl   *Acryllium vulturinum*

HOATZIN Opisthocomiformes

Hoatzin Opisthocomidae
Hoatzin   *Opisthocomus hoazin*

CRANES, RAILS AND ALLIES
Gruiformes

Mesites Mesitornithidae
White-breasted Mesite   *Mesitornis variegatus*
Brown Mesite   *Mesitornis unicolor*
Bensch's Monia   *Monias benschi*

Buttonquails Turnicidae
Small Buttonquail   *Turnix sylvaticus*
Red-backed Buttonquail   *Turnix maculosus*
Hottentot Buttonquail   *Turnix hottentottus*
Yellow-legged Buttonquail   *Turnix tanki*
Spotted Buttonquail   *Turnix ocellatus*
Barred Buttonquail   *Turnix suscitator*
Madagascar Buttonquail   *Turnix nigricollis*
Black-breasted Buttonquail   *Turnix melanogaster*
Chestnut-backed Buttonquail   *Turnix castanotus*
Buff-breasted Buttonquail   *Turnix olivii* •
Painted Buttonquail   *Turnix varius*
Luzon Buttonquail   *Turnix worcesteri*
Sumba Buttonquail   *Turnix everetti*

Red-chested Buttonquail *Turnix pyrrhothorax*
Little Buttonquail *Turnix velox*
Quail-Plover *Ortyxelos meiffrenii*

Cranes Gruidae
Gray Crowned Crane *Balearica regulorum*
Black Crowned Crane *Balearica pavonina*
Demoiselle Crane *Anthropoides virgo*
Stanley Crane *Anthropoides paradiseus*
Wattled Crane *Bugeranus carunculatus*
Siberian White Crane *Grus leucogeranus* •
Sandhill Crane *Grus canadensis*
Sarus Crane *Grus antigone*
Brolga *Grus rubicunda*
Japanese White-naped Crane *Grus vipio*
Common Crane *Grus grus*
Hooded Crane *Grus monacha*
Whooping Crane *Grus americana* •
Black-necked Crane *Grus nigricollis*
Red-crowned Crane *Grus japonensis* •
Limpkin Aramidae
Limpkin *Aramus guarauna*

Trumpeters Psophiidae
Common Trumpeter *Psophia crepitans*
Green-winged Trumpeter *Psophia viridis*
White-winged Trumpeter *Psophia leucoptera*

Rails and Coots Rallidae
White-spotted Flufftail *Sarothrura pulchra*
Buff-spotted Flufftail *Sarothrura elegans*
Red-chested Flufftail *Sarothrura rufa*
Chestnut-headed Flufftail *Sarothrura lugens*
Streaky-breasted Flufftail *Sarothrura boehmi*
Striped Flufftail *Sarothrura affinis*
Madagascar Flufftail *Sarothrura insularis*
White-winged Flufftail *Sarothrura ayresi* •
Slender-billed Flufftail *Sarothrura watersi* •
Nkulengu Rail *Himantornis haematopus*
Gray-throated Rail *Canirallus oculeus*
Madagascar Gray-throated Rail *Canirallus kioloides*
Swinhoe's Yellow Crake *Coturnicops exquisitus*
Yellow Rail *Coturnicops noveboracensis*
Darwin's Rail *Coturnicops notatus*
Ocellated Crake *Micropygia schomburgkii*
Chestnut Forest Rail *Rallina rubra*
White-striped Forest Rail *Rallina leucospila*
Forbes's Forest Rail *Rallina forbesi*
Mayr's Forest Rail *Rallina mayri*
Red-necked Crake *Rallina tricolor*
Andaman Banded Crake *Rallina canningi*
Red-legged Banded Crake *Rallina fasciata*
Slaty-legged Banded Crake *Rallina eurizonoides*
Chestnut-headed Crake *Anurolimnas castaneiceps*
Russet-crowned Crake *Anurolimnas viridis*
Black-banded Crake *Anurolimnas fasciatus*
Rufous-sided Crake *Laterallus melanophaius*
Rusty-flanked Crake *Laterallus levraudi* •
Ruddy Crake *Laterallus ruber*
White-throated Crake *Laterallus albigularis*
Gray-breasted Crake *Laterallus exilis*
Junín Rail *Laterallus tuerosi* •
Black Rail *Laterallus jamaicensis*
Galápagos Rail *Laterallus spilonotus*
Red-and-white Crake *Laterallus leucopyrrhus*
Rufous-faced Crake *Laterallus xenopterus*
Woodford's Rail *Nesoclopeus woodfordi*
Weka *Gallirallus australis*
New Caledonian Rail *Gallirallus lafresnayanus* •
Lord Howe Island Rail *Gallirallus sylvestris* •
Okinawa Rail *Gallirallus okinawae* •
Buff-banded Rail *Gallirallus philippensis*
New Britain Rail *Gallirallus insignis*
Guam Rail *Gallirallus owstoni*

Barred Rail *Gallirallus torquatus*
Calayan Rail *Gallirallus calayanensis*
Roviana Rail *Gallirallus roviana*
Slaty-breasted Rail *Gallirallus striatus*
Clapper Rail *Rallus longirostris*
King Rail *Rallus elegans*
Plain-flanked Rail *Rallus wetmorei* •
Virginia Rail *Rallus limicola*
Bogotá Rail *Rallus semiplumbeus* •
Austral Rail *Rallus antarcticus*
Water Rail *Rallus aquaticus*
African Water Rail *Rallus caerulescens*
Madagascar Rail *Rallus madagascariensis*
Luzon Rail *Lewinia mirificus*
Lewin's Rail *Lewinia pectoralis*
Auckland Islands Rail *Lewinia muelleri*
Madagascar White-throated Rail *Dryolimnas cuvieri*
African Crake *Crecopsis egregia*
Corn Crake *Crex crex*
Rouget's Rail *Rougetius rougetii*
Snoring Rail *Aramidopsis plateni*
Inaccessible Island Rail *Atlantisia rogersi*
Little Woodrail *Aramides mangle*
Rufous-necked Woodrail *Aramides axillaris*
Gray-necked Woodrail *Aramides cajanea*
Brown Woodrail *Aramides wolfi*
Giant Woodrail *Aramides ypecaha*
Slaty-breasted Woodrail *Aramides saracura*
Red-winged Woodrail *Aramides calopterus*
Uniform Crake *Amaurolimnas concolor*
Blue-faced Rail *Gymnocrex rosenbergii*
Bare-eyed Rail *Gymnocrex plumbeiventris*
Talaud Rail *Gymnocrex talaudensis* •
Brown Crake *Amaurornis akool*
Isabelline Bushhen *Amaurornis isabellina*
Plain Bushhen *Amaurornis olivacea*
White-breasted Waterhen *Amaurornis phoenicurus*
Talaud Bushhen *Amaurornis magnirostris*
Moluccan Rufous-tailed Moorhen *Amaurornis moluccana*
African Black Crake *Amaurornis flavirostra*
Olivier's Rail *Amaurornis olivieri* •
Black-tailed Crake *Amaurornis bicolor*
Little Crake *Porzana parva*
Baillon's Crake *Porzana pusilla*
Eurasian Spotted Crake *Porzana porzana*
Australian Spotted Crake *Porzana fluminea*
Sora *Porzana carolina*
Dot-winged Crake *Porzana spiloptera*
Ash-throated Crake *Porzana albicollis*
Ruddy-breasted Crake *Porzana fusca*
Band-bellied Crake *Porzana paykullii*
Spotless Crake *Porzana tabuensis*
Henderson Island Crake *Porzana atra*
Yellow-breasted Crake *Porzana flaviventer*
White-browed Crake *Porzana cinerea*
Striped Crake *Aenigmatolimnas marginalis*
Zapata Rail *Cyanolimnas cerverai*
Colombian Crake *Neocrex colombiana*
Paint-billed Crake *Neocrex erythrops*
Spotted Rail *Pardirallus maculatus*
Blackish Rail *Pardirallus nigricans*
Plumbeous Rail *Pardirallus sanguinolentus*
Drummer Rail *Habroptila wallacii*
Chestnut-bellied Rail *Eulabeornis castaneoventris*
New Guinea Flightless Rail *Megacrex inepta*
Watercock *Gallicrex cinerea*
Purple Swamphen *Porphyrio porphyrio*
Takahe *Porphyrio mantelli*
Allen's Gallinule *Porphyrio alleni*
American Purple Gallinule *Porphyrio martinica*
Azure Gallinule *Porphyrio flavirostris*
San Cristobal Mountain Rail *Gallinula silvestris* •
Tristan Moorhen *Gallinula nesiotis*

Common Moorhen *Gallinula chloropus*
Dusky Moorhen *Gallinula tenebrosa*
Lesser Moorhen *Gallinula angulata*
Spot-flanked Gallinule *Gallinula melanops*
Black-tailed Native-hen *Gallinula ventralis*
Tasmanian Native-hen *Gallinula mortierii*
Red-knobbed Coot *Fulica cristata*
Eurasian Coot *Fulica atra*
Hawaiian Coot *Fulica alai*
American Coot *Fulica americana*
Caribbean Coot *Fulica caribaea*
White-winged Coot *Fulica leucoptera*
Andean Coot *Fulica ardesiaca*
Red-gartered Coot *Fulica armillata*
Red-fronted Coot *Fulica rufifrons*
Giant Coot *Fulica gigantea*
Horned Coot *Fulica cornuta*

Sungrebes or Finfoots Heliornithidae
African Finfoot *Podica senegalensis*
Masked Finfoot *Heliopais personatus*
Sungrebe *Heliornis fulica*

Kagu Rhynochetidae
Kagu *Rhynochetos jubatus* •

Sunbittern Eurypygidae
Sunbittern *Eurypyga helias*

Seriemas Cariamidae
Red-legged Seriema *Cariama cristata*
Black-legged Seriema *Chunga burmeisteri*

Bustards Otididae
Great Bustard *Otis tarda*
Arabian Bustard *Ardeotis arabs*
Kori Bustard *Ardeotis kori*
Indian Bustard *Ardeotis nigriceps* •
Australian Bustard *Ardeotis australis*
Houbara Bustard *Chlamydotis undulata*
Macqueen's Bustard *Chlamydotis macqueenii*
Ludwig's Bustard *Neotis ludwigii*
Denham's Bustard *Neotis denhami*
Heuglin's Bustard *Neotis heuglinii*
Nubian Bustard *Neotis nuba*
White-bellied Bustard *Eupodotis senegalensis*
Blue Bustard *Eupodotis caerulescens*
Vigors's Bustard *Eupodotis vigorsii*
Rueppell's Bustard *Eupodotis rueppellii*
Little Brown Bustard *Eupodotis humilis*
Savile's Bustard *Eupodotis savilei*
Buff-crested Bustard *Eupodotis gindiana*
Red-crested Bustard *Eupodotis ruficrista*
Black Bustard *Eupodotis afra*
White-quilled Bustard *Eupodotis afraoides*
Black-bellied Bustard *Lissotis melanogaster*
Hartlaub's Bustard *Lissotis hartlaubii*
Bengal Florican *Houbaropsis bengalensis* •
Lesser Florican *Sypheotides indicus* •
Little Bustard *Tetrax tetrax*

SHOREBIRDS, GULLS, AUKS
Charadriiformes

Jacanas Jacanidae
Lesser African Jacana *Microparra capensis*
Greater African Jacana *Actophilornis africanus*
Madagascar Jacana *Actophilornis albinucha*
Comb-crested Jacana *Irediparra gallinacea*
Pheasant-tailed Jacana *Hydrophasianus chirurgus*
Bronze-winged Jacana *Metopidius indicus*
Northern Jacana *Jacana spinosa*
Wattled Jacana *Jacana jacana*

Painted Snipe Rostratulidae
Greater Painted-Snipe *Rostratula benghalensis*
American Painted-Snipe *Rostratula semicollaris*

Crab Plover Dromadidae
Crab-Plover *Dromas ardeola*

Oystercatchers Haematopodidae
Magellanic Oystercatcher *Haematopus leucopodus*
Blackish Oystercatcher *Haematopus ater*
American Black Oystercatcher *Haematopus bachmani*
American Oystercatcher *Haematopus palliatus*
African Black Oystercatcher *Haematopus moquini*
Eurasian Oystercatcher *Haematopus ostralegus*
Australian Pied Oystercatcher *Haematopus longirostris*
South Island Oystercatcher *Haematopus finschi*
Chatham Islands Oystercatcher *Haematopus chathamensis* •
Variable Oystercatcher *Haematopus unicolor*
Sooty Oystercatcher *Haematopus fuliginosus*

Ibisbill Ibidorhynchidae
Ibisbill *Ibidorhyncha struthersii*

Avocets and Stilts Recurvirostridae
Black-winged Stilt *Himantopus himantopus*
White-headed Stilt *Himantopus leucocephalus*
Black Stilt *Himantopus novaezelandiae* •
Black-necked Stilt *Himantopus mexicanus*
Black-tailed Stilt *Himantopus melanurus*
Banded Stilt *Cladorhynchus leucocephalus*
Eurasian Avocet *Recurvirostra avosetta*
American Avocet *Recurvirostra americana*
Red-necked Avocet *Recurvirostra novaehollandiae*
Andean Avocet *Recurvirostra andina*

Thick-knees Burhinidae
Water Thick-knee *Burhinus vermiculatus*
Eurasian Thick-knee *Burhinus oedicnemus*
Senegal Thick-knee *Burhinus senegalensis*
Spotted Thick-knee *Burhinus capensis*
Double-striped Thick-knee *Burhinus bistriatus*
Peruvian Thick-knee *Burhinus superciliaris*
Bush Thick-knee *Burhinus grallarius*
Great Thick-knee *Burhinus recurvirostris*
Beach Thick-knee *Esacus giganticus*

Coursers and Pratincoles Glareolidae
Egyptian Plover *Pluvianus aegyptius*
Cream-colored Courser *Cursorius cursor*
Burchell's Courser *Cursorius rufus*
Temminck's Courser *Cursorius temminckii*
Indian Courser *Cursorius coromandelicus*
Two-banded Courser *Smutsornis africanus*
Heuglin's Courser *Rhinoptilus cinctus*
Violet-tipped Courser *Rhinoptilus chalcopterus*
Jerdon's Courser *Rhinoptilus bitorquatus* •
Australian Pratincole *Stiltia isabella*
Collared Pratincole *Glareola pratincola*
Oriental Pratincole *Glareola maldivarum*
Black-winged Pratincole *Glareola nordmanni*
Madagascar Pratincole *Glareola ocularis*
Rock Pratincole *Glareola nuchalis*
Gray Pratincole *Glareola cinerea*
Small Pratincole *Glareola lactea*

Plovers Charadriidae
Northern Lapwing *Vanellus vanellus*
Long-toed Lapwing *Vanellus crassirostris*
Blacksmith Plover *Vanellus armatus*
Spur-winged Lapwing *Vanellus spinosus*
River Lapwing *Vanellus duvaucelii*

Yellow-wattled Lapwing *Vanellus malabaricus*
Black-headed Lapwing *Vanellus tectus*
White-headed Lapwing *Vanellus albiceps*
Senegal Lapwing *Vanellus lugubris*
Black-winged Lapwing *Vanellus melanopterus*
Crowned Lapwing *Vanellus coronatus*
Senegal Wattled Lapwing *Vanellus senegallus*
Spot-breasted Lapwing *Vanellus melanocephalus*
Brown-chested Lapwing *Vanellus superciliosus*
Gray-headed Lapwing *Vanellus cinereus*
Red-wattled Lapwing *Vanellus indicus*
Javanese Lapwing *Vanellus macropterus* •
Banded Lapwing *Vanellus tricolor*
Masked Lapwing *Vanellus miles*
Sociable Lapwing *Vanellus gregarius* •
White-tailed Lapwing *Vanellus leucurus*
Pied Lapwing *Vanellus cayanus*
Southern Lapwing *Vanellus chilensis*
Andean Lapwing *Vanellus resplendens*
Red-kneed Dotterel *Erythrogonys cinctus*
Pacific Golden-Plover *Pluvialis fulva*
American Golden-Plover *Pluvialis dominica*
European Golden-Plover *Pluvialis apricaria*
Gray Plover *Pluvialis squatarola*
Red-breasted Plover *Charadrius obscurus* •
Greater Ringed Plover *Charadrius hiaticula*
Semipalmated Plover *Charadrius semipalmatus*
Long-billed Plover *Charadrius placidus*
Little Ringed Plover *Charadrius dubius*
Wilson's Plover *Charadrius wilsonia*
Killdeer *Charadrius vociferus*
Piping Plover *Charadrius melodus*
Black-banded Sandplover *Charadrius thoracicus*
Kittlitz's Sandplover *Charadrius pecuarius*
St. Helena Sandplover *Charadrius sanctaehelenae*
Three-banded Plover *Charadrius tricollaris*
Forbes's Banded Plover *Charadrius forbesi*
White-fronted Plover *Charadrius marginatus*
Chestnut-banded Plover *Charadrius pallidus*
Snowy Plover *Charadrius alexandrinus*
Javan Plover *Charadrius javanicus*
Red-capped Plover *Charadrius ruficapillus*
Malaysian Sandplover *Charadrius peronii*
Collared Plover *Charadrius collaris*
Puna Plover *Charadrius alticola*
Two-banded Plover *Charadrius falklandicus*
Double-banded Plover *Charadrius bicinctus*
Lesser Sandplover *Charadrius mongolus*
Greater Sandplover *Charadrius leschenaultii*
Caspian Plover *Charadrius asiaticus*
Oriental Plover *Charadrius veredus*
Mountain Dotterel *Charadrius morinellus*
Rufous-chested Plover *Charadrius modestus*
Mountain Plover *Charadrius montanus*
Hooded Plover *Thinornis cucullatus*
New Zealand Shore Plover *Thinornis novaeseelandiae* •
Black-fronted Dotterel *Elseyornis melanops*
Inland Dotterel *Peltohyas australis*
Wrybill *Anarhynchus frontalis*
Diademed Sandpiper-Plover *Phegornis mitchellii*
Tawny-throated Dotterel *Oreopholus ruficollis*

Magellanic Plover Pluvianellidae
Magellanic Plover *Pluvianellus socialis*

Sandpipers and Snipe Scolopacidae
Eurasian Woodcock *Scolopax rusticola*
Amami Woodcock *Scolopax mira*
Bukidnon Woodcock *Scolopax bukidnonensis*
Dusky Woodcock *Scolopax saturata*
Sulawesi Woodcock *Scolopax celebensis*
Moluccan Woodcock *Scolopax rochussenii* •
American Woodcock *Scolopax minor*
Chatham Islands Snipe *Coenocorypha pusilla*

New Zealand Snipe *Coenocorypha aucklandica*
Jack Snipe *Lymnocryptes minimus*
Solitary Snipe *Gallinago solitaria*
Latham's Snipe *Gallinago hardwickii*
Wood Snipe *Gallinago nemoricola*
Pintailed Snipe *Gallinago stenura*
Swinhoe's Snipe *Gallinago megala*
African Snipe *Gallinago nigripennis*
Madagascar Snipe *Gallinago macrodactyla*
Great Snipe *Gallinago media*
Common Snipe *Gallinago gallinago*
Wilson's Snipe *Gallinago delicata*
Magellan Snipe *Gallinago paraguaiae*
Puna Snipe *Gallinago andina*
Noble Snipe *Gallinago nobilis*
Giant Snipe *Gallinago undulata*
Cordilleran Snipe *Gallinago stricklandii*
Andean Snipe *Gallinago jamesoni*
Imperial Snipe *Gallinago imperialis*
Short-billed Dowitcher *Limnodromus griseus*
Long-billed Dowitcher *Limnodromus scolopaceus*
Asian Dowitcher *Limnodromus semipalmatus*
Black-tailed Godwit *Limosa limosa*
Hudsonian Godwit *Limosa haemastica*
Bar-tailed Godwit *Limosa lapponica*
Marbled Godwit *Limosa fedoa*
Eskimo Curlew *Numenius borealis* •
Little Curlew *Numenius minutus*
Eurasian Whimbrel *Numenius phaeopus*
Bristle-thighed Curlew *Numenius tahitiensis*
Slender-billed Curlew *Numenius tenuirostris* •
Eurasian Curlew *Numenius arquata*
Long-billed Curlew *Numenius americanus*
Far-eastern Curlew *Numenius madagascariensis*
Upland Sandpiper *Bartramia longicauda*
Spotted Redshank *Tringa erythropus*
Common Redshank *Tringa totanus*
Marsh Sandpiper *Tringa stagnatilis*
Common Greenshank *Tringa nebularia*
Nordmann's Greenshank *Tringa guttifer* •
Greater Yellowlegs *Tringa melanoleuca*
Lesser Yellowlegs *Tringa flavipes*
Green Sandpiper *Tringa ochropus*
Solitary Sandpiper *Tringa solitaria*
Wood Sandpiper *Tringa glareola*
Terek Sandpiper *Xenus cinereus*
Common Sandpiper *Actitis hypoleucos*
Spotted Sandpiper *Actitis macularius*
Gray-tailed Tattler *Heterosceles brevipes*
Wandering Tattler *Heterosceles incanus*
Willet *Catoptrophorus semipalmatus*
Tuamotu Sandpiper *Prosobonia cancellata* •
Ruddy Turnstone *Arenaria interpres*
Black Turnstone *Arenaria melanocephala*
Surfbird *Aphriza virgata*
Great Knot *Calidris tenuirostris*
Red Knot *Calidris canutus*
Sanderling *Calidris alba*
Semipalmated Sandpiper *Calidris pusilla*
Western Sandpiper *Calidris mauri*
Red-necked Stint *Calidris ruficollis*
Little Stint *Calidris minuta*
Temminck's Stint *Calidris temminckii*
Long-toed Stint *Calidris subminuta*
Least Sandpiper *Calidris minutilla*
White-rumped Sandpiper *Calidris fuscicollis*
Baird's Sandpiper *Calidris bairdii*
Pectoral Sandpiper *Calidris melanotos*
Sharp-tailed Sandpiper *Calidris acuminata*
Curlew Sandpiper *Calidris ferruginea*
Dunlin *Calidris alpina*
Purple Sandpiper *Calidris maritima*
Rock Sandpiper *Calidris ptilocnemis*
Stilt Sandpiper *Calidris himantopus*

331

Spoon-billed Sandpiper   *Eurynorhynchus pygmeus* •
Broad-billed Sandpiper   *Limicola falcinellus*
Buff-Breasted Sandpiper   *Tryngites subruficollis*
Ruff   *Philomachus pugnax*
Wilson's Phalarope   *Phalaropus tricolor*
Red-necked Phalarope   *Phalaropus lobatus*
Red Phalarope   *Phalaropus fulicarius*

Plains Wanderer Pedionomidae
Plains-wanderer   *Pedionomus torquatus* •

Seedsnipe Thinocoridae
Rufous-bellied Seedsnipe   *Attagis gayi*
White-bellied Seedsnipe   *Attagis malouinus*
Gray-breasted Seedsnipe   *Thinocorus orbignyianus*
Least Seedsnipe   *Thinocorus rumicivorus*

Sheathbills Chionididae
American Sheathbill   *Chionis albus*
Black-faced Sheathbill   *Chionis minor*

Skuas or Jaegers Stercorariidae
Chilean Skua   *Stercorarius chilensis*
South Polar Skua   *Stercorarius maccormicki*
Brown Skua   *Stercorarius antarcticus*
Great Skua   *Stercorarius skua*
Pomarine Jaeger   *Stercorarius pomarinus*
Parasitic Jaeger   *Stercorarius parasiticus*
Long-tailed Jaeger   *Stercorarius longicaudus*

Gulls and Terns Laridae
Magellan Gull   *Larus scoresbii*
Pacific Gull   *Larus pacificus*
Belcher's Gull   *Larus belcheri*
Olrog's Gull   *Larus atlanticus*
Black-tailed Gull   *Larus crassirostris*
Gray Gull   *Larus modestus*
Heermann's Gull   *Larus heermanni*
White-eyed Gull   *Larus leucophthalmus*
Sooty Gull   *Larus hemprichii*
Mew Gull   *Larus canus*
Audouin's Gull   *Larus audouinii*
Ring-billed Gull   *Larus delawarensis*
Kelp Gull   *Larus dominicanus*
Californian Gull   *Larus californicus*
Greater Black-backed Gull   *Larus marinus*
Glaucous-winged Gull   *Larus glaucescens*
Western Gull   *Larus occidentalis*
Yellow-footed Gull   *Larus livens*
Glaucous Gull   *Larus hyperboreus*
Iceland Gull   *Larus glaucoides*
Thayer's Gull   *Larus thayeri*
Herring Gull   *Larus argentatus*
Lesser Black-backed Gull   *Larus fuscus*
Heuglin's Gull   *Larus heuglini*
Vega Gull   *Larus vegae*
American Herring Gull   *Larus smithsonianus*
Caspian Gull   *Larus cachinnans*
Armenian Gull   *Larus armenicus*
Steppe Gull   *Larus barabensis*
Yellow-legged Gull   *Larus michahellis*
Great Black-headed Gull   *Larus ichthyaetus*
Slaty-backed Gull   *Larus schistisagus*
Indian Black-headed Gull   *Larus brunnicephalus*
Gray-headed Gull   *Larus cirrocephalus*
Hartlaub's Gull   *Larus hartlaubii*
Silver Gull   *Larus novaehollandiae*
Red-billed Gull   *Larus scopulinus*
Black-billed Gull   *Larus bulleri* •
Brown-hooded Gull   *Larus maculipennis*
Common Black-headed Gull   *Larus ridibundus*
Slender-billed Gull   *Larus genei*
Bonaparte's Gull   *Larus philadelphia*
Saunders's Gull   *Larus saundersi*

Andean Gull   *Larus serranus*
Mediterranean Gull   *Larus melanocephalus*
Relict Gull   *Larus relictus*
Lava Gull   *Larus fuliginosus*
Laughing Gull   *Larus atricilla*
Franklin's Gull   *Larus pipixcan*
Little Gull   *Larus minutus*
Ivory Gull   *Pagophila eburnea*
Ross's Gull   *Rhodostethia rosea*
Sabine's Gull   *Xema sabini*
Swallow-tailed Gull   *Creagrus furcatus*
Red-legged Kittiwake   *Rissa brevirostris*
Black-legged Kittiwake   *Rissa tridactyla*
Gull-billed Tern   *Sterna nilotica*
Caspian Tern   *Sterna caspia*
Elegant Tern   *Sterna elegans*
Lesser Crested Tern   *Sterna bengalensis*
Sandwich Tern   *Sterna sandvicensis*
Chinese Crested Tern   *Sterna bernsteini* •
Royal Tern   *Sterna maxima*
Greater Crested Tern   *Sterna bergii*
River Tern   *Sterna aurantia*
Roseate Tern   *Sterna dougallii*
Black-naped Tern   *Sterna sumatrana*
White-fronted Tern   *Sterna striata*
South American Tern   *Sterna hirundinacea*
Common Tern   *Sterna hirundo*
Arctic Tern   *Sterna paradisaea*
Antarctic Tern   *Sterna vittata*
Kerguelen Tern   *Sterna virgata*
Forster's Tern   *Sterna forsteri*
Trudeau's Tern   *Sterna trudeaui*
Little Tern   *Sterna albifrons*
Saunders's Tern   *Sterna saundersi*
Least Tern   *Sterna antillarum*
Amazon Tern   *Sterna superciliaris*
Chilean Tern   *Sterna lorata* •
Australian Fairy Tern   *Sterna nereis*
Damara Tern   *Sterna balaenarum*
White-cheeked Tern   *Sterna repressa*
Black-bellied Tern   *Sterna acuticauda*
Aleutian Tern   *Sterna aleutica*
Gray-backed Tern   *Sterna lunata*
Black-fronted Tern   *Sterna albostriata* •
Bridled Tern   *Sterna anaethetus*
Sooty Tern   *Sterna fuscata*
Whiskered Tern   *Chlidonias hybrida*
White-winged Black Tern   *Chlidonias leucopterus*
Black Tern   *Chlidonias niger*
Large-billed Tern   *Phaetusa simplex*
Lesser Noddy   *Anous tenuirostris*
Black Noddy   *Anous minutus*
Brown Noddy   *Anous stolidus*
Blue Noddy   *Procelsterna cerulea*
Gray Noddy   *Procelsterna albivitta*
Common White Tern   *Gygis alba*
Inca Tern   *Larosterna inca*

Skimmers Rynchopidae
Black Skimmer   *Rynchops niger*
African Skimmer   *Rynchops flavirostris*
Indian Skimmer   *Rynchops albicollis*

Auks Alcidae
Little Auk   *Alle alle*
Common Murre   *Uria aalge*
Thick-billed Murre   *Uria lomvia*
Razorbill   *Alca torda*
Black Guillemot   *Cepphus grylle*
Pigeon Guillemot   *Cepphus columba*
Spectacled Guillemot   *Cepphus carbo*
Marbled Murrelet   *Brachyramphus marmoratus* •
Long-billed Murrelet   *Brachyramphus perdix*
Kittlitz's Murrelet   *Brachyramphus brevirostris* •

Xantus's Murrelet   *Synthliboramphus hypoleucus*
Craveri's Murrelet   *Synthliboramphus craveri*
Ancient Murrelet   *Synthliboramphus antiquus*
Crested Murrelet   *Synthliboramphus wumizusume*
Cassin's Auklet   *Ptychoramphus aleuticus*
Parakeet Auklet   *Aethia psittacula*
Crested Auklet   *Aethia cristatella*
Whiskered Auklet   *Aethia pygmaea*
Least Auklet   *Aethia pusilla*
Rhinoceros Auklet   *Cerorhinca monocerata*
Atlantic Puffin   *Fratercula arctica*
Horned Puffin   *Fratercula corniculata*
Tufted Puffin   *Fratercula cirrhata*

SANDGROUSE Pterocliformes

Sandgrouse Pteroclididae
Tibetan Sandgrouse   *Syrrhaptes tibetanus*
Pallas's Sandgrouse   *Syrrhaptes paradoxus*
Pin-tailed Sandgrouse   *Pterocles alchata*
Namaqua Sandgrouse   *Pterocles namaqua*
Chestnut-bellied Sandgrouse   *Pterocles exustus*
Spotted Sandgrouse   *Pterocles senegallus*
Black-bellied Sandgrouse   *Pterocles orientalis*
Yellow-throated Sandgrouse   *Pterocles gutturalis*
Crowned Sandgrouse   *Pterocles coronatus*
Black-faced Sandgrouse   *Pterocles decoratus*
Madagascar Sandgrouse   *Pterocles personatus*
Lichtenstein's Sandgrouse   *Pterocles lichtensteinii*
Double-banded Sandgrouse   *Pterocles bicinctus*
Four-banded Sandgrouse   *Pterocles quadricinctus*
Painted Sandgrouse   *Pterocles indicus*
Variegated Sandgrouse   *Pterocles burchelli*

PIGEONS Columbiformes

Doves and Pigeons Columbidae
Rock-Pigeon   *Columba livia*
Blue Hill Pigeon   *Columba rupestris*
Snow Pigeon   *Columba leuconota*
Speckled Pigeon   *Columba guinea*
White-collared Pigeon   *Columba albitorques*
Stock-Pigeon   *Columba oenas*
Yellow-eyed Pigeon   *Columba eversmanni*
Somali Pigeon   *Columba oliviae*
Common Wood-Pigeon   *Columba palumbus*
Trocaz Pigeon   *Columba trocaz*
Bolle's Pigeon   *Columba bollii*
African Wood-Pigeon   *Columba unicincta*
Laurel Pigeon   *Columba junoniae* •
African Olive Pigeon   *Columba arquatrix*
Cameroon Olive Pigeon   *Columba sjostedti*
São Tomé Olive Pigeon   *Columba thomensis*
Eastern Bronze-naped Pigeon   *Columba delegorguei*
Bronze-naped Pigeon   *Columba iriditorques*
São Tomé Bronze-naped Pigeon   *Columba malherbii*
African Lemon Dove   *Columba larvata*
São Tomé Lemon Dove   *Columba simplex*
Comoro Olive Pigeon   *Columba pollenii*
Speckled Wood-Pigeon   *Columba hodgsonii*
White-naped Pigeon   *Columba albinucha*
Ashy Wood-Pigeon   *Columba pulchricollis*
Nilgiri Wood-Pigeon   *Columba elphinstonii*
Sri Lanka Wood-Pigeon   *Columba torringtoni*
Pale-capped Pigeon   *Columba punicea*
Silvery Pigeon   *Columba argentina* •
Andaman Wood-Pigeon   *Columba palumboides*
Japanese Wood-Pigeon   *Columba janthina*
White-throated Pigeon   *Columba vitiensis*
White-headed Pigeon   *Columba leucomela*
Yellow-legged Pigeon   *Columba pallidiceps* •
White-crowned Pigeon   *Patagioenas leucocephala*
Scaly-naped Pigeon   *Patagioenas squamosa*
Scaled Pigeon   *Patagioenas speciosa*

Picazuro Pigeon *Patagioenas picazuro*
Bare-eyed Pigeon *Patagioenas corensis*
American Spotted Pigeon *Patagioenas maculosa*
Band-tailed Pigeon *Patagioenas fasciata*
Chilean Pigeon *Patagioenas araucana*
Jamaican Band-tailed Pigeon *Patagioenas caribaea*
Rufous Pigeon *Patagioenas cayennensis*
Red-billed Pigeon *Patagioenas flavirostris*
Salvin's Pigeon *Patagioenas oenops*
Plain Pigeon *Patagioenas inornata*
Plumbeous Pigeon *Patagioenas plumbea*
Short-billed Pigeon *Patagioenas nigrirostris*
Ruddy Pigeon *Patagioenas subvinacea*
Dusky Pigeon *Patagioenas goodsoni*
Mauritius Pink Pigeon *Nesoenas mayeri* •
European Turtle-Dove *Streptopelia turtur*
Dusky Turtle-Dove *Streptopelia lugens*
Pink-bellied Turtle-Dove *Streptopelia hypopyrrha*
Oriental Turtle-Dove *Streptopelia orientalis*
Island Collared-Dove *Streptopelia bitorquata*
Eurasian Collared-Dove *Streptopelia decaocto*
African Collared-Dove *Streptopelia roseogrisea*
African White-winged Dove *Streptopelia reichenowi*
Mourning Collared-Dove *Streptopelia decipiens*
Red-eyed Dove *Streptopelia semitorquata*
Ring-necked Dove *Streptopelia capicola*
Vinaceous Turtle-Dove *Streptopelia vinacea*
Red Collared-Dove *Streptopelia tranquebarica*
Madagascar Turtle-Dove *Streptopelia picturata*
Spotted Turtle-Dove *Streptopelia chinensis*
Laughing Turtle-Dove *Streptopelia senegalensis*
Barred Cuckoo-Dove *Macropygia unchall*
Large Brown Cuckoo-Dove *Macropygia phasianella*
Dusky Cuckoo-Dove *Macropygia magna*
Brown Cuckoo-Dove *Macropygia amboinensis*
Andamans Cuckoo-Dove *Macropygia rufipennis*
Philippine Cuckoo-Dove *Macropygia tenuirostris*
Ruddy Cuckoo-Dove *Macropygia emiliana*
Black-billed Cuckoo-Dove *Macropygia nigrirostris*
Mackinlay's Cuckoo-Dove *Macropygia mackinlayi*
Little Cuckoo-Dove *Macropygia ruficeps*
Great Cuckoo-Dove *Reinwardtoena reinwardtii*
Pied Cuckoo-Dove *Reinwardtoena browni*
Crested Cuckoo-Dove *Reinwardtoena crassirostris*
White-faced Cuckoo-Dove *Turacoena manadensis*
Black Cuckoo-Dove *Turacoena modesta*
Emerald-spotted Wood-Dove *Turtur chalcospilos*
Black-billed Wood-Dove *Turtur abyssinicus*
Blue-spotted Wood-Dove *Turtur afer*
White-breasted Wood-Dove *Turtur tympanistria*
Blue-headed Wood-Dove *Turtur brehmeri*
Namaqua Dove *Oena capensis*
Common Emerald Dove *Chalcophaps indica*
Stephan's Ground-Dove *Chalcophaps stephani*
New Guinea Black Bronzewing *Henicophaps albifrons*
New Britain Bronzewing *Henicophaps foersteri*
Common Bronzewing *Phaps chalcoptera*
Brush Bronzewing *Phaps elegans*
Flock Bronzewing *Phaps histrionica*
Crested Pigeon *Geophaps lophotes*
Spinifex Pigeon *Geophaps plumifera*
Squatter Pigeon *Geophaps scripta*
Partridge Pigeon *Geophaps smithii*
Chestnut-quilled Rock-Pigeon *Petrophassa rufipennis*
White-quilled Rock-Pigeon *Petrophassa albipennis*
Diamond Dove *Geopelia cuneata*
Zebra Ground-Dove *Geopelia striata*
Peaceful Dove *Geopelia placida*
Barred Dove *Geopelia maugei*
Bar-shouldered Dove *Geopelia humeralis*
Wonga Pigeon *Leucosarcia melanoleuca*
Mourning Dove *Zenaida macroura*
Socorro Dove *Zenaida graysoni*
Eared Dove *Zenaida auriculata*

Zenaida Dove *Zenaida aurita*
Galápagos Dove *Zenaida galapagoensis*
White-winged Dove *Zenaida asiatica*
West Peruvian Dove *Zenaida meloda*
Common Ground-Dove *Columbina passerina*
Plain-breasted Ground-Dove *Columbina minuta*
Ecuadorian Ground-Dove *Columbina buckleyi*
Ruddy Ground-Dove *Columbina talpacoti*
Picui Ground-Dove *Columbina picui*
Gold-billed Ground-Dove *Columbina cruziana*
Blue-eyed Ground-Dove *Columbina cyanopis* •
Inca Dove *Columbina inca*
Scaly Dove *Columbina squammata*
Blue Ground-Dove *Claravis pretiosa*
Purple-barred Ground-Dove *Claravis godefrida* •
Purple-breasted Ground-Dove *Claravis mondetoura*
Bare-faced Ground-Dove *Metriopelia ceciliae*
Bare-eyed Ground-Dove *Metriopelia morenoi*
Black-winged Ground-Dove *Metriopelia melanoptera*
Bronze-winged Ground-Dove *Metriopelia aymara*
Long-tailed Ground-Dove *Uropelia campestris*
White-tipped Dove *Leptotila verreauxi*
White-faced Dove *Leptotila megalura*
Gray-fronted Dove *Leptotila rufaxilla*
Gray-headed Dove *Leptotila plumbeiceps*
Pallid Dove *Leptotila pallida*
Brown-backed Dove *Leptotila battyi*
Grenada Dove *Leptotila wellsi* •
White-bellied Dove *Leptotila jamaicensis*
Cassin's Dove *Leptotila cassini*
Buff-bellied Dove *Leptotila ochraceiventris*
Tolima Dove *Leptotila conoveri* •
Lawrence's Quail-Dove *Geotrygon lawrencii*
Veracruz Quail-Dove *Geotrygon carrikeri*
Costa Rican Quail-Dove *Geotrygon costaricensis*
Russet-crowned Quail-Dove *Geotrygon goldmani*
Saphire Quail-Dove *Geotrygon saphirina*
Gray-faced Quail-Dove *Geotrygon caniceps*
White-fronted Quail-Dove *Geotrygon leucometopia*
Crested Quail-Dove *Geotrygon versicolor*
Rufous-breasted Quail-Dove *Geotrygon chiriquensis*
Olive-backed Quail-Dove *Geotrygon veraguensis*
White-faced Quail-Dove *Geotrygon albifacies*
Lined Quail-Dove *Geotrygon linearis*
White-throated Quail-Dove *Geotrygon frenata*
Key West Quail-Dove *Geotrygon chrysia*
Bridled Quail-Dove *Geotrygon mystacea*
Violaceous Quail-Dove *Geotrygon violacea*
Ruddy Quail-Dove *Geotrygon montana*
Blue-headed Quail-Dove *Starnoenas cyanocephala* •
Nicobar Pigeon *Caloenas nicobarica*
Luzon Bleeding-heart *Gallicolumba luzonica*
Mindanao Bleeding-heart *Gallicolumba crinigera* •
Mindoro Bleeding-heart *Gallicolumba platenae* •
Negros Bleeding-heart *Gallicolumba keayi* •
Sulu Bleeding-heart *Gallicolumba menagei* •
Cinnamon Ground-Dove *Gallicolumba rufigula*
Sulawesi Ground-Dove *Gallicolumba tristigmata*
White-breasted Ground-Dove *Gallicolumba jobiensis*
Truk Island Ground-Dove *Gallicolumba kubaryi*
Society Islands Ground-Dove *Gallicolumba erythroptera* •
White-throated Ground-Dove *Gallicolumba xanthonura*
Friendly Quail-Dove *Gallicolumba stairi*
Santa Cruz Ground-Dove *Gallicolumba sanctaecrucis* •
Thick-billed Ground-Dove *Gallicolumba salamonis*
Marquesan Ground-Dove *Gallicolumba rubescens* •
Gray-breasted Quail-Dove *Gallicolumba beccarii*
Palau Ground-Dove *Gallicolumba canifrons*
Wetar Island Ground-Dove *Gallicolumba hoedtii* •
Thick-billed Ground-Pigeon *Trugon terrestris*
Pheasant Pigeon *Otidiphaps nobilis*
Western Crowned-Pigeon *Goura cristata*

Maroon-breasted Crowned-Pigeon *Goura scheepmakeri*
Victoria Crowned-Pigeon *Goura victoria*
Tooth-billed Pigeon *Didunculus strigirostris* •
White-eared Brown-Dove *Phapitreron leucotis*
Amethyst Brown-Dove *Phapitreron amethystinus*
Tawitawi Brown-Dove *Phapitreron cinereiceps* •
Little Green-Pigeon *Treron olax*
Pink-necked Green-Pigeon *Treron vernans*
Cinnamon-headed Green-Pigeon *Treron fulvicollis*
Orange-breasted Green-Pigeon *Treron bicinctus*
Pompadour Green-Pigeon *Treron pompadora*
Thick-billed Green-Pigeon *Treron curvirostra*
Gray-cheeked Green-Pigeon *Treron griseicauda*
Sumba Green-Pigeon *Treron teysmannii*
Flores Green-Pigeon *Treron floris*
Timor Green-Pigeon *Treron psittaceus* •
Large Green-Pigeon *Treron capellei*
Yellow-footed Green-Pigeon *Treron phoenicopterus*
Bruce's Green-Pigeon *Treron waalia*
Madagascar Green-Pigeon *Treron australis*
Pemba Green-Pigeon *Treron pembaensis*
São Tomé Green-Pigeon *Treron sanctithomae*
Yellow-vented Green-Pigeon *Treron seimundi*
Pintailed Green-Pigeon *Treron apicauda*
African Green-Pigeon *Treron calvus*
Sumatran Green-Pigeon *Treron oxyurus*
Wedge-tailed Green-Pigeon *Treron sphenurus*
White-bellied Green-Pigeon *Treron sieboldii*
Whistling Green-Pigeon *Treron formosae*
Black-backed Fruit-Dove *Ptilinopus cinctus*
Black-banded Fruit-Dove *Ptilinopus alligator*
Red-naped Fruit-Dove *Ptilinopus dohertyi*
Pink-headed Fruit-Dove *Ptilinopus porphyreus*
Yellow-breasted Fruit-Dove *Ptilinopus occipitalis*
Flame-breasted Fruit-Dove *Ptilinopus marchei*
Cream-bellied Fruit-Dove *Ptilinopus merrilli*
Red-eared Fruit-Dove *Ptilinopus fischeri*
Jambu Fruit-Dove *Ptilinopus jambu*
Maroon-chinned Fruit-Dove *Ptilinopus subgularis*
Black-chinned Fruit-Dove *Ptilinopus leclancheri*
Scarlet-breasted Fruit-Dove *Ptilinopus bernsteinii*
Wompoo Fruit-Dove *Ptilinopus magnificus*
Pink-spotted Fruit-Dove *Ptilinopus perlatus*
Ornate Fruit-Dove *Ptilinopus ornatus*
Silver-shouldered Fruit-Dove *Ptilinopus tannensis*
Orange-fronted Fruit-Dove *Ptilinopus aurantiifrons*
Wallace's Fruit-Dove *Ptilinopus wallacii*
Superb Fruit-Dove *Ptilinopus superbus*
Many-colored Fruit-Dove *Ptilinopus perousii*
Purple-capped Fruit-Dove *Ptilinopus porphyraceus*
Palau Fruit-Dove *Ptilinopus pelewensis*
Rarotonga Fruit-Dove *Ptilinopus rarotongensis*
Marianas Fruit-Dove *Ptilinopus roseicapilla* •
Rose-crowned Fruit-Dove *Ptilinopus regina*
Silver-capped Fruit-Dove *Ptilinopus richardsii*
Gray-green Fruit-Dove *Ptilinopus purpuratus*
Mahatea Fruit-Dove *Ptilinopus chalcurus*
Atoll Fruit-Dove *Ptilinopus coralensis*
Grey's Fruit-Dove *Ptilinopus greyii*
Rapa Island Fruit-Dove *Ptilinopus huttoni*
White-capped Fruit-Dove *Ptilinopus dupetithouarsii*
Moustached Fruit-Dove *Ptilinopus mercierii*
Henderson Island Fruit-Dove *Ptilinopus insularis*
Lilac-capped Fruit-Dove *Ptilinopus coronulatus*
Crimson-capped Fruit-Dove *Ptilinopus pulchellus*
Blue-capped Fruit-Dove *Ptilinopus monacha*
White-bibbed Fruit-Dove *Ptilinopus rivoli*
Yellow-bibbed Fruit-Dove *Ptilinopus solomonensis*
Claret-breasted Fruit-Dove *Ptilinopus viridis*
White-headed Fruit-Dove *Ptilinopus eugeniae*
Orange-bellied Fruit-Dove *Ptilinopus iozonus*
Knob-billed Fruit-Dove *Ptilinopus insolitus*
Gray-headed Fruit-Dove *Ptilinopus hyogastrus*

Carunculated Fruit-Dove *Ptilinopus granulifrons*
Black-naped Fruit-Dove *Ptilinopus melanospilus*
Dwarf Fruit-Dove *Ptilinopus nanus*
Negros Fruit-Dove *Ptilinopus arcanus* •
Orange Dove *Ptilinopus victor*
Golden Dove *Ptilinopus luteovirens*
Yellow-headed Fruit-Dove *Ptilinopus layardi*
Cloven-feathered Dove *Drepanoptila holosericea*
Madagascar Blue-Pigeon *Alectroenas madagascariensis*
Comoro Blue-Pigeon *Alectroenas sganzini*
Seychelles Blue-Pigeon *Alectroenas pulcherrima*
Pink-bellied Imperial-Pigeon *Ducula poliocephala*
White-bellied Imperial-Pigeon *Ducula forsteni*
Mindoro Imperial-Pigeon *Ducula mindorensis*
Gray-headed Imperial-Pigeon *Ducula radiata*
Spotted Imperial-Pigeon *Ducula carola*
Green Imperial-Pigeon *Ducula aenea*
White-spectacled Imperial-Pigeon *Ducula perspicillata*
Elegant Imperial-Pigeon *Ducula concinna*
Pacific Imperial-Pigeon *Ducula pacifica*
Red-knobbed Imperial-Pigeon *Ducula rubricera*
Micronesian Imperial-Pigeon *Ducula oceanica*
Polynesian Imperial-Pigeon *Ducula aurorae* •
Nukuhiva Imperial-Pigeon *Ducula galeata* •
Spice Imperial-Pigeon *Ducula myristicivora*
Purple-tailed Imperial-Pigeon *Ducula rufigaster*
Cinnamon-bellied Imperial-Pigeon *Ducula basilica*
Finsch's Imperial-Pigeon *Ducula finschii*
Shining Imperial-Pigeon *Ducula chalconota*
Island Imperial-Pigeon *Ducula pistrinaria*
Pink-headed Imperial-Pigeon *Ducula rosacea*
Christmas Island Imperial-Pigeon *Ducula whartoni*
Gray Imperial-Pigeon *Ducula pickeringii*
Peale's Imperial-Pigeon *Ducula latrans*
Chestnut-bellied Imperial-Pigeon *Ducula brenchleyi*
Baker's Imperial-Pigeon *Ducula bakeri*
New Caledonian Imperial-Pigeon *Ducula goliath*
Pinon Imperial-Pigeon *Ducula pinon*
Black Imperial-Pigeon *Ducula melanochroa*
Collared Imperial-Pigeon *Ducula mullerii*
Banded Imperial-Pigeon *Ducula zoeae*
Mountain Imperial-Pigeon *Ducula badia*
Dark-backed Imperial-Pigeon *Ducula lacernulata*
Timor Imperial-Pigeon *Ducula cineracea* •
Pied Imperial-Pigeon *Ducula bicolor*
Australian Pied Imperial-Pigeon *Ducula spilorrhoa*
Silver-tipped Imperial-Pigeon *Ducula luctuosa*
Topknot Pigeon *Lopholaimus antarcticus*
New Zealand Fruit-Pigeon *Hemiphaga novaeseelandiae*
Sombre Pigeon *Cryptophaps poecilorrhoa*
Papuan Mountain-Pigeon *Gymnophaps albertisii*
Long-tailed Mountain-Pigeon *Gymnophaps mada*
Pale Mountain-Pigeon *Gymnophaps solomonensis*

PARROTS AND RELATIVES
Psittaciformes

Cockatoos Cacatuidae
Palm Cockatoo *Probosciger aterrimus*
Red-tailed Black-Cockatoo *Calyptorhynchus banksii*
Glossy Black-Cockatoo *Calyptorhynchus lathami*
Yellow-tailed Black-Cockatoo *Calyptorhynchus funereus*
Short-billed Black-Cockatoo *Calyptorhynchus latirostris* •
Long-billed Black-Cockatoo *Calyptorhynchus baudinii* •
Gang-gang Cockatoo *Callocephalon fimbriatum*
Galah *Eolophus roseicapilla*
Eastern Long-billed Corella *Cacatua tenuirostris*
Western Long-billed Corella *Cacatua pastinator*
Little Corella *Cacatua sanguinea*
Tanimbar Cockatoo *Cacatua goffiniana*
Philippine Islands Cockatoo *Cacatua haematuropygia* •
Yellow-crested Cockatoo *Cacatua sulphurea* •
Ducorps's Cockatoo *Cacatua ducorpsii*

Major Mitchell's Cockatoo *Cacatua leadbeateri*
Sulfur-crested Cockatoo *Cacatua galerita*
Blue-eyed Cockatoo *Cacatua ophthalmica*
Salmon-crested Cockatoo *Cacatua moluccensis*
Great White Cockatoo *Cacatua alba*
Cockatiel *Nymphicus hollandicus*

Lories Loridae
Black Lory *Chalcopsitta atra*
Duyvenbode's Lory *Chalcopsitta duivenbodei*
Yellow-streaked Lory *Chalcopsitta sintillata*
Cardinal Lory *Chalcopsitta cardinalis*
Red-and-blue Lory *Eos histrio* •
Violet-necked Lory *Eos squamata*
Red Lory *Eos bornea*
Blue-streaked Lory *Eos reticulata*
Black-winged Lory *Eos cyanogenia*
Blue-eared Lory *Eos semilarvata*
Dusky Lory *Pseudeos fuscata*
Ornate Lorikeet *Trichoglossus ornatus*
Rainbow Lorikeet *Trichoglossus haematodus*
Perfect Lorikeet *Trichoglossus euteles*
Yellow-and-green Lorikeet *Trichoglossus flavoviridis*
Mindanao Lorikeet *Trichoglossus johnstoniae*
Pohnpei Lorikeet *Trichoglossus rubiginosus*
Scaly-breasted Lorikeet *Trichoglossus chlorolepidotus*
Varied Lorikeet *Psitteuteles versicolor*
Iris Lorikeet *Psitteuteles iris*
Goldie's Lorikeet *Psitteuteles goldiei*
Chattering Lory *Lorius garrulus* •
Purple-bellied Lory *Lorius hypoinochrous*
Purple-naped Lory *Lorius domicella*
Western Black-capped Lory *Lorius lory*
White-naped Lory *Lorius albidinucha*
Yellow-bibbed Lory *Lorius chlorocercus*
Collared Lory *Phigys solitarius*
Blue-crowned Lory *Vini australis*
Kuhl's Lory *Vini kuhlii* •
Stephen's Lory *Vini stepheni*
Tahitian Lory *Vini peruviana*
Ultramarine Lory *Vini yncas* •
Musk Lorikeet *Glossopsitta concinna*
Little Lorikeet *Glossopsitta pusilla*
Purple-crowned Lorikeet *Glossopsitta porphyrocephala*
Palm Lorikeet *Charmosyna palmarum*
Red-chinned Lorikeet *Charmosyna rubrigularis*
Meek's Lorikeet *Charmosyna meeki*
Blue-fronted Lorikeet *Charmosyna toxopei* •
Striated Lorikeet *Charmosyna multistriata*
Wilhelmina's Lorikeet *Charmosyna wilhelminae*
Red-spotted Lorikeet *Charmosyna rubronotata*
Red-flanked Lorikeet *Charmosyna placentis*
Red-throated Lorikeet *Charmosyna amabilis* •
Duchess Lorikeet *Charmosyna margarethae*
Fairy Lorikeet *Charmosyna pulchella*
Josephine's Lorikeet *Charmosyna josefinae*
Papuan Lorikeet *Charmosyna papou*
Whiskered Lorikeet *Oreopsittacus arfaki*
Musschenbroek's Lorikeet *Neopsittacus musschenbroekii*
Emerald Lorikeet *Neopsittacus pullicauda*

Parrots Psittacidae
Pesquet's Parrot *Psittrichas fulgidus*
Kea *Nestor notabilis*
New Zealand Kaka *Nestor meridionalis* •
Kakapo *Strigops habroptila*
Yellow-capped Pygmy-Parrot *Micropsitta keiensis*
Geelvink Pygmy-Parrot *Micropsitta geelvinkiana*
Buff-faced Pygmy-Parrot *Micropsitta pusio*
Red-breasted Pygmy-Parrot *Micropsitta bruijnii*
Meek's Pygmy-Parrot *Micropsitta meeki*
Finsch's Pygmy-Parrot *Micropsitta finschii*

Orange-breasted Fig-Parrot *Cyclopsitta gulielmitertii*
Double-eyed Fig-Parrot *Cyclopsitta diophthalma*
Large Fig-Parrot *Psittaculirostris desmarestii*
Edwards's Fig-Parrot *Psittaculirostris edwardsii*
Salvadori's Fig-Parrot *Psittaculirostris salvadorii*
Guaiabero *Bolbopsittacus lunulatus*
Kandavu Shining-Parrot *Prosopeia splendens*
Red Shining-Parrot *Prosopeia tabuensis*
Masked Shining-Parrot *Prosopeia personata*
Horned Parakeet *Eunymphicus cornutus* •
Antipodes Green Parrot *Cyanoramphus unicolor*
Red-fronted Parakeet *Cyanoramphus novaezelandiae*
New Caledonian Parrot *Cyanoramphus saissetti*
Norfolk Island Parrot *Cyanoramphus cookii* •
Yellow-fronted Parakeet *Cyanoramphus auriceps*
Chatham Islands Parakeet *Cyanoramphus forbesi* •
Malherbe's Parrot *Cyanoramphus malherbi* •
Red-capped Parrot *Purpureicephalus spurius*
Australian Ringneck *Barnardius zonarius*
Mallee Ringneck *Barnardius barnardi*
Green Rosella *Platycercus caledonicus*
Crimson Rosella *Platycercus elegans*
Yellow Rosella *Platycercus flaveolus*
Adelaide Rosella *Platycercus adelaidae*
Northern Rosella *Platycercus venustus*
Eastern Rosella *Platycercus eximius*
Pale-headed Rosella *Platycercus adscitus*
Western Rosella *Platycercus icterotis*
Mulga Parrot *Psephotus varius*
Red-rumped Parrot *Psephotus haematonotus*
Hooded Parrot *Psephotus dissimilis*
Golden-shouldered Parrot *Psephotus chrysopterygius* •
Bluebonnet *Northiella haematogaster*
Bourke's Parrot *Neophema bourkii*
Blue-winged Parrot *Neophema chrysostoma*
Elegant Parrot *Neophema elegans*
Rock Parrot *Neophema petrophila*
Orange-bellied Parrot *Neophema chrysogaster* •
Turquoise Parrot *Neophema pulchella*
Scarlet-chested Parrot *Neophema splendida*
Swift Parrot *Lathamus discolor* •
Budgerigar *Melopsittacus undulatus*
Ground Parrot *Pezoporus wallicus*
Night Parrot *Geopsittacus occidentalis* •
Blue-rumped Parrot *Psittinus cyanurus*
Painted Tiger-Parrot *Psittacella picta*
Brehm's Tiger-Parrot *Psittacella brehmii*
Modest Tiger-Parrot *Psittacella modesta*
Madarasz's Tiger-Parrot *Psittacella madaraszi*
Red-cheeked Parrot *Geoffroyus geoffroyi*
Blue-collared Parrot *Geoffroyus simplex*
Singing Parrot *Geoffroyus heteroclitus*
Montane Racquet-tail *Prioniturus montanus*
Mindanao Racquet-tail *Prioniturus waterstradti*
Palawan Racquet-tail *Prioniturus platenae*
Green Racquet-tail *Prioniturus luconensis*
Blue-crowned Racquet-tail *Prioniturus discurus*
Blue-winged Racquet-tail *Prioniturus verticalis* •
Yellowish-breasted Racquet-tail *Prioniturus flavicans*
Golden-mantled Racquet-tail *Prioniturus platurus*
Buru Racquet-tail *Prioniturus mada*
Black-lored Parrot *Tanygnathus gramineus*
Great-billed Parrot *Tanygnathus megalorynchos*
Blue-naped Parrot *Tanygnathus lucionensis*
Müller's Parrot *Tanygnathus sumatranus*
Eclectus Parrot *Eclectus roratus*
Australian King Parrot *Alisterus scapularis*
Moluccan King Parrot *Alisterus amboinensis*
Green-winged King Parrot *Alisterus chloropterus*
Olive-shouldered Parrot *Aprosmictus jonquillaceus*
Red-winged Parrot *Aprosmictus erythropterus*
Superb Parrot *Polytelis swainsonii*
Regent Parrot *Polytelis anthopeplus*
Alexandra's Parrot *Polytelis alexandrae*

Alexandrine Parakeet *Psittacula eupatria*
Rose-ringed Parakeet *Psittacula krameri*
Mauritius Parakeet *Psittacula echo* •
Himalayan Slaty-headed Parakeet *Psittacula himalayana*
Gray-headed Parakeet *Psittacula finschii*
Plum-headed Parakeet *Psittacula cyanocephala*
Blossom-headed Parakeet *Psittacula roseata*
Malabar Parakeet *Psittacula columboides*
Layard's Parakeet *Psittacula calthropae*
Derbyan Parakeet *Psittacula derbiana*
Indian Red-breasted Parakeet *Psittacula alexandri*
Nicobar Parakeet *Psittacula caniceps*
Long-tailed Parakeet *Psittacula longicauda*
Vernal Hanging-Parrot *Loriculus vernalis*
Sri Lanka Hanging-Parrot *Loriculus beryllinus*
Philippine Hanging-Parrot *Loriculus philippensis*
Blue-crowned Hanging-Parrot *Loriculus galgulus*
Sulawesi Hanging-Parrot *Loriculus stigmatus*
Sula Hanging-Parrot *Loriculus sclateri*
Moluccan Hanging-Parrot *Loriculus amabilis*
Sangihe Hanging-Parrot *Loriculus catamene* •
Orange-fronted Hanging-Parrot *Loriculus aurantiifrons*
Green-fronted Hanging-Parrot *Loriculus tener*
Green Hanging-Parrot *Loriculus exilis*
Yellow-throated Hanging-Parrot *Loriculus pusillus*
Wallace's Hanging-Parrot *Loriculus flosculus* •
Gray-headed Lovebird *Agapornis canus*
Red-headed Lovebird *Agapornis pullarius*
Black-winged Lovebird *Agapornis taranta*
Black-collared Lovebird *Agapornis swindernianus*
Rosy-faced Lovebird *Agapornis roseicollis*
Fischer's Lovebird *Agapornis fischeri*
Yellow-collared Lovebird *Agapornis personatus*
Lilian's Lovebird *Agapornis lilianae*
Black-cheeked Lovebird *Agapornis nigrigenis*
Vasa Parrot *Coracopsis vasa*
Black Parrot *Coracopsis nigra*
African Gray Parrot *Psittacus erithacus*
Brown-necked Parrot *Poicephalus robustus*
Red-fronted Parrot *Poicephalus gulielmi*
Brown Parrot *Poicephalus meyeri*
Rueppell's Parrot *Poicephalus rueppellii*
Brown-headed Parrot *Poicephalus cryptoxanthus*
Niam-Niam Parrot *Poicephalus crassus*
Red-bellied Parrot *Poicephalus rufiventris*
Senegal Parrot *Poicephalus senegalus*
Yellow-fronted Parrot *Poicephalus flavifrons*
Hyacinthine Macaw *Anodorhynchus hyacinthinus* •
Indigo Macaw *Anodorhynchus leari* •
Little Blue Macaw *Cyanopsitta spixii* •
Blue-and-yellow Macaw *Ara ararauna*
Blue-throated Macaw *Ara glaucogularis* •
Military Macaw *Ara militaris*
Great Green Macaw *Ara ambiguus* •
Scarlet Macaw *Ara macao*
Red-and-green Macaw *Ara chloropterus*
Red-fronted Macaw *Ara rubrogenys* •
Chestnut-fronted Macaw *Ara severus*
Red-bellied Macaw *Orthopsittaca manilata*
Blue-headed Macaw *Primolius couloni* •
Blue-winged Macaw *Primolius maracana*
Golden-collared Macaw *Primolius auricollis*
Red-shouldered Macaw *Diopsittaca nobilis*
Thick-billed Parrot *Rhynchopsitta pachyrhyncha* •
Maroon-fronted Parrot *Rhynchopsitta terrisi*
Yellow-eared Parakeet *Ognorhynchus icterotis* •
Golden Conure *Guarouba guarouba*
Blue-crowned Conure *Aratinga acuticaudata*
Green Conure *Aratinga holochlora*
Pacific Conure *Aratinga strenua*
Socorro Conure *Aratinga brevipes* •
Red-throated Conure *Aratinga rubritorquis*
Red-fronted Conure *Aratinga wagleri*

Mitred Conure *Aratinga mitrata*
Red-masked Conure *Aratinga erythrogenys*
Finsch's Conure *Aratinga finschi*
White-eyed Conure *Aratinga leucophthalma*
Cuban Conure *Aratinga euops*
Hispaniolan Conure *Aratinga chloroptera*
Sulfur-breasted Parakeet *Aratinga pintoi*
Sun Conure *Aratinga solstitialis*
Jandaya Conure *Aratinga jandaya*
Golden-capped Conure *Aratinga auricapillus*
Dusky-headed Conure *Aratinga weddellii*
Brown-throated Conure *Aratinga pertinax*
Olive-throated Conure *Aratinga nana*
Orange-fronted Conure *Aratinga canicularis*
Peach-fronted Conure *Aratinga aurea*
Cactus Conure *Aratinga cactorum*
Nanday Conure *Nandayus nenday*
Golden-plumed Parakeet *Leptosittaca branickii*
Patagonian Burrowing Parrot *Cyanoliseus patagonus*
Blue-throated Conure *Pyrrhura cruentata*
Blaze-winged Parakeet *Pyrrhura devillei*
Maroon-bellied Conure *Pyrrhura frontalis*
Crimson-bellied Conure *Pyrrhura perlata*
Pearly Conure *Pyrrhura lepida*
Green-cheeked Conure *Pyrrhura molinae*
Panamanian Painted Conure *Pyrrhura eisenmanni*
Sinu Parakeet *Pyrrhura subandina*
Todd's Parakeet *Pyrrhura caeruleiceps*
Painted Conure *Pyrrhura picta*
Red-crowned Parakeet *Pyrrhura roseifrons*
Deville's Parakeet *Pyrrhura lucianii*
Hellmayr's Parakeet *Pyrrhura amazonum*
Madeira Parakeet *Pyrrhura snethlage*
Wavy-breasted Parakeet *Pyrrhura peruviana*
Fiery-shouldered Conure *Pyrrhura egregia*
Maroon-faced Conure *Pyrrhura leucotis*
Santa Marta Parakeet *Pyrrhura viridicata* •
Maroon-tailed Conure *Pyrrhura melanura*
El Oro Conure *Pyrrhura orcesi* •
Rock Conure *Pyrrhura rupicola*
White-breasted Conure *Pyrrhura albipectus*
Flame-winged Conure *Pyrrhura calliptera*
Blood-eared Conure *Pyrrhura hoematotis*
Rose-headed Parakeet *Pyrrhura rhodocephala*
Sulfur-winged Conure *Pyrrhura hoffmanni*
Austral Parakeet *Enicognathus ferrugineus*
Slender-billed Parakeet *Enicognathus leptorhynchus*
Monk Parakeet *Myiopsitta monachus*
Cliff Parakeet *Myiopsitta luchsi*
Andean Parakeet *Bolborhynchus orbygnesius*
Barred Parakeet *Bolborhynchus lineola*
Rufous-fronted Parakeet *Bolborhynchus ferrugineifrons*
Gray-hooded Parakeet *Psilopsiagon aymara*
Mountain Parakeet *Psilopsiagon aurifrons*
Mexican Parrotlet *Forpus cyanopygius*
Green-rumped Parrotlet *Forpus passerinus*
Blue-winged Parrotlet *Forpus xanthopterygius*
Spectacled Parrotlet *Forpus conspicillatus*
Dusky-billed Parrotlet *Forpus sclateri*
Pacific Parrotlet *Forpus coelestis*
Yellow-faced Parrotlet *Forpus xanthops*
Plain Parakeet *Brotogeris tirica*
Canary-winged Parakeet *Brotogeris versicolurus*
Yellow-chevroned Parakeet *Brotogeris chiriri*
Gray-cheeked Parakeet *Brotogeris pyrrhoptera* •
Orange-chinned Parakeet *Brotogeris jugularis*
Cobalt-winged Parakeet *Brotogeris cyanoptera*
Tui Parakeet *Brotogeris sanctithomae*
Golden-winged Parakeet *Brotogeris chrysoptera*
Tepui Parrotlet *Nannopsittaca panychlora*
Amazonian Parrotlet *Nannopsittaca dachilleae*
Lilac-tailed Parrotlet *Touit batavicus*
Scarlet-shouldered Parrotlet *Touit huetii*
Red-fronted Parrotlet *Touit costaricensis*

Blue-fronted Parrotlet *Touit dilectissimus*
Sapphire-rumped Parrotlet *Touit purpuratus*
Brown-backed Parrotlet *Touit melanonotus* •
Golden-tailed Parrotlet *Touit surdus*
Spot-winged Parrotlet *Touit stictopterus*
Black-headed Parrot *Pionites melanocephalus*
White-bellied Parrot *Pionites leucogaster*
Vulturine Parrot *Pionopsitta vulturina*
Bald Parrot *Pionopsitta aurantiocephala*
Brown-hooded Parrot *Pionopsitta haematotis*
Rose-faced Parrot *Pionopsitta pulchra*
Orange-cheeked Parrot *Pionopsitta barrabandi*
Saffron-headed Parrot *Pionopsitta pyrilia*
Caica Parrot *Pionopsitta caica*
Pileated Parrot *Pionopsitta pileata*
Black-eared Parrot *Hapalopsittaca melanotis*
Rusty-faced Parrot *Hapalopsittaca amazonina*
Indigo-winged Parrot *Hapalopsittaca fuertesi* •
Red-faced Parrot *Hapalopsittaca pyrrhops*
Short-tailed Parrot *Graydidascalus brachyurus*
Blue-headed Parrot *Pionus menstruus*
Red-billed Parrot *Pionus sordidus*
Scaly-headed Parrot *Pionus maximiliani*
White-crowned Parrot *Pionus senilis*
Plum-crowned Parrot *Pionus tumultuosus*
Bronze-winged Parrot *Pionus chalcopterus*
Dusky Parrot *Pionus fuscus*
Cuban Amazon *Amazona leucocephala*
Yellow-billed Amazon *Amazona collaria*
Hispaniolan Amazon *Amazona ventralis*
Puerto Rican Amazon *Amazona vittata* •
Yellow-lored Amazon *Amazona xantholora*
White-fronted Amazon *Amazona albifrons*
Black-billed Amazon *Amazona agilis*
Tucuman Amazon *Amazona tucumana*
Red-spectacled Amazon *Amazona pretrei*
Red-crowned Amazon *Amazona viridigenalis* •
Lilac-crowned Amazon *Amazona finschi*
Red-lored Amazon *Amazona autumnalis*
Blue-cheeked Amazon *Amazona dufresniana*
Red-browed Amazon *Amazona rhodocorytha* •
Red-tailed Amazon *Amazona brasiliensis*
Festive Amazon *Amazona festiva*
Yellow-faced Amazon *Amazona xanthops*
Yellow-shouldered Amazon *Amazona barbadensis*
Blue-fronted Amazon *Amazona aestiva*
Yellow-headed Amazon *Amazona oratrix* •
Yellow-crowned Amazon *Amazona ochrocephala*
Yellow-naped Amazon *Amazona auropalliata*
Kawall's Amazon *Amazona kawalli*
Orange-winged Amazon *Amazona amazonica*
Scaly-naped Amazon *Amazona mercenaria*
Mealy Amazon *Amazona farinosa*
Vinaceous Amazon *Amazona vinacea*
St. Lucia Amazon *Amazona versicolor*
Red-necked Amazon *Amazona arausiaca*
St.Vincent Amazon *Amazona guildingii*
Imperial Amazon *Amazona imperialis* •
Red-fan Parrot *Deroptyus accipitrinus*
Blue-bellied Parrot *Triclaria malachitacea*

CUCKOOS AND ALLIES Cuculiformes

Turacos Musophagidae
Great Blue Turaco *Corythaeola cristata*
Green Turaco *Tauraco persa*
Livingstone's Turaco *Tauraco livingstonii*
Schalow's Turaco *Tauraco schalowi*
Knysna Turaco *Tauraco corythaix*
Black-billed Turaco *Tauraco schuettii*
White-crested Turaco *Tauraco leucolophus*
Fischer's Turaco *Tauraco fischeri*
Yellow-billed Turaco *Tauraco macrorhynchus*
Bannerman's Turaco *Tauraco bannermani* •

Red-crested Turaco *Tauraco erythrolophus*
Hartlaub's Turaco *Tauraco hartlaubi*
White-cheeked Turaco *Tauraco leucotis*
Ruspoli's Turaco *Tauraco ruspolii*
Purple-crested Turaco *Tauraco porphyreolophus*
Ruwenzori Turaco *Ruwenzorornis johnstoni*
Violet Turaco *Musophaga violacea*
Lady Ross's Turaco *Musophaga rossae*
Bare-faced Go-away-bird *Corythaixoides personatus*
Gray Go-away-bird *Corythaixoides concolor*
White-bellied Go-away-bird *Corythaixoides leucogaster*
Western Gray Plantain-eater *Crinifer piscator*
Eastern Gray Plantain-eater *Crinifer zonurus*

Cuckoos Cuculidae
Jacobin Cuckoo *Clamator jacobinus*
Levaillant's Cuckoo *Clamator levaillantii*
Chestnut-winged Cuckoo *Clamator coromandus*
Great Spotted Cuckoo *Clamator glandarius*
Thick-billed Cuckoo *Pachycoccyx audeberti*
Sulawesi Hawk-Cuckoo *Cuculus crassirostris*
Large Hawk-Cuckoo *Cuculus sparverioides*
Common Hawk-Cuckoo *Cuculus varius*
Small Hawk-Cuckoo *Cuculus vagans*
Hodgson's Hawk-Cuckoo (Clements) *Cuculus nisicolor*
Northern Hawk-Cuckoo *Cuculus hyperythrus*
Hodgson's Hawk-Cuckoo *Cuculus fugax*
Philippine Hawk-Cuckoo *Cuculus pectoralis*
Red-chested Cuckoo *Cuculus solitarius*
Black Cuckoo *Cuculus clamosus*
Indian Cuckoo *Cuculus micropterus*
Common Cuckoo *Cuculus canorus*
African Cuckoo *Cuculus gularis*
Oriental Cuckoo *Cuculus saturatus*
Indonesian Cuckoo *Cuculus lepidus*
Horsfield's Cuckoo *Cuculus horsfieldi*
Lesser Cuckoo *Cuculus poliocephalus*
Madagascar Cuckoo *Cuculus rochii*
Pallid Cuckoo *Cuculus pallidus*
Dusky Long-tailed Cuckoo *Cercococcyx mechowi*
Olive Long-tailed Cuckoo *Cercococcyx olivinus*
Barred Long-tailed Cuckoo *Cercococcyx montanus*
Banded Bay Cuckoo *Cacomantis sonneratii*
Plaintive Cuckoo *Cacomantis merulinus*
Brush-Cuckoo *Cacomantis variolosus*
Moluccan Cuckoo *Cacomantis heinrichi*
Chestnut-breasted Cuckoo *Cacomantis castaneiventris*
Fan-tailed Brush-Cuckoo *Cacomantis flabelliformis*
Black-eared Cuckoo *Chrysococcyx osculans*
Horsfield's Bronze-Cuckoo *Chrysococcyx basalis*
Shining Bronze-Cuckoo *Chrysococcyx lucidus*
Rufous-throated Bronze-Cuckoo *Chrysococcyx ruficollis*
White-eared Bronze-Cuckoo *Chrysococcyx meyeri*
Little Bronze-Cuckoo *Chrysococcyx minutillus*
Asian Emerald Cuckoo *Chrysococcyx maculatus*
Violet Cuckoo *Chrysococcyx xanthorhynchus*
Yellow-throated Cuckoo *Chrysococcyx flavigularis*
Klaas's Cuckoo *Chrysococcyx klaas*
African Emerald Cuckoo *Chrysococcyx cupreus*
Diederik Cuckoo *Chrysococcyx caprius*
Little Long-billed Cuckoo *Rhamphomantis megarhynchus*
Asian Drongo-Cuckoo *Surniculus lugubris*
Philippine Drongo-Cuckoo *Surniculus velutinus*
White-crowned Koel *Caliechthrus leucolophus*
Dwarf Koel *Microdynamis parva*
Black-billed Koel *Eudynamys melanorhynchus*
Asian Koel *Eudynamys scolopaceus*
Australian Koel *Eudynamys cyanocephalus*
Long-tailed Koel *Eudynamys taitensis*

Channel-billed Cuckoo *Scythrops novaehollandiae*
Yellowbill *Ceuthmochares aereus*
Black-bellied Malkoha *Phaenicophaeus diardi*
Chestnut-bellied Malkoha *Phaenicophaeus sumatranus*
Blue-faced Malkoha *Phaenicophaeus viridirostris*
Large Green-billed Malkoha *Phaenicophaeus tristis*
Sirkeer Malkoha *Phaenicophaeus leschenaultii*
Raffles Malkoha *Phaenicophaeus chlorophaeus*
Red-billed Malkoha *Phaenicophaeus javanicus*
Yellow-billed Malkoha *Phaenicophaeus calyorhynchus*
Chestnut-breasted Malkoha *Phaenicophaeus curvirostris*
Red-faced Malkoha *Phaenicophaeus pyrrhocephalus*
Red-crested Malkoha *Phaenicophaeus superciliosus*
Scale-feathered Malkoha *Phaenicophaeus cumingi*
Sumatran Ground-Cuckoo *Carpococcyx viridis* •
Bornean Ground-Cuckoo *Carpococcyx radiatus*
Coral-billed Ground-Cuckoo *Carpococcyx renauldi*
Giant Coua *Coua gigas*
Coquerel's Coua *Coua coquereli*
Red-breasted Coua *Coua serriana*
Red-fronted Coua *Coua reynaudii*
Red-capped Coua *Coua ruficeps*
Running Coua *Coua cursor*
Crested Coua *Coua cristata*
Verreaux's Coua *Coua verreauxi*
Blue Coua *Coua caerulea*
Bay Coucal *Centropus celebensis*
Rufous Coucal *Centropus unirufus*
Black-faced Coucal *Centropus melanops*
Sunda Coucal *Centropus nigrorufus*
Buff-headed Coucal *Centropus milo*
Goliath Coucal *Centropus goliath*
Violet Coucal *Centropus violaceus*
Greater Black Coucal *Centropus menbeki*
New Britain Coucal *Centropus ateralbus*
Pheasant Coucal *Centropus phasianinus*
Kai Coucal *Centropus spilopterus*
Bernstein's Coucal *Centropus bernsteini*
Biak Island Coucal *Centropus chalybeus*
Short-toed Coucal *Centropus rectunguis*
Black-hooded Coucal *Centropus steerii* •
Greater Coucal *Centropus sinensis*
Brown Coucal *Centropus andamanensis*
Philippine Coucal *Centropus viridis*
Madagascar Coucal *Centropus toulou*
Black-chested Coucal *Centropus grillii*
Green-billed Coucal *Centropus chlororhynchus*
Lesser Coucal *Centropus bengalensis*
Black-throated Coucal *Centropus leucogaster*
Gabon Coucal *Centropus anselli*
Blue-headed Coucal *Centropus monachus*
Coppery-tailed Coucal *Centropus cupreicaudus*
Senegal Coucal *Centropus senegalensis*
White-browed Coucal *Centropus superciliosus*
Dwarf Cuckoo *Coccyzus pumilus*
Ash-colored Cuckoo *Coccyzus cinereus*
Black-billed Cuckoo *Coccyzus erythropthalmus*
Yellow-billed Cuckoo *Coccyzus americanus*
Pearly-breasted Cuckoo *Coccyzus euleri*
Mangrove Cuckoo *Coccyzus minor*
Cocos Island Cuckoo *Coccyzus ferrugineus*
Dark-billed Cuckoo *Coccyzus melacoryphus*
Gray-capped Cuckoo *Coccyzus lansbergi*
Great Lizard-Cuckoo *Saurothera merlini*
Puerto Rican Lizard-Cuckoo *Saurothera vieilloti*
Jamaican Lizard-Cuckoo *Saurothera vetula*
Hispaniolan Lizard-Cuckoo *Saurothera longirostris*
Chestnut-bellied Cuckoo *Hyetornis pluvialis*
Bay-breasted Cuckoo *Hyetornis rufigularis* •
Squirrel Cuckoo *Piaya cayana*
Black-bellied Cuckoo *Piaya melanogaster*
Little Cuckoo *Piaya minuta*
Greater Ani *Crotophaga major*

Smooth-billed Ani *Crotophaga ani*
Groove-billed Ani *Crotophaga sulcirostris*
Guira Cuckoo *Guira guira*
Striped Ground-Cuckoo *Tapera naevia*
Pheasant Cuckoo *Dromococcyx phasianellus*
Pavonine Cuckoo *Dromococcyx pavoninus*
Lesser Ground-Cuckoo *Morococcyx erythropygus*
Greater Roadrunner *Geococcyx californianus*
Lesser Roadrunner *Geococcyx velox*
Scaled Ground-Cuckoo *Neomorphus squamiger*
Rufous-vented Ground-Cuckoo *Neomorphus geoffroyi*
Banded Ground-Cuckoo *Neomorphus radiolosus*
Rufous-winged Ground-Cuckoo *Neomorphus rufipennis*
Red-billed Ground-Cuckoo *Neomorphus pucheranii*

OWLS Strigiformes

Barn Owls Tytonidae
Greater Sooty Owl *Tyto tenebricosa*
Lesser Sooty Owl *Tyto multipunctata*
Australian Masked-Owl *Tyto novaehollandiae*
New Britain Masked-Owl *Tyto aurantia*
Lesser Masked-Owl *Tyto sororcula*
Manus Masked-Owl *Tyto manusi*
Taliabu Masked-Owl *Tyto nigrobrunnea* •
Minahassa Masked-Owl *Tyto inexspectata*
Sulawesi Masked-Owl *Tyto rosenbergii*
Australasian Grass-Owl *Tyto longimembris*
African Grass-Owl *Tyto capensis*
Ashy-faced Barn-Owl *Tyto glaucops*
Madagascar Red Owl *Tyto soumagnei* •
Common Barn-Owl *Tyto alba*
Oriental Bay-Owl *Phodilus badius*
Congo Bay-Owl *Phodilus prigoginei* •

Owls Strigidae
White-fronted Scops-Owl *Otus sagittatus*
Andaman Scops-Owl *Otus balli*
Reddish Scops-Owl *Otus rufescens*
Serendib Scops-Owl *Otus thilohoffmanni* •
Cinnamon Scops-Owl *Otus icterorhynchus*
Sokoke Scops-Owl *Otus ireneae* •
Flores Scops-Owl *Otus alfredi* •
Mountain Scops-Owl *Otus spilocephalus*
Rajah Scops-Owl *Otus brookii*
Javan Scops-Owl *Otus angelinae*
Mentawai Scops-Owl *Otus mentawi*
Indian Scops-Owl *Otus bakkamoena*
Collared Scops-Owl *Otus lettia*
Sunda Scops-Owl *Otus lempiji*
Japanese Scops-Owl *Otus semitorques*
Wallace's Scops-Owl *Otus silvicola*
Palawan Scops-Owl *Otus fuliginosus*
Philippine Scops-Owl *Otus megalotis*
Mindanao Scops-Owl *Otus mirus*
Luzon Scops-Owl *Otus longicornis*
Mindoro Scops-Owl *Otus mindorensis*
Striated Scops-Owl *Otus brucei*
African Scops-Owl *Otus senegalensis*
Eurasian Scops-Owl *Otus scops*
Oriental Scops-Owl *Otus sunia*
Flammulated Scops-Owl *Otus flammeolus*
Moluccan Scops-Owl *Otus magicus*
Mantanani Scops-Owl *Otus mantananensis*
Elegant Scops-Owl *Otus elegans*
Sulawesi Scops-Owl *Otus manadensis*
Sangihe Scops-Owl *Otus collari*
Biak Island Scops-Owl *Otus beccarii* •
Bare-legged Scops-Owl *Otus insularis* •
Simeulue Scops-Owl *Otus umbra*
Enggaño Scops-Owl *Otus enganensis*
Nicobar Scops-Owl *Otus alius*
Pemba Scops-Owl *Otus pembaensis*

Grand Comoro Scops-Owl *Otus pauliani* •
Anjouan Scops-Owl *Otus capnodes* •
Mohéli Scops-Owl *Otus moheliensis* •
Madagascar Scops-Owl *Otus rutilus*
Torotoroka Scops-Owl *Otus madagascariensis*
Mayotte Scops-Owl *Otus mayottensis*
São Tomé Scops-Owl *Otus hartlaubi*
Western Screech-Owl *Megascops kennicottii*
Balsas Screech-Owl *Megascops seductus*
Pacific Screech-Owl *Megascops cooperi*
Whiskered Screech-Owl *Megascops trichopsis*
Eastern Screech-Owl *Megascops asio*
Tropical Screech-Owl *Megascops choliba*
Maria Koepcke's Screech-Owl *Megascops koepckeae*
West Peruvian Screech-Owl *Megascops roboratus*
Bare-shanked Screech-Owl *Megascops clarkii*
Bearded Screech-Owl *Megascops barbarus*
Rufescent Screech-Owl *Megascops ingens*
Colombian Screech-Owl *Megascops colombianus*
Cinnamon Screech-Owl *Megascops petersoni*
Cloud-forest Screech-Owl *Megascops marshalli*
Tawny-bellied Screech-Owl *Megascops watsonii*
Guatemalan Screech-Owl *Megascops guatemalae*
Vermiculated Screech-Owl *Megascops vermiculatus*
Foothill Screech-Owl *Megascops roraimae*
Rio Napo Screech-Owl *Megascops napensis*
Hoy's Screech-Owl *Megascops hoyi*
Black-capped Screech-Owl *Megascops atricapilla*
Long-tufted Screech-Owl *Megascops sanctaecatarinae*
Puerto Rican Screech-Owl *Megascops nudipes*
White-throated Screech-Owl *Megascops albogularis*
Palau Owl *Pyrroglaux podarginus*
Bare-legged Screech-Owl *Gymnoglaux lawrencii*
Northern White-faced Owl *Ptilopsis leucotis*
Southern White-faced Owl *Ptilopsis granti*
Giant Scops-Owl *Mimizuku gurneyi*
Great Horned-Owl *Bubo virginianus*
Magellanic Horned-Owl *Bubo magellanicus*
Eurasian Eagle-Owl *Bubo bubo*
Indian Eagle-Owl *Bubo bengalensis*
Pharaoh Eagle-Owl *Bubo ascalaphus*
Cape Eagle-Owl *Bubo capensis*
Spotted Eagle-Owl *Bubo africanus*
Vermiculated Eagle-Owl *Bubo cinerascens*
Fraser's Eagle-Owl *Bubo poensis*
Usambara Eagle-Owl *Bubo vosseleri*
Spot-bellied Eagle-Owl *Bubo nipalensis*
Barred Eagle-Owl *Bubo sumatranus*
Shelley's Eagle-Owl *Bubo shelleyi*
Verreaux's Eagle-Owl *Bubo lacteus*
Dusky Eagle-Owl *Bubo coromandus*
Akun Eagle-Owl *Bubo leucostictus*
Philippine Eagle-Owl *Bubo philippensis*
Snowy Owl *Bubo scandiacus*
Blakiston's Eagle-Owl *Ketupa blakistoni* •
Brown Fish-Owl *Ketupa zeylonensis*
Tawny Fish-Owl *Ketupa flavipes*
Buffy Fish-Owl *Ketupa ketupu*
Pel's Fishing-Owl *Scotopelia peli*
Rufous Fishing-Owl *Scotopelia ussheri* •
Vermiculated Fishing-Owl *Scotopelia bouvieri*
Spotted Wood-Owl *Strix seloputo*
Mottled Wood-Owl *Strix ocellata*
Brown Wood-Owl *Strix leptogrammica*
Eurasian Tawny Owl *Strix aluco*
Hume's Tawny Owl *Strix butleri*
Californian Spotted Owl *Strix occidentalis*
Northern Barred Owl *Strix varia*
Fulvous Owl *Strix fulvescens*
Rusty-barred Owl *Strix hylophila*
Rufous-legged Owl *Strix rufipes*
Chaco Owl *Strix chacoensis*
Ural Owl *Strix uralensis*
Sichuan Wood-Owl *Strix davidi*

Great Gray Owl *Strix nebulosa*
African Wood-Owl *Strix woodfordii*
Mottled Owl *Ciccaba virgata*
Black-and-white Owl *Ciccaba nigrolineata*
Black-banded Owl *Ciccaba huhula*
Rufous-banded Owl *Ciccaba albitarsus*
Crested Owl *Lophostrix cristata*
Maned Owl *Jubula lettii*
Spectacled Owl *Pulsatrix perspicillata*
Tawny-browed Owl *Pulsatrix koeniswaldiana*
Band-bellied Owl *Pulsatrix melanota*
Northern Hawk-Owl *Surnia ulula*
Eurasian Pygmy-Owl *Glaucidium passerinum*
Collared Owlet *Glaucidium brodiei*
Pearl-spotted Owlet *Glaucidium perlatum*
Californian Pygmy-Owl *Glaucidium californicum*
Mountain Pygmy-Owl *Glaucidium gnoma*
Guatemalan Pygmy-Owl *Glaucidium cobanense*
Baja Pygmy-Owl *Glaucidium hoskinsii*
Costa Rican Pygmy-Owl *Glaucidium costaricanum*
Cloud-forest Pygmy-Owl *Glaucidium nubicola*
Andean Pygmy-Owl *Glaucidium jardinii*
Colima Pygmy-Owl *Glaucidium palmarum*
Tamaulipas Pygmy-Owl *Glaucidium sanchezi*
Central American Pygmy-Owl *Glaucidium griseiceps*
Subtropical Pygmy-Owl *Glaucidium parkeri*
Yungas Pygmy-Owl *Glaucidium bolivianum*
Hardy's Pygmy-Owl *Glaucidium hardyi*
Least Pygmy-Owl *Glaucidium minutissimum*
Pernambuco Pygmy-Owl *Glaucidium mooreorum*
Ferruginous Pygmy-Owl *Glaucidium brasilianum*
Tucuman Pygmy-Owl *Glaucidium tucumanum*
Peruvian Pygmy-Owl *Glaucidium peruanum*
Austral Pygmy-Owl *Glaucidium nanum*
Cuban Pygmy-Owl *Glaucidium siju*
Red-chested Owlet *Glaucidium tephronotum*
Sjöstedt's Barred Owlet *Glaucidium sjostedti*
Asian Barred Owlet *Glaucidium cuculoides*
Javan Barred Owlet *Glaucidium castanopterum*
Jungle Owlet *Glaucidium radiatum*
Chestnut-backed Owlet *Glaucidium castanonotum*
African Barred Owlet *Glaucidium capense*
Chestnut Barred Owlet *Glaucidium castaneum*
Prigogine's Owlet *Glaucidium albertinum*
Long-whiskered Owlet *Xenoglaux loweryi* •
Elf Owl *Micrathene whitneyi*
Burrowing Owl *Athene cunicularia*
Spotted Owlet *Athene brama*
Forest Owlet *Athene blewitti* •
Little Owl *Athene noctua*
Boreal Owl *Aegolius funereus*
Northern Saw-whet Owl *Aegolius acadicus*
Unspotted Saw-whet Owl *Aegolius ridgwayi*
Buff-fronted Owl *Aegolius harrisii*
Rufous Hawk-Owl *Ninox rufa*
Powerful Owl *Ninox strenua*
Barking Hawk-Owl *Ninox connivens*
Sumba Boobook *Ninox rudolfi*
Andaman Hawk-Owl *Ninox affinis*
Morepork *Ninox novaeseelandiae*
Southern Boobook *Ninox boobook*
Sumba Hawk-owl *Ninox sumbaensis*
Brown Hawk-Owl *Ninox scutulata*
Northern Boobook *Ninox japonica*
Chocolate Boobook *Ninox randi*
White-browed Hawk-Owl *Ninox superciliaris*
Philippine Hawk-Owl *Ninox philippensis*
Ochre-bellied Hawk-Owl *Ninox ochracea*
Togian Hawk-Owl *Ninox burhani*
Cinnabar Hawk-Owl *Ninox ios*
Moluccan Hawk-Owl *Ninox squamipila*
Chrismas Island Hawk-Owl *Ninox natalis*
Jungle Hawk-Owl *Ninox theomacha*
Manus Hawk-Owl *Ninox meeki*

Speckled Hawk-Owl *Ninox punctulata*
Bismarck Hawk-Owl *Ninox variegata*
New Britain Hawk-Owl *Ninox odiosa*
Solomon Islands Hawk-Owl *Ninox jacquinoti*
Papuan Hawk-Owl *Uroglaux dimorpha*
Jamaican Owl *Pseudoscops grammicus*
Striped Owl *Pseudoscops clamator*
Stygian Owl *Asio stygius*
Northern Long-eared Owl *Asio otus*
African Long-eared Owl *Asio abyssinicus*
Madagascar Long-eared Owl *Asio madagascariensis*
Short-eared Owl *Asio flammeus*
African Marsh Owl *Asio capensis*
Fearful Owl *Nesasio solomonensis*

NIGHTJARS AND ALLIES
Caprimulgiformes

Oilbird Steatornithidae
Oilbird *Steatornis caripensis*

Owlet-nightjars *Aegothelidae*
Large Owlet-Nightjar *Aegotheles insignis*
Spangled Owlet-Nightjar *Aegotheles tatei*
Moluccan Owlet-Nightjar *Aegotheles crinifrons*
Wallace's Owlet-Nightjar *Aegotheles wallacii*
Archbold's Owlet-Nightjar *Aegotheles archboldi*
Mountain Owlet-Nightjar *Aegotheles albertisi*
New Caledonian Owlet-Nightjar *Aegotheles savesi* •
Barred Owlet-Nightjar *Aegotheles bennettii*
Australian Owlet-Nightjar *Aegotheles cristatus*

Frogmouths Podargidae
Tawny Frogmouth *Podargus strigoides*
Marbled Frogmouth *Podargus ocellatus*
Great Papuan Frogmouth *Podargus papuensis*
Large Frogmouth *Batrachostomus auritus*
Dulit Frogmouth *Batrachostomus harterti*
Philippine Frogmouth *Batrachostomus septimus*
Gould's Frogmouth *Batrachostomus stellatus*
Sri Lanka Frogmouth *Batrachostomus moniliger*
Hodgson's Frogmouth *Batrachostomus hodgsoni*
Short-tailed Frogmouth *Batrachostomus poliolophus*
Javan Frogmouth *Batrachostomus javensis*
Sunda Frogmouth *Batrachostomus cornutus*

Potoos Nyctibiidae
Great Potoo *Nyctibius grandis*
Long-tailed Potoo *Nyctibius aethereus*
Common Potoo *Nyctibius jamaicensis*
Andean Potoo *Nyctibius maculosus*
Gray Potoo *Nyctibius griseus*
White-winged Potoo *Nyctibius leucopterus*
Rufous Potoo *Nyctibius bracteatus*

Nightjars Caprimulgidae
Semi-collared Nighthawk *Lurocalis semitorquatus*
Rufous-bellied Nighthawk *Lurocalis rufiventris*
Least Nighthawk *Chordeiles pusillus*
Sand-colored Nighthawk *Chordeiles rupestris*
Lesser Nighthawk *Chordeiles acutipennis*
Common Nighthawk *Chordeiles minor*
Antillean Nighthawk *Chordeiles gundlachii*
Nacunda Nighthawk *Podager nacunda*
Band-tailed Nighthawk *Nyctiprogne leucopyga*
Bahian Nighthawk *Nyctiprogne vielliardi*
Spotted Eared-Nightjar *Eurostopodus argus*
White-throated Eared-Nightjar *Eurostopodus mystacalis*
Sulawesi Eared-Nightjar *Eurostopodus diabolicus*
Papuan Eared-Nightjar *Eurostopodus papuensis*
Archbold's Eared-Nightjar *Eurostopodus archboldi*
Malaysian Eared-Nightjar *Eurostopodus temminckii*
Great Eared-Nightjar *Eurostopodus macrotis*
Pauraque *Nyctidromus albicollis*

Common Poorwill *Phalaenoptilus nuttallii*
Least Pauraque *Siphonorhis brewsteri*
Eared Poorwill *Nyctiphrynus mcleodii*
Yucatan Poorwill *Nyctiphrynus yucatanicus*
Chocó Poorwill *Nyctiphrynus rosenbergi*
Ocellated Poorwill *Nyctiphrynus ocellatus*
Chuck-will's-widow *Caprimulgus carolinensis*
Rufous Nightjar *Caprimulgus rufus*
Cuban Nightjar *Caprimulgus cubanensis*
Hispaniolan Nightjar *Caprimulgus ekmani*
Tawny-collared Nightjar *Caprimulgus salvini*
Yucatan Nightjar *Caprimulgus badius*
Silky-tailed Nightjar *Caprimulgus sericocaudatus*
Buff-collared Nightjar *Caprimulgus ridgwayi*
Whip-poor-will *Caprimulgus vociferus*
Puerto Rican Nightjar *Caprimulgus noctitherus* •
Dusky Nightjar *Caprimulgus saturatus*
Band-winged Nightjar *Caprimulgus longirostris*
White-winged Nightjar *Caprimulgus candicans*
Pygmy Nightjar *Caprimulgus hirundinaceus*
Little Nightjar *Caprimulgus parvulus*
Spot-tailed Nightjar *Caprimulgus maculicaudus*
White-tailed Nightjar *Caprimulgus cayennensis*
Scrub Nightjar *Caprimulgus anthonyi*
Cayenne Nightjar *Caprimulgus maculosus*
Blackish Nightjar *Caprimulgus nigrescens*
Roraiman Nightjar *Caprimulgus whitelyi*
Brown Nightjar *Caprimulgus binotatus*
Red-necked Nightjar *Caprimulgus ruficollis*
Jungle Nightjar *Caprimulgus indicus*
Eurasian Nightjar *Caprimulgus europaeus*
Sombre Nightjar *Caprimulgus fraenatus*
Rufous-cheeked Nightjar *Caprimulgus rufigena*
Egyptian Nightjar *Caprimulgus aegyptius*
Nubian Nightjar *Caprimulgus nubicus*
Sykes's Nightjar *Caprimulgus mahrattensis*
Vaurie's Nightjar *Caprimulgus centralasicus*
Golden Nightjar *Caprimulgus eximius*
Large-tailed Nightjar *Caprimulgus macrurus*
Large-tailed Nightjar andamanicus *Caprimulgus andamanicus*
Mees' Nightjar *Caprimulgus meesi*
Jerdon's Nightjar *Caprimulgus atripennis*
Philippine Nightjar *Caprimulgus manillensis*
Sulawesi Nightjar *Caprimulgus celebensis*
Donaldson-Smith's Nightjar *Caprimulgus donaldsoni*
Black-shouldered Nightjar *Caprimulgus nigriscapularis*
Fiery-necked Nightjar *Caprimulgus pectoralis*
Abyssinian Nightjar *Caprimulgus poliocephalus*
Ruwenzori Nightjar *Caprimulgus ruwenzorii*
Indian Nightjar *Caprimulgus asiaticus*
Madagascar Nightjar *Caprimulgus madagascariensis*
African White-tailed Nightjar *Caprimulgus natalensis*
Plain Nightjar *Caprimulgus inornatus*
Star-spotted Nightjar *Caprimulgus stellatus*
Nechisar Nightjar *Caprimulgus solala*
Savannah Nightjar *Caprimulgus affinis*
Freckled Nightjar *Caprimulgus tristigma*
Bonaparte's Nightjar *Caprimulgus concretus*
Salvadori's Nightjar *Caprimulgus pulchellus*
Itombwe Nightjar *Caprimulgus prigoginei* •
Collared Nightjar *Caprimulgus enarratus*
Bates's Nightjar *Caprimulgus batesi*
Long-tailed Nightjar *Caprimulgus climacurus*
Slender-tailed Nightjar *Caprimulgus clarus*
Gabon Nightjar *Caprimulgus fossii*
Pennant-winged Nightjar *Macrodipteryx vexillarius*
Standard-winged Nightjar *Macrodipteryx longipennis*
Lyre-tailed Nightjar *Uropsalis lyra*
Swallow-tailed Nightjar *Uropsalis segmentata*
Ladder-tailed Nightjar *Hydropsalis climacocerca*
Scissor-tailed Nightjar *Hydropsalis torquata*
Long-trained Nightjar *Macropsalis forcipata*
Sickle-winged Nightjar *Eleothreptus anomalus*

SWIFTS AND HUMMINGBIRDS
Apodiformes

Swifts Apodidae
Tepui Swift *Cypseloides phelpsi*
Black Swift *Cypseloides niger*
White-chested Swift *Cypseloides lemosi*
Great Swift *Cypseloides rothschildi*
Sooty Swift *Cypseloides fumigatus*
White-fronted Swift *Cypseloides storeri*
Spot-fronted Swift *Cypseloides cherriei*
White-chinned Swift *Cypseloides cryptus*
Great Dusky Swift *Cypseloides senex*
Chestnut-collared Swift *Streptoprocne rutila*
White-naped Swift *Streptoprocne semicollaris*
White-collared Swift *Streptoprocne zonaris*
Biscutate Swift *Streptoprocne biscutata*
Waterfall Swift *Hydrochous gigas*
Glossy Swiftlet *Collocalia esculenta*
Linchi Swiftlet *Collocalia linchi*
Pygmy Swiftlet *Collocalia troglodytes*
Seychelles Swiftlet *Aerodramus elaphrus*
Gray-rumped Swiftlet *Aerodramus francicus*
Indian Swiftlet *Aerodramus unicolor*
Moluccan Swiftlet *Aerodramus infuscatus*
Brown-rumped Swiftlet *Aerodramus mearnsi*
Mountain Swiftlet *Aerodramus hirundinaceus*
Pacific White-rumped Swiftlet *Aerodramus spodiopygius*
Australian Swiftlet *Aerodramus terraereginae*
Himalayan Swiftlet *Aerodramus brevirostris*
Indochinese Swiftlet *Aerodramus rogersi*
Volcano Swiftlet *Aerodramus vulcanorum*
Whitehead's Swiftlet *Aerodramus whiteheadi*
Bare-legged Swiftlet *Aerodramus nuditarsus*
Mayr's Swiftlet *Aerodramus orientalis*
Palawan Swiftlet *Aerodramus palawanensis*
Uniform Swiftlet *Aerodramus vanikorensis*
Mossy-nest Swiftlet *Aerodramus salangana*
Palau Swiftlet *Aerodramus pelewensis*
Mariana Swiftlet *Aerodramus bartschi*
Caroline Islands Swiftlet *Aerodramus inquietus*
Cook Islands Swiftlet *Aerodramus sawtelli*
Tahitian Swiftlet *Aerodramus leucophaeus*
Marquesas Swiftlet *Aerodramus ocistus*
Black-nest Swiftlet *Aerodramus maximus*
Edible-nest Swiftlet *Aerodramus fuciphagus*
Oustalet's Swiftlet *Aerodramus germani*
Papuan Swiftlet *Aerodramus papuensis*
Scarce Swift *Schoutedenapus myoptilus*
Schouteden's Swift *Schoutedenapus schoutedeni*
Philippine Needletail *Mearnsia picina*
Papuan Needletail *Mearnsia novaeguineae*
Malagasy Spinetail *Zoonavena grandidieri*
São Tomé Spinetail *Zoonavena thomensis*
Indian White-rumped Spinetail *Zoonavena sylvatica*
Mottled Spinetail *Telacanthura ussheri*
Black Spinetail *Telacanthura melanopygia*
Silver-rumped Spinetail *Rhaphidura leucopygialis*
Sabine's Spinetail *Rhaphidura sabini*
Cassin's Spinetail *Neafrapus cassini*
Böhm's Spinetail *Neafrapus boehmi*
White-throated Needletail *Hirundapus caudacutus*
Silver-backed Needletail *Hirundapus cochinchinensis*
Brown-backed Needletail *Hirundapus giganteus*
Purple Needletail *Hirundapus celebensis*
Band-rumped Swift *Chaetura spinicaudus*
Costa Rican Swift *Chaetura fumosa*
Lesser Antillean Swift *Chaetura martinica*
Gray-rumped Swift *Chaetura cinereiventris*
Pale-rumped Swift *Chaetura egregia*
Chimney Swift *Chaetura pelagica*
Vaux's Swift *Chaetura vauxi*
Chapman's Swift *Chaetura chapmani*
Short-tailed Swift *Chaetura brachyura*

Tumbes Swift *Chaetura ocypetes*
Ashy-tailed Swift *Chaetura andrei*
White-throated Swift *Aeronautes saxatalis*
White-tipped Swift *Aeronautes montivagus*
Andean Swift *Aeronautes andecolus*
Antillean Palm-Swift *Tachornis phoenicobia*
Pygmy Swift *Tachornis furcata*
Fork-tailed Swift *Tachornis squamata*
Great Swallow-tailed Swift *Panyptila sanctihieronymi*
Lesser Swallow-tailed Swift *Panyptila cayennensis*
Asian Palm-Swift *Cypsiurus balasiensis*
African Palm-Swift *Cypsiurus parvus*
Alpine Swift *Tachymarptis melba*
Mottled Swift *Tachymarptis aequatorialis*
Cape Verde Swift *Apus alexandri*
Common Swift *Apus apus*
Plain Swift *Apus unicolor*
Nyanza Swift *Apus niansae*
Pallid Swift *Apus pallidus*
African Black Swift *Apus barbatus*
Forbes-Watson's Swift *Apus berliozi*
Bradfield's Swift *Apus bradfieldi*
Madagascar Black Swift *Apus balstoni*
Pacific Swift *Apus pacificus*
Dark-rumped Swift *Apus acuticauda*
Little Swift *Apus affinis*
House Swift *Apus nipalensis*
Horus Swift *Apus horus*
African White-rumped Swift *Apus caffer*
Bates's Black Swift *Apus batesi*

Tree Swifts Hemiprocnidae
Crested Treeswift *Hemiprocne coronata*
Gray-rumped Treeswift *Hemiprocne longipennis*
Whiskered Treeswift *Hemiprocne comata*
Moustached Treeswift *Hemiprocne mystacea*

Hummingbirds Trochilidae
Saw-billed Hermit *Ramphodon naevius*
White-tipped Sicklebill *Eutoxeres aquila*
Buff-tailed Sicklebill *Eutoxeres condamini*
Hook-billed Hermit *Glaucis dohrnii* •
Rufous-breasted Hermit *Glaucis hirsutus*
Bronze Hermit *Glaucis aeneus*
Band-tailed Barbthroat *Threnetes ruckeri*
Pale-tailed Barbthroat *Threnetes niger*
Broad-tipped Hermit *Anopetia gounellei*
White-whiskered Hermit *Phaethornis yaruqui*
Green Hermit *Phaethornis guy*
White-bearded Hermit *Phaethornis hispidus*
Western Long-tailed Hermit *Phaethornis longirostris*
Eastern Long-tailed Hermit *Phaethornis superciliosus*
Great-billed Hermit *Phaethornis malaris*
Tawny-bellied Hermit *Phaethornis syrmatophorus*
Koepcke's Hermit *Phaethornis koepckeae*
Needle-billed Hermit *Phaethornis philippii*
Straight-billed Hermit *Phaethornis bourcieri*
Pale-bellied Hermit *Phaethornis anthophilus*
Scale-throated Hermit *Phaethornis eurynome*
Planalto Hermit *Phaethornis pretrei*
Sooty-capped Hermit *Phaethornis augusti*
Buff-bellied Hermit *Phaethornis subochraceus*
Dusky-throated Hermit *Phaethornis squalidus*
Streak-throated Hermit *Phaethornis rupurumii*
Little Hermit *Phaethornis longuemareus*
Minute Hermit *Phaethornis idaliae*
Cinnamon-throated Hermit *Phaethornis nattereri*
Reddish Hermit *Phaethornis ruber*
White-browed Hermit *Phaethornis stuarti*
Black-throated Hermit *Phaethornis atrimentalis*
Stripe-throated Hermit *Phaethornis striigularis*
Gray-chinned Hermit *Phaethornis griseogularis*
Tooth-billed Hummingbird *Androdon aequatorialis*
Green-fronted Lancebill *Doryfera ludovicae*

Blue-fronted Lancebill   *Doryfera johannae*
Scaly-breasted Hummingbird   *Phaeochroa cuvierii*
Wedge-tailed Sabrewing   *Campylopterus curvipennis*
Long-tailed Sabrewing   *Campylopterus excellens*
Gray-breasted Sabrewing   *Campylopterus largipennis*
Rufous Sabrewing   *Campylopterus rufus*
Violet Sabrewing   *Campylopterus hemileucurus*
Rufous-breasted Sabrewing   *Campylopterus hyperythrus*
White-tailed Sabrewing   *Campylopterus ensipennis*
Lazuline Sabrewing   *Campylopterus falcatus*
Santa Marta Sabrewing   *Campylopterus phainopeplus* •
Napo Sabrewing   *Campylopterus villaviscensio*
Buff-breasted Sabrewing   *Campylopterus duidae*
Sombre Hummingbird   *Campylopterus cirrochloris*
Swallow-tailed Hummingbird   *Campylopterus macrourus*
White-necked Jacobin   *Florisuga mellivora*
Black Jacobin   *Florisuga fuscus*
Brown Violetear   *Colibri delphinae*
Green Violetear   *Colibri thalassinus*
Sparkling Violetear   *Colibri coruscans*
White-vented Violetear   *Colibri serrirostris*
Green-throated Mango   *Anthracothorax viridigula*
Green-breasted Mango   *Anthracothorax prevostii*
Black-throated Mango   *Anthracothorax nigricollis*
Veraguan Mango   *Anthracothorax veraguensis*
Antillean Mango   *Anthracothorax dominicus*
Green Mango   *Anthracothorax viridis*
Jamaican Mango   *Anthracothorax mango*
Fiery-tailed Awlbill   *Avocettula recurvirostris*
Fiery Topaz   *Topaza pyra*
Crimson Topaz   *Topaza pella*
Purple-throated Carib   *Eulampis jugularis*
Green-throated Carib   *Eulampis holosericeus*
Ruby-topaz Hummingbird   *Chrysolampis mosquitus*
Antillean Crested Hummingbird   *Orthorhyncus cristatus*
Violet-headed Hummingbird   *Klais guimeti*
Black-breasted Plovercrest   *Stephanoxis lalandi*
Emerald-chinned Hummingbird   *Abeillia abeillei*
Tufted Coquette   *Lophornis ornatus*
Dot-eared Coquette   *Lophornis gouldii*
Frilled Coquette   *Lophornis magnificus*
Short-crested Coquette   *Lophornis brachylophus* •
Rufous-crested Coquette   *Lophornis delattrei*
Spangled Coquette   *Lophornis stictolophus*
Festive Coquette   *Lophornis chalybeus*
Peacock Coquette   *Lophornis pavoninus*
Black-crested Coquette   *Lophornis helenae*
White-crested Coquette   *Lophornis adorabilis*
Wire-crested Thorntail   *Popelairia popelairii*
Black-bellied Thorntail   *Popelairia langsdorffi*
Coppery Thorntail   *Popelairia letitiae*
Green Thorntail   *Discosura conversii*
Racquet-tailed Coquette   *Discosura longicaudus*
Red-billed Streamertail   *Trochilus polytmus*
Black-billed Streamertail   *Trochilus scitulus*
Blue-chinned Sapphire   *Chlorostilbon notatus*
Blue-tailed Emerald   *Chlorostilbon mellisugus*
Golden-crowned Emerald   *Chlorostilbon auriceps*
Cozmuzel Emerald   *Chlorostilbon forficatus*
Canivet's Emerald   *Chlorostilbon canivetii*
Garden Emerald   *Chlorostilbon assimilis*
Glittering-bellied Emerald   *Chlorostilbon aureoventris*
Chirbiquete Emerald   *Chlorostilbon olivaresi*
Cuban Emerald   *Chlorostilbon ricordii*
Hispaniolan Emerald   *Chlorostilbon swainsonii*
Puerto Rican Emerald   *Chlorostilbon maugaeus*
Coppery Emerald   *Chlorostilbon russatus*
Narrow-tailed Emerald   *Chlorostilbon stenurus*
Green-tailed Emerald   *Chlorostilbon alice*
Short-tailed Emerald   *Chlorostilbon poortmani*
Fiery-throated Hummingbird   *Panterpe insignis*

White-tailed Emerald   *Elvira chionura*
Coppery-headed Emerald   *Elvira cupreiceps*
Blue-capped Hummingbird   *Eupherusa cyanophrys* •
White-tailed Hummingbird   *Eupherusa poliocerca*
Stripe-tailed Hummingbird   *Eupherusa eximia*
Black-bellied Hummingbird   *Eupherusa nigriventris*
Pirre Hummingbird   *Goethalsia bella*
Violet-capped Hummingbird   *Goldmania violiceps*
Dusky Hummingbird   *Cynanthus sordidus*
Broad-billed Hummingbird   *Cynanthus latirostris*
Blue-headed Hummingbird   *Cyanophaia bicolor*
Purple-crowned Woodnymph   *Thalurania colombica*
Mexican Woodnymph   *Thalurania ridgwayi*
Green-crowned Woodnymph   *Thalurania fannyi*
Fork-tailed Woodnymph   *Thalurania furcata*
Long-tailed Woodnymph   *Thalurania watertonii*
Violet-capped Woodnymph   *Thalurania glaucopis*
Violet-bellied Hummingbird   *Damophila julie*
Sapphire-throated Hummingbird   *Lepidopyga coeruleogularis*
Sapphire-bellied Hummingbird   *Lepidopyga lilliae* •
Shining-green Hummingbird   *Lepidopyga goudoti*
Blue-throated Goldentail   *Hylocharis eliciae*
Rufous-throated Sapphire   *Hylocharis sapphirina*
White-chinned Sapphire   *Hylocharis cyanus*
Gilded Sapphire   *Hylocharis chrysura*
Blue-headed Sapphire   *Hylocharis grayi*
Xantus's Hummingbird   *Hylocharis xantusii*
White-eared Hummingbird   *Hylocharis leucotis*
Golden-tailed Sapphire   *Chrysuronia oenone*
White-throated Hummingbird   *Leucochloris albicollis*
White-tailed Goldenthroat   *Polytmus guainumbi*
Tepui Goldenthroat   *Polytmus milleri*
Green-tailed Goldenthroat   *Polytmus theresiae*
Buffy Hummingbird   *Leucippus fallax*
Tumbes Hummingbird   *Leucippus baeri*
Spot-throated Hummingbird   *Leucippus taczanowskii*
Olive-spotted Hummingbird   *Leucippus chlorocercus*
White-bellied Hummingbird   *Leucippus chionogaster*
Green-and-white Hummingbird   *Leucippus viridicauda*
Many-spotted Hummingbird   *Leucippus hypostictus*
Rufous-tailed Hummingbird   *Amazilia tzacatl*
Chestnut-bellied Hummingbird   *Amazilia castaneiventris* •
Amazilia Hummingbird   *Amazilia amazilia*
Loja Hummingbird   *Amazilia alticola*
Buff-bellied Hummingbird   *Amazilia yucatanensis*
Cinnamon Hummingbird   *Amazilia rutila*
Plain-bellied Emerald   *Agyrtria leucogaster*
Versicolored Emerald   *Agyrtria versicolor*
Blue-fronted Emerald   *Agyrtria rondoniae*
White-chested Emerald   *Agyrtria brevirostris*
Andean Emerald   *Agyrtria franciae*
White-bellied Emerald   *Agyrtria candida*
Red-billed Azurecrown   *Agyrtria cyanocephala*
Violet-crowned Hummingbird   *Agyrtria violiceps*
Green-fronted Hummingbird   *Agyrtria viridifrons*
Sapphire-spangled Emerald   *Polyerata lactea*
Glittering-throated Emerald   *Polyerata fimbriata*
Blue-chested Hummingbird   *Polyerata amabilis*
Charming Hummingbird   *Polyerata decora*
Purple-chested Hummingbird   *Polyerata rosenbergi*
Mangrove Hummingbird   *Polyerata boucardi* •
Honduran Emerald   *Polyerata luciae* •
Steely-vented Hummingbird   *Saucerottia saucerrottei*
Indigo-capped Hummingbird   *Saucerottia cyanifrons*
Alfaros Hummingbird   *Saucerottia alfaroana*
Snowy-breasted Hummingbird   *Saucerottia edward*
Blue-tailed Hummingbird   *Saucerottia cyanura*
Berylline Hummingbird   *Saucerottia beryllina*
Green-bellied Hummingbird   *Saucerottia viridigaster*
Copper-tailed Hummingbird   *Saucerottia cupreicauda*
Copper-rumped Hummingbird   *Saucerottia tobaci*
Snowcap   *Microchera albocoronata*

Blossomcrown   *Anthocephala floriceps*
White-vented Plumeleteer   *Chalybura buffonii*
Bronze-tailed Plumeleteer   *Chalybura urochrysia*
Blue-throated Hummingbird   *Lampornis clemenciae*
Amethyst-throated Hummingbird   *Lampornis amethystinus*
Green-throated Mountain-Gem   *Lampornis viridipallens*
Green-breasted Mountain-Gem   *Lampornis sybillae*
White-bellied Mountain-Gem   *Lampornis hemileucus*
White-throated Mountain-Gem   *Lampornis castaneoventris*
Purple-throated Mountain-Gem   *Lampornis calolaemus*
Gray-tailed Mountain-Gem   *Lampornis cinereicauda*
Garnet-throated Hummingbird   *Lamprolaima rhami*
Ecuadorean Piedtail   *Phlogophilus hemileucurus*
Peruvian Piedtail   *Phlogophilus harterti*
Speckled Hummingbird   *Adelomyia melanogenys*
Brazilian Ruby   *Clytolaema rubricauda*
Gould's Jewelfront   *Heliodoxa aurescens*
Fawn-breasted Brilliant   *Heliodoxa rubinoides*
Violet-fronted Brilliant   *Heliodoxa leadbeateri*
Velvet-browed Brilliant   *Heliodoxa xanthogonys*
Black-throated Brilliant   *Heliodoxa schreibersii*
Pink-throated Brilliant   *Heliodoxa gularis*
Rufous-webbed Brilliant   *Heliodoxa branickii*
Empress Brilliant   *Heliodoxa imperatrix*
Green-crowned Brilliant   *Heliodoxa jacula*
Magnificent Hummingbird   *Eugenes fulgens*
Scissor-tailed Hummingbird   *Hylonympha macrocerca*
Violet-chested Hummingbird   *Sternoclyta cyanopectus*
White-tailed Hillstar   *Urochroa bougueri*
Chestnut-breasted Coronet   *Boissonneaua matthewsii*
Buff-tailed Coronet   *Boissonneaua flavescens*
Velvet-purple Coronet   *Boissonneaua jardini*
Shining Sunbeam   *Aglaeactis cupripennis*
White-tufted Sunbeam   *Aglaeactis castelnaudii*
Purple-backed Sunbeam   *Aglaeactis aliciae* •
Black-hooded Sunbeam   *Aglaeactis pamela*
Andean Hillstar   *Oreotrochilus estella*
Ecuadorian Hillstar   *Oreotrochilus chimborazo*
Green-headed Hillstar   *Oreotrochilus stolzmanni*
White-sided Hillstar   *Oreotrochilus leucopleurus*
Black-breasted Hillstar   *Oreotrochilus melanogaster*
Wedge-tailed Hillstar   *Oreotrochilus adela*
Mountain Velvetbreast   *Lafresnaya lafresnayi*
Bronzy Inca   *Coeligena coeligena*
Brown Inca   *Coeligena wilsoni*
Black Inca   *Coeligena prunellei* •
Gould's Inca   *Coeligena inca*
Collared Inca   *Coeligena torquata*
White-tailed Starfrontlet   *Coeligena phalerata*
Golden Starfrontlet   *Coeligena eos*
Golden-bellied Starfrontlet   *Coeligena bonapartei*
Blue-throated Starfrontlet   *Coeligena helianthea*
Buff-winged Starfrontlet   *Coeligena lutetiae*
Violet-throated Starfrontlet   *Coeligena violifer*
Rainbow Starfrontlet   *Coeligena iris*
Sword-billed Hummingbird   *Ensifera ensifera*
Great Sapphirewing   *Pterophanes cyanopterus*
Giant Hummingbird   *Patagona gigas*
Green-backed Firecrown   *Sephanoides sephaniodes*
Juan Fernández Firecrown   *Sephanoides fernandensis* •
Longuemare's Sunangel   *Heliangelus clarisse*
Orange-throated Sunangel   *Heliangelus mavors*
Amethyst-throated Sunangel   *Heliangelus amethysticollis*
Gorgeted Sunangel   *Heliangelus strophianus*
Tourmaline Sunangel   *Heliangelus exortis*
Flame-throated Sunangel   *Heliangelus micraster*
Purple-throated Sunangel   *Heliangelus viola*
Royal Sunangel   *Heliangelus regalis* •
Black-breasted Puffleg   *Eriocnemis nigrivestis* •
Glowing Puffleg   *Eriocnemis vestita*
Black-thighed Puffleg   *Eriocnemis derbyi*
Tuquoise-throated Puffleg   *Eriocnemis godini* •

Sapphire-vented Puffleg *Eriocnemis luciani*
Coppery-bellied Puffleg *Eriocnemis cupreoventris*
Coppery-naped Puffleg *Eriocnemis sapphiropygia*
Golden-breasted Puffleg *Eriocnemis mosquera*
Blue-capped Puffleg *Eriocnemis glaucopoides*
Colorful Puffleg *Eriocnemis mirabilis* •
Emerald-bellied Puffleg *Eriocnemis alinae*
Greenish Puffleg *Haplophaedia aureliae*
Buff-thighed Puffleg *Haplophaedia assimilis*
Hoary Puffleg *Haplophaedia lugens*
Purple-bibbed Whitetip *Urosticte benjamini*
Rufous-vented Whitetip *Urosticte ruficrissa*
Booted Racquet-tail *Ocreatus underwoodii*
Black-tailed Trainbearer *Lesbia victoriae*
Green-tailed Trainbearer *Lesbia nuna*
Red-tailed Comet *Sappho sparganura*
Bronze-tailed Comet *Polyonymus caroli*
Purple-backed Thornbill *Ramphomicron microrhynchum*
Black-backed Thornbill *Ramphomicron dorsale*
Bearded Mountaineer *Oreonympha nobilis*
Bearded Helmetcrest *Oxypogon guerinii*
Tyrian Metaltail *Metallura tyrianthina*
Perija Metaltail *Metallura iracunda* •
Scaled Metaltail *Metallura aeneocauda*
Fire-throated Metaltail *Metallura eupogon*
Coppery Metaltail *Metallura theresiae*
Neblina Metaltail *Metallura odomae*
Violet-throated Metaltail *Metallura baroni* •
Viridian Metaltail *Metallura williami*
Black Metaltail *Metallura phoebe*
Rufous-capped Thornbill *Chalcostigma ruficeps*
Olivaceous Thornbill *Chalcostigma olivaceum*
Blue-mantled Thornbill *Chalcostigma stanleyi*
Bronze-tailed Thornbill *Chalcostigma heteropogon*
Rainbow-bearded Thornbill *Chalcostigma herrani*
Mountain Avocetbill *Opisthoprora euryptera*
Gray-bellied Comet *Taphrolesbia griseiventris* •
Long-tailed Sylph *Aglaiocercus kingi*
Violet-tailed Sylph *Aglaiocercus coelestis*
Venezuelan Sylph *Aglaiocercus berlepschi*
Hyacinth Visorbearer *Augastes scutatus*
Hooded Visorbearer *Augastes lumachella*
Wedge-billed Hummingbird *Augastes geoffroyi*
Purple-crowned Fairy *Heliothryx barroti*
Black-eared Fairy *Heliothryx auritus*
Horned Sungem *Heliactin bilophus*
Marvellous Spatuletail *Loddigesia mirabilis* •
Plain-capped Starthroat *Heliomaster constantii*
Long-billed Starthroat *Heliomaster longirostris*
Stripe-breasted Starthroat *Heliomaster squamosus*
Blue-tufted Starthroat *Heliomaster furcifer*
Oasis Hummingbird *Rhodopis vesper*
Peruvian Sheartail *Thaumastura cora*
Sparkling-tailed Hummingbird *Tilmatura dupontii*
Slender Sheartail *Doricha enicura*
Mexican Sheartail *Doricha eliza*
Bahama Woodstar *Calliphlox evelynae*
Magenta-throated Woodstar *Calliphlox bryantae*
Purple-throated Woodstar *Calliphlox mitchellii*
Amethyst Woodstar *Calliphlox amethystina*
Slender-tailed Woodstar *Microstilbon burmeisteri*
Lucifer Hummingbird *Calothorax lucifer*
Beautiful Hummingbird *Calothorax pulcher*
Vervain Hummingbird *Mellisuga minima*
Bee Hummingbird *Mellisuga helenae*
Ruby-throated Hummingbird *Archilochus colubris*
Black-chinned Hummingbird *Archilochus alexandri*
Anna's Hummingbird *Calypte anna*
Costa's Hummingbird *Calypte costae*
Bumblebee Hummingbird *Atthis heloisa*
Wine-throated Hummingbird *Atthis ellioti*
Calliope Hummingbird *Stellula calliope*
Purple-collared Woodstar *Myrtis fanny*

Chilean Woodstar *Eulidia yarrellii* •
Short-tailed Woodstar *Myrmia micrura*
White-bellied Woodstar *Chaetocercus mulsant*
Little Woodstar *Chaetocercus bombus*
Gorgeted Woodstar *Chaetocercus heliodor*
Colombian Woodstar *Chaetocercus astreans*
Esmeraldas Woodstar *Chaetocercus berlepschi* •
Rufous-shafted Woodstar *Chaetocercus jourdanii*
Scintillant Hummingbird *Selasphorus scintilla*
Glow-throated Hummingbird *Selasphorus ardens*
Volcano Hummingbird *Selasphorus flammula*
Broad-tailed Hummingbird *Selasphorus platycercus*
Rufous Hummingbird *Selasphorus rufus*
Allen's Hummingbird *Selasphorus sasin*

COLIES OR MOUSEBIRDS Coliiformes

Mousebirds Coliidae
Speckled Mousebird *Colius striatus*
White-headed Mousebird *Colius leucocephalus*
Red-backed Mousebird *Colius castanotus*
White-backed Mousebird *Colius colius*
Blue-naped Mousebird *Urocolius macrourus*
Red-faced Mousebird *Urocolius indicus*

TROGONS Trogoniformes

Trogons Trogonidae
Narina Trogon *Apaloderma narina*
Bare-cheeked Trogon *Apaloderma aequatoriale*
Bar-tailed Trogon *Apaloderma vittatum*
Cuban Trogon *Priotelus temnurus*
Hispaniolan Trogon *Priotelus roseigaster*
Black-headed Trogon *Trogon melanocephalus*
Citreoline Trogon *Trogon citreolus*
Amazonian White-tailed Trogon *Trogon viridis*
Baird's Trogon *Trogon bairdii*
Amazonian Violaceous Trogon *Trogon violaceus*
Mountain Trogon *Trogon mexicanus*
Chocó Trogon *Trogon comptus*
Collared Trogon *Trogon collaris*
Elegant Trogon *Trogon elegans*
Orange-bellied Trogon *Trogon aurantiiventris*
Masked Trogon *Trogon personatus*
Black-throated Trogon *Trogon rufus*
Surucua Trogon *Trogon surrucura*
Blue-crowned Trogon *Trogon curucui*
Black-tailed Trogon *Trogon melanurus*
Slaty-tailed Trogon *Trogon massena*
Lattice-tailed Trogon *Trogon clathratus*
Eared Quetzal *Euptilotis neoxenus*
Resplendent Quetzal *Pharomachrus mocinno*
Crested Quetzal *Pharomachrus antisianus*
White-tipped Quetzal *Pharomachrus fulgidus*
Golden-headed Quetzal *Pharomachrus auriceps*
Pavonine Quetzal *Pharomachrus pavoninus*
Javan Trogon *Harpactes reinwardtii* •
Sumatran Trogon *Harpactes mackloti*
Malabar Trogon *Harpactes fasciatus*
Red-naped Trogon *Harpactes kasumba*
Diard's Trogon *Harpactes diardii*
Philippine Trogon *Harpactes ardens*
Whitehead's Trogon *Harpactes whiteheadi*
Cinnamon-rumped Trogon *Harpactes orrhophaeus*
Scarlet-rumped Trogon *Harpactes duvaucelii*
Red-headed Trogon *Harpactes erythrocephalus*
Orange-breasted Trogon *Harpactes oreskios*
Ward's Trogon *Harpactes wardi*

KINGFISHERS AND ALLIES
Coraciiformes

Kingfishers Alcedinidae
Blyth's Kingfisher *Alcedo hercules*

Common Kingfisher *Alcedo atthis*
Half-collared Kingfisher *Alcedo semitorquata*
Shining-blue Kingfisher *Alcedo quadribrachys*
Blue-eared Kingfisher *Alcedo meninting*
Azure Kingfisher *Alcedo azurea*
Bismarck Kingfisher *Alcedo websteri*
Blue-banded Kingfisher *Alcedo euryzona*
Indigo-banded Kingfisher *Alcedo cyanopectus*
Silvery Kingfisher *Alcedo argentata*
Malachite Kingfisher *Alcedo cristata*
Madagascar Kingfisher *Alcedo vintsioides*
White-bellied Kingfisher *Alcedo leucogaster*
Caerulean Kingfisher *Alcedo coerulescens*
Little Kingfisher *Alcedo pusilla*
Oriental Dwarf-Kingfisher *Ceyx erithaca*
Philippine Dwarf-Kingfisher *Ceyx melanurus*
Sulawesi Dwarf-Kingfisher *Ceyx fallax*
Rufous-backed Dwarf-Kingfisher *Ceyx rufidorsa*
Variable Dwarf-Kingfisher *Ceyx lepidus*
Madagascar Pygmy-Kingfisher *Ispidina madagascariensis*
African Pygmy-Kingfisher *Ispidina picta*
African Dwarf-Kingfisher *Ispidina lecontei*
Banded Kingfisher *Lacedo pulchella*
Laughing Kookaburra *Dacelo novaeguineae*
Blue-winged Kookaburra *Dacelo leachii*
Spangled Kookaburra *Dacelo tyro*
Rufous-bellied Kookaburra *Dacelo gaudichaud*
Shovel-billed Kingfisher *Clytoceyx rex*
Lilac-cheeked Kingfisher *Cittura cyanotis*
Brown-winged Stork-billed-Kingfisher *Pelargopsis amauroptera*
Brown-headed Stork-billed-Kingfisher *Pelargopsis capensis*
Celebes Stork-billed Kingfisher *Pelargopsis melanorhyncha*
Ruddy Kingfisher *Halcyon coromanda*
Chocolate-backed Kingfisher *Halcyon badia*
White-breasted Kingfisher *Halcyon smyrnensis*
Gray-headed Kingfisher *Halcyon leucocephala*
Black-capped Kingfisher *Halcyon pileata*
Javan Kingfisher *Halcyon cyanoventris*
African Mangrove Kingfisher *Halcyon senegaloides*
Woodland Kingfisher *Halcyon senegalensis*
Blue-breasted Kingfisher *Halcyon malimbica*
Brown-hooded Kingfisher *Halcyon albiventris*
Striped Kingfisher *Halcyon chelicuti*
Black-sided Kingfisher *Todiramphus nigrocyaneus*
Winchell's Kingfisher *Todiramphus winchelli*
Moluccan Kingfisher *Todiramphus diops*
Lazuli Kingfisher *Todiramphus lazuli*
Forest Kingfisher *Todiramphus macleayii*
New Britain Kingfisher *Todiramphus albonotatus*
Ultramarine Kingfisher *Todiramphus leucopygius*
Chestnut-bellied Kingfisher *Todiramphus farquhari*
Red-backed Kingfisher *Todiramphus pyrrhopygius*
Flat-billed Kingfisher *Todiramphus recurvirostris*
Micronesian Kingfisher *Todiramphus cinnamominus*
Mangrove Kingfisher *Todiramphus chloris*
Sombre Kingfisher *Todiramphus funebris*
Obscure Kingfisher *Todiramphus enigma*
Beach Kingfisher *Todiramphus saurophagus*
Timor Kingfisher *Todiramphus australasia*
Sacred Kingfisher *Todiramphus sanctus*
Tahiti Kingfisher *Todiramphus veneratus*
Mangaia Kingfisher *Todiramphus ruficollaris*
Pacific Kingfisher *Todiramphus tutus*
Marquesas Kingfisher *Todiramphus godeffroyi* •
Mangareva Kingfisher *Todiramphus gambieri*
White-rumped Kingfisher *Caridonax fulgidus*
Hook-billed Kingfisher *Melidora macrorrhina*
Moustached Kingfisher *Actenoides bougainvillei*
Rufous-collared Kingfisher *Actenoides concretus*
Spotted Kingfisher *Actenoides lindsayi*

Blue-capped Kingfisher *Actenoides hombroni*
Green-backed Kingfisher *Actenoides monachus*
Scaly-breasted Kingfisher *Actenoides princeps*
Lesser Yellow-billed Kingfisher *Syma torotoro*
Mountain Yellow-billed Kingfisher *Syma megarhyncha*
Aru Paradise-Kingfisher *Tanysiptera hydrocharis*
Common Paradise-Kingfisher *Tanysiptera galatea*
Kofiau Paradise-Kingfisher *Tanysiptera ellioti*
Biak Paradise-Kingfisher *Tanysiptera riedelii*
Numfor Paradise-Kingfisher *Tanysiptera carolinae*
Red-breasted Paradise-Kingfisher *Tanysiptera nympha*
Brown-headed Paradise-Kingfisher *Tanysiptera danae*
White-tailed Paradise-Kingfisher *Tanysiptera sylvia*
Giant Kingfisher *Megaceryle maximus*
Crested Kingfisher *Megaceryle lugubris*
Belted Kingfisher *Ceryle alcyon*
Ringed Kingfisher *Ceryle torquatus*
Lesser Pied Kingfisher *Ceryle rudis*
Amazon Kingfisher *Chloroceryle amazona*
Green Kingfisher *Chloroceryle americana*
Green-and-rufous Kingfisher *Chloroceryle inda*
American Pygmy Kingfisher *Chloroceryle aenea*

Todies Todidae
Cuban Tody *Todus multicolor*
Broad-billed Tody *Todus subulatus*
Narrow-billed Tody *Todus angustirostris*
Jamaican Tody *Todus todus*
Puerto Rican Tody *Todus mexicanus*

Motmots Momotidae
Tody Motmot *Hylomanes momotula*
Blue-throated Motmot *Aspatha gularis*
Russet-crowned Motmot *Momotus mexicanus*
Blue-crowned Motmot *Momotus momota*
Highland Motmot *Momotus aequatorialis*
Rufous Motmot *Baryphthengus martii*
Rufous-capped Motmot *Baryphthengus ruficapillus*
Keel-billed Motmot *Electron carinatum*
Broad-billed Motmot *Electron platyrhynchum*
Turquoise-browed Motmot *Eumomota superciliosa*

Bee-eaters Meropidae
Red-bearded Bee-eater *Nyctyornis amictus*
Blue-bearded Bee-eater *Nyctyornis athertoni*
Purple-bearded Bee-eater *Meropogon forsteni*
Black Bee-eater *Merops gularis*
Blue-headed Bee-eater *Merops muelleri*
Red-throated Bee-eater *Merops bulocki*
White-fronted Bee-eater *Merops bullockoides*
Little Bee-eater *Merops pusillus*
Blue-breasted Bee-eater *Merops variegatus*
Cinnamon-chested Bee-eater *Merops oreobates*
Swallow-tailed Bee-eater *Merops hirundineus*
Black-headed Bee-eater *Merops breweri*
Somali Bee-eater *Merops revoilii*
White-throated Bee-eater *Merops albicollis*
Little Green Bee-eater *Merops orientalis*
Bôhm's Bee-eater *Merops boehmi*
Blue-throated Bee-eater *Merops viridis*
Blue-cheeked Bee-eater *Merops persicus*
Madagascar Bee-eater *Merops superciliosus*
Blue-tailed Bee-eater *Merops philippinus*
Rainbow Bee-eater *Merops ornatus*
European Bee-eater *Merops apiaster*
Bay-headed Bee-eater *Merops leschenaulti*
Rosy Bee-eater *Merops malimbicus*
Carmine Bee-eater *Merops nubicus*
Southern Carmine Bee-eater *Merops nubicoides*

Rollers Coraciidae
European Roller *Coracias garrulus*
Abyssinian Roller *Coracias abyssinicus*
Lilac-breasted Roller *Coracias caudatus*

Racquet-tailed Roller *Coracias spatulatus*
Rufous-crowned Roller *Coracias noevius*
Indian Roller *Coracias benghalensis*
Purple-winged Roller *Coracias temminckii*
Blue-bellied Roller *Coracias cyanogaster*
African Broad-billed Roller *Eurystomus glaucurus*
Blue-throated Roller *Eurystomus gularis*
Dollarbird *Eurystomus orientalis*
Azure Roller *Eurystomus azureus*

Ground Rollers Brachypteraciidae
Short-legged Ground-Roller *Brachypteracias leptosomus*
Scaly Ground-Roller *Brachypteracias squamiger*
Pitta-like Ground-Roller *Atelornis pittoides*
Crossley's Ground-Roller *Atelornis crossleyi*
Long-tailed Ground-Roller *Uratelornis chimaera*

Courol or Kirombo Cuckoo Roller Leptosomatidae
Madagascar Cuckoo-Roller *Leptosomus discolor*

HOOPOES AND WOODHOOPOES
Upupiformes

Hoopoe Upupidae
Eurasian Hoopoe *Upupa epops*
Madagascar Hoopoe *Upupa marginata*

Woodhoopoes Phoeniculidae
Green Woodhoopoe *Phoeniculus purpureus*
Violet Woodhoopoe *Phoeniculus damarensis*
Black-billed Woodhoopoe *Phoeniculus somaliensis*
White-headed Woodhoopoe *Phoeniculus bollei*
Forest Woodhoopoe *Phoeniculus castaneiceps*
Black Scimitarbill *Rhinopomastus aterrimus*
Common Scimitarbill *Rhinopomastus cyanomelas*
Abyssinian Scimitarbill *Rhinopomastus minor*

HORNBILLS AND GROUND
HORNBILLS Bucerotiformes

Hornbills Bucerotidae
African White-crested Hornbill *Tockus albocristatus*
Black Dwarf Hornbill *Tockus hartlaubi*
Red-billed Dwarf Hornbill *Tockus camurus*
Monteiro's Hornbill *Tockus monteiri*
African Red-billed Hornbill *Tockus erythrorhynchus*
Eastern Yellow-billed Hornbill *Tockus flavirostris*
Southern Yellow-billed Hornbill *Tockus leucomelas*
Jackson's Hornbill *Tockus jacksoni*
Von der Decken's Hornbill *Tockus deckeni*
Crowned Hornbill *Tockus alboterminatus*
Bradfield's Hornbill *Tockus bradfieldi*
African Pied Hornbill *Tockus fasciatus*
Hemprich's Hornbill *Tockus hemprichii*
African Gray Hornbill *Tockus nasutus*
Pale-billed Hornbill *Tockus pallidirostris*
Malabar Gray Hornbill *Ocyceros griseus*
Sri Lankan Gray Hornbill *Ocyceros gingalensis*
Indian Gray Hornbill *Ocyceros birostris*
Malabar Pied Hornbill *Anthracoceros coronatus*
Oriental Pied Hornbill *Anthracoceros albirostris*
Asian Black Hornbill *Anthracoceros malayanus*
Palawan Hornbill *Anthracoceros marchei*
Sulu Hornbill *Anthracoceros montani* •
Rhinoceros Hornbill *Buceros rhinoceros*
Great Pied Hornbill *Buceros bicornis*
Rufous Hornbill *Buceros hydrocorax*
Helmeted Hornbill *Buceros vigil*
Austen's Brown Hornbill *Anorrhinus austeni*
Tickell's Brown Hornbill *Anorrhinus tickelli*
Bushy-crested Hornbill *Anorrhinus galeritus*
Luzon Hornbill *Penelopides manillae*
Mindoro Hornbill *Penelopides mindorensis* •

Visayan Taric Hornbill *Penelopides panini* •
Samar Hornbill *Penelopides samarensis*
Mindanao Hornbill *Penelopides affinis*
Sulawesi Taric Hornbill *Penelopides exarhatus*
Long-crested Hornbill *Aceros comatus*
Rufous-necked Hornbill *Aceros nipalensis*
Wrinkled Hornbill *Aceros corrugatus*
Rufous-headed Hornbill *Aceros waldeni* •
Writhed Hornbill *Aceros leucocephalus*
Red-knobbed Hornbill *Aceros cassidix*
Wreathed Hornbill *Aceros undulatus*
Narcondam Wreathed Hornbill *Aceros narcondami*
Sumba Wreathed Hornbill *Aceros everetti*
Plain-pouched Hornbill *Aceros subruficollis*
Papuan Wreathed Hornbill *Aceros plicatus*
Trumpeter Hornbill *Ceratogymna bucinator*
Piping Hornbill *Ceratogymna fistulator*
Silvery-cheeked Hornbill *Ceratogymna brevis*
Black-and-white-casqued Hornbill *Ceratogymna subcylindrica*
Brown-cheeked Hornbill *Ceratogymna cylindrica*
White-thighed Hornbill *Ceratogymna albotibialis*
Black-casqued Hornbill *Ceratogymna atrata*
Yellow-casqued Hornbill *Ceratogymna elata*
Northern Ground-Hornbill *Bucorvus abyssinicus*
Southern Ground-Hornbill *Bucorvus leadbeateri*

WOODPECKERS AND ALLIES
Piciformes

Jacamars Galbulidae
Chestnut Jacamar *Galbalcyrhynchus leucotis*
Purus Jacamar *Galbalcyrhynchus purusianus*
Dusky-backed Jacamar *Brachygalba salmoni*
Pale-headed Jacamar *Brachygalba goeringi*
Brown Jacamar *Brachygalba lugubris*
White-throated Jacamar *Brachygalba albogularis*
Three-toed Jacamar *Jacamaralcyon tridactyla*
Yellow-billed Jacamar *Galbula albirostris*
Purple-necked Jacamar *Galbula cyanicollis*
Green-tailed Jacamar *Galbula galbula*
Rufous-tailed Jacamar *Galbula ruficauda*
Coppery-chested Jacamar *Galbula pastazae*
White-chinned Jacamar *Galbula tombacea*
Bluish-fronted Jacamar *Galbula cyanescens*
Purplish Jacamar *Galbula chalcothorax*
Bronzy Jacamar *Galbula leucogastra*
Paradise Jacamar *Galbula dea*
Great Jacamar *Jacamerops aureus*

Puffbirds Bucconidae
White-necked Puffbird *Notharchus macrorhynchos*
Buff-bellied Puffbird *Notharchus swainsoni*
Black-breasted Puffbird *Notharchus pectoralis*
Brown-banded Puffbird *Notharchus ordii*
Pied Puffbird *Notharchus tectus*
Chestnut-capped Puffbird *Bucco macrodactylus*
Spotted Puffbird *Bucco tamatia*
Sooty-capped Puffbird *Bucco noanamae*
Collared Puffbird *Bucco capensis*
Barred Puffbird *Nystalus radiatus*
White-eared Puffbird *Nystalus chacuru*
Striolated Puffbird *Nystalus striolatus*
Spot-backed Puffbird *Nystalus maculatus*
Russet-throated Puffbird *Hypnelus ruficollis*
Two-banded Puffbird *Hypnelus bicinctus*
Crescent-chested Puffbird *Malacoptila striata*
White-chested Puffbird *Malacoptila fusca*
Semicollared Puffbird *Malacoptila semicincta*
Black-streaked Puffbird *Malacoptila fulvogularis*
Rufous-necked Puffbird *Malacoptila rufa*
White-whiskered Puffbird *Malacoptila panamensis*
Moustached Puffbird *Malacoptila mystacalis*
Lanceolated Monklet *Micromonacha lanceolata*

Rusty-breasted Nunlet *Nonnula rubecula*
Fulvous-chinned Nunlet *Nonnula sclateri*
Brown Nunlet *Nonnula brunnea*
Gray-cheeked Nunlet *Nonnula frontalis*
Rufous-capped Nunlet *Nonnula ruficapilla*
Chestnut-headed Nunlet *Nonnula amaurocephala*
White-faced Nunbird *Hapaloptila castanea*
Black Nunbird *Monasa atra*
Black-fronted Nunbird *Monasa nigrifrons*
White-fronted Nunbird *Monasa morphoeus*
Yellow-billed Nunbird *Monasa flavirostris*
Swallow-winged Puffbird *Chelidoptera tenebrosa*

Barbets Capitonidae
Yellow-billed Barbet *Trachyphonus purpuratus*
Crested Barbet *Trachyphonus vaillantii*
Red-and-yellow Barbet *Trachyphonus erythrocephalus*
Yellow-breasted Barbet *Trachyphonus margaritatus*
D'Arnaud's Barbet *Trachyphonus darnaudii*
Gray-throated Barbet *Gymnobucco bonapartei*
Sladen's Barbet *Gymnobucco sladeni*
Bristle-nosed Barbet *Gymnobucco peli*
Naked-faced Barbet *Gymnobucco calvus*
White-eared Barbet *Stactolaema leucotis*
Whyte's Barbet *Stactolaema whytii*
Anchieta's Barbet *Stactolaema anchietae*
Green Barbet *Stactolaema olivacea*
Speckled Tinkerbird *Pogoniulus scolopaceus*
Eastern Green Tinkerbird *Pogoniulus simplex*
Moustached Green Tinkerbird *Pogoniulus leucomystax*
Western Green Tinkerbird *Pogoniulus coryphaeus*
Red-rumped Tinkerbird *Pogoniulus atroflavus*
Yellow-throated Tinkerbird *Pogoniulus subsulphureus*
Yellow-rumped Tinkerbird *Pogoniulus bilineatus*
Red-fronted Tinkerbird *Pogoniulus pusillus*
Yellow-fronted Tinkerbird *Pogoniulus chrysoconus*
Yellow-spotted Barbet *Buccanodon duchaillui*
Hairy-breasted Barbet *Tricholaema hirsuta*
Red-fronted Barbet *Tricholaema diademata*
Miombo Barbet *Tricholaema frontata*
Pied Barbet *Tricholaema leucomelas*
Spot-flanked Barbet *Tricholaema lacrymosa*
African Black-throated Barbet *Tricholaema melanocephala*
Banded Barbet *Lybius undatus*
Vieillot's Barbet *Lybius vieilloti*
White-headed Barbet *Lybius leucocephalus*
Chaplin's Barbet *Lybius chaplini*
Red-faced Barbet *Lybius rubrifacies*
Black-billed Barbet *Lybius guifsobalito*
Black-collared Barbet *Lybius torquatus*
Brown-breasted Barbet *Lybius melanopterus*
Black-backed Barbet *Lybius minor*
Double-toothed Barbet *Lybius bidentatus*
Bearded Barbet *Lybius dubius*
Black-breasted Barbet *Lybius rolleti*
Brown Barbet *Calorhamphus fuliginosus*
Fire-tufted Barbet *Psilopogon pyrolophus*
Great Barbet *Megalaima virens*
Red-vented Barbet *Megalaima lagrandieri*
Brown-headed Barbet *Megalaima zeylanica*
Lineated Barbet *Megalaima lineata*
White-cheeked Barbet *Megalaima viridis*
Green-eared Barbet *Megalaima faiostricta*
Brown-throated Barbet *Megalaima corvina*
Gold-whiskered Barbet *Megalaima chrysopogon*
Red-crowned Barbet *Megalaima rafflesii*
Red-throated Barbet *Megalaima mystacophanos*
Black-banded Barbet *Megalaima javensis*
Sri Lanka Yellow-fronted Barbet *Megalaima flavifrons*
Golden-throated Barbet *Megalaima franklinii*
Black-browed Barbet *Megalaima oorti*
Blue-throated Barbet *Megalaima asiatica*
Moustached Barbet *Megalaima incognita*

Mountain Barbet *Megalaima monticola*
Yellow-crowned Barbet *Megalaima henricii*
Flame-fronted Barbet *Megalaima armillaris*
Golden-naped Barbet *Megalaima pulcherrima*
Blue-eared Barbet *Megalaima australis*
Bornean Barbet *Megalaima eximia*
Crimson-fronted Barbet *Megalaima rubricapillus*
Coppersmith Barbet *Megalaima haemacephala*
Scarlet-crowned Barbet *Capito aurovirens*
Scarlet-banded Barbet *Capito wallacei*
Spot-crowned Barbet *Capito maculicoronatus*
Orange-fronted Barbet *Capito squamatus*
White-mantled Barbet *Capito hypoleucus* •
Black-girdled Barbet *Capito dayi*
Brown-chested Barbet *Capito brunneipectus*
Black-spotted Barbet *Capito niger*
Gilded Barbet *Capito auratus*
Five-colored Barbet *Capito quinticolor*
Lemon-throated Barbet *Eubucco richardsoni*
Red-headed Barbet *Eubucco bourcierii*
Scarlet-hooded Barbet *Eubucco tucinkae*
Versicolored Barbet *Eubucco versicolor*
Prong-billed Barbet *Semnornis frantzii*
Toucan Barbet *Semnornis ramphastinus*

Toucans Rhamphastidae
Wagler's Toucanet *Aulacorhynchus wagleri*
Emerald Toucanet *Aulacorhynchus prasinus*
Blue-throated Toucanet *Aulacorhynchus caeruleogularis*
Violet-throated Toucanet *Aulacorhynchus cognatus*
Santa Marta Toucanet *Aulacorhynchus lautus*
Andean Toucanet *Aulacorhynchus albivitta*
Black-throated Toucanet *Aulacorhynchus atrogularis*
Groove-billed Toucanet *Aulacorhynchus sulcatus*
Chestnut-tipped Toucanet *Aulacorhynchus derbianus*
Crimson-rumped Toucanet *Aulacorhynchus haematopygus*
Yellow-browed Toucanet *Aulacorhynchus huallagae* •
Blue-banded Toucanet *Aulacorhynchus coeruleicinctis*
Guianan Toucanet *Selenidera culik*
Tawny-tufted Toucanet *Selenidera nattereri*
Golden-collared Toucanet *Selenidera reinwardtii*
Gould's Toucanet *Selenidera gouldii*
Spot-billed Toucanet *Selenidera maculirostris*
Yellow-eared Toucanet *Selenidera spectabilis*
Gray-breasted Mountain-Toucan *Andigena hypoglauca*
Hooded Mountain-Toucan *Andigena cucullata*
Plate-billed Mountain-Toucan *Andigena laminirostris*
Black-billed Mountain-Toucan *Andigena nigrirostris*
Saffron Toucanet *Baillonius bailloni*
Green Araçari *Pteroglossus viridis*
Lettered Araçari *Pteroglossus inscriptus*
Red-necked Araçari *Pteroglossus bitorquatus*
Ivory-billed Araçari *Pteroglossus azara*
Black-necked Araçari *Pteroglossus aracari*
Chestnut-eared Araçari *Pteroglossus castanotis*
Many-banded Araçari *Pteroglossus pluricinctus*
Collared Araçari *Pteroglossus torquatus*
Fiery-billed Araçari *Pteroglossus frantzii*
Curl-crested Araçari *Pteroglossus beauharnaesii*
Red-breasted Toucan *Ramphastos dicolorus*
Keel-billed Toucan *Ramphastos sulfuratus*
Choco Toucan *Ramphastos brevis*
Channel-billed Toucan *Ramphastos vitellinus*
Toco Toucan *Ramphastos toco*
Red-billed Toucan *Ramphastos tucanus*
Black-mandibled Toucan *Ramphastos ambiguus*

Honeyguides Indicatoridae
Cassin's Honeybird *Prodotiscus insignis*
Eastern Green-backed Honeybird *Prodotiscus zambesiae*
Wahlberg's Honeybird *Prodotiscus regulus*

Zenker's Honeyguide *Melignomon zenkeri*
Yellow-footed Honeyguide *Melignomon eisentrauti*
Dwarf Honeyguide *Indicator pumilio*
Willcocks's Honeyguide *Indicator willcocksi*
Pallid Honeyguide *Indicator meliphilus*
Least Honeyguide *Indicator exilis*
Thick-billed Honeyguide *Indicator conirostris*
Lesser Honeyguide *Indicator minor*
Spotted Honeyguide *Indicator maculatus*
Scaly-throated Honeyguide *Indicator variegatus*
Yellow-rumped Honeyguide *Indicator xanthonotus*
Malaysian Honeyguide *Indicator archipelagicus*
Greater Honeyguide *Indicator indicator*
Lyre-tailed Honeyguide *Melichneutes robustus*

Woodpeckers Picidae
Eurasian Wryneck *Jynx torquilla*
Red-throated Wryneck *Jynx ruficollis*
Speckled Piculet *Picumnus innominatus*
Bar-breasted Piculet *Picumnus aurifrons*
Orinoco Piculet *Picumnus pumilus*
Lafresnaye's Piculet *Picumnus lafresnayi*
Golden-spangled Piculet *Picumnus exilis*
Black-dotted Piculet *Picumnus nigropunctatus*
Ecuadorian Piculet *Picumnus sclateri*
Scaled Piculet *Picumnus squamulatus*
White-bellied Piculet *Picumnus spilogaster*
Guianan Piculet *Picumnus minutissimus*
Spotted Piculet *Picumnus pygmaeus*
Speckle-chested Piculet *Picumnus steindachneri*
Varzea Piculet *Picumnus varzeae*
White-barred Piculet *Picumnus cirratus*
Ocellated Piculet *Picumnus dorbignyanus*
Ochre-collared Piculet *Picumnus temminckii*
White-wedged Piculet *Picumnus albosquamatus*
Rusty-necked Piculet *Picumnus fuscus*
Rufous-breasted Piculet *Picumnus rufiventris*
Tawny Piculet *Picumnus fulvescens*
Ochraceous Piculet *Picumnus limae*
Mottled Piculet *Picumnus nebulosus*
Plain-breasted Piculet *Picumnus castelnau*
Fine-barred Piculet *Picumnus subtilis*
Olivaceous Piculet *Picumnus olivaceus*
Grayish Piculet *Picumnus granadensis*
Chestnut Piculet *Picumnus cinnamomeus*
African Piculet *Sasia africana*
Rufous Piculet *Sasia abnormis*
White-browed Piculet *Sasia ochracea*
Antillean Piculet *Nesoctites micromegas*
White Woodpecker *Melanerpes candidus*
Lewis' Woodpecker *Melanerpes lewis*
Guadeloupe Woodpecker *Melanerpes herminieri*
Puerto Rican Woodpecker *Melanerpes portoricensis*
Red-headed Woodpecker *Melanerpes erythrocephalus*
Acorn Woodpecker *Melanerpes formicivorus*
Black-cheeked Woodpecker *Melanerpes pucherani*
Golden-naped Woodpecker *Melanerpes chrysauchen*
Yellow-tufted Woodpecker *Melanerpes cruentatus*
Yellow-fronted Woodpecker *Melanerpes flavifrons*
White-fronted Woodpecker *Melanerpes cactorum*
Hispaniolan Woodpecker *Melanerpes striatus*
Jamaican Woodpecker *Melanerpes radiolatus*
Golden-cheeked Woodpecker *Melanerpes chrysogenys*
Gray-breasted Woodpecker *Melanerpes hypopolius*
Yucatan Woodpecker *Melanerpes pygmaeus*
Red-crowned Woodpecker *Melanerpes rubricapillus*
Gila Woodpecker *Melanerpes uropygialis*
Red-bellied Woodpecker *Melanerpes carolinus*
Great Red-bellied Woodpecker *Melanerpes superciliaris*
Golden-fronted Woodpecker *Melanerpes aurifrons*
Hoffmann's Woodpecker *Melanerpes hoffmannii*

Yellow-bellied Sapsucker *Sphyrapicus varius*
Red-naped Sapsucker *Sphyrapicus nuchalis*
Red-breasted Sapsucker *Sphyrapicus ruber*
Williamson's Sapsucker *Sphyrapicus thyroideus*
Cuban Green Woodpecker *Xiphidiopicus percussus*
Fine-spotted Woodpecker *Campethera punctuligera*
Nubian Woodpecker *Campethera nubica*
Bennett's Woodpecker *Campethera bennettii*
Reichenow's Woodpecker *Campethera scriptoricauda*
Golden-tailed Woodpecker *Campethera abingoni*
Mombasa Woodpecker *Campethera mombassica*
Knysna Woodpecker *Campethera notata*
Little Green Woodpecker *Campethera maculosa*
Green-backed Woodpecker *Campethera cailliautii*
Fine-banded Woodpecker *Campethera tullbergi*
Buff-spotted Woodpecker *Campethera nivosa*
Brown-eared Woodpecker *Campethera caroli*
Ground Woodpecker *Geocolaptes olivaceus*
Little Gray Woodpecker *Dendropicos elachus*
Speckle-breasted Woodpecker *Dendropicos poecilolaemus*
Abyssinian Golden-backed Woodpecker *Dendropicos abyssinicus*
Cardinal Woodpecker *Dendropicos fuscescens*
Melancholy Woodpecker *Dendropicos lugubris*
Gabon Woodpecker *Dendropicos gabonensis*
Stierling's Woodpecker *Dendropicos stierlingi*
Bearded Woodpecker *Dendropicos namaquus*
Fire-bellied Woodpecker *Dendropicos pyrrhogaster*
Yellow-crested Woodpecker *Dendropicos xantholophus*
Elliot's Woodpecker *Dendropicos elliotii*
Gray Woodpecker *Dendropicos goertae*
Gray-headed Woodpecker *Dendropicos spodocephalus*
Olive Woodpecker *Dendropicos griseocephalus*
Brown-backed Woodpecker *Dendropicos obsoletus*
Sulawesi Pygmy-Woodpecker *Dendrocopos temminckii*
Philippine Woodpecker *Dendrocopos maculatus*
Brown-capped Woodpecker *Dendrocopos moluccensis*
Gray-capped Woodpecker *Dendrocopos canicapillus*
Pygmy-Woodpecker *Dendrocopos kizuki*
Lesser Spotted Woodpecker *Dendrocopos minor*
Brown-fronted Woodpecker *Dendrocopos auriceps*
Fulvous-breasted Woodpecker *Dendrocopos macei*
Stripe-breasted Woodpecker *Dendrocopos atratus*
Yellow-crowned Woodpecker *Dendrocopos mahrattensis*
Arabian Woodpecker *Dendrocopos dorae*
Rufous-bellied Woodpecker *Dendrocopos hyperythrus*
Crimson-breasted Woodpecker *Dendrocopos cathpharius*
Darjeeling Pied Woodpecker *Dendrocopos darjellensis*
Middle Spotted Woodpecker *Dendrocopos medius*
White-backed Woodpecker *Dendrocopos leucotos*
Great Spotted Woodpecker *Dendrocopos major*
Syrian Woodpecker *Dendrocopos syriacus*
White-winged Woodpecker *Dendrocopos leucopterus*
Sind Woodpecker *Dendrocopos assimilis*
Himalayan Woodpecker *Dendrocopos himalayensis*
Striped Woodpecker *Picoides lignarius*
Chequered Woodpecker *Picoides mixtus*
Nuttall's Woodpecker *Picoides nuttallii*
Ladder-backed Woodpecker *Picoides scalaris*
Downy Woodpecker *Picoides pubescens*
Red-cockaded Woodpecker *Picoides borealis*
Strickland's Woodpecker *Picoides stricklandi*
Arizona Woodpecker *Picoides arizonae*
Hairy Woodpecker *Picoides villosus*
White-headed Woodpecker *Picoides albolarvatus*
Eurasian Three-toed Woodpecker *Picoides tridactylus*
Northern Three-toed Woodpecker *Picoides dorsalis*

Black-backed Three-toed Woodpecker *Picoides arcticus*
Scarlet-backed Woodpecker *Veniliornis callonotus*
Yellow-vented Woodpecker *Veniliornis dignus*
Bar-bellied Woodpecker *Veniliornis nigriceps*
Smoky-brown Woodpecker *Veniliornis fumigatus*
Little Woodpecker *Veniliornis passerinus*
Dot-fronted Woodpecker *Veniliornis frontalis*
White-spotted Woodpecker *Veniliornis spilogaster*
Blood-colored Woodpecker *Veniliornis sanguineus*
Red-rumped Woodpecker *Veniliornis kirkii*
Chocó Woodpecker *Veniliornis chocoensis*
Golden-collared Woodpecker *Veniliornis cassini*
Red-stained Woodpecker *Veniliornis affinis*
Yellow-eared Woodpecker *Veniliornis maculifrons*
Rufous-winged Woodpecker *Piculus simplex*
Stripe-cheeked Woodpecker *Piculus callopterus*
Lita Woodpecker *Piculus litae*
White-throated Woodpecker *Piculus leucolaemus*
Yellow-throated Woodpecker *Piculus flavigula*
Golden-green Woodpecker *Piculus chrysochloros*
White-browed Woodpecker *Piculus aurulentus*
Gray-crowned Woodpecker *Piculus auricularis*
Golden-olive Woodpecker *Piculus rubiginosus*
Crimson-mantled Woodpecker *Piculus rivolii*
Black-necked Woodpecker *Colaptes atricollis*
Spot-breasted Woodpecker *Colaptes punctigula*
Green-barred Woodpecker *Colaptes melanochloros*
Northern Flicker *Colaptes auratus*
Gilded Flicker *Colaptes chrysoides*
Fernandina's Flicker *Colaptes fernandinae*
Chilean Flicker *Colaptes pitius*
Andean Flicker *Colaptes rupicola*
Campo Flicker *Colaptes campestris*
Rufous Woodpecker *Celeus brachyurus*
Cinnamon Woodpecker *Celeus loricatus*
Scaly-breasted Woodpecker *Celeus grammicus*
Waved Woodpecker *Celeus undatus*
Chestnut-colored Woodpecker *Celeus castaneus*
Chestnut Woodpecker *Celeus elegans*
Pale-crested Woodpecker *Celeus lugubris*
Blond-crested Woodpecker *Celeus flavescens*
Cream-colored Woodpecker *Celeus flavus*
Rufous-headed Woodpecker *Celeus spectabilis*
Ringed Woodpecker *Celeus torquatus*
Helmeted Woodpecker *Dryocopus galeatus*
Pileated Woodpecker *Dryocopus pileatus*
Lineated Woodpecker *Dryocopus lineatus*
Black-bodied Woodpecker *Dryocopus schulzi*
White-bellied Woodpecker *Dryocopus javensis*
Andaman Woodpecker *Dryocopus hodgei*
Black Woodpecker *Dryocopus martius*
Powerful Woodpecker *Campephilus pollens*
Crimson-bellied Woodpecker *Campephilus haematogaster*
Red-necked Woodpecker *Campephilus rubricollis*
Robust Woodpecker *Campephilus robustus*
Pale-billed Woodpecker *Campephilus guatemalensis*
Crimson-crested Woodpecker *Campephilus melanoleucos*
Guayaquil Woodpecker *Campephilus gayaquilensis*
Cream-backed Woodpecker *Campephilus leucopogon*
Magellanic Woodpecker *Campephilus magellanicus*
Imperial Woodpecker *Campephilus imperialis* •
Ivory-billed Woodpecker *Campephilus principalis* •
Banded Woodpecker *Picus mineaceus*
Lesser Yellownape *Picus chlorolophus*
Crimson-winged Woodpecker *Picus puniceus*
Greater Yellownape *Picus flavinucha*
Chequer-throated Woodpecker *Picus mentalis*
Streak-breasted Woodpecker *Picus viridanus*
Laced Woodpecker *Picus vittatus*
Streak-throated Green Woodpecker *Picus xanthopygaeus*
Common Scaly-bellied Woodpecker *Picus squamatus*

Japanese Green Woodpecker *Picus awokera*
Eurasian Green Woodpecker *Picus viridis*
Levaillant's Green Woodpecker *Picus vaillantii*
Red-collared Woodpecker *Picus rabieri*
Black-headed Woodpecker *Picus erythropygius*
Gray-headed Green Woodpecker *Picus canus*
Olive-backed Woodpecker *Dinopium rafflesii*
Himalayan Flameback *Dinopium shorii*
Common Goldenback *Dinopium javanense*
Black-rumped Flameback *Dinopium benghalense*
Greater Flameback *Chrysocolaptes lucidus*
White-naped Woodpecker *Chrysocolaptes festivus*
Pale-headed Woodpecker *Gecinulus grantia*
Bamboo Woodpecker *Gecinulus viridis*
Okinawan Woodpecker *Sapheopipo noguchii*
Maroon Woodpecker *Blythipicus rubiginosus*
Bay Woodpecker *Blythipicus pyrrhotis*
Orange-backed Woodpecker *Reinwardtipicus validus*
Buff-rumped Woodpecker *Meiglyptes tristis*
Black-and-buff Woodpecker *Meiglyptes jugularis*
Buff-necked Woodpecker *Meiglyptes tukki*
Gray-and-buff Woodpecker *Hemicircus concretus*
Heart-spotted Woodpecker *Hemicircus canente*
Ashy Woodpecker *Mulleripicus fulvus*
Sooty Woodpecker *Mulleripicus funebris*
Great Slaty Woodpecker *Mulleripicus pulverulentus*

PERCHING BIRDS Passeriformes

Broadbills Eurylimidae
African Broadbill *Smithornis capensis*
Gray-headed Broadbill *Smithornis sharpei*
Rufous-sided Broadbill *Smithornis rufolateralis*
Lesser Green Broadbill *Calyptomena viridis*
Hose's Broadbill *Calyptomena hosii*
Whitehead's Broadbill *Calyptomena whiteheadi*
Black-and-red Broadbill *Cymbirhynchus macrorhynchos*
Long-tailed Broadbill *Psarisomus dalhousiae*
Silver-breasted Broadbill *Serilophus lunatus*
Banded Broadbill *Eurylaimus javanicus*
Black-and-yellow Broadbill *Eurylaimus ochromalus*
Wattled Broadbill *Eurylaimus steerii*
Visayan Wattled Broadbill *Eurylaimus samarensis*
Dusky Broadbill *Corydon sumatranus*
African Green Broadbill *Pseudocalyptomena graueri*

Asities Philepittidae
Velvet Asity *Philepitta castanea*
Schlegel's Asity *Philepitta schlegeli*
Common Sunbird Asity *Neodrepanis coruscans*
Yellow-bellied Sunbird Asity *Neodrepanis hypoxanthus*

Pittas *Pittidae*
Eared Pitta *Pitta phayrei*
Blue-naped Pitta *Pitta nipalensis*
Blue-rumped Pitta *Pitta soror*
Rusty-naped Pitta *Pitta oatesi*
Schneider's Pitta *Pitta schneideri*
Giant Pitta *Pitta caerulea*
Blue Pitta *Pitta cyanea*
Banded Pitta *Pitta guajana*
Bar-bellied Pitta *Pitta elliotii*
Gurney's Pitta *Pitta gurneyi* •
Blue-headed Pitta *Pitta baudii*
Superb Pitta *Pitta superba*
Ivory-breasted Pitta *Pitta maxima*
Blue-banded Pitta *Pitta arquata*
Garnet Pitta *Pitta granatina*
Black-and-crimson Pitta *Pitta ussheri*
Graceful Pitta *Pitta venusta*
African Pitta *Pitta angolensis*
Green-breasted Pitta *Pitta reichenowi*
Azure-breasted Pitta *Pitta steerii*
Hooded Pitta *Pitta sordida*

Whiskered Pitta *Pitta kochi*
Red-bellied Pitta *Pitta erythrogaster*
Sula Pitta *Pitta dohertyi*
Indian Pitta *Pitta brachyura*
Fairy Pitta *Pitta nympha*
Blue-winged Pitta *Pitta moluccensis*
Mangrove Pitta *Pitta megarhyncha*
Elegant Pitta *Pitta elegans*
Noisy Pitta *Pitta versicolor*
Black-faced Pitta *Pitta anerythra*
Rainbow Pitta *Pitta iris*

Ovenbirds Furnariidae
Campo Miner *Geobates poecilopterus*
Common Miner *Geositta cunicularia*
Slender-billed Miner *Geositta tenuirostris*
Short-billed Miner *Geositta antarctica*
Grayish Miner *Geositta maritima*
Coastal Miner *Geositta peruviana*
Dark-winged Miner *Geositta saxicolina*
Puna Miner *Geositta punensis*
Rufous-banded Miner *Geositta rufipennis*
Creamy-rumped Miner *Geositta isabellina*
Thick-billed Miner *Geositta crassirostris*
Scale-throated Earthcreeper *Upucerthia dumetaria*
White-throated Earthcreeper *Upucerthia albigula*
Plain-breasted Earthcreeper *Upucerthia jelskii*
Buff-breasted Earthcreeper *Upucerthia validirostris*
Striated Earthcreeper *Upucerthia serrana*
Rock Earthcreeper *Upucerthia andaecola*
Straight-billed Earthcreeper *Upucerthia ruficaudus*
Bolivian Earthcreeper *Ochetorhynchus harterti*
Chaco Earthcreeper *Ochetorhynchus certhioides*
Band-tailed Earthcreeper *Eremobius phoenicurus*
Crag Chilia *Chilia melanura*
Stout-billed Cinclodes *Cinclodes excelsior*
Royal Cinclodes *Cinclodes aricomae* •
Bar-winged Cinclodes *Cinclodes fuscus*
Cordoba Cinclodes *Cinclodes comechingonus*
Long-tailed Cinclodes *Cinclodes pabsti*
Olrog's Cinclodes *Cinclodes olrogi*
Gray-flanked Cinclodes *Cinclodes oustaleti*
Dark-bellied Cinclodes *Cinclodes patagonicus*
Peruvian Seaside Cinclodes *Cinclodes taczanowskii*
Chilean Seaside Cinclodes *Cinclodes nigrofumosus*
Blackish Cinclodes *Cinclodes antarcticus*
White-winged Cinclodes *Cinclodes atacamensis*
White-bellied Cinclodes *Cinclodes palliatus* •
Pale-legged Hornero *Furnarius leucopus*
Pale-billed Hornero *Furnarius torridus*
Lesser Hornero *Furnarius minor*
Rufous Hornero *Furnarius rufus*
Crested Hornero *Furnarius cristatus*
Tail-banded Hornero *Furnarius figulus*
Curve-billed Reedhaunter *Limnornis curvirostris*
Straight-billed Reedhaunter *Limnornis rectirostris*
Wren-like Rushbird *Phleocryptes melanops*
Thorn-tailed Rayadito *Aphrastura spinicauda*
Mas Afuera Rayadito *Aphrastura masafuerae* •
Brown-capped Tit-Spinetail *Leptasthenura fuliginiceps*
Tawny Tit-Spinetail *Leptasthenura yanacensis*
Tufted Tit-Spinetail *Leptasthenura platensis*
Plain-mantled Tit-Spinetail *Leptasthenura aegithaloides*
Striolated Tit-Spinetail *Leptasthenura striolata*
Rusty-crowned Tit-Spinetail *Leptasthenura pileata*
White-browed Tit-Spinetail *Leptasthenura xenothorax* •
Streaked Tit-Spinetail *Leptasthenura striata*
Andean Tit-Spinetail *Leptasthenura andicola*
Araucaria Tit-Spinetail *Leptasthenura setaria*
Bay-capped Wren Spinetail *Spartonoica maluroides*
Des Murs's Wiretail *Sylviorthorhynchus desmursii*
Perijá Thistletail *Schizoeaca perijana* •
Ochre-browed Thistletail *Schizoeaca coryi*
White-chinned Spinetail *Schizoeaca fuliginosa*

Mouse-colored Thistletail *Schizoeaca griseomurina*
Eye-ringed Thistletail *Schizoeaca palpebralis*
Vilcabamba Thistletail *Schizoeaca vilcabambae*
Puna Thistletail *Schizoeaca helleri*
Black-throated Thistletail *Schizoeaca harterti*
Itatiaia Spinetail *Oreophylax moreirae*
Chotoy Spinetail *Schoeniophylax phryganophilus*
Rufous-capped Spinetail *Synallaxis ruficapilla*
Bahia Spinetail *Synallaxis cinerea*
Pinto's Spinetail *Synallaxis infuscata* •
Gray-bellied Spinetail *Synallaxis cinerascens*
Silvery-throated Spinetail *Synallaxis subpudica*
Sooty-fronted Spinetail *Synallaxis frontalis*
Azara's Spinetail *Synallaxis azarae*
Apurimac Spinetail *Synallaxis courseni*
Pale-breasted Spinetail *Synallaxis albescens*
Dark-breasted Spinetail *Synallaxis albigularis*
Chicli Spinetail *Synallaxis spixi*
Cinereous-breasted Spinetail *Synallaxis hypospodia*
Ruddy Spinetail *Synallaxis rutilans*
Chestnut-throated Spinetail *Synallaxis cherriei*
Rufous Spinetail *Synallaxis unirufa*
Black-throated Spinetail *Synallaxis castanea*
Rusty-headed Spinetail *Synallaxis fuscorufa*
Rufous-breasted Spinetail *Synallaxis erythrothorax*
Slaty Spinetail *Synallaxis brachyura*
Blackish-headed Spinetail *Synallaxis tithys* •
White-bellied Spinetail *Synallaxis propinqua*
MacConnell's Spinetail *Synallaxis macconnelli*
Dusky Spinetail *Synallaxis moesta*
Cabanis' Spinetail *Synallaxis cabanisi*
Marañón Spinetail *Synallaxis maranonica*
Plain-crowned Spinetail *Synallaxis gujanensis*
White-lored Spinetail *Synallaxis albilora*
Ochre-cheeked Spinetail *Synallaxis scutata*
White-whiskered Spinetail *Synallaxis candei*
Hoary-throated Spinetail *Synallaxis kollari*
Stripe-breasted Spinetail *Synallaxis cinnamomea*
Russet-bellied Spinetail *Synallaxis zimmeri* •
Necklaced Spinetail *Synallaxis stictothorax*
Chinchipe Spinetail *Synallaxis chinchipensis*
Great Spinetail *Siptornopsis hypochondriaca*
Red-shouldered Spinetail *Gyalophylax hellmayri*
White-browed Spinetail *Hellmayrea gularis*
Marcapata Spinetail *Cranioleuca marcapatae*
Light-crowned Spinetail *Cranioleuca albiceps*
Rusty-backed Spinetail *Cranioleuca vulpina*
Parker's Spinetail *Cranioleuca vulpecula*
Sulfur-bearded Spinetail *Cranioleuca sulphurifera*
Crested Spinetail *Cranioleuca subcristata*
Stripe-crowned Spinetail *Cranioleuca pyrrhophia*
Bolivian Spinetail *Cranioleuca henricae* •
Olive Spinetail *Cranioleuca obsoleta*
Pallid Spinetail *Cranioleuca pallida*
Gray-headed Spinetail *Cranioleuca semicinerea*
Creamy-crested Spinetail *Cranioleuca albicapilla*
Red-faced Spinetail *Cranioleuca erythrops*
Tepui Spinetail *Cranioleuca demissa*
Streak-capped Spinetail *Cranioleuca hellmayri*
Ash-browed Spinetail *Cranioleuca curtata*
Line-cheeked Spinetail *Cranioleuca antisiensis*
Baron's Spinetail *Cranioleuca baroni*
Speckled Spinetail *Cranioleuca gutturata*
Scaled Spinetail *Cranioleuca muelleri*
Yellow-chinned Spinetail *Certhiaxis cinnamomeus*
Red-and-white Spinetail *Certhiaxis mustelinus*
Striated Softtail *Thripophaga macroura*
Orinoco Softtail *Thripophaga cherriei*
Plain Softtail *Thripophaga fusciceps*
Russet-mantled Softtail *Thripophaga berlepschi*
Canyon Canastero *Asthenes pudibunda*
Rusty-fronted Canastero *Asthenes ottonis*
Iquico Canastero *Asthenes heterura*
Cordilleran Canastero *Asthenes modesta*

Cactus Canastero *Asthenes cactorum*
Streak-throated Canastero *Asthenes humilis*
Streak-backed Canastero *Asthenes wyatti*
Puna Canastero *Asthenes sclateri*
Austral Canastero *Asthenes anthoides*
Hudson's Canastero *Asthenes hudsoni*
Line-fronted Canastero *Asthenes urubambensis*
Many-striped Canastero *Asthenes flammulata*
Junin Canastero *Asthenes virgata*
Scribble-tailed Canastero *Asthenes maculicauda*
Lesser Canastero *Asthenes pyrrholeuca*
Dusky-tailed Canastero *Asthenes humicola*
Creamy-breasted Canastero *Asthenes dorbignyi*
Dark-winged Canastero *Asthenes arequipae*
Pale-tailed Canastero *Asthenes huancavelicae*
Berlepsch's Canastero *Asthenes berlepschi*
Chestnut Canastero *Asthenes steinbachi*
Short-billed Canastero *Asthenes baeri*
Cipó Canastero *Asthenes luizae*
Patagonian Canastero *Asthenes patagonica*
Common Thornbird *Phacellodomus rufifrons*
Little Thornbird *Phacellodomus sibilatrix*
Streak-fronted Thornbird *Phacellodomus striaticeps*
Freckle-breasted Thornbird *Phacellodomus striaticollis*
Chestnut-backed Thornbird *Phacellodomus dorsalis*
Greater Thornbird *Phacellodomus ruber*
Spot-breasted Thornbird *Phacellodomus maculipectus*
Red-eyed Thornbird *Phacellodomus erythrophthalmus*
Canebrake Groundcreeper *Clibanornis dendrocolaptoides*
Firewood-gatherer *Anumbius annumbi*
Lark-like Brushrunner *Coryphistera alaudina*
Spectacled Prickletail *Siptornis striaticollis*
Orange-fronted Plushcrown *Metopothrix aurantiaca*
Double-banded Graytail *Xenerpestes minlosi*
Equatorial Graytail *Xenerpestes singularis*
Pink-legged Graveteiro *Acrobatornis fonsecai*
Rusty-winged Barbtail *Premnornis guttuligera*
Spotted Barbtail *Premnoplex brunnescens*
White-throated Barbtail *Premnoplex tatei*
Roraiman Barbtail *Roraimia adusta*
Ruddy Treerunner *Margarornis rubiginosus*
Star-chested Treerunner *Margarornis stellatus*
Beautiful Treerunner *Margarornis bellulus*
Pearled Treerunner *Margarornis squamiger*
Caatinga Cachelote *Pseudoseisura unirufa*
Rufous Cacholote *Pseudoseisura cristata*
Brown Cacholote *Pseudoseisura lophotes*
White-throated Cacholote *Pseudoseisura gutturalis*
Buffy Tuftedcheek *Pseudocolaptes lawrencii*
Streaked Tuftedcheek *Pseudocolaptes boissonneautii*
Point-tailed Palmcreeper *Berlepschia rikeri*
Scaly-throated Foliage-gleaner *Anabacerthia variegaticeps*
Montane Foliage-gleaner *Anabacerthia striaticollis*
White-browed Foliage-gleaner *Anabacerthia amaurotis*
Guttulated Foliage-gleaner *Syndactyla guttulata*
Lineated Foliage-gleaner *Syndactyla subalaris*
Buff-browed Foliage-gleaner *Syndactyla rufosuperciliata*
Rufous-necked Foliage-gleaner *Syndactyla ruficollis*
Peruvian Recurvebill *Simoxenops ucayalae*
Bolivian Recurvebill *Simoxenops striatus*
Chestnut-winged Hookbill *Ancistrops strigilatus*
Eastern Woodhaunter *Hyloctistes subulatus*
Rufous-tailed Foliage-gleaner *Philydor ruficaudatum*
Slaty-winged Foliage-gleaner *Philydor fuscipenne*
Rufous-rumped Foliage-gleaner *Philydor erythrocercum*
Chestnut-winged Foliage-gleaner *Philydor erythropterum*
Ochre-breasted Foliage-gleaner *Philydor lichtensteini*
Alagoas Foliage-gleaner *Philydor novaesi* •
Black-capped Foliage-gleaner *Philydor atricapillus*

Buff-fronted Foliage-gleaner *Philydor rufum*
Cinnamon-rumped Foliage-gleaner *Philydor pyrrhodes*
Russet-mantled Foliage-gleaner *Philydor dimidiatum*
Bamboo Foliage-gleaner *Anabazenops dorsalis*
White-collared Foliage-gleaner *Anabazenops fuscus*
Pale-browed Treehunter *Cichlocolaptes leucophrus*
Uniform Treehunter *Thripadectes ignobilis*
Streak-breasted Treehunter *Thripadectes rufobrunneus*
Black-billed Treehunter *Thripadectes melanorhynchus*
Striped Treehunter *Thripadectes holostictus*
Streak-capped Treehunter *Thripadectes virgaticeps*
Flammulated Treehunter *Thripadectes flammulatus*
Buff-throated Treehunter *Thripadectes scrutator*
Buff-throated Foliage-gleaner *Automolus ochrolaemus*
Olive-backed Foliage-gleaner *Automolus infuscatus*
Para Foliage-gleaner *Automolus paraensis*
White-eyed Foliage-gleaner *Automolus leucophthalmus*
Brown-rumped Foliage-gleaner *Automolus melanopezus*
White-throated Foliage-gleaner *Automolus roraimae*
Ruddy Foliage-gleaner *Automolus rubiginosus*
Chestnut-crowned Foliage-gleaner *Automolus rufipileatus*
Henna-hooded Foliage-gleaner *Hylocryptus erythrocephalus*
Chestnut-capped Foliage-gleaner *Hylocryptus rectirostris*
Tawny-throated Leaftosser *Sclerurus mexicanus*
Short-billed Leaftosser *Sclerurus rufigularis*
Scaly-throated Leaftosser *Sclerurus guatemalensis*
Black-tailed Leaftosser *Sclerurus caudacutus*
Gray-throated Leaftosser *Sclerurus albigularis*
Rufous-breasted Leaftosser *Sclerurus scansor*
Sharp-tailed Streamcreeper *Lochmias nematura*
Sharp-billed Xenops *Heliobletus contaminatus*
Rufous-tailed Xenops *Xenops milleri*
Slender-billed Xenops *Xenops tenuirostris*
Plain Xenops *Xenops minutus*
Streaked Xenops *Xenops rutilans*
Great Xenops *Megaxenops parnaguae*
White-throated Treerunner *Pygarrhichas albogularis*

Woodcreepers Dendrocolaptidae
Tyrannine Woodcreeper *Dendrocincla tyrannina*
Plain-brown Woodcreeper *Dendrocincla fuliginosa*
Thrush-like Woodcreeper *Dendrocincla turdina*
Tawny-winged Woodcreeper *Dendrocincla anabatina*
White-chinned Woodcreeper *Dendrocincla merula*
Ruddy Woodcreeper *Dendrocincla homochroa*
Long-tailed Woodcreeper *Deconychura longicauda*
Spot-throated Woodcreeper *Deconychura stictolaema*
Olivaceous Woodcreeper *Sittasomus griseicapillus*
Wedge-billed Woodcreeper *Glyphorynchus spirurus*
Scimitar-billed Woodcreeper *Drymornis bridgesii*
Long-billed Woodcreeper *Nasica longirostris*
Cinnamon-throated Woodcreeper *Dendrexetastes rufigula*
Red-billed Woodcreeper *Hylexetastes perrotii*
Uniform Woodcreeper *Hylexetastes uniformis*
Brigida's Woodcreeper *Hylexetastes brigidai*
Bar-bellied Woodcreeper *Hylexetastes stresemanni*
Strong-billed Woodcreeper *Xiphocolaptes promeropirhynchus*
Carajas Woodcreeper *Xiphocolaptes carajaensis*
White-throated Woodcreeper *Xiphocolaptes albicollis*
Moustached Woodcreeper *Xiphocolaptes falcirostris*
Great Rufous Woodcreeper *Xiphocolaptes major*
Northern Barred Woodcreeper *Dendrocolaptes sanctithomae*
Amazon Barred Woodcreeper *Dendrocolaptes certhia*
Hoffmanns's Woodcreeper *Dendrocolaptes hoffmannsi*
Black-banded Woodcreeper *Dendrocolaptes picumnus*

Planalto Woodcreeper *Dendrocolaptes platyrostris*
Lesser Woodcreeper *Xiphorhynchus fuscus*
Tschudi's Woodcreeper *Xiphorhynchus chunchotambo*
Ocellated Woodcreeper *Xiphorhynchus ocellatus*
Chestnut-rumped Woodcreeper *Xiphorhynchus pardalotus*
Spix's Woodcreeper *Xiphorhynchus spixii*
Elegant Woodcreeper *Xiphorhynchus elegans*
Jurua Woodcreeper *Xiphorhynchus juruanus*
Striped Woodcreeper *Xiphorhynchus obsoletus*
Buff-throated Woodcreeper *Xiphorhynchus guttatus*
Lafresnaye's Woodcreeper *Xiphorhynchus guttatoides*
Cocoa Woodcreeper *Xiphorhynchus susurrans*
Ivory-billed Woodcreeper *Xiphorhynchus flavigaster*
Black-striped Woodcreeper *Xiphorhynchus lachrymosus*
Spotted Woodcreeper *Xiphorhynchus erythropygius*
Olive-backed Woodcreeper *Xiphorhynchus triangularis*
Straight-billed Woodcreeper *Dendroplex picus*
Zimmer's Woodcreeper *Dendroplex kienerii*
Narrow-billed Woodcreeper *Lepidocolaptes angustirostris*
White-striped Woodcreeper *Lepidocolaptes leucogaster*
Lineated Woodcreeper *Lepidocolaptes albolineatus*
Spot-crowned Woodcreeper *Lepidocolaptes affinis*
Montane Woodcreeper *Lepidocolaptes lacrymiger*
Streak-headed Woodcreeper *Lepidocolaptes souleyetii*
Scaled Woodcreeper *Lepidocolaptes squamatus*
Scalloped Woodcreeper *Lepidocolaptes falcinellus*
Greater Scythebill *Campylorhamphus pucherani*
Black-billed Scythebill *Campylorhamphus falcularius*
Curve-billed Scythebill *Campylorhamphus procurvoides*
Red-billed Scythebill *Campylorhamphus trochilirostris*
Brown-billed Scythebill *Campylorhamphus pusillus*

Typical Antbirds Thamnophilidae
Fasciated Antshrike *Cymbilaimus lineatus*
Bamboo Antshrike *Cymbilaimus sanctaemariae*
Spot-backed Antshrike *Hypoedaleus guttatus*
Giant Antshrike *Batara cinerea*
Large-tailed Antshrike *Mackenziaena leachii*
Tufted Antshrike *Mackenziaena severa*
Black-throated Antshrike *Frederickena viridis*
Undulated Antshrike *Frederickena unduligera*
Great Antshrike *Taraba major*
Black-crested Antshrike *Sakesphorus canadensis*
Silvery-cheeked Antshrike *Sakesphorus cristatus*
Collared Antshrike *Sakesphorus bernardi*
Black-backed Antshrike *Sakesphorus melanonotus*
Band-tailed Antshrike *Sakesphorus melanothorax*
Glossy Antshrike *Sakesphorus luctuosus*
White-bearded Antshrike *Biatas nigropectus*
Barred Antshrike *Thamnophilus doliatus*
Chapman's Antshrike *Thamnophilus zarumae*
Bar-crested Antshrike *Thamnophilus multistriatus*
Lined Antshrike *Thamnophilus tenuepunctatus*
Chestnut-backed Antshrike *Thamnophilus palliatus*
Rufous-winged Antshrike *Thamnophilus torquatus*
Rufous-capped Antshrike *Thamnophilus ruficapillus*
Black-hooded Antshrike *Thamnophilus bridgesi*
Black Antshrike *Thamnophilus nigriceps*
Cocha Antshrike *Thamnophilus praecox*
Blackish-gray Antshrike *Thamnophilus nigrocinereus*
Castelnau's Antshrike *Thamnophilus cryptoleucus*
White-shouldered Antshrike *Thamnophilus aethiops*
Uniform Antshrike *Thamnophilus unicolor*
Plain-winged Antshrike *Thamnophilus schistaceus*
Mouse-colored Antshrike *Thamnophilus murinus*
Upland Antshrike *Thamnophilus aroyae*
Western Slaty Antshrike *Thamnophilus atrinucha*
Guianan Slaty Antshrike *Thamnophilus punctatus*
Peruvian Slaty Antshrike *Thamnophilus leucogaster*
Natterer's Slaty Antshrike *Thamnophilus stictocephalus*

Bolivian Slaty Antshrike *Thamnophilus sticturus*
Planalto Slaty Antshrike *Thamnophilus pelzelni*
Sooretama Slaty Antshrike *Thamnophilus ambiguus*
Amazonian Antshrike *Thamnophilus amazonicus*
Streak-backed Antshrike *Thamnophilus insignis*
Variable Antshrike *Thamnophilus caerulescens*
Acre Antshrike *Thamnophilus divisorius*
Spot-winged Antshrike *Pygiptila stellaris*
Black Bushbird *Neoctantes niger*
Recurve-billed Bushbird *Clytoctantes alixii* •
RondÙnia Bushbird *Clytoctantes atrogularis* •
Pearly Antshrike *Megastictus margaritatus*
Speckled Antshrike *Xenornis setifrons*
Russet Antshrike *Thamnistes anabatinus*
Spot-breasted Antvireo *Dysithamnus stictothorax*
Plain Antvireo *Dysithamnus mentalis*
Streak-crowned Antvireo *Dysithamnus striaticeps*
Spot-crowned Antvireo *Dysithamnus puncticeps*
Rufous-backed Antvireo *Dysithamnus xanthopterus*
White-streaked Antvireo *Dysithamnus leucostictus*
Plumbeous Antvireo *Dysithamnus plumbeus*
Bicolored Antvireo *Dysithamnus occidentalis*
Dusky-throated Antshrike *Thamnomanes ardesiacus*
Saturnine Antshrike *Thamnomanes saturninus*
Cinereous Antshrike *Thamnomanes caesius*
Bluish-slate Antshrike *Thamnomanes schistogynus*
Pygmy Antwren *Myrmotherula brachyura*
Griscom's Antwren *Myrmotherula ignota*
Guianan Streaked Antwren *Myrmotherula surinamensis*
Amazonian Streaked Antwren *Myrmotherula multostriata*
Pacific Streaked Antwren *Myrmotherula pacifica*
Cherrie's Antwren *Myrmotherula cherriei*
Klages's Antwren *Myrmotherula klagesi*
Stripe-chested Antwren *Myrmotherula longicauda*
Sclater's Antwren *Myrmotherula sclateri*
Yellow-throated Antwren *Myrmotherula ambigua*
Rufous-bellied Antwren *Myrmotherula guttata*
Plain-throated Antwren *Myrmotherula hauxwelli*
Star-throated Antwren *Myrmotherula gularis*
Brown-bellied Antwren *Myrmotherula gutturalis*
Checker-throated Antwren *Myrmotherula fulviventris*
White-eyed Antwren *Myrmotherula leucophthalma*
Foothills Antwren *Myrmotherula spodionota*
Stipple-throated Antwren *Myrmotherula haematonota*
Yasuní Antwren *Myrmotherula fjeldsaai*
Ornate Antwren *Myrmotherula ornata*
Rufous-tailed Antwren *Myrmotherula erythrura*
White-flanked Antwren *Myrmotherula axillaris*
Slaty Antwren *Myrmotherula schisticolor*
Río Suno Antwren *Myrmotherula sunensis*
Salvadori's Antwren *Myrmotherula minor*
Ihering's Antwren *Myrmotherula iheringi*
Rio de Janeiro Antwren *Myrmotherula fluminensis* •
Plain-winged Antwren *Myrmotherula behni*
Ashy Antwren *Myrmotherula grisea*
Unicolored Antwren *Myrmotherula unicolor*
Alagoas Antwren *Myrmotherula snowi* •
Long-winged Antwren *Myrmotherula longipennis*
Band-tailed Antwren *Myrmotherula urosticta*
Gray Antwren *Myrmotherula menetriesii*
Leaden Antwren *Myrmotherula assimilis*
Banded Antwren *Dichrozona cincta*
Stripe-backed Antbird *Myrmorchilus strigilatus*
Spot-backed Antwren *Herpsilochmus dorsimaculatus*
Pileated Antwren *Herpsilochmus pileatus*
Black-capped Antwren *Herpsilochmus atricapillus*
Caatinga Antwren *Herpsilochmus sellowi*
Creamy-bellied Antwren *Herpsilochmus motacilloides*
Ash-throated Antwren *Herpsilochmus parkeri* •
Colombian Antwren *Herpsilochmus dugandi*
Spot-tailed Antwren *Herpsilochmus sticturus*
Roraiman Antwren *Herpsilochmus roraimae*

Yellow-breasted Antwren   *Herpsilochmus axillaris*
Ancient Antwren   *Herpsilochmus gentryi*
Todd's Antwren   *Herpsilochmus stictocephalus*
Large-billed Antwren   *Herpsilochmus longirostris*
Pectoral Antwren   *Herpsilochmus pectoralis*
Rufous-winged Antwren   *Herpsilochmus rufimarginatus*
Dot-winged Antwren   *Microrhopias quixensis*
Narrow-billed Antwren   *Neorhopias iheringi*
Paraná Antwren   *Formicivora acutirostris*
White-fringed Antwren   *Formicivora grisea*
Serra Antwren   *Formicivora serrana*
Restinga Antwren   *Formicivora littoralis* •
Black-bellied Antwren   *Formicivora melanogaster*
Rusty-backed Antwren   *Formicivora rufa*
Black-hooded Antwren   *Formicivora erythronotos* •
Ferruginous Antbird   *Drymophila ferruginea*
Bertoni's Antwren   *Drymophila rubricollis*
Rufous-tailed Antbird   *Drymophila genei*
Ochre-rumped Antbird   *Drymophila ochropyga*
Dusky-tailed Antbird   *Drymophila malura*
Scaled Antbird   *Drymophila squamata*
Striated Antbird   *Drymophila devillei*
Long-tailed Antbird   *Drymophila caudata*
Streak-capped Antwren   *Terenura maculata*
Orange-bellied Antwren   *Terenura sicki* •
Rufous-rumped Antwren   *Terenura callinota*
Chestnut-shouldered Antwren   *Terenura humeralis*
Yellow-rumped Antwren   *Terenura sharpei* •
Ash-winged Antwren   *Terenura spodioptila*
Blackish Antbird   *Cercomacra nigrescens*
Willis's Antbird   *Cercomacra laeta*
Dusky Antbird   *Cercomacra tyrannina*
Parker's Antbird   *Cercomacra parkeri*
Black Antbird   *Cercomacra serva*
Gray Antbird   *Cercomacra cinerascens*
Rio de Janeiro Antbird   *Cercomacra brasiliana*
Rio Branco Antbird   *Cercomacra carbonaria*
Jet Antbird   *Cercomacra nigricans*
Mato Grosso Antbird   *Cercomacra melanaria*
Manu Antbird   *Cercomacra manu*
Bananal Antbird   *Cercomacra ferdinandi*
White-backed Fire-eye   *Pyriglena leuconota*
Fringe-backed Fire-eye   *Pyriglena atra* •
White-shouldered Fire-eye   *Pyriglena leucoptera*
Slender Antbird   *Rhopornis ardesiacus* •
White-browed Antbird   *Myrmoborus leucophrys*
Ash-breasted Antbird   *Myrmoborus lugubris*
Black-faced Antbird   *Myrmoborus myotherinus*
Black-tailed Antcreeper   *Myrmoborus melanurus*
Warbling Antbird   *Hypocnemis cantator*
Yellow-browed Antbird   *Hypocnemis hypoxantha*
Black-chinned Antbird   *Hypocnemoides melanopogon*
Band-tailed Antbird   *Hypocnemoides maculicauda*
Black-and-white Antbird   *Myrmochanes hemileucus*
Bare-crowned Antbird   *Gymnocichla nudiceps*
Silvered Antbird   *Sclateria naevia*
Black-headed Antbird   *Percnostola rufifrons*
Allpahuayo Antbird   *Percnostola arenarum*
Slate-colored Antbird   *Percnostola schistacea*
Spot-winged Antbird saturata   *Percnostola saturata*
Spot-winged Antbird   *Percnostola leucostigma*
Caura Antbird   *Percnostola caurensis*
White-lined Antbird   *Percnostola lophotes*
Yapacana Antbird   *Myrmeciza disjuncta*
Gray-headed Antbird   *Myrmeciza griseiceps*
White-bellied Antbird   *Myrmeciza longipes*
Chestnut-backed Antbird   *Myrmeciza exsul*
Ferruginous-backed Antbird   *Myrmeciza ferruginea*
Scalloped Antbird   *Myrmeciza ruficauda* •
White-bibbed Antbird   *Myrmeciza loricata*
Squamate Antbird   *Myrmeciza squamosa*
Dull-mantled Antbird   *Myrmeciza laemosticta*
Esmeraldas Antbird   *Myrmeciza nigricauda*
Stub-tailed Antbird   *Myrmeciza berlepschi*

Gray-bellied Antbird   *Myrmeciza pelzelni*
Chestnut-tailed Antbird   *Myrmeciza hemimelaena*
Northern Chestnut-tailed Antbird   *Myrmeciza castanea*
Plumbeous Antbird   *Myrmeciza hyperythra*
Goeldi's Antbird   *Myrmeciza goeldii*
White-shouldered Antbird   *Myrmeciza melanoceps*
Sooty Antbird   *Myrmeciza fortis*
Immaculate Antbird   *Myrmeciza immaculata*
Black-throated Antbird   *Myrmeciza atrothorax*
Spotted Antbird   *Hylophylax naevioides*
Spot-backed Antbird   *Hylophylax naevius*
Dot-backed Antbird   *Hylophylax punctulatus*
Scale-backed Antbird   *Hylophylax poecilinotus*
Wing-banded Antbird   *Myrmornis torquata*
White-plumed Antbird   *Pithys albifrons*
White-masked Antbird   *Pithys castaneus*
Bicolored Antbird   *Gymnopithys leucaspis*
Rufous-throated Antbird   *Gymnopithys rufigula*
White-throated Antbird   *Gymnopithys salvini*
Lunulated Antbird   *Gymnopithys lunulatus*
Bare-eyed Antbird   *Rhegmatorhina gymnops*
Harlequin Antbird   *Rhegmatorhina berlepschi*
White-breasted Antcatcher   *Rhegmatorhina hoffmannsi*
Hairy-crested Antcatcher   *Rhegmatorhina melanosticta*
Chestnut-crested Antcatcher   *Rhegmatorhina cristata*
Pale-faced Antbird   *Skutchia borbae*
Black-spotted Bare-eye   *Phlegopsis nigromaculata*
Reddish-winged Bare-eye   *Phlegopsis erythroptera*
Ocellated Antbird   *Phaenostictus mcleannani*

Antthrushes and Antpittas Formicariidae

Rufous-capped Antthrush   *Formicarius colma*
Mexican Antthrush   *Formicarius monileger*
Black-faced Antthrush   *Formicarius analis*
Black-headed Antthrush   *Formicarius nigricapillus*
Rufous-fronted Antthrush   *Formicarius rufifrons*
Rufous-breasted Antthrush   *Formicarius rufipectus*
Short-tailed Antthrush   *Chamaeza campanisona*
Striated Antthrush   *Chamaeza nobilis*
Brazilian Antthrush   *Chamaeza ruficauda*
Such's Antthrush   *Chamaeza meruloides*
Scalloped Antthrush   *Chamaeza turdina*
Barred Antthrush   *Chamaeza mollissima*
Spotted Antpitta   *Hylopezus macularius*
Masked Antpitta   *Hylopezus auricularis*
Streak-chested Antpitta   *Hylopezus perspicillatus*
Fulvous-bellied Antpitta   *Hylopezus dives*
White-lored Antpitta   *Hylopezus fulviventris*
Amazonian Antpitta   *Hylopezus berlepschi*
White-browed Antpitta   *Hylopezus ochroleucus*
Speckle-breasted Antpitta   *Hylopezus nattereri*
Thrush-like Antpitta   *Myrmothera campanisona*
Tepui Antpitta   *Myrmothera simplex*
Great Antpitta   *Grallaria excelsa*
Giant Antpitta   *Grallaria gigantea*
Undulated Antpitta   *Grallaria squamigera*
Variegated Antpitta   *Grallaria varia*
Scaled Antpitta   *Grallaria guatimalensis*
Moustached Antpitta   *Grallaria alleni*
Táchira Antpitta   *Grallaria chthonia* •
Plain-backed Antpitta   *Grallaria haplonota*
Tawny Antpitta   *Grallaria quitensis*
Rufous-faced Antpitta   *Grallaria erythrotis*
Brown-banded Antpitta   *Grallaria milleri* •
Bicolored Antpitta   *Grallaria rufocinerea*
Stripe-headed Antpitta   *Grallaria andicolus*
Cundinamarca Antpitta   *Grallaria kaestneri*
Santa Marta Antpitta   *Grallaria bangsi*
White-throated Antpitta   *Grallaria albigula*
Red-and-white Antpitta   *Grallaria erythroleuca*
Bay Antpitta   *Grallaria capitalis*
Black-crowned Antpitta   *Pittasoma michleri*

Rufous-crowned Antpitta   *Pittasoma rufopileatum*
Ochre-striped Antpitta   *Grallaria dignissima*
Elusive Antpitta   *Grallaria eludens*
Chestnut-crowned Antpitta   *Grallaria ruficapilla*
Watkins's Antpitta   *Grallaria watkinsi*
Chestnut-naped Antpitta   *Grallaria nuchalis*
Jocotoco Antpitta   *Grallaria ridgelyi* •
Pale-billed Antpitta   *Grallaria carrikeri*
Yellow-breasted Antpitta   *Grallaria flavotincta*
White-bellied Antpitta   *Grallaria hypoleuca*
Rusty-tinged Antpitta   *Grallaria przewalskii*
Gray-naped Antpitta   *Grallaria griseonucha*
Rufous Antpitta   *Grallaria rufula*
Chestnut Antpitta   *Grallaria blakei*
Ochre-breasted Antpitta   *Grallaricula flavirostris*
Rusty-breasted Antpitta   *Grallaricula ferrugineipectus*
Scallop-breasted Antpitta   *Grallaricula loricata*
Hooded Antpitta   *Grallaricula cucullata*
Peruvian Antpitta   *Grallaricula peruviana*
Ochre-fronted Antpitta   *Grallaricula ochraceifrons* •
Slate-crowned Antpitta   *Grallaricula nana*
Crescent-faced Antpitta   *Grallaricula lineifrons*

Gnateaters (or antpipits) Conopophagidae

Chestnut-belted Gnateater   *Conopophaga aurita*
Black-cheeked Gnateater   *Conopophaga melanops*
Rufous Gnateater   *Conopophaga lineata*
Hooded Gnateater   *Conopophaga roberti*
Ash-throated Gnateater   *Conopophaga peruviana*
Slaty Gnateater   *Conopophaga ardesiaca*
Chestnut-crowned Gnateater   *Conopophaga castaneiceps*
Black-bellied Gnateater   *Conopophaga melanogaster*

Tapaculos Rhinocryptidae

Chestnut-throated Huet-huet   *Pteroptochos castaneus*
Black-throated Huet-huet   *Pteroptochos tarnii*
Moustached Turca   *Pteroptochos megapodius*
White-throated Tapaculo   *Scelorchilus albicollis*
Chucao Tapaculo   *Scelorchilus rubecula*
Crested Gallito   *Rhinocrypta lanceolata*
Sandy Gallito   *Teledromas fuscus*
Rusty-belted Tapaculo   *Liosceles thoracicus*
Ocellated Tapaculo   *Acropternis orthonyx*
Ochre-flanked Tapaculo   *Eugralla paradoxa*
Tall-grass Wetland Tapaculo   *Scytalopus iraiensis* •
Mouse-colored Tapaculo   *Scytalopus speluncae*
Brasília Tapaculo   *Scytalopus novacapitalis*
White-breasted Tapaculo   *Scytalopus indigoticus*
Bahia Tapaculo   *Scytalopus psychopompus* •
Southern White-crowned Tapaculo   *Scytalopus bolivianus*
Northern White-crowned Tapaculo   *Scytalopus atratus*
Santa Marta Tapaculo   *Scytalopus sanctaemartae*
Peruvian Rufous-vented Tapaculo   *Scytalopus femoralis*
Equatorial Rufous-vented Tapaculo   *Scytalopus micropterus*
Narino Tapaculo   *Scytalopus vicinior*
Stiles' Tapaculo   *Scytalopus stilesi*
Ecuadorian Tapaculo   *Scytalopus robbinsi*
Chocó Tapaculo   *Scytalopus chocoensis*
Tacarcuna Tapaculo   *Scytalopus panamensis*
Silvery-fronted Tapaculo   *Scytalopus argentifrons*
Caracas Tapaculo   *Scytalopus caracae*
Mérida Tapaculo   *Scytalopus meridanus*
Brown-rumped Tapaculo   *Scytalopus latebricola*
Spillmann's Tapaculo   *Scytalopus spillmanni*
Chusquea Tapaculo   *Scytalopus parkeri*
Gray Tapaculo   *Scytalopus parvirostris*
Sharp-billed Tapaculo   *Scytalopus acutirostris*
Lara Tapaculo   *Scytalopus fuscicauda*
Unicolored Tapaculo   *Scytalopus unicolor*
Rufous-rumped Tapaculo   *Scytalopus griseicollis*
Páramo Tapaculo   *Scytalopus canus*

Ancash Tapaculo *Scytalopus affinis*
Elfin Forest Tapaculo *Scytalopus altirostris*
Cuzco Tapaculo *Scytalopus urubambae*
Diademed Tapaculo *Scytalopus schulenbergi*
Andean Tapaculo *Scytalopus simonsi*
Zimmer's Tapaculo *Scytalopus zimmeri*
White-browed Tapaculo *Scytalopus superciliaris*
Magellanic Tapaculo *Scytalopus magellanicus*
Dusky Tapaculo *Scytalopus fuscus*
Blackish Tapaculo *Scytalopus latrans*
Large-footed Tapaculo *Scytalopus macropus*
Ash-colored Tapaculo *Myornis senilis*
Stresemann's Bristlefront *Merulaxis stresemanni* •
Slaty Bristlefront *Merulaxis ater*
Spotted Bamboowren *Psilorhamphus guttatus*
Collared Crescentchest *Melanopareia torquata*
Olive-crowned Crescentchest *Melanopareia maximiliani*
Marañon Crescentchest *Melanopareia maranonica*
Elegant Crescentchest *Melanopareia elegans*

Sharpbill Oxyruncidae
Sharpbill *Oxyruncus cristatus*

Plantcutters Phytotomidae
Peruvian Plantcutter *Phytotoma raimondii* •
White-tipped Plantcutter *Phytotoma rutila*
Rufous-tailed Plantcutter *Phytotoma rara*

Cotingas Cotingidae
Black-necked Red-Cotinga *Phoenicircus nigricollis*
Guianian Red-Cotinga *Phoenicircus carnifex*
Shrike-like Cotinga *Laniisoma elegans*
Swallow-tailed Cotinga *Phibalura flavirostris*
Black-and-gold Cotinga *Tijuca atra*
Gray-winged Cotinga *Tijuca condita*
Hooded Berryeater *Carpornis cucullata*
Black-headed Berryeater *Carpornis melanocephala*
Red-crested Cotinga *Ampelion rubrocristatus*
Chestnut-crested Cotinga *Ampelion rufaxilla*
Chestnut-bellied Cotinga *Doliornis remseni*
Bay-vented Cotinga *Doliornis sclateri*
White-cheeked Cotinga *Zaratornis stresemanni*
Green-and-black Fruiteater *Pipreola riefferii*
Band-tailed Fruiteater *Pipreola intermedia*
Barred Fruiteater *Pipreola arcuata*
Golden-breasted Fruiteater *Pipreola aureopectus*
Orange-breasted Fruiteater *Pipreola jucunda*
Black-chested Fruiteater *Pipreola lubomirskii*
Masked Fruiteater *Pipreola pulchra*
Fiery-throated Fruiteater *Pipreola chlorolepidota*
Scarlet-breasted Fruiteater *Pipreola frontalis*
Handsome Fruiteater *Pipreola formosa*
Red-banded Fruiteater *Pipreola whitelyi*
Scaled Fruiteater *Ampelioides tschudii*
Buff-throated Purpletuft *Iodopleura pipra*
White-browed Purpletuft *Iodopleura isabellae*
Dusky Purpletuft *Iodopleura fusca*
Kinglet Calyptura *Calyptura cristata* •
Gray-tailed Piha *Snowornis subalaris*
Olivaceous Piha *Snowornis cryptolophus*
Dusky Piha *Lipaugus fuscocinereus*
Chestnut-capped Piha *Lipaugus weberi* •
Scimitar-winged Piha *Lipaugus uropygialis*
Screaming Piha *Lipaugus vociferans*
Rufous Piha *Lipaugus unirufus*
Cinnamon-vented Piha *Lipaugus lanioides*
Rose-collared Piha *Lipaugus streptophorus*
Purple-throated Cotinga *Porphyrolaema porphyrolaema*
Lovely Cotinga *Cotinga amabilis*
Turquoise Cotinga *Cotinga ridgwayi*
Blue Cotinga *Cotinga nattererii*
Plum-throated Cotinga *Cotinga maynana*

Purple-breasted Cotinga *Cotinga cotinga*
Banded Cotinga *Cotinga maculata* •
Spangled Cotinga *Cotinga cayana*
Pompadour Cotinga *Xipholena punicea*
White-tailed Cotinga *Xipholena lamellipennis*
White-winged Cotinga *Xipholena atropurpurea* •
Black-tipped Cotinga *Carpodectes hopkei*
Yellow-billed Cotinga *Carpodectes antoniae* •
Snowy Cotinga *Carpodectes nitidus*
Black-faced Cotinga *Conioptilon mcilhennyi*
Bare-necked Fruitcrow *Gymnoderus foetidus*
Crimson Fruitcrow *Haematoderus militaris*
Purple-throated Fruitcrow *Querula purpurata*
Red-ruffed Fruitcrow *Pyroderus scutatus*
Long-wattled Umbrellabird *Cephalopterus penduliger*
Amazonian Umbrellabird *Cephalopterus ornatus*
Bare-necked Umbrellabird *Cephalopterus glabricollis*
Capuchinbird *Perissocephalus tricolor*
Three-wattled Bellbird *Procnias tricarunculatus*
White Bellbird *Procnias albus*
Bearded Bellbird *Procnias averano*
Bare-throated Bellbird *Procnias nudicollis*
Guianan Cock-of-the-rock *Rupicola rupicola*
Andean Cock-of-the-rock *Rupicola peruvianus*

Manakins Pipridae
Jet Manakin *Chloropipo unicolor*
Olive Manakin *Chloropipo uniformis*
Green Manakin *Chloropipo holochlora*
Yellow-headed Manakin *Chloropipo flavicapilla*
White-collared Manakin *Manacus candei*
Orange-collared Manakin *Manacus aurantiacus*
Golden-collared Manakin *Manacus vitellinus*
White-bearded Manakin *Manacus manacus*
White-throated Manakin *Corapipo gutturalis*
White-ruffed Manakin *Corapipo altera*
Lance-tailed Manakin *Chiroxiphia lanceolata*
Long-tailed Manakin *Chiroxiphia linearis*
Blue-backed Manakin *Chiroxiphia pareola*
Yungas Manakin *Chiroxiphia boliviana*
Swallow-tailed Manakin *Chiroxiphia caudata*
Crimson-hooded Manakin *Pipra aureola*
Band-tailed Manakin *Pipra fasciicauda*
Wire-tailed Manakin *Pipra filicauda*
Golden-headed Manakin *Pipra erythrocephala*
Red-capped Manakin *Pipra mentalis*
Red-headed Manakin *Pipra rubrocapilla*
Round-tailed Manakin *Pipra chloromeros*
Scarlet-horned Manakin *Pipra cornuta*
White-crowned Manakin *Dixiphia pipra*
Orange-bellied Manakin *Lepidothrix suavissima*
White-fronted Manakin *Lepidothrix serena*
Blue-crowned Manakin *Lepidothrix coronata*
Opal-crowned Manakin *Lepidothrix iris*
Blue-rumped Manakin *Lepidothrix isidorei*
Golden-crowned Manakin *Lepidothrix vilasboasi*
Snow-capped Manakin *Lepidothrix nattereri*
Cerulean-capped Manakin *Lepidothrix coeruleocapilla*
Helmeted Manakin *Antilophia galeata*
Araripe Manakin *Antilophia bokermanni* •
Golden-winged Manakin *Masius chrysopterus*
Pin-tailed Manakin *Ilicura militaris*
Fiery-capped Manakin *Machaeropterus pyrocephalus*
Striped Manakin regulus *Machaeropterus regulus*
Striped Manakin *Machaeropterus striolatus*
Club-winged Manakin *Machaeropterus deliciosus*
Black Manakin *Xenopipo atronitens*
Yellow-crested Manakin *Heterocercus flavivertex*
Orange-crested Manakin *Heterocercus aurantiivertex*
Flame-crested Manakin *Heterocercus linteatus*
Saffron-crested Tyrant-Manakin *Neopelma chrysocephalum*
Sulfur-bellied Tyrant-Manakin *Neopelma sulphureiventer*

Pale-bellied Tyrant-Manakin *Neopelma pallescens*
Wied's Tyrant-Manakin *Neopelma aurifrons*
Wied's Tyrant-Manakin chrysolophum *Neopelma chrysolophum*
Dwarf Tyrant-Manakin *Tyranneutes stolzmanni*
Tiny Tyrant-Manakin *Tyranneutes virescens*
Black-capped Piprites *Piprites pileata*
Gray-headed Piprites *Piprites griseiceps*
Wing-barred Piprites *Piprites chloris*
Broad-billed Sapayoa *Sapayoa aenigma*
Várzea Schiffornis *Schiffornis major*
Thrush-like Schiffornis *Schiffornis turdina*
Greenish Schiffornis *Schiffornis virescens*

Tyrant Flycatchers Tyrannidae
White-lored Tyrannulet *Ornithion inerme*
Yellow-bellied Tyrannulet *Ornithion semiflavum*
Brown-capped Tyrannulet *Ornithion brunneicapillus*
Northern Beardless Tyrannulet *Camptostoma imberbe*
Southern Beardless Tyrannulet *Camptostoma obsoletum*
Mouse-colored Tyrannulet *Phaeomyias murina*
Cocos Island Flycatcher *Nesotriccus ridgwayi*
Yellow Tyrannulet *Capsiempis flaveola*
Yellow-crowned Tyrannulet *Tyrannulus elatus*
Forest Elaenia *Myiopagis gaimardii*
Foothill Elaenia *Myiopagis olallai*
Gray Elaenia *Myiopagis caniceps*
Pacific Elaenia *Myiopagis subplacens*
Yellow-crowned Elaenia *Myiopagis flavivertex*
Jamaican Elaenia *Myiopagis cotta*
Greenish Elaenia *Myiopagis viridicata*
Gray-and-white Tyrannulet *Pseudelaenia leucospodia*
Caribbean Elaenia *Elaenia martinica*
Large Elaenia *Elaenia spectabilis*
Yellow-bellied Elaenia *Elaenia flavogaster*
Noronha Elaenia *Elaenia ridleyana*
White-crested Elaenia *Elaenia albiceps*
Small-billed Elaenia *Elaenia parvirostris*
Slaty Elaenia *Elaenia strepera*
Olivaceous Elaenia *Elaenia mesoleuca*
Mottle-backed Elaenia *Elaenia gigas*
Brownish Elaenia *Elaenia pelzelni*
Plain-crested Elaenia *Elaenia cristata*
Rufous-crowned Elaenia *Elaenia ruficeps*
Lesser Elaenia *Elaenia chiriquensis*
Mountain Elaenia *Elaenia frantzii*
Highland Elaenia *Elaenia obscura*
Great Elaenia *Elaenia dayi*
Sierran Elaenia *Elaenia pallatangae*
Greater Antillian Elaenia *Elaenia fallax*
Torrent Tyrannulet *Serpophaga cinerea*
Sooty Tyrannulet *Serpophaga nigricans*
River Tyrannulet *Serpophaga hypoleuca*
White-crested Tyrannulet *Serpophaga subcristata*
White-bellied Tyrannulet *Serpophaga munda*
Ochre-bellied Flycatcher *Mionectes oleagineus*
Streak-necked Flycatcher *Mionectes striaticollis*
Olive-striped Flycatcher *Mionectes olivaceus*
Gray-hooded Flycatcher *Mionectes rufiventris*
MacConnell's Flycatcher *Mionectes macconnelli*
Rufous-breasted Leptopogon *Leptopogon rufipectus*
Inca Leptopogon *Leptopogon taczanowskii*
Sepia-capped Leptopogon *Leptopogon amaurocephalus*
Slaty-capped Leptopogon *Leptopogon superciliaris*
Bronze-olive Pygmy-Tyrant *Pseudotriccus pelzelni*
Hazel-fronted Pygmy-Tyrant *Pseudotriccus simplex*
Rufous-headed Pygmy-Tyrant *Pseudotriccus ruficeps*
Variegated Bristle-Tyrant *Pogonotriccus poecilotis*
Chapman's Bristle-Tyrant *Pogonotriccus chapmani*
Marbled-faced Bristle-Tyrant *Pogonotriccus ophthalmicus*
Southern Bristle-Tyrant *Pogonotriccus eximius*
Spectacled Bristle-Tyrant *Pogonotriccus orbitalis*

Venezuelan Bristle-Tyrant   *Pogonotriccus venezuelanus*
Antioquia Bristle-Tyrant   *Pogonotriccus lanyoni* •
Black-fronted Tyrannulet   *Phylloscartes nigrifrons*
Ecuadorean Tyrannulet   *Phylloscartes gualaquizae*
Rufous-lored Tyrannulet   *Phylloscartes flaviventris*
Cinnamon-faced Tyrannulet   *Phylloscartes parkeri*
Minas Gerais Tyrannulet   *Phylloscartes roquettei* •
São Paulo Tyrannulet   *Phylloscartes paulista*
Oustalet's Tyrannulet   *Phylloscartes oustaleti*
Restinga Tyrannulet   *Phylloscartes kronei*
Serra do Mar Tyrannulet   *Phylloscartes difficilis*
Alagoas Tyrannulet   *Phylloscartes ceciliae* •
Mottle-cheeked Tyrannulet   *Phylloscartes ventralis*
Bahia Tyrannulet   *Phylloscartes beckeri*
Yellow-green Tyrannulet   *Phylloscartes flavovirens*
Olive-green Tyrannulet   *Phylloscartes virescens*
Rufous-browed Tyrannulet   *Phylloscartes superciliaris*
Bay-ringed Tyrannulet   *Phylloscartes sylviolus*
Planalto Tyrannulet   *Phyllomyias fasciatus*
Rough-legged Tyrannulet   *Phyllomyias burmeisteri*
Greenish Tyrannulet   *Phyllomyias virescens*
Reiser's Tyrannulet   *Phyllomyias reiseri*
Urich's Tyrannulet   *Phyllomyias urichi* •
Sclater's Tyrannulet   *Phyllomyias sclateri*
Gray-capped Tyrannulet   *Phyllomyias griseocapilla*
Sooty-headed Tyrannulet   *Phyllomyias griseiceps*
Plumbeous-crowned Tyrannulet   *Phyllomyias plumbeiceps*
Black-capped Tyrannulet   *Phyllomyias nigrocapillus*
Ashy-headed Tyrannulet   *Phyllomyias cinereiceps*
Tawny-rumped Tyrannulet   *Phyllomyias uropygialis*
Paltry Tyrannulet   *Zimmerius vilissimus*
Venezuelan Tyrannulet   *Zimmerius improbus*
Bolivian Tyrannulet   *Zimmerius bolivianus*
Red-billed Tyrannulet   *Zimmerius cinereicapilla*
Mishana Tyrannulet   *Zimmerius villarejoi*
Slender-footed Tyrannulet   *Zimmerius gracilipes*
Peruvian Tyrannulet   *Zimmerius viridiflavus*
Golden-faced Tyrannulet   *Zimmerius chrysops*
Dusky Flycatcher   *Sublegatus obscurior*
Northern Scrub-Flycatcher   *Sublegatus arenarum*
Southern Scrub-Flycatcher   *Sublegatus modestus*
Campo Suiriri Flycatcher   *Suiriri affinis*
Chapada Flycatcher   *Suiriri islerorum*
White-throated Tyrannulet   *Mecocerculus leucophrys*
White-tailed Tyrannulet   *Mecocerculus poecilocercus*
Buff-banded Tyrannulet   *Mecocerculus hellmayri*
Rufous-winged Tyrannulet   *Mecocerculus calopterus*
Sulfur-bellied Tyrannulet   *Mecocerculus minor*
White-banded Tyrannulet   *Mecocerculus stictopterus*
Slender-billed Inezia   *Inezia tenuirostris*
Plain Inezia   *Inezia inornata*
Amazonian Inezia   *Inezia subflava*
Pale-tipped Inezia   *Inezia caudata*
Lesser Wagtail-Tyrant   *Stigmatura napensis*
Greater Wagtail-Tyrant   *Stigmatura budytoides*
Agile Tit-Tyrant   *Anairetes agilis*
Unstreaked Tit-Tyrant   *Anairetes agraphia*
Ash-breasted Tit-Tyrant   *Anairetes alpinus* •
Marañón Tit-Tyrant   *Anairetes nigrocristatus*
Pied-crested Tit-Tyrant   *Anairetes reguloides*
Yellow-billed Tit-Tyrant   *Anairetes flavirostris*
Juan Fernandez Tit-Tyrant   *Anairetes fernandezianus*
Tufted Tit-Tyrant   *Anairetes parulus*
Many-colored Rush Tyrant   *Tachuris rubrigastra*
Sharp-tailed Tyrant   *Culicivora caudacuta*
Bearded Tachuri   *Polystictus pectoralis*
Gray-backed Tachuri   *Polystictus superciliaris*
Crested Doradito   *Pseudocolopteryx sclateri*
Dinelli's Doradito   *Pseudocolopteryx dinelliana*
Subtropical Doradito   *Pseudocolopteryx acutipennis*
Warbling Doradito   *Pseudocolopteryx flaviventris*
Tawny-crowned Pygmy-Tyrant   *Euscarthmus meloryphus*

Rufous-sided Pygmy-Tyrant   *Euscarthmus rufomarginatus*
White-bellied Pygmy-Tyrant   *Myiornis albiventris*
Eared Pygmy-Tyrant   *Myiornis auricularis*
Black-capped Pygmy-Tyrant   *Myiornis atricapillus*
Short-tailed Pygmy-Tyrant   *Myiornis ecaudatus*
Scale-crested Pygmy-Tyrant   *Lophotriccus pileatus*
Double-banded Pygmy-Tyrant   *Lophotriccus vitiosus*
Long-crested Pygmy-Tyrant   *Lophotriccus eulophotes*
Helmeted Pygmy-Tyrant   *Lophotriccus galeatus*
Pale-eyed Pygmy-Tyrant   *Atalotriccus pilaris*
Northern Bentbill   *Oncostoma cinereigulare*
Southern Bentbill   *Oncostoma olivaceum*
Rufous-crowned Tody-Tyrant   *Poecilotriccus ruficeps*
Lulu's Tody-Tyrant   *Poecilotriccus luluae*
White-cheeked Tody-Tyrant   *Poecilotriccus albifacies*
Black-and-white Tody-Tyrant   *Poecilotriccus capitalis*
Buff-cheeked Tody-Flycatcher   *Poecilotriccus senex*
Ruddy Tody-Flycatcher   *Poecilotriccus russatus*
Ochre-faced Tody-Flycatcher   *Poecilotriccus plumbeiceps*
Smoky-fronted Tody-Flycatcher   *Poecilotriccus fumifrons*
Rusty-fronted Tody-Flycatcher   *Poecilotriccus latirostris*
Slaty Tody-Flycatcher   *Poecilotriccus sylvia*
Golden-winged Tody-Flycatcher   *Poecilotriccus calopterus*
Black-backed Tody-Flycatcher   *Poecilotriccus pulchellus*
Black-chested Tyrant   *Taeniotriccus andrei*
Snethlage's Tody-Tyrant   *Hemitriccus minor*
Boat-billed Tody-Tyrant   *Hemitriccus josephinae*
Flammulated Bamboo Tyrant   *Hemitriccus flammulatus*
Drab-breasted Bamboo Tyrant   *Hemitriccus diops*
Brown-breasted Bamboo Tyrant   *Hemitriccus obsoletus*
White-eyed Tody-Tyrant   *Hemitriccus zosterops*
White-bellied Tody-Tyrant   *Hemitriccus griseipectus*
Zimmer's Tody-Tyrant   *Hemitriccus minimus*
Eye-ringed Tody-Tyrant   *Hemitriccus orbitatus*
Johannes' Tody-Tyrant   *Hemitriccus iohannis*
Stripe-necked Tody-Tyrant   *Hemitriccus striaticollis*
Hangnest Tody-Tyrant   *Hemitriccus nidipendulus*
Yungas Tody-Tyrant   *Hemitriccus spodiops*
Pearly-vented Tody-Tyrant   *Hemitriccus margaritaceiventer*
Pelzeln's Tody-Tyrant   *Hemitriccus inornatus*
Black-throated Tody-Tyrant   *Hemitriccus granadensis*
Buff-throated Tody-Tyrant   *Hemitriccus rufigularis*
Cinnamon-breasted Tody-Tyrant   *Hemitriccus cinnamomeipectus*
Buff-breasted Tody-Tyrant   *Hemitriccus mirandae*
Kaempfer's Tody-Tyrant   *Hemitriccus kaempferi* •
Fork-tailed Tody-Tyrant   *Hemitriccus furcatus*
Spotted Tody-Flycatcher   *Todirostrum maculatum*
Yellow-lored Tody-Flycatcher   *Todirostrum poliocephalum*
Short-tailed Tody-Flycatcher   *Todirostrum viridanum*
Black-headed Tody-Flycatcher   *Todirostrum nigriceps*
Painted Tody-Flycatcher   *Todirostrum pictum*
Common Tody-Flycatcher   *Todirostrum cinereum*
Yellow-browed Tody-Flycatcher   *Todirostrum chrysocrotaphum*
Ringed Antpipit   *Corythopis torquatus*
Southern Antpipit   *Corythopis delalandi*
Brownish Flycatcher   *Cnipodectes subbrunneus*
Large-headed Flatbill   *Ramphotrigon megacephalum*
Dusky-tailed Flatbill   *Ramphotrigon fuscicauda*
Rufous-tailed Flatbill   *Ramphotrigon ruficauda*
Eye-ringed Flatbill   *Rhynchocyclus brevirostris*
Pacific Flatbill   *Rhynchocyclus pacificus*
Olivaceous Flatbill   *Rhynchocyclus olivaceus*
Fulvous-breasted Flatbill   *Rhynchocyclus fulvipectus*
Yellow-olive Flatbill   *Tolmomyias sulphurescens*
Zimmer's Flatbill   *Tolmomyias assimilis*
Gray-crowned Flatbill   *Tolmomyias poliocephalus*
Orange-eyed Flatbill   *Tolmomyias traylori*

Ochre-lored Flatbill   *Tolmomyias flaviventris*
Cinnamon-crested Spadebill   *Platyrinchus saturatus*
Stub-tailed Spadebill   *Platyrinchus cancrominus*
Yellow-throated Spadebill   *Platyrinchus flavigularis*
Golden-crowned Spadebill   *Platyrinchus coronatus*
White-throated Spadebill   *Platyrinchus mystaceus*
White-crested Spadebill   *Platyrinchus platyrhynchos*
Russet-winged Spadebill   *Platyrinchus leucoryphus*
Northern Royal-Flycatcher   *Onychorhynchus mexicanus*
Amazonian Royal-Flycatcher   *Onychorhynchus coronatus*
Pacific Royal-Flycatcher   *Onychorhynchus occidentalis*
Ornate Flycatcher   *Myiotriccus ornatus*
Flavescent Flycatcher   *Myiophobus flavicans*
Orange-crested Flycatcher   *Myiophobus phoenicomitra*
Roraiman Flycatcher   *Myiophobus roraimae*
Unadorned Flycatcher   *Myiophobus inornatus*
Handsome Flycatcher   *Myiophobus pulcher*
Orange-banded Flycatcher   *Myiophobus lintoni*
Ochraceous-breasted Flycatcher   *Myiophobus ochraceiventris*
Bran-colored Flycatcher   *Myiophobus fasciatus*
Olive-chested Flycatcher   *Myiophobus cryptoxanthus*
Ruddy-tailed Flycatcher   *Terenotriccus erythrurus*
Tawny-breasted Flycatcher   *Myiobius villosus*
Sulfur-rumped Flycatcher   *Myiobius sulphureipygius*
Whiskered Flycatcher (Clements)   *Myiobius barbatus*
Whiskered Flycatcher   *Myiobius mastacalis*
Black-tailed Flycatcher   *Myiobius atricaudus*
Cinnamon Neopipo   *Neopipo cinnamomea*
Cinnamon Flycatcher   *Pyrrhomyias cinnamomeus*
Cliff Flycatcher   *Hirundinea ferruginea*
Fuscous Flycatcher   *Cnemotriccus fuscatus*
Euler's Flycatcher   *Lathrotriccus euleri*
Gray-breasted Flycatcher   *Lathrotriccus griseipectus*
Tawny-chested Flycatcher   *Aphanotriccus capitalis*
Black-billed Flycatcher   *Aphanotriccus audax*
Belted Flycatcher   *Xenotriccus callizonus*
Pileated Flycatcher   *Xenotriccus mexicanus*
Northern Tufted-Flycatcher   *Mitrephanes phaeocercus*
Olive Tufted-Flycatcher   *Mitrephanes olivaceus*
Olive-sided Flycatcher   *Contopus cooperi*
Greater Pewee   *Contopus pertinax*
Dark Pewee   *Contopus lugubris*
Smoke-colored Pewee   *Contopus fumigatus*
Ochraceous Pewee   *Contopus ochraceus*
Western Wood Pewee   *Contopus sordidulus*
Eastern Wood Pewee   *Contopus virens*
Tropical Pewee   *Contopus cinereus*
Blackish Pewee   *Contopus nigrescens*
Cuban Pewee   *Contopus caribaeus*
Jamaican Pewee   *Contopus pallidus*
Hispaniolan Peewee   *Contopus hispaniolensis*
Lesser Antillean Pewee   *Contopus latirostris*
White-throated Pewee   *Contopus albogularis*
Yellow-bellied Flycatcher   *Empidonax flaviventris*
Acadian Flycatcher   *Empidonax virescens*
Alder Flycatcher   *Empidonax alnorum*
Willow Flycatcher   *Empidonax traillii*
White-throated Flycatcher   *Empidonax albigularis*
Least Flycatcher   *Empidonax minimus*
Hammond's Flycatcher   *Empidonax hammondii*
Gray Flycatcher   *Empidonax wrightii*
American Dusky Flycatcher   *Empidonax oberholseri*
Pine Flycatcher   *Empidonax affinis*
Pacific-slope Flycatcher   *Empidonax difficilis*
Cordilleran Flycatcher   *Empidonax occidentalis*
Yellowish Flycatcher   *Empidonax flavescens*
Buff-breasted Flycatcher   *Empidonax fulvifrons*
Black-capped Flycatcher   *Empidonax atriceps*
Eastern Phoebe   *Sayornis phoebe*
Black Phoebe   *Sayornis nigricans*
Say's Phoebe   *Sayornis saya*

Vermilion Flycatcher *Pyrocephalus rubinus*
Crowned Chat-Tyrant *Ochthoeca frontalis*
Peruvian Chat-Tyrant *Ochthoeca spodionota*
Jelski's Chat-Tyrant *Ochthoeca jelskii*
Yellow-bellied Chat-Tyrant *Ochthoeca diadema*
Golden-browed Chat-Tyrant *Ochthoeca pulchella*
Slaty-backed Chat-Tyrant *Ochthoeca cinnamomeiventris*
Maroon-chested Chat-Tyrant *Ochthoeca thoracica*
Piura Chat-Tyrant *Ochthoeca piurae*
D' Orbigny's Chat-Tyrant *Ochthoeca oenanthoides*
Rufous-breasted Chat-Tyrant *Ochthoeca rufipectoralis*
Brown-backed Chat-Tyrant *Ochthoeca fumicolor*
White-browed Chat-Tyrant *Ochthoeca leucophrys*
Tumbes Tyrant *Tumbezia salvini*
Patagonian Tyrant *Colorhamphus parvirostris*
Drab Water-Tyrant *Ochthornis littoralis*
Red-rumped Bush-Tyrant *Cnemarchus erythropygius*
Streak-throated Bush-Tyrant *Myiotheretes striaticollis*
Santa Marta Bush-Tyrant *Myiotheretes pernix* •
Smoky Bush-Tyrant *Myiotheretes fumigatus*
Rufous-bellied Bush-Tyrant *Myiotheretes fuscorufus*
Fire-eyed Diucon *Xolmis pyrope*
Gray Monjita *Xolmis cinereus*
Black-crowned Monjita *Xolmis coronatus*
White-rumped Monjita *Xolmis velatus*
White Monjita *Xolmis irupero*
Rusty-backed Monjita *Xolmis rubetra*
Salinas Monjita *Xolmis salinarum*
Black-and-white Monjita *Xolmis dominicanus*
Chocolate-vented Tyrant *Neoxolmis rufiventris*
Black-billed Shrike-Tyrant *Agriornis montanus*
White-tailed Shrike-Tyrant *Agriornis andicola*
Great Shrike-Tyrant *Agriornis lividus*
Gray-bellied Shrike-Tyrant *Agriornis micropterus*
Lesser Shrike-Tyrant *Agriornis murinus*
Rufous-webbed Bush-Tyrant *Polioxolmis rufipennis*
Spot-billed Ground-Tyrant *Muscisaxicola maculirostris*
Little Ground-Tyrant *Muscisaxicola fluviatilis*
Dark-faced Ground-Tyrant *Muscisaxicola maclovianus*
Cinnamon-bellied Ground-Tyrant *Muscisaxicola capistratus*
Rufous-naped Ground-Tyrant *Muscisaxicola rufivertex*
Puna Ground-Tyrant *Muscisaxicola juninensis*
White-browed Ground-Tyrant *Muscisaxicola albilora*
Plain-capped Ground-Tyrant *Muscisaxicola alpinus*
Plain-capped Ground-Tyrant griseus *Muscisaxicola griseus*
Cinereous Ground-Tyrant *Muscisaxicola cinereus*
White-fronted Ground-Tyrant *Muscisaxicola albifrons*
Ochre-naped Ground-Tyrant *Muscisaxicola flavinucha*
Black-fronted Ground-Tyrant *Muscisaxicola frontalis*
Short-tailed Field Tyrant *Muscigralla brevicauda*
Andean Negrito *Lessonia oreas*
Patagonian Negrito *Lessonia rufa*
Cinereous Tyrant *Knipolegus striaticeps*
Hudson's Black Tyrant *Knipolegus hudsoni*
Amazonian Black Tyrant *Knipolegus poecilocercus*
Andean Tyrant *Knipolegus signatus*
Blue-billed Black Tyrant *Knipolegus cyanirostris*
Rufous-tailed Tyrant *Knipolegus poecilurus*
Riverside Tyrant *Knipolegus orenocensis*
White-winged Black Tyrant *Knipolegus aterrimus*
Caatinga Black-Tyrant *Knipolegus franciscanus*
Velvety Black Tyrant *Knipolegus nigerrimus*
Crested Black Tyrant *Knipolegus lophotes*
Spectacled Tyrant *Hymenops perspicillatus*
Pied Water-Tyrant *Fluvicola pica*
Black-backed Water-Tyrant *Fluvicola albiventer*
Masked Water-Tyrant *Fluvicola nengeta*
White-headed Marsh Tyrant *Arundinicola leucocephala*
Cock-tailed Tyrant *Alectrurus tricolor*
Strange-tailed Tyrant *Alectrurus risora*
Streamer-tailed Tyrant *Gubernetes yetapa*

Yellow-browed Tyrant *Satrapa icterophrys*
Long-tailed Tyrant *Colonia colonus*
Cattle Tyrant *Machetornis rixosa*
Shear-tailed Gray Tyrant *Muscipipra vetula*
Rufous-tailed Attila *Attila phoenicurus*
Cinnamon Attila *Attila cinnamomeus*
Ochraceous Attila *Attila torridus*
Citron-bellied Attila *Attila citriniventris*
Bright-rumped Attila *Attila spadiceus*
White-eyed Attila *Attila bolivianus*
Gray-hooded Attila *Attila rufus*
Speckled Cotinga *Laniocera rufescens*
Cinereous Cotinga *Laniocera hypopyrra*
Rufous Casiornis *Casiornis rufa*
Ash-throated Casiornis *Casiornis fusca*
Eastern Sirystes *Sirystes sibilator*
Rufous Mourner *Rhytipterna holerythra*
Grayish Mourner *Rhytipterna simplex*
Pale-bellied Mourner *Rhytipterna immunda*
Rufous Flycatcher *Myiarchus semirufus*
Yucatan Flycatcher *Myiarchus yucatanensis*
Sad Flycatcher *Myiarchus barbirostris*
Dusky-capped Flycatcher *Myiarchus tuberculifer*
Swainson's Flycatcher *Myiarchus swainsoni*
Venezuelan Flycatcher *Myiarchus venezuelensis*
Panama Flycatcher *Myiarchus panamensis*
Short-crested-Flycatcher *Myiarchus ferox*
Pale-edged Flycatcher *Myiarchus cephalotes*
Sooty-crowned Flycatcher *Myiarchus phaeocephalus*
Apical Flycatcher *Myiarchus apicalis*
Ash-throated Flycatcher *Myiarchus cinerascens*
Nutting's Flycatcher *Myiarchus nuttingi*
Great Crested-Flycatcher *Myiarchus crinitus*
Brown-crested Flycatcher *Myiarchus tyrannulus*
Grenada Flycatcher *Myiarchus nugator*
Galápagos Flycatcher *Myiarchus magnirostris*
Rufous-tailed Flycatcher *Myiarchus validus*
La Sagra's Flycatcher *Myiarchus sagrae*
Stolid Flycatcher *Myiarchus stolidus*
Lesser Antillian Flycatcher *Myiarchus oberi*
Puerto Rican Flycatcher *Myiarchus antillarum*
Flammulated Flycatcher *Deltarhynchus flammulatus*
Lesser Kiskadee *Philohydor lictor*
Greater Kiskadee *Pitangus sulphuratus*
Boat-billed Flycatcher *Megarynchus pitangua*
Rusty-margined Flycatcher *Myiozetetes cayanensis*
Social Flycatcher *Myiozetetes similis*
Gray-capped Flycatcher *Myiozetetes granadensis*
Dusky-chested Flycatcher *Myiozetetes luteiventris*
White-ringed Flycatcher *Conopias albovittatus*
Three-striped Flycatcher *Conopias trivirgatus*
Yellow-throated Flycatcher *Conopias parvus*
Lemon-browed Flycatcher *Conopias cinchoneti*
Golden-bellied Flycatcher *Myiodynastes hemichrysus*
Golden-crowned Flycatcher *Myiodynastes chrysocephalus*
Baird's Flycatcher *Myiodynastes bairdii*
Streaked Flycatcher *Myiodynastes maculatus*
Sulfur-bellied Flycatcher *Myiodynastes luteiventris*
Piratic Flycatcher *Legatus leucophaius*
White-bearded Flycatcher *Phelpsia inornata*
Variagated Flycatcher *Empidonomus varius*
Crowned Slaty Flycatcher *Griseotyrannus aurantioatrocristatus*
Sulfury Flycatcher *Tyrannopsis sulphurea*
Snowy-throated Kingbird *Tyrannus niveigularis*
White-throated Kingbird *Tyrannus albogularis*
Tropical Kingbird *Tyrannus melancholicus*
Couch's Kingbird *Tyrannus couchii*
Cassin's Kingbird *Tyrannus vociferans*
Thick-billed Kingbird *Tyrannus crassirostris*
Western Kingbird *Tyrannus verticalis*
Eastern Kingbird *Tyrannus tyrannus*
Gray Kingbird *Tyrannus dominicensis*

Loggerhead Kingbird *Tyrannus caudifasciatus*
Giant Kingbird *Tyrannus cubensis* •
Scissor-tailed Flycatcher *Tyrannus forficatus*
Fork-tailed Flycatcher *Tyrannus savana*
White-naped Xenopsaris *Xenopsaris albinucha*
Chestnut-crowned Becard *Pachyramphus castaneus*
Green-backed Becard *Pachyramphus viridis*
Yellow-cheeked Becard *Pachyramphus xanthogenys*
Barred Becard *Pachyramphus versicolor*
Cinnamon Becard *Pachyramphus cinnamomeus*
White-winged Becard *Pachyramphus polychopterus*
Gray-collared Becard *Pachyramphus major*
Black-and-white Becard *Pachyramphus albogriseus*
Black-capped Becard *Pachyramphus marginatus*
Glossy-backed Becard *Pachyramphus surinamus*
Cinereous Becard *Pachyramphus rufus*
Slaty Becard *Pachyramphus spodiurus* •
Pink-throated Becard *Pachyramphus minor*
Jamaican Becard *Pachyramphus niger*
Rose-throated Becard *Pachyramphus aglaiae*
One-colored Becard *Pachyramphus homochrous*
Crested Becard *Pachyramphus validus*
Black-tailed Tityra *Tityra cayana*
Masked Tityra *Tityra semifasciata*
Black-crowned Tityra *Tityra inquisitor*

Scrubbirds Atrichornithidae
Rufous Scrubbird *Atrichornis rufescens*
Noisy Scrubbird *Atrichornis clamosus*

Lyrebirds Menuridae
Prince Albert's Lyrebird *Menura alberti*
Superb Lyrebird *Menura novaehollandiae*

New Zealand Wrens Xenicidae
Rifleman *Acanthisitta chloris*
Bush Wren *Xenicus longipes*
Rock Wren *Xenicus gilviventris*

Larks Alaudidae
Monotonous Lark *Mirafra passerina*
Western Singing Bushlark *Mirafra cantillans*
Eastern Singing Bushlark *Mirafra javanica*
Melodious Lark *Mirafra cheniana*
Northern White-tailed Lark *Mirafra albicauda*
Hova Lark *Mirafra hova*
Kordofan Lark *Mirafra cordofanica*
Williams's Lark *Mirafra williamsi*
Friedmann's Lark *Mirafra pulpa*
Red-winged Lark *Mirafra hypermetra*
Somali Long-billed Lark *Mirafra somalica*
Ash's Lark *Mirafra ashi* •
Angolan Lark *Mirafra angolensis*
Rufous-naped Lark *Mirafra africana*
Flappet Lark *Mirafra rufocinnamomea*
Clapper Lark *Mirafra apiata*
Eastern Clapper Lark *Mirafra fasciolata*
Collared Lark *Mirafra collaris*
Indian Bushlark *Mirafra erythroptera*
Gillett's Lark *Mirafra gilletti*
Rufous-winged Bushlark *Mirafra assamica*
Jerdon's Bushlark *Mirafra affinis*
Indochinese Bushlark *Mirafra erythrocephala*
Burmese Bushlark *Mirafra microptera*
Rusty Bushlark *Mirafra rufa*
Degodi Lark *Mirafra degodiensis*
Pink-breasted Lark *Calendulauda poecilosterna*
Sabota Lark *Calendulauda sabota*
Fawn-colored Lark *Calendulauda africanoides*
Abyssinian Lark *Calendulauda alopex*
Ferruginous Lark *Calendulauda burra*
Karoo Lark *Calendulauda albescens*
Barlow's Lark *Calendulauda barlowi*
Dune Lark *Calendulauda erythrochlamys*

Rufous-rumped Lark   *Pinarocorys erythropygia*
Dusky Lark   *Pinarocorys nigricans*
Archer's Long-clawed Lark   *Heteromirafra archeri* •
Sidamo Lark   *Heteromirafra sidamoensis*
Rudd's Lark   *Heteromirafra ruddi*
Cape Long-billed Lark   *Certhilauda curvirostris*
Angulhas Long-billed Lark   *Certhilauda brevirostris*
Eastern Long-billed Lark   *Certhilauda semitorquata*
Benguela Long-billed Lark   *Certhilauda benguelensis*
Karoo Long-billed Lark   *Certhilauda subcoronata*
Short-clawed Lark   *Certhilauda chuana*
Spike-heeled Lark   *Chersomanes albofasciata*
Spike-heeled Lark beesleyi   *Chersomanes beesleyi*
Black-eared Sparrow-Lark   *Eremopterix australis*
Chestnut-backed Sparrow-Lark   *Eremopterix leucotis*
Black-crowned Sparrow-Lark   *Eremopterix nigriceps*
Gray-backed Sparrow-Lark   *Eremopterix verticalis*
Chestnut-headed Sparrow-Lark   *Eremopterix signatus*
Fischer's Sparrow Lark   *Eremopterix leucopareia*
Ashy-crowned Sparrow-Lark   *Eremopterix griseus*
Bar-tailed Lark   *Ammomanes cinctura*
Rufous-tailed Lark   *Ammomanes phoenicura*
Desert Lark   *Ammomanes deserti*
Gray's Lark   *Ammomanopsis grayi*
Greater Hoopoe-Lark   *Alaemon alaudipes*
Lesser Hoopoe-Lark   *Alaemon hamertoni*
Thick-billed Lark   *Ramphocoris clotbey*
Calandra Lark   *Melanocorypha calandra*
Bimaculated Lark   *Melanocorypha bimaculata*
Long-billed Calandra Lark   *Melanocorypha maxima*
Mongolian Lark   *Melanocorypha mongolica*
White-winged Lark   *Melanocorypha leucoptera*
Black Lark   *Melanocorypha yeltoniensis*
Greater Short-toed Lark   *Calandrella brachydactyla*
Blanford's Lark   *Calandrella blanfordi*
Erlanger's Short-toed Lark   *Calandrella erlangeri*
Hume's Short-toed Lark   *Calandrella acutirostris*
Lesser Short-toed Lark   *Calandrella rufescens*
Red-capped Lark   *Calandrella cinerea*
Asian Short-toed Lark   *Calandrella cheleensis*
Sandlark   *Calandrella raytal*
Somali Short-toed Lark   *Calandrella somalica*
Pink-billed Lark   *Spizocorys conirostris*
Botha's Lark   *Spizocorys fringillaris* •
Sclater's Lark   *Spizocorys sclateri*
Obbia Lark   *Spizocorys obbiensis*
Masked Lark   *Spizocorys personata*
Stark's Lark   *Spizocorys starki*
Dunn's Lark   *Eremalauda dunni*
DuPont's Lark   *Chersophilus duponti*
Crested Lark   *Galerida cristata*
Thekla Lark   *Galerida theklae*
Malabar Crested Lark   *Galerida malabarica*
Sun Lark   *Galerida modesta*
Sykes Lark   *Galerida deva*
Large-billed Lark   *Galerida magnirostris*
Short-tailed Lark   *Pseudalaemon fremantlii*
Woodlark   *Lullula arborea*
Eurasian Skylark   *Alauda arvensis*
Oriental Skylark   *Alauda gulgula*
Razo Lark   *Alauda razae* •
Horned-Lark   *Eremophila alpestris*
Temminck's Horned-Lark   *Eremophila bilopha*

Swallows and Martins Hirundinidae

African River-Martin   *Pseudochelidon eurystomina*
White-eyed River-Martin   *Pseudochelidon sirintarae* •
Brown-chested Martin   *Progne tapera*
Purple Martin   *Progne subis*
Cuban Martin   *Progne cryptoleuca*
Caribbean Martin   *Progne dominicensis*
Sinaloa Martin   *Progne sinaloae*
Gray-breasted Martin   *Progne chalybea*

Southern Martin   *Progne elegans*
Galápagos Martin   *Progne modesta*
Peruvian Martin   *Progne murphyi*
Tree Swallow   *Tachycineta bicolor*
Mangrove Swallow   *Tachycineta albilinea*
Tumbes Swallow   *Tachycineta stolzmanni*
White-winged Swallow   *Tachycineta albiventer*
White-rumped Swallow   *Tachycineta leucorrhoa*
Chilean Swallow   *Tachycineta meyeni*
Golden Swallow   *Tachycineta euchrysea*
Violet-green Swallow   *Tachycineta thalassina*
Bahama Swallow   *Tachycineta cyaneoviridis*
Blue-and-white Swallow   *Notiochelidon cyanoleuca*
Brown-bellied Swallow   *Notiochelidon murina*
Pale-footed Swallow   *Notiochelidon flavipes*
Black-capped Swallow   *Notiochelidon pileata*
White-banded Swallow   *Atticora fasciata*
Black-collared Swallow   *Atticora melanoleuca*
White-thighed Swallow   *Neochelidon tibialis*
Andean Swallow   *Haplochelidon andecola*
Tawny-headed Swallow   *Alopochelidon fucata*
Northern Rough-winged Swallow   *Stelgidopteryx serripennis*
Southern Rough-winged Swallow   *Stelgidopteryx ruficollis*
White-backed Swallow   *Cheramoeca leucosterna*
Common Sand-Martin   *Riparia riparia*
Pale Sand-Martin   *Riparia diluta*
Brown-throated Sand-Martin   *Riparia paludicola*
Congo Sand-Martin   *Riparia congica*
Banded Sand-Martin   *Riparia cincta*
Mascarene Martin   *Phedina borbonica*
Congo Martin   *Phedina brazzae*
American Cliff Swallow   *Petrochelidon pyrrhonota*
Chestnut-collared Swallow   *Petrochelidon rufocollaris*
West Indian Cave Swallow   *Petrochelidon fulva*
Red Sea Swallow   *Petrochelidon perdita*
Preuss's Swallow   *Petrochelidon preussi*
Angolan Cliff Swallow   *Petrochelidon rufigula*
South African Cliff Swallow   *Petrochelidon spilodera*
Tree Martin   *Petrochelidon nigricans*
Streak-throated Swallow   *Petrochelidon fluvicola*
Fairy Martin   *Petrochelidon ariel*
Forest Cliff Swallow   *Petrochelidon fuliginosa*
Gray-rumped Swallow   *Pseudhirundo griseopyga*
Eurasian Crag Martin   *Ptyonoprogne rupestris*
Rock Martin   *Ptyonoprogne fuligula*
Dusky Crag Martin   *Ptyonoprogne concolor*
Barn Swallow   *Hirundo rustica*
Red-chested Swallow   *Hirundo lucida*
Ethiopian Swallow   *Hirundo aethiopica*
Angolan Swallow   *Hirundo angolensis*
White-throated Swallow   *Hirundo albigularis*
Pacific Swallow   *Hirundo tahitica*
Welcome Swallow   *Hirundo neoxena*
Wire-tailed Swallow   *Hirundo smithii*
White-throated Blue Swallow   *Hirundo nigrita*
Black-and-rufous Swallow   *Hirundo nigrorufa*
Blue Swallow   *Hirundo atrocaerulea*
Pied-winged Swallow   *Hirundo leucosoma*
White-tailed Swallow   *Hirundo megaensis*
Pearl-breasted Swallow   *Hirundo dimidiata*
Greater Striped Swallow   *Cecropis cucullata*
Lesser Striped Swallow   *Cecropis abyssinica*
Rufous-chested Swallow   *Cecropis semirufa*
Mosque Swallow   *Cecropis senegalensis*
Red-rumped Swallow   *Cecropis daurica*
Striated Swallow   *Cecropis striolata*
Striated Swallow badia   *Cecropis badia*
Common House-Martin   *Delichon urbicum*
Asian House-Martin   *Delichon dasypus*
Nepal House-Martin   *Delichon nipalense*
Square-tailed Sawwing   *Psalidoprocne nitens*

Cameroon Mountain Sawwing   *Psalidoprocne fuliginosa*
White-headed Sawwing   *Psalidoprocne albiceps*
Black Sawwing   *Psalidoprocne pristoptera*
Fanti Sawwing   *Psalidoprocne obscura*

Wagtails and Pipits Motacillidae

Forest Wagtail   *Dendronanthus indicus*
White Wagtail   *Motacilla alba*
Mekong Wagtail   *Motacilla samveasnae*
Black-backed Wagtail   *Motacilla lugens*
Japanese Pied Wagtail   *Motacilla grandis*
White-browed Wagtail   *Motacilla madaraspatensis*
African Pied Wagtail   *Motacilla aguimp*
Cape Wagtail   *Motacilla capensis*
Madagascar Wagtail   *Motacilla flaviventris*
Citrine Wagtail   *Motacilla citreola*
World Yellow Wagtail   *Motacilla flava*
Yellow Wagtail   *Motacilla tschutschensis*
Gray Wagtail   *Motacilla cinerea*
Mountain Wagtail   *Motacilla clara*
Golden Pipit   *Tmetothylacus tenellus*
Yellow-throated Longclaw   *Macronyx croceus*
Fülleborn's Longclaw   *Macronyx fuelleborni*
Ethiopian Longclaw   *Macronyx flavicollis*
Orange-throated Longclaw   *Macronyx capensis*
Rosy-breasted Longclaw   *Macronyx ameliae*
Pangani Longclaw   *Macronyx aurantiigula*
Grimwood's Longclaw   *Macronyx grimwoodi*
Sharpe's Longclaw   *Hemimacronyx sharpei* •
Yellow-breasted Pipit   *Hemimacronyx chloris*
Striped Pipit   *Anthus lineiventris*
African Rock Pipit   *Anthus crenatus*
Mountain Pipit   *Anthus hoeschi*
Jackson's Pipit   *Anthus latistriatus*
Woodland Pipit   *Anthus nyassae*
Paddyfield Pipit   *Anthus rufulus*
Australasian Pipit (Clements)   *Anthus novaeseelandiae*
Plain-backed Pipit   *Anthus leucophrys*
Long-tailed Pipit   *Anthus longicaudatus*
Richard's Pipit   *Anthus richardi*
Buffy Pipit   *Anthus vaalensis*
Grassland Pipit   *Anthus cinnamomeus*
Long-legged Pipit   *Anthus pallidiventris*
Malindi Pipit   *Anthus melindae*
Kimberley Pipit   *Anthus pseudosimilis*
Tawny Pipit   *Anthus campestris*
Blyth's Pipit   *Anthus godlewskii*
Long-billed Pipit   *Anthus similis*
Berthelot's Pipit   *Anthus berthelotii*
Short-tailed Pipit   *Anthus brachyurus*
Bush Pipit   *Anthus caffer*
Sokoke Pipit   *Anthus sokokensis* •
Eurasian Tree Pipit   *Anthus trivialis*
Olive-backed Pipit   *Anthus hodgsoni*
Pechora Pipit   *Anthus gustavi*
Meadow Pipit   *Anthus pratensis*
Red-throated Pipit   *Anthus cervinus*
Rosy Pipit   *Anthus roseatus*
Rock Pipit   *Anthus petrosus*
Water Pipit   *Anthus spinoletta*
Upland Pipit   *Anthus sylvanus*
Buff-bellied Pipit   *Anthus rubescens*
Nilgiri Pipit   *Anthus nilghiriensis*
Correndera Pipit   *Anthus correndera*
South Georgia Pipit   *Anthus antarcticus*
Sprague's Pipit   *Anthus spragueii*
Short-billed Pipit   *Anthus furcatus*
Hellmayr's Pipit   *Anthus hellmayri*
Paramo Pipit   *Anthus bogotensis*
Yellowish Pipit   *Anthus lutescens*
Chaco Pipit   *Anthus chacoensis*
Ochre-breasted Pipit   *Anthus nattereri*
New Guinea Pipit   *Anthus gutturalis*

Cuckooshrikes Campephagidae
Ground Cuckooshrike *Coracina maxima*
Large Cuckooshrike *Coracina macei*
Sunda Cuckooshrike *Coracina larvata*
Javan Cuckooshrike *Coracina javensis*
Slaty Cuckooshrike *Coracina schistacea*
Wallacean Cuckooshrike *Coracina personata*
Melanesian Cuckooshrike *Coracina caledonica*
Black-faced Cuckooshrike *Coracina novaehollandiae*
Stout-billed Cuckooshrike *Coracina caeruleogrisea*
Bar-bellied Cuckooshrike *Coracina striata*
Pied Cuckooshrike *Coracina bicolor*
Moluccan Cuckooshrike *Coracina atriceps*
Buru Island Cuckooshrike *Coracina fortis*
Caerulean Cuckooshrike *Coracina temminckii*
Yellow-eyed Cuckooshrike *Coracina lineata*
White-lored Cuckooshrike *Coracina boyeri*
White-rumped Cuckooshrike *Coracina leucopygia*
White-bellied Cuckooshrike *Coracina papuensis*
Hooded Cuckooshrike *Coracina longicauda*
Halmahera Cuckooshrike *Coracina parvula*
Pygmy Cuckooshrike *Coracina abbotti*
New Caledonian Cuckooshrike *Coracina analis*
White-breasted Cuckooshrike *Coracina pectoralis*
Blue Cuckooshrike *Coracina azurea*
Gray Cuckooshrike *Coracina caesia*
Grauer's Cuckooshrike *Coracina graueri*
Madagascar Cuckooshrike *Coracina cinerea*
Mauritius Cuckooshrike *Coracina typica*
Réunion Cuckooshrike *Coracina newtoni* •
Slender-billed Graybird *Coracina tenuirostris*
Blackish Cuckooshrike *Coracina coerulescens*
Sumba Cicadabird *Coracina dohertyi*
Sula Cicadabird *Coracina sula*
Kai Cicadabird *Coracina dispar*
Black-bibbed Cicadabird *Coracina mindanensis*
Sulawesi Cicadabird *Coracina morio*
Bale Cicadabird *Coracina ceramensis*
Papuan Cicadabird *Coracina incerta*
Gray-headed Cuckooshrike *Coracina schisticeps*
New Guinea Cuckooshrike *Coracina melas*
Black-bellied Graybird *Coracina montana*
Solomon Islands Cuckooshrike *Coracina holopolia*
McGregor's Cuckooshrike *Coracina mcgregori*
Indochinese Cuckooshrike *Coracina polioptera*
White-winged Cuckooshrike *Coracina ostenta*
Black-winged Cuckooshrike *Coracina melaschistos*
Lesser Cuckooshrike *Coracina fimbriata*
Black-headed Cuckooshrike *Coracina melanoptera*
Orange Cuckooshrike *Campochaera sloetii*
Black-and-white Triller *Lalage melanoleuca*
Pied Triller *Lalage nigra*
White-rumped Triller *Lalage leucopygialis*
White-shouldered Triller *Lalage sueurii*
Australian Triller *Lalage tricolor*
Rufous-bellied Triller *Lalage aurea*
Tanimbar Triller *Lalage moesta*
Varied Triller *Lalage leucomela*
Black-browed Triller *Lalage atrovirens*
Samoan Triller *Lalage sharpei*
Polynesian Triller *Lalage maculosa*
Long-tailed Triller *Lalage leucopyga*
Petit's Cuckooshrike *Campephaga petiti*
African Black Cuckooshrike *Campephaga flava*
Red-shouldered Cuckooshrike *Campephaga phoenicea*
Purple-throated Cuckooshrike *Campephaga quiscalina*
Western Cuckooshrike *Campephaga lobata*
Eastern Cuckooshrike *Campephaga oriolina*
Rosy Minivet *Pericrocotus roseus*
Swinhoe's Minivet *Pericrocotus cantonensis*
Ashy Minivet *Pericrocotus divaricatus*
Small Minivet *Pericrocotus cinnamomeus*

Ryukyu Minivet *Pericrocotus tegimae*
Fiery Minivet *Pericrocotus igneus*
Flores Minivet *Pericrocotus lansbergei*
White-bellied Minivet *Pericrocotus erythropygius*
Long-tailed Minivet *Pericrocotus ethologus*
Short-billed Minivet *Pericrocotus brevirostris*
Sunda Minivet *Pericrocotus miniatus*
Scarlet Minivet *Pericrocotus flammeus*
Gray-chinned Minivet *Pericrocotus solaris*
Bar-winged Flycatcher-Shrike *Hemipus picatus*
Black-winged Flycatcher-Shrike *Hemipus hirundinaceus*

Bulbuls Pycnonotidae
Crested Finchbill *Spizixos canifrons*
Collared Finchbill *Spizixos semitorques*
Straw-headed Bulbul *Pycnonotus zeylanicus*
Striated Bulbul *Pycnonotus striatus*
Cream-striped Bulbul *Pycnonotus leucogrammicus*
Spot-necked Bulbul *Pycnonotus tympanistrigus*
Black-and-white Bulbul *Pycnonotus melanoleucos*
Gray-headed Bulbul *Pycnonotus priocephalus*
Black-headed Bulbul *Pycnonotus atriceps*
Black-crested Bulbul *Pycnonotus melanicterus*
Styan's Bulbul *Pycnonotus taivanus*
Scaly-breasted Bulbul *Pycnonotus squamatus*
Gray-bellied Bulbul *Pycnonotus cyaniventris*
Red-whiskered Bulbul *Pycnonotus jocosus*
Brown-breasted Bulbul *Pycnonotus xanthorrhous*
Light-vented Bulbul *Pycnonotus sinensis*
Garden Bulbul *Pycnonotus barbatus*
African Red-eyed Bulbul *Pycnonotus nigricans*
Cape Bulbul *Pycnonotus capensis*
White-spectacled Bulbul *Pycnonotus xanthopygos*
White-eared Bulbul *Pycnonotus leucotis*
White-cheeked Bulbul *Pycnonotus leucogenys*
Red-vented Bulbul *Pycnonotus cafer*
Sooty-headed Bulbul *Pycnonotus aurigaster*
Puff-backed Bulbul *Pycnonotus eutilotus*
Blue Wattled Bulbul *Pycnonotus nieuwenhuisii*
Yellow-wattled Bulbul *Pycnonotus urostictus*
Orange-spotted Bulbul *Pycnonotus bimaculatus*
Stripe-throated Bulbul *Pycnonotus finlaysoni*
Yellow-throated Bulbul *Pycnonotus xantholaemus*
Yellow-eared Bulbul *Pycnonotus penicillatus*
Flavescent Bulbul *Pycnonotus flavescens*
White-browed Bulbul *Pycnonotus luteolus*
Yellow-vented Bulbul *Pycnonotus goiavier*
Olive-winged Bulbul *Pycnonotus plumosus*
Streak-eared Bulbul *Pycnonotus blanfordi*
Cream-vented Bulbul *Pycnonotus simplex*
Red-eyed Bulbul *Pycnonotus brunneus*
Spectacled Bulbul *Pycnonotus erythropthalmos*
Cameroon Mountain Greenbul *Andropadus montanus*
Shelley's Greenbul *Andropadus masukuensis*
Little Greenbul *Andropadus virens*
Gray Greenbul *Andropadus gracilis*
Ansorge's Greenbul *Andropadus ansorgei*
Plain Greenbul *Andropadus curvirostris*
Slender-billed Greenbul *Andropadus gracilirostris*
Zanzibar Sombre Greenbul *Andropadus importunus*
Yellow-whiskered Greenbul *Andropadus latirostris*
Gray-throated Greenbul *Andropadus tephrolaemus*
Mountain Greenbul *Andropadus nigriceps*
Stripe-cheeked Greenbul *Andropadus milanjensis*
Golden Greenbul *Calyptocichla serina*
Honeyguide Greenbul *Baeopogon indicator*
Sjöstedt's Honeyguide Greenbul *Baeopogon clamans*
Spotted Greenbul *Ixonotus guttatus*
Simple Greenbul *Chlorocichla simplex*
Yellow-throated Greenbul *Chlorocichla flavicollis*
Yellow-necked Greenbul *Chlorocichla falkensteini*
Yellow-bellied Greenbul *Chlorocichla flaviventris*
Joyful Greenbul *Chlorocichla laetissima*

Prigogine's Greenbul *Chlorocichla prigoginei* •
Swamp Palm Bulbul *Thescelocichla leucopleura*
Common Leaflove *Phyllastrephus scandens*
Cabanis' Greenbul *Phyllastrephus cabanisi*
Fischer's Greenbul *Phyllastrephus fischeri*
Terrestrial Brownbul *Phyllastrephus terrestris*
Northern Brownbul *Phyllastrephus strepitans*
Pale-olive Greenbul *Phyllastrephus fulviventris*
Gray-olive Greenbul *Phyllastrephus cerviniventris*
Baumann's Olive Greenbul *Phyllastrephus baumanni*
Toro Olive Greenbul *Phyllastrephus hypochloris*
Cameroon Olive Greenbul *Phyllastrephus poensis*
Sassi's Olive Greenbul *Phyllastrephus lorenzi*
Yellow-streaked Greenbul *Phyllastrephus flavostriatus*
Gray-headed Greenbul *Phyllastrephus poliocephalus*
Tiny Greenbul *Phyllastrephus debilis*
White-throated Greenbul *Phyllastrephus albigularis*
Icterine Greenbul *Phyllastrephus icterinus*
Liberian Greenbul *Phyllastrephus leucolepis* •
Xavier's Greenbul *Phyllastrephus xavieri*
Common Tetraka *Phyllastrephus madagascariensis*
Short-billed Tetraka *Phyllastrephus zosterops*
Appert's Tetraka *Phyllastrephus apperti*
Dusky Tetraka *Phyllastrephus tenebrosus*
Gray-crowned Tetraka *Phyllastrephus cinereiceps*
Common Bristlebill *Bleda syndactylus*
Green-tailed Bristlebill *Bleda eximius*
Lesser Bristlebill *Bleda notatus*
Gray-headed Bristlebill *Bleda canicapillus*
Western Nicator *Nicator chloris*
Eastern Nicator *Nicator gularis*
Yellow-throated Nicator *Nicator vireo*
Red-tailed Greenbul *Criniger calurus*
Western Bearded Greenbul *Criniger barbatus*
Eastern Bearded Greenbul *Criniger chloronotus*
Yellow-bearded Greenbul *Criniger olivaceus*
White-bearded Greenbul *Criniger ndussumensis*
Finsch's Bearded Bulbul *Alophoixus finschii*
White-throated Bulbul *Alophoixus flaveolus*
Puff-throated Bulbul *Alophoixus pallidus*
Ochraceous Bulbul *Alophoixus ochraceus*
Gray-cheeked Bearded Bulbul *Alophoixus bres*
Yellow-bellied Bulbul *Alophoixus phaeocephalus*
Golden Bulbul *Alophoixus affinis*
Hook-billed Bulbul *Setornis criniger*
Hairy-backed Bulbul *Tricholestes criniger*
Olive Bulbul *Iole virescens*
Gray-eyed Bulbul *Iole propinqua*
Buff-vented Bulbul *Iole olivacea*
Yellow-browed Bulbul *Iole indica*
Sulfur-bellied Bulbul *Ixos palawanensis*
Philippine Bulbul *Ixos philippinus*
Zamboanga Bulbul *Ixos rufigularis*
Streak-breasted Bulbul *Ixos siquijorensis* •
Asian Brown-eared Bulbul *Ixos amaurotis*
Yellowish Bulbul *Ixos everetti*
Mountain Bulbul *Ixos mcclellandii*
Sunda Bulbul *Ixos virescens*
Streaked Bulbul *Ixos malaccensis*
Ashy Bulbul *Hemixos flavala*
Chestnut Bulbul *Hemixos castanonotus*
Madagascar Black Bulbul *Hypsipetes madagascariensis*
Seychelles Bulbul *Hypsipetes crassirostris*
Comoros Black Bulbul *Hypsipetes parvirostris*
Réunion Bulbul *Hypsipetes borbonicus*
Mauritius Bulbul *Hypsipetes olivaceus*
Black Bulbul *Hypsipetes leucocephalus*
Nicobar Bulbul *Hypsipetes virescens*
White-headed Bulbul *Hypsipetes thompsoni*
Black-collared Bulbul *Neolestes torquatus*

Kinglets Regulidae
Golden-crowned Kinglet *Regulus satrapa*
Ruby-crowned Kinglet *Regulus calendula*

European Goldcrest   *Regulus regulus*
Tenerife Goldcrest   *Regulus teneriffae*
Flamecrest   *Regulus goodfellowi*
Eurasian Firecrest   *Regulus ignicapilla*

Leafbirds Chloropseidae
Philippine Leafbird   *Chloropsis flavipennis*
Yellow-throated Leafbird   *Chloropsis palawanensis*
Greater Green Leafbird   *Chloropsis sonnerati*
Lesser Green Leafbird   *Chloropsis cyanopogon*
Blue-winged Leafbird   *Chloropsis cochinchinensis*
Golden-fronted Leafbird   *Chloropsis aurifrons*
Orange-bellied Leafbird   *Chloropsis hardwickii*
Blue-masked Leafbird   *Chloropsis venusta*

Ioras Aegithinidae
Common Iora   *Aegithina tiphia*
Marshall's Iora   *Aegithina nigrolutea*
Green Iora   *Aegithina viridissima*
Great Iora   *Aegithina lafresnayei*

Silky flycatchers Ptilognatidae
Black-and-yellow Silky-Flycatcher   *Phainoptila melanoxantha*
Gray Silky-Flycatcher   *Ptilogonys cinereus*
Long-tailed Silky-Flycatcher   *Ptilogonys caudatus*
Phainopepla   *Phainopepla nitens*

Waxwings Bombycillidae
Bohemian Waxwing   *Bombycilla garrulus*
Cedar Waxwing   *Bombycilla cedrorum*
Japanese Waxwing   *Bombycilla japonica*

Hypocolius Hypocoliidae
Hypocolius   *Hypocolius ampelinus*

Palmchat Dulidae
Palmchat   *Dulus dominicus*

Dippers Cinclidae
White-throated Dipper   *Cinclus cinclus*
Brown Dipper   *Cinclus pallasii*
American Dipper   *Cinclus mexicanus*
White-capped Dipper   *Cinclus leucocephalus*
Rufous-throated Dipper   *Cinclus schulzi*

Wrens Troglodytidae
Donacobius   *Donacobius atricapilla*
White-headed Cactus-Wren   *Campylorhynchus albobrunneus*
Band-backed Cactus-Wren   *Campylorhynchus zonatus*
Gray-barred Cactus-Wren   *Campylorhynchus megalopterus*
Giant Cactus-Wren   *Campylorhynchus chiapensis*
Rufous-naped Cactus-Wren   *Campylorhynchus rufinucha*
Spotted Cactus-Wren   *Campylorhynchus gularis*
Boucard's Cactus-Wren   *Campylorhynchus jocosus*
Yucatan Cactus-Wren   *Campylorhynchus yucatanicus*
Northern Cactus-Wren   *Campylorhynchus brunneicapillus*
Bicolored Cactus-Wren   *Campylorhynchus griseus*
Thrush-like Cactus-Wren   *Campylorhynchus turdinus*
Stripe-backed Cactus-Wren   *Campylorhynchus nuchalis*
Fasciated Cactus-Wren   *Campylorhynchus fasciatus*
Gray-mantled Wren   *Odontorchilus branickii*
Tooth-billed Wren   *Odontorchilus cinereus*
American Rock Wren   *Salpinctes obsoletus*
Canyon Wren   *Catherpes mexicanus*
Sumichrast's Wren   *Hylorchilus sumichrasti*
Nava's Wren   *Hylorchilus navai*
Rufous Wren   *Cinnycerthia unirufa*
Sharpe's Wren   *Cinnycerthia olivascens*

Peruvian Wren   *Cinnycerthia peruana*
Fulvous Wren   *Cinnycerthia fulva*
Black-throated Wren   *Thryothorus atrogularis*
Sooty-headed Wren   *Thryothorus spadix*
Black-bellied Wren   *Thryothorus fasciatoventris*
Inca Wren   *Thryothorus eisenmanni*
Whiskered Wren   *Thryothorus mystacalis*
Plain-tailed Wren   *Thryothorus euophrys*
Moustached Wren   *Thryothorus genibarbis*
Coraya Wren   *Thryothorus coraya*
Happy Wren   *Thryothorus felix*
Spot-breasted Wren   *Thryothorus maculipectus*
Rufous-breasted Wren   *Thryothorus rutilus*
Speckle-breasted Wren   *Thryothorus sclateri*
Riverside Wren   *Thryothorus semibadius*
Black-capped Wren   *Thryothorus nigricapillus*
Stripe-breasted Wren   *Thryothorus thoracicus*
Stripe-throated Wren   *Thryothorus leucopogon*
Banded Wren   *Thryothorus pleurostictus*
Carolina Wren   *Thryothorus ludovicianus*
Rufous-and-white Wren   *Thryothorus rufalbus*
Sinaloa Wren   *Thryothorus sinaloa*
Plain Wren   *Thryothorus modestus*
Buff-breasted Wren   *Thryothorus leucotis*
Nicéforo's Wren   *Thryothorus nicefori* •
Superciliated Wren   *Thryothorus superciliaris*
Fawn-breasted Wren   *Thryothorus guarayanus*
Long-billed Wren   *Thryothorus longirostris*
Gray Wren   *Thryothorus griseus*
Bewick's Wren   *Thryomanes bewickii*
Socorro Wren   *Thryomanes sissonii*
Zapata Wren   *Ferminia cerverai* •
Northern Wren   *Troglodytes troglodytes*
House Wren   *Troglodytes aedon*
Clarión Island Wren   *Troglodytes tanneri*
Cobb's Wren   *Troglodytes cobbi*
Rufous-browed Wren   *Troglodytes rufociliatus*
Ochraceous Wren   *Troglodytes ochraceus*
Santa Marta Wren   *Troglodytes monticola*
Mountain Wren   *Troglodytes solstitialis*
Tepui Wren   *Troglodytes rufulus*
Short-billed Marsh-Wren   *Cistothorus platensis*
Apolinar's Marsh-Wren   *Cistothorus apolinari* •
Paramo Wren   *Cistothorus meridae*
Marsh-Wren   *Cistothorus palustris*
White-bellied Wren   *Uropsila leucogastra*
Timberline Wren   *Thryorchilus browni*
White-breasted Wood-Wren   *Henicorhina leucosticta*
Gray-breasted Wood-Wren   *Henicorhina leucophrys*
Munchique Wood-Wren   *Henicorhina negreti*
Bar-winged Wood-Wren   *Henicorhina leucoptera*
Northern Nightingale Wren   *Microcerculus philomela*
Southern Nightingale Wren   *Microcerculus marginatus*
Flutist Wren   *Microcerculus ustulatus*
Wing-banded Wren   *Microcerculus bambla*
Song Wren   *Cyphorhinus phaeocephalus*
Chestnut-breasted Wren   *Cyphorhinus thoracicus*
Musician Wren   *Cyphorhinus arada*

Mockingbirds and Thrashers Mimidae
Gray Catbird   *Dumetella carolinensis*
Black Catbird   *Melanoptila glabrirostris*
Bahaman Mockingbird   *Mimus gundlachii*
Northern Mockingbird   *Mimus polyglottos*
Tropical Mockingbird   *Mimus gilvus*
Chalk-browed Mockingbird   *Mimus saturninus*
Patagonian Mockingbird   *Mimus patagonicus*
Brown-backed Mockingbird   *Mimus dorsalis*
White-banded Mockingbird   *Mimus triurus*
Long-tailed Mockingbird   *Mimus longicaudatus*
Chilean Mockingbird   *Mimus thenca*
Galapogos Mockingbird   *Nesomimus parvulus*
Charles Mockingbird   *Nesomimus trifasciatus* •
Hood Mockingbird   *Nesomimus macdonaldi*

San Cristobal Mockingbird   *Nesomimus melanotis* •
Sage Thrasher   *Oreoscoptes montanus*
Socorro Thrasher   *Mimodes graysoni*
Brown Thrasher   *Toxostoma rufum*
Long-billed Thrasher   *Toxostoma longirostre*
Cozumel Thrasher   *Toxostoma guttatum* •
Gray Thrasher   *Toxostoma cinereum*
Bendire's Thrasher   *Toxostoma bendirei*
Ocellated Thrasher   *Toxostoma ocellatum*
Curve-billed Thrasher   *Toxostoma curvirostre*
California Thrasher   *Toxostoma redivivum*
Crissal Thrasher   *Toxostoma crissale*
Le Conte's Thrasher   *Toxostoma lecontei*
Vizcaino Thrasher   *Toxostoma arenicola*
White-breasted Trembler   *Ramphocinclus brachyurus* •
Blue Mockingbird   *Melanotis caerulescens*
Blue-and-white Mockingbird   *Melanotis hypoleucus*
Gray Trembler   *Cinclocerthia gutturalis*
Brown Trembler   *Cinclocerthia ruficauda*
Scaly-breasted Thrasher   *Allenia fusca*
Pearly-eyed Thrasher   *Margarops fuscatus*

Accentors Prunellidae
Alpine Accentor   *Prunella collaris*
Altai Accentor   *Prunella himalayana*
Robin Accentor   *Prunella rubeculoides*
Rufous-breasted Accentor   *Prunella strophiata*
Siberian Accentor   *Prunella montanella*
Radde's Accentor   *Prunella ocularis*
Yemen Accentor   *Prunella fagani*
Brown Accentor   *Prunella fulvescens*
Black-throated Accentor   *Prunella atrogularis*
Mongolian Accentor   *Prunella koslowi*
Hedge Accentor   *Prunella modularis*
Japanese Accentor   *Prunella rubida*
Maroon-backed Accentor   *Prunella immaculata*

Thrushes and Chats Turdidae
Rufous Flycatcher-Thrush   *Neocossyphus fraseri*
Finsch's Flycatcher-Thrush   *Neocossyphus finschii*
Red-tailed Antthrush   *Neocossyphus rufus*
White-tailed Antthrush   *Neocossyphus poensis*
Forest Rock-Thrush   *Pseudocossyphus sharpei*
Benson's Rock-Thrush   *Pseudocossyphus bensoni*
Littoral Rock-Thrush   *Pseudocossyphus imerinus*
Cape Rock-Thrush   *Monticola rupestris*
Sentinel Rock-Thrush   *Monticola explorator*
Short-toed Rock-Thrush   *Monticola brevipes*
Miombo Rock-Thrush   *Monticola angolensis*
Rufous-tailed Rock-Thrush   *Monticola saxatilis*
Little Rock-Thrush   *Monticola rufocinereus*
Blue-capped Rock-Thrush   *Monticola cinclorhynchus*
White-throated Rock-Thrush   *Monticola gularis*
Chestnut-bellied Rock-Thrush   *Monticola rufiventris*
Blue Rock-Thrush   *Monticola solitarius*
Sri Lanka Whistling-Thrush   *Myophonus blighi* •
Shiny Whistling-Thrush   *Myophonus melanurus*
Sunda Whistling-Thrush   *Myophonus glaucinus*
Brown-winged Whistling-Thrush   *Myophonus castaneus*
Sunda Whistling-Thrush borneensis   *Myophonus borneensis*
Malaysian Whistling-Thrush   *Myophonus robinsoni*
Malabar Whistling-Thrush   *Myophonus horsfieldii*
Taiwan Whistling-Thrush   *Myophonus insularis*
Blue Whistling-Thrush   *Myophonus caeruleus*
Geomalia   *Geomalia heinrichi*
Slaty-backed Ground-Thrush   *Zoothera schistacea*
Moluccan Ground-Thrush   *Zoothera dumasi*
Moluccan Thrush joiceyi   *Zoothera joiceyi*
Chestnut-capped Ground-Thrush   *Zoothera interpres*
Chestnut-capped Thrush leucolaema   *Zoothera leucolaema*
Chestnut-backed Ground-Thrush   *Zoothera dohertyi*

Red-backed Ground-Thrush   *Zoothera erythronota*
Rusty-backed Thrush mendeni   *Zoothera mendeni*
Pied Ground-Thrush   *Zoothera wardii*
Ashy Ground-Thrush   *Zoothera cinerea*
Orange-sided Thrush   *Zoothera peronii*
Orange-headed Ground-Thrush   *Zoothera citrina*
Everett's Ground-Thrush   *Zoothera everetti*
Siberian Ground-Thrush   *Zoothera sibirica*
Abyssinian Ground-Thrush   *Zoothera piaggiae*
Kivu Ground-Thrush   *Zoothera tanganjicae*
Crossley's Ground-Thrush   *Zoothera crossleyi*
Orange Ground-Thrush   *Zoothera gurneyi*
Black-eared Ground-Thrush   *Zoothera cameronensis*
Gray Ground-Thrush   *Zoothera princei*
Oberlaender's Ground-Thrush   *Zoothera oberlaenderi*
Spotted Ground-Thrush   *Zoothera guttata* •
Spot-winged Ground-Thrush   *Zoothera spiloptera*
Sunda Ground-Thrush   *Zoothera andromedae*
Plain-backed Thrush   *Zoothera mollissima*
Long-tailed Thrush   *Zoothera dixoni*
White's Ground-Thrush   *Zoothera dauma*
Fawn-breasted Thrush   *Zoothera machiki*
Bassian Thrush   *Zoothera lunulata*
Russet-tailed Thrush   *Zoothera heinei*
Northern Melanesian Ground-Thrush   *Zoothera talaseae*
San Cristobal Ground-Thrush   *Zoothera margaretae*
Long-billed Thrush   *Zoothera monticola*
Dark-sided Thrush   *Zoothera marginata*
Sulawesi Mountain Thrush   *Cataponera turdoides*
Tristan Thrush   *Nesocichla eremita*
Forest Thrush   *Cichlherminia lherminieri*
Eastern Bluebird   *Sialia sialis*
Western Bluebird   *Sialia mexicana*
Mountain Bluebird   *Sialia currucoides*
Townsend's Solitaire   *Myadestes townsendi*
Brown-backed Solitaire   *Myadestes occidentalis*
Cuban Solitaire   *Myadestes elisabeth*
Rufous-throated Solitaire   *Myadestes genibarbis*
Black-faced Solitaire   *Myadestes melanops*
Varied Solitaire   *Myadestes coloratus*
Slate-colored Solitaire   *Myadestes unicolor*
Andean Solitaire   *Myadestes ralloides*
Kama'o   *Myadestes myadestinus*
Oloma'o   *Myadestes lanaiensis* •
Omao   *Myadestes obscurus*
Puaiohi   *Myadestes palmeri* •
Rufous-brown Solitaire   *Cichlopsis leucogenys*
White-eared Solitaire   *Entomodestes leucotis*
Black Solitaire   *Entomodestes coracinus*
Orange-billed Nightingale-Thrush   *Catharus aurantiirostris*
Slaty-backed Nightingale-Thrush   *Catharus fuscater*
Russet Nightingale-Thrush   *Catharus occidentalis*
Black-billed Nightingale-Thrush   *Catharus gracilirostris*
Ruddy-capped Nightingale-Thrush   *Catharus frantzii*
Black-headed Nightingale-Thrush   *Catharus mexicanus*
Spotted Nightingale-Thrush   *Catharus dryas*
Veery   *Catharus fuscescens*
Gray-cheeked Thrush   *Catharus minimus*
Bicknell's Thrush   *Catharus bicknelli*
Swainson's Thrush   *Catharus ustulatus*
Hermit Thrush   *Catharus guttatus*
Wood Thrush   *Hylocichla mustelina*
Pale-eyed Thrush   *Platycichla leucops*
Yellow-legged Thrush   *Platycichla flavipes*
Groundscraper Thrush   *Psophocichla litsipsirupa*
Yemen Thrush   *Turdus menachensis*
Olive Thrush   *Turdus olivaceus*
Olivaceous Thrush   *Turdus olivaceofuscus*
Comoros Thrush   *Turdus bewsheri*
Kurrichane Thrush   *Turdus libonyanus*
African Thrush   *Turdus pelios*

African Bare-eyed Thrush   *Turdus tephronotus*
Gray-backed Thrush   *Turdus hortulorum*
Tickell's Thrush   *Turdus unicolor*
Black-breasted Thrush   *Turdus dissimilis*
Japanese Gray Thrush   *Turdus cardis*
White-collared Blackbird   *Turdus albocinctus*
Ring Ouzel   *Turdus torquatus*
Gray-winged Blackbird   *Turdus boulboul*
Common Blackbird   *Turdus merula*
Island Thrush   *Turdus poliocephalus*
Chestnut Thrush   *Turdus rubrocanus*
Kessler's Thrush   *Turdus kessleri*
Gray-sided Thrush   *Turdus feae*
Eyebrowed Thrush   *Turdus obscurus*
Pale Thrush   *Turdus pallidus*
Brown-headed Thrush   *Turdus chrysolaus*
Izu Islands Thrush   *Turdus celaenops*
Dark-throated Thrush   *Turdus ruficollis*
Dusky Thrush   *Turdus naumanni*
Fieldfare   *Turdus pilaris*
Redwing   *Turdus iliacus*
Common Song Thrush   *Turdus philomelos*
Chinese Song Thrush   *Turdus mupinensis*
Mistle Thrush   *Turdus viscivorus*
Red-legged Thrush   *Turdus plumbeus*
Chiguanco Thrush   *Turdus chiguanco*
Sooty Thrush   *Turdus nigrescens*
Great Thrush   *Turdus fuscater*
Black Thrush   *Turdus infuscatus*
Glossy-black Thrush   *Turdus serranus*
Andean Slaty Thrush   *Turdus nigriceps*
Eastern Slaty Thrush   *Turdus subalaris*
Black-hooded Thrush   *Turdus olivater*
Plumbeous-backed Thrush   *Turdus reevei*
Marañón Thrush   *Turdus maranonicus*
Chestnut-bellied Thrush   *Turdus fulviventris*
Rufous-bellied Thrush   *Turdus rufiventris*
Austral Thrush   *Turdus falcklandii*
Pale-breasted Thrush   *Turdus leucomelas*
Creamy-bellied Thrush   *Turdus amaurochalinus*
American Mountain Thrush   *Turdus plebejus*
Black-billed Thrush   *Turdus ignobilis*
Lawrence's Thrush   *Turdus lawrencii*
Cocoa Thrush   *Turdus fumigatus*
Pale-vented Thrush   *Turdus obsoletus*
Hauxwell's Thrush   *Turdus hauxwelli*
Clay-colored Thrush   *Turdus grayi*
American Bare-eyed Thrush   *Turdus nudigenis*
Ecuadorean Thrush   *Turdus maculirostris*
Unicolored Thrush   *Turdus haplochrous*
White-eyed Thrush   *Turdus jamaicensis*
White-throated Thrush   *Turdus assimilis*
White-necked Thrush   *Turdus albicollis*
Rufous-backed Thrush   *Turdus rufopalliatus*
Rufous-collared Thrush   *Turdus rufitorques*
American Robin   *Turdus migratorius*
La Selle Thrush   *Turdus swalesi* •
White-chinned Thrush   *Turdus aurantius*
Varied Thrush   *Ixoreus naevius*
Aztec Thrush   *Ridgwayia pinicola*
Black-breasted Fruithunter   *Chlamydochaera jefferyi*
Rusty-bellied Shortwing   *Brachypteryx hyperythra*
Gould's Shortwing   *Brachypteryx stellata*
White-bellied Shortwing   *Brachypteryx major*
Lesser Shortwing   *Brachypteryx leucophrys*
White-browed Shortwing   *Brachypteryx montana*
Greater Shortwing   *Heinrichia calligyna*
Brown-chested Alethe   *Alethe poliocephala*
Red-throated Alethe   *Alethe poliophrys*
Cholo Mountain Alethe   *Alethe choloensis* •
White-chested Alethe   *Alethe fuelleborni*
White-tailed Alethe   *Alethe diademata*

Cisticolas Cisticolidae

Red-faced Cisticola   *Cisticola erythrops*
Singing Cisticola   *Cisticola cantans*
Whistling Cisticola   *Cisticola lateralis*
Chattering Cisticola   *Cisticola anonymus*
Trilling Cisticola   *Cisticola woosnami*
Bubbling Cisticola   *Cisticola bulliens*
Chubb's Cisticola   *Cisticola chubbi*
Hunter's Cisticola   *Cisticola hunteri*
Black-lored Cisticola   *Cisticola nigriloris*
Rock-loving Cisticola   *Cisticola aberrans*
Boran Cisticola   *Cisticola bodessa*
Rattling Cisticola   *Cisticola chiniana*
Ashy Cisticola   *Cisticola cinereolus*
Red-pate Cisticola   *Cisticola ruficeps*
Dorst's Cisticola   *Cisticola dorsti*
Tinkling Cisticola   *Cisticola rufilatus*
Gray-backed Cisticola   *Cisticola subruficapilla*
Wailing Cisticola   *Cisticola lais*
Tana River Cisticola   *Cisticola restrictus*
Churring Cisticola   *Cisticola njombe*
Winding Cisticola   *Cisticola galactotes*
Chirping Cisticola   *Cisticola pipiens*
Carruthers's Cisticola   *Cisticola carruthersi*
Levaillant's Cisticola   *Cisticola tinniens*
Stout Cisticola   *Cisticola robustus*
Croaking Cisticola   *Cisticola natalensis*
Piping Cisticola   *Cisticola fulvicapilla*
Aberdare Cisticola   *Cisticola aberdare* •
Tabora Cisticola   *Cisticola angusticauda*
Slender-tailed Cisticola   *Cisticola melanurus*
Siffling Cisticola   *Cisticola brachypterus*
Rufous Cisticola   *Cisticola rufus*
Foxy Cisticola   *Cisticola troglodytes*
Tiny Cisticola   *Cisticola nana*
Zitting Cisticola   *Cisticola juncidis*
Socotra Cisticola   *Cisticola haesitatus*
Madagascar Cisticola   *Cisticola cherina*
Desert Cisticola   *Cisticola aridulus*
Spotted Cloud Cisticola   *Cisticola textrix*
Black-necked Cisticola   *Cisticola eximius*
Cloud-scraping Cisticola   *Cisticola dambo*
Pectoral-patch Cisticola   *Cisticola brunnescens*
Pale-crowned Cisticola   *Cisticola cinnamomeus*
Wing-snapping Cisticola   *Cisticola ayresii*
Golden-headed Cisticola   *Cisticola exilis*
White-browed Chinese Warbler   *Rhopophilus pekinensis*
Socotra Warbler   *Incana incanus*
Streaked Scrub-Warbler   *Scotocerca inquieta*
Rufous-vented Prinia   *Prinia burnesii*
Swamp Prinia   *Prinia cinerascens*
Striated Prinia   *Prinia crinigera*
Javan Brown Prinia   *Prinia polychroa*
Hill Prinia   *Prinia atrogularis*
Gray-crowned Prinia   *Prinia cinereocapilla*
Rufous-fronted Prinia   *Prinia buchanani*
Rufescent Prinia   *Prinia rufescens*
Gray-breasted Prinia   *Prinia hodgsonii*
Bar-winged Prinia   *Prinia familiaris*
Graceful Prinia   *Prinia gracilis*
Jungle Prinia   *Prinia sylvatica*
Yellow-bellied Prinia   *Prinia flaviventris*
Ashy Prinia   *Prinia socialis*
Tawny-flanked Prinia   *Prinia subflava*
Plain-colored Prinia   *Prinia inornata*
Pale Prinia   *Prinia somalica*
River Prinia   *Prinia fluviatilis*
Black-chested Prinia   *Prinia flavicans*
Karoo Prinia   *Prinia maculosa*
Saffron-breasted Prinia   *Prinia hypoxantha*
White-breasted Prinia   *Prinia substriata*
São Tomé Prinia   *Prinia molleri*
Roberts's Prinia   *Prinia robertsi*
Banded Prinia   *Prinia bairdii*

Red-winged Warbler *Prinia erythroptera*
Sierra Leone Prinia *Schistolais leontica*
White-chinned Prinia *Schistolais leucopogon*
Rufous-eared Prinia *Malcorus pectoralis*
Red-winged Gray Warbler *Drymocichla incana*
Green Longtail *Urolais epichlorus*
Cricket Longtail *Spiloptila clamans*
Black-collared Apalis *Apalis pulchra*
Collared Apalis *Apalis ruwenzorii*
Bar-throated Apalis *Apalis thoracica*
Black-capped Apalis *Apalis nigriceps*
Black-throated Apalis *Apalis jacksoni*
White-winged Apalis *Apalis chariessa*
Masked Apalis *Apalis binotata*
Mountain Masked Apalis *Apalis personata*
Yellow-breasted Apalis *Apalis flavida*
Rudd's Apalis *Apalis ruddi*
Sharpe's Apalis *Apalis sharpii*
Buff-throated Apalis *Apalis rufogularis*
Bamenda Apalis *Apalis bamendae*
Gosling's Apalis *Apalis goslingi*
Chestnut-throated Apalis *Apalis porphyrolaema*
Chapin's Apalis *Apalis chapini*
Black-headed Apalis *Apalis melanocephala*
Chirinda Apalis *Apalis chirindensis*
Gray Apalis *Apalis cinerea*
Brown-headed Apalis *Apalis alticola*
Karamoja Apalis *Apalis karamojae*
Red-faced Warbler *Urorhipis rufifrons*
Oriole Warbler *Hypergerus atriceps*
Gray-capped Warbler *Eminia lepida*
Green-backed Camaroptera *Camaroptera brachyura*
Yellow-browed Camaroptera *Camaroptera superciliaris*
Olive-green Camaroptera *Camaroptera chloronota*
Pale Wren-Warbler *Calamonastes undosus*
Gray Wren-Warbler *Calamonastes simplex*
Thornbush Barred Wren-Warbler *Calamonastes fasciolatus*
Cinnamon-breasted Warbler *Euryptila subcinnamomea*

Old World Warblers Sylviidae
Chestnut-headed Tesia *Tesia castaneocoronata*
Javan Tesia *Tesia superciliaris*
Slaty-bellied Tesia *Tesia olivea*
Gray-bellied Tesia *Tesia cyaniventer*
Russet-capped Tesia *Tesia everetti*
Timor Stubtail *Urosphena subulata*
Bornean Stubtail *Urosphena whiteheadi*
Asian Stubtail *Urosphena squameiceps*
Manchurian Bush-Warbler *Cettia canturians*
Pale-footed Bush-Warbler *Cettia pallidipes*
Japanese Bush-Warbler *Cettia diphone*
Philippine Bush-Warbler *Cettia seebohmi*
Palau Bush-Warbler *Cettia annae*
Shade Warbler *Cettia parens*
Fiji Bush-Warbler *Cettia ruficapilla*
Tanimbar Bush-Warbler *Cettia carolinae*
Brown-flanked Bush-Warbler *Cettia fortipes*
Sunda Bush-Warbler *Cettia vulcania*
Chestnut-crowned Bush-Warbler *Cettia major*
Aberrant Bush-Warbler *Cettia flavolivacea*
Yellow-bellied Bush-Warbler *Cettia acanthizoides*
Gray-sided Bush-Warbler *Cettia brunnifrons*
Cetti's Bush-Warbler *Cettia cetti*
Little Rush Warbler *Bradypterus baboecala*
Dja River Warbler *Bradypterus grandis*
White-winged Scrub-Warbler *Bradypterus carpalis*
Grauer's Swamp-Warbler *Bradypterus graueri* •
Bamboo Warbler *Bradypterus alfredi*
Knysna Scrub-Warbler *Bradypterus sylvaticus*
Cameroon Scrub-Warbler *Bradypterus lopezi*
African Scrub-Warbler *Bradypterus barratti*

Bangwa Forest Warbler *Bradypterus bangwaensis*
Cinnamon Bracken Warbler *Bradypterus cinnamomeus*
Victorin's Scrub-Warbler *Bradypterus victorini*
Spotted Bush-Warbler *Bradypterus thoracicus*
Long-billed Bush-Warbler *Bradypterus major*
Chinese Bush-Warbler *Bradypterus tacsanowskius*
Russet Bush-Warbler *Bradypterus seebohmi*
Brown Bush-Warbler *Bradypterus luteoventris*
Taiwan Bush-Warbler *Bradypterus alishanensis*
Sri Lanka Bush-Warbler *Bradypterus palliseri*
Friendly Bush-Warbler *Bradypterus accentor*
Long-tailed Bush-Warbler *Bradypterus caudatus*
Chestnut-backed Bush-Warbler *Bradypterus castaneus*
Brown Emutail *Dromaeocercus brunneus*
Gray Emutail *Dromaeocercus seebohmi*
Black-headed Rufous Warbler *Bathmocercus cerviniventris*
Black-faced Rufous Warbler *Bathmocercus rufus*
Mrs Moreau's Warbler *Bathmocercus winifredae*
Anjouan Brush-Warbler *Nesillas longicaudata*
Madagascar Brush-Warbler *Nesillas typica*
Comoro Brush-Warbler *Nesillas brevicaudata*
Moheli Brush-Warbler(ss) *Nesillas mariae*
Aldabra Brush-Warbler *Nesillas aldabranus*
Thamnornis Warbler *Thamnornis chloropetoides*
African Moustached Warbler *Melocichla mentalis*
Cape Grassbird *Sphenoeacus afer*
Lanceolated Warbler *Locustella lanceolata*
Common Grasshopper-Warbler *Locustella naevia*
Pallas's Grasshopper-Warbler *Locustella certhiola*
Middendorff's Grasshopper-Warbler *Locustella ochotensis*
Pleske's Grasshopper-Warbler *Locustella pleskei*
Eurasian River Warbler *Locustella fluviatilis*
Savi's Warbler *Locustella luscinioides*
Gray's Grasshopper-Warbler *Locustella fasciolata*
Stepanyan's Grasshopper-Warbler *Locustella amnicola*
Moustached Warbler *Acrocephalus melanopogon*
Aquatic Warbler *Acrocephalus paludicola*
Sedge Warbler *Acrocephalus schoenobaenus*
Streaked Reed-Warbler *Acrocephalus sorghophilus*
Black-browed Reed-Warbler *Acrocephalus bistrigiceps*
Paddyfield Warbler *Acrocephalus agricola*
Blunt-winged Warbler *Acrocephalus concinens*
Eurasian Reed-Warbler *Acrocephalus scirpaceus*
South African Reed-Warbler *Acrocephalus baeticatus*
Blyth's Reed-Warbler *Acrocephalus dumetorum*
European Marsh Warbler *Acrocephalus palustris*
Great Reed-Warbler *Acrocephalus arundinaceus*
Oriental Great Reed-Warbler *Acrocephalus orientalis*
Clamorous Reed-Warbler *Acrocephalus stentoreus*
Large-billed Reed-Warbler *Acrocephalus orinus*
Basra Reed-Warbler *Acrocephalus griseldis* •
Australian Reed-Warbler *Acrocephalus australis*
Nightingale Reed-Warbler *Acrocephalus luscinius* •
Caroline Reed-Warbler *Acrocephalus syrinx*
Nauru Reed-Warbler *Acrocephalus rehsei*
Laysan Millerbird *Acrocephalus familiaris* •
Polynesian Reed-Warbler *Acrocephalus aequinoctialis*
Long-billed Reed-Warbler *Acrocephalus caffer*
Tuamotu Reed-Warbler *Acrocephalus atyphus*
Rimatara Reed-Warbler *Acrocephalus rimitarae*
Pitcairn Reed-Warbler *Acrocephalus vaughani*
Henderson Island Reed-Warbler *Acrocephalus taiti*
Marquesan Reed-Warbler *Acrocephalus mendanae*
Cook Islands Reed-Warbler *Acrocephalus kerearako*
Greater Swamp-Warbler *Acrocephalus rufescens*
Cape Verde Islands Warbler *Acrocephalus brevipennis* •
Lesser Swamp-Warbler *Acrocephalus gracilirostris*
Madagascar Swamp-Warbler *Acrocephalus newtoni*
Thick-billed Warbler *Acrocephalus aedon*
Rodriguez Brush-Warbler *Acrocephalus rodericanus* •

Seychelles Brush-Warbler *Acrocephalus sechellensis*
Booted Warbler *Hippolais caligata*
Sykes's Warbler *Hippolais rama*
Western Olivaceous Warbler *Hippolais opaca*
Eastern Olivaceous Warbler *Hippolais pallida*
‹pcher's Warbler *Hippolais languida*
Olive-tree Warbler *Hippolais olivetorum*
Melodious Warbler *Hippolais polyglotta*
Icterine Warbler *Hippolais icterina*
African Yellow Warbler *Chloropeta natalensis*
Mountain Yellow Warbler *Chloropeta similis*
Papyrus Yellow Warbler *Chloropeta gracilirostris*
Buff-bellied Warbler *Phyllolais pulchella*
African Tailorbird *Orthotomus metopias*
Long-billed Tailorbird *Orthotomus moreaui* •
Mountain Tailorbird *Orthotomus cuculatus*
Common Tailorbird *Orthotomus sutorius*
Rufous-headed Tailorbird *Orthotomus heterolaemus*
Dark-necked Tailorbird *Orthotomus atrogularis*
Philippine Tailorbird *Orthotomus castaneiceps*
Rufous-fronted Tailorbird *Orthotomus frontalis*
Gray-backed Tailorbird *Orthotomus derbianus*
Rufous-tailed Tailorbird *Orthotomus sericeus*
Ashy Tailorbird *Orthotomus ruficeps*
Olive-backed Tailorbird *Orthotomus sepium*
Yellow-breasted Tailorbird *Orthotomus samarensis*
Black-headed Tailorbird *Orthotomus nigriceps*
White-eared Tailorbird *Orthotomus cinereiceps*
White-tailed Warbler *Poliolais lopezi*
Grauer's Warbler *Graueria vittata*
Salvadori's Eremomela *Eremomela salvadorii*
Yellow-vented Eremomela *Eremomela flavicrissalis*
Yellow-bellied Eremomela *Eremomela icteropygialis*
Smaller Green-backed Eremomela *Eremomela pusilla*
Green-backed Eremomela *Eremomela canescens*
Green-capped Eremomela *Eremomela scotops*
Karoo Green Eremomela *Eremomela gregalis*
Rufous-crowned Eremomela *Eremomela badiceps*
Turner's Eremomela *Eremomela turneri* •
Black-necked Eremomela *Eremomela atricollis*
Burnt-necked Eremomela *Eremomela usticollis*
Rand's Warbler *Randia pseudozosterops*
Dark Newtonia *Newtonia amphichroa*
Common Newtonia *Newtonia brunneicauda*
Archbold's Newtonia *Newtonia archboldi*
Red-tailed Newtonia *Newtonia fanovanae*
Cryptic Warbler *Cryptosylvicola randriansoloi*
Green Crombec *Sylvietta virens*
Lemon-bellied Crombec *Sylvietta denti*
White-browed Crombec *Sylvietta leucophrys*
Northern Crombec *Sylvietta brachyura*
Somali Short-billed Crombec *Sylvietta philippae*
Red-capped Crombec *Sylvietta ruficapilla*
Red-faced Crombec *Sylvietta whytii*
Somali Long-billed Crombec *Sylvietta isabellina*
Long-billed Crombec *Sylvietta rufescens*
Neumann's Warbler *Hemitesia neumanni*
Kemp's Longbill *Macrosphenus kempi*
Yellow Longbill *Macrosphenus flavicans*
Gray Longbill *Macrosphenus concolor*
Pulitzer's Longbill *Macrosphenus pulitzeri* •
Kretschmer's Longbill *Macrosphenus kretschmeri*
São Tomé Shorttail *Amaurocichla bocagei*
Green Hylia *Hylia prasina*
White-browed Tit-Warbler *Leptopoecile sophiae*
Crested Tit-Warbler *Leptopoecile elegans*
Red-faced Woodland-Warbler *Phylloscopus laetus*
Laura's Woodland-Warbler *Phylloscopus laurae*
Yellow-throated Woodland-Warbler *Phylloscopus ruficapilla*
Uganda Woodland-Warbler *Phylloscopus budongoensis*
Brown Woodland-Warbler *Phylloscopus umbrovirens*
Black-capped Woodland-Warbler *Phylloscopus herberti*

Willow-Warbler *Phylloscopus trochilus*
Canary Islands Chiffchaff *Phylloscopus canariensis*
Common Chiffchaff *Phylloscopus collybita*
Iberian Chiffchaff *Phylloscopus ibericus*
Mountain Chiffchaff *Phylloscopus sindianus*
Plain Leaf-Warbler *Phylloscopus neglectus*
Eastern Bonelli's Warbler *Phylloscopus bonelli*
Western Bonelli's Warbler *Phylloscopus orientalis*
Wood Warbler *Phylloscopus sibilatrix*
Dusky Warbler *Phylloscopus fuscatus*
Smoky Warbler *Phylloscopus fuliginventer*
Tickell's Leaf-Warbler *Phylloscopus affinis*
Buff-throated Warbler *Phylloscopus subaffinis*
Sulfur-bellied Warbler *Phylloscopus griseolus*
Yellow-streaked Leaf-Warbler *Phylloscopus armandii*
Radde's Warbler *Phylloscopus schwarzi*
Buff-barred Warbler *Phylloscopus pulcher*
Ashy-throated Leaf-Warbler *Phylloscopus maculipennis*
Pallas's Leaf-Warbler *Phylloscopus proregulus*
Kansu Leaf-Warbler *Phylloscopus kansuensis*
Lemon-rumped Warbler *Phylloscopus chloronotus*
Sichuan Leaf-Warbler *Phylloscopus forresti*
Chinese Leaf-Warbler *Phylloscopus yunnanensis*
Brooks's Leaf-Warbler *Phylloscopus subviridis*
Yellow-browed Leaf-Warbler *Phylloscopus inornatus*
Hume's Leaf-Warbler *Phylloscopus humei*
Arctic Warbler *Phylloscopus borealis*
Greenish Warbler *Phylloscopus trochiloides*
Pale-legged Leaf-Warbler *Phylloscopus tenellipes*
Sakhalin Leaf-Warbler *Phylloscopus borealoides*
Large-billed Leaf-Warbler *Phylloscopus magnirostris*
Tytler's Leaf-Warbler *Phylloscopus tytleri*
Western Crowned Leaf-Warbler *Phylloscopus occipitalis*
Eastern Crowned Leaf-Warbler *Phylloscopus coronatus*
Ijima's Leaf-Warbler *Phylloscopus ijimae*
Blyth's Leaf-Warbler *Phylloscopus reguloides*
Hainan Leaf-Warbler *Phylloscopus hainanus*
Emei Leaf-Warbler *Phylloscopus emeiensis*
White-tailed Leaf-Warbler *Phylloscopus davisoni*
Yellow-vented Warbler *Phylloscopus cantator*
Sulfur-breasted Warbler *Phylloscopus ricketti*
Lemon-throated Leaf-Warbler *Phylloscopus cebuensis*
Mountain Leaf-Warbler *Phylloscopus trivirgatus*
Sulawesi Leaf-Warbler *Phylloscopus sarasinorum*
Timor Leaf-Warbler *Phylloscopus presbytes*
Island Leaf-Warbler *Phylloscopus poliocephalus*
Philippine Leaf-Warbler *Phylloscopus olivaceus*
San Cristobal Leaf-Warbler *Phylloscopus makirensis*
Kulambangra Leaf-Warbler *Phylloscopus amoenus*
Golden-spectacled Warbler *Seicercus burkii*
Gray-crowned Warbler *Seicercus tephrocephalus*
Eastern Golden Spectacled Warbler *Seicercus soror*
Whistler's Warbler *Seicercus whistleri*
Bianchi's Warbler *Seicercus valentini*
Gray-hooded Warbler *Seicercus xanthoschistos*
White-spectacled Warbler *Seicercus affinis*
Gray-cheeked Warbler *Seicercus poliogenys*
Chestnut-crowned Warbler *Seicercus castaniceps*
Yellow-breasted Warbler *Seicercus montis*
Sunda Warbler *Seicercus grammiceps*
Rufous-faced Warbler *Abroscopus albogularis*
Yellow-bellied Warbler *Abroscopus superciliaris*
Black-faced Warbler *Abroscopus schisticeps*
Broad-billed Warbler *Tickellia hodgsoni*
Yellow-bellied Hyliota *Hyliota flavigaster*
Southern Yellow-bellied Hyliota *Hyliota australis*
Usambara Hyliota *Hyliota usambarae* •
Violet-backed Hyliota *Hyliota violacea*
Japanese Swamp-Warbler *Megalurus pryeri*
Tawny Grassbird *Megalurus timoriensis*
Little Grassbird *Megalurus gramineus*

Striated Grassbird *Megalurus palustris*
Fly River Grassbird *Megalurus albolimbatus*
New Zealand Fernbird *Megalurus punctatus*
Brown Songlark *Cincloramphus cruralis*
Rufous Songlark *Cincloramphus mathewsi*
Spinifexbird *Eremiornis carteri*
Buff-banded Grassbird *Buettikoferella bivittata*
New Caledonian Grassbird *Megalurulus mariei*
Bismarck Thicketbird *Megalurulus grosvenori*
Bougainville Thicketbird *Megalurulus llaneae*
Guadalcanal Thicketbird *Megalurulus whitneyi*
Rusty Thicketbird *Megalurulus rubiginosus*
Long-legged Thicketbird *Trichocichla rufa* •
Bristled Grassbird *Chaetornis striata*
Rufous-rumped Grassbird *Graminicola bengalensis*
Broad-tailed Grassbird *Schoenicola platyurus*
Fan-tailed Grassbird *Schoenicola brevirostris*
Wrentit *Chamaea fasciata*
Yemen Warbler *Sylvia buryi*
Blackcap *Sylvia atricapilla*
Garden Warbler *Sylvia borin*
Barred Warbler *Sylvia nisoria*
Desert Lesser Whitethroat *Sylvia minula*
Margelanic Lesser Whitethroat *Sylvia margelanica*
Hume's Lesser Whitethroat *Sylvia althaea*
Western Orphean Warbler *Sylvia hortensis*
Eastern Orphean Warbler *Sylvia crassirostris*
Desert Warbler *Sylvia nana*
Common Whitethroat *Sylvia communis*
Lesser Whitethroat *Sylvia curruca*
African Desert Warbler *Sylvia deserti*
Arabian Warbler *Sylvia leucomelaena*
Cyprus Warbler *Sylvia melanothorax*
Ménétries' Warbler *Sylvia mystacea*
Spectacled Warbler *Sylvia conspicillata*
Tristram's Warbler *Sylvia deserticola*
Dartford Warbler *Sylvia undata*
Marmora's Warbler *Sylvia sarda*
Balearic Warbler *Sylvia balearica*
Rueppell's Warbler *Sylvia rueppelli*
Subalpine Warbler *Sylvia cantillans*
Sardinian Warbler *Sylvia melanocephala*
Layard's Tit-Warbler *Parisoma layardi*
Southern Tit-Warbler *Parisoma subcaeruleum*
Brown Sylvia *Parisoma lugens*
Banded Tit-Warbler *Parisoma boehmi*

Gnatcatchers Polioptilidae
Collared Gnatwren *Microbates collaris*
Tawny-faced Gnatwren *Microbates cinereiventris*
Straight-billed Gnatwren *Ramphocaenus melanurus*
Blue-gray Gnatcatcher *Polioptila caerulea*
Cuban Gnatcatcher *Polioptila lembeyei*
California Gnatcatcher *Polioptila californica*
Black-tailed Gnatcatcher *Polioptila melanura*
Iquitos Gnatcatcher *Polioptila clementsi*
Black-capped Gnatcatcher *Polioptila nigriceps*
White-lored Gnatcatcher *Polioptila albiloris*
Guianan Gnatcatcher *Polioptila guianensis*
Tropical Gnatcatcher *Polioptila plumbea*
Creamy-bellied Gnatcatcher *Polioptila lactea*
Slate-throated Gnatcatcher *Polioptila schistaceigula*
Masked Gnatcatcher *Polioptila dumicola*

Old World Flycatchers Muscicapidae
Silverbird *Empidornis semipartitus*
Pale Flycatcher *Bradornis pallidus*
Chat Flycatcher *Bradornis infuscatus*
Marico Flycatcher *Bradornis mariquensis*
African Gray Flycatcher *Bradornis microrhynchus*
Angolan Slaty Flycatcher *Melaenornis brunneus*
White-eyed Slaty Flycatcher *Melaenornis fischeri*
Abyssinian Slaty Flycatcher *Melaenornis chocolatinus*
Northern Black-Flycatcher *Melaenornis edolioides*

Southern Black-Flycatcher *Melaenornis pammelaina*
Yellow-eyed Black-Flycatcher *Melaenornis ardesiacus*
Nimba Flycatcher *Melaenornis annamarulae*
African Forest-Flycatcher *Fraseria ocreata*
White-browed Forest-Flycatcher *Fraseria cinerascens*
Fiscal Flycatcher *Sigelus silens*
Streaky-breasted Jungle-Flycatcher *Rhinomyias additus*
Russet-backed Jungle-Flycatcher *Rhinomyias oscillans*
Brown-chested Jungle-Flycatcher *Rhinomyias brunneatus*
Gray-chested Jungle-Flycatcher *Rhinomyias umbratilis*
Fulvous-chested Jungle-Flycatcher *Rhinomyias olivaceus*
Rufous-tailed Jungle-Flycatcher *Rhinomyias ruficauda*
Henna-tailed Jungle-Flycatcher *Rhinomyias colonus*
Eyebrowed Jungle-Flycatcher *Rhinomyias gularis*
White-browed Jungle-Flycatcher *Rhinomyias insignis*
White-throated Jungle-Flycatcher *Rhinomyias albigularis* •
Slaty-backed Jungle-Flycatcher *Rhinomyias goodfellowi*
Spotted Flycatcher *Muscicapa striata*
Gambaga Flycatcher *Muscicapa gambagae*
Gray-streaked Flycatcher *Muscicapa griseisticta*
Siberian Flycatcher *Muscicapa sibirica*
Asian Brown Flycatcher *Muscicapa dauurica*
Brown-streaked Flycatcher *Muscicapa williamsoni*
Ashy-breasted Flycatcher *Muscicapa randi*
Sumba Brown Flycatcher *Muscicapa segregata*
Rusty-tailed Flycatcher *Muscicapa ruficauda*
Brown-breasted Flycatcher *Muscicapa muttui*
Ferruginous Flycatcher *Muscicapa ferruginea*
Ussher's Flycatcher *Muscicapa ussheri*
African Sooty Flycatcher *Muscicapa infuscata*
Bôhm's Flycatcher *Muscicapa boehmi*
Swamp Flycatcher *Muscicapa aquatica*
Olivaceous Flycatcher *Muscicapa olivascens*
Chapin's Flycatcher *Muscicapa lendu*
African Dusky Flycatcher *Muscicapa adusta*
Little Gray Flycatcher *Muscicapa epulata*
Yellow-footed Flycatcher *Muscicapa sethsmithi*
Dusky Blue-Flycatcher *Muscicapa comitata*
Tessmann's Flycatcher *Muscicapa tessmanni*
Cassin's Flycatcher *Muscicapa cassini*
Ashy Flycatcher *Muscicapa caerulescens*
Gray-throated Tit-Flycatcher *Myioparus griseigularis*
Gray Tit-Flycatcher *Myioparus plumbeus*
Fairy Warbler *Stenostira scita*
Grand Comoro Flycatcher *Humblotia flavirostris* •
European Pied Flycatcher *Ficedula hypoleuca*
Atlas Pied Flycatcher *Ficedula speculigera*
Collared Flycatcher *Ficedula albicollis*
Semi-collared Flycatcher *Ficedula semitorquata*
Yellow-rumped Flycatcher *Ficedula zanthopygia*
Narcissus Flycatcher *Ficedula narcissina*
Beijing Flycatcher *Ficedula beijingnica*
Mugimaki Flycatcher *Ficedula mugimaki*
Slaty-backed Flycatcher *Ficedula hodgsonii*
Rufous-gorgeted Flycatcher *Ficedula strophiata*
Red-breasted Flycatcher *Ficedula parva*
Taiga Flycatcher *Ficedula albicilla*
Kashmir Flycatcher *Ficedula subrubra*
Snowy-browed Flycatcher *Ficedula hyperythra*
White-gorgeted Flycatcher *Ficedula monileger*
Rufous-browed Flycatcher *Ficedula solitaris*
Rufous-chested Flycatcher *Ficedula dumetoria*
Rufous-throated Flycatcher *Ficedula rufigula*
Cinnamon-chested Flycatcher *Ficedula buruensis*
Little Slaty Flycatcher *Ficedula basilanica*
Damar Flycatcher *Ficedula henrici*
Sumba Flycatcher *Ficedula harterti*
Palawan Flycatcher *Ficedula platenae*
Cryptic Flycatcher *Ficedula crypta*
Furtive Flycatcher *Ficedula disposita*
Lompobatang Flycatcher *Ficedula bonthaina* •

Little Pied Flycatcher *Ficedula westermanni*
Ultramarine Flycatcher *Ficedula superciliaris*
Slaty-blue Flycatcher *Ficedula tricolor*
Black-and-orange Flycatcher *Ficedula nigrorufa*
Sapphire Flycatcher *Ficedula sapphira*
Black-banded Flycatcher *Ficedula timorensis*
Blue-and-white Flycatcher *Cyanoptila cyanomelana*
Verditer Flycatcher *Eumyias thalassinus*
Dull Blue-Flycatcher *Eumyias sordidus*
Island Flycatcher *Eumyias panayensis*
Nilgiri Flycatcher *Eumyias albicaudatus*
Indigo Flycatcher *Eumyias indigo*
Large Niltava *Niltava grandis*
Small Niltava *Niltava macgrigoriae*
Fujian Niltava *Niltava davidi*
Rufous-bellied Niltava *Niltava sundara*
Rufous-vented Niltava *Niltava sumatrana*
Vivid Niltava *Niltava vivida*
Matinan Blue-Flycatcher *Cyornis sanfordi* •
Blue-fronted Blue-Flycatcher *Cyornis hoevelli*
Timor Blue-Flycatcher *Cyornis hyacinthinus*
White-tailed Flycatcher *Cyornis concretus*
Rueck's Blue-Flycatcher *Cyornis ruckii* •
Blue-breasted Flycatcher *Cyornis herioti*
Hainan Blue-Flycatcher *Cyornis hainanus*
White-bellied Blue-Flycatcher *Cyornis pallipes*
Pale-chinned Blue-Flycatcher *Cyornis poliogenys*
Pale Blue-Flycatcher *Cyornis unicolor*
Blue-throated Flycatcher *Cyornis rubeculoides*
Hill Blue-Flycatcher *Cyornis banyumas*
Large-billed Blue-Flycatcher *Cyornis caerulatus*
Malaysian Blue-Flycatcher *Cyornis turcosus*
Palawan Blue-Flycatcher *Cyornis lemprieri*
Bornean Blue-Flycatcher *Cyornis superbus*
Tickell's Blue-Flycatcher *Cyornis tickelliae*
Mangrove Blue-Flycatcher *Cyornis rufigastra*
Sulawesi Blue-Flycatcher *Cyornis omissus*
Pygmy Blue-Flycatcher *Muscicapella hodgsoni*
Gray-headed Canary Flycatcher *Culicicapa ceylonensis*
Citrine Canary Flycatcher *Culicicapa helianthea*
White-starred Bush-Robin *Pogonocichla stellata*
Swynnerton's Bush-Robin *Swynnertonia swynnertoni*
Forest-Robin *Stiphrornis erythrothorax*
Bocage's Akalat *Sheppardia bocagei*
Whiskered Akalat *Sheppardia cyornithopsis*
Equatorial Akalat *Sheppardia aequatorialis*
Sharpe's Akalat *Sheppardia sharpei*
East Coast Akalat *Sheppardia gunningi*
Gabela Akalat *Sheppardia gabela* •
Usambara Akalat *Sheppardia montana* •
Iringa Akalat *Sheppardia lowei*
Rubeho Akalat *Sheppardia aurantiithorax*
European Robin *Erithacus rubecula*
Japanese Robin *Erithacus akahige*
Ryukyu Robin *Erithacus komadori*
Rufous-tailed Robin *Luscinia sibilans*
Thrush Nightingale *Luscinia luscinia*
Rufous Nightingale *Luscinia megarhynchos*
Siberian Rubythroat *Luscinia calliope*
White-tailed Rubythroat *Luscinia pectoralis*
Bluethroat *Luscinia svecica*
Rufous-headed Robin *Luscinia ruficeps*
Blackthroat *Luscinia obscura*
Firethroat *Luscinia pectardens*
Indian Blue Robin *Luscinia brunnea*
Siberian Blue Robin *Luscinia cyane*
Red-flanked Bluetail *Tarsiger cyanurus*
Golden Bush-Robin *Tarsiger chrysaeus*
White-browed Bush-Robin *Tarsiger indicus*
Rufous-breasted Bush-Robin *Tarsiger hyperythrus*
Collared Bush-Robin *Tarsiger johnstoniae*
White-throated Robin *Irania gutturalis*
White-bellied Robinchat *Cossyphicula roberti*
Mountain Robinchat *Cossypha isabellae*

Archer's Robinchat *Cossypha archeri*
Olive-flanked Robinchat *Cossypha anomala*
Cape Robinchat *Cossypha caffra*
White-throated Robinchat *Cossypha humeralis*
Blue-shouldered Robinchat *Cossypha cyanocampter*
Gray-winged Akalat *Cossypha polioptera*
Rueppell's Robinchat *Cossypha semirufa*
White-browed Robinchat *Cossypha heuglini*
Red-capped Robinchat *Cossypha natalensis*
Chorister Robinchat *Cossypha dichroa*
White-headed Robinchat *Cossypha heinrichi*
Snowy-headed Robinchat *Cossypha niveicapilla*
White-crowned Robinchat *Cossypha albicapilla*
Angola Cave-Chat *Xenocopsychus ansorgei*
Collared Palm Thrush *Cichladusa arquata*
Rufous-tailed Palm Thrush *Cichladusa ruficauda*
Spotted Palm Thrush *Cichladusa guttata*
Forest Scrub-Robin *Cercotrichas leucosticta*
Eastern Bearded Scrub-Robin *Cercotrichas quadrivirgata*
Miombo Bearded Scrub-Robin *Cercotrichas barbata*
Brown Scrub-Robin *Cercotrichas signata*
Brown-backed Scrub-Robin *Cercotrichas hartlaubi*
White-browed Scrub-Robin *Cercotrichas leucophrys*
Rufous-tailed Scrub-Robin *Cercotrichas galactotes*
Kalahari Scrub-Robin *Cercotrichas paena*
African Scrub-Robin *Cercotrichas minor*
Karoo Scrub-Robin *Cercotrichas coryphaeus*
Black Scrub-Robin *Cercotrichas podobe*
Herero Chat *Namibornis herero*
Madagascar Magpie-Robin *Copsychus albospecularis*
Oriental Magpie-Robin *Copsychus saularis*
White-rumped Shama *Copsychus malabaricus*
Seychelles Magpie-Robin *Copsychus sechellarum* •
White-crowned Shama *Copsychus stricklandii*
White-browed Shama *Copsychus luzoniensis*
White-vented Shama *Copsychus niger*
Black Shama *Copsychus cebuensis* •
Rufous-tailed Shama *Trichixos pyrropygus*
Indian Robin *Saxicoloides fulicatus*
Ala Shan Redstart *Phoenicurus alaschanicus*
Eversmann's Redstart *Phoenicurus erythronotus*
Blue-capped Redstart *Phoenicurus caeruleocephala*
Black Redstart *Phoenicurus ochruros*
Eurasian Redstart *Phoenicurus phoenicurus*
Hodgson's Redstart *Phoenicurus hodgsoni*
White-throated Redstart *Phoenicurus schisticeps*
Daurian Redstart *Phoenicurus auroreus*
Moussier's Redstart *Phoenicurus moussieri*
Güldenstadt's Redstart *Phoenicurus erythrogastrus*
Blue-fronted Redstart *Phoenicurus frontalis*
White-capped Water-Redstart *Chaimarrornis leucocephalus*
Plumbeous Water-Redstart *Rhyacornis fuliginosa*
Luzon Water-Redstart *Rhyacornis bicolor*
White-bellied Redstart *Hodgsonius phaenicuroides*
White-tailed Robin *Cinclidium leucurum*
Sunda Robin *Cinclidium diana*
Blue-fronted Robin *Cinclidium frontale*
Grandala *Grandala coelicolor*
Little Forktail *Enicurus scouleri*
Sunda Forktail *Enicurus velatus*
Chestnut-naped Forktail *Enicurus ruficapillus*
Black-backed Forktail *Enicurus immaculatus*
Slaty-backed Forktail *Enicurus schistaceus*
White-crowned Forktail *Enicurus leschenaulti*
Spotted Forktail *Enicurus maculatus*
Purple Cochoa *Cochoa purpurea*
Green Cochoa *Cochoa viridis*
Sumatran Cochoa *Cochoa beccarii*
Javan Cochoa *Cochoa azurea*
Whinchat *Saxicola rubetra*
Stoliczka's Bushchat *Saxicola macrorhynchus*
Hodgson's Bushchat *Saxicola insignis*

Fuerteventura Chat *Saxicola dacotiae* •
Common Stonechat *Saxicola rubicola*
Siberian Stonechat *Saxicola maurus*
African Stonechat *Saxicola torquatus*
Réunion Stonechat *Saxicola tectes*
White-tailed Stonechat *Saxicola leucurus*
Pied Stonechat *Saxicola caprata*
Jerdon's Bushchat *Saxicola jerdoni*
Gray Bushchat *Saxicola ferreus*
White-bellied Bushchat *Saxicola gutturalis*
Buff-streaked Chat *Saxicola bifasciatus*
White-crowned Black Wheatear *Oenanthe leucopyga*
Hooded Wheatear *Oenanthe monacha*
Hume's Wheatear *Oenanthe albonigra*
Black Wheatear *Oenanthe leucura*
Mountain Wheatear *Oenanthe monticola*
Somali Wheatear *Oenanthe phillipsi*
Northern Wheatear *Oenanthe oenanthe*
Mourning Wheatear *Oenanthe lugens*
Finsch's Wheatear *Oenanthe finschii*
Variable Wheatear *Oenanthe picata*
Red-rumped Wheatear *Oenanthe moesta*
Pied Wheatear *Oenanthe pleschanka*
Cyprus Pied Wheatear *Oenanthe cypriaca*
Black-eared Wheatear *Oenanthe hispanica*
Red-tailed Wheatear *Oenanthe xanthoprymna*
Desert Wheatear *Oenanthe deserti*
Capped Wheatear *Oenanthe pileata*
Isabelline Wheatear *Oenanthe isabellina*
Red-breasted Wheatear *Oenanthe bottae*
Heuglin's Wheatear *Oenanthe heuglini*
Sicklewinged Chat *Cercomela sinuata*
Karoo Chat *Cercomela schlegelii*
Tractrac Chat *Cercomela tractrac*
Red-tailed Chat *Cercomela familiaris*
Brown-tailed Chat *Cercomela scotocerca*
Brown Rockchat *Cercomela fusca*
Sombre Rockchat *Cercomela dubia*
Blackstart *Cercomela melanura*
Alpine Chat *Cercomela sordida*
Congo Moorchat *Myrmecocichla tholloni*
Northern Anteater Chat *Myrmecocichla aethiops*
Southern Anteater Chat *Myrmecocichla formicivora*
Sooty Chat *Myrmecocichla nigra*
Rueppell's Chat *Myrmecocichla melaena*
White-fronted Blackchat *Myrmecocichla albifrons*
White-headed Blackchat *Myrmecocichla arnotti*
Mocking Cliffchat *Thamnolaea cinnamomeiventris*
White-winged Cliffchat *Thamnolaea semirufa*
Boulder Chat *Pinarornis plumosus*

Wattle-eyes and Puff-back Flycatchers
Platysteiridae
African Shrike-Flycatcher *Megabyas flammulatus*
Black-and-white Shrike-Flycatcher *Bias musicus*
Ward's Flycatcher *Pseudobias wardi*
Scarlet-spectacled Wattle-eye *Platysteira cyanea*
White-fronted Wattle-eye *Platysteira albifrons*
Black-throated Wattle-eye *Platysteira peltata*
Bamenda Wattle-eye *Platysteira laticincta* •
Chestnut Wattle-eye *Platysteira castanea*
White-spotted Wattle-eye *Platysteira tonsa*
Red-cheeked Wattle-eye *Platysteira blissetti*
Black-necked Wattle-eye *Platysteira chalybea*
Jameson's Wattle-eye *Platysteira jamesoni*
Yellow-bellied Wattle-eye *Platysteira concreta*
Margaret's Batis *Batis margaritae*
Forest Batis *Batis mixta*
Ruwenzori Batis *Batis diops*
Cape Batis *Batis capensis*
Woodwards's Batis *Batis fratrum*
Chinspot Batis *Batis molitor*
Pale Batis *Batis soror*
Pririt Batis *Batis pririt*

Senegal Batis *Batis senegalensis*
Gray-headed Batis *Batis orientalis*
Black-headed Batis *Batis minor*
Pygmy Batis *Batis perkeo*
Verreaux's Batis *Batis minima*
Ituri Batis *Batis ituriensis*
Fernando Po Batis *Batis poensis*
West African Batis *Batis occulta*
Angola Batis *Batis minulla*
White-tailed Shrike *Lanioturdus torquatus*

Fantails Rhipiduridae
Yellow-bellied Fantail *Rhipidura hypoxantha*
Blue Fantail *Rhipidura superciliaris*
Blue-headed Fantail *Rhipidura cyaniceps*
Rufous-tailed Fantail *Rhipidura phoenicura*
Black-and-cinnamon Fantail *Rhipidura nigrocinnamomea*
White-throated Fantail *Rhipidura albicollis*
Spot-breasted Fantail *Rhipidura albogularis*
White-bellied Fantail *Rhipidura euryura*
White-browed Fantail *Rhipidura aureola*
Northern Fantail *Rhipidura rufiventris*
Pied Fantail *Rhipidura javanica*
Spotted Fantail *Rhipidura perlata*
Willie Wagtail *Rhipidura leucophrys*
Brown-capped Fantail *Rhipidura diluta*
Cinnamon-tailed Fantail *Rhipidura fuscorufa*
Cockerell's Fantail *Rhipidura cockerelli*
Friendly Fantail *Rhipidura albolimbata*
Chestnut-bellied Fantail *Rhipidura hyperythra*
Sooty Thicket-Fantail *Rhipidura threnothorax*
Black Thicket-Fantail *Rhipidura maculipectus*
White-bellied Thicket-Fantail *Rhipidura leucothorax*
Black Fantail *Rhipidura atra*
Mangrove Fantail *Rhipidura phasiana*
Brown Fantail *Rhipidura drownei*
Dusky Fantail *Rhipidura tenebrosa*
Rennell Fantail *Rhipidura rennelliana*
Gray Fantail *Rhipidura albiscapa*
New Zealand Fantail *Rhipidura fuliginosa*
Streaked Fantail *Rhipidura spilodera*
Kandavu Fantail *Rhipidura personata*
Samoan Fantail *Rhipidura nebulosa*
Dimorphic Rufous Fantail *Rhipidura brachyrhyncha*
Rusty-bellied Fantail *Rhipidura teysmanni*
Tawny-backed Fantail *Rhipidura superflua*
Streaky-breasted Fantail *Rhipidura dedemi*
Long-tailed Fantail *Rhipidura opistherythra*
Palau Fantail *Rhipidura lepida*
Gray-breasted Rufous Fantail *Rhipidura rufidorsa*
St Matthias Fantail *Rhipidura matthiae*
New Britain Fantail *Rhipidura dahli*
Malaita Fantail *Rhipidura malaitae*
Manus Fantail *Rhipidura semirubra*
Rufous Fantail *Rhipidura rufifrons*
Arafura Fantail *Rhipidura dryas*
Ponapé Fantail *Rhipidura kubaryi*

Monarchs Monarchidae
Chestnut-capped Flycatcher *Erythrocercus mccallii*
Little Yellow Flycatcher *Erythrocercus holochlorus*
Livingstone's Flycatcher *Erythrocercus livingstonei*
African Blue-Flycatcher *Elminia longicauda*
White-tailed Blue-Flycatcher *Elminia albicauda*
Dusky Crested-Flycatcher *Elminia nigromitrata*
White-bellied Crested-Flycatcher *Elminia albiventris*
White-tailed Crested-Flycatcher *Elminia albonotata*
Blue-headed Crested-Flycatcher *Trochocercus nitens*
African Crested-Flycatcher *Trochocercus cyanomelas*
Short-crested Monarch *Hypothymis helenae*
Black-naped Monarch *Hypothymis azurea*
Pacific Small Monarch *Hypothymis puella*
Celestial Monarch *Hypothymis coelestis*

Cerulean Paradise-Flycatcher *Eutrichomyias rowleyi* •
Red-bellied Paradise-Flycatcher *Terpsiphone rufiventer*
Bedford's Paradise-Flycatcher *Terpsiphone bedfordi*
Rufous-vented Paradise-Flycatcher *Terpsiphone rufocinerea*
Bates's Paradise-Flycatcher *Terpsiphone batesi*
African Paradise-Flycatcher *Terpsiphone viridis*
São Tomé Paradise-Flycatcher *Terpsiphone atrochalybeia*
Madagascar Paradise-Flycatcher *Terpsiphone mutata*
Seychelles Paradise-Flycatcher *Terpsiphone corvina* •
Mascarene Paradise-Flycatcher *Terpsiphone bourbonnensis*
Black Paradise-Flycatcher *Terpsiphone atrocaudata*
Blue Paradise-Flycatcher *Terpsiphone cyanescens*
Rufous Paradise-Flycatcher *Terpsiphone cinnamomea*
Asian Paradise-Flycatcher *Terpsiphone paradisi*
Elepaio *Chasiempis sandwichensis* •
Rarotonga Monarch-Flycatcher *Pomarea dimidiata* •
Tahiti Monarch-Flycatcher *Pomarea nigra* •
Allied Flycatcher *Pomarea iphis*
Marquesas Flycatcher *Pomarea mendozae* •
Large Monarch *Pomarea whitneyi* •
Ogea Monarch *Mayrornis versicolor*
White-tipped Slaty Flycatcher *Mayrornis lessoni*
Small Slaty Monarch *Mayrornis schistaceus*
Buff-bellied Monarch *Neolalage banksiana*
Southern Shrikebill *Clytorhynchus pachycephaloides*
Rennell Shrikebill *Clytorhynchus hamlini*
Fiji Shrikebill *Clytorhynchus vitiensis*
Black-throated Shrikebill *Clytorhynchus nigrogularis*
Truk Monarch *Metabolus rugensis* •
Black Monarch *Monarcha axillaris*
Rufous Monarch *Monarcha rubiensis*
Island Monarch *Monarcha cinerascens*
Black-winged Monarch *Monarcha frater*
Black-faced Monarch *Monarcha melanopsis*
Bougainville Monarch *Monarcha erythrostictus*
Chestnut-bellied Monarch-Flycatcher *Monarcha castaneiventris*
Richards's Monarch *Monarcha richardsii*
White-naped Monarch *Monarcha pileatus*
Loetoe Monarch *Monarcha castus*
White-eared Monarch *Monarcha leucotis*
Spot-winged Monarch *Monarcha guttulus*
Black-bibbed Monarch *Monarcha mundus*
Spectacled Monarch *Monarcha trivirgatus*
Flores Mountain Monarch *Monarcha sacerdotum* •
White-tipped Monarch *Monarcha everetti* •
Black-tipped Monarch *Monarcha loricatus*
Black-chinned Monarch *Monarcha boanensis* •
White-tailed Monarch *Monarcha leucurus*
Kofiau Monarch *Monarcha julianae*
Black-and-white Monarch *Monarcha manadensis*
Biak Monarch *Monarcha brehmii* •
Admiralty Islands Monarch *Monarcha infelix*
White-breasted Monarch *Monarcha menckei*
New Britain Pied Monarch *Monarcha verticalis*
Kulambangra Monarch *Monarcha browni*
San Cristobal Monarch *Monarcha viduus*
Solomon Islands Pied Monarch *Monarcha barbatus*
Yap Island Monarch *Monarcha godeffroyi*
Tinian Island Monarch *Monarcha takatsukasae*
Black-and-yellow Monarch *Monarcha chrysomela*
Australian Frilled Monarch *Arses telescophthalmus*
Frill-necked Monarch *Arses lorealis*
Rufous-collared Monarch *Arses insularis*
Australian Pied Monarch *Arses kaupi*
Mangrove Flycatcher *Myiagra erythrops*
Ponapé Flycatcher *Myiagra pluto*
Micronesian Flycatcher *Myiagra oceanica*
Black Myiagra-Flycatcher *Myiagra atra*
Helmeted Flycatcher *Myiagra galeata*
Leaden Flycatcher *Myiagra rubecula*

Solomons Flycatcher *Myiagra ferrocyanea*
San Cristobal Myiagra-Flycatcher *Myiagra cervinicauda*
Melanesian Flycatcher *Myiagra caledonica*
Vanikoro Flycatcher *Myiagra vanikorensis*
Samoan Flycatcher *Myiagra albiventris*
Blue-crested Flycatcher *Myiagra azureocapilla*
Broad-billed Myiagra *Myiagra ruficollis*
Satin Myiagra-Flycatcher *Myiagra cyanoleuca*
Restless Flycatcher *Myiagra inquieta*
Paperback Flycatcher *Myiagra nana*
Shining Myiagra-Flycatcher *Myiagra alecto*
Dull Flycatcher *Myiagra hebetior*
Silktail *Lamprolia victoriae*
Black-breasted Boatbill *Machaerirhynchus nigripectus*
Yellow-breasted Boatbill *Machaerirhynchus flaviventer*

Australasian Robins Petroicidae
Greater New Guinea Thrush *Amalocichla sclateriana*
Lesser New Guinea Thrush *Amalocichla incerta*
River Flycatcher *Monachella muelleriana*
Jacky Winter *Microeca fascinans*
Tanimbar Microeca Flycatcher *Microeca hemixantha*
Lemon-bellied Flycatcher *Microeca flavigaster*
Yellow-legged Flyrobin *Microeca griseoceps*
Olive Microeca *Microeca flavovirescens*
Papuan Microeca *Microeca papuana*
Garnet Robin *Eugerygone rubra*
Forest Robin-Flycatcher *Petroica bivittata*
Rock Robin-Flycatcher *Petroica archboldi*
Pacific Robin *Petroica multicolor*
New Zealand Tomtit *Petroica macrocephala*
Red-capped Robin *Petroica goodenovii*
Flame Robin-Flycatcher *Petroica phoenicea*
Rose Robin-Flycatcher *Petroica rosea*
Pink Robin-Flycatcher *Petroica rodinogaster*
New Zealand Robin *Petroica australis*
Chatham Islands Robin *Petroica traversi* •
Hooded Robin *Melanodryas cucullata*
Dusky Robin *Melanodryas vittata*
White-faced Robin *Tregellasia leucops*
Pale-yellow Robin *Tregellasia capito*
Eastern Yellow Robin *Eopsaltria australis*
Western Yellow Robin *Eopsaltria griseogularis*
Yellow-bellied Robin *Eopsaltria flaviventris*
White-breasted Robin *Eopsaltria georgiana*
Mangrove Robin *Eopsaltria pulverulenta*
Black-chinned Robin *Poecilodryas brachyura*
Black-sided Robin *Poecilodryas hypoleuca*
White-browed Robin *Poecilodryas superciliosa*
Olive-yellow Robin *Poecilodryas placens*
Black-throated Robin *Poecilodryas albonotata*
White-winged Robin *Peneothello sigillata*
Smoky Robin *Peneothello cryptoleuca*
White-rumped Robin *Peneothello bimaculata*
Blue-gray Robin *Peneothello cyanus*
Gray-headed Robin *Heteromyias albispecularis*
Green-backed Robin *Pachycephalopsis hattamensis*
Eastern White-eyed Robin *Pachycephalopsis poliosoma*
Northern Scrub-Robin *Drymodes superciliaris*
Southern Scrub-Robin *Drymodes brunneopygia*

Whistlers and allies Pachycephalidae
Whitehead *Mohoua albicilla*
Yellowhead *Mohoua ochrocephala* •
New Zealand Brown Creeper *Mohoua novaeseelandiae*
Eastern Shrike-Tit *Falcunculus frontatus*
Crested Bellbird *Oreoica gutturalis*
Mottled Whistler *Rhagologus leucostigma*
Golden-faced Pachycare *Pachycare flavogriseum*
Olive-flanked Whistler *Hylocitrea bonensis*
Maroon-backed Whistler *Coracornis raveni*
Rufous-naped Whistler *Aleadryas rufinucha*

Olive Whistler *Pachycephala olivacea*
Red-lored Whistler *Pachycephala rufogularis*
Gilbert's Whistler *Pachycephala inornata*
Mangrove Whistler *Pachycephala grisola*
Green-backed Whistler *Pachycephala albiventris*
White-vented Whistler *Pachycephala homeyeri*
Island Whistler *Pachycephala phaionota*
Rusty Whistler *Pachycephala hyperythra*
Brown-backed Whistler *Pachycephala modesta*
Bornean Mountain Whistler *Pachycephala hypoxantha*
Sulfur-bellied Whistler *Pachycephala sulfuriventer*
Vogelkop Whistler *Pachycephala meyeri*
Yellow-bellied Whistler *Pachycephala philippinensis*
Gray-headed Whistler *Pachycephala griseiceps*
Fawn-breasted Whistler *Pachycephala orpheus*
Gray Whistler *Pachycephala simplex*
Common Golden Whistler *Pachycephala pectoralis*
Sclater's Whistler *Pachycephala soror*
Lorentz's Whistler *Pachycephala lorentzi*
Mangrove Golden Whistler *Pachycephala melanura*
New Caledonian Whistler *Pachycephala caledonica*
Yellow-fronted Whistler *Pachycephala flavifrons*
Tongan Whistler *Pachycephala jacquinoti*
Schlegel's Whistler *Pachycephala schlegelii*
Bare-throated Whistler *Pachycephala nudigula*
Hooded Whistler *Pachycephala implicata*
Yellow-backed Whistler *Pachycephala aurea*
Drab Whistler *Pachycephala griseonota*
Wallacean Whistler *Pachycephala arctitorquis*
Black-headed Whistler *Pachycephala monacha*
White-bellied Whistler *Pachycephala leucogastra*
Rufous Whistler *Pachycephala rufiventris*
White-breasted Whistler *Pachycephala lanioides*
Sooty Shrike-Thrush *Colluricincla umbrina*
Little Shrike-Thrush *Colluricincla megarhyncha*
Sangihe Shrike-Thrush *Colluricincla sanghirensis* •
Bower's Shrike-Thrush *Colluricincla boweri*
Sandstone Shrike-Thrush *Colluricincla woodwardi*
Gray Shrike-Thrush *Colluricincla harmonica*
Morningbird *Colluricincla tenebrosa*
Hooded Pitohui *Pitohui dichrous*
White-bellied Pitohui *Pitohui incertus*
Rusty Pitohui *Pitohui ferrugineus*
Crested Pitohui *Pitohui cristatus*
Variable Pitohui *Pitohui kirhocephalus*
Black Pitohui *Pitohui nigrescens*
Wattled Shrike-Tit *Eulacestoma nigropectus*

Rockfowl Picathartidae
White-necked Picathartes *Picathartes gymnocephalus*
Gray-necked Picathartes *Picathartes oreas*

Babblers Timaliidae
Malia *Malia grata*
Ashy-headed Laughingthrush *Garrulax cinereifrons*
Sunda Laughingthrush *Garrulax palliatus*
Rufous-fronted Laughingthrush *Garrulax rufifrons*
Masked Laughingthrush *Garrulax perspicillatus*
White-throated Laughingthrush *Garrulax albogularis*
White-crested Laughingthrush *Garrulax leucolophus*
Lesser Necklaced Laughingthrush *Garrulax monileger*
Greater Necklaced Laughingthrush *Garrulax pectoralis*
Black Laughingthrush *Garrulax lugubris*
Striated Laughingthrush *Garrulax striatus*
White-necked Laughingthrush *Garrulax strepitans*
Black-hooded Laughingthrush *Garrulax milleti*
Gray Laughingthrush *Garrulax maesi*
Rufous-necked Laughingthrush *Garrulax ruficollis*
Chestnut-backed Laughingthrush *Garrulax nuchalis*
Black-throated Laughingthrush *Garrulax chinensis*
White-cheeked Laughingthrush *Garrulax vassali*
Yellow-throated Laughingthrush *Garrulax galbanus*
Wynaad Laughingthrush *Garrulax delesserti*

Rufous-vented Laughingthrush *Garrulax gularis*
Plain Laughingthrush *Garrulax davidi*
Snowy-cheeked Laughingthrush *Garrulax sukatschewi*
Moustached Laughingthrush *Garrulax cineraceus*
Rufous-chinned Laughingthrush *Garrulax rufogularis*
Chestnut-eared Laughingthrush *Garrulax konkakinhensis*
Spotted Laughingthrush *Garrulax ocellatus*
Barred Laughingthrush *Garrulax lunulatus*
White-speckled Laughingthrush *Garrulax bieti*
Giant Laughingthrush *Garrulax maximus*
Gray-sided Laughingthrush *Garrulax caerulatus*
Rusty Laughingthrush *Garrulax poecilorhynchus*
Chestnut-capped Laughingthrush *Garrulax mitratus*
Spot-breasted Laughingthrush *Garrulax merulinus*
Hwamei *Garrulax canorus*
White-browed Laughingthrush *Garrulax sannio*
Nilgiri Laughingthrush *Garrulax cachinnans* •
Gray-breasted Laughingthrush *Garrulax jerdoni*
Streaked Laughingthrush *Garrulax lineatus*
Striped Laughingthrush *Garrulax virgatus*
Scaly Laughingthrush *Garrulax subunicolor*
Brown-capped Laughingthrush *Garrulax austeni*
Blue-winged Laughingthrush *Garrulax squamatus*
Elliot's Laughingthrush *Garrulax elliotii*
Variegated Laughingthrush *Garrulax variegatus*
Brown-cheeked Laughingthrush *Garrulax henrici*
Black-faced Laughingthrush *Garrulax affinis*
White-whiskered Laughingthrush *Garrulax morrisonianus*
Chestnut-crowned Laughingthrush *Garrulax erythrocephalus*
Golden-winged Laughingthrush *Garrulax ngoclinhensis*
Collared Laughingthrush *Garrulax yersini* •
Red-winged Laughingthrush *Garrulax formosus*
Red-tailed Laughingthrush *Garrulax milnei*
Mount Omei Shan Liocichla *Liocichla omeiensis*
Steere's Liocichla *Liocichla steerii*
Red-faced Liocichla *Liocichla phoenicea*
Spot-throat *Modulatrix stictigula*
Dappled Mountain Robin *Arcanator orostruthus*
White-chested Jungle-Babbler *Trichastoma rostratum*
Sulawesi Jungle-Babbler *Trichastoma celebense*
Ferruginous Jungle-Babbler *Trichastoma bicolor*
Bagobo Babbler *Trichastoma woodi*
Abbott's Babbler *Malacocincla abbotti*
Horsfield's Babbler *Malacocincla sepiaria*
Short-tailed Babbler *Malacocincla malaccensis*
Ashy-headed Babbler *Malacocincla cinereiceps*
Brown-capped Jungle-Babbler *Pellorneum fuscocapillus*
Marsh Babbler *Pellorneum palustre*
Buff-breasted Babbler *Pellorneum tickelli*
Temminck's Babbler *Pellorneum pyrrogenys*
Spot-throated Babbler *Pellorneum albiventre*
Puff-throated Babbler *Pellorneum ruficeps*
Black-capped Jungle-Babbler *Pellorneum capistratum*
Melodious Babbler *Malacopteron palawanense*
Moustached Tree-Babbler *Malacopteron magnirostre*
Sooty-capped Tree-Babbler *Malacopteron affine*
Scaly-crowned Tree-Babbler *Malacopteron cinereum*
Rufous-crowned Tree-Babbler *Malacopteron magnum*
Gray-breasted Babbler *Malacopteron albogulare*
Damara Rockjumper *Chaetops pycnopygius*
Cape Rockjumper *Chaetops frenatus*
Orange-breasted Rockjumper *Chaetops aurantius*
Blackcapped Illadopsis *Illadopsis cleaveri*
Scaly-breasted Illadopsis *Illadopsis albipectus*
Rufous-winged Illadopsis *Illadopsis rufescens*
Puvel's Illadopsis *Illadopsis puveli*
Pale-breasted Illadopsis *Illadopsis rufipennis*
Brown Illadopsis *Illadopsis fulvescens*
Mountain Illadopsis *Illadopsis pyrrhoptera*
Gray-chested Illadopsis *Kakamega poliothorax*
African Hill Babbler *Pseudoalcippe abyssinica*

Spotted Thrush-Babbler *Ptyrticus turdinus*
Large Scimitar-Babbler *Pomatorhinus hypoleucos*
Spot-breasted Scimitar-Babbler *Pomatorhinus erythrocnemis*
Rusty-cheeked Scimitar-Babbler *Pomatorhinus erythrogenys*
Indian Scimitar-Babbler *Pomatorhinus horsfieldii*
White-browed Scimitar-Babbler *Pomatorhinus schisticeps*
Chestnut-backed Scimitar-Babbler *Pomatorhinus montanus*
Streak-breasted Scimitar-Babbler *Pomatorhinus ruficollis*
Red-billed Scimitar-Babbler *Pomatorhinus ochraceiceps*
Coral-billed Scimitar-Babbler *Pomatorhinus ferruginosus*
Slender-billed Scimitar-Babbler *Xiphirhynchus superciliaris*
Short-tailed Scimitar-Babbler *Jabouilleia danjoui*
Long-billed Wren-Babbler *Rimator malacoptilus*
Bornean Wren-Babbler *Ptilocichla leucogrammica*
Striated Wren-Babbler *Ptilocichla mindanensis*
Falcated Wren-Babbler *Ptilocichla falcata*
Striped Wren-Babbler *Kenopia striata*
Large Wren-Babbler *Napothera macrodactyla*
Rusty-breasted Wren-Babbler *Napothera rufipectus*
Black-throated Wren-Babbler *Napothera atrigularis*
Marbled Wren-Babbler *Napothera marmorata*
Limestone Wren-Babbler *Napothera crispifrons*
Streaked Wren-Babbler *Napothera brevicaudata*
Mountain Wren-Babbler *Napothera crassa*
Rabor's Wren-Babbler *Napothera rabori*
Eyebrowed Wren-Babbler *Napothera epilepidota*
Scaly-breasted Wren-Babbler *Pnoepyga albiventer*
Nepal Wren-Babbler *Pnoepyga immaculata*
Pygmy Wren-Babbler *Pnoepyga pusilla*
Rufous-throated Wren-Babbler *Spelaeornis caudatus*
Rusty-throated Wren-Babbler *Spelaeornis badeigularis*
Bar-winged Wren-Babbler *Spelaeornis troglodytoides*
Spotted Wren-Babbler *Spelaeornis formosus*
Long-tailed Wren-Babbler *Spelaeornis chocolatinus*
Tawny-breasted Wren-Babbler *Spelaeornis longicaudatus*
Wedge-billed Wren-Babbler *Sphenocichla humei*
Madagascar Jery *Neomixis tenella*
Southern Green Jery *Neomixis viridis*
Stripe-throated Jery *Neomixis striatigula*
Wedge-tailed Jery *Hartertula flavoviridis*
Deignan's Babbler *Stachyris rodolphei*
Buff-chested Babbler *Stachyris ambigua*
Rufous-fronted Babbler *Stachyris rufifrons*
Rufous-capped Babbler *Stachyris ruficeps*
Black-chinned Babbler *Stachyris pyrrhops*
Golden Tree-Babbler *Stachyris chrysaea*
Pygmy Tree-Babbler *Stachyris plateni*
Golden-crowned Babbler *Stachyris dennistouni*
Black-crowned Babbler *Stachyris nigrocapitata*
Rusty-crowned Babbler *Stachyris capitalis*
Flame-templed Babbler *Stachyris speciosa* •
Chestnut-faced Babbler *Stachyris whiteheadi*
Luzon Striped Babbler *Stachyris striata*
Panay Striped Babbler *Stachyris latistriata*
Negros Striped Babbler *Stachyris nigrorum* •
Palawan Striped Babbler *Stachyris hypogrammica*
White-breasted Babbler *Stachyris grammiceps*
Sooty Tree-Babbler *Stachyris herberti*
Gray-throated Babbler *Stachyris nigriceps*
Gray-headed Babbler *Stachyris poliocephala*
Snowy-throated Babbler *Stachyris oglei*
Spot-necked Babbler *Stachyris striolata*
White-necked Babbler *Stachyris leucotis*
Black-throated Babbler *Stachyris nigricollis*
White-bibbed Babbler *Stachyris thoracica*
Chestnut-rumped Babbler *Stachyris maculata*
Chestnut-winged Babbler *Stachyris erythroptera*

Crescent-chested Babbler *Stachyris melanothorax*
Tawny-bellied Babbler *Dumetia hyperythra*
Dark-fronted Babbler *Rhopocichla atriceps*
Striped Tit-Babbler *Macronous gularis*
Gray-cheeked Tit-Babbler *Macronous flavicollis*
Gray-faced Tit-Babbler *Macronous kelleyi*
Brown Tit-Babbler *Macronous striaticeps*
Fluffy-backed Tit-Babbler *Macronous ptilosus*
Miniature Tit-Babbler *Micromacronus leytensis*
Red-capped Babbler *Timalia pileata*
Oriental Yellow-eyed Babbler *Chrysomma sinense*
Jerdon's Babbler *Chrysomma altirostre*
Rufous-tailed Babbler *Chrysomma poecilotis*
Spiny Babbler *Turdoides nipalensis*
Iraq Babbler *Turdoides altirostris*
Common Babbler *Turdoides caudata*
Striated Babbler *Turdoides earlei*
White-throated Babbler *Turdoides gularis*
Slender-billed Babbler *Turdoides longirostris*
Large Gray Babbler *Turdoides malcolmi*
Arabian Babbler *Turdoides squamiceps*
Fulvous Babbler *Turdoides fulva*
Scaly Chatterer *Turdoides aylmeri*
Rufous Chatterer *Turdoides rubiginosa*
Rufous Babbler *Turdoides subrufa*
Jungle-Babbler *Turdoides striata*
Orange-billed Babbler *Turdoides rufescens*
White-billed Babbler *Turdoides affinis*
Blackcap Babbler *Turdoides reinwardtii*
Dusky Babbler *Turdoides tenebrosa*
Sharpe's Pied Babbler *Turdoides sharpei*
Angola Babbler *Turdoides hartlaubii*
Black-lored Babbler *Turdoides melanops*
Scaly Babbler *Turdoides squamulata*
White-rumped Babbler *Turdoides leucopygia*
Southern Pied Babbler *Turdoides bicolor*
Northern Pied Babbler *Turdoides hypoleuca*
Hinde's Pied Babbler *Turdoides hindei*
White-headed Babbler *Turdoides leucocephala*
African Brown Babbler *Turdoides plebejus*
Arrow-marked Babbler *Turdoides jardineii*
Bare-cheeked Babbler *Turdoides gymnogenys*
Chinese Babax *Babax lanceolatus*
Giant Babax *Babax waddelli*
Tibetan Babax *Babax koslowi*
Silver-eared Mesia *Leiothrix argentauris*
Red-billed Leiothrix *Leiothrix lutea*
Cutia *Cutia nipalensis*
Black-headed Shrike-Babbler *Pteruthius rufiventer*
White-browed Shrike-Babbler *Pteruthius flaviscapis*
Green Shrike-Babbler *Pteruthius xanthochlorus*
Black-eared Shrike-Babbler *Pteruthius melanotis*
Chestnut-fronted Shrike-Babbler *Pteruthius aenobarbus*
White-hooded Babbler *Gampsorhynchus rufulus*
Rusty-fronted Barwing *Actinodura egertoni*
Spectacled Barwing *Actinodura ramsayi*
Black-crowned Barwing *Actinodura sodangorum*
Hoary-throated Barwing *Actinodura nipalensis*
Streak-throated Barwing *Actinodura waldeni*
Streaked Barwing *Actinodura souliei*
Taiwan Barwing *Actinodura morrisoniana*
Blue-winged Minla *Minla cyanouroptera*
Chestnut-tailed Minla *Minla strigula*
Red-tailed Minla *Minla ignotincta*
Golden-breasted Fulvetta *Alcippe chrysotis*
Gold-fronted Fulvetta *Alcippe variegaticeps*
Yellow-throated Fulvetta *Alcippe cinerea*
Rufous-winged Fulvetta *Alcippe castaneceps*
White-browed Fulvetta *Alcippe vinipectus*
Chinese Fulvetta *Alcippe striaticollis*
Spectacled Fulvetta *Alcippe ruficapilla*
Streak-throated Fulvetta *Alcippe cinereiceps*
Brown-throated Fulvetta *Alcippe ludlowi*
Rufous-throated Fulvetta *Alcippe rufogularis*

Dusky Fulvetta *Alcippe brunnea*
Rusty-capped Fulvetta *Alcippe dubia*
Brown Fulvetta *Alcippe brunneicauda*
Brown-cheeked Fulvetta *Alcippe poioicephala*
Gray-cheeked Fulvetta *Alcippe morrisonia*
Javan Fulvetta *Alcippe pyrrhoptera*
Mountain Fulvetta *Alcippe peracensis*
Nepal Fulvetta *Alcippe nipalensis*
Bush Blackcap *Lioptilus nigricapillus*
White-throated Mountain-Babbler *Kupeornis gilberti* •
Red-collared Mountain-Babbler *Kupeornis rufocinctus*
Chapin's Mountain-Babbler *Kupeornis chapini*
Dôhrn's Thrush-Babbler *Horizorhinus dohrni*
Abyssinian Catbird *Parophasma galinieri*
Capuchin Babbler *Phyllanthus atripennis*
Gray-crowned Crocias *Crocias langbianis* •
Spotted Crocias *Crocias albonotatus*
Rufous-backed Sibia *Heterophasia annectens*
Rufous Sibia *Heterophasia capistrata*
Gray Sibia *Heterophasia gracilis*
Black-backed Sibia *Heterophasia melanoleuca*
Black-eared Sibia *Heterophasia desgodinsi*
White-eared Sibia *Heterophasia auricularis*
Beautiful Sibia *Heterophasia pulchella*
Long-tailed Sibia *Heterophasia picaoides*
Striated Yuhina *Yuhina castaniceps*
Chestnut-crested Yuhina *Yuhina everetti*
White-naped Yuhina *Yuhina bakeri*
Whiskered Yuhina *Yuhina flavicollis*
Burmese Yuhina *Yuhina humilis*
Stripe-throated Yuhina *Yuhina gularis*
White-collared Yuhina *Yuhina diademata*
Rufous-vented Yuhina *Yuhina occipitalis*
Taiwan Yuhina *Yuhina brunneiceps*
Black-chinned Yuhina *Yuhina nigrimenta*
White-bellied Yuhina *Yuhina zantholeuca*
Fire-tailed Myzornis *Myzornis pyrrhoura*
White-throated Oxylabes *Oxylabes madagascariensis*
Yellow-browed Oxylabes *Crossleyia xanthophrys*
Crossley's Babbler *Mystacornis crossleyi*

Pomastomus babblers Pomatostomidae
Isidor's Rufous Babbler *Pomatostomus isidorei*
Gray-crowned Babbler *Pomatostomus temporalis*
White-browed Babbler *Pomatostomus superciliosus*
Hall's Babbler *Pomatostomus halli*
Chestnut-crowned Babbler *Pomatostomus ruficeps*

Parrotbills Paradoxornithidae
Bearded Parrotbill *Panurus biarmicus*
Great Parrotbill *Conostoma oemodium*
Brown Parrotbill *Paradoxornis unicolor*
Gray-headed Parrotbill *Paradoxornis gularis*
Three-toed Parrotbill *Paradoxornis paradoxus*
Black-breasted Parrotbill *Paradoxornis flavirostris*
Spot-breasted Parrotbill *Paradoxornis guttaticollis*
Spectacled Parrotbill *Paradoxornis conspicillatus*
Vinous-throated Parrotbill *Paradoxornis webbianus*
Brown-winged Parrotbill *Paradoxornis brunneus*
Ashy-throated Parrotbill *Paradoxornis alphonsianus*
Gray-hooded Parrotbill *Paradoxornis zappeyi*
Rusty-throated Parrotbill *Paradoxornis przewalskii*
Fulvous Parrotbill *Paradoxornis fulvifrons*
Black-throated Parrotbill *Paradoxornis nipalensis*
Golden Parrotbill *Paradoxornis verreauxi*
Short-tailed Parrotbill *Paradoxornis davidianus*
Black-browed Parrotbill *Paradoxornis atrosu
  perciliaris*
Greater Rufous-headed Parrotbill *Paradoxornis
  ruficeps*
Reed Parrotbill *Paradoxornis heudei*

Logrunners Orthonychidae
Northern Logrunner *Orthonyx novaeguineae*

Southern Logrunner *Orthonyx temminckii*
Spalding's Logrunner *Orthonyx spaldingii*

Whipbirds and quail-thrushes Eupetidae
Papuan Whipbird *Androphobus viridis*
Eastern Whipbird *Psophodes olivaceus*
Western Whipbird *Psophodes nigrogularis*
Chiming Wedgebill *Psophodes occidentalis*
Chirruping Wedgebill *Psophodes cristatus*
Spotted Quail-Thrush *Cinclosoma punctatum*
Chestnut Quail-Thrush *Cinclosoma castanotum*
Chestnut-breasted Quail-Thrush *Cinclosoma
  castaneothorax*
Cinnamon Quail-Thrush *Cinclosoma cinnamomeum*
Ajax Quail-Thrush *Cinclosoma ajax*
Spotted Jewel-Babbler *Ptilorrhoa leucosticta*
Lowland Jewel-Babbler *Ptilorrhoa caerulescens*
Chestnut-backed Jewel-babbler *Ptilorrhoa castanonota*
Malaysian Rail-Babbler *Eupetes macrocerus*
Ifrita *Ifrita kowaldi*

Long-tailed Tits Aegithalidae
Eurasian Long-tailed-Tit *Aegithalos caudatus*
White-cheeked Long-tailed-Tit *Aegithalos leucogenys*
Black-throated Long-tailed-Tit *Aegithalos concinnus*
White-throated Long-tailed-Tit *Aegithalos niveogularis*
Rufous-fronted Long-tailed-Tit *Aegithalos iouschistos*
Sooty Long-tailed-Tit *Aegithalos fuliginosus*
Plain Bushtit *Psaltriparus minimus*
Pygmy Tit *Psaltria exilis*

Fairywrens Maluridae
Orange-crowned Fairywren *Clytomyias insignis*
Wallace's Fairywren *Sipodotus wallacii*
Broad-billed Fairywren *Malurus grayi*
White-shouldered Fairywren *Malurus alboscapulatus*
Red-backed Fairywren *Malurus melanocephalus*
White-winged Fairywren *Malurus leucopterus*
Superb Fairywren *Malurus cyaneus*
Splendid Fairywren *Malurus splendens*
Variegated Fairywren *Malurus lamberti*
Lovely Fairywren *Malurus amabilis*
Red-winged Fairywren *Malurus elegans*
Blue-breasted Fairywren *Malurus pulcherrimus*
Purple-crowned Fairywren *Malurus coronatus*
Emperor Fairywren *Malurus cyanocephalus*
Southern Emuwren *Stipiturus malachurus*
Rufous-crowned Emuwren *Stipiturus ruficeps*
Mallee Emuwren *Stipiturus mallee*
Thick-billed Grasswren *Amytornis textilis*
Dusky Grasswren *Amytornis purnelli*
Kalkadoon Grasswren *Amytornis ballarae*
Black Grasswren *Amytornis housei*
Striated Grasswren *Amytornis striatus*
White-throated Grasswren *Amytornis woodwardi*
Carpentarian Grasswren *Amytornis dorotheae*
Short-tailed Grasswren *Amytornis merrotsyi*
Gray Grasswren *Amytornis barbatus*
Eyrean Grasswren *Amytornis goyderi*

Thornbills and Flyeaters Acanthizidae
Western Bristlebird *Dasyornis longirostris*
Eastern Bristlebird *Dasyornis brachypterus* •
Rufous Bristlebird *Dasyornis broadbenti*
Pilotbird *Pycnoptilus floccosus*
Rock-Warbler *Origma solitaria*
Australian Fernwren *Oreoscopus gutturalis*
Rusty Mouse-Warbler *Crateroscelis murina*
Black-backed Mouse-Warbler *Crateroscelis nigrorufa*
Mountain Mouse-Warbler *Crateroscelis robusta*
Yellow-throated Sericornis *Sericornis citreogularis*
White-browed Sericornis *Sericornis frontalis*
Tasmanian Sericornis *Sericornis humilis*
Atherton Sericornis *Sericornis keri*

Tropical Scrubwren   *Sericornis beccarii*
Perplexing Sericornis   *Sericornis virgatus*
Large Sericornis   *Sericornis nouhuysi*
Large-billed Sericornis   *Sericornis magnirostra*
Vogelkop Sericornis   *Sericornis rufescens*
Buff-faced Sericornis   *Sericornis perspicillatus*
Papuan Sericornis   *Sericornis papuensis*
Gray-green Sericornis   *Sericornis arfakianus*
Pale-billed Sericornis   *Sericornis spilodera*
Scrubtit   *Acanthornis magna*
Redthroat   *Pyrrholaemus brunneus*
Speckled Warbler   *Pyrrholaemus sagittatus*
Rufous Calamanthus   *Calamanthus campestris*
Western Fieldwren   *Calamanthus montanellus*
Striated Calamanthus   *Calamanthus fuliginosus*
Chestnut-rumped Hylacola   *Hylacola pyrrhopygia*
Shy Hylacola   *Hylacola cauta*
Papuan Thornbill   *Acanthiza murina*
Buff-rumped Thornbill   *Acanthiza reguloides*
Western Thornbill   *Acanthiza inornata*
Slender-billed Thornbill   *Acanthiza iredalei*
Mountain Thornbill   *Acanthiza katherina*
Brown Thornbill   *Acanthiza pusilla*
Tasmanian Thornbill   *Acanthiza ewingii*
Broad-tailed Thornbill   *Acanthiza apicalis*
Yellow-rumped Thornbill   *Acanthiza chrysorrhoa*
Chestnut-rumped Thornbill   *Acanthiza uropygialis*
Slaty-backed Thornbill   *Acanthiza robustirostris*
Yellow Thornbill   *Acanthiza nana*
Striated Thornbill   *Acanthiza lineata*
Brown Weebill   *Smicrornis brevirostris*
Gray Gerygone   *Gerygone cinerea*
Green-backed Gerygone   *Gerygone chloronota*
Fairy Gerygone   *Gerygone palpebrosa*
Biak Gerygone   *Gerygone hypoxantha* •
White-throated Gerygone   *Gerygone olivacea*
Yellow-bellied Gerygone   *Gerygone chrysogaster*
Large-billed Gerygone   *Gerygone magnirostris*
Dusky Gerygone   *Gerygone tenebrosa*
Brown Gerygone   *Gerygone mouki*
Golden-bellied Gerygone   *Gerygone sulphurea*
Plain Gerygone   *Gerygone inornata*
Rufous-sided Gerygone   *Gerygone dorsalis*
Treefern Gerygone   *Gerygone ruficollis*
Western Gerygone   *Gerygone fusca*
Mangrove Gerygone   *Gerygone levigaster*
Norfolk Island Gerygone   *Gerygone modesta*
New Zealand Gray Gerygone   *Gerygone igata*
Chatham Islands Gerygone   *Gerygone albofrontata*
Fan-tailed Gerygone   *Gerygone flavolateralis*
Southern Whiteface   *Aphelocephala leucopsis*
Chestnut-breasted Whiteface   *Aphelocephala pectoralis*
Banded Whiteface   *Aphelocephala nigricincta*

Australian chats Epthianuridae
Crimson Chat   *Epthianura tricolor*
Orange Chat   *Epthianura aurifrons*
Yellow Chat   *Epthianura crocea*
White-fronted Chat   *Epthianura albifrons*
Gibberbird   *Ashbyia lovensis*

Sittellas Neosittidae
Black Sittella   *Neositta miranda*
Varied Sittella   *Neositta chrysoptera*

Australian Creepers Climacteridae
Papuan Treecreeper   *Cormobates placens*
White-throated Treecreeper   *Cormobates leucophaea*
White-browed Treecreeper   *Climacteris affinis*
Red-browed Treecreeper   *Climacteris erythrops*
Brown Treecreeper   *Climacteris picumnus*
Black-tailed Treecreeper   *Climacteris melanurus*
Rufous Treecreeper   *Climacteris rufus*
Tits and Chickadees Paridae

Sombre Tit   *Poecile lugubris*
Marsh Tit   *Poecile palustris*
Black-bibbed Marsh Tit   *Poecile hypermelaenus*
Caspian Tit   *Poecile hyrcana*
Willow Tit   *Poecile montana*
Songar Tit   *Poecile songara*
Carolina Chickadee   *Poecile carolinensis*
Black-capped Chickadee   *Poecile atricapillus*
Mountain Chickadee   *Poecile gambeli*
Mexican Chickadee   *Poecile sclateri*
White-browed Tit   *Poecile superciliosa*
Rusty-breasted Tit   *Poecile davidi*
Chestnut-backed Chickadee   *Poecile rufescens*
Boreal Chickadee   *Poecile hudsonica*
Siberian Chickadee   *Poecile cincta*
Coal Tit   *Periparus ater*
Rufous-naped Black Tit   *Periparus rufonuchalis*
Rufous-vented Tit   *Periparus rubidiventris*
Spot-winged Black Tit   *Periparus melanolophus*
Yellow-bellied Tit   *Pardaliparus venustulus*
Elegant Tit   *Pardaliparus elegans*
Palawan Tit   *Pardaliparus amabilis*
Crested Tit   *Lophophanes cristatus*
Gray-crested Tit   *Lophophanes dichrous*
White-winged Black Tit   *Melaniparus leucomelas*
Northern Black Tit   *Melaniparus guineensis*
Southern Black Tit   *Melaniparus niger*
Carp's Tit   *Melaniparus carpi*
White-bellied Tit   *Melaniparus albiventris*
White-backed Black Tit   *Melaniparus leuconotus*
Rufous-bellied Tit   *Melaniparus rufiventris*
Dusky Tit   *Melaniparus funereus*
Red-throated Tit   *Melaniparus fringillinus*
Stripe-breasted Tit   *Melaniparus fasciiventer*
Northern Gray Tit   *Melaniparus thruppi*
Miombo Gray Tit   *Melaniparus griseiventris*
Ashy Tit   *Melaniparus cinerascens*
Southern Gray Tit   *Melaniparus afer*
Great Tit   *Parus major*
Turkestan Great Tit   *Parus bokharensis*
Green-backed Tit   *Parus monticolus*
White-naped Black Tit   *Parus nuchalis*
Black-lored Yellow-Tit   *Parus xanthogenys*
Yellow-cheeked Tit   *Parus spilonotus*
Yellow Tit   *Macholophus holsti*
Blue Tit   *Cyanistes caeruleus*
African Blue Tit (Clements)   *Cyanistes teneriffae*
Azure Tit   *Cyanistes cyanus*
Yellow-breasted Tit   *Cyanistes flavipectus*
White-fronted Tit   *Sittiparus semilarvatus*
Varied Tit   *Sittiparus varius*
Bridled Titmouse   *Baeolophus wollweberi*
Oak Titmouse   *Baeolophus inornatus*
Juniper Titmouse   *Baeolophus ridgwayi*
Tufted Titmouse   *Baeolophus bicolor*
Black-crested Titmouse   *Baeolophus atricristatus*
Yellow-browed Tit   *Sylviparus modestus*
Sultan Tit   *Melanochlora sultanea*
Hume's Ground-Jay   *Pseudopodoces humilis*

Nuthatches Sittidae
Chestnut-bellied Nuthatch   *Sitta castanea*
European Nuthatch   *Sitta europaea*
Chestnut-vented Nuthatch   *Sitta nagaensis*
Kashmir Nuthatch   *Sitta cashmirensis*
White-tailed Nuthatch   *Sitta himalayensis*
White-browed Nuthatch   *Sitta victoriae* •
Pygmy Nuthatch   *Sitta pygmaea*
Brown-headed Nuthatch   *Sitta pusilla*
Corsican Nuthatch   *Sitta whiteheadi*
Algerian Nuthatch   *Sitta ledanti* •
Kruper's Nuthatch   *Sitta krueperi*
Chinese Nuthatch   *Sitta villosa*
Yunnan Nuthatch   *Sitta yunnanensis*

Red-breasted Nuthatch   *Sitta canadensis*
White-cheeked Nuthatch   *Sitta leucopsis*
White-breasted Nuthatch   *Sitta carolinensis*
Western Rock Nuthatch   *Sitta neumayer*
Eastern Rock Nuthatch   *Sitta tephronota*
Velvet-fronted Nuthatch   *Sitta frontalis*
Yellow-billed Nuthatch   *Sitta solangiae*
Sulfur-billed Nuthatch   *Sitta oenochlamys*
Blue Nuthatch   *Sitta azurea*
Giant Nuthatch   *Sitta magna*
Beautiful Nuthatch   *Sitta formosa*

Wallcreeper Tichodromidae
Wallcreeper   *Tichodroma muraria*

Creepers Certhiidae
Eurasian Treecreeper   *Certhia familiaris*
Sichuan Treecreeper   *Certhia tianquanensis*
American Treecreeper   *Certhia americana*
Short-toed Treecreeper   *Certhia brachydactyla*
Bar-tailed Treecreeper   *Certhia himalayana*
Rusty-flanked Treecreeper   *Certhia nipalensis*
Brown-throated Treecreeper   *Certhia discolor*
Spotted Creeper   *Salpornis spilonotus*

Philippine Creepers Rhabdornithidae
Stripe-sided Rhabdornis   *Rhabdornis mysticalis*
Long-billed Rhabdornis   *Rhabdornis grandis*
Stripe-breasted Rhabdornis   *Rhabdornis inornatus*

Penduline Tits Remizidae
Verdin   *Auriparus flaviceps*
Eurasian Penduline-Tit   *Remiz pendulinus*
Black-headed Penduline-Tit   *Remiz macronyx*
White-crowned Penduline-Tit   *Remiz coronatus*
Chinese Penduline-Tit   *Remiz consobrinus*
Sennar Penduline-Tit   *Anthoscopus punctifrons*
Mouse-colored Penduline-Tit   *Anthoscopus musculus*
Yellow Penduline-Tit   *Anthoscopus parvulus*
Forest Penduline-Tit   *Anthoscopus flavifrons*
African Penduline-Tit   *Anthoscopus caroli*
Cape Penduline-Tit   *Anthoscopus minutus*
Fire-capped Tit   *Cephalopyrus flammiceps*
Tit-Hylia   *Pholidornis rushiae*

Sunbirds and spiderhunters Nectariniidae
Ruby-cheeked Sunbird   *Chalcoparia singalensis*
Scarlet-tufted Sunbird   *Deleornis fraseri*
Gray-headed Sunbird   *Deleornis axillaris*
Plain-backed Sunbird   *Anthreptes reichenowi*
Anchieta's Sunbird   *Anthreptes anchietae*
Plain Sunbird   *Anthreptes simplex*
Brown-throated Sunbird   *Anthreptes malacensis*
Red-throated Sunbird   *Anthreptes rhodolaemus*
Mouse-brown Sunbird   *Anthreptes gabonicus*
Western Violet-backed Sunbird   *Anthreptes longuemarei*
Kenya Violet-backed Sunbird   *Anthreptes orientalis*
Ulluguru Violet-backed Sunbird   *Anthreptes neglectus*
Violet-tailed Sunbird   *Anthreptes aurantium*
Little Green Sunbird   *Anthreptes seimundi*
Green Sunbird   *Anthreptes rectirostris*
Banded Sunbird   *Anthreptes rubritorques*
Collared Sunbird   *Hedydipna collaris*
Western Pygmy Sunbird   *Hedydipna platura*
Nile Valley Sunbird   *Hedydipna metallica*
Amani Sunbird   *Hedydipna pallidigaster* •
Purple-naped Sunbird   *Hypogramma hypogrammicum*
Reichenbach's Sunbird   *Anabathmis reichenbachii*
Príncipe Sunbird   *Anabathmis hartlaubii*
Newton's Yellow-breasted Sunbird   *Anabathmis newtonii*
São Tomé Giant Sunbird   *Dreptes thomensis*
Orange-breasted Sunbird   *Anthobaphes violacea*

Green-headed Sunbird *Cyanomitra verticalis*
Bannerman's Sunbird *Cyanomitra bannermani*
Blue-throated Brown Sunbird *Cyanomitra cyanolaema*
Cameroon Sunbird *Cyanomitra oritis*
Blue-headed Sunbird *Cyanomitra alinae*
Eastern Olive Sunbird *Cyanomitra olivacea*
Western Olive Sunbird *Cyanomitra obscura*
Mouse-colored Sunbird *Cyanomitra veroxii*
Buff-throated Sunbird *Chalcomitra adelberti*
Carmelite Sunbird *Chalcomitra fuliginosa*
Green-throated Sunbird *Chalcomitra rubescens*
Amethyst Sunbird *Chalcomitra amethystina*
Scarlet-chested Sunbird *Chalcomitra senegalensis*
Hunter's Sunbird *Chalcomitra hunteri*
Socotra Sunbird *Chalcomitra balfouri*
Purple-rumped Sunbird *Leptocoma zeylonica*
Crimson-backed Sunbird *Leptocoma minima*
Purple-throated Sunbird *Leptocoma sperata*
Black Sunbird *Leptocoma sericea*
Copper-throated Sunbird *Leptocoma calcostetha*
Bocage's Sunbird *Nectarinia bocagei*
Purple-breasted Sunbird *Nectarinia purpureiventris*
Tacazze Sunbird *Nectarinia tacazze*
Bronze Sunbird *Nectarinia kilimensis*
Malachite Sunbird *Nectarinia famosa*
Red-tufted Malachite Sunbird *Nectarinia johnstoni*
Golden-winged Sunbird *Drepanorhynchus reichenowi*
Olive-bellied Sunbird *Cinnyris chloropygius*
Tiny Sunbird *Cinnyris minullus*
Miombo Double-collared Sunbird *Cinnyris manoensis*
Southern Double-collared Sunbird *Cinnyris chalybeus*
Neergaard's Sunbird *Cinnyris neergaardi*
Stuhlmann's Sunbird *Cinnyris stuhlmanni*
Prigogine's Sunbird *Cinnyris prigoginei*
Montane Double-collared Sunbird *Cinnyris ludovicensis*
Northern Double-collared Sunbird *Cinnyris reichenowi*
Greater Double-collared Sunbird *Cinnyris afer*
Regal Sunbird *Cinnyris regius*
Rockefeller's Sunbird *Cinnyris rockefelleri*
Eastern Double-collared Sunbird *Cinnyris mediocris*
Moreau's Sunbird *Cinnyris moreaui*
Loveridge's Sunbird *Cinnyris loveridgei* •
Beautiful Sunbird *Cinnyris pulchellus*
Mariqua Sunbird *Cinnyris mariquensis*
Shelley's Sunbird *Cinnyris shelleyi*
Congo Black-bellied Sunbird *Cinnyris congensis*
Red-chested Sunbird *Cinnyris erythrocercus*
Smaller Black-bellied Sunbird *Cinnyris nectarinioides*
Purple-banded Sunbird *Cinnyris bifasciatus*
Tsavo Sunbird *Cinnyris tsavoensis*
Kenya Violet-breasted Sunbird *Cinnyris chalcomelas*
Pemba Sunbird *Cinnyris pembae*
Orange-tufted Sunbird *Cinnyris bouvieri*
Palestine Sunbird *Cinnyris osea*
Shining Sunbird *Cinnyris habessinicus*
Splendid Sunbird *Cinnyris coccinigastrus*
Johanna's Sunbird *Cinnyris johannae*
Superb Sunbird *Cinnyris superbus*
Rufous-winged Sunbird *Cinnyris rufipennis*
Oustalet's Sunbird *Cinnyris oustaleti*
Southern White-bellied Sunbird *Cinnyris talatala*
Yellow-bellied Sunbird *Cinnyris venustus*
Dusky Sunbird *Cinnyris fuscus*
Fernando Po Sunbird *Cinnyris ursulae*
Bates's Sunbird *Cinnyris batesi*
Coppery Sunbird *Cinnyris cupreus*
Purple Sunbird *Cinnyris asiaticus*
Olive-backed Sunbird *Cinnyris jugularis*
Apricot-breasted Sunbird *Cinnyris buettikoferi*
Flame-breasted Sunbird *Cinnyris solaris*
Souimanga Sunbird *Cinnyris souimanga*
Madagascar Green Sunbird *Cinnyris notatus*

Seychelles Sunbird *Cinnyris dussumieri*
Humblot's Sunbird *Cinnyris humbloti*
Anjouan Sunbird *Cinnyris comorensis*
Mayotte Sunbird *Cinnyris coquerellii*
Loten's Sunbird *Cinnyris lotenius*
Gray-hooded Sunbird *Aethopyga primigenia*
Apo Sunbird *Aethopyga boltoni*
Lina's Sunbird *Aethopyga linaraborae*
Flaming Sunbird *Aethopyga flagrans*
Metallic-winged Sunbird *Aethopyga pulcherrima*
Elegant Sunbird *Aethopyga duyvenbodei* •
Lovely Sunbird (Clements) *Aethopyga shelleyi*
Lovely Sunbird *Aethopyga bella*
Mrs Gould's Sunbird *Aethopyga gouldiae*
Green-tailed Sunbird *Aethopyga nipalensis*
White-flanked Sunbird *Aethopyga eximia*
Fork-tailed Sunbird *Aethopyga christinae*
Black-throated Sunbird *Aethopyga saturata*
Western Crimson Sunbird *Aethopyga vigorsii*
Crimson Sunbird *Aethopyga siparaja*
Javan Sunbird *Aethopyga mystacalis*
Temminck's Sunbird *Aethopyga temminckii*
Fire-tailed Sunbird *Aethopyga ignicauda*
Little Spiderhunter *Arachnothera longirostra*
Thick-billed Spiderhunter *Arachnothera crassirostris*
Long-billed Spiderhunter *Arachnothera robusta*
Spectacled Spiderhunter *Arachnothera flavigaster*
Yellow-eared Spiderhunter *Arachnothera chrysogenys*
Naked-faced Spiderhunter *Arachnothera clarae*
Gray-breasted Spiderhunter *Arachnothera modesta*
Streaky-breasted Spiderhunter *Arachnothera affinis*
Streaked Spiderhunter *Arachnothera magna*
Whitehead's Spiderhunter *Arachnothera juliae*

Berrypeckers Melanocharitidae
Obscure Berrypecker *Melanocharis arfakiana*
Black Berrypecker *Melanocharis nigra*
Mid-mountain Berrypecker *Melanocharis longicauda*
Fan-tailed Berrypecker *Melanocharis versteri*
Streaked Berrypecker *Melanocharis striativentris*
Spotted Berrypecker *Melanocharis crassirostris*
Yellow-bellied Longbill *Toxorhamphus novaeguineae*
Slaty-chinned Longbill *Toxorhamphus poliopterus*
Gray-bellied Longbill *Toxorhamphus iliolophus*
Pygmy Longbill *Toxorhamphus pygmaeum*

Tit berrypeckers Parymythiidae
Tit Berrypecker *Oreocharis arfaki*
Crested Berrypecker *Paramythia montium*

Flowerpeckers Dicaeidae
Olive-backed Flowerpecker *Prionochilus olivaceus*
Yellow-breasted Flowerpecker *Prionochilus maculatus*
Crimson-breasted Flowerpecker *Prionochilus percussus*
Palawan Flowerpecker *Prionochilus plateni*
Yellow-rumped Flowerpecker *Prionochilus xanthopygius*
Scarlet-breasted Flowerpecker *Prionochilus thoracicus*
Golden-rumped Flowerpecker *Dicaeum annae*
Thick-billed Flowerpecker *Dicaeum agile*
Brown-backed Flowerpecker *Dicaeum everetti*
Whiskered Flowerpecker *Dicaeum proprium*
Yellow-vented Flowerpecker *Dicaeum chrysorrheum*
Yellow-bellied Flowerpecker *Dicaeum melanoxanthum*
Legge's Flowerpecker *Dicaeum vincens*
Yellow-sided Flowerpecker *Dicaeum aureolimbatum*
Olive-capped Flowerpecker *Dicaeum nigrilore*
Flame-crowned Flowerpecker *Dicaeum anthonyi*
Bicolored Flowerpecker *Dicaeum bicolor*
Cebu Flowerpecker *Dicaeum quadricolor* •
Red-striped Flowerpecker *Dicaeum australe*
Visayan Flowerpecker *Dicaeum haematostictum*

Scarlet-collared Flowerpecker *Dicaeum retrocinctum*
Orange-bellied Flowerpecker *Dicaeum trigonostigma*
Buzzing Flowerpecker *Dicaeum hypoleucum*
Pale-billed Flowerpecker *Dicaeum erythrorhynchos*
Plain Flowerpecker *Dicaeum concolor*
Pygmy Flowerpecker *Dicaeum pygmaeum*
Crimson-crowned Flowerpecker *Dicaeum nehrkorni*
Flame-breasted Flowerpecker *Dicaeum erythrothorax*
Ashy Flowerpecker *Dicaeum vulneratum*
Olive-crowned Flowerpecker *Dicaeum pectorale*
Red-capped Flowerpecker *Dicaeum geelvinkianum*
Louisiade Flowerpecker *Dicaeum nitidum*
Red-banded Flowerpecker *Dicaeum eximium*
Solomon Islands Flowerpecker *Dicaeum aeneum*
San Cristobal Flowerpecker *Dicaeum tristrami*
Black-fronted Flowerpecker *Dicaeum igniferum*
Red-chested Flowerpecker *Dicaeum maugei*
Fire-breasted Flowerpecker *Dicaeum ignipectum*
Black-sided Flowerpecker *Dicaeum monticolum*
Gray-sided Flowerpecker *Dicaeum celebicum*
Blood-breasted Flowerpecker *Dicaeum sanguinolentum*
Mistletoebird *Dicaeum hirundinaceum*
Scarlet-backed Flowerpecker *Dicaeum cruentatum*
Scarlet-headed Flowerpecker *Dicaeum trochileum*

Pardalotes Pardalotidae
Spotted Pardalote *Pardalotus punctatus*
Forty-spotted Pardalote *Pardalotus quadragintus* •
Red-browed Pardalote *Pardalotus rubricatus*
Yellow-tipped Pardalote *Pardalotus striatus*

White-eyes Zosteropidae
Black-capped Speirops *Speirops lugubris*
Mount Cameroon Speirops *Speirops melanocephalus*
Fernando Po Speirops *Speirops brunneus*
Príncipe Speirops *Speirops leucophoeus*
African Yellow White-eye *Zosterops senegalensis*
Broad-ringed White-eye *Zosterops poliogastrus*
White-breasted White-eye *Zosterops abyssinicus*
Cape White-eye *Zosterops pallidus*
Pemba White-eye *Zosterops vaughani*
Mayotte White-eye *Zosterops mayottensis*
Madagascar White-eye *Zosterops maderaspatanus*
Comoro White-eye *Zosterops mouroniensis*
Príncipe White-eye *Zosterops ficedulinus*
Annobón White-eye *Zosterops griseovirescens*
Réunion Gray White-eye *Zosterops borbonicus*
Réunion Olive White-eye *Zosterops olivaceus*
Mauritius Olive White-eye *Zosterops chloronothos* •
Seychelles White-eye *Zosterops modestus* •
Sri Lanka White-eye *Zosterops ceylonensis*
Chestnut-flanked White-eye *Zosterops erythropleurus*
Oriental White-eye *Zosterops palpebrosus*
Japanese White-eye *Zosterops japonicus*
Lowland White-eye *Zosterops meyeni*
Enggano White-eye *Zosterops salvadorii*
Bridled White-eye *Zosterops conspicillatus* •
Caroline White-eye *Zosterops semperi*
Plain White-eye *Zosterops hypolais*
Black-capped White-eye *Zosterops atricapilla*
Everett's White-eye *Zosterops everetti*
Golden-green White-eye *Zosterops nigrorum*
Mountain White-eye *Zosterops montanus*
Christmas Island White-eye *Zosterops natalis*
Javan White-eye *Zosterops flavus*
Lemon-bellied White-eye *Zosterops chloris*
Australian Pale White-eye *Zosterops citrinella*
Pearl-bellied White-eye *Zosterops grayi*
Golden-bellied White-eye *Zosterops uropygialis*
Pale-bellied White-eye *Zosterops consobrinorum*
Black-ringed White-eye *Zosterops anomalus*
Yellow-spectacled White-eye *Zosterops wallacei*
Black-crowned White-eye *Zosterops atrifrons*

Sangihe White-eye   *Zosterops nehrkorni* •
Seram White-eye   *Zosterops stalkeri*
Creamy-throated White-eye   *Zosterops atriceps*
New Guinea Black-fronted White-eye   *Zosterops minor*
White-throated White-eye   *Zosterops meeki*
Black-headed White-eye   *Zosterops hypoxanthus*
Biak White-eye   *Zosterops mysorensis*
Yellow-bellied Mountain White-eye   *Zosterops fuscicapilla*
Buru Island White-eye   *Zosterops buruensis*
Ambon White-eye   *Zosterops kuehni*
New Guinea White-eye   *Zosterops novaeguineae*
Australian Yellow White-eye   *Zosterops luteus*
Louisiades White-eye   *Zosterops griseotinctus*
Rennell Island White-eye   *Zosterops rennellianus*
Banded White-eye   *Zosterops vellalavella*
Ganongga White-eye   *Zosterops splendidus*
Splendid White-eye   *Zosterops luteirostris* •
Yellow-throated White-eye   *Zosterops metcalfii*
Solomon Islands White-eye   *Zosterops rendovae*
Kulambangra Mountain White-eye   *Zosterops murphyi*
Gray-throated White-eye   *Zosterops ugiensis*
Malaita White-eye   *Zosterops stresemanni*
Santa Cruz White-eye   *Zosterops santaecrucis*
Large Lifou White-eye   *Zosterops inornatus*
Green-backed White-eye   *Zosterops xanthochroa*
Small Lifou White-eye   *Zosterops minutus*
Lord Howe Island White-eye   *Zosterops tephropleurus*
Slender-billed White-eye   *Zosterops tenuirostris* •
White-chested White-eye   *Zosterops albogularis* •
Layard's White-eye   *Zosterops explorator*
Silvereye   *Zosterops lateralis*
Yellow-fronted White-eye   *Zosterops flavifrons*
Samoan White-eye   *Zosterops samoensis*
Dusky White-eye   *Zosterops finschii*
Gray White-eye   *Zosterops cinereus*
Yap Olive White-eye   *Zosterops oleagineus*
Great Truk White-eye   *Rukia ruki* •
Ponapé White-eye   *Rukia longirostra*
Golden White-eye   *Cleptornis marchei* •
Bicolored White-eye   *Tephrozosterops stalkeri*
Rufous-throated White-eye   *Madanga ruficollis* •
Javan Gray-throated White-eye   *Lophozosterops javanicus*
Streak-headed White-eye   *Lophozosterops squamiceps*
Gray-hooded White-eye   *Lophozosterops pinaiae*
Black-masked White-eye   *Lophozosterops goodfellowi*
Yellow-browed White-eye   *Lophozosterops superciliaris*
Crested White-eye   *Lophozosterops dohertyi*
Pygmy White-eye   *Oculocincta squamifrons*
Thick-billed White-eye   *Heleia crassirostris*
Spot-breasted White-eye   *Heleia muelleri*
Mountain Black-eye   *Chlorocharis emiliae*
Bare-eyed White-eye   *Woodfordia superciliosa*
Sanford's White-eye   *Woodfordia lacertosa*
Large Palau White-eye   *Megazosterops palauensis*
Cinnamon Ibon   *Hypocryptadius cinnamomeus*

Sugarbirds Promeropidae
Gurney's Sugarbird   *Promerops gurneyi*
Cape Sugarbird   *Promerops cafer*

Honeyeaters Meliphagidae
Olive Straightbill   *Timeliopsis fulvigula*
Tawny Straightbill   *Timeliopsis griseigula*
Long-billed Honeyeater   *Melilestes megarhynchus*
Bougainville Honeyeater   *Stresemannia bougainvillei*
Green-backed Honeyeater   *Glycichaera fallax*
Scaly-crowned Honeyeater   *Lichmera lombokia*
Olive Honeyeater   *Lichmera argentauris*
Brown Honeyeater   *Lichmera indistincta*
Indonesian Honeyeater   *Lichmera limbata*
Dark-brown Honeyeater   *Lichmera incana*
White-tufted Honeyeater   *Lichmera squamata*

Silver-eared Honeyeater   *Lichmera alboauricularis*
Buru Honeyeater   *Lichmera deningeri*
Seram Honeyeater   *Lichmera monticola*
Yellow-eared Honeyeater   *Lichmera flavicans*
Black-chested Honeyeater   *Lichmera notabilis*
White-streaked Honeyeater   *Trichodere cockerelli*
Drab Myzomela   *Myzomela blasii*
White-chinned Myzomela   *Myzomela albigula*
Red-throated Myzomela   *Myzomela eques*
Ashy Myzomela   *Myzomela cineracea*
Dusky Myzomela   *Myzomela obscura*
Red Myzomela   *Myzomela cruentata*
Papuan Black Myzomela   *Myzomela nigrita*
Olive-yellow Myzomela   *Myzomela pulchella*
Crimson-hooded Myzomela   *Myzomela kuehni*
Red-headed Myzomela   *Myzomela erythrocephala*
Sumba Myzomela   *Myzomela dammermani*
Mountain Myzomela   *Myzomela adolphinae*
Sulawesi Myzomela   *Myzomela chloroptera*
Wakolo Myzomela   *Myzomela wakoloensis*
Banda Myzomela   *Myzomela boiei*
New Caledonian Myzomela   *Myzomela caledonica*
Scarlet Myzomela   *Myzomela sanguinolenta*
Micronesian Myzomela   *Myzomela rubratra*
Cardinal Myzomela   *Myzomela cardinalis*
Rotuma Myzomela   *Myzomela chermesina*
Scarlet-bibbed Myzomela   *Myzomela sclateri*
Bismarck Black Myzomela   *Myzomela pammelaena*
Scarlet-naped Myzomela   *Myzomela lafargei*
Yellow-vented Myzomela   *Myzomela eichhorni*
Red-bellied Myzomela   *Myzomela malaitae*
Black-headed Myzomela   *Myzomela melanocephala*
Sooty Myzomela   *Myzomela tristrami*
Orange-breasted Myzomela   *Myzomela jugularis*
Black-bellied Myzomela   *Myzomela erythromelas*
Red-rumped Myzomela   *Myzomela vulnerata*
Red-collared Myzomela   *Myzomela rosenbergii*
Banded Honeyeater   *Certhionyx pectoralis*
Black Honeyeater   *Certhionyx niger*
Pied Honeyeater   *Certhionyx variegatus*
Forest White-eared Honeyeater   *Meliphaga montana*
Large Spot-breasted Honeyeater   *Meliphaga mimikae*
Hill-forest Honeyeater   *Meliphaga orientalis*
Scrub White-eared Honeyeater   *Meliphaga albonotata*
Puff-backed Honeyeater   *Meliphaga aruensis*
Mimic Honeyeater   *Meliphaga analoga*
Tagula Honeyeater   *Meliphaga vicina*
Graceful Honeyeater   *Meliphaga gracilis*
Yellow-spotted Honeyeater   *Meliphaga notata*
Yellow-gaped Honeyeater   *Meliphaga flavirictus*
Lewin's Honeyeater   *Meliphaga lewinii*
White-lined Honeyeater   *Meliphaga albilineata*
Streak-breasted Honeyeater   *Meliphaga reticulata*
Guadalcanal Honeyeater   *Guadalcanaria inexpectata*
Wattled Honeyeater   *Foulehaio carunculatus*
Black-throated Honeyeater   *Lichenostomus subfrenatus*
Obscure Honeyeater   *Lichenostomus obscurus*
Bridled Honeyeater   *Lichenostomus frenatus*
Eungella Honeyeater   *Lichenostomus hindwoodi*
Yellow-faced Honeyeater   *Lichenostomus chrysops*
Varied Honeyeater   *Lichenostomus versicolor*
Mangrove Honeyeater   *Lichenostomus fasciogularis*
Singing Honeyeater   *Lichenostomus virescens*
Yellow Honeyeater   *Lichenostomus flavus*
White-gaped Honeyeater   *Lichenostomus unicolor*
White-eared Honeyeater   *Lichenostomus leucotis*
Yellow-throated Honeyeater   *Lichenostomus flavicollis*
Yellow-tufted Honeyeater   *Lichenostomus melanops*
Purple-gaped Honeyeater   *Lichenostomus cratitius*
Gray-headed Honeyeater   *Lichenostomus keartlandi*
Yellow-tinted Honeyeater   *Lichenostomus flavescens*
Fuscous Honeyeater   *Lichenostomus fuscus*
Gray-fronted Honeyeater   *Lichenostomus plumulus*
Yellow-plumed Honeyeater   *Lichenostomus ornatus*

White-plumed Honeyeater   *Lichenostomus penicillatus*
Tawny-breasted Honeyeater   *Xanthotis flaviventer*
Spotted Honeyeater   *Xanthotis polygrammus*
Macleay's Honeyeater   *Xanthotis macleayanus*
Kadavu Honeyeater   *Xanthotis provocator*
Orange-cheeked Honeyeater   *Oreornis chrysogenys*
Bonin Islands White-eye   *Apalopteron familiare*
White-naped Honeyeater   *Melithreptus lunatus*
Black-headed Honeyeater   *Melithreptus affinis*
White-throated Honeyeater   *Melithreptus albogularis*
Black-chinned Honeyeater   *Melithreptus gularis*
Strong-billed Honeyeater   *Melithreptus validirostris*
Brown-headed Honeyeater   *Melithreptus brevirostris*
Stitchbird   *Notiomystis cincta*
Plain Honeyeater   *Pycnopygius ixoides*
Marbled Honeyeater   *Pycnopygius cinereus*
Streak-headed Honeyeater   *Pycnopygius stictocephalus*
White-streaked Friarbird   *Melitograis gilolensis*
Meyer's Friarbird   *Philemon meyeri*
Timor Friarbird   *Philemon inornatus*
Gray Friarbird   *Philemon kisserensis*
Brass's Friarbird   *Philemon brassi*
Dusky Friarbird   *Philemon fuscicapillus*
Little Friarbird   *Philemon citreogularis*
Black-faced Friarbird   *Philemon moluccensis*
Gray-necked Friarbird   *Philemon subcorniculatus*
Helmeted Friarbird   *Philemon buceroides*
White-naped Friarbird   *Philemon albitorques*
New Britain Friarbird   *Philemon cockerelli*
New Ireland Friarbird   *Philemon eichhorni*
Silver-crowned Friarbird   *Philemon argenticeps*
Noisy Friarbird   *Philemon corniculatus*
New Caledonian Friarbird   *Philemon diemenensis*
Leaden Streaked Honeyeater   *Ptiloprora plumbea*
Olive-streaked Honeyeater   *Ptiloprora meekiana*
Rufous-sided Honeyeater   *Ptiloprora erythropleura*
Mayr's Honeyeater   *Ptiloprora mayri*
Rufous-backed Honeyeater   *Ptiloprora guisei*
Black-backed Streaked Honeyeater   *Ptiloprora perstriata*
Sooty Melidectes   *Melidectes fuscus*
Bismarck Melidectes   *Melidectes whitemanensis*
Short-bearded Melidectes   *Melidectes nouhuysi*
Long-bearded Melidectes   *Melidectes princeps*
Cinnamon-browed Melidectes   *Melidectes ochromelas*
Vogelkop Melidectes   *Melidectes leucostephes*
Belford's Melidectes   *Melidectes belfordi*
Yellow-browed Melidectes   *Melidectes rufocrissalis*
Huon Wattled Melidectes   *Melidectes foersteri*
Ornate Melidectes   *Melidectes torquatus*
San Cristobal Melidectes   *Melidectes sclateri*
Arfak Melipotes   *Melipotes gymnops*
Common Melipote   *Melipotes fumigatus*
Huon Melipotes   *Melipotes ater*
Dark-eared Myza   *Myza celebensis*
White-eared Myza   *Myza sarasinorum*
Green Honeyeater   *Gymnomyza viridis*
Black-breasted Honeyeater   *Gymnomyza samoensis* •
Red-faced Honeyeater   *Gymnomyza aubryana* •
Kaua'i O'o   *Moho braccatus*
Bishop's O'o   *Moho bishopi*
Crescent Honeyeater   *Phylidonyris pyrrhopterus*
New Holland Honeyeater   *Phylidonyris novaehollandiae*
White-cheeked Honeyeater   *Phylidonyris niger*
White-fronted Honeyeater   *Phylidonyris albifrons*
Barred Honeyeater   *Phylidonyris undulatus*
New Hebrides Honeyeater   *Phylidonyris notabilis*
Tawny-crowned Honeyeater   *Phylidonyris melanops*
Brown-backed Honeyeater   *Ramsayornis modestus*
Bar-breasted Honeyeater   *Ramsayornis fasciatus*
Striped Honeyeater   *Plectorhyncha lanceolata*
Rufous-banded Honeyeater   *Conopophila albogularis*
Rufous-throated Honeyeater   *Conopophila rufogularis*

Gray Honeyeater   *Conopophila whitei*
Painted Honeyeater   *Grantiella picta*
Regent Honeyeater   *Xanthomyza phrygia* •
Eastern Spinebill   *Acanthorhynchus tenuirostris*
Western Spinebill   *Acanthorhynchus superciliosus*
Blue-faced Honeyeater   *Entomyzon cyanotis*
Bell Miner   *Manorina melanophrys*
Noisy Miner   *Manorina melanocephala*
Yellow-throated Miner   *Manorina flavigula*
Black-eared Miner   *Manorina melanotis* •
New Zealand Bellbird   *Anthornis melanura*
Spiny-cheeked Honeyeater   *Acanthagenys rufogularis*
Red Wattlebird   *Anthochaera carunculata*
Brush Wattlebird   *Anthochaera chrysoptera*
Western Wattlebird   *Anthochaera lunulata*
Yellow Wattlebird   *Anthochaera paradoxa*
Tui   *Prosthemadera novaeseelandiae*

Orioles Oriolidae
Olive-brown Oriole   *Oriolus melanotis*
Black-eared Oriole   *Oriolus bouroensis*
Gray-collared Oriole   *Oriolus forsteni*
Dusky Oriole   *Oriolus phaeochromus*
Brown Oriole   *Oriolus szalayi*
Olive-backed Oriole   *Oriolus sagittatus*
Australian Yellow Oriole   *Oriolus flavocinctus*
Dark-throated Oriole   *Oriolus xanthonotus*
White-lored Oriole   *Oriolus albiloris*
Philippine Oriole   *Oriolus steerii*
Isabela Oriole   *Oriolus isabellae* •
Eurasian Golden Oriole   *Oriolus oriolus*
African Golden Oriole   *Oriolus auratus*
Black-naped Oriole   *Oriolus chinensis*
Slender-billed Oriole   *Oriolus tenuirostris*
Green-headed Oriole   *Oriolus chlorocephalus*
São Tomé Oriole   *Oriolus crassirostris*
Western Black-headed Oriole   *Oriolus brachyrhynchus*
Dark-headed Oriole   *Oriolus monacha*
African Black-headed Oriole   *Oriolus larvatus*
Montane Oriole   *Oriolus percivali*
Black-winged Oriole   *Oriolus nigripennis*
Black-hooded Oriole   *Oriolus xanthornus*
Black Oriole   *Oriolus hosii*
Black-and-crimson Oriole   *Oriolus cruentus*
Maroon Oriole   *Oriolus traillii*
Silver Oriole   *Oriolus mellianus*
Wetar Figbird   *Sphecotheres hypoleucus*
Green Figbird   *Sphecotheres viridis*
Australasian Figbird   *Sphecotheres vieilloti*

Fairy-bluebirds Irenidae
Asian Fairy-Bluebird   *Irena puella*
Philippine Fairy-Bluebird   *Irena cyanogastra*

Shrikes Laniidae
Tiger Shrike   *Lanius tigrinus*
Bull-headed Shrike   *Lanius bucephalus*
Red-backed Shrike   *Lanius collurio*
Isabelline Shrike   *Lanius isabellinus*
Brown Shrike   *Lanius cristatus*
Burmese Shrike   *Lanius collurioides*
Emin's Shrike   *Lanius gubernator*
Souza's Shrike   *Lanius souzae*
Bay-backed Shrike   *Lanius vittatus*
Long-tailed Shrike   *Lanius schach*
Gray-backed Shrike   *Lanius tephronotus*
Mountain Shrike   *Lanius validirostris*
Loggerhead Shrike   *Lanius ludovicianus*
Great Gray Shrike   *Lanius excubitor*
Southern Gray Shrike   *Lanius meridionalis*
Lesser Gray Shrike   *Lanius minor*
Chinese Gray Shrike   *Lanius sphenocercus*
Gray-backed Fiscal   *Lanius excubitoroides*
Long-tailed Fiscal   *Lanius cabanisi*

Taita Fiscal   *Lanius dorsalis*
Somali Fiscal   *Lanius somalicus*
Mackinnon's Shrike   *Lanius mackinnoni*
Common Fiscal   *Lanius collaris*
Newton's Fiscal   *Lanius newtoni* •
Masked Shrike   *Lanius nubicus*
Woodchat Shrike   *Lanius senator*
Yellow-billed Shrike   *Corvinella corvina*
Magpie Shrike   *Corvinella melanoleuca*
Northern White-crowned Shrike   *Eurocephalus rueppelli*
Southern White-crowned Shrike   *Eurocephalus anguitimens*

Bushshrikes Malaconotidae
Brubru   *Nilaus afer*
Northern Puffback   *Dryoscopus gambensis*
Pringle's Puffback   *Dryoscopus pringlii*
Black-backed Puffback   *Dryoscopus cubla*
Red-eyed Puffback   *Dryoscopus senegalensis*
Pink-footed Puffback   *Dryoscopus angolensis*
Sabine's Puffback   *Dryoscopus sabini*
Marsh Tchagra   *Tchagra minutus*
Black-crowned Tchagra   *Tchagra senegalus*
Brown-crowned Tchagra   *Tchagra australis*
Three-streaked Tchagra   *Tchagra jamesi*
Southern Tchagra   *Tchagra tchagra*
Red-naped Bushshrike   *Laniarius ruficeps*
Lüehder's Bushshrike   *Laniarius luehderi*
Orange-breasted Bushshrike   *Laniarius brauni* •
Amboim Bushshrike   *Laniarius amboimensis* •
Bulo Burti Boubou   *Laniarius liberatus* •
Turati's Boubou   *Laniarius turatii*
Tropical Boubou   *Laniarius aethiopicus*
Gabon Boubou   *Laniarius bicolor*
Southern Boubou   *Laniarius ferrugineus*
Yellow-crowned Gonolek   *Laniarius barbarus*
Black-headed Gonolek   *Laniarius erythrogaster*
Crimson-breasted Gonolek   *Laniarius atrococcineus*
Papyrus Gonolek   *Laniarius mufumbiri*
Yellow-breasted Boubou   *Laniarius atroflavus*
Slate-colored Boubou   *Laniarius funebris*
Sooty Boubou   *Laniarius leucorhynchus*
Mountain Sooty Boubou   *Laniarius poensis*
Füelleborn's Black Boubou   *Laniarius fuelleborni*
Rosy-patched Bushshrike   *Rhodophoneus cruentus*
Bokmakierie Bushshrike   *Telophorus zeylonus*
Gray-green Bushshrike   *Telophorus bocagei*
Sulfur-breasted Bushshrike   *Telophorus sulfureopectus*
Rufous-breasted Bushshrike   *Telophorus olivaceus*
Many-colored Bushshrike   *Telophorus multicolor*
Black-fronted Bushshrike   *Telophorus nigrifrons*
Mount Kupé Bushshrike   *Telophorus kupeensis* •
Perrin's Bushshrike   *Telophorus viridis*
Doherty's Bushshrike   *Telophorus dohertyi*
Fiery-breasted Bushshrike   *Malaconotus cruentus*
Lagden's Bushshrike   *Malaconotus lagdeni*
Green-breasted Bushshrike   *Malaconotus gladiator*
Gray-headed Bushshrike   *Malaconotus blanchoti*
Monteiro's Bushshrike   *Malaconotus monteiri*
Uluguru Bushshrike   *Malaconotus alius* •

Helmetshrikes Prionopidae
White Helmetshrike   *Prionops plumatus*
Gray-crested Helmetshrike   *Prionops poliolophus*
Yellow-crested Helmetshrike   *Prionops alberti*
Red-billed Helmetshrike   *Prionops caniceps*
Gabon Helmetshrike   *Prionops rufiventris*
Retz's Helmetshrike   *Prionops retzii*
Angola Helmetshrike   *Prionops gabela* •
Chestnut-fronted Helmetshrike   *Prionops scopifrons*
Large Woodshrike   *Tephrodornis gularis*
Common Woodshrike   *Tephrodornis pondicerianus*
Rufous-winged Philentoma   *Philentoma pyrhoptera*
Maroon-breasted Philentoma   *Philentoma velata*

Vanga Shrikes Vangidae
Red-tailed Vanga   *Calicalicus madagascariensis*
Red-shouldered Vanga   *Calicalicus rufocarpalis*
Rufous Vanga   *Schetba rufa*
Hook-billed Vanga   *Vanga curvirostris*
Lafresnaye's Vanga   *Xenopirostris xenopirostris*
Van Dam's Vanga   *Xenopirostris damii* •
Pollen's Vanga   *Xenopirostris polleni*
Sickle-billed Vanga   *Falculea palliata*
White-headed Vanga   *Artamella viridis*
Chabert Vanga   *Leptopterus chabert*
Madagascar Blue Vanga   *Cyanolanius madagascarinus*
Bernier's Vanga   *Oriolia bernieri* •
Helmet Vanga   *Euryceros prevostii*
Tylas Vanga   *Tylas eduardi*
Nuthatch Vanga   *Hypositta corallirostris*

Drongos Dicruridae
Pygmy Drongo   *Chaetorhynchus papuensis*
Square-tailed Drongo   *Dicrurus ludwigii*
Shining Drongo   *Dicrurus atripennis*
Common Drongo   *Dicrurus adsimilis*
Velvet-mantled Drongo   *Dicrurus modestus*
Aldabra Drongo   *Dicrurus aldabranus*
Comoro Drongo   *Dicrurus fuscipennis* •
Crested Drongo   *Dicrurus forficatus*
Mayotte Drongo   *Dicrurus waldenii* •
Black Drongo   *Dicrurus macrocercus*
Ashy Drongo   *Dicrurus leucophaeus*
White-bellied Drongo   *Dicrurus caerulescens*
Crow-billed Drongo   *Dicrurus annectans*
Bronzed Drongo   *Dicrurus aeneus*
Lesser Racquet-tailed Drongo   *Dicrurus remifer*
Hair-crested Drongo   *Dicrurus hottentottus*
Balicassio   *Dicrurus balicassius*
Sulawesi Drongo   *Dicrurus montanus*
Sumatran Drongo   *Dicrurus sumatranus*
Wallacean Drongo   *Dicrurus densus*
New Ireland Drongo   *Dicrurus megarhynchus*
Spangled Drongo   *Dicrurus bracteatus*
Andaman Drongo   *Dicrurus andamanensis*
Greater Racquet-tailed Drongo   *Dicrurus paradiseus*

Wattlebirds Callaeidae
Kokako   *Callaeas cinereus* •
Saddleback   *Philesturnus carunculatus*

Magpie Larks Grallinidae
Magpie-Lark   *Grallina cyanoleuca*
Torrent-Lark   *Grallina bruijni*

Australian Mud Nesters Corcoracidae
White-winged Chough   *Corcorax melanorhamphos*
Apostlebird   *Struthidea cinerea*

Wood Swallows Artamidae
Ashy Woodswallow   *Artamus fuscus*
Fiji Woodswallow   *Artamus mentalis*
Ivory-backed Woodswallow   *Artamus monachus*
Papuan Woodswallow   *Artamus maximus*
White-breasted Woodswallow   *Artamus leucorhynchus*
Bismarck Woodswallow   *Artamus insignis*
Masked Woodswallow   *Artamus personatus*
White-browed Woodswallow   *Artamus superciliosus*
Black-faced Woodswallow   *Artamus cinereus*
Dusky Woodswallow   *Artamus cyanopterus*
Little Woodswallow   *Artamus minor*

Bristlehead Pityriaseidae
Bornean Bristlehead   *Pityriasis gymnocephala*

Butcher Birds Cracticidae
Mountain Peltops   *Peltops montanus*
Lowland Peltops   *Peltops blainvillii*

Black-backed Butcherbird *Cracticus mentalis*
Gray Butcherbird *Cracticus torquatus*
Silver-backed Butcherbird *Cracticus argenteus*
Hooded Butcherbird *Cracticus cassicus*
Tagula Butcherbird *Cracticus louisiadensis*
Pied Butcherbird *Cracticus nigrogularis*
Black Butcherbird *Cracticus quoyi*
Australasian Magpie *Gymnorhina tibicen*
Pied Currawong *Strepera graculina*
Black Currawong *Strepera fuliginosa*
Gray Currawong *Strepera versicolor*

Birds-of-Paradise Paradisaeidae
Loria's Bird-of-Paradise *Cnemophilus loriae*
Crested Bird-of-Paradise *Cnemophilus macgregorii*
Yellow-breasted Bird-of-Paradise *Loboparadisea sericea*
Macgregor's Bird-of-Paradise *Macgregoria pulchra*
Paradise-Crow *Lycocorax pyrrhopterus*
Glossy-mantled Manucode *Manucodia ater*
Jobi Manucode *Manucodia jobiensis*
Crinkle-collared Manucode *Manucodia chalybatus*
Curl-crested Manucode *Manucodia comrii*
Australian Trumpetbird *Manucodia keraudrenii*
Long-tailed Paradigalla *Paradigalla carunculata*
Short-tailed Paradigalla *Paradigalla brevicauda*
Arfak Astrapia *Astrapia nigra*
Splendid Astrapia *Astrapia splendidissima*
Ribbon-tailed Astrapia *Astrapia mayeri*
Princess Stephanie's Astrapia *Astrapia stephaniae*
Huon Astrapia *Astrapia rothschildi*
Western Parotia *Parotia sefilata*
Queen Carola's Parotia *Parotia carolae*
Lawes's Parotia *Parotia lawesii*
Wahnes's Parotia *Parotia wahnesi*
King of Saxony's Bird-of-Paradise *Pteridophora alberti*
Magnificent Riflebird *Ptiloris magnificus*
Paradise Riflebird *Ptiloris paradiseus*
Victoria's Riflebird *Ptiloris victoriae*
Superb Bird-of-Paradise *Lophorina superba*
Black Sicklebill *Epimachus fastuosus*
Brown Sicklebill *Epimachus meyeri*
Black-billed Sicklebill *Epimachus albertisi*
Pale-billed Sicklebill *Epimachus bruijnii*
Magnificent Bird-of-Paradise *Cicinnurus magnificus*
Wilson's Bird-of-Paradise *Cicinnurus respublica*
King Bird-of-Paradise *Cicinnurus regius*
Wallace's Standardwing *Semioptera wallacii*
Twelve-wired Bird-of-Paradise *Seleucidis melanoleucus*
Lesser Bird-of-Paradise *Paradisaea minor*
Greater Bird-of-Paradise *Paradisaea apoda*
Raggiana Bird-of-Paradise *Paradisaea raggiana*
Goldie's Bird-of-Paradise *Paradisaea decora*
Red Bird-of-Paradise *Paradisaea rubra*
Emperor's Bird-of-Paradise *Paradisaea guilielmi*
Blue Bird-of-Paradise *Paradisaea rudolphi*
Lesser Melampitta *Melampitta lugubris*
Greater Melampitta *Melampitta gigantea*

Bowerbirds Ptilonorhynchidae
White-eared Catbird *Ailuroedus buccoides*
Spotted Catbird *Ailuroedus melanotis*
Green Catbird *Ailuroedus crassirostris*
Tooth-billed Catbird *Ailuroedus dentirostris*
Archbold's Bowerbird *Archboldia papuensis*
Sanford's Bowerbird *Archboldia sanfordi*
Vogelkop Gardener-Bowerbird *Amblyornis inornata*
Macgregor's Gardener-Bowerbird *Amblyornis macgregoriae*
Streaked Bowerbird *Amblyornis subalaris*
Golden-fronted Bowerbird *Amblyornis flavifrons*
Newton's Golden Bowerbird *Prionodura newtoniana*
Flame Bowerbird *Sericulus aureus*
Fire-maned Bowerbird *Sericulus bakeri*
Regent Bowerbird *Sericulus chrysocephalus*

Satin Bowerbird *Ptilonorhynchus violaceus*
Western Bowerbird *Chlamydera guttata*
Spotted Bowerbird *Chlamydera maculata*
Great Gray Bowerbird *Chlamydera nuchalis*
Yellow-breasted Bowerbird *Chlamydera lauterbachi*
Fawn-breasted Bowerbird *Chlamydera cerviniventris*

Crows and Jays Corvidae
Crested Jay *Platylophus galericulatus*
Black Jay *Platysmurus leucopterus*
Siberian Jay *Perisoreus infaustus*
Sichuan Jay *Perisoreus internigrans*
Gray Jay *Perisoreus canadensis*
Steller's Jay *Cyanocitta stelleri*
Blue Jay *Cyanocitta cristata*
Black-throated Magpie-Jay *Calocitta colliei*
White-throated Magpie-Jay *Calocitta formosa*
Tufted Jay *Cyanocorax dickeyi*
Black-chested Jay *Cyanocorax affinis*
Inca Jay *Cyanocorax yncas*
Brown Jay *Cyanocorax morio*
Bushy-crested Jay *Cyanocorax melanocyaneus*
San Blas Jay *Cyanocorax sanblasianus*
Yucatan Jay *Cyanocorax yucatanicus*
Beechey's Jay *Cyanocorax beecheii*
Purplish Jay *Cyanocorax cyanomelas*
Azure Jay *Cyanocorax caeruleus*
Violaceous Jay *Cyanocorax violaceus*
Curl-crested Jay *Cyanocorax cristatellus*
Azure-naped Jay *Cyanocorax heilprini*
Cayenne Jay *Cyanocorax cayanus*
Plush-crested Jay *Cyanocorax chrysops*
White-naped Jay *Cyanocorax cyanopogon*
White-tailed Jay *Cyanocorax mystacalis*
Black-collared Jay *Cyanolyca armillata*
Turquoise Jay *Cyanolyca turcosa*
White-collared Jay *Cyanolyca viridicyanus*
Azure-hooded Jay *Cyanolyca cucullata*
Beautiful Jay *Cyanolyca pulchra*
Black-throated Jay *Cyanolyca pumilo*
Dwarf Jay *Cyanolyca nana*
Silvery-throated Jay *Cyanolyca argentigula*
White-throated Jay *Cyanolyca mirabilis*
Florida Scrub-Jay *Aphelocoma coerulescens*
Island Scrub-Jay *Aphelocoma insularis*
Western Scrub-Jay *Aphelocoma californica*
Gray-breasted Jay *Aphelocoma ultramarina*
Unicolored Jay *Aphelocoma unicolor*
Pinyon Jay *Gymnorhinus cyanocephalus*
Eurasian Jay *Garrulus glandarius*
Black-headed Jay *Garrulus lanceolatus*
Purple Jay *Garrulus lidthi*
Azure-winged Magpie *Cyanopica cyanus*
Sri Lanka Blue-Magpie *Urocissa ornata*
Taiwan Blue-Magpie *Urocissa caerulea*
Yellow-billed Blue-Magpie *Urocissa flavirostris*
Red-billed Blue-Magpie *Urocissa erythrorhyncha*
White-winged Magpie *Urocissa whiteheadi*
Green-Magpie *Cissa chinensis*
Indochinese Green-Magpie *Cissa hypoleuca*
Short-tailed Green-Magpie *Cissa thalassina*
Rufous Treepie *Dendrocitta vagabunda*
Gray Treepie *Dendrocitta formosae*
Sumatran Treepie *Dendrocitta occipitalis*
Bornean Treepie *Dendrocitta cinerascens*
White-bellied Treepie *Dendrocitta leucogastra*
Collared Treepie *Dendrocitta frontalis*
Andaman Treepie *Dendrocitta bayleyi*
Black Racquet-tailed Treepie *Crypsirina temia*
Hooded Racquet-tailed Treepie *Crypsirina cucullata*
Ratchet-tailed Treepie *Temnurus temnurus*
Common Magpie *Pica pica*
Black-billed Magpie *Pica hudsonia*
Yellow-billed Magpie *Pica nuttalli*

Stresemann's Bush-Crow *Zavattariornis stresemanni* •
Mongolian Ground-Jay *Podoces hendersoni*
Xinjiang Ground-Jay *Podoces biddulphi*
Pander's Ground-Jay *Podoces panderi*
Pleske's Ground-Jay *Podoces pleskei*
Clark's Nutcracker *Nucifraga columbiana*
Spotted Nutcracker *Nucifraga caryocatactes*
Red-billed Chough *Pyrrhocorax pyrrhocorax*
Yellow-billed Chough *Pyrrhocorax graculus*
Piapiac *Ptilostomus afer*
Eurasian Jackdaw *Corvus monedula*
Daurian Jackdaw *Corvus dauuricus*
House Crow *Corvus splendens*
New Caledonian Crow *Corvus moneduloides*
Slender-billed Crow *Corvus enca*
Piping Crow *Corvus typicus*
Flores Crow *Corvus florensis* •
Marianas Crow *Corvus kubaryi* •
Long-billed Crow *Corvus validus*
White-billed Crow *Corvus woodfordi*
Bougainville Crow *Corvus meeki*
Brown-headed Crow *Corvus fuscicapillus*
Gray Crow *Corvus tristis*
Cape Crow *Corvus capensis*
Eurasian Rook *Corvus frugilegus*
American Crow *Corvus brachyrhynchos*
Northwestern Crow *Corvus caurinus*
Cuban Palm Crow *Corvus minutus* •
Hispaniolan Palm Crow *Corvus palmarum*
Cuban Crow *Corvus nasicus*
White-necked Crow *Corvus leucognaphalus*
Jamaican Crow *Corvus jamaicensis*
Tamaulipas Crow *Corvus imparatus*
Sinaloa Crow *Corvus sinaloae*
Fish Crow *Corvus ossifragus*
Hawaiian Crow *Corvus hawaiiensis*
Chihuahuan Raven *Corvus cryptoleucus*
Carrion Crow *Corvus corone*
Hooded Crow *Corvus cornix*
Large-billed Crow *Corvus macrorhynchos*
Torresian Crow *Corvus orru*
Little Crow *Corvus bennetti*
Australian Raven *Corvus coronoides*
Little Raven *Corvus mellori*
Forest Raven *Corvus tasmanicus*
Collared Crow *Corvus torquatus*
African Pied Crow *Corvus albus*
Brown-necked Raven *Corvus ruficollis*
Dwarf Raven *Corvus edithae*
Fan-tailed Raven *Corvus rhipidurus*
White-naped Raven *Corvus albicollis*
Thick-billed Raven *Corvus crassirostris*
Common Raven *Corvus corax*

Starlings Sturnidae
Metallic Starling *Aplonis metallica*
Grant's Starling *Aplonis mystacea*
Singing Starling *Aplonis cantoroides*
Tanimbar Starling *Aplonis crassa*
Atoll Starling *Aplonis feadensis*
Rennell Island Starling *Aplonis insularis*
Long-tailed Starling *Aplonis magna*
White-eyed Glossy-Starling *Aplonis brunneicapillus* •
Large Glossy-Starling *Aplonis grandis*
San Cristobal Starling *Aplonis dichroa*
New Hebrides Starling *Aplonis zelandica*
Striated Starling *Aplonis striata*
Santo Mountain Starling *Aplonis santovestris*
Asian Glossy-Starling *Aplonis panayensis*
Island Starling *Aplonis mysolensis*
Short-tailed Glossy-Starling *Aplonis minor*
Micronesian Starling *Aplonis opaca*
Ponapé Starling *Aplonis pelzelni* •
Polynesian Starling *Aplonis tabuensis*

Samoan Starling *Aplonis atrifusca*
Rarotonga Starling *Aplonis cinerascens*
Yellow-faced Myna *Mino dumontii*
Golden-breasted Myna *Mino anais*
Long-tailed Myna *Mino kreffti*
Sulawesi Crested Myna *Basilornis celebensis*
Helmeted Myna *Basilornis galeatus*
Long-crested Myna *Basilornis corythaix*
Mount Apo Myna *Basilornis mirandus*
Coleto *Sarcops calvus*
White-necked Myna *Streptocitta albicollis*
Bare-eyed Myna *Streptocitta albertinae*
Fiery-browed Myna *Enodes erythrophris*
Finch-billed Myna *Scissirostrum dubium*
Spot-winged Starling *Saroglossa spiloptera*
Madagascar Starling *Saroglossa aurata*
Golden-crested Myna *Ampeliceps coronatus*
Common Hill-Myna *Gracula religiosa*
Southern Hill-Myna *Gracula indica*
Engganno Hill-Myna *Gracula enganensis*
Nias Hill-Myna *Gracula robusta*
Sri Lanka Myna *Gracula ptilogenys*
White-vented Myna *Acridotheres grandis*
Crested Myna *Acridotheres cristatellus*
Javan Myna *Acridotheres javanicus*
Pale-bellied Myna *Acridotheres cinereus*
Jungle Myna *Acridotheres fuscus*
Collared Myna *Acridotheres albocinctus*
Bank Myna *Acridotheres ginginianus*
Common Myna *Acridotheres tristis*
Vinous-breasted Myna *Acridotheres burmannicus*
Black-winged Myna *Acridotheres melanopterus*
Bali Myna *Leucopsar rothschildi* •
Black-collared Starling *Gracupica nigricollis*
Asian Pied Starling *Gracupica contra*
Daurian Starling *Sturnia sturnina*
Chestnut-cheeked Starling *Sturnia philippensis*
White-shouldered Starling *Sturnia sinensis*
Chestnut-tailed Starling *Sturnia malabarica*
White-headed Starling *Sturnia erythropygia*
White-faced Starling *Sturnia albofrontata*
Brahminy Starling *Temenuchus pagodarum*
Rosy Starling *Pastor roseus*
Red-billed Starling *Sturnus sericeus*
White-cheeked Starling *Sturnus cineraceus*
Common Starling *Sturnus vulgaris*
Spotless Starling *Sturnus unicolor*
Wattled Starling *Creatophora cinerea*
Red-shouldered Glossy-Starling *Lamprotornis nitens*
Blue-eared Glossy-Starling *Lamprotornis chalybaeus*
Lesser Blue-eared Glossy-Starling *Lamprotornis chloropterus*
Bronze-tailed Glossy-Starling *Lamprotornis chalcurus*
Splendid Glossy-Starling *Lamprotornis splendidus*
Príncipe Glossy-Starling *Lamprotornis ornatus*
Iris Glossy-Starling *Lamprotornis iris*
Purple Glossy-Starling *Lamprotornis purpureus*
Rueppell's Long-tailed Glossy-Starling *Lamprotornis purpuroptera*
Northern Long-tailed Glossy-Starling *Lamprotornis caudatus*
Golden-breasted Starling *Lamprotornis regius*
Meves's Glossy-Starling *Lamprotornis mevesii*
Burchell's Glossy-Starling *Lamprotornis australis*
Sharp-tailed Glossy-Starling *Lamprotornis acuticaudus*
Black-bellied Glossy-Starling *Lamprotornis corruscus*
Superb Starling *Lamprotornis superbus*
Hildebrandt's Starling *Lamprotornis hildebrandti*
Shelley's Starling *Lamprotornis shelleyi*
Chestnut-bellied Starling *Lamprotornis pulcher*
Purple-headed Glossy-Starling *Lamprotornis purpureiceps*
Copper-tailed Glossy-Starling *Lamprotornis cupreocauda*

Violet Starling *Cinnyricinclus leucogaster*
African Pied Starling *Spreo bicolor*
Fischer's Starling *Spreo fischeri*
Ashy Starling *Spreo unicolor*
White-crowned Starling *Spreo albicapillus*
Red-winged Starling *Onychognathus morio*
Slender-billed Chestnut-winged Starling *Onychognathus tenuirostris*
Common Chestnut-winged Starling *Onychognathus fulgidus*
Waller's Chestnut-winged Starling *Onychognathus walleri*
Somali Starling *Onychognathus blythii*
Socotra Starling *Onychognathus frater*
Tristram's Starling *Onychognathus tristramii*
Pale-winged Starling *Onychognathus nabouroup*
Bristle-crowned Starling *Onychognathus salvadorii*
White-billed Starling *Onychognathus albirostris*
Neumann's Starling *Onychognathus neumanni*
Narrow-tailed Starling *Poeoptera lugubris*
Stuhlmann's Starling *Poeoptera stuhlmanni*
Kenrick's Starling *Poeoptera kenricki*
Sharpe's Starling *Pholia sharpii*
Abbott's Starling *Pholia femoralis*
White-collared Starling *Grafisia torquata*
Magpie Starling *Speculipastor bicolor*
White-winged Starling *Neocichla gutturalis*
Red-billed Oxpecker *Buphagus erythrorhynchus*
Yellow-billed Oxpecker *Buphagus africanus*

Old World Sparrows Passeridae
Saxaul Sparrow *Passer ammodendri*
House Sparrow *Passer domesticus*
Spanish Sparrow *Passer hispaniolensis*
Sind Sparrow *Passer pyrrhonotus*
Somali Sparrow *Passer castanopterus*
Cinnamon Sparrow *Passer rutilans*
Plain-backed Sparrow *Passer flaveolus*
Dead Sea Sparrow *Passer moabiticus*
Iago Sparrow *Passer iagoensis*
Socotra Sparrow *Passer insularis*
Southern Rufous Sparrow *Passer motitensis*
Kenya Rufous Sparrow *Passer rufocinctus*
Rufous Sparrow shelleyi *Passer shelleyi*
Rufous Sparrow cordofanicus *Passer cordofanicus*
Cape Sparrow *Passer melanurus*
Gray-headed Sparrow *Passer griseus*
Swainson's Sparrow *Passer swainsonii*
Parrot-billed Sparrow *Passer gongonensis*
Swahili Sparrow *Passer suahelicus*
Southern Gray-headed Sparrow *Passer diffusus*
Desert Sparrow *Passer simplex*
Eurasian Tree Sparrow *Passer montanus*
Sudan Golden Sparrow *Passer luteus*
Arabian Golden Sparrow *Passer euchlorus*
Chestnut Sparrow *Passer eminibey*
Yellow-spotted Petronia *Petronia pyrgita*
Yellow-throated Petronia *Petronia xanthocollis*
South African Petronia *Petronia superciliaris*
Bush Petronia *Petronia dentata*
Rock Petronia *Petronia petronia*
Pale Rock-Sparrow *Carpospiza brachydactyla*
White-winged Snowfinch *Montifringilla nivalis*
Tibetan Snowfinch *Montifringilla adamsi*
White-rumped Snowfinch *Montifringilla taczanowskii*
Père David's Snowfinch *Montifringilla davidiana*
Rufous-necked Snowfinch *Montifringilla ruficollis*
Plain-backed Snowfinch *Montifringilla blanfordi*
Theresa's Snowfinch *Montifringilla theresae*

Weavers and Sparrows Ploceidae
White-billed Buffalo-Weaver *Bubalornis albirostris*
Red-billed Buffalo-Weaver *Bubalornis niger*
White-headed Buffalo-Weaver *Dinemellia dinemelli*

Speckle-fronted Weaver *Sporopipes frontalis*
Scaly Weaver *Sporopipes squamifrons*
White-browed Sparrow-Weaver *Plocepasser mahali*
Chestnut-crowned Sparrow-Weaver *Plocepasser superciliosus*
Chestnut-mantled Sparrow-Weaver *Plocepasser rufoscapulatus*
Donaldson-Smith's Sparrow-Weaver *Plocepasser donaldsoni*
Rufous-tailed Weaver *Histurgops ruficauda*
Gray-capped Social-Weaver *Pseudonigrita arnaudi*
Black-capped Social-Weaver *Pseudonigrita cabanisi*
Common Social-Weaver *Philetairus socius*
Bannerman's Weaver *Ploceus bannermani* •
Bates's Weaver *Ploceus batesi*
Black-chinned Weaver *Ploceus nigrimentus*
Baglafecht Weaver *Ploceus baglafecht*
Bertrand's Weaver *Ploceus bertrandi*
Slender-billed Weaver *Ploceus pelzelni*
Loango Weaver *Ploceus subpersonatus*
Little Weaver *Ploceus luteolus*
Lesser Masked-Weaver *Ploceus intermedius*
Spectacled Weaver *Ploceus ocularis*
Black-necked Weaver *Ploceus nigricollis*
Black-billed Weaver *Ploceus melanogaster*
Strange Weaver *Ploceus alienus*
Bocage's Weaver *Ploceus temporalis*
Cape Weaver *Ploceus capensis*
African Golden-Weaver *Ploceus subaureus*
Holub's Golden-Weaver *Ploceus xanthops*
Príncipe Golden-Weaver *Ploceus princeps*
Orange Weaver *Ploceus aurantius*
Golden Palm Weaver *Ploceus bojeri*
Taveta Golden-Weaver *Ploceus castaneiceps*
Southern Brown-throated Weaver *Ploceus xanthopterus*
Northern Brown-throated Weaver *Ploceus castanops*
Kilombero Weaver *Ploceus burnieri*
Rueppell's Weaver *Ploceus galbula*
Heuglin's Masked-Weaver *Ploceus heuglini*
Northern Masked-Weaver *Ploceus taeniopterus*
Southern Masked-Weaver *Ploceus velatus*
Vitelline Masked-Weaver *Ploceus vitellinus*
Tanzanian Masked-Weaver *Ploceus reichardi*
Ruwet's Masked-Weaver *Ploceus ruweti*
Katanga Masked-Weaver *Ploceus katangae*
Village Weaver *Ploceus cucullatus*
Giant Weaver *Ploceus grandis*
Speke's Weaver *Ploceus spekei*
Fox's Weaver *Ploceus spekeoides*
Vieillot's Black Weaver *Ploceus nigerrimus*
Weyns's Weaver *Ploceus weynsi*
Clarke's Weaver *Ploceus golandi* •
Yellow-backed Weaver *Ploceus melanocephalus*
Salvadori's Weaver *Ploceus dichrocephalus*
Jackson's Golden-backed Weaver *Ploceus jacksoni*
Cinnamon Weaver *Ploceus badius*
Chestnut Weaver *Ploceus rubiginosus*
Golden-naped Weaver *Ploceus aureonucha* •
Yellow-mantled Weaver *Ploceus tricolor*
Maxwell's Black Weaver *Ploceus albinucha*
Nelicourvi Weaver *Ploceus nelicourvi*
Sakalava Weaver *Ploceus sakalava*
Streaked Weaver *Ploceus manyar*
Baya Weaver *Ploceus philippinus*
Asian Golden-Weaver *Ploceus hypoxanthus*
Finn's Weaver *Ploceus megarhynchus*
Black-breasted Weaver *Ploceus benghalensis*
Dark-backed Weaver *Ploceus bicolor*
Western Golden-backed Weaver *Ploceus preussi*
Yellow-capped Weaver *Ploceus dorsomaculatus*
Usambara Weaver *Ploceus nicolli* •
Olive-headed Weaver *Ploceus olivaceiceps*
Brown-capped Weaver *Ploceus insignis*

Bar-winged Weaver   *Ploceus angolensis*
São Tomé Weaver   *Ploceus sanctithomae*
Yellow-legged Malimbe   *Ploceus flavipes*
Compact Weaver   *Pachyphantes superciliosus*
Red-crowned Malimbe   *Malimbus coronatus*
Black-throated Malimbe   *Malimbus cassini*
Gola Malimbe   *Malimbus ballmanni* •
Rachel's Malimbe   *Malimbus racheliae*
Red-vented Malimbe   *Malimbus scutatus*
Ibadan Malimbe   *Malimbus ibadanensis* •
Red-bellied Malimbe   *Malimbus erythrogaster*
Gray's Malimbe   *Malimbus nitens*
Crested Malimbe   *Malimbus malimbicus*
Red-headed Malimbe   *Malimbus rubricollis*
Red-headed Anaplectes   *Anaplectes rubriceps*
Bob-tailed Weaver   *Brachycope anomala*
Cardinal Quelea   *Quelea cardinalis*
Red-headed Quelea   *Quelea erythrops*
Red-billed Quelea   *Quelea quelea*
Madagascar Red Fody   *Foudia madagascariensis*
Red Forest Fody   *Foudia eminentissima*
Forest Fody   *Foudia omissa*
Mauritius Fody   *Foudia rubra* •
Seychelles Fody   *Foudia sechellarum*
Rodrigues Fody   *Foudia flavicans*
Yellow-crowned Bishop   *Euplectes afer*
Fire-fronted Bishop   *Euplectes diadematus*
Black Bishop   *Euplectes gierowii*
Black-winged Red Bishop   *Euplectes hordeaceus*
Northern Red Bishop   *Euplectes franciscanus*
Southern Red Bishop   *Euplectes orix*
Zanzibar Bishop   *Euplectes nigroventris*
Golden-backed Bishop   *Euplectes aureus*
Yellow Bishop   *Euplectes capensis*
Fan-tailed Widowbird   *Euplectes axillaris*
Yellow-mantled Widowbird   *Euplectes macroura*
White-winged Widowbird   *Euplectes albonotatus*
Red-collared Widowbird   *Euplectes ardens*
Hartlaub's Marsh Widowbird   *Euplectes hartlaubi*
Buff-shouldered Widowbird   *Euplectes psammocromius*
Long-tailed Widowbird   *Euplectes progne*
Jackson's Widowbird   *Euplectes jacksoni*
Grosbeak Weaver   *Amblyospiza albifrons*

Waxbills Estrildidae
Jameson's Antpecker   *Parmoptila rubrifrons*
Jameson's Antpecker jamesoni   *Parmoptila jamesoni*
Woodhouse's Antpecker   *Parmoptila woodhousei*
White-breasted Negrofinch   *Nigrita fusconotus*
Chestnut-breasted Negrofinch   *Nigrita bicolor*
Pale-fronted Negrofinch   *Nigrita luteifrons*
Gray-headed Negrofinch   *Nigrita canicapillus*
White-collared Oliveback   *Nesocharis ansorgei*
Fernando Po Oliveback   *Nesocharis shelleyi*
Gray-headed Oliveback   *Nesocharis capistrata*
Orange-winged Pytilia   *Pytilia afra*
Lineated Pytilia   *Pytilia phoenicoptera*
Red-winged Pytilia lineata   *Pytilia lineata*
Green-winged Pytilia   *Pytilia melba*
Red-faced Pytilia   *Pytilia hypogrammica*
Green-backed Twinspot   *Mandingoa nitidula*
Red-faced Crimsonwing   *Cryptospiza reichenovii*
Ethiopian Crimsonwing   *Cryptospiza salvadorii*
Dusky Crimsonwing   *Cryptospiza jacksoni*
Shelley's Crimsonwing   *Cryptospiza shelleyi*
Crimson Seedcracker   *Pyrenestes sanguineus*
Black-bellied Seedcracker   *Pyrenestes ostrinus*
Lesser Seedcracker   *Pyrenestes minor*
Grant's Bluebill   *Spermophaga poliogenys*
Western Bluebill   *Spermophaga haematina*
Red-headed Bluebill   *Spermophaga ruficapilla*
Brown Twinspot   *Clytospiza monteiri*
Red-throated Twinspot   *Hypargos niveoguttatus*

Rosy Twinspot   *Hypargos margaritatus*
Dybowski's Twinspot   *Euschistospiza dybowskii*
Dusky Twinspot   *Euschistospiza cinereovinacea*
Bar-breasted Firefinch   *Lagonosticta rufopicta*
Brown Firefinch   *Lagonosticta nitidula*
Red-billed Firefinch   *Lagonosticta senegala*
Black-bellied Firefinch   *Lagonosticta rara*
African Firefinch   *Lagonosticta rubricata*
Pale-billed Firefinch   *Lagonosticta landanae*
Jameson's Firefinch   *Lagonosticta rhodopareia*
Kulikoro Firefinch   *Lagonosticta virata*
Rock Firefinch   *Lagonosticta sanguinodorsalis*
Black-throated Firefinch   *Lagonosticta larvata*
Reichenow's Firefinch   *Lagonosticta umbrinodorsalis*
Blue-cheeked Cordonbleu   *Uraeginthus angolensis*
Red-cheeked Cordonbleu   *Uraeginthus bengalus*
Blue-capped Cordonbleu   *Uraeginthus cyanocephalus*
Purple Grenadier   *Uraeginthus ianthinogaster*
Common Grenadier   *Uraeginthus granatinus*
Lavender Waxbill   *Estrilda caerulescens*
Black-tailed Lavender Waxbill   *Estrilda perreini*
Cinderella Waxbill   *Estrilda thomensis*
Yellow-bellied Waxbill   *Estrilda quartinia*
Swee Waxbill   *Estrilda melanotis*
Fawn-breasted Waxbill   *Estrilda paludicola*
Anambra Waxbill   *Estrilda poliopareia*
Orange-cheeked Waxbill   *Estrilda melpoda*
Arabian Waxbill   *Estrilda rufibarba*
Crimson-rumped Waxbill   *Estrilda rhodopyga*
Black-rumped Waxbill   *Estrilda troglodytes*
Common Waxbill   *Estrilda astrild*
Black-lored Waxbill   *Estrilda nigriloris*
Black-crowned Waxbill   *Estrilda nonnula*
Black-headed Waxbill   *Estrilda atricapilla*
Kandt's Waxbill   *Estrilda kandti*
Black-faced Waxbill   *Estrilda erythronotos*
Red-rumped Waxbill   *Estrilda charmosyna*
Red Avadavat   *Amandava amandava*
Zebra Waxbill   *Sporaeginthus subflavus*
Green Avadavat   *Sporaeginthus formosus*
Black-chinned Quailfinch   *Ortygospiza gabonensis*
African Quailfinch fuscocrissa   *Ortygospiza fuscocrissa*
African Quailfinch   *Ortygospiza atricollis*
Common Locustfinch   *Paludipasser locustella*
Painted Finch   *Emblema pictum*
Beautiful Firetail   *Stagonopleura bella*
Red-eared Firetail   *Stagonopleura oculata*
Diamond Firetail   *Stagonopleura guttata*
Crimson-sided Mountain-Finch   *Oreostruthus fuliginosus*
Red-browed Firetail   *Neochmia temporalis*
Crimson Finch   *Neochmia phaeton*
Star Finch   *Neochmia ruficauda*
Plum-headed Finch   *Neochmia modesta*
Zebra Finch   *Taeniopygia guttata*
Chestnut-eared Finch   *Taeniopygia castanotis*
Double-barred Finch   *Taeniopygia bichenovii*
Masked Finch   *Poephila personata*
Long-tailed Finch   *Poephila acuticauda*
Black-throated Finch   *Poephila cincta*
Tawny-breasted Parrotfinch   *Erythrura hyperythra*
Pin-tailed Parrotfinch   *Erythrura prasina*
Green-faced Parrotfinch   *Erythrura viridifacies*
Three-colored Parrotfinch   *Erythrura tricolor*
Blue-faced Parrotfinch   *Erythrura trichroa*
Red-eared Parrotfinch   *Erythrura coloria*
Papuan Parrotfinch   *Erythrura papuana*
Red-throated Parrotfinch   *Erythrura psittacea*
Fiji Parrotfinch   *Erythrura pealii*
Red-headed Parrotfinch   *Erythrura cyaneovirens*
Royal Parrotfinch   *Erythrura regia*
Pink-billed Parrotfinch   *Erythrura kleinschmidti*
Gouldian Finch   *Chloebia gouldiae* •
African Silverbill   *Euodice cantans*

Indian Silverbill   *Euodice malabarica*
Gray-headed Silverbill   *Odontospiza griseicapilla*
Bronze Mannikin   *Spermestes cucullatus*
Black-and-white Mannikin   *Spermestes bicolor*
Magpie Munia   *Spermestes fringilloides*
Madagascar Munia   *Lonchura nana*
White-rumped Munia   *Lonchura striata*
Javan White-bellied Munia   *Lonchura leucogastroides*
Dusky Munia   *Lonchura fuscans*
Black-faced Munia   *Lonchura molucca*
Black-throated Munia   *Lonchura kelaarti*
Scaly-breasted Munia   *Lonchura punctulata*
White-bellied Munia   *Lonchura leucogastra*
Streak-headed Mannikin   *Lonchura tristissima*
Black-headed Munia   *Lonchura malacca*
Chestnut Munia   *Lonchura atricapilla*
White-capped Munia   *Lonchura ferruginosa*
Chestnut-and-white Munia   *Lonchura quinticolor*
White-headed Munia   *Lonchura maja*
Pale-headed Munia   *Lonchura pallida*
Great-billed Munia   *Lonchura grandis*
Gray-banded Mannikin   *Lonchura vana*
Gray-crowned Munia   *Lonchura nevermanni*
New Britain Mannikin   *Lonchura spectabilis*
Gray-headed Mannikin   *Lonchura caniceps*
Hunstein's Munia   *Lonchura hunsteini*
New Ireland Munia   *Lonchura forbesi*
New Hanover Munia   *Lonchura nigerrima*
Yellow-rumped Munia   *Lonchura flaviprymna*
Chestnut-breasted Munia   *Lonchura castaneothorax*
Black Mannikin   *Lonchura stygia*
Grand Valley Munia   *Lonchura teerinki*
Snow Mountain Munia   *Lonchura montana*
Eastern Alpine Munia   *Lonchura monticola*
Thick-billed Munia   *Lonchura melaena*
Pictorella Finch   *Heteromunia pectoralis*
Java Sparrow   *Padda oryzivora*
Timor Dusky Sparrow   *Padda fuscata*
Cut-throat Finch   *Amadina fasciata*
Red-headed Finch   *Amadina erythrocephala*

Indigobirds Viduidae
Village Indigobird   *Vidua chalybeata*
Jambandu Indigobird   *Vidua raricola*
Baka Indigobird   *Vidua larvaticola*
Jos Plateau Indigobird   *Vidua maryae*
Quailfinch Indigobird   *Vidua nigeriae*
Variable Indigobird   *Vidua funerea*
Twinspot Indigobird   *Vidua codringtoni*
Purple Indigobird   *Vidua purpurascens*
Pale-winged Indigobird   *Vidua wilsoni*
Cameroon Indigobird   *Vidua camerunensis*
Steel-blue Whydah   *Vidua hypocherina*
Straw-tailed Whydah   *Vidua fischeri*
Shaft-tailed Whydah   *Vidua regia*
Pin-tailed Whydah   *Vidua macroura*
Togo Paradise-Whydah   *Vidua togoensis*
Long-tailed Paradise-Whydah   *Vidua interjecta*
Eastern Paradise-Whydah   *Vidua paradisaea*
Northern Paradise-Whydah   *Vidua orientalis*
Broad-tailed Paradise-Whydah   *Vidua obtusa*
Parasitic Weaver   *Anomalospiza imberbis*

Vireos Vireonidae
Slaty Vireo   *Vireo brevipennis*
White-eyed Vireo   *Vireo griseus*
Thick-billed Vireo   *Vireo crassirostris*
Mangrove Vireo   *Vireo pallens*
Cozumel Vireo   *Vireo bairdi*
St Andrew Vireo   *Vireo caribaeus*
Jamaican White-eyed Vireo   *Vireo modestus*
Cuban Vireo   *Vireo gundlachii*
Puerto Rican Vireo   *Vireo latimeri*
Flat-billed Vireo   *Vireo nanus*

Bell's Vireo   *Vireo bellii*
Black-capped Vireo   *Vireo atricapilla*
Dwarf Vireo   *Vireo nelsoni*
Gray Vireo   *Vireo vicinior*
Blue Mountain Vireo   *Vireo osburni*
Yellow-throated Vireo   *Vireo flavifrons*
Plumbeous Vireo   *Vireo plumbeus*
Cassin's Vireo   *Vireo cassinii*
Blue-headed Vireo   *Vireo solitarius*
Carmiol's Vireo   *Vireo carmioli*
Hutton's Vireo   *Vireo huttoni*
Eastern Warbling Vireo   *Vireo gilvus*
Brown-capped Vireo   *Vireo leucophrys*
Philadelphia Vireo   *Vireo philadelphicus*
Red-eyed Vireo   *Vireo olivaceus*
Chocó Vireo   *Vireo masteri* •
Golden Vireo   *Vireo hypochryseus*
Yellow-green Vireo   *Vireo flavoviridis*
Noronha Vireo   *Vireo gracilirostris*
Black-whiskered Vireo   *Vireo altiloquus*
Yucatan Vireo   *Vireo magister*
Rufous-crowned Greenlet   *Hylophilus poicilotis*
Gray-eyed Greenlet   *Hylophilus amaurocephalus*
Lemon-chested Greenlet   *Hylophilus thoracicus*
Gray-chested Greenlet   *Hylophilus semicinereus*
Ashy-headed Greenlet   *Hylophilus pectoralis*
Tepui Greenlet   *Hylophilus sclateri*
Buff-cheeked Greenlet   *Hylophilus muscicapinus*
Brown-headed Greenlet   *Hylophilus brunneiceps*
Dusky-capped Greenlet   *Hylophilus hypoxanthus*
Rufous-naped Greenlet   *Hylophilus semibrunneus*
Olivaceous Greenlet   *Hylophilus olivaceus*
Scrub Greenlet   *Hylophilus flavipes*
Tawny-crowned Greenlet   *Hylophilus ochraceiceps*
Golden-fronted Greenlet   *Hylophilus aurantiifrons*
Lesser Greenlet   *Hylophilus decurtatus*
Chestnut-sided Shrike-Vireo   *Vireolanius melitophrys*
Green Shrike-Vireo   *Vireolanius pulchellus*
Yellow-browed Shrike-Vireo   *Vireolanius eximius*
Slaty-capped Shrike-Vireo   *Vireolanius leucotis*
Rufous-browed Peppershrike   *Cyclarhis gujanensis*
Black-billed Peppershrike   *Cyclarhis nigrirostris*

Finches Fringillidae
European Chaffinch   *Fringilla coelebs*
Blue Chaffinch   *Fringilla teydea*
Brambling   *Fringilla montifringilla*
Jamaican Euphonia   *Euphonia jamaica*
Plumbeous Euphonia   *Euphonia plumbea*
Scrub Euphonia   *Euphonia affinis*
Purple-throated Euphonia   *Euphonia chlorotica*
Yellow-crowned Euphonia   *Euphonia luteicapilla*
Trinidad Euphonia   *Euphonia trinitatis*
Velvet-fronted Euphonia   *Euphonia concinna*
Orange-crowned Euphonia   *Euphonia saturata*
Finsch's Euphonia   *Euphonia finschi*
Violaceous Euphonia   *Euphonia violacea*
Thick-billed Euphonia   *Euphonia laniirostris*
Yellow-throated Euphonia   *Euphonia hirundinacea*
Green-chinned Euphonia   *Euphonia chalybea*
Elegant Euphonia   *Euphonia elegantissima*
Blue-hooded Euphonia   *Euphonia musica*
Golden-rumped Euphonia   *Euphonia cyanocephala*
Spot-crowned Euphonia   *Euphonia imitans*
Fulvous-vented Euphonia   *Euphonia fulvicrissa*
Olive-backed Euphonia   *Euphonia gouldi*
Bronze-green Euphonia   *Euphonia mesochrysa*
White-lored Euphonia   *Euphonia chrysopasta*
White-vented Euphonia   *Euphonia minuta*
Tawny-capped Euphonia   *Euphonia anneae*
Orange-bellied Euphonia   *Euphonia xanthogaster*
Rufous-bellied Euphonia   *Euphonia rufiventris*
Golden-sided Euphonia   *Euphonia cayennensis*
Chestnut-bellied Euphonia   *Euphonia pectoralis*

Yellow-collared Chlorophonia   *Chlorophonia flavirostris*
Blue-naped Chlorophonia   *Chlorophonia cyanea*
Chestnut-breasted Chlorophonia   *Chlorophonia pyrrhophrys*
Blue-crowned Chlorophonia   *Chlorophonia occipitalis*
Golden-browed Chlorophonia   *Chlorophonia callophrys*
São Tomé Grosbeak   *Neospiza concolor* •
Oriole Finch   *Linurgus olivaceus*
Golden-winged Grosbeak   *Rhynchostruthus socotranus*
Golden-winged Grosbeak louisae   *Rhynchostruthus louisae*
Hodgson's Mountain-Finch   *Leucosticte nemoricola*
Brandt's Mountain-Finch   *Leucosticte brandti*
Sillem's Mountain-Finch   *Leucosticte sillemi*
Arctic Rosy-Finch   *Leucosticte arctoa*
Gray-crowned Rosy-Finch   *Leucosticte tephrocotis*
Black Rosy-Finch   *Leucosticte atrata*
Brown-capped Rosy-Finch   *Leucosticte australis*
Pine Grosbeak   *Pinicola enucleator*
Red-headed Rosefinch   *Pinicola subhimachala*
Blanford's Rosefinch   *Carpodacus rubescens*
Dark Rosefinch   *Carpodacus nipalensis*
Common Rosefinch   *Carpodacus erythrinus*
Cassin's Finch   *Carpodacus cassinii*
Purple Finch   *Carpodacus purpureus*
House Finch   *Carpodacus mexicanus*
Beautiful Rosefinch   *Carpodacus pulcherrimus*
Stresemann's Rosefinch   *Carpodacus eos*
Pink-browed Rosefinch   *Carpodacus rodochroa*
Vinaceus Rosefinch   *Carpodacus vinaceus*
Dark-rumped Rosefinch   *Carpodacus edwardsii*
Sinai Rosefinch   *Carpodacus synoicus*
Pallas's Rosefinch   *Carpodacus roseus*
Three-banded Rosefinch   *Carpodacus trifasciatus*
Spot-winged Rosefinch   *Carpodacus rhodopeplus*
White-browed Rosefinch   *Carpodacus thura*
Tibetan Rosefinch   *Carpodacus roborowskii*
Red-mantled Rosefinch   *Carpodacus rhodochlamys*
Eastern Great Rosefinch   *Carpodacus rubicilloides*
Caucasian Great Rosefinch   *Carpodacus rubicilla*
Red-breasted Rosefinch   *Carpodacus puniceus*
Parrot Crossbill   *Loxia pytyopsittacus*
Scottish Crossbill   *Loxia scotica*
Common Crossbill   *Loxia curvirostra*
Hispaniolan Crossbill   *Loxia megaplaga* •
White-winged Crossbill   *Loxia leucoptera*
Himalayan Greenfinch   *Carduelis spinoides*
Vietnamese Greenfinch   *Carduelis monguilloti*
European Greenfinch   *Carduelis chloris*
Black-headed Greenfinch   *Carduelis ambigua*
Common Redpoll   *Carduelis flammea*
Arctic Redpoll   *Carduelis hornemanni*
Eurasian Siskin   *Carduelis spinus*
Pine Siskin   *Carduelis pinus*
Black-capped Siskin   *Carduelis atriceps*
Black-headed Siskin   *Carduelis notata*
Andean Siskin   *Carduelis spinescens*
Yellow-faced Siskin   *Carduelis yarrellii*
Thick-billed Siskin   *Carduelis crassirostris*
Hooded Siskin   *Carduelis magellanica*
Yellow-bellied Siskin   *Carduelis xanthogastra*
Saffron Siskin   *Carduelis siemiradzkii*
Olivaceous Siskin   *Carduelis olivacea*
Red Siskin   *Carduelis cucullata* •
Antillean Siskin   *Carduelis dominicensis*
Lesser Goldfinch   *Carduelis psaltria*
Lawrence's Goldfinch   *Carduelis lawrencei*
Black-chinned Siskin   *Carduelis barbata*
Black Siskin   *Carduelis atrata*
Yellow-rumped Siskin   *Carduelis uropygialis*
American Goldfinch   *Carduelis tristis*
European Goldfinch   *Carduelis carduelis*
Oriental Greenfinch   *Carduelis sinica*

Twite   *Carduelis flavirostris*
Eurasian Linnet   *Carduelis cannabina*
Yemeni Linnet   *Carduelis yemenensis*
Warsangli Linnet   *Carduelis johannis* •
Ankober Serin   *Carduelis ankoberensis*
Red-fronted Serin   *Serinus pusillus*
European Serin   *Serinus serinus*
Syrian Serin   *Serinus syriacus*
Canary   *Serinus canaria*
Citril Finch   *Serinus citrinella*
Corsican Finch   *Serinus corsicanus*
Tibetan Siskin   *Serinus thibetanus*
Yellow-crowned Canary   *Serinus canicollis*
Cape Canary flavivertex   *Serinus flavivertex*
Abyssinian Siskin   *Serinus nigriceps*
African Citril   *Serinus citrinelloides*
Western Citril   *Serinus frontalis*
East African Citril   *Serinus hyposticutus*
Black-faced Canary   *Serinus capistratus*
Papyrus Serin   *Serinus koliensis*
Forest Canary   *Serinus scotops*
White-rumped Seedeater   *Serinus leucopygius*
Arabian Yellow-rumped Serin   *Serinus rothschildi*
Yellow-throated Serin   *Serinus flavigula* •
Salvadori's Serin   *Serinus xantholaemus*
Southern Yellow-rumped Seedeater   *Serinus atrogularis*
Kenyan Yellow-rumped Seedeater   *Serinus reichenowi*
Abyssinian Yellow-rumped Seedeater   *Serinus xanthopygius*
Lemon-breasted Seedeater   *Serinus citrinipectus*
Yellow-fronted Serin   *Serinus mozambicus*
Abyssinian Grosbeak Canary   *Serinus donaldsoni*
Kenya Grosbeak Canary   *Serinus buchanani*
White-bellied Serin   *Serinus dorsostriatus*
Yellow Canary   *Serinus flaviventris*
Brimstone Serin   *Serinus sulphuratus*
Stripe-breasted Serin   *Serinus reichardi*
White-throated Canary   *Serinus albogularis*
Streaky-headed Serin   *Serinus gularis*
Black-eared Serin   *Serinus mennelli*
Brown-rumped Serin   *Serinus tristriatus*
Yemen Serin   *Serinus menachensis*
Streaky Serin   *Serinus striolatus*
Yellow-browed Seedeater   *Serinus whytii*
Thick-billed Serin   *Serinus burtoni*
Kipengere Seedeater   *Serinus melanochrous*
Príncipe Seedeater   *Serinus rufobrunneus*
White-winged Seedeater   *Serinus leucopterus*
Mountain Serin   *Serinus estherae*
Cape Siskin   *Pseudochloroptila totta*
Drakensberg Siskin   *Pseudochloroptila symonsi*
Black-headed Canary   *Alario alario*
Damara Canary   *Alario leucolaemus*
Brown Bullfinch   *Pyrrhula nipalensis*
Philippine Bullfinch   *Pyrrhula leucogenis*
Orange Bullfinch   *Pyrrhula aurantiaca*
Red-headed Bullfinch   *Pyrrhula erythrocephala*
Beavan's Bullfinch   *Pyrrhula erythaca*
Common Bullfinch   *Pyrrhula pyrrhula*
Hawfinch   *Coccothraustes coccothraustes*
Evening Grosbeak   *Coccothraustes vespertinus*
Hooded Grosbeak   *Coccothraustes abeillei*
Chinese Grosbeak   *Eophona migratoria*
Japanese Grosbeak   *Eophona personata*
Black-and-yellow Grosbeak   *Mycerobas icterioides*
Collared Grosbeak   *Mycerobas affinis*
Spotted-winged Grosbeak   *Mycerobas melanozanthos*
White-winged Grosbeak   *Mycerobas carnipes*
Gold-naped Finch   *Pyrrhoplectes epauletta*
Red-browed Finch   *Callacanthis burtoni*
Crimson-winged Finch   *Rhodopechys sanguineus*
Mongolian Finch   *Rhodopechys mongolicus*
Trumpeter-Finch   *Bucanetes githagineus*

Desert-Finch *Rhodospiza obsoletus*
Long-tailed Rosefinch *Uragus sibiricus*
Scarlet Finch *Haematospiza sipahi*

Hawaiian Honeycreepers Drepanididae
Laysan Finch *Telespiza cantans*
Nihoa Finch *Telespiza ultima* •
O'u *Psittirostra psittacea* •
Palila *Loxioides bailleui* •
Maui Parrotbill *Pseudonestor xanthophrys* •
Hawaii Amakihi *Hemignathus virens*
O'ahu Amakihi *Hemignathus flavus*
Kaua'i Amakihi *Hemignathus kauaiensis*
Anianiau *Hemignathus parvus*
Greater Akialoa *Hemignathus ellisianus*
Nukupu'u *Hemignathus lucidus* •
Akiapolaa'u *Hemignathus munroi* •
Akikiki *Oreomystis bairdi* •
Hawaii Creeper *Oreomystis mana* •
O'ahu 'Alauahio *Paroreomyza maculata* •
Maui Alauahio *Paroreomyza montana* •
Akeke'e *Loxops caeruleirostris* •
Akepa *Loxops coccineus* •
Iiwi *Vestiaria coccinea*
Akohekohe *Palmeria dolei* •
Apapane *Himatione sanguinea*
Po'o-uli *Melamprosops phaeosoma* •

Olive Warbler Peucedramidae
Olive Warbler *Peucedramus taeniatus*

New World Warblers Parulidae
Bachman's Warbler *Vermivora bachmanii* •
Blue-winged Warbler *Vermivora pinus*
Golden-winged Warbler *Vermivora chrysoptera*
Tennessee Warbler *Vermivora peregrina*
Orange-crowned Warbler *Vermivora celata*
Nashville Warbler *Vermivora ruficapilla*
Virginia's Warbler *Vermivora virginiae*
Colima Warbler *Vermivora crissalis*
Lucy's Warbler *Vermivora luciae*
Flame-throated Warbler *Parula gutturalis*
Crescent-chested Warbler *Parula superciliosa*
Northern Parula *Parula americana*
Tropical Parula *Parula pitiayumi*
Golden Warbler *Dendroica petechia*
Chestnut-sided Warbler *Dendroica pensylvanica*
Magnolia Warbler *Dendroica magnolia*
Cape May Warbler *Dendroica tigrina*
Black-throated Blue Warbler *Dendroica caerulescens*
Yellow-rumped Warbler *Dendroica coronata*
Black-throated Gray Warbler *Dendroica nigrescens*
Golden-cheeked Warbler *Dendroica chrysoparia* •
Black-throated Green Warbler *Dendroica virens*
Townsend's Warbler *Dendroica townsendi*
Hermit Warbler *Dendroica occidentalis*
Blackburnian Warbler *Dendroica fusca*
Yellow-throated Warbler *Dendroica dominica*
Olive-capped Warbler *Dendroica pityophila*
Grace's Warbler *Dendroica graciae*
Adelaide's Warbler *Dendroica adelaidae*
Barbuda Warbler *Dendroica subita*
St Lucia Warbler *Dendroica delicata*
Pine Warbler *Dendroica pinus*
Kirtland's Warbler Dendroica kirtlandii •
Prairie Warbler *Dendroica discolor*
Vitelline Warbler *Dendroica vitellina*
Palm Warbler *Dendroica palmarum*
Bay-breasted Warbler *Dendroica castanea*
Blackpoll Warbler *Dendroica striata*
Cerulean Warbler *Dendroica cerulea*
Plumbeous Warbler *Dendroica plumbea*
Arrowhead Warbler *Dendroica pharetra*
Elfin Woods Warbler *Dendroica angelae*

Whistling Warbler *Catharopeza bishopi* •
Black-and-white Warbler *Mniotilta varia*
American Redstart *Setophaga ruticilla*
Prothonotary Warbler *Protonotaria citrea*
Worm-eating Warbler *Helmitheros vermivorum*
Swainson's Warbler *Limnothlypis swainsonii*
Ovenbird *Seiurus aurocapilla*
Northern Waterthrush *Seiurus noveboracensis*
Louisiana Waterthrush *Seiurus motacilla*
Kentucky Warbler *Oporornis formosus*
Connecticut Warbler *Oporornis agilis*
Mourning Warbler *Oporornis philadelphia*
MacGillivray's Warbler *Oporornis tolmiei*
Common Yellowthroat *Geothlypis trichas*
Belding's Yellowthroat *Geothlypis beldingi* •
Altamira Yellowthroat *Geothlypis flavovelata*
Bahama Yellowthroat *Geothlypis rostrata*
Olive-crowned Yellowthroat *Geothlypis semiflava*
Black-polled Yellowthroat *Geothlypis speciosa* •
Masked Yellowthroat *Geothlypis aequinoctialis*
Gray-crowned Yellowthroat *Geothlypis poliocephala*
Hooded Yellowthroat *Geothlypis nelsoni*
Green-tailed Ground-Warbler *Microligea palustris*
Yellow-headed Warbler *Teretistris fernandinae*
Oriente Warbler *Teretistris fornsi*
Semper's Warbler *Leucopeza semperi* •
Hooded Warbler *Wilsonia citrina*
Wilson's Warbler *Wilsonia pusilla*
Canada Warbler *Wilsonia canadensis*
American Red-faced Warbler *Cardellina rubrifrons*
Red Warbler *Ergaticus ruber*
Pink-headed Warbler *Ergaticus versicolor*
Painted Whitestart *Myioborus pictus*
Slate-throated Whitestart *Myioborus miniatus*
Tepui Whitestart *Myioborus castaneocapilla*
Brown-capped Whitestart *Myioborus brunniceps*
Paria Whitestart *Myioborus pariae* •
White-faced Whitestart *Myioborus albifacies*
Guaiquinima Whitestart *Myioborus cardonai*
Collared Whitestart *Myioborus torquatus*
Spectacled Whitestart *Myioborus melanocephalus*
Golden-fronted Whitestart *Myioborus ornatus*
White-fronted Whitestart *Myioborus albifrons*
Yellow-crowned Whitestart *Myioborus flavivertex*
Neotropic Fan-tailed Warbler *Euthlypis lachrymosa*
Gray-and-gold Warbler *Basileuterus fraseri*
Two-banded Warbler *Basileuterus bivittatus*
Golden-bellied Warbler *Basileuterus chrysogaster*
Chocó Warbler *Basileuterus chlorophrys*
Pale-legged Warbler *Basileuterus signatus*
Citrine Warbler *Basileuterus luteoviridis*
Black-crested Warbler *Basileuterus nigrocristatus*
Gray-headed Warbler *Basileuterus griseiceps* •
Santa Marta Warbler *Basileuterus basilicus*
Gray-throated Warbler *Basileuterus cinereicollis*
White-lored Warbler *Basileuterus conspicillatus*
Russet-crowned Warbler *Basileuterus coronatus*
Golden-crowned Warbler *Basileuterus culicivorus*
Three-banded Warbler *Basileuterus trifasciatus*
White-bellied Warbler *Basileuterus hypoleucus*
Rufous-capped Warbler *Basileuterus rufifrons*
Golden-browed Warbler *Basileuterus belli*
Black-cheeked Warbler *Basileuterus melanogenys*
Pirre Warbler *Basileuterus ignotus*
Three-striped Warbler *Basileuterus tristriatus*
White-rimmed Warbler *Basileuterus leucoblepharus*
White-striped Warbler *Basileuterus leucophrys*
Flavescent Warbler *Basileuterus flaveolus*
Buff-rumped Warbler *Basileuterus fulvicauda*
Neotropical River Warbler *Basileuterus rivularis*
Wrenthrush *Zeledonia coronata*
Yellow-breasted Chat *Icteria virens*
Red-breasted Chat *Granatellus venustus*
Gray-throated Chat *Granatellus sallaei*

Rose-breasted Chat *Granatellus pelzelni*
White-winged Warbler *Xenoligea montana*

Bananaquit Coerebidae
Bananaquit *Coereba flaveola*

Tanagers Thraupidae
Chestnut-vented Conebill *Conirostrum speciosum*
White-eared Conebill *Conirostrum leucogenys*
Bicolored Conebill *Conirostrum bicolor*
Pearly-breasted Conebill *Conirostrum margaritae*
Cinereous Conebill *Conirostrum cinereum*
Tamarugo Conebill *Conirostrum tamarugense*
White-browed Conebill *Conirostrum ferrugineiventre*
Rufous-browed Conebill *Conirostrum rufum*
Blue-backed Conebill *Conirostrum sitticolor*
Capped Conebill *Conirostrum albifrons*
Giant Conebill *Oreomanes fraseri*
Brown Tanager *Orchesticus abeillei*
Cinnamon Tanager *Schistochlamys ruficapillus*
Black-faced Tanager *Schistochlamys melanopis*
White-banded Tanager *Neothraupis fasciata*
White-rumped Tanager *Cypsnagra hirundinacea*
Black-and-white Tanager *Conothraupis speculigera*
Cone-billed Tanager *Conothraupis mesoleuca* •
Magpie Tanager *Cissopis leverianus*
Red-billed Pied Tanager *Lamprospiza melanoleuca*
Grass-green Tanager *Chlorornis riefferii*
Scarlet-throated Tanager *Compsothraupis loricata*
White-capped Tanager *Sericossypha albocristata*
Puerto Rican Tanager *Nesospingus speculiferus*
Common Bush-Tanager *Chlorospingus ophthalmicus*
Tacarcuna Bush-Tanager *Chlorospingus tacarcunae*
Pirre Bush-Tanager *Chlorospingus inornatus*
Dusky Bush-Tanager *Chlorospingus semifuscus*
Sooty-capped Bush-Tanager *Chlorospingus pileatus*
Yellow-whiskered Bush-Tanager *Chlorospingus parvirostris*
Yellow-throated Bush-Tanager *Chlorospingus flavigularis*
Yellow-green Bush-Tanager *Chlorospingus flavovirens*
Ashy-throated Bush-Tanager *Chlorospingus canigularis*
Gray-hooded Bush-Tanager *Cnemoscopus rubrirostris*
Three-striped Hemispingus *Hemispingus trifasciatus*
Black-capped Hemispingus *Hemispingus atropileus*
White-browed Hemispingus *Hemispingus auricularis*
Orange-browed Hemispingus *Hemispingus calophrys*
Parodi's Hemispingus *Hemispingus parodii*
Superciliaried Hemispingus *Hemispingus superciliaris*
Black-headed Hemispingus *Hemispingus verticalis*
Drab Hemispingus *Hemispingus xanthophthalmus*
Rufous-browed Hemispingus *Hemispingus rufosuperciliaris*
Slaty-backed Hemispingus *Hemispingus goeringi*
Piura Hemispingus *Hemispingus piurae*
Oleaginous Hemispingus *Hemispingus frontalis*
Black-eared Hemispingus *Hemispingus melanotis*
Gray-capped Hemispingus *Hemispingus reyi*
Chestnut-headed Tanager *Pyrrhocoma ruficeps*
Fulvous-headed Tanager *Thlypopsis fulviceps*
Rufous-chested Tanager *Thlypopsis ornata*
Brown-flanked Tanager *Thlypopsis pectoralis*
Orange-headed Tanager *Thlypopsis sordida*
Buff-bellied Tanager *Thlypopsis inornata*
Rust-and-yellow Tanager *Thlypopsis ruficeps*
Guira Tanager *Hemithraupis guira*
Rufous-headed Tanager *Hemithraupis ruficapilla*
Yellow-backed Tanager *Hemithraupis flavicollis*
Black-and-yellow Tanager *Chrysothlypis chrysomelas*
Scarlet-and-white Tanager *Chrysothlypis salmoni*
Hooded Tanager *Nemosia pileata*
Cherry-throated Tanager *Nemosia rourei* •
Black-crowned Palm-Tanager *Phaenicophilus palmarum*

Gray-crowned Palm-Tanager *Phaenicophilus poliocephalus*
Western Chat-Tanager *Calyptophilus tertius*
Eastern Chat-Tanager *Calyptophilus frugivorus*
Rosy Thrush-Tanager *Rhodinocichla rosea*
Dusky-faced Tanager *Mitrospingus cassinii*
Olive-backed Tanager *Mitrospingus oleagineus*
Carmiol's Tanager *Chlorothraupis carmioli*
Lemon-spectacled Tanager *Chlorothraupis olivacea*
Ochre-breasted Tanager *Chlorothraupis stolzmanni*
Olive-green Tanager *Orthogonys chloricterus*
Gray-headed Tanager *Eucometis penicillata*
Fulvous Shrike-Tanager *Lanio fulvus*
White-winged Shrike-Tanager *Lanio versicolor*
Black-throated Shrike-Tanager *Lanio aurantius*
White-throated Shrike-Tanager *Lanio leucothorax*
Rufous-crested Tanager *Creurgops verticalis*
Slaty Tanager *Creurgops dentatus*
Sulfur-rumped Tanager *Heterospingus rubrifrons*
Scarlet-browed Tanager *Heterospingus xanthopygius*
Flame-crested Tanager *Tachyphonus cristatus*
Yellow-crested Tanager *Tachyphonus rufiventer*
Fulvous-crested Tanager *Tachyphonus surinamus*
White-shouldered Tanager *Tachyphonus luctuosus*
Tawny-crested Tanager *Tachyphonus delatrii*
Ruby-crowned Tanager *Tachyphonus coronatus*
White-lined Tanager *Tachyphonus rufus*
Red-shouldered Tanager *Tachyphonus phoenicius*
Black-goggled Tanager *Trichothraupis melanops*
Red-crowned Ant-Tanager *Habia rubica*
Red-throated Ant-Tanager *Habia fuscicauda*
Sooty Ant-Tanager *Habia gutturalis*
Black-cheeked Ant-Tanager *Habia atrimaxillaris* •
Crested Ant-Tanager *Habia cristata*
Rose-throated Tanager *Piranga roseogularis*
Hepatic Tanager *Piranga flava*
Scarlet Tanager *Piranga olivacea*
Summer Tanager *Piranga rubra*
Western Tanager *Piranga ludoviciana*
Flame-colored Tanager *Piranga bidentata*
White-winged Tanager *Piranga leucoptera*
Red-headed Tanager *Piranga erythrocephala*
Red-hooded Tanager *Piranga rubriceps*
Vermilion Tanager *Calochaetes coccineus*
Crimson-collared Tanager *Ramphocelus sanguinolentus*
Masked Crimson Tanager *Ramphocelus nigrogularis*
Crimson-backed Tanager *Ramphocelus dimidiatus*
Huallaga Tanager *Ramphocelus melanogaster*
Silver-beaked Tanager *Ramphocelus carbo*
Brazilian Tanager *Ramphocelus bresilius*
Passerini's Tanager *Ramphocelus passerinii*
Cherrie's Tanager *Ramphocelus costaricensis*
Flame-rumped Tanager *Ramphocelus flammigerus*
Western Spindalis *Spindalis zena*
Puerto Rican Spindalis *Spindalis portoricensis*
Hispaniolan Spindalis *Spindalis dominicensis*
Jamaican Spindalis *Spindalis nigricephala*
Blue-gray Tanager *Thraupis episcopus*
Glaucous Tanager *Thraupis glaucocolpa*
Sayaca Tanager *Thraupis sayaca*
Azure-shouldered Tanager *Thraupis cyanoptera*
Golden-chevroned Tanager *Thraupis ornata*
Blue-capped Tanager *Thraupis cyanocephala*
Blue-and-yellow Tanager *Thraupis bonariensis*
Yellow-winged Tanager *Thraupis abbas*
Palm Tanager *Thraupis palmarum*
Blue-backed Tanager *Cyanicterus cyanicterus*
Blue-and-gold Tanager *Bangsia arcaei*
Black-and-gold Tanager *Bangsia melanochlamys*
Golden-chested Tanager *Bangsia rothschildi*
Moss-backed Tanager *Bangsia edwardsi*
Gold-ringed Tanager *Bangsia aureocincta* •
Hooded Mountain-Tanager *Buthraupis montana*
Black-chested Mountain-Tanager *Buthraupis eximia*

Golden-backed Mountain-Tanager *Buthraupis aureodorsalis* •
Masked Mountain-Tanager *Buthraupis wetmorei*
Orange-throated Tanager *Wetmorethraupis sterrhopteron*
Santa Marta Mountain-Tanager *Anisognathus melanogenys*
Lacrimose Mountain-Tanager *Anisognathus lacrymosus*
Scarlet-bellied Mountain-Tanager *Anisognathus igniventris*
Blue-winged Mountain-Tanager *Anisognathus somptuosus*
Black-chinned Mountain-Tanager *Anisognathus notabilis*
Diademed Tanager *Stephanophorus diadematus*
Purplish-mantled Tanager *Iridosornis porphyrocephalus*
Yellow-throated Tanager *Iridosornis analis*
Golden-collared Tanager *Iridosornis jelskii*
Golden-crowned Tanager *Iridosornis rufivertex*
Yellow-scarfed Tanager *Iridosornis reinhardti*
Buff-breasted Mountain-Tanager *Dubusia taeniata*
Chestnut-bellied Mountain-Tanager *Delothraupis castaneoventris*
Fawn-breasted Tanager *Pipraeidea melanonota*
Glistening-green Tanager *Chlorochrysa phoenicotis*
Orange-eared Tanager *Chlorochrysa calliparaea*
Multicolored Tanager *Chlorochrysa nitidissima*
Plain-colored Tanager *Tangara inornata*
Turquoise Tanager *Tangara mexicana*
Azure-rumped Tanager *Tangara cabanisi* •
Gray-and-gold Tanager *Tangara palmeri*
Paradise Tanager *Tangara chilensis*
Seven-colored Tanager *Tangara fastuosa*
Green-headed Tanager *Tangara seledon*
Red-necked Tanager *Tangara cyanocephala*
Brassy-breasted Tanager *Tangara desmaresti*
Gilt-edged Tanager *Tangara cyanoventris*
Blue-whiskered Tanager *Tangara johannae*
Green-and-gold Tanager *Tangara schrankii*
Emerald Tanager *Tangara florida*
Golden Tanager *Tangara arthus*
Silver-throated Tanager *Tangara icterocephala*
Golden-eared Tanager *Tangara chrysotis*
Saffron-crowned Tanager *Tangara xanthocephala*
Flame-faced Tanager *Tangara parzudakii*
Yellow-bellied Tanager *Tangara xanthogastra*
Spotted Tanager *Tangara punctata*
Speckled Tanager *Tangara guttata*
Dotted Tanager *Tangara varia*
Rufous-throated Tanager *Tangara rufigula*
Bay-headed Tanager *Tangara gyrola*
Rufous-winged Tanager *Tangara lavinia*
Burnished-buff Tanager *Tangara cayana*
Black-backed Tanager *Tangara peruviana*
Lesser Antillean Tanager *Tangara cucullata*
Chestnut-backed Tanager *Tangara preciosa*
Scrub Tanager *Tangara vitriolina*
Green-capped Tanager *Tangara meyerdeschauenseei*
Rufous-cheeked Tanager *Tangara rufigenis*
Golden-naped Tanager *Tangara ruficervix*
Metallic-green Tanager *Tangara labradorides*
Blue-browed Tanager *Tangara cyanotis*
Blue-necked Tanager *Tangara cyanicollis*
Golden-hooded Tanager *Tangara larvata*
Masked Tanager *Tangara nigrocincta*
Spangle-cheeked Tanager *Tangara dowii*
Green-naped Tanager *Tangara fucosa*
Beryl-spangled Tanager *Tangara nigroviridis*
Blue-and-black Tanager *Tangara vassorii*
Black-capped Tanager *Tangara heinei*
Sira Tanager *Tangara phillipsi*
Silver-backed Tanager *Tangara viridicollis*
Straw-backed Tanager *Tangara argyrofenges*
Black-headed Tanager *Tangara cyanoptera*

Opal-rumped Tanager *Tangara velia*
Opal-crowned Tanager *Tangara callophrys*
Yellow-collared Tanager *Iridophanes pulcherrimus*
Turquoise Dacnis *Pseudodacnis hartlaubi*
White-bellied Dacnis *Dacnis albiventris*
Black-faced Dacnis *Dacnis lineata*
Yellow-bellied Dacnis *Dacnis flaviventer*
Black-legged Dacnis *Dacnis nigripes*
Scarlet-thighed Dacnis *Dacnis venusta*
Blue Dacnis *Dacnis cayana*
Viridian Dacnis *Dacnis viguieri*
Scarlet-breasted Dacnis *Dacnis berlepschi*
Green Honeycreeper *Chlorophanes spiza*
Short-billed Honeycreeper *Cyanerpes nitidus*
Shining Honeycreeper *Cyanerpes lucidus*
Purple Honeycreeper *Cyanerpes caeruleus*
Red-legged Honeycreeper *Cyanerpes cyaneus*
Tit-like Dacnis *Xenodacnis parina*
Swallow-Tanager *Tersina viridis*
Plushcap *Catamblyrhynchus diadema*
Tanager Finch *Oreothraupis arremonops*
Black-backed Bush-Tanager *Urothraupis stolzmanni*
Pardusco *Nephelornis oneilli*

Przewalski's Rosefinch Urocynchramidae
Przewalski's Rosefinch *Urocynchramus pylzowi*

Buntings Emberizidae
Crested Bunting *Melophus lathami*
Slaty Bunting *Latoucheornis siemsseni*
Yellowhammer *Emberiza citrinella*
Pine Bunting *Emberiza leucocephalos*
Cirl Bunting *Emberiza cirlus*
Koslov's Bunting *Emberiza koslowi*
Rock Bunting *Emberiza cia*
Godlewski's Bunting *Emberiza godlewskii*
Siberian Meadow Bunting *Emberiza cioides*
Jankowski's Bunting *Emberiza jankowskii*
Gray-necked Bunting *Emberiza buchanani*
Cinereous Bunting *Emberiza cineracea*
Ortolan Bunting *Emberiza hortulana*
White-capped Bunting *Emberiza stewarti*
Cretzschmar's Bunting *Emberiza caesia*
Striolated Bunting *Emberiza striolata*
Lark-like Bunting *Emberiza impetuani*
Cinnamon-breasted Bunting *Emberiza tahapisi*
Socotra Bunting *Emberiza socotrana*
Cape Bunting *Emberiza capensis*
Cape Bunting vincenti *Emberiza vincenti*
Ochre-rumped Bunting *Emberiza yessoensis*
Tristram's Bunting *Emberiza tristrami*
Chestnut-eared Bunting *Emberiza fucata*
Little Bunting *Emberiza pusilla*
Yellow-browed Bunting *Emberiza chrysophrys*
Rustic Bunting *Emberiza rustica*
Yellow-throated Bunting *Emberiza elegans*
Yellow-breasted Bunting *Emberiza aureola*
Golden-breasted Bunting *Emberiza flaviventris*
Somali Golden-breasted Bunting *Emberiza poliopleura*
Brown-rumped Bunting *Emberiza affinis*
Cabanis' Bunting *Emberiza cabanisi*
Chestnut Bunting *Emberiza rutila*
Black-headed Bunting *Emberiza melanocephala*
Red-headed Bunting *Emberiza bruniceps*
Japanese Yellow Bunting *Emberiza sulphurata*
Black-faced Bunting *Emberiza spodocephala*
Gray Bunting *Emberiza variabilis*
Pallas's Bunting *Emberiza pallasi*
Common Reed-Bunting *Emberiza schoeniclus*
Corn Bunting *Emberiza calandra*
Coal-crested Finch *Charitospiza eucosma*
Black-masked Finch *Coryphaspiza melanotis*
Many-colored Chaco-Finch *Saltatricula multicolor*
Gray Pileated-Finch *Coryphospingus pileatus*

Red Pileated-Finch *Coryphospingus cucullatus*
Crimson-breasted Finch *Rhodospingus cruentus*
Black-hooded Sierra-Finch *Phrygilus atriceps*
Peruvian Sierra-Finch *Phrygilus punensis*
Gray-hooded Sierra-Finch *Phrygilus gayi*
Patagonian Sierra-Finch *Phrygilus patagonicus*
Mourning Sierra-Finch *Phrygilus fruticeti*
Plumbeous Sierra-Finch *Phrygilus unicolor*
Red-backed Sierra-Finch *Phrygilus dorsalis*
White-throated Sierra-Finch *Phrygilus erythronotus*
Carbonated Sierra-Finch *Phrygilus carbonarius*
Band-tailed Sierra-Finch *Phrygilus alaudinus*
Ash-breasted Sierra-Finch *Phrygilus plebejus*
Canary-winged Finch *Melanodera melanodera*
Yellow-bridled Finch *Melanodera xanthogramma*
Black-crested Finch *Lophospingus pusillus*
Gray-crested Finch *Lophospingus griseocristatus*
Long-tailed Reed-Finch *Donacospiza albifrons*
Gough Island Finch *Rowettia goughensis*
Nightingale Finch *Nesospiza acunhae*
Wilkins's Finch *Nesospiza wilkinsi*
White-winged Diuca-Finch *Diuca speculifera*
Common Diuca-Finch *Diuca diuca*
Short-tailed Finch *Idiopsar brachyurus*
Cinereous Finch *Piezorhina cinerea*
Slender-billed Finch *Xenospingus concolor*
Great Inca Finch *Incaspiza pulchra*
Rufous-backed Inca Finch *Incaspiza personata*
Gray-winged Inca Finch *Incaspiza ortizi*
Buff-bridled Inca Finch *Incaspiza laeta*
Little Inca Finch *Incaspiza watkinsi*
Bay-chested Warbling-Finch *Poospiza thoracica*
Bolivian Warbling-Finch *Poospiza boliviana*
Plain-tailed Warbling-Finch *Poospiza alticola* •
Rufous-sided Warbling-Finch *Poospiza hypochondria*
Cinnamon Warbling-Finch *Poospiza ornata*
Rusty-browed Warbling-Finch *Poospiza erythrophrys*
Black-and-rufous Warbling-Finch *Poospiza nigrorufa*
Black-and-chestnut Warbling-Finch *Poospiza whitii*
Red-rumped Warbling-Finch *Poospiza lateralis*
Rufous-breasted Warbling-Finch *Poospiza rubecula* •
Cochabamba Mountain-Finch *Poospiza garleppi* •
Tucumán Mountain-Finch *Poospiza baeri*
Chestnut-breasted Mountain-Finch *Poospiza caesar*
Collared Warbling-Finch *Poospiza hispaniolensis*
Ringed Warbling-Finch *Poospiza torquata*
Black-capped Warbling-Finch *Poospiza melanoleuca*
Cinereous Warbling-Finch *Poospiza cinerea*
Blue-black Grassquit *Volatinia jacarina*
Buffy-fronted Seedeater *Sporophila frontalis*
Temminck's Seedeater *Sporophila falcirostris*
Slate-colored Seedeater *Sporophila schistacea*
Plumbeous Seedeater *Sporophila plumbea*
Caquetá Seedeater *Sporophila murallae*
Gray Seedeater *Sporophila intermedia*
Wing-barred Seedeater *Sporophila americana*
Variable Seedeater *Sporophila corvina*
White-collared Seedeater *Sporophila torqueola*
Rusty-collared Seedeater *Sporophila collaris*
Lesson's Seedeater *Sporophila bouvronides*
Lined Seedeater *Sporophila lineola*
Black-and-white Seedeater *Sporophila luctuosa*
Yellow-bellied Seedeater *Sporophila nigricollis*
Dubois' Seedeater *Sporophila ardesiaca*
Hooded Seedeater *Sporophila melanops* •
Double-collared Seedeater *Sporophila caerulescens*
White-throated Seedeater *Sporophila albogularis*
Drab Seedeater *Sporophila simplex*
Gray-backed Seedeater *Sporophila leucoptera*
Parrot-billed Seedeater *Sporophila peruviana*
Black-and-tawny Seedeater *Sporophila nigrorufa*
Capped Seedeater *Sporophila bouvreuil*
Ruddy-breasted Seedeater *Sporophila minuta*
Tawny-bellied Seedeater *Sporophila hypoxantha*

Dark-throated Seedeater *Sporophila ruficollis*
Marsh Seedeater *Sporophila palustris* •
Chestnut-bellied Seedeater *Sporophila castaneiventris*
Rufous-rumped Seedeater *Sporophila hypochroma*
Chestnut Seedeater *Sporophila cinnamomea*
Narosky's Seedeater *Sporophila zelichi*
Black-bellied Seedeater *Sporophila melanogaster*
Chestnut-throated Seedeater *Sporophila telasco*
Tumaco Seedeater *Sporophila insulata*
Nicaraguan Seed-Finch *Oryzoborus nuttingi*
Large-billed Seed-Finch *Oryzoborus crassirostris*
Black-billed Seed-Finch *Oryzoborus atrirostris*
Great-billed Seed-Finch *Oryzoborus maximiliani*
Lesser Seed-Finch *Oryzoborus angolensis*
Thick-billed Seed-Finch *Oryzoborus funereus*
Blackish-blue Seedeater *Amaurospiza moesta*
Blue Seedeater *Amaurospiza concolor*
Carrizal Seedeater *Amaurospiza carrizalensis*
Cuban Bullfinch *Melopyrrha nigra*
White-naped Seedeater *Dolospingus fringilloides*
Band-tailed Seedeater *Catamenia analis*
Plain-colored Seedeater *Catamenia inornata*
Paramo Seedeater *Catamenia homochroa*
Dull-colored Grassquit *Tiaris obscurus*
Cuban Grassquit *Tiaris canorus*
Yellow-faced Grassquit *Tiaris olivaceus*
Black-faced Grassquit *Tiaris bicolor*
Sooty Grassquit *Tiaris fuliginosus*
Yellow-shouldered Grassquit *Loxipasser anoxanthus*
Orangequit *Euneornis campestris*
St Lucia Black Finch *Melanospiza richardsoni* •
Puerto Rican Bullfinch *Loxigilla portoricensis*
Greater Antillean Bullfinch *Loxigilla violacea*
Lesser Antillean Bullfinch *Loxigilla noctis*
Lesser Antillean Bullfinch barbadensis *Loxigilla barbadensis*
Cocos Island Finch *Pinaroloxias inornata*
Slaty Finch *Haplospiza rustica*
Uniform Finch *Haplospiza unicolor*
Peg-billed Finch *Acanthidops bairdii*
Cinnamon-bellied Flowerpiercer *Diglossa baritula*
Slaty Flowerpiercer *Diglossa plumbea*
Rusty Flowerpiercer *Diglossa sittoides*
Venezuelan Flowerpiercer *Diglossa venezuelensis* •
Chestnut-bellied Flowerpiercer *Diglossa gloriosissima* •
White-sided Flowerpiercer *Diglossa albilatera*
Glossy Flowerpiercer *Diglossa lafresnayii*
Moustached Flowerpiercer *Diglossa mystacalis*
Merida Flowerpiercer *Diglossa gloriosa*
Black Flowerpiercer *Diglossa humeralis*
Black-throated Flowerpiercer *Diglossa brunneiventris*
Gray-bellied Flowerpiercer *Diglossa carbonaria*
Scaled Flowerpiercer *Diglossa duidae*
Greater Flowerpiercer *Diglossa major*
Indigo Flowerpiercer *Diglossopis indigoticus*
Golden-eyed Flowerpiercer *Diglossopis glaucus*
Bluish Flowerpiercer *Diglossopis caerulescens*
Masked Flowerpiercer *Diglossopis cyaneus*
Puna Yellow-Finch *Sicalis lutea*
Saffron Yellow-Finch *Sicalis flaveola*
Grassland Yellow-Finch *Sicalis luteola*
Stripe-tailed Yellow-Finch *Sicalis citrina*
Bright-rumped Yellow-Finch *Sicalis uropygialis*
Citron-headed Yellow-Finch *Sicalis luteocephala*
Greater Yellow-Finch *Sicalis auriventris*
Greenish Yellow-Finch *Sicalis olivascens*
Patagonian Yellow-Finch *Sicalis lebruni*
Orange-fronted Yellow-Finch *Sicalis columbiana*
Raimondi's Yellow-Finch *Sicalis raimondii*
Sulfur-throated Finch *Sicalis taczanowskii*
Wedge-tailed Grass-Finch *Emberizoides herbicola*
Duida Grass-Finch *Emberizoides duidae*
Lesser Grass-Finch *Emberizoides ypiranganus*
Pale-throated Sierra-Finch *Embernagra longicauda*

Great Pampa-Finch *Embernagra platensis*
Yellow Cardinal *Gubernatrix cristata* •
Red-crested Cardinal *Paroaria coronata*
Red-cowled Cardinal *Paroaria dominicana*
Red-capped Cardinal *Paroaria gularis*
Crimson-fronted Cardinal *Paroaria baeri*
Yellow-billed Cardinal *Paroaria capitata*
Sooty-faced Finch *Lysurus crassirostris*
Olive Finch *Lysurus castaneiceps*
Yellow-thighed Finch *Pselliophorus tibialis*
Yellow-green Finch *Pselliophorus luteoviridis*
Large-footed Finch *Pezopetes capitalis*
White-naped Brushfinch *Atlapetes albinucha*
Pale-naped Brushfinch *Atlapetes pallidinucha*
Rufous-naped Brushfinch *Atlapetes latinuchus*
Vilcabamba Brushfinch *Atlapetes terborghi*
Black-faced Brush-Finch *Atlapetes melanolaemus*
Bolivian Brushfinch *Atlapetes rufinucha*
Slaty Brushfinch *Atlapetes schistaceus*
Cusco Brushfinch *Atlapetes canigenis*
White-rimmed Brushfinch *Atlapetes leucopis*
Rufous-capped Brushfinch *Atlapetes pileatus*
Santa Marta Brushfinch *Atlapetes melanocephalus*
Olive-headed Brushfinch *Atlapetes flaviceps* •
Dusky-headed Brushfinch *Atlapetes fuscoolivaceus*
Tricolored Brushfinch *Atlapetes tricolor*
Moustached Brushfinch *Atlapetes albofrenatus*
Bay-crowned Brushfinch *Atlapetes seebohmi*
Rusty-bellied Brushfinch *Atlapetes nationi*
White-winged Brushfinch *Atlapetes leucopterus*
White-headed Brushfinch *Atlapetes albiceps*
Pale-headed Brushfinch *Atlapetes pallidiceps* •
Rufous-eared Brushfinch *Atlapetes rufigenis*
Black-spectacled Brushfinch(ss)(forbesi) *Atlapetes forbesi*
Black-spectacled Brushfinch *Atlapetes melanopsis* •
Ochre-breasted Brushfinch *Atlapetes semirufus*
Fulvous-headed Brushfinch *Atlapetes fulviceps*
Tepui Brushfinch *Atlapetes personatus*
Yellow-striped Brushfinch *Atlapetes citrinellus*
Chestnut-capped Brushfinch *Buarremon brunneinucha*
Green-striped Brushfinch *Buarremon virenticeps*
Stripe-headed Brushfinch *Buarremon torquatus*
Orange-billed Sparrow *Arremon aurantiirostris*
Pectoral Sparrow *Arremon taciturnus*
Half-collared Sparrow *Arremon semitorquatus*
Golden-winged Sparrow *Arremon schlegeli*
Black-capped Sparrow *Arremon abeillei*
Saffron-billed Sparrow *Arremon flavirostris*
Olive Sparrow *Arremonops rufivirgatus*
Tocuyo Sparrow *Arremonops tocuyensis*
Green-backed Sparrow *Arremonops chloronotus*
Black-striped Sparrow *Arremonops conirostris*
Rusty-crowned Ground-Sparrow *Melozone kieneri*
Prevost's Ground-Sparrow *Melozone biarcuata*
White-eared Ground-Sparrow *Melozone leucotis*
Green-tailed Towhee *Pipilo chlorurus*
Collared Towhee *Pipilo ocai*
Socorro Towhee *Pipilo socorroensis*
Eastern Towhee *Pipilo erythrophthalmus*
Spotted Towhee *Pipilo maculatus*
California Towhee *Pipilo crissalis*
Canyon Towhee *Pipilo fuscus*
Abert's Towhee *Pipilo aberti*
White-throated Towhee *Pipilo albicollis*
Bridled Sparrow *Aimophila mystacalis*
Black-chested Sparrow *Aimophila humeralis*
Stripe-headed Sparrow *Aimophila ruficauda*
Cinnamon-tailed Sparrow *Aimophila sumichrasti*
Stripe-capped Sparrow *Aimophila strigiceps*
Tumbes Sparrow *Aimophila stolzmanni*
Bachman's Sparrow *Aimophila aestivalis*
Botteri's Sparrow *Aimophila botterii*
Cassin's Sparrow *Aimophila cassinii*

Rufous-crowned Sparrow *Aimophila ruficeps*
Rufous-winged Sparrow *Aimophila carpalis*
Five-striped Sparrow *Aimophila quinquestriata*
Oaxaca Sparrow *Aimophila notosticta*
Rusty Sparrow *Aimophila rufescens*
Striped Sparrow *Oriturus superciliosus*
Zapata Sparrow *Torreornis inexpectata* •
American Tree Sparrow *Spizella arborea*
Chipping Sparrow *Spizella passerina*
Clay-colored Sparrow *Spizella pallida*
Brewer's Sparrow *Spizella breweri*
Field Sparrow *Spizella pusilla*
Worthen's Sparrow *Spizella wortheni* •
Black-chinned Sparrow *Spizella atrogularis*
Vesper Sparrow *Pooecetes gramineus*
Lark Sparrow *Chondestes grammacus*
Black-throated Sparrow *Amphispiza bilineata*
Sage Sparrow *Amphispiza belli*
Lark Bunting *Calamospiza melanocorys*
Savannah Sparrow *Passerculus sandwichensis*
Seaside Sparrow *Ammodramus maritimus*
Nelson's Sharp-tailed Sparrow *Ammodramus nelsoni*
Saltmarsh Short-tailed Sparrow *Ammodramus caudacutus*
Le Conte's Sparrow *Ammodramus leconteii*
Henslow's Sparrow *Ammodramus henslowii*
Baird's Sparrow *Ammodramus bairdii*
Grasshopper Sparrow *Ammodramus savannarum*
Grassland Sparrow *Ammodramus humeralis*
Yellow-browed Sparrow *Ammodramus aurifrons*
Red Fox-Sparrow *Passerella iliaca*
Sierra Madre Sparrow *Xenospiza baileyi* •
Song Sparrow *Melospiza melodia*
Lincoln's Sparrow *Melospiza lincolnii*
Swamp Sparrow *Melospiza georgiana*
White-crowned Sparrow *Zonotrichia leucophrys*
White-throated Sparrow *Zonotrichia albicollis*
Golden-crowned Sparrow *Zonotrichia atricapilla*
Rufous-collared Sparrow *Zonotrichia capensis*
Harris's Sparrow *Zonotrichia querula*
Dark-eyed Junco *Junco hyemalis*
Yellow-eyed Junco *Junco phaeonotus*
Guadalupe Junco *Junco insularis* •
Volcano Junco *Junco vulcani*
McCown's Longspur *Calcarius mccownii*
Lapland Longspur *Calcarius lapponicus*
Smith's Longspur *Calcarius pictus*
Chestnut-collared Longspur *Calcarius ornatus*
Snow Bunting *Plectrophenax nivalis*
McKay's Bunting *Plectrophenax hyperboreus*
Large Ground-Finch *Geospiza magnirostris*
Medium Ground-Finch *Geospiza fortis*
Small Ground-Finch *Geospiza fuliginosa*
Sharp-beaked Ground-Finch *Geospiza difficilis*
Small Cactus Finch *Geospiza scandens*
Large Cactus Finch *Geospiza conirostris*
Vegetarian Finch *Camarhynchus crassirostris*
Mangrove Finch *Camarhynchus heliobates* •
Large Insectivorous Tree-Finch *Camarhynchus psittacula*
Small Insectivorous Tree-Finch *Camarhynchus parvulus*
Medium Tree-Finch *Camarhynchus pauper*
Woodpecker Finch *Camarhynchus pallidus*
Warbler Finch *Certhidea olivacea*

Cardinals and Grosbeak Cardinalidae
Red-and-black Grosbeak *Periporphyrus erythromelas*
Lesser Antillean Saltator *Saltator albicollis*
Streaked Saltator *Saltator striatipectus*
Grayish Saltator *Saltator coerulescens*
Buff-throated Saltator *Saltator maximus*
Black-headed Saltator *Saltator atriceps*
Slate-colored Grosbeak *Saltator grossus*
Black-throated Grosbeak *Saltator fuliginosus*

Black-winged Saltator *Saltator atripennis*
Green-winged Saltator *Saltator similis*
Orinocan Saltator *Saltator orenocensis*
Black-cowled Saltator *Saltator nigriceps*
Golden-billed Saltator *Saltator aurantiirostris*
Thick-billed Saltator *Saltator maxillosus*
Masked Saltator *Saltator cinctus*
Black-throated Saltator *Saltator atricollis*
Rufous-bellied Saltator *Saltator rufiventris*
Black-faced Grosbeak *Caryothraustes poliogaster*
Yellow-green Grosbeak *Caryothraustes canadensis*
Yellow-shouldered Grosbeak *Parkerthraustes humeralis*
Crimson-collared Grosbeak *Rhodothraupis celaeno*
Vermilion Cardinal *Cardinalis phoeniceus*
Northern Cardinal *Cardinalis cardinalis*
Pyrrhuloxia *Cardinalis sinuatus*
Mexican Yellow Grosbeak *Pheucticus chrysopeplus*
Southern Yellow Grosbeak *Pheucticus chrysogaster*
Black-thighed Grosbeak *Pheucticus tibialis*
Black-backed Grosbeak *Pheucticus aureoventris*
Rose-breasted Grosbeak *Pheucticus ludovicianus*
Black-headed Grosbeak *Pheucticus melanocephalus*
Ultramarine Grosbeak *Cyanocompsa brissonii*
Blue Bunting *Cyanocompsa parellina*
Blue-black Grosbeak *Cyanocompsa cyanoides*
Indigo Grosbeak *Cyanoloxia glaucocaerulea*
Blue Grosbeak *Passerina caerulea*
Lazuli Bunting *Passerina amoena*
Indigo Bunting *Passerina cyanea*
Rose-bellied Bunting *Passerina rositae*
Orange-breasted Bunting *Passerina leclancherii*
Varied Bunting *Passerina versicolor*
Painted Bunting *Passerina ciris*
Blue Finch *Porphyrospiza caerulescens*
Dickcissel *Spiza americana*

New World Blackbirds Icteridae
Bobolink *Dolichonyx oryzivorus*
Saffron-cowled Blackbird *Xanthopsar flavus*
Tawny-shouldered Blackbird *Agelaius humeralis*
Yellow-shouldered Blackbird *Agelaius xanthomus* •
Red-winged Blackbird *Agelaius phoeniceus*
Tricolored Blackbird *Agelaius tricolor* •
Red-shouldered Blackbird *Agelaius assimilis*
Yellow-eyed Blackbird *Agelasticus xanthophthalmus*
Unicolored Blackbird *Agelasticus cyanopus*
Yellow-winged Blackbird *Agelasticus thilius*
Chestnut-capped Blackbird *Chrysomus ruficapillus*
Yellow-hooded Blackbird *Chrysomus icterocephalus*
Jamaican Blackbird *Nesopsar nigerrimus* •
Red-breasted Blackbird *Sturnella militaris*
White-browed Blackbird *Sturnella superciliaris*
Peruvian Meadowlark *Sturnella bellicosa*
Pampas Meadowlark *Sturnella defilippii*
Long-tailed Meadowlark *Sturnella loyca*
Eastern Meadowlark *Sturnella magna*
Western Meadowlark *Sturnella neglecta*
Yellow-headed Blackbird *Xanthocephalus xanthocephalus*
Cuban Blackbird *Dives atroviolaceus*
Melodious Blackbird *Dives dives*
Scrub Blackbird *Dives warszewiczi*
Rusty Blackbird *Euphagus carolinus*
Brewer's Blackbird *Euphagus cyanocephalus*
Boat-tailed Grackle *Quiscalus major*
Common Grackle *Quiscalus quiscula*
Great-tailed Grackle *Quiscalus mexicanus*
Nicaraguan Grackle *Quiscalus nicaraguensis*
Greater Antillean Grackle *Quiscalus niger*
Lesser Antillean Grackle *Quiscalus lugubris*
Bay-winged Cowbird *Molothrus badius*
Screaming Cowbird *Molothrus rufoaxillaris*
Shiny Cowbird *Molothrus bonariensis*

Bronzed Cowbird *Molothrus aeneus*
Brown-headed Cowbird *Molothrus ater*
Giant Cowbird *Molothrus oryzivorus*
Moriche Oriole *Icterus chrysocephalus*
Epaulette Oriole *Icterus cayanensis*
Yellow-backed Oriole *Icterus chrysater*
Yellow Oriole *Icterus nigrogularis*
Jamaican Oriole *Icterus leucopteryx*
Orange Oriole *Icterus auratus*
Yellow-tailed Oriole *Icterus mesomelas*
Orange-crowned Oriole *Icterus auricapillus*
White-edged Oriole *Icterus graceannae*
Spot-breasted Oriole *Icterus pectoralis*
Altamira Oriole *Icterus gularis*
Streak-backed Oriole *Icterus pustulatus*
Hooded Oriole *Icterus cucullatus*
Troupial *Icterus icterus*
Campo Troupial *Icterus jamacaii*
Orange-backed Troupial *Icterus croconotus*
Baltimore Oriole *Icterus galbula*
Bullock's Oriole *Icterus bullockii*
Abeillé's Oriole *Icterus abeillei*
Orchard Oriole *Icterus spurius*
Fuerte's Oriole *Icterus fuertesi*
Central American Black-cowled Oriole *Icterus prosthemelas*
Greater Antillean Oriole *Icterus dominicensis*
Black-vented Oriole *Icterus wagleri*
St Lucia Oriole *Icterus laudabilis*
Martinique Oriole *Icterus bonana*
Montserrat Oriole *Icterus oberi* •
Audubon's Oriole *Icterus graduacauda*
Bar-winged Oriole *Icterus maculialatus*
Scott's Oriole *Icterus parisorum*
Yellow-billed Cacique *Amblycercus holosericeus*
Yellow-rumped Cacique *Cacicus cela*
Red-rumped Cacique *Cacicus haemorrhous*
Subtropical Cacique *Cacicus uropygialis*
Selva Cacique *Cacicus koepckeae*
Golden-winged Cacique *Cacicus chrysopterus*
Southern Mountain Cacique *Cacicus chrysonotus*
Ecuadorian Cacique *Cacicus sclateri*
Solitary Cacique *Cacicus solitarius*
Yellow-winged Cacique *Cacicus melanicterus*
Russet-backed Oropendola *Psarocolius angustifrons*
Dusky-green Oropendola *Psarocolius atrovirens*
Chestnut-headed Oropendola *Psarocolius wagleri*
Crested Oropendola *Psarocolius decumanus*
Montezuma Oropendola *Gymnostinops montezuma*
Para Oropendola *Gymnostinops bifasciatus*
Band-tailed Oropendola *Ocyalus latirostris*
Casqued Oropendola *Psarocolius oseryi*
Green Oropendola *Psarocolius viridis*
Black Oropendola *Psarocolius guatimozinus*
Baudó Oropendola *Gymnostinops cassini* •
Oriole Blackbird *Gymnomystax mexicanus*
Yellow-rumped Marshbird *Pseudoleistes guirahuro*
Brown-and-yellow Marshbird *Pseudoleistes virescens*
Scarlet-headed Blackbird *Amblyramphus holosericeus*
Red-bellied Grackle *Hypopyrrhus pyrohypogaster* •
Austral Blackbird *Curaeus curaeus*
Forbes Blackbird *Curaeus forbesi* •
Chopi Blackbird *Gnorimopsar chopi*
Bolivian Blackbird *Agelaioides oreopsar*
Velvet-fronted Grackle *Lampropsar tanagrinus*
Tepui Mountain Grackle *Macroagelaius imthurni*
Colombian Mountain Grackle *Macroagelaius subalaris* •

The World Checklist of Birds is based on the Clements Birds of the World Checklist, and is reproduced with the kind permission of Karen Clements and Cornell University Press.

GLOSSARY

Altrical chicks blind and naked at hatching.

Dimorphic sexes different.

Jizz the general impression of a bird in the field.

Lek an assembly ground or gathering of birds for communal display.

Monomorphic sexes alike.

Monotypic descended from a single common ancestral group.

Pelagic found out at sea when not breeding.

Polyandrous females having more than one male breeding partner in the same season.

Polygynous males have more than one female breeding partner in the same season.

Polymorphic having more than one plumage form in the same species, independent of sex.

Polyphyletic descended from more than one ancestral group.

Precocial chicks highly developed at hatching.

Syndactyl toes joined.

Zygodactyl two toes pointing forward and two pointing backward.

ABOUT THE AUTHORS

Prof Christopher Perrins (Foreword) is Emeritus Professor of Ornithology at the Edward Grey Institute of Field Ornithology at Oxford University and is one of the foremost bird scientists in the United Kingdom.

Dr Andrew Gosler (General Editor) is a Research Lecturer in Oxford University's Edward Grey Institute of Field Ornithology. He has published more than 50 scientific papers, and his other books include *The Great Tit* (1993) and contributions to *Birds of the Western Palearctic*, and *Bird Ecology and Conservation* (2004). Since 2002 he has been a member of the International Ornithological Committee of the International Ornithological Congress; he is also President of the Oxford Ornithological Society.

Prof Edward H. Burrt (Nearctic) is Professor of Zoology at Ohio Wesleyan University, and the Vice President of the American Ornithologists Union.

Martin Kelsey (Neotropical) OBE completed a doctorate at the Edward Grey Institute before working in Colombia with the British Ornithologists' Union. He was head of the Americas Division for BirdLife International.

Malcolm Ogilvie (Palaearctic) is a freelance writer and editor specializing in ornithology and natural history. He worked for the Wildfowl and Wetlands Trust as a research scientist and, since 1986, has lived on the island of Islay, Inner Hebrides, Scotland, where he has continued his studies of geese and raptors.

Prof Luc Lens (Afrotropical) is Professor and Head of the Terrestrial Ecology Unit at Ghent University (Belgium). He originally studied territorial behavior of temperate zone *Parus* species, but became fascinated by tropical ornithology when residing in Kenya.

Hilde Eggermont (Afrotropical) is a post-doctoral fellow with the Fund for Scientific Research, Flanders (Belgium).

Martin W. Woodcock (Oriental) is a bird artist who has specialized in illustrating family monographs, field guides and handbooks, mainly of African and Asian birds. He painted most of the color plates for the seven-volume *Birds of Africa* series.

Hugh Ford (Australasian) is Professor of Zoology in the School of Environmental Science and Natural Resources Management at the University of New England, New South Wales. His main research interests are the behavior and ecology of nectar-feeding birds and ecology and conservation of woodland birds. He is a member of the Research and Conservation Committee of Birds Australia.

The illustrations in Bird Families of the World are by the following artists:
Martin Woodcock: pages 18, 19, 20, 21, 24, 25, 26, 27, 30, 31, 32, 33, 36, 37, 42, 43. Robert Morton/Bernard Thorton Artists: pages 22, 23, 28, 29, 34, 35, 40, 41, 46, 47. Jan Wilczure: pages 32, 38, 39, 44, 45.

INDEX

ACKNOWLEDGEMENTS

Note; the numbers of the pages on which the photographs occur are followed by letters indicating the position of the photographs on the particular page, moving horizontally across from left to right.

Academy of Natural Sciences 99I/P. Alden 131G/A.M. Bada 105I/J.R. Blake 117C, 121J/Erik N. Breden 73J/P. Canevari 105C/B. Chudieigh 295J/H.Clarke 77J, 83J/H. Cruickshank 61G/P. Davey 193I/R. Dierrebaard 105G/J. Dunning 97B, 97D, 101A, 107C, 107E, 107F, 111D, 113I, 115C, 115G, 117I, 121B, 121K, 121L, 123A, 123C, 123F, 123K, 125C, 125E, 125I, 127A, 127C, 127D, 127E, 127G, 127H, 127I, 127J, 127K, 127L, 129A, 129C, 131F, 131K, 133A, 133B, 133C, 133E, 133F, 133H, 133I, 135A, 135C, 135J, 135K, 137A, 137B, 137H, 137K, 139H/C.H. Greenewalt 107L, 119B, 119D, 119E, 119F, 119I, 119J, 119L, 123G, 125J, 125K, 129I, 135D, 135F, 139B, 139C, 139E, 139G, 299C, 301G, 301I, 311B, 319B, 319D, 319E, 323C, 323E/Steven Holt 79E, 89H, 139I/M.P. Kahl 295C, 295I/E.F. Knights 245E/S. Lafrance 51F/S.J. Lans 77D/S. Lipschutz 131A, 131D/A. Morris 77I, 87G/C.Munn 105J/J.P. Myers 111E/J. Olsen 291E/P. O'Neill 129G/W.S. Peckover 269I, 291D, 303H, 309C, 315I, 317C, 319H, 323C, 323F, 323G/D.S. Pettingill Jr. 315G/M.J. Rauzon 69I, 283I/G. Reynard 313A/R. Ridgely 121C, 125D, 133K, 245A/D. Roby & K. Brink 99E/F.K. Schleicher 63A/B. Schorre 83K, 85A, 85D, 87B, 87D, 87H, 87J/T. Schulenberg 129F/Johann Schumacher 83B/R. Shallenberber 99C/N.B. Smith 115I, 137G/C. Speeble 251D/P.W. Sykes Jr. 103G/P. Tomkovich 251F/Doug Wechsler 71B, 131B, 125A, 263G, 265K/D.K. Wheeler 105A/D. and M. Zimmerman 73G, 83C, 87C, 103B, 109F; P. Alden 73I, 117H; Aquila/G. & G. Attwell 229B, 231J/G.G.& L.M. Bates 181G/J.B. Blossom 57H, 103E, 199B, 241G, 289C, 289H, 289I, 289K, 293G/J.J. Brooks 79I, 101F, 137I, 137J, 201C, 203A, 215C, 217A, 217G, 219C, 219F, 223G, 225G, 225H, 225I, 231G, 231K, 233J, 275I, 283A, 287C, 287G, 287I, 289E, 289G, 291C, 291I, 293A, 293C, 299D, 299E, 299F, 301C, 301I, 303D, 305I, 311C, 315D, 315F, 319C, 321C, 321K/Abraham Cardwell 147C/Kevin Carlson 293E/J.F. Carlyon 105F, 191A, 193J, 195A, 209H, 213B, 217B, 217E, 221F, 225A/J.F. Carlyon & M. Wilson 195K/Anthony Cooper 147C/Dr J. Davies 289F, 289J, 293D, 295C, 295F, 295G, 295J, 297A, 297F, 301F, 301H, 303B, 303C, 307B, 307D, 321A, 321D/Paul Doherty 165G, 189F/Hanne & Jens Eriksen 93K, 251C, 275A, 289B, 305I, 319I/C. Haus Geblus 175B/K. Ghani 251H/R.Gill 283G, 285F/R. Glover 149H, 291A, 297D/Conrad Greaves 69C, 99F, 111J, 203I, 203K, 249D, 251A, 253B, 257G, 267I, 291B, 311E/Brian Hawkes 59G, 67H, 69H, 111I/S.F. Horton 257H, 291J, 299B, 299G, 299H, 307F, 321B, 321F, 321J, 323A/Edgar T. Jones 55G, 65F, 71I, 85G, 87A/Edgar T. Jones & Gary R. Jones 63H/Gary R. Jones 59J/Mike Lane 55F, 169G/Wayne Lankinen foreword, 51A, 51B, 51J, 55C, 55D, 55H, 55I, 55J, 57A, 57B, 57C, 57G, 57I, 59H, 59I, 61A, 61B, 61C, 61D, 61F, 61I, 63F, 63G, 63K, 65A, 65C, 65F, 65K, 67A, 67B, 67D, 67G, 67I, 67K, 71J, 71K, 73A, 73B, 75C, 75F, 75G, 75H, 75I, 75J, 75F, 77B, 77E, 79D, 79F, 79K, 81D, 81F, 83F, 83H, 85B, 85E, 85I, 85J, 89A, 89B, 89D, 89J, 89K, 89L, 91B, 91C, 91D, 91H, 91I, 91J, 93A, 93B, 93C, 93D, 93E, 93F, 93G, 93J, 93L/Graham M. Lenton 255C/Ed Mackrill 99J, 103J, 107D, 231F/Geoff McIlleron 191F, 205I, 207A, 209G, 215H, 225J, 229F/J.Mills 277G, 287G, 295D, 299A, 301A/Richard T.Mills 65G/A.T. Moffett 167A/D.K. Richards 197H, 199C, 201A, 207G/J. Lawton Roberts 169E/Bryan L. Sage 51D, 51F, 53D, 89F, 287B/Anup Shah 189J, 195D, 209A, 215B, 219H, 225F, 239D, 239G, 241F, 243C, 247F, 251B, 255D, 265G, 267F, 269B, 297J/Philip Shaw 297J/R. Stevens 221K/C.T. Stuart 231C/Ray Tipper 81B, 251F, 253D, 253I, 257B, 277C, 297F/Gary Weber 287F, 295H, 305C, 305G, 305H, 309A, 309B, 309F, 309J, 311A, 311I, 313D, 313E, 313G, 313H, 315F, 317H, 319F, 319G, 319J, 321I/P.J. White 117D/M.C. Wilkes 51I, 53G, 53H, 53I, 53K, 63B, 63J, 65I, 65F, 67J, 69F, 71F, 79C, 83G, 187D, 187F, 189G, 189H, 189I, 191B, 193B, 193C, 193G, 195B, 197G, 199A, 199F, 199F, 201F, 201F, 201I, 203H, 207J, 209I, 209K, 211H, 213F, 217H, 219F, 225F, 227B, 231I, 233F, 233I, 235D/G.D. Wilson 297C; Ardea 105L, 293F/Dennis Avon 113J, 139B, 273E, 301J/Hans & Judy Beste 313C/Brian Bevan 303D/John Cancalosi 73L/Graeme Chapman 303F, 309G, 317J/John S. Dunning 113D, 123B, 125F, 135H, 137L, 139C, 139E, 139H/Kenneth W. Fink 75B, 259B, 261G/A. Greensmith 109A/Joanna Van Gruisen 257E, 247G/Don Hadden 293G, 293H, 305E, 307C, 307G, 311H, 311F, 313B, 317E, 321H, 323J/Irene Neufelot 267G/George Reszeter 265A/Wolfgang Wagner 247E/C. Bradshaw 261H, 269J; Corbis/Rick Price 141; David Bakewell 271I; Jose Colon 121F; Simon Cook 101D, 109F; P. Cotton 125F; R.S. Daniell 105K, 121H, 205K, 207I, 209C, 209B, 213A, 213C, 215J, 219B, 219K, 221J, 225D, 227H, 227K, 231A, 231H, 233B, 235I; I.R. Dean 257F, 259G, 263C; Devashish Deb 259F; Nik Devasar 269C, 269K; 271B, 271E, 271G 275F; Sue Earl 269C, 277A, 393F, 323I; Michael Fogden 101E, 105D, 107G, 107H, 109G, 109H, 111B, 117A, 117F, 117F, 117G, 119A, 121A, 129F, 131F, 135F; Michael & Patricia Fogden 129H; S.J.M. Gantlett 101C, 243G, 261F, 315B; John Holmes 247G, 259F, 269A, 273A, 273B, 273D, 275B; Eric Hosking 109D, 137F, 253E, 253F, 257F, 261C, 279G; Eric & David Hosking 51G, 57J, 99D, 115B, 115D, 115F, 123H, 139A, 239F, 245C, 247C, 257A, 257D, 283D, 291H, 291I, 305B, 315C; David Hosking 111F, 111H, 247B; M.G. Kelsey 103A, 107B, 113D, 113H, 117C, 125B, 125F, 125I, 129B, 133D, 135G, 137F; Frank Lane Picture Agency/Ronald Austing 59E, 59L, 71D, 73H, 81F, 81I, 87I/Hans Dieter Brandl 75D/C.Carvalhd 113F/W.S. Clark 63C, 103H, 107A, 255F, 257C, 271D/Eichhorn & Zingel 183D, 243F, 253G/W.Elison 101J/Tom & Pam Gardner 101G, 241D, 285G, 285H, 293F, 297B, 311G, 311J, 317F, 323B/K. Ghani 103F, 239A/A.R. Hamblin 71A, 79A/Hannu Hautala 75K/R. Jones 311G/John Karmali 235H/Frank W. Lane 103C, 105H, 107J, 107K,

121G, 123F, 137C, 139D, 211D, 239I, 243H, 245D, 249F, 259C, 259D, 265C, 267B, 267F, 271A, 271C, 273F/Steve Maslowski 71F, 73F, 77F, 77H, 79H, 81G, 83A, 85C, 87F, 89C, 89I/S.S. Menon 263B/Geoff Moon 283C, 287D, 293B, 307A, 313F/Mark Newman 101I/R. Van Nostrand 261A/Mandal Ranjit 239H, 241I, 249B, 253H, 277H/Len Robinson 283B, 295F, 30A3A, 303I, 305A, 305D, 307F, 309E, 309F, 309I, 315A, 315H, 315J, 317A/Leonard Lee Rue 61H, 69G, 73D, 97I/Len Rue Jr. 59F/Hanz Schrempp 139F, 265B/Silvestris 177J/Irene Vandermolen 79B/L. West 83D, 85K/Terry Whittaker 245G/Roger Wilmshurst 241E/Dieter Zingel 151B, 245B/Dr T.S.U. de Zylva 255A, 255B, 261B, 265J, 267C, 271D, 279D; Tim Loseby 255F, 265E; Clement Martin 269E, 269F, 271J, 275C, 275G; C. Mubguiney 307I, 309D, 317B; Nature Photographers Ltd/T. Andrewartha 153C, 153B, 161F, 163F, 165F, 181B/S.C. Bisserot 103I, 109B, 243A, 277F, 289D/F.V. Blackburn frontispiece, 151B, 153D, 153F, 161F, 167F, 169A, 169C, 171D, 175D, 175F, 179G/Mark Bolton 151L, 157C, 163K, 181I/Derick Bonsall 161B, 171A, 175A/L.H. Brown 12-13, 93H, 153H, 187I, 189D, 189E, 189F, 191F, 199F, 203B/N.A. Callow 241C/Kevin Carlson 59D, 63F, 85H, 91A, 91F, 105I, 137F, 145B, 145C, 145F, 145G, 151D, 151I, 153A, 153B, 155B, 155E, 155F, 157F, 157H, 159G, 159B, 161C, 161I, 167I, 169H, 169J, 171H, 173H, 173F, 175H, 177F, 177H, 179H, 179K, 183F, 201D, 213G, 219B, 223F, 223H, 223I, 233B, 280, 287A, 319A/Colin Carver 147I, 159B, 159H, 165C, 171F, 173B, 173F, 173K, 175C, 175F, 177D, 177F, 179J, 181F, 183B, 183K/R.J. Chandler 163C, 181I, 203C/Hugh Clark 53B, 113F, 167D, 169I, 177J, 247D/Andrew Cleave 53F, 61J, 143K, 163F/R.S. Daniell 101B, 115J, 121J, 139J, 184, 187D, 187G, 189B, 193A, 195H, 197C, 197I, 199D, 201B, 201G, 201H, 201K, 205A, 205J, 207B, 207D, 207F, 211B, 211E, 211F, 215D, 215H, 217F, 221B, 221D, 221F, 221H, 223D, 225B, 225C, 227A, 227C, 229G, 231F, 233F, 235A, 289A, 307H/Peter Davey 209B/A.K. Davies 177B/Thomas Ennis 183/Richard Fairbank 109I, 133J, 249F, 251B, 263H/Michael Gore 97A, 97H, 99B, 115A, 121D, 121F, 140-141, 151K, 159A, 161K, 167K, 175K, 179K, 179F, 181B, 187A, 187C, 191C, 191G, 193K, 195C, 195G, 197D, 197F, 199G, 199H, 199K, 203D, 205C, 205D, 205G, 211A, 211I, 213D, 213I, 215F, 217D, 219D, 219I, 221J, 223A, 223F, 225K, 227E, 227F, 227G, 227I, 227J, 229A, 229C, 229D, 229F, 231B, 231D, 231F, 235F, 263F, 279A, 283F, 297I/James A. Hancock 48, 53F, 59C, 69A, 97F, 111A, 111C, 123J, 135B, 139K, 155H, 203F, 207F, 207H, 221A, 235F, 239F, 247C, 287K/M.P.Harris 8-9, 53C, 69J, 97F, 97J, 99F, 163G, 187B, 283F, 283H, 283J, 285A, 285B, 285C, 285D, 285F/Dr M.R. Hill 59K, 63D, 63F, 99I, 119G, 149G, 161J, 171D, 181C, 236, 239B, 239C, 241B, 243B, 261D, 263F, 265H, 279F, 279I, 287J/David Hutton 179F, 197F/E.A. Janes 55A, 55B, 69F, 91G, 147H, 147K, 151F, 165H, 165I, 165K, 181F, 183G, 187A, 201K, 209D, 209F, 235B/John Karmali 97G, 189A, 189C, 189K, 191I, 191K, 195F, 197J, 205B, 205E, 205F, 205H, 209F, 211K, 213H, 215A, 215F, 221C, 223C, 229H, 229I, 229J, 233A, 233C, 233D, 233G, 235C, 235J, 235K/Paul Knight 145J/Chris & Jo Knights 151E, 155K/E.C.G. Lemon 51H, 285I/B. Mearns 157G, 157I, 161D, 183K/R. Mearns 65B/Hugh Miles 147D, 245F/M. Muller & H.Wohlmuth 151H, 255D/C.K. Mylne 143C, 279F/Philip J. Newman 51C, 71H, 143B, 151G, 171I, 173A, 173G, 175F, 177G/D. Osborn 99K/William S. Paton 59B, 71G, 73C, 111G, 147A, 149D, 151A, 157A, 167G, 179A, 179F, 187J, 227D, 233H/J.F. Reynolds 157B, 159I, 159K, 195I, 195J, 199I, 211C, 213F, 219A, 221G, 223B, 233F, 235G/Peter Roberts 99A/J. Russell 147G, 155C, 167C, 183H/Don Smith 71C, 73F, 77A, 77G, 79B, 79G, 81J, 83F, 89G, 151C, 153E, 153I, 161A, 167B, 171C, 197B, 207C, 211G/Paul Sterry 53L, 55K, 57D, 57F, 57J, 59A, 63I, 65D, 65J, 67C, 67E, 67F, 69B, 77C, 81C, 81H, 81K, 85F, 89F, 91F, 93I, 95, 107I, 109C, 113C, 113G, 115F, 115H, 119H, 119K, 123D, 127D, 127B, 131C, 131H, 131I, 131J, 133G, 135I, 137D, 143F, 143G, 143H, 143I, 145F, 145H, 147E, 147F, 149A, 149C, 149F, 149J, 155D, 155G, 155I, 157J, 159E, 159F, 163A, 163B, 163J, 165A, 165D, 167H, 167J, 171F, 173E, 175G, 175J, 181D, 183J, 191B, 191D, 215G/Roger Tidman 11, 53A, 53J, 57F, 61E, 65H, 67F, 69D, 81A, 87F, 91J, 103D, 105B, 143F, 143J, 145I, 147B, 147J, 149B, 149F, 149I, 153G, 155A, 155J, 157D, 157F, 159C, 159D, 159F, 161G, 161H, 163F, 165B, 165J, 167E, 169D, 169F, 171B, 171G, 171J, 175I, 177C, 183A, 191H, 193D, 193E, 193F, 195F, 197A, 199J, 203B, 203E, 203F, 217C, 219G/E.K. Thompson 55F, 143A/Maurice K. Walker 143D, 169B, 171C, 173I, 173J, 177A, 177I, 179B, 179C, 179D, 181A, 183F/Derek Washington 163I/Dave Watts 297H/Jonathan Wilson 145A, 145D, 179I; NHPA 119C/A.N.T. Photo Library 285J, 321E/Bill Coster 323H/Gerald Cubit 301B, 321C/Stephen Dalton 229E/Nick Garbutt 247H/K. Ghani 245E, 265B/Martin Harvey 189A/Hellio & Van Ingen 287H/Ralph & Daphne Keller 267H, 283K/Mike Lane 133I, 295A/Lacz Lemoine 273B/ Haroldo Paro Jnr 129I/Otto Pfister 243H/Mandal Ranjit 241A/E. Hanumantha Rao 247F, 259A, 259B, 261G/Kevin Schafer 139I/Eric Soder 247J/Taketomo Shiratori 239C/Morten Strange 249A, 249C, 255I, 255I, 257H, 259F, 263A, 263D, 265A, 255E, 277D, 277F, 279C/David Tomlinson 111E, 265I/Alan Williams 145E/James Warwick 121E; Martin Wendler 101G; Daniel Zupanc 301E; William S. Paton 163F; G. Seywald 253C, 265D, 267A, 267D, 269H, 271F, 273F, 273G, 275D, 277B, 279B, 279H; Ong Kiem Sian 259H; David Tipling 249H, 253A; Ray Tipper 249G, 261F, 265F, 269G, 275J; Alan Tye 113B, 123I, 125G, 127F, 129D, 135H; Hilary Tye 97C, 101H, 109E, 113A, 119C; Martin Williams 243D, 255G, 267G.